Fourth Edition

THE AMERICAN POLITICAL EXPERIENCE
An Introduction to Government

David V. Edwards

The University of Texas at Austin

PRENTICE HALL, Englewood Cliffs, New Jersey 07632

Library of Congress Cataloging-in-Publication Data

Edwards, David V.
   The American political experience.

   Includes bibliographies and index.
   1. United States—Politics and government.
I. Title.
JK274.E45 1988   320.973   87-17433
ISBN 0-13-028482-3

To Sandy
For Everything
With Love and Admiration

Editorial/production supervision: Linda B. Pawelchak
Cover and interior design: Jayne Conte
Manufacturing buyer: Margaret Rizzi
Page layout: Meg Van Arsdale
Photo research: Ilene Cherna
Photo editor: Lorinda Morris-Nantz
Acquisitions editor: Karen Horton
Cover photo: John Aikins/Uniphoto

Chapter Opening Photo Credits: (1) Fred J. Maroon/Photo Researchers (2) Kay Chernush/The Image Bank (3) Michael McDermott/Black Star (4) Erich Hartmann/Magnum Photos (5) Dennis Brack/Black Star (6) John Ficara/Woodfin Camp & Associates (7) Bob Daemmrich/Uniphoto (8) Mark S. Reinstein/Uniphoto (9) AP/Wide World Photos (10) Teresa Zabala/Uniphoto (11) Wesley Bocxe/Photo Researchers (12) Randy Taylor/Black Star (13) Bill Anderson/Monkmeyer (14) Paul Conklin/Monkmeyer (15) Sloan/Gamma-Liaison (16) Elliot Erwitt/Magnum Photos (17) C. Vergara/Photo Researchers (18) Fred Ward/Black Star (19) Bpivet-Duclos-Simon/Gamma-Liaison

© 1988, 1985, 1982, 1979 by Prentice Hall
A Division of Simon & Schuster
Englewood Cliffs, New Jersey 07632

Printed in the United States of America

10 9 8 7 6 5 4 3 2 1

ISBN 0-13-028482-3 01

Prentice-Hall International (UK) Limited, *London*
Prentice-Hall of Australia Pty. Limited, *Sydney*
Prentice-Hall Canada Inc., *Toronto*
Prentice-Hall Hispanoamericana, S.A., *Mexico*
Prentice-Hall of India Private Limited, *New Delhi*
Prentice-Hall of Japan, Inc., *Tokyo*
Simon & Schuster Asia Pte. Ltd., *Singapore*
Editora Prentice-Hall do Brasil, Ltda., *Rio de Janeiro*

CONTENTS

2

THE POLITICS OF FEDERALISM:
The States in a Nation of Cities
and Regions 49

PART TWO
Who Cares about Politics?

Perspective

THE POLITICS OF PRESIDENTIAL
ELECTIONS: The Case of 1984 76

3

VOTERS, NONVOTERS,
AND POLITICAL ACTIVISTS 93

7

THE MASS MEDIA 186

PART THREE
Who Decides in Government?

Perspective

THE POLITICS OF THE BUDGET:
The Deficit and Gramm-Rudman-
Hollings 210

8

THE PRESIDENCY 229

9

THE FEDERAL BUREAUCRACY 269

10

CONGRESS 304

Epilogue

THE FUTURE POSSIBILITIES OF AMERICAN POLITICS 600

PREFACE

To the Student

This introductory textbook will tell you the essential things you need to know to be an informed observer of, and an effective citizen in, our American political system. As its author, that is my commitment to you. It is up to you to decide what commitments you wish to make—both to learning about American government and to living your life in this political system. As a student and a citizen, you can commit yourself to understanding what happens in American politics, why it happens, and what effect it has on your life. As a citizen, you can also commit yourself to being an active and effective participant in American politics, should you wish to do so.

More than any other political system in the world, ours is grounded in, kept alive by, and reinvigorated by commitments. The founders of this nation made their commitment very clear when they concluded their Declaration of Independence from Britain in 1776 with these words: "For the support of this Declaration, with a firm reliance on the protection of divine Providence, we mutually pledge to each other our lives, our fortunes, and our sacred honor." (You'll find the whole text of the Declaration of Independence reprinted on pp. 28–29 of this book.) Eighty-seven years later, at another critical moment in the struggle to determine the political futures of all Americans, President Abraham Lincoln reinvigorated that pledge in an address consecrating a cemetery for Civil War soldiers at Gettysburg. He called on citizens to "highly resolve . . . that this nation, under God, shall have a new birth of freedom; and that government of the people, by the people, for the people, shall not perish from the earth."

The history of the United States and its politics has been a story of efforts by leaders and citizens to make and keep such commitments in the face of challenges to these commitments both at home and abroad. The record is a very mixed one at best, as we shall see in this book. Still, both leaders and citizens continue to commit themselves to those efforts. You too have that choice.

Leaders and citizens make decisions about how to act based, in part, on common experience. Much of that common experience derives from the fact that we all encounter American government in hundreds of ways every day of our lives. We pay taxes. We obey laws. We buy and use products that are regulated by the government for our safety or health. At the same time, we all study American government, whether casually or rigorously, most of our lives. Some of that study occurs formally in high school and college classes. Other study is less formal: watching the news on television or discussing current affairs with friends, for example. Unfortunately, American government and politics are now so complex that all of us need help if we are just to understand what is happening, let alone act effectively as citizens to affect what happens.

To understand American government we must know about its institutions, such as the presidency, the bureaucracy, the Congress, and the courts, just as we must know about its political processes, such as voting and lobbying. To help you to understand these topics, we shall focus, to a greater extent than most textbooks do, on the activities of the people who are involved. And once we have studied the major institutions and processes, we shall examine specific issues and common concerns—not abstractly, but as concrete problems. For example, in the latter part of the book, we shall give special attention to minority groups (blacks, Mexican-Americans, Puerto Ricans, Cuban Americans, Native American Indians, and the various groups of Asian Americans) and to women, the young, the elderly, and the handicapped. In doing so, we shall examine the varying needs and desires of these groups, as well as the government's responses to them. And we shall find that even when these needs, desires, and responses are distinctive, they often reflect the kinds of problems that are common to all of us. Among the concerns that we shall examine are economic issues such as poverty, taxes, and government regulation of the economy; and policy problems such as human rights, energy, the environment, education, and foreign relations. In examining both special groups and more general policy problems, we shall really be looking at the American political experience from the human side as well as the institutional side. That human side often seems to reflect weakness, either in people's characters or in the way the system operates. In this book we'll see examples of both. But the human side can also reflect strength, either of political actors or of the system and its institutions. We'll also see examples of these.

We do live in difficult times. Our leaders often seem to have difficulty making commitments to us, and we citizens often have difficulty believing those commitments when they are made. In this book you will learn some important reasons why. You will also learn what you must know to be able to make and keep commitments to our system or to its improvement; it will be up to you to decide whether you wish to do so. The fact that you have the privilege—which is your right in our system—to make these decisions for yourself makes you very unusual among the five billion people in the world today.

You have that same right—people living in most other systems might call it a privilege—to decide how much of a commitment you wish to make to learning about American government. If you choose to commit yourself to learning how our system works, you will find the important information here. I have done my best to write the book to maximize your effectiveness in learning that information. The book has many features intended to do exactly that.

- It is up-to-date.
- It emphasizes experience, rather than just institutions such as Congress or processes such as policy making. We generally learn best when we can relate what we are studying to our own experience and when we can put ourselves in the place of other people. To make this possible, we shall examine the experience of political actors such as the president, the members of Congress, and the bureaucrats as well as that of citizens such as you and I.
- Each of the five parts opens with a *perspective*—a case study or overview that gives a sense of what politics is really like, while it introduces the major ideas, questions, and topics that will be discussed in the chapters of that part.
- Throughout the book are clear and helpful diagrams, thought-provoking photographs, boxed quotations, and informative tables and charts that expand on, and give added meaning to, the text discussion.
- Key terms are highlighted in boldface where they first appear. They are also defined and explained clearly both in the text and in the glossary at the back of the book.

- Each chapter begins with a brief introduction and ends with a summary of its main points.
- Following each chapter summary are suggestions for further reading and study that describe various books, magazines, and other sources you can use to learn more about topics discussed in the chapter.
- The book also contains Action Units. These inserts, which appear at relevant points in the text and are listed in the Table of Contents, tell you how to perform a wide range of political activities, such as effectively lobbying your representative in Congress, finding out what information about you the government has stored in its files, organizing to protect human rights, and so on. You'll find that these Action Units enable you to broaden your knowledge and understanding by practical action.

I have also written a companion volume, called a Learning Guide, designed to help you further. It includes the following:

- Suggestions on how to study effectively
- Outline summaries of each chapter and perspective, together with definitions of key terms
- Questions on the material in each chapter and perspective to be used to test your comprehension
- Questions for you to think about in order to deepen your understanding of topics discussed
- A guide to political dictionaries and other research sources
- A guide to political science journals and political opinion magazines
- Information on how you might get an internship to work in Washington, perhaps during summer vacation, so that you might learn about American government by seeing it in day-to-day operation from the inside
- A discussion of jobs you may eventually be able to get if you decide to continue your studies in political science

Of course, the book can always be improved. This fourth edition benefited from contributions by students in my classes in American government at the University of Texas at Austin over the past twenty years, as well as from comments, criticisms, and suggestions from students around the country who used the earlier editions of the book. This is a much better book now than it was in previous editions, in large part because students like you shared with me their experiences of using the book to study American government or to act effectively as citizens. I would very much appreciate it if you would do the same. I hope to hear from you at the address below. I will do my best to take account of your views as I write the fifth edition.

David V. Edwards
Department of Government
The University of Texas at Austin
Austin, TX 78712

To the Professor

This introduction to American politics was written with today's students and their committed teachers very much in my mind. Its first three editions, published in 1979, 1982, and 1985, were used as textbooks in classes at some five hundred colleges and universities in the United States and abroad. As a result, I have received comments, criticisms, and suggestions from many students and professors that have been very helpful, and I have tried to take account of them in doing this revision.

This fourth edition follows the same chapter structure as the third, because virtually every reader found it very helpful. One innovative feature of all editions of this book has been the perspectives—case studies that open each of the five parts of the book. Each one describes an important event or issue that involves the actors and the kinds of politics that will be the focus of the chapters in that part of the book. Each new edition provides new perspectives. Perspective One focuses on the 1986 tax reform as an introduction to the nature of politics and the structure and functioning of our system. This edition includes a detailed account of the 1984 presidential election as Perspective Two. Perspective Three examines the politics of the budget in terms of the Gramm-Rudman-Hollings act and the dispute over the deficit.

This fourth edition retains all the special pedagogical features that made the earlier editions so popular. The book has also been improved in many ways. First of all, much has happened in the three years since the third edition was written. In rewriting the text, I have updated every chapter extensively, also taking account of much important new research by political scientists. I have also updated and retained the perspectives on shoe-import policy and on the education rights of the children of illegal aliens.

One thing that has not changed is the basic philosophy that guided the writing of the first three editions. As you well know, everyone experiences reality somewhat differently—especially the reality of American politics. Some see it largely in terms of the dictates of the Constitution. With these high expectations, the more one learns about what really goes on, the more disillusioned one is likely to become. Others see American politics largely in terms of the actions of self-interested politicians and powerful special interests acting behind the scenes in opposition to the public interest. Those who depend on the mass media for their knowledge and understanding may tend toward this view. They are also less likely to become disillusioned—but only because they lost their illusions, and often their sense of possibilities as well, long ago.

My own experience of politics, both in school and in the "real world," suggests that neither of these extreme views is very accurate. I have been active in politics from time to time at various levels and in various ways. And I have taught the introductory course in American government at the University of Texas for more than two decades. Over the years, my image of American political reality has changed considerably—as has American politics.

This book reflects my present image of American political reality. It also reflects my present beliefs about how an American government course is best taught—beliefs that have also changed considerably over these years. But I have written this book with an awareness that everyone does indeed experience reality somewhat differently. This means that everyone teaches American government somewhat differently, and that everyone learns American government somewhat differently, regardless of what the textbook says. I have therefore designed and written this text in a way that I hope will be interesting and helpful to you as a teacher as well as to your students. Together we have a wide variety of interests and orientations, but we share a common humanity and much common experience. I have tried hard to build upon them in writing and revising this book. For a description of some of this book's special features and pedagogical aids, see the Preface to the Student.

For this new edition, Michael Digby, Georgia College, has thoroughly revised the accompanying Teaching Guide, available to you on request from the publisher. It has two basic objectives. First, it is designed to free you from the more routine chores often associated with preparing a course such as this. Second, it is designed to share with you insights I have gained in my years of teaching American government and developing the text and the Learning Guide. The first section:

- Suggests teaching strategies for the course
- Describes various special approaches to, and analyses of, teaching that I have found helpful
- Lists sources of available audiovision materials and simulations that you might wish to use to supplement the text

The next section presents, for each chapter and perspective,

- a list of specific learning objectives
- a comprehensive outline of the major contents of the chapter
- suggested supplementary lecture topics
- ways of overcoming student learning obstacles
- questions for student reflection and for class discussion
- topics for student research projects deriving from the chapter or perspective

The complete listing of supplements available for the fourth edition of THE AMERICAN POLITICAL EXPERIENCE include:

TEACHING GUIDE, authored by Michael F. Digby of Georgia College.

LEARNING GUIDE, authored by David Edwards, which is described fully in the Preface to the Student.

TEST ITEM FILE, over 1000 true-false, multiple choice, short answer, and essay questions prepared by Timothy J. O'Brien of Marquette University.

TELEPHONE TEST PREPARATION SERVICE, provides test preparation and typing of items contained in the Test Item File, on bond paper or ditto master, complete with a page-referenced answer key. 24 hour turn-around time.

FLOPPY DISK TESTING, the questions from the Test Item File are also available upon adoption on floppy disk for both the IBM-PC and the Apple II, IIE, and II +; includes master program disk and instruction booklet.

GRADEBOOK/CLASS RECORD FILE, a computer program on a floppy disk that is available on adoption for Apple or IBM configurations. It allows the instructor to keep class records, compute class statistics, average grades, print graphs, sort by student name, and more.

FULL COLOR TRANSPARENCIES, 50 charts and diagrams selected from this and other Prentice Hall American Government texts, available free upon adoption. A sample transparency is enclosed.

FREE VIDEOS/FILM RENTALS, high quality, award winning documentaries and docudramas are available free upon adoption. The adoption must be for at least 100 copies to qualify. Contact your local PH representative for details.

If you wish to examine or learn more about any part of supplementary package, please contact your local PH representative, or write directly to Richard Hunter, College Operations, Prentice Hall, Englewood Cliffs, NJ 07632.

These materials—however you select and combine them—should enable you to teach your course in American government in a way that suits your own preferences and maximizes the benefits students receive from it.

Acknowledgments

My students at the University of Texas have encouraged me to develop this approach to teaching American government in many ways. They have patiently tested my various experiments. They have made regular critiques of many aspects of the courses. And they have frequently offered helpful suggestions for improvements, many of which I have used in writing and revising this book. I wish to thank them all for this.

Many of my fellow political scientists have provided challenging and helpful criticisms and suggestions during the writing and revising stages. For their assistance and interest, I would especially like to thank the following:

John T. Barnard, Green River Community College; Alice Fleetwood Bartee, Southwest Missouri State University; Paul D. Blanchard, Eastern Kentucky University; Robert L. Bock, Western New England College; Christopher J. Bosso, Northeastern University; Ronald Brecke, Syracuse University; Ken August Brunner, Georgia State University; David S. Calihan, Longwood College; David Caputo, Purdue University; Joseph Cepuran, University of Michigan; Allen J. Cigler, University of Kansas; Stanley E. Clark, California State College—Bakersfield; Peter Colby, University of Central Florida; Nelda Cook, Tarrant County Junior College; Rita W. Cooley, New York University; A. Michael Corbett, Ball State University; Robert Craig, University of New Hampshire; Douglas L. Crane, Jr., DeKalb Community College; Arthur Daniel, Alvin Community College; J. Patrick Do-

bel, University of Michigan; William M. Downer, Thiel College; Robert Elias, Tufts University; Jerry Franks, Midland College; H. Richard Friman, Marquette University; James A. Funkhouser, Edison State Community College; Darwin Gamble, Arkansas State University; Joel Goldstein, University of Louisville; George J. Gordon, Illinois State University; Calvin E. Harris, University of Texas; Gale A. Harrison, Floyd Junior College; Charles W. Hartwig, Arkansas State University; Andrea R. C. Helms, University of Alaska; Arthur C. Hill, Minneapolis Community College; Laurie Holland, University of Utah; D. L. Hughes, Texas Tech University; James L. Hutter, Iowa State University; Richard Jackson, West Texas State University; Mary Grisez Kweit, University of North Dakota; Robert Langran, Villanova University; Harlan Lewin, San Diego State University; Richard Loverd, Villanova University; Eugene A. Mawhinney, University of Maine; William J. McCoy, University of North Carolina; Edward H. McGee, Sacred Heart College; Carroll R. McKibbin, California Polytechnic Institute; Michael A. Maggiotto, University of South Carolina; Howard Neighbor, University of Texas; Joseph A. Pike, University of Delaware; Don Racheter, Central College; Don Ranish, Antelope Valley College; Bradley R. Rice, Clayton Junior College; Patricia Bayer Richard, Ohio University; Byron Robinson, Technical College of Alamance; Walter A. Rosenbaum, University of Florida; David H. Rosenbloom, Syracuse University; Robert S. Ross, California State University; Stuart A. Ross, University of Southern California; Robert C. Sahr, Purdue University; Roger Schaeffer, Texas Tech University; Stephen L. Schechter, Russell Sage College; John N. Short, University of Arkansas; Sanford R. Silverburg, Catawba College; T. McN. Simpson, University of Tennessee; Jeffrey N. Stafford, Community College of Beaver County; Donald H. Threlkeld, Troy State University; Stephen Wainscott, Clemson University; and James Ward, University of Massachusetts—Boston.

Special thanks are due to the excellent professionals of my publisher. Martin Tenney, the Prentice Hall representative in Austin, first saw promise in the project and recommended it to Prentice Hall. Stan Wakefield, as political science editor, coordinated the project in its first three editions. Karen Horton, his successor, has brought to the task of coordinating all aspects of the book's development enthusiasm and a commitment to making this the best possible American government textbook. Raymond Mullaney of Prentice Hall's College Book Editorial Development Department contributed in major and imaginative ways to every aspect of the project, personally shepherding the first and second editions through the various editorial and production stages. The design of this new edition was developed by Jayne Conte. Under the supervision of Ann Marie McCarthy, production was undertaken by Linda Pawelchak, who handled these many complexities with skill and sensitivity. The text benefited considerably from attentive and considerate copyediting by Shirley Stone. Photo research was provided by Ilene Cherna and Lorinda Morris-Nantz.

Only an author can know and fully appreciate these professional contributions. As a reader of this book, you will share the benefits of them.

Finally, and especially, thanks and much more are due to Alessandra Lippucci, who believed in the project from the start, who enthusiastically and helpfully discussed much of it with me at its various stages, and who first suggested many of its best features.

In conclusion, let me note that a book like this is never really finished, even when it is published. I hope that you will remember this as you read and use it and that you will write to me with your comments, criticisms, and suggestions for the fifth edition.

David V. Edwards
Department of Government
The University of Texas at Austin
Austin, Texas 78712

Perspective

THE STRUGGLE OVER TAX REFORM:
The Politics of Principles and Interests

In 1789 Ben Franklin, one of the founders of the United States, wrote to a friend: "Our Constitution is in actual operation; everything appears to promise that it will last; but in this world nothing is certain but death and taxes."

Two hundred years have passed since Franklin wrote those words. Time has proved him right. The Constitution has indeed lasted—with the addition of 26 major amendments. It is still the fundamental law of the land. Modern science hasn't abolished death—but advancing technology has extended the average life expectancy from about 35 years of age in Franklin's time to 75 years today. And our governments, at all levels, have expanded the scope of taxation from the original customs duties on imports in 1789 to a complex collection of federal, state, and local taxes on everything from income to spending. In fact, one of those 26 amendments to the Constitution—the 16th, ratified in 1913—made the personal income tax constitutional.

THE POLITICS OF TAXATION

The Constitution is the highest law of the land. Whatever it says must guide the president and Congress when they decide what policies to adopt. If some person or some organization charges that something the government is doing violates the Constitution, the courts decide whether it does.

The Evolution of the Income Tax

During the American Civil War, in 1862, the Congress passed a law putting a tax on incomes to help finance the war. It was repealed, or ended, ten years later. In 1894, when Congress needed extra money, it put a 2 percent tax on incomes over $4000 a year. That was a very large income in those days. Only 5 percent of the people were affected. When

1

this law was challenged, the Supreme Court concluded that it was virtually a tax on property. The Court then ruled it unconstitutional on the grounds that Article I, section 2, paragraph 3 prohibited such a tax.[1]

The government was still depending on tariffs charged on imported goods for its revenue. As government got bigger and more expensive, it raised the tariffs. Eventually, politicians favoring freer trade and progressives supporting the interests of "the common man" over those of the rich banded together to tax income. Congress in 1909 passed a 1 percent tax on profits of business corporations and a proposed amendment to the Constitution to allow a personal income tax. By 1913 the required three-quarters of the states had approved the amendment.

Congress then passed a new income tax law as a part of a new tariff in 1913. The rate was 1 percent for most taxpayers and 7 percent for the very rich. It was thus what we call a **progressive tax**—one that taxes higher income at a higher percentage rate. A year later, war broke out in Europe. By the time the United States entered the war against Germany in 1917, the corporate tax had been raised to 12 percent and the top rate for individuals to a staggering 77 percent.[2]

After the First World War, rates were lowered. During the Second World War (1941–1945), rates were raised again. The same thing happened during the Korean War (1950–1953). In the 1960s and 1970s many reductions and special "tax breaks" for both individuals and corporations were passed. Still, by 1980 the "tax bite" had risen so high that the average American was paying one dollar in every four of his or her income in taxes.[3]

The Reagan Tax Cuts

Ronald Reagan, like many other politicians, thought this tax burden was too high. Some economists agreed. They argued that the rates on the

Pres. Ronald Reagan speaks to the nation on his 1981 tax proposals. (Larry Downing/Woodfin Camp & Associates)

rich were so high that they had very little incentive to be more productive. By 1980 people making over $40,000 a year had to pay 50 percent of any additional income in federal income taxes. Those making over $108,000 had to pay 70 percent. At this time, the nation's economy was in its deepest recession in 40 years, with very high unemployment. So everyone wanted to do something to stimulate new economic growth.

Reagan, as his first major act upon becoming president in 1981, proposed cutting everyone's tax rates by 30 percent over three years. The immediate effect of this would be to reduce government income substantially. That was a problem because the government was then spending $60 billion more a year than it was getting in taxes and other fees.

But Reagan and some economists argued that lower tax rates would result in more government income in the long run. This would happen, they said, for two reasons. First, with lower tax rates, people would have an incentive to work harder and so make more income and profit on which to pay taxes. They would pay *a lower rate on a much bigger sum*, so the government would end up with more money. Second, people would save and invest the extra income they would be able to keep, and that would stimulate economic growth.

Reagan submitted this proposal to Congress, which must approve any change in taxes. He also urged the American people to tell their senators and representatives that they supported his proposal. Many did. Congress responded by approving a tax

[1]You'll find the full text of the Constitution at the back of this book. What this part of the Constitution says is, in effect, that direct taxes must be apportioned among the states by population. The Court, by very complicated reasoning, interpreted this to prevent a direct tax on individual property by the federal government. The ruling, a very controversial one, was by a five-to-four vote of the Justices.

[2]For the history, see Jerold L. Waltman, *Political Origins of the U.S. Income Tax* (Jackson: Univ. Press of Mississippi, 1985).

[3]For a comprehensive study of the whole tax system, see Joseph A. Pechman, *Federal Tax Policy*, 5th ed. (Washington, D.C.: Brookings, 1987). This edition has been revised to include the 1986 reform.

rate cut of 25 percent over three years. Most Democrats and some Republicans in Congress were not sure that the cuts would produce the economic benefits Reagan promised, but they couldn't withstand the popular pressure for lower taxes.

The name of the new tax law, the Economic Recovery Act of 1981, emphasized the long-term economic benefits everyone hoped for rather than the short-term revenue losses that were certain.

The Question of Tax "Loopholes"

The U.S. income tax is supposed to be "progressive"—that is, you pay taxes at a higher rate if you make more money because you are better able to afford that than someone living in poverty. But studies showed that in 1980 those making $5000 to $10,000 a year actually paid 27 percent of their income in taxes, while those making over a million dollars paid only 21 percent. In other words, the *actual* tax bite in percentage terms was higher for the poor than for the very rich.[4] Indeed, Congressional investigators found that thousands of millionaires were paying no income taxes at all.

The reason for this situation was that Congress over the years had created thousands of special exemptions and deductions from taxable income for particular groups of people and for particular types of expenditures. Why? The purpose of tax policy is not only to raise money to finance government but also to encourage certain behaviors by citizens and discourage others. The special provisions have been intended to encourage or reward certain behaviors, such as investing in energy development or in the stock market. We call these provisions **tax loopholes** because people fit their income safely through them. The government officially calls them **tax expenditures**. The official reason for this name is that the effect of the loopholes on tax revenue is the same as if Congress had spent the money due in taxes by giving it back to the privileged people as a kind of subsidy. The actual reason government calls them that is that everyone can understand the term *loophole* but very few can understand *tax expenditures*. Nobody in government wants to be thought to favor certain people over everybody else. But that is, in fact, what government has been doing with most of the tax expenditures, or **tax**

preferences as they are also sometimes called. The fact that there were so many loopholes benefiting special interests was a major reason for the drive to reform the tax law.

Through the years, some of these loopholes have been granted to rather ordinary people. An example is the loophole that lets people deduct from their taxable income the interest they pay on home mortgages—money they borrowed to buy a house. Before tax reform, another let people deduct interest paid on credit-card balances. Yet another let people deduct from the taxes they owed some of the money they gave to political candidates. And another allowed deduction of unusually high medical expenses. But many of the special benefits went to rich investors in stocks and bonds and real estate. Table P1.1 lists the major tax expenditures for individual citizens before tax reform. Other loopholes have benefited business in order to stimulate economic development. Table P1.2 lists benefits before tax reform. (See p. 4 for tables.)

Over the decades, the many changes made the tax code, as the 1700 pages of tax laws is called, very complicated. The income tax began in 1913 with a single sheet of instructions. In 1986 every taxpayer got a 48-page booklet of instructions on how to fill out up to 28 different forms, for which there were also dozens of other instruction booklets. Indeed, the code was so difficult to understand that 40 million of the 100 million income tax returns that the Internal Revenue Service got each year were done by the 100,000 private businesses (such as H&R Block) that people paid to fill out their tax forms. In addition, the IRS answered 50 million telephone questions each year plus hundreds of thousands of personal inquiries in its 400 branches around the country.

Everyone found the tax code very complicated for obvious reasons. Most Americans—experts and ordinary citizens alike—also found it very unfair.

THE POLITICS OF TAX REFORM

There were two different motives behind efforts to change the tax laws. One was the desire of a particular group—or "interest"—to get favorable treatment, usually in the form of its own special tax loophole. Often these groups, or "special interests," ended up competing for "preferential" treatment in what we might call the politics of interests.

---

[4]See Joseph Pechman, *Who Paid the Taxes, 1966–1985* (Washington, D.C.: Brookings, 1985).

TABLE P1.1

Major Tax Expenditures, or Subsidies, for Individual Citizens

INCOME NOT TAXED	ESTIMATED ANNUAL TAX LOSS ($ MILLIONS)	PERSONAL DEDUCTIONS AND CREDITS	ESTIMATED ANNUAL TAX LOSS ($ MILLIONS)
Pension plans—company contributions plus annual earnings of plan investments	$59,195	Mortgage interest on owner-occupied homes	$29,560
Capital gains treatment of income	29,390	State, local income and sales taxes	25,025
Company-paid insurance, other non-wage benefits	26,345	Energy credits and deductions	21,010
		Interest on consumer debt	18,735
Deferral of capital gains on home sales	20,090	Charitable contributions	14,290
Social Security benefits	19,545	Property tax on owner-occupied homes	10,865
Individual Retirement Accounts	15,885	Deduction for working married couples	8,155
Dividend and interest exclusion	3,990	Medical expenses	3,950
Interest on life-insurance savings	3,415	Tax credit for the elderly	3,755
Investment credit	3,230	Credit for child and dependent-care expenses	3,235
Workers' compensation benefits	2,570	Parent's exemption for students 19 or over	1,345
Pension contributions of self-employed, others	2,365	Credit and deductions for political contributions	295
Military benefits and allowances	2,210	Casualty losses	290
Veterans' benefits	2,045	Earned-income credit	285
Income earned abroad by U.S. citizens	1,580		
Student fellowship and scholarship income	995		
Capital gain on home sale for persons 55 and over	990		
Unemployment-insurance benefits	945		
Railroad retirement-system benefits	465		

Source: These totals, for 1987, were calculated from figures from the Office of Management and Budget, *The Budget for Fiscal Year 1987,* pp. 6-42 to 6-46.

TABLE P1.2

Major Tax Expenditures, or Subsidies, for Business

Investment credit	$24,505
Accelerated depreciation on equipment	22,880
Accelerated depreciation on buildings	7,145
Special corporate income tax reduction	5,885
Research and development spending	3,025
Employee stock ownership contributions	2,585
Capital gains	1,710
Charitable contributions	1,400
Special life insurance company tax reduction	900
Exclusion of interest on airports & sports facilities	795
Energy deductions	780
Natural resource deductions	500
Job program credits	245
Agriculture deductions	120

Source: These totals, for 1987, were calculated from figures from the Office of Management and Budget, *The Budget for Fiscal Year 1987,* pp. 6-42 to 6-46.

The second motive behind efforts to change the tax laws was the desire of scholars, politicians, and public opinion generally to make the tax system as a whole more fair.[5] But because people found it difficult to agree on just how to make the tax system fairer, they got involved in what we might call instances of the politics of principles.

The Politics of Principles

Virtually every American is in favor of fairness—not just in taxes but in sports and human relations generally. But what is fair? What would be

<hr>

[5]For a critique of a wide range of proposals, see Joseph J. Minarik, *Making Tax Choices* (Washington, D.C.: Urban Institute, 1985).

a fair way to tax people in order to raise the revenue the government needs to do what citizens want it to do?

The Question of Fairness

How about an income tax system that takes the *same amount of dollars* from everyone, regardless of wealth or income? Would such an across-the-board tax system be fair? Most states charge fees for registering autos and taxes on gasoline, for example, that are the same for everybody. But no state taxes income this way because it doesn't seem fair to take the same amount from the very poor and the very rich.

Then how about a tax system that takes the *same percentage* from everyone regardless of wealth or income? The Treasury Department in 1986 calculated that such a "flat tax" with a tax rate of only 6.7 percent but without any special tax breaks would produce the same revenue as the current system. Would that be fair? Sales taxes work this way, at least for every dollar one spends. But such a tax applied to the purchase of necessities such as food or medicine will take a bigger share of the poor's income because everyone has to buy the necessities. So many people think such a flat sales tax is not really fair and would be even less fair if it were on income.

Then how about a tax that takes *a bigger percentage of income from those making more money*? That has been the basic principle of our federal "progressive" tax on income. If you think that's fair, then how much more should taxes take from those with large incomes than those with small incomes? The U.S. system long had 14 "brackets," or ranges of income, each taxed at a higher percentage than the one below it. But what are fair percentages? And at what levels of income should the bracket lines be drawn to be fair? These things have been changed from time to time over the decades. Table P1.3 shows the percentages in 1986. Are they fair? How should we decide?

The difficulty we have in agreeing on these questions suggests that perhaps this isn't the right way to go about it. Perhaps we should tax people in terms of the *benefits* they get from government rather than their *ability to pay*. Government protects all of us from foreign threats, so perhaps we all owe something for that. But government makes

TABLE P1.3

Federal Income Tax Rates in 1986

TAXABLE INCOME LEVEL	PERCENT TAX RATE
$ 0– 2,000	0
2,000– 4,000	11
4,000– 5,000	12
5,000– 7,000	14
7,000– 9,000	15
9,000–12,000	16
12,000–14,000	18
14,000–16,000	20
16,000–20,000	23
20,000–25,000	26
25,000–31,000	30
31,000–37,000	34
37,000–45,000	38
45,000–60,000	42
60,000–88,000	48
88,000 up	50

Note: Annual income figures are rounded off. The percentage tax is the marginal tax rate—that paid on the income exceeding the lower figure on the line. These rates are for an unmarried individual.

some policies on economic matters—such as regulating the stock market—that benefit the rich but not the poor. It also funds welfare programs that benefit the poor more than others. Maybe, then, the rich and the poor should be taxed more than the middle class since they each get special benefits from government. But the poor would not have the money to pay or at least would suffer much more if they had to pay. Perhaps then the rich should pay more because the real benefits of national defense and domestic protection provide the most benefits to those with the most to lose.

The Question of Equality

These complications may suggest that the principle of fairness, however much we believe in it, can't answer the question of how to tax. What, then, about the principle of *equality*? That seems to be more specific. The problem is that there are many different ideas of equality. Most ideas of equality go deeper than those we've just considered: the same number of dollars or even an equal percentage from each person. Most argue for *equality of opportunity*. That might mean special treatment for those who are sick, handicapped, or otherwise unable to have an equal chance to succeed in life. Perhaps we should also include those who, because

The Net Worth of the American People

ASSETS	PERCENT OF TOTAL	DOLLAR VALUE
Tangible Assets		
Owner-occupied housing	19%	$ 2,128,000,000
Consumer durable goods (appliances, autos, etc.)	10	1,120,000,000
Land	6	672,000,000
Other	2	224,000,000
Financial Assets		
Bank deposits	17	1,904,000,000
Bonds, mortgages, etc.	6	672,000,000
Noncorporate businesses	17	1,904,000,000
Life insurance and pension funds	10	1,120,000,000
Stocks in corporations	12	1,344,000,000
Other	1	112,000,000
Total		$11,200,000,000

Source: These figures, for 1982, were calculated from percentages supplied by the Federal Reserve and published by the *Washington Post,* November 13, 1983.

they are orphaned or less educated, have had fewer economic opportunities. Perhaps these groups should pay fewer taxes. However, some people have done well economically despite these limitations, so perhaps we should focus on actual wealth.

How about those born rich or with large inheritances? Perhaps taxes should be based on wealth instead of income. That way, the tax system could eventually *create* more equality by transferring wealth from the rich to those less well-off.

The problem is that there are many different ideas of just what equality is or should be. Although equality appears to be a simple principle in the abstract, applying it in concrete, complex situations is very difficult.[6]

The Question of Economic Efficiency

If we can't agree on either fairness or equality as the basic principle for a tax system, perhaps we should be more "practical." Perhaps we should focus on using the tax system to make the economic system more efficient. A more efficient economy might produce sufficient tax revenue with less pain for the people. It might even produce more benefits for everyone.

What would such an emphasis on economic efficiency recommend? Suppose we focused on favoring the *people* who make the greatest contributions to stimulating economic growth. People

who earn their income are contributing to economic growth, which is supposed to benefit the economy and society as a whole. Perhaps the basic principle for taxation should be to tax most heavily the people who are contributing the least. Some of the rich don't work very hard if at all, choosing instead to live off their wealth. If we taxed away their wealth instead of the income of the hard-working people, maybe our economy would be in better shape.

There is a lot of wealth in our society. The total of all private wealth was recently estimated at $11.2 billion, as Table P1.4 reveals.[7] But the rich do not hold enough wealth to pay the enormous costs of our federal budget. In fact, neither do the American people as a whole. Our federal government now spends over a trillion dollars every year. (We'll learn how in Perspective 3.) To pay its bills, it needs contributions every year from virtually everybody, including especially the vast working middle class. Indeed, it gets almost 45 percent of the revenue it needs from the individual income tax, as Figure P1.1 shows.

So even if we agree on taxing the least productive (other than those who can't work) at the highest rate, we still need a principle to determine who among the productive should pay how much for government. Some people call for equal taxation in terms of ability to pay or for taxation in terms of benefits received, which would tend to penalize

---

[6]See Douglas Rae et al., *Equalities* (Cambridge: Harvard Univ. Press, 1981), p. 150.

[7]We'll study the distribution of wealth and income in Chapter 16.

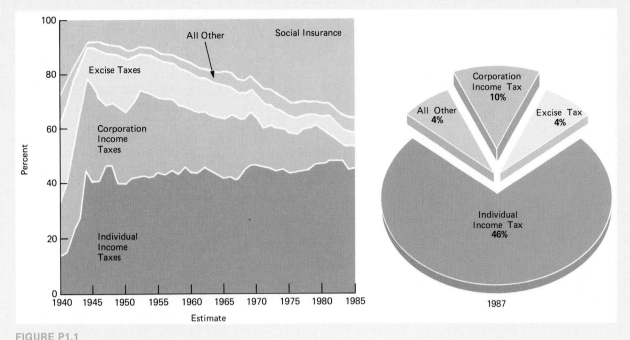

FIGURE P1.1
Where the Government Gets Its Money.
Source: Office of Management and Budget, *U.S. Budget in Brief, Fiscal Year 1987.*

those people who own a lot of property. Those with property protest that equal taxation in these senses is unfair. They claim it violates their right to property. Private property is an essential element of capitalism, and our economic system is based on capitalism, as we'll see in Chapter 15. So a tax system based on ability to pay could tend to undermine our economic system, according to this view. Interestingly, surveys show that most Americans, including many of those who own little or nothing, agree on this.

In addition, it is often argued that the health of our economy—and therefore the welfare even of the poor—depends on the *economic efficiency of our system* as a whole rather than directly on the economic efficiency of individuals. Some economic theorists argue that taxes are in themselves bad because they distort or even prevent the operation of the market forces of supply and demand. The market, these people argue, is the best judge of what should happen. Taxes take money out of the marketplace and allocate it inefficiently, they say. But others respond that the marketplace doesn't have armed forces to defend the country, nor does it take care of the sick, the handicapped, orphans, and others who cannot pay their own way. Taxes are used by governments to provide

these "public goods." So arguments based on the economic efficiency of the system have their problems too.

We can begin to see that no principle—fairness, equality, benefit, productivity, efficiency, or whatever—provides guidelines for taxation that are clear and generally acceptable to all the people.[8] So questions of how to tax are always difficult for government to decide on principle.[9] But taxes must be levied, and politicians must decide how and on whom. The fact is, politicians have to make such decisions, in practical terms, every time they pass a tax bill—something they've been doing almost every year for the past two decades. However, such questions of principle are not always uppermost on politicians' minds. They are usually too busy listening to the things they are being told by representatives of special interests—businesses, labor unions, or consumer groups, for example. These representatives are often called **lobbyists** because they have tended to hang around in the lobbies of the Capitol building waiting to talk to members of

[8]See William E. Connolly, *The Terms of Political Discourse*, 2d ed. (Princeton, N.J.: Princeton Univ. Press, 1983). Connolly calls these "essentially contested" terms.

[9]For an analysis of the debate, see Harold Groves, *Tax Philosophies* (Madison: Univ. of Wisconsin Press, 1970).

Congress as they come and go, trying to influence their votes.

In fact, most of these special interests—many thousands of them, from the Apple Institute to Zero Population Growth—were especially interested in proposed changes in the tax laws. Why? Every law, and every change in the law, makes winners and losers—those who pay few taxes and those who pay a lot of taxes.

These competing special interests made it very difficult to change the tax laws in any way except cutting taxes across the board (for everyone), as Reagan and the Congress did in 1981. Indeed, special interests had so many special loopholes to protect that almost all the experts believed that a general overhaul of the tax code designed to make taxes fairer would be impossible.[10] Experts were saying this right up until Congress passed and President Reagan signed into law the Tax Reform Act of 1986—a major, massive overhaul of the whole tax code. How did that happen? How could the experts have been so wrong?

The Politics of the Tax Reform Act of 1986

Opinion polls showed for decades that a large majority of the people believed that the federal income tax system was unfair and too complex. Special-interest groups favoring lower taxes or tax reform had long appealed for public support by issuing studies showing that many rich individuals and large corporations had been paying little or no tax year after year.

The Interests Involved

While tax reform was being debated in 1985, a study by a labor-funded group called Citizens for Tax Justice reported that 40 large corporations that made profits totaling over $10 billion in 1984 paid no federal taxes that year. The reason? Loopholes written into the tax law. The same study found that 129 large companies paid no taxes in at least one of the years from 1981 through 1984 even though their profits in those no-tax years totaled over $66 billion. The law also allowed 118 of these com-

panies at the same time to get money back from the government that they had paid in taxes in previous years.[11] Studies such as this one increased the interest in fundamental tax reform. But reform was opposed by many thousands of businesses favored by the existing tax code. Most of these were industrial firms that benefited from special tax deductions for investment in new factories and machinery. Companies involved in retail sales—computer firms, department stores, and food producers, for example—did not have as many special tax breaks. They therefore tended to favor any tax reform that would lower the basic corporate tax rate. Thousands of businesses and many business groups such as the Chamber of Commerce got involved, some on one side and some on the other.

Hundreds of nonbusiness groups were also arguing for particular tax reforms that would benefit their concerns. Among these were groups concerned with problems of the poor and the hungry (for example, Bread for the World), of children (Children's Defense Fund), of working women, (Women's Equity Action League), and of the environment (Environmental Action). Many of these groups also lobbied.

But special interests were not alone in their concern with tax reform. They were joined by some scholars and many politicians. Scholars had been studying the tax code for decades. Some showed how nonprogressive it had been in practice. Others showed how its economic effects had limited economic productivity.

Since 1978 various members of Congress, too, had proposed major tax reform. A 1978 proposal for large tax cuts developed by Representative Jack Kemp (Republican of New York) and Senator William Roth (Republican of Delaware) formed the basis of Reagan's 1981 program. In 1982 Senator Bill Bradley (Democrat of New Jersey) and Representative Richard Gephardt (Democrat of Missouri) proposed a Fair Tax Act. It cut the top tax rate from 50 percent to 28 percent and replaced the existing 14 brackets with only 2. It was designed, however, so that by eliminating many loopholes it would produce the same revenue for government as the existing tax law. It was, as the saying goes, **revenue neutral**—it would neither increase nor decrease revenue. Some other members of Congress offered their own proposals as well.

[10]David G. Davies, *U.S. Taxes and Tax Policy* (New York: Cambridge Univ. Press, 1986), p. 287. Davies is endorsing the analysis of another expert, John F. Witte, *The Politics and Development of the Federal Income Tax* (Madison: Univ. of Wisconsin Press, 1985), pp. 18–19.

[11]Laurie McGinley, "No U.S. Income Taxes Were Paid in '84 By 40 Big, Profitable Firms, Study Says," *Wall Street Journal*, August 29, 1985.

Sen. Bill Bradley (D-NJ) and Rep. Richard Gephardt (D-MO) present their tax reform proposals. (Wally McNamee/Woodfin Camp & Associates)

The Political Considerations

Senator Bradley chaired the Democratic party's task force on tax reform. With a presidential election coming up in 1984, Republicans feared that Democrats would seize the issue of tax reform. After all, Jimmy Carter had done just that in his successful campaign in 1976, calling the tax system "a disgrace to humanity."

To preempt the Democrats, Reagan announced in January 1984 that he was creating a special commission in the Treasury Department to develop a proposed new tax structure. However, to keep the issue out of the campaign, he asked it to make its report in late November, just after the election. The Democratic presidential nominee, Walter Mondale, decided not to try to make tax reform an issue. Instead, citing the growing federal deficit, he said he'd have to raise taxes if elected—and warned that Reagan would too. Reagan pledged not to do so and won reelection by a landslide.

After the election, Reagan told Congress that tax reform was his highest domestic priority:

> Over the years, the entire tax system has come to mirror Washington itself: a complicated, frustrating, unfair mystery of legalistic gobbledegook and loopholes never designed, it seems, to help everyday wage earners, only those who can afford high-priced attorneys and accountants.

This rhetoric was supposed to appeal to citizens—to get them to tell their representatives in Congress to support tax reform. Yet, strangely, the people did not seem much interested in tax reform. Perhaps this was because politicians had long

promised basic reform but never delivered. Maybe they were satisfied with the Reagan-Kemp-Roth cuts of 1981 through 1984. Whatever the reason, Reagan decided to press ahead. In May he sent his own proposal to Congress and made a television speech calling it the Second American Revolution. He then undertook a "fall offensive" of seven speaking trips to sell the program to the people.

But Reagan had a problem. To get tax reform, he had to have Democratic support. The Democrats had a majority in the House of Representatives and Democratic representative Dan Rostenkowski of Chicago chaired the committee that would have to recommend any tax reform bill. So Reagan gave mild, nonpartisan (politically neutral) speeches criticizing special interests who benefited from the unfair system. However, he didn't mention these targeted interests by name. That would have stirred them to active opposition. Besides, these "special interests" were businesses, and most of the people who led these businesses and most of those who owned them were Republicans and regularly gave campaign contributions to Republicans in Congress. If these people turned against tax reform, many Republicans—especially in the Senate, where Republicans were a small voting majority—might decide to oppose the bill. So Reagan's speeches were gentle, and most people found them boring.

Meanwhile, Democrats in Congress had to decide what position to take. Few were enthusiastic about tax reform, for several reasons. One was that Reagan's proposal was slanted in favor of members of the upper middle class, who tend to vote Republican anyway. Another was that the budget deficit was leading to more and more cuts in domestic spending programs for cities, welfare, health, and other issues that benefited Democratic voters. So Democrats generally favored a tax rise rather than a "revenue-neutral" reform such as Reagan had proposed. Nonetheless, Democrats were afraid to oppose tax reform, for fear that Reagan would be able to blame them for killing tax relief for the middle class.

The Political Struggle

The Democrats in the House of Representatives decided to prepare their own tax-reform proposal and try to substitute it for Reagan's. The bill they produced differed from Reagan's in that it shifted more of the tax burden to high-income individuals and

The Struggle Over Tax Reform 9

Lobbyists hoping for a chance to influence decisions camp out at the door to the House Ways and Means Committee as it considers the tax reform bill. (Dennis Brack/ Black Star)

corporations. The estimates were that the Reagan bill would cut middle-class taxes by $15 billion and those of families earning over $200,000 by $39 billion. The House bill would have cut middle-class taxes by $67 billion and those over $200,000 by only $21 billion while raising corporate taxes by $30 billion.

These changes upset most House Republicans and some Democrats, so there weren't enough votes to pass the Democratic bill. The president wanted a bill—even what he thought was a bad bill— passed by the House. He assumed that the Senate, controlled by the Republicans, would pass a much better bill. Then a compromise could be worked out that would result in the sort of tax reform he favored. So Reagan pressured his own party members in the House to support the Democratic bill, promising that if the bill was not later improved by the Senate he would veto it. In the end, the House voted overwhelmingly for the Democratic bill.

Action then shifted to the Senate. In March the Republican chair of the Finance Committee, Bob Packwood of Oregon, presented his own proposal. It followed the general outlines of the Reagan proposal but restored a number of important tax breaks for business. After almost two months of de-

bate and maneuvering, the committee approved a modified bill with a top individual tax rate of only 27 percent and few special tax breaks. In late June the Senate approved the bill by a vote of 97 to 3.

When each house of Congress passes a different bill on the same subject, a special conference committee is appointed. Key members concerned about the subject from each house serve on that committee. They negotiate a compromise, which is normally then approved routinely by both houses. That sends the bill to the president for his approval. When he signs the bill, it becomes law.

In this case, many special interests were scheduled to lose tax breaks according to provisions of one version of the bill or the other. They were upset and so tried to convince members of the conference committee to change the bill in their favor. The halls outside the room where the conference committee met were packed with their lobbyists during the month of its deliberations.

Finally, the conferees reached agreement on the Tax Reform Act of 1986. Among its key provisions are these:

- Two basic brackets, 15 and 28 percent, replace the 14 tax-rate brackets ranging from 11 percent to 50 percent.

Members of the Senate Finance Committee debate tax reform proposals. (Wally McNamee/Woodfin Camp & Associates)

- Six million poor people no longer have to pay any federal income tax.
- Fifteen percent of those with very high incomes have to pay more taxes.
- Most tax loopholes are closed, but certain favorites are retained, among them deduction from taxable income of mortgage payments on regular and vacation homes, of state and local income tax payments, and of most contributions to charity.
- The top corporate tax rate is lowered from 46 percent to 40 percent, but many tax preferences for business (especially for investment in factories and machinery) are eliminated, so that business tax revenues will increase by $120 million over five years—the same amount that individual payments will decrease.

On September 25, 1986, the House approved the compromise by a vote of 292 to 136, with a majority of each party in favor. Two days later, the Senate approved it by 74 to 23. On October 22 the president signed the Tax Reform Act of 1986, calling it "the best antipoverty bill, the best profamily measure, and the best job-creation program ever to come out of the Congress of the United States."

The Interplay of Principles and Interests

It would be easy to conclude from this case that interests dominated principles in determining the outcome. Clearly, the partisan political interests of the president and members of Congress were major factors in shaping the actual terms of the final bill.

Still, the bill upset many more special interests than it pleased. If the major motivation of political figures were satisfying special interests who pestered them and who made vital campaign contributions, we would expect tax reform to have failed. Indeed, all the expert observers of politics, including most advocates of major tax reform, *did* expect the effort to fail. But, as we have seen, they were wrong.

Why, then, did the tax-reform effort succeed? Apparently, a concern with principles was also a factor in the decisions of many key actors, from the president to the Congress to many of the lobbying interest groups.

The case of President Reagan is especially interesting. His unofficial biographer, Lou Cannon, who has "covered" him for the *Washington Post* throughout his presidency, reported that friends of Reagan had heard him condemn income taxes on principle as far back as his days as a Hollywood movie actor.[12]

Furthermore, the basic principle of the Reagan administration has been to reduce the role of government in American life. At the national level, it sought to do this in two ways. One was to control spending on domestic programs—something it did by budget cuts we'll examine in Perspective 3. The other was to cut federal tax revenue so that government would have to do less—which it achieved

---

[12]See Lou Cannon, *Reagan* (New York: Putnam, 1982).

Sen. Bob Packwood (R-OR) and Senate Majority Leader Robert Dole (R-KS) examine documents concerning the proposed tax bill. (Dennis Brack/Black Star)

by the original tax cuts. To preserve this effect, Reagan insisted successfully that tax reform be revenue neutral.

He even tried to extend this effect to the state and local levels by changing the relations among our three levels of government. (We will examine this relationship, which we call federalism, in Chapter 2.) In fact, his tax-reform proposal called for prohibiting citizens from deducting their state and local taxes from their federally taxable income. That would have made state and local taxes more painful for citizens and thus would have encouraged them to try to cut down the activities of these governments as well. However, members of Congress tend to be more sensitive than the president to the interests of the states and localities from which they are elected and to the interests of taxpayers who vote in those areas. So they refused to accept Reagan's proposal and preserved the federal tax deduction for such state and local property and income taxes, although they did agree to eliminate the deduction for sales taxes.

Reagan's efforts here were heavily influenced by principles in which he believed strongly. So were the actions of the members of the House and Senate in pursuing major tax reform in the face of strong opposition from so many special interests as well as apparent public indifference.

Therefore, to understand why political figures act as they do we must take note of both consid-

erations: political interests and principles. Their calculations of their political interests—especially in relation to the special interests of those who vote and those who make campaign contributions—are almost always important. But so, in many cases, are their beliefs about what is in the public interest or what will make good public policy. We'll return to these questions in Chapter 5.

THE POLITICS OF GOVERNANCE

The question of tax reform is just one of thousands of issues that arise in American government. But it is a vital issue because taxes play a major role in shaping what government does and how it does these things. As a consequence, tax reform stimulates major conflicts, as we have seen. These conflicts demonstrate the politics of governance because they concern how the government works. To understand what happens in these cases more generally, we must study three different aspects of American government: institutions, processes, and policies. That's what we'll be doing in this book.

The Nature of Government

Our word **government** comes from an ancient Greek word meaning "to direct a ship." People still speak sometimes of "the ship of state" that government must captain. When we use the term *government*, we most often mean the public bodies that direct public affairs. The word *public* means "of the people," and public affairs are the concerns of all the people. In this sense, then, government directs all the people over whom it has power.

The Aspects of Government

The diagram, or organization chart, as it is often called, that is Figure P1.2 tells us important things about the government. It shows that there are three branches—legislative, executive, and judicial—and that all three are subordinate to, or ruled by, the United States Constitution. It also shows us the various parts of each branch, such as the president, the Executive Office of the President, the cabinet departments, and the "independent agencies" in the executive branch—all of which we often call the bureaucracy. The ways the connecting lines are

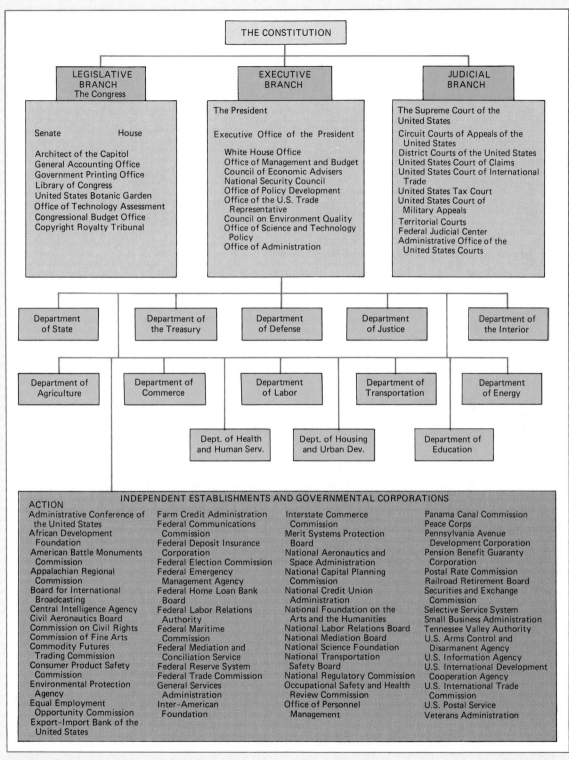

FIGURE P1.2
The Government of the United States—the Official View
Source: Adapted from *U.S. Government Manual 1986* (Washington, DC: Government Printing Office, 1986).

drawn report "who orders whom around." In the executive branch, for example, the president sits on top of everything else, and all the departments and agencies report to him through his Executive Office.

The Constitution and also the formal structure of the government are extremely important. They create the *institutions*—such as Congress, the president, the courts, and the bureaucracy—that make up the government. But we cannot really understand these **institutions** apart from the *processes* of government. By **processes** we mean the elections, with their campaigning and voting, the lobbying and other forms of influence that citizens and groups in and out of government use to try to affect the outcomes or outputs of the institutions, and the various other types of politicking we find in government as the various parts of the government cooperate and compete with each other. We've just seen how some of these processes operated in the case of tax reform.

This brings us to the third and final major focus of our study: the *policies* that the institutions develop and implement. Government is constantly developing **policies**—decisions about what government will do. A glance at the evening news or at the morning paper reminds us of how controversial many policies are. We will examine some of these controversial policies in coming chapters—especially toward the end of the book. Some of these policies deal with the claims to rights and liberties and special programs made by various groups, and others are policies intended to cope with economic, urban, and foreign problems. The debate over tax reform, which raised questions of fairness and of rights to equality and property, is but one example of the sorts of controversial policies we will be dealing with.

As we study institutions, processes, and policies, let us not forget that we, the people, have our own vital role to play in the practice of government. Abraham Lincoln, in his famous Gettysburg Address in 1863, described ours as a "government of the people, by the people, for the people." We must remember—even when the politicians forget and need to be reminded—that we are the *subjects* of government ("government of the people"), as well as the participants ("by the people") and the objects or targets ("for the people"). But when these principles are converted into practice, we discover

that each aspect of our relationship with government is controversial. For example, when the federal government creates tax incentives, it is telling you how it prefers that you spend your money. And when it tells you how much of your income you must turn over to it, it is getting very close to you. Over its 200-year history, our government has moved further and further in this direction, expanding its sphere of activity or operation—its domain—at the same time. These two tendencies are big departures from the intentions of the country's founders.

Limitations on Governance

The colonists who declared their independence from England in 1776 were fearful of too strong a government. Many of their ancestors had come to this country to escape from European governments that were so close to the people that they were even able to dictate what religion the people should practice. And at the time of the American Revolution, the British government was close enough to the American colonists, even though it was located an ocean away in London, to dictate what taxes the colonists had to pay, without even consulting them.

The colonists feared that a central government might be so powerful that it would curtail the liberties they valued. So when they established a national ruling power, they devised a new type of central government—one prohibited from getting too close to the people. We shall examine what they did and how they did it in Chapter 1. For the moment, however, we must note three limitations on ruling power that they imposed.

Rights are the first such limitation. Some countries have a central government that has total power over every aspect of life. We call them dictatorships because they can dictate to the people what can and cannot be done. Our central government, however, is a *limited government*—limited in two important ways. First, the document that created it, our *Constitution*, says specifically what the government can and cannot do. It declares that we as citizens have certain rights the government cannot infringe upon or take away. For example, the Constitution prohibits Congress from passing a law declaring something a crime *ex post facto* ("after the fact" or "after the deed"). As a result, citizens cannot be punished for doing something that was not a crime when they did it. This may not seem like much but only because we take it for granted. And we can take it for granted only because this prohibition is in the Constitution, and the Constitution has legitimacy. Most of the other rights we take for granted are guaranteed to us by the first ten amendments to the Constitution—the Bill of Rights. Among them are freedom of speech and religion and trial by jury. We shall examine these limitations in Chapter 1 as we study how we got our Constitution and what it does for us.

The *federal division of powers* is a second limitation on national ruling power. This limitation, also found in the Constitution, is as important as the first. Our government is divided into many different parts, each of which has some power granted to it alone, so that no other part can destroy or dominate it. This limitation works in several ways.

First, it breaks up governing power into *levels*. The Constitution *divides* powers among the *national* government (what we call the federal level) and the *state* governments (the state level)—and then reserves still other powers to the people. We call this division of powers **federalism**. The national government is a federal government—a federation of states that have given up some powers to the central government and kept others for themselves. (The states have also granted some of their powers to their cities, creating yet another level of government—but one wholly dependent on the states for its powers.) We shall describe this division of powers further in Chapter 1, and in Chapter 2 we shall see how American federalism has developed.

The *separation of powers* is a third limitation on national ruling power. This breaking up of powers into pieces occurs at each level of government. *Powers are separated* into three branches in order to further limit the danger of a too powerful government. As we saw in Figure P1.2, at the national level we have the **executive branch**, headed by the president and including a large bureaucracy; the **legislative branch**, consisting of Congress; and the **judicial branch**, at the top of which is the United States Supreme Court. Congress has the power to make laws. The president has the power to enforce these laws. The courts interpret the laws to see whether what the president does is correct and whether the laws Congress makes are consistent with the Constitution, which is the highest law of the land. The states, too, have separation of powers in their governments.

And so the Constitution limits the ruling power in our system to guarantee that no one level and no one branch within any one level can dominate the others. But all these limits are so complicated, and all these pieces are so jumbled, that things rarely work in practice exactly as they are outlined in theory. Thus, the task of governing is complex, and the way it is done is always controversial.

The Politics of Domain

A major area of controversy is the question of the appropriate sphere of governmental activity—or "the politics of **domain**." Over the past 200 years, commonly accepted notions of what government *could* do and what it *must* do for its people have been transformed. One striking example has been the growing and changing involvement of the government in matters of health. But there are many others, from controlling the economy to combating poverty to protecting consumers, as we shall see in Parts 4 and 5 of this book.

Each of these is a controversial area in two senses. First, the very *fact* of government involvement is opposed by some and supported by others. President Reagan has led the opposition to some of these programs, as we shall see. Second, the *actual types* of involvement the government undertakes are controversial. Debates over whether government should act in a given area are instances of the politics of domain—disputes over what domains or realms government should enter.

The Politics of Policy

When government does decide to make policy in a given area, it is usually responding to desires of, or pressures from, organized groups having a special interest in that area. The politics of policy concerns which decisions are to be made on a given question. It involves questions concerning the objectives and calculations of actors as well as debates between advocates of various proposals. In the case of tax policy, for example, some assert a right to property—to keep what one makes. Others assert a right to government services and therefore recognize the right of government to collect taxes to pay for them. All of these claims or assertions can be thought of as competing assertions about rights. Other debates involve the question of the appropriate criteria for decisions about whom to tax at what rates—criteria such as individual and economic efficiency. Such disputes may involve many different areas but are aspects of the politics of policy, which will be our focus in Parts 4 and 5.

The Politics of Participation

The founders debated not only what the government should do but also who should be involved in its activities. Who, in other words, should act as the government for the people? We'll examine that debate in Chapter 1, and we'll see in Chapter 3 how participation has expanded throughout our history.

Controversy always invites participation because there is room for great debate as to how things should be done. But complexity tends to discourage participation by all but those with a special interest in what the government does. The special interests have always been the most active participants in American politics. But this large role for special interests has also been controversial, for there was, and is, little agreement on the answer to two other key questions.

How Much Should the People Be Involved in Government?

One of the strongest cries of the rebellious colonists was "No taxation without representation." And so the founders began with the assumption that the people should have representation in the government. But what form was that to take?

Today, the most obvious form of participation is voting. But, as we shall see in Chapter 3, the right to vote belonged only to adult white male property owners in the early years of this country. It has been a long and difficult struggle to extend that right first to adult white males without property, then to black males, then to women and to Native American Indians, and finally to 18-to-20-year-olds.

This movement toward **democracy** (from a Greek word meaning "rule by the people") has also helped to open up to more people other types of participation, such as running for office and serving in appointed government positions. But even this has not resolved the basic questions of who shall rule and who shall have influence.

How Should People Be Involved in Government?

In the making of tax policy, you probably did not play a role. Nor, in fact, did I. Nor, indeed, did most of the American people. But each of us could have, had we chosen to do so, because the key decisions were made in Congress. The people who did play key roles were representing special interests. They did so by trying to influence representatives. How? By providing information about their views on the issues and arguments in support of them. Also, they commonly contributed to representatives' campaign funds. Such activities are examples of the politics of influence in the policy process. We'll encounter many more in coming chapters.

THE POLITICS OF EXPERTISE

There is another sort of politics, in addition to disputes over domain, policy, and participation. It gets less attention from citizens and even scholars than it deserves. It is the politics of **expertise**.

We live in a world that is very complex and often difficult to understand. As a result, we—both citizens and politicians—depend upon the advice of experts in many areas. For example, we turn to experts to learn the likely effects of various proposals, what can be done and what should be done to achieve particular objectives as well as how what we wish to do can be done.

We usually turn to experts because we have no other choice. We cannot specialize as experts can, so we cannot know the answers that experts know. Of course, experts aren't always right.

In the case of taxes, almost all the experts argued that major tax reform was impossible. The Tax Reform Act of 1986 proved them wrong. How did it happen? A popular president made it his highest domestic policy priority and pressured members of his own party to support it even though they feared opposition from business. Democrats supported it for fear they would be blamed by many Americans if they opposed tax relief. But, equally important, the groundwork for it had been laid by the hard work of tax scholars and by politicians such as Bradley and Gephardt, who had developed the proposal of a "fair tax" that was generally similar to what Reagan eventually proposed. These ideas were ready, just waiting for the right moment—which Reagan provided.

Bradley in fact had managed to shape the actual tax-reform debate by combining in his own proposal both lower tax rates—a traditional conservative, Republican desire—and the elimination of unfair loopholes—a traditional liberal, Democratic program. This combination was eventually coupled with Reagan's insistence on revenue neutrality. Most taxpayers come from the middle class, which produces most of the income tax revenue. If the rates the middle class pays are cut, the only way to obtain the same revenue is to raise the rates on other taxpayers. Eliminating loopholes helped somewhat but left some $120 billion in lost revenue over five years. The only other place that this money could come from was business. Business tax rates were also to be cut, which meant that even more tax breaks for business had to go as well. Among these were special deductions for investment in new machinery. The result was that some parts of business supported the proposal while other parts opposed it.

The same sort of split occurred among other special interests. One reason was that even the experts disagreed over what the long-term effects of the reform would turn out to be.

The president, we recall, said it would produce new jobs and fight poverty. Most experts agreed that the poor would benefit because so many of them would no longer have to pay taxes. They calculated that the average family in poverty would save about $1000 a year.

The tax experts also calculated that about 60 percent of taxpayers would receive a tax cut. However, for most of them the loss of deductions for such things as interest on credit-card debt and sales taxes would probably wipe out much of the gain from lower rates.

Experts had the greatest difficulty agreeing on the likely effects of the tax reform on various businesses. Take the case of real estate. Ownership of land and buildings has long been one of the most "tax-advantaged" activities. Speculators received major tax advantages for borrowing money to hold land for later development or for building offices and stores and homes for later occupancy. The tax

A Summary of the Tax Bill
• a distillation of all that has been written and said about it.

CATEGORY	EFFECT
Lower Incomes	Huge percentage decrease. Dollar amount insignificant.
Middle Incomes	It depends. How do you define middle? What are your deductions? Are you married? Why? Net effect will be about the same.
Upper Incomes	You could get clobbered. But you won't.
Super-Rich	Nothing mortals do applies to you.
Business	Very anti-business, except the pro-growth nature of the bill will offset this.
The Economy	Best thing ever for the economy, though canceled out by the anti-business provisions.
Accountants	Will be put out of work. Right into lavish retirement.

ONWARD TO THE DEFICIT!

(By Toles for *The Buffalo News*. Reprinted by permission of Universal Press Syndicated.)

reform removed most of these advantages. In fact, the rich investors in real estate stand to lose $50 billion in benefits over the first five years of the reform. This explains why real estate lobbyists fought the bill ferociously. Martin Feldstein, originally President Reagan's chief economist, wrote that rents on apartments would go up markedly because of the loss of special deductions.[13] But George Gilder, a journalist specializing in economics, argued that the reform would "shift the balance of power in real estate from the owners of land to the improvers of it." The result would be better buildings, including lower-cost housing. "The strong movement in the real-estate industry away from tax dodge properties foreshadows a major shift in the entire economy toward the creation of real income and value as opposed to [financial] wheeling and dealing. . . . Americans who know how to create and deliver goods and services—especially housing—will prosper as never before."[14]

So the experts disagreed about real estate. They also disagreed about the effects of tax reform on other parts of the economy and on the economy as a whole. Feldstein argued that "the changes in business investment rules . . . will hurt productivity-increasing investments in plant and equipment. That decline in investment will . . . reduce economic growth in the longer run." On the other

[13]Martin Feldstein, "Rents Will Rise," *Washington Post National Weekly Edition*, September 15, 1986, p. 29.
[14]George Gilder, "Tax-Reform Critics Should Have Second Thoughts," *Wall Street Journal*, May 29, 1986.

hand, economist Michael Evans argued that "the longer-term implications of tax reform are positive for both real growth and productivity." And Allen Sinai, an economist for an investment banker, concluded that "because the tax bill is approximately revenue-neutral over a five-year period, it is likely to be 'growth-neutral' as well."[15] These examples of differing expert judgments could be multiplied many times.

What are we to make of such disagreements among experts? You and I aren't economists. I don't know the truth about the effects of the tax-reform act, and neither do you. Neither did the politicians who voted it into law. In fact, the House committee that developed the first reform bill had over 400 studies of the economic effects of various tax changes to rely on. Of course, these studies disagreed with each other too. And so did the lobbyists for the various special interests. They didn't know either. In fact, neither did the economists.[16] But this is just the kind of problem we always seem to face on controversial issues in politics. When experts disagree, we have to make up our own minds anyway because we have to decide how to live our own lives and which positions to take on questions of what the government should do.

In the face of such disagreement among the actors and often among the experts, what does the average citizen—or the politician—do? He or she has to decide whom to believe. Each side takes a position. Each side cites the views of experts. At first, the contest is one between two views: one which says that tax reform will be good for the economy and the other which says that it won't. What happens, though, is that when experts disagree, the argument tends to shift to the question of whose experts should be believed. Which experts are more expert? In other words, each side begins to make claims to authority for its experts. Each side claims that you should believe its experts rather than the other side's experts. Thus, we have a case of the politics of expertise—of expert opinion or commentary.

One tactic in such disputes is to focus on the *qualifications* of the experts: where they work, where they studied, what research they've pub-

lished, which commissions they've served on, and so on. Another strategy is to question the motivations of the other side's experts. Experts used by the real estate interests are criticized as being in the pay of investors and so not really impartial. Experts on the other side may be criticized because they are paid by, or their research is financed by, others who may stand to benefit from the new law or even by the government.

In other words, each side uses arguments and research findings to support its claims, and each attacks the other for the arguments and evidence it offers. Each side wants to convince the other to let *it* decide what should be done about tax policy. Each claims the authority to decide not only for the other but also for the rest of us what government policy will be on taxes. This sort of dispute—in which each party claims the authority to decide the question for others, and both sides disagree—is what we always find in politics. When it involves experts and their claims about reality, we can refer to it as an instance of the politics of expertise. But even when experts are not involved, such conflicts among images of reality are instances of politics.

THE NATURE OF POLITICS

A political question arises any time two people or groups or institutions disagree about something, when each claims the authority to decide the question, to resolve the dispute, as he, she, or it sees fit.

Politics, in other words, is *dispute over claims to the authority to decide what some part of reality is or should be*.

We get the term *politics* from the ancient Greeks. It comes from their word *polis*, which referred to "the city," the largest political unit the Greeks had. But the word really referred to the whole people and how they lived their lives together. A leading expert on ancient Greece, H. D. F. Kitto, wrote that the polis was

. . . so much more than a form of political organization. The polis was a living community, based on kinship, real or assumed—a kind of extended family, turning as much as possible of life into family life, and of course having its family quarrels, which were the more bitter because they were family quarrels. . . . In the winning of his livelihood, [the Greek] was essentially individualistic; in the filling of his life he was essentially "communist." Religion, art, games, the discussion of things—all these were needs of life

[15]These quotes are from "Tax Bill Assessment," *Austin American-Statesman*, September 28, 1986.
[16]Economists rarely agree. See Bruno S. Frey et al., "Consensus and Dissension among Economists: An Empirical Inquiry," *American Economic Review* 74 (1984), 986–94.

that could be fully satisfied only through the polis—not, as with us, through voluntary associations of like-minded people, or through entrepreneurs appealing to individuals. . . . Moreover, he wanted to play his own part in running the affairs of the community.[17]

Power and Authority

Any ruler, no matter how he or she becomes ruler, will have power, or else he or she will not last long in office. As we noted above, by power we mean the capacity to make people act in accord with one's own wishes when they would rather act differently. **Power** thus is the ability to change people's behavior.[18]

Guns can give you power. So can money. So, sometimes, can a loud voice, if it makes it possible for you to be heard and to be convincing in your commands. But power, raw power, is not really very efficient in governing, as rulers in dictatorships quickly find out. The problem with power is that you have to keep using it in order to get your way. This is very costly in term of energy, bullets and bombs, money, vocal chords, or whatever you are using to make people obey you.

Governments rarely have enough resources—soldiers, police, spies, plus money and goods—to rule by power alone. How long, after all, can one hold an entire population at gunpoint? They must instead rule by **authority**. If we say, "He's an authority on how to play split end," or "She's an authority on the Civil War," we mean that the person knows so much about the subject that we should take his or her word for it. Authorities are people who are known to be able to do something and are accepted as having that ability. In this sense, a football authority in sports is like a ruling authority in government. People know his or her power and accept it. They know a football authority has the power to describe the pass patterns a split end runs and to explain why they work or don't work against particular defenses. People also know a ruling or governmental authority has the power to make

them do what he or she orders them to do. The authority may perhaps call out the police to jail a lawbreaker or order a bureaucrat to perform some duty. The fact that we know certain people are authorities on certain things means that we do not have to keep testing them but instead can take their word for it.

In politics, therefore, authority is recognized or accepted power. We often speak of the power of the president. Many people say the president has become too powerful; many say that President Nixon abused his power as president. But most of the time we really mean *authority* rather than just *power*, when we speak this way. Most governments, and most officials, operate most of the time with authority rather than with raw, direct power. And this is where elections come in. We can think of our system of elections as a *way of creating and maintaining political*, or ruling, *authority* in our political system.

When we elect someone to office, we grant him or her power, of course. A president, once elected, can use the army and the FBI, just as a mayor can use the local police, to influence or control people's behavior. But even more important, *election grants someone authority* because we all recognize that elections are the way we choose our rulers.

In later chapters, we shall see how politics arises in elections, how it arises in Congress, how it arises in policy making—and even how it arises in our everyday lives. Our greatest interest in this book will be in the governmental politics that involves citizens as candidates, as voters, as activists, and as leaders.

Most of the time in life there will be disputes over claims to authority. Parties who are disputing will tend to make appeals—to voters, to judges, to the president, to Congress, or whatever. Often these appeals will be accepted, in which cases the political dispute is over and things can go on without further political struggle. But when such appeals are rejected or contested, we're back to politics as usual. Voters may reject a candidate, or another candidate may appear to contest the election. Judges may reject an argument in court, or a loser in court may contest a judgment and appeal to a higher court. Congress may reject a bill proposed by the president by refusing to pass it, or the president may reject a bill passed by Congress by vetoing it.

Thus, in our system disputes over claims to au-

---

[17]H. D. F. Kitto, *The Greeks* (Baltimore: Penguin, 1951), p. 78.

[18]Political scientists and philosophers are still debating about how best to define power. The definition we use here is a clear, simple version of that which is now most widely accepted. For discussions of the problem of definition and examples of many different approaches to the study of power, see Roderick A. Bell, David V. Edwards, and R. Harrison Wagner, eds., *Political Power: A Reader in Theory and Research* (New York: Free Press, 1969).

thority are resolved through politics. People preferring different answers to a question meet and compete in politics, and one side wins. At that point, the question is answered—at least until the next election or the next vote in Congress or the next constitutional amendment. But this view is a bit too simple.

Basic questions are rarely conclusively answered in our system, even when one candidate wins a landslide victory in an election. Here is where the division of power between levels and the separation of power between branches become so important. Questions are not answered by elections so much as they are by legislation. But they are not even answered by legislation until that legislation is implemented or executed. That requires the participation of the president and the millions of bureaucrats who make up the executive branch—and often state and local governments as well. Further, the courts may also intervene and change the answer if someone appeals to them.

No two people see things quite the same, and so everybody thinks and acts somewhat differently. These differences, these disputes and their resolutions—however temporary they prove to be—are what make politics interesting and frustrating and important—and a challenge to study. It is on these sorts of disputes and their resolutions that we'll be focusing throughout the rest of the book.

Because we shall focus on disputes among political actors concerning who should decide what is to be done, we shall need to know how these political actors—including, often, citizens like us—see the world. This means we must learn about their *images of reality*—the pictures they have in their minds. It also means we must try to understand their *experiences* in the political world. To learn what it is like to act in politics, we shall examine, for example, a day in the life of the president. We shall also cover a day in the life of a member of the United States Congress—Senator Bill Bradley,[19] a father of tax reform—and look at the typical experience of other political figures as well. Much of our attention, in other words, will be on the images of reality that shape the behavior of people active in politics. We shall also focus on the experiences of these activists—and the experiences we would likely have should we decide to involve ourselves. These will be our special concerns as we study American political institutions, processes, and policies in order to understand the nature and prospects of American politics.

To give us the background necessary for such study, we shall first examine briefly, in Chapter 1, how our present government developed from a written Constitution and the uncertain hopes of a few million people on an underdeveloped continent two centuries ago. Then, in Chapter 2, we shall see how it grew to be a federal system of some 82,000 different governments ruling some 242 million citizens in a world of over 5 billion people.

[19]For an interesting "behind-the-scenes" account of Bradley's role, see Dale Russakoff, "Bill Bradley Takes His Shot," *Washington Post National Weekly Edition*, February 23, 1987, pp. 6–9.

1

THE POLITICS OF THE ANCESTORS:
The Founders and the Constitution

The United States was born two centuries ago. The birth was slow and difficult, beginning with a war and political turmoil. The country replaced 13 colonies of Britain, which together declared their independence and then set about establishing their own government. In this chapter we'll encounter the people who founded the new country and learn what they did, why they did it, and what happened afterward. Along the way, we'll learn who our national ancestors were and why they are still important both to us and to our government. We'll also learn about the basic challenges any government must confront: controlling its people; running its political institutions, such as the Congress and the executive branch; and making policy on the important problems that face it, such as rebellions at home, military threats from other countries, and protection of hard-won liberties. ∎

THE POLITICS OF CONTROL

Any small group of people can declare itself the government of another group. However, to be taken seriously, the governing group must have the obedience of the group it claims to govern. Indeed, any would-be government must first be concerned about obedience before it can effectively make policy. We call this the politics of control. Some sort of government always exists where people are gathered into groups. It may be weak in its ability to control its own people. It may be contested by some of the people it is trying to rule. It may be grounded in tradition rather than in the sort of formal laws we are used to—but it is a government nonetheless.

When the 13 colonies declared their independence from Britain in 1776, they were rejecting the government that ruled them—a government they had previously accepted and obeyed. When the earliest colonists came to what they called the New World early in the 17th century, they encountered existing governments created by the people already there, whom we tend to call Indians. These colonists were also at the time citizens of various European states ruled by kings and queens. Some of the colonists were even sponsored and supported by their governments back home, which wanted to stake a claim to the land and resources of this "new" continent.

All of American history—almost 400 years—has been a chronicle of governments concerned with controlling their citizens. At certain key points, such as during the American Revolution or during the Civil War, there were struggles between competing governments seeking the loyalty, or **allegiance,** of a people. Government is always about control, and when control is contested, we find politics. To understand what happened two centuries ago and how politics eventually produced the government we have today, we must look briefly at the vital stages in the founding of the United States of America.

THE POLITICS OF THE FOUNDING OF THE UNITED STATES

The Colonial Origins of American Government

The Creation of Governments

The first Europeans to settle in the New World were a group of farmers sent over to establish a trading post at what they called Jamestown, in what we call Virginia. The charter their backers got from the king of England gave them "full power and authority to . . . make . . . laws . . . for the good and welfare" of the settlement and to choose their own officials. They set up a repre-

The signing of the Mayflower Compact. (The Bettmann Archive)

sentative assembly. The venture was not a commercial success, but it set the precedent for government making that was to characterize all subsequent colonial ventures here.

Thirteen years later, in 1620, a group of English Puritans called Pilgrims, who had left England for Holland, came on the *Mayflower* to the New World to set up a colony. They landed at what they called Plymouth, in what we call Massachusetts. On the way over, the male adults aboard drew up the *Mayflower Compact*, by which they constituted themselves "a civill body politick." Never before had a group of people (most of them with little education) come together to create their own government from scratch. Although the document was unknown to the king as well as to others who followed in their wake, it "proves the determination of the small group of English emigrants to live under a rule of law, based on the consent of the people, and to set up their own civil government."[1]

The Puritans of the Massachusetts Bay Company who arrived in 1629 were responsible for the first written constitutions in the New World: the *Fundamental Orders of Connecticut* (1639) and the *Massachusetts Body of Liberties* (1641). In the following century or so each of the 13 colonies came to have its own written constitution.

The Place of Constitutions

A **constitution** is a statement of the fundamental rules or laws of an organization. The word is of Latin origin, meaning "to set up, or establish, together." A constitution thus sets up or founds a political body such as a state. A **state** is a government (composed of rulers and ruled) embedded or institutionalized in a structure. To be effective, a state must have institutions that are strong enough to be accepted by the people, or the ruled, and to survive changes in the government, or the rulers. The constitutions of American states provide for governors, legislatures, and courts. Similarly, the national government has the presidency, a Congress, and a court system. The U.S. Constitution describes the structure of these institutions—how they are formed and how they relate to each other.

---

[1]Samuel Eliot Morison, "The Mayflower Compact," in *An American Primer*, ed. Daniel J. Boorstin (Chicago: Univ. of Chicago Press, 1966), p. 19. For an account of the early migrations and the development of the colonies into states, see D. W. Meinig, *The Shaping of America*, vol. 1: *Atlantic America, 1492–1800* (New Haven, CT: Yale Univ. Press, 1986).

A constitution creates the institutions of the state that will be used by the rulers and (if they are allowed to participate) the ruled. We generally think of constitutions as good things. Indeed, politicians, judges, and lawyers often talk as if such documents are almost sacred. We may therefore tend to assume that any constitution will be accepted by those who live under it. In fact, however, all constitutions are potentially controversial. They benefit some people and hurt others. They give some people what they want and deny benefits to others. Thus, even a constitution can be the subject of political battles—indeed, our national constitution has been debated throughout our history.

The situation in the colonial years was quite similar. The colonies had constitutions that established their own governments. However, each such constitution had to be approved by the colonies' master, Britain.

The Grievances

King George III and his Parliament viewed the colonies primarily as markets for goods Britain produced or purchased from its other colonies. The colonists had no representatives in the British Parliament, and yet Parliament made laws binding on them. Conflicts developed with Parliament when it imposed taxes on the colonies to help pay the costs

Samuel Adams by J. S. Copley. (Museum of Fine Arts, Boston)

of protecting them against the French and the Indians. The Stamp Act of 1765 placed taxes on newspapers, legal documents, and playing cards. Protest in the colonies led to repeal of the act the next year. In 1767, however, the Townshend Revenue Act imposed duties on tea, glass, paints, lead, and paper. Protests over the next three years resulted in the repeal of all but the duty on tea.

In 1722 Samuel Adams, in a town meeting in Boston, proposed that a "Committee of Correspondence" be established to state the rights of the colonists and correspond with other towns in New England. Within a few months, Virginians set up another such committee to correspond with the other colonies. These groups and the connections they made laid the intellectual groundwork for the growth of revolutionary sentiment.

Meanwhile, in 1773 the British government agreed to cancel all duties on tea exported by the British East India Company to the American colonies. This enabled it to undercut American tea merchants, even though the import tax of three pence per pound was retained. The result was that on December 16 Boston radicals dressed as Indians boarded British tea ships and dumped 342 chests of tea into the harbor. To punish Boston, Parliament in 1774 (1) ordered the city's port closed until the colony paid the cost of the tea, (2) banned unauthorized public meetings, and (3) required colonists to put up British troops in their homes if asked or ordered.

The First Continental Congress

Following the enactment of what the colonists called the Intolerable Acts, Rhode Island, Pennsylvania, and New York proposed the convening of a colonial congress. The Massachusetts House of Representatives then asked all colonies to hold special conventions to select delegates to be sent to Philadelphia for what became the First Continental Congress, held in September–October 1774. That Congress rejected by one vote a conservative proposal to create a grand colonial council to share governing power with the British Parliament. Instead, the Congress eventually passed resolutions calling on the colonies to send a petition to King George III, to raise their own troops (the Minutemen), and to boycott all British trade. "On a fateful October day," writes historian Roy Nichols, "these delegates agreed upon the first political organization and regulation for what they called 'our country.'"[2] They declared that a committee was to "be chosen in every county, city, and town, by those who are qualified to vote for representatives in the legislature." The duty of these committees would be to "observe the conduct of all persons" and to report in the press any violators of the trade ban. Thus, the first act of cooperation among the colonies was based on the democratic principle of election. And that act of cooperation in 1774 was the first move of the Continental Congress toward becoming, in a sense, the first national government in America—nearly two years before the Declaration of Independence.

The British, fearful of these early revolutionary developments, took preventive military action against the colonial militias at Lexington, near Boston, on April 19, 1775. Their attack provoked Paul Revere's famous warning. "The British are coming," as well as the patriots' response—later called "the shot heard around the world."

The Second Continental Congress

By the time the Second Continental Congress convened, in May 1775, the Revolution was in fact under way. Rather than creating a new continental army, the Congress simply "adopted" the army then gathering around Boston for "the general defense of the right of America." It designated Virginia Congressman George Washington as commander in chief. Still, the Congress continued to seek peaceful settlement of its grievances with Parliament, and on July 6, 1775, it declared: "We have not raised armies with ambitious designs of separating from Great Britain, and establishing independent States."

But compromise was not politically attainable, and the military encounters became both more frequent and more serious. Conflict that had been triggered largely by economic grievances became increasingly political in the public debates, with battle cries such as "No taxation without representation," referring to the absence of colonial representatives in the British Parliament.

In January 1776 a pamphlet appeared in Philadelphia bookstores that galvanized popular sentiment for independence instead of reconciliation. Written by a recent immigrant from England named Tom Paine, the pamphlet, entitled *Com-*

---

[2]Roy F. Nichols, *American Leviathan* (New York: Harper & Row, 1966), p. 47.

Thomas Paine. (Independence National Historic Park, Philadelphia)

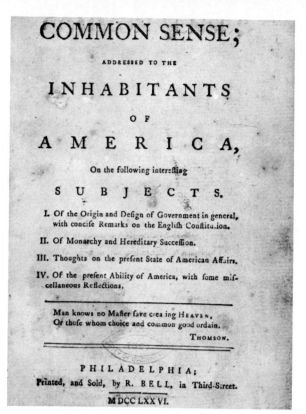

(Library of Congress)

mon Sense, rapidly spread throughout the colonies. It sold some 150,000 copies within a year—at a time when the entire colonial population (excluding slaves) was only about 3,700,000. Paine attacked hereditary rule and monarchy and argued for establishment of a republic: "A government of our own is a natural right," he argued. "There is something very absurd in supposing a continent to be perpetually governed by an island." Instead, Paine's new republic would become "an asylum for mankind" in a world in which "every spot of the old world is overrun with oppression." The genius of Paine's pamphlet was not its arguments, which were very much in the air at the time. Rather, it was his rhetorical style. Instead of the usual style of arguing with legal precedents and citing authorities, he used language "as plain as the alphabet" and offered "nothing more than simple facts, main arguments, and common sense."[3]

The Deliberations of the Founders

The Resolution of Independence

That "common sense" captured opinion in the colonies. In March the colony of South Carolina created its own constitution, thereby separating from

[3]See Eric Foner, "A Volcanic Pamphlet," *New York Times*, January 9, 1976.

Britain. On April 6, 1776, the Congress voted to open American ports to commerce with all nations except Britain—which in effect constituted a declaration of independence. In May the Congress advised all colonies to form new state governments unconnected to Britain. And then, on July 2, it adopted a Resolution of Independence: "RESOLVED, That these United Colonies are, and of right ought to be, free and independent States, that they are absolved from allegiance to the British Crown, and that all political connection between them and the State of Great Britain is, and ought to be, totally dissolved."

Americans have long thought of this step as the culmination of a deep desire for independence as such. The historical record, however, offers a somewhat different picture. The reproduction here of the full text of the resolution as it was drafted by Richard Henry Lee shows three parts: (1) a resolution of independence; (2) a call for forming foreign alliances; and (3) the charge that "a plan of confederation be prepared and transmitted to the respective colonies for their consideration and approbation."

"About the motive for declaring independence there can be no doubt," writes Garry Wills.

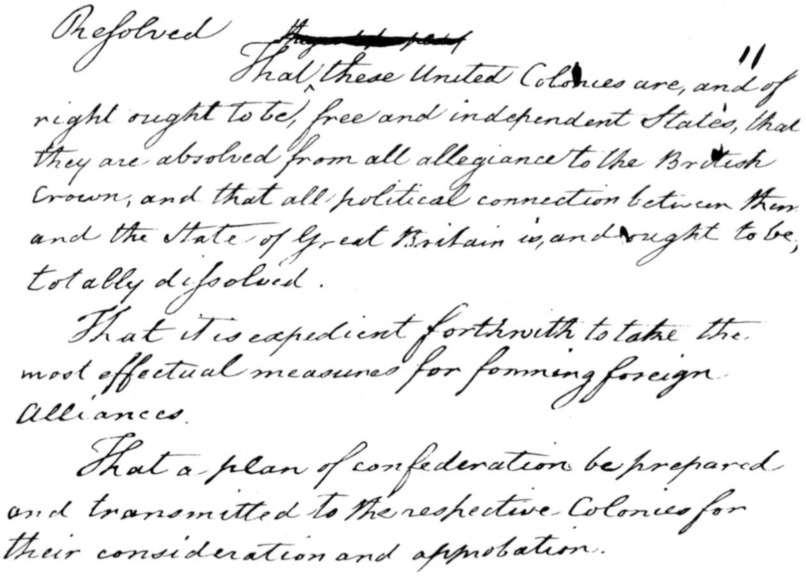

Resolved

That these United Colonies are, and of right ought to be, free and independent States, that they are absolved from all allegiance to the British Crown; and that all political connection between them and the State of Great Britain is, and ought to be, totally dissolved.

That it is expedient forthwith to take the most effectual measures for forming foreign Alliances.

That a plan of confederation be prepared and transmitted to the respective Colonies for their consideration and approbation.

FIGURE 1.1

The Resolution of Independence Introduced by Richard Henry Lee and Passed by the Continental Congress on July 2, 1776.
Source: The National Archives.

The testimony is ample and unanimous. It was not done to found a new nation—the colonies took special measures to prevent that [by their written instructions to their delegates]. It was not done to make the colonies self-governing—they were already that in fact. . . . No, there was only one motive, dwelt on repeatedly by both friends and foes of the move, that made declaring independence look attractive. It was a necessary step for the securing of foreign aid in the ongoing war effort.

. . . The colonies were in dire need of supplies and cordial relations with France, to keep their army in the field and their hopes of prevailing alive. But it was hard to get any major or continuing commitment while the colonies lacked international legal standing. They were not a corporate body that could enter into a contract. In international law they were still parts of England, engaged in a civil war.[4]

The colonies needed legitimacy in the eyes of other states. They had to become independent of Britain for that. But then they also had to form a league among themselves that would enable their joint Congress to commit all of them by treaty to an alliance with France for aid in their war effort against Britain. Thus began the drafting of a proposal for a league of the former colonies that were now self-declared independent states.

---

[4]Garry Wills, *Inventing America: Jefferson's Declaration of Independence* (New York: Random House, 1978), p. 325.

The Declaration of Independence

Once the independence resolution was passed, Thomas Jefferson argued that "a decent respect to the opinions of mankind requires that they should declare the causes which impel them to the separation." Thus, as the leader of a congressional committee Jefferson drafted a declaration of independence enumerating the major grievances. It was amended and passed on July 4, 1776. To impress and gain the support of the rest of the world, Congress sought unanimous approval of the document by the colonies. This meant that Jefferson's condemnation of slavery would have to be eliminated in order to satisfy South Carolina and Georgia. On July 19 the draft became "The Unanimous Declaration of the Thirteen United States of America." It was carefully written by hand on parchment paper by a scribe and on August 2 was signed by members of the Continental Congress. The first printed version of the Declaration is shown in Figure 1.2 (pp. 28–29) and carries only the printed signatures of John Hancock (president) and Charles Thompson (secretary).

We date the birth of the United States from July 4, 1776, but this account indicates that that is not really accurate. The Resolution of Independence on July 2 and the Declaration on July 4 formally

"The Unanimous Declaration of the Thirteen United States of America, in Congress, July 4, 1776." John Trumbell. (Architect of the Capitol)

broke the ties with Britain, but the effective break came with the April 6 closing of the ports to Britain and opening of them to others. Here Congress for the first time represented the increasingly united colonies externally. It acted for them in shaping their foreign relations and in effect established a United States able to act in the world of other states. In one sense, April 6 was the birth date of the United States.

Viewed another way, that birth occurred the previous summer, when the Continental Congress convened and "adopted" the army forming around Boston. The Revolutionary War was intended to solidify the independence of what were at first called the United Colonies and later the United States. But the rebels were united not by a common desire to join together as a unified state—for they did not feel that—but rather by their desire for independence from England. Hostilities ended in 1782, and when a peace treaty was signed on September 3, 1783, there were 13 independent states rather than 13 colonies unified by the colonial domination of Britain.

The Need for Legitimate Ruling Power

During the Revolutionary War the states tended to cooperate as if they were united into one country. In this period the Congress was at work on a formal document that would create a ruling structure for the states. This ruling power would have to be strong enough to command the respect and acceptance of the states yet limited enough in its power so that it would not scare those who still remembered the abuses of the British crown. The challenge was to create a structure with enough power to have ruling *authority* yet one limited enough to have *legitimacy*.

Thomas Jefferson by Chappell. (The Bettmann Archive)

In CONGRESS, July 4, 1776.

A DECLARATION

By the REPRESENTATIVES of the
UNITED STATES OF AMERICA,
In GENERAL CONGRESS assembled.

WHEN in the Course of human Events, it becomes necessary for one People to dissolve the Political Bands which have connected them with another, and to assume among the Powers of the Earth, the separate and equal Station to which the Laws of Nature and of Nature's God entitle them, a decent Respect to the Opinions of Mankind requires that they should declare the causes which impel them to the Separation.

WE hold these Truths to be self-evident, that all Men are created equal, that they are endowed by their Creator with certain unalienable Rights, that among these are Life, Liberty, and the Pursuit of Happiness—That to secure these Rights, Governments are instituted among Men, deriving their just Powers from the Consent of the Governed, that whenever any Form of Government becomes destructive of these Ends, it is the Right of the People to alter or to abolish it, and to institute new Government, laying its Foundation on such Principles, and organizing its Powers in such Form, as to them shall seem most likely to effect their Safety and Happiness. Prudence, indeed, will dictate that Governments long established should not be changed for light and transient Causes; and accordingly all Experience hath shewn, that Mankind are more disposed to suffer, while Evils are sufferable, than to right themselves by abolishing the Forms to which they are accustomed. But when a long Train of Abuses and Usurpations, pursuing invariably the same Object, evinces a Design to reduce them under absolute Despotism, it is their Right, it is their Duty, to throw off such Government, and to provide new Guards for their future Security. Such has been the patient Sufferance of these Colonies; and such is now the Necessity which constrains them to alter their former Systems of Government.

The History of the present King of Great-Britain is a History of repeated Injuries and Usurpations, all having in direct Object 'the Establishment of an absolute Tyranny over these States. To prove this, let Facts be submitted to a candid World.

HE has refused his Assent to Laws, the most wholesome and necessary for the public Good.

HE has forbidden his Governors to pass Laws of immediate and pressing Importance, unless suspended in their Operation till his Assent should be obtained; and when so suspended, he has utterly neglected to attend to them.

HE has refused to pass other Laws for the Accommodation of large Districts of People, unless those People would relinquish the Right of Representation in the Legislature, a Right inestimable to them, and formidable to Tyrants only.

HE has called together Legislative Bodies at Places unusual, uncomfortable, and distant from the Depository of their public Records, for the sole Purpose of fatiguing them into Compliance with his Measures.

HE has dissolved Representative Houses repeatedly, for opposing with manly Firmness his Invasions on the Rights of the People.

HE has refused for a long Time, after such Dissolutions, to cause others to be elected; whereby the Legislative Powers, incapable of Annihilation, have returned to the People at large for their exercise; the State remaining in the mean time exposed to all the Dangers of Invasion from without, and Convulsions within.

HE has endeavoured to prevent the Population of these States; for that Purpose obstructing the Laws for Naturalization of Foreigners; refusing to pass others to encourage their Migrations hither, and raising the Conditions of new Appropriations of Lands.

HE has obstructed the Administration of Justice, by refusing his Assent to Laws for establishing Judiciary Powers.

HE has made Judges dependent on his Will alone, for the Tenure of their Offices, and the Amount and Payment of their Salaries.

HE has erected a Multitude of new Offices, and sent hither Swarms of Officers to harrass our People, and eat out their Substance.

HE has kept among us, in Times of Peace, Standing Armies, without the consent of our Legislatures.

HE has affected to render the Military independent of and superior to the Civil Power.

He

FIGURE 1.2

The First Printed Version of the Declaration of Independence.

Many hoped that with independence each former colony could go its own way in its internal governance, developing its own form of government, maintaining or abolishing slavery as it saw fit, and so on. But concerning its external, or "foreign," relations, there were grave doubts. Victory over Britain did not guarantee peaceful relations with that country or with France and Spain, the other states with longstanding interests on the American continent. Nor did it guarantee peaceful relations with the native Indian tribes with whom the states shared the continent. The 13 states depended for their safety on the goodwill of the European powers. For their well-being they depended on commerce, which required protection for the merchant fleet. But the states were small and weak. As a result, a great debate arose over whether they should attempt to unite and, if so, on what terms and in what way.

Each state had drafted its own constitution. Eight of these included a "bill of rights" designed to protect citizens against the transgressions of their own independent and sovereign governments. And all of them mandated the separation of the legislative, executive, and judicial powers to protect against **tyranny**. But in every case, the legislature was predominant, even electing the executive or governor in most states. That was done so that there could be no repetition of the experience of domination at the hands of an executive with royal pretensions.

These state constitutions took care—with varying degrees of success—of the problem of **internal representation** by creating governments to represent the citizens effectively within state borders. But something more was needed to handle problems of **external representation**. Who was to represent the states in their relations with each other on matters of commerce or when disputes arose? Who was to handle relations with foreign powers—including, of course, the conduct of the Revolutionary War?

He has combined with others to subject us to a Jurisdiction foreign to our Constitution, and unacknowledged by our Laws; giving his Assent to their Acts of pretended Legislation:

For quartering large Bodies of Armed Troops among us:

For protecting them, by a mock Trial, from Punishment for any Murders which they should commit on the Inhabitants of these States:

For cutting off our Trade with all Parts of the World:

For imposing Taxes on us without our Consent:

For depriving us, in many Cases, of the Benefits of Trial by Jury:

For transporting us beyond Seas to be tried for pretended Offences:

For abolishing the free System of English Laws in a neighbouring Province, establishing therein an arbitrary Government, and enlarging its Boundaries, so as to render it at once an Example and fit Instrument for introducing the same absolute Rule into these Colonies:

For taking away our Charters, abolishing our most valuable Laws, and altering fundamentally the Forms of our Governments:

For suspending our own Legislatures, and declaring themselves invested with Power to legislate for us in all Cases whatsoever.

He has abdicated Government here, by declaring us out of his Protection and waging War against us.

He has plundered our Seas, ravaged our Coasts, burnt our Towns, and destroyed the Lives of our People.

He is, at this Time, transporting large Armies of foreign Mercenaries to compleat the Works of Death, Desolation, and Tyranny, already begun with circumstances of Cruelty and Perfidy, scarcely paralleled in the most barbarous Ages, and totally unworthy the Head of a civilized Nation.

He has constrained our fellow Citizens taken Captive on the high Seas to bear Arms against their Country, to become the Executioners of their Friends and Brethren, or to fall themselves by their Hands.

He has excited domestic Insurrections amongst us, and has endeavoured to bring on the Inhabitants of our Frontiers, the merciless Indian Savages, whose known Rule of Warfare, is an undistinguished Destruction, of all Ages, Sexes and Conditions.

In every stage of these Oppressions we have Petitioned for Redress in the most humble Terms: Our repeated Petitions have been answered only by repeated Injury. A Prince, whose Character is thus marked by every act which may define a Tyrant, is unfit to be the Ruler of a free People.

Nor

Nor have we been wanting in Attentions to our British Brethren. We have warned them from Time to Time of Attempts by their Legislature to extend an unwarrantable Jurisdiction over us. We have reminded them of the Circumstances of our Emigration and Settlement here. We have appealed to their native Justice and Magnanimity, and we have conjured them by the Ties of our common Kindred to disavow these Usurpations, which, would inevitably interrupt our Connections and Correspondence. They too have been deaf to the Voice of Justice and of Consanguinity. We must, therefore, acquiesce in the Necessity, which denounces our Separation, and hold them, as we hold the rest of Mankind, Enemies in War, in Peace, Friends.

We, therefore, the Representatives of the UNITED STATES OF AMERICA, in GENERAL CONGRESS, Assembled, appealing to the Supreme Judge of the World for the Rectitude of our Intentions, do, in the Name, and by Authority of the good People of these Colonies, solemnly Publish and Declare, That these United Colonies are, and of Right ought to be, FREE AND INDEPENDENT STATES; that they are absolved from all Allegiance to the British Crown, and that all political Connection between them and the State of Great-Britain, is and ought to be totally dissolved; and that as FREE AND INDEPENDENT STATES, they have full Power to levy War, conclude Peace, contract Alliances, establish Commerce, and to do all other Acts and Things which INDEPENDENT STATES may of right do. And for the support of this Declaration, with a firm Reliance on the Protection of divine Providence, we mutually pledge to each other our Lives, our Fortunes, and our sacred Honor.

Signed by ORDER *and in* BEHALF *of the* CONGRESS,

JOHN HANCOCK, PRESIDENT.

ATTEST.

CHARLES THOMSON, SECRETARY.

PHILADELPHIA: PRINTED BY JOHN DUNLAP.

The Articles of Confederation

The Second Continental Congress spent two and a half years developing a proposed form of government for the new states. The document finally developed was called The Articles of Confederation and Perpetual Union. The term **confederation** was chosen because it emphasized that the states were joined with (*con-*) each other, or *federated together*, to act together as the limited government to achieve certain limited common purposes.

Our present system, by contrast, is called a **federation,** or *federal system*, because it creates a national government that has the power to act on (or has power over) the states. When the southern states attempted to withdraw from the United States at the time of the Civil War, they called themselves the Confederacy to emphasize that they wished to reassert states' rights against the central government—something of a throwback to the period of the Articles of Confederation.

The government proposed by the Articles was characterized by its drafters as a "firm league of friendship." It established a one-house legislature in which each state would have one vote regardless of size, in which major legislation required a two-thirds majority, and in which there would be *no single executive*, so that there could be no would-be monarch. The Congress had virtually no major *internal* responsibilities or authority beyond establishing post offices and regulating the coinage of money. While it did have *external* powers of war and peace, in fact, it could not raise troops because it could not levy taxes. Because it had to depend on voluntary payments from member states and could not regulate commerce, it was still largely at the mercy of the states. And finally, any amendments to the Articles required the approval of all member states.[5] Figure 1.3 (p. 30) depicts the structure of government under the Articles.

[5]Merrill Jensen, *The Articles of Confederation* (Madison: Univ. of Wisconsin Press, 1940).

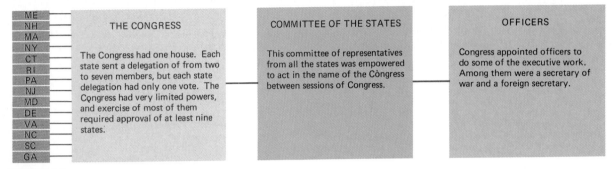

FIGURE 1.3

The Structure of Government under the Articles of Confederation.

The Experience of the New Confederate State

Despite all these constraints, designed to protect the member states against domination by the central government, it took until March 1, 1781, for the states to ratify the Articles so that Congress could proclaim the "United States of America." But no sooner had the Articles been ratified and the Revolutionary War won than the confederacy began to disintegrate. Indeed, the Congress could not even get enough of the states represented in Congress to ratify the peace treaty with Britain within the stipulated six months.

As the war came to a close, Tom Paine once again sought to rally opinion to unification. In the last issue of his periodical *The American Crisis*, he wrote:

> We have no other national sovereignty than as United States. . . . Individuals, or individual states, may call themselves what they please; but the world, and especially the world of enemies, is not to be held in awe by the whistling of a name. Sovereignty must have power to protect all the parts that compose and constitute it; and as UNITED STATES we are equal to the importance of the title, but otherwise we are not.

Abroad, American diplomats found that other powers would not make agreements on trade and other matters because they did not believe that the Congress could compel the states to abide by them. The Congress simply could not represent the confederation adequately in a world of states that were represented by monarchs and governments with effective ruling power. The Articles had failed at what they were primarily intended to do: represent the states united in the confederation to the outside world. The primary reason for this failure of external representation was the incapacity of the Congress to do what in fact it was not intended to do: represent the government of the confederation effectively to its own people by legislating, regulating commerce, levying taxes, and raising forces from the states for a national army. In other words, effective external representation required that very sort of effective internal representation that the former colonies resisted because they feared reemergence of the monarchy they had rebelled against.

THE POLITICS OF THE FRAMING OF THE CONSTITUTION

A nation—the United States—had been founded. But neither the institutions provided for by the Articles nor the government established by the founders worked well enough or proved strong enough. The nation's experience under the Articles of Confederation led eventually to a decision to refound the United States by creating yet another document—a new constitution. But first, those favoring a stronger national government sought a way to amend the Articles.

The Call to a Convention

Because amendment required unanimity, the call to a constitutional convention did not come from the Congress, which could not achieve unanimity on anything by that time. Instead, the Virginia legislature in January 1786 called for a meeting of all the states. That meeting, held in Annapolis in September but attended by only five states, then called for a new convention to meet in Philadelphia in May 1787. Once the Congress saw, in February 1787, that the meeting would take place, it hesitantly approved such a convention "for the sole and express purpose of revising the Articles of Confederation."

Delegates to the Convention

The states appointed 74 men to attend the new convention. The 55 who actually attended averaged 42 years of age, were generally college educated (something very rare at the time), and were predominantly lawyers (42 of them), businessmen, and farmers. Many of them had served as soldiers in the Revolutionary War. Generally, they represented wealthy property owners rather than the working class.

This fact has led to sustained debate among historians over the ultimate significance of the Revolution and the Constitution. In 1913 historian Charles A. Beard wrote a very influential historical study, *An Economic Interpretation of the Constitution*, which emphasized the overriding importance to the framers of achieving economic stability and creating opportunities for their own financial gain.[6] It is true that wealth was overrepresented, largely because in many states the right to vote was restricted to property owners. At the same time, the expectations of the poor, many of whom had participated enthusiastically in the Revolution, were being disappointed by the failure of the states and the Articles to assist debtors and to foster social reform. By the time the convention met, as historian Jesse Lemisch has found, there were "waves of bitterness sweeping through the bottom layers of the population," whose members had concluded that the emerging government did not care about them and their concerns. Indeed, on the eve of the convention, following a long history of unfair taxation, Massachusetts farmers whose land was being seized for failure to pay their mortgage debts united behind Daniel Shays, a Revolutionary War veteran, and stormed an arsenal to seize weapons. They were defeated by the militia, but their daring and desperate act raised fears of popular rebellion in the minds of many in

America and Europe. In addition, this action strengthened opposition to popular participation in politics among conservative elements of the population and increased support for a strong central government able to suppress rebellion and preserve the peace. Shays's Rebellion came at a time when more and more merchants and artisans, like farmers, were becoming increasingly disaffected with political domination by those with economic power.

"The things that were suggested by artisans and shopkeepers," says historian Gary B. Nash, "would make people's hair stand on end—limits on income, redistribution of property, rights of women, abolition of slavery."[7] It was as if the people—or at least a fair fraction of them—had taken seriously the argument of the Declaration: "We hold these Truths to be self-evident, that all Men are created equal, that they are endowed by their Creator with certain unalienable Rights, that among these are Life, Liberty, and the Pursuit of Happiness."

The Decision to Refound

The Declaration continued:

> That to secure these Rights, Governments are instituted among Men, deriving their just Powers from the Consent of the Governed, that whenever any Form of Government becomes destructive of these Ends, it is the Right of the People to alter or to abolish it, and to institute new Government, laying its Foundation on such Principles and organizing its Powers in such Form, as to them shall seem most likely to effect their Safety and Happiness.

Those men meeting in Philadelphia—eight of whom had signed the Declaration—were in fact once again following the dictates of their consciences. They were appointed to revise the Articles, but they immediately decided instead to start from scratch and draft a new constitution—something they had to do in secrecy because it was "extralegal" (that is, not within their legal powers).

Thus, instead of being amenders, they became what we call **framers**. They framed, or conceived and wrote, a new constitution.

[6]Charles Beard, *An Economic Interpretation of the Constitution* (New York: Macmillan, 1913). But see also the critiques of Beard's work: Robert E. Brown, *Charles Beard and the Constitution* (New York: Norton, 1956); Forrest McDonald, *We the People: The Economic Origins of the Constitution* (Chicago: Univ. of Chicago Press, 1958); and Lee Benson, *Turner and Beard* (Glencoe, IL: Free Press, 1960).

[7]These quotations come from Israel Shenker, "Historians Still Debating the Meaning of the American Revolution—If It Was a Revolution," *New York Times*, July 6, 1976, p. 13. See also Nash's book, *The Urban Crucible: Social Change, Political Consciousness, and the Origins of the American Revolution* (Cambridge, MA: Harvard Univ. Press, 1979).

George Washington presides over the signing of the Constitution. Painting by Thomas Rossitier. (Independence National Historic Park, Philidelphia)

Concerns of the Framers

The framers of the Constitution sought to establish a new ruling power that was limited enough so that individual rights and states' rights would survive. Still, it had to be powerful enough to achieve effective internal and external representation for a *United* States of America to succeed the United *States* of America. The framers sought to establish political liberty for the population in the face of four serious threats.

1. Foreign enemies. The most immediate threat to the newly independent states was posed by hostile powers abroad—especially Britain, which was expected to seek to reimpose its will whenever possible. Coping with this threat required a government with strong powers of external representation. That government would have to be able to act so as to earn legitimacy in foreign relations.

2. State factionalism. The states disagreed among themselves about almost everything—from taxes to regulation of trade, and from foreign affairs to slavery. They also disagreed about how strong the government needed to be and how it should be structured. They all had the experience of living under the Articles, both before the latter were ratified (when they were observed largely because the states were at war) and after ratification. All recognized that they were inadequate, and all agreed rather quickly that the new government must have a broader set of powers over the states.

The common experience of the war had laid the groundwork for this. But the prospect of **national supremacy** raised in many minds the third threat.

3. A tyrannical central government. Some of the framers feared *all* government because in their experience governments tended to claim too much power and use it against the citizens. They feared the return to a monarchy, something they had only recently overthrown. They were afraid that any single executive would tend to become a tyrant. Thus, they believed it necessary to build in checks or limits on the government.

4. Human nature. Underlying all the other threats in the minds of the framers was a fourth and fundamental threat: human nature. They saw love of power as a natural human attribute and feared that any monopoly over the instruments of power would lead to tyranny. But this view was not one of despair. It was, instead, as Samuel Beer has written, "a workable pessimism . . . which held that if control over these instruments were properly divided and balanced, power could be made to check power so that it would be used only for the common good."[8]

The story of the Constitutional Convention is the story of the efforts of the framers to come to terms with these four obstacles by compromising their personal differences and controlling the powers they granted to the government.

---

[8]Samuel Beer, "Federalism, Nationalism and Democracy in America," *American Political Science Review* 72, no. 1 (March 1978), 12–13.

Major Debates at the Constitutional Convention

Electoral Powers

The framers set about determining who would *control* the national government—who would have ruling power. The first specific question was whether the number of representatives in Congress would be determined on the basis of population or would be equal for each state. The large states, not surprisingly, favored population, as proposed in the Virginia Plan. The small states favored the equality prescribed in the New Jersey Plan. That dispute was settled by the Connecticut Compromise. This provided for two houses of Congress: the House of Representatives, in which the size of each state's delegation would be determined on the basis of population, and the Senate, in which each state would have equal representation. The power to elect senators was then given to the state legislatures. (The Seventeenth Amendment, ratified in 1913, finally gave this power to the citizens of the states.)

The power to elect the president was granted to a novel creation, the **electoral college**, which was to be made up of citizens from each state, chosen as each state legislature specified.

The states thus received major roles in selecting both senators and the president. Yet many of the framers, as we have noted, were concerned about tendencies toward factionalism. They thus decided to grant the power to elect representatives directly to the people within each state, according to population. The reasoning behind this decision was significant. It was argued by some who favored greater democracy that representatives should have very small districts so that they could come to know and accurately reflect the particular interests of their constituents. However, the majority view was that districts should be moderately large so that representatives would not be parochial. Borrowing an argument from the Scottish philosopher David Hume (1711–1776), they claimed that larger districts would enable—or even force—representatives to refine the interests and opinions of voters in their districts. Indeed, James Madison explicitly commended the greater social and economic diversity in the makeup of such larger districts be-

cause it would counter tendencies toward narrow factionalism in the states and enable the common interest to prevail.[9]

Slavery and Representation

Another major struggle occurred over slavery. Slavery was not outlawed by the Constitution, as delegates from some northern states advocated. Indeed, Article I, Section 9, specifically prohibited any law ending the importation of slaves before 1808. But slaves, who made up 30 percent of the population in five southern states, were not counted as full persons for congressional representation, as southern states sought. Instead, another compromise provided that slaves were to be counted as "**three-fifths persons**" for both apportionment of congressional seats and apportionment of direct federal taxes among the states.[10]

The Underlying Issue

All these major battles reflected the basic underlying issue: whether this new sovereign government was to be a government of (over) the states (like the Congress set up by the Articles, only stronger) or a government of (over) the people. Although they were appointed by state legislatures, the framers did not derive their authority from the existing government of the states, which they were flatly (but secretly) contravening. They believed that government *should*, although it rarely did, derive its authority from the people. By providing that their draft constitution be ratified by special state conventions rather than by the Congress or the state legislatures, they sought to institutionalize this "consent of the governed." At the same time they would bypass the supporters of the Articles of Confederation in the state legislatures.[11]

---

[9]See Jean Yarbrough, "Representation and Republicanism: Two Views," *Publius*, 10 (Spring 1979), pp. 77–98.

[10]The southern states did not, of course, accept the logical extension of their argument that if slaves should be counted as persons for representation in Congress, they should also be allowed to vote for those representatives. Indeed, at this time, as we shall see in Chapter 3, only adult white males owning property were generally thought to be suitable voters.

[11]For an account of the origins and development of the notion of popular sovereignty, see Paul K. Conkin, *Self-Evident Truths* (Bloomington: Indiana Univ. Press, 1974), p. 1.

The Politics of Participation: A Republic or a Democracy?

Although the Preamble to the Constitution begins with the words "We the People of the United States . . . do ordain and establish this Constitution for the United States of America," the framers did not intend that the people play a major role in the day-to-day affairs of the government.

Their support was not for a **democracy.** The people scared them. The poor might be stampeded into governmental plunder of the rich; the rich might tend to exploit the rest by seizing control of the governmental machinery and using it for their own benefit. Thus, the people or, more exactly, those who met voting requirements—would be allowed to vote only for members of the House of Representatives once they had ratified the Constitution. Should it be necessary, they might also vote on amendments to the Constitution to renew popular consent.

But at the same time, the framers feared the chief executive, who might become another despotic king. They sought to avoid a **monarchy,** in which authority resides in a crown, and instead wanted to establish a republic. The term *republic* comes from the Latin words *res* ("thing") and *publica* ("public") and so refers to a "public thing," or "public domain," as contrasted with "royal domain" in a monarchy. A **republic** is a nonmonarchical government whose authority resides ultimately in the people, who delegate this power to their elected officials. The republic the founders designed[12] became a *democratic* republic in the current sense only very gradually. This change occurred as the Bill of Rights was ratified, as the right to vote was extended, and as the people achieved the right to elect their senators and, indirectly, their president. As Martin Diamond has written: "For the founding generation it was liberty that was the comprehensive good, the end against which political things had to be measured; and democracy was only a form of government which, like any other

form of government, had to prove itself adequately instrumental to the securing of liberty."[13]

In this manner the framers resolved, temporarily, the dispute we now call the politics of participation. The people were to have a limited role in this government. But where, then, was the ruling power to reside?

The Disposition of Power

The task, as the framers saw it, was to design the institutions of the republic so that they would meet two different criteria. In terms of internal ruling power, the institutions had to be powerful enough to preserve order without compromising individual freedom. In terms of external ruling power, they had to be powerful enough to preserve the independence and security of the country in its foreign relations. How could this be achieved? The framers developed a constitutional system characterized by a unique combination of three qualities: division, separation, and confrontation of powers.

Division of Powers

Division of powers or division of capabilities among the national government, the state governments, and the people. The federal structure made it possible for the framers of the system, in the Tenth Amendment of the Bill of Rights, to *reserve all powers not delegated* to the national government, plus all powers prohibited to it, to the states and the people.

Separation of Powers

Separation of powers or separation of functions in the national government among three branches: the executive branch, the legislative branch, and the judicial branch.

Confrontation of Powers

Confrontation of powers or confrontation of responsibilities via **checks and balances** among the branches and between both houses of Congress.

---

[12]For interesting studies of the founders' views and disagreements, see the special Spring 1979 issue of *Publius* on "Republicanism, Representation, and Consent: Views of the Founding Era." See also Samuel H. Beer, "The Rule of the Wise and the Holy," *Political Theory* 14, no. 3 (August 1986), 391–422, for an analysis of the revolutionary break that the choice of republicanism was.

[13]Martin Diamond, "The Declaration and the Constitution: Liberty, Democracy, and the Founders," in *The American Commonwealth 1976,* ed. Nathan Glazer and Irving Kristol (New York: Basic Books, 1976), p. 47. See also a reprint of other writings by Diamond, *The Founding of the Democratic Republic* (Itasca, IL: Peacock, 1981).

Each of the three branches had its own functions, but no one branch could act alone for long if one or both of the other branches were troubled by its actions. The executive branch needs a budget passed by Congress to carry out its functions. Major presidential appointments and all treaties made by the president must be approved by the Senate.

On the other hand, both houses of Congress must reach agreement on a bill before that bill can pass. For the bill to become law, the president must sign it. There are many other examples, as we'll see in Part 3. (The major ones are summarized in Figure 1.4.) Thus, each branch can *check*, or delay the action of, another branch. Further, two branches

FIGURE 1.4
The Separation and Confrontation of Powers in the Three Branches of National Government.

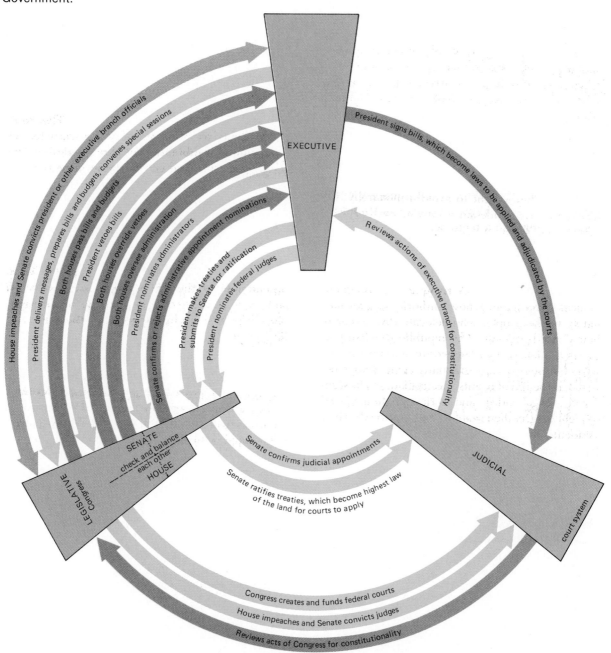

in conflict have powers that can result in *balances*, or stalemates, until one convinces the other or they reach a compromise.

Checks and balances can be important in the operation of our government. For example, consider relations between the president and the Congress. In two centuries the president has vetoed some 2400 bills passed by Congress. Congress was able to override or overcome only about 100 of these vetoes by once again approving the bill in question, this time by a two-thirds vote. The Senate has also rejected 8 cabinet and 27 Supreme Court nominations made by the president. These totals are relatively small, considering the vast number of bills passed and nominations made. However, it is important to realize that the very existence of the checks-and-balances system may lead a president to refrain from nominating someone unlikely to be confirmed. Likewise, anticipation of a presidential veto may lead Congress to decide to modify a bill in advance. And belief that Congress will override a veto may lead presidents to sign bills they don't like. As so often happens in politics, existence of a particular structure creates *expectations that modify behavior in advance*. Thus, the formal record of vetoes, overrides, and refusals to confirm will not reveal the true role of checks and balances in influencing outcomes.

The qualities of division, separation, and confrontation of powers satisfied most citizens that the president would not be either strong enough or independent enough to threaten their liberties. At the same time, however, these qualities satisfied the framers that the chief executive would be strong enough to govern the country despite the obvious powers of the legislative branch—including its checks on presidential actions. They believed that the president's capacity to check Congress's actions and so create a balance of stalemate would induce Congress to compromise when important national interests were at stake.[14]

The Mixture of Powers

The practical effect of these three qualities turned out to be more complicated than anyone expected. As we shall see, there have been periods in which the legislative branch predominated and others in which the executive was more powerful. But throughout our history our government has been characterized by a fourth quality, which we might call the *mixture of powers*. In other words, each branch inevitably gets involved in doing the other branches' primary functions to some degree. The president has become the chief legislator, in the sense that the chief executive proposes most of the major bills Congress passes—as we shall see in Chapter 8. Congress has become an executor of the law by specifying just how the executive branch should act and by checking up to see that it does so—as we shall see in Chapter 10. And the Supreme Court has immersed itself in legislation and execution to extents undreamed of by the founders—as we shall see in Chapter 11.

The Distinctiveness of the Disposition of Power

The combination of these three provisions—division, separation, and confrontation of powers—gave the Constitution its distinctive character. Nothing like it had ever been developed before. Not that each component, each underlying idea, was new—far from it. The emphasis on liberty can be traced to the writings of the British philosopher John Locke (1632–1704), which most of the framers had read. The finely developed attention to the structure of the government—down to its checks and balances—reflects the influence of the French political philosopher Montesquieu (1689–1755). Others, such as the English legal theorist Blackstone, the French social theorist Rousseau, and the English political theorist Hobbes, were also "present in spirit" to influence the framers.[15] Historian Bernard Bailyn, after studying the writings of American authors and activists in the revolutionary era, concluded: "The theory of politics that emerges from the political literature of the pre-Revolutionary years rests on the belief that what lay behind every political scene, the ultimate explanation of every political controversy, was *the*

---

[14]For an interesting discussion on the origins of these ideas, see Conkin, *Self-Evident Truths*, chap. 7. See also E. P. Panagopoulos, *Essays on the History and Meaning of Checks and Balances* (Lanham, MD: Univ. Press of America, 1985).

[15]The major relevant works are Locke, *Two Treatises of Government*; Montesquieu, *The Spirit of the Laws*; Blackstone, *Commentaries on the Laws of England*; Rousseau, *The Social Contract*; and Hobbes, *Leviathan*. See Donald S. Lutz, "The Relative Influence of European Writers on Late Eighteenth-Century American Political Thought," *American Political Science Review* 78 (March 1984), 189–97.

Alexander Hamilton by John Trumbull. (National Portrait Gallery, Smithsonian Institution)

the convention's deliberations. Furthermore, the Federalists were in large part merchants, bankers, lawyers, planters, and speculators. Living in urban areas with superior transport and communication, they were able to organize and campaign successfully to elect Federalists to the state conventions.

Despite these advantages, a great national debate arose in and around the state conventions. Out of that great debate came a series of essays written by Alexander Hamilton, James Madison, and John Jay. These essays were published anonymously, under the name "Publius" (Latin for "public man"), in newspapers and later in book form. In form, the essays were rather like the pieces by current columnists such as James Reston and Anthony Lewis. But in content they were much more philosophical, carrying to the people the argument for a strong political union—a *federation* (the concept that gave the papers their name) rather than the previous weak *confederation*. Known as **The Federalist Papers**, they are to this day an outstanding example of political theorizing.[18]

The Federalist Papers have received more attention than any other American theoretical writings. However, the opponents of ratification also produced lucid statements of their position. These writers generally favored republican government organized in rather small units. They wanted a government responsive to the majority in each region. Opposing the creation of the powerful central government favored by the Federalists, they came to be known as *Anti-Federalists*.[19]

As the debate between the supporters and the opponents of the new constitution developed, ratification became more difficult. Delaware ratified first, and unanimously, on December 7, 1787. Five days later Pennsylvania ratified, followed six days later by New Jersey. Georgia and Connecticut ratified in early January 1788, but there were bitter struggles in Massachusetts before it agreed. Mary-

disposition of power."[16] This constant focus on "the disposition of power" led the founders to combine ideas from philosophers and experience from the Articles of Confederation into "an elaborate and complicated division of newly created power."[17]

The Struggle over Ratification

When the Constitutional Convention completed its work on September 17, 1787, it sent the document to the Continental Congress in New York. Although it was signing its own death warrant, the Congress passed the draft on to the state legislatures, which then passed laws authorizing election of delegates to state conventions that were to vote on it.

Since communication and travel were very slow in those days, the **Federalists**—supporters of the new constitution—had a great advantage over their opponents. They knew what was being done in secret and could prepare for the political battle over ratification, whereas opponents knew nothing of

[16]Bernard Bailyn, *The Ideological Origins of the American Revolution* (Cambridge, MA: Harvard University Press, 1973), p. 55. Emphasis added. For further interesting studies, see Forrest McDonald, *Novus Ordo Seclorum: The Intellectual Origins of the Constitution* (Lawrence: Univ. Press of Kansas, 1985), and Michael Kammen, *Spheres of Liberty: Changing Perceptions of Liberty in American Culture* (Madison: Univ. of Wisconsin Press, 1986), chap. 1.

[17]Nichols, *American Leviathan*, p. 51.

[18]There are many editions of *The Federalist Papers*. The most accessible is that of Clinton Rossiter (New York: New American Library, Mentor paperback, 1961). Also helpful is the version edited by Benjamin F. Wright (Cambridge, MA: Harvard Univ. Press, 1961). For a listing and analysis of other writings by supporters of the Constitution, see Herbert J. Storing, "The 'Other' Federalist Papers," *Political Science Reviewer* 6 (Fall 1976), 215–47. And for an analytical commentary, see Morton White, *Philosophy*, The Federalist, *and the Constitution* (New York: Oxford Univ. Press, 1987).

[19]For writings by 88 opponents, see Herbert J. Storing, ed., *The Complete Anti-Federalist* (Chicago: Univ. of Chicago Press, 1981), published in seven volumes. Storing's 73-page introduction to this work has been issued as a separate paperback, *What the Anti-Federalists Were For* (Chicago: Univ. of Chicago Press, 1981).

THE

FEDERALIST:

A COLLECTION

OF

E S S A Y S,

WRITTEN IN FAVOUR OF THE

NEW CONSTITUTION,

AS AGREED UPON BY THE FEDERAL CONVENTION,
SEPTEMBER 17, 1787.

IN TWO VOLUMES.

VOL. I.

NEW-YORK:

PRINTED AND SOLD BY J. AND A. M'LEAN;
No. 41, HANOVER-SQUARE,
M.DCC,LXXXVIII.

(The Bettmann Archive)

land and South Carolina followed, and on June 21, New Hampshire became the ninth state to ratify. That was enough to put the Constitution into effect formally. But Virginia and New York were such important states that their acceptance was essential. After desperate struggles, both ratified during the summer. North Carolina did not ratify for another 15 months, and Rhode Island became the last state to agree, on May 29, 1790.

Meanwhile, Washington was elected the first president and was inaugurated on April 30, 1789. He was designated by "electors" chosen by direct elections in Pennsylvania, Maryland, Virginia, and Delaware, and by state legislatures, rather than by the people, in the other states. As it happens, the Constitution was ratified by conventions of representatives selected by only 160,000 of the 4 million citizens. So the birth of America was not very democratic—except compared to those of all other countries at that time. Nor was it very harmonious—almost immediately, strong support arose for limits on the power of the government.

Throughout this period in American history the pendulum swung between strengthening the national government—as required by the demands of internal and external representation (or by the development of effective ruling power)—and preserving and even expanding the rights and liberties of the people. The Declaration, the Revolution, and the Articles together can be seen as a movement toward liberty; the Constitution as drafted marked a return swing of the pendulum toward more effective ruling power, which inevitably threatened to curtail the individual liberty protected formally in the Articles. But this development was so novel (and so sudden and so troubling) to many citizens that it immediately stimulated a backward swing toward individual liberty. This swing was quickly expressed in the first efforts to amend the new Constitution: creation of the Bill of Rights.

THE POLITICS OF REFORM

Amending the Constitution

The Constitution was written to last. It was intended to provide continuity—a sense of national identity—after the founders were gone. Still, as Washington wrote just after its drafting:

> The warmest friends and the best supporters the Constitution has do not contend that it is free from imperfections; but they found them unavoidable, and are sensible, if evil is likely to arise therefrom, the remedy must come hereafter; . . . and as there is *a constitutional door open for it*, I think the people (for it is with them to judge), can, as they will have the advantage of experience on their side, decide with as much propriety on the alterations and amendments which are necessary, as ourselves.[20]

The "constitutional door open for it" is Article V.[21] In effect, it grants the ultimate power to amend to the states, although the process is some-

_____
[20]George Washington, letter to Bushrod Washington, November 10, 1787.
[21]For a discussion of constitutional amendment in our system and other federal systems, see William S. Livingston, *Federalism and Constitutional Change* (Oxford: Clarendon, 1956), esp. chap. 5.

Proposal	Ratification
Either: Congress proposes an amendment by passing it by a two-thirds vote in each house. It also states a time limit for completion of ratification (if it chooses to) and which of two possible ways of ratification will be used.	**Route One** Three-quarters of the state legislatures must vote favorably on it, but each can decide whether to require a simple majority vote or an unusual majority such as two-thirds in favor. **Route Two** Special conventions are called in each state, and three-quarters of them vote favorably on it.
Or: The legislatures of two-thirds of the states request a convention for proposing amendments, at which point Congress is obliged to call such a convention. The national convention then proposes an amendment for ratification by whichever of two routes Congress specified.	**Route Three** Three-quarters of the state legislatures must vote favorably on it, but each can decide whether to require a simple majority vote or an unusual majority such as two-thirds in favor. **Route Four** Special conventions are called in each state, and three-quarters of them vote favorably on it.

In practice, routes three and four have never been used; route two was used only for the Twenty-first Amendment; thus the normal route has turned out to be route one. Note also that a state cannot legally rescind (or "take back") its ratification, but it can change its mind by voting to ratify after first rejecting an amendment. After ratification by whichever route, the amendment is automatically in force—"valid to all intents and purposes, as part of this Constitution," in the language of Article V.

FIGURE 1.5
Amending the Constitution.

what more complex, as Figure 1.5, which shows the four possible ways of amending the Constitution, reveals.

The Processes of Amendment

Amendment was not meant to be easy. On certain issues, such as the outlawing of slavery by the Thirteenth Amendment (1865), the repeal of prohibition of alcoholic beverages by the Twenty-first Amendment (1933), and the extension of the vote to 18- to 20-year-olds by the Twenty-sixth Amendment (1971), the process has gone quickly. More often it takes years to get the required three-fourths of state legislatures to ratify an amendment once the Congress has proposed it by a two-thirds vote in both houses. And often Congress refuses to propose an amendment that is widely supported by public opinion—as on the question of banning school busing. Because of the large majorities required in Congress and among the states, amendments that pass tend to be concerns "whose time has come."

The Patterns of Amendment

The expansion of citizenship rights—especially suffrage, the right to vote—has been the subject of eight amendments:

- Thirteenth—abolition of slavery (1865)
- Fourteenth—citizenship rights not to be abridged by states (1868)
- Fifteenth—black suffrage (1870)
- Seventeenth—direct election by the people of their senators (1913)
- Nineteenth—women's suffrage (1920)
- Twenty-third—suffrage in presidential elections for District of Columbia residents (1960)
- Twenty-fourth—the poll tax outlawed in federal elections (1964)
- Twenty-sixth—suffrage for all citizens 18 or older (1971)

"What the people have done to the Constitution has been to make it a far more democratic document than the one they inherited from their ancestors," writes Alan Grimes. "The amendments have

. . . brought the values articulated in the Declaration of Independence into American constitutional law."[22]

But the growth of democracy has not been the only common thread running through the amendments. The growth of the role and power of central government figured especially in the Sixteenth Amendment (income tax, 1913) and the Eighteenth Amendment (prohibition of alcoholic beverages, 1919—repealed by the Twenty-first Amendment in 1933). But it also enters into most other amendments in that they generally conclude with the provision: "Congress shall have power to enforce this article by appropriate legislation."

As a result of the lengthy and demanding ratification process, only 26 amendments have been passed in some 190 years. And if we set aside the 10 amendments of the Bill of Rights, the total is only 16.

The Bill of Rights

The strongest opposition to the Constitution after it was proposed in 1787 focused on the absence of a bill of rights. Bills of rights had originated in 1689 in England with the demands of English lords that the king observe certain rights claimed by the noblemen. Eight of the new state constitutions had bills of rights designed to guarantee various individual liberties, some of them almost identical to those sought by British citizens a century earlier. The framers of the U.S. Constitution generally believed such a listing of limitations on government power to be unnecessary; they believed they were creating a government of strictly limited "enumerated" powers. But popular memories of British tyrants were still fresh in some minds. Furthermore, the Constitution did create a government with direct power over the people rather than only over the states (as was the case under the Articles). Thus, state after state demanded a bill of rights as the price for ratifying the Constitution.

In 1789, two years after the Constitution was drafted, 12 amendments were proposed and approved by the new Congress when the required two-thirds majority in each house of Congress approved them. The most important prohibited laws limiting freedom of speech, of the press, of reli-

gion, of assembly, and of protest and stated a wide range of rights of the accused. Two years later, in 1791, ratification of the first 10 amendments by the required three-fourths of the states was complete, and the new nation had what became known as the Bill of Rights.[23] We will discuss its contents in more detail in Chapter 12.

Adapting the Constitution

The Tenth Amendment, the last in the Bill of Rights, declared that "the powers not delegated to the United States by the Constitution, nor prohibited by it to the States, are reserved to the States respectively or to the people." That was a formal attempt to limit the growth of national ruling power in favor of state powers. Nonetheless, inevitably, when the first constitutional government came to power in 1789, it began to establish precedents for a strong central government. This pendulum swing in the opposite direction from the Bill of Rights was an instance of informal reform, or *adaptation*.

The Federalist Era

The Federalist Era, as the years under George Washington and John Adams came to be called, was characterized by establishment of effective *external* ruling power: Treaties were negotiated with Spain, England, and France, and financial credit with European countries was established. Effective internal ruling power, as we have noted, usually increases a state's effectiveness in dealing with other states. Here, too, America's success abroad was due largely to the fact that the government was exercising its internal ruling power directly over the people with strength and authority.

However, effective internal government was sometimes achieved at the expense of popular expectations about individual liberties and states' rights. The result was growing opposition from those who wished to limit central governmental power and expand the country westward through the admission of new states to the Union. These forces united behind the presidential candidacy of Thomas Jefferson in 1800.

---

[22]Alan P. Grimes, *Democracy and the Amendments to the Constitution* (Lexington, MA: Lexington Books, 1978), p. xi.

[23]The two that were never ratified by a sufficient number of states dealt with apportionment of the House of Representatives and the pay of senators and representatives.

John Adams by John Trumbell. (National Portrait Gallery, Smithsonian Institution)

Jefferson and the Louisiana Purchase

Ironically, it was Jefferson who presided over what may have been the most important event in the growth of centralized ruling power: the Louisiana Purchase. To understand its impact we must backtrack a bit. In 1787 while the convention in Philadelphia was drafting the Constitution, the Congress in New York was drafting the Northwest Ordinance. This law provided that the land on the frontier to the west was to be organized first into territories and then into three to five states. Each of these would be admitted to the Union as equals of the original states once it had 5000 or more residents. In other words, the new nation, instead of getting colonies like the old nations of Europe, would get new member states. Furthermore, these new states were expected to develop their own forms of self-government. This "was to be one of the important instruments that maintained experimentation in developing the capacity for self-government in the midst of the nation's spectacular ex-

The signing of the Louisiana Purchase authorization. (New York Public Library Picture Collection)

pansion of wealth and power. It gave elasticity to an organism that might otherwise have become rigid."[24]

In 1803 Jefferson's ministers in France arranged to purchase the whole Louisiana Territory—on the French condition that the land would be "incorporated into the Union" and its inhabitants made citizens. The Louisiana Purchase doubled the land mass of the United States and created great economic opportunities on that new frontier. It also offered new ground for the struggle between the proslavery and antislavery forces in the Congress, which by Article IV, Section 3, had the power to admit new states into the Union.

Experiments in self-government in the "territories," where there were no property limits on the right to vote, accelerated the trend toward greater democracy in America—a trend we will trace in Chapter 3. The admission of new states into the Union—10 by 1821, 37 to date—made certain that the territory and the economy of America would grow. It also meant that the government itself would expand in ways the founders could not have foreseen. That expansion would require more national ruling power than the Constitution provided and more governmental changes than the difficulty of constitutional amendment requirements would allow.

Opportunities for Adaptation

Jefferson had always favored **strict construction** (or literal reading) of the Constitution. He opposed the liberal or loose reading favored by those seeking to strengthen the central government. But when he was confronted with the possibility of purchasing the entire Louisiana Territory, he found nothing in the Constitution that specifically allowed such a transaction. He wrote privately that the purchase was "an act beyond the Constitution," but he overcame his constitutional scruples, and so did the Congress. In Jefferson's words, "as new discoveries are made, new truths disclosed, and manners and opinions changed . . . institutions must advance also, and keep pace with the times."

When constitutional amendment was too difficult or too time consuming, other forms of adaptation had to be found.[25] The Constitution offered three major options: First, *much constitutional language is very general*. This makes it subject to further development and interpretation. For example, its instruction to the president to "take care that the laws be faithfully executed" has allowed for most of the expansion of presidential power from George Washington onward, a subject we shall discuss in Chapter 8.

Second, *the Constitution is silent on important matters*. For example, it does not specifically grant the Supreme Court the power of "judicial review"—reviewing, and even declaring unconstitutional, lower-court decisions and laws. We shall see in Chapter 11 that this judicial review has been an important factor in American political development. The Constitution is also silent on the role of political parties (Chapter 4) and of cities (Chapter 17), both of which have gained importance partly because they were not constricted by explicit constitutional limitations.

Third, *words used in the Constitution have changed meanings* with the times. We will see in Chapter 12, for example, that the language in the Bill of Rights forbidding "unreasonable searches" has been easily redefined to include the use of electronic spying equipment, which was unimaginable in the days of the framers.

Our Use and Abuse of the Ancestors

Generalities specified, silences filled in by practice, and words redefined have been important tools in adapting the Constitution to a changing world. Jefferson had declared that "the Constitution belongs to the living and not to the dead," and his actions proved it. Yet all the time there was—and still is—a countervailing power working against such adaptation. That power is the concept of "the intent of the framers." Strict constructionists and political conservatives try to figure out what the framers really meant by the words they wrote in the document. They do so first by examining the records we have of the debates in the Constitutional Convention.[26] If that is inconclusive, they

---

[24]Nichols, *American Leviathan*, p. 58.
[25]For an interesting discussion of adaptation, see Gerald Garvey, *Constitutional Bricolage* (Princeton, NJ: Princeton Univ. Press, 1971).

[26]If you'd like to try that, the best place to start is the classic work edited by Max Ferrand, *The Records of the Federal Convention of 1787* (New Haven, CT: Yale Univ. Press, 1911; rev. ed. 1937), which comes in four volumes. Or you might prefer to start with Ferrand's own summary account, *The Framing of the Constitution of the United States* (New Haven, CT: Yale Univ. Press, 1913). An easier route, though less reliable, is to read *The Federalist Papers*. For a survey including the text of many documents, see Page Smith, *The Constitution: A Documentary and Narrative History* (New York: Morrow, 1978).

ask what the founders would say and do if they were alive today.

Our attachment to our ancestors is obvious. There are monuments to Washington and Jefferson in Washington—and the capital is itself named for the first president. There are statues of various founders all around the country. Cities, streets, and even individuals are named for them. Their faces appear on our money and our stamps. Why all this obsession with ancestors? Is it a quest for our "roots" as a nation, like Alex Haley's quest for his roots as a black Afro-American,[27] or is it our own interest in "climbing our family tree"?

When the country was founded, George Washington had such stature as a political and military leader that his presidency served to *legitimize* the new country and its government. He had **charisma**—magnetic appeal—that helped establish a sense of unity among the people. He was also able to unify the leaders of the various factions in the

This 1800 portrait of George Washington is an example of ancestor worship. (Courtesy, The Henry Francis du Pont Winterthur Museum)

government while allowing them the freedom to develop their followers into what would become the political parties that would help stabilize governance when he retired. In other words, he was overseeing the creation of "legal authority" out of "charismatic authority," so that the government would be able to function well without him.[28]

Washington once remarked: "I do not think we are more inspired, have more wisdom, or possess more virtue, than those who will come after us."[29] But there is always a kind of magic in the founding—and in the founders—that those who come later cannot hope to equal. We may—and do—attempt to have periodic "refoundings" with "new ancestors," such as the popular image of the restoration of the Union under Abraham Lincoln or of the escape from the Great Depression under Roosevelt's New Deal. But in times of trouble, we look to the original founders for guidance.

The underlying reason for this unending return to the words of the ancestors seems to be that without them, anything goes—which means there is no compelling answer to the question of how politics should be conducted. The authority of the ancestors appeals to everyone—especially the leaders, who hope some of this authority will rub off on them.

But the danger is that despite the amendments and adaptations we will become too tied to old ways of seeing and doing things as we face new problems. Some 70 years after Washington, Abraham Lincoln, in the throes of the Civil War, remarked that "the dogmas of the quiet past are inadequate to the stormy present. The occasion is piled high with difficulty, and we must rise with the occasion. As our case is new, so we must think anew, and act anew. We must disenthrall ourselves, and then we shall save our country."[30]

THE POLITICS OF DOMAIN: CHANGING DEMANDS AND EXPECTATIONS

The debates over ratification of the Constitution and over the expansion of the Union raised questions of **domain**. Into which areas of life should

---

[27]See Alex Haley, *Roots* (Garden City, NY: Doubleday, 1976).

[28]See Marcus Cunliffe, *George Washington: Man and Monument* (New York: New American Library, 1960), for a fascinating account of the American hero worship and ancestor worship of Washington.

[29]George Washington, letter to Bushrod Washington.

[30]Quoted in Nichols, *American Leviathan*, pp. 278–79.

government be allowed to extend its power? Over which areas of the continent should the government extend its rule? Such questions have arisen frequently in our nation's history. They continue to arise today: Should the government regulate abortion or school prayer? Should it plan to "colonize" outer space?

The history of the country can be viewed as the history of the government expanding its domain—or the realm it governs—both geographically and substantively. Some critics claim that government does this against the wishes of the people. Careful reflection, however, will reveal that the wishes of the people have expanded along with—and perhaps ahead of—expansions in the government's domain.

The Growth of Government

The government has grown immensely since 1789.[31] The First Congress (1789–1791) had 65 legislators, each of whom represented 30,000 constituents; the Ninety-ninth Congress (1985–1986) had 435, each representing over half a million citizens. The members of the First Congress introduced a total of 144 bills and passed 82 percent; members of the Ninety-ninth Congress introduced 11,602 bills but passed fewer than 4 percent.

Even more revealing of the breadth of governmental activity is the size of the federal government's budget—the total amount of money it spends. In the years 1789–1791, that sum was $4,269,000, and it produced a $150,000 surplus of funds received over funds spent. In 1987 the budget was just under a trillion dollars, or about 900,000 times as much as the average annual expenditure in the years 1789–1791. And by that time the federal debt had increased to $2 trillion—over $8,100 for each citizen.

Massive increases like this in the scope and cost of governmental activity do not just happen. They result partly from the sheer growth of the country, from a population of 3,893,635 in 1790 to 215,667,979 in 1976 and 242,000,000 in 1987. Such

an increase requires more governmental officials and so costs more money. But even more important has been the change in how the population lives. In 1790 only 5 percent of the people lived in cities, and the biggest American city, New York, had only 33,131 residents. By 1987 the country contained four times as much land, yet 75 percent of the people lived in cities. Over 400 cities are now larger than New York was in 1790. Such massive urbanization of the country created many new demands on the government, as we shall see in Chapter 17.

Changes in Citizen Expectations

Even the trend toward urbanization does not account for most of the growth in the size and activities of government. We might get a better indication of the causes of that growth from another statistical comparison. In 1790 the average American could expect to live only until age 35. Today the average life expectancy has more than doubled. The causes of this doubling are many, but major credit must go to governmental programs to promote and protect public health. The government conducts vaccination programs; provides health care; and tests the food we eat, the water we drink, and the medicines we take.

Such government programs result from public demands that the government undertake major new efforts "to promote the general Welfare." Our ancestors who inscribed those words at the top of the Constitution would probably envy us our long life expectancy. But they would no doubt be astonished—and probably quite alarmed—at the extent to which we rely on the government for so many services.

Two hundred years ago government was generally thought of as a necessary evil. It was something people had to have in order "to insure domestic tranquility" (we would say "law and order") and "to provide for the common defense" ("national security"). If the government maintained law and order and guaranteed national security, it was believed, the other stated objectives—justice, welfare, and liberty—would follow almost as a matter of course.

But in the late 19th century people began to change their minds about all that. They saw a series of economic depressions that did not simply cure themselves and that took a terrible human toll.

---

[31]On the occasion of the bicentennial the U.S. Census Bureau, which has been counting Americans and their activities ever since 1790, issued a special two-volume report, *Historical Statistics of the United States: Colonial Times to 1970* (Washington, DC: GPO, 1976), on which much of the following account relies. For more current figures see the *Statistical Abstract of the United States, 1987*, 107th ed. (Washington, DC: Bureau of the Census, 1987). A new edition is published each year.

Symbols of American identity. (© 1975 Staples & Charles Ltd.)

They saw economic interests grow into monopolies. They saw political "machines" come to dominate life in the growing cities. As a result, people increasingly demanded that the government intervene in the economy. Some also called for the government to take action to restore opportunities for political competition. The consequence of these new demands was government regulation of the economy and the polity—something the founders thought unnecessary and even dangerous.

The immediate effects of this growing role of government were manifest in more government workers and bigger budgets. The longer-run effects were reflected in changes in popular conceptions of the state itself. The old conception of limited government has been called the negative state, because the state was expected to protect citizens *against* internal disorder and foreign threats. This view was increasingly replaced by a new conception of a more active government, which has come to be called the positive state. In this view the state is expected to take positive action to guarantee people economic opportunity, welfare, and equality.

This shift, in other words, was from government providing *freedom from* domestic disorder and foreign threats to government providing *freedom to* live a better life through measures that would control economic exploitation; expand political opportunities; and increase the health, education, and welfare of all citizens.

From Expectations to Demands on Government

Today we expect the government to provide education up to the limit of each citizen's capacity to learn (or, perhaps still, capacity to pay). We expect the government to guarantee employment to everyone able and desiring to work, or at least to provide unemployment insurance for those unable to find work. We expect government to provide old-age insurance pensions (Social Security, we call it). And increasingly we expect government to guarantee us health care.

A hundred years ago no Americans expected their government to provide these goods and services. Today, however, many Americans believe that they *should* get them, and increasingly they demand them from their government. Further, they expect government to guarantee that they can *purchase*, if they wish, pure water, electric light and power, heat, and even air conditioning, anywhere they choose to settle. Similarly, they expect the government to see to it that they can receive information and entertainment of their own choice via the mass media. They expect to be able to travel by air or highway (if no longer by sea or rail) anywhere they wish, anytime they wish, merely for payment of a fee. How did this change in expectations come about?

The Politics of the Ancestors 45

When the country was founded, most human needs were met in and by the family unit. According to the Census Bureau, in 1790 half of all households contained six or more people, and only a tenth consisted of one or two people living alone. People generally earned—or won by struggle—their livelihood directly from the land as farmers, hunters, and foresters. Gradually, however, livelihoods shifted toward providing services to other people as life and work became more specialized. And then, inevitably, those services were increasingly provided by institutions (supermarkets, dairies, construction companies, factories, and so on) instead of by individuals (merchants, farmers, carpenters, and other artisans). People came to gain their livelihood, as well as their goods and services, from those institutions rather than from other people. Through this evolution the virtually self-sufficient large household unit gave way to the small family. Today only one in ten households has six or more people, and half of all Americans live alone or with just one other person.[32] More and more responsibilities that once fell naturally on the family unit have gradually become demands on the government.

Indeed, these specific demands increasingly became parts of more general demands. In the area of economics, following the Great Depression in the 1930s, the people and the Congress (in the Full Employment Act of 1946) demanded that the federal government ("with assistance and cooperation of industry, agriculture, labor, and state and local governments") prevent future depressions and seek "to promote maximum employment, production, and purchasing power."

From Demands on Government to Demands on Citizens

Citizens demand services that require large government. But the people working in big government also develop their own notions about other things that should be done. The result is that big government becomes even bigger. It begins to seem inefficient and unresponsive to the citizens who first made demands for more services. And so citizens demand that there be *less* government—especially when they find that large government makes large demands on its citizens.

Americans have never much liked demands made on them by government. In fact, the Constitution and the Bill of Rights contain what one observer has called "45 no's and not's circumscribing governmental power."[33] Only reluctantly, under the impact of World War I, did Americans, after the ratification of the Sixteenth Amendment in 1913, finally accept an income tax to pay for strongly desired services.

This ever-growing need for money brings about but one of the demands governments impose today. In wartime (and until recently in peacetime as well) the state drafts its young male citizens to serve as soldiers. More and more, the government has also demanded that its citizens submit to standardized "identity routines"—from obtaining a Social Security card before beginning to work, to carrying a draft card while eligible for military service, to carrying a passport when traveling outside the country, to presenting a voter registration card at the polls. It also insists that we fill out growing numbers of forms for purposes of taxation and business activity. We also need to have a birth certificate to prove what we claim about our origins. As a result, we now have a Federal Paperwork Commission to study ways of curtailing these and other such requirements on citizens and business. In addition, Congress has passed a Right to Privacy Act to curtail governmental abuse of the information so obtained.

The Challenge to the Constitution

We shall encounter such happenings—such challenges—time and again in coming chapters. The growing demands of citizens on the government are matched by growing demands of the government on the citizens. Such mutual demands not only cause resentment in many citizens but also place strains on the institutions and processes of government. Looking back on the bicentennial of the Declaration of Independence in 1976 and forward to the bicentennial of the Constitution in 1987, historian Richard B. Morris remarked:

---

[32]For a recent account of the current characteristics of Americans, see Bryant Robey, *The American People* (New York: Dutton, 1985).

[33]Leonard Read, "The Heritage We Owe Our Children," *Notes from the Foundation for Economic Education*, September 1976, p. 3.

I don't think we can afford to take this system for granted. It's obvious that the Constitution was constructed in a different time frame and to meet an entirely different set of problems in an era when the national purpose was conceived of quite differently from the present day. Now—to underscore the differences—our nation is confronted with a serious decline in popular participation in, and a pervasive distrust of, government. We need to find out if the Constitution can continue to function effectively against this background of corrosive distrust in government at almost every level of our society—a distrust perhaps far deeper than in any previous period.[34]

The Constitution has been increasingly criticized as outmoded and inadequate. For example, Harvey Wheeler concluded an assessment of the Constitution with these harsh words:

Its Gothic territorial federalism no longer conforms to the associational realities and the community needs of our times. Its tripartite provision for governmental powers [legislative, executive, and judicial] is woefully inadequate [in an era when more demands on government require more governmental powers], and its mechanistic paradigm [of checks and balances] has become self-contradictory.[35]

But before we decide whether to accept or reject such a harsh judgment, we must examine both the participation of citizens and the operation of our institutions—both of which are strongly shaped by our Constitution, for better or for worse. And to do that we must first look in more detail at the politics of federalism in our system. As Roy Nichols observed, "American democracy had its origin and its experimental grounds in the local units, colonies, territories and states."[36]

SUMMARY

The earliest colonists came to what we now call the United States almost 400 years ago. Immediately they had to create governments. These governments had to master the politics of control: getting and keeping the loyalty of the citizens. When the British government imposed more limits on the freedom of the colonists, the latter rebelled. After declaring independence in 1776, they fought a long war with Britain under the direction of a weak government, which operated under the Articles of Confederation. When the war ended in victory, the former colonies saw the need for a stronger central government to protect their newly won independence. The result was the Constitution—a compromise among large and small states that helped the colonies overcome four threats: foreign enemies, state factionalism, a tyrannical central government, and a power-loving human nature.

The Constitution created a federal republic of states rather than a democracy. Its disposition of power was unique. It had three key features: division of powers among the national government, the state governments, and the people; separation of powers among the legislative, executive, and judicial branches; and confrontation of powers via checks and balances among the branches and between both houses of Congress. In practice, there developed a mixing of powers among the branches. The struggle over ratification resulted in the victory of the Federalists in 1788. *The Federalist Papers*, which argued the case for the Constitution, were an important factor in that victory. The opponents did succeed in obtaining a Bill of Rights— 10 amendments protecting civil liberties. Subsequently, 16 other amendments have been added, with Congress proposing by a two-thirds vote in each house and three-quarters of the states ratifying each amendment.

The Constitution has also been *adapted*, or informally reformed, through innovations such as the Louisiana Purchase of 1803. Jefferson and Lincoln, along with Washington, played important roles as leaders and are still looked to as authorities—especially in helping us interpret the Constitution.

Through its 200-year history, the United States has faced growing demands from, and expectations by, its people. As a result, the domain of government has increased. In turn, government has come to place greater demands on its citizens. Debates over the proper role of government and the adequacy of the Constitution continue to this day.

---

[34]Interview in *U.S. News & World Report*, July 4, 1977, p. 63.

[35]Harvey Wheeler, "Constitutionalism," in *Handbook of Political Science*, vol. 5, ed. Fred I. Greenstein and Nelson Polsby (Reading, MA: Addison-Wesley, 1975), p. 78.
[36]Nichols, *American Leviathan*, p. 58.

Suggestions for Further Reading and Study

By now the literature on early American history is positively massive. Probably the best guide to it is the *Harvard Guide to American History*, ed. Frank Freidel (Cambridge, MA: Harvard University Press, 1974). Volume 1 of this selective listing of book and periodical writings is arranged by topic, whereas volume 2 is chronological. A less comprehensive bibliographical guide is Eugene R. Fingerhut, *The Fingerhut Guide* (Santa Barbara, CA: ABC-Clio, 1973). The footnotes to this chapter will lead you to many of the most helpful studies.

Among more recent works of interest are Garry Wills, *Inventing America: Jefferson's Declaration of Independence* (New York: Random House paperback, 1978), and his *Explaining America: The Federalist* (Garden City, NY: Doubleday, 1981); Clinton Rossiter, *Seedtime of the Republic* (New York: Harcourt, Brace, 1953); Robert A. Rutland, *The Birth of the Bill of Rights, 1776–1791* (Chapel Hill: Univ. of North Carolina Press, 1955); Daniel J. Boorstin, *The Americans: The Colonial Experience* (New York: Random House paperback, 1958); and Broadus Mitchell and Louise Pearson Mitchell, *A Biography of the Constitution* (New York: Oxford Univ. Press, 1961). An interesting and provocative analysis, accompanied by generous excerpts from documents, is Page Smith, *The Constitution: A Documentary and Narrative History* (New York: Morrow paperback, 1978). The definitive collection of documents bearing on the Constitution from the 17th through the 19th century is Philip B. Kurland and Ralph Lerner, eds., *The Founders' Constitution*, 5 vols. (Chicago: Univ. of Chicago Press, 1987).

The very interesting studies that concentrate on the political and social theories underlying the great American experiment include Bernard Bailyn, *The Ideological Origins of the American Revolution* (Cambridge, MA: Harvard Univ. Press paperback, 1967), which relates American thought to the European liberal tradition; Louis Hartz, *The Liberal Tradition in America* (New York: Harcourt, Brace paperback, 1955); Gordon Wood, *Creation of the American Republic 1776–1787* (New York: Norton paperback, 1972); and Roy F. Nichols, *American Leviathan: The Evolution and Process of Self-Government in the United States* (New York: Harper Colophon paperback, 1963), which was originally published under the title *Blueprints for Leviathan: American Style;* and Forrest McDonald, *Novus Ordo Seclorum* (Lawrence: Univ. of Kansas Press, 1985).

2

THE POLITICS OF FEDERALISM:
The States in a Nation of Cities and Regions

The fact that we have a federal system affects your life in many ways every day. Most pervasive is the fact that you have several sets of laws—and several sets of police officers—to obey. You also have several sets of laws and police officers to protect you. Our federal system divided authority between the national government and the states, as we saw in the last chapter. That is why we have federal law and state law—why we have the Federal Bureau of Investigation (along with other federal police agencies concerned with drugs, firearms, and alcohol, for example) plus state police. Each state in turn grants some authority to the cities and counties within its borders. That's why we have city police and county sheriffs enforcing laws passed by these local governments. This means that when you go from one city to another—or even cross the city limits into a neighboring county—you have to obey different local laws and different law officers but the same state and federal laws. And if you cross into another state, the state law you must obey changes again.

This may seem like a needlessly complicated way of organizing law and order. We saw in the last chapter that federalism was a compromise to ensure a strong central government while insulating citizens from full central control. We'll see in this chapter that the federal system has other effects, such as offering a citizen who loses his or her claims in local or state courts the possibility of appealing to courts on another level. That is precisely what happened to William James Rummel. ■

THE CASE
OF WILLIAM JAMES RUMMEL

On January 31, 1973, William James Rummel was convicted of a felony in San Antonio, Texas. He had received and cashed a check for $120.75 to fix an air conditioner at a local tavern but had failed to do the work. The Texas court sentenced him to life in prison.

That seems like a stiff sentence for such a small crime, but Rummel's record showed previous convictions for buying $80 worth of tires with a false credit card in 1964 and for forging a check for $28.36 to pay a hotel bill in 1969. A Texas law passed in 1856 gives the local prosecutor the option of charging anyone convicted of three felonies as a "habitual offender." Such a charge carries a mandatory sentence of life imprisonment. So Rummel got life for three thefts totaling $229.11—even though he'd already served a total of three and a half years for the prior convictions.

The American Civil Liberties Union, a national group of citizens concerned about protecting civil liberties, took an interest in the case. As Matthew Myers, chief counsel of its National Prison Project, remarked: "Texas is not alone in having drafted statutes as oversimplistic as this habitual-offender law to reach types of individuals who, certainly, no rational person would put away for life. This case is important because it symbolizes . . . examples of states' sentencing . . . which are so over-reaching [as to] shock the conscience of anybody familiar with the criminal justice system."[1]

The sentence was appealed, but Rummel stayed in jail during the long appeal process because he was too poor to post bond. Finally, in May 1979 the U.S. Supreme Court agreed to hear the case on appeal. The lawyer appointed by the court to represent Rummel claimed that the Texas habitual-offender law was unconstitutional. Speaking before the Supreme Court in January 1980, lawyer Scott Atlas said that the life sentence was "too much for too little." It therefore violated the Eighth Amendment's ban on "cruel and unusual punish-

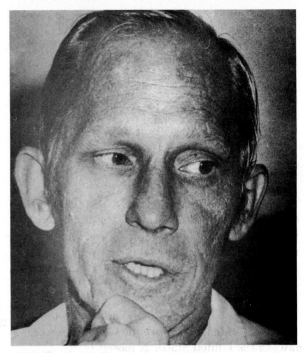

William James Rummel. (San Antonio Light)

ment." The state of Texas disagreed. Assistant Attorney General Douglas Becker told the Court that the state was entitled to determine prison sentences without interference from the national government.

The case was important not just for Rummel but for many others. At that moment there were 2593 persons in Texas prisons serving such sentences under the habitual-offender law. Furthermore, 16 other states had similar laws requiring life in prison for a combination of offenses that singly would not entail so severe a punishment. If the Supreme Court ruled the Texas law unconstitutional, that would, in effect, instruct lower courts to make the same rulings about other states' laws when similar cases came before them.

After hearing arguments on the case in January 1980, the Supreme Court considered the case. In March it issued its decision. By a 5-to-4 vote it found the Texas law constitutional. In the words of Justice William H. Rehnquist, setting the length of prison terms "is purely a matter of legislative prerogative." So Rummel's life sentence had been upheld by the Supreme Court not because it was fair or just but because under our Constitution, the Texas legislature has the power to make whatever laws it wishes in order to set penalties for violation of state laws. That is a power of the states, the Court held, and so it was none of the national gov-

---

[1]Quoted in William J. Choyke, "Texas Statute Faces Challenge in High Court," *Austin American-Statesman*, January 14, 1980. For accounts of subsequent developments, see the Associated Press dispatch from San Antonio, November 14, 1980 (*Austin American-Statesman*, November 15, 1980), and Jim Mann, "Freed Convict Waits 6 Long Hours for Release," *Austin American-Statesman*, November 16, 1980. And also see Maurice de G. Ford, "The Law: Collect $230 and Go to Jail," *The Atlantic*, July 1980, pp. 14–18.

ernment's business. Thus, Rummel had to continue serving his life sentence, even though Supreme Court Justice Lewis Powell declared that his sentence "would be viewed as unjust by virtually every lawyer and layman."

The Rummel Case and American Federalism

The Rummel case shows us federalism in action. Each state passes its own laws on matters other than "federal offenses," such as treason against the United States. This means that laws about what is illegal can and do vary from one state to another. Similarly, penalties for the same offenses can be different from state to state. As we noted, 17 states have one or another sort of habitual-offender law. The other 33 have none. Such variation is legal, so long as no state laws violate the Constitution or the laws of the United States as passed by Congress.

Our federal system was set up by the founders in part to preserve such *diversity*. They had various reasons for doing this. Some argued that the states would understand their own problems best because they would be closest to them and would therefore be able to make better laws and develop better policies. Others emphasized the value of having an *experiment* tried in just one state. If it worked there, it could be adopted by other states or even by the nation as a whole. If it failed, only one state need suffer the consequences. Most, however, focused on the belief that if *two sovereignties*—two sources of law—were created, each could protect the citizens against abuses by the other. (See the box on the impacts of federalism, p. 52.)

The Rummel case reminds us that this system doesn't always work to everyone's liking. The national government did not protect Rummel—nor the many thousands of others in Texas and sixteen other states sentenced under habitual-offender laws—from a sentence that seemed extreme. The federal system did, however, allow Rummel to appeal his state sentence. Sometimes such appeals are successful.

The Rummel Resolution

In Rummel's case the Supreme Court's refusal to grant him relief focused national attention on the problem in general and on his case in particular.

The result was yet another appeal on other grounds. When he lost his claim that his life sentence violated the Eighth Amendment, he appealed on grounds that his original court-appointed lawyer in 1973 had not defended him properly. That appeal went first to the U.S. district court—a lower federal court in San Antonio.

In October 1980 Judge Dorwin W. Suttle overturned Rummel's conviction on grounds that his lawyer had not investigated potential witnesses before his trial for theft in January 1973. That ruling was in a sense based on a technicality because the Supreme Court decision prevented any further dispute of the sentence itself. But it had much the same effect that a favorable Supreme Court ruling would have had for Rummel. It entitled him to a new trial. This time his new lawyer, Scott Atlas, worked out a deal with the prosecutor: a **plea bargain.** Rummel pleaded guilty in a Texas district court to the charge of failing to fix the air conditioner, and in return the prosecutor dropped the habitual-offender charge. The judge accepted the deal and sentenced Rummel to 7 years in prison for the offense. But because Rummel had already served 7 years, 9 months, and 15 days of his previous life sentence, the judge declared him free. He left prison that evening, November 14, 1980, a free man at last after serving 11 years in prison for crimes worth $229.11.

Because we have a federal system Rummel was finally able to get freedom on **appeal** to a U.S. district court. Because the U.S. Supreme Court refused to rule that habitual-offender laws violate the Eighth Amendment, our federal system allows 17 states, including Texas, to keep such laws on the books. Thus, Rummel's eventual victory was a victory for him alone among the thousands similarly sentenced. It could also be seen, however, as a victory for our federal system. The federal system made possible his appeal and at the same time preserved the power of the states to make whatever laws they wish in order to deal with repeat offenders. In recent decades challenges to such state powers have been growing. On the other hand, calls for, and moves toward, strengthening the powers of the states against the national government have also increased. We shall find many instances of these two conflicting trends as we examine the federal system. The question of which trend will prevail is at the heart of many struggles in Washington these days.

The Impacts of Federalism on the American Political System

Territoriality

The most striking impact of federalism on our politics is seen in the fact that state lines and territoriality, instead of population or special interests, or particular functions like transportation or environmental protection, dominate and shape so much of our politics.

Two Sovereignties

A second effect is the creation of a second sovereignty, or source of law, beyond the national government. In fact, because states have delegated some powers to cities and counties we have three or four sources of law. But only two are sovereign; only two can make laws that the others cannot overturn. This makes life much more complex, especially for businesses, many of which operate in several states as well as under U.S. jurisdiction.

Diversity Preserved

The federal structure protects diversity among the states in many ways. This diversity is prominent in matters such as citizen rights. States have different laws on drugs and abortion, for example. It is also present in questions of the proper role of the government. For example, some states, but not others, control loan sharks who charge outrageous interest rates, taking advantage of people who need to borrow money. More generally, the diversity extends to most areas of crime and punishment. The only exceptions are those realms where federal law predominates.

This preserved diversity usually benefits some groups at the expense of others. The federal structure was what preserved slavery in the southern states for 75 years after a majority of the country opposed it. Federalism also sheltered racist acts in both the South and the North up to recent years. On both slavery and racism the Supreme Court long ago ruled that state policies and practices are protected from federal meddling. The same thing has been true of sexism. We shall see more of such preserved diversity and its effects on minorities and "outsiders" in Chapters 13 and 14.

Limitations on Government's Economic Role

Much the same sort of limitation on federal and state intervention occurred in the area of economic regulation in the interests of the poor, small business, and the consumer. For 150 years the Supreme Court rather consistently ruled against such intervention. Only when the Great Depression of the 1930s threatened the very survival of capitalism did the Court relent. We will learn more of this in Chapter 15.

Creativity and Innovation

A fifth effect of federalism is more benign. The 50 states can sometimes serve as 50 laboratories in which policy innovations can be developed and tested. Once lessons are learned at a state level, a national program may be developed. One state innovation is the bottle deposit law that Oregon pioneered to foster recycling. When this program worked in Oregon, other states and cities decided to try it. It may yet become a national policy.

In a world, and a nation, of growing complexity, bureaucracy, and political stalemate at the national level, such local experiments can prove especially useful.

Insulation of the Cities from the National Government

The final major effect of federalism has been the insulation of the cities—and their problems—from the national government. We shall see in more detail in Chapter 17 how cities derive their powers from the states and how this dependence long kept the federal government out of urban affairs, sometimes for the better and sometimes for the worse.

OUR SYSTEM OF FEDERALISM

The essence of our federal system is the special role of the states. There are two key aspects to this. The first is the division of powers between the national government and the states. The second is the special roles the states have in the ratification and amendment of the Constitution and in the selection of the president and senators.

How did we come to have such a system? The early version, we know, was created by the founders in drafting the Constitution. It has, of course, changed its nature considerably in the last 200 years. Still, we cannot understand either the nature of the federal system or its development without first seeing what the founders had in mind in creating it.[2]

The Origins of Federalism

The origins of federalism, like the origins of politics (as we saw in Perspective 1), can be found in ancient Greece. The Greeks believed that the good life could be lived only in a small independent "city-state," or *polis.* There the citizens could know each other, recognize the public problems, and join together in solving them. They could do so by practicing direct democracy, in which everyone votes on public questions. They knew, however, that a small polis would sometimes have difficulty defending itself against threats from outside. So they saw *polis-federalism* as a way to create alliances in foreign affairs. Indeed, the word *federal* is related to the Latin word for *faith,* as applied to a league or contract. To the Greeks, federalism was intended to promote external defense rather than internal governance.

This view persisted until the time of the French political philosopher Montesquieu (1689–1755). We have already encountered him as the author of the concept of the separation of powers among the branches of government. He argued that republics—governments without monarchs, in which the people hold the ultimate authority and delegate it to their representatives—had to be small. He saw two reasons for that: First, a large state would necessarily require a despotic authority, an emperor, as ruler. Second, in a small republic the people would be patriotic and tend to be good citizens—virtuous rather than narrowly self-interested. The primary reason for smallness of the country, Montesquieu said, is not, as the Greeks believed, to make it possible to live the good life but rather to make it possible to preserve republican virtue in the citizens and thereby to guarantee republican liberty.

The shift from polis-federalism to *small-republic federalism*[3] is important because it weakens the

French philosopher Montesquieu. (New York Public Library Picture Collection)

argument against enlarging the national, or central, authority. If one can still protect republican liberty while increasing centralized government, that is permissible.

The genius of James Madison was to argue *not just* that greater size was *compatible with* preserving liberty and government by consent *but* that it was *essential to* that preservation. We saw in the last chapter that Madison adapted Scottish philosopher David Hume's analysis of larger districts. He asserted that larger size brought greater diversity, and diversity brought conflicts among special interests (such as farmers, merchants, and manufacturers) that would tend to prevent any one segment from dominating. As a result, citizens and their representatives would come to see and to seek the public interest that transcended these special interests.

Madison's experience in the period of the Articles of Confederation had shown him that the states as relatively independent political units had been quarrelsome and had threatened liberty. He thus proposed originally that the national—or "consolidated"—government should have an absolute veto over all state actions.[4] He settled for a division of

---

[2]See Michael P. Zuckert, "Federalism and the Founding: Toward a Reinterpretation of the Constitutional Convention," *Review of Politics* 48 (Spring 1986), 166–210, for a description of six different concepts of federalism considered by the framers.

[3]The terms are Martin Diamond's. So is much of the analysis in this section. See his article "The Ends of Federalism." in *The Federal Polity,* ed. Daniel J. Elazar (New Brunswick, NJ: Transaction Books, 1974), pp. 129–52.

[4]See Max Farrand, ed., *The Records of the Federal Convention,* vol. 1 (New Haven, CT: Yale Univ. Press. 1937), pp. 27, 165. See also Jean Yarbrough, "Federalism in the Foundation and Preservation of the American Republic." *Publius* 7 (Summer 1976), 43–60, and Charles F. Hobson, "The Negative on State Laws: James Madison, the Constitution, and the Crisis of Republican Government," *William and Mary Quarterly* 36 (April 1979), 215–35.

David Hume. (New York Public Library)

James Madison. (National Portrait Gallery, Smithsonian Institution)

powers. The national government was to have supreme power in certain spheres (such as foreign relations, interstate and foreign commerce, coining money, and creating a postal service), and state governments were to have supreme power in certain other spheres (such as conducting elections, regulating commerce within the state's borders, and creating local governments)—provided that the exercise of these powers did not overstep the bounds set by the Constitution. Table 2.1 lists some powers granted and some powers denied to each level of government by the Constitution.

The system we have, in other words—the words, in fact, of James Madison in *Federalist* no. 39—"is in strictness neither a national nor a federal constitution; but a composition of both." There are two basic reasons for this. The first is that the Constitution was a political compromise between advocates of a strong national government and advocates of states' rights. The second reason is more basic. "Federalism is always an arrangement pointed in two contrary directions or aimed at securing two contrary ends," Martin Diamond observed. "One end is always found in the reason why the member units do not simply consolidate themselves into one large unitary country; the other end is always found in the reason why the member units do not choose to remain simply small wholly autonomous countries."[5] The desire for defense against enemies abroad and for orderly conduct of

commerce suggested union. The desire for protection against centralized tyranny and for preservation of local interest and customs (including slavery) suggested federation.

The continued belief in federalism, although thus attenuated, obliged the leading Framers, all nationalists, to consent to the grafting on to the Constitution of some authentically federal features. And their opponents, seeing in federalism, no longer the full-blown traditional reasons for autonomous republics, but only one among many possible means for securing liberty, were contented with the modest degree of federalism they achieved. The compromise over federalism created "an incomplete national government, which is neither exactly national nor exactly federal."[6]

We have seen that the foremost feature of our federalist government is the complex distribution of powers between the national and the state governments. The other key feature is the special role of the states in the national government. This role has three aspects.

First, the states had special roles in the *formation* of the Union. Each state had a voluntary choice as to whether or not to join the Union, and only when 9 of the 13 states ratified the Constitution did the Union come into existence. In addition, it was out of that state ratification process that the demand for a Bill of Rights emerged.

Second, the states had key roles in the *structure*

[5]Diamond, "The Ends of Federalism," p. 130.

[6]Ibid., p. 135. The concluding phrase is from the astute French observer Alexis de Tocqueville. See his *Democracy in America*, vol. 1 (New York: Vintage, 1944; originally published in 1835), p. 164.

TABLE 2.1
Distribution of Powers According to the Constitution

SOME POWERS GRANTED	SOME POWERS PROHIBITED
National government:	
Delegated powers	
To regulate commerce with foreign nations and among the states	To tax articles exported from one state to another
To declare war	To pass laws violating the Bill of Rights (first ten amendments)
To coin money	
To establish post offices	
To establish courts inferior to the Supreme Court	
To raise and support an army	
To provide and maintain a navy	
To make laws necessary and proper to carry out the foregoing powers	
State government:	
Reserved powers	
To conduct elections	To enter into any treaty, alliance, or confederation
To establish local governments	To coin money
To regulate commerce within the state	To impair the obligations of contracts
To ratify amendments to the federal Constitution	To abridge the privileges of immunities of citizens (Fourteenth Amendment)
To exercise powers the Constitution does not grant to the national government nor prohibit the states from exercising (Tenth Amendment)	
National and state government:	
Concurrent powers[a]	
To tax	To grant titles of nobility
To borrow money	To permit slavery (Thirteenth Amendment)
To pass and enforce laws	To deny citizens the right to vote because of race, color, or previous condition of servitude (Fifteenth Amendment)
To spend money for the general welfare	To deny citizens the right to vote because of their sex (Nineteenth Amendment)
To take private property for public purposes, with just compensation	To deny citizens eighteen years of age or older the right to vote (Twenty-sixth amendment)

[a]State authority to exercise these five powers comes from state constitutions just as the federal government's authority to exercise them comes from the national Constitution.

of the central government. The Senate represented the states in two ways. First, the state legislature originally selected senators; second, each state had equal representation—two senators—regardless of its population. This contrasted with the House of Representatives, which represented the people by population size and districts. The presidency also had a federal aspect in that each state received electoral votes equal in number to its total membership in the House (which was by population) and the Senate (which was by state).[7]

Third, the *extent of powers* of the national government is somewhat federal in that the states retain some powers to themselves and share others with the national government. (See Table 2.1.) The national government does have some powers that it alone can exercise, and when it exercises them, these powers reach not only to the states but also directly to the citizens, as we all know. But for it to be a full-fledged national government, it would have to have all power over both states and citizens. Because it doesn't Madison called it "a composition" of national and federal elements, and today we call it a federal system.[8]

[7]See William H. Riker, "The Heresthetics of Constitution-making," *American Political Science Review* 78 (March 1984), 1–16.

[8]For Madison's reply to critics who said the Constitution went too far away from federalism toward a "consolidated" national form, see *Federalist* no. 39. See also Martin Diamond, "The Federalist on Federalism: Neither a National Nor a Federal Constitution, But a Composition of Both," *Yale Law Journal* 86 (1977), 1273–85.

The Source of Authority

Our government can thus be seen as *a system of shared authority.* The national government and the state governments share the authority to rule us. And because they share ruling authority they often dispute which level should predominate in a given domain, such as welfare, pollution control, or education. So there are always political struggles between the levels—struggles we describe as *intergovernmental*. These are instances of the politics of federalism.

When Washington and one or more state capitals disagree over who should decide or control a certain program, who should decide which level of government prevails? This question has arisen time and again. In the short run, on particular questions, the courts make these decisions. And when they do, they refer to the statement in Article VI of the Constitution that

> this Constitution, and the Laws of the United States which shall be made in Pursuance thereof; and all Treaties made, or which shall be made, under the Authority of the United States, shall be the supreme Law of the Land; and the Judges in every State shall be bound thereby, any Thing in the Constitution or Laws of any State to the Contrary notwithstanding.

This clause is often called the key to the Constitution, for it binds the parts—the states—into the whole. The language originally adopted by the framers—unanimously, we should remember—termed the laws and treaties "the supreme law of the States." This was later changed at the Constitutional Convention to read "the supreme Law of the Land." The change seemed to emphasize that the Constitution was the work of the whole—of the people—and not of the states. In a similar way, the Preamble to the Constitution as first drafted began "We the people of the States of New Hampshire [and so on through the list of states] . . . " It was later changed to read "We the People of the United States. . . . "

Still, there continues to be debate over the source of the authority of the new government. Was it the people or the states? Two theories have been set forth: the compact theory and the national theory.

The Compact Theory versus the National Theory

- The **compact theory** argues that the colonies became separate, independent states when they declared independence and won the war that followed. It asserts that these states came together, through their chosen representatives in the convention, and created a new constitution. This document was then ratified by representatives of these same states in special conventions. Thus, the national government received—and still receives—its authority from its member states, which created that government by making a compact.

- The **national theory** examines the same historical events but reaches a different conclusion. According to this theory, a single sovereign power, the people, created both the national and the state governments. In so doing they delegated a certain, specified, limited authority to each level of government.

This may sound like an unimportant academic debate, but it's not. If you believe the compact theory, you also believe that the states can withdraw the authority they granted to the national government when they don't like what it does. Historically, southern states used this view to justify continuation of slavery, among other matters, via **nullification** of national laws and **secession** at the time of the Civil War. In recent years advocates of greater states' rights have appealed to this compact theory. And in his inaugural address, Ronald Reagan declared that he wishes to reinstitute the nation as "a federation of sovereign states." He even used the classic phrase "*These* United States *are* . . ."

The Civil War and a long string of Supreme Court rulings have given the victory, at least for now, to the national theory over the compact theory. Many scholars would agree. As Samuel Beer has written:

> The national theory . . . is a superior interpretation of what actually happened, an interpretation incidentally which has been given further powerful support by recent historical research. The important thing, however . . . is that the men who conceived and elaborated [the original design of American federalism] worked from the premises of the national theory. Their federalism presupposes their nationalism. In their view the constituent power was one people, the nation. What they sought to produce in the constitution of the new polity was a scheme by which that nation would act not only as the constituent power, but also as the continuous controlling and directing influence in the political life of the new polity.[9]

---

[9]Samuel Beer, "Federalism, Nationalism, and Democracy in America," *American Political Science Review* 72, no. 1 (March 1978), 12.

State Sovereignty, *Garcia*, and Preemption

Through the country's history, the extent of state sovereignty has frequently been an issue. The framers had established supremacy for the national government within the realm of the authority specifically delegated to it in the Constitution. The Tenth Amendment, however, had declared: "The powers not delegated to the United States by the Constitution, nor prohibited by it to the States, are reserved to the States respectively, or to the people."

Over time it became increasingly difficult for the Congress or the courts to draw the line between the appropriate powers of Congress and the protected powers of the states. In general, the historical process seemed to favor the federal government. But in 1976 the Supreme Court, in *National League of Cities* v. *Usery,* held that a law passed by Congress to extend federal wage regulations to all employees of states and cities was unconstitutional. It argued that states have a "freedom to structure integral operations in the areas of traditional governmental services."

But what are "the areas of traditional governmental services"? The Supreme Court didn't say, and neither states nor Congress could tell. Thus lower courts tended to ignore the decision. Eventually the Supreme Court realized that its ruling could not be implemented. And so, eight years later, it reversed itself. In *Garcia* v. *San Antonio Metropolitan Transit Authority* in 1985 the Court concluded that while states do retain sovereign authority, that authority is protected by the structure of the federal government itself—especially the representative structure of Congress—rather than by the extension of constitutional immunity to state action.[10] In other words, to protect their powers states have to rely on their ability to influence their representatives in Congress rather than on the Tenth Amendment.

And yet, Congress itself was increasingly taking actions designed to preempt state authority in various realms. Starting in 1965, it passed various laws specifically declaring that they preempted or overruled whatever laws any states might have passed in a given area. In general, such federal laws are favored by business when they set a single national standard—for example, on flammable babies' pajamas—to replace up to 50 different state standards. On the other hand, when states have taken action more extreme than the federal government's, they resent being preempted by what they see as insufficient governmental regulation.[11]

Such disputes will never be settled by Supreme Court rulings, any more than they will by Congressional or state legislation. They will, however, continue to raise theoretical disputes over the appropriate division of sovereign powers between the national and the state governments.

A Layer Cake or a Marble Cake?

Whatever the theoretical basis, we live today in a country with a strong national government—but a country that also has increasingly strong state governments. The desire to further increase the powers and resources of the states is widespread and growing among a large segment of the people as well as among officials of the states. However, efforts to do so today are complicated by the complexity of relations among the various levels in our federal system.

At one time, people describing the federal system used the metaphor of a layer cake. The top layer was the national government, the next layer the state government, and at the bottom was the local government. The local layer may include sublayers such as the county, the city, and the school district. As experts studied the federal system more carefully, however, they found that in fact, most governmental functions are shared by different levels of government. For example, as we shall see in Perspective 4, public education is financed by a combination of local property taxes, state grants, and programs of federal aid to education. Again, if you are convicted in a local court of breaking a local law, you may decide to appeal the conviction. You could go to a state appeals court on grounds that the law violates the state constitution, or to a state or federal court if you think the law or your court treatment violated your rights as an American citizen. This, of course, is just what Rummel did. By the same token, the Constitution

---

[10]See James R. Alexander, "State Sovereignty in the Federal System," *Publius* 16 (Spring 1986), 1–15.

[11]See Joseph F. Zimmerman, "Federal Preemption of State and Local Activities," paper delivered at the annual meeting of the American Political Science Association in Washington, August 1986.

says that federal law is supreme in the areas of powers granted to the national government. Thus, Congress can pass laws that are binding on state and local governments.

In addition, and probably most important, each level of government has some power directly over all citizens living within its borders. Thus, you must obey laws of your city, your county, your state, and the nation—and so must state, local, and national officials.

The result, in the words of political scientist Morton Grodzins, is this:

> The federal system is not accurately symbolized by a neat layer cake of three distinct and separate planes. A far more realistic symbol is that of the marble cake. Wherever you slice through it you reveal an inseparable mixture of differently colored ingredients. . . . Vertical and diagonal lines almost obliterate the horizontal ones, and in some places there are unexpected whirls and an imperceptible merging of colors, so that it is difficult to tell where one ends and the other begins. So it is with federal, state, and local responsibilities in the chaotic marble cake of American government.[12]

In other words, in a federal governmental system, there must be several levels or layers of government that rule over the same people, each of which is supreme or sovereign in some spheres. As William Riker, a longtime student of the subject, puts it: "Federalism is a political organization in which the activities of government are divided between regional governments and a central government in such a way that each kind of government has some activities on which it makes final decisions."[13]

But as Grodzins reminds us, in today's world most functions are shared among Washington and the states and the cities. Each level has certain special responsibilities and certain superior capabilities. The result of this sharing, or interdependence, is that political relations between the levels often produce conflict and involve efforts by one level to influence the other. Such intergovernmental relations are rarely harmonious. It is as if no level is fully content with the marble cake structure of intergovernmental relations. Thus, each level struggles to recreate a layer cake—but each level wants to be the top layer. The consequence is that each level seeks more economic resources (through taxes and grants) and more political authority (through lawmaking and policing). The result is that the cake becomes even more marbled.

If our American system is in this sense a marble cake, so, in a sense, is each one of us—for our governments operate in and through each of us, making and enforcing laws and providing services. To understand this better we must sort out the components or ingredients of the marble cake. We must examine how they have developed, why they are important, and what is happening to them in this complex and challenging era. We must study the ways in which we as citizens, not only of America but also of our state and community, may play constructive roles in politics and government at various levels.

We shall first examine these ingredients here, where our focus will be on the states in their relations with Washington. In Chapter 17 we shall see many of the same trends from the perspective of local governments.

THE CONSTITUTIONAL BASES OF FEDERALISM

The states are referred to some 50 times in the 45 separate sections of the Constitution. The system of federalism is established in three key places. (You can find them in the text of the Constitution printed at the back of this book.) The first is Article I, which describes limited national powers. The second is Article III, which recognizes a dual court system—national and state. The third is Article IV, which establishes dual citizenship—national and state—for Americans.[14]

Expansion of the Union

The Constitution (Article IV, Section 3) provides that "new States may be admitted by the Congress into this Union." Beyond the original 13 "charter

[12]Morton Grodzins, "Centralization and Decentralization in the American Federal System," in *A Nation of States*, ed. Robert A. Goldwin (Chicago: Rand McNally, 1963), pp. 3–4. The term *marble cake* was used earlier by Joseph E. McLean.

[13]W. H. Riker, "Federalism," in *Handbook of Political Science*, ed. Fred I. Greenstein and Nelson Polsby (Reading, MA: Addison-Wesley, 1975), p. 101.

[14]See Donald S. Lutz, "The Founding of Popular Government in America: The United States Constitution as an Incomplete Text," paper presented at the 1980 annual meeting of the American Political Science Association in Washington, DC.

members," 37 additional states have been admitted (see Table 2.2). This growth raised problems as it occurred.

The new states were more democratic than the original colonies, as we noted in Chapter 1. They experimented with self-government as territories even before they became states, and they allowed all adult white males to vote whether or not they owned property. The new states generally supported the Democratic-Republicans, the antifederalist party led by Thomas Jefferson. As we noted previously, the Louisiana Purchase more than doubled the land mass of the United States. It also guaranteed continued political dominance for the Jeffersonians by adding more democratically inclined populations to the American citizenry.

Expansion continued over the coming decades—but it became more controversial: The southern states, which maintained the institution of slavery, insisted that slavery be allowed in enough of the new states to prevent the national government from outlawing it. A series of compromises did just that until the Civil War, in the 1860s, finally ended slavery. States continued to be admitted from time to time (see Table 2.2) until

TABLE 2.2
The Growth of the Union

THE ORIGINAL MEMBERS AND YEAR CONSTITUTION RATIFIED

Delaware	1787	South Carolina	1788
Pennsylvania	1787	New Hampshire	1788
New Jersey	1787	Virginia	1788
Georgia	1788	New York	1788
Connecticut	1788	North Carolina	1789
Massachusetts	1788	Rhode Island	1790
Maryland	1788		

STATES AND YEAR ADMITTED

Vermont	1791	Oregon	1859
Kentucky	1792	Kansas	1861
Tennessee	1796	West Virginia	1863
Ohio	1803	Nevada	1864
Louisiana	1812	Nebraska	1867
Indiana	1816	Colorado	1876
Mississippi	1817	North Dakota	1889
Illinois	1818	South Dakota	1889
Alabama	1819	Montana	1889
Maine	1820	Washington	1889
Missouri	1821	Idaho	1890
Arkansas	1836	Wyoming	1890
Michigan	1837	Utah	1896
Florida	1845	Oklahoma	1907
Texas	1845	New Mexico	1912
Iowa	1846	Arizona	1912
Wisconsin	1848	Alaska	1959
California	1850	Hawaii	1959
Minnesota	1858		

FIGURE 2.1
Population Centers.

Source: U.S. Bureau of the Census, *Census of Population: 1980*, vol. 1, p. 7.

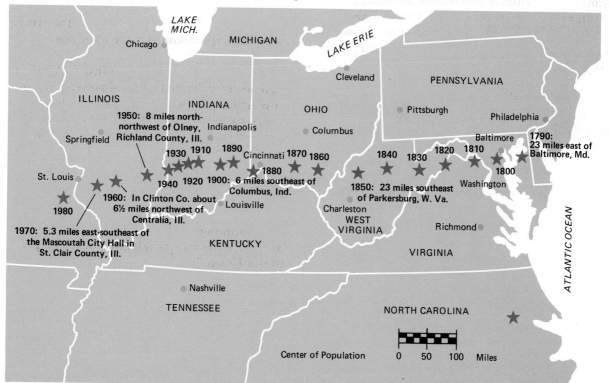

the entire 48 contiguous (or "touching") states were incorporated with the admission of Arizona and New Mexico in 1912. It was not until 1959 that Alaska and Hawaii, after much political bickering, became the 49th and 50th states. Today there is some discussion concerning statehood for Puerto Rico. This controversial issue will be discussed in Chapter 13.

Expansion of the Powers of the National Government

Physical expansion of the Union was the most obvious development in the early decades of America. But expansion of the powers of the national government, which often came at the expense of the states, was more important for the future of American federalism.

Delegated Powers and Reserved Powers

The Constitution **delegated** certain enumerated (or "stated") **powers** to the national government. Among these were the power to make treaties, declare war, coin money, establish post offices, establish national courts, and regulate interstate commerce. It **reserved** all other **powers** to the states and the people. But as soon as the government began to operate, it started acting in ways that served to expand its powers. And almost immediately that expansion was challenged in the courts.

Implied Powers and the Case of McCulloch v. Maryland

The landmark case that resolved an early attempt to expand government power was *McCulloch* v. *Maryland* (1819). The national government had established a Bank of the United States and had opened a branch in Maryland. It argued that its power to do so was implied by the explicitly stated power to coin money or control the currency. The state of Maryland had imposed a tax on the bank, and James W. McCulloch, the bank cashier, had refused to pay. Maryland argued before the Supreme Court that the United States had no right to establish a bank because the Constitution did not explicitly permit it to do so. In its argument, Maryland also claimed that in any case it had the right

to tax such a bank because the power to tax is a power reserved to the states by the Constitution.

The Court unanimously decided against Maryland and for the bank on two grounds, thus laying the foundation for the continuing growth of the national government at the expense of the states. Chief Justice John Marshall wrote in his opinion: "We must never forget that it is a *constitution* we are expounding. . . . [A] constitution intended to endure for ages to come, and consequently, to be adapted to the various crises of human affairs." He first set forth, in defense of Congress's establishing the bank, words that would become known as the **doctrine of implied powers:** "Let the end be legitimate, let it be within the scope of the Constitution, and all means which are appropriate, which are plainly adapted to that end, which are not prohibited, but consist with the letter and spirit of the Constitution are Constitutional." The clause under which this doctrine was justified, Article I, Section 8, gives Congress power "to make all laws which shall be necessary and proper for carrying into execution the foregoing powers, and all other powers vested by this constitution in the government of the United States, or in any department or officer thereof." It thus became known as the **necessary and proper clause,** or, less formally, as the **elastic clause,** because it could be stretched to include so much.

Marshall then set forth the related *doctrine of national supremacy* in asserting that Maryland could not tax the bank: "The power to tax involves the power to destroy. . . . If the right of the states to tax the means employed by the general government be conceded, the declaration that the Constitution, and the laws made in pursuance thereof, shall be the supreme law of the land, is empty and unmeaning declamation."

The McCulloch case established the principle of implied powers. A related case, *Osborn* v. *Bank of the U.S.* (1824), allowed a state official who was violating the law to be sued. This case established the principle that the national government could enforce federal law against the states. Together, these two cases clearly asserted the supremacy of the Constitution and national law over state law. Thus, the groundwork was established for national domination in this phase of the struggle for ruling power.

TABLE 2.3
Types of Powers in our Federal System

TYPE OF POWER	ORIGIN OF THE POWER	EXAMPLES
Enumerated (national government)	Constitution	Power to make war, to establish post office, to regulate interstate and foreign commerce
Implied (national government)	Constitution, as interpreted in *McCulloch* v. *Maryland*	Any power that is an appropriate, nonprohibited means to a legitimate end
Inherent (national government)	Supreme Court in *U.S.* v. *Curtiss-Wright*	Power to acquire territory by exploration, to regulate arms sales
Reserved (state governments)	Constitution	Power to establish state and local governments, to conduct elections, to police
Concurrent (shared by national and state governments)	Traditional practice	Power to tax, to spend, to build roads, to regulate business

Inherent Powers and the Case of U.S. v. Curtiss-Wright

It was more than a century before the third part of the "triangle of powers" of the national government was explicitly developed in a Supreme Court opinion in *U.S.* v. *Curtiss-Wright Export Corp.* (1936). That company had sold arms to Bolivia after Congress had empowered the president to forbid such sales by issuing a proclamation making them a crime. The question was whether Congress could delegate such legislative power to the president in the area of international relations. The court said yes, ruling that the national government has the powers any nation-state must have, not only to declare war and make treaties (which the Constitution explicitly grants it) but also, for example, to acquire territory by exploration (which the Constitution does not mention). These powers are termed **inherent powers** because they are "necessary concomitants of its nationality." Thus, such powers inhere in the United States as a nation-state, regardless of what the Constitution does or does not say.

Concurrent Powers

The special constitutional powers of the national government, as they have developed, are the express or enumerated powers, the implied powers, and the inherent powers. The special constitutional powers of the state governments are the reserved powers. The most commonly exercised powers, however, are called the **concurrent**, or shared,

powers. These powers are exercised at both levels, national and state, so long as they do not conflict. Among the important concurrent powers are the power to collect taxes, the power to spend, the power to build roads, and the power to regulate commerce within each state. The development of the types of ruling power is summarized in Table 2.3.

The power to regulate commerce was eventually to become the focus for more dispute between the national government and the states. But for the first century and a half of America's history, the courts interpreted the **commerce clause**[15] as a license for Congress to subsidize trade and prevent discriminatory treatment of goods by different states—both of which policies made major contributions to the economic development of America. As we shall see in Chapter 15, when movements for limitation of child labor and for what we now call consumer protection gained great strength, there were major struggles in the courts over the appropriate extent of national regulation of commerce.

Over the years the long-term movement has been toward more extensive national powers and more limited state powers. When it involved the question of slavery, this struggle led to the Civil War but only after a conservative-leaning Supreme Court had reaffirmed the constitutionality of slavery in *Dred Scott* v. *Sandford* (1857). In that case,

---

[15]Article I, Section 8: "The Congress shall have power . . . to regulate commerce with foreign nations, and among the several states, and with the Indian tribes."

Dred Scott. (Courtesy of Missouri Historical Society)

a slave named Dred Scott, who had been moved by his owner to Illinois—where, by state law, slavery was illegal—sued in court for his freedom. But the Supreme Court, dominated by southern judges, made two important rulings. The first was that, as a black man, Scott could not be a citizen of the United States and so had no right to sue in court at all. The Court reached this conclusion and applied it to Scott in Illinois, even though blacks had long been considered citizens in most northern states, including Illinois, and so had such a right. The second ruling was that the Compromise of 1820, an act passed by Congress outlawing slavery, was unconstitutional because it deprived citizens of their property (slaves) without due process of law.

The Civil War settled not only the question of slavery but also the question of whether states had the right to secede from the Union, as the South had tried to do. In the Reconstruction era after the war, radical northerners dominated southern politics and passed progressive legislation in some southern states as well as civil-rights enforcement laws in the Congress. They also passed and ratified three constitutional amendments: The Thirteenth (1865) outlawed slavery; the Fourteenth (1868) guaranteed all persons "equal protection of the laws" and protection against any state's efforts to "deprive any person of life, liberty, or property, without due process of law"; and the Fifteenth (1870) prohibited denying the right to vote "on account of race, color, or previous condition of servitude."

The pendulum then swung back toward states' rights. But the second decade of the 20th century, dominated by Woodrow Wilson's presidency, saw major new programs of national aid to states and localities for agriculture, vocational education, and highway construction. These programs inevitably increased federal control over the states.

The Depression of the 1930s resulted in a massive increase in national programs under the New Deal. Some of these programs were so controversial in their shift of power from the states to Washington that the Supreme Court ruled many of them unconstitutional.

THE EVOLUTION OF AMERICAN FEDERALISM

The first problems in governing, as we have seen, are establishing obedience to political authority and achieving stability over time. This stability was gained in the American case by elections and constitutional amendment. The next two problems for America have involved expansion and extension. These processes have tended to occur together in our history.

The national government *expanded* its authority over geographical space and the peoples of that space as the country extended its borders from the East Coast to the Pacific. At the same time, it *extended* its authority over more and more realms of life or *domains*. Both processes strengthened the power of the national government in relation to the states, changing the nature of our federalism.

The Era of Dual Federalism

With the passing of John Marshall, who served as chief justice of the Supreme Court until his death in 1835, the nationalist tide ebbed. The Jacksonian era, which began with Andrew Jackson's two terms as president (1829–1837), was characterized by a renewed focus on states' rights. It was an era of great economic growth, especially in the years between the Jackson administration and the Civil War. New economic interests emerged and often sought assistance from government. If they wanted subsidies or tax breaks, they were likely to go to their state governments. If they sought tariffs to protect them from competition from cheap imports, they had to go to the national government.

Roger B. Taney. (New York Public Library Picture Collection)

At the same time, however, there was political development under Jacksonian leadership. As we will see in detail in Chapter 3, the vote was extended to new groups, and political participation increased. This changing political pattern "shifted influence away from business elites aware of the nationalizing trends and toward farmers and working men whose economic position made them less directly implicated in the nationalizing economy."[16]

The consequence was an era often characterized as dual federalism. In 1835 Roger B. Taney (1777–1864) succeeded Marshall as chief justice. Taney saw the Court's position as standing outside and above both the national government and the states. He saw its role as arbitrator between these two centers of diverse yet equally sovereign power. "This judicial power," he wrote in a decision issued just before the Civil War, "was justly regarded as indispensable, not merely to maintain the supremacy of the laws of the United States, but also to guard the States from any encroachment upon their reserved rights by the general [national] government."[17]

The era of dual federalism is generally said to have extended until the New Deal years of the 1930s. However, research by Daniel J. Elazar has shown that this is not really an accurate description of political reality in this period. In fact, national and state governments were cooperating in such areas as railroad construction and banking as early as the mid-19th century, and in canals and ports as early as the late 18th century.[18] There was an important element of partnership or cooperation throughout this era in which the overall pattern was once again one of centralization of power. Thus, we might refer to the period between 1861 and 1932 as dual federalism II.

This pattern of centralization became clear only when it was widely recognized that ending the Great Depression of the 1930s would require more than cooperation between the states and Washington—and more than mediation between them by the Supreme Court.

This era saw such new departures as the Social Security Act of 1935 (which we shall discuss in Chapter 16). That act included national grants for state and local unemployment and welfare programs. The 1930s also saw the first national involvement in local public housing (the Housing Act of 1937). As federal relations became more centralized, the role of money provided by Washington became more important.

The Era of Cooperative Federalism

Most scholars use the term **cooperative federalism** to describe the system operating during the period since the New Deal. "By the cooperative conception of the federal relationship," wrote constitutional expert Edward S. Corwin in 1953, "the States and the National Government are regarded as mutually complementary parts of a single governmental mechanism all of whose powers are intended to realize the current purposes of government according to their applicability to the problem in hand."[19]

As we shall see, and as Table 2.4 shows, there have been important differences among recent administrations, and each administration has cho-

---

[16]Samuel Beer, "The Modernization of American Federalism," in *The Federal Polity*, ed. Daniel J. Elazar, p. 62.

[17]*Abelman* v. *Booth* (1859).

[18]See Daniel J. Elazar, *The American Partnership* (Chicago: Univ. of Chicago Press, 1962).

[19]Edward S. Corwin, *The Constitution of the United States of America: Analysis and Interpretation* (Washington, DC: GPO, 1953), p. x. The term was coined by Jane Perry Clark in her book *The Rise of a New Federalism* (New York: Russell, 1938). For a competing view asserting that it has been less a matter of cooperation and more a matter of centralization, see Harry N. Scheiber, *The Condition of American Federalism: An Historian's View* (Washington, DC: GPO, 1966).

TABLE 2.4

Stages in American Federalism

PERIOD	NAME	POPULAR METAPHOR	CHARACTERISTICS
1. Until 1860	Dual Federalism	legal federalism	National government limited to enumerated powers within their own spheres; the states and the national government are sovereign and therefore equal; the relation between the states and the national government is one of tension rather than collaboration
2. 1861–1932	Dual Federalism II	layer cake	Dual-federal characteristics persist, but national government gains strength because of role in promoting economic growth; era of land grants
3. 1930–1960	Cooperative Federalism	cooperative	Federal-state-local sharing of responsibilities for almost all functions; steady growth of national government's powers, especially regulation
4. 1960–1968	Creative Federalism	cooperative	President Johnson's emphasis on partnership of national government, states, cities, counties, school districts, nonprofit organizations; many new programs with many grants made directly to cities
5. 1968–1976	New Federalism I	marble cake	President Nixon's emphasis on decentralization
6. 1977–1980	New Partnership Federalism	picket fence	President Carter's emphasis on partnership, urban problems, devolution of responsibility, and fiscal caution coupled with tighter management
7. 1981–	New Federalism II	picket fence	President Reagan's emphasis on cutting back federal government's role and increasing managerial efficiency

Source: This chart has been developed from various scholarly accounts, the most useful of which have been David B. Walker, *Toward a Functioning Federalism* (Cambridge, MA: Winthrop, 1981), and Raymond A. Shapek, *Managing Federalism: The Evolution and Development of the Grants-in-Aid System* (Charlottesville, VA: Community Collaborators, 1981).

sen a name to characterize its program. All have emphasized cooperation between Washington and the states and cities. But this cooperation has been very uneven, largely because of the controversial and varying roles played by money and regulation.

The Fiscal and Regulatory Aspects of Federalism

Many of the things governments do involve making rules, and most of the things they do involve money—either spending it or collecting it. Experts now call the issues concerning money fiscal federalism and those concerning rules made to govern the conduct of business and industry—and of states and cities—regulatory federalism.

The national government has made grants of money to states ever since its creation.[20] The first instance was the decision by the new government to grant money to pay the debts the states had in-curred during the struggle for independence. That was done to establish the financial authority of the country and its national government.[21] The next instance of such **grants-in-aid** was an 1802 law providing that revenue from the sale of public lands was to be shared with the states. In 1836 Congress voted to divide a budgetary surplus with the states. But from this point on, programs tended to become more specific. Such **categorical grants** required that lands granted be used or funds given be spent for particular programs in particular ways.

Such programs were developed because certain important activities, such as education and welfare, were not express or implied powers of the national government, according to the Constitution, but were reserved to the states. Thus, if the national government wanted to encourage such activities, all it could do was give money to the other levels of government so that they could do these things themselves. This federal money is raised by taxation, which became an express power of the

---

[20]For a brief history of fiscal federalism, see George F. Break, "Fiscal Federalism in the U.S.: The First 200 Years, Evolution and Outlook," in Conference on the Future of Federalism, *The Future of Federalism in the 1980s* (Washington, DC: Advisory Commission on Intergovernmental Relations, 1981), chap. 3.

[21]It was a controversial policy, opposed by the states that had already paid off their debts. The compromise reached included a provision that the national government would reimburse those states.

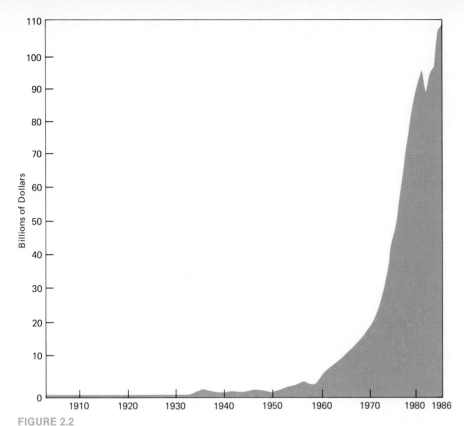

FIGURE 2.2

The Growth of Federal Aid to State and Local Governments.

Source: Office of Management and Budget.

national government by virtue of the Sixteenth Amendment.[22] With the "carrot" of funds has come the "stick" of rules and regulations. When the national government provided funds, it also tended to specify how they were to be spent. In other words, the grants came with strings attached.

The great enforcement device in intergovernmental relations today is the threat to withhold federal funds. It can be used to force states and cities to take steps to achieve anything from greater racial equality to highway beautification. Until the Depression, the level of federal financial aid to states and localities was low enough so that no real dependency was involved. Figure 2.2 shows the rapid growth of federal aid in recent decades; Table 2.5 shows federal aid as a percentage of total state and local revenue. It shows that the percentage peaked at the end of Carter's administration and began to decline under Reagan before rising again. To see how fiscal federalism and regulatory federalism have evolved hand in hand, we must review what recent administrations have done.

[22]For a concise history, see George E. Hale and Marian Lief Palley, *The Politics of Federal Grants* (Washington, DC: Congressional Quarterly Press, 1981).

TABLE 2.5

Federal Aid as a Percentage of Total State and Local Revenue from Own Sources

YEAR	PERCENT
1955	11.8
1960	16.8
1965	17.7
1970	22.9
1975	29.1
1980	30.5
1982	25.0
1984	20.0
1985	24.0

Source: Data from Advisory Commission on Intergovernmental Relations.

The Era of Creative Federalism

How has this great growth in national aid to state and local governments come about? The first important innovation came from the Democrats. It began with Roosevelt's New Deal in 1933 but flowered most fully in Lyndon Johnson's Great Society (1963–1968). The number of grant programs grew from about 50 in 1961 to some 420 by the time

Johnson left office. Johnson called his program Creative Federalism, and it certainly created many new categorical grant programs, complete with regulations as to how they were to be carried out by the states and cities. One result was growing national dominance in policy making. Another result, however, was a growing desire by states and cities for more discretion in how they spent federal grant funds.

Nixon's New Federalism

The Politics of Revenue Sharing

In a message to Congress on February 4, 1971, President Nixon noted that most federal assistance took the form of "highly restricted programs of categorical grants-in-aid. . . . The major difficulty is that States and localities are not free to spend these funds on their own needs as they see them. The money is spent instead for the things Washington wants and in the way Washington orders. . . . State and local governments need Federal . . . money to spend, but they also need greater freedom in spending it."

So Congress passed the State and Local Fiscal Assistance Act of 1972, which called for revenue sharing. Nixon had declared that his program would bring about "a historic and massive reversal of the flow of power in America" because it would provide grants of funds that could be spent in whatever ways states and localities saw fit.

The political struggle that surrounded revenue sharing reveals much about the politics of federalism today. The first proposals for revenue sharing had come eight years earlier, when it became obvious that states and cities could no longer rely on state and local taxes to finance needed services and programs. Governmental experts expected then that continued economic growth would increase federal revenues year by year and that the war in Vietnam would come to a speedy end, so that the federal government would have surplus funds. Some suggested that these surplus funds should therefore be transferred to the states and cities.

The proposal stimulated a major debate in Congress, where the various interests were well represented, both by congressional supporters and by lobbyists. President Nixon and state governors favored the plan. Governor Nelson Rockfeller of New York formed a National Citizens Committee for

TABLE 2.6
Number of Local Units of Government

Counties	3,041
Municipalities	19,076
Townships	16,734
School districts	14,851
Special districts[a]	28,588
Total	82,290

[a]These special districts are established to provide firefighting, water, transit, and other local or regional services.
Source: U.S. Bureau of the Census, *1982 Census of Governments,* published August 1983.

Revenue Sharing to lobby Congress in the spring of 1971. Its 33 state affiliates, composed of business people, academics, and church groups, did more lobbying. Less enthusiastic were Democratic liberals and members of Congress from large urban areas. They feared that it would end the categorical grants that required spending for the poor and disadvantaged.

Any issue that promises to affect strongly all levels of government will bring out strong representation of America's many governments.[23] There are over 82,000 governments in America, according to the Census Bureau's survey, reported in Table 2.6. All of these governments were to be affected in one way or another by the revenue-sharing program. The National Governors' Conference lobbied; and so did the National League of Cities, the U.S. Conference of Mayors, and the International City Management Association. So too did the National Association of Counties.

The end result was passage of the bill in 1972. We shall discuss some of the effects of the $30 billion spent over the first six-year period when we examine urban problems (Chapter 17). The program remained so controversial that when it expired in 1976, it took a great struggle to get it renewed for four more years and an appropriation of $26 billion.

Still, revenue sharing remained very popular with state and local governments—especially those local governments with decreasing tax bases, such as northern cities. It came up for renewal again in 1980, and its sledding was even rougher then. After long debates in Congress—two and a half months after the program had lapsed and after the con-

---

[23]For an account of state and local lobbying, see Donald Haider, *When Governments Come to Washington* (New York: Free Press, 1974).

President Nixon signing the State and Local Fiscal Assistance Act of 1972 which established revenue sharing. (AP/Wide World Photos)

servative tide in the 1980 election but before the new Congress took office—the program was renewed for three years. It provided $4.6 billion each year for local governments. The states, however, were excluded totally. In 1983 it was extended for three more years at the same level of $4.6 billion a year. Once again, states were excluded. Finally, in 1986, at a time of obsession with the enormous federal deficit, revenue sharing was allowed to die despite a major lobbying effort by the same coalition.

The Politics of Other Federal Aid Programs

Most federal aid programs are still of the old, categorical type: aid for specific programs. About three-quarters of all funds granted to states and localities fall into this category. Originally, these programs were developed to create greater equality among the various parts of the nation in areas such as education and public transportation. In 1972 political scientist Michael Reagan, a staunch advocate of such programs, forecast that

> the fundamental trend in the development of our intergovernmental system will be the continued further development of the notion of a national community and a further ideological acceptance of the corollary proposition that it is proper for the goals and standards of public service to be set by the national gov-

ernment as a basis for uniform rights for citizens no matter where they live.[24]

But has the result been common national goals and standards? More and more observers have their doubts.[25] One concluded in 1980 that "instead of bringing clear-cut federal control, it has resulted in a mishmash of federal-state-local authority with a resultant loss of efficiency, accountability, and public confidence."[26]

One of many such examples of overlap is the case of fire protection. Until recently, this was thought to be the most local of functions. But in 1972 Congress passed the Rural Development Act, which provided for grants to rural communities with poor fire protection. Two years later, the Federal Fire Prevention and Control Act was passed. It set up the U.S. Fire Administration, now a part of the Federal Emergency Management Agency. While this unit is supposed to coordinate federal fire-protection efforts, it is only one of 49 federal agencies now involved. In fact, agencies within all federal cabinet departments except State and Defense,

---

[24]Michael Reagan, *The New Federalism* (New York: Oxford Univ. Press, 1972), p. 11. (This Reagan is no relation to Ronald Reagan.)

[25]From the point of view of local governments, the situation is complicated by the fact that the states also impose a great many regulations on them.

[26]John Shannon, "The End of a Fiscal Era—Uncle Sam Loses His Trump Cards," *Intergovernmental Perspective* (Fall 1980), 31.

along with 11 other independent federal agencies, are involved in fire-related activities that affect state and local governments. In addition, there are 52 grant-in-aid programs administered by 24 of these agencies to help such governments fight fire.[27] In 1960 the only federal involvement in this realm was through a Forest Service program.

The primary cause of growing national dominance, as Corwin put it three decades ago, was that

> when two cooperate, it is the stronger member of the combination who usually calls the tunes. Resting as it does primarily on the superior fiscal resources of the National Government, Cooperative Federalism has been, at least to date, a short expression for a constantly increasing concentration of power at Washington in the stimulation and supervision of local policies.[28]

This fiscal dominance increased in the 1960s and 1970s. In 1960 there were only 50 programs of federal aid to states and cities. Today there are over 500, despite the Reagan administration's attempts to combine and cut back programs. In 1986 the states and localities received over $100 billion in federal aid, up from $7 billion in 1960. That amount was between a fifth and a quarter of these governments' budgets. In some programs the percentage is much higher. Fully 85 percent of all state and local spending on housing comes from Washington, as does almost 60 percent of welfare spending, for example.

The Politics of Regulatory Federalism

With money has come regulation. Until recently, most federal regulation concerned labor and businesses such as railroads, trucking, radio, and television. But in the past two decades, the national government has undertaken new programs of social regulation in fields such as civil rights, consumer protection, health and safety, and environmental quality. These national laws have sought goals favored by state and local governments and by the people—as well as by Washington. But because they have been drafted in Washington the laws contain general rules intended to apply to all states and cities. Further, many of the laws are supposed to be applied and enforced by the states or the cities. In fact, by 1980 there were 223 sets

of direct federal orders regulating states or cities and another 1036 sets that were conditions of fiscal aid.

By the 1970s opposition to such regulation had mounted, and there were calls for strengthening the states in their relations with Washington. Revenue sharing was the first program from Washington to recognize this new direction. But even before it was developed, there was new thinking in the Nixon White House. In fact, one Nixon aide, William Safire, drafted and circulated a long document, which began:

> We like the blessings of strong central government: a clear direction toward social goals, a willingness to counteract economic freezings and overheatings, a single voice in world affairs. But we are repelled by centralization's side effects: ineffective administration that breeds resentment, inflexible bureaucracy that breeds alienation. We also like the blessings of decentralization or "home rule," with its respect for diversity, its ready response to local demands, its personality tailored to its constituents. But we are repelled by frequent local unwillingness or inability to meet human needs. Local authority will now regain the right to meet local needs itself, and again an additional right to Federal financial help; but it will not regain the right it once held to neglect the needs of its citizens. States' rights are now more accurately described as States' duties; this is a fundamental change in Federalism, removing its great fault without undermining its essential local-first character, and [it] provides the New Federalists with two of their prime causes: the cause of regaining control, and the cause of fairness.[29]

Safire entitled his memo "New Federalist Paper No. 1" and signed it Publius.

Nixon's New Federalism, while recognizing local concerns, in fact tended to shift *ultimate* power even further toward Washington. Carter's program focused on urban problems and on better management. Most observers found his approach of only limited effectiveness.[30]

Reagan's New Federalism

As we shall see time and again in this book, Ronald Reagan took office pledging a revolution in government that would reduce the role of the national

---

[27]See *The Federal Role in Local Fire Protection* (Washington, DC: Advisory Commission on Intergovernmental Relations, 1980).

[28]Corwin, *Constitution of the United States*, p. xiv.

[29]Publius, "New Federalist Paper No. 1," reprinted in *Publius* 3 (Spring 1972), 99–100.

[30]We'll examine his efforts to develop an urban policy in Chapter 17. For an assessment of his policy on federalism, see David B. Walker, *Toward a Functioning Federalism* (Cambridge, MA: Winthrop, 1981), pp. 113–23.

government. In this area, he called his revolution by the same name Nixon had used.

In his first year he successfully cut levels of federal aid, enacted nine new block grants, and began to cut back federal regulations of industry so that states could reclaim that power. There had been growing unhappiness in business and industry over the press of federal regulations. This unhappiness was compounded by the fact that these regulations were sometimes enforced inconsistently from state to state or from city to city. This feeling contributed to the widespread support for Reagan's policies.[31] When this cutback occurred, many states did indeed step in and pass new regulations. But in some states politically powerful labor unions got state legislatures to pass new, strong laws protecting worker safety and health.

The "Reagan revolution" was intended to free business and industry from control by government. The actual effect, however, was often to confront business with different rules in different states. This situation so complicated life for big businesses operating in many states that they increasingly called for a return to national regulation. Reagan's reform proposals were not limited to regulatory federalism. In his second year he called for drastic cutbacks in federal spending for state and local programs. But with the economy in recession and many states and cities near bankruptcy, Congress refused to accept the proposals.

Reagan's proposals in later years were even more modest. He sought consolidation of programs and limits on revenue sharing, but Congress did not agree. The final result was a continuation of programs as usual. There was, however, one important change. By Reagan's fourth year, states and cities had stopped expecting Washington to solve their problems for them. Instead, they had turned their efforts to coping with their own problems as their own resources increased while the federal budget deficit did likewise. That shift was certainly a success for Reagan's New Federalism.[32]

But why did the Reagan program have little

success beyond this? Thomas Anton offers three reasons. First, it was developed without consulting the governors and mayors who would have to implement it. Second, it neglected the fact that most programs are supported by coalitions of different interests. This meant that a decision to cut back a program would affect many different groups. For example, Reagan proposed cuts in funds for reconstructing local communities. This program was supported by residents, by local businesses, by builders and contractors, and by mayors. These groups joined together locally and then coordinated their lobbying nationally. They were a large and powerful national coalition—and they won.

Yet another failure of the Reagan administration, according to Anton, was ignoring the different ways its proposals would affect different regions. For example, Reagan proposed to cut general block grants and instead turn back to each state the money raised within the state by federal taxes on alcohol, telephones, and gasoline. The problem is that more than half of this money comes from less than a half-dozen states. In each case, then, a handful of states would get significantly more money while the other 40-odd states would get much less. Those who would have lost out under this system formed a coalition and beat the proposal.[33]

The states—and the cities—*are* different. They benefit in different ways from federal programs, and they pay different amounts in taxes to Washington. Realization of this fact has produced strong political movements for regional power in some areas of the country in the last decade or so. It has also renewed appreciation of the diversity that federalism helps to preserve, as we shall now see.

RECENT TRENDS IN FEDERALISM

Conservative opposition to Washington's dominance has been consistent. Thus, President Reagan's program caused no surprise. Conservatives have always argued for less federal control—even when they were accepting federal funds for their states and cities. Recently, however, both conservatives and liberals in some states have taken important new policy initiatives.

---

[31]See *Regulatory Federalism: Policy, Process, Impact and Reform* (Washington, DC: Advisory Commission on Intergovernmental Relations, 1983).

[32]For interesting evaluations of Reagan's New Federalism, see the articles in *Publius* 16 (Winter 1986). And for an argument that it cannot overcome the fundamental centralized nature of intergovernmental relations, see John E. Chubb, "Federalism and the Bias for Centralization," chap. 10 in Chubb and Paul E. Peterson, eds., *The New Direction in American Politics* (Washington, DC: Brookings, 1985).

[33]See Thomas J. Anton, "Decay and Reconstruction in the Study of American Intergovernmental Relations," *Publius* 15 (Winter 1985), 65–97.

State Initiatives

There have been important initiatives at the state level in recent years. A survey done by the National Governors' Association found some 60 programs that, it said, reaffirmed the states' historic role as "laboratories of democracy." Among them:

- Georgia's Family Farm Bond Program helps family farmers obtain land through low-interest loans. Other states now have similar programs.
- California has a program to help renters become owners of buildings or mobile-home parks being converted to cooperatives or condominiums.
- Minnesota developed a Comprehensive Child Health Screening Program.
- Iowa has a Railroad Rehabilitation Program.[34]

In addition, more and more states are proving to be innovators in providing economic incentives to new and redeveloping businesses. In the past, states have given tax breaks to new businesses. Now some also offer special job-training aid, new transportation systems, and plant-site development assistance as well as special low-interest loans.

State Modernization

The growth in state initiatives is but one consequence of the modernization of state governments. The box summarizing such modernization between 1960 and 1980 specifies some of the important changes in state institutions. Before these changes occurred, most state governments were regarded by many observers as outdated, inefficient, and unresponsive to the problems and challenges facing them. That is one reason why the national government took on so many new functions and gained so much power. Recent developments such as these innovations have led Leon Epstein to conclude:

> By most measures . . . the states are thriving within the federal system. Their constitutional durability is in little doubt, their activities are greatly expanded, their capacity and their authority are increasingly more impressive in relation to those of local governments, they are changing their institutional structures so as to be more effective as agencies of government. . . . [35]

Education Reform

The current state initiatives with the greatest long-term importance will be the efforts to improve education. The Reagan administration cut federal contributions to spending on education from 9.2 percent in 1980 to 6.4 percent in 1986. It called for greater state and local roles. In the early 1980s many states mandated state exams to test high school students' competencies. Then in 1986 the National Governors' Association issued a report including 65 proposals for improving teaching and learning. Meanwhile, every state in the union was developing new programs to improve undergraduate education. Among these have been new core curricula, remedial education, and teacher education reforms. Such changes will be slow to take effect but could have profound impact on the economic strength of a state—and even on the political skills of its citizens.[36]

Although the states as a whole have recently gained in power and assumed more responsibility, some states have benefited more than others. Because there is a geographical pattern to these differences some observers believe we are becoming a nation of regions rather than a nation of states.[37]

FEDERALISM AND REGIONALISM: SUNBELT AND SNOWBELT

In recent decades there has been a large population shift from the older states of the Northeast, the Midwest, and the Northwest (the **Snowbelt**) to the states of the South and the Southwest (the **Sunbelt**). A line across the middle of the United States leaving Virginia in the southern half forms the usual dividing line between Sunbelt and Snowbelt. From 1970 to 1980 the U.S. population grew by 11 percent, but that growth was concentrated in the Sunbelt, which grew by more than 20 percent. Figure 2.3 shows the percentage changes state by state in this decade. From 1980 to 1986 the U.S. growth was 3.3 percent, but 91 percent of that was in the Sunbelt. These figures remind us that al-

---

[34]See *Governors' Policy Initiatives: Meeting the Challenges of the 1980s* (Washington, DC: National Governors' Association, 1980).

[35]Leon Epstein, "The Old States in a New System," in *The New American Political System*, ed. Anthony King (Washington, DC: American Enterprise Institute, 1978), p. 366.

[36]For accounts of such efforts, see *State Education Leader*, published quarterly by the Education Commission of the States, and Ellen Hoffman, "Reform's Second Wave," *National Journal*, Sept. 13, 1986, pp. 2165–69.

[37]It is worth remembering, however, that such regional imbalances are not a new phenomenon.

The Modernization of State Institutions: 1960–1980

Eleven state constitutions were overhauled.

Fifteen states in 1960 limited their governors to two-year terms, as against only four now; and 16 prohibited their chief executives from succeeding themselves, compared to 50 in 1980.

Twenty-three major executive-branch reorganizations between 1965 and 1979, however, achieved a significant lowering in the number of independent administrative agencies. Connecticut's 1977–1979 reorganization, for example, reduced its number of such units from 210 to 22.

All but 5 state legislatures in 1960 were heavily malapportioned (and at least two dozen of the 99 separate bodies—Nebraska being unicameral—were placed beyond the reapportionment process by state constitutional provisions); whereas at present all the legislatures are apportioned according to the "one person, one vote" principle, thanks chiefly to *Baker* v. *Carr* and its follow-up decisions.

While two decades ago 31 legislatures operated primarily on a biennial session basis, today only 14 function in this fashion, and these frequently are called into special session in the second year.

Over half the state constitutions then restricted regular legislative sessions to 60 legislative or calendar days or less. At this point the figure is 19.

Source: Adapted from David B. Walker, "The States and the System: Changes and Choices," *Intergovernmental Perspective* 6 (Fall 1980), 7.

though the Snowbelt still has almost twice as many people, the rate of change has recently favored the Sunbelt.

Such population shifts do not simply happen. They are related to other developments. In the last 25 years many industries in the northern states have either moved south or closed down. One reason is high labor costs in the North, where unions are stronger. Another is outmoded industrial machinery in older northern factories that are expensive to modernize. In addition, states have offered special tax breaks to lure industry. Both Sunbelt and

FIGURE 2.3

U.S. Population Growth, 1970–1980—Sunbelt versus Snowbelt.

Source: U.S. Bureau of the Census, *Census of Population: 1970*, vol. 1, chap. A (PC80–1A).

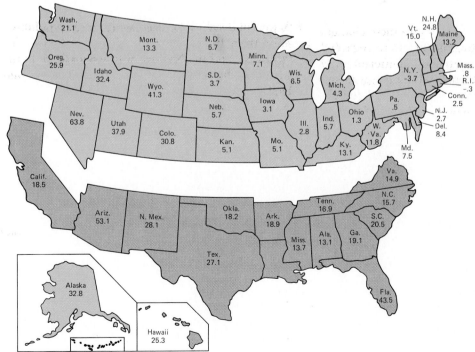

Snowbelt states now do so. This shift of industry has meant more jobs in the South and West and fewer jobs in the North. People tend to move where the jobs are. In turn, this means that per capita (per person) income in each region has changed, too. In 1940, for example, the average income in the Northeast was 131 percent of the national average, while in the South it was only 66 percent. By 1980 the Northeast was down to only 106 percent of the national average, while the South was up to 91 percent. In other words, the people in the South remain poorer on the average than those in the Northeast, but the gap is closing.

This closing of the gap was hastened by the sharp increases in the prices of food and fuel following the energy crisis of 1973–1974 and by the high inflation of the early 1970s. Since many states in the Sunbelt have surpluses of energy and food, prices are lower there. Furthermore, they need less energy because of the warmer climate. So costs are yet another reason why both citizens and industries from the Snowbelt have been moving south and west.

Related to these developments has been a shift in federal government spending toward the Sunbelt states. Defense and space-program industries have tended to set up plants in the states with lower labor costs and taxes—those in the Sunbelt—so government dollars have increasingly been spent in these states. Furthermore, special government antipoverty programs have tended to concentrate on the urban poor, and Sunbelt cities such as Houston, Atlanta, and Los Angeles have been among the major targets.

From 1975 to 1979, for example, the people and businesses of the 18 Snowbelt states of the Northeast and Midwest areas paid $165 billion more in federal taxes than they received from Washington in grants and government spending. The 32 Sunbelt states, by contrast, got $112 billion more back than they paid in taxes. Figure 2.4 shows how much tax money the federal government collects in each state for each dollar it spends in aid to the state.

As a consequence of these varied factors, long-standing regional differences are declining. A study

FIGURE 2.4

Federal Aid to States, 1982–1984—Sunbelt versus Snowbelt.

Source: Intergovernmental Perspective, Spring/Summer, 1985, p. 19.

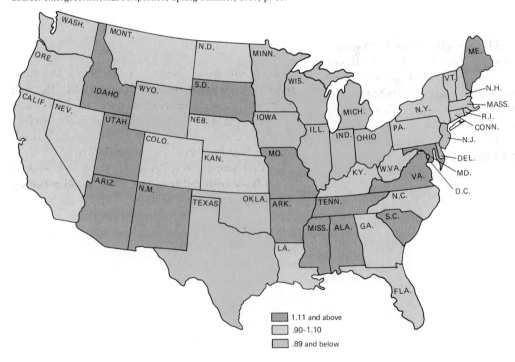

1.11 and above
.90–1.10
.89 and below

by the Advisory Commission on Intergovernmental Relations (ACIR) found that "per capita income and ratios of federal revenues and expenditures by state are converging over the long pull—at rates which have slowed considerably in the past few years. At the same time, there has been a definite decentralization of economic activity away from earlier industrialized states, toward the 'newer,' less developed sections of the country."[38] A consequence of this trend has been a reduction in the longstanding poverty so characteristic of the South. Some experts conclude that these declining differences are good for the country as a whole.

> To a large extent, migration of people and jobs is occurring in response to real economic forces affecting the costs of production and service delivery. The result has been to improve overall economic efficiency in the national economy. Furthermore, the dramatic declines in poverty rates in the fast-growing southern states suggest that *rapid economic development may provide the best hope for achieving social equity policy goals.*[39]

Even if this is so, the states that are declining have not welcomed the trend in the short run. It is not surprising that different growth rates have led to a political struggle between the Sunbelt and Snowbelt for jobs, people, and capital. Battles over how federal funds should be spent have been fought increasingly along regional lines in recent years, and it appears this regional conflict will intensify in coming years.[40] When results of the 1980 census were used to reapportion the 435 seats in the House of Representatives among the 50 states, the states gaining the most population gained seats from those falling behind. These changes shifted 17 seats from the Snowbelt states to the Sunbelt states, as Table 2.7 shows. This shift gives the South and West a majority for the first time.

Another recent Census Bureau study projects changes likely to occur in the next two censuses. It forecasts the shift of another 19 seats from the East and Midwest to the South and West after the 1990 census, and another 19 seats after the 2000 census. The big gainers would be California (up from 45

TABLE 2.7
Congressional Reapportionment Resulting from the 1980 Census

State	Change	State	Change
Alabama	—	Nebraska	—
Arizona	+1	Nevada	+1
Arkansas	—	New Hampshire	—
California	+2	New Jersey	−1
Colorado	+1	New Mexico	+1
Connecticut	—	New York	−5
Delaware	—	North Carolina	—
D. C.	—	North Dakota	—
Florida	+4	Ohio	−2
Georgia	—	Oklahoma	—
Idaho	—	Oregon	+1
Illinois	−2	Pennsylvania	−2
Indiana	−1	Rhode Island	—
Iowa	—	South Carolina	—
Kansas	—	South Dakota	−1
Kentucky	—	Tennessee	+1
Louisiana	—	Texas	+3
Maine	—	Utah	+1
Maryland	—	Vermont	—
Massachusetts	−1	Virginia	—
Michigan	−1	Washington	+1
Minnesota	—	West Virginia	—
Mississippi	—	Wisconsin	—
Missouri	−1	Wyoming	—
Montana	—		

Figures indicate number of seats each state gained or lost.

to 50), Texas (from 27 to 34), and Florida (from 19 to 28). The biggest losers would be New York (down from 34 to 24) and Pennsylvania (from 23 to 18). However, these projections depend on continued migration from the Northeast and Midwest to the South and West.

In recent years, many northeastern states have achieved economic revitalization, largely through a growth in high-technology industry. The major factors have been innovative economic-development programs plus the presence of strong schools and universities and the availability of a well-educated work force. Meanwhile, many Sunbelt states have suffered from a decline in oil refining, chemicals, steel, and textiles. And when the price of oil collapsed from $35 a barrel to under $10 in 1986, the states with economies highly dependent upon oil—Texas, Louisiana, Oklahoma, and Colorado—suffered major setbacks. Workers lost jobs, businesses lost customers, and states lost tax revenues.[41]

[38]Janet Rothenberg Park, "Frostbelt and Sunbelt: Convergence over Time," *Intergovernmental Perspective* 4 (Fall 1978), 8.

[39]Bernard L. Weinstein and John Rees, "Sunbelt/Frostbelt Confrontation?" *Society* 17 (May–June 1980), 21.

[40]See Robert Goodman, *The Last Entrepreneurs: America's Regional Wars for Jobs and Dollars* (New York: Simon & Schuster, 1979).

[41]See Bernard Weinstein et al., *Regional Growth and Decline in the United States*, 2d ed. (New York: Praeger, 1985).

The Politics of Federalism 73

Economic developments such as these are very hard to forecast. They are very dependent on developments in the world economy that no government can control. They affect the flow of population and of federal funds as well. Thus the future of the regions of the United States remains to be determined. So does the future of federalism.

THE FUTURE OF AMERICAN FEDERALISM

Because of changing policies in Washington and changing economic conditions, federalism is now experiencing a rebirth in the minds of many politicians and citizens alike. "The hard test of any federal system," Stephen L. Schechter has written, "is whether it can formulate and implement national policies for problems that require national solutions, but in ways that are sensitive to the constitutional balance between general (federal) and constituent (state) governments *and* to the reasons for wanting that balance."[42]

For the states to play an active role, they must have greater power to act and more resources with which to act. That will depend on cooperation, first among the states and then between the states and the central government. It will also depend on the effects of the major changes now occurring in America. The changes over the past 25 years that seem most important are summarized in Table 2.8. The political impact and outcome of such changes will depend in part on shifts in population, capital, and political power. Developments involving food, energy, and the economy, both domestic and international, are very hard to predict. In addition, it is still not clear how solidly the states within each region will cooperate or how different regional objectives will become.

There are signs of growing cooperation among the states in certain areas, as we have seen. In addition, most states have now modernized their governments so that they can operate more effectively, alone or together, in dealing with the federal government and with their own cities. Our federal system is intended to facilitate both efforts. As Daniel J. Elazar writes: "The virtue of the federal system lies in its ability to develop and maintain mecha-

[42]Stephen L. Schechter, "The State of American Federalism: 1979," *Publius*, Winter 1980, p. 7.

TABLE 2.8
Key Trends in the Federal System over the Past Twenty-five Years

1. Growth in government and expansion of governmental roles into many areas formerly limited to the private sector
2. Massive growth in the size, scope, and intrusiveness of federal aid
3. Troubled cities and urban areas
4. Increasingly significant role of the courts in intergovernmental areas, accompanying a concern for equity in the system
5. Growing dependence of local government (particularly cities) on state and federal aid
6. Strengthened states in general and more powerful state revenue systems in particular
7. Disaffection with government and growing concern for government accountability
8. Increased intergovernmental lobbying—governments lobbying government
9. Increasing numbers of regional bodies
10. Emergence of the Frostbelt-Sunbelt regional competition
11. New state emphasis on reforming public education at secondary and college levels

Source: Adapted and updated from Advisory Commission on Intergovernmental Relations, *Intergovernmental Perspective* (Winter 1980), 8.

nisms vital to the perpetuation of the unique combination of governmental strength, political flexibility, and individual liberty, which has been the central concern of American politics."[43]

"The future of American federalism," Richard H. Leach has suggested, "depends first of all on the satisfaction the American people feel about its performance now and in the past."[44] Elazar concludes that "the American people are known to appreciate their political tradition and the Constitution. Most important, they seem to appreciate the partnership, too, in some unreasoned way, and have learned to use all its elements to reasonably satisfy their claims on government."[45]

The discontent and disinterest so apparent in the minds and actions of many Americans in recent years may lead us to wonder whether Elazar is too optimistic. To find out, we shall next examine how the American people use the elements of our federal system in making claims on government.

[43]Daniel J. Elazar, *American Federalism: A View from the States*, 3d ed. (New York: Harper & Row, 1984), p. 227.
[44]Richard H. Leach, *American Federalism* (New York: Norton, 1970), p. 221.
[45]Elazar, *American Federalism*, p. 227.

SUMMARY

Our federal system has two key features. One is the division of powers between the states and the national government. This system is better described in practice as a marble cake rather than a layer cake, because functions are so mixed among the levels. The other feature is the special roles the states play in ratifying and amending the Constitution and in selecting the president and senators. Despite these roles, the source of authority in the system is best understood as the people—as the national theory argues—rather than as the states—as is argued by the compact theory.

Federalism has important impacts on our politics, for better or for worse: It emphasizes the role of territory as against population, special interests, or functions; it creates two sovereignties; it preserves variety; it limits government's economic role; it allows for creativity and innovation; and it tends to insulate the cities and their problems from the national government.

The development of American federalism began with the expansion of the Union, which reached fifty states in 1959. Meanwhile, the powers of the national government also expanded. The Constitution delegated certain (*enumerated*) powers to the central government and *reserved* all others to the states and the people. The Supreme Court then expanded the national powers in two ways. First

were those *implied* by the Constitution (*McCulloch* v. *Maryland*, 1819). Second were those *inherent* in the fact of being a state (*U.S.* v. *Curtiss-Wright*, 1936). The *concurrent powers* are those exercised by both levels.

The major periods in American federalism have been the era of dual federalism (until 1932), in which the states and the national government were equally sovereign, and the era of cooperative federalism. Recent presidents have made major changes in the practice of federalism. Johnson expanded categorical grants-in-aid, Nixon developed revenue sharing, and Reagan emphasized regulatory federalism. Each of these approaches has been politically controversial.

In recent decades many state governments have been strengthened. A regional split has also developed between the Sunbelt, which grew economically after lagging in previous eras, and the Snowbelt. It is hard to predict what the long-term impact of such changes will be. If the states continue to gain strength and to increase their cooperation, they may be able to limit, if not reverse, the long-term trend toward the concentration of power at the national level. If that happens, it will be the existence of a federal system that makes it possible.

Suggestions for Further Reading and Study

On the theory of federalism: William Riker, *Federalism: Origin, Operation, Significance* (Boston: Little, Brown, 1964), which is historical, comparative, and critical of American federalism.

The most innovative study of American federalism is Daniel J. Elazar, *American Federalism: A View from the States*, 3d ed. (New York: Harper & Row, 1984). For other helpful views, see Morton Grodzins, *The American System* (Chicago: Rand McNally, 1966), which Elazar edited; Richard H. Leach, *American Federalism* (New York: Norton, 1970); and Michael Reagan and John G. Sanzone, *The New Federalism*, 2d ed. (New York: Oxford Univ. Press, 1981).

A recent study of the governments in our federal system is Michael N. Danielson et al., *One Nation, So Many Governments* (Lexington, MA: Lexington Books, 1977). On the allocation of powers among states and the federal government, see David E. Engdahl, *Constitutional Power: Federal and State* (St. Paul: West, 1974). Efforts to solve state problems politically are the subject of Donald Haider, *When Governments Come to Washington:*

Governors, Mayors and Intergovernmental Lobbying (New York: Free Press, 1974).

Intergovernmental relations are surveyed in George E. Hale and Marian Lief Palley, *The Politics of Federal Grants* (Washington, DC: Congressional Quarterly Press, 1981); Arnold Howitt, *Managing Federalism* (Washington: CQ Press, 1984); Deil S. Wright, *Understanding Intergovernmental Relations*, 2d ed. (Belmont, CA: Brooks/Cole, 1982); David B. Walker, *Toward a Functioning Federalism* (Cambridge, MA: Winthrop, 1981); and the annual reports since 1960 of the U.S. Advisory Commission on Intergovernmental Relations and its quarterly journal, *Intergovernmental Perspective*. The Advisory Commission on Intergovernmental Relations also publishes special studies on important topics from time to time.

Finally, the quarterly academic journal *Publius* often publishes interesting analyses of aspects of federalism in America and elsewhere and every year devotes one issue to a survey of the state of American federalism.

Perspective

THE POLITICS OF PRESIDENTIAL ELECTIONS:
The Case of 1984

Over 91 million Americans—53 percent of those of voting age—went to their local polling places on November 6, 1984, to elect someone to be president of the United States for the next four years. Or so they thought. Almost all of them thought they were voting for Ronald Reagan or Walter Mondale or one of the less well-known candidates, such as Sonia Johnson of the Citizens party or David Bergland of the Libertarian party. And when they heard the vote totals on television from Dan Rather, Peter Jennings, or Tom Brokaw that evening, almost all of them thought that they had collectively reelected Ronald Reagan president.

In fact, none of these beliefs was true. The real presidential election occurred not on November 6 but on December 17. The votes that were cast by over 91 million Americans on November 6 were not cast for Reagan or Mondale, but rather for slates of **presidential electors** whose names were not even on most of the ballots. The electors were "pledged"

to vote for Reagan or Mondale (or another designated candidate) when the chosen electors of each state (collectively referred to as the **electoral college**) met in the 50 state capitals on December 17 to elect the president. The votes they cast were counted on January 7, 1985, by a special session of the U.S. Congress in Washington. *That* was the moment when Ronald Reagan was officially reelected president.

All this may seem like an unimportant legal technicality. After all, Reagan received 53,428,357 votes, 59 percent of those cast on November 6, while Mondale received 36,930,923, or 41 percent. And Reagan, having won a plurality of the votes of the people, did immediately begin acting like a reelected president, reorganizing his cabinet and staff and making plans for new proposals to submit to Congress when it convened in January. And he was indeed sworn in for his second term on January 21, 1985, just as American voters expected.

WHY THE ELECTORAL COLLEGE MATTERS

Before we decide to dismiss the electoral college as insignificant and look only at the popular vote cast on election day, we should note that there have been instances in which a candidate got more popular votes than his opponent but not enough elec- toral votes to become president. In the 1976 election, Jimmy Carter had a popular vote plurality (margin) of 1,680,974 votes over Gerald Ford, and an electoral vote margin of 297 to 241, as Figure P2.1 shows. Even so, the election was so close that a shift of only about 5000 votes in Ohio and Hawaii would have given Ford the majority of electoral votes and a new term as president. Carter, with

FIGURE P2.1
Results of Recent Presidential Elections.

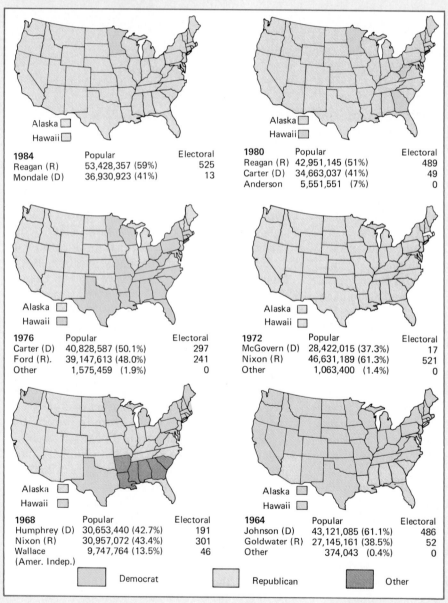

1984	Popular	Electoral
Reagan (R)	53,428,357 (59%)	525
Mondale (D)	36,930,923 (41%)	13

1980	Popular	Electoral
Reagan (R)	42,951,145 (51%)	489
Carter (D)	34,663,037 (41%)	49
Anderson	5,551,551 (7%)	0

1976	Popular	Electoral
Carter (D)	40,828,587 (50.1%)	297
Ford (R).	39,147,613 (48.0%)	241
Other	1,575,459 (1.9%)	0

1972	Popular	Electoral
McGovern (D)	28,422,015 (37.3%)	17
Nixon (R)	46,631,189 (61.3%)	521
Other	1,063,400 (1.4%)	0

1968	Popular	Electoral
Humphrey (D)	30,653,440 (42.7%)	191
Nixon (R)	30,957,072 (43.4%)	301
Wallace (Amer. Indep.)	9,747,764 (13.5%)	46

1964	Popular	Electoral
Johnson (D)	43,121,085 (61.1%)	486
Goldwater (R)	27,145,161 (38.5%)	52
Other	374,043 (0.4%)	0

Democrat   Republican   Other

The results of the 1980 presidential election are made official by the electoral college, presided over by then vice president Mondale and former House Speaker O'Neill.

some 1,675,000 more votes than Ford, would not have become president.

Furthermore, nothing guarantees that all the electors chosen in November will vote as they are pledged in December. In 1976 only one elector bolted, voting for Ronald Reagan instead of Ford. But if 29 Democratic electors had for some reason bolted from Carter to Ford, Ford would again have been president.

So the electoral college is important in its potential impact on the outcome of an election after the people vote. And because it can be important afterward, it is also important before the election. It influences the strategies employed by the major parties because, in effect, some votes—in large, closely contested states—are more important to the outcome than others. This is true even though we usually think that in our system of "one person, one vote," all votes are equal.

To understand how the electoral college influences elections today, let us consider how it came to exist at all and how it has been changed through the years.

The founders did not trust the people to elect their own president. They provided instead that each state would choose distinguished representatives (as many as it had members of Congress) who would meet as the electoral college to elect the best candidate president and the runner-up vice-presi-

dent. At that time there still were no political parties as we know them today, and so there was reason to hope that the choice would indeed be a free choice of the best two candidates. Thus George Washington was chosen our first president in what we call a nonpartisan (nonparty) election. But by 1800 parties had emerged, as we'll see in Chapter 4, and narrowed the field of candidates, so electors increasingly represented parties rather than the states in which they were chosen.

In 1800 there was a tie in the electoral college between Thomas Jefferson and Aaron Burr. The election had to be decided, as the Constitution provides in such cases, in the House of Representatives, where each state's delegation is allowed only one vote, regardless of how many representatives it has. Jefferson finally won. In 1824 in a similar situation, the House elected John Quincy Adams president, even though Andrew Jackson had outpolled him. The controversy this caused abated somewhat when, in the next election, Jackson won a landslide victory. But electoral trouble arose once more in 1876 and again in 1888, when presidents who had not won the popular vote were elected by the electoral college. The situation in 1876 was very complex; the election was eventually decided in February 1877 by an electoral commission set up by Congress.

To this day, every time there is a close election,

ELECTORAL COLLEGE VOTING STRENGTH

Alabama	9	Montana	4
Alaska	3	Nebraska	5
Arizona	5	Nevada	3
Arkansas	6	New Hampshire	4
California	45	New Jersey	17
Colorado	7	New Mexico	4
Connecticut	8	New York	41
Delaware	3	N. Carolina	13
Florida	17	N. Dakota	3
Georgia	12	Ohio	25
Hawaii	4	Oklahoma	8
Idaho	4	Oregon	6
Illinois	26	Pennsylvania	27
Indiana	13	Rhode Island	4
Iowa	8	S. Carolina	8
Kansas	7	S. Dakota	4
Kentucky	9	Tennessee	10
Louisiana	10	Texas	26
Maine	4	Utah	4
Maryland	10	Vermont	3
Massachusetts	14	Virginia	12
Michigan	21	Washington	9
Minnesota	10	W. Virginia	6
Mississippi	7	Wisconsin	11
Missouri	12	Wyoming	3

such as that of 1976, there is fear that a candidate will win the electoral vote but not the popular vote. That fear is compounded by the fact that electors in most states are not legally bound to vote for the candidate they are pledged to. In others, they face no legal penalty for bolting.

THE POLITICS OF THE ELECTORAL COLLEGE

Why then, if the electoral college creates such fears in so many minds, don't we abolish it in favor of simple popular election? The answer reveals much about political power and strategy in America.

In almost every session of Congress an effort is made to abolish the electoral college by constitutional amendment. President Carter, following his close victory, himself proposed such a change only two months after his inauguration. Thus far, all efforts have failed, primarily because many believe that the electoral college favors two different interest groups. One is the *small states* like Alaska. Such states get "extra representation" in the electoral college because each state gets two electors for its two senators, regardless of its size. This is in addition to the number of electors the state gets to match its House membership (a number deter-

mined by the size of its population). But the more important special interest that many believe is favored by the electoral college is *big urban states* that have the most electoral votes. In these states, the swing vote is usually concentrated in the major cities, which therefore get extra attention—and promises—from the candidates. So the small rural states and the large urban states tend to unite against the middle to preserve the electoral college.

Whether or not this is an accurate picture of the effects of the electoral college is still being debated by the experts. One study of the effects in the 1960s and 1970s concluded that

> the electoral college has countervailing biases, which result in a net advantage to large states, and a disadvantage to states with 4 to 14 electoral votes. The electoral college also favors inhabitants of the Far West and the East, as well as central city and urban citizen-voters. In contrast, it discriminates against inhabitants of the Midwest, South, and Mountain states as well as blacks and rural residents.[1]

Specifically, one recent study found that a citizen voting in California has two and one-half times the potential for influencing the outcome of the presidential election than a voter in the District of Columbia, which is the most disadvantaged area.[2]

What, then, would be the alternative? Some suggest a simple popular-vote election, in which all votes count equally, wherever they are cast. In that case, candidates would probably tend to use even more national television and reduce personal appearances, even in areas of heavy voter concentration where most such efforts are now focused. **Direct popular election,** as this proposal is called, would be much more democratic than our present system, in which all of a state's electoral votes go to the winner, even if he or she receives only one more popular vote than the loser. This means that those who vote for the loser in a given state get no representation in the electoral college, for the whole slate of state electors is supposed to vote unanimously for the person who won the state vote.

The normal effect of this provision is to widen the margin of the winner in the electoral college in comparison to the popular vote margin. Notice, for

[1]John H. Yunker and Lawrence D. Longley, *The Electoral College: Its Biases Newly Measured for the 1960s and 1970s* (Beverly Hills, CA: Sage, 1976), p. 44.

[2]Lawrence D. Longley, "Minorities and the 1980 Electoral College" (paper delivered at the annual meeting of the American Political Science Association, Washington, DC, August 1980).

example, that although Reagan's popular vote margin over Mondale was 59–41 percent, his electoral vote margin was 98–2 percent. Some supporters of the electoral college say it helps lessen the likelihood of a disruptive transition of power in a close election. Others discount this argument, pointing out that few citizens pay any attention to electoral vote totals anyway.[3]

HOW THE ELECTORAL COLLEGE WORKS

Just who are these electors who have been the focus of such controversy, and what do they actually do? Traditionally, they have been party workers whose reward for their labors was the honor of being an elector. But recently efforts have been made, especially in the Democratic party, to democratize the selection of electors and make them more representative of the state's population or at least of its party supporters.

All the electors gather at the 50 state capitals on the first Monday after the second Wednesday in December of each election year. There they cast their votes, sign the official rolls, and send the certified votes on to the president of the Senate in Washington, who opens these votes in a joint session of Congress on January 6 or 7 and declares a president elected. This happens just 14 days before the president is to be inaugurated.

So it was in January 1985, as it had been with occasional slight modifications throughout American history. But we still think of the popular election as the *real* election, and when we study politics we generally concentrate on the November election.

THE POLITICS OF THE 1984 ELECTION

The Setting

Few Americans were surprised by Ronald Reagan's victory on November 6, 1984. Polls had shown him to have a very large lead from the time Mondale

won the Democratic nomination. Indeed, the **incumbent** (the person already holding an office) has traditionally won reelection if he sought it. This tendency is called *the incumbency effect*, or the advantage of incumbency. However, the two previous incumbents had been beaten by outsiders. Democrat Jimmy Carter beat incumbent Gerald Ford in 1976, and then challenger Reagan beat President Carter in 1980.

When many people are dissatisfied, incumbency tends to become a disadvantage. In 1984, although he was no longer an incumbent, Mondale suffered from what might be called the liability of incumbency because he had been Carter's vice-president. A vice-president is expected to support his or her president, and when that president becomes unpopular, as Carter did, it reflects on his vice-president. Thus, Mondale carried some negative baggage into the 1984 campaign.

The Development of the Campaign

The results, as we've noted, surprised virtually nobody on election night. Even Mondale himself revealed the next day that he thought his chances of an upset vanished after the second debate with Reagan. Many people had long since forgotten that as recently as January 1984 surveys had found Mondale and Reagan neck and neck. (Figure P2.2 shows how public preferences between the two candidates evolved throughout 1984.) From that point, Mondale dropped in the polls as he faced the primary challenge of Gary Hart. Hart argued that Mondale represented the failed policies of the Carter-Mondale administration, and he claimed that his own "new ideas" would make him better able to solve the nation's problems and thus better able to defeat President Reagan. Meanwhile, Reagan gained relative to both Mondale and Hart as the economy improved through the spring and early summer.

There were two moments in the general election campaign when the Democratic ticket picked up new support. The first was at its July convention. For that week it dominated television—something that usually benefits a party. And then Mondale chose Representative Geraldine Ferraro as his running mate. His choice of the first woman ever to be nominated by a major party electrified activist women's groups and excited many others. Mon-

[3]For a sample of the extensive literature discussing the electoral college and its effects, see Harvey Zeidenstein, *Direct Election of the President* (Lexington, MA: Lexington Books, 1973), and Paul M. Perkins, "What's Good about the Electoral College?" *Washington Monthly* (April 1977), pp. 40–41.

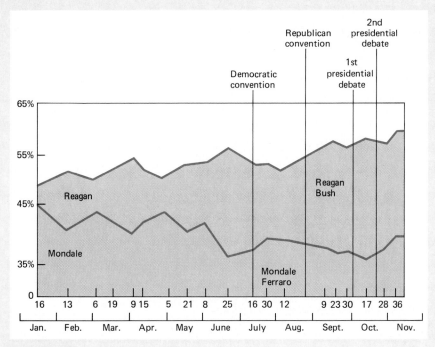

FIGURE P2.2
Presidential Preferences during the 1984 Campaign.
Source: Christian Science Monitor, November 8, 1984.

dale's rating increased. However, the Reagan-Bush ticket still held a 15-point lead at that stage, and it resumed its climb in the polls almost immediately as questions arose about Ferraro's personal and political finances.

After the first debate, in which Reagan struck many observers as unsure of himself and tired, people began to raise "the age issue." Was Reagan, at 73, too old to serve four more years? The Mondale-Ferraro ticket began to gain ground again, but by

Walter Mondale and Gary Hart debate during their quests for the Democratic party nomination. (Dennis Brack/Gamma Liaison)

Geraldine Ferraro, Democratic vice presidential candidate, campaigning. (Forrest Anderson/ Gamma Liaison)

then it was very late in the campaign, and the gap in the preference polls remained enormous. In the final days, as the remaining "undecideds" committed themselves, it was already over for the Democratic ticket. Reagan had captured a popular vote margin comparable to those of Democrat Lyndon Johnson in 1964 and Republican Richard Nixon in 1972. His electoral vote margin was even greater, second only to that of Democrat Franklin Delano Roosevelt in 1936. How was this avalanche created?

The Factors in the Outcome

Walter Mondale explained the extent of his defeat to the press the day after the election this way: "I was running against an incumbent President, with the strength of incumbency, who is very popular personally, very well liked, in the midst of what is perceived as good economic times, and with diminished international tensions . . . and with an electorate that was anxious for some continuity." Reagan, on the other hand, told the press that same day: "I feel that the people made it very plain that they approved what we've been doing and we're going to continue what we've been doing. . . . "

And yet, experts were quick to point out that while Reagan was winning his enormous victory, the Republicans suffered a net loss of 2 seats in the Senate, where their margin fell to 53 to 47. And in the House they won a net increase of only 14 seats, after losing 26 in the 1982 midterm elections. This left the Democrats with a margin of 253 to 182 in the House—easily enough for control on most issues. Thus, the voters generally supported incumbent congressional Democrats along with the incumbent president, even though those Democrats often opposed the president. To most observers, including some of the president's closest advisers, this hardly seemed like a strong mandate to continue the conservative direction for which the first Reagan administration was known.

Thus, the candidates disagreed with each other in their explanations of why people voted as they did. At the same time, experts generally disagreed with both candidates' public explanations of the outcome. Studying the patterns of the vote, most experts rapidly reached general agreement on how Reagan had won such a landslide victory.

Electoral victories are fashioned out of money, organization, and strategy—all within the context of current circumstances (see Table P2.1). To understand how Reagan beat Mondale—and why he won by so much—we shall examine each of these aspects of both candidates' campaigns.

How to Become President of the United States

1. *Preliminaries*
   a. Make sure you're eligible: a natural-born American citizen, at least 35, have lived in the United States for at least 14 years.
   b. Decide to run.
   c. Decide which party's nomination you will seek—or whether you will found your own.
   d. Formulate a general campaign strategy.
   e. Register as a candidate with the Federal Election Commission.
   f. Begin your campaign a year or even two before election.
   g. Announce your candidacy.
   h. Make yourself known to party leaders around the country.

2. *Organizing your campaign*
   a. Develop a fund-raising program.
   b. Apply for federal matching funds from taxpayers' contributions.
   c. Organize a staff to prepare campaign literature, do research, write speeches, do your campaign scheduling, and handle your relations with the media.
   d. Establish a headquarters.
   e. Develop separate strategies for states that select convention delegates by primaries and states that select them by local, district, and state conventions.
      (1) *For the states with primaries that you want to enter that are scheduled for February through June*
         (a) Get your name or a slate of delegates pledged to you on the ballot by registering with each state's chief election official and submitting petitions signed by supporters; or, in some states, by being a "nationally recognized candidate."
         (b) Campaign in each state until the primary date.
            Schedule visits in accordance with the importance of the state to you and your likely strength there. Remember that victories in the early primaries will give a psychological boost to your candidacy.
            Note that some primaries select delegates who may or may not have presidential preferences to the national convention; some instruct delegates about voters' presidential preferences ("advisory presidential-preference primaries"); some will be "winner-take-all-the-delegates" primaries; and some will be "proportional-representation" primaries in which delegates are apportioned to the candidates by the vote percentages.
      (2) *For the states with conventions or caucuses that you choose to enter that are scheduled from January through July*
         (a) Organize supporters by local areas such as voting precincts or townships so they will attend conventions and vote for you or your delegates.
         (b) Campaign in each state, seeking to reach individuals who will attend local conventions.
         (c) Once local conventions select delegates to county or congressional-district conventions, campaign among the delegates personally.
         (d) At the district conventions, get as many delegates to the state convention pledged to you as possible.
         (e) At the state conventions, do the same for delegates to the national party convention, and get your supporters chosen as state party officers. This will make sure the state party organization works hard for your election once you win the nomination.

3. *The national convention*
   a. Continue your general campaigning nationally.
   b. But concentrate your efforts on wooing uncommitted delegates individually.
   c. Aim to capture more than half of the delegates (the total needed for nomination).
      (1) Challenge the credentials of delegates supporting your opponent, on grounds they were wrongly selected and should be replaced by your people.
      (2) Bargain with other, weaker candidates, especially over your vice-presidential selection. (You might want to offer that office to an opponent whose delegates would put you over the top if added to yours.)
      (3) In the weeks before the convention, see that your supporters play major roles in drafting the party platform on which you will run. Then try to gain delegate strength by agreeing to compromise planks in the platform.
   d. Have yourself nominated, and your nomination seconded, by various prominent people representing different segments of the party and the population.
   e. When you win, urge your chief opponent to ask his or her supporters to move that your nomination be made unanimous to begin the effort to unify the party behind your candidacy.
   f. Make your choice for vice-president, if you haven't already had to make it to get needed delegate votes, and announce it.
   g. On the last night of the convention, let your running mate make a brief speech and then make your acceptance speech, setting forth the themes of your coming campaign.

4. *The general election campaign*
   a. Plan your final strategy with your best advisors.
   b. Decide whether you want to raise your own funds or accept federal funds from taxpayers. (You can't have both.)
   c. Expand your staff to include previous supporters of your opponents to further unify the party.
   d. Get the backing of major interest groups sympathetic to you.

(table continues)

   e. On Labor Day launch your campaign formally at a big rally in an important city.
   f. Challenge your opponent to debates if you need the publicity or believe you will benefit from them.
   g. Concentrate your efforts on the key states critical to getting a majority of the electoral college—270 of the 538 electoral votes.
   h. Organize special drives to get out the sympathetic voters on Election Day, again emphasizing the key states.
   i. Don't stop running till the Tuesday immediately after the first Monday in November: Election Day.
   j. Watch the votes come in and the computerized projections by television networks with the rest of the nation.
   k. Accept your victory, once your opponent concedes, in a spirit of unifying the country behind you.

5. *After the election*
   a. Pick your own White House staff, cabinet officers, and other key officials.
   b. With them begin to develop the programs you will be proposing as well as the changes you will be suggesting to Congress regarding the budget the incumbent has prepared to go into effect the next fall.
   c. Note that the electors meet in their state capitals in mid-December and send their votes to the president of the Senate (who is also the departing vice-president) in Washington—and hope and pray that the electors pledged to you actually vote for you.
   d. Note that the members of the Senate and the House meet in special session in the House chamber at 1 P.M., January 6,* to count the electoral votes and declare you elected president.
   e. Attend your own swearing-in ceremony at the Capitol on January 20* around noon, at which you take the oath and deliver your inaugural address.
   f. Begin being president.

One day later if this date falls on a Sunday.

Note: These guidelines have been derived from the efforts and successes of recent presidential candidates. Obviously, no one could actively follow all of them. Nonetheless, to be successful, a candidate would have to follow most of them as best as his or her circumstances allow. For more detail, see Stephen J. Wayne, *The Road to the White House: The Politics of Presidential Elections,* rev. ed. (New York: St. Martin's Press, 1981); John Kessel, *Presidential Campaign Politics: Coalition Strategies and Citizen Response* (Homewood, IL: Dorsey, 1980); John H. Aldrich, *Before the Convention: Strategies and Choices in Presidential Nomination Campaigns* (Chicago: Univ. of Chicago Press, 1980); Burt Neuborne and Arthur Eisenberg, *The Rights of Candidates and Voters,* rev. ed. (New York: Avon, 1980); and Nelson W. Polsby and Aaron Wildavsky, *Presidential Elections: Strategies of American Electoral Politics,* 6th ed. (New York: Scribner's, 1984).

Money

Money is often referred to as "the mother's milk of politics." Traditionally, candidates have depended primarily on large contributions from wealthy individuals who sought favors in return for their contributions. They may have sought special legislation or a favorable ruling by a government agency on a commercial venture they were undertaking or even an ambassadorship to a foreign country.

The cost of presidential elections has skyrocketed in recent decades. In 1956, for example, the two candidates together spent over $13 million, but in 1960 Richard Nixon alone spent over $10 million in losing, while John Kennedy spent almost as much in winning. In 1966 Nixon spent over $25 million to beat Humphrey's $11 million. And in 1972 Nixon used $61 million against McGovern's $30 million.

The 1972 election was the occasion of corrupt activities by Nixon's Committee to Re-Elect the President. As a result, the Federal Election Campaign Act of 1971, which became effective part way through the campaign, was strengthened by amendment. Among the provisions that came into effect with the 1976 election were the following:

- *Public disclosure* of contributions during and after the campaign so the voters could know who was supporting whom
- *Limits on expenditures* to help equalize the resources available to both major parties—especially important to Democrats, who are almost always outspent by Republicans
- *Restrictions on contributions,* including a limit of $1000 from any one individual to a candidate
- An offer of *government funding* or subsidization of presidential campaigns from funds contributed by citizens on their income tax returns

Since 1976 major party candidates have chosen to accept federal subsidies for the presidential contest and thereby agreed to spend no more than that sum. In addition, they and their opponents have accepted federal matching funds to complement money they raised during their party primaries. Table P2.2 summarizes the actual limits on cam-

Political Campaign Contribution Limits

| | RECIPIENT | | | |
CONTRIBUTOR	CANDIDATES OR CANDIDATE CAMPAIGN COMMITTEES	MULTICANDIDATE COMMITTEES (POLITICAL ACTION COMMITTEES)	PARTY COMMITTEES— NATIONAL, STATE, CONGRESSIONAL	TOTAL LIMIT
Candidates themselves	Unlimited (except for presidential candidates who accept public funds)	Same as other individuals	Same as other individuals	Same as other individuals for contributions to other candidates and committees
Other individuals	$1000 per candidate per election	$5000 per year	$20,000 per year	$25,000 per year
Multicandidate committees (political action committees)	$5000 per candidate per election	$5000 per year	$15,000 per year	No limit
Party committees (national, state, congressional)	Senate: $17,500 per year House: $5000 per election	Not applicable	No limit	No limit
Corporations, unions	Not allowable	Administrative and fundraising costs of political action committees	Not allowable	Not applicable

Source: League of Women Voters Education Fund. Reprinted with permission.

paign contributions that apply.[4] The sum provided by the government to the two major party candidates for the 1984 general election was $34 million. It was larger than that of four years earlier to compensate for inflation. This money comes primarily from funds designated by taxpayers on their income tax returns. Each person can earmark $1 of his or her tax to this fund each year. In recent years an average of 37 million Americans have done so. (Interestingly, one who did not do so was Ronald Reagan. However, he still decided to accept the federal funding for his campaigns.)

This total is only part of the actual federal subsidy to the major parties, however. The government also grants them over $3 million each to help pay the costs of their conventions and gives another $3.5 million to each city in which a convention is held to pay for security. It also allows the parties to pay only 3.5¢ per letter mailed—a special postal rate normally reserved for nonprofit organizations—rather than the regular rate in force at the time. This postal subsidy alone was estimated to cost the government over $21 million in 1980.[5] Small parties and independent candidates lack the same advantages.

No major campaign gets by on federal funding alone. There are two other important sources of support. One is contributions of time and energy by supporters; such contributions are not limited by the new laws. In the 1984 campaign organized labor distributed millions of pieces of literature, made more than 10 million phone calls to voters, and furnished thousands of volunteers to register new voters, get out the vote, and run car pools to the polls. Such labors, had they been purchased, would have cost some $40 million, according to experts. Despite this, union households went for Mondale by only a 52 to 48 percent margin, down from 47 to 44 in 1980, and 59 to 39 in 1976. Because union households are 26 percent of the elec-

[4]America's leading expert on campaign finance is Herbert E. Alexander, long the director of the Citizens' Research Foundation, which has studied campaign finance figures and practices for more than a decade. The best introduction to the subject is his book *Financing Politics: Money, Elections, and Political Reform*, 2d ed. (Washington, DC: Congressional Quarterly Press, 1980). See also Michael J. Malbin, ed., *Parties, Interest Groups, and Campaign Finance Laws* (Washington, DC: American Enterprise Institute, 1981), for an interesting collection of essays by scholars and practitioners.

[5]See Mary Meehan, "How the Donkey and the Elephant Turned into Pigs," *Inquiry*, July 7 and 21, 1980, pp. 11–15.

Campaign memorabilia. (© 1975 Staples & Charles Ltd.)

torate the drop off has been very damaging indeed to recent Democratic nominees.

Republicans got the greater benefit in 1984, as in previous elections, of the other supplement to federal funding: contributions by independent political action committees (PACs). Over 4000 PACs contributed close to $300 million in the 1984 election, most of it for congressional races, according to the Federal Election Commission. These PACs have always given Republicans more money than Democrats. That pattern held in the 1984 election, although Democrats in Congress received more PAC money than in previous elections.

Organization

The development and coordination of a national campaign is a very complex task. It involves thousands of paid workers and tens of thousands of volunteers. It requires the development of campaign themes—issues and positions—into a message that is coherent and appealing. That message must then be spread by campaign events and by media coverage and advertising.

The Reagan camp was very well prepared for the 1984 campaign. Reagan faced no competition for renomination—as Carter had from Edward Kennedy in 1980 and as Ford had from Reagan in 1976. His campaign had plenty of money. It also added a new high-technology program: 26 computer operators and analysts. They collected 75,000 quotations from Mondale, along with his voting record in the Senate. All this was computerized by subject so that it could be retrieved instantly for use in the campaign, and Reagan and Bush's campaign airplanes could plug directly into this data bank. Reagan and Bush used it over and over again to attack Mondale on the basis of his past.[6]

The Mondale campaign, by contrast, was often disorganized. Mondale had to fight off challenges from seven fellow Democrats in a bitterly fought battle for the nomination. During this battle his staff had little time to plan ahead for the general election campaign. Once nominated, Mondale got widely varying advice from fellow Democrats about how to campaign, and his staff often seemed unsure of what to do. Mondale and his staff also made key decisions on campaign strategy that many experts consider major mistakes.

Strategy and Circumstances

The two campaigns adopted drastically different strategies. As the incumbent, Reagan had an advantage as long as circumstances were favorable. After taking office in 1981, he had achieved passage by Congress of a 25 percent cut in personal income taxes. The economy was weak when he came to power: The inflation rate was 12 percent; unemployment was 7.5 percent; interest rates were 21 percent. In 1981–1982 the country underwent the worst recession since the 1930s, but then the economy began improving. Massive increases in military spending plus the tax cuts led to unprecedented budget deficits of close to $200 billion a year—rather than the balanced budget candidate Reagan had promised to achieve by 1983. However, by the fall campaign, inflation was down to under 5 percent; interest rates had been cut in half,

---

[6]Associated Press, "Secret Reagan Weapon in Race: Computer," *New York Times*, November 13, 1984.

while unemployment had dropped to 7.5 percent from a recession high of 10.7 percent in 1982. Thus, most Americans found the economy improving, which always favors the incumbent.

In foreign affairs, the record was less impressive. Reagan had been unable to achieve an arms-control agreement with the Soviet Union—the first president to fail to do so in 30 years. His efforts to mediate in the Arab-Israeli conflict in the Middle East had been unsuccessful and had cost the lives of 241 U.S. Marines he had stationed in Lebanon. In Central America, he supported the conservative government of El Salvador, guilty of large-scale human-rights violations, against leftist rebels; and in Nicaragua he supported conservative rebels against the leftist government. Both efforts met resistance at home as well as abroad. He also ordered an armed invasion of the small Caribbean island of Grenada to overthrow its Marxist government a year before the election. That move proved popular with most Americans; Mondale also supported it.

Reagan's foreign affairs record was patchy at best, but many Americans interpreted it—and the massive growth in the military budget—as signs that the United States was again proud and assertive in the world. Coming after the humiliation of American diplomats being held as hostages by Iranian students in the Carter years, this shift led a majority of Americans to decide that the Republicans were better able to handle foreign policy than were the Democrats.

Thus, the Reagan campaign emphasized economic progress and renewed patriotism. Reagan carefully avoided committing himself to any specific programs for his second term, saying simply, "You ain't seen nothin' yet." His managers were careful to limit his appearances. He held no news conferences between the party convention and the election. He capitalized on the ceremonial activities of being president: receiving foreign leaders, signing laws and proclamations, and making speeches to selected organizations. His only significant spontaneous appearances were the two televised "debates" with Mondale. But even these were carefully controlled by Reagan's negotiators. The ground rules they insisted on required that reporters ask questions of the candidates, rather than letting the candidates interrogate each other.

The result of this careful management of Reagan's campaign was that, in the words of two generally sympathetic columnists,

Reagan bluffed his way to reelection in an antiseptic, stagey and shallow campaign in which both the man and his plans for the next four years were very carefully sheltered from the voters and the accompanying

Walter Mondale and Ronald Reagan debate during the 1984 campaign. (Chris Cross/ UNIPHOTO)

news media. . . . Reagan campaigned from a roving isolation booth, playing cheerleader at slickly orchestrated political pep rallies and reducing the voters to extras in a Cecil B. DeMille crowd scene and reporters to spear-carriers.[7]

In the face of this White House strategy and the accompanying widespread popular support for Reagan's economic and foreign policy, Mondale faced a very difficult challenge. Still, he managed to weaken his situation further by various strategic miscalculations:

- He spent the month between the Democratic and Republican conventions at home in Minnesota, resting and fishing and planning the fall campaign. He could instead have campaigned during those weeks to capitalize on the momentum the convention and his choice of Geraldine Ferraro had generated.

- He decided to spend much of his effort early in the fall campaign in the South and in Reagan's home state of California—places experts said he had virtually no chance of carrying. He could instead have concentrated on solidifying his "natural political base" in the Northeast and the Midwest, both regions with serious economic problems. His failure to do so probably contributed to his losing all the states in these potentially supportive regions. As a result, he carried only the District of Columbia and his home state of Minnesota, as Figure P2.1 indicates.

- He failed to select and emphasize a few key issues that would give his campaign a theme. As late as 60 days before the election, he and his aides were still trying to decide what issues and proposals to emphasize in the campaign. As a result, voters were often unsure of what his candidacy offered and unimpressed by his capacity for leadership. By contrast, Reagan had always been known to stand for certain positions on major issues. Surveys showed consistently that a majority of people disagreed with Reagan on many of these issues, such as abortion and the Equal Rights Amendment (both of which he opposed). Yet they saw him as a leader—in large part, it seems, because he was clearly identified with certain policies and positions. Mondale was clearly identified with only one proposal: raising taxes.

- Mondale had announced in his convention acceptance speech that he would raise taxes to help cut the deficit. His proposal was to increase taxes on those in the upper-middle and higher income brackets, and on corporations. But few voters like to hear promises of increased taxes, and many of those whose support Mondale needed feared that

they would fall into the group being hit with higher taxes. Reagan responded by pledging not to raise taxes and thus was able to label Mondale a typical "tax-and-spend Democrat." Mondale chose not to endorse tax reform as a way of raising taxes on those benefiting from unfair loopholes. Most political observers thought this was a major mistake.

Thus, most observers concluded that Mondale's own strategic decisions doomed an already difficult candidacy to a disastrous avalanche. The campaign he designed and conducted couldn't overcome its own miscalculations, the outstanding Republican campaign organization, the massive Republican financial advantage, and Reagan's favorable image in the eyes of a majority of voters happy with his economic and foreign policies.

The Determinants of the Vote

In the end, a presidential election is an effort to win a plurality of votes in states with a majority of electoral votes. As we shall see in the next chapter, scholars look to three key factors as possible determinants of voting decisions: party, issues, and candidate image or personal character. Let's see how each figured in this election.

Party

In recent elections, party membership has seemed less important than it used to be. Nonetheless, fewer people who say they are Democrats voted for Reagan in 1984 (16 percent in 1984 versus 26 percent in 1980). More Republicans voted for Reagan (97 percent in 1984 versus 86 percent in 1980). These two shifts suggest that party may again be important to voters, but as changes in the totals from 1980, they virtually cancelled each other out.

The big shift from 1980 was among those who call themselves independents. In 1980, 55 percent of them voted for Reagan, and 29 percent voted for Carter. In 1984, 67 percent voted for Reagan, and 33 percent voted for Mondale. One difference was that in 1980 John Anderson, a Republican congressman, ran as a moderate independent candidate and got 14 percent of independents' votes. There was no such independent candidate in 1984 to draw the independents' votes; instead, Reagan seemed to.

By 1984 more voters called themselves inde-

---

[7]Jack W. Germond and Jules Witcover, "On Reagan's Second-Term Plans, the Public 'Ain't Heard Nothin' Yet,'" *National Journal*, November 10, 1984, p. 2176.

pendents (36 percent) than Democrats (34 percent) or Republicans (30 percent). Thus, they held the balance of power between the two parties. Independents tend to split their tickets, voting for Republicans for president (as a majority of them have every election since 1968) and for Democrats for the Senate, the House of Representatives, and governor. But in 1984 even Republicans were splitting their votes. One in every five Republicans who voted for Reagan split his or her ticket.[8]

A related factor was new voters. Fully 16 percent of those who voted in 1984 had never been registered before. Some were blacks, who registered at the urging of Jesse Jackson, a black activist minister who was defeated for the Democratic nomination and then supported Mondale. Others were Hispanics, who were encouraged to register by both parties. And even more were white Protestants—mostly fundamentalists—who were encouraged to register by the Republican party and by the activist conservative "religious right." Of those who registered for the first time in 1984, 61 percent voted for Reagan and 39 percent for Mondale.[9]

Issues

Many observers contend that the 1984 election offered voters a clearer choice "on the issues" than any since 1964, when liberal Lyndon Johnson faced conservative Barry Goldwater and won by 60 to 39 percent. But the signs are that voters are not using issues to decide whom to vote for. Polls throughout the campaign consistently showed that the public agreed with Mondale more than Reagan on most issues, yet preferred Reagan to Mondale. Election day surveys of voters confirmed this. Among these interesting voting patterns were:

- 8 percent of the voters called themselves "very liberal," but 40 percent of them voted for Reagan.
- 40 percent of the poorest voters picked Reagan, while one-third of the richest voted for Mondale.[10]

On the other hand, when asked whether they were better off under Reagan than they had been under Carter, 41 percent said yes. They voted for Reagan, 81 percent to 19. Of the 19 percent who said they were "worse off," 73 percent voted for Mondale and 27 percent for Reagan. Those saying "about the same" split their vote, 51 to 49 for Reagan. Thus, voting in this election correlated highly with people's own sense of self-interest.[11]

When pollsters asked voters what the most important issue was to them, those voting for Reagan were most likely to say inflation, taxes, government spending, or foreign relations. Those voting for Mondale tended to pick civil rights, nuclear arms control, or unemployment. (For the full results, see Table P2.3.)

Candidate Image or Character

But when voters were asked why they had voted for their candidate, many more (28 percent) picked "He has strong qualities of leadership" than any other reason. These people voted for Reagan by 86 to 14 percent. Another 18 percent picked "He is more capable." They chose Reagan by 71 to 29 percent. Nineteen percent picked "He cares about people like me," and they went for Mondale by a two-to-one ratio. (These results are also reported in Table P2.3.) Asked why they voted against Mondale, many criticized him as a weak leader.[12]

Thus, according to many experts the image of a candidate's character seemed more important to voters than issues or party. Pat Caddell, who did polling for Gary Hart and then for Walter Mondale, explained his view that

> in a political system where very few people seem to believe very much, Reagan is viewed as a man of great conviction, whether people agree with him or not. It's his bedrock. His leadership comes from believing in something and trying to accomplish something, and the ease with which that allows him to be President.[13]

John Sears, a political consultant who ran Reagan's 1980 campaign for the Republican nomination for several months, emphasized the impact that Reagan's perceived personality has in triggering a positive response among Americans.

> Blindly optimistic, fiercely patriotic and unbending in his loyalty, even to some who may not have deserved it, he is the embodiment of a peculiar kind of

[8]These figures are based on NBC exit polls. See Haynes Johnson, "Voters Sent Up Caution Flags," *Washington Post*, November 8, 1984.

[9]William Schneider, "An Uncertain Consensus," *National Journal*, November 10, 1984, p. 2130.

[10]These results are based on NBC exit polls. See Richard Harwood, "Explaining the Voter," *Washington Post*, November 8, 1984.

[11]These results were based on *Los Angeles Times* exit polls. See Schneider, "An Uncertain Consensus," p. 2132.

[12]Ibid.

[13]Quoted in Steven R. Weisman, "The Politics of Popularity," *New York Times*, November 8, 1984.

How Voters Explained Their Vote

	PERCENT VOTING FOR	
	REAGAN	MONDALE
Reason for vote		
He has strong qualities of leadership (28%)	86%	14%
He cares about people like me (19)	32	68
He is more capable (18)	71	29
He has a clearer vision of the future (15)	48	52
He impressed me during the debates (7)	27	73
He's my party's candidate (6)	32	68
He has a better Vice President (4)	56	44
He'll stand up to the Russians (3)	93	7
Most important issue		
Government spending (14%)	69%	31%
The federal budget deficit (12)	48	52
Foreign relations (12)	67	33
Inflation (11)	83	17
Nuclear arms control (11)	33	67
Taxes (11)	80	20
Unemployment (9)	42	58
No issues, really (7)	75	25
Civil rights (7)	26	74
Environmental protection (3)	26	74
Farm problems (3)	54	46
Those favorable to		
Further reductions in domestic spending (49%)	79%	21%
Reductions in military spending (38)	37	63
Tax increases (13)	40	60

Source: Los Angeles Times exit polls, Nov. 6, 1984, as reported in William Schneider, "An Uncertain Consensus," *National Journal*, November 10, 1984, p. 2131.

American virtue that says that all things are possible if you will just make them so. . . . We Americans live in the future and, therefore, such things as hope, expectation, and confidence mean more to us than mere reason. To get to the future, one must be willing to take a leap into nowhere, not knowing . . . exactly where you will land.[14]

Such characterizations invariably exaggerate. Still, the fact is that Reagan won the votes of a majority of virtually every group except blacks (9 percent), the unemployed (31 percent), Jews (32 percent), Hispanics (33 percent), big-city residents (36 percent), and union members (41 percent). For statistics that show how these and other voting blocs voted in every election since 1952, see Table 3.5 on pp. 106–7.

Reagan gained a majority of the votes of:

■ Both men (61 percent) and women (57 percent)
■ Whites (66 percent)
■ People of all levels of education

■ White Protestants (73 percent) and Catholics (55 percent)
■ All households with incomes over $12,500
■ All age groups, including those under 30 (58 percent—a group usually heavily Democratic)
■ Students, teachers, homemakers, veterans, government employees, and the retired.[15]

In this broad appeal, Reagan's reelection triumph was unusual. But the Congressional election results in 1986, which yielded important Democratic gains, suggest that Reagan's triumph was his own, rather than a sign of a major shift in voter allegiance. What is clear is that the Reagan campaign succeeded in convincing a large majority of Americans to vote for a candidate with whom many of them disagreed on many issues. This achievement, as we've seen, depended on a campaign strategy that was carefully crafted to ensure

[14]John Sears, "What the Glass May Hold for '88," *New York Times*, November 13, 1984.

[15]These statistics are from the *New York Times*/CBS News exit polls. See "Portrait of the Electorate," *New York Times*, November 8, 1984. For more details, see Gerald Pomper et al., *The Election of 1984* (Chatham, NJ: Chatham House, 1985) and Paul Abramson et al., *Change and Continuity in the 1984 Elections* (Washington, DC: CQ Press, 1986).

that the people developed an image of Reagan—and of Mondale—that led them to favor Reagan's reelection despite their disagreements with him.

THE ESSENCE OF ELECTIONS IN POLITICS

"The link between campaign strategy and citizen response is information," wrote John Kessel. "Broadly speaking, the aim of the entire campaign is to transmit persuasive information to the electorate. The citizen's response is similarly based on knowledge."[16] How is this citizen knowledge created? By the authority of the candidate. Indeed, it can be created only if the candidate has authority in the minds of the citizens. Authority is what every election is all about. Ultimately, what is at issue is the authority to rule. A candidate who seems likely to be a good ruler will make a good candidate. Thus, the 1984 election, like all elections, was a contest for authority—in this case, for presidential authority. Reagan and Mondale, and the minor party candidates as well, were competing for the authority to run the country—for the authority to decide what should be done by our government.

In a more general sense, each candidate was offering to the voters his or her own image of reality. Each was offering an image of the present state of things at home and abroad, an image of what should be done to improve things, an image of his or her own competence to make those changes and run the country. The voters had to choose which image to accept as true or better.

As the incumbent seeking reelection, Reagan could list his accomplishments as arguments for his own image, while Mondale could list problems that had not been solved by Reagan as arguments for *his* own image. But what the two candidates were really doing was competing for victory in the election. That victory would give one of them the authority to define reality to the American people for four years. Because the president has authority the chances are most of the people will be influenced by the definitions of reality that the president offers—at least until the next election, when they have a choice again. In addition, the president has the authority to describe reality—or American be-

liefs about reality which he symbolizes and expresses—to the rest of the world. This is so because the rest of the world, too, knows that the president is elected by the people to represent them and their image of reality to the rest of the world.

To get this authority, this ruling authority, a candidate must first convince the voters that they should accept his image of reality. Usually, each starts out by giving arguments for his view. In the 1984 election, Reagan was saying, in effect, "I know how to solve our economic problems and keep the peace. I've had experience." Mondale, on the other hand, was saying, in effect, "The Republicans don't understand the problems of the people. Unemployment is still much too high, and the deficits will cause economic disaster if they are not controlled soon. In addition, the nuclear arms race threatens all life on earth if it is not soon controlled. Much remains to be done, and my proposals are the best way to get the improvements we need."

As always happens, the candidates disagree, and voters need to know why they should believe one rather than the other—why they should accept one's image of reality rather than the other's. So the focus of the campaign almost always tends to shift from policy issues and assertions about programs toward statements about personal qualifications. Candidates spend little time arguing about the issues and presenting the proposals. Instead, they emphasize their own special qualifications for the office—their talents, their knowledge, their experience.

In the 1984 election, Reagan attempted to appear "presidential." He implied that we as voters should believe his views about the state of the nation and about the best ways to solve its problems because he is an authority on politics and an authority on national problems. In other words, he used his experience as a *claim to authority*. Mondale, on the other hand, sought to play down his experience as Carter's vice-president because voters generally had unfavorable images of the Carter years. Thus, Mondale emphasized his lifelong experience in politics as a *claim to authority*. At the same time, he was challenging Reagan's claim to authority by saying that Reagan had proved himself to be ignorant of the complexities of issues such as arms control. He also claimed that Reagan was so removed from the daily aspects of policy making that he was not really in control of his own ad-

---

[16]John Kessel, *Presidential Campaign Politics: Coalition Strategies and Citizen Response* (Homewood, IL: Dorsey, 1980), p. 173.

ministration. The question was, as he said in the second debate, Who's in charge?

Each candidate, in other words, was making *claims to authority to define or interpret the nature of reality* in America for Americans, as any president does. And each was disputing the other's claims to this authority by running against him and debating with him during the campaign. Each wanted to use his personal authority as an impressive candidate to gain the institutional authority of the presidency. Once there, he would use the authority of the presidency to describe or interpret the nature of reality to the American people and to the rest of the world, just as authorities always do. We can, therefore, conclude that the essence of elections is dispute between candidates concerning their claims to the authority to define or interpret the nature of reality for the voters.

When we as voters discuss our political preferences, we tend to do the same thing. We may start by describing reality—the candidates and the issues as we see them. But when we disagree among ourselves, we are likely to shift to making claims to authority, such as: "I read in *Newsweek* that . . ." or "I heard him speak at . . ." or "Everyone I know agrees. . . ." These are claims that we are able to make because of our own experiences.

Candidates dispute over claims to authority.

Voters do the same. And so do public officials when they disagree among themselves. Two members of Congress may disagree on how to vote on a bill; President Reagan and the leader of the Soviet Union may disagree on an arms-limitation proposal or on an issue of human rights.

The important point, as we will see time and again in coming chapters, is that this *dispute over claims to the authority to define and interpret reality is the essence of all politics.* People often refer to politics as "a struggle for power." In a sense, of course, it is. But we have seen that beneath that obvious competition for power is a dispute over claims to authority.

If we remember this, we shall be better able to understand how politics really works, what politicians are really trying to do, why some people are more successful at it than others, and what we ourselves can do to avoid being fooled by politics and politicians. Such an understanding will help us to be effective in politics ourselves.

In the chapters that follow, we shall examine the many ways to be politically active: in voting, in political parties, or in interest groups. We shall also examine the role of public opinion in politics. And we shall study carefully the growing impact of the mass media on all these activities and on politics in general.

3

VOTERS, NONVOTERS, AND POLITICAL ACTIVISTS

Did you vote in the 1984 election? If so, you were one of just over half the people old enough to vote who actually did so. That might make you wonder why almost half didn't vote. If you didn't vote, perhaps it was because you weren't yet 18. It's more likely, however, that you had trouble registering or voting because you were away at school. Or even more likely, you decided it wasn't worth the trouble, either because you didn't think your vote would matter or because you didn't really like either of the major party candidates.

Whatever your decision, in this chapter you'll learn how it compares to those of others. You'll learn why so many Americans don't vote and how those who do vote decide whom to vote for. You'll also learn that voting is only one of many ways of acting in politics and what roles political participation actually plays in our system. ∎

In the presidential election on November 6, 1984, 92 million Americans voted—more people than had ever voted in any election in American history! And yet this turnout was only 53 percent of the voting-age population. A low turnout in percentage terms was nothing new; the percentage of age-eligible people actually voting has been dropping rather steadily in recent elections. This was the seventh straight decline, and it reached a level lower than any year since 1948, as Table 3.1 reveals. The announcement of the turnout, shortly after the election, brought new expressions of concern in many quarters that the American people were becoming more apathetic about politics, more hostile toward candidates, less trustful of government, and less confident of their own abilities to make a difference in elections.

If these assertions are true, American democracy may be in real trouble. If, on the other hand, many people don't vote simply because they are content with things as they are, then there may be little reason for concern.

Which of these images of the American voter—alienated or contented—is more accurate? Until recently, we would have had no way of knowing except from our own impressions based on our conversations with our friends and other voters, along with our study of voting results. In the past few decades, however, pollsters, political scientists, and the Census Bureau have made regular careful studies of citizen opinion and voting. As a result, we now know a great deal about who votes, who doesn't vote, and how those who do vote cast their ballots. We can also answer with growing confidence questions about why they vote as they do and even about why many don't vote. In this chapter, we shall survey what experts have learned about voting, nonvoting, and other forms of political activity by the American people.

As mentioned, the *official* turnout figure in 1984 was only 53 percent. In other words, only a bit over half of the *voting-age population* actually voted in 1984, according to the Census Bureau. However, experts on population and turnout point out that the figure for voting-age population is misleading in several ways. It includes aliens, who are not eligible to vote because they are not citizens. It also includes those in prison or in mental institutions,

TABLE 3.1

Voters and Nonvoters in Presidential Elections, 1920–1984

YEAR	PERCENT VOTING FOR			PERCENT NOT VOTING[a]	ELIGIBLE VOTERS (IN MILLIONS)
	Democratic candidate	Republican candidate	Other candidates		
1920	15.1	26.6	2.5	55.8	61.6
1924	12.8	24.0	8.0	55.6	65.6
1928	21.3	30.4	0.5	47.7	70.4
1932	30.4	21.0	1.6	47.1	75.0
1936	35.0	21.0	1.5	42.5	79.4
1940	32.7	26.7	0.3	40.4	83.5
1944	28.6	24.6	0.4	46.4	89.5
1948	25.6	23.3	2.8	48.4	94.5
1952	27.6	34.3	0.3	37.8	99.0
1956	25.1	34.4	0.4	40.1	103.6
1960	31.7	31.6	0.2	36.5	108.0
1964	37.9	23.9	0.3	38.0	113.9
1968	26.1	26.5	8.5	39.0	120.9
1972	20.9	33.8	1.0	44.3	139.6
1976	26.7	24.9	1.7	45.6	150.0
1980	22.1	27.4	4.4	46.1	160.5
1984	21.6	31.1	0.3	47.2	174.0

[a]Voters and nonvoters do not always total to 100 percent due to rounding.

Source: Adapted from Paul R. Abramson, *Generational Change in American Politics* (Lexington, MA: Lexington Books, 1975), p. 5, and updated to include 1976–1984 election data.

many of whom are therefore not eligible. It includes those who have died or moved away since the last time the voting registers were reviewed. For all these reasons, the official figure for the voting-age population really overstates the number of people who are eligible to vote. Furthermore, in calculating the number of voters, the Census Bureau counts only the votes cast for president. Many Americans who vote do not vote for any presidential candidate; others spoil their ballots either purposely or accidentally. Thus, the *actual* percentage of *eligible voters who vote* may be much higher.[1]

The figures for the 1984 election are particulary disappointing because both major parties as well as other groups made a special effort to register new voters. The Democrats had concluded that they were unlikely to win unless 100 million people voted. They therefore worked hard to register new voters—particularly blacks and Hispanics, who they thought would be more likely to vote Democratic. Republicans, fearing that Democrats might gain an important advantage, launched a similar campaign aimed at citizens likely to be conservative.

These voter-registration programs cost some $20 million. They succeeded in raising registration to a total of about 127 million Americans. But when it came time to vote, most of those newly registered did not do so. Only 8 percent of all who did vote were voting for the first time, and they voted for Reagan by 60 to 39 percent—a margin virtually identical to that for the electorate as a whole. Thus, the turnout among actually registered voters fell from 75 percent in 1980 to about 72 percent in 1984.[2] It appears that even presidential elections continue to be unattractive to many potential American voters.

But the presidential election is but one of about 525,000 races decided by popular vote every fourth year. In addition, many elections for other state and local offices are held in the so-called off years.[3] As our governments—national, state, and local—have grown, the number of offices for which citizens can run, and for which they are urged to vote, has ballooned. In some areas of the country, even dogcatchers are elected.

Why so many elections? Elections serve very important functions in our political system. First, they are the way we select most of our leaders. Second, they are a kind of public referendum on the incumbents and their policies, revealing public approval and disapproval. They may also reveal public desires for change. Third, they are a way of involving the people in the government. They keep people tied to the system without letting them interfere in daily decision making.

But the importance of elections in our system goes deeper.[4] Perhaps the most important answer to the question of why we have so many elections in America is that we define democracy in terms of elections.

When our political units are small enough, all citizens can participate in the actual making of decisions. This is the principle of the town meetings by which much of New England was long governed. Some small cities are still governed by debates and votes taken by all citizens in regular public meetings. We call this system *pure democracy* because it is *direct rule by the people*.

But most of our cities long ago became too large to be governed this way. So they switched to *representative democracy*. In such a system, most decisions are made by officials who are elected at regular intervals by the people and who represent the people when they make decisions for them. Thus, voting seems to be the most important way in which citizens can participate in the governing of a democracy such as ours. Why, then, do some choose to participate while others do not? It is to this question that we now turn.

---

[1]Ronald Moe of the Library of Congress studied the case of California's turnout in 1976. He found 9,980,488 registered voters, of whom 7,867,043 voted for one of the presidential candidates. That was a voting rate of 78.8 percent for registered voters. But 8,137,202 people turned up at the polls and signed in. These additional voters didn't cast legal votes for president, but they did vote; so the actual turnout was 81.5 percent of registered voters. If we then deduct 6 percent from the voter rolls as an estimate of those who moved away or died in the two years since the rolls of registered voters were last reviewed, the actual turnout figure hits 87.5 percent of really eligible voters. Moe's estimate for the whole nation in 1976, arrived at in a similar way, is 88 percent. See Ronald C. Moe, *"The Empty Voting Booth: Fact or Fiction," Commonsense* (Winter 1979), summarized in the *Wilson Quarterly* 3 (Summer 1979).

[2]According to an exit poll. See David E. Rosenbaum, "Surveys Provide a Portrait of Expanded American Electorate," *New York Times*, November 7, 1984.

[3]In "off years" (years in which there is no presidential election, also known as midterm election years), voter turnout generally drops by 10 to 15 percentage points. In general, turnout is lowest for state and local races. See William J. Crotty and Gary C. Jacobson, *American Parties in Decline* (Boston: Little, Brown, 1980), chap. 1. In the 1986 off-year elections, turnout was only 37 percent.

[4]See Benjamin Ginsberg, *Consequences of Consent: Elections, Citizen Control, and Popular Acquiescence* (Reading, MA: Addison-Wesley, 1982).

A town meeting today. (Ivan Massar/Black Star)

WHY SOME PEOPLE DO NOT VOTE

The number of people eligible to vote has been expanding regularly for four main reasons. First, the population has continued to grow. Second, recent civil-rights laws have allowed blacks to vote more extensively in the South. Third, the rules and regulations surrounding registration to become eligible to vote have been simplified and reduced in most parts of the country. And fourth, those 18 through 20 years old can now vote.

Registration Requirements as Obstacles

To vote, one still must register first in every state but North Dakota, which has no system of registration. In the past, one could register only at an official building and there only during normal

(UPI/Bettmann Archive)

working hours. In recent years, more and more states and cities have added mobile registrars, who open booths in schools, shopping centers, and neighborhoods as elections near. Almost half the states now allow registration by postcard. Nonetheless, the very fact that Americans must register to vote—often well in advance of an election, before they are interested—is cited by experts as one reason for the generally low turnout in American elections.

Why Do We Require Registration?

Some argue that registration was established primarily to control fraud. The system does keep people from voting several times in the same contest. It also helps prevent people from voting in the name of people who are dead or who have moved away. Registration requirements, along with the requirement that one be a citizen to be eligible to vote, were introduced toward the end of the 19th century. Some believe their original purpose was to protect business interests against political controls that might be imposed if the emerging industrial working class were to vote in large numbers. Many also feared the new immigrant citizens would simply "vote as they were told" by big-city political bossses.

Alternatives

Registration regulations persist to this day and seriously limit the extent of participation, particularly among the poor and less educated. Some have proposed a national registration system, conducted by the federal government, as a way of standardizing procedures and overcoming present discrim-

A voter registration drive in North Carolina. (© 1984 Charles Gupton/UNIPHOTO)

inatory provisions. One such plan, proposed by Jimmy Carter shortly after he took office, called for registration on election day, perhaps right at the polling place. Such proposals remain controversial, not least because the Constitution reserves the right to determine voting eligibility to individual states rather than the federal government.[5]

The debate over these proposals continues. On one side are people who fear that the vote will become meaningless if it is made too easy. Some also say that fraud will increase and that a new bureaucracy will be needed to supervise the new process. Those favoring greater effort to enroll more voters believe such reforms essential. In the 1976 election, the Census Bureau interviewed voters and nonvoters nationally, and analysis of the results suggested that election-day registration could increase the turnout by perhaps 10 percent. In that election, both Minnesota and Wisconsin used the system and got turnouts of 72 and 66 percent, respectively, without evidence of fraud.[6]

These findings strengthened the claims of supporters, many of whom agree with former Attorney General Ramsey Clark's assessment:

> Those that wield political power today don't want to share it. They don't understand the frustrations of being utterly powerless in America. Politics is a source of power. And if we revitalize democracy in this country and share power with the people, create new constituencies for our representatives, . . . we'll see America flourish. We'll see our people included in this system. We'll see a commitment to the rule of law because they participate in its making.[7]

Legal Restraints as Obstacles

In the past, legal restraints were an important obstacle to voting. Most Americans were not actually "included in the system" by being allowed to vote until recently. In the early days of the Republic, women and slaves and those men who did not own property or were not of the proper religion were not allowed to vote. That left perhaps as little as 5 or 10 percent of the adult population as voters. By the middle of the 19th century, the growth of democratic sentiment and the expansion of the frontier westward to incorporate new states combined to remove religious and property-owning qualifications generally. Still, many states continued to require that one pay a poll tax—a fee, usually several dollars—when registering. That provision did not disappear in some parts of the country until the Twenty-fourth Amendment prohibited it in national elections in 1964 and then the Supreme Court outlawed it for all elections in 1966.

Once those not owning property were granted the franchise (a common term for the right to vote that derives from a French word for freedom or for frankness, and perhaps, therefore, for free expression), the former black male slaves freed as a result of the Civil War were the next-intended beneficiaries. The Fifteenth Amendment (1870) affirmed that "the right of citizens of the United States to vote shall not be denied or abridged by the United States or by any State on account of race, color, or previous condition of servitude." But within a half-dozen years the North had abandoned the freedmen, as they were called, to renewed domination by white southerners. It was not until the Civil

---

[5]For a comprehensive survey and hostile analysis of proposals for registration reform, see Kevin P. Phillips and Paul H. Blackman, *Electoral Reform and Voter Participation* (Washington, DC: American Enterprise Institute, 1975). But see also, for a more favorable view, William J. Crotty, *Political Reform and the American Experiment* (New York: Crowell, 1977), chaps. 2, 3.

[6]Warren Weaver, "Voting Day Registration," *New York Times*, May 25, 1977, p. 18.

[7]Clark made this statement on a public television program called "The Advocates," November 3, 1970.

Rights Acts of 1957, 1960, and 1964 and the Voting Rights Act of 1965 (see Table 3.2) that blacks were able to register and vote in appreciable numbers across the South.

In the intervening years, blacks and often poor whites as well were kept **disfranchised** by a series of special state laws and regulations. One of these was the so-called **white primary,** in which only whites could vote. Contests were usually decided in these primaries because there were no serious Republican opponents to Democrats then. The votes of blacks in the general election thus had little meaning. Another was the **grandfather clause,** which provided that only those who could demonstrate that their father or grandfather had voted were exempt from strict literacy tests and property requirements. Special language and literacy laws, often unfairly administered, existed in many states until outlawed by the Voting Rights Act Amendments passed by Congress in 1970 and 1975.

Women fared somewhat better than southern blacks in their efforts to get the vote. The campaign for women's **suffrage** was conducted by growing and well-organized groups called suffra-gettes. (*Suffrage* is another term for voting, this one deriving from an old church term for intercessionary or petitionary prayer, suggesting that the voter acts to try to change the outcome of something.) The suffragettes lobbied, picketed, paraded, and organized strikes to demand political equality with men, until they finally won the right to vote with the ratification in 1920 of the Nineteenth Amendment. We shall examine the roles of women in politics in Chapter 14.

Native Americans (Indians) finally got the right to vote in 1924. This left young people as the remaining group of disfranchised citizens. Many thought it strange that men could be sent to war at age 18 but could not vote until they were 21 in most states. During World War II, Georgia had lowered its voting age to 18, and by the time the Vietnam War was at its peak, when the argument for the 18-year-old vote was at its strongest, Kentucky and Alaska had lowered theirs. In the 1970 elections, voters in Maine, Massachusetts, Montana, and Nebraska approved the 18-year-old vote. Sentiment grew so strong that in that same year the Congress, which had refused to propose constitu-

TABLE 3.2
The Legal Extension of the Right to Vote

YEAR	ACTION	IMPACT
1870	Fifteenth Amendment	Prohibited voter discrimination because of race.
1920	Nineteenth Amendment	Prohibited voter discrimination because of sex.
1924	Act of Congress	Granted citizenship to Native American Indians.
1944	*Smith* v. *Allwright*	Supreme Court decision prohibited the "white primary."
1957	Civil Rights Act of 1957	Authorized Justice Department to go to court to protect voting rights.
1960	Civil Rights Act of 1960	Authorized courts to appoint referees to assist voter registration.
1961	Twenty-third Amendment	Extended right to vote in presidential elections to residents of District of Columbia
1964	Twenty-fourth Amendment	Prohibited poll tax in national elections.
1965	Voting Rights Act of 1965	Suspended literacy tests and authorized federal voter registrars in seven southern states.
1966	*Harper* v. *Virginia State Board of Elections*	Supreme Court decision prohibited poll taxes in any election.
1970	Voting Rights Act Amendments of 1970	Lowered minimum voting age for federal elections to 18; abolished state literacy tests; required uniform rules for absentee voting; in effect imposed a maximum 30-day residency requirement for presidential elections.
1971	Twenty-sixth Amendment	Lowered the minimum voting age to 18 for all elections.
1972	*Dunn* v. *Blumstein*	Supreme Court decision shortened residency requirements for voting in all elections.
1975	Voting Rights Act Amendments of 1975	Authorized federal voter registrars in ten more states; provided for use of ballots printed in more than one language.
1982	Voting Rights Act Amendments of 1982	Extended provisions of 1970 and 1975 amendments; allowed private parties to prove violations.

TABLE 3.3

Reasons People Give for Not Voting

REASON	PERCENT CITING REASON				
	1984	1980	1976	1972	1968
Not registered	31	42%	38%	28%	34%
Didn't like candidates	10	17	14	10	12
No particular reason	8	10	10	13	8
Not interested in politics	8	5	10	4	7
Illness	7	8	7	11	15
Not an American citizen	6	5	4	—[a]	—[a]
New resident	6	4	4	8	10
Traveling out of town	5	3	3	5	6
Working	7	3	2	7	3
No way to get to polls	3	1	2	—[a]	—[a]
Didn't get absentee ballot	1	—[a]	1	1	2
Miscellaneous other reasons	1	2	5	13	3

[a]Less than 1 percent.

Source: The Gallup Poll 1984 (Washington, DC: Scholarly Resources, 1985), p. 259.

tional amendments lowering the voting age for several decades, finally passed a *law* (not a constitutional amendment) lowering the age to 18 for *all elections*. But the Supreme Court then ruled (in *Oregon* v. *Mitchell*) that Congress had the power to legislate the requirement only for federal elections—those for president and Congress. So, at last, the Congress proposed a constitutional amendment in March 1971 lowering the age to 18 for all elections. The required three-fourths of the state legislatures had ratified the Twenty-sixth Amendment by July 1971.

Legal restraints on the right to vote are now therefore largely a thing of the past for all citizens 18 or over. Table 3.2 summarizes the major amendments, laws, and Supreme Court decisions that have brought this about. *Legal limits on the ease of voting* persist. Registration provisions are one type which limits turnout in elections. Residency requirements that demand someone reside in a given district for a specified period of time, supposedly to become familiar with the district and the candidates, are another factor limiting turnout in other than presidential elections.[8]

However, their actual impact on the outcomes may be limited. Raymond Wolfinger and Steven Rosenstone studied the 1972 and 1974 elections and found that if every state had had registration laws

as permissive as those in the most permissive state, turnout would have been about 9 percentage points higher. However, they found that these additional voters would have been very similar to those who did vote in terms of party, ideology, sex, age, and economic status. So the effect on the outcome would probably have been minimal.[9]

Citizen Attitudes as Obstacles

There is some evidence that by now the major obstacles to voting are psychological rather than legal. Following the legal progress just recounted, Penn Kimball studied "the disconnected" (his term for nonparticipants) in Newark, New Jersey. "The key difference between voters and nonvoters," Kimball noted, "seemed to be their own opinion of themselves, whether or not they felt they possessed the aptitudes for politics, whether or not they felt that the participation of one individual like themselves would make any difference."[10]

The ominous thing for the future of democratic elections in America is that more and more Americans seem to be concluding that their participation is not worthwhile. Table 3.3 shows the reasons nonvoters gave for their failure to vote in various

---

[8]For a detailed account of "The Evolution of the Franchise," see Crotty, *Political Reform*, chap. 1.

[9]Raymond E. Wolfinger and Steven J. Rosenstone, *Who Votes?* (New Haven, CT: Yale Univ. Press, 1980), chap. 4.

[10]Penn Kimball, *The Disconnected* (New York: Columbia Univ. Press, 1972), p. 295.

recent presidential elections. They include not being registered (31 percent in 1984) and not liking the candidates (10 percent), along with various indicators of disinterest and statements of obstacles.

In 1984, as in previous elections, the poor, the less well educated, those under 30, and blue-collar workers (those with nonprofessional, general-manual jobs) were less likely than others to vote. These are the segments of the population with the least status in contemporary America. Thus, they are the people least likely to feel effective or powerful in politics.

Of course, it is difficult to conclude that one's own vote matters much in any case. It is a very rare election, at any level of government, that is actually decided by a plurality (or margin) of one vote. Still, 21 of our presidential elections have been so close that the results would have been changed if only one in every hundred votes had shifted.[11] In some of those less close, like the 1976 presidential election, the existence of the electoral college makes it possible that a shift of several thousand votes in several states could change the outcome.

Nonetheless, some may think of voting as "costly" in that it takes time and effort, especially if one attempts to be well informed. And others offer still another argument for not voting: They assert that voting for unimpressive candidates "only encourages the bums" and contributes to the acceptance of elections and the dominant parties as an adequate way of seeking political change.

WHY SOME PEOPLE DECIDE TO VOTE

Having looked at who does not vote, let's examine what types of people do vote. Wolfinger and Rosenstone's study of Census Bureau findings for the 1972 and 1974 election turnouts enabled them to compare voters to the entire adult population. They found education the most important factor differentiating voters from nonvoters, followed by age and then by being married. Interestingly, neither higher income nor a high-status job made one more likely to vote. How then do voters compare with

the whole population? One way of comparing is to list the characteristics of people who are a larger percentage of those who vote than they are of the whole population. Wolfinger and Rosenstone found that "people who are white, well educated, well-to-do, middle-aged, married, Northerners, government employees, and residentially stable account for a proportion of voters larger than their share of the population."[12] On the other hand, "The most underrepresented Americans include those who are disadvantaged . . . the poor, the uneducated, and racial minorities," along with youths and people who are single or have recently moved.[13]

Wolfinger and Rosenstone also found that in terms of views on particular issues, both liberals and conservatives are somewhat overrepresented. The only group underrepresented among voters is those people who lack opinions. If those findings are accurate, perhaps those who decide to vote do so because of their views on issues. If so, they rarely say so when asked. For example, a survey of voters in 1976 found that 53 percent voted because they viewed voting as their "civic duty." Only 10 percent thought their vote would make a difference. About 16 percent gave as their reason strong feelings for their candidate, and 17 percent cited their belief that it was "a very important election."[14]

WHY PEOPLE VOTE AS THEY DO

Every person is unique. Each has his or her own biography, a body and mind shaped by a unique genetic endowment at birth, and a unique set of experiences through life. Still, we have much in common with each other, especially when it comes to political life and action. For everyone's opportunities for experience in politics are shaped by the existing political system and the elections it conducts as well as the decisions it confronts.

This common opportunity makes it possible for political scientists to study "the American voter" and generalize about the underlying influences on

[11]Neal R. Peirce, *The People's President* (New York: Simon & Schuster, 1968), pp. 317–21.

[12]Wolfinger and Rosenstone, *Who Votes?*, p. 105.
[13]Ibid., p. 108.
[14]Robert Reinhold, "Poll Links Sense of Powerlessness, Not Disillusionment, to Low Vote," *New York Times*, November 16, 1976, p. 33. For an assessment of our limited ability to explain why people do decide to vote, see John H. Aldrich and Dennis M. Simon, "Turnout in American National Elections," in *Research in Micropolitics*, vol. 1, ed. Samuel Long (Westport CT: JAI Press, 1986), pp. 271–301.

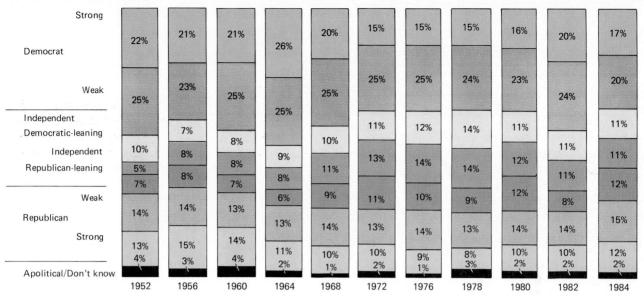

	Strong	22%	21%	21%		20%	15%	15%	15%	16%	20%	17%
Democrat					26%							
	Weak	25%	23%	25%		25%	25%	25%	24%	23%		20%
											24%	
					25%							
Independent Democratic-leaning		10%	7%	8%		10%	11%	12%	14%	11%		11%
Independent Republican-leaning		5%	8%	8%	9%		13%	14%	14%	12%	11%	11%
		7%	8%	7%	8%	11%					11%	12%
	Weak	14%	14%	13%	6%	9%	11%	10%	9%	12%	8%	15%
Republican					13%							
	Strong	13%	15%	14%		14%	13%	14%	13%	14%	14%	
					11%							12%
Apolitical/Don't know		4%	3%	4%	2%	10% 1%	10% 2%	9% 1%	8% 3%	10% 2%	10% 2%	2%
		1952	1956	1960	1964	1968	1972	1976	1978	1980	1982	1984

FIGURE 3.1
Changes in Expressed Partisanship, 1952–1984.

Source: Computed from data from the American National Election Studies, Center for Political Studies, University of Michigan.

the views and behavior of each segment of the population. There are various common approaches to such voting studies.

Conscious Reasons

The first and most common approach is simply to ask the voter. The reasons given by individuals will reflect their beliefs about, and perceptions and images of, the parties (partisanship), the issues, and the candidates among which they select.

Partisanship

In the 1950s most Americans were little interested in politics. They seemed basically satisfied with the operation of the political system and generally identified themselves as supporters or members of the Democratic or the Republican party. When they voted, they tended to vote for the candidate of their party. The result was a politics that involved little struggle over issues. Americans elected Dwight D. Eisenhower, a popular retired military general who had led the allied forces in Europe in World War II, by large margins in 1952 and again in 1956, in elections that were not notable for issue conflicts. Then in 1960 they elected John Kennedy over Eisenhower's vice-president, Richard Nixon, in a very close election characterized by little at-

tention to issues and much more concern with the images of the candidates.[15]

After the 1964 Johnson-Goldwater election, **partisanship**—the tendency of citizens to call themselves members or supporters of a party—declined drastically. Figure 3.1 shows a consistent decline in the percentage of people calling themselves members of either major party. There are still many more Democrats than Republicans, but there are now about as many independents as Democrats.

The impact of partisanship on voting also shows a long-term decrease. Fewer than half of the people who still call themselves Democrats and Republicans have always voted for their own party's presidential nominee. This percentage was once higher, when **party loyalty** was still encouraged by candidates and felt by voters.

Traditionally, party preference was passed from one generation to the next. The children of Democratic parents tended to become Democrats and to stay Democrats, and the same was true for Republicans. But since the 1960s more and more new voters have tended to call themselves independents, regardless of their parents' partisanship. And

---

[15]For a helpful discussion of these elections and those following through 1972, incorporating summaries of most voting studies, see Norman Nie, Sidney Verba, and John Petrocik, *The Changing American Voter* (Cambridge, MA: Harvard Univ. Press, 1976).

TABLE 3.4
Election-Year Key Issues and Election Results

YEAR	KEY ISSUE[a]	CITIZENS' VIEWS ON WHICH PARTY CAN BEST HANDLE KEY ISSUE[a]	PRESIDENTIAL-ELECTION RESULTS
1956	Fear of war	Republican	Republican Eisenhower defeats Democrat Stevenson
1960	International relations	Democratic	Democrat Kennedy defeats Republican Nixon
1964	International relations	Democratic	Democrat Johnson defeats Republican Goldwater
1968	Vietnam	Republican	Republican Nixon defeats Democrat Humphrey
1972	Vietnam and inflation	Republican	Republican Nixon defeats Democrat McGovern
1976	Inflation	Democratic	Democrat Carter defeats Republican Ford
1980	Inflation	Republican	Republican Reagan defeats Democrat Carter
1984	International relations	Republican	Republican Reagan defeats Democrat Mondale

[a]Determined by Gallup Poll that asked Americans what they considered to be the main problem facing the nation and which political party they thought could deal with it better.
Source: Data from *Gallup Polls.*

thus party preference, which used to be an important influence on presidential voting, has lost much of its impact.[16] Nonetheless, research shows that it "remains the single most important influence on the vote in most presidential elections."[17]

Issues

The 1960s were years of civil-rights protests followed by controversy over the war in Vietnam. In those years, the importance of party as an influence on voting seemed to decline. One reason may have been the fact that the parties themselves were split on these issues. Another no doubt was that the issues were very important to many voters. As a result, they seemed to be influenced in their voting by the issue stands taken by candidates—and occasionally by the parties. This trend persisted in the 1972 election, most likely because candidates were offering distinctive alternatives in response to social and political crises. In 1976 studies showed that party identification again increased in importance while issues declined somewhat. In 1980, however, party declined once again, and greater attention was paid by voters to the candidates' characters and

leadership qualities. In 1984 both party and issues played important roles.[18]

Gallup Polls over the past 35 years have asked voters which issue they considered most important and which party they believed best able to handle that issue. As Table 3.4 shows, in presidential-election years voters have selected the candidate of the party that more of them believed was better able to handle the major issue. As experts note, however, there are many issues raised in any campaign.

What then are we to conclude about the degree or extent of "issue voting"? "When issues are on the voters' mind, as in 1964, 1968, and 1972, they tend to displace party loyalties as the source of the vote," argues Bruce Campbell.[19] But it is not easy for voters to use issues in deciding how to vote, as Herbert Asher reminds us:

Issue voting requires information, and the acquisition of information involves costs for the citizen. These costs are probably less for citizens with the cognitive skills (e.g., education) that facilitate the collection and evaluation of information. Thus, one might expect that the increase in American education levels may gradually lead to a citizenry better able to be informed about politics and elections. . . . In conclusion, while the amount of issue voting may still not be impressively high, . . . the electorate is capable of

---

[16]For studies of this phenomenon, see Burnham, *Critical Elections,* chap. 5; Nie et al., *The Changing American Voter;* Gerald Pomper, *Voter's Choice* (New York: Dodd, Mead, 1975), chap. 2; and William J. Crotty and Gary C. Jacobson, *American Parties in Decline* (Boston: Little, Brown, 1980).

[17]James E. Campbell, Mary Munro, John R. Alford, and Bruce A. Campbell, "Partisanship and Voting," in *Research in Micropolitics,* vol. 1, ed. Long, pp. 99–126 at 115.

[18]See Paul R. Abramson, John H. Aldrich, and David W. Rohde, *Change and Continuity in the 1984 Elections* (Washington, DC: CQ Press, 1986).

[19]Bruce A. Campbell, *The American Electorate* (New York: Holt, Rinehart & Winston, 1979), p. 265.

making issue-related decisions, especially when the candidates and parties fashion issue appeals to the electorate.[20]

Unfortunately for those who believe that democracy is best served by clear electoral choices on the issues, research shows that this is rarely the case. As Benjamin Page has argued, in general "candidates' policy proposals are highly ambiguous. They are infrequent, inconspicuous, and non-specific. . . . The great bulk of campaign rhetoric concerns goals, problems, and past performance."[21]

Thus, it can be very difficult for voters to make judgments about the issue positions of a candidate in a campaign. To do so, they often must make inferences from the positions a party has taken in the past or from the views they already know prominent party leaders hold. Otherwise, the "information cost" of finding out directly what a candidate believes or stands for may be too great for most voters.[22] The other possibility for the voter is to go beyond issues to images of the candidates.

Candidate Images

Opposing candidates for political office often have very different backgrounds and personalities and sometimes differ greatly in terms of knowledge and experience. Voters often base their decisions on these qualities in choosing the candidate they feel they can best trust to carry out campaign promises and to manage the government. Jeffrey Smith has argued: "The evidence is clear and substantial that the matter of candidate trustworthiness is on the minds of most voters in every election."[23] As the salience of issues faded in the 1970s, voters did indeed seem to take greater note of these various qualities that we call candidate images—the personal characteristics of the candidates.

In general, voters are especially interested in a candidate's perceived strength, integrity, and empathy. By the time he ran for reelection in 1980, Jimmy Carter had a record and an image that were well developed in the minds of most voters. That image often hurt him in comparison to Ronald Reagan.[24] By the time *he* ran for reelection in 1984, Reagan too had a well-developed image. But it served him well in 1984, running as a popular incumbent.

Unconscious or Psychological Reasons

The importance of these three sets of factors—party, issues, and images of the candidates—is uncovered in voting studies by asking voters the reasons for their votes. Although it is rare that a voter will say, "I don't know why I voted for Candidate X," sometimes we may find his or her answer doubtful or too superficial. We may therefore decide to move on to the second approach to the study of voter behavior: *looking for deeper, unconscious reasons* for the choice.[25] We might find, for example, that one unconscious reason for a person's voting decision is his or her underlying attitude toward authority—whether he or she tends to defer to strong-willed people, for instance. Alternately, a voter's experience—such as a family tradition of voting for a particular party, which he or she feels unwilling or unable to break—may be a factor. The big difficulty with such a search for unconscious psychological reasons is that the voter cannot tell us what these reasons are because he or she is not conscious of them. Thus, we must infer them from other things we know about the voter's personality or about the behavior of other, similar people. And when we do so, we cannot test the accuracy of our conclusions by checking with the subject of our study.

---

[20]Herbert Asher, *Presidential Elections and American Politics*, rev. ed. (Homewood, IL: Dorsey, 1980), pp. 129–31. A 1981 Gallup Poll found that half of those who did not vote in 1980 said they would have been more likely to vote had they also been able to vote on major issues facing the nation.

[21]Benjamin I. Page, *Choices and Echoes in Presidential Elections: Rational Man and Electoral Democracy* (Chicago: Univ. of Chicago Press, 1978), pp. 279–80.

[22]See Stanley Feldman and Pamela Johnston Conover, "Candidates, Issues and Voters: The Role of Inference in Political Perception," *Journal of Politics* 45 (1983), 810–39.

[23]Jeffrey A. Smith, *American Presidential Elections: Trust and the Rational Voter* (New York: Praeger, 1980), p. 136.

[24]See Paul R. Abramson, John H. Aldrich, and David W. Rohde, *Change and Continuity in the 1980 Elections* (Washington, DC: CQ Press, 1982), esp. chap. 7. This is an instance of what political scientists call retrospective voting—evaluating a candidate's past. See Morris P. Fiorina, *Restrospective Voting in American National Elections* (New Haven, CT: Yale Univ. Press, 1981).

[25]The pioneering work on various psychological aspects of voting has been carried on since 1948 by a team at the University of Michigan. Their first book was Angus Campbell, Philip E. Converse, Warren E. Miller, and Donald E. Stokes, *The American Voter* (New York: Wiley, 1960). For subsequent works, see the suggested readings at the end of this chapter.

The third way to study voting behavior is to *look for social factors*. In this approach, we find regularities in the combination of basic characteristics of individuals—their age, race, religion, sex, education, and so on—and the way they vote. We assume that the fact that there are regularities implies a connection between these characteristics and voting behavior.

It has tended to be true as a general rule, for example, that poor people vote Democratic and rich people vote Republican. But if we ask them why, they usually do not connect their economic status with their votes. Nonetheless, the combination is so common that we suspect there is a connection. In the researcher's terms, we hypothesize that wealth tends to cause Republican voting, and poverty tends to cause Democratic voting. The more evidence we find of such connections, the more we are inclined to believe we have found a *causal relationship* or *correlation* between economic status and party vote.

Such a correlation may turn out to be *spurious*. That is, the two factors may not, in fact, be connected as cause and effect; instead, both may be caused by some third factor. For example it is no doubt true that people who wear business suits to work tend to vote Republican, whereas people who wear overalls at work tend to vote Democratic. It would be misleading to conclude from this correlation that party preference is caused by one's type of dress at work, however; the truth is that both party choice and mode of work dress are traceable to economic status.

So we must be careful about the conclusions we reach on the basis of correlations. We must realize that they are really hypotheses, or educated guesses. And we must remember that they become understandable only when we are able to connect them to the conscious reasons people give for their actions. Our observed correlation between economic status and party preference becomes plausible when we consider that Republican policy tends to favor the interests and to respond to the concerns of business and professional people. In contrast, Democratic policy proposals tend to pay special attention to the needs and desires of organized labor. There are exceptions to both generalizations, as there are to most generalizations about American politics. But on the whole, over

time, they have been true enough that we can establish a plausible connection in terms of the beliefs and images of American business executives and workers that give them reasons for their voting behavior.

Once we have discovered such a correlation, we can sometimes predict voting from it. We know, for example, that people of high economic status not only tend to vote Republican but also tend to vote more regularly than those of lower economic status, who we also know tend to vote Democratic. We also know that there are many more low-income Americans than high-income Americans. This means that the outcome of a presidential election may depend, in a sense, on the turnout: If it is large, the Democrat is usually more likely to win; if small, the Republican's chances are improved. Turnout, in turn, is affected by everything from the personalities of the candidates, to the get-out-the-vote efforts of organized labor, to the weather on election day. The more we know about such causes of voter activity and voter choice, the better we can be at forecasting election outcomes.

Intensive studies of social factors and voting may be concentrated on a particular community that is thought to be representative of the electorate in general, or researchers may use a "sample" of the entire population that represents the major types of Americans in accurate proportions.[26] Because such studies have been conducted for several decades they provide a great range of information about Americans in general and their attitudes and voting behavior in particular. Some of the most revealing conclusions they have reached are discussed in the following sections.

Socioeconomic Status

Because we spend so many of our waking hours working it would not be surprising if our occupation correlated with our voting decisions. Furthermore, because our income affects the way we live and what sort of neighborhood we live in as well as our social standing we would not be surprised to find correlations here also. These factors—oc-

---

[26]The latter approach is the basis for the famous Gallup Poll and the Harris Survey as well as for the foremost political science project, the "American Voter" studies, from which most of the poll data we use are derived. The former approach was pioneered by researchers at Columbia University in the 1940s. See Paul F. Lazarsfeld, Bernard Berelson, and Hazel Gaudet, *The People's Choice* (New York: Columbia Univ. Press, 1944).

cupation, income, social class—are often lumped together as **socioeconomic status** (or **SES**) characteristics.

In the years of the Great Depression of the 1930s, voting did correlate very strongly with SES. The poor, the working class, and low-income Americans generally voted Democratic while the wealthy, professional, and white-collar, higher-income Americans voted Republican.

But in subsequent years, America underwent several major transformations. Women entered the work force in larger numbers. They generally performed nonmanual labor and added a second income to their households. This made their families somewhat more middle class—even if their husbands continued to do manual labor themselves (as 58 percent of nonagricultural working males did as late as 1972).[27] Meanwhile, the family farm was being replaced by large corporate farms. As a result, poor whites from the Midwest and the South and southern blacks increasingly headed for the cities of the North. The resulting racial conflict led to greater Democratic voting by newly enfranchised blacks and less Democratic voting by whites both in and outside the South, so that, on balance, *the class basis of voting declined.*

Age

Much of the explanation for the decline of SES as a determinant of voting behavior can be found in the fact that new voters have come along less tied to parties. At each election, about 8 percent of the electorate has newly come of age. These new voters have different experiences and memories and less contact with influential elders than used to be the case. Young voters recently have emphasized issues more than their elders and at the same time have voted less often. This is probably because they generally feel both disillusioned and politically powerless, as we have already noted.

The Special Case of the Generational Vote

There were signs in the 1984 campaign that this age-related difference among younger voters is gaining strength. Gary Hart built his campaign for

Sen. Gary Hart campaigns among Yuppie voters.
(David Burnett/Woodfin Camp & Associates)

the Democratic presidential nomination on the claim that it was time for a new generation of leadership. Hart, although himself 47, knew that there was a large group of people under 40 who had never—or only rarely—voted, largely because they felt alienated from the politicians. Population figures support this. The period between 1946 and 1964 is called the baby-boom era because soldiers back from World War II settled down and had children. In those 18 years, 76 million people were born—half again as many as in any similar time period. Today there are now 25 million households headed by people under 35—up from 16 million in 1970.

The baby boomers who supported Hart came to be called Yuppies during the 1984 primaries—for "young, urban professionals." During his campaign, Hart explained:

This is a generation that grew up in 20 of the worst years this country has ever seen, starting with Nov. 22, 1963 [the assassination of President Kennedy]. In that 20-year span, there was a wave of assassinations unprecedented in our nation's history [Robert Kennedy and black leaders Malcolm X and Martin Luther King, Jr., as well as attempts on George Wallace and President Reagan], the most divisive war since the Civil War [Vietnam], the biggest political scandal of our nation's history [Watergate], and a period of the worst economic crisis since the Great Depression. All we've had for 20 years is bad news. . . . There were reasons for these people not to get involved in politics. I believe there is a latent idealism in the

---

[27]These figures can be found annually in the United States Department of Labor's *Manpower Report of the President* (Washington, DC: GPO). My account owes much to Paul R. Abramson, *Generational Change in American Politics* (Lexington, MA: Lexington Books, 1975).

TABLE 3.5
Vote by Groups in Presidential Elections since 1952

	1952		1956		1960		1964	
	Stevenson	Eisenhower	Stevenson	Eisenhower	Kennedy	Nixon	Johnson	Goldwater
National	44.6%	55.4%	42.2%	57.8%	50.1%	49.9%	61.3%	38.7%
Sex								
Male	47	53	45	55	52	48	60	40
Female	42	58	39	61	49	51	62	38
Race								
White	43	57	41	59	49	51	59	41
Nonwhite	79	21	61	39	68	32	94	6
Education								
College	34	66	31	69	39	61	52	48
High school	45	55	42	58	52	48	62	38
Grade school	52	48	50	50	55	45	66	34
Occupation								
Prof.-business	36	64	32	68	42	58	54	46
White collar	40	60	37	63	48	52	57	43
Manual	55	45	50	50	60	40	71	29
Age								
Under 30	51	49	43	57	54	46	64	36
30–49	47	53	45	55	54	46	63	37
Over 50	39	61	39	61	46	54	59	41
Religion								
Protestant	37	63	37	63	38	62	55	45
Catholic	56	44	51	49	78	22	76	24
Politics								
Republican	8	92	4	96	5	95	20	80
Democrat	77	23	85	15	84	16	87	13
Independent	35	65	30	70	43	57	56	44
Region								
East	45	55	40	60	53	47	68	32
Midwest	42	58	41	59	48	52	61	39
South	51	49	49	51	51	49	51	48
West	42	58	43	57	49	51	60	40
Members of labor union families	61	39	57	43	65	35	73	27

Not all figures total 100% because of rounding.

[a]1976 and 1980 results do not include vote for minor party candidates.

[b]Less than 1 percent.

American people, a need to serve something other than their own interests. When it isn't tapped, people get cynical.[28]

Whether these young professionals continue to be politically active in coming campaigns probably depends most of all on whether the parties offer candidates sensitive to their experiences and to their concerns. And, of course, not all baby boomers are Hart-style Yuppies—many are religious fundamentalists, and many are less educated members of minority groups, for example. Both parties know that people between 25 and 44 years of age are now 41.5 percent of the eligible electorate. Like all other sectors, they will not vote as a solid bloc. But whichever candidates can get them to the polls will gain major new support.

Education

As a general rule, people with more formal education are more likely to vote Republican while those who stopped going to school earlier are more likely to vote Democratic. Table 3.5 clearly shows this tendency. But it also reminds us that even this tendency may be overcome by particularly popular candidates, such as Lyndon Johnson in 1964, Rich-

---

[28]Quoted by David Shribman, "A Closer Look at the Hart Generation," *New York Times Magazine*, May 27, 1984, p. 34. His article is also the source of the statistics in this section.

1968			1972		1976[a]			1980[a]			1984	
Humphrey	Nixon	Wallace	McGovern	Nixon	Carter	Ford	McCarthy	Carter	Reagan	Anderson	Reagan	Mondale
43.0%	43.4%	13.6%	38%	62%	50%	48%	1%	41%	51%	7%	59%	41%
41	43	16	37	63	53	45	1	38	53	7	61	37
45	43	12	38	62	48	51	—[b]	44	49	6	57	42
38	47	15	32	68	46	52	1	36	56	7	66	34
85	12	3	87	13	85	15	—	86	10	2	14	86
37	54	9	37	63	42	55	2	35	53	10	60	39
42	43	15	34	66	54	46	—	43	51	5	60	39
52	33	15	49	51	58	41	1	54	42	3	50	49
34	56	10	31	69	42	56	1	33	55	10	62	37
41	47	12	36	64	50	48	2	40	51	9	59	40
50	35	15	43	57	58	41	1	48	46	5	53	46
47	38	15	48	52	53	45	1	47	41	7	58	41
44	41	15	33	67	48	49	2	38	52	8	59	41
41	47	12	36	64	52	48	—	41	54	4	62	31
35	49	16	30	70	46	53	—	39	54	6	75	24
59	33	8	48	52	57	42	1	46	47	6	55	44
9	86	5	5	95	9	91	—	8	86	5	92	7
74	12	14	67	33	82	18	—	69	26	4	26	73
31	44	25	31	69	38	57	4	29	55	14	63	35
50	43	7	42	58	51	47	1	43	47	9	52	47
44	47	9	40	60	48	50	1	41	51	7	61	38
31	36	33	29	71	54	45	—	44	52	3	63	36
44	49	7	41	59	46	51	1	35	54	9	59	40
56	29	15	46	54	63	36	1	50	43	5	45	53

Source: Data for 1952–1980 from *Gallop Opinion Index* no. 183, December 1980; 1984 data calculated from *New York Times*/CBS News exit polls, summarized in "Portrait of the Electorate," *New York Times,* November 8, 1984.

ard Nixon in 1972, and Ronald Reagan in 1984, each of whom won a majority of votes among each educational level of voters.

Sex

Because sex is an obvious physical and social difference between people, we might expect a significant difference in the way men and women vote. But research shows that there is now usually little voting difference between the sexes. General rates of participation for both sexes are comparable, as are attitudes on almost all issues, including women's rights. The only significant difference is in attitudes toward the use of force, which women tend to oppose more than men, both in foreign affairs and in dealing with urban unrest. Apparently as a result of this attitude, in the Vietnam era, women tended to vote Democratic more than men.[29]

Religion and Ethnic Background

Traditionally, Catholics and Jews have voted Democratic while Protestants have tended to be Republicans. In addition, Irish, Italian, Polish, eastern European, and Slavic voters have generally supported Democrats while northern European

[29]See Marjorie Lansing and Sandra Baxter, *Woman and Politics: The Invisible Majority* (Ann Arbor: Univ. of Michigan Press, 1980), and Lansing, "Women's Power," *The New York Times,* September 25, 1980.

and Anglo-Saxon voters have voted Republican. These parallels are hardly surprising because Anglo-Saxons tend to be Protestant, and the other ethnic groups tend to be Catholic and Jewish. Recent elections, however, have disrupted some of these patterns. Richard Nixon, for example, got only 33 percent of the Catholic vote in 1968 but 52 percent of it in 1972. And Carter got 57 percent of Catholics in 1976 but only 46 percent of Protestants.

These various tendencies of differing, somewhat overlapping population groups in America can be portrayed graphically by comparing voting behavior over a series of elections. Poll data for the presidential elections from 1952 to 1984 are shown in Table 3.5.

VOTING AND POLITICAL ACTION

In previous periods, a study of social characteristics was a valuable way to try to understand and explain voting behavior in America. The American voter then was thought of as what Gerald Pomper has called the dependent voter. Voters seemed to pay little attention to political events and issues. Instead, they referred to their social group and their party membership for cues as to how to vote— if they voted at all. Voters, in other words, were dependent on their social and economic situation for cues on how to vote.[30]

It was not a very flattering picture of the American voter—nor, for that matter, of American democracy as we had always conceived it. One result was a tendency for some people to argue that it is better that such people not vote. Voting should be left to those who are informed and care enough to take the trouble to learn and to vote. Perhaps democracy should be redefined, some said, to emphasize rule by an expert elite elected by a knowledgeable fragment of the population. Others suggested that perhaps campaigns should be run differently, to emphasize the appearance or image of the candidates, rather than the issues.

One result of these studies has been the development of new styles of campaigning and new types of elections—the "merchandising of candidates."[31] Many fear that this new trend is a grave threat to the strength and viability of democracy in America, as we shall see in our study of the mass media in Chapter 7. Another, even more important consequence, which we discuss later in this chapter, has been a growing debate over the nature of democracy and the desirability and justification of various forms of political participation beyond voting.

Voting and campaigning are types of political participation that occur in the electoral process. These are, however, a small fraction of the types of political action a citizen can take. Many of the others involve collective activities intended to demonstrate the interests of a certain group. We'll look in more detail at this category of political action in Chapter 5. We'll also see various forms of it in action elsewhere in this book. For example, we'll survey neighborhood action groups in Chapter 17 on urban politics and policy. In the rest of this chapter we'll focus most of our attention on the various ways in which individual citizens can and do participate in politics beyond the electoral process.

How many Americans are political activists? Only about half of all voting-age Americans actually vote in presidential elections, and even fewer vote in state and local elections. Only 15 percent of all Americans have ever written a letter to a public official, and two-thirds of all letters written to officials come from only 3 percent of the population.

Facts like these have led many observers to conclude that Americans are not really politically active and that they may not even care much about politics. Some observers fear this may doom democracy in America. Others, as we shall see, are reassured by it, arguing that too much participation might make our system unworkable. However we may feel about the desirability of mass participation in politics, it is difficult to challenge the conclusion that Americans are apathetic if we accept voting and letter writing as the major types of political participation available to ordinary citizens.

But studies of political behavior increasingly suggest that this conception of participation is too narrow. There are in fact a great many other types of activities that are political. These range from

---

[30]See Pomper, *Voters' Choice*, p. 7. For a further development of his views, see Pomper and Susan Lederman, *Elections in America*, 2d ed. (New York: Longman, 1980), chap. 4.

[31]See Joe McGinniss, *The Selling of the President 1968* (New York: Trident, 1969).

signing a petition to rioting, from going to court to contest a government ruling to going to Canada to escape the draft. And some would even argue that not voting is itself a political act because it signifies a rejection of the system or of the candidates and their parties. This rejection may have political implications for the future of the country that prove more serious than the actual election results.

To discover what opportunities we may have to take part in politics and to understand how our system works and the context within which decision makers act, we need to know three things. First, what types of political activities are available to us and to American citizens generally? Second, how widely and how often do citizens engage in such activities? Third, what effects do these activities have—on the people who undertake them as well as on those in authority?

We shall find that citizen action is going on in all parts of our politics, concerning all aspects of policy. We shall refer to it in chapter after chapter. Sometimes it will appear as a factor in current decisions. Other times it will appear as a possible strategy for political change. Always it will be serving as a linkage or connection between the rulers and the ruled. This linkage, in its various forms, is an essential—perhaps the essential—aspect of effective and responsive democracy. This is a lesson all citizens must learn. It is also a lesson citizens must, from time to time, teach to wayward politicians who seem to prefer that citizens leave politics to them.

THE TYPES OF POLITICAL ACTION

Political participation need not be successful. It need not be organized. It need not employ legitimate methods. Any action intended to influence the choice of public policies, the administration of public affairs, or the choice of political leaders is political. Because a wide range of activities qualifies as political participation it may be helpful to do some categorizing.

We can divide the types of political action into five groups: (1) working *around* politics, (2) working *in* politics, (3) working *with* politics, (4) working *against* politics, and (5) working *beyond* politics. Having named our categories, let us look in more detail at the types of political activities that can be grouped under each heading. (They are summarized in Table 3.6.)

Working around Politics

Working around politics includes activities that demonstrate support for the political system. Some of these actions *provide patriotic support or ceremony.* Examples include saluting the flag, singing the "Star-Spangled Banner" before a football game, and saying the "Pledge of Allegiance." We might even include paying taxes as a support activity because without that revenue the government could not function.

TABLE 3.6
Types of Political Action

TYPE	EXAMPLES
1. Working *around* politics	Providing patriotic support or ceremony (e.g., flag salute) Keeping informed about public issues and governmental activity
2. Working *in* politics	Voting Doing party and campaign work Serving in government as an elected official or an appointed bureaucrat
3. Working *with* politics	Lobbying Consulting or advising government Sending letters, telegrams, etc., to officials
4. Working *against* politics	Pressure activities (litigating in court, investigating for exposure in the media, organizing political support for a movement, writing letters to the editor) Obstructive activities (strikes, slowdowns, Alinsky direct action) Civil disobedience Uncivil disobedience (riot, arson, assassination, terrorism)
5. Working *beyond* politics	Expressions or assertions to the public rather than to political actors Extragovernmental problem solving

Working in Politics

Three types of activism fall under the heading of "working in politics." The first two are those we are most familiar with: *voting* and *doing party and campaign work.* We distingush between these two types of electoral activities because, as we saw above, people generally vote out of feelings of civic duty, while those who do party and campaign work are usually more committed to a cause and expect their actions to be effective. The other type of "working in politics" is *serving in government as an elected official or an appointed bureaucrat.* Rulers and servers are political activists.

Working with Politics

Our third category, "working with politics" (or working with politicians), incorporates the various "informational" activities of *lobbying* for legislation or for favorable administrative decisions by government. (We shall examine this in detail in Chapter 5.) It also includes *consulting*—advising the government. And it includes individual citizens informing the government or politicians of their views via *letters, telegrams, telephone calls, and so on, to officals.* In all these cases, people themselves furnish information directly to politicians or to the government.

ACTION UNIT 3.1

How to Write an Effective Letter to the Editor

Here are some suggestions that can help you to write the kind of letter most likely to receive favorable consideration by the editorial desk:

1. If possible, *use a typewriter* and double-space the lines.
2. *Plan your first sentence carefully.* Try to make it short and interesting. If you begin with a reference to a news item, editorial, or letter in the paper addressed, your letter immediately has added interest for the editor. . . .

   If you write to criticize, *begin with a word of appreciation, agreement, or praise.* Don't be merely critical; make constructive suggestions.
3. *Deal with only one topic in a letter.* It should be timely and newsworthy. Be sure your meaning is clear. Use simple and short words, short sentences, and paragraphs. Your letter will be easier to read.
4. *Express your thoughts as clearly and concisely as possible.* Check your local paper for the average length of a letter and try not to exceed it.
5. *Avoid violent language or sarcasm.*
6. *Help supply facts* that may be omitted or slanted in presentation of the news or editorials. You can render a valuable service to the public by presenting views that may ordinarily be given little or no attention by the press. . . .
7. *Don't hesitate to use a relevant personal experience* to illustrate a point.
8. *Bring moral judgments to bear* upon issues confronting the nation and the world. Appeal to readers' sense of fair play, justice, and mercy. Challenge them to respond to the issue.
9. *Try to be hopeful and practical.* Out of fear and despair, people may avoid the most pressing issues of the day. But they may take action when given a possible response and reason to believe that there is hope for a solution.
10. You can make appropriate changes in your letter and *send it to editors of newspapers in other cities.* When doing so, always send first copies, never carbons or photocopies. As a rule, do not send exactly the same letter to different papers in the same city: [Many] papers have a policy against publishing letters which are also sent to other papers.
11. *Always sign your name* and give your address and telephone number. You can use a pen name or initials for publication, but the editor must know the source of the letter.
12. Don't give up looking for your letter too soon. It may not appear for ten days or even longer. **Don't be discouraged if your letter is not printed.** You have given the editor the benefit of your thinking. . . . Try again. If one letter in ten is accepted, you have reached an audience large enough to make your effort worthwhile. (But your score will probably be better than that!)

Adapted from "How-to-Write a Letter to the Editor," published by the Friends Committee on National Legislation.

Working against Politics

The fourth category, "working against politics"—and against politicians—includes a wide range of activities. The first type is *pressure activities* designed to compel desired responses from government. Among the pressure activities are litigating (going to court to force the government to act as you wish); investigating for exposure, such as journalists do; organizing political support for a movement; making threats to withdraw, or promises to encourage, support for political figures; and appealing to others for support through such acts as writing letters to the editor of a newspaper. (See Action Unit 3.1.)

A second type of "working against politics" is *obstructive activities* designed to make the functioning of the government or another public organization difficult or even impossible. Unions traditionally organize strikes or slowdowns or boycotts to force companies to give in to their demands. The same sort of tactics can be used by public employees and citizen groups. For example, in 1977 citizens living near New York City's Kennedy Airport objected to a court decision to allow the British-French Concorde supersonic transport plane to

(AP/Wide World Photos)

(© 1975 Staples & Charles, Ltd.)

land. Because they had lost in the courts they decided to try to force a reversal of the decision by other means. On certain days, they all piled into their cars and drove to the airport access roads, where they then moved as slowly as possible. The traffic congestion that resulted stranded some travelers in the airport and blocked others from ever getting to the airport. In this instance, the action was a legal obstruction designed to force government to change its policy or position. Such activities are becoming more and more possible as our society becomes more and more dependent on technology that is easily disrupted. They are also becoming more and more common.

Not all such activities depend on high technology, however. Many are undertaken by the powerless and technology-less. The most imaginative designer of such activities was the late Saul Alinsky, an urban organizer based in Chicago who spent his life helping the powerless gain greater political clout. The box on page 113 contains his ac-

count of one of his more imaginative—or outrageous—programs for "direct action" of an obstructive sort.

All programs of obstructive activity have one thing in common: They are legal. The same cannot be said for the next two categories of "working against politics": civil disobedience and uncivil disobedience.

Civil disobedience has a long history in our country. The most recent frequent instances were parts of the civil-rights movement of the 1960s and the antiwar movement during the years of Vietnam. People who commit civil disobedience break a law in order to call attention to the alleged injustice of the law or to a policy they believe seriously wrong. Being apprehended and punished for the lawbreaking is an essential part of the action. It emphasizes one's commitment to the cause and generates pressure against the system. In cases of civil disobedience, the action is nonviolent, and the punishment is accepted as part of the protest.

ACTION UNIT 3.2

How to Work in and around Politics

The root of political influence lies in political activity organized at the local level—whether within or outside official party organization. The long-term task of political education is a vital part of the process of political influence in which you can play a major role.

1. Help those around you to become aware of the ways in which decisions made by their representatives affect them. You can encourage others to join or form new discussion and action groups in their own communities, expanding participation and activity wherever possible.

2. Set up a small informal library in your area with information about your representatives, their backgrounds, and voting records, as well as with materials on current political issues.

3. Help others to register and vote.

4. Arrange a "telephone tree" for rapid communication among individuals and groups in your area. This can be helpful in informing one another about future activities and meetings, but it is especially useful when urgent messages to your representatives are needed to show support for a particular piece of legislation.

5. Arrange meetings with individual senators and representatives when they are at home. You may want to get local news coverage of some sessions.

6. Several persons can have a session with your representative in his or her legislative office together over the phone by means of a conference call. (For more information call your local operator.)

7. You may find that no prospective candidate seems to represent your beliefs and interests. If so, consider whether you or someone else in your area might be the potential candidate meeting those requirements.

8. Support the candidate of your choice by organizing appearances for him or her at group meetings and public debates before local citizens. Campaign and make financial contributions.

Adapted from "How to Work in Politics," a guide prepared by the Friends Committee on National Legislation.

To get more ideas about what to do, read the books on activism cited at the end of this chapter and special magazines, including *Citizen Participation* and *Campaigns and Elections*, available in libraries or by subscription.

Saul Alinsky on Direct Action

I have emphasized and re-emphasized that tactics means you do what you can with what you've got, and that power in the main has always gravitated towards those who have money and those whom people follow. The resources of the Have-Nots are (1) no money and (2) lots of people. All right, let's start from there. People can show their power by voting. What else? Well, they have physical bodies. How can they use them? Now a melange of ideas begins to appear. Use the power of the law by making the establishment obey its own rules. Go outside the experience of the enemy, stay inside the experience of your people. Emphasize tactics that your people will enjoy. . . .

[One] tactic involving the bodily functions developed in Chicago during the days of the Johnson-Goldwater campaign. Commitments that were made by the authorities to the Woodlawn ghetto organization were not being met by the city. The political threat that had originally compelled these commitments was no longer operative. The community organization had no alternative but to support Johnson, and therefore the Democratic administration felt the political threat had evaporated. It must be remembered here that not only is pressure essential to compel the establishment to make its initial concession, but the pressure must be maintained to make the establishment deliver. The second factor seemed to be lost to the Woodlawn Organization.

Since the organization was blocked in the political arena, new tactics and a new arena had to be devised.

O'Hare Airport became the target. To begin with, O'Hare is the world's busiest airport. Think for a moment of the common experience of jet travelers. Your stewardess brings you your lunch or dinner. After eating, most people want to go to the lavatory. However, this is often inconvenient because your tray and those of your seat partners are loaded down with dishes. So you wait until the stewardess has removed the trays. By that time those who are seated closest to the lavatory have got up and the "occupied" sign is on. So you wait. And in these days of jet travel the seat belt sign is soon flashed, as the airplane starts it landing approach. You decide to wait until after landing and use the facilities in the terminal. . . .

With this in mind, the tactic becomes obvious—we tie up the lavatories. In the restrooms you drop a dime, enter, push the lock on the door—and you can stay there all day. Therefore the occupation of the sit-down toilets presents no problem. It would take just a relatively few

The late Saul Alinsky addressing a crowd. (AP/Wide World Photos)

people to walk into these cubicles armed with books and newpapers, lock the doors, and tie up all the facilities. What are the police going to do? Break in and demand evidence of legitimate occupancy? Therefore, the ladies' restrooms could be occupied completely; the only problem in the men's lavatories would be the stand-up urinals. This, too, could be taken care of, by having groups busy themselves around the airport and then move in on the stand-up urinals to line up four or five deep whenever a flight arrived. An intelligence study was launched to learn how many sit-down toilets for both men and women, as well as stand-up urinals, there were in the entire O'Hare Airport complex and how many men and women would be necessary for the nation's first "shit-in."

The consequences of this kind of action would be catastrophic in many ways. People would be desperate for a place to relieve themselves. One can see children yelling at their parents, "Mommy, I've got to go," and desperate mothers surrendering, "All right—well, do it. Do it right here." O'Hare would soon become a shambles. The whole scene would become unbelievable and the laughter and ridicule would be nationwide. It would probably get a front page story in the London *Times*. It would be a source of great mortification and embarrassment to the city administration. . . .

The threat of this tactic was leaked . . . back to the administration, and within forty-eight hours the Woodlawn Organization found itself in conference with the authorities who said that they were certainly going to live up to their commitments and they could never understand where anyone got the idea that a promise made by Chicago's City Hall would not be observed.

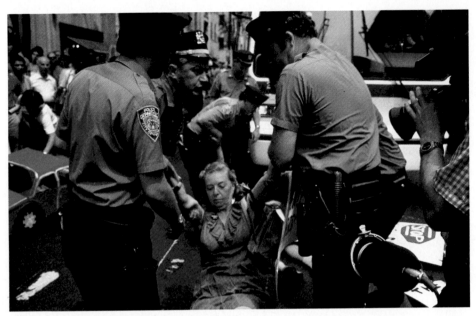

A civil disobedience action. (Tannenbaum/Sygma)

Other instances of "working against politics" are quite different, and might be termed *uncivil disobedience*. Instances of rioting, arson, assassination, terrorist acts, and other forms of violence are one category. Bribery of public officials, ideologically based shoplifting or other theft (assertedly intended to "strike a blow against capitalism"), and other nonviolent deeds constitute another category. They have in common, however, an effort to circumvent the law and to avoid paying the consequences for the act. Their flagrant challenge to the law automatically makes them instances of political activism. The effort to escape punishment makes them all the more dangerous to the existing order in general and to the rule of law in particular. But it may also make them less likely to win public support.

Working beyond Politics

Our final category, "working beyond politics," also poses particular challenges to the existing order but in a somewhat different way. We are all familiar with protest demonstrations, negative bumper stickers (such as "Register criminals, not guns"), and popular protest songs. Such actions and statements differ from "working with politics" in that they do not have a particular target. These actions and statements are often called *expressive or asser-*

tive acts. They express concerns but are intended for consumption not so much—or at least not directly—by politicians as by the public generally.

The other major category of "working beyond politics" is *extragovernmental problem solving*. In this century, Americans have tended increasingly to look to the government to solve their major problems. But people are losing confidence that government can solve problems. More and more, they are attempting to regain control over their own lives by doing for themselves what government has previously tried to do. A theme of the Reagan administration, this return to self-help, or self-reliance, began much earlier.

Examples range from private schools to vigilante groups organized by citizens to police their own neighborhoods. "Working beyond politics" is itself a form of political activity because it challenges the authority of the government. More and more Americans are engaging in it.

WHO PARTICIPATES— AND HOW MUCH?

We have just examined briefly a variety of general types of political activity. To some degree, these various activities are open to any American, al-

TABLE 3.7
Ways Citizens Relate to the Government

GROUP	ACTIVITIES OF GROUP AND PERCENT OF POPULATION TAKING PART IN GIVEN ACTIVITY
Protesters	Join in public street demonstrations (3%) Riot if necessary (2%) Protest vigorously if government does something morally wrong (26%) Attend protest meetings (6%) Refuse to obey unjust laws (16%) (Protesters also take part in activities of other groups)
Community activists	Work with others on local problems (30%) Form a group to work on local problems (14%) Active membership in community organizations (8%) Contact officials on social issues (14%) (Activists also vote fairly regularly)
Party and campaign workers[a]	Actively work for party or candidate (26%) Persuade others how to vote (28%) Attend meetings, rallies (19%) Give money to party or candidate (13%) Join and support political party (35%) Be a candidate for office (3%) (Workers also vote regularly)
Communicators	Keep informed about politics (67%) Engage in political discussions (42%) Write letters to newspaper editors (9%) Send support or protest messages to political leaders (15%) (Communicators also vote fairly regularly)
Contact specialists	Contact local, state, and national officials on particularized problems (4%) (Specialists are inactive otherwise)
Voters and patriots	Vote regularly in elections (63%) Love my country (94%) Show patriotism by flying the flag, attending parades, etc. (70%) Pay all taxes (94%)
Nonparticipants	No voting, no other activity (22%) No patriotic inputs (3–5%)

[a]Percentages for the party campaign worker category are based mostly on a national survey of the American public conducted in 1967 and reported by Sidney Verba and Norman Nie, *Participation in America* (New York: Harper & Row, 1972). Percentages for the remaining modes are based on the Buffalo Survey (1968) by Milbrath.

Source: Adapted from Lester Milbrath and M. L. Goel, *Political Participation*, 2d ed., pp. 18–19. Copyright © 1977 Houghton Mifflin Company. Adapted with permission.

though few have the opportunity to lobby, and relatively few have the occasion to engage in civil or not-so-civil disobedience. But if this wide range of activities is possible for any American, how probable is participation in them? To find out, we can examine the results of some recent surveys that asked representative groups of Americans what types of political activities they engaged in from time to time and what types they had ever engaged in. None of these surveys asked about the whole range of activities we have examined. Nor did they describe those they did ask about in identical ways. For these reasons, the best approach is to examine each study separately.

The most recent comprehensive effort to summarize research on political participation is that of Lester Milbrath and M. L. Goel.[32] They combine results from Milbrath's own survey of the population of Buffalo, New York, with those from a nationwide survey developed by Sidney Verba and Norman Nie. Their findings are summarized in Table 3.7.

The survey reported by Milbrath and Goel describes the types of activities of each active segment of the population, but it does not tell us which

[32]Lester Milbrath and M. L. Goel, *Political Participation*, 2d ed. (Chicago: Rand McNally, 1977).

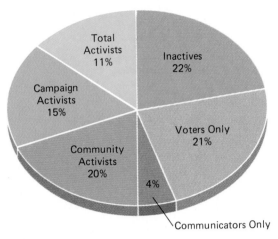

FIGURE 3.2

Six Types of Participants in American Politics.

Note: These figures come from Sidney Verba and Norman Nie, *Participation in America* (New York: Harper & Row, 1972), pp. 79–80. The figures do not add to 100 percent because Verba and Nie could not classify 7 percent of the people. The names they assign to groups have been changed to correspond to our discussion.

groups within the population tend to take which action. To get a better sense of this, we must look more closely at this aspect of Verba and Nie's study.[33]

Verba and Nie divide the population into six groups, as shown in Figure 3.2. The first group, the *inactives* (22 percent of population), tend to be of lower socioeconomic status (SES). In this group, blacks, the young, the elderly, and women are all overrepresented. Another 21 percent of the population are in the second group; they *vote but do nothing else.* They, too, tend to be of lower SES. The elderly and city dwellers are overrepresented here, whereas those living in rural areas are underrepresented.

The third group are people who *contact officials on particular concerns* but are otherwise inactive; they make up only 4 percent of the population. They tend to live in big cities and are usually Catholics rather than Protestants, whites rather than blacks, and of lower SES. The fourth group (20 percent of the population) are those who *contact officials on broader concerns, cooperate to solve local problems, and usually vote.* They tend to live

in rural areas and small towns and are usually of upper SES, Protestant rather than Catholic, and white rather than black.

The fifth group (about 15 percent of the population) not only *vote* but are heavily *active in campaigns.* They tend to live in big cities and suburbs, have higher SES, and are little involved in community problem solving. They include unusual percentages of blacks and Catholics.

The final group are those *active in all these ways.* About all that can be said of this 11 percent of the population is that upper SES people are overrepresented, whereas the old and the young are underrepresented.[34]

This study indicates that certain social groups tend to participate more actively than others. It also suggests there is considerable overlap among types of activity: That is, the same people tend to take different types of political actions. The Verba and Nie survey also examined the extent of this multiple participation.

They found, for example, that 64 percent of the population reported it voted regularly. (We know this is an overstatement; people always tend to overstate their voting rate when asked.) They also found that 25 percent scored high on campaign participation. But almost everyone who participates in a campaign also votes. Only 4 percent do not. This means that 32 percent of the population admits that it neither votes nor works in campaigns.[35]

Three major conclusions can be drawn from a survey of participation studies. First, fewer Americans are politically active than we might expect. Second, those who do more than just vote tend to be active in a variety of ways. Many tend to concentrate on campaign activities, some on community activities, and fewer still on protest activities. Third, certain groups in our society are more likely to be active: the college educated and those with higher incomes, especially. Blacks, women, the young, and the old are less likely to be active, but these differences are less pronounced and are declining. We shall have more to say about this in Chapters 13 and 14.

---

[33]Sidney Verba and Norman Nie, *Participation in America* (New York: Harper & Row, 1972).

[34]Seven percent of the population could not be classified in these categories and so are omitted. See Verba and Nie, *Participation in America*, pp. 118–19.

[35]Ibid., pp. 36–37.

WHY PEOPLE RUN
FOR POLITICAL OFFICE

Voting is a relatively easy and common form of political activity. Running for and serving in office, on the other hand, is one rarely undertaken—by a maximum of 3 percent of the population according to the Milbrath study. Why, then, do people run for office?

We could cast this question in various ways. In casual terms, we could ask whether politicians are born, self-made, chosen, or made by upbringing and other circumstances. People sometimes say of someone: "He's a *born politician*," just as they speak of "born athletes." Studies have shown that the firstborn in a family tends to be more assertive and more venturesome—qualities generally valuable to a politician, of course. But we really have no evidence directly relating political activity to one's genetic inheritance. Nor can we link much other behavior to genes.

The model of the *self-made politician* fits better in some cases, as it does in the case of Richard Nixon (whom we shall discuss in more detail in coming chapters). It may also fit other cases if it is understood to focus on the conscious reasons an individual has for choosing a political career.

Conscious Reasons

One possible reason for people to enter and remain in politics is that they have strong policy interests. Politicians tend to give answers in terms of policy interests, as well as service, when asked why they are in politics. Observers, however, are often doubtful that such answers constitute the whole truth.

They might be pardoned for being somewhat skeptical. For large egos and politicians seem to inhabit the same always-on-the-run bodies. One result of this skepticism has been development of what is sometimes called ambition theory. It explains the behavior of politicians in terms of another set of conscious reasons: immediate personal success in elections.

Politicians, in other words, often have their eyes not on the voters who elected them to their present offices but rather on the voters who could elect them to higher offices should they become available.[36] Yet, if ambition of this sort were truly the major motivating force in elections, it would be difficult to explain why there are so many candidates running for Congress, for example. There has never been a turnover rate higher than 26 percent in any congressional election year since 1932. It is rare that more than 15 percent of incumbents seeking reelection are defeated. "By almost any standards," one scholar observes,

> the opportunity structure of the House of Representatives is restricted; few elective institutions in American political life have achieved the degree of stability which since the depression has characterized membership in the House. Given the limited oportunity structure, why do candidates participate?[37]

Perhaps the answer is that ambition, or "the power motive" more generally, is less important than we might suspect. Or perhaps we must look beneath the conscious reasons of candidates and other activists to unconscious reasons or motives.

Unconscious Reasons

When someone's behavior does not seem rational, we often look to unconscious factors as possible explanations. Politics is no exception. Some 40 years ago, Harold Lasswell, a leading political scientist, wrote a book called *Power and Personality*, which argued that the politician "pursues power as a means of compensation against deprivation. *Power is expected to overcome low estimates of the self.*"[38] Because certain political people feel personally inadequate, Lasswell argued, they regard power as "compensation against estimates of the self as weak, contemptible, immoral, unloved," and so their "motives are displaced onto public targets and rationalized in the name of public good."[39]

This very negative conception of political participators has not been confirmed by subsequent

---

[36]Joseph Schlesinger, *Ambition and Politics: Political Careers in the United States* (Chicago: Rand McNally, 1966), pp. 1–2, 6. For interesting critiques, see Dwaine Marvick, "Continuities in Recruitment Theory and Research," in *Elite Recruitment in Democratic Politics*, ed. Heinz Eulau and Moshe Czudnowski (New York: Sage/Wiley, 1976), pp. 29–44.

[37]Jeff Fishel, *Party and Opposition: Congressional Challenges in American Politics* (New York: McKay, 1973), p. 31.

[38]H. D. Lasswell, *Power and Personality* (New York: Norton, 1948), p. 39.

[39]Ibid., p. 58.

research. For example, Paul Sniderman studied delegates to the 1956 national party conventions, 60 percent of whom held elective offices. He found that they had *higher self-esteem* than American adults in general, and in particular much higher "feelings of interpersonal competence." They had, in other words, the ability "to feel at ease and self-assured when in the company of others, to be articulate and persuasive, to take the initiative frequently, to be outgoing, active, forceful."[40]

"The available evidence suggests," according to Milbrath and Goel, "that persons with great neurotic or psychotic problems are not attracted to normal democratic political action. The chaotic, rough-and-tumble environment of competitive politics carries few rewards for thin-skinned, neurotic personalities." Political activists, they conclude,

> are persons who are particularly well equipped to deal with their environment. They feel personally competent; they know themselves and feel confident of their knowledge and skills; their egos are strong enough to withstand blows; they are not burdened by a load of anxiety and internal conflict; they can control their impulses; they are astute, sociable, self-expressive, and responsible.[41]

Sound like pretty nice people, don't they? Probably rather like the rest of us, only perhaps a bit more effective. If it is true that they are no different from the rest of us, then we may have to conclude that the motivations of political activists are more complex than any of these theories suggest. In this, too, politicians are probably quite like the rest of us. It seems, then, that political activists are neither born nor self-made nor chosen. Perhaps the real difference between activists and nonactivists is primarily circumstance—circumstance that limits the opportunities for many of us to participate actively in politics.

LIMITS ON POPULAR PARTICIPATION

The major limitation on participation in politics, especially running for office, is resources—particularly money and time. We noted in Perspective 2

that current campaign finance laws limit somewhat the role of "big money" in presidential politics. But to run for other offices—or to run for nomination for president in the primaries—you still must raise large sums of money. It can cost hundreds of thousands of dollars just to run for the House and millions to run for the Senate. Running for other offices is less costly but still out of reach for most Americans, with or without the help of their friends and supporters.

But the limitations go deeper than just the cost of being elected. Once elected, you must be able to afford to serve. For most people in state or national posts, that immediately requires maintaining two residences—one in the home district and another in the state capital or in Washington, depending on the job. Furthermore, a politician is expected to be well dressed and to entertain fashionably if not lavishly. He or she must also support two office staffs (one at home and one in the capital) that generally cost more than his or her "office allotment" of expense funds allows. This means most politicians must either be independently wealthy or constantly raising funds by public speaking and writing books and articles—or by accepting favors from special interests. Most of us probably cannot afford to run for office, nor could many of us afford to win.

Furthermore, most of us cannot afford to do much party and campaign work because of our other responsibilities. So the roster of political activists is further limited this way. To some extent, energy and imagination may substitute for money and time. But even so, few Americans have energy and imagination left over for political work once they meet their normal responsibilities.

What this means is that most of the channels by which ordinary citizens could make known their concerns are actually left to **elites**—lobbyists and leaders of protest movements, for example. Malcontents are therefore aced with two options: infiltrating the elites to get their views represented or developing new channels through which to protest.

There is evidence that various social groups are slowly *infiltrating the elites*. In the years since FDR's New Deal in the 1930s, there has been a gradual broadening of the recruitment base of high officials in government. Most such officials used to be upper-middle-class Protestants from the Northeast and the Midwest. Now more and more come

---

[40]Paul Sniderman, *Personality and Democratic Politics* (Berkeley, CA: Univ. of California Press, 1975).

[41]Milbrath and Goel, *Political Participation*, p. 85.

from other classes, other religions, and other regions. A major part of this change has been a shift toward people with specialized technical skills.[42]

Of course, such changes are very slow, and it is always possible that by the time these new elements make it into government they will have been so well trained, so well "socialized" that they will think and act rather like everyone else who is already there. Such fears and suspicions encourage the *development of new channels of influence.* In a sense, the George Wallace (1968, 1972), Eugene McCarthy (1968, 1976), and John Anderson (1980) campaigns might be thought of as efforts to redevelop the "protest vote" as a new channel—a channel to "send a message to Washington," in Wallace's memorable phrase. These new channels nonetheless in a sense reflect yet another limitation on political activism by citizens: The government itself is a political participant, and it after all has more resources than anyone else.

The Government as a Political Activist

The government's chief role in political action is to encourage—and sometimes to compel—citizens to act in certain ways in politics. Besides requiring that we pay taxes, serve in the armed forces when called, and so on, the government tries to get citizens involved in policy making. In the 1930s the Department of Agriculture and the Tennessee Valley Authority led efforts to involve citizens in rural and agricultural development. Such efforts by the government are now common, especially since President Carter issued Executive Order 12044, which called on agencies to involve the public in policy making from its early stages.[43] Stuart Langton points out that

> while many citizens have organized to influence and improve government, many officials have attempted to make government more accessible and responsive to citizens. Consequently, two citizen-participation movements have grown simultaneously in the last decade. The citizen-initiated movement . . . has included grassroots organizations, public-interest groups, consumer groups, voluntary service organizations, and the like. The government-initiated

movement has stressed the importance of involving citizens in improving and gaining support for administrative decisions and government programs.[44]

We still usually think of the government as a political responder rather than as a political activist. We hear our political system described as one of "government of the people, by the people, and for the people." Such a phrase suggests that the government will be responsive to the wishes and actions of the people. The leaders, after all, are *from* the people—representatives of the people. They are expected to act *for* the people, in accordance with their needs and wishes.

But this is not a fully accurate description of what happens. Our government is indeed a government *of* the people, but it is a government *by only some* of the people and often *for only some.* The government responds more readily to some political activists than to others—as we shall see in Chapter 5 when we discuss the roles of various interests in politics. And even when government tries to respond positively, the results may be the opposite of those intended—for reasons we shall examine in Part 3. This selective responsiveness is itself a form of political action.

Furthermore, the government can make various responses to demands. Among these responses, when government does not agree with activists seeking to influence policy, five are common: (1) *delay;* (2) *tokenism*—doing only a little of what is asked and thereby seeming to be more responsive than it actually is; (3) *discrediting* the request as being unrepresentative of popular will—as judged by the leaders—or as being impractical, too expensive, or otherwise undesirable; (4) *suppressing* the request by punishing the requesters, jailing them, or keeping them from public attention; and (5) *ignoring* or pretending not to hear the request or demand.

Even when it is responding to people, however, the government may be playing even more of a role as a political activist. The government makes most of the news we read and see. Governmental leaders make most of the speeches we hear, and governmental officials take most of the regulating actions that affect our lives. These governmental acts are prominent and convincing because they are official

---

[42]Kenneth Prewitt and William McAllister, "Changes in the American Executive Elite, 1930–1970," in *Elite Recruitment,* ed. Eulau and Czudnowski, pp. 105–32.

[43]For a survey, see *Citizen Participation in the American Federal System* (Washington, DC: Advisory Commission on Intergovernmental Affairs, 1979).

[44]Stuart Langton, "Citizen Participation in America: Current Reflections on the State of the Art," in *Citizen Participation,* ed. Langton, pp. 1–2.

acts of a government and because we still think of that government as representing us, the people, and deriving its authority from us, the people.

What effect do the big role and large influence of government have on the ideas we hold about what government should do? One stark view is offered by political scientist Murray Edelman:

> If legislative, administrative, and judicial procedures significantly influence how people see leaders, issues, and themselves and therefore what they will accept, what they want, and what they demand, then those procedures are less likely to express the people's will than to shape it. More precisely, they reflect it only after they shape it.[45]

What Effects Does Participation Have?

What, then, are the consequences of participation on those who participate and on the political system? Edelman concludes that available ways of acting usually help to legitimize the regime and to bring potential dissenters into the system. In some cases, however, they foster discontent and protest. "In either case they significantly influence people's roles, self-concepts, and willingness to accept their own statuses and the official rules. They affect not so much who gets what as who is satisfied or dissatisfied with what he gets and with who orders him around."[46]

So there seems to be a kind of circle. The people elect representatives and in a sense instruct them from time to time by engaging in political activism. These representatives then turn around and use their authority to help instruct the people on how to see the world, how to define political reality. Eldelman notes

> the remarkable degree of support official governmental acts and policies enjoy even when they bring serious deprivations to their supporters and to others: economic, welfare, civil rights, and regulatory policies that are manifestly tokens or that perpetuate inequalities; virtually continuous wars fought in the name of a peace that appears only intermittently and precariously.[47]

Edelman's assessment may well be too harsh. We shall have to wait until we examine these various policy problems and government efforts to solve

them, in Part 5, before we can decide. But even if he exaggerates, his point is an important one. It calls to our attention the extent to which our political participation does generally support the status quo. When we vote, especially when we vote for one of two rather comparable candidates, our action tends to reinforce the status quo. When we decide not to vote, perhaps because we do not like the choice we are offered, we thereby strengthen the existing system by concealing the extent of our discontent. The same seems often to be true for party and campaign work and even for letter writing or demonstrations.

Is Participation Good or Bad?

If it is true that political participation does generally reinforce the system, then we would expect to find supporters of the system glad to see more political participation by more people.

But that is not always the case. The strongest advocates of increased participation now are on the political left, where many call for "participatory democracy." By this they mean a system in which citizens play greater roles in deciding the things that affect their lives. At the other extreme are those—many of them regular advisors of the government in Washington—who now argue that increased participation may make democracies ungovernable. They fear that it will produce further disillusionment and so disrespect for authority, when the government is unresponsive to the wishes and demands of the activists.[48] Throughout this book, we shall be studying the possibilities for, and the effects of, participation. Then, in the epilogue, we shall return to the debate over its desirability.

In the meantime, we are left wondering. The current situation is one in which a relatively small segment of the population rules and participates in other ways. Does it necessitate a government responsive to, and controlled by, "some of the people" instead of "all of the people"? In the next three chapters, we shall examine the roles of parties, interest groups, and public opnion in our politics.

---

[45]Murray Edelman, *Politics as Symbolic Action* (Chicago: Markham, 1971), p. 179.
[46]Ibid., p. 179
[47]Ibid., pp. 175–76.

[48]For example, compare Daniel C. Kramer, *Participatory Democracy: Developing Ideals of the Political Left* (Cambridge, MA: Schenkman, 1972), with Michel Crozier, Samuel P. Huntington, and Joji Watanuki, *The Crisis of Democracy: Report on the Government of Democracies* (New York: New York Univ. Press, 1975). And see the excerpts from statements on both sides reprinted in the Epilogue to this book.

SUMMARY

Voter turnout in the United States has always been low. Among the factors are registration requirements, legal restraints (most of which, such as the poll tax and the white primary, have been abolished), and dislike of the candidates. If we remember that few elections are decided by only one vote, we may even wonder why people bother to vote; most see it as their civic duty.

Experts explain why people vote as they do in terms of conscious reasons (partisanship, issues, and candidate images), unconscious reasons (attitude toward authority), and social factors (socioeconomic status, age, education, sex, religion, and ethnic background). The influence of each of these is summarized in the text and tables of this chapter.

Citizens may take many other types of political action. This action includes working *around* politics (patriotic support, keeping informed), working *in* politics (voting, doing party and campaign work, and running for or serving in office), working *with* politics (lobbying, consulting, contacting officials), working *against* politics (pressure, obstruction, civil disobedience, uncivil disobedience), and working *beyond* politics (expressions to the public and extragovernmental problem solving). Figures show that about one-fifth of the population only vote, another fifth both vote and are community activists, 15 percent vote and work in campaigns, 11 percent do many different types of actions, 4 percent only communicate, and 22 percent are totally inactive.

Most choose to run for office because of strong policy interests or ambition for higher office. Some people have argued that politicians have weak characters and seek to compensate for them, but research shows that most political activists are psychologically healthy.

Participation is limited by the need for the twin resources of time and money. Thus, it is usually done by elites. But the traditional privileged elites have been infiltrated by various new types of people since the 1930s. Government sometimes encourages people to participate. At other times it will delay, or else ignore, discredit, or suppress requests. Or it may engage in tokenism. In each case, it will itself be acting in politics and influencing citizens. Both government and experts disagree over whether citizen participation is usually good or bad for American politics, as we'll see in coming chapters.

Suggestions for Further Reading and Study

If you want to know how people voted in a particular national election, the official source is *Statistics of the Presidential and Congressional Election*, published regularly by the government. A comparable source is *America Votes*, edited by Richard Scammon and published every two years by CQ Press in Washington.

The question of why people voted as they did is more complicated and controversial. There are important classic studies cited in the text. On presidential elections generally, see the comprehensive study by Nelson W. Polsby and Aaron Wildavsky, *Presidential Elections*, 6th ed. (New York: Scribner, 1984). For popular accounts of each election from 1960 through 1972, see the series of books written by Theodore H. White and published by Atheneum entitled *The Making of the President*.

Gerald Pomper is the author of an interesting study of voting that focuses on the impacts of party, class, sex, youth, and race: *Voters' Choice* (New York: Dodd, Mead, 1975). Another effort to reexamine the findings of voting studies over several decades is Norman H. Nie, Sidney Verba, and John R. Petrocik, *The Changing American Voter*, enlarged ed. (Cambridge, MA: Harvard Univ. Press, 1979). See also Herbert Asher, *Presidential Elections and American Politics*, 3d ed. (Homewood, IL: Dorsey, 1984). For an examination of the impact of elections on policy, see Gerald Pomper and Susuan Lederman, *Elections in America: Control and Influence in Democratic Politics*, 2d ed. (New York: Longman, 1980).

There is no end to the literature on activism—nor will there be an end to our discussion of it until we have finished the final chapter of this book. Among the stimulating general discussions of participation in politics are E. E. Schattschneider, *Semisovereign People: A Realist's View of Democracy in America* (New York: Holt, Rinehart & Winston, 1960); Robert Lane, *Political Life* (New York: Free Press, 1959), which examines attitudes and other factors affecting political participation; and two books by Murray Edelman: *Symbolic Uses of Politics* (Urbana: Univ. of Illinois Press, 1964) and *Politics as Symbolic Action* (Chicago: Markham, 1971).

The most comprehensive surveys of participation in America are cited in this chapter. See also two collections of helpful articles edited by Stuart Langton: *Citizen Participation in America* (Lexington, MA: Lexington Books, 1978) and *Citizen Participation Perspectives*

(Medford, MA: Lincoln Filene Center, 1979). See also the newsletter published by the Lincoln Filene Center, *Citizen Participation*. And see M. Margaret Conway, *Political Participation in the United States* (Washington: CQ Press, 1985).

For discussion of various aspects of working with politics, see Michael Walzer, *Political Action: A Practical Guide to Movement Politics* (New York: Quadrangle, 1971); Dick Simpson and George Beam, *Strategies for Change: How to Make the American Political Dream Work* (Chicago: Swallow, 1976), a book that is actually more comprehensive than this categorization suggests, based as it is on Simpson's experience as a renegade local politician in Chicago as well as a professor of political science; Donald Ross, *A Public Citizen's Action Manual* (New York: Grossman, 1973), and Center for Study of Responsive Law, *Working on the System: A Comprehensive Manual for Citizen Access to Federal Agencies* (New York: Basic Books, 1974), both products of Ralph Nader's public-interest organizations; and Jeffrey M. Berry, *Lobbying for the People* (Princeton, NJ: Princeton Univ. Press, 1977), a study of various public-interest lobbies.

On direct action, see the two classics by Saul Alinsky, *Reveille for Radicals* (New York: Vintage, 1946) and *Rules for Radicals* (New York: Vintage, 1972); and a handbook by Martin Oppenheimer and George Lakey, *A Manual for Direct Action* (Chicago: Quadrangle, 1964).

On nonviolence, see Joan Bondurant, *Conquest of Violence: The Gandhian Philosophy of Conflict* (Berkeley: Univ. of California Press, 1965); Martin Luther King, *Why We Can't Wait* (New York: Signet, 1963), about the civil-rights struggle in Birmingham; Richard B. Gregg's classic, *The Power of Nonviolence* (Nyack, NY: Fellowship, 1959); and Gene Sharp, *The Politics of Nonviolent Action* (Boston: Porter Sargent, 1973), a monumental book that analyzes 198 different methods of nonviolent action.

Among books dealing with working beyond politics are John Hunefeld, *The Community Activist's Handbook: A Guide to Organizing, Financing, and Publicizing Community Campaigns* (Boston: Beacon, 1970); the O. M. Collective, *The Organizer's Manual* (New York: Bantam, 1971); and George Lakey, *Strategy for a Living Revolution* (San Francisco: Freeman, 1973).

4

POLITICAL PARTIES

Our elections are fought by candidates picked by political parties. While many of us tend to associate ourselves with a particular party, large numbers of voters call themselves independents. The same two parties have been dominant in our system for some 130 years. Many experts think our system needs two strong parties—parties stronger than those we have today. In this chapter, we'll study the various roles our parties play in shaping our politics and the reasons for the dominance of these two parties. We'll also see how the parties have changed in recent years and why some experts think they are on the way out while others see signs of rebirth. At the end, you'll have a better basis on which to understand our elections—and on which to identify with one of our parties or to favor an alternative system. ■

"THE TELEVISION PARTY"

When John Anderson decided to run for president in the summer of 1980 after failing to get the Republican nomination, he ran as an independent. He decided not to create his own party. Why? It would have been difficult to do in a short time, of course. But George Wallace had created the American Independent party when he decided to run outside his own Democratic party in 1968. Anderson said he believed in the two-party system. He just didn't believe that the alternatives it offered in 1980—Carter or Reagan—adequately represented the concerns of the people.

At the time he began his independent—or "national unity"—campaign, Anderson and some experts believed he had a chance to win. One of the reasons for this belief was the weakness of the existing parties. That weakness itself may have suggested to Anderson that he didn't really need a party. All the surveys, as we've seen, showed voters' party identification to be very weak. In addition, major party candidates have increasingly depended on their own organizations rather than on their parties in running and financing their campaigns. In any case, most experts now believe that the news media are more important than the parties in deciding elections. Indeed, the *New York Times* (September 14, 1980) editorialized that Anderson, the candidate without a party, was really the first candidate of "the television party" because

John Anderson, independent presidential candidate in the 1980 election. (Wally McNamee/Woodfin Camp & Associates)

his success had depended so heavily on media coverage.

Anderson's nonparty effort in 1980 was a failure, as we know. He did get 7 percent of the popular vote, but as he didn't carry any states, he didn't win any electoral votes.

Then three years later, on November 8, 1983—a year before the next presidential election—Anderson announced he and some supporters were forming a new political party—the National Unity party. It would be built by a steering committee of 30 members from 14 states, with appeals to be sent to 40,000 people who worked for Anderson or gave money in 1980. Anderson said he would accept this party's nomination for president if asked, but he added: "I am not declaring myself a candidate, because I am trying to focus attention specifically on what I think at this point is the important consideration, and that is that we get a party . . . established."[1] His effort failed, and there was no National Unity party ticket in the 1984 election. There were, however, tickets run by ten parties other than the Democratic and the Republican parties, as Table 4.1 shows.

Why had Anderson changed his mind and his strategy—twice? Why did so many others choose to run as party candidates? Experts, for more than a decade, had been saying that parties were weak and were growing weaker, and many observers had become worried that the weakening of the two major parties was undermining politics and government. One group of some 50 social scientists, government officials, and politicians declared in 1982 that political parties "provide some measure of continuity, stability, and orderliness in politics." The group argued that parties needed to be strengthened in order to attain "a healthier, stronger government."[2]

Thus, both observers and candidates now see parties as valuable yet endangered organizations. But just what are these parties—and are they really an endangered species? To find out, we must see what they do in our system and how they and their roles have been changing.

---

[1] Associated Press dispatch, printed in the *New York Times*, November 9, 1983. Several months later, Anderson decided that the National Unity party would not run a presidential candidate in 1984 because its highest priority was the defeat of Ronald Reagan, and a NUP candidate would tend to split the anti-Reagan vote.

[2] Michael Oreskes, "Stronger U.S. Political Parties Urged," *New York Times*, April 19, 1982. For the text of papers pesented at this American Assembly conference, see Joel L. Fleishman, ed., *The Future of American Political Parties* (Englewood Cliffs, NJ: Prentice-Hall, 1982).

TABLE 4.1

Minor Party Presidential and Vice-Presidential Candidates in 1984

PARTY	OCCUPATION
American	
Delmar Dennis (Tenn.)	Book publisher
Traves Brownlee (Del.)	Head of Americans for Constitutional Taxation
Citizens	
Sonia Johnson (Va.)	Women's rights activist
Richard Walton (R.I.)	Free-lance writer
Communist	
Gus Hall (N.Y.)	Party general secretary
Angela Davis (Calif.)	Political science teacher, author
Independent	
Lyndon H. LaRouche (Va.)	Self-described economist
Billy Davis (Miss.)	Lawyer and farmer
Independent Alliance	
Dennis L. Serrette (N.J.)	Phone technician, union organizer
Nancy Ross (N.Y.)	Former schoolteacher
Libertarian	
David Bergland (Calif.)	Lawyer
Jim Lewis (Conn.)	Bookbinding sales representative
Populist	
Bob Richards (Texas)	Lecturer and real estate developer
Maureen Kennedy Salaman (Calif.)	President of the National Health Federation
Prohibition	
Earl F. Dodge (Colo.)	National party chairman
Warren C. Martin (Kan.)	Farmer and businessman
Socialist Workers	
Mel Mason (Calif.)	Ex-Seaside, Calif., city councilor
Andrea Gonzalez (N.Y.)	Young Socialist Alliance chairperson
Workers World	
Larry Holmes (N.Y.)	Black activist
Gloria La Riva (Calif.)	Political activist

Source: Congressional Quarterly Weekly Report, November 3, 1984, 2851. Reprinted with permission from Congressional Quarterly, Inc.

WHAT A PARTY IS

Parties are generally defined, in the words of one political scientist, as "enduring coalitions of more or less like-minded individuals who engage in various sorts of party activity: giving substantial sums of money, running party organizations, canvassing precincts, or just declaring loyalty to a party and voting for its candidates."[3] The dictionary tells us that our term *party* actually derives from an old Latin term meaning "a division" or "a part"—a body or group of persons on one side of a contest maintaining an opinion or a cause against another such part or group. In this sense, the more people participate in other ways besides political party

membership, the more lively American politics is likely to become. But before we decide to abandon our parties as they are or to reject our present system of two dominant parties in favor of other forms of political participation, we need to know what effects our parties have on our politics.

America today has two major parties—the Democratic party and the Republican party—and a number of smaller parties. These parties nominate candidates for office and campaign to get votes for those candidates. But what or who actually *does* these things? Are the citizens who actually work for the party the heart of the party? And who are more important? The candidates? The voters who declare themselves Democrats or Republicans? "The organization"—the party officials whose role is to keep things going between elections and to see that arrangements are made so that primary elections are held, conventions are convened, funds are

---

[3]Benjamin I. Page, *Choices and Echoes in Presidential Elections* (Chicago: Univ. of Chicago Press, 1978), p. 62.

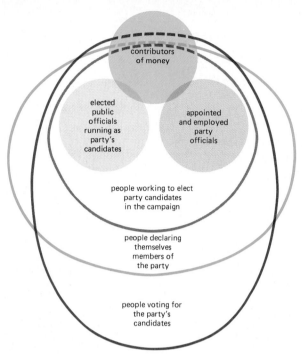

FIGURE 4.1

The Elements of a Political Party.

Note: The sizes of these groups are not to scale in this figure. In fact, the total number of appointed party officials is smaller than that of elected public officials; there are many thousands more contributors of money and of labor in campaigns; declared members number in the millions; voters are the largest group, but vary considerably with the party and election.

raised, and so on? (These various elements of a political party are depicted in Figure 4.1.)

Why is this important? You can, in a sense, have a party without workers if someone simply announces that he or she is running for office on a particular ticket. You can have voters who declare themselves Democrats yet always vote Republican. Many southerners now do this. You can even have parties that do not run candidates. Republican parties in some areas of the South that remain overwhelmingly Democratic still tend to do this.

This look at the real-world political party has expanded the dictionary definition given earlier, but we still do not know exactly what a party is. Perhaps a look at the *function* of parties—at what parties actually do—will help. Political scientists often define parties as groups that organize to win elections by selecting candidates and running campaigns.

WHAT A PARTY DOES

But parties play other roles and serve other functions in American politics besides (1) recruiting candidates and (2) competing with each other to get candidates elected to office. They also (3) attract popular attention to elections by campaigning publicly for votes. They (4) tend to focus that popular attention on the particular issues they emphasize in the campaign to make that choice easier for citizens. These effects often result in yet another function: (5) educating the people about politics and issues generally. These last three are important information functions.

In addition, the fact that the parties are seeking to get a majority vote makes them likely to try to (6) integrate various groups (races, classes, and so on) and opinions (liberal, moderate, conservative) in the electorate behind a single candidate. In other words, they form **coalitions.** This may tend to unify or stabilize what otherwise could be divisive differences in public opinion.

Once the election is over, the parties (7) serve as links between popular sentiment and interest groups *outside* the government and policy made *within* the government. Ways in which these *linkages* are established and maintained will be a major focus of coming chapters. Finally, the party may (8) help to coordinate the actions of various public officials. For example, party unites the president with some members of Congress and separates the president from others. These functions are summarized in Table 4.2.

Providing linkages between people with opinions on the one hand and officials with power on the other, or between various officials, is the func-

TABLE 4.2
Functions of Political Parties

Recruiting candidates
Competing to elect candidates
Campaigning for votes
Focusing attention on issues
Educating people about politics
Forming coalitions of groups of voters
Linking people and groups outside the government with those inside
Coordinating actions of officials in the same party

ACTION UNIT 4.1

How to Work in a Political Party

Local organization is important within the political party. Active involvement in a party will probably mean that you will have more say in choosing candidates for local offices and in defining the policies and issues discussed in a campaign.

Your influence can be crucial. Numerous elections have been won or lost by less than one vote per precinct.

Register to vote. List yourself as a member of the political party of your choice (or as an independent), you do not have to support anyone of whom you disapprove.

Secure names and addresses of party leaders in your local area from the election commission, party, or newspapers.

Contact your precinct leader or local political party leader, in person if possible. Volunteer your services.

Find out when precinct or club meetings and state and local caucuses are held. Ask to be notified about them regularly so that you can plan to attend.

Learn parliamentary procedure. This will enable you to follow what occurs in meetings and to find the best way to bring issues before the group.

Become an expert on one or two issues so that you can express your views in meetings, in debates, and on resolutions committees. Others will soon come to depend on your expertise.

Be willing to knock on doors. Your assignments may include going from door to door in your own area or another neighborhood. This includes canvassing, fund raising, finding voters who will need absentee ballots or assistance in getting to the polls, and getting out the vote.

For further information contact the various political parties at their local, state, or national headquarters. [Addresses are in Action Unit 4.2.]

Adapted and reprinted from "How to Work in Politics," a guide prepared by the Friends Committee on National Legislation, 245 Second St. NE, Washington, DC 20002.

---

tion of *the party in office*—in the presidency or in the Congress or in a state governorship or state legislature. The other six functions are carried out by *the party organization*, which is made up of party officials and party activists. But they can do their job only with the help of the voters. Voters, therefore, form the third element of the party, which is sometimes called *the-party-in-the-electorate*.[4] To understand the roles of parties better, we must know more about both their organization membership and their electorate membership.

WHO BELONGS TO OUR PARTIES?

In some countries you pay dues to join a party, and the party gives you a membership card to carry in exchange. In America all you have to do is say, "I'm a Democrat" or "I'm a Republican" to be one. Nei-

ther party even demands party loyalty—that members vote for its candidates at election time. There are, in other words, no real responsibilities that go along with party membership. But there are opportunities—opportunities to participate in the nominating process, to contribute time or money, to help get out the vote on election day, and to celebrate on election night. Action Unit 4.1 describes such opportunities. Few Americans actually take advantage of these opportunities for active party work—most estimates and surveys suggest that only 5 to 10 percent of our citizens participate in this way. This means that most party work is done either by professional, paid employees or by a small group of regular volunteers.

Differences between the Parties

Because that is the case, we might expect to find little difference between the activists of one party and those of the other. And yet there are differ-

[4]The term is Frank Sorauf's. See chap. 2, "Political Parties and Political Analysis," in *The American Party System*, ed. William N. Chambers and Walter Dean Burnham (New York: Oxford Univ. Press, 1967).

(Tony Ayth, *The Philadelphia Inquirer*)

ences. A look at both party conventions is enough to demonstrate this difference. Or you could take the word of an expert such as the late conservative political scientist Clinton Rossiter, who observed:

A gathering of Democrats is more sweaty, disorderly, offhand, and rowdy than a gathering of Republicans; it is also more likely to be more cheerful, imaginative, tolerant of dissent, and skillful at the game of give and take. A gathering of Republicans is more respectable, sober, purposeful, and businesslike than a gathering of Democrats; it is also likely to be more self-righteous, pompous, cut-and-dried, and just plain boring.[5]

This generalization, written in 1960, still seems valid.[6] Our two parties really are different, not only in the policy positions they take and the economic groups that support them (as we shall see shortly) but also in the social backgrounds of those who identify with them. The box on distinguishing characteristics of Democrats and Republicans presents one lighthearted set of contrasts. More seriously, Democrats are much more likely to be people of lower socioeconomic status, city dwellers, members of labor unions, Catholics or Jews, and members of one or another ethnic minority. Republicans, by contrast, are more likely to be white, well educated and with prestigious jobs and high incomes, suburbanites, businesspersons or professionals, Protestant, and Anglo-Saxons.[7]

Professionals and Amateurs

Although the party members differ in these ways, both parties have as part of their activist ranks both professionals and amateurs, or regulars and purists, as they are sometimes called. The professionals tend to place the greatest emphasis on the survival and success of the party as an institution. The amateurs tend to be most concerned with particular candidates and/or special issues, win or lose. The differences in perspective are well represented by the following description by Arthur Miller, professional playwright and amateur politician:

The professionals . . . see politics as a sort of game in which you win sometimes and sometimes you lose. Issues are not something you feel, like morality, like good and evil, but something you succeed or fail to make use of. To these men an issue is a segment of public opinion which you either capitalize on or at-

[5]Clinton Rossiter, *Parties and Politics in America* (Ithaca, NY: Cornell Univ. Press, 1960), p. 117.

[6]For an interesting study of changes in party composition in the last half-century, see John R. Petrocik, *Party Coalitions: Realignments and the Decline of the New Deal Party System* (Chicago: Univ. of Chicago Press, 1981).

[7]For a detailed study of the electorate in terms of party in 1980, see Sheldon Kamieniecki, *Party Identification, Political Behavior, and the American Electorate* (Westport, CT: Greenwood Press, 1985).

How to Tell Democrats from Republicans: One View

1. Democrats buy most of the books that have been banned somewhere. Republicans form censorship committees and read them as a group.
2. Republicans consume three-fourths of all the rutabaga produced in this country. The remainder is thrown out.
3. Republicans usually wear hats and almost always clean their paint brushes.
4. Democrats give their worn-out clothes to those less fortunate. Republicans wear theirs.
5. Republicans employ exterminators. Democrats step on the bugs.
6. Democrats name their children after currently popular sports figures, politicians, and entertainers. Republican children are named after their parents or grandparents, according to where the most money is.
7. Democrats keep trying to cut down on smoking but are not successful. Neither are Republicans.
8. Republicans tend to keep their shades drawn, although there is seldom any rea-

son why they should. Democrats ought to, but don't.
9. Republicans study the financial pages of the newspaper. Democrats put them in the bottom of the bird cage.
10. Most of the stuff you see alongside the road has been thrown out of the car window by Democrats.
11. Republicans raise dahlias, Dalmatians and eyebrows. Democrats raise Airedales, kids and taxes.
12. Democrats eat the fish they catch. Republicans hang them on the wall.
13. Republican boys date Democratic girls. They plan to marry Republican girls, but feel they're entitled to a little fun first.
14. Democrats make up plans and then do something else. Republicans follow the plans their grandfathers made.
15. Republicans sleep in twin beds—some even in separate rooms. That is why there are more Democrats.

Source: *Florence Morning News*, February 16, 1975.

tempt to assuage according to the present interests of the party. To the amateurs . . . an issue is first of all moral, and embodies a vision of the country, even of man, and is not a counter in a game.[8]

Austin Ranney, political scientist and Democratic party activist, gives the professional's view:

The professionals are people who have a substantial commitment to the party itself. They have served it before the nomination contest and expect to serve it after the election. . . . The professionals seek a candidate whose style they think will appeal to the voters they need to win, not necessarily to party leaders. They judge a candidate by how well or badly he runs in the election and by how much he has helped or hurt the rest of the ticket. And they see negotiation, compromise, and accommodation not as hypocrisy or immorality but as the very essense of what keeps parties—and nations—from disintegrating.[9]

If the parties contained only professionals, they would rarely stimulate much public interest. If, on the other hand, they were composed primarily of amateur-purists, politics would be fascinating, but parties would come and go with special issues. The fact that the parties contain both elements helps explain their viability. But other factors are even more important.

WHAT SUSTAINS OUR PARTIES

At any given time, one or the other of our major parties seems to be in serious disarray. Yet the Democratic party has existed since 1828 and can trace its roots back to around 1800, while the Republican party dates from 1854. What explains their long lives and their periodic returns from the shadow of death? Observers cite four major factors: constitutional provisions, historical developments, the federal structure of the parties, and party reform.

[8]Arthur Miller, "The Battle of Chicago: From the Delegates' Side," *New York Times Magazine*, September 15, 1968, p. 29. Even then, although Miller's language does not reveal it, women were important actors in politics.

[9]Austin Ranney, *Curing the Mischiefs of Faction: Party Reform in America* (Berkeley: Univ. of California Press, 1975), pp. 140–41. For another view of these distinctions, see Gary R. Orren, "The Changing Styles of American Party Politics," in Joel L. Fleishman, ed., *The Future of American Political Parties*, chap. 1.

Constitutional Provisions

In most cases, survival of political institutions can be traced to constitutional provisions that create and protect them. But the Constitution doesn't even mention political parties. The founders, as we saw in Chapter 1, were generally fearful of parties and hoped to be able to do without them. In his farewell address, George Washington warned the country against "the baneful effects of the spirit of party." His successor, John Adams, wrote: "There is nothing I dread so much as the division of the Republic into two great parties, each under its leader."

Despite the wishes of the founders, and despite the omission of parties from the Constitution, political parties developed quickly and grew stronger—in large part because of certain constitutional provisions. Foremost among these is the requirement that public officials be elected regularly: representatives every two years, the president every four years, and senators every six years. Competing in regular elections requires organization. This task is handled in our system by political parties. Such parties might be weak, however, in the absence of two guarantees in the First Amendment of the Constitution: freedom of speech and freedom of assembly. Taken together, these three constitutional provisions virtually guaranteed that parties would become a standard feature of our political system.

They did not, however, guarantee that our present two parties would survive as long as they have. To understand their long lives, we must examine both their development and their operation.

Historical Developments

Federalists, Democratic-Republicans, and Whigs

In the early years American politics was in flux. The first people to organize a party were called Federalists. The Federalist party was established to encourage development of a strong and effective central government able to protect the new country from foreign enemies and to foster commercial economic development, largely for the benefit of bankers and traders. To oppose this emphasis on commerce and banking, Thomas Jefferson soon organized the Republican party among farmers, frontier dwellers, and debtors hostile to banks. This party, which favored weaker central government, dominated politics for a quarter of a century following Jefferson's election as president in 1800. In those years it came to be known as the Democratic-Republican party. One faction within it supported greater democratization of the political system. When Andrew Jackson, a strong supporter of greater party democracy, became party leader and then in 1828 was elected president, the faction suspicious of democratization left the party. This faction, known as the National Republicans, favored a stronger legislature rather than a dominant popular president. It eventually joined with fragments of the old Federalists favoring commerce, industry, and finance to form the Whig party in 1832. (The Whigs took their name from a comparable British party of the period.) The faction of the Democratic-Republicans that remained loyal to Jackson eventually became known as the Democratic party.

"Out of the conflict of Democrats and Whigs" during the next 25 years, observed Clinton Rossiter, "emerged the American political system—complete with such features as two major parties, a sprinkle of third parties, national nominating conventions, state and local bosses, patronage, popular campaigning, and the Presidency as the focus of politics."[10]

Democrats and Republicans

But the party system we have to this day, dominated by the Democratic and Republican parties, did not emerge until the Whigs were badly beaten in 1852. At that time the issue of extending slavery to new states was shattering both parties. The Democrats, with their strong southern base, were unable to wrestle with the issue. Antislavery Whigs left that party in 1854 to form the Republican party, which opposed the extension of slavery into the new western territories then seeking admission to the Union. With Lincoln's election as president in 1860, the Republicans began a period of national dominance that was interrupted only three times until 1932 (see Figure 4.2).

---

[10]Rossiter, *Parties and Politics*, pp. 73–74.

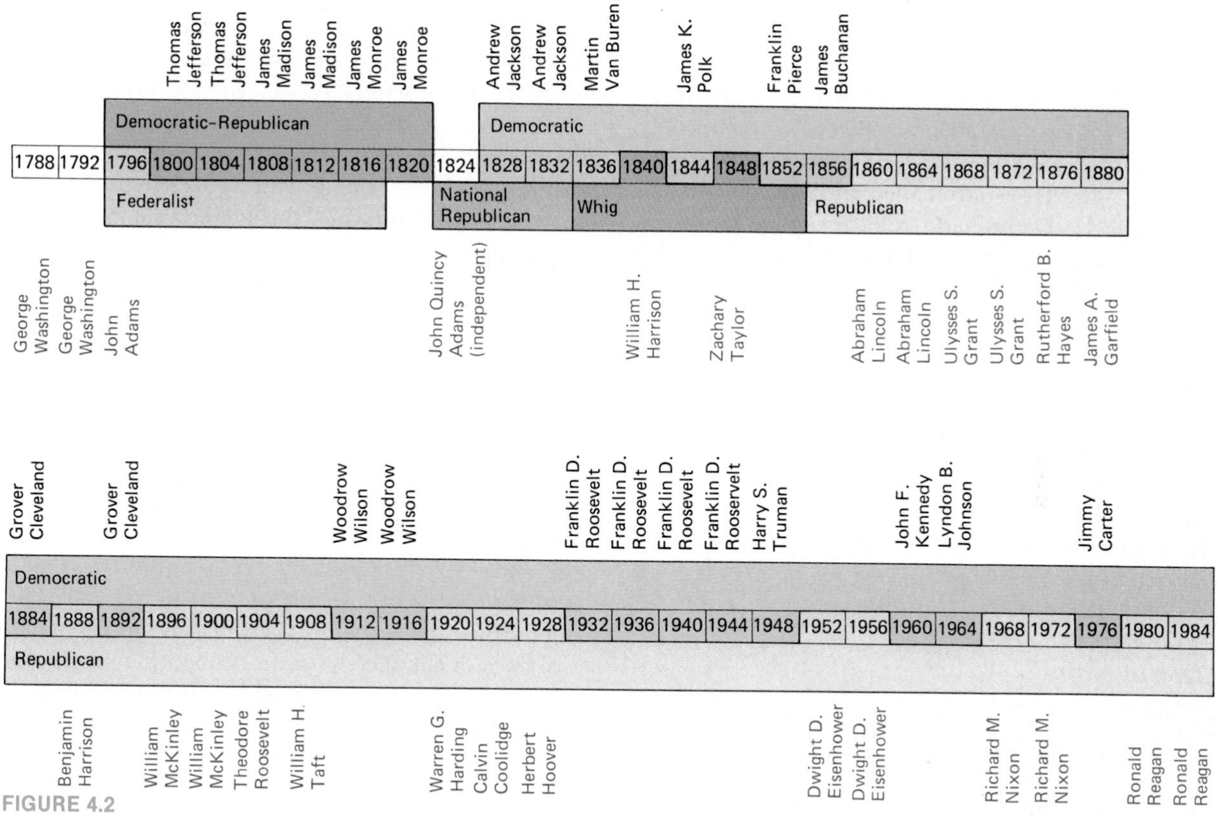

Thomas Jefferson · Thomas Jefferson · James Madison · James Madison · James Monroe · James Monroe · Andrew Jackson · Andrew Jackson · Martin Van Buren · James K. Polk · Franklin Pierce · James Buchanan

Democratic-Republican									Democratic														
1788	1792	1796	1800	1804	1808	1812	1816	1820	1824	1828	1832	1836	1840	1844	1848	1852	1856	1860	1864	1868	1872	1876	1880

Federalist · National Republican · Whig · Republican

George Washington · George Washington · John Adams · John Quincy Adams (independent) · William H. Harrison · Zachary Taylor · Abraham Lincoln · Abraham Lincoln · Ulysses S. Grant · Ulysses S. Grant · Rutherford B. Hayes · James A. Garfield

Grover Cleveland · Grover Cleveland · Woodrow Wilson · Woodrow Wilson · Franklin D. Roosevelt · Franklin D. Roosevelt · Franklin D. Roosevelt · Franklin D. Roosevelt · Harry S. Truman · John F. Kennedy · Lyndon B. Johnson · Jimmy Carter

Democratic																									
1884	1888	1892	1896	1900	1904	1908	1912	1916	1920	1924	1928	1932	1936	1940	1944	1948	1952	1956	1960	1964	1968	1972	1976	1980	1984

Republican

Benjamin Harrison · William McKinley · William McKinley · Theodore Roosevelt · William H. Taft · Warren G. Harding · Calvin Coolidge · Herbert Hoover · Dwight D. Eisenhower · Dwight D. Eisenhower · Richard M. Nixon · Richard M. Nixon · Ronald Reagan · Ronald Reagan

FIGURE 4.2
President and Parties, 1792–1984

Populism

In the forty years following the Civil War, there was one major new political movement—Populism, a term derived from the Latin word for "the people." A People's party was formed to protect the interests of farmers against the railroads (which were exploiting the monopoly they had in transporting farm goods to city markets) and the banks (which were seizing farms for nonpayment of mortgage debts).[11] The small Populist parties such as the Greenback party (1876–1884) and the People's party (1892–1908) never won the presidency. However, they did influence the politics of the two major parties, especially the Democratic party, and they succeeded in weakening this party by cutting into its voting strength.

As a result, the Democrats remained dependent for support on the more Populist South and West, where the population was relatively constant. They lost strength in the industrial Northeast, where population was growing because of the wave of European immigrants coming to work in the factories. The consequence was that from 1896 on, the Democrats lost seven of the next nine presidential elections.

The Democratic New Deal Coalition

This losing record did not change until the Great Depression, which created so much economic hardship that it forced a major political realignment. Democrat Franklin Roosevelt replaced Republican Herbert Hoover in 1933, pledging to the American people a "New Deal"—a metaphor that suggests both a new hand of cards in a risky game and a new set of "terms of trade" between govern-

[11]See Lawrence Goodwyn, *The Populist Moment* (New York: Oxford Univ. Press, 1978).

ment and the people. As we shall see in Chapter 15, both implications were realized.

In terms of American party politics, the New Deal turned out to mean a new Democratic dominance. Roosevelt was able to win four straight presidential elections by establishing and maintaining what is usually called the New Deal coalition or the Democratic coalition. This political grouping was based on what we referred to in the last chapter as class voting—voting by economic status rather than along geographical lines.

Roosevelt continued to pay heed to the needs of the many small farmers—the traditional political base of the Democrats. But he began to support legislation to strengthen labor unions and so began to polarize politics along class lines. The poorer classes and the workers increasingly became Democratic; the rich and much of the professional middle class voted Republican; and the farmers tended to vote according to their most recent harvest.

Recent Shifts

In the elections since the New Deal years of 1932–1945, the Republicans have fared best when they could break up this class polarization. Dwight Eisenhower won in 1952 by attacking corruption in Democrat Harry Truman's government and pledging to use his experience as a career military man to end America's fighting in the Korean War. Both of these were nonclass issues. Ike, as he was affectionately known to the American people, won reelection by a landslide in 1956 on a platform citing "peace, prosperity, and progress"—achievements that also cut across class lines.

But that prosperity turned into recession (an economic decline or slowdown), and the man who had been Eisenhower's vice-president, Richard Nixon, lost narrowly in 1960 to Democrat John Kennedy, who pledged to "get this country moving again." Kennedy's vice-president, Lyndon Johnson, became president when Kennedy was assassinated on November 22, 1963. Johnson then emphasized economic issues—the problems of the poor in particular—in winning the 1964 election. By arguing that he had "a secret plan" to achieve peace in Vietnam—another nonclass issue—Nixon barely defeated Johnson's vice-president, Hubert Humphrey, in 1968. Nixon's reelection in 1972 was built even further on nonclass issues. In foreign affairs, he cited the "winding down" of the war in Vietnam. In domestic affairs, he appealed to what he called the silent majority—meaning primarily middle-class Republicans and traditionally Democratic urban ethnic groups and workers. These voting groups supported his "law and order" campaign against student radicals and against agitation for major new progress on racial integration through school busing and "reverse discrimination"—issues that split the traditional New Deal coalition.

The Carter victory in 1976 showed some signs of rebuilding that traditional coalition. One such sign was renewed Democratic success in the South. As a southerner, Carter was able to achieve this success by combining white and black support. The other major sign was the return to the fold of those concerned about economic issues—America had just been through the worst recession since the 1930s. But in 1980 economic issues were important in once again shattering the traditional Democratic power base. And when Ronald Reagan won a landslide reelection in 1984, it was largely on the strength of the success of his economic reform program in lowering taxes and curbing inflation—achievements that appealed to voters across class lines. Thus, most observers agree that the major parties can neither expect nor rely upon class-based party voting in a country that has become more and more middle class.

The Federal Structure of the Parties

We tend to think of our parties as national organizations. It is true each party runs a single candidate for president across the entire nation. It is also true that each party has a national committee that is supposed to conduct or supervise party affairs from a national perspective. But these national committees are made up largely of representatives selected by the party organizations in each state. And in each state the party organization is dominated by one or more regions (mainly cities or counties) in which the party is traditionally dominant.

Furthermore, within most states one party is permanently dominant over the other. This party domination is found not so much in the presidential vote, which may vary from election to election, but rather in party strength in state legislatures. The situation there has been such that, "Within a large proportion of the states only by the most gen-

FIGURE 4.3

Party Competition in the States. This map shows the degree of competition between the Democratic and Republican parties in each of the states in the period from 1974 through 1980.

Source: From John F. Bibby et al., "Parties in State Politics." Copyright © 1983 by John F. Bibby, Cornelius P. Cotter, James L. Gibson, and Robert J. Huckshorn, in Virginia Gray, Herbert Jacob, and Kenneth R. Vines, eds., *Politics in the American States: A Comparative Analysis,* 4th ed., Reprinted by permission of Little, Brown and Company.

erous characterization may it be said that political parties compete for power."[12] This party predominance derives largely from strength in particular state legislative districts, in many of which one party will run no opponent at all or at most only a token opponent. It extends also to mayoral races in cities and to races for the U.S. Congress as well.

The latest detailed study of party competition found 22 states in which there is real two-party competition. It found 19 in which the Democratic party tends to dominate but only one where the Republican party holds sway.[13] The map in Figure 4.3 shows how each state was classified.

Political parties at the local and state levels tend to be more than parties. We normally think of a party as a group of candidates, organizers, and voters who combine to support a group of candidates in an election. But at local and state levels, a dominant party is sometimes more like a "political machine"—a well-entrenched organization of leaders and followers who are able in one way or another to control nominations, if not always elections.

Machines, as we shall see in Chapter 17, are able to maintain power through a wide variety of devices. One way is through **patronage**—jobs given to political supporters. Another way is through **reapportionment** (redrawing boundaries of legislative districts as populations change); this can be used to strengthen the party in its home base by carving up sections to exclude areas of strong support for an opposing party from districts the machine controls and vice versa. Yet another device is *electoral fraud,* made possible by the fact that state law usually gives parties the major responsibility for conducting and policing elections.

[12]V. O. Key, quoted in Walter Karp, *Indispensable Enemies* (Baltimore: Penguin, 1974), p. 7.

[13]The study was based on elections from 1974 through 1980. See John F. Bibby, Cornelius P. Cotter, James L. Gibson, and Robert J. Huckshorn, "Parties in State Politics," in *Politics in the American States,* 4th ed., Virginia Gray, Herbert Jacob, and Kenneth R. Vines, eds. (Boston: Little, Brown, 1983). For a study of the evolution of party organizations state by state, see David R. Mayhew, *Placing Parties in American Politics* (Princeton, NJ: Princeton Univ. Press, 1986).

Party Reform

The tendency toward party dominance at the state and local level has been lessened somewhat over the years by reforms that have curtailed the influence of party organizations. In doing so, they have tended to weaken the traditional bases of party strength. However, the reforms have made the parties more attractive to potential supporters by granting them greater opportunities for participation. Thus, these reforms have probably helped to perpetuate, as well as to change, our major parties.

One such reform is the use of **nonpartisan elections**—in which candidates run without party identification—at the local level. Even more important are use of the "direct primary" and the reform of political conventions.

Electoral Reforms

In the heyday of machine politics, the party bosses openly controlled candidate selection. Local party clubs and organizations would nominate local candidates and select delegates to state and national conventions, where other candidates were chosen.

The **direct primary** began to be used more frequently around the turn of the century, when efforts were made to weaken the machines. Under this system voters (only party members if it is a "closed" primary; all voters if it is "open") choose a candidate from among those who have signed up or submitted nominating petitions with a specified number of signatures. The name *primary* comes from the Latin word *primus*, "the first": A primary is the first election, to be followed by the **general election**, in which candidates from all parties compete.

The direct primary made control of candidate selection more difficult for party bosses. But the bosses were still generally able to control presidential nominations because they were able to dominate selection of national convention delegates. Increasingly, however, such delegates have themselves been selected by a primary—an **indirect primary**, in that it picks delegates who then meet to pick the candidates in a party convention.

Convention Reforms

However, even the selection of national convention delegates by primary was not enough to take away control from the bosses. They still ran their candidates and generally "worked the process" better because they knew it better. Nevertheless, in 1968 discontended Democrats achieved passage of a resolution at the national convention to open up the selection of delegates to the 1972 convention. A Commission on Party Structure and Delegate Selection, cochaired by Senator George McGovern and Representative Donald Fraser, resulted in three major reforms:

1. *Procedural reforms* (fair-play rules, as they were soon to be called) to ensure that party meetings were open to all members, were announced in advance, were held in public places, allowed only those actually in attendance to vote, and had written rules (something new to ten states).
2. *Broadened participation* by minorities, women, and youths "in reasonable relationship to their presence in the state's population" because all had been underrepresented previously.
3. *Altered delegate-selection* procedures by which delegates would be selected within a year of the election with at least 75 percent selected in state primaries or local conventions. (Many delegates had been selected even before candidates had announced, most by the state committee.)

These reform proposals were adopted by the national committee and enforced on the state parties in 1972, when they were used effectively by McGovern himself in his successful drive for the nomination. However, when the Democrats lost the election, opponents succeeded in watering down the reforms.

After the widespread Democratic defeats of 1980, there were further efforts to strengthen the role of party professionals over that of amateurs. In 1984 14 percent of the Democratic convention delegates were either party officials or elected officials who were to go to the convention uncommitted. These "superdelegates" were added to the 55 percent chosen in primaries and 31 percent chosen in caucuses, with the intention of adding more professional judgment to convention decisions.

Thus, the role of grassroots activists declined somewhat in 1984. But the Democratic party remains a relatively open party. It is certainly much more open than the Republican party, which hasn't changed its rules in a decade and which has much less participation by women and minorities.[14]

---

[14]For fascinating accounts of the changes and their consequences, see Byron E. Shafer, *Quiet Revolution: The Struggle for the Democratic Party and the Shaping of Post-Reform Politics* (New York: Russell Sage Foundation, 1983), and Nelson W. Polsby, *Consequences of Party Reform* (New York: Oxford Univ. Press, 1983).

THE NATURE OF OUR PARTY SYSTEM

In national terms, the United States has had a two-party system since 1800. We have seen that smaller parties have come and gone as their special issues—from prohibition of alcohol to socialism—have risen and fallen in public interest. But since the Civil War, our politics have been dominated, in somewhat alternating fashion, by the Democratic and Republican parties.

How Our Major Parties Are Similar

These parties have been loose national confederations of state and local units. Their members have really been more like "supporters" in comparison to party members in other countries, for they do not pay dues and are not compelled, or often even expected, to demonstrate party loyalty. The result of this decentralized two-party structure has been parties that are, in Clinton Rossiter's terms, "creatures of compromise, coalitions of interest in which principle is muted and often even silenced. They are vast, gaudy, friendly umbrellas under which all Americans, whoever and wherever and however minded they may be, are invited to stand for the sake of being counted in the next election."[15]

The major parties have thus lacked consistent and strong ideological positions and programs and have often competed with each other for the support of the same groups of voters. Their leaders and candidates have often been virtually indistinguishable. Some experts have suggested that our political figures are more influenced in their attitudes and policy positions by their locations in the political structure than by either their own beliefs or those of the constituents or voters who elected them. This may explain the frequent difficulty a Democratic president has in getting a Democratic Congress to accept and adopt the chief executive's legislative program. But not all congressional Democrats agree among themselves.

As a general rule, in recent decades the members of each party in the Senate have tended to be somewhat more liberal than those of each party in the House. But in each body there have been conservative and liberal members of each party, sometimes differentiated by their geographical origins.

How Our Major Parties Differ

The parties draw their basic support from different social groups. Republicans tend to be richer and Protestant, for example, while Democrats include larger segments of union workers, Catholics and Jews, members of ethnic minority groups, and southerners.

Supporters of each party do tend to have relatively similar or highly overlapping political philosophies. But candidates, officeholders, and activists differ significantly by party. In general, studies show that Democratic activists tend to favor government action to cope with problems of poverty, injustice, and inequality. Republican activists, by contrast, tend to rely on the competitive economic system and the personal character of citizens to cope with such problems. Similar differences are also found in surveys of national, state, and local party leaders.[16]

Members of Congress, too, generally show significant agreement with fellow party members except when there are strong pressures in another direction from their own constituents or from strong interest groups in their districts. Congressional voting studies also reveal significant differences between the ways in which the majority of Democrats vote and the ways in which the majority of Republicans vote. These differences are comparable to those found among party activists.

Further, the same sort of differences emerge when national convention delegates of each party are compared with ordinary citizens who call themselves Democrats or Republicans. Figure 4.4 shows how delegates, party supporters, and the American population as a whole described themselves in 1980. It indicates that more Democratic delegates called themselves liberal than did Democrats as a whole. But Democrats as a whole called themselves liberal more than did the American people as a whole. In the same way, Republican

---

[15]Rossiter, *Parties and Politics*, p. 11.

[16]See, for example, a survey of attitudes of American political leaders conducted by the Harvard Center for International Affairs and the *Washington Post*, reported in the *Washington Post*, September 27, 1976, p. 1.

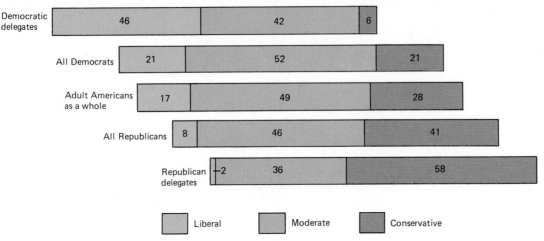

FIGURE 4.4

The Political Orientation of Convention Delegates, Party Supporters, and the American People. This figure shows how delegates to the 1980 party conventions described their own political views, and how these descriptions compare with the self-descriptions of party supporters and of the public as a whole.

Source: New York Times–CBS News Poll, August 1980, reported in the *New York Times*, August 13, 1980. Copyright © 1980 by the New York Times Company. Reprinted by permission.

convention delegates called themselves conservative more than did Republicans as a whole. But Republicans in general called themselves conservative more than did the American people as a whole.[17]

WHAT OUR TWO-PARTY SYSTEM DOES TO OUR POLITICS

At the national level, a major effect of the two-party system is to encourage both parties to move toward the center in order to gain enough support to win elections. Some of this support will come from people who usually support the other party but who are disenchanted with its current candidate. More of it will come from voters who declare themselves independents and who hold moderate or middle-of-the-road views.

The Spectrum of Political Positions

To explain this point, it may help to use an illustration, even though all such illustrations oversimplify. Imagine that we can categorize likely voters as liberals, moderates, or conservatives. Just what

position each group takes on specific issues will vary over time, of course. In Figure 4.5 the so-called bell-shaped curve represents independent voters. We can then add curves for normally Democratic and Republican supporters, who with the independent voters make up the electorate. Now we can add a curve representing the views of Democratic politicians and activists, which tends toward the liberal left, and another for Republican activists and politicians, which tends toward the conservative right. But notice that they overlap. We can then, using a series of dots, note where various presidential candidates might be located, from Barry Goldwater on the extreme Republican right to George McGovern on the left liberal side, with Ronald Reagan, Gerald Ford, Richard Nixon, Jimmy Carter, and Lyndon Johnson in between.

Most of the population is clustered around the middle of the political spectrum. Because there are only two major candidates in most elections after the primaries, presidential candidates will assume they can hold the votes of everyone from their point over in the direction away from the opponent. This usually means that the Democratic candidate gets the liberals and the Republican, the conservatives. Each candidate also expects to get the support of most people who think of themselves as members of or supporters of his or her party—indicated on our diagram as Democratic or Republican supporters. That is usually true even though the voters

[17]For a comprehensive study, see John S. Jackson III, Barbara Leavitt Brown, and David Bositis, "Herbert McClosky and Friends Revisited: Party Elites Compared to the Mass Public," *American Politics Quarterly* 10 (April 1982), 158–80.

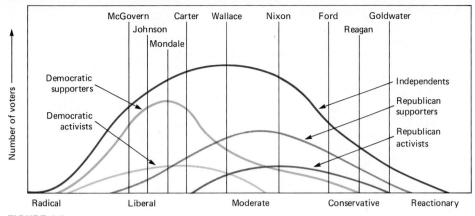

FIGURE 4.5

The Spectrum of Political Positions.

Competition for the Middle

No candidate can win, however, without also getting substantial support from the independents. And each will hope to get defectors from the other party. Thus, in the campaign each party will tend to move toward the center in order to pick up these

may in fact be more conservative than their Democratic candidate or more liberal than their Republican candidate.

necessary additional votes. This *competition for the middle* is a consequence of our two-party structure.

If we did not have two-party dominance, there might be a radical party, a liberal party, a conservative party, and a reactionary party, and each might emphasize its distinctiveness in campaigning. After the election in such a multiparty (or "many party") system, there would be several possible developments: There could be a runoff election between the top two vote getters to determine the winner of a ruling majority. Or there might be

bargaining between the parties to form a coalition government made up of several parties in the legislature. Or there might be a "minority government" in which the leading vote getter ruled even without a majority.

Two-party dominance prevents the uncertainty and instability that may arise in a multiparty system. But it also reduces the obvious differences between candidates and parties, for both parties tend to converge on the middle, competing for moderate votes. A two-party system is, therefore, likely to disappoint voters who want "a choice, not an echo" (to use Barry Goldwater's characterization of his conservative candidacy in 1964).

MAJOR AND MINOR PARTIES IN OUR SYSTEM

If many voters are unhappy with the two available major party choices in a given election, they can, of course, attempt to form a new party that reflects their views better. American history, we have noted, is full of such efforts. Table 4.3 lists various examples. But no such third party—as it is usually called—has ever won a presidential election, and few have lasted longer than several elections before giving up in discouragement.

Usually, if the new party reflects a major new view, one or the other major party will tend to adopt that position and so woo the unhappy voters to its camp. In the years of Populism, which we discussed above, the Democratic party became more and more Populist, and the People's party faded away. In the Depression, the Socialist party campaigned for government intervention in the economy on grounds that capitalism had collapsed. Roosevelt's New Deal eventually adopted major portions of its program, and a party that once won over a million votes in a single election became a very minor party again. Similarly, George Wallace's American independent party polled well on a law-and-order and anti-school-busing platform (14 percent and 46 electoral votes in 1968) until the Republicans under Nixon adopted much of its program. (Wallace's crippling by a would-be assassin in the 1972 campaign was also a factor, of course.)

Eugene McCarthy's independent campaign in the 1976 election was less an issue campaign than one based on his own character and on widespread

TABLE 4.3
Minor Parties: Types and Examples

Ideological parties
Offer an ideology or comprehensive world view that is significantly different from that presented by the major parties
 Socialist party (1901 to the present)
 Communist party (1920s to the present)
 Libertarian party (1972 to the present)

Single-issue parties
Present one issue of paramount importance to them and generally ignore other issues
 Prohibition party (for prohibition of alcoholic beverages—1869 to the present)
 Right-to-Life party (against abortion—1980)
 Green party (ecology—1984)

Regional economic-protest parties
Represent regional protest—most often by farmers
 Greenback party (1876–1884)
 People's (Populist) party (1892–1908)

Factional parties
Created by a section of an existing party that splits off from the major party, usually in objection to its presidential candidate
 "Bull Moose" Progressive party (1912—from the Republican party, led by Teddy Roosevelt)
 Progressive party (1924—from the Republican party, led by "Fighting Bob" LaFollette)
 Progressive party (1948—from the Democratic party, led by Henry Wallace)
 American Independent Party (1968—from the Democratic party, led by George Wallace)

Sonia Johnson, Citizens party, presidential candidate, 1984. (UPI/Bettmann Newsphotos)

Gus Hall, Communist party, presidential candidate, 1984. (UPI/Bettmann Newsphotos)

David Bergland, Libertarian party, presidential candidate, 1984. (Lee Connelly)

lack of enthusiasm for either Ford or Carter, particularly among left-wing students. It was, therefore, less likely to have a policy impact on either party. But it does seem to have shifted a handful of key states into the Republican column by taking votes that would otherwise have gone to Carter. McCarthy may thereby have come very close to changing the election's outcome, even though he hadn't founded a party.

John Anderson's independent campaign in 1980 had less impact on the election, in that there were no states that Carter would have carried had he received all the votes cast for Anderson. Nonetheless, Anderson received many more votes in 1980 (5.5 million) that McCarthy did in 1976 (0.75 million). Anderson's greatest effect may be that he made it easier for independent and minor party candidates to get on future ballots. In order to get on the ballot in all 50 states, he had to contest state laws making ballot access hard for minor parties. Because of his efforts many of those laws were ruled unconstitutional. We may therefore see more minor parties on the ballot in future elections.

Of course, there already are many minor parties. Some of them come and go, while others such as the Prohibition (of alcoholic beverages) party have been running without electoral success for many decades. Action Unit 4.2 lists the major and

minor parties alive in the mid-1980s and indicates how you can contact them to learn more about their party positions and candidates.[18]

WHAT SUSTAINS OUR TWO-PARTY SYSTEM?

In seeking to explain what sustains our two-party system, political observers have offered four major theories.

Some have cited the fact that in the early years there was a *political split* between the northern industrialists, commercialists, and financiers (the Federalists/Whigs/Republicans) and the southern farmers and western frontier dwellers (the Jeffersonian Republicans/Jacksonian Democrats). A two-party system developed then, and perhaps its persistence has been a combination of habit and inertia based on this early situation.[19]

Another argument notes that there was a general *social homogeneity* in the parties in the early

---

[18]The most comprehensive studies of minor parties are Daniel Mazmanian, *Third Parties in Presidential Elections* (Washington, DC: Brookings Institution, 1974), and Frank Smallwood, *The Other Candidates: Third Parties in Presidential Elections* (Hanover, NH: Univ. Press of New England, 1983).

[19]See, for example, the argument of V. O. Key in *Politics, Parties, and Pressure Groups*, 5th ed. (New York: Crowell, 1964), pp. 229ff.

How to Contact American Political Parties

This list includes the major and minor national political parties in America as of the 1984 presidential election. There are, in addition, many smaller parties with a local or scattered membership.

American Independent party (PO Box 373 Simi Valley, CA 93063). Founded in 1968 with the candidacy of George Wallace, this national organization continues to run conservative candidates for president and certain state offices. In 1980 a faction split off and ran its own candidate for president as the **American party.**

Citizens party (2000 P St. NW, Washington, DC 20036). Founded in 1980 as, in the words of its leader, ecologist Barry Commoner, "a broad-based coalition of all the millions of Americans who feel disenfranchised by the backwardness, timidity, and corporate control of the present political establishment." Commoner received 220,000 votes and was on the ballot of 30 states. He campaigned for drastic economic change, solar energy, abortion rights, and other issues.

Communist Party of the United States of America (239 W. 23rd St., New York, NY 10011). Founded in 1919, this party has several thousand members who claim to be "representatives of the American working class." It seeks establishment of "the dictatorship of the proletariat" and the construction of socialism as the political and economic system in the U.S., and it favors détente with the Soviet Union; it publishes the *Daily World* and a monthly, *Political Affairs;* and it runs presidential candidates. In 1980 it was on 25 state ballots. Its ticket included Gus Hall and Angela Davis.

Democratic party (1625 Massachusetts Ave. NW, Washington, DC 20036). Founded in its present form in 1848.

Libertarian party (2300 Wisconsin Ave. NW, Washington, DC 20007). Founded in 1971, this is a radical conservative party that has about 4000 members and hopes to establish a voluntary society of free markets and free enterprise, in which the role of the government is limited to protecting citizens from the initiation of force against the person and his or her property and in which there are no draft, no taxes, and no foreign involvements; its presidential candidate in 1980 was Ed Clark, who received almost 900,000 votes and was on every state ballot.

National Socialist White People's party, formerly called the **American Nazi party** (2507 North Franklin Rd., Arlington, VA 22201). This extreme right-wing party was founded in 1959 and is composed of people who describe themselves as "White Americans of Aryan descent who accept the National Socialist teachings of Adolf Hitler without reservation and are willing to submit themselves to Party discipline." Its program calls for "A White America; White World Solidarity; A New Social Order; An Honest Economy; White Self-Defense; Government by Leaders; A Spiritual Rebirth; An Aryan Culture; A Healthy Environment; A Better Race."

National States' Rights party (PO Box 1211, Marietta, GA 30061). Founded in 1948, this party advocates racial segregation and state sovereignty against the federal government; it includes 12,000 "White Gentile Americans of voting age" and publishes the monthly newspaper *Thunderbolt.*

National Unity party (2233 Wisconsin Ave. NW, Washington, DC 20007), founded by John Anderson in 1983 after his nonparty campaign for the presidency in 1980.

Progressive Labor party (GPO Box 808, Brooklyn, NY 11201). Founded in 1962, this party seeks to establish socialism through a revolution to overthrow the governments of the "bosses" and establish the dictatorship of the working class, guided by Marxism-Leninism.

Prohibition National Committee (P.O. Box 2635, Denver, CO 80201). Founded in 1869, this is the administrative body of the Prohibition party, which still runs presidential candidates and advocates "repeal of all laws which legalize the liquor traffic and the enactment and rigorous enforcement of new laws which prohibit the manufacture, distribution and sale of alcoholic beverages," but criticizes the income tax and federal aid to education.

Republican party (310 First St. SE, Washington, DC 20003). Founded in 1854.

Social Democrats, U.S.A. (275 Seventh Ave, New York, NY 10001). Founded in 1901, this moderate, socialist party was an important political force during the depression and still runs presidential candidates. Its 1980 candidate, David McReynolds, was on the ballots of 10 states.

Socialist Labor party (PO Box 50218, Palo Alto, CA 94303). Founded in 1891, this party seeks "the peaceful abolition of capitalism via the ballot, backed up by an industrial organization," runs various candidates nationally and locally, and publishes the newspaper *Weekly People.*

Socialist Workers party (14 Charles Lane, New York, NY 10014). Founded in 1938, this party takes a Trotskyite approach to socialism and emphasizes issues of racism and feminism as well as economic revolution. Its presidential candidate was on 29 state ballots in 1980.

U.S.A. Green party (1710 Connecticut Ave., Washington, DC 20036). Founded in 1972 to emphasize environmental issues with the slogan "We do not inherit the earth from our parents, we borrow it from our children."

agrarian years of the Republic, perhaps largely because those without property were also without a vote. Possibly this social consensus has tended to persist even as the franchise has widened. The overlap we found in the attitudes of Republicans and Democrats is cited in support of this view.

A third theory argues that, like our British ancestors, we have always been *"politically mature."* We understand the virtues of stability and the essential role that compromise or accommodation plays in maintaining stability. A two-party system in this view is a sensible, conscious selection.

The explanation that convinces most observers is the *institutional* view. Our legal system provides for single-member districts: Only one person may represent a district in Congress. We also have winner-take-all elections: A **plurality**, or one vote more than that received by the second highest candidate, is all that is required to win. In systems where a *majority* is required to win, parties and candidates tend to take extreme stands in a first election and then compromise their stands in a runoff. In a plurality system, they don't have this opportunity, so they tend to avoid taking extreme stands altogether. Thus, there is little hope for success for extremist parties and positions, and only two parties are likely to survive. In addition, our Constitution provides for a single national executive, the president, and each state has a single governor. This means that a minor party cannot run a minority candidate and then become part of a coalition-cabinet government, as often happens in Europe's multiparty systems. Furthermore, the Electoral College system for election of the president requires that a successful candidate in fact win separate elections in a large number of states around the country. This makes it impossible for a candidate whose support is only regional, or not sufficiently national, to win. It also encourages those seeking to control the presidency to seek first to dominate an existing major party.

There is no way of proving that any one of these theories is correct and adequate in explaining why we have a two-party system. Perhaps all four theories point to important factors in the shaping of American party politics.[20] But do they thereby guarantee that the American system will continue as is in the coming years?

WILL—AND SHOULD—OUR TWO-PARTY SYSTEM SURVIVE?

Many political activists and observers have long been unhappy with the way our present party system operates. Some favor greater diversity of the sort that a multiparty system would allow or even foster. Others favor development of a system of party government, by which parties would be made more responsible to the electorate.

The Party Government Alternative

We have seen that our parties are decentralized and heterogeneous. This makes it difficult to know just what each stands for when we vote. It also makes it difficult for a president or even the majority party leaders in Congress to get the Congress to pass promised legislation. The suggestion has been made, therefore, that parties should be made to pledge particular programs. The winning party should then compel its members to vote for those programs or "discipline" them. It might do this by expelling deviants, by denying them committee assignments, or by either refusing to give them financial help in their next campaign or running another candidate in opposition.

Such a system of party government would make the parties more ideological and the government more responsible to the electorate. Voters would know in advance what they were getting. If voters did not get what they expected and could collectively vote a ruling party out at the next election by defeating the members of Congress up for reelection, American politics would become more issue oriented.

Some observers, however, believe that instability and confrontation would result from such a system, and they fear that Congress would become less flexible. They also fear that its members, who are now able to be relatively independent and deliberative, would lose this freedom, rendering them less able to help develop constructive legislation. Furthermore, special interests of various sorts, good or bad, would lose the important role they now have.

---

[20]Frank Sorauf, one of America's leading experts on parties, suggests that this is so, following his presentation of all four theories. See Sorauf, *Party Politics in America*, 5th ed. (Boston: Little, Brown), pp. 37–41.

The debate over the desirability of such party government has been carried on for decades and will no doubt continue.[21] Meanwhile, advocates of change have suggested that a more likely, and perhaps safer, route to the same sort of issue-oriented responsible politics is party realignment. Other observers endorse movement toward a multiparty system. These suggestions result from the fact that voters are, after all, less and less inclined to identify with a particular party, while they increasingly split their tickets when they vote, picking some candidates from one party and some from the other. Furthermore, some join special-interest groups that reflect their policy views and lobby to achieve them. Some observers take these developments as signs that our traditional parties do not and cannot any longer express the views and interests of most Americans. If this analysis is correct, one possible outcome is the splintering of the two parties into many smaller parties or at least creation of a strong third party.

The Third-Party or Multiparty Alternative

Pointing to the failure of our present two-party system to furnish clear alternatives and coherent policies, some experts argue that a viable third party would be beneficial. According to Theodore Lowi:

> The presence of a real third party with a real electoral base and a real presence in state legislatures, in Congress and in the Electoral College, could clarify the policies, programs and accountability of the two major parties by reducing their need to appear to be all things to all people. . . . Parties could present real choices, especially once everyone recognizes that compromises would take place after the election in the legislature.[22]

The Party Realignment Alternative

Another possibility, however, is realignment within the existing two-party system. One possible basis for realignment would be social or economic class.

This might produce an upper-class party of wealthy business people and professionals and a working-class party of labor and intellectuals.[23] Yet another possibility would be a realignment by which conservatives would be grouped in a new conservative party and liberals in another party.

When Ronald Reagan lost his struggle for the Republican nomination in 1976, a number of conservative leaders asserted that it was time to form a new national conservative party. They claimed that if it could take the conservative South away from the Democrats, this could be the new majority party in America.[24] When Reagan won both the nomination and the presidency in 1980, many of these same people thought that such a conservative-liberal realignment was underway—but within the traditional parties. Discontented liberals had their doubts, however. They thought Carter too conservative and were suspicious of efforts by party leaders to restore the influence of professionals within the party. Yet at the same time, they saw how poorly the more liberal John Anderson and the more radical Barry Commoner had done with new organizations, and they felt they had nowhere to turn but to the Democratic party. The contest for control of the party resumed—just as had happened in the Republican party after it lost the White House in 1976.

At first some analysts suggested that the 1980 election would prove to be a realigning election—but most experts disagree. Major realignments have occurred five times in American history: 1800 (the Jeffersonian Republicans), 1828 (the Jacksonian Democrats), 1860 (the Lincoln Republicans), 1896 (the Bryan Populist Democrats), and 1932 (the Roosevelt New Deal). These critical elections, as they are often called, came at times of political turmoil and had effects that lasted between 30 and 40 years. By such calculation, a realignment may be overdue in America.

For the 1980 election to qualify, its outcome would have to set a new and lasting pattern. This means that the future must bring "permanent electoral changes favoring a party and sustained con-

[21]For a discussion of the arguments, see Sorauf, *Party Politics*, chap. 16. The stimulus for the debate was a report prepared by a group of political scientists: Committee on Political Parties of the American Political Science Association, *Toward a More Responsible Two-Party System* (New York: Rinehart, 1950).

[22]Theodore J. Lowi, "Toward a More Responsible Three-Party System: The Mythology of the Two-Party System and the Prospects for Reform" *PS* (published by the American Political Science Association), Fall 1983, 699–706 at 705.

[23]For examination of one such suggestion, see David Broder, *The Party's Over* (New York: Harper & Row, 1972).

[24]For the background analyses for this argument, see Kevin Phillips, *The Emerging Republican Majority* (New Rochelle, NY: Arlington House, 1969), and his modification in *Mediacracy* (Garden City, NY: Doubleday, 1975); see also William Rusher, *The Making of the New Majority Party* (Mission, KS: Sheed Andrews & McMeel, 1975).

trol of policy-making institutions by that party."[25] In the cases of 1860, 1896, and 1932, the shifts in voting behavior lasted through later elections, and the same party got and held control not only of the presidency but also of both houses of Congress. What seems to have happened in each case is that voters felt there was a crisis and so voted differently than usual. They then saw the party newly in power passing new programs to deal with the crisis. Therefore, they continued to vote for that party.

Did 1980 mark the beginning of a realignment? The fact that the Republicans did not capture control of the House suggested that it did not. So did the fact that so many supporters of each presidential candidate said they were voting for their candidate primarily to keep the other contender out. So too did the fact that turnout declined once again. It appears that the people had not been politicized enough by the circumstances to vote in large numbers. Instead, they seemed even more alienated, and perhaps what we saw was further decomposition of basic party strength. The elections of 1982, 1984, and 1986 can also be read to suggest dealignment rather than realignment.

Most experts believe that if there has been any major realignment, it is only at the presidential level, where the voters have picked Republicans in four of the last five elections.[26] These presidential victories reflected what some have come to call a Republican lock on the electoral college. As we saw in Chapter 2, population has been shifting from the Democratic strongholds of the Northeast and Midwest to the South and West. The Democrats used to carry the South regularly; it was even called the Solid South. But it was the conservative wing of the party that dominated the South. That wing had long opposed civil rights for blacks, but the Democrats under President Lyndon Johnson of Texas passed major civil-rights laws in the 1960s. The South then started moving more toward the Republican party, especially in presidential voting. Since then, the South has supported the Democratic presidential candidate only once, when Jimmy Carter of Georgia ran in 1976. Even Carter couldn't hold the South in his unsuccessful bid for reelection in 1980. Meanwhile, Republican strength has grown in the West. The result of these various developments has been that Republican presidential candidates have won easily in the South and West and have also tended to win in the Midwest and often in the East as well. Thus, there has been a significant change in the pattern of presidential voting, but it is a change different from what is generally meant by political realignment.

Furthermore, the Republicans continue to show weakness in Congress. In the 1986 elections, the Democrats gained a net of 8 Senate seats to regain control with a commanding 55–45 margin. In the House, they gained a net of only 5 seats, but that left them with an 81-seat advantage. The story at the gubernatorial level was reversed, however. There, the Republicans gained 8 governorships, cutting the Democratic margin to 2. There are now 26 Democratic and 24 Republican governors.

What does this mean? Journalist Kevin Phillips has argued that a "split-level realignment" has already taken place. The country, he argues, now has a normal Republican majority at the presidential level, a competitive system in the Senate, and a Democratic system in the House and below the federal level.[27] Whether Phillips proves to be correct or not will only become clear with further elections. In the meantime, it seems clear that we have not had the sort of comprehensive realignment that some commentators have suspected.

Some Trends to Watch

There are trends that bear watching for their still unpredictable implications.[28] Foremost among these is *the decline in party identification* (mem-

[25]Walter Dean Burnham, Jerome M. Clubb, and William H. Flanigan, "Partisan Realignment: A Systemic Perspective," in *The History of American Electoral Behavior*, ed. Joel H. Silbey et al. (Princeton, NJ: Princeton Univ. Press, 1978), p. 49.

[26]The literature analyzing party realignment is growing. The classic argument is V. O. Key, "A Theory of Critical Elections," *Journal of Politics* 27 (February 1955), 3–18. See also Walter Dean Burnham, *Critical Elections and the Mainsprings of American Politics* (New York: Norton, 1970); James J. Sundquist, *Dynamics of the Party System* (Washington, DC: Brookings Institution, 1973); and the chapter by Kristi Andersen (chap. 5) in Norman H. Nie, Sidney Verba, and John R. Petrocik, *The Changing American Voter*, enlarged ed. (Cambridge, MA: Harvard Univ. Press, 1979). For more recent studies, see the collection of essays by Bruce A. Campbell and Richard J. Trilling, *Realignment in American Politics: Toward a Theory* (Austin: Univ. of Texas Press, 1980); and Jerome M. Clubb, Wiliam H. Flanigan, and Nancy H. Zingale, *Partisan Realignment: Voters, Parties, and Government in American History* (Beverly Hills, CA: Sage, 1980).

[27]See Phillips's newsletter, *The American Political Report*, January 11, 1985.

[28]For a recent survey, see Austin Ranney, "The Political Parties: Reform and Decline," chap. 6 in *The New American Political System*, ed. Anthony King (Washington, DC: American Enterprise Institute, 1978).

bership), discussed in the last chapter. Fewer and fewer Americans are "open Democrats" (as distinguished from "closed Democrats," who claim to be independents but still vote Democratic when they get to the polling place) and "open Republicans." This continuing decline in party identification may be a facet of what Walter Dean Burnham has called "the onward march of party decomposition."[29]

On the other hand, it is possible that the parties will find ways of arresting the decline. Or they may compensate for it by attracting new members from among the groups long excluded from active party roles, especially ethnic minorities (in all but big-city machines) and the young.[30] The Democrats have made some headway among the former groups, while the Republicans have gained among the young.

To some extent, recent elections have stimulated the rebirth of our major parties. After their loss in 1976, Republicans set about to rebuild their party. They emphasized raising money and computerizing their communications systems and conducted special seminars to train candidates and campaign managers. When that approach resulted in victory for Ronald Reagan and Republican control of the Senate, the Democratic party set out to do the same thing. That produced victory in the 1982 midterm elections. Since then both parties have remained active in fund raising and training as well as in voter registration.

Such developments may herald the resurgence of our major parties as organizations and as influences on election outcomes. But whether they will also attract new supporters or "party identifiers"— especially among the nonpartisan and alienated young—remains to be seen. If they do not, the "parties-in-the-electorate" will continue to atrophy.

"We do need the kinds of services that only strong, autonomous party organizations can provide," writes Everett Carll Ladd, Jr.:

> By substantially removing party from nominee selection almost everywhere, we have eliminated the one institution able to practice political planning. By removing party from governance, we have aided the already strong centrifugal forces working against coherence in public policy. And even in the area of representation, where the reformers have made their proudest claims, it is at least arguable that the machinery of party achieved results superior to those of the putatively more democratic procedures that have been erected in their stead.[31]

But suppose that parties, whatever their virtues, continue to decline. We may well wonder what would replace them as organizers of citizen opinion into forms that can shape political outcomes. Interest groups, which we shall examine in Chapter 5, perform some of the same functions. But interest groups do not generally select and run candidates for office. Nor indeed do those other leading political organizers, protest groups. So it is not at all clear what would or could step in to fill the void that would be left by the collapse of our parties. People would still have opinions on issues, and so would special interests. The media would still influence elections. Could public opinion, interest groups, and the media replace parties in our politics? Before we can answer such a question, we must examine each of these in turn. We shall do this in the next three chapters.

SUMMARY

Experts generally agree that our system requires strong parties to function well, and many think our parties should be stronger than they are now. Parties are coalitions of individuals that serve eight important functions in our system: recruiting candidates, competing to elect them, campaigning for votes, focusing attention on issues, educating people about politics, forming coalitions of voting groups, linking outside people and groups to the government, and coordinating the actions of officials belonging to the same party. As such, parties include both amateurs and professionals, or "regulars."

---

[29]See Burnham, *Critical Elections*, and his updating article, "American Politics in the 1970s: Beyond Party?" in *The Future of Political Parties*, ed. Louis Maisel and Paul M. Sachs (Beverly Hills, CA: Sage, 1975), pp. 238–77.

[30]See Nie et al., *Changing American Voter*, chap. 5, and Paul Beck, "A Socialization Theory of Partisan Realignment," in *New Views of Children and Politics*, ed. Richard Niemi (San Francisco: Jossey-Bass, 1974).

[31]Ladd, *Where Have All the Voters Gone?* p. 72. See also Robert Harmel and Kenneth Janda, *Parties and Their Environments: Limits to Reform* (New York: Longman, 1982).

Our parties have survived for a long time, for a variety of reasons: constitutional provisions for regular elections, freedom of speech, and freedom of assembly; their federal structure, which enables them to be strong in one region while weak in another; and reforms that have emphasized grassroots participation—especially in the Democratic party. The two parties do differ, with Democrats more liberal and Republicans more conservative. But their memberships overlap ideologically. This fact encourages parties to "compete for the middle," and in turn helps to preserve the two-party system. Minor parties tend to come and go, sometimes influencing a major party to adopt their programs. Minor parties are not likely to become major because our system has plurality voting in elections.

There are, however, several alternatives to a two-party system, each of which has some adherents. One is party government, in which parties would adopt fixed programs and implement them if elected. Another is a multiparty system, in which voters would have more choice and parties would compromise in the legislature. A third is realignment, by which parties would become more consistent—for example, liberal versus conservative. None of these alternatives now seems likely to occur, in part because our parties seem to be regaining vitality. Nevertheless, the future of our parties remains unclear.

Suggestions for Further Reading and Study

Parties have been with us since the beginning, and so, it often seems, have books about American party politics. Our listing here merely skims the surface and picks those that are most likely to help you develop your understanding. The classic historical treatment is Wilfred Binkley, *American Political Parties*, 4th ed. (New York: Knopf, 1963), which emphasizes formation of coalitions. More recent books with strong historical analysis include James L. Sundquist, *Dynamics of the Party System*, 2d ed. (Washington, DC: Brookings, 1983); Everett Carll Ladd, Jr., *American Political Parties: Social Change and Political Response* (New York: Norton, 1970); Everett Carll Ladd, Jr., and Charles Hadley, *Transformations of the American Party System*, 2d ed. (New York: Norton, 1978); the papers edited by William Chambers and Walter Dean Burnham, *The American Party System*, 2d ed. (New York: Oxford Univ. Press, 1975).

There is a large and interesting literature on party reform, in addition to the works on realignment cited in this chapter. It starts with the classic books by E. E. Schattschneider, *Party Government* (New York: Holt, 1942), and *The Struggle for Party Government* (College Park: Univ. of Maryland Press, 1948). Studies focusing on reforms include John S. Saloma and Frederick H. Sontag, *Parties: The Real Opportunity for Effective Citizen Politics* (New York: Knopf, 1972); Austin Ranney, *Curing the Mischiefs of Faction: Party Reform in America* (Berkeley: Univ. of California Press, 1975); William J. Crotty, *Political Reform and the American Experi-ment* (New York: Crowell, 1977); Walter Karp, *Indispensable Enemies* (Baltimore: Penguin, 1974); Gerald M. Pomper, ed., *Party Renewal in America: Theory and Practice* (New York: Praeger, 1980); Robert Harmel and Kenneth Janda, *Parties and Their Environments: Limits to Reform* (New York: Longman, 1982); Joel L. Fleishman, ed., *The Future of American Political Parties* (Englewood Cliffs, NJ: Prentice-Hall, 1982); Nelson Polsby, *The Consequences of Party Reform* (New York: Oxford Univ. Press, 1983); and David E. Price, *Bringing Back the Parties* (Washington: CQ Press, 1984).

Parties are, of course, found elsewhere. For comparative perspective, see two classics: Maurice Duverger, *Political Parties: Their Organization and Activity in the Modern State* (New York: Wiley, 1954), and Leon Epstein, *Political Parties in Western Democracies* (New York: Praeger, 1967). See also two newer comprehensive analyses: Giovanni Sartori, *Parties and Party Systems* (New York: Cambridge Univ. Press, 1976); and Kenneth Janda, *Political Parties: A Cross-National Survey* (New York: Free Press, 1980).

And finally, if there is something else you want to know about parties, try the most comprehensive text, Frank Sorauf, *Party Politics in America*, 5th ed. (Boston: Little, Brown, 1984); William J. Crotty and Gary C. Jacobson, *American Parties in Decline* (Boston: Little, Brown paperback, 1980); or Samuel J. Eldersveld, *Political Parties in American Society* (New York: Basic Books, 1982).

5

THE INTERESTS:
Public, Special, and Vested

Who do you think matters in American politics? Which groups generally get what they want? Is what they get what we—the public—want or what we should want? We will consider these questions as we look at the roles of interest groups. Some of the answers may surprise you. You may not think of yourself as a member of an interest group—at least, not in your role as a student. But our first case study will show students at work in a coalition with school officials and parents, lobbying the Congress to get what they want. We will see that almost anyone can be a member of an interest group, and almost any group can try to influence what happens in politics. But some will be more successful than others, and we'll learn why—and how to be an effective lobbyist—in this chapter. ■

TABLE 5.1
Major Federal Student Aid Programs

PROGRAM	NATURE	YEAR ESTABLISHED	BUDGETED COST IN FY83	NUMBER OF STUDENTS BENEFITING
1. National direct student loans	Federal gov't. provides 90%, college 10% for loans to needy students at 5% interest	1958	$ 179,000,000	266,000
2. College work-study	Federal gov't. pays 80% of wages of low-income students employed by colleges	1964	528,000,000	915,000
3. Supplemental educational opportunity grants	Federal grants to colleges to give to very needy students	1965	278,000,000	615,000
4. Guaranteed student loans	Federal gov't. insures private bank loans to students and pays difference between 9% interest and current rate charged; $25,000 family income limit removed in 1978; $30,000 limit imposed in 1981	1965	3,900,000,000	3,500,000
5. State student incentive grants	Federal gov't. gives money to states, which add an equal amount and give all to colleges to give to needy students	1972	74,000,000	300,000
6. Pell (basic economic opportunity) grants	Federal gov't. grants from $200 to $1670 based on need (until 1978), to students with family incomes below $15,000; then, below $27,000; most goes to those below $9000.	1972	2,389,000	2,800,000
			4,961,389,000	8,396,000*

*Some students receive two or more types of federal aid.
Source: National Journal, April 17, 1982, p. 1263

THE CASE OF FEDERAL SCHOLARSHIPS

The odds are good that you are receiving some sort of federal aid to attend your college or university. Almost half of all students now do—and there are about 12,400,000 students in colleges and universities today. The federal government now spends almost $9 billion on such financial aid each year, or more than $50 for every man, woman, and child in the United States. But large though this sum is, it is still small compared to the total cost of education, from kindergarten through graduate school, in the United States. That total was $230 billion for the 1983–1984 school year.

Obviously, education is a big, big business. Indeed, one of every three Americans is either in school or working for an educational institution. But the 57 million Americans now in school pay far less than one-quarter of the cost of their education in tuition and fees. The other three-quarters comes from their governments: local, state, and federal.

Because education is the central activity of so many Americans perhaps it is not surprising that Washington pays almost a tenth of the bill. But until recently that was not the case. Indeed, the first of the basic loan programs from which almost half of all college students now benefit was created as recently as 1958, and it applied only to graduate students.[1]

As Table 5.1 shows, the federal government's student aid programs are recent creations. The major ones, however, have grown rapidly and have become very costly.

Programs that aid so many people are not usually challenged. Instead, they tend to grow with

---

[1] An earlier program, begun in 1944, provided scholarship aid to veterans, and a small program begun in 1952 provided aid to certain science students. For a history and critique of the entire range of programs, see Denis P. Doyle and Terry W. Hartle, "Student Aid Muddle," *Atlantic,* Feb. 1986, pp. 30–34.

the years. Federal aid to students was no exception. Until 1978 most aid went to students from poor families. Pell grants—named after the senator from Rhode Island, Claiborne Pell, who first proposed them—were limited to families whose income was less than $15,000 a year. Loans that were guaranteed at low interest rates were limited to families making no more than $25,000. In the 1970s, however, tuition and other costs rose rapidly, and many middle-class families sought help. They turned to Congress, which responded in 1978 by raising these income ceilings.

However, when Ronald Reagan was elected president in 1980, he argued that education should be the concern primarily of state and local government rather than of the federal government. When he took office in 1981, he called for cutbacks in almost all domestic programs. With widespread political support, he got most of the cuts he desired, including a 10 percent cut in student aid for 1981. The next year Congress had trouble deciding what to do and ended up cutting almost all domestic spending. Federal student aid programs went down another 5.4 percent.

The Reagan administration then proposed more drastic cuts. It argued that millions of students who didn't need the aid were taking it anyway and that in any case, provision of such aid is not the federal government's responsibility. Therefore, Reagan proposed cutting funds from $6.4 billion to $4.3 billion. Included in this proposal was complete abolition of the programs numbered 1, 3, and 5 in Table 5.1—the programs that provided grants to very needy students.

The Reagan proposals created a major political battle in Washington, where thousands of organizations work to influence what the government does. Some of these **interest groups**, as they are called, work for or represent colleges and universities. Among them are the American Association of Community and Junior Colleges and the Association of American Universities. Others represent student groups around the country. Among them are the National Organization of Black University and College Students and the U.S. Student Association. Altogether, 49 higher-education interest groups have headquarters or offices in Washington. When these groups saw the president's proposed budget for 1983, they went into action.

First they formed a special group, the Action Committee for Higher Education, to begin an all-out public relations campaign. The committee prepared information on the potential impact of the proposed cuts and gave it to its members. The latter then passed it on to *their* members—schools, faculty, and students. It also prepared special reports for the TV networks and the news services to alert them to the proposal and its effects—and to let them know that opposition was being mobilized. This campaign made the federal student aid budget a public issue in the newspapers and on the evening news.

The committee then prepared a special report for each member of Congress showing how the proposed changes would affect the people in his or her district. Congress would have to vote on the Reagan proposals in the summer—just before the 1982 November elections in which all 435 members of the House of Representatives and one-third of the 100 senators would be facing the voters.

At the same time, a group in Washington called the National Coalition of Independent College and University Students organized a National Student Lobby Day. It brought students from schools all over the country to Washington. Each one visited the member of Congress from his or her district to protest the proposed cuts. This activity is called lobbying because it used to occur in the lobby outside the chamber where the House of Representatives meets. Now it usually occurs in the member's office in the Capitol.

In addition, middle-class parents got word of the proposed cuts from the media, and many of them wrote their representatives opposing the president.

Members of Congress know, as we saw in Chapter 3, that middle-class adults and college students are among those most likely to vote. Thus, they could see that if they voted for the president's proposed cuts, they might well lose the votes of the thousands of people in their districts who were in college or who had children in college.

The result was that Reagan's proposals lost by a wide margin. Congress voted to continue funding of the programs at the 1982 levels, and even to increase funds for the two largest programs, guaranteed loans and Pell grants. Even most conservative Republicans who supported Reagan's budget cutting in Congress voted for federal aid to students.

What had happened? Students, parents, teach-

Rep. Stewart McKinney (R-Conn.) speaking with students who came to his office to lobby for federal scholarship programs. (Art Stein/Photo Researchers)

ers, schools, and other interested parties had united in a special coalition to influence what the government would decide to do. They used whatever resources they had—their votes in the coming election, their information on how to influence Congress, their ability to get access to their representatives, and the money needed to get to Washington to lobby. They also used arguments. Some of the arguments were about what was good for their representatives—who wanted to be reelected. Some of the arguments were about what was good for them—continued federal aid for students. And some of the arguments were about what was good for the country—helping young people become well educated so that they could become good citizens and productive members of society.

In making these arguments, the lobbyists were taking issue with their president. They were claiming that they were better judges of their interests, their representatives' interests, and what we usually call the public interest than the president himself. In this case, these *claims to authority* worked, and Congress voted with the special interests—the students (and their parents and schools)—rather than with the president. Does this mean that the president was wrong in his view of the public interest? Or that the lobbyists were right in their

view? Or that Congress decides what is in the public interest?

INTERESTS IN AMERICA

What are we to make of these disputes over what is in "the public interest"? If people and groups disagree so much on specific cases, can we look to a general definition to find out who is right? Unfortunately, political scientists and philosophers also disagree on what the public interest is and even on whether or not it exists.[2]

Private Interests and Special Interests

Everyone grants that there are **private interests**—the interests of individuals. When a number of people—as individuals or perhaps as one of the groups that lobbied on student loans—have the

[2]For a discussion of concepts of the common good and the public interest, see Glendon Schubert, *The Public Interest* (Glencoe, IL: Free Press, 1960); Richard Flathman, *The Public Interest* (New York: Wiley, 1966); the symposium on interests in *Political Theory* 3, no. 3 (August 1975); J. D. B. Miller, *The Nature of Politics* (London: Duckworth, 1962), chap. 4; and Barry M. Mitnick, "A Typology of Conceptions of the Public Interest," *Administration and Society* 8, no. 1 (May 1976); 5–28.

same private interest, we may refer to this as a **special interest**—an interest "shared by only a few people or a fraction of the community." Special interests "*exclude* others and may be *adverse* to them."[3]

In politics, two things can make a special interest especially important. One is that those sharing the same special interest can *organize into a special-interest group* in order to increase their chances of getting what they want. When we speak of special interests in politics, we often refer to organized special-interest groups or "pressure groups," such as the National Association of Manufacturers (NAM), the AFL-CIO, or the U.S. Student Association. Political scientists generally define an interest group as an organized group whose members have common views about certain policies or actions and so undertake activities to influence government officials and policies.[4]

Vested Interests

A special interest is especially important in politics if it is *vested*. The term *vested* comes from the French word for a cloak or garment in which one is wrapped for protection, and we still use it to refer to an article of clothing. In politics, it refers to an interest wrapped in, or protected by, the status quo—the distribution of wealth or privilege, for example—or benefiting from a particular program. The defense industries and some labor unions benefit from a large defense budget; thus, we may refer to them as vested interests when the subject of defense spending is being debated. **Vested interests**, in other words, are special interests that are already getting their way—already benefiting specially from the way things are—and that thus usually seek to preserve the status quo.

The Public Interest

What, then, about the "common interest," the "general interest," or, as it is most often called, the **public interest?** Here there is no agreement. Before

the term *public interest* became widely used, it was generally believed that there were truths about human beings—their needs, and their values—that existed beyond time and place, beyond specific individuals. The common good, as it was then usually called, was the body of basic truths or principles by which politics and policy could be judged to see whether they were right. But as the growth of science and the spread of revolution shattered belief in this shared world view, it became more difficult for many people to believe the notion that there was a single, eternal common good.

Politics therefore became more individualistic, more conflictual, less stable. As this occurred, people began to think of politics not as a way of achieving an ideal order but rather as a way of expressing and reconciling or compromising individual differences without resorting to violence. So the focus shifted from the common good to that of individual interests. A second notion of the public interest, as some cumulation or compromising of a wide range of private interests, gradually began to spread.

Since then we have had several centuries of pragmatic, individualistic politics. But with rare exceptions, there has been no evidence that the concept of the public interest as a cumulation of private interests can unite a fragmented society behind constructive programs. The old belief was that if every person pursued his or her own private interests, the general good or the public interest would be served in the longer run. This view, which we will encounter again in coming chapters, argued that there was "an invisible hand" that would make things turn out that way. It followed that government should intervene as little as possible in the economy and in society. But time has shown "the invisible hand" to be quite arthritic. New notions of the public interest, most agree, must include the interests of the weak as well as the strong, of the poor as well as the rich, of women as well as men, and of the yet unborn as well as the living.

It is a big order—a big challenge to our thinkers and an even bigger one to our politicians. Our thinkers can try to develop a notion without worrying about immediate problems and decisions. But our politicians must develop and use such a notion in the day-to-day struggles we call politics while being buffeted by special interests on all sides.

E. E. Schattschneider observed that:

---

[3]These words belong to the late E. E. Schattschneider, but the concept has been found in political writings since the ancient Greeks. See Schattschneider, *The Semi-Sovereign People* (New York: Holt, Rinehart & Winston, 1960), pp. 23–24.

[4]For a discussion emphasizing the role of groups in politics—a role that has been very influential in political science—see David B. Truman, *The Governmental Process*, 2d ed. (New York: Knopf, 1971), chap. 2.

Perfect agreement within a community is not always possible, but an interest may be said to have become public when it is shared so widely as to be substantially universal.[5]

But this insight does not solve the problem of the political leader. For, as J. D. B. Miller has written, in practice the common interest "is something which manifests itself from time to time, but is neither constant nor reliable. It is more applicable to ends than to means; it may dissolve under the pressure of arguments about how it is to be served."[6]

The result is that debates about public policy often cite the public interest. But the debates are conducted under the influence of special interests—often, those that are vested. To understand American politics, we must know who these special interests are and how they operate. We can then examine with more clarity their impact on American politics and decide what this tells us about the place of interests in American government.

AMERICANS AND INTEREST GROUPS

Washington columnist George Will once offered his readers Will's rule of informed citizenship. "If you want to understand your government," it says, "don't begin by reading the Constitution. . . . Instead read selected portions of the Washington Telephone Directory . . . which contain listings for all the organizations with titles beginning with the word 'National.'" There are more than a thousand such organizations. They range from such well-known giants as the National Association of Manufacturers to much less well-known groups like the National Fishmeal and Oil Association. As Will explains, these special-interest groups portray "a picture of the government and the economy inextricably intertwined." For example, the National Limestone Institute is concerned both with federal mining safety regulations and with the federal highway construction program.

Lest we think that these organizations do not represent us, there are such groups as the U.S. Student Association and the National Student Lobby, as we saw at the beginning of this chapter. And when we add Washington telephone listings

---

A few of the listings under *National* in the Washington Telephone Directory.

beginning with the word *American*, we include the American Association of University Professors and the American Political Science Association as well as the American Association of University Women.[7]

It once was thought that virtually all Americans belonged to at least one such organization and that most belonged to several. We now know that this is not true. Indeed, a study by Robert Salisbury found that, including churches, only about 75 percent of Americans belong to any organizations, and just under half belong to more than one.[8] Table 5.2 reports the results of Salisbury's survey, broken down by percentages belonging to the various types of organizations.[9]

---

[7]See George F. Will, "Government by Association," *Washington Post,* April 8, 1976, p. A19. Another way to find such groups is to look in the Washington Yellow Pages under "Associations," where you'll find 30 columns—8 pages—of societies, councils, institutes, alliances, leagues, federations, committees, and so on—some 1600 listings in all. *Washington Representatives,* a directory published annually in Washington by Columbia Books, lists some 10,000 advocates of special interests and causes.

[8]Robert Salisbury, "Overlapping Memberships, Organizational Interactions, and Interest Group Theory," paper delivered at the 1976 annual meeting of the American Political Science Association, Chicago.

[9]See also Carol S. Greenwald, *Group Power: Lobbying and Public Policy* (New York: Praeger, 1977), pp. 38–39.

---

[5]Schattschneider, *Semi-Sovereign People,* p. 24.
[6]Miller, *Nature of Politics,* p. 83.

TABLE 5.2
Organizational Memberships of Americans

TYPE OF ORGANIZATION	PERCENTAGE OF AMERICANS BELONGING TO ORGANIZATION
Church	41.8
Sports	17.5
School service	17.5
Fraternal	13.7
Professional	13.0
Youth	10.3
Literary, art, study	9.2
Hobby	9.6
Veterans	8.9
Service	8.9
Political	4.4
Farm	4.2
Nationality	3.5
Percent of Americans belonging to an organization	74.5
Percent belonging to two organizations	18.9
Percent belonging to three or more organizations	29.9

Source: Robert Salisbury, "Overlapping Memberships, Organizational Interactions, and Interest Group Theory," p. 4. These figures are for 1974.

Some of these organizations include as members most of those who would be eligible. Others include only a small percentage. For example, the National Consumers League, a consumer action group, has only about 15,000 actual members, although in a sense, all 242 million Americans are consumers and so are potential members.[10]

Why Groups Arise and Why People Join

Why do we decide to join—or not to join—interest groups? Experts disagree. Traditionally, the emphasis was on the political benefits of membership. Interest groups arise, it was said, because people have common interests to seek or protect.[11] In the last several decades, there has been a growing tendency to analyze political behavior in terms of rational decision making. If you assume that people

are rational, well informed, and economically self-interested, you may conclude that people with the same interests may *refuse to join* an interest group. Why? Because joining and participating cost time and money, and most of the things the group achieves become available to you whether or not you join. A law passed by Congress applies to everyone in similar circumstances. Clean air achieved by environmental-protection advocates is there for everyone to breathe. Both laws that apply to everyone and laws that apply to such things as clean air are now often called **collective goods.** Once a goal is gained, each person can share in its benefits whether or not he or she joined the interest group that helped get it.

Thus, Mancur Olson argues:

> If the members of a large group rationally seek to maximize their personal welfare, they will *not* act to advance their common or group objectives unless there is coercion to force them to do so, or unless some separate incentive, distinct from the achievement of common or group interest, is offered to the members of the group individually on the condition that they help bear the costs or burdens involved in the achievement of the group objectives.[12]

According to this analysis, the decision to join and/or to act depends *not* on common political interests *nor* even on feelings of solidarity with fellow members. Rather, economic self-interest is said to be the key. However, many people have traditionally joined groups seeking things in which they have no direct economic interest. For example, whites join black civil-rights organizations such as the National Association for the Advancement of Colored People (NAACP), and citizens of New York State join organizations seeking to protect the Alaskan wilderness. Also, many people give funds to groups they do not join and that do not speak for their own interests.

Why We Have So Many Interest Groups

Even though many Americans belong to no political interest groups, there has been a large increase in the number of such groups since the early 1960s.

[10]See Truman, *Governmental Process*, p. 511. For lists of such groups and further information on them, see Mary Wilson Pair, ed., *Encyclopedia of Associations*, 15th ed. (Detroit: Gale Research Co., 1981), which lists 14,726 national organizations. See also *Washington Information Directory 1986–87* (Washington: CQ Press, 1986), which lists those with offices in the Washington area.

[11]See, for example, Truman, *Governmental Process*, and Earl Latham, *The Group Basis of Politics* (Ithaca, NY: Cornell Univ. Press, 1972).

[12]Mancur Olson, Jr., *The Logic of Collective Action* (Cambridge, MA: Harvard Univ. Press, 1965), p. 2. For a somewhat critical expansion of Olson's analysis, see Terry M. Moe, *The Organization of Interests* (Chicago: Univ. of Chicago Press, 1980).

Why? America has long had the diversity that makes such groups flourish because of immigration and conflicts between people of different economic levels. It has also had the protections such groups require in the Constitution's First Amendment guarantees of free speech, free association, and the right to petition the government for redress of grievances. The decentralization of government functions resulting from federalism also creates opportunities for more interest groups at each level.

But what has happened in recent decades to spur the growth of new groups? Four things. First, the government has expanded its activities into many new areas of concern to citizens, such as environment, energy, consumer affairs, and medical care. Second, as we have noted in previous chapters, voting has declined, and parties have weakened. So the traditional routes for participation have declined while the range of citizen interests has been increasing. The result has been new organizations to fill this gap. Third, businesses, universities, professional groups, and recipients of governmental services have become more active politically. Some of them are even paid by the federal government for participating in the policy-making process. Others—especially citizens' groups—have even been given federal contracts to support their organizing. The Reagan administration has tried to "defund" such groups, but once formed they tend to continue acting with or without federal funds. And fourth, new laws have fostered new groups organized as political action committees (PACs) to give contributions to political candidates.[13]

Politics within Interest Groups

The decision to join or not to join, or to give money or not—like other instances of political participation that we examined in Chapter 3—may have various motives. This may suggest that the activities of an interest group will reflect the mixed motives of its members. In fact, however, most such groups are run by leaders who often are not in close touch with their members. They are likely to have their own plans. They will also have to work with their staff employees, with government officials, and with others. In other words, there will be politics within such interest groups, just as there will be politics between the groups and other organizations. Accordingly, what the interest groups actually do may not always correspond to the views of even a majority of members, let alone of all of them.

THE MAJOR SPECIAL-INTEREST GROUPS

The most common term for special-interest-group representatives is **lobbyist.** The term arose, as we noted above, because these activists originally hung around the lobbies of the House and Senate waiting for chances to talk with the legislators about their concerns. Today most of them do many other things as well, as we will see in detail later in this chapter. Indeed, some never set foot in the congressional lobbies. Take, for example, the case of the leading Washington lawyers.

The Washington Lawyers

Some observers would claim that the most powerful lobbyists in Washington now are the individuals and law firms known collectively as the superlawyers.[14] These are people who know the ropes in Washington and are available for hire by anyone who can afford their help. Many of them once worked in the government. Some are retired or defeated politicians. All have the advantage of operating independently, so they do not have the problems of attempting to run interest groups composed of often conflicting interests while trying to influence decisions in Washington. The number of lawyers working in Washington is now close to 40,000. Many of them are engaged in lobbying, working for the 300 out-of-town law firms with Washington branch offices. But such Washington lawyers are the exception among lobbyists. Most common of all are the trade and professional associations that George Will referred to.

[13]See Burdett A. Loomis and Allan J. Cigler, "The Changing Nature of Interest Group Politics," in *Interest Group Politics*, 2d ed., ed. Cigler and Loomis (Washington: CQ Press, 1986), chap. 1.

[14]See Joseph Goulden, *The Superlawyers* (New York: Dell, 1973) and Robert H. Salisbury, "Washington Lobbyists: A Collective Portrait," in *Interest Group Politics*, 2d ed., ed. Cigler and Loomis, chap. 8.

Trade and Professional Associations

Trade associations top the list in terms of political activity. The oldest trade association still in business is the New York Chamber of Commerce, formed by 20 merchants in 1768. In the century following, only a dozen or so national groups were formed. Today, another century later, however, the Commerce Department reports 20,000 national and international associations, 25,000 regional and state associations, and perhaps 400,000 local associations. There are so many such groups that there is even a group made up only of officers of such groups—the American Society of Association Executives, established in 1920, with 9500 members (including 2000 in Washington).

Trade organizations exist to provide services to their members. Many of those services are things that would fall under the various lobbying activities we discussed above. That is why more than 2000 of the 4700 largest national trade groups have headquarters in Washington, where they spend perhaps a billion dollars a year and employ some 50,000 persons, many of whom might qualify as lobbyists, according to our broad definition.[15] The Washington location is becoming essential. As William Utz of the National Shrimp Congress explains it: "The reaction time to new rules and regulations is faster if the headquarters is based in Washington. If you have an ear here, you can translate things as they happen."[16]

In fact, it is not so much an ear as a mouth, or a mouthpiece, that special interests want in Washington. A pocketbook is also helpful. The most effective lobbies tend to combine all three elements: gathering information, dispensing information, and dispersing resources where they will do the most good.

The following have been among the most effective lobbies through the years: the AFL-CIO, representing most labor unions; the United States Chamber of Commerce, the National Association of Manufacturers, and the Business Roundtable, representing business; and Common Cause and Ralph Nader's Public Citizen groups, representing what they assert is the public interest.

---

[15]Robert D. Hershey, Jr., "Washington Watch: The Magnet for Lobbyists," *New York Times*, August 18, 1980.
[16]Quoted in Greenwald, *Group Power*, p. 65.

Labor Lobbies

The American Federation of Labor-Congress of Industrial Organizations (created by a merger of the AFL and the CIO in 1955) consists of some 110 unions with about 14 million members. Of course, it lobbies for special labor concerns. It also lobbies for social programs, such as national health insurance and tax reform, in cooperation with other liberal lobbies. Further, it lobbies for high defense spending and new technological projects such as the supersonic transport (SST) and the Alaska oil pipeline, in cooperation with business lobbies, partly because these programs promise more jobs, and partly because AFL-CIO leadership is generally conservative in its attitudes toward foreign affairs.

Many of the larger unions also maintain their own lobbyists in Washington. While these lobbyists usually work in tandem with the AFL-CIO lobbyists, they occasionally take independent action when their positions differ. Among the large independent unions that lobby actively are the United Mine Workers and the Teamsters.

Big-Business Lobbies

The lobby for big business includes thousands of trade organizations—but these groups are dominated by three powerful coalitions. The first is the United States Chamber of Commerce, which represents about 225,000 businesses, including 3500 local chambers of commerce and trade associations. The leading segments include manufacturers (26 percent); retail trade (14 percent); construction (13 percent); and finance, insurance, and real estate (11 percent). Dues produce a budget of over $65 million a year. The National Chamber, as it is called, with a staff of 1400, uses this money to lobby on Capitol Hill, where it has been a prominent opponent of a consumer-protection agency, of stronger antitrust legislation, and of national health insurance. Its effectiveness is partly a product of its Congressional Action System, a network of 100,000 business people who contact members of Congress directly. It has also established an organization called Citizen's Choice, designed to mobilize "Americans who resent high taxes, inflation, and increasing government interference in their lives," so that they too will lobby for chamber objectives. In 1977 the chamber established the Na-

A lobbyist talks to Democractive Representative Jim Wright of Texas, new Speaker of the House. (Dennis Brack/Black Star)

tional Chamber Litigation Center (NCLC), which it calls a public-interest law firm. Citizen's Choice seems to be an alternative to Common Cause, while the NCLC is a counter to the Nader operation—both of which we shall discuss shortly.

The second major business lobby is the National Association of Manufacturers, which represents some 14,000 corporations and collects about $7 million a year in dues. It represents primarily the bigger corporations. But the country's largest corporations are represented by the Business Roundtable, the third of the business coalitions. This group of the chief executives of nearly 200 of the largest corporations in America is based in New York but operates actively in Washington—using personal contacts with the president as well as with members of Congress. It has taken a special interest in opposing creation of a consumer-protection agency and obstructing passage of laws designed to curb monopolies and break up large corporations.[17]

Small-Business Lobbies

The "big three" tend to focus their efforts on concerns of big business. Smaller businesses are represented by several major groups. The biggest is the

National Federation of Independent Business. It employs 600 people nationwide and represents 605,000 small-business owners. It regularly polls its members and reports results of its surveys to Congress. It also rates members of Congress on how they vote on issues of interest to small businesses. The other leading advocate for small business is the National Small Business Association, which represents 50,000 members but acts through an executive committee rather than by polling its members.

Historically, small business has had relatively little influence on government. In recent years, however, economists have discovered that when it prospers, small business creates large numbers of jobs in the economy. As a result, politicians have become more sympathetic to its appeals.

Corporation Lobbies

In addition to these coalitions made up of businesses, almost 500 corporations have their own offices in Washington to lobby directly for their own specific interests. These offices typically consist of half a dozen people, whose average salary is now

Neal Knox of the National Rifle Association , which lobbies against gun control. (Dennis Brack/Black Star)

---

[17]For a study of the history and current operation of business lobbies in Washington, see Sar A. Levitan and Martha Cooper, *Business Lobbies: The Public Good and the Bottom Line* (Baltimore: Johns Hopkins Univ. Press, 1983).

about $70,000 a year. The employees monitor news developments and attend hearings held by Congress and press conferences held by government agencies. They then report back to their company's headquarters. They also arrange for corporate officials to contact government officials and to testify at hearings, and they issue reports and statements on topics of concern to their company.[18]

Agricultural Lobbies

There are four main farm groups that lobby. The American Farm Bureau Federation, which represents larger farmers, is strongest in the South and Midwest. It opposes federal regulations on agriculture and tends to support conservative Republicans. The National Farmers Union is more liberal. It is strongest among grain farmers in the Midwest and favors the government's subsidies to farmers and tends to support Democrats. The National Farmers Organization consists of cattle farmers, and the American Agricultural Movement consists of family farmers. Both tried to organize boycotts and strikes in the 1970s to increase farm incomes. Thereafter, they became more conventional lobbying groups.

Religious Lobbies

In recent years, certain religious special-interest groups have taken a very active role in politics. Most prominent among them have been groups often called the Christian Right, which took a very active role in the 1980 election. Perhaps the most visible has been Moral Majority. It was founded in late 1978 by the Reverend Jerry Falwell, star of television's "Old Time Gospel Hour." Within a year it had developed chapters in all fifty states, with a mailing list of half a million people and a budget of over a million dollars. It has a lobbying office in Washington called the Liberty Federation, which tries to influence Congress to pass bills such as constitutional amendments outlawing abortion and permitting school prayer. The Religious Roundtable, based in Dallas, is another such group. Founded by evangelical television preacher James Robison, it concentrates on training leaders for

A tractorcade demonstration in Washington sponsored by the American Agricultural Movement. (© A. Pierce Bounds/UNIPHOTO)

Bible-based political action, with a budget of about a million dollars a year.

Christian Voice, a group of several hundred thousand members, publishes ratings of members of Congress and a "hit list" of liberals to be defeated, and lobbies Congress; it has a budget of about $1.5 million. On the Sunday before election day, it distributes leaflets against incumbents it opposes outside churches across the country. It also has a PAC that contributes funds to conservative candidates.

The visible role of these and other parts of the Christian right in the 1984 elections should not distract attention from other religious groups, many of them more liberal. The Washington Interfaith Staff Council includes representatives of 30 major denominations and religious groups, each of which

---

[18]See Beth Brophy, "Would You Want Your Daughter to Marry a Lobbyist?" *Washingtonian*, August 1980, pp. 115–22.

has an office in Washington. These groups have played important roles in battles in Congress by supporting the food-stamp program and human-rights issues in foreign policy, for example. Many denominations are also directly represented in Washington by organizations such as the U.S. Catholic Conference, the United Methodist Board of Church and Society, and the Jewish B'nai Brith. Traditionally, these groups have tended to take liberal positions on public issues. Their activities have not been widely publicized.

The groups of the Christian Right have rapidly become much more active. Among their tactics, in addition to direct lobbying, have been the following: massive voter-registration drives centering on the churches; "moral action committees" organized in churches to study candidates and legislation; state and regional training seminars in political tactics; newsletters that "simplify" and "clarify" political issues from a scriptural point of view; and a communications network of "telephone trees" that can notify supporters to contact members of Congress with their views when a bill is up for a vote—a system used by other effective interest groups.

The potential political significance of this new movement is noteworthy for two reasons. First, many Americans consider themselves strict believers in the Bible and are thus potential members or

Rev. Pat Robertson announces his campaign for the 1988 Republican presidential nomination. (John Ficara/Woodfin Camp & Associates)

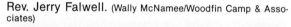

Rev. Jerry Falwell. (Wally McNamee/Woodfin Camp & Associates)

supporters. A Gallup Poll found the number to be 20 percent of all Americans—or 30 million voters. Another 21 million voters consider themselves "born again" Christians. In general, these people have not been very active politically until now. If the Christian Right can mobilize them effectively, their votes and letters may indeed affect who wins elections and what bills get passed. A second factor that may contribute to the movement's political impact is money. Christian evangelicals can capitalize upon the large-scale contributions ($150 million a year to the three top TV preachers) from supporters of their telecasts on the Christian Broadcasting Network and the PTL (Praise the Lord) Network, as well as contributions made directly to the lobbying groups. These broadcasts regularly reach millions of viewers. Thus, they are seen as an instant political force. Their messages are generally conservative—for example, against arms-control agreements with the Soviet Union, against abortion, against the Equal Rights Amendment, and against gay rights.

The Interests 157

Public-Interest Lobbies

The interests of consumers and of ordinary citizens are represented primarily by Common Cause and by various "public-interest" law and lobbying organizations, many of them under the guidance of Ralph Nader.[19]

Public-interest organizations representing the concerns of those without great economic power or influential political position are nothing new in America. Other such groups include the organizations that worked to expand the right to vote, which we discussed in Chapter 3; the various civil-rights movements designed to improve the lot of the blacks; and the union movement in its earlier phases. The Anti-Saloon League and the more general prohibition movement to outlaw alcoholic beverages would also qualify, as would Planned Parenthood and the American Civil Liberties Union.

These organizations have sought to change the dominant conception of the public interest—and have sometimes succeeded. They have operated on the principle that government should protect citizens from unjust practices of all sorts. And they have relied upon the First Amendment guarantee of "the right of the people . . . to petition the government for a redress of grievances."

Some of these groups have emphasized lobbying, while others have relied primarily upon appeals to the courts. Still others have used research and distribution of their findings to generate popular interest in their crusades. John Guinther observes:

> Many of these organizations can point to successes, some legislative, some judicial. In many instances, however, the significant contribution has been a [philosophical] one. By its propagandizing, over the years the organization implants in the public consciousness a general perception of right and wrong which the people come to believe in and sometimes act upon.[20]

The actual membership of such organizations is difficult to determine, but one study found that 51

John Gardner, founder of Common Cause. (UPI/Bettmann Archive)

Washington-based public-interest groups together had 3.5 million members.[21]

Common Cause

Common Cause is a national citizens' lobby with a membership of about a quarter of a million people. It has focused its attention on Congress, lobbying for campaign-finance reform, including abolition of PACs, and laws requiring that lobbies disclose their gifts to politicians and the sources of their funds. It has also drafted and supported "sunset" laws providing that government agencies self-destruct after a given period of time if they cannot demonstrate their continued usefulness. It has favored creation of ombudsmen to help make bureaucracy more responsive. And it has supported various congressional reforms such as altering the seniority system. It was founded in 1970 by John Gardner, who had been a foundation executive and secretary of the Department of Health, Education, and Welfare (HEW) under Lyndon Johnson. Not only has it grown in membership but it has

[19]See Jeffrey M. Berry, *Lobbying for the People: The Political Behavior of Public Interest Groups* (Princeton, NJ: Princeton Univ. Press, 1977).

[20]John Guinther, *Moralists and Managers: Public Interest Movements in America* (New York Anchor paperback, 1976), p. xv.

[21]See Jeffrey M. Berry, "Public Interest vs. Party System," *Society* 17 (May–June 1980), pp. 42–48. This figure counts several times those who are members of several groups. On the other hand, it omits those who are members of the thousands of other groups with similar objectives and activities on the state and local levels.

spawned branches in various states that have turned their attention to reforming state government as well.

The Nader Groups

Ralph Nader, then a young lawyer, got his start in the early 1960s when he accused General Motors of making unsafe cars. When GM hired a "private eye" to snoop on his private life, Nader won a court judgment against GM. He used that money to establish what has become a kind of conglomerate of public-interest research, lobbying, and litigating groups. His Public Citizen raises money for these projects. His Center for the Study of Responsive Law produces research on how to make the law and the legal system more responsive to public concerns. Other research on special topics is done by the Health Research Group, the Tax Reform Research Group, and Public Interest Research Groups (PIRGs) in many states and universities. In addition, Congress Watch studies congressional activity on issues of consumer, environmental, and other public-interest concerns. Other subsidiaries come and go with the issues and activities they focus on.

Nader and his colleagues have been very influential on a wide variety of issues, from auto safety to antismoking regulations and from opposition to nuclear power plants as unsafe to support of congressional reform. Although many business officials have resented and opposed his activities, some observers have pointed out that he is far from being the revolutionary troublemaker business people tend to see him as. He seems instead to be devoted to making our existing capitalist economic system and our present political system more responsive to public concerns, so that they will not be undone by their own faults and weaknesses.

Lobbyists in Government

These groups began by examining specific problems and then proposing and lobbying for laws to cope with them. When the Carter administration came to power, it hired as policy makers many of the leaders of these groups. By some counts, at least 50 public-interest activists took important jobs in government under Carter. Once in government, they sought to implement policies they had advocated while outside. With the advent of the Reagan administration, however, these people were replaced with others more sympathetic to the interests of business and industry—who then tried, in general, to roll back or undo many of the things

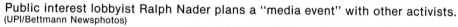

Public interest lobbyist Ralph Nader plans a "media event" with other activists. (UPI/Bettmann Newsphotos)

the Carter appointees had done. Many of the Reagan appointees came from newer lobbying groups created by business, industry, and other groups opposed to the existing public-interest groups.

The fact that so many lobbyists take jobs in government when given the opportunity is hardly surprising, for their goals have been to shape governmental policy. The fact that the government hires so many lobbyists need not surprise us either. After all, each bureau within the executive branch has to lobby within that branch for its budget request and for presidential support for its favorite proposals. Once that is assured, it must lobby Congress to get its budget and programs actually approved. Thus much of the day-to-day work done within government resembles the lobbying done outside government.

Lobbyists and the Public Interest

What interests are all these lobbyists within as well as outside government actually serving? Most will tell you it's "the public interest." And yet, of course, many of them will disagree among themselves about just what that is. How can, or should, we define "the public interest"?

Jeffrey Berry insists on two criteria in determining if a group serves the public interest: First, *the group must seek a "collective good."* An example cited above is clean air, which we all benefit from whether or not we have joined the antipollution groups that struggle to get it. Another example is national defense, which we all get equally whether or not we are in the armed forces or paying the taxes that finance them. The second criterion is that the *achievement of the good must not selectively and materially benefit the group's members or activists.* These criteria would rule out the American Medical Association, whose opposition to national health insurance specifically benefits its member doctors, and the National Rifle Association, whose opposition to gun control specially benefits its gun-using members.[22]

Now that we have learned something about who the interests are, we must examine the specific ways in which they operate.

HOW SPECIAL INTERESTS OPERATE

The Life of the Lobbyist

It should be clear that interest groups vary immensely in membership, in clout, and in lobbying activities, within and outside the government. The most comprehensive study of Washington lobbyists, by Lester Milbrath, found that lobbyists spend most of their time receiving and sending communications—mostly in their own offices. Personal conversations with members of Congress or other governmental officials are important but not very time consuming, Milbrath found. Even less useful, and less frequent, is the stereotypical lobbying activity, entertainment. Much more important, the lobbyists said, is time spent traveling around visiting local groups in order to improve communication with the people and groups who support them and "to stimulate a flow of communications from the grass roots to governmental decision-makers."[23] Thus, we could not describe a typical day in the life of a typical lobbyist.[24] But it is clear that we couldn't imagine a day in American politics without lobbies or lobbyists.

Lobbyists and Congress

No one knows just how many representatives of special interests there now are in Washington. One recent directory suggests about 10,000.

Providing Information

In dealing with Congress, lobbyists use a variety of tactics. First, they *provide information* to legislators and their assistants on how the special interest views the matter in question and often even on what is in question. Senator John F. Kennedy described this role of lobbyists clearly some five years before he became president:

[23]Lester Milbrath, *The Washington Lobbyists* (Chicago: Rand McNally, 1963), p. 121.

[24]For two fascinating accounts of one lobbyist, see "Charlie," a portrait of Charls E. Walker originally published in *The New Yorker* in 1978 and reprinted in *Interest Group Politics*, 1st ed., ed. Cigler and Loomis, as chap. 10; and "Charls Walker: External Revenue Service," in Ralph Nader and William Taylor, *The Big Boys: Power and Position in American Business* (New York: Pantheon, 1986), pp. 244–91.

[22]Berry, *Lobbying for the People*, pp. 6–11.

Lobbyists are in many cases expert technicians and capable of explaining complex and difficult subjects in a clear, understandable fashion. They engage in personal discussions with Members of Congress in which they can explain in detail the reason for positions they advocate. Lobbyists prepare briefs, memorandums, legislative analysis, and draft legislation for use by committees and Members of Congress: they are necessarily masters of their subject and, in fact, they frequently can provide useful statistics and information not otherwise available.[25]

But, as Senator Kennedy added, a legislator must be on guard to see that the information is accurate, if not necessarily balanced and fair.

Kennedy's emphasis on the *authority* of lobbyists as experts in their subject describing their image of reality to politicians highlights the political nature of lobbyists' activity. It also reminds us of how necessary lobbyists are. As the late Senator Lee Metcalf (Democrat of Montana) remarked during a congressional debate on revision of the lobbying law: "We would have to multiply our staffs fourfold or fivefold if it were not for the information that the lobbyists give us . . . upon which we can act."[26] In other words, information is power. And the lobbyists who can provide the most comprehensive and seemingly accurate information are likely to be powerful and effective. There is nothing secret about the basic technique. Charls E. Walker, once a high-level official in the Treasury Department and now a leading lobbyist, describes it succinctly: "We translate legislative proposals into jobs, payrolls, or economic growth for the Congressman's district or the Senator's state. We leave a briefing paper behind and then mail out a follow-up letter a few days later."[27]

Providing Support or Enticements

But the lobbyists' actions in Congress are not all of such a purely informational nature. Another category of action involves *support*. Lobbyists will often *promise support* (in the form of campaign contributions, for example[28]), or they may threaten

to *withdraw support* when necessary. Furthermore, where information and campaign support are inadequate, they may also *offer enticements*—from fancy dinners and tickets to Washington Redskins football games to sexual favors from available call girls.

On occasion, lobbyists may "*go partisan,*" openly supporting an opponent of someone who votes against their interests. This step is unusual. The common practice is to contribute to both candidates in a race, on the theory that whoever wins, you win, because you helped fund his or her campaign.

The limits on campaign contributions, according to current law, were listed in Table P2.3. Lobby contributions to congressional campaigns have recently risen sharply. In 1975, according to Common Cause, they totaled $12,525,586. By the 1984 congressional elections, the figure was up to $112.6 million. And recently, PACs have gotten around legal limits on the campaign contributions they can

(Copyright © 1982 by Herblock in *The Washington Post*)

[25]John F. Kennedy, quoted in Congressional Quarterly, *The Washington Lobby*, 2d ed. (Washington, DC: CQ Press, 1974), p. 6.

[26]Congressional Record, 94th Cong., 2d sess., p. S-9269.

[27]Quoted in "The Hidden Army of Washington Lobbyists," *U.S. News & World Report*, July 25, 1977, p. 30.

[28]See Herbert E. Alexander, *Financing Politics: Money, Elections, and Political Reform*, 2d ed. (Washington, DC: CQ Press, 1980); and Michael J. Malbin, ed., *Parties, Interest Groups, and Campaign Finance Laws* (Washington, DC: American Enterprise Institute, 1980).

make to an individual candidate by running their own advertising campaigns for the candidates they favor. The Supreme Court has held that PACs can spend unlimited funds supporting someone so long as they don't collaborate directly with the candidate's own campaign. Many of these contributions are "targeted" to reach members—usually from both parties—of Senate and House committees that handle bills of special interest to the special-interest group.[29]

In other cases, where the whole body of the Congress will decide issues of concern to a group, conbributions may be directed to most members. For example, in 1982 the Federal Trade Commission (FTC) proposed a new regulation that would have required used-car dealers to disclose to buyers any known defects in the cars they were selling. The car dealers opposed the rule. Their political action committee, the National Automobile Dealers Association PAC (NADA-PAC), contributed more than a million dollars to members of the 1982 Congress. In May 1982 Congress voted to kill the rule. House members who voted to defeat it had received five times more money in contributions from NADA-PAC than those who voted against the used-car dealers. In the Senate those who voted with the dealers had received twice as much as those who did not.[30]

Forming Coalitions

Some cases affect only one or several organized interests, and the group that acts is powerful enough to win on its own. More often, however, many organized interests are involved—on opposite sides of the issue. In such cases, the route to success usually lies in forming a **coalition**. A coalition is a temporary alliance created to facilitate joint action for a specific objective.

Lobbying coalitions have become especially important in the Reagan years, particularly over budgetary issues—and they have often involved strange partnerships. One example is the case of the Clinch River breeder reactor program, which involved a nuclear power plant to be built in Tennessee by the federal government. It was to produce—or "breed"—more fuel than it consumed. Advocates of energy growth and supporters of nuclear power loved the idea. Environmentalists, on the other hand, believed it would do grave damage. Planning took a dozen years, and each year the cost estimates grew—until ultimately many people thought it could never be economical. Still, it had strong support in Congress—especially because the Senate majority leader, Howard Baker, was from Tennessee. Many senators continued voting for it as a favor to him—perhaps expecting that he would then do them favors in return on other issues. But finally, in October 1983 the active environmental lobbies, such as the Sierra Club and the National Resources Defense Council (see Action Unit 18.1), joined forces with the lobbying groups, such as the National Taxpayers Union and the Heritage Foundation, which supported cutbacks in the federal government's economic role and in federal spending. As a result, funds for the breeder reactor were deleted from the budget by a vote of 56 to 40, and the breeder reactor project was dead—after a dozen years. Such coalitions of liberal and conservative interest groups against expensive projects are becoming more common as huge federal deficits persist. But coalitions as such are as old as lobbying itself.[31]

Lobbyists and the Public

Lobbyists also often *"go public,"* engaging in advertising campaigns and other public relations activities for their cause. They do this to develop public support that will be conveyed to officials in Washington by citizens and other interests. Also, such activities may help to control what is often called the public agenda—the list of topics considered appropriate for government action. Interests may attempt to keep something *off* the public agenda—as the American Medical Association has tried to keep government-funded medical care off the public agenda since 1935. Or they may attempt to get something *on* the public agenda by making

[29]For a study of PACs, see Ann B. Matasar, *Corporate PACs and Federal Campaign Financing Laws* (Westport, CT: Quorum, 1986). For summary statistics, see Michael Barone et al., *Almanac of American Politics 1986* (Washington, DC: National Journal, 1985), pp. 1502–15. And see Edward Roeder, *PACs Americana: A Directory of PACs and Their Interests* (Washington, DC: Sunshine Services, 1986) for detailed information on all currently operating PACs.

[30]See the Common Cause pamphlet "People against PACs," 1983, pp. 8–10. For a study of the problem as a whole, see Elizabeth Drew, *Politics and Money: The New Road to Corruption* (New York: Macmillan, 1983).

[31]See Burdett A. Loomis, "Coalitions of Interests: Building Bridges in the Balkanized State," in *Interest Group Politics*, 2d ed., ed. Cigler and Loomis, chap. 14.

it of interest to public opinion—as environmentalists did in the 1960s.

In addition, once an issue is on the public agenda, interests will attempt to build the record or set the context within which the issue is defined and debated. They can do this by testifying publicly before Congress and by becoming recognized as leading authorities on the issue itself, not just on their own special-interest conception or definition of it.[32]

Such "grassroots lobbying" is now being transformed by new technologies. Computers can take census data about the United States and divide the population in terms of thousands of different characteristics. Special interests can then develop or buy and use mailing lists produced from such data to contact and mobilize only those people or groups most likely to agree with them. Well-financed groups can also create their own private closed-circuit television networks to inform and mobilize their members. The Chamber of Commerce already has such a program under way, and other wealthy special-interest groups are sure to follow.[33]

Lobbyists and the Bureaucracy

Lobbyists do not confine their efforts to Congress and to the public, of course. They also "go to the bureaucracy" to influence the development and implementation of programs. Prime examples of this are the ways in which lobbyists combine with bureaucrats and congressional leaders to make decisions in private, outside the ordinary channels. We shall discuss these activities in detail in Chapter 9. Special interests maintain access to government in part by hiring former politicians and bureaucrats as their lobbyists or as their officials, as we have noted in previous chapters, or by getting the government to hire their own officials as policy makers.

Lobbyists and the Courts

The special interests may also "go to court" to seek favorable judicial rulings when they can't get satisfaction elsewhere. One of the clearest instances of this approach occurred when the National Association for the Advancement of Colored People went to court to challenge segregation in public schools. This move was finally successful in the case of *Brown* v. *Board of Education* in 1954, as we shall see in Chapter 12.

Seeking Direct Popular Legislation

Interest groups may sometimes bypass lobbying to achieve direct legislation by the voters. Some states and localities have constitutional provisions for the **initiative.** If a required percentage of the voters signs petitions requesting it, a proposed law is put on the ballot for a vote by the general public. If it passes, it becomes law even though the legislature or city council has refused to pass it. Twenty-three states now have this provision—most of them in the West. Related to the initiative is the **referendum,** whereby action by the legislature or council is put to a popular vote for ratification (approval). The legislature may decide on its own to call for a referendum or may be prompted to do so by citizen petition. If an interest group finds the legislature dominated by hostile interests, it may choose to utilize the initiative—as environmentalists often do, for example, on bills to abolish or tax throwaway bottles and cans. Figure 5.1 shows which states have one or both devices.

Over the years both initiative and referendum have been used in most states and many cities by labor unions, farm groups, education organizations, groups supporting the aged, and religious and civic groups. Business groups have been especially fond of referenda as ways of canceling legislation of which they disapprove. One major appeal of this approach is that there can be no amendment of the proposal. A legislative body can amend a bill to satisfy enough interest groups to get it passed, but the voters must say either yes or no to a referendum, and so it is usually easier to unite opponents of a measure.[34]

---

[32] See Roger W. Cobb and Charles D. Elder, *Participation in American Politics: The Dynamics of Agenda Building* (Boston: Allyn & Bacon, 1972).

[33] See Burdett A. Loomis, "A New Era: Groups and the Grass Roots," in *Interest Group Politics*, 1st ed., ed. Cigler and Loomis, chap. 8. For the history of such efforts, see Kay Lehman Schlozman and John T. Tierney, "More of the Same: Washington Pressure Group Activity in a Decade of Change," *Journal of Politics* 45, no. 2 (May 1983), 351–77.

[34] For a discussion of such "direct legislation," see Joseph F. Zimmerman, *Participatory Democracy: Populism Revived* (New York: Praeger, 1986).

FIGURE 5.1
States with Initiative or Referendum.

Legend:
- Initiative
- Referendum
- Initiative and Referendum

INTEREST GROUPS IN AMERICAN POLITICS

Regulating Interest Groups

Special interests play such a large role in our politics that many believe they should be strictly regulated. But so far such efforts have had limited success. Congress passed the Federal Regulation of Lobbying Act in 1946. But the act was carelessly drafted and hurriedly passed; as a result, it has never been effective in controlling lobbying. It applies only to individuals and groups who are paid for the principal purpose of influencing legislation by direct contact with individuals in Congress. Such groups are required to register with the House and Senate and to file quarterly reports of their own spending. But in fact, many do not register—and those who do rarely file full spending totals. Supreme Court decisions have upheld this limited interpretation of the requirements of the law. All observers agree that the law is inadequate.[35]

After Watergate, a new bill with stricter registration and reporting provisions supported by Common Cause almost passed Congress. It died in the closing hours of the session under attack from business, labor, and Ralph Nader. *National Journal* explained this rare split among the public-interest lobbying groups this way:

> Common Cause is more interested in issues of governmental and political procedures than it is in the substance of policy, while the Nader groups are more concerned with the policy questions. As a result, Common Cause is anxious that an improved lobbying law be adopted, while the Nader organization worries that such a law might limit its influence on policy issues that are important to it.[36]

Others worry that strict regulation may violate the "right to petition for redress of grievances," which is an important part of the First Amendment. Some civil libertarians fear that laws requiring even small groups of citizens advocating a particular policy to register with the government will deter many individuals and groups from even entering the lobbying process.

---

[35]See Congressional Quarterly, *Washington Lobby*, for background.

[36]*National Journal*, July 31, 1976, p. 1076.

The situation now is that some interests are more vested than others in American politics. Some advocates of democracy argue that this is undemocratic because it weights the political process in favor of the status quo. Others, as we have seen, believe that the system allows those who really care enough, or have the most to lose, to express their concerns effectively. In this sense, ours is indeed a politics of special interests. It is doubtful that a large, diversified country's politics could function any other way.

Is this fact of special-interest politics unfortunate? That depends on your views about what function special interests actually play in our politics and your view of what role they should play.

The Basic Function of Interest Groups

The real function of the interest group is to offer its own view or image of reality—of how the world is and how it ought to be—in an effort to convince citizens and policy makers that they should accept it themselves. To encourage them to do so, lobbyists who represent special interests may use information, arguments, threats, promises, favors, or any other resource at their disposal. Ultimately, such groups are making *claims to authority*—authority to interpret the public interest, to express special interests, and to predict the political future of those they seek to influence. Representatives of special interests, then, are politicians just as much as elected officials are.

THE BASIC EFFECTS OF INTEREST GROUPS

There is, however, another consideration. When interest groups are too effective, there is a real danger that government may tend toward paralysis. The framers sought to control the excesses of a dominant or "majority faction" by using a complex disposition of power, as we saw in Chapter 1.[37] Now, however, the United States contains thousands of minority factions, or special-interest groups—perhaps hundreds of which can have real power on issues of great concern to them.

Political parties have tended to unite various factions under a broader "umbrella." Special-interest groups, in contrast, tend to fracture policy making into many separate subject areas, raising the specter that American government may increasingly resemble what Andrew McFarland calls "a confederation of oligarchies"—a loose grouping of small ruling powers. When this happens effective governance becomes more difficult. Making unified national policy across a broad range of economic issues, for example, would upset so many minority factions that a coalition of them would effectively be able to block action. Working in the opposite direction, however, is a trend toward more social movements that involve larger numbers of less powerful people in politics. Examples include the women's movement and the environmental movement. These movements tend to integrate larger numbers of people over a broad range of issues, usually against the efforts and wishes of narrower special interests.[38]

In American politics, these varying interests often clash. Sometimes the clash is between special interests and a broad social movement, as when environmentalists oppose industrial polluters. At other times, it is between different special interests, as when labor opposes business on laws requiring a minimum wage. Occasionally, two social movements may clash, as when the civil-rights and the women's movements differed over whether priority should be given to wage discrimination against blacks or that against women.

Some people argue that these interests diverge, conflict, and compete in ways that countervail each other and generally make it possible for the public interest to emerge through competition and compromise. People with this view are often called *pluralists*. Others believe this is a mirage. These "elitist theorists" point out that the major special interests in our system are vested interests, with special benefits in the status quo that they seek to protect and expand. They get their way more often because they have more money and occupy more positions of authority and power. The public interest is therefore a victim more often than not, according to this view.

---

[37]See *Federalist No. 10*, written by James Madison.

[38]See Andrew S. McFarland, "Public Interest Lobbies Versus Minority Faction," in *Interest Group Politics*, 1st ed., ed. Cigler and Loomis, chap. 14.

PLURALISM VERSUS ELITISM—
THE GREAT DEBATE

No one now disputes that interest groups are important influences on Amerian politics. There is, however, a continuing debate over whether what happens in American politics is primarily determined by a large collection of different groups competing with each other or by a relatively small collection of powerful individuals. The former view is called **pluralism**, the latter, **elitism.**

Pluralists argue that there are many interests—a "plurality" of interests—competing to influence politics. These interests—political, economic, and social—today tend to be organized into groups that try to influence policy. They may do so directly, by lobbying, or indirectly, by campaigning for candidates likely to favor their desires or by influencing opinion, which then influences policy makers. According to pluralist theorists, various groups compete to influence policy on a given issue. For example, business and labor compete on economic issues. Further, different groups are effective on different issues, so that no one interest group actually runs or dominates the government. In our example, business may dominate on tax policy, but labor dominates on minimum-wage laws. Politics, in other words, is a continuing competition among a number of special interests, no one of which is able to dominate by itself. The main reason for this failure of any one group to dominate, according to pluralists, is that government is itself fragmented because of separation of powers, division of powers, and checks and balances. These safeguards make bargaining and compromise essential, and no group can have its way completely. In our example, members of Congress sympathetic to labor and those who are probusiness compromise somewhat on the issue less important to them.[39]

But is the pluralist image an accurate picture of how American politics really works? Many experts doubt it.[40] Foremost among the doubters are the elite theorists. They argue that the real power in America is held and shared by a small group of people who either hold important political positions or control politics by controlling economic resources. According to this view, these elites may compete with each other for power, but most people—and most organizations—never have a real chance at influence. Why? "In theory, whenever needs or wants are felt strongly enough new groups will form to make their influence felt," wrote former senator and 1972 Democratic presidential nominee George McGovern.

> But it is not that easy. Incumbency with interest groups, as with officeholders, is a powerful weapon. If some Americans are born joiners and organizers, others are not. If some groups are wise to the ways of Washington, others are not. If some groups communicate internally, others are isolated and cannot. And the consequence is . . . the public opinion surveys telling us that most Americans feel that government represents someone other than them.[41]

But whom does government represent, if not "the people"? Ruling-elite theorists argue that it is the most powerful interests that get their way. Who are they? On this point, elite theorists disagree among themselves. The late sociologist C. Wright Mills wrote of a "power elite" consisting of the corporate rich, political insiders, and military leaders, each at the top of their sector of society, and each sharing power with the others.[42]

Others, however, point out that there are thousands of such leaders, many of whom do not know each other and do not consult with each other on politics and policy. Furthermore, many of them disagree among themselves on many matters. This suggests that although there is indeed an elite, it is not a *ruling* elite as such. On the other hand, the *absence* of a ruling elite does not necessarily imply the *presence* of a truly democratic system in which the public interest is reflected in policy made by

---

[39]The classic statement of the pluralist theory is Robert A. Dahl, *Who Governs? Democracy and Power in an American City* (New Haven, CT: Yale Univ. Press, 1961). See also his "Critique of the Ruling Elite Model," *American Political Science Review* 52, no. 2 (June 1958), 463–69. For his current view, see *Dilemmas of Pluralist Democracy: Autonomy vs. Control* (New Haven, CT: Yale Univ. Press, 1982).

[40]See Andrew McFarland, *Power and Leadership in Pluralist Systems* (Stanford, CA: Stanford Univ. Press. 1969), chap. 2.

[41]George McGovern, "Pluralist Structures or Interest Groups?" *Society* 14 (January–February, 1977), 13–15.

[42]Wright Mills, *The Power Elite* (New York: Oxford Univ. Pres, 1956). For a survey of subsequent debates, see the introduction to *Power Structure Research*, ed. G. William Domhoff (Beverly Hills, CA: Sage, 1980).

political representatives of the people as a whole. No one argues that this description accurately depicts American politics today—or at any time in our history.

What then can we say about the nature of our political system in terms of interests, groups, and elites? Perhaps G. David Gerson put it best in asserting that "American politics are neither the marketplace of group theory nor the conspiracy of simple elite theorists. If America is elitist, it is elitist in a pluralistic way, or, if pluralist, then pluralist in a way that benefits an elite."[43] Gerson argues that the system is *elitist* with respect to *ends*. Elites set or limit the agenda of our politics because they dominate our institutions and most of our interest groups.

Nonetheless, the system is *pluralist* with respect to *means*. Groups struggle with one another over how our government, our society, and we citizens should reach the ends. Thomas Dye wrote:

> The federal law-making process involves bargaining, competition, persuasion, and compromise, as generally set forth in "pluralist" political theory. But this interaction occurs *after* the agenda for policy making has been established and the major directions of policy changes have already been determined.[44]

This may be true most of the time. Still, we shall see time and again in coming chapters that decisions about the agenda are influenced by special interests both inside and outside government. One such influence is public opinion. It is to an examination of this that we now turn.

SUMMARY

Individuals have *private interests*. A group of individuals with the same private interest is called a *special interest*. If that group benefits from the status quo and seeks to preserve it, we call it a *vested interest*. Groups in politics generally seek to achieve their special interests, but many claim that this is in *the public interest*. Both political actors and experts usually disagree over just what the public interest really is.

People join groups or give them funds for various reasons. They also may decide for rational reasons not to join at all, if the group seems likely to succeed without their assistance and they will benefit from the group's success because the group seeks a *collective good*. Only three-quarters of Americans belong to any organization, and less than half belong to more than one.

More politically active groups now have offices in Washington run by professional staffs. Among the most important groups are the Washington lawyers; trade and professional organizations; labor lobbies; big-business lobbies; small-business lobbies; corporation lobbies; religious lobbies; and public-interest lobbies such as Common Cause, Ralph Nader's Public Citizen, and similar groups with more rightwing orientations.

Lobbyists in Washington converse with government officials, communicate with their member groups, and occasionally entertain. They deal with Congress (to whose members they contribute funds) and the bureaucracy and occasionally appeal issues to the courts. They also increasingly mobilize public opinion through "grassroots lobbying" using new communications technology. They may also use *initiative* and *referendum* where these are available.

Interest groups are regulated—quite inadequately—by laws. Members of Congress usually appreciate lobbyists as a source of information, with the latter presenting their image of reality in political terms.

While effects of interest groups on our politics are still a matter of debate, it is clear that they tend to fragment decision making. Pluralist theorists believe that the groups tend to compete effectively and so balance each other out, creating compromise. Elite theorists believe that leaders of important groups dominate and shape political outcomes. Expert observers disagree as to the dominance of powerful groups but agree that their role tends to limit the direct effect of public opinion in politics.

---

[43]G. David Gerson, *Group Theories of Politics* (Beverly Hills, CA: Sage, 1978), p. 207.

[44]Thomas R. Dye, *Who's Running America?* 2d ed. (Englewood Cliffs, NJ: Prentice-Hall, 1979), p. 245.

Suggestions for Further Reading and Study

The footnotes to this chapter will lead you to some interesting and helpful case studies of lobbies in action. For more general studies see V. O. Key, *Politics, Parties, and Pressure Groups*, 5th ed. (New York: Crowell, 1964); E. E. Schattschneider, *The Semi-Sovereign People* (New York: Holt, Rinehart & Winston, 1960); and David B. Truman, *The Governmental Process*, 2d ed. (New York: Knopf, 1971)—all classics. For a different theory of interest groups, see Mancur Olson, Jr., *The Logic of Collective Action: Public Goods and the Theory of Groups*, rev. ed. (Cambridge, MA: Harvard Univ. Press, 1971), which uses economic analysis of individual self-interest and analyzes the size of coalitions.

Among more recent surveys are Jeffrey M. Berry, *The Interest Group Society* (Boston: Little, Brown, 1984); and Kay Lehman Schlozman and John T. Tierney, *Organized Interests and American Democracy* (New York: Harper & Row, 1986). And for a survey emphasizing public policy effects, see Carol S. Greenwald, *Group Power: Lobbying and Public Policy* (New York: Praeger, 1977).

Finally, for futher information on how interest groups operate, see Lester Milbrath, *The Washington Lobbyists* (Chicago: Rand McNally, 1963); James Deakin, *The Lobbyists* (Washington, DC: Public Affairs Press, 1966), which is anecdotal; Lewis A. Dexter, *How Organizations Are Represented in Washington* (Indianapolis:

Bobbs-Merrill, 1969), which is practical; and Bobby Baker, *Wheeling and Dealing: Confessions of a Capitol Hill Operator* (New York: Norton, 1978), which is autobiographical.

To pursue the longstanding debate between elitist and pluralist theorists beyond the sources cited in the footnotes of this chapter, you might consult the following: Peter Bachrach, *The Theory of Democratic Elitism: A Critique* (Boston: Little, Brown, 1967); Robert Dahl, *Pluralist Democracy in the United States: Conflict and Consensus* (Chicago: Rand McNally, 1967); and Thomas Dye and Harmon Ziegler, *The Irony of Democracy*, 7th ed. (Belmont, CA: Wadsworth, 1986). Among academic analysts there has been developing what might be termed a postpluralist analysis, often applied in a comparative perspective to various democracies. Among the major contributions to it thus far are these: Daniel Bell, *The Coming of Post-Industrial Society* (New York: Basic Books, 1973); Anthony Giddens, *The Class Structure of the Advanced Societies* (New York: Harper & Row, 1973); Arend Lijphart, *Democracy in Plural Societies: A Comparative Exploration* (New Haven, CT: Yale Univ. Press, 1977), which analyzes "consociational democracy"; and Reginald J. Harrison, *Pluralism and Corporatism: The Political Evolution of Modern Democracies* (London: Allen & Unwin, 1980).

6

PUBLIC OPINION

You have opinions about lots of things, just as everyone else does. Most of those opinions have nothing to do with politics. Some of them may concern politics but may be views you wouldn't express to politicians or pollsters. All of these we call private opinions. But some of your opinions that concern political questions may be ones that you are happy to tell anyone—politician or pollster—about. Those are your part of what we call public opinion. Of course, just because you and the rest of us have such opinions doesn't mean that this public opinion will matter in politics. In this chapter we'll find out how we get such opinions, how they get "mobilized" so that political actors become aware of them, and how—if at all—they influence what happens in politics. ■

THE CASE OF THE NUCLEAR FREEZE MOVEMENT

When Ronald Reagan took office in 1981, he committed the United States to a massive increase in the military budget, much of it to go to new nuclear weapons systems. Opinion polls showed that a majority of Americans believed that the Soviet Union was ahead in the "arms race" at that time and that the United States should increase defense spending. But as the Reagan program was implemented, more and more people became worried that the danger of nuclear war was increasing.

In 1979 a young scientist in Boston named Randall Forsberg decided to launch a campaign in support of what she termed a nuclear freeze. Her proposal called on both sides—the United States and the Soviet Union—to "freeze" the levels of nuclear weapons they had: Neither side could thereby add more of the types they had, nor could either side test, produce, or install new types. This freeze was to be negotiated by the two superpowers.

With others of like mind, she organized what quickly became the National Nuclear Weapons Freeze Campaign. Working at the grassroots level, advocates sought to mobilize public opinion behind the idea of a freeze. They began by collecting signatures on petitions. To do so, they enlisted the help of thousands of existing local and national or-

ganizations. This network then sought three different objectives. The first was to put the question of a freeze on the ballots of local and state elections, to let voters express their views. At the same time, efforts were made to lobby local and state

Nuclear freeze rallies in New York City (1982) and Washington, DC (1985). (Below, Susan Meiselas/Magnum Photos; right, John Ficara/Woodfin Camp & Associates)

governments to pass resolutions endorsing a freeze. Third, senators and representatives in Washington were lobbied to vote for a resolution calling for a freeze. The hope was that this three-pronged effort would pressure the administration into trying to negotiate a nuclear freeze with the Soviet Union.

Public opinion polls consistently showed about three-quarters of the people in favor of the idea of a freeze. In two years profreeze resolutions were passed by over 400 New England town meetings, by several hundred city councils across the nation, and by 7 state legislatures. In the 1982 elections, in places where the question was on the ballot, the voters of 9 out of 10 states and the District of Columbia and those of 35 out of 38 cities passed freeze resolutions. By this time, one in every four American voters had had the opportunity to vote on the question, and large majorities had voted yes almost everywhere.

Finally, in 1983 Congress began to respond to public opinion. In May the House of Representatives voted for a nuclear freeze by 278 to 149, after having defeated it by two votes the previous August. Public pressure continued to mount. The Reagan administration strongly and publicly opposed the freeze proposal because it would prevent the buildup Reagan was undertaking. Then, after much lobbying by both sides, the Senate rejected the proposal in October 1983 by a vote of 58 to 40.

By this time four of every five Americans favored the proposal. It had been endorsed by 11 state legislatures, 56 county councils, 320 city councils, and hundreds of national organizations. Public opinion was clear. But it was not influential enough in the Senate, let alone in the Executive Office. So the members of the National Nuclear Weapons Freeze Campaign decided to create a new program, Freeze Voter '84, to support political candidates in the 1984 elections who favored the freeze and oppose those who opposed it. Their principle was, if you can't change the minds of your representatives, change your representatives. Their efforts did help some profreeze candidates win, but the nuclear freeze as an issue receded once the Reagan administration took a more active role in trying to negotiate arms control with the Soviet Union.

The story of the nuclear freeze movement reveals important aspects of the role of public opinion in the United States. Public opinion grows out of basic attitudes, such as concern for military security and fear of nuclear war. It can be organized—and sometimes created or strengthened—by movements that recognize these concerns and enable people to express their views with votes, contributions of money and time, or efforts to lobby the government. It can influence the decisions of politicians and sometimes even end or begin political careers. But even when it is successful at these activities, it may not be able to shape national policy. In this chapter we shall see why.

THE NATURE OF PUBLIC OPINION

Each of us has what could be called a small piece of public opinion—the collection of views we have on public questions, such as how well presidents are doing their job, whether our political system is really democratic, whether or not marijuana should be legalized, and indeed anything else that concerns government or politics. More specifically, public opinion is generally taken to include preferences about candidates, policies, and party, and political knowledge and ideology (or set of general beliefs and values with which to interpret things). To be public opinion rather than private opinion, in the way these terms are generally used, a view must concern a public question and must be held by more than one person. These public views are sometimes studied by politicians looking for guidance on how they should act or as indications of the risks they run if they act unpopularly. Public opinion is also studied by observers such as pollsters, who sometimes report to politicians, business leaders, and other interested groups on what the public believes and wants. At other times, various polling organizations report their findings to the people themselves so that the people can determine what they as a whole are thinking.

People who study public opinion, whether they are politicians or political scientists, usually break the population down into various categories. By doing so, they can study and compare the opinions held by the elites (business executives, for example, or professors or members of Congress) and those held by the masses or by segments of them (workers, for example, or the poor or the young). In this way they can talk about the opinions of various "special publics" as well as those of the general public. And they can act, if they are politicians, in ways designed to affect the views of a certain segment.

As a result of studies of what people actually believe, experts have come to question whether there really is any such group as "the public." Studies show that it is very difficult to find any topic on which everyone has an opinion of any sort, let alone the same opinion. Nonetheless, politicians still talk about what "the public" wants, what public opinion on a given question is, and what "the people" will or won't stand for. And so, particularly in a democracy, it is important to know not just what public opinion is but how it is shaped, how it is uncovered and measured, and what role it plays in politics. These are the major questions we will examine in this chapter.

Where do we get our opinions or beliefs? The easy answer is that we get them from our experience in the world. We experience our environment, which generally consists first of family, then of friends, then of schools, then of a work situation, and—from the early years of childhood—the media. All of these aspects of our lives act or operate to shape our views of things in certain geographical locations and circumstances. Among other factors that may influence us are religion and various groups of people. We have seen, in our discussion of voting in Chapter 3, some of the ways in which these factors matter. In terms of our own lives, the first influential factor is socialization. So

let's look at how it shapes and reshapes our political attitudes and thereby tends to determine our public opinions.

GETTING ATTITUDES: SOCIALIZATION

The Nature of Socialization

We often hear that a human being is by nature a social animal. When a child is born, the animal part seems dominant. The child has bodily needs for food and affection and demonstrates them immediately. The social part develops as the child gets a sense of other people and of his or her relations with and feelings toward them. Social scientists refer to this process of learning as **socialization**.

During this process, children learn ways of relating to other people. They may learn to be friendly or aggressive, for example. They may learn to be trusting or suspicious. They learn to obey authority—at least under certain conditions. They learn how best to get their own way when that is important to them and how to help and hurt, love and hate both other children and adults. When they have learned these sorts of things, we say they have been socialized. The attitudes and behaviors

School children recite the pledge of allegiance—an element in their political socialization. (Charles Gupton/Uniphoto)

they have learned may be either good or bad for society, in our judgment.

Children, then, begin to learn about politics as a part of this socialization process. They seem to learn attitudes toward our leaders as well as attitudes toward the country. And they also begin to learn to "play politics"—to campaign for a leadership role, as we would say of an adult, or to lead other people. Learning these things helps prepare children to participate in politics later on. But *just what they learn* may be very important in determining whether they become obedient citizens who fulfill their responsibilities (voting, obeying the law) regularly or whether they become discontented dropouts or even revolutionaries.

To find out how important childhood experiences are in later political behavior, we study **political socialization**—the process by which we learn about politics and by which we then teach our friends, children, and students about politics. We try to determine what factors are most important in shaping the political opinions and behavior of adults. How important is the family? Schools and teachers? Peer groups (friends and others of the same age or group)? What roles do government itself and the mass media play? And how does this political socialization happen?

Unfortunately, studies are still at an early stage, and there is little certainty about how to answer these questions.[1] Perhaps the basic problem is that we still can't answer with certainty the basic question of how socialization happens.

Theories of Socialization

The first and most obvious explanation is that we learn about politics bit by bit, fact by fact, belief by belief. These bits accumulate into the image of political reality that we hold when we act politically. There are two major problems with this account. First, it doesn't tell us why we learn some of the political facts we come upon but not others. Nor does it tell us how we come to have feelings and make judgments about various political figures such as the president. Thus, this approach, which is sometimes called the *accumulation* explanation, doesn't really explain what we want to understand. Experts have therefore turned to various theories to try to explain why people develop the attitudes they do. No single theory seems adequate, but there are three that seem to help.

Interpersonal Transfer

When they are young, children tend to learn certain attitudes toward authority from their parents. As they grow up, however, in the words of one expert, their experiences often lead them "to demote their parents in their scale of values and to look for other heroes and ideal figures farther from home."[2] What they do then is to displace important feelings to people who are admired in the world outside the family, such as the president.

Identification

According to social learning theory, as it is called, a child learns rules of behavior by imitating, or "identifying with," a model. Usually, the model is a parent, but it can be anyone the child admires, such as a teacher. Most often the child learns the attitude because it is rewarded by praise or appreciation from the model.

Cognitive Development

The interpersonal transfer and identification theories seem to assume that anyone can learn anything anytime, so long as the conditions are right. But many experts on the ways children learn now believe that there are limits to what one can learn at a given stage. The third view is a theory of the way our thought capabilities develop. It holds that what you can learn depends on how much you already know plus how well developed your capacity to think abstractly is. The more you know about politics, the better you can learn about the differences in candidates' positions, for example. And the better you are at abstract thinking, the more you can learn about the differences in political ideologies such as liberalism and conservatism, which are quite abstract.[3]

[1]For a summary of research findings, see Stanley A. Renshon, ed., *Handbook of Political Socialization* (New York: Free Press, 1977).

[2]Martha Wolfenstein, "Death of a Parent and Death of a President: Children's Reactions to Two Kinds of Loss," in *Children and the Death of a President*, ed. Martha Wolfenstein and Gilbert Kliman (Magnolia, MA: Peter Smith Publisher, 1971), p. 75.

[3]These theories are summarized by two experts on political socialization, Robert D. Hess and Judith V. Torney, *The Development of Political Attitudes in Children* (Chicago: Aldine, 1967). For a comprehensive survey, see Richard E. Dawson, Kenneth Prewitt, and Karen S. Dawson, *Political Socialization*, 2d ed. (Boston: Little, Brown, 1977). For a helpful explanation see Bruce A. Campbell, *The American Electorate: Attitudes and Action* (New York: Holt, Rinehart & Winston, 1979), chap. 4.

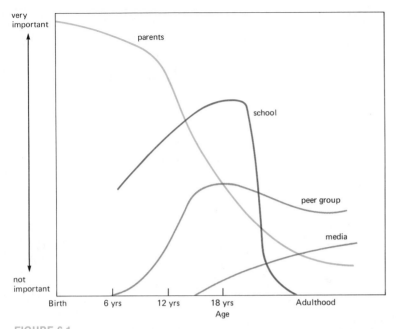

FIGURE 6.1

The Importance of Various Socialization Influences at Each Stage in Life.

Source: Adapted from *The American Electorate* by Bruce A. Campbell. Copyright © 1979 by Holt, Rinehart and Winston. Reprinted by permission of Holt, Rinehart and Winston, CBS College Publishing.

Each of these theories seems helpful in examining and explaining a part of the political socialization we undergo. Studies have found that children's initial attachment is to their political community or nation. The child's first emotional reaction to the system is favorable, and his or her attitude toward its leader tends to be trusting. Between the ages of 12 and 15, a young person's image of political reality usually becomes deeper, clearer, and more precise. He or she tends to connect issues with political parties, to think of the nation as more than the president, and to assess politics and the government more realistically.[4]

Agents of Socialization

We might then assume that the major authority figures (parents and teachers) and institutions (family, school, and the mass media) in the lives of children are important influences. But there is reason to believe that the wider social and political environment—the government, social groups such as labor unions and private organizations, and even the general atmosphere in a given period—may also be quite important. Figure 6.1 shows the relative importance of each major influence at each stage in life. The general notion of what forms of political participation are possible or of what a citizen's political obligation is may be influential, even though these notions are not taught by parents and schools. Also, parents may be less influential than we might suppose. In these times of rapid change, they may themselves be "going through changes" in the stages of their lives at the very time they are supposed to be setting clear authoritative examples for their children. These factors may help explain why children do not simply turn out to believe the things their parents do—or the things the schools teach—about politics.[5]

We are not born with our opinions. Nor do we think them up from scratch—otherwise there

---

[4]For a summary, see Judith V. Torney, A. N. Oppenheim, and Russell F. Farnen, *Civic Education in Ten Countries* (New York: Wiley, 1975), esp. pp. 24–32.

[5]See Neal E. Cutler, "Toward a Generational Conception of Political Socialization," in *New Directions in Political Socialization*, ed. David C. Schwartz and Sandra Kenyon Schwartz (New York: Free Press, 1975).

TABLE 6.1

American Support for the Values of the Free Society

	MEAN SUPPORT FOR VALUES			
Value	1935–1945	1946–1955	1956–1970	1971–1976
1. National unity	—	94%	88%	87%
2. Community trust	66%	66	77	67[a]
3. National anthem symbol	65	—	—	—
4. Popular rule and elections	—	86	79	91[a]
5. Legislative predominance	71	62	78	80
6. Federalism	65	—	65	72
7. Decentralized parties	62	69	73	56
8. The home	68	—	—	80
9. Liberty	72	72	68	81[b]
10. Political equality	98	—	85	—
11. Property	60	66	66	66[b]
12. Achievement	74	—	86	73[a]
13. Belief in God	96	95	98	94[c]
14. Religion	70	72	73	71[a]
15. Altruism	—	—	73	58[b]
Mean support for political culture by era	74	76	78	75

[a]Survey Research Center–Center for Political Studies (SRC) *1982 Election Study* from Inter-University Consortium for Political Research (ICPR); *Gallup Opinion Index* (December 1973), p. 12; *Confidence and Concern: Citizens View American Government* (Washington, DC: Senate Subcommittee on Intergovernmental Relations,, 1973), p. 66; *Gallup Opinion Index* (February 1975), p. 15; Institute of Life Insurance Poll in *Current Opinion* (June 1974), p. 64.

[b]Harris Poll in *Current Opinion* (October 1973), p. 102.

[c]AIPO (Gallup) Poll in *Current Opinion* (August 1976), p. 85.

Source: Donald J. Devine, *The Political Culture of the United States* (Boston: Little, Brown, 1972), pp. 92, 99. For 1971–1976: *Current Opinion* (May 1974), 50.

would be some 242 million images of political reality held by the American people. Our knowledge and opinions do not simply come from our parents, our schools, or other early influences. Our adult experiences with peers and at work are also important, because socialization is a continuing process. But what makes us susceptible to these various influences? And why are we more susceptible to some influences than to others? One way of answering these questions is to look at what experts call our political culture.

POLITICAL CULTURE IN AMERICA

The National Political Culture

As a result of our socialization, each of us develops a set of attitudes toward, and beliefs about, politics, our leaders, and our institutions. Donald Devine has examined opinion poll data to see whether there are beliefs held in common by most Americans. He refers to these beliefs as being the "American political culture"—the values held by most citizens that influence their political and social attitudes and behavior.[6] Devine found a group of fifteen key values in the American political culture.[7] They include *liberty, equality,* and *property*—the three central values in the beliefs of the British philosopher John Locke, who influenced Jefferson, Madison, and other founders. Two other values Devine found are *belief in God* and *support for religion.* There was also strong support for *altruistic (self-sacrificial) community service.* An *emphasis on achievement* was a seventh widely held value. In addition, there were four qualities of politics supported in surveys: *popular rule* including elections; *predominance of the legislative branch; a federal structure of government*—national, state, and local; and *decentralized political parties* responsive to local needs and desires. The average rate of support for these values and for several others in the various polls Devine examined in each of four periods is given in Table 6.1.

---

[6]The concept was developed by Gabriel Almond and employed by Almond and Sidney Verba in their influential book *The Civic Culture* (Boston: Little, Brown, 1963), where it is defined as "attitudes toward the political system and its various parts, and attitudes toward the role of the self in the system."

[7]Donald Devine, *Political Culture of the United States* (Boston: Little, Brown, 1972); and *Does Freedom Work? Liberty and Justice in America* (Ottawa, IL: Caroline House Books/Green Hill, 1978).

Political Subcultures

Studies find strong differences in the attitudes and political knowledge of different parts of the population. This argues for further studies that break the political culture down into what social scientists call *subcultures*, or parts of the culture. In earlier chapters, we indicated that geographical region, religion, nationality or ethnic groupings, social class, and rural-versus-urban location can affect what people believe and how they vote. We cannot examine all these subcultures again here, but several studies will indicate what we may find.[8]

Throughout American history, the North-South sectional or regional conflict has been dominant. But the South has changed in recent decades.

One factor contributing to changes in the South has been the large number of northerners moving to the Sunbelt—as we saw in Chapter 2. Distinctions between North and South are very general and may conceal more than they reveal about a particular matter. Some experts, therefore, have sought to uncover regional differences that are more precise.[9]

But it is worth remembering, as Norman Ornstein points out, that

> America's culture and its economic sectors have become increasingly homogeneous. One can drive down a street in Montgomery, Alabama or Athens, Georgia, and see the same record stores, clothing shops, and restaurants as in Indianapolis, Indiana or Ann Arbor, Michigan. . . . Television programming, cable channels, movies, music—all are national now, with few regional distinctions, fads, or trends.[10]

How Political Culture Influences Public Opinion

Whatever impact political culture has on public opinion is somewhat indirect. One observer, Walter A. Rosenbaum, has suggested that political culture may influence opinion in three basic ways: defining the context, screening information, and shaping expectations.[11]

1. *Defining the context*—First, political culture may define the general context within which opinions are developed and expressed. It does this by teaching a person how to form his or her political opinions, how to express them, and to which offices or institutions to address them. Our political culture emphasizes the importance of the presidency, for example. This encourages citizens to look to the president for guidance in forming their views and to express these views to the president when they seem to be desired or needed.

2. *Screening information*—Second, the political culture helps the citizen screen political information so that he or she need only pay attention to what is real and meaningful. What is believable is usually determined for most citizens by leaders and other members of the political elite whose roles are given importance by the political culture—from the president to the anchors on a TV network news program.

3. *Shaping expectations*—Third, the political culture shapes expectations about government "inputs" (demands on government from people and interests) and "outputs" (policies and actions adopted by government). It does this by defining what is an appropriate matter for government to act upon and what is not. We now believe, for example, that governments should create and run public schools—where once we did not. On the other hand, we do not believe the government should dictate what types of art and music are "American" and what are "un-American"—although we seem somewhat undecided about the question of pornography. All these views are shaped by values that are part of our dominant political culture.

GETTING OPINIONS: POLITICS, EXPERIENCE, AND AUTHORITY

How Politics Influences Opinions

It is clear that our politics influences our political culture. As long as things are going well, we tend to accept the values underlying our system (our po-

---

[8]Alan D. Monroe, *Public Opinion in America* (New York: Dodd, Mead, 1975), chap. 6.

[9]For one such attempt, see Daniel Elazar's study of "cultural streams" in *Cities of the Prairie: The Metropolitan Frontier and American Politics* (New York: Basic Books, 1970). The most interesting recent effort is by Joel Garreau of the *Washington Post*. He argues that North America is best understood as a collection of nine nations that cut across not only state but also national boundaries. The state of Texas, for example, according to his analysis, is really divided into—or is being fought over by—three such nations: "Mexamerica," which includes Mexico and much of the Southwest; "The Breadbasket," which is the Midwest region where wheat and other grains are grown; and "Dixie," the old Deep South. See Joel Garreau, *The Nine Nations of North America* (Boston: Houghton Mifflin, 1981). For more specific studies, see the special Spring 1980 issue of *Publius*, entitled "The Study of American Political Culture and Its Subcultures."

[10]Norman Ornstein, "What Political Dreams Are Made Of," *Public Opinion*, September–October 1986, p. 14.

[11]Walter A. Rosenbaum, *Political Culture* (New York: Praeger, 1975), pp. 121–28.

litical culture) without very much questioning. On the other hand, when we are disappointed and disillusioned by our politics, our political culture may undergo changes.

But politics influences our opinions more directly as well. When we discussed political participation in Chapter 3, we described the role of the government as a political participant that often actively shapes people's political thoughts. In Chapter 7, when we discuss the mass media, we shall cite instances of government efforts to manipulate public opinion by using and abusing the media.

We tend to take for granted many of the ways in which politics influences opinions. Some of them simply fall under the category of "leadership"—opinion leadership by those better informed than we are. But many of them are not necessarily what we would expect to find in a democracy, according to democratic theorists.

The opportunity to exert such political influence on our opinions can be traced to the fact that we often experience political figures as authorities. None of us is likely to know enough about politics—or about a controversial political question such as taxes or defense—to make up our own mind without help. After all, we live in a very complex world.

How Authority Influences Opinions

In a complex world, everyone depends on experts for decisions and opinions about many difficult questions in which the experts specialize. For people who take the views of these experts seriously, the experts have authority. Authority, as we have noted earlier, is a recognized or believed capacity to describe something accurately, to reach a judgment about something that is sensible or compelling, or to give good reasons for one's views if asked. Because people grant such authority to other people, or believe that those experts have earned such authority, experts play a major role in shaping public opinion.

Each of us has a unique set of *genes* and a unique *biography* of life experiences as well as a different *perspective* on the world. We might therefore expect to hear 242 million private, individual opinions on each and every topic. The thing that prevents this from happening is the fact that we all grant authority to others to describe, interpret, and explain large areas of reality to us and for us. Public opinion is shaped by teachers who teach about politics, by authors who write about politics, and also by movie stars and sports heroes who endorse candidates—as well as by politicians themselves, as we noted in Perspective 2.

Indeed, as we have already seen, one way of understanding what happens in politics is to think of politics as *disputes over claims to the authority to describe, interpret, explain, or influence the nature of reality.* Because people see reality differently they are constantly disagreeing about what reality is as well as about what should be done. In other words, people are always disputing about the nature of reality. Consequently, and because real agreement is so hard to achieve on important questions, people must select individuals to decide and act for them. This is the function politics plays in a democracy: It provides opportunities for people to select authorities to resolve their differences by reinterpreting reality or influencing reality for them. Thought of in this way, the essence of everyday life is dispute over various aspects of the nature of reality. The *essence of politics*, however, in these terms, is *dispute over claims to authority* to interpret and influence reality. In our politics, as we saw in Perspective 2, candidates dispute before the voters about which one deserves the authority to act for the people by running the government. As the basis for his or her claim, a candidate may cite or emphasize personal character, experience, education, party membership, physical appearance, or almost any other quality. If the people prefer one candidate's claims to authority to those of a rival, they designate him or her as their authority.

The same sort of politics, as we already know, occurs in the government as well. Members of Congress dispute with each other for the votes of their fellow legislators in the same way, and the president may dispute with the Congress or the bureaucracy over who should have the authority to interpret and change reality. And so on, throughout the government.[12]

Thinking of politics in this way—as dispute over claims to the authority to describe, interpret, ex-

---

[12]And, indeed, throughout the rest of life as well. This general definition of politics enables us to see and better understand the politics in, for example, relations between a parent and children, where politics may arise over the question of what rules children should obey or whether a child should go to college, and if so, to which one. Politics also arises between a teacher and students, or between two students disagreeing over a point, or between books that dispute each other's arguments.

plain, and influence the nature of reality—can be especially helpful in studying the role of public opinion in politics; for public opinion gets shaped by authorities who define reality for others, whether or not those who are the shaping authorities are politicians. In authoritarian or dictatorial systems, authority comes only from the top down, from the leader to the people. In democracies, some authority goes from the bottom up, from the people to the leader, as in elections, lobbying, and other expressions of public opinion that are strongest in a functioning democracy.

How Experience Influences Opinions

Analysis of the impact of authority may suggest that one's actual experience isn't really very important in shaping one's views. To see whether that is true, experts look at the same factors that are thought to have an effect on voting behavior, such as socioeconomic status (SES), race, and age. They find that these factors do not usually influence opinions *directly*. They do, however, help determine the kinds of experiences a person has and the way a person interprets those experiences. These experiences and interpretations then influence opinions.[13]

THE OPINIONS WE HOLD

When studying politics, we usually use the term *opinion* to refer to someone's belief about something, whether or not it is accurate. Research shows that most Americans are not very well informed about politics, nor are they very attentive to what is happening in politics.

The Extent of Citizen Ignorance

Polls show conclusively that many Americans are quite ignorant of important facts about our political system. For example, during the bicentennial celebration a Gallup Poll found that 28 percent could not identify the important event that occurred in this country in 1776.[14]

If we hope that younger Americans, who are

getting more education and have greater access to the media, will do better, we seem likely to be disappointed. A recent Gallup Poll of 17- and 18-year-olds found that one-quarter did not know where the Declaration of Independence was signed, 16 percent didn't know when the United States declared its independence, only 11 percent could name their state's two U.S. senators, and only 4 percent could identify the three presidents who preceded Gerald Ford.[15] These figures must certainly trouble both those who believe that public opinion is important in American politics and those who believe that it should be. We do not have fully comparable results testing the American people as a whole, but Table 6.2 summarizes some results from national polls over the years.

Perhaps the closest equivalent surveys conducted rather regularly are those by Gallup and other pollsters asking whether citizens know the name of their member of Congress. The results have been rather consistent over time. For example, in 1966 some 46 percent said they did while in 1970 the figure was 53 percent. In 1973 it dropped to 46 percent. But even more interesting is the *distribution* of that knowledge among different groups in the population. Surveys find that males are more likely to know than females, whites are more likely to know than blacks, and those with higher levels of education, income, and occupation are more likely to know than others.[16] This ignorance tends to be even greater in the area of foreign affairs.

The Attentiveness of Citizens

Ignorance varies tremendously from one person to the next. For this reason, experts who study public opinion in more detail often begin by distinguishing between the *elites* (those people who dominate major areas such as politics, business, labor, and the professions) and the *masses* (everyone else). For most purposes, this distinction is still too general, and so scholars usually follow Gabriel Almond in making two further distinctions: dividing the "elites" category into "leaders" and "elites," and dividing the "masses" category into the "attentive public" and the "general public." A recent survey

---

[13]Scholars often distinguish here between interpersonal factors such as SES, race, and age and intrapersonal factors such as perceptions and interpretations. Each category may be important. See, for example, Campbell, *The American Electorate*, chaps. 8, 9.

[14]Gallup Poll reported in the *New York Times*, November 30, 1975.

[15]The nationwide poll was conducted in 1979 for the National Municipal League.

[16]For further results and analysis, see Norval Glenn, "The Distribution of Political Knowledge in the U.S.," in *Political Attitudes and Public Opinion*, ed. Dan Nimmo and Charles Bonjean (New York: McKay, 1972), pp. 272–83.

TABLE 6.2
The Level of Political Information among the Adult Public

		YEAR	SOURCE
94%	Know the capital city of United States	1945	AIPO
94%	Know the president's term is four years	1951	AIPO
93%	Recognize photograph of the current president	1948	AIPO
89%	Can name governor of their home state	1973	Harris
80%	Know meaning of term "veto"	1947	AIPO
79%	Can name the current vice president	1978	NORC
78%	Know what initials "FBI" stand for	1949	AIPO
70%	Can name their mayor	1967	AIPO
69%	Know which party has most members in U.S. House of Representatives	1978	NORC
68%	Know that president is limited to two terms	1970	CPS
63%	Have some understanding of term "conservative"	1960	SRC
52%	Know that there are two U.S. senators from their state	1978	NORC
46%	Can name their congressman	1973	Harris
39%	Can name both U.S. senators from their state	1973	Harris
38%	Know Russia is not a NATO member	1964	AIPO
34%	Can name the current secretary of state	1978	NORC
30%	Know term of U.S. House member is two years	1978	NORC
28%	Can name their state senator	1967	AIPO
23%	Know which two nations are involved in SALT talks	1979	CBS/NYT

Source: Adapted from Robert S. Erickson, Norman R. Luttbeg, and Kent L. Tedin, *American Public Opinion: Its Origins, Content, and Impact,* 2d ed. (New York: Wiley, 1980), p. 19. Used by permission. Data from American Institute of Public Opinion (Gallup); Center for Political Studies; Lou Harris and Associates; National Opinion Research Center; CBS/*New York Times.*

found that 36 percent of Americans claim to follow what is happening in government and public affairs most of the time while only 10 percent say "hardly at all." Another 36 percent say "some of the time" while 18 percent say "only now and then."[17]

An earlier, more detailed study measured attention to politics by signs of interest in politics generally, interest in national election campaigns, talking about politics, self-exposure to political information, engaging in political activities, and caring about elections and politics. This study concluded that the people most likely to be attentive to politics were those with high-status occupations, higher incomes, and more education, although one-fifth of those who didn't finish high school qualified as attentive, and half of the high school graduates were attentive. Attentiveness did not vary greatly with sex, race, or age.[18]

The Ideologies of Citizens

If we wish to probe political opinions further, we can study political ideologies. To scholars, an **ideology** is a coherent set of beliefs about politics and public policy.[19] We saw in Chapter 3 that voters today tend to be more issue oriented than they were in the 1950s and even in the 1960s. In our present terms, many of them have more developed political ideologies. Bruce Campbell examined the results of the many opinion surveys over time on questions concerning domestic economic issues, civil rights, abortion, foreign policy, and other issues. He concluded: "In the United States most important issues are consensus issues, with most people grouped loosely around a central, neutral position."[20] Why? There are probably two main reasons. First, the issues of the day tend to reflect the widely held views that we call the political culture. If we looked at less common issues, we would likely find less consensus. Second, most people are neither well informed about politics nor much interested in them most of the time. Their attitudes are therefore likely to be weakly held, and such views are rarely extreme.

Liberalism and Conservatism

Does this mean, then, that there is a common American public opinion after all? To find out, we may wish to examine evidence about the extent of

[17]National Opinion Research Center survey, reported in *Public Opinion,* October–November 1982, p. 28.

[18]Donald J. Devine, *The Attentive Public* (Chicago: Rand McNally, 1970). For a comprehensive study, see W. Russell Neuman, *The Paradox of Mass Politics: Knowledge and Opinion in the American Electorate* (Cambridge, MA: Harvard Univ. Press, 1986).

[19]For an elaboration, see Robert E. Lane, *Political Ideology* (New York: Free Press, 1962), pp. 13–16.

[20]Campbell, *American Electorate,* p. 206.

the two major ideologies in the United States, liberalism and conservatism.[21] In general, a person who believes that the federal government should play a strong role in the economy and in social questions, such as enforcing civil rights and protecting civil liberties, is called a liberal. A conservative is one who favors individual initiative and private actions instead of big government.[22]

In recent years, however, more and more liberals have come to attack big government as inefficient, while certain types of conservatives have endorsed abortion and other traditionally liberal positions. Many observers interpreted the results of the 1980 elections as a "conservative tide." Yet many of those who voted for Ronald Reagan and other conservative candidates disagreed with Reagan's stands on issues such as tax cuts and the Equal Rights Amendment. Indeed, a 1986 Gallup Poll found people terming themselves liberal (20 percent), moderate (45), and conservative (28) in almost exactly the same percentages as ten years earlier.[23] What seems to be the case, as Everett Carll Ladd argues in the box on page 181 is that most Americans hold a number of different policy views, some of which have long been thought of as conservative while others have been called liberal. The people, in short, are not very ideological—and are becoming less so.[24]

DISCOVERING OPINIONS: POLLING

How do we get all this information about public opinion? The most common means is public opinion polls. You've probably taken a public opinion poll—or at least a semipublic one—some time in your life. Just asking some of your friends whom they plan to vote for or how they feel about abortion or who they think will win the Super Bowl could count as an opinion poll. But the results of

such a poll probably wouldn't be very interesting to anyone besides those interviewed because no one would expect your friends to be representative of the public at large, or of any other group except perhaps the group, "your friends."

Candidates often say, "The only poll that counts is on election day," and they are right in a sense. But both candidates and voters seem to be influenced by the results of the numerous polls taken during every major campaign. Many people even believe that poll reports may create a "sympathy vote" for the underdog or a "bandwagon" effect for the leader. Research on this is inconclusive.

How Opinion Polls Are Taken

A **poll** is a survey of a few people that is supposed to represent with considerable accuracy how everyone involved thinks. No one can afford to poll everyone, and so pollsters have developed ways to pick small numbers of people whose views should somehow be typical of the ones who aren't asked. This process of *sampling* the population is the reason why you almost certainly have never been interviewed, say, by the Gallup Poll and probably never will be in your entire life, even though the Gallup organization is always polling all year round on all sorts of subjects. In fact, it interviews only about 350,000 people each decade.

If they never ask you, me, or most other Americans, how can the major pollsters be so accurate in predicting election outcomes? There are two important considerations. First, they generally use *random samples*. Second, they pick a sample size large enough to give *a low probability of error*. Let us see how this works in practice.

The Sample

A **random sample** is a group—in polls, a group of people—for which each individual within the whole population being surveyed has an equal chance of being selected. Most major national polls interview about 1500 people to represent the American adult population of about 140 million people. These people form a probability sample. The way the sample is "drawn" is too complex to describe in detail here. (But see the suggested readings at the end of this chapter for more detailed sources.) Briefly, a polling organization picks people by where they live. It may start with counties

[21]For an argument, based on opinion data, that liberalism and conservatism are not polar opposites but rather separate and independent sets of beliefs, see Fred N. Kerlinger, *Liberalism and Conservatism: The Nature and Structure of Social Attitudes* (Hillsdale, NJ: Erlbaum, 1984). And for an interesting study of current opinion, see Thomas Ferguson and Joel Rogers, *Right Turn: The Decline of the Democrats and the Future of American Politics* (New York: Hill and Wang, 1986).

[22]For a recent history, see Sidney Blumenthal, *The Rise of the Counter-Establishment: From Conservative Ideology to Political Power* (New York: Times Books, 1986).

[23]Gallup Report no. 249, June 1986.

[24]For interesting studies, see Everett Carll Ladd, Jr., *Where Have All the Voters Gone?* (New York: Norton, 1978), and Thomas Exter and Frederick Barber, "The Age of Conservatism," *American Demographics*, Nov. 1986, pp. 30–37. And see Ladd's regular articles in *Public Opinion*.

Is There a New Conservatism among Americans?

The General Social Surveys conducted by the National Opinion Research Center (NORC) show a slight increase since the mid-1970's in the number of self-described conservatives. Gallup, on the other hand, has found conservative ranks declining slightly over this period. While contrasting question wording accounts for some of these differences, the prime factor is the mushiness of the categories themselves. Most people just are not conservatives or liberals in any wide-ranging ideological sense. When the reality is soft, measures of it necessarily vary greatly.

Within the general public, people who call themselves conservatives are consistently more likely to take conservative stands on various issues—but not that much more likely. Take the question of an amendment to the Constitution to permit prayers in the public schools as an example. In late March 1980, 87 percent of conservatives favored such an amendment, but so did 77 percent of liberals. . . .

Conservative politicians and writers are much more in favor of cuts in governmental expenditure than are their liberal counterparts. Within the public at large, though, conservatives are only modestly less in favor of government spending than liberals. In its annual General Social Survey, NORC asks respondents whether they think spending is "too much," "too little," or "about right" in eleven different policy areas. . . . Only on foreign aid and welfare, among the eleven areas explored, did the public think spending was excessive—and here majorities of conservatives and liberals were on the same side.

There are reasons why some people call themselves conservatives while others prefer the liberal label; the choice of one tag or the other is not random or meaningless. But *the reasons are not ideological.* That is, they do not, for the most part, involve adherence to a formal package of political ideas and prescriptions. Instead, they are generally narrow, specific, and individualistic. Because of this, conservatives and liberals are not sharply different overall in their political views.

There are clear class differences in the meanings of conservatism, too. . . . Thus, two-thirds of conservatives with grade school educations do not believe a woman should be able to obtain a legal abortion "if she is married and does not want any more children," while two-thirds of the postgraduate conservatives favor abortions in this instance. On this issue, the class differences—whether measured by education, income, or occupation—are greater than the differences between liberals and conservatives of the same class. . . .

Applying a general ideological category like conservatism to the public at large carries with it wonderful possibilities for confusion and obfuscation. Most Americans are not conservatives or liberals; they do not apply "overarching conceptual dimensions" to give order and coherence to a variety of specific public policy stands.

Reprinted by permission of *Public Opinion* from "Conservatism: A National Review," by Everett Carll Ladd, Jr., *Public Opinion,* February–March 1981, p. 19. Copyright 1981 by American Enterprise Institute.

or election precincts and break them down to neighborhoods, streets, and buildings and then down to, say, the person living there who has the longest first name. The goal is to get people from all over the country in all sorts of living conditions, so that in fact their views will represent the views of the population because they themselves—as a group—are generally like the population. In the old days, polls of samples drawn from telephone directories were often used. They were also often wrong because at that time rich people were much more likely to have phones, so their opinions were overrepresented in the sample. That is why census tracts—which show who lives in every house and apartment in the nation and which are updated every ten years—are now commonly used.

The Margin of Error

Once the pollsters have a sample, they know the probability of error because the laws of statistical probability tell how likely a certain size sample is to be typical. The 1500-person sample of the population gives a range of accuracy of plus or minus 3 percentage points 95 percent of the time. What does this actually mean? Let's take a few actual examples.

In the 1976 campaign, the final Gallup Poll, taken the week before the election, reported Ford with 47 percent of the votes and Carter with 46 percent, with 4 percent undecided, so Gallup said the race was too close to call; its sampling error of plus or minus 3 percent meant that "Ford 47–

ALL RIGHT— 17% OF US THINK WE WERE ASKING THE WRONG PEOPLE, 17% THINK WE WERE ASKING THE WRONG QUESTIONS AND 66% WONDER WHY ANYBODY EVER TRUSTED US ANYWAY....

(Ben Sargent. © *The Austin American Statesman*)

Carter 46" could also be "Ford 50–Carter 43" or "Carter 49–Ford 44," and the Gallup Poll would still be "right" within its stated margin of error. And in 5 out of every 100 polls, it could be even farther off. Nonetheless, since a major disaster in 1948, when all the polls were wrong, the major polls have on average predicted the presidential vote within 2 percent of the actual totals—an impressive performance.

Still, the matter of the allowable margin of error points out why it is important to read poll results carefully, if at all. They rarely actually mean what they appear to say, although we seldom are reminded of this fact except when a poll gets something wrong, as Gallup seemed to in 1976.

Poll results include a number of important judgment calls as well as the probability error. A pollster has to try to determine how likely each respondent is to vote on election day and then somehow build that into his or her final total. Also, a pollster may allocate to the various candidates those "undecideds" who seem likely to vote in the election. This may be done on the basis of how the trend seems to be going—as it seemed to be going to Ford in 1976, for example.

In the 1980 election, the pollsters appeared to fail miserably. Reagan beat Carter by 51 to 41 percent, but no final national poll came anywhere near these figures. Indeed, most found the election too close to call. One reason for this was the margin of error. Another was uncertainty as to turnout, which pollsters must estimate for each potential voter. The third was the large percentages who said they were undecided very late in the campaign. Averaging the five leading polls shows 40 percent for Carter and 8 percent for Anderson—almost exactly the outcome of 41 and 7 actually achieved. The big failure, then, was the Reagan vote, which turned out to be 8 percent more than the 43 percent average in the final polls. It appears that many undecided voters went for Reagan at the last minute. This is something the polls cannot handle because they are usually completed some days before election day.

Pollsters performed better in the 1984 election, in that all major polls just before election day showed Ronald Reagan winning handily over Walter Mondale. However, they varied widely in the size of the margin they reported. NBC's poll showed Reagan with a lead of 24 percent. The CBS/*New York Times* poll predicted 22 percent. Gallup reported 18 percent, which turned out to be correct, as Reagan won by 59 to 41 percent. But the ABC/*Washington Post* poll called it 14 points, and the Harris Poll said 12 while Roper said 10.

Why such large differences? The NBC poll underestimated the size of Mondale's vote, perhaps because it did not press those who said they were undecided. Other differences seemed to result from ways of estimating the likelihood that each person polled would actually vote. The Roper poll, which found the race much closer than it turned out to be, does not consider whether a person has voted in previous elections; most other polls do, and they were more accurate.

In any event, there were more national polls doing regular interviewing and reporting in the 1984 election than ever before, and politicians seemed to be paying more attention to them in adjusting their campaigns. But there can be dangers in too great a reliance on polls, as even pollsters point out.

Strengths and Weaknesses of Polls

Polls on issues may be affected by the way in which questions are asked. A loaded question with emotional language or a complex question with only yes-or-no answers allowed, may produce a result that doesn't really reflect the opinions of the people being interviewed.

Polls often do not find out the *direction* of an opinion. Often a person's opinion on a given issue is not a simple yes-or-no matter but can range from "strongly in favor" through "indifferent" to "strongly opposed." They also may not reflect the *strength or intensity* with which an opinion is held. Nor will they reflect an opinion's *stability or fluidity* unless they are repeated over a period of time. Furthermore, they rarely reveal the *relevance or salience*—the importance—of an opinion to the people who hold it.

So there is much to be learned about public opinion beyond what the pollsters usually tell us— even when what they tell us proves to be accurate despite the use of their own judgment in processing their own data. Some of what is missing can be learned from in-depth interviews of the sort we relied on in our study of voting in Chapter 3.

How to Evaluate Polls

Most experts on polls and polling urge caution in reading and interpreting polls and suggest that the following questions be asked:

- *Who was interviewed*? Was it a national sample or a special population group? Was it a random sample (generally the most reliable kind) or some other type?
- *How big was the sample*? For any large population group, reliability declines markedly as the sample size drops below 1500.
- *What questions were asked and in what order*? Could you have answered them confident that your answers would accurately reflect your views?
- *How were the interviews conducted*? Those done in people's homes are usually most reliable. Telephone comes next, with mail and street-corner polls not reliable.
- *When were the interviews conducted* in relation to opinion-influencing events or elections?
- *Who did the polling*? A reliable firm such as Gallup, Harris, Roper, the National Opinion Research Center? Or an unknown (or, worse, an unmentioned) firm?
- *Who sponsored it—and why*? Was it sponsored by a political candidate to show his or her strength? Or by newspapers without any particular vested interest in the outcome? Or by an academic research organization such as the University of Michigan's Survey Research Center?

Bearing in mind questions like these, you can judge a poll in ways that can make its information useful.[25]

USING OPINIONS

Whatever their information content, opinion polls can be used in various ways by various people. We might expect them to influence politicians in their campaigns and in their decisions on public policy. Do they?

Do Opinions Influence Politics?

Our system, we well know, is not a pure democracy. The people don't themselves together make the decisions. There are too many of us to do that and too many decisions as well, as we have noted. Instead, we have a representative democracy. The people choose individuals who make decisions for them.

But do public officials really take public opinion seriously? How do they even know what it is? Elections may reveal something—but only half or fewer of the citizens vote. Letters, telegrams, and other messages may also help—but very few Americans ever send such messages.

This leaves our politicians with opinion polls as their major source of information on public opinion over and above their own hunches. We are told that politicians are always examining polls—but these are usually polls about their own popularity rather than polls about popular opinion on public issues. When they do examine polls on public issues, what do they learn?

"For many years, philosophers and political scientists dealt with public opinion as though it represented . . . one force among many in the complex flux of politics," writes Leo Bogart.

These forces were like currents of the air or ocean, constantly changing in their contours and directions. The public opinion survey method requires that these elusive currents be treated as though they were static, that we define and measure what was formerly undefinable and unmeasurable. Once this is done, and done over and over again, it is easy to succumb to the illusion that the measurements represent reality rather

[25]You might also read I. A. Lewis and William Schneider, "Is the Public Lying to the Pollsters?" *Public Opinion*, April–May 1982, pp. 42–47, and Evans Witt, "Reporting Polls: The Writer's Job from Stats to Story," *Washington Journalism Review*, April 1984, pp. 19–21.

than a distorted, dim, approximate reflection of a reality that alters its shape when seen from different angles.[26]

Do Opinions Influence Policy?

Still, experts study the extent to which these public opinions are related to government policy—*congruent with* is the term they use. Robert Weissberg made an extensive study of opinion-policy congruence on domestic issues (defense spending, health care, income tax rates, racial integration, religion in the schools, gun control, and the death penalty) and foreign policy questions (Vietnam, foreign aid, and admission of China to the United Nations) over 40 years. He concluded that opinion-policy congruence does occur, but it varies with the topic and the time period, and there are frequent instances of incongruity. For example, the majority agreed with government action on the question of Communist China's admission to the United Nations for a period of 20 years. Yet public opinion has disagreed totally with court rulings and government actions prohibiting prayer in the public schools. Other cases vary from year to year—capital punishment for murder, for example.[27] Other experts would agree with Weissberg that there is no clear pattern of congruence between opinion and policy.

When Alan Monroe studied another wide range of cases, he found that two-thirds of them demonstrated such congruence or consistency. "Public desires are not perfectly satisfied," he found, "but the political system eventually produces acceptable policies most of the time. And it should be emphasized that a majority of policy outcomes were in accordance with public preferences in most categories of policy." The major reason that there was not more consistency, he concluded, was

> the tendency of the political system to find it [harder] to pass publicly approved policy changes than to maintain the status quo . . . political decision makers are usually disposed to act in accordance with public opinion, but . . . institutional structures and the press of so many decisions to be made cause decisions to be long delayed and sometimes forgotten.[28]

The problem is not that public opinion is fickle. A study of survey results from 1935 to 1979 on both domestic and foreign policy questions found remarkable stability in Americans' policy preferences. Most views changed hardly at all from year to year, and most of the changes that did occur were small. Major changes almost always occurred at times of major events. For example, opposition to impeaching President Nixon plummeted when it was revealed that he was covering up the Watergate scandal.[29]

Thus, policy clearly is not simply based upon, or a reflection of, public opinion. Why then do we do so much polling? Perhaps the polls serve as substitutes for information that politicians used to get from local party workers when parties were stronger. Or perhaps, as Bogart suggests,

> opinion surveys have become a mechanism through which the public becomes sensitized to its own needs and self-conscious about its own collective stance. . . . An entire generation of Americans now has grown up accepting polling as a commonplace institution and poll findings as part of the normal daily flow of expected information.[30]

By this reasoning, polls may be more important to us, the people, than to them, the politicians.

Opinion surveys, Bogart reminds us, "are often dubious indicators of actual behavior because they do not, and perhaps cannot, measure the seething, changing character of the public tempers. They generally fail to embody the rich context of motivation and cross-communication out of which opinions arise and activate people in the mass.[31]

The motivations that "activate people in the mass"—that is, in large groups—create interest groups out of "special publics." The cross-communication that makes possible this organizing of opinion now depends heavily on the media. Opinions without communication can have little influence on people. Opinions without action of the sort we examined in the last chapter can have little influence on politics. Thus, to get to a fuller understanding of the interplay of public opinion and politics, we must also examine the media. This will be our topic in the next chapter.

[26]Leo Bogart, *Silent Politics: Polls and the Awareness of Public Opinion* (New York: Wiley, 1972), p. 15.

[27]Robert Weissberg, *Public Opinion and Popular Government* (Englewood Cliffs, NJ: Prentice-Hall, 1976), chaps. 8–11, esp. p. 244.

[28]Alan D. Monroe, "Consistency between Public Preferences and National Policy Decisions," *American Politics Quarterly* 7 (January 1979), 17. For an interesting argument that polling has actually decreased public influence over policy, see Benjamin Ginsberg, *The Captive Public: How Mass Opinion Promotes State Power* (New York: Basic Books, 1986).

[29]See Benjamin I. Page and Robert Y. Shapiro, "Changes in Americans' Policy Preferences, 1935–1979," *Public Opinion Quarterly* 46 (Spring 1982), 24–42.

[30]Bogart, *Silent Politics*, p. 15.

[31]Ibid., pp. 17–18.

SUMMARY

Public opinion is opinion held by more than one person that concerns a public question. In fact, there are almost always many different publics holding differing opinions on any question. Attitudes underlie opinions, and we get our attitudes from socialization. There are three major theories of how socialization occurs: through interpersonal transfer, identification, or cognitive development. The major agents of socialization, both authorities and institutions, are parents, school, peer group, and the media. Their importance varies with one's age, as is shown in Figure 6.1.

Experts speak of our beliefs about politics, leaders, and institutions as our political culture. There are 15 key values that are endorsed in the American political culture, including liberty, equality, property, belief in God, support for religion, altruistic community service, emphasis on achievement, popular rule, legislative predominance, federalism, and decentralized parties. These values enjoy widespread political support. Experts also find differences in political culture in different regions of the country, and therefore speak of political subcultures. Political culture influences public opinion in three ways: defining the context, screening information, and shaping expectations.

Politics influences opinions because we think of political figures as authorities. One reason we do is that most of us are quite ignorant of politics. Indeed, most Americans are not members of the "attentive public." Citizens do have political ideologies—coherent sets of beliefs about politics and public policy. Some people have claimed that Americans are becoming more conservative, but evidence suggests that the old labels *conservative* and *liberal* no longer fit most Americans very well.

Experts discover the views of Americans by public opinion polling. Polls use random samples to enable them to generalize from a small group of people who are representative of the population as a whole. Because of this method, however, polls always have margins of error. Besides taking into account the margin of error, we should evaluate any poll carefully in terms of the questions raised in the text before placing confidence in it.

While politicians often pay attention to polls, other factors also enter into their decisions about how to act. Studies on the impact of opinions on policy suggest that it varies from time to time and from issue to issue. Although public opinion is usually quite constant over the years, the political system often has difficulty responding to it, even when politicians are interested in being responsive. Thus, the significance of public opinion for politics is often limited.

Suggestions for Further Reading and Study

For a good general introduction to the study of public opinion, three already classic pieces can be recommended: V. O. Key, *Public Opinion and American Democracy* (New York: Knopf, 1961); Gabriel Almond, *The American People and Foreign Policy* (New York: Praeger, 1960); and Philip Converse, "The Nature of Belief Systems in Mass Publics," in *Ideology and Discontent*, ed. David Apter (New York: Free Press, 1964), pp. 206–61. Among the more recent and comprehensive texts are Bernard Hennessey, *Public Opinion*, 3d ed. (Belmont, CA: Wadsworth, 1981); and Paul R. Abramson, *Political Attitudes in America: Formation and Change* (San Francisco: Freeman, 1983).

On socialization, a good overview is Richard E. Dawson, Kenneth Prewitt, and Karen S. Dawson, *Political Socialization*, 2d ed. (Boston: Little, Brown paperback, 1977). For more specialized pieces summarizing recent research, see Stanley Allen Renshon, ed., *Handbook of Political Socialization* (New York: Free Press, 1977).

On polls, in addition to the works cited in the text, see Leo Bogart, *Polls and the Awareness of Public Opinion* (New Brunswick, NJ: Transaction, 1985), and H. L. Nieburg, *Public Opinion: Tracking and Targeting* (New York: Praeger, 1984).

Summary presentations of the major findings of the University of Michigan's Center for Political Studies can be found in Philip E. Converse, Jean D. Dotson, Wendy J. Hoag, and William H. McGee III, *American Social Attitudes Data Sourcebook 1947–1978* (Cambridge, MA: Harvard Univ. Press, 1980).

For current reports, see the "Opinion Roundup" section in each issue of the bimonthly magazine *Public Opinion*. Relevant scholarly studies can also be found in *Public Opinion Quarterly*.

7

THE MASS MEDIA

If you're a typical American, you have a television set. Over 99 percent of American households do, and the average set is on more than 7 hours every day. Further, by your late teens you will have seen some 350,000 commercials on television. The average high school student will have seen 13,000 killings on television—for there are, on average, 7 killings in every hour of television programming. And by age 17 most children will have spent more hours in front of the television screen than they have in the classroom.

You probably think of TV viewing as entertainment. To most of us, this entertainment is what comes to mind when people talk about "the mass media." Of course, on TV and radio this entertainment is interrupted occasionally for brief news reports. And about a third of all Americans watch a news program on TV on any given day—just as almost two-thirds read at least part of a newspaper each day.

Some of these experiences seem nonpolitical. But in its ultimate effects, crime is political, and so is our economic activity. The media, which portray these things, thus may have political effects even when they are not reporting political news. In this chapter we'll examine the politics of the mass media as they affect us, as they affect politics, and as politicians and the government try to affect them—in order to affect us. We'll also learn how we can play a more active role in the media as consumers and citizens, should we wish to. ∎

At 8 P.M. Eastern Standard Time on November 6, 1984, a presidential election was in progress in the United States. Polls were still open in 26 of the 50 states. In those states where polls were closed, about 1 percent of the total vote had been counted. At that moment, CBS anchor Dan Rather announced to the nationwide television audience that Ronald Reagan had been reelected because he had already won at least 280 electoral votes.

How did Rather know this if only 1 in every 100 votes had been counted? CBS employees had been conducting exit polls in "key precincts" in each state, asking tens of thousands of voters as they left the polls whom they had voted for. Interviewers also gathered information about each voter and his or her views and reasons for voting. With this information, they constructed a representative sample of the voters in each state, and on that basis they projected the winner of each state's electoral votes. Because of this exit polling CBS was certain that Reagan had won long before the polls had closed in any state, but it chose to wait to declare the victor in each state until the polls in that state had closed.

A television network exit poll in process. (© Bob Daemmrich/UNIPHOTO)

The same thing had happened in 1980 when at 8:15 P.M. Eastern Standard Time—5:15 Pacific Standard Time—NBC had declared Reagan the victor over Jimmy Carter in a landslide. About the same time, President Carter called Reagan to congratulate him, and an hour and a half later, Carter made a public concession speech. Many people who heard these reports on their way to the polls in the 26 states where voting was not yet finished then decided not to vote. Some Democratic members of Congress in the West who lost to Republican challengers attributed their losses to this resignation by the electorate that was fostered by exit poll projections.

Whatever the extent of television's influence on voter turnout in 1980 and 1984, we know that the media are now very powerful in American politics. Politicians know it too. The day after his loss in the 1984 presidential election, Walter Mondale told a news conference:

> Modern politics requires television. . . . I've never really warmed up to television, and in fairness to television, it's never really warmed up to me. . . . I don't believe it's possible any more to run for president without the capacity to build confidence and communications every night. It's got to be done that way.

The Reagan camp certainly knew that. Reagan's aides and advisors had carefully controlled his limited appearances during the campaign. By so doing they avoided misstatements and prevented people from seeing the president when he was tired or in a bad mood or ill informed. They also prevented the press from asking him questions that might be embarrassing—especially when his domestic or foreign policy was not going well.[1] The media have great power in today's politics, but they can also be used very effectively—even against their will—by some politicians.

OUR EXPERIENCE OF THE MASS MEDIA

Our everyday life is permeated by media. But most of the media that deal with public affairs and offer entertainment programs are owned outside our communities and programmed largely from New

---

[1]For a fascinating account of how this is done, based on interviews with Reagan administration officials and media figures, see Mark Hertsgaard, "How Reagan Seduces Us: Inside the President's Propaganda Factory," *Village Voice*, September 25, 1984, p. 1.

York and Washington via giant networks and news wire services. We are remarkably unaware of the impact *national* media such as CBS-TV or the Associated Press or *Time* magazine have, not just on our image of politics but on our image of reality in general. And our image of reality to a great extent shapes our lives by determining our action.

Every day some 65 million Americans watch the news on one of three major television networks: CBS, NBC, and ABC. Still others watch it on the Cable News Network. When asked, "Where do you usually get most of your news about what's going on in the world today?" 59 percent mention television; 44 percent say newspapers; 18 percent, radio; 5 percent, magazines; and 5 percent, other people. And surveys consistently show that the people, by large margins, believe that the media are usually more truthful than high government officials.[2]

But just what sort of information do we—or can we—actually get from the media? The average report of a major event by a correspondent on the nightly television news lasts 60 to 90 seconds. On radio, spot reports are often even briefer. Do we really believe such brief accounts can tell us what actually happened? And can they possibly tell us why? When, where, and how do we—or can we—get the background that makes such reports meaningful?

We often say that democracy is based upon, depends upon, an informed citizenry. But in fact democracy is based upon, or depends upon, only a voting electorate—and it doesn't even take a majority vote to sustain the process, as we have noted. The political system goes on whether or not the citizenry is well-informed. In the same way, the news shows go on and the newspapers are published, whether or not they are accurate and informative—and whether or not the people are paying attention.

The mass media in America have become so important that they are often referred to as the fourth branch of government—or, in terms borrowed from the French Revolution, the Fourth Estate. Some suggest that the media are even more important than that. Editor Edward Hunter has argued that "the press is now the Third Estate and the Congress is the Fourth Estate. Our legislators—and the Administration—first determine what the press will or will not use and set policy accordingly."[3]

Perhaps this view overstates the case. Certainly the media's status as a part of government is not official. But in this chapter, we shall see how the media have grown, what has made them "mass" media, and how the media and the government are intertwined. This will prepare us to ask what responsibilities the media should have, not only to the government but to us as citizens.

WHY WE CALL THEM MEDIA

A *medium* (plural, *media*) is a means of transmission. The term basically means "middle." The same word is used for a newspaper and for a mystic who claims to be able to put people in touch with the spirits of their departed loved ones. In each case and many others, the medium makes communication possible. This communication requires four things: a *source*, a *message*, a *medium* to transmit the message from the source, and a *receiver* to which the message comes.

It is easy to see how television, newspapers, books, the telephone, and radio are communications media. So are person-to-person speech, letter writing, junk mail, records, movies, and so on. But our communications experiences are much broader than just these. A Columbia University professor asked his students to keep a log of the communications media they were exposed to in a 24-hour period. The results, shown in Table 7.1, though probably not typical of the American people as a whole, help us realize how much of the time we are engaged in communication.

Today we depend on the media for information vital to most aspects of our lives. We look primarily to the media to provide us with the information we need to act as responsible citizens—and to get the government to act responsibly. The media are able to provide more information to more people than ever before because they have indeed become "mass" media.

---

[2]Figures from a Roper Poll conducted in 1981, cited in Lawrence W. Lichty, "Video Versus Print," *Wilson Quarterly*, special issue, 1982, pp. 53–54.

[3]Quoted by Kevin Phillips, "Busting the Media Trusts," *Harper's*, July 1977, pp. 23–34.

CBS anchor Dan Rather covering the 1984 Democratic convention. (Dennis Brack/Black Star)

TABLE 7.1

The Average Student's Daily Exposure
to Communications Media

MEDIA CHANNEL	EXPOSURE (MINUTES)
Television	63
Newspapers	53
Radio	78
Magazines	30
Books	149
Records	15
Movies	3
Posters, etc	19
Conversations lasting under 5 minutes	144
Conversations lasting over 5 minutes	125
Lectures	140
Other	13

Source: W. Phillips Davison, James Boylan, and Frederick Yu, *Mass Media* (New York: Praeger, 1976), p. 105.

WHY WE CALL THEM "MASS"

Communication, we noted above, requires a source, a message, a medium, and a receiver. Such contact can be on a small scale, as when I write a message to you through the medium of a letter. But it can also be on a very large scale, as when Prentice Hall sends this message to you and your fellow readers by editing, printing, and distributing this book. Book publishing has become a mass medium, just as television, radio, newspapers, and magazines have.

Why do we call them "mass" media? First, because they now *reach large masses* of people. Second, because all aspects of this communication have been *standardized* to reach the mass audiences. And third, because the ownership and control of these media have become increasingly *concentrated*, or massed.

Mass Audiences

There are now more television sets in America than there are telephones or toilets. Over 99 percent of American homes have at least one set (a third have two or more, and a tenth have three or more). The average set is on over seven hours a day, with the average viewer watching for almost three hours, and the average child between ages 6 and 17 watching more than four. In winter and spring some 75 million Americans on the average watch television on any given night. In addition, spot checks show that about 85 percent of our population over the age of 12 listens to the radio at some point on any given day.[4] And some 62 million

---

[4]These statistics on mass audiences come from Edwin Diamond, *The Tin Kazoo* (Cambridge, MA: MIT Press, 1975), pp. 13, 14, 16.

The Mass Media   **189**

newspapers are bought every day, many of them read by several people.[5] The audiences, or recipients, of the messages sent by the media in America today are clearly of enormous size.

To reach these mass publics, the media attempt to standardize as many aspects of communication as possible. They use *standardized production equipment*, such as printing presses and radio and television tape and film systems. They use *standardized content*: Reports from national news services such as Associated Press (AP), United Press International (UPI), the New York Times News Service, and radio and television network programs are "fed" to local stations from New York. They use *standardized transmission* via telegraph, telephone, satellite, and other electronic hookups. And they use *standardized reception* by our radios, televisions, and even our ears, eyes, and brains—all of which are "built" to receive the same messages in about the same ways.

Concentrated Ownership and Control

There are a great many message senders in this country: 9026 commercial radio stations; 1161 commercial television stations; and 1701 daily newspapers.[6] In reality, however, the news the media distribute comes primarily from two major news or wire services: AP and UPI. Many of those 9026 commercial radio stations are linked into four large radio networks: CBS, NBC, ABC, and Mutual, while the 322 noncommercial stations form National Public Radio. The 1161 commercial television stations are affiliated for the most part with the three large networks: CBS, NBC, and ABC, while 322 noncommercial stations form the Public Broadcasting Service. And the daily papers have increasingly been bought by "chains" such as Gannett, which owns 78 daily papers across the country; Thomson, with 57; Knight-Ridder, which owns 44 different papers; and Newhouse, which owns 31. In recent years, chains have been merging with each other to create even bigger chains.

Another aspect of this concentration is the disappearance of competition, as happened with newspapers. In 1910 there were 100 million Americans and 2400 daily newspapers. Today there are 245 million Americans but only 1701 papers. Yet even these figures tell only part of the story. In 98 percent of the cities with daily papers today, there is only one newspaper publisher, even though sometimes it owns and publishes several seemingly competing papers. In 1920 there were 700 cities with competing papers, but today there are fewer than 50.

In 1930 chains owned 43 percent of the circulation of daily papers in the United States. In 1960 the figure was 46 percent—today it is over 70 percent. As a result of this trend, many now fear the end of the independent daily paper. Such changes are ominous because they will limit the media that are independent minded and that reflect the needs and interests of the local regions in which they operate.

Competition among media is also becoming limited. A Federal Communications Commission study found that there are 72 cities and towns in which the only local newspaper owns the only local radio station. It also found that in another 180 cities, a daily paper owned one of the broadcasting stations. Perhaps even more ominous is the recent growth of "media conglomerates"—companies that own newspapers, TV stations, radio stations, magazines, and even book publishers. Sometimes media conglomerates even own quite different businesses as well; for example, RCA, the electronics corporation, owns a carpet factory, a food company, and a car rental company—as well as NBC and a large book publisher; and RCA itself is owned by the giant conglomerate General Electric. Table 7.2 lists the media and other businesses owned by the Times Mirror Company, another major media conglomerate.

The result of this "massification" of ownership and control, some observers believe, is that we as consumers get *choice without diversity*. The giant corporations tend to aim for the "middle" just as our giant political parties do, and so picking between NBC and CBS or between *Time* and *Newsweek* today may be much like picking between Carter and Ford in 1976. Furthermore, this tendency toward appealing to the middle is intensified by the fact that all these mass media depend for their profits on advertising revenue. In 1985 the

[5]*Statistical Abstract of the United States, 1986* (Washington, DC: GPO, 1986), p. 550.

[6]Ibid., pp. 547, 550. There are also about 10,000 other newspapers, including 40 foreign-language dailies, 90 specialist dailies, and 8000 papers published less frequently. See Benjamin M. Compaine, *Who Owns the Media? Concentration of Ownership in the Mass Communications Industry*, 2d ed. (White Plains, NY: Knowledge Industry Publications, 1982), p. 29.

TABLE 7.2

Principal Operations of the Times Mirror Company, a Media Conglomerate (Total Sales in 1986: $4 billion, with profits of over $240 million)

Newspapers

Los Angeles Times
Baltimore Sun
Denver Post
Newsday (Long Island, NY)
Hartford Courant
Greenwich Time (Connecticut)
The Advocate (Stamford, CT)
Morning Call (Allentown, PA)

Magazines

Broadcasting
Popular Science
Diamond Popular Science (Japanese)
Golf
Ski
Outdoor Life
National Journal
Sporting News
Sporting Goods Dealer
Sports, Inc.

Cable Television

Seventh-largest operator in the United States, with 50 cable systems, about 823,000 subscribers in some 300 communities in 15 states.

Book Publishing Companies

Harry N. Abrams (art books)
Learning International (training programs)
Southwestern (home reference and religious books)
Matthew Bender & Co. (law books)
C. V. Mosby Co. (nursing and medical books)
Year Book Medical Publishers
Mirror Systems (computer software)

Broadcasting

Owns four VHF TV stations (Dallas/Ft. Worth, Austin, St. Louis, Birmingham

Other Businesses

Times Mirror National Marketing
National Education Marketing Services
Jeppesen Sanderson (flight information services)
Times Mirror Press (phone books)
Times Mirror Land and Timber Company

---

three TV networks made over $1 billion profit on $9 billion in advertising revenue.[7] Except in the case of cable television, which we'll discuss shortly, we listeners and viewers don't pay for our radio and TV programs at all. And to take another example, the cost of printing and mailing a news magazine—let alone the cost of paying the staff to write for it—is more than we pay per copy for it. Advertising makes up the difference and accounts for the profits.

Recently, however, there have been attempts to make at least some of the media less controlled from above and more responsive to local needs. Attempts include *underground* papers created, written, and published to meet the needs of some people for specialized information and assistance; *city magazines*, such as *New York* and *Los Angeles*, published in and for the people of a city rather than for a national audience; *state magazines*, such as *Texas Monthly* and *California*; citizen organizations to improve broadcasting that monitor the media and lobby for better coverage (see Action Unit 7.1, p. 192); *local journalism reviews* in more than

a dozen cities that criticize the performance of the press and other media, using a magazine format; *truth-in-advertising* groups that have achieved important checks on media advertising; *feedback columns in newspapers* that have opened the pages of some newspapers to citizens; and *news ombudsmen* hired by almost three dozen papers to listen to and write for their readers about the papers' accuracy and fairness.

THE POLITICS OF COMMUNICATION

Information is essential to all aspects of living. But it is especially vital to political action because politics usually takes place beyond our own direct experience. In other words, we depend upon authorities for political information more regularly than we do for information about the cost of living, for example, because we experience the cost of living personally whenever we shop. We must be aware of the influences that shape the news we receive, as is suggested by Action Unit 7.2, p. 194, "How to Watch the Evening News."

---

[7]*Channels 1987 Field Guide to the Electronic Environment*, p. 24.

How to Talk Back to Your TV Set

There are now many citizen action organizations seeking to improve broadcasting in various ways. You can form your own local organization to influence local programming—or even to threaten to challenge a local station's license when it comes up for renewal every third year—if you believe it is not living up to its public service obligations as a free user of the public airwaves.

Such license challenges are sometimes based on programming (percentage of time given to news and public affairs) and sometimes on hiring practices and the station's failure to use women and minorities on the air. To find out specifically what a local station does do and how other citizens react to it, go to the station's headquarters and ask to see its "public file," which by law must be available free to the public during regular business hours.

For more detailed instructions on how to appeal to the Federal Communications Commission, see Chapter 7 of James R. Michael, ed., *Working on the System* (New York: Basic Books, 1974); and for encouragement and guidance, see the book by Nicholas Johnson, a former renegade FCC commissioner, entitled *How to Talk Back to Your Television Set* (New York: Bantam paperback, 1970). The following groups represent various perspectives, and one or more might be helpful to you in lobbying.

Accuracy in Media, AIM (1275 K St. NW, Washington, DC 20005), was founded in 1969 as a nonprofit educational organization to combat what it considers inaccuracies and distorted reporting by the major media. It publishes *AIM Report*.

Action for Children's Television, ACT (46 Austin St., Newtonville, MA 02160), was founded in 1968 to make networks more responsive to the desires of parents and teachers concerning television programming for children.

American Women in Radio and Television (1101 Connecticut Ave. NW, Washington, DC 20036) works for equal status for women in media jobs.

Citizens Communications Center (25 E St. NW, Washington, DC 20036) is a public-interest law firm that specializes in communications regulatory policy.

Media Access Project (1609 Connecticut Ave. NW, Washington, DC, 20009) is a public-interest law firm founded in 1972 that represents individuals and citizens' groups in efforts to increase public access to the mass media. Much help has been given to minorities, gays, environmentalists, and consumers.

National Black Media Coalition (38 New York Ave. NE, Washington, DC 20002) is made up of over 70 local black organizations, each dedicated to eliminating racism from radio and television.

National Organization for Women, NOW (1776 K St. NW, Washington, DC 20006), has a *Media Project* that gives technical assistance and advice to those working to promote both the employment and the image of women in broadcasting.

"Beyond our limited daily experience," observes media expert Robert Stein,

> it is television, radio, newspapers, magazines and books—the media—that furnish our consciousness with the people, places, and events that we agree to call reality. But reality, in a literal sense, is what happens to three and a half billion people all over the world twenty-four hours a day. Out of that teeming experience, the media can only give us, in words and pictures, a representation of tiny fragments that are deemed significant or suggestive.[8]

[8]Robert Stein, *Media Power: Who Is Shaping Your Picture of the World?* (Boston: Houghton Mifflin, 1972), p. xi. For a sociological analysis, see Gaye Tuchman, *Making News: A Study in the Construction of Reality* (New York: Free Press, 1978). For a political one, see W. Lance Bennett, *News: The Politics of Illusion* (New York: Longman, 1983).

We have now new authorities (those in the media) who are able to compete with our traditional authorities (those in the government), as Stein argues in the box on media power. They also compete with each other, as network "anchor persons" do, or as television and the newspapers do. But the most important competition is over claims to the authority to represent reality for us that the media and the government sometimes wage with each other. So we must now examine the politics of communication as it arises at each stage in the process: source, message, medium, receiver. We can then consider the impact of, and controls upon, our media on our politics, and the controls our politics puts on our media.

Media Power

In the past, our picture of the world was largely shaped by the established institutions of the society. Most vital information was, at least for a time, the exclusive property of government officials, military men, and business leaders. News, with rare exceptions, was what they wanted us to know. Throughout most of its history, journalism was limited to mediating between the public and those who held power. Like education, journalism was concerned with describing and cataloguing our condition rather than questioning and changing it, and like education, operated largely within the received values of the society.

Now, in little more than a generation, technology has changed this situation. In making it possible for the media to give us more words and pictures than ever before and to give them to us instantaneously, television and transistors have, at the same time, loosened the grip of authority on our consciousness. In an era of instant and almost universal communication, such control is hardly possible. . . .

. . . If knowledge is power, it is no longer concentrated in the hands of the powerful. From thousands of sources every day, information bypasses those in authority and flows directly to the media, and, in the case of television, not just information but experience: the raw sights and sounds of conflict and pain. As substantial control over what we know has passed from established institutions, a new force has emerged in American life: Media Power. By shaping our picture of the world on an almost minute-to-minute basis, the media now largely determine what we think, how we feel and what we do about our social and political environment.

From Robert Stein, *Media Power: Who Is Shaping Your Picture of the World?* pp. xi-xii. Copyright © 1972 by Robert Stein. Reprinted by permission of Houghton Mifflin Company.

The Politics of the Source and the Message

The major original sources of media messages are still governments, in large part because what governments and their officers do is what is considered news. More specifically, studies show that networks get most of their material from the national wire services, which in turn get most of their material from officials. Local stations get half or more of their stories from press releases from public figures and public relations handouts from businesses, while the rest comes from police and fire department radio monitors.[9]

A study of the nation's leading papers, the *New York Times* and the *Washington Post*, found that of their front-page stories, about half came from U.S. government officials, a quarter came from foreign or international officials, and 15 percent came from other U.S. citizens. Leon Sigal examined all stories in both papers for their origins and divided them into "routine" (for public statements and official events), "informal" (for briefings, leaks, and so on), and "enterprise" (for cases where reporters used their own initiative to get the story).

Table 7.3 shows the breakdown. A recent survey of Washington correspondents found that almost half rely on middle-level officials who are more anonymous and more insulated. As far as the most productive sources of news are concerned, one-third prefer personal interviews, and another third rely on a combination of personal interview and confidential source information.[10]

TABLE 7.3
Channels of Information for 2850 front-page stories in the *New York Times* and the *Washington Post*

Routine (58.2%)
   Official proceedings (12.0%)
   Press conferences (24.2%)
   Nonspontaneous events (4.5%)
Informal (15.7%)
   Background briefings (7.9%)
   Leaks (2.3%)
   Nongovernmental proceedings (1.5%)
   News reports, editorials (4.0%)
Enterprise (25.8%)
   Interviews (23.7%)
   Spontaneous events (1.2%)
   Reporter's own analysis (0.9%)
Not ascertainable (0.3%)

Source: Leon V. Sigal, *Reporters and Officials: The Organization and Politics of Newsmaking* (Lexington, MA: Heath, 1973), p. 121.

---

[9]David Altheide, *Creating Reality: How TV News Distorts Events* (Beverly Hills, CA: Sage, 1976), p. 16.

[10]Charles S. Steinberg, *The Information Establishment: Our Government and the Media* (New York: Hastings House, 1980), p. 77.

How to Watch the Evening News

The Washington news that gets to us via the evening news on TV or in the morning paper has already been "processed" at least three times: first by the source in government, second by the reporter, and third by the editors in New York who prepare it for television, for *the New York Times*, or for the Associated Press or United Press International. This means that you probably shouldn't take this news at face value, for such news usually means something more than, or different from, what it seems to say. How then should we interpret it? There are no hard-and-fast rules, but here are some general guidelines:

1. Don't mistake a "trial balloon" for a fully developed, agreed-upon, official policy or course of action. Often an official will "leak" a proposal to find out what popular reaction would be were it to become policy.

2. Don't mistake a "hostile leak" for a "trial balloon." Often an opponent of a particular policy proposal will leak it to stimulate hostile reactions that would encourage its advocates to withdraw it—a bureaucrat's strategy we shall encounter in Chapter 9.

3. Remember that there is always a time lag between an erroneous accusation and a correction, and furthermore, that denials and corrections usually get less "play" than accusations. So don't assume that what you hear at first is true.

4. Pay careful attention to the type of denial that is made. A quick "blanket denial" of a fast-breaking story is usually made by a low-level official who wouldn't be in a position to know whether it was true or not—such as a press secretary—in hopes that the whole thing will blow over. As soon as the involved officials "get their act together," they are likely to issue a "cover story" designed to be a plausible explanation of what happened. Such stories may in fact cover up the truth, as was the case with the Nixon White House's handling of the Watergate break-in. So it's best to suspend judgment until more facts are in.

5. A "no comment" response usually means that the accusation or account is true. The involved officials think it so likely that a particular story will be confirmed by events or study that they don't dare risk denying it.

6. What day it is may make a big difference in how believable or how important an account is. Sunday is a slow news day, so officials are likely to make statements—either privately or on interview shows like "Meet the Press" or "Face the Nation"—that aren't really that important but will be inflated by reporters and editors seeking news to report in Monday's paper. Such a story is often called a Monday-morning plant because it is designed to appear in the Monday news.

7. On the other hand, very little really important news is released on Friday because people tend to be away from their TV screens Friday night, and hardly anybody reads the paper on Saturday.

8. By contrast, the Sunday papers have the largest newspaper audiences, so outsiders such as government critics or activists have developed a successful strategy of releasing their major news on Saturday in what can be called a Sunday-morning plant.

9. Most news is not as bad as reporters make it out to be. Usually it's less serious than it seems. The problem is that reporters have an understandable tendency to make a story seem more important than it is so that it—and they—will get more attention.

10. However, the really bad stories are almost always worse than reports suggest. Hardened reporters have difficulty believing that issues like Vietnam and Watergate can be as bad as they are, and because they're often afraid they'll lose their access to important public official sources if they overstate such matters, they're cautious.

In sum, when you hear or read what seems to be an important story, it usually helps to ask first who would benefit from, and who would be hurt by, people's believing the report. Then, in the coming days, you should watch for reports of the activities and statements of both parties. It is also worthwhile to keep your own scorecard.

See Austin Kiplinger, *Washington NOW* (New York: Harper & Row, 1975), pp. 270–72, where points 1, 3, 4, 5, 6, and 9 above are presented and developed. For a more detailed study, see Stephen Hess, *The Washington Reporters* (Washington, DC: Brookings Institution, 1981). And for a behind-the-scenes account, see Av Westin, *Newswatch: How TV Decides the News* (New York: Simon & Schuster, 1983).

In a ten-year study of the news operations of *Time, Newsweek,* and the CBS and NBC networks, sociologist Herbert Gans concluded that although anyone can be a source of news, in practice almost all sources are "knowns" rather than "unknowns." He found that some 70 to 85 percent of all news comes from "knowns," such as political, economic, social, or cultural celebrities. Fully 20 percent of all domestic news, he found, comes from the president, and another 20 percent comes from the cabinet.[11]

"Presidents have considerable leverage with which to manipulate part of the press," writes Lyndon Johnson's one-time press secretary George Reedy,

> and all try to do so with varying degrees of success. The principal source of the leverage is the unusual position of the President as one of the very few figures in public life who has in his exclusive possession a type of news virtually indispensable to the social and economic security of any reporter assigned to cover the White House full time. This category of newsworthy material consists of the President himself—his thoughts, his relationship with his friends and employees, his routine habits, his personal likes and dislikes, his intimate moments with his family and his associates. The fact that these things constitute "news" of a front page variety gives the President a trading power with individual newsmen of such magnitude that it must be seen at close quarters to be credited.[12]

Many of the things a president—or another official—says and does may be what historian Daniel Boorstin has called pseudo-events.[13] Pseudo-events, according to Boorstin, are not spontaneous but rather happen because someone planned, planted, staged, or incited them. The major reason for their being planned or planted is so that they can be reported, and they are therefore arranged to occur for the convenience of the media. Events such as press conferences, news leaks, campaign debates, the public signing of proclamations or of newly passed bills—all are pseudo-events in Boorstin's terms.

In recent years, antigovernment activists have learned this approach from politicians. The result has been a flood of pseudo-events—now more often called media events—such as demonstrations, marches, and instances of civil disobedience. These pseudo-events or media events are designed primarily to "make news" and thereby advance a cause. In the era of media events, you don't have to be a political figure, nor do you even have to have any sort of usable political power, to "make news"—to be a source and, in a sense, to create or even almost become a message in the media. But studies such as Gans's show that you may have to resort to such pseudo-events as breaking the law or causing civil disturbances to make news or to get any attention if you are an unknown. The media have what in the trade are called news routines—principles of selection and rejection by which they decide which events to cover and report and which to ignore.

Todd Gitlin was a leader of Students for a Democratic Society in the 1960s when it led the movement for civil rights and then the one against the Vietnam War. He later became a sociology professor and wrote a book recounting and analyzing his activist experiences. "In the late twentieth century," he wrote,

> political movements feel called upon to rely on large-scale communications in order to *matter*, to say who they are and what they intend to publics they want to sway; but in the process they become "newsworthy" only by submitting to the implicit rules of newsmaking, by conforming to journalistic notions . . . of what a "story" is, what an "event" is, what a "protest" is. . . . Mass media define the public significance of movement events or, by blanking them out, actively deprive them of larger significance. . . . For what defines a movement as "good copy" is often flamboyance, often the presence of a media-certified celebrity-leader . . . but these qualities of the image are not what movements intend to be their projects, their identities, their goals.[14]

Thus, the emphasis on the newsworthy event distorts the activities of newsmakers, both in government and in opposition. It also tends to prevent coverage of much of what really matters in Washington and elsewhere, especially by television, which tends to depend on cameras. "TV focuses

---

[11]See Herbert J. Gans, *Deciding What's News* (New York: Pantheon, 1979).

[12]George Reedy, *The Twilight of the Presidency* (New York: World, 1970), pp. 100–101.

[13]Daniel J. Boorstin, *The Image: A Guide to Pseudo-Events in America* (New York: Harper, 1964). It is also worth noting that not just the events but also the analysis—even that by political scientists—may be "pseudo." See, for a lively argument, Dan Nimmo and James E. Combs, *Subliminal Politics: Myths and Mythmakers in America* (Englewood Cliffs, NJ: Prentice-Hall, 1980).

[14]Todd Gitlin, *The Whole World Is Watching: Mass Media in the Making and Unmaking of the New Left* (Berkeley: Univ. of California Press, 1980), pp. 3–4.

almost entirely on the 'visible' Government in Washington—the President, Congress, the Cabinet departments and the Supreme Court," observed Ron Nessen, long a TV newsman and then President Ford's press secretary.

> Television virtually ignores the "hidden" Government that is responsible for much of what happens here—the 3200 lawyers, the 2500 trade associations, the innumerable lobbyists, foundations, Washington representatives and consultants. . . . In fact, just about the only time the 'hidden' Government ever attracts the attention of the cameras is when someone breaks the rules and gets caught, for bribery, conspiracy or peddling influence. Otherwise, for TV, it's not a story. But, oh, what stories there are to tell![15]

The Politics of the Medium and the Receiver

The camera is a medium by which television conveys news. So too is the reporter. So too are the newspapers and the television and radio stations that carry the news reports to us over the airwaves. Any medium, whether it be human or technological, will tend to affect the message it carries. Each can therefore be politically imporant.

Herbert Gans has concluded that one can best view

> news as information which is transmitted from sources to audiences, with journalists—who are both employees of bureaucratic commercial organizations and members of a profession—summarizing, refining, and altering what becomes available to them from sources in order to make the information suitable for their audiences. Because news has consequences, however, journalists are susceptible to pressure from groups and individuals (including sources and audiences) with power to hurt them, their organizations, and their firms.[16]

A journalist may conceive of his or her role as that of *neutral or objective observer and reporter*. Edward R. Murrow, one of the great broadcast journalists of all time, once remarked that "the communication system . . . is totally neutral. It has no conscience, no principle, no morality. . . . It will broadcast filth or inspiration with equal facility." But he went on to say that "it is, in sum, no more or no less than the men and women who

Edward R. Murrow. (UPI/Bettmann Archive)

use it."[17] An NBC News pamphlet asserts that a reporter has an obligation "to put news into perspective, to interpret and to analyze," because "the bare statement of a development may confuse and mislead when it is divorced from essential background and context."[18] Many observers believe that the less a reporter interprets the news in this sense, the more likely it is that he or she will be used by public officials in ways that distort the news. When an official says something, it's news whether it's true or not. But an interpretive journalist would also claim that the fact that an official's statement is false is equally newsworthy and should be reported.

However, this view tends to shift the reporter from a position of neutrality to one where he or she is a *participant reporter*. As such he or she may be *the representative of the people*, seeking the truth and providing information to the public, and guarding the public interest. Alternately, the reporter may be a *critic of government*. But the reporter as critic may tend toward a third participant role—that of *policy maker* or actor in the policy process, something to which few reporters would claim to aspire. Some, however, will take a

[15]Ron Nessen, "The Washington You Can't See on Television," *TV Guide*, September 20, 1980, p. 10.
[16]Gans, *Deciding What's News*, p. 80.

[17]Quoted in I. E. Fang, *Television News* (New York: Hastings House, 1968), p. 218.
[18]Quoted by Robert M. Batscha, *Foreign Affairs News and the Broadcast Journalist* (New York: Praeger, 1975), pp. 30–31.

fourth role: that of *advocate of policy* via editorial or commentary.[19]

Newspeople differ not only in their concepts of the role they should play but also in their notion of what actually is the news. But they do tend to agree that people in authority make news. Edward R. Murrow once referred critically to this: "The bias I refer to is in the direction of authority, and in this case authority means anything which is organized, which has a name, and which gives speeches. . . . In covering the news . . . the press tends . . . to take its cues from established authority."[20] That happens in the White House press room, and it happens in any city.[21]

We may be influenced by the authority we grant to correspondents just as they may be influenced by the authority they grant to established individuals or organizations. These kinds of influence are effects of the personal media—the people themselves. But what of the mechanical media? Do the peculiar features of the mass media themselves—newspapers, radio, and especially television—affect us as well? Many believe they do.

Television as a medium tends to *fragment* information. The news on television consists of a rapid-fire series of unrelated items lasting only seconds apiece. Furthermore, the news is regularly interrupted by commercials. Finding meaning in all this may be difficult indeed.

Information on television is also *immediate*. Instant reporting is an essential feature of television news as we have come to view it. This, too, limits the meaning in the news by limiting its pattern, or structure, in the minds of its recipients.

Furthermore, television tends to make the viewer passive. Just as with parades, spectator sports, movies, and radio, once you're there you tend to take what comes. The most you are likely to do with television is switch channels. To prevent

such switching, even the news may be tailored to suit viewers' tastes.[22]

All in all, the combination of fragmentation, immediacy of information, and passivity of viewers may have important effects on what we learn from television. Some argue that television tends to destroy or prevent the development of the experience and skills essential to the effective functioning of our democratic politics. Jarol Manheim has conclded that

> as the reliance on television as a teaching/learning device (in the largest sense) increases, many interpretive and interactive skills may fall into disuse and decay. And since human interaction is the very heart and soul of the political process, a general decline in the analytical and expressive skills which characterize that interaction in the society as a whole cannot help but be reflected in the polity as well.[23]

Others are more optimistic. For example, critic Edwin Diamond, noting Nixon's inability to use the medium well to cover up his involvement in the Watergate scandal and the failures of many recent "media" election campaigns, concluded that

> it just may be that television is no longer as potent a political tool as the textbook wisdom holds. Or, to put the same heretical thought in another way, it may be that the audience—the political consumer . . . has changed in some critical ways. . . . Perhaps viewers are simply smarter, more sophisticated, or more skeptical.[24]

Increasingly, however, the electronic media seem to be homogenizing us, the receivers, by giving us one standardized message that we must take or leave. And if we choose to "leave" it by changing channels, we are quite likely to find something approximately the same awaiting us elsewhere around the dial. The media may also be doing the same to our politics, according to some critics.

IMPACT OF THE MEDIA ON POLITICS

The media, especially television, have had wide-ranging effects on politics in general. In the 1960s television news programs publicized the civil rights and antiwar movements. In the 1970s the media

[19]For a description of the major columnists and commentators—and their biases—see Carl Kalvelage and Morley Segal, *Research Guide in Political Science*, 2d ed. (Morristown, NJ: General Learning Press, 1976), chap. 6.

[20]Quoted in Louis M. Lyons, ed., *Reporting Television News* (Cambridge, MA: Harvard Univ. Press, 1965), p. 154. For a comprehensive study of concepts of news and objectivity by a widely experienced newsperson, see Bernard Roshco, *Newsmaking* (Chicago: Univ. of Chicago Press, 1975).

[21]See Michael B. Grossman and Martha J. Kumar, *Portraying the President: The White House and the News Media* (Baltimore: Johns Hopkins Univ. Press, 1981), and Stephen Hess, *Washington Reporters* (Washington, DC: Brookings Institution, 1981). See also James M. Perry, *Us & Them* (New York: Clarkson Potter, 1973), an account of press coverage of presidential campaigns by one who was a member of "the pack" in 1972.

[22]This practice is also discussed by Diamond in *The Tin Kazoo*, pp. 23–25.

[23]Jarol B. Manheim, "Can Democracy Survive Television?" *Journal of Communication*, Spring 1976, p. 85.

[24]Diamond, *The Tin Kazoo*, p. 8.

not only focused on but helped to generate (in the views of some) a widespread disenchantment with politics and government.[25] However, the media usually have their most immediate impact on elections and political campaigns.

The first political commercials on TV appeared in the 1952 presidential campaign, along with the first televising of the party conventions. There were then only about 15 million sets in American homes—a total that climbed to about 54 million in 1960, 93 million in 1970, and well over 100 million since then. The impact of television on elections has, understandably, grown with the spread of TV sets throughout the population.[26]

Research indicates that, in general, roughly a third of the voters decide whom to vote for before the conventions, another third during the conventions, and a final third during the fall campaign. Television is the major information source on both conventions and campaigns, and so it probably plays an important role in these voting decisions, even though voters rarely attribute such influence to television itself.[27]

Two political scientists, Thomas Patterson and Robert McClure, studied the influence of television on voters in the 1972 presidential election. They reported their study in a book whose title gives away their conclusion: *The Unseeing Eye: The Myth of Television Power in National Elections.*[28] They found that

> the only noticeable effect of network campaign news is an increased tendency among voters to view politics in the same trivial terms that the newscasters depict it. Regular viewers of network news are likely to describe an election campaign as a lot of nonsense rather than a choice between fundamental issues.[29]

What does reach viewers, they found, is political advertising, which actually has more issue content than do network newscasts. But their research discovered that advertising is almost as likely to benefit one's opponent as it is to benefit the one who is paying for it because viewers tend to see in it what they want to see.

Patterson then did a follow-up study of the 1976 campaign. This time he concentrated on media coverage and voters' experiences of it. He found that the media coverage tended to focus on the "horse-race" aspects of the campaign instead of on the important substantive questions of the issues, the candidates' policy positions, the candidates' characters and abilities, their public records, and their personal backgrounds.

"The press can never give the voters what many of them really want," he concluded,

> which is the "truth" about the candidates. . . . But the press could give the voters more facts, so that their opinions will be informed. If they chose to do so, reporters could place more emphasis on what the candidates are saying on the issues, on their public records, on their qualifications, and so on. The horse race does not have to occupy 50 percent or more of the news space.[30]

But it has continued to do so in subsequent campaign coverage.

IMPACT OF THE MEDIA ON THE GOVERNMENT

We have seen that the media tend to standardize their reports. We noted earlier that they also tend to standardize their audiences. It is important to remember that one of the media's important audiences is the government itself. The government, too, increasingly finds the media stereotyping it— and perhaps thereby homogenizing it as well. Researchers studying media effects have concluded that "the audience is not so malleable as merely to follow in the ways advocated on the editorial pages of newspapers or in the commentaries of the networks. But its members do take their cues about the nature of the world about them from the media. And these cues influence what they do."[31] The

[25]See Michael J. Robinson, "Television and American Politics: 1956–1976," *Public Interest* 48 (Summer 1977), 3–39.

[26]See Edwin Diamond and Stephen Bates, *The Spot: The Rise of Political Advertising on Television* (Cambridge, MA: MIT Press, 1984).

[27]See research reports summarized in Sidney Kraus and Dennis Davis, *The Effects of Mass Communication on Political Behavior* (University Park, PA: Pennsylvania State Univ. Press, 1976), chap. 3.

[28](New York: Putnam, 1976).

[29]Ibid., p. 22. Patterson and McClure studied every newscast of all three networks in the 1972 campaign and interviewed 2000 viewers as well. For another view of the same campaign, see C. Richard Hofstetter, *Bias in the News: Network Television Coverage of the 1972 Election Campaign* (Columbus, OH: Ohio State Univ. Press, 1976). And for a study of coverage of a later campaign, see Michael J. Robinson and Margaret A. Sheehan, *Over the Wire and on TV: CBS and UPI in Campaign '80* (New York: Russell Sage, 1984).

[30]Thomas E. Patterson, "The Media Muffed the Message," *Washington Post*, December 5, 1976, p. 1. Patterson presented his findings in more detail in *The Mass Media Election: How Americans Choose Their President* (New York: Praeger, 1980).

[31]Lee B. Becker, Maxwell E. McCombs, and Jack M. McLeod, "The Development of Political Cognitions," in *Political Communication*, ed. Steven H. Chaffee (Beverly Hills, CA: Sage, 1975), p. 58. See Kraus and Davis, *Effects of Mass Communication on Political Behavior*, chap. 6.

media, in other words, may "set the agenda" for the public. Much the same might be said about the government as an audience. No politician can long afford to ignore the media.

Of course, no politician does. Studies have found that the press often plays a major part in "setting the agenda" in public affairs.[32] A study of opinion leaders by C. H. Weiss found that the media actually serve to link leaders in various sectors of government and society better than, for example, private meetings do. A study by W. P. Davison found that even diplomats get most of their information about world developments from the media, despite the fact that they have access to diplomatic and intelligence channels.[33] Everyone seems to depend on the media, and everyone is subject to whatever influence the media exert.

IMPACT OF GOVERNMENT ON THE MEDIA

The influence process works the other way too, of course. We've already seen the extent to which government, as the primary source of most political news, may "manage" the news in its own interests. However, there are more subtle and often more important ways in which the government attempts to influence or control the media.

"Disinforming" the Media and the People

In some instances, the government uses the media to misinform the public. One controversial instance of misinformation occurred in the summer of 1986. The Reagan administration had bombed Col. Moamar Quadhafi's Libya in April in retaliation for its alleged support of terrorism against Americans abroad. In August members of the administration made statements to the press that Quadhafi was undertaking new terrorist strikes. They warned that the United States might not wait for new instances of terrorism before striking Libya again. The *Wall Street Journal* printed a long article reporting these assertions as truth. Some weeks later, the president's press secretary, Larry Speakes, repeated these assertions. But officials in the State Department and the Defense Department publicly disagreed, saying that the evidence against Quadhafi was growing but not "hard." Speakes then said that there was "hard evidence," citing as his source the National Security Advisor, Admiral John Poindexter. The *Washington Post* later learned that Poindexter had written a memo to the president asserting that Quadhafi was doing nothing, but nonetheless advocating a policy of "disinformation" in the American press concerning Libyan terrorist intentions and actions. Disinformation is a term that the Reagan administration and others had been using in statements attacking actions by the Soviet Union in "planting" inaccurate reports in the Western press. So the Reagan administration had secretly adopted the policy it had been criticizing the Soviets for. When the *Washington Post* uncovered the strategy, Speakes admitted that he sometimes used his press briefings to "shape" events in foreign countries on a range of issues.[34] And Secretary of State George Shultz said that "leaked" disinformation was an appropriate tactic if it advanced the administration's foreign policy goals.

Regulation of the Media: The First Amendment and the FCC

The First Amendment protects freedom of the press, and so government's efforts to control the print media directly often fail. Laws concerning publication or distribution of pornography have fared better, and so have prohibitions against libel—defaming someone's character in print.[35]

The First Amendment says nothing about radio and television, of course, for radio was invented in 1896 and television came into public use some five decades later. When radio began operating, the secretary of commerce laid down certain restrictions on broadcast frequencies. (Frequencies are the levels of broadcast signals that determine where on your dial you get a station. Regulations control them so that each signal is clear and not mixed with another, so that you can hear it.) In 1926 a court ruled that the secretary of commerce had no such power, and competitors then began to use signals that overlapped and interfered with each other.

---

[32]See Michael Bruce MacKuen et al., *More Than News* (Beverly Hills, CA: Sage, 1981), part 1.

[33]These two and other studies are summarized in William L. Rivers, Susan Miller, and Oscar Gandy, "Government and the Media," in *Political Communication*, ed. Chaffee, pp. 217–36.

[34]See Leslie H. Gelb, "Speakes Defines His Role in Shaping Events," *New York Times*, October 10, 1986.

[35]For a survey of the legal field, see Harvey L. Zuckman and Martin J. Gaynes, *Mass Communications Law* (St. Paul, MN: West, 1977).

When the broadcast industry protested, Congress passed the Radio Act of 1927. That bill created the Federal Radio Commission (FRC) and gave it power to regulate frequencies. In 1934 the FRC was combined into the new Federal Communications Commission (FCC). The new agency was given broader powers to regulate in order to achieve "a fair, efficient, and equitable" broadcasting system responsive to the "public interest, convenience, or necessity."

Over the years the FCC developed three primary guidelines: first, that the basic purpose of broadcasting is "the development of an informed public opinion through the public dissemination of news and ideas concerning the vital public issues of the day"; second, that the news and information should come from "diverse and antagonistic sources"; and third, that radio and television should be basically local institutions, reflecting local needs and desires. The FCC can issue licenses to stations to use the "public airwaves"—but there are few frequencies still available. It can also revoke or re-fuse to renew licenses when they come due every three years—but it does so only very rarely, in cases of extreme violations of its guidelines. Further, it can make regulations on how stations should serve the public interest—without censoring what is broadcast. The FCC developed the **fairness doctrine**, which requires a station to broadcast a range of public affairs opinions, to avoid monopolistic control of content.[36] It has also limited ownership of multiple broadcast stations in an area by a single company as well as ownership of television stations by newspapers in the same city.

As an independent regulatory agency, the FCC is supposed to be removed from politics. But the president, with the approval of the Senate, appoints a new member whenever a term expires. This means that interest groups—both citizen

---

[36]A debate among media people is now emerging over whether the fairness doctrine is necessary or desirable. See Hugh Carter Donahue, "The Fairness Doctrine Is Shackling Broadcast," *Technology Review*, Nov.–Dec. 1986, pp. 45–52, and David Bollier, "The Strange Politics of 'Fairness,'" *Channels*, Jan.–Feb. 1986, pp. 46–52.

Mark S. Fowler, Reagan appointee, chairs a meeting of the Federal Communications Commission, which he led until 1987. (John Troha/Black Star)

groups and industrial interests—can play a role. Also, FCC decisions can be appealed to the courts—which adds yet another political dimension.[37] In addition, the FCC, like other regulatory agencies, must receive a budgetary appropriation every year from Congress. Congress recently has taken to attaching *riders* to these bills prohibiting particular actions it does not like. This adds still another political consideration. Further, the FCC may disagree with other agencies of government as to what should or should not be done.

Deregulation of the Media

The politics of media regulation became especially active in the Reagan years. Reagan appointed a former disc jockey turned communications lawyer, Mark Fowler, to head the FCC. He also appointed other members sympathetic to cutting back regulation. Fowler announced that he favored abolishing both the fairness doctrine and the equal-time rule. Indeed, he favored total deregulation of television. "It's just another appliance—it's a toaster with pictures," he said. Before Fowler resigned in 1987, the FCC did abolish rules limiting the num-

ber of radio commercials as well as regulations requiring radio public affairs programming. The FCC was less successful with television and cable, however, where its deregulation efforts were blocked in the House of Representatives. Fowler argued that there are now so many stations, including the new cable broadcasters, that the marketplace can provide enough diversity as well as sufficient protection of minority interests. But many others suspected that the profit motive would not protect unpopular views. Some also feared greater political domination of media content by conservative owners in the absence of FCC rules. These issues are now being decided in the courts.

Control of the Media

Political influence on the media—and even efforts to dominate them—are nothing new. Sometimes government itself seeks such control. The Nixon administration made various efforts to influence the media. Through budgetary controls, it sought to change programming on the largely government-funded Public Broadcasting Service, which provides certain programs to the nation's 322 noncommercial stations and which Nixon believed to be too liberal in its programming content. (The Reagan administration was later much more successful in altering PBS's direction by cutting its

[37]For accounts of regulations, see Erwin G. Krasnow, Lawrence D. Longley, and Herbert A. Terry, *The Politics of Broadcast Regulation*, 3d ed. (New York: St. Martin's Press, 1982); Edward Jay Epstein, *News from Nowhere*; and Doris A. Graber, *Mass Media and American Politics* (Washington, DC: CQ Press, 1980).

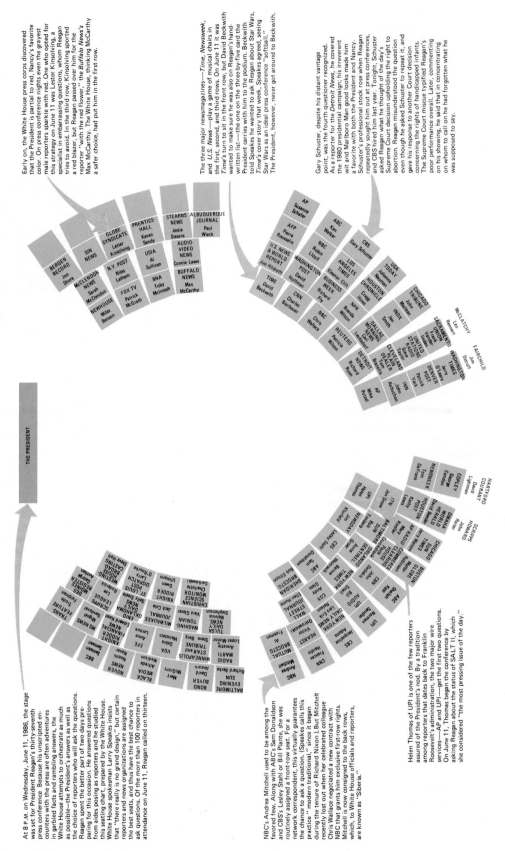

At 8 P.M. on Wednesday, June 11, 1986, the stage was set for President Reagan's thirty-seventh press conference. Because his unscripted encounters with the press are often adventures in garbled facts and rambling answers, the White House attempts to orchestrate as much as possible—the President's answers as well as the choice of reporters who will ask the questions. Reagan spent the better part of two days preparing for this occasion. He answered questions from aides posing as reporters and he studied this seating chart, prepared by the White House. White House spokesman Larry Speakes insists that "there really is no grand design," but certain reporters and news organizations are assigned the best seats, and thus have the best chance to ask questions. Of the more than 100 reporters in attendance on June 11, Reagan called on thirteen.

NBC's Andrea Mitchell used to be among the favored few. Along with ABC's Sam Donaldson and CBS's Lesley Stahl or Bill Plante, she was routinely assigned a front-row seat. For a network correspondent, this virtually guarantees the chance to ask a question. (Speakes calls this practice "modern traditional," since it began during the tenure of Richard Nixon.) But Mitchell recently lost out when her celebrated colleague Chris Wallace negotiated a new contract with NBC that grants him exclusive first-row rights. Mitchell is now consigned to the back rows, which, to White House officials and reporters, are known as "Siberia."

Helen Thomas of UPI is one of the few reporters assured of the President's nod. By a tradition among reporters that dates back to Franklin Roosevelt's administration, the two major wire services—AP and UPI—get the first two questions. On June 11, Thomas began the conference by asking Reagan about the status of SALT II, which she considered "the most pressing issue of the day."

Early on, the White House press corps discovered that the President is partial to red, Nancy's favorite color. On press conference nights even the gravest male reporters sparkle with red. One who opted for this strategy on June 11 was Lester Kinsolving, a specialist in embarrassing questions, whom Reagan tries to avoid. In the third row, Kinsolving sported a red blazer, but Reagan passed over him for the reporter "with the red flower," the Buffalo News's Max McCarthy. The White House, thinking McCarthy a safer choice, had put him in the first row.

The three major newsmagazines—Time, Newsweek, and U.S. News—play a game of musical chairs in the first, second, and third rows. On June 11 it was Time's turn to sit in the front row, but David Beckwith wanted to make sure he was also on Reagan's handwritten list—the one on the three-by-five card the President carries with him to the podium. Beckwith told Speakes he wanted to ask Reagan about Star Wars, Time's cover story that week. Speakes agreed, seeing Star Wars as an ideal press conference "softball." The President, however, never got around to Beckwith.

Gary Schuster, despite his distant vantage point, was the fourth questioner recognized. As a reporter for the Detroit News, he covered the 1980 presidential campaign; his irreverent wit and Marlboro Man good looks made him a favorite with both the President and Nancy. Schuster's professional stock rose when Reagan repeatedly sought him out at press conferences, and CBS hired him last year. Tonight, Schuster asked Reagan what he thought of the day's Supreme Court decision upholding the right to abortion. Reagan misunderstood the question even though he asked Schuster to repeat it, and gave his response to another Court decision concerning the rights of handicapped infants. The Supreme Court miscue typified Reagan's poor performance overall. Later, commenting on his showing, he said that in concentrating on whom to call on he had forgotten what he was supposed to say.

The Politics of the President's News Conference. (Adapted from Eleanor Clift, "All the President's Nods." Harper's Magazine, September 1986, pp. 54-55. Reproduced with permission.)

Male as well as female journalists wear red in order to be called upon at President Reagan's news conference. (© Mark Reinstein/UNIPHOTO)

budget and appointing conservatives to its board of directors.) The Nixon administration also used the courts to try to force reporters to reveal the confidential sources of their exposés, with some success.[38]

Even when political pressure is not applied, there are factors at work that tend to inhibit the media—especially those representatives who cover the White House. The White House press corps covers the president from comfortable quarters paid for by the taxpayers and travels with him as well. One member of that group wrote of the strong temptation to become part of the president's "court"—"to depict the president as larger than life, to assume an air of self-importance and to view the White House as the center of the universe."[39]

However, the White House usually tends to see the networks as offering coverage that is too critical of it.[40] CBS News is often cited by White House officials as being the most critical organization. To test this perception, TV Guide studied all three networks' coverage of a randomly selected week, May 1–7, 1983. It concluded that

CBS broadcast more stories about the Reagan Administration and the ways its policies affect the Nation than its competitors. . . . And when the President was mentioned, CBS, by a margin of more than 7 to 1, tended to cast the Reagan Administration in a more negative light than either ABC or NBC. . . . However . . . the reason for CBS's aggressiveness is not personal bias against Mr. Reagan. It is, instead, CBS's specific vision of what news is and how it should be presented.

TV Guide went on to characterize the CBS objective as "a populist newscast" and said that

---

[38]For an account of these and other efforts, see William E. Porter, *Assault on the Media: The Nixon Years* (Ann Arbor: Univ. of Michigan Press, 1976).

[39]John Herbers, *No Thank You, Mr. President* (New York: Norton, 1976). See also the memoirs of a man who served in the White House press corps for 25 years, James Deakin, *Straight Stuff: The Reporters, the White House and the Truth* (New York: Morrow, 1984); and Stephen Hess, *The Washington Reporters*. For further pictures of this tendency and the cynicism it can breed, see Timothy Crouse's book on the press corps in the 1972 election, *The Boys on the Bus* (New York: Random House, 1973). The same phenomenon can occur in coverage of Congress, too. For an account of the perquisites of the Capitol press, see Charles Peters, *How Washington Really Works* (Reading, MA: Addison-Wesley, 1980), pp. 18–20.

[40]For the most recent such criticism, see the book by Carter's press secretary, Jody Powell: *The Other Side of the Story* (New York: Morrow, 1984). And for a report of a survey of journalists that found "a dominant perspective" that is "liberal and alienated from traditional norms and institutions" and argues that journalists tend to project their own assumptions onto the news, see S. Robert Lichter, Stanley Rothman, and Linda S. Lichter, *The Media Elite: America's New Powerbrokers* (New York: Adler & Adler, 1986). But see also the view that the media report in a way that tends to support the status quo and "delegitimate" movements for significant change in American institutions, as summarized in Robert E. Denton, Jr., and Gary C. Woodward, *Political Communication in America* (New York: Praeger, 1985), chap. 6.

this vision of America . . . that is adversarial toward Government . . . lies behind CBS's toughness toward the Reagan Administration and CBS's tendency to personalize the news. CBS enhances the conflict between Americans and their government by laying the responsibility for much of what goes on directly at Mr. Reagan's feet.[41]

CBS News anchor Dan Rather responded:

Part of our job—whether it's a Democratic or a Republican Administration—is to say to our audience, "All right, this is what the President says is happening. Now we're going to go out and see whether, in fact, this is what is happening." When it is, we say so. When it isn't, we say so. That kind of coverage gets you a reputation at anybody's White House of being The Enemy.[42]

Rather later told the *New York Times* that he and his network were subject to frequent, "unrelenting" criticism and pressure in the form of phone calls from Reagan White House officials before he went on the air, as well as afterwards. He said this criticism was much more sophisticated and so, more difficult to resist, than that from the Nixon administration. Reagan officials, he said, are "slicker and smarter and therefore more dangerous and more effective."[43]

Network news gets such attention from the White House because it is still the major source of news for most Americans. However, that will probably change as more and more Americans take advantage of new information technologies and new media. The key to this development is the question of media access.

MEDIA ACCESS FOR THE PUBLIC

Rules and Practices Concerning Access

Journalist A. J. Liebling used to say that "freedom of the press belongs to the man who owns one." We have already discussed evidence of broader access to the print media. Increasingly, the courts in the past decade have agreed that citizens should have more access to the broadcast media as well because commercial stations are private businesses using the public airwaves for profit and sometimes for news coverage and editorial statements that affect citizens' interests. There are four key rules concerning access that apply to broadcasters.

- *The fairness doctrine* requires that a broadcaster give air time to opposing spokespersons to present their views on controversial issues.
- *The personal-attack rule* gives individuals or groups a right to reply if they are maligned on the air.
- *The political-editorial rule* gives candidates whose election is opposed by a station editorial the right to reply.
- *The equal-time rule* gives a candidate the right to the same air time that his or her opponent gets.

Not all access is forced by rules, of course.[44] Sometimes it is invited by editors and directors seeking out varying views. At other times it comes about through the "newsworthiness" of citizens or groups and their activities. However, Edie Goldenberg has noted that "resource-rich" news sources, such as established business and social groups, are in a much stronger position to bargain with reporters and to manage the news than are "resource-poor" groups. Resource-rich groups are usually thought to be more newsworthy; they are more often a part of a reporter's regular beat, or specialization, and they can more easily help the reporter in collecting the news. "Resource-poor sources are at a disadvantage both in initiating contacts with the press and in regularizing them," she concludes. Yet, as Goldenberg observes, such contacts can carry the message of resource-poor groups to policy makers and can strengthen a group's position in the political arena.[45]

---

[41]John Weisman, "Who's Toughest on the White House—And Why," *TV Guide*, August 27, 1983, pp. 4–13.

[42]Ibid., p. 11.

[43]Sally Bedell Smith, "Rather Finds 'Unrelenting' Criticism from the Reagan Administration," *New York Times*, November 11, 1983.

[44]The FCC (until the Reagan administration) and the courts have been developing regulations and procedures for giving citizens access to the media. This has created a new field within the law. For summaries of its development as it concerns television and other media, see Benno C. Schmidt, Jr., *Freedom of the Press vs. Public Access* (New York: Praeger, 1976). See also Fred A. Friendly, *The Good Guys, the Bad Buys, and the First Amendment* (New York: Random House, 1976). And for a handbook that will be valuable should you wish to secure access rights, see Andrew O. Shapiro, *Media Access: Your Rights to Express Your Views on Radio and Television* (Boston: Little, Brown, 1976). You may also get further guidance on media access from the organizations described in Action Unit 7.1.

[45]Edie Goldenberg, *Making the Papers: The Access of Resource-Poor Groups to the Metropolitan Press* (Lexington, MA: Lexington Books, 1975), p. 145. See also Roshco, *Newsmaking*, chap. 6, "Being a News Source vs. Becoming a News Source."

Access and the New Media Technologies

Information is power—or at least it creates the possibility of power. Nowhere is this clearer than in the case of the media. We get almost all our information through the communications media, rather than through our own personal, direct experience. Our communication is increasingly electronic—via telephone, television, and computer—rather than personal. Thus, control over the communications media brings the possibility of great power—for good or for ill.

Many people fear this new electronic technology. It is strange and hard to understand, and some of it is hard to use. In 1984 many authors wrote of the threat to liberty and privacy posed by such new media, for *1984* is also the title of a famous novel written by George Orwell in 1948, which deals with electronic political control.[46] Orwell's "Big Brother," the state, policed everybody with two-way television screens. Such "interactive television" was actually developed from 1977 to 1984 in Columbus, Ohio, on an experimental basis. There, with the "Qube" cable system, TV pictures went only one way, but viewers could communicate with headquarters via a little key-pad. With it they could vote in opinion polls, tell the mayor what they thought he or she should do, take educational quizzes, play in game shows, shop, and so on. The same system has also been tried in Cincinnati, Pittsburgh, Dallas, Houston, and suburbs of St. Louis.

This is but one example of new communications technology that may eventually transform our lives—and probably our politics—in ways we can't yet predict.[47] There are three important trends here that we must recognize—and that we can then help to shape.[48]

The most basic trend is the *proliferation of technologies*, many of which are becoming competitive. Many people can now use their telephones to pay bills through their banks instead of using the mails. Increasingly, we will be able to use our own televisions to receive text (by processes called Teletext and Videotex)[49] such as books, magazines, and shopping catalogs. The millions of citizens who have personal computers can now hook them to phone lines with devices called modems and send and receive "electronic mail" instantly. They can also get the text of newspaper and magazine articles and other data. Someday students like you will probably read a subsequent edition of this book by sitting at their computer terminals and calling it up page by page as they want it. Such "electronic publishing," or "publishing on demand," now already occurs in technical subject areas where facts change very quickly and are expensive to publish in "hard copy" (that is, on paper). This system will make it possible to tailor a textbook to the particular needs and desires of an individual reader. Thus, these new technologies diversify our sources of information and our means of communication.

Technology, then, is *decentralizing access to both information and transmission lines*. Still, all this new technology decentralizes access only for those who can afford to buy the technology and pay the fees for such access. Thus, the well-off will have increasing access, but the poor will not.

These joint trends of proliferation of technologies and decentralization of access could result in tendencies toward powerful information monopolies. This monopolization could happen if one or a few "common carriers" (as telephone companies and other communications services are called) get control over the technology. It could also happen if the FCC deregulates the television industry so that it no longer has to allow public access through rules such as equal time and the fairness doctrine. It could also result if the technology remains too expensive for most citizens. Finally, it could occur if the dispensers of information choose to "stan-

---

[46]Orwell's novel is still in print. For an example of such recent warnings, see David Burnham, *The Rise of the Computer State: The Threat to Our Freedoms, Our Ethics, and Our Democratic Processes* (New York: Random House, 1983).

[47]Among others are Low Power TV, Satellite Master-Antenna TV, and Direct Broadcast Satellite TV (to "dishes" in viewers' backyards). For descriptions of these and a concise survey of all elements of the electronic media, see *Essential Field Guide to the Electronic Environment*, published each year by *Channels* magazine and available in most libraries.

[48]These and other important trends are analyzed in Ithiel de Sola Pool, *Technologies of Freedom* (Cambridge, MA: Harvard Univ. Press, 1983), chap. 9.

[49]"Teletext" is a one-way technology that telecasts text and graphics to TV sets equipped with special decoders. "Videotex" is an interactive technology, such as the "Qube" system described above, in which the viewer may use a computer and phone lines or a two-way cable to communicate with a central station. Experimental versions of both are now in operation in various cities around the country, as well as abroad.

dardize" the messages they transmit to national audiences in the same way the TV networks have.

On the other hand, if the decentralization of the technology, and so of access, proceeds at a rapid pace, there could be much more diversity in the messages we recieve. Cable television offers the prospect of dozens of channels of programming. As of today some 40 million Americans subscribe to a local cable service. Forty-eight percent of Americans receive cable programming. There are almost 6000 cable systems serving 33 million homes. This gives viewers access to the major networks and to over 100 national satellite channels. (Table 7.4 lists the major ones. Most cable systems also offer one or more pay—mostly movie—channels, such as Home Box Office, Cinemax, and The Disney

Channel.) But already there is a trend toward concentration in the cable business. The ten largest cable companies already serve half of all cable subscribers. Furthermore, almost all these large companies are owned by media conglomerates such as TIME Inc., Warner Communications, Times Mirror Co. (see Table 7.2), Cox, and Storer. Thus, greater diversity of choice for viewers is being provided by firms that are decreasing the diversity of cable companies through their purchase of independent systems. Furthermore, many of the cable programming systems listed in Table 7.4 are themselves owned by cable system companies, such as Warner or TIME Inc., or by networks, such as ABC and CBS.

But while cable networks and cable systems are

TABLE 7.4
Major Satellite Cable Channels

NAME	LAUNCH DATE	HOMES REACHED (MILLIONS)	CONTENT
ESPN (Entertainment and Sports Programming Network)	1979	39	Sports events and sports news
CNN (Cable News Network)	1980	35	Continuous news reporting
USA Network	1977	33	Sports and features
CBN (Christian Broadcasting Network)	1977	32	"Family programming stressing positive values"
MTV (Music Television)	1981	30	Video version of rock radio
Nickelodeon	1979	29	Children's programming
Nashville Network	1983	28	Country-oriented entertainment
Lifetime	1984	26	Health, science, better living
C-SPAN (Cable Satellite Public Affairs Network)	1979	25	Live coverage of U.S. House of Representatives, other governmental events
Financial News Network	1981	23	National business news
The Weather Channel	1982	23	Continuous weather news
CNN Headline News	1982	21	
Arts and Entertainment Network	1981	20	Cultural programming
Score	1985	19	Sports news and events
VH-1 (Video Hits 1)	1985	14	Top 40 music videos
PTL Network	1978	14	Christian programming
BET (Black Entertainment Television)	1980	13	Black-oriented programming
Tempo Television	1979	13	International programming
Discovery Channel	1985	11	Nonfiction programming
C-SPAN II	1986	8	Live coverage of U.S. Senate, etc.
TLC (The Learning Channel)	1980	8	Educational programming
The Silent Network	1984	7	Deaf and hearing-impaired programming
EWTN (Eternal Word Television Network)	1981	5	Catholic programming
ACTS Satellite Network	1984	5	Southern Baptist programming
SIN (Spanish International Network)	1979	4	Spanish-language programming

Source: Channels, 1987 Field Guide to the Electronic Environment. Reprinted by permission of Channels magazine.

becoming more concentrated in ownership terms, decentralization and diversity in content are being strengthened by public access cable. Public access cable is nonprofit programming furnished by a local cable company. It provides the air time and usually a studio and equipment, but it does not control program content. The FCC made public access a requirement in all cable franchise agreements between cities and cable companies in 1972. In 1979 the Supreme Court voided this rule, but most local companies continue to offer public access. Thus, if your city has cable, you may be able to make your own cable programs with the company's help, and see yourself on local television.

This proliferation of new technologies and program providers has outstripped current regulations. But experts disagree on what to do about this. The Reagan administration's FCC has sought to abolish all regulation in order to let market forces determine what we can see and how we can use the technology. An opposite view has been argued by consumer advocate Ralph Nader, who offers the following principles as the basis of protection of citizen access:

- Every electronic communications technology must be operated in the interest of all citizens.
- The literacy that is the people's birthright must also include media literacy (the teaching of the use of video equipment and computers).
- Every citizen has the right to an opportunity to reach an audience.
- Every citizen has the right to all the information necessary to make rational choices as a voter and as a consumer.[50]

Others say we will need new codes of ethics to protect our rights to privacy and to see that the new technology serves only desirable purposes.[51]

Meanwhile, various new technologies are allowing the individual new opportunities through novel types of "public access." For example, citizen-band (CB) radio has done for radio what the copying machine has done for the press. They have given every person the opportunity to be his or her own broadcaster and publisher. Video cassette recorders (VCRs), now owned by over 40 percent of all households, offer individuals the opportunity to become their own TV programmers—and even

their own "telecasters" if they exchange cassettes with others or find local stations with "public access" programs. Courts have held that noncommercial use of such VCRs to record TV programs is legal. The greater interest for many, however, is in creating their own programs with inexpensive camera equipment. Not surprisingly, these inexpensive technologies have also created new citizen action groups. For example, the National Federation of Local Cable Programmers links people developing and using new methods of gaining and holding operator support for community TV and distributes programs developed by local citizen groups.[52] Some are even calling for a "public-interest satellite" to transmit nonprofit programming. This, however, would require further government regulation.[53] Indeed, various types of governmental involvement, by courts, by Congress, and by regulatory agencies, seem inevitable. Meanwhile, the Public Interest Video Network uses a Public Broadcasting System (PBS) satellite to transmit its own TV programs, such as those covering antinuclear demonstrations. It is able to do so at a low fee because of the 1978 Public Telecommunications Financing Act passed by Congress.[54]

THE QUESTION OF MEDIA RESPONSIBILITY IN DEMOCRATIC POLITICS

With these opportunities have come new questions concerning the responsibilities of the media, of the government, and increasingly, of the public—the audience that seems more and more to be turning into sources of messages, with growing opportunities for influencing the development of new media or channels.

What is the responsibility of the media in democratic politics? Should they be objective reporters or interpreters or critics? Should they inform or entertain or both?[55] Should they give the public what it needs or what it wants? Should the media be run as businesses? One television magnate, Lord

---

[50]Ralph Nader, "A Citizen's Communication Agenda," *Citizen Participation*, May–June 1980, p. 3.

[51]See "August Bequai, Fighter for Ethics," *Computerworld*, May 21, 1984, pp. ID1–ID14.

[52]See Tim Onosko, "Grassroots Television: Programming by the People" *Video*, February, 1981.

[53]See Douglas Davis, "Open Up the Satellites," *Newsweek*, November 3, 1980.

[54]See Rich Wilson, "Instant Network!" *Videography*, August 1979.

[55]One question gaining prominence recently is that of libel. For a fascinating analysis of libel cases filed by Gen. William Westmoreland against CBS-TV and by Israeli defense minister Ariel Sharon against *Time* magazine, see Renata Adler, *Reckless Disregard* (New York: Knopf, 1986).

Thomson, characterized a television station's license as "a license to print money," and broadcasters often refer to the business as "failure-proof" because it is so profitable even for poorly run stations.[56] The press also is usually highly profitable. "Both its power and its role come from one source: the Constitution's protection of press freedom," according to journalist-critic Charles Seib. "That's the only constitutional protection given a private business. It carries with it awesome responsibilities."[57] These responsibilities—uncertain and under debate as they still are—also extend to the government, which regulates the media.

And what of the citizens? Experts increasingly refer to the prospect of "the wired city." But the same technology that makes information from around the world and around the corner available in one's own home may separate people from each other even further. Critic Erik Barnouw warns:

What disturbs me is that the writer, the teacher, or the communicator is getting further away from the audience. . . . The viewer, meanwhile, is becoming more and more isolated. Tomorrow, he won't have to go to the polling place any more. He'll be able to vote by pushing buttons. He doesn't have to attend class; he can take the course from home. . . . The result is that people are getting out of touch with humanity. Everything is pretended participation.[58]

Furthermore, the same technology that brings messages to us can be used—by the government or by private interests—to eavesdrop on our daily lives and even perhaps to dictate our behavior. So there are important questions of civil liberties raised by the very advances that can also promise to increase our civil rights. The mass media have thus become much more than an influence on governmental decision making. They have become as well a promise of greater liberty and at the same time a challenge to our liberty.[59] We shall examine the politics of liberty in Chapter 12. Meanwhile, we must turn our attention more directly to the governmental actors that play major roles not only in the media but in our own daily lives.

SUMMARY

Most Americans rely on television for most of the news they get. Television and newspapers are the most important mass media in America today. Media are means of transmission of information. We call them "mass" media because they reach large audiences, their communications have been standardized, and their ownership is concentrated. We usually rely on the mass media for information about things that are beyond our own experience. In other words, the media are authorities for us. This makes them political actors. They attempt to shape our images of political reality. They do so by choosing what to tell us and by selecting a political role for themselves (objective observer, interpreter, critic, or policy advocate). Special features of television also affect its message: a tendency to fragment information, the immediacy of information, the passivity of viewers, and its total dependence on advertising for revenue.

The media have played important roles in shaping issues such as civil rights, the antiwar movement, and disenchantment with government. They also influence the way campaigns are conducted and the impact campaigns have on voters—especially by emphasizing the "horse-race" aspects of campaigns rather than issues and character. In addition, the media often set the agenda for government.

Government also influences the media. It is the source of most media reports. The Federal Communications Commission regulates television through limits on multiple ownership, requirements concerning public service broadcasting, and imposition of four rules: fairness, personal attack, political-editorial, and equal time. The Reagan administration has sought complete deregulation of television but has had only partial success.

New technologies—such as various types of cable, interactive television, and computer-based communication—are proliferating and decentralizing access to both information and communica-

---

[56]Les Brown, "Television Becomes the 'Failure-Proof Business,'" *New York Times*, March 15, 1976.

[57]Charles B. Seib, "Journalistic Conflicts," *Washington Post*, November 26, 1976, p. A23.

[58]Interview in *U.S. News & World Report*, March 1, 1976, pp. 27–29. See also Richard Hollander, *Video Democracy: The Vote-From-Home Revolution* (Mt. Airy, MD: Lomond, 1985).

[59]For a stimulating analysis of the complex challenge, see Ithiel de Sola Pool, *Technologies of Freedom*, chap. 9, on "policies for freedom."

tion lines. These could prove to be "technologies of freedom," or they could result in further monopolization of communications. Local public access programming in cable systems is diversifying content. All these developments raise anew the question of media responsibility in democratic politics.

Suggestions for Further Reading and Study

The best and most current study of this subject is Doris A. Graber, *Mass Media and American Politics* (Washington, DC: CQ Press, 1980). Graber has also edited an excellent selection of articles, *Media Power in Politics* (Washington, DC: CQ Press, 1984). The topic is put in its broader context in Robert G. Meadow, *Politics as Communication* (Norwood, NJ: Ablex, 1980), a book that surveys and summarizes many other studies. A survey of research on political aspects with helpful annotated bibliographies attached to each chapter is Sidney Kraus and Dennis Davis, *The Effects of Mass Communication on Political Behavior* (University Park, PA: Pennsylvania State Univ. Press, 1976). For reprints of the best research, see the *Mass Communication Review Yearbook*, published each year by Sage, Beverly Hills, CA. For a discussion of the Washington media, see Austin Kiplinger, *Washington Now* (New York: Harper & Row, 1975), chap. 20, and Timothy Crouse's often riotous yet troubling account of reporters in the 1972 campaign, *The Boys on the Bus* (New York: Bantam, 1973), as well as the works cited in chapter footnotes. For a more far-reaching study of the major news media, see David Halberstam, *The Powers That Be* (New York: Knopf, 1979), on the *Los Angeles Times*, the *Washington Post, Time*, and CBS. For a very critical perspective, see Michael Parenti, *Inventing Reality: The Politics of the Mass Media* (New York: St. Martin's Press, 1986). See also W. Lance Bennett, *News: The Politics of Illusion* (New York: Longman, 1983). And on television's development see Erik Barnouw's interesting account, *Tube of Plenty: The Evolution of American Television* (New York: Oxford Univ. Press, 1975). On the potential of the new technologies, see the fascinating study of the interplay of technology and politics by Ithiel de Sola Pool, *Technologies of Freedom* (Cambridge, MA: Harvard Univ. Press, 1983).

To keep up with current developments in the communications industry, the trade journal *Broadcasting* is helpful. In addition, interesting articles on a wide variety of media topics appear in the *Journal of Communication, Journalism Quarterly, Channels*, the *Columbia Journalism Review*, and the *Washington Journalism Review*.

Perspective

THE POLITICS OF THE BUDGET:
The Deficit
and Gramm-Rudman-Hollings

The United States government now spends more than a trillion dollars a year. That's 1 with 12 zeros after it. Or a million millions. If you figure the business day is eight hours long, that means the federal government spends $136,700 every second, or almost $4 billion every single business day of the year.

You may have some trouble even *imagining* that, but the government doesn't seem to have much trouble *doing* it. Of course, there are some three million employees engaged in the task.

What the government *does* have trouble doing is *raising* that much money. It gets most of its money from taxes, as we saw in Perspective 1. In recent years, it has come up short by something like $200 billion, give or take a few dozen billion, each year.

Each time it comes up short in its fund raising, it has to borrow money. That borrowing creates the **national debt**: The current national debt passed $2 trillion in 1986. When you or I go into debt by borrowing money, those who lend us the money require that we regularly pay off part of the debt, the *principle*, along with the *interest*, the fee for using that money. Nobody requires that of the federal government.

Who has lent all this money to our government? In the old days, it was mainly Americans. The government sold savings bonds to the people and Treasury bonds to businesses with money to spare. But in recent years, the government has needed much more money than Americans could lend it. So it has borrowed from foreigners and from their governments. The result is that in 1986 the United States became a debtor nation. This means that foreigners have lent so much money to our government and also bought ownership of so many American companies that our net foreign debt is now over $250 billion. In other words, foreign loans to, and investments in, the United States are that much greater than everything American banks, multinational corporations, and individuals own or have lent abroad.

The interest alone on this foreign debt totals $20

billion a year. This means we must export $20 billion worth of goods each year just to "service" (pay the interest on) our debt without even reducing it.

In fact, we are exporting lots of goods and services—over $200 billion worth in 1986—but we are now importing close to $170 billion more than we export each year. We have gone from being the world's biggest creditor to the world's biggest debtor in half a dozen years. Thus, we as a country have two enormous deficits—a budget deficit and a trade deficit.

So what? Is this anything to be concerned about? Some fear that foreigners owning extensive assets in the United States could interfere in our economy at some point and even jeopardize our national security. But so far it's the national deficit that bothers most people.

Deficits are nothing new in America. The government hasn't been "in the black" (taking in more money than it spends) since 1969. In fact, it's been "in the red" for all but 1 of the last 30 years. But the deficits have never been so large until recently,

"YES, SON, SOMEDAY ALL THIS WILL BE YOURS!"

(By permission of Field Newspaper Syndicate)

nor have they grown so fast, as Figure P3.1 reveals. When Ronald Reagan took office, the total national debt was just under a trillion dollars. In five years it doubled under the Reagan policies of large tax cuts plus large increases in defense spending and social security. This meant that the government had to borrow a trillion dollars more.

FIGURE P3.1
The Annual Federal Budget Deficit.
Source: Statistical Abstract of the United States 1987.

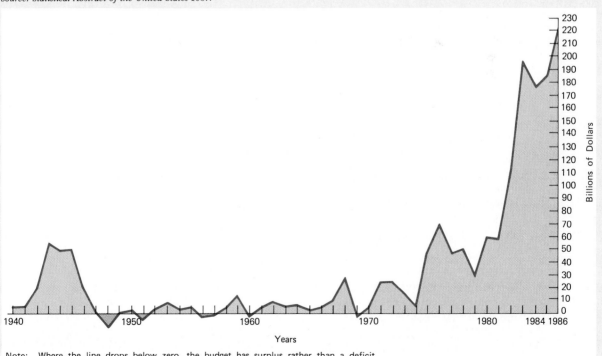

Note: Where the line drops below zero, the budget has surplus rather than a deficit.

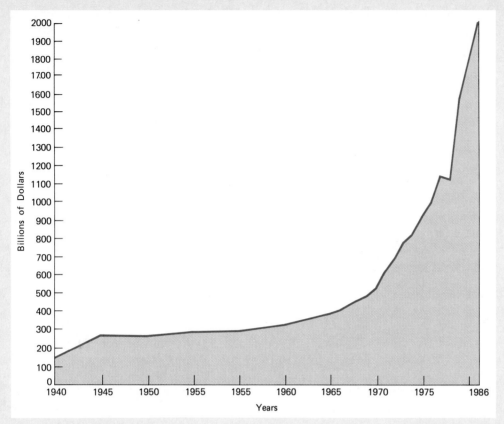

FIGURE P3.2
The National Debt.
Source: Statistical Abstract of the United States 1987.

THE STRANGE CASE
OF GRAMM-RUDMAN-HOLLINGS

When the government needs to borrow more money to meet its budgetary obligations, Congress has to pass a bill raising the official "ceiling" on the national debt. Figure P3.2 shows how the national debt has grown over the years. The debt has been growing so fast under Reagan that Congress has had to do this every year. No one likes to vote for such a bill, but without it the United States would go into bankruptcy—would "go out of business." So it must be done. Usually, when the latest debt-ceiling bill comes up for consideration, members of Congress make speeches attacking the deficit vociferously for a few hours—and then pass the bill. After all, it's all the spending bills they've passed—and all the tax increases they haven't passed—that make the rise necessary.

On October 3, 1985, in the middle of the usual Senate debate on the latest debt-ceiling bill—one to raise the limit past $2 trillion—three Senators

suddenly proposed an amendment that Senator Phil Gramm (Republican of Texas) called "an emergency program to deal with an economic emergency." He was joined in proposing the amendment by Senators Warren Rudman (Republican of New Hampshire) and Ernest Hollings (Democrat of South Carolina).

Three days earlier, fiscal year 1985 had ended with a deficit of $185 billion.[1] Of that $130 billion was interest payments on the national debt of $1.8 trillion. The budget Reagan had proposed for fiscal year 1986 foresaw an increase in that debt of another $181 billion, and Congress's own estimate of the FY86 deficit was $212 billion.

Most thought something drastic had to be done. Some in Congress wanted to slash the defense budget. Others wanted to increase taxes. Still others wanted to do both. But the administration re-

---

[1] A fiscal year is different from a calendar year. For budgeting convenience, it begins on October 1 and ends on the following September 30, and it is numbered for the calendar year in which it ends. The common abbreviation for fiscal year 1987 is FY87.

Sen. Phil Gramm (R-TX, center), Sen. Warren Rudman (R-NH, left), and Sen. Ernest Hollings discussing their Balanced Budget Act. (UPI/Bettmann Newsphotos)

fused to do either. Its proposal, as usual, was to cut domestic spending. But almost everyone in Congress thought there was little or nothing that could be cut from the domestic budget after the cuts it had sustained in each of the previous five years at Reagan's urging. The result was stalemate. And every day the national debt was increasing by $500 million.

The Gramm-Rudman-Hollings amendment (GRH) set maximum allowable deficits for the next five years. It was designed to result in a balanced budget in 1991 by forcing a series of budget cuts over those five years. The stunning thing about it was, it didn't say where these cuts would be made. Instead, it provided that if Congress and the president couldn't agree on $36 billion of cuts in a given year, the president would be authorized to impose the cuts "across the board"—the same percentage cut in every program except Social Security, defense contracts, and national-debt interest payments. The cuts, in other words, would be automatic.

GRH caused a virtual panic. Most Republicans decided to support it, and many Democrats did too, fearing that otherwise they would be blamed by voters for whatever long-term bad effects the deficit had. But the real panic was among lobbyists for various special interests and their Congressional supporters. Many special interests had succeeded thus far in protecting their favorite programs from major cuts. They would not be protected from automatic cuts.

The Senate approved GRH, with 22 of 47 Democrats in favor, in October. The House quickly passed a somewhat similar bill. Then came two months of negotiation between the two houses in conference committee. There were two main debates.

One debate was over which programs would be exempt from the automatic cuts, or **sequestrations**,

Pres. Reagan signing the GRH Balanced Budget Act, December 1985. (UPI/Bettmann Newsphotos)

as they were called. The House insisted that cuts be split evenly between defense (which the Senate had exempted) and domestic programs. It also insisted that unemployment compensation and welfare programs be exempt. Thus, at the end, over 70 percent of all government spending (which meant 85 percent of all nondefense spending) was either exempt or subject to special protective rules. (This meant, although nobody seems to have noticed it at the time, that the biggest "hits" would be taken by such programs as the Federal Bureau of Investigation's anticrime work and the Federal Aviation Administration's air traffic control work—not a comforting thought to anyone who flies.)

The second debate was over who would decide the exact nature of the automatic cuts. The Senate gave this power to the president in its bill. The House insisted that it be someone more independent. They compromised on the comptroller general. He is the head of the General Accounting Office, the body which makes reports to Congress about how effective government programs are. The comptroller general is appointed by the president but can be removed by Congress if it so wishes. The bill specified that the Congressional Budget Office and the president's Office of Management and Budget would together determine the scale of the deficit problem each year and therefore the depth of the required cuts.

The compromise version of GRH was finally passed by both houses on December 11, 1985. President Reagan signed it on December 12. Its official name was the Balanced Budget and Emergency Deficit Control Act.

Sen. Pete Domenici and Rep. William Gray of Senate and House Budget Committees negotiating (Terry Ashe/UNIPHOTO)

Even before it passed, people were questioning its constitutionality. The Constitution, in Article III, says that "the judicial power shall extend to all cases . . . arising under this Constitution, the laws of the United States, and treaties. . . . " Since the early history of the country, as we'll see in detail in Chapter 11, the courts have claimed and sometimes exercised the power to rule on the constitutionality of laws and actions of government, even when this involved limiting the powers of another branch.

Once GRH passed, Representative Mike Synar, Democrat of Oklahoma, got assistance from a public-interest lawyer and filed suit in federal court claiming that it was unconstitutional. His argument was that Congress was evading its legislative responsibility to make spending decisions. The federal court ruled on February 7 that the provision for making automatic cuts was indeed unconstitutional. However, it rejected Synar's claim. Instead it based its decision on the fact that the program would infringe on *executive* power because it involved the comptroller general, who could be fired by the legislative branch.

The decision was immediately appealed to the Supreme Court. It heard oral argument by both sides in the case in April and announced its decision in *Bowsher* v. *Synar* on July 7.[2] It held that the GRH mechanism was indeed unconstitutional because the Constitution "does not contemplate an active role for Congress in the supervision of officers charged with the execution of the laws it enacts." In short, it agreed with the lower court.[3]

The result was that Congress still had the deficit-reduction target of GRH to meet but without the "club" of threatened automatic cuts to encourage a budgetary compromise between the Congress and the president. No such compromise occurred. Congress still had to make enough cuts in the FY87 budget to get the deficit down to the specified range of $144 to $154 billion.

Congress succeeded in reaching a projected deficit of $151 by a rather unusual set of actions. First, it held defense spending virtually constant and cut spending for foreign aid. But that only saved $6.5

[2]Bowsher was the comptroller general, in whose name the case was fought against Synar.

[3]The decision was controversial, in part because it seemed to challenge the legality of congressional oversight of executive agencies, something that has been going on for 200 years. We'll examine it in Chapter 10.

billion. Miscellaneous cuts throughout the budget saved another billion, but that left $12 billion to be saved somehow. So Congress ordered the Treasury department's Internal Revenue Service to collect an extra $5 billion in back taxes and penalties and then announced it would sell to private businesses various government assets, including Conrail, the rail freight system, and various outstanding loans. This "asset sale" was supposed to raise about $8 billion and thereby cut the deficit by that amount.

In this way, the GRH target figure was met for FY87. But observers pointed out that selling assets would gain revenue immediately but reduce the revenue government would have gotten in later years when people paid off their loans and when Conrail was paid by firms using its freight operations. Thus, present GRH success was bought at the price of guaranteed larger-future-deficit problems.

This whole GRH approach to the politics of the deficit is interesting because it shows us Congress dealing with a complicated and important issue—the budget deficit—in an unusual way. In the normal legislative process, a bill intended to change the budget process would be handled in a very deliberate fashion by Congress. It would be "introduced" by its sponsors and "referred" to the committee that specializes in the area. The committee would "refer" it to the appropriate subcommittee, which would study it and hold "hearings" on it at which interested people would be allowed to "testify" or comment on it. If the subcommittee thought the bill should be passed, it would then "mark up" or change the bill in whatever ways it thought desirable and send it back up to the whole committee. The committee would then decide whether to make any further changes and then, if it approved the bill, send it to "the floor," the whole House or Senate, where it would be debated and voted upon.

That, in brief, is the standard procedure. It provides for careful deliberation, usually over many months, before a bill is passed. And once it is passed by one house, for it to become law, the other house must go through much the same process, either on the bill referred to it by the first house or on its own proposal. (We'll look at this process in detail in Chapter 10.)

What has just been described, for example, was what happened in the case of the tax-reform bills that we examined briefly in Perspective 1. There, as usually happens, different bills passed by each house had to be compromised in a conference committee before a common version was finally passed by each house and sent to the president for his signature or veto.

GRH, as we have seen, went through virtually none of these standard procedures. As such, it provides a very interesting case of what is sometimes called fast-track legislating. What Congress then did with the president's proposed FY87 budget was also unlike the official ordinary budgetary process, but in a way it was more an instance of "slow-track" legislating, as we'll see once we examine the basics of the budgetary process.

THE BASICS OF THE BUDGET

What Is a Budget?

The federal budget—as a glance at the photo nearby will reveal—is an enormous document. It runs over 1000 telephone-book-sized pages of small type. It contains both words and figures that pro-

These books contain the FY86 budget submitted to Congress by the president. (Dennis Brack/Black Star)

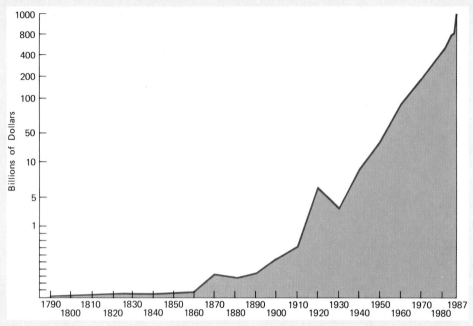

FIGURE P3.3

The Growth of the Federal Budget. In order to represent the massive increase in the budget within the limits of this page, the units in the vertical scale have been compressed toward the top of the figure. If the scale used for the years before 1910 were used for the entire figure, the line for the growth of the budget would be almost one hunderd feet high by 1987.

Source: For 1790–1970, *Historical Statistics, Colonial Times to 1970* (Washington, DC: Census Bureau, 1976); from 1971 on, *Statistical Abstract of the United States 1987* (Washington, DC: Census Bureau, 1987).

pose how money is to be spent for certain purposes and items. It also indicates where that money is expected to come from. In slightly more technical terms, a budget is concerned with the translation of financial resources into human purposes.[4] As Figure P3.3 shows, the federal budget has grown tremendously over the past 200 years.

The federal budget is proposed by the president after it has been "worked up" by the bureaucracy for one year. Once proposed, however, it must be approved by Congress before it becomes the actual budget for the U.S. government. That approval is a long, involved process, as we'll soon see.

Money as the "Energy of Government"

Money is, we might say, the "energy of government" in several important senses. First, money fuels the machinery, which has continued to expand in size and in realms of operation. Second,

money motivates the people. For politicians, money provides rewards to give. For bureaucrats, it provides salaries. For special interests, it provides rewards in the form of government contracts, programs, and payments.

Money and Politics

The Political Development of Money

Like other forms of energy, money must be found or generated. There are several ways the government can do this. One is by taxation (see Perspective 1). Another is by borrowing—from American citizens or businesses or foreigners. The third way government gets money is by "generating" it—by printing enough additional money to pay the bills resulting from government spending.

The Political Allocation of Money

Once money is found or generated, it must be allocated. This is where the politics of the budget really comes into play. Every decision about the

---

[4]See Aaron Wildavsky, *The Politics of the Budgetary Process*, 4th ed. (Boston: Little, Brown, 1984), p. 1.

budget requires two essential things: information and authority. There must be information on needs and wants in the form of proposed programs and on economic conditions past, present, and (as estimates) future. Those making the decisions must also have authority to make the hard choices and make them stick. Decisions are difficult, and authority is essential because all decisions are contested by interests both inside the government (bureaucrats and members of Congress) and outside it (lobbyists, experts, and ordinary concerned citizens). To understand how this happens, we must look at the budgetary process as it operates both in theory and in practice.

THE STAGES OF THE BUDGETARY PROCESS, FY87

Until 1921 each government agency gave its budget requests to the secretary of the treasury, who put them all in a Book of Estimates and sent it to Congress without comment or revision. Both the extent of government activity and the cost increased enormously during and after World War I, and it became clear that a more systematic budget process was needed. In 1921 a Bureau of the Budget (BOB) was created within the Treasury Department to involve the president in the process and thereby promote economy and efficiency in government.[5]

The world kept getting more complex, however, and government kept getting bigger as well as more complex. It was hard for the BOB to keep pace, and harder still for the president to keep track. So in 1939 the president transferred the BOB to the newly created Executive Office of the President, where he could have closer relations with it. Within one hundred days of the transfer, World War II broke out. It was the BOB that helped the president manage the war effort. It became his chief staff agency. It continued as such until the Eisenhower administration (1953–1961), when its role declined as government became somewhat less active.

[5]For a history of the budgetary process, see Percival Flack Brundage, *The Bureau of the Budget* (New York: Praeger, 1970), and Larry Borman, *The Office of Management and Budget and the Presidency 1921–1979* (Princeton, NJ: Princeton Univ. Press, 1979), along with Louis Fisher, *Presidential Spending Power* (Princeton, NJ: Princeton Univ. Press, 1975), especially chaps. 1, 2. For a fascinating behind-the-scenes account of budgetary politics in the first five years of the Reagan administration, see the memoirs of the head of OMB, David Stockman, *The Triumph of Politics* (New York: Harper & Row, 1986).

With the activist presidencies of Kennedy (1961–1963) and Johnson (1963–1969), the BOB once again had an important role. The demands on it were so great, however—developing the budget and coordinating programs—that it was inadequate to the tasks. The Nixon administration, seeking to gain better control over the government, converted the BOB into the Office of Management and Budget (OMB), giving it more responsibility for managing the enormous and complicated executive branch and its programs. Since then its importance has continued to grow.

In the Executive Branch

Because of its management responsibility, the Office of Management and Budget is often involved in efforts to reorganize the government to make it more efficient. Its greatest power, however, derives from its greatest responsibility: preparing the budget. That process continues throughout the entire year. In fact, preparation for a budget begins some 19 months before the fiscal year starts.

The fiscal year 1987 officially began October 1, 1986. However, the FY87 budget was born, in a sense, in March 1985 when some OMB staff members began developing projections of likely global and national developments, revenues, and program needs. Those guidelines and instructions from the president went to the various agencies (such as the Department of Housing and Urban Development and the National Aeronautics and Space Administration) later that spring. The agencies then developed their own proposals with these guidelines in mind and submitted them to OMB in September 1985. Meanwhile, OMB was monitoring developments in the outside world and advising the agencies about changes in their proposals ordered by the president or by OMB itself. December is usually a month of great budget struggles, including appeals by various agency heads to the president or the director of OMB when OMB slashes a valued program. Figure P3.4 (p. 219) depicts all the stages in the preparation of the budget. The top section depicts the stages for the executive, or presidential, budget.

On February 5, 1986 President Reagan sent to Congress his proposed budget for FY87. It called for spending $994 billion, even though it estimated that the government would take in only about $850

President Reagan presents Congressional leaders with copies of the administration's FY87 budget proposal. (Jose R. Lopez/The New York Times)

billion in revenues. That meant a likely 1987 deficit of $144 billion. Figure P3.5 (p. 220) shows how the administration estimated revenue sources and expenditure categories.

In his first five years in office, Reagan had sought major cuts in antipoverty programs, in federal loans and grants to college students (as we saw in Chapter 5), in government regulation of business, and in other social programs. He had also sought major cuts in personal income tax rates to stimulate the economy. He got most of his tax cuts and many of the social-spending cuts approved by Congress. He also sought massive increases in military spending, and he got most of what he wanted here too. The result was that government income went down when taxes were decreased, but the defense-spending increases were so much greater than the social-program cuts that government spending expanded enormously, producing larger and larger federal deficits.

The year 1986 was an election year for one-third of the Senate and for the entire House of Representatives. Republican control of the Senate was at stake. A shift of four seats there would give the Democrats control. This, combined with continuing Democratic control of the House, would make it very difficult for Reagan to get anything controversial through Congress.

The FY87 budget that Reagan submitted called for major cuts in social programs such as Medicare, mass transit, and loans for students, home buyers, farmers, and small businesses. It also called for an increase of 12 percent in military spending.

Why in an election year did the president call for major cuts in popular social programs? He knew most Democrats strongly supported those programs, and many Republicans favored them as well. The reason was that he was absolutely committed to a continuing increase in military spending and he still opposed new taxes. Thus, he had to slash social programs because he was forced to propose a budget with a deficit no larger than $144 billion by the Gramm-Rudman-Hollings deficit-reduction targets. While GRH was going through the courts, Reagan's budget was going through Congress.

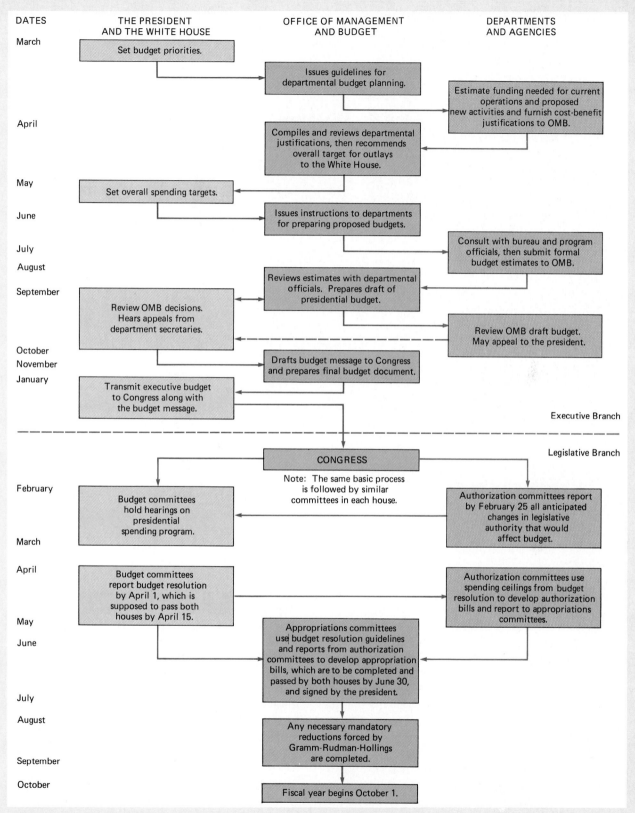

DATES	THE PRESIDENT AND THE WHITE HOUSE	OFFICE OF MANAGEMENT AND BUDGET	DEPARTMENTS AND AGENCIES
March	Set budget priorities.	Issues guidelines for departmental budget planning.	Estimate funding needed for current operations and proposed new activities and furnish cost-benefit justifications to OMB.
April		Compiles and reviews departmental justifications, then recommends overall target for outlays to the White House.	
May	Set overall spending targets.		
June		Issues instructions to departments for preparing proposed budgets.	
July August			Consult with bureau and program officials, then submit formal budget estimates to OMB.
September	Review OMB decisions. Hears appeals from department secretaries.	Reviews estimates with departmental officials. Prepares draft of presidential budget.	Review OMB draft budget. May appeal to the president.
October November		Drafts budget message to Congress and prepares final budget document.	
January	Transmit executive budget to Congress along with the budget message.		

Executive Branch

- -

Legislative Branch

CONGRESS

Note: The same basic process is followed by similar committees in each house.

February	Budget committees hold hearings on presidential spending program.		Authorization committees report by February 25 all anticipated changes in legislative authority that would affect budget.
March			
April	Budget committees report budget resolution by April 1, which is supposed to pass both houses by April 15.		Authorization committees use spending ceilings from budget resolution to develop authorization bills and report to appropriations committees.
May June		Appropriations committees use budget resolution guidelines and reports from authorization committees to develop appropriation bills, which are to be completed and passed by both houses by June 30, and signed by the president.	
July			
August		Any necessary mandatory reductions forced by Gramm-Rudman-Hollings are completed.	
September			
October		Fiscal year begins October 1.	

FIGURE P3.4

The New Executive and Congressional Budget Process. This diagram depicts the process as it has been modified by Gramm-Rudman-Hollings, which instructs Congress to observe the indicated deadlines.

Source: Executive branch data adapted from Richard Pious, *American Politics and Government* (New York: McGraw-Hill, 1986), p. 490.

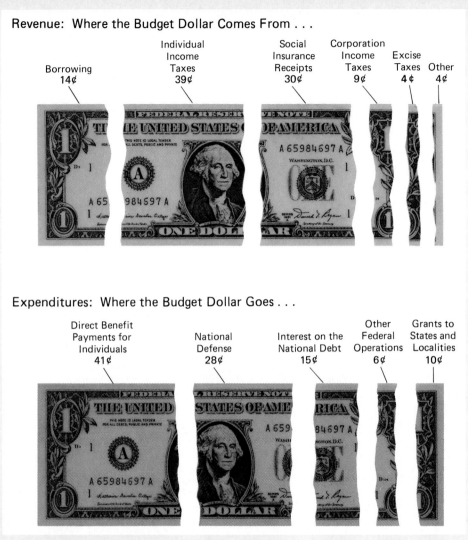

Revenue: Where the Budget Dollar Comes From . . .

Borrowing 14¢ — Individual Income Taxes 39¢ — Social Insurance Receipts 30¢ — Corporation Income Taxes 9¢ — Excise Taxes 4¢ — Other 4¢

Expenditures: Where the Budget Dollar Goes . . .

Direct Benefit Payments for Individuals 41¢ — National Defense 28¢ — Interest on the National Debt 15¢ — Other Federal Operations 6¢ — Grants to States and Localities 10¢

FIGURE P3.5
The Reagan Budget Estimates for Fiscal Year 1987.
Source: Office of Management and Budget, February 1986.

In the Congress

Once the White House has prepared and submitted its recommendations, Congress takes on the primary decision-making role. The president's budget is really a collection of requests that Congress grant to the executive branch certain funds to use for certain purposes. Congress responds to those requests in three basic stages. The bottom section of Figure P3.4 depicts this process in detail.

First, each house of Congress develops and both houses pass a joint budget resolution—according to law, by May 15, but in practice often later. This resolution sets targets for spending in all areas of government activity. It is a compromise between the bills developed by each house's Budget Committee, based on both the president's budget message and reports from its own committees on likely revenues and expenditures. It must be passed by both houses in identical form.

Second, Congress authorizes expenditures of certain specified sums for programs or agencies over the coming year. This decision of how much to authorize for what is made by a committee specializing in the subject. The House Foreign Affairs Committee and the Senate Foreign Relations Committee, for example, prepare and recommend an authorization bill for our foreign aid program, for our contributions to the United Nations, and for the running of our diplomatic embassies around the world and the State Department here at home. The whole House and the whole Senate then must approve the authorization bill. But the **authorization**, despite its name, doesn't really authorize or allow the agency to actually spend the money. Instead, it sets a kind of limit, or ceiling, as to how much may eventually be appropriated, and it establishes short-run policy principles and guidelines for the bureaucracy to follow.

Then comes the third stage of funding, the **appropriations** phase. Each house of Congress has an Appropriations Committee. Its job is to gather together all the authorizations and, taking a broader view of the financial state of things, to decide how much of what has been authorized can actually be spent.

The Constitution requires that all revenue bills originate in the House, and precedent makes all appropriations bills originate there too. The reason for this is that the House is closer to the people because its members are elected every two years from smaller districts. The hope of the founders was that the House would be less willing to spend money than the Senate because the House would recognize that the people would dislike the higher taxes that higher spending would require. So appropriations bills originate in the House and then go to the Senate for approval or modification. Of course, if the Senate makes changes—as it always does—another conference committee must develop a compromise, which then must be passed in identical form by both houses.

By law, all appropriations bills are supposed to have been finished by the start of the new fiscal year, October 1. In fact, that is less and less often the case now. If Congress has not decided by then, it passes temporary laws, called **continuing resolutions**. These bills usually allow agencies to continue to operate at last year's levels until the appropriations bills are finally passed. In recent years, however, they have tended to replace regular appropriations bills altogether.

THE STRUGGLES OF THE FY87 BUDGETARY PROCESS

Congress has not succeeded in passing a complete budget by the October 1 start of the fiscal year since 1978. Each year the budget has been so controver-sial that Congress has had to resort to a continuing resolution instead.

The whole budget is divided into 13 separate bills, each dealing with a particular area—such as defense, agriculture, transportation, or foreign affairs. In FY86 Congress was able to pass six of these budget bills, or appropriations, but had to pass a continuing resolution to cover the other seven areas for the year.

In the case of FY87, the situation was even worse. Congress passed the budget resolution, the first stage of the process, on June 26—but only after a month of negotiations between the Senate and the House. It provided for budget authority of $1093 billion and outlays (actual spending) of $995 billion. However, as the new fiscal year began on October 1, Congress had not passed a single one of the 13 major appropriations bills; nor had it passed the authorization bills that are supposed to follow the budget resolution. To prevent the government from having to shut down, it passed a "stopgap" one-week continuing resolution. When the House and Senate couldn't reach agreement during that extra week, they passed another continuing resolution. When deadlock persisted, they passed yet another. Finally, on October 17, facing the Congressional elections in just three weeks, Congress passed a continuing resolution to last the whole fiscal year, funding all government programs requiring annual appropriations. The bill rejected Reagan's calls for large cuts in domestic programs, holding them constant. It also cut Reagan's defense-spending request by $25 billion, granting a net increase of only $3.5 billion over the FY85 total. Nonetheless, the president signed the bill.

The ultimate compromise took three temporary continuing resolutions because of persistent disputes between the Democratic-controlled House and the Republican-controlled Senate. Foremost among them were the questions of arms control and aid to the *Contras*, rebels fighting to overthrow the Marxist government in Nicaragua. (We'll discuss these questions in Chapter 19.) Reagan wanted the Contra aid approved. The Senate agreed but the House opposed it.

On arms control, the House wanted a requirement that the government continue to abide by the terms of the SALT II agreement with the Soviet Union. This treaty was never ratified, but both sides had observed its limits on increasing nuclear missile systems since the Carter administration signed it in 1979. Reagan had recently decided to exceed the limits in December. The House sought to prevent this by including such a prohibition in the continuing resolution. In the middle of the budget debate over the continuing resolutions, Reagan announced that he would soon go to Iceland for a minisummit meeting with the Soviet leader. Aides said the House-proposed prohibition would tie his hands in negotiations. Rather than give in, however, Congress waited to reach a budget compromise until after the summit. The language finally approved expressed support of the SALT II limits but was not binding on the president. Thus, Reagan won on the Contras and arms control but lost on defense and domestic spending.

Why did the stalemate persist so long? The answer is that neither side wanted to compromise its basic commitments until the last moment. If Congress had included prohibitions on arms buildups or Contra aid in a separate defense-appropriations bill, the president could have vetoed it. The same holds for controversial domestic questions. By waiting for one big final continuing resolution (CR), Congress forces the president to take or leave the whole appropriation. If he vetoes it, the government must shut down all but essential services, and negotiation must begin again—not just between the president and Congress but between the House and Senate as well.

Knowing this, representatives often try to attach favorite bills or special provisions to the CR—bills that might not otherwise pass both houses or that might be vetoed if they had to stand alone. This final CR had hundreds of extraneous items attached. Included by the House was an antidrug initiative. Added by the Senate were programs for child nutrition, aviation safety, and AIDS medical research. Both houses supported adding a special new program to control Defense Department **procurement**, or buying of weapons.[6] This was a new effort to control cost overruns and mismanagement in the defense budget, sought because cost overruns are such a large fraction of the budget and the largest part of the deficit.

THE POLITICS OF EXPERTISE IN THE BUDGETARY PROCESS

More than most subjects, understanding the budgetary process requires expertise. Two types of expertise are important: expert knowledge of the subject areas being debated and expert knowledge of the budgetary process itself. In theory, the process is designed to maximize the effective use by Congress of both types of expertise. The authorization committees, the specialists on particular policy areas (for example, the Armed Services Committees on defense), are supposed to evaluate the president's proposals and then make their own. They are supposed to take account of expertise on the economy and society and the world in deciding what programs should be funded. The newer budget committees are supposed to take the much broader financial view of the whole budget in its economic context and coordinate program proposals in all areas.

But when Congress slips into a pattern of relying on continuing resolutions, as it recently has, the substantive-area authorization committees lose most of their role. Indeed, the real focus has shifted away from the economy and budget as a whole—the traditional area of the appropriations committees—and toward deficit policy.

The result is that experts in estimating revenues and costs tend to become the dominant authorities. They are the ones who can force the Congress to change direction under the Gramm-Rudman-Hollings deficit-reduction umbrella.

To get an idea of how important this can be, consider the case of interest rates. They rise or fall depending on a number of factors, including government spending, government borrowing, foreign borrowing, and consumer confidence in the economy. Each of these factors is hard enough to predict with any accuracy. No one really knows just how they influence each other or how, taken together, they shape interest rates. Yet both OMB and CBO have to make interest-rate forecasts as part of their regular estimates of the deficit for the coming year. Those estimates are averaged to become guidelines for GRH-required cuts in spending. If OMB and CBO estimate that interest rates will go up by a mere 1 percent, that will increase the estimated budget by about $6 billion—largely because the national debt is so high and the government has to borrow money at higher rates to pay

---

[6]For the background, see Richard A. Stubbing, *The Defense Game* (New York: Harper & Row, 1986) and Richard Halloran, *To Arm a Nation* (New York: Macmillan, 1986).

the interest on the debt. GRH requires that such projected debt increases be met by spending cuts and that half of each cut come out of defense spending. More than a third of the "cuttable" defense spending goes to military personnel. To cut personnel spending by just over a billion dollars would necessitate reducing our armed forces by more than 50,000 people. Such a reduction would have significant implications for our global military posture.

The point is that such a decision to reduce troop levels would come about not on its merits, not even on its relative merits in relation to other military spending programs, not even on changes in world affairs or in U.S. military doctrine. Instead, it would occur because of changing estimates of U.S. interest rates made by anonymous technical analysts in OMB and CBO. The same phenomenon of reliance on technical experts for substantive policy decisions will occur in every aspect of governmental policy making as a result of the new focus on the deficit. Is this wise? Is the deficit all that dangerous? Or are we now overly concerned about the deficit?

The Question of the Deficit's Danger

The truth is, the experts disagree about how dangerous our enormous deficits are. Until recently—that is, until after the 1984 presidential election—the Reagan administration argued that they hardly mattered. Economic growth was supposed to solve our deficit problems over time by increasing tax revenue. Now, the administration echoes the grave warnings of many economists.

But some economists disagree. They point out that the debt is only about 40 percent of the total output of our economy (the gross national product, or GNP). In 1945, at the end of World War II, the debt was more than double this, relative to GNP. Not only that, the federal government's assets—the land and buildings and equipment it owns and the other resources it holds—total over $2 trillion, or just about what its liabilities total.[7] And some government spending—on roads, bridges, harbors, and airports, for example—creates debt but is really an investment in our future. So is spending on education. So, it could be argued, is spending

on national defense. Some of this deficit spending *does* stimulate economic growth—as the Reagan deficit budgets in the early years amply showed.

The Reagan deficits have ranged from 5 to 6 percent of GNP. That is higher than those of previous administrations but a small percentage nonetheless. On the other hand, only about 12 percent of the federal budget is spent on investments such as dams and buildings. Most of it goes to such items as wages, subsidies to farmers, and grants to cities and states. Ultimately, then, such debt compounds over the years and eventually forces cuts in spending or higher taxes to pay the holders of the debt—who include more and more foreigners.[8]

So, what are we to conclude about the deficit? How dangerous is it? What should be done about it? As on so many questions, such as the tax reform that we examined in Perspective 1, the experts disagree. The disagreement makes it fundamentally *a political question*. As such, it will be answered by our political system. Indeed, it is being answered just that way, as we have seen in our account of the FY87 budget. But some are calling for further deficit-control measures. Let's see what some of these measures are.

Proposed Solutions to the Problem of Deficits

The Reagan administration endorsed passage of a proposed constitutional amendment that would require that the federal budget be balanced except in the event of an emergency. Many politicians endorsed this amendment in principle. In practice, however, everyone in Washington knows that there is no way the president could now achieve a balanced budget, given the current commitments to ongoing defense spending and to Social Security and Medicare.

Still, 32 states have petitioned Congress to call a special convention to consider such a balanced-budget amendment. As we saw in Chapter 1, the framers provided that if two-thirds of the state legislatures make such a request, Congress must do so. That means 34 states (two-thirds of 50 states) are required. However, 3 of the 32 states that have petitioned did so in 1975, and 8 did so in 1976. Most

[7]See Robert Eisner, *How Real Is the Federal Deficit?* (New York: Free Press, 1986), p. 200. See also Bernard D. Nossiter, "Debunking the Deficit," *Nation*, January 10, 1987, pp. 12–16.

[8]For this case against the deficit, see Harold Hovey, *Red Ink: A Guide to Understanding the Deficit* (Washington, DC: Roosevelt Center, 1985).

constitutional experts think that such requests "expire" after 7 years. Thus, we're not likely to have such a convention soon—let alone an amendment, which would have to be ratified by three-fourths of the states if the convention approved it.[9]

The Reagan administration also endorsed the **line-item veto**, allowing the president to veto any item in an appropriations bill without vetoing the whole bill. Forty-three states give their governors this power. But it would take a constitutional amendment to give the president this power, and Congress is very unlikely to go along. The reason is that now Congress can put things into the budget it wants but the president doesn't. The only way the president can stop such spending is by vetoing the whole bill, in which case there is no budget and hence no government. And Congress can override the veto by a two-thirds vote of both houses, so that the budget becomes law anyway. Thus, the line-item veto would strengthen the president's hand in dealings with Congress.

But in any case, the line-item veto might not help cut budget deficits very much—many parts of the budget can't be "line-itemed." Among them are interest on the national debt and entitlement programs such as Social Security, Medicare, and farm subsidies. Therefore, most experts believe the line-item veto impossible to obtain and unlikely to help much even if it were obtained.[10]

If such special devices to control deficits are impossible or impractical, that means that the only hope is politics. But we do not really know yet whether the political process can control deficits.

The fact is that both the deficit and the national debt are also questions of foreign policy, tax policy, and domestic policy, as we have seen. All of these issues are politically controversial. In each of them, experts disagree not only over solutions but even over just what the problem is. We can expect the politics of the deficit to take on even greater importance in coming years, as the national debt grows. Even without large deficits, however, the whole budgetary process is always controversial because it is essentially political.

[9]For an interesting account of the politics behind the balanced-budget effort, see Tom Alexander, "The Grass-Roots Revolt against Federal Deficits," *Fortune*, November 28, 1983, pp. 51–58.

[10]Some argue that the framers would approve of such an amendment because Congress has perverted the legislative process by attaching its favorite questionable bills as amendments, or riders, to bills necessary for the operation of the government in order to prevent a presidential veto. See Judith A. Best, "The Line-Item Veto: Would the Founders Approve?" *Presidential Studies Quarterly*, Spring 1984, pp. 183–88.

THE CONTINUING POLITICS OF THE BUDGET

Budgetary Outcomes: What's In?

But is the budgetary process just politics like all other politics, or is there something peculiar to budgetary politics? To answer that question we must look at several major theories of budgeting.[11]

Rational Budgeting

The standard theory sees budgeting as a rational process in which one ranks goals (for example, an active foreign policy versus domestic economic growth), compares the alternative ways of spending funds toward those ranked goals (for example, spending on "guns," or military forces, versus spending on "butter," or domestic business subsidies, job programs, and so on), and then chooses the spending pattern that maximizes attainment of the ranked goals (the proper mix of guns and butter).

Yet, as we have seen in our account of FY87, this theory isn't a very good account of what actually happens in government. Experts outside government saw that long ago, although many argued it was what *should* go on.

Incremental Budgeting

When they began studying how budgets were actually made, more and more scholars concluded that the process was incremental. Officials did not sit down with a set of objectives, rank them, and examine alternatives. Instead, they inherited a series of programs and agencies. There was a "general expectation among participants that programs will be carried on at close to the going level of expenditures." As a result:

> Budgeting is incremental, not comprehensive. The beginning of wisdom about an agency budget is that it is almost never actively reviewed as a whole every year in the sense of reconsidering the value of all existing programs as compared to all possible alternatives. Instead, it is based on last year's budget with special attention given to a narrow range of increases or decreases. Thus, the men who make the budget are concerned with relatively small increments to an existing base.[12]

[11]The classic study is David J. Ott and Attiat F. Ott, *Federal Budget Policy*, 3rd ed. (Washington, DC: Brookings, 1977). Another helpful study is Dennis S. Ippolito, *The Budget and National Politics* (San Francisco: Freeman, 1978).

[12]Wildavsky, *Budgetary Process*, p. 17.

Most of what happened in the FY87 budget is best described as the executive branch coping with inflation by adding only small increments to certain agencies and programs, and Congress accepting these measures after making its own small changes here and there. There was, in other words, an appearance of **incrementalism** in FY87. Indeed, there always is. One reaction has been an effort to create new budget procedures that bring greater rational control over the process.

Rational-Control Budgeting

Critics of the way budgets have been made make two important points. First, there is a need for more *long-range planning* in the development of budget objectives because the world is changing rapidly, and governments tend to change only slowly unless they are forced to plan. In budgeting, this planning should result in new programs linked clearly to the long-range goals and built into the annual budgets. If you want to be able to deploy ground forces in the Persian Gulf rapidly, you have to start many years in advance developing those forces and the means of transporting them there quickly. Incremental changes will not be adequate.

The result of this criticism of incrementalism was a new budgeting approach, which was called the **planning-programming-budgeting system** (PPBS). The Bureau of the Budget officially adopted it in 1968. Those involved in the new system, however, often found it was not much different from the old. Meanwhile, government continued to get bigger and more expensive. So a second major criticism of the incremental approach took on greater urgency: the argument that the process never really questioned the *base* but only fiddled with the increments. The result was yet another approach: zero-base budgeting.

Zero-Base Budgeting

If you want to cut waste and make an agency more efficient, you should force it to justify everything it does regularly, critics said. You must, in other words, *challenge the base* as well as the possible increment. The leading advocate of this approach was candidate Jimmy Carter in the 1976 presidential election. He had used a form of **zero-based budgeting** (ZBB) as governor of Georgia. It called on agencies to begin each budget cycle assuming a *zero base*—that is, starting from scratch with no

ongoing programs or funds—and so each agency had to justify *all* aspects of its request each year. On January 23, 1978, President Carter unveiled his first budget with a message saying he had used ZBB in preparing it. Observers, however, generally found it "the most incremental financial statement" in memory because it "hardly terminates or curtails anything of significance, continues most spending at inflation-adjusted levels, and offers few program initiatives."[13] Subsequent Carter budgets looked much the same.[14] Interest in ZBB seemed to disappear when Carter left office.

Political Budgeting: Top-Wise, Bottom-Wise, and Side-Wise

What is the lesson of all this? "Let's look at it this way," writes Aaron Wildavsky, the intellectual father of the incrementalist analysis of budgeting.

> If you are in a spending agency, whether defense or large domestic, and you think a budget can be made from your bottom-up viewpoint, you must be told that there are fiscal limits placed at the top which effectively limit your discretion. If you sit where the president does . . . however, and you think you can impose a fixed ceiling from the top down, then you must be told that the millions below and the multitudes outside have a great deal to say about how far you can go. I cannot argue with those who believe that the budget is made upside-down or downside-up, but I feel secure in saying that it is made top-wise, bottom-wise, and side-wise, as well. Budgets are planned . . . by mutual adaptation.[15]

Political Budgeting: Economy-Outward

We should not get the impression that this incremental process prevents effective political budgeting, however. Richard Nixon as vice-president under Dwight Eisenhower (1953–1961) saw that there were recessions just before the congressional elections of 1954 and 1958 as Eisenhower tried to control government spending and balance the budget. In these elections, Republicans suffered big defeats. Then, when Nixon ran for president against Kennedy in 1960, there was yet another preelection recession. Nixon later wrote that

> the economy started to move up in November—after it was too late to affect the election returns. In October, usually a month of rising employment, the job-

---

[13]Allen Shick, "The Road from ZBB," *Public Administration Review*, March–April 1978, p. 177.
[14]Agency officials reported on FY81 that although ZBB was used, it did not change any important administration decisions.
[15]Wildavsky, *Budgetary Process*, p. xviii.

less rolls increased by 452,000. All the speeches, television broadcasts, and precinct work in the world could not counteract that one hard fact.[16]

Nixon lost the election by just over 100,000 votes, but he learned a lesson he was to put to good use.

As Nixon's own presidential reelection campaign approached in 1972, the Nixon budget produced an unemployment rate in November lower than that in all of the preceding 24 months. In October Social Security benefit checks were increased by a new 20 percent cost-of-living adjustment. The checks arrived just before the election, and enclosed with each was a note saying that the increase was due to a new law "enacted by the Congress and signed into law by President Richard M. Nixon." The text of that note had been reviewed personally by Nixon. The rise in Social Security deductions from paychecks to cover the increased payout was not scheduled to begin until the following January.[17]

But that was not all. As Nixon aide Patrick Buchanan later recounted,

> Anxious not to enter a presidential year with the economy running at less than breakneck speed, the Republicans in 1971 and 1972 opened the sluices and the dollars flowed. Back-to-back $23 billion deficits were run in the two years preceding the election in 1972. To control the unpleasant side effects, such as a rising consumer price index, the GOP went down to the Democratic barn and stole the bridle of wage-and-price controls.[18]

Political manipulation of the economy for electoral purposes is not unusual. The extent of it under Nixon has never been duplicated, however. Indeed, facing his 1976 election battle with Carter, Gerald Ford rejected such a strategy when the economy faltered in early fall. A key advisor remarked at the time: "We considered the use of stimulus . . . but the president didn't want anything to do with a short-term view."[19] For all his restraint, Ford lost a close election to Carter.

In 1980 Carter lost in a landslide to Reagan. Carter had first proposed a budget for FY81 with a deficit of $16 billion, then recalled it and offered one with a projected surplus of $16.5 billion. By the time Congress finished its work in that election year, the projected deficit was $27 billion. But the economy was slipping into recession, and although Reagan called for and got many cuts in the original Carter budget when he took office, the final deficit in FY81 was $65 billion.

The lesson seems to be twofold. As Edward Tufte has shown in the Nixon case and others, "incumbents may seek to determine the *location* and the *timing* of economic benefits in promoting the fortunes of their party and friends."[20] But on the other hand, the best laid plans of presidents and their strategists—despite the enormous influence they have over the budget and other economic programs—may be torn asunder by uncontrollable developments at home and abroad.

"Nonpolitical" Budgeting: The "Uncontrollables"

The budget is full of what officials choose to call **uncontrollables**—spending commitments neither the president nor Congress can do anything about. About three-quarters of the federal budget is now "uncontrollable" without changes in the law. It includes what are called **entitlements**—programs providing benefits to individuals who have an established legal right to them. Among these are Social Security, pensions for retired government workers and military personnel, Medicare, Medicaid, and veterans' benefits. Another item in the budget that is beyond control is interest on the national debt. Because that debt is now over $2 trillion, as we have noted, the interest is enormous; and it grows higher as interest rates rise. Yet another uncontrollable part of the budget is loans the government makes or guarantees to citizens for home mortgages through the Federal Housing Administration (FHA) and the Veterans Administration (VA), to businesses such as Lockheed and Chrysler, to farmers, and even to students (for college expenses).

"Why has so much of the budget become uncontrollable?" George Shultz and Kenneth Dam both asked after each directed OMB for a time under Nixon.

> The prime reason is that advocates of particular programs want to place their outlays beyond the reach of the annual budget process. They believe strongly in their programs and want to keep money grubbers in the OMB or on the appropriations committees from chiseling away at the program in order to achieve

[16]Richard Nixon, *Six Crises* (Garden City, NY: Doubleday, 1962), pp. 310–11.

[17]See Edward R. Tufte, *Political Control of the Economy* (Princeton, NJ: Princeton Univ. Press, 1978), pp. 21, 29–33.

[18]Patrick J. Buchanan, *Conservative Votes, Liberal Victories* (New York: Quadrangle, 1975), pp. 119–20.

[19]William Seidman, quoted in the *New York Times*, October 26, 1976.

[20]Tufte, *Political Control*, p. 4.

some arbitrary spending total completely unrelated to the merits of the program. . . . Legislative committees seek protection from appropriations committees, and departments seek protection from the president's budgetary apparatus.[21]

Other programs are so dependent on external factors that they are virtually uncontrollable. When unemployment grows, government outlays for jobless benefits, welfare, and food stamps rise rapidly. When the weather is good, farm output increases and prices tend to fall, resulting in government food-price-support payments to farmers.

"Antipolitical" Budgeting: Supplementals under the Table

The budget as originally proposed is not very revealing in another sense. Not only do new developments cause new spending later on; in addition, new programs are added later in the year, and that cost must be added to the budget eventually. The press rarely notices such developments once the fascination with the original budget proposal dies down. George Schultz examined presidential proposals for FY73 after he left OMB and found that Nixon had proposed 99 new or expanded programs, but only 45 of them were in the original budget. "The other 44," he writes, "emerged during the course of the year either in response to new problems or as an outlet for the fertile creativity of the federal bureaucracy."[22]

For these and other contingencies, the law provides that the president send Congress an update on the budgetary situation every three months. Congress then obliges with supplemental appropriations throughout the year. As economist Lester Thurow wrote after Carter's first FY81 budget was released:

> The president, Congress, and events will modify the budget so much both before and during the fiscal year that begins next October that what goes into place often has little to do with what was first proposed. . . . Whenever difficult choices have to be made, this process gives every president an incentive to have an under-the-table as well as an on-the-table budget. While that budget cannot be prepared in secret, it is much less noticed. Even more important, the hard decisions can be postponed for many months until an election or another inconvenience is safely past.[23]

On the other hand, a president seeking to cut the budget can do the opposite. Reagan has often made effective use of **recision**—cutbacks in budgets already approved. Such an approach requires that Congress agree to such cutbacks within 45 days of the president's proposal of them.

Budgetary Implementation: What's Out?

As we saw earlier, Richard Nixon in 1972 took major economic initiatives before the election to maximize economic activity and win popular support. He knew all along, however, that he couldn't keep up deficit spending without doing severe damage to the economy. After the election, he resorted to massive use of **impoundment**—refusal of the executive branch to spend money appropriated by Congress. This effort tells us important things, not just about budgetary politics but also about relations between the branches of government.

Budgetary Impoundment as a Presidental Strategy

Impoundment has been practiced at times by various presidents since Ulysses Grant (1868–1876), but it never became a common practice until the Nixon administration. Sometimes a president would partially implement a program, withholding a small percentage of funds. During World War II Franklin Roosevelt occasionally canceled certain construction programs to increase resources available for the war effort. Presidents Truman and Eisenhower impounded certain military funds. All these efforts were limited and occasional.

Nixon's impoundment program was unique in that it was much larger and contravened explicit congressional instructions to spend the money appropriated. He claimed a formal constitutional power to impound, on the basis of the *executive power* and *commander-in-chief* clauses that describe the presidential roles in the Constitution.[24]

Impoundment in the Courts

Some of those who would have received funds had Nixon not impounded them began going to federal court to contest impoundment in 1971. In virtually every case, the lower-level courts upheld their claims. The case that went furthest concerned the

[21]George P. Shultz and Kenneth W. Dam, *Economic Policy Beyond the Headlines* (New York: Norton, 1977), p. 29.

[22]Ibid., p. 31.

[23]Lester Thurow, "Secrets of the Budget," *New Republic*, February 9, 1980, p. 16.

[24]See James P. Pfiffner, *The President, the Budget, and Congress: Impoundment and the 1974 Budget Act* (Boulder, CO: Westview, 1979), especially chap. 3.

Federal Water Pollution Control Act Amendments of 1972. This bill authorized commitments to spend $25 billion by 1983 for cleaning up the nation's waters. Congress passed the bill easily, but Nixon vetoed the bill, claiming it would be inflationary. Congress then overrode his veto, as the Constitution empowers it to do, making the bill law despite Nixon's opposition. The president, however, directed the head of the Environmental Protection Agency not to allot the full amounts of money authorized by the bill to states and localities, and the EPA obeyed. This led various states, cities, interest groups, and individuals to sue the EPA for the allotment of funds the bill promised.

The cases began at the district court level—the lowest level of federal courts in our system. Most district courts upheld the suitors, so the federal government appealed the cases to the courts of appeals in the various *circuits*, or areas of the country where the district courts were located. When the Circuit Court of Appeals for New York upheld the district court rulings in several cases, the government appealed to the U.S. Supreme Court for a final decision by the highest court in the land. It lost there too.

The net effect of the various court decisions was to affirm that Congress has "the power of the purse," and that the president and his bureaucracy were illegally impinging upon that power by impounding funds.[25]

Impoundment and the Congress

At the same time that opposition to impoundment was being pursued in the courts, Congress was attempting to outlaw impoundment while improving its ability to handle the budgetary process effectively. The result was the Congressional Budget and Impoundment Control Act of 1974. This act attempted to control impoundment by providing that if the president sought to impound appropriated funds, either house of Congress could veto the effort. This "legislative veto" was ruled unconstitutional by the Supreme Court in 1983 (as we'll see in Chapter 10) on grounds similar to those used in the GRH case. The Reagan administration then resumed impoundment to cut the budget. But in 1987 the courts ruled that the 1983 decision in effect barred both the impoundment and the legislative-veto sections of the 1974 act.

The second purpose of that act was to set up the system of budget committees that we encountered in our study of the FY87 budget. This new budget system was designed to do two important things. First, it enabled Congress to develop a budget proposal independent of the executive branch, so Congress wouldn't be totally dependent on OMB for overall budget policy. Second, it enabled Congress to make general budget-policy decisions each year somewhat outside the influence of the special interests that tend to dominate the authorization and appropriations committees.[26]

The Unending Budgetary Process

Whether the 1974 reforms have achieved their objectives is still very much a matter of debate. In 1986 Congress spent about 60 percent of its time on the budget and still couldn't complete the process as the law specifies. As one expert noted, "In giving Congress more control over the budget, these procedures have increased internal conflict."[27]

But if there is now more internal conflict within Congress over the budget, so too is there more within the executive branch. The situation is made even more difficult by the fact that the budgetary process requires the executive branch to be working on at least *three different budgets* at any one time: the budget in force, which is subject to revision every quarter; the budget soon to be presented to Congress or currently under debate in Congress; and the budget to be presented to Congress the following year.

Thus, budgetary politics always involves three budgets and three branches of government. It also involves the three levels of government because federal funds are always important parts of the budgets of states and cities as well.

And of course, it always involves us—the people and the interest groups into which we organize ourselves to attempt to influence the outcomes of budgetary politics. In this part of the book, one of the things we focus on is how the three branches of the federal government operate on "the energy of government"—the money they receive from the budgetary process that we have been exploring in this perspective.

[25]For an account and an analysis of these cases in the courts, see Pfiffner, *The President, the Budget, and Congress,* chap. 5.

[26]For a comprehensive study, see Allen Schick, *Congress and Money* (Washington, DC: Urban Institute, 1980). See also Dennis Ippolito, *Congressional Spending* (Ithaca, NY: Cornell Univ. Press, 1982).

[27]John W. Ellwood, "Budget Controls in a Redistributive Environment," chap. 3 in *Making Economic Policy in Congress* (Washington, DC: American Enterprise Institute, 1983), p. 95.

8

THE PRESIDENCY

The president personifies the country, representing the government to the people, and the country, the government, and the people to the rest of the world. As such, whatever the president does is news. Some of the president's duties, such as meeting a visiting foreign leader or proclaiming a certain week to be World Trade Week, are functions of a head of state. Most countries have a king or queen or an elected president to do these things. Most also have a prime minister to run the government. We combine both these roles—and many others, as we'll see—in the presidency. How our overworked chief executive selects and organizes the thousands of assistants who comprise the White House Office is a critical factor in determining how effective that president will be.

In this chapter, we'll learn what the life of the president is like and about the president's roles and powers. We'll also see how the chief executive's success is affected by such factors as personality, organization of the White House, and relations with Congress and the public. ■

THE QUESTION
OF PRESIDENTIAL AUTHORITY

At 2:30 P.M. on March 30, 1981, after completing a speech to a labor group at a Washington hotel, President Ronald Reagan was shot as he entered his limousine. The entire event was captured by television film crews and shown within minutes to the entire nation. In the apparent confusion, viewers could see a man behind the president dash from the scene carrying a black bag. At first glance, some observers thought him an accomplice of the apparent attacker, who had been immediately subdued. But as the mystery man left the scene for the hospital, it became clear to experts that he was "the man with the football."

The "football," as aides and journalists alike have come to call it, is a code satchel. It contains

Ronald Reagan is rushed into the presidential limousine by Secret Service agents after being shot outside a Washington hotel. (AP/Wide World Photos)

authentication codes—intricate cryptic numbers that make it possible for the president to order a nuclear strike anywhere in the world from wherever he is at any time. The "football," carried by a military aide, goes with the president wherever he goes. On March 30, 1981, this aide followed the president to the hospital and stayed with him even as he underwent two hours of surgery. During the surgery, presidential aides at the hospital were in constant touch with other aides at the White House in the "situation room," where national security intelligence information is constantly monitored. Secretary of State Alexander Haig had rushed there upon hearing of the assassination attempt, and so had the president's national security advisor, Richard V. Allen. Haig held a press conference in the White House press room shortly after 4 P.M. while the president was in surgery. A reporter asked him, "Who is making the decisions?" He replied: "Constitutionally, gentlemen, you have the president, the vice-president, and the secretary of state, in that order. And should the president decide he wants to transfer the helm to the vice-president, he will do so. He has not done that. As of now, I am in control here in the White House, pending return of the vice-president, and am in close touch with him. [Vice-President Bush had been speaking in Texas and so was in flight back to Washington.] If something came up, I would check with him, of course."

Those concerned that the world know that governmental authority was intact and functioning may have been reassured by Secretary Haig's assertion. Those who knew the law, however, might have been somewhat disquieted. Article II, Section 5, of the Constitution declares that presidential authority shall "devolve" on the vice-president if the president is removed or resigns, or in the event of his death or "inability to discharge the powers and duties" of his office. It also allows Congress to determine who would succeed the vice-president were he also unable to serve. The Twenty-fifth Amendment, ratified in 1967, gives the vice-president the authority to step in as acting president if either the president or a majority of the cabinet declares that the president cannot serve. Contrary to Haig's assertion, however, the Constitution says nothing about the further succession. Instead, it is the Presidential Succession Act of 1947 that determines an order: president, vice-president, speaker of the House of Representatives, president pro tempore of

Former Secretary of State Alexander Haig speaking to reporters after President Reagan was injured. (Karl Schumacher, The White House)

the Senate, and then the secretaries of state, treasury, and defense, followed by others in the order in which their departments were established.

Thus, Haig's account was in error, both constitutionally and legally. Still, the matter was of no real consequence. There were no extraordinary challenges to the United States from abroad during the crisis, and President Reagan recovered from the wound and his surgery quickly enough to resume limited duties in several days. He was thus able to reassume the exercise of both internal and external ruling power.

Internal ruling power—to govern the people in America—and external ruling power—to represent America in the world—are the twin parts of the responsibility of the president in our system, as we saw when examining the founding of the United States in Chapter 1. But while those twin responsibilities fall to the president in our system, the *powers* needed to fulfill them do not. Some of those powers, we have already noted, are *divided* between the national level and the states, while others are reserved to the people. Further, the powers allocated to the national level are *separated* among

the branches: executive, legislative, and judicial. So while the president has the responsibility *to lead the nation at home and abroad*, doing this effectively means leading the federal government and the people. The story of the presidency in our system is always the story of a person trying *to develop the powers of the office of president* and *to mold the organization of the executive branch* so that the whole government will do what the president asks. We shall see in this chapter—and again in the coming chapter on the bureaucracy—how the president tries to achieve these twin objectives. That has never been an easy task, but it is probably more difficult now than ever before, as the experience of recent presidents clearly shows.

John F. Kennedy, elected in 1960, presided less than 1000 days—frustrating days, most of them—before being gunned down by an assassin. Lyndon Johnson, his successor, then tried to combine an activist foreign policy (dominated by the war in Vietnam) with an innovative domestic presidency (epitomized by the "War on Proverty") and was forced to retire after little more than five years, with neither objective successfully achieved. Richard Nixon then won two elections, only to see his efforts at reconstruction in foreign policy plagued by the continuing tragedy of Vietnam and his programs for domestic reform so discredited by Watergate that he was forced to resign in disgrace.

Gerald Ford, nominated to be vice-president by Nixon and confirmed by Congress when Spiro Agnew was forced to resign because of corruption, picked up the pieces and, as Jimmy Carter said at the beginning of his inaugural address, did much "to heal our land." But his efforts at developing policies and programs were so unimpressive that—for only the eighth time in the nation's 200 years—the voters turned an incumbent president seeking reelection out of office and picked instead a relatively unknown candidate. Then, four short years later, the public did the same to Carter, replacing him with a man who had spent most of his professional life as an actor and whose only political experience had been as governor of California. Only Ronald Reagan, victor by a landslide in his quest for reelection in 1984, seemed positioned to escape the unhappy fate of recent presidents. But he faced intractable problems as the oldest president ever to serve. And half way through his second term his administration became embroiled in the Iran-Contra scandal that we'll discuss shortly.

THE LIFE OF THE PRESIDENT

All presidents face the same basic challenges. They must manage and strengthen the American economy while spreading its benefits to more people at home; and they must strengthen the peace while preserving America's place in the world abroad. The presidential inauguration combines domestic and foreign aspects in the taking of the oath and the passing of the code box. So does most presidential policy making. For example, the strength of our economy and its impact on both rich and poor depend on the price of foreign oil and other vital imports. So too do American jobs and profits at home. At the same time, the world economy is heavily influenced by the economic condition of the world's largest trader, the United States.

The life of the president is therefore a constant combination of domestic and foreign activities (see the box "A Day in the Life of President Reagan," pp. 233–34). To understand more fully what the president does and why, we must examine the roles of the president, the powers of the office, and the resources the occupant uses. We shall then be able to see the importance of organization as well as presidential skills and personality in the conduct of American politics.

THE ROLES AND POWERS OF THE PRESIDENT

According to the Constitution

To find out what our presidents are supposed to do and how they are meant to do it, we look first at the Constitution. Article II begins: "The executive power shall be vested in a president of the United States of America." Sections 2 and 3 then list the president's major constitutional roles and the powers they imply or convey.

- "The President shall be commander in chief of the army and navy of the United States. . . . "—and now, of course, of the air force too. In other words, the president is *chief officer* in the armed forces of the United States.

- " . . . he may require the opinion, in writing, of the principal officer in each of the executive departments . . . and he shall nominate, and by and with the advice and consent of the senate, shall appoint . . . public ministers . . . and all other officers of the United States . . . " and "he shall take care that the laws be faithfully executed. . . . " In other words the president is *chief administrator* of the government.[1]

- "He shall have the power, by and with the advice and consent of the senate, to make treaties, provided two-thirds of the senators present concur. . . . " In other words, the president is the *chief diplomat*, conducting America's foreign relations.

- "He shall from time to time give the Congress information of the state of the union, and recommend to their consideration such measures as he shall judge necessary and expedient. . . . " In other words, the president is the *chief legislator*, proposing new laws to the Congress for it to pass or not and signing or vetoing laws passed by Congress.

- " . . . he . . . shall appoint ambassadors . . . and . . . receive ambassadors and other public ministers" from other countries. In other words, the president is *chief of state*, conducting formal relations with other countries in order to represent the nation.

There were strong debates among the framers of the Constitution in 1787 over whether to have a president at all. One alternative was a king—perhaps an "elective kingship" in which an individual would be elected but then would rule as a king without the limitations that were eventually written into the Constitution. Another was what is called a plural executive—a committee—which would rule collectively, perhaps by majority vote. The framers were attempting to avoid the abuses they had endured while under the rule of George III before the American Revolution. At the same time, they sought to overcome the weakness of the first government established after the Revolution, under the Articles of Confederation of 1781, which provided only for a "Committee of the States" to rule when the Congress was not in session.[2] The decision to have a president was a compromise that created considerable debate as the states considered whether or not to ratify, or approve, the new Constitution.

---

[1] What does it mean to be responsible for the execution of the laws of the United States? Those laws are contained in the U.S. Code, which organizes all the laws in force by subject matter and is updated regularly. The index alone to its 49 "titles" and 1507 "chapters" is 26 pages long. You will probably find the many-volumed Code, published by the government, or a more useful annotated version, published privately, in your college or university library.

[2] A helpful brief account is C. Herman Pritchett, "The President's Constitutional Position," in *Rethinking the Presidency*, ed. Thomas E. Cronin (Boston: Little, Brown, 1982), pp. 117–38. The classic account of the debate and the decision is Charles C. Thach, Jr., *The Creation of the Presidency: 1775–1789* (Baltimore: Johns Hopkins Univ. Press, 1923; reprinted 1969).

A Day in the Life of President Reagan

The daily life of the president is full of challenges, but rarely are any two days alike. President Reagan's schedule for February 10, 1981, contained many of the "typical" activities of a "typical" day, but it also included such unusual activities as a meeting with governors and attendance at a dance performance.

Like most days, this one began with a brief staff meeting with the men who were then the president's chief advisors: Counsellor Edwin Meese III, Chief of Staff James A. Baker III, and Assistant to the President Michael K. Deaver. After a working breakfast meeting—this with a group of labor leaders—there followed the usually daily national security briefing by the assistant to the president for national security affairs, Richard V. Allen.

There are usually then various meetings with other public officials. On this day the president met with his cabinet in midmorning. Early in his term the cabinet met several times a week, but six months after Reagan's inauguration, that frequency was down to once every several weeks. Between the cabinet meeting and a meeting with the Executive Committee of the National Governors Association came forty minutes of "personal staff time" during which the president could read, write, and telephone, thereby taking care of other matters.

Lunch is often a matter of business and sometimes one of ceremony. This day the governors were luncheon guests of the president in the White House.

The afternoon included another meeting with a second group of labor leaders, whose support Reagan was seeking for his "economic recovery program" of tax and spending cuts. Then, following more staff time, there was a videotaped interview with NBC's David Brinkley.

Dinner is often ceremonial. On this day, however, the Reagans had dinner alone before going to the Kennedy Center to watch a performance of the Dance Theatre of Harlem from the special "presidential box" in the opera house there. Following the performance, the Reagans went backstage, as scheduled, to greet the cast. They then returned to the White House and retired for the night.

The formal schedule on p. 234 does not report the briefer informal meetings with White House aides. There may be as many as a dozen a day, usually including meetings with the counsellor, the press secretary, and, when Congress is in session, the person in charge of relations with Congress. Nor does this schedule reveal the memos the president reads during his morning staff time and between meetings.

When he is not working, and if the weather is nice, the president may choose to swim in the outdoor White House pool; otherwise, he may decide to see a film in the White House movie theater. Were he a tennis player, he could play on the White House court, as Jimmy Carter did several times a week. He could also bowl in the White House bowling alley.

These special facilities are part of the 132 rooms and 18 acres that make up the White House. They are tended by a staff that numbers over 80 indoors, including 6 butlers, 7 maids, 6 cooks, 11 operating engineers, 4 electricians, 6 carpenters, 2 plumbers, 2 painters, 4 floral designers, a laundress, a seamstress, an accountant, and 3 doormen. Another 13 workers maintain the grounds. The salaries of these and other White House staffers exceed $1.2 million every year, and maintenance costs exceed another $2 million—including a White House electricity bill of more than $200,000 a year.

The president also has a fleet of a dozen limousines and several smaller cars for use by him and his most important assistants. One limousine has armor-plating as a security measure; when the president travels, this limousine is often flown ahead for his use. When he travels, the president has what amounts to his own airline: 5 Boeing 747s and 707s, 11 Lockheed Jetstars, 5 KC-135 tankers, 3 DC-9s, 4 Convair jetprops, and a Beechcraft King Air light plane, plus 2 helicopters. In addition, the president can use any military aircraft he wishes. He flies long distances on a 747, which is called Air Force One when he's on board and costs over $2000 an hour to fly with its crew of 17. This plane is actually a small hotel-office, equipped with desks, chairs, and even a bedroom, as well as special communications equipment.

Everywhere he goes, the president is protected by the Secret Service, as are other members of his family. This protection is provided by some 1650 agents who are assisted from time to time by people borrowed from other law enforcement agencies. The cost of this protection is well over $100 million a year.

Such special facilities and protection have led some to conclude that although the president sees many people every day he is really very insulated and lives a life more like that of a king or an emperor than that of a citizen who happens to be president. And many wonder what effects the insulation, protection, and special treatment have on the attitudes and behavior of a president. Even the president himself may not know.

8:00 A.M.—"Staff time" meeting with closest aides in the Oval Office.

8:15 A.M.—Breakfast with a group of labor leaders in the family dining room.

10:00 A.M.—Cabinet meeting in the cabinet room.

11:00 A.M.—"Personal staff time" in the Oval Office.

Noon—Luncheon with the National Governors Association in the family dining room.

10:00 P.M.—Meeting with the cast and officials of the Dance Theatre of Harlem backstage at the Kennedy Center.

White House photos courtesy of Fan Snodgrass.

THE PRESIDENT'S SCHEDULE:
TUESDAY, FEBRUARY 10, 1981

8:00 A.M.	Staff time—Oval Office	1:15 P.M.	Personal staff time—Oval Office
8:15	Breakfast with group of labor leaders—first floor family dining room	3:00	Meeting with second group of labor leaders—Oval Office
9:30	National Security Briefing—Oval Office	3:30	Staff time
9:45	Meeting with staff members—Oval Office	5:45	Videotaped interview with NBC's David Brinkley
10:00	Cabinet meeting—cabinet room	6:15	Dinner in the White House—first floor family dining room
11:00	Personal staff time—Oval Office	8:00	Attend performance by the Dance Theatre of Harlem—Kennedy Center Opera House
11:40	Meeting with Executive Committee of the National Governors Association—Roosevelt Room		
12:00 Noon	Luncheon with the governors—first floor family dining room	10:45	Arrive back at the White House—to the private quarters

---

The emphasis in these debates was on "competent," or effective, powers. Words in the Constitution describing the powers of the president are just that: words—until they have been made "competent" by the way the president utilizes the office.

Because the Constitution defined presidential roles and powers in broad general statements, there was great uncertainty as to just how the president would perform the roles and exercise the specific powers. Only experience would tell.

Since the birth of the Republic in 1787, many presidents have contributed to the strengthening of the executive branch, to make it more "competent." The major contributions, most experts would agree, have been those of Presidents George Washington, Thomas Jefferson, Andrew Jackson, Abraham Lincoln, Theodore Roosevelt, Woodrow Wilson, and Franklin Delano Roosevelt. Each of them ruled in difficult times and acted decisively, so all are known as strong presidents.[3] Let us look briefly at what these seven strong presidents did to develop the roles and powers of the presidency.

George Washington

George Washington is called the father of his country for his service as our military leader during the Revolution and as our first president. He could also be called the father of the presidency, for his presidency was crucial in defining the actual powers of the office. As the first occupant of the office, he set vital **precedents**—actions or statements that established a new approach or pattern and set an example for the future.

The Constitution gives the president the right to appoint officials with senatorial approval, but it says nothing about removal of officials. Knowing that the executive power would mean little if he could not fire those of whose work he disapproved, Washington took control of firing as well as hiring. He also established the practice of meeting regularly with the heads of the three departments created by the first Congress (state, war, and treasury) plus the attorney general. These secretaries of departments formed what we now call the **cabinet**—something not provided for in the Constitution.

In addition, Washington began the practice of *submitting proposed legislation* to the Congress and, through the efforts of Alexander Hamilton, his secretary of the treasury, getting support for it in the Congress. Many had expected Congress to take the lead in developing policy via legislation. Washington's strong initiative as chief legislator set a precedent that has lasted to this day.

---

[3]A helpful recent summary of presidential powers and their evolution is William F. Mullen, *Presidential Power and Politics* (New York: St. Martin's Press, 1976), esp. chaps. 1 and 2. For an account with more attention to legal aspects, see Arthur S. Miller, *Presidential Power* (St. Paul, MN: West, 1977).

Washington also began the practice of vetoing (or negating—a word we derive from the Latin term for "I forbid") legislation of which he did not approve or which he believed to be unconstitutional. The Constitution made this legal—provided a two-thirds majority of both houses did not vote to override the veto. Washington made it an effective presidential power.

In another blow to congressional dominance, Washington withheld from Congress his own papers and documents on a matter of diplomacy on grounds that Congress was not constitutionally entitled to them. This precedent became an important protection of presidential power from the prying eyes of political opponents. Some 150 years later it was labeled **executive privilege.** In the Watergate affair, Nixon claimed that executive privilege entitled him to keep his White House tapes and other materials from Congress, and even to prevent his officials from testifying before Congress. The controversy that followed was finally resolved against the president by the Supreme Court, as we shall see in Chapter 11. But the principle of limited executive privilege, established by the first president, survives to this day.

As *commander in chief,* Washington used troops to put down a rebellion in Pennsylvania. As *chief diplomat,* he made foreign policy without consulting Congress. This precedent surprised Congress and laid the groundwork for our long history of active foreign policy making by the president, whether for good or ill.

These varied efforts to solidify the powers of the presidency were probably Washington's chief contribution to the establishment of a legitimate government for the former colonies. But at the time many thought his greatest contribution was his *voluntary resignation* after serving two terms of four years each. The decision to resign made certain that the office would not become a lifetime possession of any one person—an "elective kingship," as it was called. Washington's two-term service set a precedent observed by all his successors until Franklin Roosevelt, who was elected during the Depression and then World War II to four straight terms. Roosevelt's shattering of the precedent was so controversial that it resulted in passage of the Twenty-second Amendment, ratified in 1951, which limits a president to two terms.

This two-term limitation is also important for the power of the presidency, because a president once reelected becomes a **lame duck** ("lame," in that the president can no longer run). Such presidents lose clout with party members, who know they won't have to deal with them much longer and won't have to run on the same ticket with them next election. Even worse, members of their party may begin jockeying for position to succeed them. On the other hand, such presidents may feel freer to attempt innovations in their second term because they need not fear losing potential support for the next campaign. At this time they may be more concerned about "making their mark" in the history books.

Thomas Jefferson

Thomas Jefferson's major contribution to the development of the presidency was to add a sixth role to those the Constitution established: that of *party leader*. As we saw in Chapter 4, by the time of his administration (1801–1809), the Federalists who had written the Constitution and dominated the government had lost power to the opposition, organized into the Republican party by Jefferson. Jefferson then established close ties with his supporters in Congress and proved a very effective politician as leader of his party. Since that time, relations between the executive and the legislative branches have always been influenced by party politics, for better or for worse. Presidents have been expected to lead their party—something particularly difficult when a president of one party faces a Congress controlled by the other.

Andrew Jackson

The framers had always assumed that Congress would be more representative of the people than the president would. Senators were expected to be attentive to the interests of the states whose legislatures elected them. Representatives were expected to reflect the interests of the people of their congressional districts. The presidency probably was less representative of the people through the time when John Quincy Adams lost the popular vote to Andrew Jackson in 1824 but won the election nonetheless in the electoral college. However, when Jackson beat Adams overwhelmingly in the rematch of 1828, in the first election in which most white males, regardless of property holdings, were allowed to vote, he proclaimed himself the "people's president." His support came largely from small farmers, frontier dwellers, and the emerging industrial working class—all of whom believed that the government had been serving the rich and propertied interests.

This transformation of the president into a *representative of the people* added a seventh role and was a major step in the evolution of American democratic politics. At the same time, Jackson brought two innovations to the "administrative politics" of the executive branch. By firing many of the long-serving and mostly unrepresentative bureaucrats and replacing them with people loyal to him (a development we'll examine in more detail in Chapter 9), he sought to make the bureaucracy more responsive to his new policy directions. And by relying for advice less on the department heads who formed the official cabinet and more on his own informal advisors (often called his **Kitchen Cabinet** because they worked behind the scenes), he received greater loyalty and support. Both these precedents strengthened the political and policy powers of the president and so contributed to the success of Jackson's efforts to democratize the presidency.

Abraham Lincoln

Thus far, the expansion of presidential powers had been in the realm of domestic affairs. The contributions of Abraham Lincoln, Theodore Roosevelt, and Woodrow Wilson expanded the president's war powers. Lincoln, confronting the prospect of a civil war, took important actions while Congress was not in session. He suspended certain constitutional liberties, spent funds that had not yet been appropriated by Congress, blockaded southern ports, and banned "treasonable correspondence" from the U.S. mails. All these acts were, at the very least, of doubtful constitutionality. All were done in the name of his powers as commander in chief and his responsibility to "take care that the laws be faithfully executed" and to "preserve, protect and defend the Constitution." He was, in sum, the father of the emergency powers that have since been such an important part of the eighth role of the president: *mobilizer of the government for war*. Lincoln's actions preserved the Union during the Civil War. But eventually there was a strong reaction in Congress—a reaction that reestablished congressional supremacy until the next period of crisis, at the turn of the century.

Theodore Roosevelt

In some ways, the modern presidency can trace its ancestry to the contributions of Theodore ("Teddy") Roosevelt (1901–1909) and Woodrow Wilson (1913–1921). In retrospect, Roosevelt's major contribution to the growth of presidential powers was probably his addition of a ninth role: *mobilizer of the people* to increase the influence of public opinion on government. To that end, he took advantage of the emerging mass-audience newspapers and magazines by inventing the "press conference." He used it effectively to generate popular support for programs he sought to push through Congress. But he also began to develop the tenth presidential role: that of *world leader exercising American power* in world affairs. Capitalizing on America's new-found enthusiasm for empire and its traditional endorsement of "rugged individualism," he developed the policy of "gunboat diplomacy." Under his leadership American armed forces were used to police the politics of other (particularly Latin American) countries in order to protect American lives and business interests.

Woodrow Wilson

In a sense, Woodrow Wilson further developed the role of world leader at the same time that he fostered the eleventh presidential role: that of *manager of the economy* influencing development through governmental action. Originally a political science professor, Wilson combined Jefferson's skill at party leadership with TR's activist conception of the office to forge a highly successful legislative record. Among its major achievements were a lowered tariff for freer international trade, a new antitrust (antimonopoly) law, and establishment of new federal regulation of banking and business. Most important of all, he achieved the introduction of the income tax on wealthy individuals (which first required passage of the Sixteenth Amendment, ratified in 1913) and the passage during World War I of the Overman Act (1918), which gave him virtually dictatorial power over the economy.

These measures and the world war transformed the president into an economic manager while they transformed America into a modern nation-state. World War I was the first war to be fought not just between military forces but also between industrial productive forces. It was, in other words, total war between countries.

The United States adopted universal military conscription (by which all able-bodied males were to be drafted into the armed forces) and used the massive new revenue from the income tax to finance military mobilization for the world's first total war. Wilson's new authority over the economy was used to reconstruct industry in the service of the state. It was the end of the period of wide-ranging economic **laissez faire** (a French term meaning, roughly, "let it be"), or nonregulation of

THE FATES OF RECENT PRESIDENTS

Harry S Truman. Declined to run for reelection. (UPI/Bettmann Newsphotos)

Dwight D. Eisenhower. Two inactive terms; health problems while in office. (AP/Wide World Photos)

John F. Kennedy. Assassinated. (AP/Wide World Photos)

Lyndon B. Johnson. Declined to run for reelection. (AP/Wide World Photos)

Richard M. Nixon. Resigned under threat of impeachment. (AP/Wide World Photos)

Gerald R. Ford. Defeated in quest for election. (AP/Wide World Photos)

Jimmy Carter. Defeated by landslide in quest for reelection. (AP/Wide World Photos)

Ronald Reagan. Reelected by landslide, but then beseiged over Iran-Contra affair. (Michael Evans/The White House)

business and industry. Further, it was the end of the limited government that had been the chief intent of the framers of the Constitution.

Wilson, in contrast to Lincoln, used his outstanding skills as party leader to get Congress to give by law to the executive branch the authority to marshal, develop, and coordinate business, industry, and the population at large in the service of the state. As is often the case, these changes, once made by law in time of war, were never to be reversed. They set the stage for the bureaucratization not only of the government but also of the American economy and other institutions. Even Congress became bureaucratized as it struggled vainly to keep up with the executive branch.[4]

Wilson laid the groundwork for the large and powerful executive branch we have today but at the price of the old efficiency and personal mastery that had been the primary attribute of the administrations of active presidents until that time. The combination of the new revenue generated by the income tax and the new demands and opportunities that government assumed because of American involvement in World War I ballooned the federal budget from a normal $800 million a year to over $18 billion in 1919. A president who before the war

(according to the chief usher at the White House), "worked but three or four hours a day and spent much of his time happily and quietly, sitting around with his family,"[5] found himself increasingly preoccupied with affairs of state both grand and trivial in a way that would soon characterize all presidencies.

Franklin Delano Roosevelt

Franklin Delano Roosevelt was an excellent orator and an effective campaigner who could fully exploit the new national radio networks in marshaling public support for his programs. He was also an innovative organizer, and he immediately drew to himself two special groups of assistants: a team of specialists from the universities to develop new policies and legislation (called the brain trust) and an informal set of political advisors and assistants (another Kitchen Cabinet). His advisors helped to develop the broad range of programs that culminated in the irreversible governmental domination of the economy under the guidance of the president in an eleventh role, one that Wilson had begun to develop, that of *economic manager*. Indeed, many would say that his presidency drew together all the previous elements and so became the first modern presidency. It created the expectation that presidents would exercise all their powers to shape national and world affairs.

[4]For a more comprehensive account of this transformation, see Roderick A. Bell and David V. Edwards, *American Government: The Facts Reorganized* (Morristown, NJ: General Learning Press, 1974), esp. chaps. 5 and 6. See also Lawrence C. Dodd and Richard L. Schott, *Congress and the Administrative State* (New York: Wiley, 1979).

[5]Irvin H. Hoover, *Forty-two Years in the White House* (Boston: Houghton Mifflin, 1934), p. 266.

ROLES REQUIRE POWERS, AND POWERS REQUIRE EXERCISE

We have seen the roles of the president grow from the 5 specified in the Constitution to 12. Table 8.1 (p. 240) summarizes these roles and their emergence. We have also seen the powers of the presidency grow along with the roles. Such powers as appointment, treaty making, the veto, and the right to pardon were specifically provided in the Constitution. Other powers have been established by laws passed by Congress. These are called **statutory powers** because they are found in statutes, or laws. They include developing the budget (for congressional approval), governing by special powers in times of emergency, such as a war or an economic crisis, and reorganizing the executive branch for greater efficiency or competence.

In a sense, however, the greatest growth in presidential powers has been through what are often called the **inherent powers**—the powers inherent in any executive branch. The Constitution says that "the executive power shall be vested in a president." Ever since those words were ratified, presidents have been engaged in *defining through practice* just what those words imply. The president is supposed to "take care that the laws be faithfully executed." This executive responsibility has been the justification for executive privilege and for the issuance of over 12,000 executive orders supposedly based on powers derived from the Constitution and statutes. These executive orders are the means by which most things are done by the president.

In the words of constitutional lawyer Arthur S. Miller:

> Presidential power . . . is a process, a flow of decisions open-ended and ever-changing, rather than a closed, internally consistent body of rules or principles. Its sources are in the Constitution and partially in the statutes; but they transcend both—they may be found in the customs or conventions which have been built up through the years as accepted (and constitutionally acceptable) patterns of behavior.[6]

The powers that derive from customs or conventions can be lost if they are not exercised. President Eisenhower followed two activists in office— Roosevelt and Truman. Because of his temperament and political philosophy he believed that

[6]Miller, *Presidential Power*, p. 9.

President Nixon says goodbye to his White House staff before resigning.   (Wally McNamee/Woodfin Camp & Associates)

strict limits should be placed on the exercise of presidential power. He was particularly hesitant to use federal power to enforce racial integration in the public schools after the 1954 Supreme Court decision declaring segregation unconstitutional. It thereby became all the more difficult for those who came afterwards to do so.

The exercise of presidential power can also be overdone, of course, as happened during the Nixon years. President Nixon was accused of "abuse of power" in Article II of the Resolution of Impeachment passed by the House Judiciary Committee just before he resigned. That article began with this charge:

> Using the powers of the office of President of the United States, Richard M. Nixon . . . has repeatedly engaged in conduct violating the constitutional rights of citizens, impairing the due and proper administration of justice and the conduct of lawful inquiries, or contravening the laws governing agencies of the executive branch and the purposes of these agencies.

The article then specifically accused Nixon of a number of such abuses of power. One was meddling with the Internal Revenue Service by trying to get confidential information on citizens' tax returns and then ordering the IRS to investigate certain citizens' returns. Another was ordering illegal wiretapping of certain citizens. It also accused Nixon of maintaining a secret spy unit in the office of the president—and it cited his efforts to cover up the Watergate violations. These violations and the case that emerged from them, which we have come to call Watergate, are summarized in the box on Watergate and the Nixon presidency.

TABLE 8.1
The Roles of the President

INFORMAL TITLE	RESPONSIBILITY	SOURCE OR PRIME ORIGINATOR	OCCASION FOR THE INNOVATION OR EXPERIENCE ENCOURAGING IT	WHERE ELSE IN THIS BOOK ORIGINS AND/OR DEVELOPMENT ARE DISCUSSED
1. Commander in chief	Leading our military forces	Constitution, Article II, Section 2	Experience of Revolutionary War	Chapter 1
2. Chief administrator	Managing the executive branch and enforcing the law	Constitution, Article I, Article II, Sections 2 and 3	Experience under Articles of Confederation	Chapter 1
3. Chief of state	Representing the American people externally	Constitution, Article II, Section 3	Experience under Articles of Confederation	Chapters 1, 19
4. Chief legislator	Proposing bills to Congress and signing or vetoing bills passed by Congress	Constitution, Article I, Section 7, Article II, Section 3, and Washington	Creating the first administration	Chapter 10
5. Chief diplomat	Making and implementing foreign policy	Constitution, Article II, Section 2, and Washington	Creating the first administration	Chapters 1, 19
6. Party leader	Titular head at least, possibly selecting officials to run the party and organizing party support for the presidential program	Jefferson	Rise of political parties	Chapter 4
7. Representative of the people	Voicing the concerns of the people in the government	Jackson	First popular election of a president with universal white adult male suffrage	Chapter 9
8. Mobilizer of the government	Organizing and exercising the governmental powers needed to fight wars	Lincoln and Wilson	Civil War and World War I	Chapters 9, 19
9. Mobilizer of the people	Organizing the power of public opinion to influence government	Theodore Roosevelt	Development of the "press conference" for new mass dailies and use of the presidency as a "bully pulpit"	Chapters 3, 5, 7
10. World leader	Exercising American power in world affairs	Theodore Roosevelt and Wilson	Emergence of America as a world power in Western Hemisphere (following Spanish-American War) and in Europe (following World War I)	Chapter 19
11. Manager of the economy	Influencing economic developments through governmental action	Wilson and Franklin Roosevelt	Passage of the income tax amendment, conduct of World War I, and fighting the Depression	Chapters 15, 16, 18
12. Social reformer	Developing and implementing programs to solve social problems	Lyndon B. Johnson	The "Great Society" programs including especially civil rights and "War on Poverty"	Chapters 12, 13, 14, 16

Watergate and the Nixon Presidency

On June 17, 1972, five men were arrested in the Democratic party offices in the Watergate office building in Washington. The following January the seven men eventually indicted for the break-in were tried. Five confessed and the other two were found guilty by the jury. Federal Judge John Sirica gave long sentences to the group. This led one of the men, James McCord, to write Sirica a letter saying that the men were under political pressure to plead guilty, that some had lied during the trial, and that the break-in had been approved by higher-ups. Sirica read the letter aloud in court, and that in effect reopened the case.

One result was the beginning of hearings on the affair by a Senate select committee, which began May 17, 1973, and ended several months later. Another result was Nixon's appointment of Archibald Cox as special Watergate prosecutor. Cox took over the Justice Department's investigation on May 18, 1973, and served until he was fired in what was called the "Saturday Night Massacre" of October 20. Yet another result was greater investigation by the media. That investigation was hampered by what came to be called a cover-up by the White House. Dan Rather, then CBS's White House correspondent, termed it "the deadly daily diet of deceit sent us from the White House. . . . They lied, schemed, threatened, and cajoled to prevent network correspondents from getting a handle on the story. And they succeeded" ("Watergate on TV," *Newsday,* December 16, 1973).

As the scandal unfolded—despite the cover-up—Nixon aides increasingly claimed that the president was being "hounded from office" by the press. However, the conventional account of Watergate as primarily a media achievement is at best only partially true. Indeed, readers of Bob Woodward and Carl Bernstein's memoir, *All the President's Men* (New York: Simon & Schuster, 1974), are well aware of the importance not only of Judge Sirica's role but also—especially—of the contribution of "Deep Throat." "Deep Throat" was the source of major leaks to "Woodstein," as the pair came to be known. His identity is still not publicly known. The common supposition is that he was a government bureaucrat close enough to the parties involved to be very well informed but far enough away to escape suspicion.

Other members of the executive branch were also important. Clearly, Special Prosecutor Cox and his successor, Leon Jaworski, played vital roles in pursuing the case in the face of White House resistance and obstruction. John Dean, once the president's counsel and then a leading witness against his White House colleagues before the Senate Watergate Committee, was also important. Another important figure was Alexander Butterfield, previously a Nixon aide, who revealed in his Senate testimony that Nixon had installed a system to tape all his conversations. Many still believe that without this knowledge and the texts of tapes that were eventually obtained, Nixon would have been able to serve his full term as president.

But those tapes would never have reached the special prosecutor or the Congress and the public were it not for the federal courts, which ruled that Nixon had to turn the tapes over once they were subpoenaed (see Chapter 11).

Even after the court rulings, the media revelations, and the bureaucratic leaks, Nixon was still president—with two and a half years left to serve. Why did he then resign? While all this was going on, Nixon's popularity was taking a severe beating. By the time he resigned, only one in four Americans approved of his conduct in the presidency.

Some have therefore concluded that it was the pressure of public opinion on Congress that forced the issue that summer. But does a drastic decline in popularity explain Nixon's fall? Lyndon Johnson had slipped to a 35 percent favorable rating in 1968 and managed at least to survive the rest of his term. And Harry Truman in 1951 and 1952 had plummeted to a 25 percent rating, comparable to Nixon's, but even more sustained through time.

Why, then, did Nixon have to go? Was it his Watergate crimes? The articles of impeachment that the House Judiciary Committee voted on through those final days were an appalling indictment. Article I cited the "cover-up," an illegal obstruction of justice on a grand scale. It was passed by a vote of 27 to 11 on July 27, 1974. Article II covered "abuse of power," with emphasis on a wide range of violations of citizens' constitutional rights. It passed by a vote of 28 to 10 on July 29. Article III cited Nixon's defiance of congressional subpoenas commanding him to turn over tapes and documents. It passed the next day. The committee then rejected a proposed article concerning the illegal concealment of the bombing of Cambodia during the Vietnam War and another alleging income tax fraud by the president by identical votes of 12 to 26.

This is a stunning bill of particulars, of "high crimes and misdemeanors" (as the Constitution defines impeachable offenses). But offenses rather similar to these had been committed at one time or another by other presidents. Indeed, Nixon's record in this regard may not be much different as a whole from those of Truman and Johnson and is probably better than those of Wilson and FDR—let alone Lincoln.

Still, Nixon's presidency had been one in which people in and around the White House had been guilty of breaking and entering, illegal wiretapping, theft of private documents, lying to a grand jury, falsifying records presented to a grand jury, and various violations of campaign-finance laws.

All these and many other acts during the Nixon administration were illegal. A study by Ralph Nader's Corporate Accountability Research Group found that appeals courts had ruled 897 acts by federal agencies illegal in the period from January 1971 to August 1974. These acts, ranging from Nixon's illegal impoundment of sewer funds to illegal tax charges by the Internal Revenue Service, included none of the Watergate misdeeds. Thus, the "tone" of the Nixon administration was not one to foster concern for legality among its own employees. And Nixon himself escaped trial and punishment for his own role in Watergate and its cover-up; he was pardoned by Gerald Ford, the very man whom he had chosen to be vice-president when Spiro Agnew was forced to resign because of corruption.

Some would say that Nixon's fall was the result of his administration's perpetration of so many misdeeds at the same time, and at such high levels, and of discovery of his own involvement in these affairs. Still others would point to his having ignored Congress, alienated the bureaucracy, downgraded the cabinet, ceased to attend adequately to the special-interest groups, and lost the support of the Republican party by running for reelection on his own. (See Nicholas von Hoffman, "The Breaking of a President," *Penthouse*, March 1977.) As a result, this analysis goes, he had lost the political base that is essential to effective governance. The best explanation of his fall may be this unique combination of transgression and erosion in an era when politics is very visible and public expectations of leaders remain high.

The abuse-of-power charges were but one of three sets of charges against Nixon when he resigned. The general assertion that Nixon had overstepped the legal limits in using certain powers of the presidency contrasts with the criticism that Eisenhower had made too little use of presidential power.[7] To what can we attribute such utterly different attitudes toward presidential power in two men who worked together in the same administration from 1953 to 1961? The political and economic climates of their presidencies were somewhat different, it is true. But many observers believe the key difference was in the specific personalities of the two men.

PRESIDENTIAL PERSONALITY AND EXPERIENCE

Prepresidential Experience

Presidents are no exception to the rule that people act in accordance with their personality and experience. For most people coming to the presidency, the political experience is relatively typical. (Figure 8.1 portrays the routes taken by all major-

party presidential nominees of the past 40 years.) This is not because the Constitution requires a certain type of experience. Quite the contrary, it sets only three formal requirements: One must be a native-born citizen of the United States; one must be at least 35 years old; and one must have lived in the United States for at least 14 years. However, political practice or custom has always set other "requirements." These are usually taken seriously until they are successfully broken. For example, until John Kennedy—a Roman Catholic—was victorious, it was widely believed that a Catholic could not be elected president and so should not even be nominated. The same is still believed about Jews and atheists as well as about blacks and women. In addition, it used to be said that "outsiders"—those not experienced in federal governmental service—were not electable. But then "outsider" Carter beat "insider" Ford, at a time when public confidence in government was on the decline and "outsider" status suddenly seemed an advantage. In 1980 Reagan did the same thing to Carter.

Normally, whatever differences there may be in upbringing and education, we expect to find the work experience of presidents rather similar. Usually presidents work their way up through politics—most often through a governorship or Congress. Eisenhower, who was a retired military general serving as a college president when nomi-

---

[7]Some scholars argue that Eisenhower was more directive and assertive than he appeared. His style was not confrontational, however, for he preferred to work behind the scenes. See Fred I. Greenstein, *The Hidden-Hand Presidency* (New York: Basic Books, 1982).

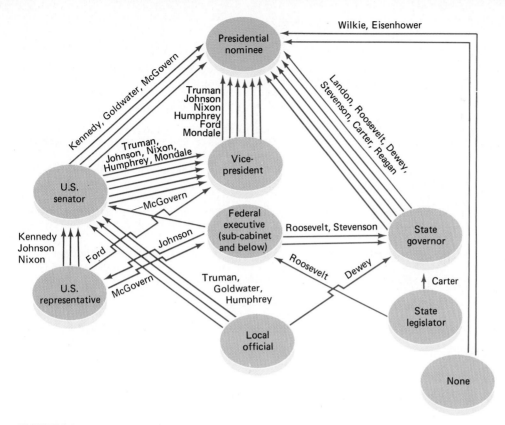

FIGURE 8.1
Routes to the Presidential Nomination.
Source: Adapted and updated from Donald R. Matthews, "Presidential Nominations," in *Choosing the President*, ed. James David Barber. © 1974 by The American Assembly, Columbia University (Englewood Cliffs, NJ: Prentice-Hall, Inc., 1973), p. 46.

nated, was an exception. Interestingly, Johnson and Nixon, with long national political careers, were probably our best prepared recent presidents, according to the conventional wisdom. And yet each overstepped political bounds in ways that terminated his career prematurely. These are conspicuous cases of the failure of previous political experience to prevent disastrous presidential mistakes such as Vietnam and Watergate. They have led observers to wonder whether perhaps personality is more important than it once was thought to be.[8]

By personality, we mean psychological predis-

positions or character and temperament—such features as one's need for privacy, one's sense of self-esteem, and one's need for power or for achievement. We have no direct way of discovering the nature of a president's personality. Rather, we have to examine the way presidents do a job and how they feel about it. We also refer to psychological theories about personality and try to apply them to the people we study. This approach is now often referred to as the study of presidential character.

The Presidential Character

The leading student of presidential character is political scientist James David Barber. He studies presidents' style, character, and world view, as well as their childhood experience, to predict their likely performance under the stress of the office. Barber divides all presidents along two dimensions in two ways, as Table 8.2 reveals. First, he separates those he calls the "actives," who devote a lot of energy to the job, from the "passives," who seldom take

[8]See the many "psychobiographies" of recent presidents: Fawn Brodie, *Richard Nixon: The Shaping of His Character* (New York: Norton, 1981); Bruce Mazlish, *In Search of Nixon* (New York: Basic Books, 1972); Doris Kearns, *Lyndon Johnson and the American Dream* (New York: Harper & Row, 1976); Bruce Mazlish and Edwin Diamond, *Jimmy Carter: A Character Portrait* (New York: Simon & Schuster, 1979); Lloyd deMause and Henry Ebel, eds., *Jimmy Carter and American Fantasy: Psychohistorical Explorations* (New York: Psychohistory Press, 1977); Betty Glad, *Jimmy Carter: In Search of the Great White House* (New York: Norton, 1980). For less psychohistorical studies of Reagan, see Lou Cannon, *Reagan* (New York: Putnam, 1982); Laurence I. Barrett, *Gambling with History: Ronald Reagan in the White House* (Garden City, NY: Doubleday, 1983); and Garry Wills, *Reagan's America: Innocents at Home* (Garden City, NY: Doubleday, 1987).

TABLE 8.2
Presidential Character Types

		EMOTIONAL ATTITUDE TOWARD THE PRESIDENCY	
		Positive	Negative
ENERGY LEVEL IN DOING THE JOB	Active	Tends to show confidence, flexibility, a focus on producing results through rational mastery	Tends to emphasize ambitious striving, aggressiveness, a focus on the struggle for power against a hostile environment
		Examples: Jefferson, Franklin Roosevelt, Truman, Kennedy, Ford, Carter	Examples: John Adams, Wilson, Hoover, Johnson, Nixon
	Passive	Tends to show receptiveness, compliance, other-directedness, plus a superficial hopefulness masking inner doubt	Tends to withdraw from conflict and uncertainty and to think in terms of vague principles of duty and regular procedure
		Examples: Madison, Taft, Harding, Reagan	Examples: Washington, Coolidge, Eisenhower

Source: Developed from James David Barber, *The Presidential Character,* 3d ed. (Englewood Cliffs, NJ: Prentice-Hall, 1985).

initiatives. And second, he divides all of them into the categories of "positives," who seem generally happy and optimistic, and "negatives," who seem sad or irritable.[9] These two distinctions can be combined to yield four categories of presidents, each with a unique character and approach to the office.

This pioneering effort to uncover the most important determinants of presidential performance has proved very provocative. Barber warns that those of the "active-negative" type may have difficulty controlling their aggressiveness because they are motivated by anxieties and guilt and tend to confuse their own ambitions and psychological needs with national policy. The result may be fixation on a disastrous policy (Vietnam for Johnson, Watergate for Nixon, and the League of Nations for Wilson).

Some have argued that equating these three presidents is indefensible. Alexander George, author of a psychobiography of Woodrow Wilson, emphasizes that Wilson's uncompromising behavior was based on strong moral principles, whereas Nixon's was based on personal ambition. Recognizing this difference, Barber grants that Nixon may deserve a special subcategory of "active-negative" for those threatened not by defeat of their moral principles but rather by attacks on their independence.

But if Nixon deserves a special subcategory for

this reason, so too do Hoover and Johnson—for other reasons, according to George. All these men differed in their motives and goals, and in their ability to cast their motives in ways that might attain their goals—even though all essentially failed to attain these goals.[10] While some experts believe we may need a different set of primary categories for assessing our presidents' characters and predicting their likely performance, all seem to have been stimulated by Barber's efforts. So far no one has produced an alternative that seems more satisfactory.

The Psychological Effects of the Presidential Experience

The focus on presidential character tends to imply that if only we select the right person for the job, things will go well. Experience, however, suggests that that is not necessarily so. Bruce Buchanan has studied the effects of the job on its occupants in recent decades. He finds four effects that may have serious psychological impacts:

- Stress from the overwhelming demands of the job may be so severe as to bring one to a physical and/or emotional breaking point.
- Deference by colleagues to one's own views may tend to nurture systematic distortions in one's perception of oneself and of the environment.

---

[9]James David Barber, *The Presidential Character,* 3d ed. (Englewood Cliffs, NJ: Prentice-Hall, 1985).

[10]See Alexander George, "Assessing Presidential Character," *World Politics* 26 (January 1974), 234–82.

Photos of President Carter taken early and late in his term show the effect of stress. (Left, UPI/Bettmann Newsphotos; right, AP/Wide World Photos)

■ Frustration at the difficulties of succeeding may be so great as to erode personal values and scruples (as seemed to happen to Nixon in Watergate).

■ Dissonance—a conflict of views within one's own mind—may encourage equivocation and lying.

The results, Buchanan fears, may be decisions based on faulty, distorted information or wishful thinking, battles with other legitimate power centers such as Congress or the courts, and even actions risking war to save face.[11]

The Dangers of Psychological Interpretations of the Presidency

We have already seen that some experts take issue with the particular psychological assessments of presidents made by other experts. Still others object to the whole enterprise. "This interest is what our presidents are really like leads to a political fatalism which seems to assume that once we elect someone president, he is beyond our control," writes Martin Levin.

> This . . . in turn tends to legitimize quiescence and political passivity on the part of citizens, organizations, and institutions in the face of presidential power. . . . Most importantly, it is refuted by recent history which indicates that we can influence a president's policy and that this satisfies democratic values and indeed often improves policies through error detection and correction.[12]

While observers disagree about how much attention should be given to the character of the pres-

---

[11]See Bruce Buchanan, *The Presidential Experience* (Englewood Cliffs, NJ: Prentice-Hall, 1978).

[12]Martin A. Levin, "A Call for a Politics of Institutions, Not Men," *Society* 18 (November–December 1978), 51.

ident as distinguished from the institution of the presidency, no one denies that presidential personality may be one important influence on presidential action.

EXERCISE OF POWER REQUIRES RESOURCES

While personality can be an important asset—or a serious liability—to a president, it is no substitute for resources. In essence, the powers we have listed are permissions. A president is only one person, and there are severe limits to what any one person can do, even when there is no real opposition. In politics, of course, there is almost always opposition, and often much of it. In our system of divided, separated, and shared powers, it is all the more necessary—and difficult—to get others to do what they must do in order for one's own presidential word or deed to have effect. What can a president do to encourage others to support his programs? The president can use resources—such as jobs, budgetary monies, access, personal support, and information—to encourage others to support presidential programs. It is particularly important to have usable and relevant resources in dealing with Congress, the bureaucracy, the courts, and the media.

Jobs: Presidential Appointments

The Constitution gives the president the power to appoint. As we'll see in some detail in Chapter 9, the civil service system has gradually whittled down that power. Thus, when Ronald Reagan took office, there were only about 2000 jobs—out of about 2.8 million in the executive branch—that he could fill. Of these jobs only about a thousand are "policy" jobs (as distinguished from "supporting" jobs such as secretary or chauffeur). Still, those thousand jobs are a source of great power to new presidents, for they can appoint not only their own political friends and supporters but also the friends of people they want to become their friends and supporters, such as influential members of Congress. In fact, all presidents, during the transition between administrations, find it difficult to select only their own friends and acquaintances, since they don't know enough reliable people. John Kennedy, faced with the task, is said to have com-

The Presidency 245

One Insider's View of the Ideal Presidential Personality

The demand for loyalty is the paramount characteristic of every presidential personality. Ideally it will be accompanied by a sufficiently mature sense of security to permit loyal dissent and disagreement. Similarly, the egocentricity that leads men to conclude they can be a better president than anyone else should be tempered by the kind of curiosity and flexibility that instructs changes of view and informs perspective.

Persistence, occasionally to the point of stubbornness, is essential to the achievement of most controversial presidential objectives. Unyielding, "I'm-from-Missouri-you've-got-to-show me" skepticism is critical to the intelligent analysis and selection of policy options. So is the sense of security that comes from a well-balanced ego that makes a president personally comfortable in testing policy alternatives on a variety of aides, government officials, outside experts, special interest representatives, casual office visitors, and opponents. The difficulty in having the relevant facts before a presidential decision is made and the need to take most presidential decisions without all the relevant facts make these particularly desirable personality traits.

All these qualities are likely to be accompanied in most presidential personalities by full measures of shrewd calculation, secretiveness, and pragmatic detachment.

From Joseph A. Califano, *A Presidential Nation* (New York: Norton, 1975), p. 244. Reprinted with permission.

---

plained that he didn't know any people—all he knew were politicians. Like his predecessors, Reagan finally appointed a good many people suggested by others. This tactic does, of course, produce "political IOUs" from supporters, which can be cashed in when the president's program needs support in Congress, for example.

The traditional name for such appointments is **patronage**—something given by one's patron or boss in exchange for support.[13] It is important to remember that in most major instances, the appointment power is shared with Congress, which must approve the president's nominations. But even when Congress is controlled by the opposition party, it approves virtually every presidential appointee.[14]

Money: Budgetary Allocations

Congress is involved in appointments, but it is immersed in the budget, as we saw in Perspective 3. The president has a special ability to use the decisions on money as political resources. That is because the president proposes the budget in the first place, and fellow executive-branch employees are the ones who ultimately spend it.

For this reason, most presidents attempt to develop new approaches to budgeting. Johnson adopted the Program Planning Budgeting System (PPBS), designed to assess and compare various programs throughout the government in terms of their cost effectiveness. Nixon, as we saw in Perspective 3, made much greater use of impoundment than his predecessors—so much so that Congress outlawed it. Carter attempted zero-base budgeting (ZBB), according to which, each agency must start with a zero budget and justify each program with its claim for money each year. Reagan greatly expanded the use of recisions, or cutbacks, in previously approved spending. In each case, the president was using the resource of money to increase his political power.

Access: The Opportunity to Get Word to the President

Whatever the subject, from appointments to budgets, and whoever the person, from member of Congress to lobbyist or even bureaucrat, no one gets anything from the president without first having access to the Oval Office. Access is the opportunity to see the president, or to phone and talk to the president, or to write the president a letter and know he will receive it. This may not seem all that difficult—until we consider how many people

---

[13]If you're curious about these jobs, which pay up to $81,300 a year and are located around the world as well as in Washington, the official list—which is informally called the plum book because it lists "political plums" ripe for the picking—is *Policy and Supporting Positions*, published by the Government Printing Office just after each presidential election.

[14]See Calvin MacKenzie, *The Politics of Presidential Appointments* (New York: Free Press, 1980).

probably want access to the president: 100 senators and 435 representatives; 50 state governors; a good number of those 1000 policy-making officials appointed when the president took office; the chief representatives of the special interests, thousands of them, many of whom probably gave money to the president's campaign hoping for such access later; and the president's own staff—over 500 in the White House Office alone when Reagan took over. And this doesn't even include the heads of 150 or so other countries, let alone the rest of the American people—more than a million of whom write the president every year. Viewed in these terms, we shouldn't be surprised that access is very difficult to get and even harder to keep.

Support: The Opportunity to Get Something from the President

Politicians always want to demonstrate to their constituents their White House access. It's a good argument for their reelection: "Keep Jones in Congress; she gets things done for you because she's the president's friend." Such support can be demonstrated by a "Dear Joan" letter, or a "photo opportunity" in which the president is photographed with Jones, or even a speech by the president in Jones's district. The greatest "gift" from a president, of course, is a program desired by the politician for his or her constituents. But any instance of support is appreciated, and this makes support a valuable presidential resource. As Larry O'Brien, whom many term the most successful congressional lobbyist in White House history on the basis of his work for Kennedy and Johnson, observes:

> A President can't whip members of Congress into line. All he can do is work out a relationship with the members that is comfortable for them and that keeps the lines of communication open. It's a very fragile thing, and it can break apart so easily if you lose touch with each other. The little things are so important—returning their phone calls and setting aside time on the President's schedule for informal, off-the-record meetings with members; getting their constituents on the White House VIP tours; helping them get publicity and speakers in their districts; . . . answering their questions; getting them information that lets them justify their support for something the President wants to do.[15]

Information: The Knowledge for Effective Action

Perhaps the most important resource of any active individual is information. The more you know about your circumstances and those of your friends and adversaries, the more likely you are to be able to act effectively. Presidents have potential access to more information than any other individuals. They not only have their own "vantage point," as Lyndon Johnson called it; they also have a personal staff that reads the papers and watches TV and prepares summaries of all that for them. They have access to the reports on issues and proposals developed by the thousands of members of the executive branch involved in policy making. Further, they get regular reports from the government's special "intelligence" organizations: the FBI on domestic matters and the CIA and other agencies on foreign affairs. Further, friends and advisors are always ready to offer information and advice; and the American people write, wire, and phone them—and reach an assistant—regularly.

Presidents can use this information in various ways. They can rely on it in making decisions. They can keep it from those they wish to punish or penalize, such as their political enemies or even members of their own party who have not proved cooperative. They can release it for political purposes: Presidents develop favorite channels—usually trusted sympathetic journalists—which they use to "leak" confidential information to gain support for an action they are taking or to mobilize opposition to something someone else is planning. In addition, presidents may be tempted to use such sources to develop damaging or embarrassing information on their political opponents—as Johnson and Nixon were caught doing with FBI, CIA, and Internal Revenue Service files. And, of course, they can—and do—use information to shape—or manipulate—public opinion.[16]

In practical terms, however, the president's situation is always difficult. Although presidents can use information to increase their political power, they have access to *too much information* on virtually everything to be able to absorb it, let alone to use it well themselves. Yet, here is the observa-

---

[15]Quoted in David Broder, "The Teachings of Larry O'Brien," *Washington Post*, November 24, 1976. See also O'Brien's book, *No Final Victories* (Garden City, NY: Doubleday, 1974).

[16]For a survey of ways in which this can be done, see George C. Edwards III, "Presidential Manipulation of Public Opinion," in *Rethinking the Presidency*, ed. Cronin, pp. 200–217.

tion of William D. Carey, former assistant budget director, in 1969:

> What a President does not know about the activities under way in Defense, State and CIA, to say nothing of the Office of Education and the Bureau of Indian Affairs is uncalculable. There he sits, overworked and making the best of a bad situation, while all around him his princes and serfs are doing and undoing in thousands of actions the work of his administration without him having a clue.[17]

A president is thus forced to depend on others for sifting and coordinating "paper."

Sometimes the system doesn't work very well. In March 1980, for example, President Carter received inadequate information from the State Department about a resolution on Israel and the Middle East being debated in the United Nations. On the basis of this information, he authorized a favorable vote. Forty-eight hours after that vote was cast, Carter saw the actual resolution for the first time and realized that vote had been a serious mistake. It was, however, too late to do anything but admit the mistake. This did neither Carter nor his administration any good.[18]

At other times the system may work too well. One day President Carter's young daughter, Amy, came home from school with a homework problem concerning the Industrial Revolution. She didn't know how to do it, so she took it to her mother, Rosalyn. Mrs. Carter couldn't understand it either, so she asked one of her aides to call the Department of Labor to get help. The next afternoon a truck arrived at the White House full of computer printouts giving a complete answer to the question. Someone in Labor had taken the query from Mrs. Carter's aide to be a serious inquiry by the president. Because it was a weekend, Labor put a full computer team to work overtime to answer it. The cost of this overreaction was hundreds of thousands of dollars.[19]

To prevent either of these types of problems, the Carter Administration developed a new White House Information Center. It could deliver overnight all the information the government has stored away about any particular problem or question. But even that was not sufficient. The Reagan White House thus developed a computer-based communications network to replace memos and bulletin boards for all senior executives. EOPNET (for Executive Office of the President Network) allows officials to send messages electronically, receive news reports from AP and UPI and other "data bases," and get information about the federal budget and current policy positions on dozens of topics instantly.[20] But of course people still have to request and read all this information and then decide which of it the president needs to know. So once again the ultimate resource is people.

EFFECTIVE USE OF RESOURCES REQUIRES PERSONNEL AND ORGANIZATION

The Vice-President

We might expect the vice-president to be an assistant president. But that is not what has happened. In the early years the vice-president was the runner-up in the race for the presidency, and so the two were sometimes political adversaries. The Twelfth Amendment, ratified in 1804, changed that. The Twenty-fifth Amendment (1967) allowed the vice-president, in cooperation with the cabinet, of which the vice-president is a member, to declare a president disabled and then to replace the president—as "acting president"—or to temporarily assume the powers and duties of a president who feels unable to perform the duties of office. The same amendment also provided that a vice-president who dies, leaves office (as Spiro Agnew did), or becomes president (as Gerald Ford did) is to be replaced by someone nominated by the president and confirmed by a majority vote of both houses of Congress. If both the president and the vice-president should die at the same time, the Speaker of the House would become president. Next in line is the president pro tempore of the Senate, followed by various cabinet officers. As mentioned at the beginning of this chapter, this line of succession was established by the Presidential Succession Act of 1947. Table 8.3 lists permanent or temporary successions by vice-presidents.

[17]Quoted in Richard Rose, *Managing Presidential Objectives* (New York: Free Press, 1976), p. 117.

[18]See Carter's account of this affair in his memoirs, *Keeping Faith* (New York: Bantam, 1981), pp. 492–94.

[19]See "Homework Costs a Lot," *Daily Texan*, February 10, 1981.

[20]Brad Lemley, "All the President's PCs," *PC Magazine*, May 29, 1984, pp. 139–44. PC stands for "personal computer."

TABLE 8.3
Vice-Presidential Successions to the Presidency

VICE-PRESIDENT	DATE	CIRCUMSTANCES
Permanent Successions		
John Tyler	1841	Death of President William Henry Harrison
Millard Fillmore	1850	Death of President Zachary Taylor
Andrew Johnson	1865	Assassination of President Abraham Lincoln
Chester A. Arthur	1881	Assassination of President James A. Garfield
Theodore Roosevelt	1901	Assassination of President William McKinley
Calvin Coolidge	1923	Death of President Warren G. Harding
Harry S Truman	1945	Death of President Franklin D. Roosevelt
Lyndon B. Johnson	1963	Assassination of President John F. Kennedy
Gerald Ford	1974	Resignation of President Richard M. Nixon
Unofficial Temporary Successions		
Thomas R. Marshall	17 months, 1919–1921	President Woodrow Wilson suffering from a stroke that disabled him; Wilson's wife Edith was actually in control
Richard M. Nixon	1955	President Dwight Eisenhower had a heart attack
Richard M. Nixon	1956	President Eisenhower had an ileitis operation
Richard M. Nixon	1957	President Eisenhower had a brief cerebral blockage
George Bush	1 month, 1981	President Ronald Reagan was recovering from a gunshot wound following unsuccessful assassination attempt

Source: Adapted from "Past Presidential Assassination Attempts," *Congressional Quarterly Weekly Report,* April 4, 1981, p. 582.

Until recently the vice-president has been, in Nelson Rockefeller's words, "standby equipment." As president, Gerald Ford began to change that by assigning more responsibility to Rockefeller. But it fell to Carter to make the first major addition to the vice-president's constitutional powers of presiding over the Senate and succeeding a president who dies or quits or is removed from office.

Walter Mondale assumed unprecedented responsibilities once Carter took office. In his own characterization, he was "to be President Carter's general advisor, to be privy to all of the information that he has, to sit in on the crucial meetings, to serve on the central policy-advisory groups, to troubleshoot, and to have foreign assigments as well as domestic. . . . "[21] As a former member of Congress, he also took on special lobbying duties when major bills were in trouble in the Congress, and after the first year took responsibility for coordinating the legislative program.[22] To facilitate his exercising these responsibilities, Mondale received an office very near Carter's—another major change, for previously vice-presidents were exiled to the neighboring Executive Office Building.

George Bush's role as Reagan's vice-president has been somewhat different. Bush came from the Republican party's moderate wing and so is looked upon with suspicion by Reagan's conservative followers. He has thus chosen to be less conspicuous than Mondale was, hoping to disarm the conservatives and position himself to get the Republican nomination for the presidency in 1988. In addition, Bush's experience was in foreign affairs, as United Nations ambassador, CIA director, and envoy to China. He has not had his own "agenda" of policy goals in the domestic realm. Thus, he became head of Reagan's campaign to decrease government regulation of business (a goal conservatives favor) and has helped lobby Congress (in which he served for four years) to pass Reagan's tax cuts and budget changes. He has continued Mondale's role of advising the president but does this very quietly.

Experience such as Mondale and Bush have received across a broad range of presidential activities best prepares a vice-president to succeed to the presidency on short notice—on the death or resignation of a president—or through later election. It may also help ease the strain on the president or increase his effectivenes. So should the cabinet and the White House staff—but do they?

---

[21]Interview, *U.S. News & World Report,* March 28, 1977. See also Brock Brower, "The Remaking of the Vice President," *New York Times Magazine,* June 5, 1977, pp. 38–48.

[22]For an interesting account of the evolution of vice-presidential responsibilities, which focuses on Rockefeller and Mondale, see Paul C. Light, *Vice-Presidential Power: Advice and Influence in the White House* (Baltimore: Johns Hopkins Univ. Press, 1984).

President Reagan's Cabinet. (Mark S. Reinstein/UNIPHOTO)

The Cabinet

Although the cabinet was not mentioned in the Constitution, it has remained a fixture since Washington's administration.[23] Table 8.4 depicts its departmental evolution since 1789. It usually includes the heads of the various executive departments plus the president and vice-president. The president may assign other officers "cabinet rank" and may also invite other interested parties to attend cabinet meetings.

In theory, cabinet meetings have two major functions. They allow presidents to express their interests and wishes to the people who run the 13 departments that employ 1.5 million people. And they make it possible for these 13 administrative experts and other high presidential aides to discuss policy questions, many of which cross normal departmental lines.

In fact, things rarely work out this way—at least, not once the administration is settled. As Charles G. Dawes, a vice-president and the first director of the Budget Bureau, once remarked: "Cabinet members are vice presidents in charge of spending, and as such they are the natural enemies of the presidents."[24]

President Nixon stated after a term in office: "It is inevitable when an individual has been in a Cabinet position or, for that matter, holds any position

TABLE 8.4

The Evolution of the President's Cabinet Departments

State	1789
Treasury	1789
War (Army)[a]	1789
Attorney General[b]	1789
Navy[a]	1798
Interior	1849
Justice	1870
Post Office[c]	1872
Agriculture	1889
Commerce and Labor[d]	1903
Commerce	1913
Labor	1913
Defense	1949
Health, Education, and Welfare[e]	1953
Housing and Urban Development	1965
Transportation	1966
Energy	1977
Health and Human Serivces[e]	1980
Education	1980

[a]Consolidated with air force into National Military Establishment in 1947. Became Defense Department in 1949.
[b]Became Justice Department in 1870.
[c]Became independent federal agency in 1970.
[d]Split into two separate departments in 1913.
[e]HEW was split into HHS and Education departments by a law passed in 1979, which became effective in 1980.

in government, after a certain length of time he becomes an advocate of the status quo; rather than running the bureaucracy, the bureaucracy runs him."[25] Or, as Nixon aide John Ehrlichman remarked, somewhat more picturesquely: After the administration appoints key officials to high offices and they have their pictures taken with the presi-

---

[23]See R. Gordon Hoxie, "The Cabinet in the American Presidency, 1789–1984," *Presidential Studies Quarterly* 14 (1984), 209–30.

[24]Quoted in Kermit Gordon, "Reflections on Spending," in *Public Policy*, vol. 15, ed. J. D. Montgomery and Arthur Smithies (Cambridge, MA: Harvard Univ. Press, 1966), p. 15.

[25]Quoted in the *New York Times*, November 28, 1972, p. 40C.

dent, "we only see them at the annual White House Christmas party; they go off and marry the natives."[26] The more the cabinet members think in terms of the interests and needs of their departments instead of those of the president, the less likely the president is to rely on cabinet meetings. This then puts more of a policy burden on the White House staff.

The White House Staff and the Executive Office of the President

Around 1900 the White House Office consisted of a few presidential assistants, bookkeepers, messengers, secretaries, cooks, and household staff. By 1932 it included only 37 people. But under Franklin Roosevelt, it began to grow rapidly as it tried to develop and then oversee the many new programs designed to overcome the Great Depression.

As such programs multiplied and the government grew, the president's bureaucracy proved unable to keep up. Roosevelt proposed a major reorganization of the executive branch. Congress passed a watered-down version that nonetheless revolutionized the presidency. It created the Executive Office of the President (EOP) to help Roosevelt oversee and coordinate the bureaucracy. It also moved the Bureau of the Budget out of the Treasury Department and into the EOP, where it would be more responsive to Roosevelt's wishes. The old maxim that "he who controls the purse strings controls everything else" began to be confirmed once again.

When the White House office grew so large that much of it was moved across the street—literally as well as figuratively—into the Executive Office Building, in its place, inevitably, grew up a new White House staff. This new staff, which came to be called the White House Office, was formally a part of the EOP. It was intended to coordinate relations between the president and Congress, and between the president and the rest of the government.

By the Truman years (1945–1953), World War II (1941–1945) had bloated the military establishment, and the Cold War that followed reemphasized the continuing importance of foreign affairs.

As a result, the National Security Act of 1947 reorganized the Departments of the Army and the Navy into the National Military Establishment (renamed the Department of Defense in 1949) to coordinate the army, the navy, and the new air force. The same act also established a new National Security Council (NSC) in the EOP. There it joined the new Council of Economic Advisors (CEA). The CEA had been created in 1946 to oversee the transition from a wartime economy to a peacetime economy and to advise the president on how to foster economic stability and full employment so that the United States would never suffer another depression.

Truman, like Roosevelt, had a staff organized like a circle with himself at the hub. Eisenhower, a retired general, replaced that system with a pyramid: He stood at its tip, aided by a powerful chief of staff who had a still-growing bureaucracy beneath him.

Kennedy and Johnson, both activists, returned to a version of the Roosevelt model, adding more special agencies to do things under presidential guidance that were not being done satisfactorily under cabinet supervision. Nixon then took that approach even further. The result was a return to what is generally called the personalized and centralized presidency.

One expert on executive organization, who eventually helped President Carter organize his own staff, described its operation and its limitations this way:

> The personalized presidency largely depends on the leader's ability to mobilize public opinion to put pressure on the government to perform as he desires and to support what he believes is right. If the President lacks this skill, he cannot compensate in the long run by relying on the inherent strength of the office. The centralized presidency largely depends on the leader's ability to keep lines open to those outside his immediate circle and to resist minutiae. If the President is suspicious of cabinet members and relies too heavily on overworked assistants, he is apt to lose perspective and even his sense of reality.[27]

Many observers attribute the Vietnam disaster and the Watergate catastrophe to the failure of the centralized personalized presidencies of Johnson and Nixon, different though they were in significant respects.

---

[26]Quoted in Richard P. Nathan, *The Plot That Failed: Nixon and the Administrative Presidency* (New York: Wiley, 1975), p. 40.

[27]Stephen Hess, *Organizing the Presidency* (Washington, DC: Brookings Institution, 1976), p. 8.

Both presidencies were products of the long-term trend toward larger and larger White House staffs, with the resulting weakening of the cabinet. The argument for this centralization has been that most important policy questions transcend the narrow foci of the departments, so that the required co-ordination is best achieved in the less specialized EOP. During the Nixon and Johnson years, virtually all major policy was developed at the White House. Foreign policy was developed by the NSC, with perhaps 100 employees. Domestic policy was developed by the Domestic Council, established by President Nixon in 1970 and employing about 50 persons. Once policy was made, it then had to be "sold," as the common expression goes. First the president's staff had to convince the president. Then policy had to be "sold" to Congress (as always) and to the segments of the public that might then support it or oppose it through lobbying. But in addition, policy now had to be sold to the executive-branch bureaucracy itself.

This transformation, in other words, created *a little government* (some 600 or so in the White House Office and over 1000 more in the rest of the Executive Office of the President) *within a government* (about 2.8 million employees in the executive-branch bureaucracy). This placed an even greater burden upon the power of the president—not just to move the nation but also to move Congress and the president's own bureaucracy.

The Carter Compromise

Before he took office, Carter had been warned by his advisors on government organization of the dangers posed by this centralization of policy making in the White House. As president, he sought to shrink the numbers and powers of the White House staff, abolishing some EOP agencies in order to increase the policy role of the department secretaries—the cabinet.

Carter developed a system he called cabinet administration. He convened regular cabinet meetings. He also let the cabinet secretaries pick their own subordinates rather than forcing his own political choices on them. And he let them administer their departments, generally without interference from the White House staff. Furthermore, he generally used cabinet officers as his primary policy advisors.

Like his predecessors, however, Carter finally became frustrated with the operation of his cabinet and the White House Office. After 31 months he suddenly asked for the resignations of all department heads and senior staff. He then accepted those of a handful of the most vocal critics of his policies and shifted the positions of several others. In addition, for the first time he appointed a chief of staff to oversee the activities of cabinet heads and other assistants, all of whom would have to report to the chief of staff rather than to the president. This meant a shift in the form of White House organization. The old Carter system was like the Truman and Roosevelt systems—a wheel with the president at the hub and cabinet heads and other key aides as spokes. The new system was more of a pyramid, with everyone reporting upward toward the chief of staff, Hamilton Jordan, who policed their contacts with the president.[28]

The Reagan Variant

The Carter administration was widely criticized for ineffectiveness—after the reorganization as much as before it. Thus, the Reagan team determined to do things differently, as new administrations usually do.[29]

It began by hiring very slowly—only after the political and ideological loyalty of candidates had been thoroughly checked. It also fired virtually all the holdovers in the White House—even the secretaries and clerical workers—in an unusually thorough housecleaning. Further, it shifted many of the career civil servants, who might be attached to the existing programs, to other jobs.

It then adopted an approach that Reagan called cabinet government. He told his cabinet appointees that he wanted to have regular cabinet meetings in which all would speak freely. However, his aides made it clear to cabinet officers that they were to function as loyal lieutenants dedicated to the pursuit of Reagan's objectives rather than of those of their agencies. As part of Reagan's new economic program, cabinet officers were com-

---

[28]See the special issue of *Presidential Studies Quarterly* 16 (Fall 1986) for articles on presidential leadership, management, and organization.

[29]See Colin Campbell, *Managing the Presidency: Carter, Reagan, and the Search for Executive Harmony* (Pittsburgh: Univ. of Pittsburgh Press, 1986).

pelled to participate in drastic budget cutting even before they had had any experience working with the permanent bureaucracies of their agencies.

Reagan's preference for decentralizing authority appealed to many of his cabinet members and White House assistants. However, the fact that he was generally removed and distant from the daily business of government tended to lessen his effectiveness with Congress and the bureaucracy as his administration evolved. The dangers of this detached style of administration did not become clear until halfway through his second term, when the Iran-Contra scandal, summarized in the accompanying box, erupted.

The Lessons of Personnel and Organization

Despite all the reorganizations discussed above, no one has yet found effective way of organizing the executive branch. Figure 8.2 depicts the formal

FIGURE 8.2

The Organization of the Executive Branch as It Varied under Recent Presidents.

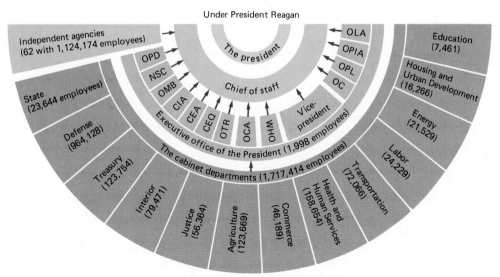

Key

CAU = Central Administrative Unit
CEA = Council of Economic Advisors
CEQ = Council on Environmental Quality
CIA = Central Intelligence Agency
CWPS = Council on Wage and Price Stability
DPG = Domestic Policy Group
EOP = Executive Office of the President

NSC = National Security Council
OMB = Office of Management and Budget
OPD = Office of Policy Development
OSTP = Office of Science and Technology Policy
OSTR = Office of Trade Representative
SRTN = Special Representative for Trade Negotiations
WHO = White House Office

OCA = Office of Cabinet Affairs
OF = Office of Communications
OPL = Office of Public Liaison
OPIA = Office of Political and
      Intergovernmental Affairs
OLA = Office of Legislative Affairs

The Iran-Contra Affair and the Reagan Administration

Riding the crest of his landslide reelection and continuing high popularity, President Reagan in 1985 sought a major foreign policy success to guarantee his place in history.

People working in the president's National Security Council (NSC) staff proposed selling arms to Iran. The United States sells weapons to many countries. But Iran had been denied such weapons for years because it sponsored terrorist attacks on Americans and its allies in the Middle East were holding a handful of American citizens as hostages. The arms sales were apparently intended to secure the release of these hostages.

At the same time, the president wanted to continue giving military aid to rebels (called "Contras") fighting to overthrow the Marxist-leaning government of Nicaragua. Congress had lost patience with this policy and in 1984 passed "the Boland amendment" to a budget bill prohibiting sending military aid to the Contras.

NSC staffers thus developed a new policy proposal: selling arms to Iran and using profits from these sales to help finance the Contras. But because both actions were contrary to announced U.S. policy, and also violated certain U.S. laws, they were to be done covertly—under cover. The arms were to be shipped to Iran via other countries, and the profits were to be passed to the Contras via secret bank accounts in various countries.

Somebody approved the plan. (President Reagan later denied that it was he. Secretary of State George Shultz and Secretary of Defense Caspar Weinberger both opposed it when they heard it proposed, and so were excluded from further planning sessions.) Lt. Col. Oliver North, a Marine assigned to the NSC, supervised its execution. He had the assistance of some employees of the Central Intelligence Agency (CIA) as well as various private citizens. The program continued for a year until a newspaper in Lebanon "blew its cover," revealing that the U. S. was engaged in trading arms to Iran for hostages.

That revelation caused an outcry in the United States. The Reagan administration first claimed it was only selling the arms to strengthen the position of moderates in the Iranian government, so that they would be more friendly toward the United States in the future.

A quick investigation in November 1986 by Attorney General Edwin Meese 3d revealed, however, that arms sale profits were diverted to the Contras. This caused greater outcry because Congress had expressly prohibited such military aid. So the administration set up a special commission headed by former Senator John Tower (Republican of Texas) to investigate the operation of the NSC. It also appointed a special prosecutor to determine whether anyone involved should be charged with illegal conduct in what soon came to be called "Irangate" or "Contragate."

But Congress was not satisfied by these measures, so each house set up its own special investigating committee. The Tower Commission reported its conclusion that "The president did not seem to be aware of the way in which the operation was implemented and the full consequences of U.S. participation." However, to discover how the policy had been developed and who was responsible for it, the Congressional committees held combined hearings in the summer of 1987.

In all, there were 40 days of public hearings (many of them nationally telecast) and 4 days of closed or secret sessions. The 28 witnesses testified for 250 hours. The committees also examined 1,059 documents supplied by the participants in the affair.

What was concluded?

1. The president had denied that he knew about the Contra fund diversion, and no witness contradicted that. Former NSC head Rear Adm. John Poindexter, who was forced to resign when the scandal broke, said that he approved the program but didn't raise the matter with the president because he assumed Reagan would have approved it.

2. The Reagan administration's policy process worked very badly on this affair. Small groups of people, in and out of government, acting in secrecy against the will of Congress and violating the law, created and implemented policies that hurt the United States' standing in the Middle East and around the world when they were revealed. Nor did those policies actually achieve their objectives of freeing the hostages and strengthening the Contras.

3. Foreign policy should be made with the participation of the Department of State (which was excluded from the debate over the Iran-Contra affair) and executed by the State Department and other official representatives with operational experience, rather than by staff members of the NSC and the CIA plus interested private citizens.

4. Reagan's management style of giving blanket authority to subordinates and not checking up on what they did helped to create these developments. This was an important failure in presidential leadership.

and actual relations between the president and the latter's advisors and assistants—both in the cabinet and in the White House staff, as they have developed from Franklin Roosevelt to Ronald Reagan. We'll return to some of these problems when we analyze bureaucratic politics in the next chapter.[30]

For the moment, we must remember that inevitably the president and the executive staff must constantly attempt to find ways of motivating those in the executive branch to do the president's bidding, even when they'd rather not. The power of the president has always depended on ability to get people to follow orders if they refuse to follow suggestions. But the government has become so big that the chief executive cannot possibly even *issue* orders to most bureaucrats, let alone *follow up* to see that they are carried out. Thus, more than ever, the power of the president has become *the power of persuasion.*

PRESIDENTIAL POWER

As Persuasion

"People talk about the powers of a President, all the powers that a Chief Executive has, and what he can do. Let me tell you something—from experience!" Harry Truman remarked after three years on the job.

> The President may have a great many powers given to him in the Constitution and may have certain powers under certain laws which are given to him by the Congress of the United States; but the principal power that the President has is to bring people in and try to persuade them to do what they ought to do without persuasion. That's what the powers of the President amount to.[31]

Most of the important things a president wants to do require the cooperation of other parts of government. The Congress must pass legislation and appropriate money to establish and fund programs. The various parts of the bureaucracy must follow orders to develop and carry out the pro-

grams. The courts, if asked, must rule on whether the programs and the laws are constitutional. And the people must accept the programs and the president who proposes them.

The president, according to the Constitution and tradition, has a wide range of powers as commander in chief, chief legislator, chief diplomat, and so on, as we and Harry Truman noted above. But in fact presidents share these powers with other officials and other branches. They depend on others for cooperation. Of course, the other officials will depend on the president from time to time for assistance with various of their own projects, and so the chief executive's power is more than simply that of charm, charisma, or powerful reasoning. It also includes the resources detailed above: jobs, money, access, support, and information.

But presidents cannot simply impose their wishes on others, as we noted in our discussion of authority in Perspective 1. They must persuade these others to accept their position, their definition of the situation, their policy proposals. As Richard Neustadt once said:

> The essence of a President's persuasive task with congressmen and everybody else is to induce them to believe that what he wants of them is what their own appraisal of their own responsibilities requires them to do in their interest, not his. Because men may differ in their views on public policy, because differences in outlook stem from differences in duty—duty to one's office, one's constituents, oneself—that task is bound to be more like collective bargaining than like a reasoned argument. . . . [32]

Even the "collective bargaining" image may sometimes be misleading. Presidents must often find devious ways of getting information to officials without appearing to be imposing their will on them. Joseph Califano, secretary of health, education and welfare under Carter, once told an amusing but revealing story of how Lyndon Johnson, whom Califano assisted in the White House, operated in this devious way as president (see the box on persuasion in action). It emphasizes the importance not only of occasional deviousness but also of an understanding of structures and roles and their impact on the effectiveness of persuasion.

[30]By now there is a large literature on government organization and reorganization. The standard source on the present formal structure is the *United Sates Government Manual*, published each year by the Government Printing Office.

[31]Harry S Truman, *Public Papers of the President 1948* (Washington, DC: GPO, 1949), p. 247.

[32]Richard Neustadt, *Presidential Power*, 2d ed. (New York: Wiley, 1976), p. 114. Emphasis deleted.

The Presidential Power of Persuasion in Action

One of the best examples in the Johnson administration involved Treasury Secretary Henry (Joe) Fowler and House Banking Committee Chairman Wright Patman. Fowler was one of Johnson's favorites in the cabinet and Patman had been the president's friend and political ally for a generation, beginning during the New Deal. To stem increases in the prime rate by the major banks in early 1966, Johnson wanted to turn loose the power of his administration and to deposit federal funds in banks that held down interest rates (as well as to remove such funds from banks that increased them). Although generally inclined to use executive power to hold down prices and wages, Fowler opposed the particular jawboning and action program Johnson sought to put into effect. Johnson requested and received an analysis of interest rates for the period Fowler had been treasury secretary and discovered that, in percentage terms, those rates had risen more during Fowler's brief tenure than during that of any previous secretary in the twentieth century. Johnson immediately called Wright Patman and said, "Wright, there's something you've just got to know. Interest rates have risen faster under Joe Fowler than under any secretary in the century."

Patman was appalled. "Something's got to be done about that, Mr. President," he said.

"That's why I'm telling you," Johnson continued, "If I were you, I'd send him a blistering letter and have him up to testify. You've got to build a fire under him."

"You're absolutely right, Mr. President." By now Patman was getting angry.

"You know, Wright, unless Fowler starts moving on these banks, the New York bankers will just keep hiking the interest rates and rolling in the money. Your committee can't stand for that."

"I'll write him today, Mr. President. We'll call him to testify this week."

By the time Johnson hung up, Patman was sputtering mad. When Fowler received Patman's scathing letter, he called the White House. Johnson passed the word that Fowler had "better tell Patman you'll turn loose some pressure on the banks or else he'll turn your hearing into a Texas barbecue." Fowler agreed and Johnson got a jawboning program with the banks off the ground. Fond as he was of Fowler, Johnson was sufficiently detached to realize that he had to give him a hard shove to get him moving.

From Joseph A. Califano, *A Presidential Nation* (New York: Norton, 1975), pp. 206-7. Reprinted with permission.

As Leadership

Emphasizing persuasion as the basic tool of presidential power can be misleading in two important ways. First, as we saw earlier, the president *does* have various instruments that can be used to influence others' conduct—especially appointments, budgetary monies, access, and support. But second, possibilities are often severely limited by *circumstances* beyond the president's control. In recent decades first the Cold War and then economic competition from abroad have set the context for the chief executive's activities in foreign affairs and have gravely limited the range of possibilities. At home racial division and economic stagnation coupled with inflation have had similar effects. In addition, certain *general trends* have tended to weaken the president's ability to govern. The lists of key trends vary somewhat from one expert to the next, but most would probably agree with that offered by Bert Rockman:

The growth of the electronic media . . . has affected politics everywhere, but it has undoubtedly hastened the decomposition of a not very sturdy political party system. The growth in political awareness, itself hastened by the impact of television according to some accounts, has narrowed the deference shown to and thus the latitude for political authority. Most of all, the growth of knowledge and the rise of issue specialists have denied us the joys of certainty which earlier could be brought to government. The old bromides fade in the face of the intricate connection of issues and the delicate trade-offs to be made among them. Hugh Heclo, in his superb analysis of this phenomenon, notes that in the old days the primary problem of government was to do what was right, whereas now it is to know what is right.[33]

Today the federal government is doing more things than ever before, and each thing it does af-

[33]Bert A. Rockman, "Carter's Troubles," *Society* 17 (July–August 1980), 34. The piece Rockman cites is Hugh Heclo, "Issue Networks and the Executive Establishment," in *The New American Political System*, ed. Anthony King (Washington, DC: American Enterprise Institute, 1978), pp. 87–124.

fects many other things. Look, for example, at the building of highways. Thirty years ago, when the Interstate Highway System was developed, a highway-building program was concerned with highway building, pure and simple. Now it also raises questions of mass transit (an urban alternative), energy efficiency (cars are big consumers of expensive oil), environmental impact (cars pollute), urban effects (highways destroy neighborhoods), and jobs (who should build them)—as well as who should pay for the highways. Each of these issues is of strong concern to certain special interests who are politically active. Therefore, a president seeking a new program must design it so as to get the support of many different single-interest groups, who must then build a coalition in order to get it approved by Congress.[34]

Even so, some presidents are able to be effective leaders, at least some of the time. Occasionally, it is by offering a vision of a desirable future that followers are attracted. More often, it is by the astute use of resources in what we sometimes call political bargaining or transactional leadership. This approach can help the president lead the executive and legislative branches.

But often neither of these approaches works. At that point, the president is likely to try what Samuel Kernell calls "going public." This involves promoting policies in Washington by appealing directly to the American people for support. Put another way, it usually involves going over the heads of members of Congress to get their constituents to put pressure on them. Every president since Woodrow Wilson has used this tactic occasionally. Nixon often did so on Vietnam; Carter did so on energy; Reagan regularly did so on both budget cuts and foreign policy.[35]

Even so, most of the president's activities involve bargaining. "It is a virtue that presidential leadership depends so heavily on securing the cooperation of others," writes Barbara Kellerman. ". . . [T]here is merit to a system that tends to stall unless the governor consents to negotiate with representatives of the governed. At its considerable best, politics admits change while at the same time

"The question is, do we want to emphasize foreign policy to take the people's minds off domestic policy, or emphasize domestic policy to take the people's minds off foreign policy?" (Drawing by Dana Fradon; ©1979 The New Yorker Magazine, Inc.)

imposing on our public life an order in keeping with the democratic ideal that power be shared."[36]

As Coalition Building

Part of this sharing occurs in coalitions. Coalition building is essential to the success of any political actor in a system of several parties, many interest groups, and cross-cutting issues. By the time presidents take office, they have already developed two different coalitions of voters: one to win their party's nomination and another to win the general election. The second one be broader than the first. Once in office, presidents must then develop a third group: a governance coalition.[37]

A governance coalition is a collection of groups or special interests that generally support the president's program. It will exist in the public at large as well as in Congress. If it is strong and cohesive enough, the president will tend to be successful. Its strength usually depends initially on how broad the president's support in the electorate was and on whether members of Congress wish to support the

[34]See Huge Heclo, "One Executive Branch or Many?" in *Both Ends of the Avenue: The Presidency, the Executive Branch and Congress in the 1980s*, ed. Anthony King (Washington, DC: American Enterprise Institute, 1983), pp. 96–136.

[35]Samuel Kernell, *Going Public: New Strategies of Presidential Leadership* (Washington, DC: CQ Press, 1986).

[36]Barbara Kellerman, *The Political Presidency: Practice of Leadership from Kennedy through Reagan* (New York: Oxford Univ. Press, 1984), p. 256. See also George C. Edwards III and Stephen J. Wayne, *Presidential Leadership: Politics and Policy Making* (New York: St. Martin's Press, 1985).

[37]See Lester G. Seligman, "Electoral Governing Coalitions in the Presidency," *Congress and the Presidency*, 10, no. 2 (Autumn 1983), 125–46.

President Reagan speaks to a joint session of Congress. (John Fucara/Woodfin Camp & Associates)

chief executive or at least whether they fear popular disapproval—and even defeat—if they do not.

Once in office, presidents can often attract new support for their programs, especially if they use the resources of the office effectively. Mobilizing public opinion and negotiating effectively with Congress can contribute further to success. But at the same time, presidents who desire to run again must preserve their two electoral coalitions.

To successfully implement their programs, even with a strong governing coalition, presidents must limit their objectives and set priorities among them, so that they can use what power they have efficiently—especially in dealings with Congress.[38]

THE PRESIDENT AND CONGRESS

Most of a president's relations with Congress involve attempting to achieve change by putting together coalitions of people and interests by compromise and accommodation. This sort of leadership is also common in Congress itself; and not surprisingly, it characterized the presidencies of former congressional leaders Johnson and Ford.[39]

The president is, after all, the chief legislator, as the Constitution allows and as the complexity of contemporary national challenges at home and abroad requires. In his study of "the legislative presidency," Stephen Wayne noted:

Under our system, the president can provide that leadership probably better than the Congress on many controversial, large-impact issues. Having a national constituency, superior resources, and a more supportive internal structure makes it easier for the president, through the presidency, to solicit, synthesize, and sell national policy objectives to the Congress than for the Congress to do this itself. Moreover, a president's ability to shape public opinion and generate external support, especially for innovative domestic proposals, provides the muscle for coalition building that Congress so often lacks.[40]

Still, presidents have difficulty getting their way in Congress. It is not surprising that presidents receive more support in Congress from members of their own party than from the opposition. But because presidents often face one or even both houses of Congress controlled by the other party, and because they cannot count on full support from members of their own party, presidents must seek bipartisan support for their legislative programs. They may get such support in several ways.[41] One is to help members of Congress with their constituents' problems. Another is patronage: appointing

[38]For this and other pieces of advice, see the articles in Arnold J. Meltsner, ed., *Politics and the Oval Office: Towards Presidential Governance* (San Francisco: Institute for Contemporary Studies, 1981). See also Paul C. Light, *The President's Agenda* (Baltimore: Johns Hopkins Univ. Press, 1983).

[39]James Macgregor Burns in his book *Leadership* (New York: Harper & Row, 1978) calls this transactional leadership. He contrasts it with the much rarer type, transformational leadership, in which the leader attempts to change minds or stir people to action through the appeal to purposes that raise both leader and followers to new levels of motivation.

[40]Stephen J. Wayne, *The Legislative Presidency* (New York: Harper & Row, 1978), p. 24.

[41]For an interesting brief survey of presidents from Johnson through Reagan, see Charles O. Jones, "Presidential Negotiation with Congress," in *Both Ends of the Avenue*, ed. Anthony King, pp. 96–130. See also Stephen A. Shull, *Domestic Policy Formation: Presidential-Congressional Partnership?* (Westport, CT: Greenwood Press, 1983).

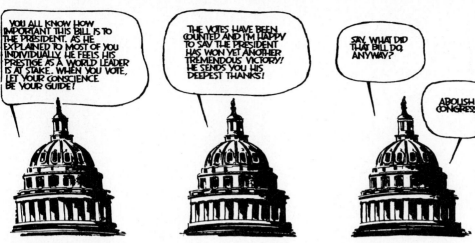

(By Wright for *The Miami News*)

to federal jobs people who are designated by members of Congress. Yet another is adopting a program proposed or favored by a legislator. All presidents do these things. Some presidents also campaign for members of their party at election time. All presidents sometimes appeal directly to the citizens to influence the votes of their own members of Congress and more often mobilize special interests to influence Congress.

Presidents who have served in Congress are more likely to be effective there because they know how Congress works and what is likely to have an impact. "Outsider" presidents are especially likely to have difficulty in their relations with Congress, as did Jimmy Carter. In his first several years, he did not consult often enough with Congress, he often refused to bargain and compromise, and some of his liaison people were not well respected on Capitol Hill. In his last several years in office, his relations with Congress improved. Even so, he was more successful than Republicans who faced Democrat-controlled Congresses but less successful than fellow Democrats Kennedy and Johnson, who like Carter dealt with Democratic Congresses.[42]

Presidents seem to face what Paul Light views as two cycles of influence. The first is the *"cycle of increasing effectiveness."* Over time presidents and their staffs become more effective in managing their scarce opportunities. But at the same time, presidents tend to lose opportunities through the

"cycle of decreasing influence." During the term, public approval tends to drop, and party seats in Congress decline in the midterm election, costing presidents opportunities for influence. Thus, as Light notes, "Even though they become more effective at finding opportunities for ideas, Congress and the public become less interested."[43]

Reagan had greater success than Carter in his first year, although he too was an outsider. In later years, his success declined to levels typical of presidents facing a Congress with at least one house controlled by the opposition. Even so, many continued to praise Reagan's skill at communicating. Effective leadership does seem to depend to some extent on effective communication, which usually relies upon a kind of eloquence and the use of important symbols. As Bruce Miroff reminds us:

> Presidents employ dramatic symbols in order to cast their actions in the most effective terms—e.g., to gratify important electoral blocs and to touch vital nerves in American ideology. Often the goal of White House symbolism is to recast the president's own image, as a way of masking the limitations upon presidential effectiveness or countering persistent criticisms in the mass media. With history and myth—aided by a substantial public-relations apparatus in the White House—working for them, presidents have power on this symbolic plane that usually exceeds their power in Washington politics. And such power is far from negligible; in modern America it is presidential symbolism, more than any other single factor, that shapes the prevailing imagery and popular consciousness of politics.[44]

---

[42]A president's legislative success is usually measured by the percentages of presidential victories on Congressional votes where the president took clear-cut positions. Johnson's reached 93 percent in his second year—the highest ever recorded. Eisenhower's ranged from 89 percent in his first year to 52 percent (the lowest ever recorded) in his seventh year. Reagan's was 82 percent in his first year, but fell to 56 percent in his sixth year. See *Congressional Quarterly Weekly Report*, October 25, 1986, p. 2687.

[43]Paul Light, "The Presidential Policy Streams," in *The Presidency and the Political System*, ed. Michael Nelson (Washington, DC: CQ Press, 1984), pp. 423–48 at 445. See also Light's book *The President's Agenda* (Baltimore: Johns Hopkins Univ. Press, 1983).

[44]Bruce Miroff, "Beyond Washington," *Society* 17 (July–August 1980), p. 70.

Fear of terrorist attacks has recently resulted in special barricades surrounding the White House. (Wally McNamee/Woodfin Camp & Associates)

THE PRESIDENT AND THE PEOPLE

In order "to move a nation," in former presidential advisor Roger Hilsman's words, presidents must move the people.[45] Sometimes presidents ask the people to support their program by lobbying their members of Congress. At other times presidents seek adoption of their program, such as the energy conservation urged by Presidents Nixon, Ford, and Carter. In general, the president tries to satisfy 245 million people making up various interest groups. This task is made especially difficult by the fact that different people want different things, and resources are always scarce.

The Problem of Popular Confidence

Surveys since the mid-1960s have consistently revealed a general decline in public confidence in government. One reason was, of course, Watergate. Another was Vietnam and the "credibility gap" of the Johnson years, in which even presidential statements and pledges became suspect. John-

son, after all, had campaigned against Barry Goldwater in 1964 by painting his opponent as a militarist or "war hawk" and pledging that he would not commit American fighting forces in Vietnam—a pledge he broke just months after the inauguration, in what turned out to be but the first of a series of misleading assertions.

The result has been that the American people came to value "honesty" and "trustworthiness" as the most important characteristics in a presidential candidate—ahead of concern for people, experience, leadership ability, intelligence, and education.[46]

In recent years the public view seems to have changed, probably in response to the difficulties Ford and Carter had. In a recent Gallup Poll, strength, forcefulness, and decisiveness were high on the list of valued traits. Furthermore, political savvy was thought to be important—a change from the years just after Watergate, when people generally feared such skills in a president.[47]

---

[45]See Hillsman's memoir of the Kennedy years, *To Move a Nation* (Garden City, NY: Doubleday, 1967).

[46]See Melvin D. Field, "Public Opinion and Presidential Response," in *The Effective President*, ed. John C. Hoy and Melvin H. Bernstein (Pacific Palisades, CA: Palisades Publishers, 1976), pp. 59–77. See also Bruce Buchanan, *The Citizen's Presidency* (Washington, DC: CQ Press, 1987).

[47]See Stephen J. Wayne, "Great Expectations: What People Want from Presidents," in *Rethinking the Presidency*, ed. Thomas E. Cronin, pp. 185–99.

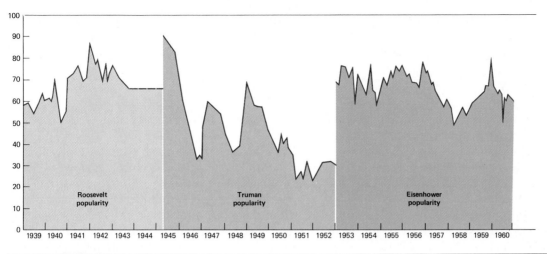

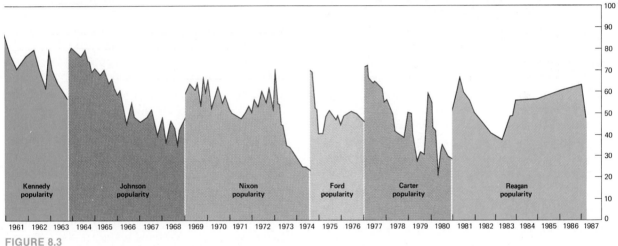

FIGURE 8.3

The Evolution of Popular Approval Ratings of Recent Presidents.

Source: Gallup Opinion Index, Oct.–Nov. 1980, Dec. 1983, Sept. 1986.

The Expressions of Popular Views

Public attitudes are often expressed in communication with the president, whether by letter, telegram, or phone call. This communication between the people and the president, indirect though it be, happens whether or not presidents encourage it—especially when they do something that upsets people. Today the president gets from 35,000 to 75,000 letters a week, depending upon current events. Such communications rarely if ever reach the president directly. But 20 or so White House staff members prepare summaries of opinions expressed and single out typical or unusual messages for the president to see and occasionally to respond to.[48]

---

[48]See Gustofson, "The President's Mail."

WHAT INFLUENCES THE PRESIDENT?

Does public opinion really affect a president's behavior? How do presidents decide what to do? Presidents deal with so many different questions, domestic and foreign, that it is difficult even to specify the relative importance of possible influences on their decisions. We know that presidents interested in being reelected are likely to be concerned about the general assessment the public gives their work. But is it likely to matter much what position they take on one particular issue? Perhaps not, although occasionally particular issues—such as President Ford's pardon of Nixon—do make a difference.

Does this mean that the views of presidential advisors will matter more? Those advisors are more likely to be watching either political implications or technical aspects of a question—but rarely both, as a president must. What about the cabinet and other senior officials? Presidents know each has his or her own special interests, and so they are not likely to take a specific cabinet secretary's recommendation without question. And Congress? Presidents must be concerned about congressional reaction, but they know that members of Congress represent narrow constituencies and that Congress expects them to offer national leadership, since their constituency is the entire country. What about vested interests? Or foreign nations, if it is a foreign policy question? Or what about the role of intelligence agencies—the FBI domestically and the CIA internationally? Or will a president's own past experience and personality prove more influential than these momentary suggestions and considerations?

The answer to all these questions is, unfortunately, that no one knows for sure. Presidents themselves may not know, even in retrospect, at least if we can judge by reading their memoirs. When Gerald Ford was asked about the relative influence on his decisions of pressure groups, the Congress, and his own conscience, he responded:

> It is hard to be totally certain whether conscience or some other factor matters most. Some subjective feelings about certain things or certain issues are bound to play a part. In my case, I had a combination of what I thought were good recommendations from people in the administration and my own background and personal convictions. It was a combination of the two—options that came to me and my own experience and convictions—that ended up in whatever decision I made.[49]

If there are no clear and major outside influences on presidential decisions, does this suggest that the office is, or has become, too powerful?

IS THE PRESIDENT TOO POWERFUL?

"The tyranny of the legislature is really the danger most to be feared, and will continue so for many years to come," Thomas Jefferson wrote to James Madison just before George Washington was inaugurated as our first president. "The tyranny of the executive power will come in its turn, but at a more distant period."

The Use of Executive Orders

The Constitution makes the president commander in chief and charges the chief executive to "take care that the laws be faithfully executed." This charge has required presidents to act alone and often quickly, especially in national emergencies. The major instrument developed by presidents for such action has been the **executive order**, a proclamation requiring agencies or individuals to take certain specific actions without Congress having first passed a law on the subject.

All presidents have found executive orders an essential tool in carrying out their oath to "faithfully execute the office of president," even though the Constitution makes no mention of that specific power. From time to time, certain executive orders have been challenged in court on the grounds that they overstep the president's authority. But the courts have upheld the president's power to issue executive orders even when they have declared a specific order unconstitutional.

Presidents Johnson and Nixon significantly extended the use of the executive order. In doing so, Johnson managed to fight a war in Vietnam without having Congress first declare it. Nixon managed, with mixed success, to abolish programs and agencies established by Congress without Congress's approval. Both presidents also used their powers less openly to involve bureaus like the FBI and the CIA in domestic spying and violation of the civil liberties of citizens. The peak of these violations came with the Watergate affair.[50]

One major result of Vietnam and Watergate was a widespread conclusion—by politicians, observers, and ordinary citizens alike—that the president had gained too much power. It was time, many argued, to dismantle or at least limit what historian Arthur Schlesinger termed "the imperial presidency."[51]

---

[49]*A Discussion with Gerald R. Ford: The American Presidency* (Washington, DC: American Enterprise Institute, 1977), p. 19.

[50]See Phillip J. Cooper, "By Order of the President: Administration by Executive Order and Proclamation," *Administration and Society*, 18 (August 1986), 233–62.

[51]See Arthur Schlesinger, *The Imperial Presidency* (Boston: Houghton Mifflin, 1973).

The Relativity of Presidential Power

Power is a relative thing in any system. If presidents seem to have too much power, it may be because Congress and the courts have too little power to restrain them or to counter their power. In other cases, Congress or the courts may choose not to resist presidential initiatives. This was the case during the Vietnam War. In the Watergate activities, however, much of what Nixon and his administration did was done in secret. The same was true of the Iran-Contra activities during the Reagan administration. In such a case, neither Congress nor the courts know enough about the president's actions to be able to resist at the time.

There are, then, three different possibilities: (1) inadequate countervailing power; (2) insufficient will to counteract the president; and (3) incomplete knowledge of the president's use (and abuse) of presidential powers. The problem of presidential power is thus more complex than is sometimes argued. The real danger may be the power to evade the law in ways that are kept secret.

Congressional Limitations on Presidential Power

Vietnam and Watergate appear to have changed all that—or at least some of the most dangerous abuses. Congress in 1973 passed the War Powers Resolution, which permits the president to use armed forces in an emergency without prior declaration of war by Congress but requires that the president inform Congress immediately and allows Congress to recall the forces after 60 days. President Nixon thought the bill so limiting that he vetoed it, but Congress then passed it over his veto.

Shortly thereafter, Congress held extensive hearings on abuses by intelligence agencies and established new procedures with special oversight committees to supervise the agencies. Because the agencies operate in secret it is difficult to know how effective such "oversight" actually is. But greater investigative efforts by both Congress and the press, as well as by nongovernmental groups such as the American Civil Liberties Union and the Center for National Security Studies, seem to be keeping the agencies more honest. This in turn limits the possibilities for abuse of power by the president—or by the agencies acting independently.

Other Congressional action in the 1970s limited the president's ability to impound, or refuse to spend, funds it had appropriated, as we saw in Perspective 3. Yet another sought to limit the president's power to make secret executive agreements with other countries.

The Impact of Recent Presidents

Gerald Ford

It may be, however, that the greatest contributions to limitations on presidential abuse of power have come from recent presidents. Gerald Ford made a major contribution. He exercised less power as president than Johnson or Nixon, for several reasons.

First, he was an *unelected* president, taking up the office when Nixon was forced to resign. Indeed, he hadn't even been elected vice-president, but instead was appointed to that post when Nixon's original vice-president, Spiro Agnew, was forced to resign owing to allegations of corrupt behavior. Never having been elected by the American people as a whole, Ford did not have a public mandate to act as a strong president.

Second, as a Republican facing a Congress strongly controlled by the Democrats, his opportunities for strong leadership, like those of Nixon, were limited. Third, and perhaps even more important, Ford's philosophy of government emphasized reliance on private enterprise rather than on the federal government; and so on most matters he was not so inclined to be a strong president in the Johnson or Carter mold.

Furthermore, he came into office just when the Congress was trying to recover from its failure to assert itself over Vietnam and Watergate. As a result, it had passed the War Powers Resolution and had established the new budgetary system (discussed in Perspective 3). Further, it had begun to conduct more and stronger investigations into the activities of the executive branch. All these reassertions of congressional power came at the expense of presidential power.

Jimmy Carter

Ford often criticized Carter during the latter's term. So did much of the press and many political figures. Experts disagree about how many of Carter's difficulties should be ascribed to his character and conduct and how many to the difficult times in which he had to govern.

As Carter left office, *Newsweek* columnist Meg Greenfield remarked that "public relations got Jimmy Carter—the tireless and doomed pursuit of an effective image, a winning voice, the right set of symbols, to project. . . . Carter worked at it like the devil, but he could never acquire that quality of authenticity in his communications with others from which Presidential authority flows." She went on to explain:

> Presidents can't make many things happen. They can make news and noise, but these merely create an illusion of achievement, and when they subside not much will have changed. Arguably, in fact, Jimmy Carter may ultimately have more impact on this country through the Federal judges he appointed than by anything else he did. But what little a President can do in the realm of foreign, economic, defense and social policy requires as a precondition that he speak with plausibility and authority to the country and to those it does business with.[52]

Ronald Reagan

Effective communication, most observers agreed, proved to be the greatest strength of Ronald Reagan as president. But conservative columnist George Will wrote:

> His strength is not that he is a great communicator. He is not. He is terrific at making people feel good about themselves and their country. That talent is necessary for any president—necessary, but not sufficient. A great communicator communicates ideas as well as moods, including complicated and sometimes distressing ideas."[53]

The fact that Reagan tended to create moods rather than communicate ideas and transmit ideology meant that his political success with Congress was ultimately limited. Furthermore, his own belief that government should play less of a role in the economy and do less regulating of business and industry led him to focus his use of the powers of office on his limited agenda of higher military spending, lower domestic spending, and tax cuts.

Thus, he was generally seen as using the inherent powers of the office effectively rather than as striving to increase those powers.[54] The sole exception to this was the wide range of foreign policy initiatives in Central America and the Middle East undertaken covertly but eventually revealed in the Iran-Contra affair.

So each of the presidents since Nixon has acted in ways that have made the presidency less imperial and less dangerous—and thereby limited its power. Hugh Heclo has concluded that over the last 20 years,

> presidential power has increased by becoming more extended, scattered, and shared; it has decreased by becoming less of a prerogative, less unilateral, and less closely held by the man himself. The right word for what has happened to the power of the office is diffusion, not dissipation. This condition exists, not basically because Congress or other groups have made successful grabs at the president's power, but because of the very nature of modern policymaking and the growth of federal activity.[55]

These trends and the experience of recent presidents, who have found it so difficult to cope effectively with economic and foreign policy challenges, have led many observers to argue that the presidency should be transformed. But the proposals they make vary widely.

POSSIBLE REFORMS

Strengthening Decision Systems

There is always a need to strengthen presidential information and decision-making systems. Many of the reorganizations we've described have been intended to do just that. One major concern is ensuring that a wide range of options and viewpoints is presented. Some people, therefore, propose what is called a multiple advocacy system. As Alexander George describes it, a neutral aide would take steps

[52]Meg Greenfield, "Carter and the PR Trap," *Newsweek*, January 26, 1981, p. 84.

[53]George Will, "Hollings One Reagan Should Watch," *Austin American-Statesman*, February 16, 1984.

[54]For an interesting analysis, see James W. Ceaser, "The Theory of Governance of the Reagan Administration," in Lester M. Salamon and Michael S. Lund, eds., *The Reagan Presidency and the Governing of America* (Washington, DC: Urban Institute, 1985), pp. 57–87.

[55]Heclo, "The Changing Presidential Office," in *Politics and the Oval Office*, ed. Arnold Meltsner, pp. 172–73.

The Oval Office. (Llewellyn/UNIPHOTO)

to see that whenever an issue comes up, those arguing for different positions get equal chances and resources to present their views.[56]

A Plural Presidency

Another proposal sometimes made is that we have a plural executive—a group of two or more people serving as president. Observers have often asserted that there is little necessary connection between the foreign policy tasks of the president and the domestic tasks, even though, as we noted at the beginning of the chapter, both are entwined in the role of president as it exists. Yet each of these twin

roles is large enough to be a full-time job. Therefore, some propose that we have two presidents, one for each set of responsibilities. Others, such as Senator Mark Hatfield (Republican of Oregon), have proposed splitting the domestic responsibilities into several elected offices—in effect, election of a cabinet. But such a move might just increase the political struggles within the executive branch, to the detriment of efficient administration. Furthermore, critics point out that increasing the number of major officers who must be selected and then elected would only increase the difficulty of electing good people.

Electing Better People

In general, most observers seem to think that America has gotten surprisingly good presidents, considering what candidates must go through to get elected. Experts note that many who would make excellent presidents simply cannot undergo the rigors of the selection process—from long campaigning (Jimmy Carter campaigned nonstop for 21 months, making the staggering sum of 1495 speeches) through hard political bargaining for convention delegates. This would not be a problem, except that the qualities that make one a good campaigner bear little resemblance to those that make one a good president.

In 1975 Senator Walter Mondale withdrew from the presidential race, saying:

> I do not have the overwhelming desire to be president which is essential for the kind of campaign that is required. . . . I like to ponder issues, sit down with knowledgeable people and talk about them, chew them over, read a book, let them rest a little, reach a conclusion that I'm comfortable with and go to work. All of that's out the window in a Presidential campaign, and I'd never get a chance to think ideas over. . . . Nationally, it's more theater than the politics I know. I kept getting constant suggestions that I needed to buy different clothes and go to speech instructors and spend two days in Hollywood with a videotape machine. I hated that.[57]

Some have suggested holding but one national primary or several staggered regional primaries to replace the present contests spread across the states

---

[56]See Alexander George, "The Case for Multiple Advocacy in Making Foreign Policy," *American Political Science Review* 66 (September 1972), 751–85. George develops this argument further in his subsequent book, *Presidential Decisionmaking in Foreign Policy: The Effective Use of Information and Advice* (Boulder, CO: Westview, 1980). See also Irving L. Janis, *Victims of Groupthink* (Boston: Houghton Mifflin, 1972), for a study of the problem in such policy cases as Vietnam.

[57]Quoted in the *New York Times*, December 1, 1974.

from New Hampshire to California and across the months from February through June. Others emphasize the importance of avoiding the selection of people such as Nixon who turn out to be unsuited to the job. Barber's study of presidential character was undertaken to help in this challenge. But even if there were agreement among observers as to the ideal character, there is no way to prevent the wrong type from gaining nomination and election.

Even greater concern is evidenced over vice-presidential selections, which are usually made on political rather than presidential grounds. Nixon's choice of Agnew put a corrupt politician next in the line of succession. McGovern's choice of Senator Thomas Eagleton (Democrat of Missouri) designated someone with a history of mental illness. Carter's choice of Mondale seemed based largely on the question of his suitability for the presidency. But it was exceptional—and was only possible because Carter already had the nomination sewed up when selection time came, which is infrequent. The same criterion may have operated in Reagan's choice of George Bush. But also considered was the contribution Bush could make to broadening the political base of the ticket. As a solution to the problem of vice-presidential selection, some suggest that such choices be made by the presidential nominees well after the convention, after possible candidates have been thoroughly investigated, rather than by the convention the day after the presidential candidate is nominated.

Disposing of the Mistakes

The fact that it took the certainty of impeachment and removal before Nixon consented to resign highlights the difficulty of correcting mistakes in the election of presidents. To increase the opportunity, some have suggested the possibility of a *recall* procedure. Some states and many cities require a popular vote on whether to remove an official from office if a certain percentage of voters sign a petition demanding it. But there are serious problems with this idea when applied to the presidency. Our system does not produce new candidates quickly. And, presidents who face a recall threat will be tempted to do things that placate the voters but may not be in the interest of the country. And there is no agreement on how many signatures should be required to start recall proceedings.

Toward a Parliamentary Government

These difficulties have led some in Congress to propose that there be a way for Congress to take a "vote of confidence" on the president, with provision that a two-thirds negative vote would remove the chief executive from office. A new election would then perhaps be held to pick a successor—and, some urge, to elect a new Congress, so that voters could in effect express their views on the action by the Congress.[58]

Such a move would approach the *parliamentary* system, where the head of government is elected by the legislature, in the same way that he or she is replaced. Some have seen merit in this more radical step, for it would tend to unite the president and Congress behind a common legislative program.[59]

One Six-Year Term

But many others believe that the problem now is that presidents already tend to be too sensitive to public opinion and too obsessed with reelection. They therefore propose that the president be elected to a six-year term (which would provide sufficient time to develop and implement a program) but only one (so that there will be no incentive to worry about reelection). Various public officials, such as Lyndon Johnson and former Senator Mike Mansfield, have advocated this plan. As Johnson remarked in his memoirs:

> The growing burdens of the office exact an enormous physical toll on the man himself and place incredible demands on his time. Under these circumstances the old belief that a President can carry out the responsibilities of the office and at the same time undergo the rigors of campaigning is, in my opinion, no longer valid.[60]

---

[58]See James L. Sundquist, "Needed: A Workable Check on the Presidency," *Brookings Bulletin* 10, no. 4 (Spring 1974).

[59]Remember in this connection our discussion of party government in Chapter 4. For discussion of this and other aspects of increased accountability, see Charles Hardin, *Presidential Power and Accountability* (Chicago: Univ. of Chicago Press, 1974). See also the article by Lloyd Cutler, who served as counsel to President Carter and then wrote "To Form a Government—On the Defects of Separation of Powers," *Foreign Affairs* 49 (Fall 1980), 126–43. Also see the panel transcript *President vs. Congress: Does the Separation of Powers Still Work?* (Washington, DC: American Enterprise Institute, 1981).

[60]Lyndon B. Johnson, *The Vantage Point* (New York: Holt, Rinehart & Winston, 1971), p. 344.

One six-year term might indeed ease the physical burden of the office. But there is widespread doubt that it would really reduce the role of politics in the White House. Furthermore, many believe that such an effect—making the president a "lame duck" from the moment of election—would be a big mistake. This case is made strongly by former presidential aid and long-time president watcher Thomas Cronin:

> The presidency must be a highly political office, and the president an expert practitioner of the art of politics. Quite simply, there is no other way for presidents to negotiate favorable coalitions within the country, Congress, and the executive branch and to gather the authority needed to translate ideas into accomplishments. A president who remains aloof from politics, campaigns, and partisan alliances does so at the risk of becoming the prisoner of events, special interests, or his own whims.[61]

Indeed, for these reasons others have advocated repealing the Twenty-second Amendment so that the president could use the prospect of running for a third term to gain more congressional support during the second term.

Looking to the Congress— Or the Bureaucracy

As this survey of proposed reforms reveals, there are no reforms with broad enough support to be instituted now. Indeed, there is very little agreement among observers of the presidency and its difficulties as to what reforms are desirable.[62] Some seek to make the presidency more powerful while others seek to make it more accountable. Some believe that any reforms should improve decision making within the bureaucracy while others believe reforms should increase cooperation with the Congress. We will better understand why some observers believe such changes are desirable once we examine how the bureaucracy and the Congress function. This will be our project in the next two chapters.

SUMMARY

The president has both internal and external ruling power. The Constitution gives the president the executive power, and that power has been developed over two centuries by strong presidents: Washington, Jefferson, Jackson, Lincoln, Theodore Roosevelt, Wilson, and Franklin Roosevelt. Today the president has 12 roles: commander in chief, chief administrator, chief of state, chief legislator, chief diplomat, party leader, representative of the people, mobilizer of the government, mobilizer of the people, world leader, manager of the economy, and social reformer. The president uses both statutory and inherent powers in exercising these roles. Also available are various resources—among them jobs, budgetary allocations, access, support, and information. Presidents must rely on persuasion, leadership, and coalition building to be successful in their relations with Congress and the public. Presidential personality may be an important factor in the success or failure of a president. Also important are the roles given the vice-president and the cabinet as well as organization of the president's staff. Presidents vary in these matters, and no single approach has proved most effective.

Many people found the presidency too powerful under Johnson and Nixon, especially because of extensive use of executive orders. Since then, Congress has set limits such as the War Powers Resolution, and subsequent presidents have been less dominant. As a result, many now belive the office is too weak; and they have proposed various reforms. Among these are strengthened decision systems, a plural presidency, electing better people, recall of bad rulers, parliamentary government, and one six-year term. But so far, no such reform has gathered much support.

[61]Thomas E. Cronin, *The State of the Presidency* (Boston: Little, Brown, 1975), p. 301.

[62]For discussions of various reforms, see James L. Sundquist, *Constitutional Reform and Effective Government* (Washington: Brookings, 1986); Cronin, *State of the Presidency*, chaps. 10, 11; Hardin, *Presidential Power and Accountability*; William W. Lammers, *Presidential Politics: Patterns and Prospects* (New York: Harper & Row, 1976), chap. 14; among many other works.

Among the most helpful general studies of the presidency, all available in paperback editions, are these: Clinton Rossiter, *The American Presidency*, rev. ed. (New York: Harcourt Brace Jovanovich, 1960), which is especially good on the roles of the president; Arthur Schlesinger, *The Imperial Presidency* (Boston: Houghton Mifflin, 1973), which puts the presidency into historical perspective and focuses on foreign affairs aspects; Thomas E. Cronin, *The State of the Presidency*, 2d ed. (Boston: Little, Brown, 1980), a contemporary study based on many interviews as well as the standard literature; and Richard M. Pious, *The American Presidency* (New York: Basic Books, 1979).

Several classic studies of the powers of the presidency still merit study. One is Edward S. Corwin, *The President: Office and Powers*, 4th ed. (New York: New York Univ. Press, 1957), which focuses on constitutional and legal aspects, and the other is Richard Neustadt's *Presidential Power*, rev. ed. (New York: Wiley, 1980, first published in 1960).

Three fascinating paperback studies of White House decision making in relation to the rest of the executive branch are Richard P. Nathan, *The Plot That Failed: Nixon and the Administrative Presidency* (New York: Wiley, 1975), by someone who was there; John Kessel, *The Domestic Presidency: Decision-Making in the White House* (North Scituate, MA: Duxbury, 1975), by a scholar who talked to those who were there; and Paul C. Light, *The President's Agenda: Domestic Policy Choice from Kennedy to Carter* (Baltimore: Johns Hopkins Univ. Press, 1983).

Among the interesting studies of particular presidencies are the following: Robert J. Donovan, *The Inside Story* (Garden City, NY: Doubleday, 1956), a study of the Eisenhower administration based on cabinet notes; Arthur Schlesinger, *A Thousand Days* (Boston: Houghton Mifflin, 1965), and Theodore Sorensen, *Kennedy* (New York: Harper & Row, 1965), both insider accounts of the Kennedy administration; Bruce Miroff, *Pragmatic Illusions: The Presidential Politics of John F. Kennedy* (New York: McKay, 1976); Rowland Evans and Robert Novak, *Lyndon B. Johnson: The Exercise of Power* (New York: New American Library, 1966); Doris Kearns, *Lyndon Johnson and the American Dream* (New York: Harper & Row, 1976); Merle Miller, *Lyndon: An Oral Biography* (New York: Putnam, 1980); William Safire, *Before the Fall: An Inside View of the Pre-Watergate White House* (Garden City, NY: Doubleday, 1975); John Dean, *Blind Ambition* (New York: Simon & Schuster, 1976); Robert T. Hartmann, *Palace Politics: An Inside Account of the Ford Years* (New York: McGraw-Hill, 1980); Joseph A. Califano, *Governing America* (New York: Simon & Schuster, 1981), by a Carter cabinet secretary; and Hamilton Jordan, *Crisis: The Last Year of the Carter Presidency* (New York: Putnam, 1982), by Carter's chief aide.

For an extensive annotated bibliography, see Robert U. Goehlert and Fenton S. Martin, *The Presidency: A Research Guide* (Santa Barbara, CA: ABC-Clio, 1985). Finally for regular coverage of the presidency, there are no substitutes for two weekly journals: *National Journal* and *Congressional Quarterly's Weekly Report*, available in many academic and reference libraries, and *Presidential Studies Quarterly*.

9

THE FEDERAL BUREAUCRACY

People are always complaining about bureaucrats and the rules they make. You may have done so, too—perhaps when you found you had to get a Social Security card before you could start work or a passport before you could travel abroad. Or when you had to file an income tax return or register for classes and pay your fees. Or perhaps you are or have been a bureaucrat, working for a large organization in the summer, or part time. If so, you may well have been on the receiving end of these complaints. Not all bureaucrats work for the government, of course—but some 16 million Americans do, for the federal, state and local governments. What do they do? How much do they matter? Those are the questions we shall address in this chapter. ■

THE CASE OF THE CHALLENGER AND THE BUREAUCRACY

At 11:38 A.M. on January 28, 1986, the Space Shuttle Challenger took off from its Cape Canaveral launch pad in Florida, carrying its crew of seven astronauts and its commercial and scientific payload. Seconds later, the craft blew up, scattering wreckage for hundreds of miles across the Atlantic. It was the first accident in 25 flights of the four space shuttles.

The disaster was first seen as a national tragedy, especially because it took the lives of two amateur astronauts, schoolteacher Christa McAuliffe and engineer Gregory Jarvis, along with those of the five professional astronauts. The National Aeronautics and Space Administration (NASA), which runs the federal government's space program, announced that it would investigate to find out what went wrong. So did Congress.

As investigations progressed, it became clear that the national tragedy was also a bureaucratic dis-

aster. Inspectors for NASA told a Congressional hearing that they had warned that the cold weather—24° F the night before and only 36° at launch time—had caused ice to form on the craft, and they thought it might break off and damage the booster rockets in flight. Indeed, the "ice team" at the launch site had told NASA's launch director "the only choice you've got today is not to go."

Independently, officials of Rockwell International, which built the shuttle itself, had expressed to NASA fears that ice shaken loose at liftoff might damage the craft. And the night before, engineers for Morton Thiokol, the company that built the booster rockets, argued vigorously that the cold weather could cause the O-rings (rubber gaskets that seal the joints between large pieces of the booster rocket) to fail, letting hot gasses enter the fuel tank and blow up the craft.

Why then did NASA decide to launch Challenger that morning? Fearing that NASA's own investigation might not probe deeply enough, President Reagan appointed a special commission, headed by William P. Rogers, secretary of state in

The Space Shuttle *Challenger* crew: (left to right, front row) Astronauts Michael J. Smith, Francis R. (Dick) Scobee, and Ronald E. McNair; (back row) Ellison S. Onizuka, Sharon Christa McAuliffe, Gregory Jarvis, and Judith A. Resnik. McAuliffe and Jarvis were payload specialists representing the Teacher in Space Project and Hughes Co., respectively. (NASA)

the Nixon administration, to investigate. It consisted of 13 members—mainly astronauts, officials of NASA contractors, and NASA consultants. It held hearings and reported its findings four months later.

The commission learned that Morton Thiokol engineers had been concerned about the O-rings for years because they had shown damage after most of the previous flights. And NASA engineers had been concerned about them two years before the first shuttle flight. Indeed, NASA engineers were scheduled to meet with two top NASA officials to discuss the problems in May 1984, but the meeting was cancelled when one of the officials left to become head of the Strategic Defense Initiative program and the other went out of town to discuss a new job. Although he returned to serve for three more months, he considered himself a "lame duck" and never rescheduled the meeting. Meanwhile, no flights had exploded, so NASA officials and Morton managers (not engineers) ceased to be concerned.

Any changes in the rings would have required redesigning the rocket, which would have cost both time and money. NASA was behind schedule in its launching of shuttles already. That schedule had been established for economic reasons—to make the four shuttles "pay their way" as commercial cargo carriers by putting commercial satellites into orbit for fees paid by communications companies such as RCA and AT&T. As part of his effort to cut federal spending, President Reagan had signed a special order—National Security Decision Directive No. 144—on August 15, 1984, ordering NASA to develop "a fully operational and cost effective" shuttle program by August 1, 1988. This would require NASA to launch a shuttle every two weeks year-round. But it was still taking close to two months to repair each shuttle for the next flight on its return from orbit. This meant that every delay in a particular launch set back the whole program and made it harder to meet budget targets. Thus, NASA had a strong incentive to go ahead with launches—as quickly as possible.

Still, when there was strong reason to think that launching might result in disaster, NASA postponed launches. Indeed, this flight of Challenger had already been delayed twice. The flight just before it had been delayed seven times. In fact, at virtually every launch engineers had had last-minute reservations. But this time, the senior Morton engineer present at the launch site refused to OK the launch. This had never happened before. So NASA officials at the Marshall Space Flight Center in Alabama talked to Morton managers in

(By MacNelly for the *Chicago Tribune*)

Utah by conference call, told them to "put on your management hats," and got them to overrule the company's engineers and agree to the launch.

No one told NASA officials in Washington or at mission control in Houston of this extraordinary override before the final "go" decision was made. But then, the head of NASA, James M. Beggs, had just resigned weeks earlier to fight in court charges he had cheated the government in billing on a defense contract when he had worked for General Dynamics. He had been replaced as acting NASA administrator by his deputy, William R. Grahame. Grahame, a weapons technologist, had only recently been appointed Beggs's deputy by President Reagan, even though Beggs had opposed him as being unqualified for the job of deputy. In any event, Grahame was absent in Washington when the final decision to launch was made, unlike all previous administrators, who had been at Kennedy or in Houston for launches.

NASA's office of space flight in Washington had to coordinate the activities of the Kennedy Space Center in Florida, where the launches took place, the Johnson Space Center in Houston, where the shuttle program is directed, and the Marshall Space Flight Center in Alabama, which is in charge of rockets for the shuttle. As *Fortune* magazine summarized the Challenger disaster,

Source: Paul Conrad, *Los Angeles Times,* Los Angeles Times Syndicate.

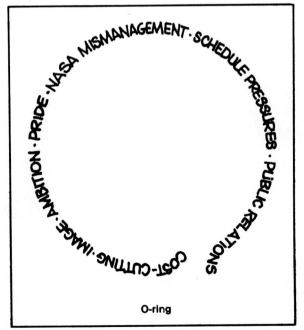

O-ring

It was the almost predictable result of a pattern of mismanagement that has spread throughout the agency since the glory days of the Apollo moon landings. The people at the top ended up isolated. . . .
The agency's leaders have been preoccupied with raising money for NASA from Congress. To win over the politicians, they have set goals for the shuttle program totally out of sync with the resources at their command. Organizational components that were supposed to work closely together—the Marshall, Kennedy, and Johnson space centers—have behaved like quasi-independent baronies, uncommunicative with one another and with the top. Watching the agency's fortunes decline, employees have tended to act like cowed bureaucrats. The result: an organization in which the flow of vital information up and down was as flawed as the now notorious O-rings.[1]

Developments such as these give bureaucracy a bad name. Presidents and other senior officials in government depend on the bureaucracy not only to take their orders and carry them out but also to make prudent decisions when running programs like the shuttle and to pass vital information up to them when something is dangerously wrong. Yet particular bureaus don't always act as the president hopes they will—or orders them to.

Presidents often express discontent with the bureaucracy on which they depend, and frequently presidents try to reform that bureaucracy. President Reagan came into office having pledged to abolish 2 of the 13 cabinet departments in the bureaucracy: Energy and Education. He found that pledge impossible to keep. He did, however, manage to control the growth of the bureaucracy temporarily by imposing a partial freeze on the hiring of replacements for bureaucrats who resigned or retired. But by 1985 the bureaucracy was bigger than it had been in 15 years. President Carter came into office having pledged to reduce the number of bureaucratic agencies from 2000 to 200. He found that reorganization an impossible task and, indeed, presided over creation of the two new de-

[1]Michael Brody, "NASA's Challenge: Ending Isolation at the Top," *Fortune,* May 12, 1986, pp. 26–32 at 26. See also David E. Sanger, "How See-No-Evil Doomed Challenger," *New York Times,* June 29, 1986; William J. Broad, "NASA Official Advised Against Liftoff," *New York Times,* Nov. 5, 1986; and David E. Sanger, "Top NASA Aides Knew of Shuttle Flaw in '84," *New York Times,* Dec. 21, 1986. The official report on the disaster is *Report to the President by the Presidential Commission on the Space Shuttle Challenger Accident,* 5 vols. (Washington, DC: GPO, 1986). For accounts of the political factors driving the U.S. space program, see Walter A. McDougall, *The Heavens and the Earth: A Political History of the Space Age* (New York: Basic Books, 1986); and Malcolm McConnell, *Challenger: A Major Malfunction* (Garden City, NY: Doubleday, 1987).

Members of the commission investigating the Challenger disaster inspect the external fuel tank and solid fuel boosters of the sister shuttle Atlantis. (UPI/Bettmann Newsphotos)

partments Reagan later sought to abolish. But Carter did manage to reorganize the civil service system in important ways, as we shall see in more detail shortly.

Every president wrestles with the bureaucracy, and every president reforms it to some degree—but every president also depends on the bureaucracy to carry out orders. Consequently, presidents cannot even attempt the kind of bureaucratic reform that they advocated when they were candidates. While it is still popular to campaign against "big government" and "bureaucratic red tape," it is no longer so easy to get away with broadside criticisms of bureaucrats because all of us depend on bureaucrats—and because more and more Americans are themselves bureaucrats. They key question for politics thus becomes: Who should control the federal bureaucracy? The president believes he should because it is part of the executive branch, and the president depends on it to provide information and carry out the chief executive's policies and programs. But Congress, too, thinks it should play a major role in controlling the bureaucracy. After all, it passes the laws the bureaucrats execute, and it modifies and approves the budget that funds both the bureaucracy and the programs. Increasingly, even the courts get involved. They are often asked to decide whether the rules and actions of bureaucrats are legal or even constitutional.[2]

So as we'll see in this chapter, concern about the bureaucracy is really concern about who should influence government and about what principles government should be operating on. These are questions for all of us.

THE BUREAUCRACY AND US

One of every six employed Americans works for the government—federal, state or local—and so might be classed as one of the 16 million governmental bureaucrats. If we include the 2 million people on active duty with the armed forces, 5 million Americans work for the federal government. Thus, 5 million of us are, in a sense, part of this "Washington bureaucracy" that is so often attacked as bloated, wasteful, and unresponsive to people's needs, even though relatively few actually work in the Washington area.[3]

---

[2]See David H. Rosenbloom, "Public Administrative Theory and the Separation of Powers," *Public Administration Review* 43 (May–June 1983), 219–26.

[3]Indeed, only about 200,000 federal bureaucrats work in Washington itself, with 362,000 in the Washington metropolitan area. Over 300,000 work in California, along with 150,000 each in New York State and Texas.

Joseph Wright, Deputy Director of the Office of Management and Budget under President Reagan, tells a press briefing that the elimination of "costly, redundant and superfluous publications" would save the government about $21 million in printing and distribution costs over the next two years. (UPI/ Bettmann Newsphotos)

Most of us encounter the bureaucracy on paper more than in person. We fill out a form to get a Social Security card when we start to work, and we fill out a set of forms to file an income tax return every year. We also fill out a form if we want to get a passport so that we can travel abroad. And we may occasionally write a letter to Washington to request a government publication. The superintendent of documents, the bureaucrat who runs the Government Printing Office, the largest publisher in America, currently offers over 60,000 publications for sale, with titles ranging from *The Department of Agriculture Yearbook* to a *Pocket Guide to Babysitting*. Sales total over 800 million copies a year.[4] The government also publishes hundreds of magazines, with titles such as *Postal Life*, *Plant Disease Reporter*, and *Driver* (this one, complete with pinups, is published by the air force, which calls it "the traffic-safety magazine for the military driver").[5]

---

[4]When the Reagan administration took office, it eliminated nearly 2000 publications as an economy measure and raised the prices of most of the others.

[5]Donald Lambro, "Henry Luce on the Potomac," *Washingtonian*, February 1977. One of the publications is *Consumers Guide to Federal Publications*; you may get a free copy by writing to the U.S. Government Printing Office, Washington, DC 20402, or the Consumer Information Center, Pueblo, CO 81009.

The federal bureaucrat we are most likely to encounter delivers our mail—one of 683,000 people the Postal Service employs. Only the Defense Department, which accounts for over 3 million, or 65 percent of federal bureaucrats—two-thirds of them soldiers and one-third civilians—employs more people.

But whether or not we personally encounter any federal bureaucrats, our lives are affected many times every day by regulations made and enforced by bureaucrats.

Bureaucrats play a big role in our breakfast. Any meat we eat will almost certainly have been inspected—whether carefully or not—by federal agents. The price of milk is influenced by federal "price supports" designed to increase the income of dairy farmers at the expense of the rest of us. The price of the grain that goes into our bread and cereal is influenced by decisions of the Agriculture Department, which makes America's "farm policy," and by the Commerce and State departments, which determine how much grain can be sold abroad—something that lowers supply at home and so raises prices for us. And all the fine print concerning vitamins and minerals on the cereal box, like that on cans of fruit and vegetables, results from regulations made by the Federal Trade Commission and the Food and Drug Administration. This list could go on and on—as long as our appetites hold out.

Then as we set off for school, the bureaucrats are involved again. Federal regulations determine safety standards for buses, just as they require seatbelts in cars. In school, just who our teachers are and what equipment they have to teach with may be influenced by federal regulations prohibiting discrimination in hiring designed to increase the number of minority employees, and by federal grants-in-aid to colleges and universities for certain specified purchases. What we learn and what teachers teach are still unregulated by Washington. But if we eventually decide we want to work for the government ourselves, we may have to pass a civil service exam or the foreign service exam developed and administered by the government.

Furthermore, every time we turn on a radio or television, we are getting a message over airwaves that are formally regulated by the Federal Communications Commission. The advertisements that finance commercial TV and radio are sometimes screened by the Federal Trade Commission in an attempt to protect us from lies and misleading statements. But if we tune in "public television," what we see may be subject ultimately to approval by—and may also be funded by—the Corporation for Public Broadcasting, which is federally chartered and receives appropriations from Congress as well as private gifts.

And so it goes from breakfast through school, at work and at play, from shopping through travel, and even in sleep,for mattresses and pillows are regulated (as is revealed by those little tags that list the contents and say "not to be removed"), and children's pajamas must meet federal standards of resistance to fire. Some of these federal regulations reassure us, such as the stamp on meat saying "Inspected by U.S. Dept. of Agriculture." Others may annoy us, such as the requirement that warning buzzers must sound in autos to warn us to fasten our seatbelts. Most of them may pass unnoticed most of the time.

But federal regulation never passes unnoticed by business, which must spend considerable time, effort, and money abiding by regulations and reporting to Washington. That fact is reflected not only in great safety precautions in our jobs and surrounding our foods but also in higher consumer prices to cover the costs of the safety measures and of filling out the reports.

As we shall see in Chapter 15, most business officials and many citizens believe there is too much bureaucratic regulation. But few would wish to return to the days when we might well have gotten food poisoning when we ate, gone without com-

pensation when we were disabled at work, been victimized by false advertising without any recourse, and had no one to complain to when we felt cheated or ill-treated by business or by government.

All these things—the beneficial, the precautionary, the annoying, and the wasteful—are the result of the growth of the government's role in our everyday lives. All these things are done by bureaucrats—whether they are done for us or to us. Many Americans now say they find government—and especially big government in Washington—unresponsive to their needs. But before we can decide whether government really is too big or too unresponsive, we must understand how big it actually is. We must learn who the bureaucrats are, where they work, what they do, and how it got that way. Then we should be able to understand both the public attitudes toward government and the bureaucrats' actions toward the public. Perhaps then we may also be able to find ways in which "Washington" can be made more efficient and more responsive.

WHAT THE BUREAUCRACY IS

Today the term *bureaucracy* usually has a negative connotation. Nobody campaigns for office on a platform calling for a bigger bureaucracy, although candidates do make promises that would in fact require more employees. Hardly anybody working for the government likes to be called a bureaucrat. Government employees prefer to be called civil servants—people who serve the public. But the term *bureaucracy*, which came from the French word meaning first "a writing desk" and later "an office," once meant simply the group of government officials.

The Nature of Bureaucracy

An organization may be termed a bureaucracy if it includes three important features of larger organizations. First, there is *specialization* among officials. Second, the offices or positions in the organization are arranged in a *hierarchy*, so that there are superiors and subordinates, and the superiors give orders to the subordinates. And third, the basis for this giving of orders, or for this authority, is *the law* rather than the personal qualities of the superiors and the subordinates or the dictatorial assertions of the chief of government.

In other societies, the authority to give orders may come from the leader's superior strength in battle, from his or her personal charisma, from a popular belief that he or she has been chosen by God, or as in ours, from having been elected by the people. But bureaucrats are not necessarily stronger than those under them, nor are they elected by those they govern. Instead, they are appointed, generally after being assessed for their competence in a competitive exam or screening procedure. Therefore, they are supposed to be experts who could be replaced by other experts who have the same skills, regardless of their other personal qualities. These experts are supposed to obey and enforce the law rather than the dictates of a charismatic leader or the expressed wishes of the public.

Democracy and Bureaucracy

Already we can see the roots of popular discontent with bureaucrats. Bureaucrats are not chosen by the people, nor are they supposed simply to do the will of the people—not, at least, until that will is translated into law.

Thus, bureaucracy is by its nature *nondemocratic*; and in our democratic society, it tends to be *antidemocratic* as well, for two important reasons. First, it replaces the traditional arrangement in which the people volunteer their time to decide what should be done and then do it. This system of pure democracy is still practiced in some small organizations, but it is impossible where matters are so complex that they require experts who *specialize* in one aspect or another. In other words, in a modern bureaucracy, specialist professionals replace amateurs, and democracy is thereby curtailed.[6]

Second, bureaucracy tends to be antidemocratic because the more efficient it is technically, the more it concentrates expertise, or specialized knowledge, in the middle-level administrators. This makes the people being administered less and less able to in-

fluence decisions. They often cannot even understand the problems, let alone the possible solutions proposed by the experts on such matters as new forms of energy, auto-safety regulations, or pesticide controls.

There is, in sum, a basic "tension between the needs of democratic government and the dominant tendencies of bureaucratic government," in the words of Samuel Krislov and David H. Rosenbloom.[7]

The chief advantage of bureaucracy is its tendency to standardize everything. Even *the bureaucrats themselves are in a sense standardized*. Those who work at the upper level, as professional administrators, receive generalized training so that they are interchangeable. Because their authority derives from their role, that is, from their responsibilities rather than from their personalities, they can always be replaced by others with similar training. Their replacements, in theory, should do the job just as well—and even the same way.

Similarly, bureaucrats are supposed to treat every individual they deal with alike, regardless of personality, race, or political views, for example. In other words, *bureaucrats standardize their clients*. We can see how this will tend to alienate citizens, each of whom is likely to believe that his or her own case is special and requires—and merits—exceptional treatment. Nevertheless, it was this quality of standardized treatment of all citizens that made creation of our modern bureaucracy, the civil service, so attractive to reformers who sought to abolish discrimination and preferential treatment in our government.

HOW THE BUREAUCRACY DEVELOPED

The early leaders of our nation were men of aristocratic origin. They were "born to rule" and "bred to rule" as well, and they took their dominant role in America for granted. What made them qualified rulers was their "fitness of character"—their virtue and public reputation—rather than passing

---

[6]For an argument that bureaucracy is nonetheless associated with democracy and extended freedom of choice, see Anthony Downs, *Inside Bureaucracy* (Boston: Little, Brown, 1967).

[7]Samuel Krislov and David H. Rosenbloom, *Representative Bureaucracy and the American Political System* (New York: Praeger, 1981), p. 14. See also Michael Nelson, "A Short, Ironic History of American National Bureaucracy," *Journal of Politics* 44 (1982), 747–78. For an argument that individual responsibility can reconcile bureaucracy and democracy, see John P. Burke, *Bureaucratic Responsibility* (Baltimore: Johns Hopkins Univ. Press, 1986).

TABLE 9.1

The Conflicting Requirements of Democracy and Bureaucracy

DEMOCRACY REQUIRES	BUT	BUREAUCRACY REQUIRES
Equality		Hierarchy
Rotation in office		Seniority
Freedom		Command
Pluralism		Unity
Citizen participation		Participation based on expertise
Openness		Secrecy
Community		Impersonality
Legitimacy based on elections		Legitimacy based on expertise

Source: Reprinted from Samuel Krislov and David H. Rosenbloom, *Representative Bureaucracy and the American Political System* (New York: Praeger, 1981), p. 15

marks in a competitive exam, as is now generally required. These aristocrats readily became professional public servants and generally continued to serve in office regardless of who was president. But over the years, there grew a new public sentiment favoring broader participation in government.

Andrew Jackson and the "Spoils System"

Finally, in the 1828 election, Andrew Jackson—a popular general and self-proclaimed "man of the people"—was elected president.

Historians credit President Jackson with the first major change in the government bureaucracy: firing many of the holdovers from previous administrations and replacing them with men loyal to him. This action was attacked by his adversaries but endorsed by his supporters, who cited the old maxim, "to the victor belong the spoils." Thus was born the **spoils system**, in which a winner rewards political workers with jobs. This practice is now more often referred to as patronage because it is provided by the boss, or patron, to loyal workers.

The spoils system was not, strictly speaking, a Jacksonian invention, for President Thomas Jefferson had practiced the same patronage on a more limited scale. The objective in both instances was less a matter of rewarding supporters than a way of guaranteeing that officials would be loyal to their superiors and would carry out their wishes.

But Jackson, like most of his successors, found that changing the personnel alone, via the spoils system, was not enough to get the government to act as he wished. Accordingly, he began the first major effort to reorganize the structure of the government into permanent offices to be filled by ro-

tating employees, so that officials would be more responsive to his will. In the first 40 years of the government, the organization of the bureaucracy had remained virtually unchanged. In Jackson's 8 years, almost every bureau or department was restructured, some a number of times.

Such reorganizations had become possible only because the functions or roles of offices were gradually becoming "separated" from the personal qualities of the individuals who performed them. This separation, developed and implemented by the president usually criticized for originating the spoils system, was the necessary first step toward creation of a modern bureaucracy. It made the impersonal, formal, standardized specification of a job's responsibilities possible, so that the job or office would continue regardless of who occupied it and so that any generally competent individual could perform it.

Modernizing a bureaucracy means writing down job specifications, telling just what the individual officeholder must do and can do and what resources he or she has to work with. Specifications also indicate which other job is superior to that particular job (the person to whom the worker therefore reports and from whom orders are received) and which jobs belong to subordinates (the persons who report to that worker and take that individual's orders). Once this formal description has been achieved, it becomes possible to draw clearer diagrams of the chain of command in an organization. Such diagrams, like that in Figure P1.2 in Perspective 1, represent such relationships graphically without needing to mention the actual individuals who may be serving in the various jobs or their personal relationships as friends or confidants.

Buildings, Bodies, and Budgets

In Jackson's time, the executive branch was located entirely in four drab buildings located at the four corners of the lot on which the White House stood. Today the executive branch is located in 470,400 buildings scattered not only all over Washington but all over the nation and around the world as well. Indeed, the government now owns 2.6 billion square feet of office space (which cost $40 billion to build) and rents another 206 million square feet (for rental fees of $700 million a year). These are staggering figures. But perhaps we can begin to grasp their scale and significance if we compare them to figures for a big office building.

The biggest office building in the world today is the Sears Tower in downtown Chicago. It is 1454 feet tall (about the length of five football fields), has 110 stories, and contains 4.5 million square feet of office space. The U.S. government owns the

The Sears Tower. (George Kufrin, Click/Chicago)

TABLE 9.2
The Growth of the Federal Bureaucracy

YEAR	NUMBER OF EMPLOYEES
1816	4,837
1851	26,274
1871	51,020
1901	239,476
1921	561,142
1931	609,746
1941	1,437,682
1945	3,816,310
1946	2,696,529
1951	2,482,666
1961	2,435,804
1966	2,759,019
1971	2,860,000
1976	2,842,000
1981	2,865,000
1982	2,848,000
1983	2,875,000
1984	2,942,000
1985	3,021,000

Source: 1790–1970, *Historical Statistics, Colonial Times to 1970* (Washington, DC: Census Bureau, 1976); 1971 on, *Statistical Abstract of the United States* (Washington, DC: Census Bureau, 1986), p. 294, and Census Bureau.

equivalent of 564 of these buildings in office space and rents the equivalent of 49 more, for a total of 613 superskyscrapers.

But if the physical size of the government has changed so drastically in these 150 years, so has the number of people employed—from about 5000 when James Monroe was elected president in 1816 to the present 3 million. (See Table 9.2.) The figures in the table include all civilian federal employees, wherever they are located and whether full time or intermittent, except for employees of the Central Intelligence Agency. In a typical year, the federal government now hires about 600,000 new people, and a slightly smaller number quit, retire, or die. As a result, the bureaucracy has tended to grow at a slow but steady rate.

The Reagan administration did, however, have some partial success in cutting back the size of the bureaucracy in its first two years. Most of the cuts were achieved by not replacing people who retired or resigned, rather than by firing people. As Table 9.2 shows, the number of federal employees began to grow again in 1983.

Over time, the total of federal workers has tended to grow as the formal structure of the government has swelled to include more bureaus at lower levels and more cabinet-level departments at the top. Among the most important elements in this burgeoning of the bureaucracy have been the expansion of America's military forces and the development of the independent regulatory agencies, which we will examine later in this chapter.

One of the primary effects of all this growth has been the expansion of the federal budget—the total sum spent by the federal government. The total budget for the first three years of George Washington's administration was $4,269,000—an average of $1,423,000 per year. In the first year of Jackson's presidency, it was $15,203,000. By 1986 it was just under a trillion dollars. Current figures work out to about $1,800,000 *a minute*. Thus, the entire year's budget for Washington's time would finance less than a minute of the government's operation today, and that of Jackson's less than nine minutes.[8]

The federal government now spends a billion dollars every ten hours, more or less. How much is that? It is 53 tons of $20 bills—about the weight of 50 Volkswagen Beetles. Or, put another way, if you started to count a billion dollars in $1 bills at the rate of one bill per second, eight hours a day, it would take you 95 years.

Despite the enormous cost of keeping up the government's 470,400 buildings and of purchasing and maintaining military installations, weapons, and ammunition, much of the federal budget goes just to pay the salaries of government employees. The 3 million civilian bureaucrats now earn over $54 billion per year.

The Merit System

Efforts to control the size of this federal expenditure, and with it the size of the bureaucracy, are unlikely to make much headway, for most bureaucrats have what amounts to guaranteed jobs for life. For despite Jackson's institution of the spoils system, public unhappiness with the quality of government service, and indignation over the assassination of President James Garfield by a disgruntled office seeker in 1881 resulted in the passage of the Pendleton Act—the Civil Service Act of 1883—which began the movement to replace the

spoils system with a permanent career civil service. The bill established a bipartisan Civil Service Commission to supervise competitive exams to fill certain federal jobs—about 10 percent of them at that time.

Since then, the competitive **merit system** has been extended by various congressional acts, so that now at least 85 percent of the bureaucracy is part of the civil service. Furthermore, many of the remaining 450,000 jobs not considered part of the civil service are nonetheless competitive, because they fall under merit systems operated by such agencies as the Foreign Service (for diplomats) or the Federal Bureau of Investigation (for FBI agents). The result is that the number of patronage jobs a new president can fill now totals little more than 2000. This is a smaller number than existed at the time of Andrew Jackson, and of these, only a half to two-thirds have special importance in policy responsibility and salary. Furthermore, as we noted in Chapter 8, every administration feels compelled to hire various experts who do not have any real loyalty to it for many of these jobs. In the case of the Carter administration, many jobs went to former Carter opponents because Carter allowed his cabinet choices to do their own staffing, and most of those in the cabinet had other political ties.[9] Reagan was more careful, but this care took much time, effort, and money and resulted in his administration's getting off to a slow start in many areas. Indeed, many important jobs remained unfilled in Reagan's fourth year and were only filled once he won reelection.

The Growing Yearning for "Spoils"

Whatever happens in the "spoils" appointments at the top, the merit system, as it actually operates, continues to protect the jobs of the competent and the incompetent, the needed and the unneeded, alike. One critic, Charles Peters, recounts the incident of an Internal Revenue Service employee who was fired for repeatedly reporting for work dead drunk. His union got his dismissal overturned. How? By arguing that the IRS was negligent in not establishing programs to detect and treat alcoholism among IRS employees. "With that

---

[8]However, these figures are not adjusted for the impact of inflation; in fact, Washington's and Jackson's dollars bought much more then than ours do now. Still, even in current dollars there would be a very massive difference.

[9]See Robert G. Kaiser, "The 2,000 Carter Jobs: Who Got Them?" *Washington Post*, June 6, 1977.

The Difficulty of Firing a Federal Bureaucrat—
And How an Official Copes with It

From an interview with Frank C. Carlucci, former Deputy Secretary of Defense:

"Q. *What can be done about firing incompetent* [federal bureaucrats]?"

"A. That is a problem. There have been instances where I have tried to either fire people or move them out, and I have learned that the amount of effort you have to put forth to do it just isn't worth it. It can easily be a year-long process—very expensive in man-hours.

"In theory, you can fire a government worker, but you have to document the record so carefully and there are so many routes of appeal that it is terribly time-consuming. And then there are grievance mechanisms that can be used to frustrate the process."

Q. *So what does an executive do in that case?"*

"A. You tend to look for ways to bypass the employee, maybe a promotion to get him or her out of the way. This often happens. I think we have to redress the imbalance between the rights of the individual and the responsibilities of the manager. In my judgment, we've gone overboard in protecting the individual employee and frustrating the manager in accomplishing his mission. You should also be able to provide greater incentives and rewards for the more talented and more industrious employee."

Source: U.S. News & World Report, April 4, 1983, p. 65.

kind of thing the likely product of a series of hearings and appeals that could last for years," Peters concludes, "it is the rare administrator who will attempt to fire anyone."[10]

Firings are rare. Of the 3 million bureaucrats in the executive branch, somewhere between 12,000 and 30,000 are dismissed for all causes each year. Of these, fewer than 250 are fired for incompetence. The difficulty in firing incompetents is described by a former high official in the box on this page. It is one reason why many now oppose the merit system on administrative grounds. But there are other grounds as well. One aide to Lyndon Johnson explained his view to Thomas Cronin this way:

> You can't really be an administrator at the White House. You have to get top personnel to carry things out—and that is literally impossible to do with this venal Civil Service system. Frankly, I would abolish it and rather live with a spoils system. You need to be able to make far more appointees than you can now. Civil Service officials can play very tough politics with their senior friends in Congress, and they can resist the White House constantly.[11]

---

[10]Charles Peters, "A Kind Word for the Spoils System," *Washington Monthly*, September 1976.

[11]Quoted in Thomas Cronin, *The State of the Presidency*, 2d ed. (Boston: Little, Brown, 1980), p. 171.

Limiting "Spoils"

In recent years, the Supreme Court has further limited the use of the spoils system by elected officials. A 1976 decision, *Elrod* v. *Burns*, declared it unconstitutional for a new sheriff to fire all noncivil service employees of his office who did not belong to his political party. In his opinion in the case, Justice William J. Brennan, Jr., argued that "political beliefs and association constitute the core of those activities protected by the First Amendment."

Then in *Branti* v. *Finkel* (1980), the Court once again held that the First Amendment protects a public employee from being fired solely because of his or her political beliefs as manifest in party membership. The Court did say that "if an employee's private political beliefs would interfere with the discharge of his public duties, his First Amendment rights may be required to yield to the state's vital interest in maintaining governmental effectiveness and efficiency." But it specified that "the question is whether the hiring authority can demonstrate that party affiliation is an appropriate requirement for the effective performance of the public office involved." However, Ronald Reagan found this decision no obstacle when he replaced the approximately 2000 political appointees of the

Budget Director James McIntyre pointing out the steps it takes to fire one government employee. (Dennis Brack/Black Star)

previous administration. Thus, the impact of the case on presidential control has been less than was originally anticipated.

The Persisting Problem with "Spoils"

Still, a president seeking to maintain control over the top level of the bureaucracy—the officials the president does appoint—remains great. "It is inevitable when an individual has been in a Cabinet position or, for that matter, holds any position in government," President Nixon remarked as he completed his first term, "[that] after a certain length of time he becomes an advocate of the status quo; rather than running the bureaucracy, the bureaucracy runs him."[12] Thus, curtailing the extent of the merit system in favor of more spoils may not make much difference, unless appointees are moved about regularly from one agency to another.

But moving officials around can raise a different set of problems. It takes time for an official newly in place to learn the job well enough to be effective. As Frederic V. Malek, who served President Nixon by selecting top appointees for the executive branch, has noted: "A characteristic of the vast and unwieldy government structure is the short time

---

[12]Quoted in the *New York Times*, November 28, 1972.

available to achieve results because of rapid turnover at top levels and the inchworm pace of policy implementation at lower levels."[13]

The Carter Reforms and the Reagan Aftermath

There are, then, two major problems facing any administration: selecting the right personnel and organizing the government to operate effectively. Every president comes into office pledging to increase efficiency by reforming the bureaucracy. Few achieve much in this realm. Jimmy Carter, however, did achieve passage of the 1978 Civil Service Reform Act.

Personnel Reform

Critics of the federal bureaucracy had long argued that it was difficult to assemble teams of highly competent officials to implement new programs, because of limitations on salary and on transferring managers.

---

[13]Quoted in Michael Thoryn, "The Turnover Two-Step," *Nation's Business*, March 1980, p. 75. See also Malek's *Washington's Hidden Tragedy: The Failure to Make Government Work* (New York: Free Press, 1978).

To overcome these and other problems, Carter—along with the head of the Civil Service Commission, social scientist Alan K. Campbell—developed a package of reform proposals. After a major struggle in Congress, the reform bill was passed in 1978. Its major provisions were these:

- Creation of a Senior Executive Service (SES) of some 8500 top civil servants who would be eligible for large cash bonuses for good work but also liable to transfer among jobs or to demotion
- Provision that raises for middle-level bureaucrats, other than those for cost-of-living increases, must be based strictly on merit rather than being virtually automatic, as had been the case
- Legal recognition of the right of nonsupervisory government employees to join unions and bargain collectively
- Streamlining of the appeals process for bureaucrats who are fired, so that firing for incompetence can be more quickly sustained if it is justified
- Division of the Civil Service Commission into (1) an Office of Personnel Management (OPM) to manage the federal work force by setting pay scales and selection procedures and (2) a Merit Systems Protection Board (MSPB) to hear appeals of employees charging mistreatment
- Prohibition of reprisals against **whistle blowers**—employees who disclose evidence of gross mismanagement by the government

This reform package did allow the Reagan administration to transfer good managers to key jobs, in an effort to gain more control over the bureaucracy while implementing new policies—something previous presidents had found difficult. Many of the senior bureaucrats who were removed or transferred by Reagan have challenged the legality of the shifts, and others have gotten Congress to force their reinstatement. Over all, the impact of the reforms during the first five years of their existence has not been impressive. As Alan Campbell has concluded: "The line between political appointees and career officials remains an obstacle to responsiveness, effective management, and intelligent policy formulation."[14]

Structural Reform

It is one thing to reorganize personnel to make them more responsive. It is quite another to restructure the bureaucratic agencies to make them more efficient. Almost every president attempts this restructuring. Harry Truman (1945–1953) achieved important reforms centralizing authority in the hands of the people responsible for managing programs. He also presided over reorganization of the defense establishment (see Chapter 19) and the economic policy agencies (see Chapters 15 and 16). But as his term proceeded, he lost some of his earlier enthusiasm for reorganization. As one historian has explained:

> Truman had learned, as did later presidents, that reorganization proposals faced such strong opposition that expenditures of time, energy, and political resources ordinarily make them too costly to be undertaken on a large scale. The combined opposition from executive agencies, congressional committees, and pressure groups [was] almost impossible to overcome, especially in the case of plans that were most desirable to the executive.[15]

Eisenhower (1953–1961) learned much the same thing. So later did Nixon. Each proposed major restructuring that came to naught. Still, Carter undertook a similar project, designed to combine programs in similar policy areas located in various departments, independent agencies, and the White House Office into four major new departments. The proposal, as rational as could be and as likely to make government more efficient as any reforms that might be proposed, never received serious consideration. It was killed by the combined opposition of those bureaus that would lose functions, the special interests comfortable with the present system, and the congressional committees in charge of these agencies as they had been set up. This defeat for restructuring was just one instance of the strength of the "subgovernments" or "iron triangles" that we have encountered in many political struggles and will examine in more detail later in this chapter.

Carter was successful in creating two new departments—Energy and Education—as we saw in the last chapter. Indeed, a glance at Table 8.4, which shows when each cabinet department was established, will reveal that this kind of success is achieved from time to time. Such success tends to be possible when an area suddenly becomes very

---

[14]Alan K. Campbell, "The Bureaucrats and Politicians Need a Treaty," *Washington Post*, January 16, 1983, p. B8.

[15]William E. Pemberton, *Bureaucratic Politics: Executive Reorganization During the Truman Administration* (Columbia, MO: Univ. of Missouri Press, 1979), p. 176.

important and the government's means of dealing with it are fragmented and subordinated. That was the case with energy in 1977. It may also occur when an interest group becomes so strong that it can command enough support in Congress and with the president to get its program taken out of an existing department and set up independently. This was the case with education in 1980.

President Reagan soon found out why these two new departments had been set up. During his campaign, he had called for their abolition on the grounds that (1) they were unnecessary and (2) they meddled with things the government should stay out of as much as possible. When he took office, he found that most of the special interests concerned with these topics liked having separate departments. So did Congress. Thus, he was unable to abolish them. He did, however, succeed in weakening the Department of Energy by refusing to make many new appointments and by transferring important civil service employees to insignificant jobs.

When Reagan proposed a structural reorganization that would make administration more rational, he had the same problems as his predecessors. He called for the creation of a new department for international trade and industry. Its purpose would be to strengthen America's efforts to compete in international markets with the Japanese and others. The new department was to include most of the existing Commerce Department (except for the Census Bureau and the National Oceanic and Atmospheric Administration) plus the Office of the U.S. Trade Representative, located in the White House. It seemed a sensible reorganization in terms of efficiency and rationality. However, most of the special interests involved in trade preferred the existing structure because they knew how to operate effectively within it. The same thing was true of Congress. As a result, no new department was created.

Thus, major reorganizations are quite rare. Nonetheless, minor reorganizations go on all the time. Congress regularly extends the president's authority to reorganize the executive branch by means of executive orders. To prevent major change, it has attached a "legislative veto" providing that the plan goes into effect if neither house of Congress votes against the plan within 60 days. Under this authority, since the Reorganization Act was first passed in 1949, presidents have submitted 103 plans to Congress, 83 of which have been implemented.[16]

In 1983, however, the Supreme Court ruled the legislative veto unconstitutional, so Congress had to develop other ways of controlling minor reorganizations. (We will examine the question of legislative vetoes in the next chapter.)

Throughout all this turmoil of reorganization—proposed, if rarely implemented—life goes on for the federal bureaucrats. Let's see what that life is like.

THE BUREAUCRATS AND THEIR EXPERIENCE

Where They Are and What They Do

The 3 million federal bureaucrats work in some 83 major government bureaus, administering 1040 different domestic programs and various foreign programs as well. Their responsibilities range from running the government (which is done generally by the 13 executive departments that constitute the president's cabinet and by the 9 bureaus in the Executive Office of the President) to regulating business, industry, and other segments of the private sector (which is done primarily by 55 so-called independent agencies).[17]

But just where are all these government employees, these bureaucrats, located? In addition to the 2.1 million members of the armed services, the Pentagon employs almost a million civilians around the world. Another 220,000 work for the Veterans Administration and are located throughout the country. The Postal Service employs about 192,000 letter carriers among its 683,000-person work force. Smaller numbers are engaged in activities that have long been governmental responsibilities, such as building dams and highways and managing federal lands. Land management is a surprisingly large task because the federal government owns 776 million acres—one-third of all the land in the United States—including 98.5 percent of Alaska,

[16]See "Congress Clears Legislation Extending President's Power to Revamp Executive Branch," *Congressional Quarterly Weekly Report,* April 5, 1980, p. 935.

[17]See *The Government Manual* 1984 (Washington, DC: GPO, 1984); and *Organization of Federal Executive Departments and Agencies* (Washington, DC: U.S. Senate Committee on Governmental Affairs, 1984). The figures include 39,000 employees of the legislative branch and 16,000 of the judicial branch.

87 percent of Nevada, 66 percent of Utah, 64 percent of Idaho, and even 45 percent of California; in these areas the tasks include tending the forests, which requires 14,500 foresters.

Much of the growth in the federal bureaucracy has resulted from new demands on the government: to regulate and manage the economy (there are over 100,000 regulators in the federal government, overseeing everything from the environment to consumer goods); to foster scientific research and technological development (NASA employs 25,000, for example); and to maintain America's dominant role in world affairs. Indeed, the government employs 132,000 civilians overseas, working in some 3600 buildings in 136 foreign nations; in addition, 480,000 armed services personnel are stationed in 305 American military bases outside the United States.

The budget for all governmental activities totals almost one-quarter of the entire American output of goods and services. Bureaucrats write an average of 100 checks every second to pay the bills. These same bureaucrats supervise the filling out by American citizens and businesses of 4500 different federal forms. This produces enough paperwork—66 billion sheets—to fill the Washington

ACTION UNIT 9.1

How to Become a Bureaucrat: Getting a Government Job

There are two basic ways to get a job with the federal government. The first involves going to your nearest office of the U.S. Office of Personnel Management (OPM)—check the phone book under "U.S. Government"—and applying. At the office, you will talk with a specialist about the sorts of jobs you'd be best suited to and then fill out the appropriate application forms. You may also have to take a written test if the job you are seeking is typing, stenography, sales store clerk and checker, or cardpunch operator. Whether or not you take an exam, you will be rated by the OPM, and in about six weeks you will be notified whether it finds you qualified for the job you are seeking. If you are found qualified, you go on the "register" of qualified applicants. You then wait until your name is matched to an opening.

In the old days, this approach usually worked eventually. But now there are more than 75 applicants for every opening. More than one-and-a-quarter-million people every year take a government exam hoping to be hired; only about 10 percent are successful—so unless you're in an area of the country where for some special reason the demand is small, this approach is no longer likely to work.

The second approach is to become a "name request." Most hiring above the level of secretaries and clerks takes the form of name requests. The agency seeking someone sends in a specific name to the OPM along with the job description. It writes the job description in such a way that, most likely, the only person who can fit it is the one it names. If no one else comes up in the OPM computer's register, the job goes to the person whose name was sent in.

Apparently, the secret to getting a government job these days is to become a name request. There are two ways to do this. The first is to know someone already working in the agency you want to work in. He or she will be among the first to know about coming job openings and may be able to tailor the description to fit you and only you and then to propose you as the candidate.

The other way to become a name request is to get the help of your member of Congress. If you worked in his or her campaign or contributed money to it, visit the member and ask for help. The representative can pressure the agency you want to work in to make you a name request. If he or she does so, your application will be circulated in that agency with "must hire" written on it, and the odds are good that you'll soon be one of our 3 million federal bureaucrats.

The alternative is to try state or local government agencies, which are still expanding and so have more openings. Probably, the approaches there as well as the jobs and their rewards will be rather similar.

For more details see the OPM's *Federal Career Directory: A Guide for College Students* (available in libraries, or from the Superintendent of Documents, Government Printing Office, Washington, DC 20402). You can also get a free copy of the pamphlet *Working for the USA* from the Office of Personnel Management, Washington, DC 20415, or from one of the Federal Job Information Centers it operates in major cities.

Monument 11 times each year—or to make 48 trips to the moon if the sheets were laid end to end. More than 5000 "information specialists" also spend some $2.5 billion annually in what might be called propaganda activities: advertising, making films, putting out press releases, and so on.[18]

But such figures don't really tell us much about what working life is really like for most bureaucrats. In fact, it is usually not much different from life in a large business establishment—paperwork, telephoning (the 140 agencies in the Washington area alone have 240,000 telephones), and conferences. The only major difference is that, as we have noted, a governmental official is somewhat less likely to be fired.

What They Get

Relative job security is not the only attraction of government jobs. There are other important privileges—**perquisites** (or **perks** as they are called). Bureaucrats get 20 days of paid vacation every year after 3 years on the job and 26 days after 15 years as well as 13 days of sick leave every year. They also get 9 regular holidays a year. They have extensive health insurance, including a psychiatric care, on which the government pays half the premium. And they may have large life insurance policies, a third of the cost paid by the government. They may retire at age 55 with a pension of up to 56 percent of their highest salary if they worked for 30 years—with a cost-of-living increase that regularly adjusts for the effects of inflation. For this they contribute 7 percent of their salary.

In any event, perquisites, coupled with relative job security, have made civil service jobs very attractive, both for white-collar (professional and managerial positions or desk jobs—so called because traditionally such people wore white shirts and ties to the office) and blue-collar workers (the latter are those in labor occupations—so called after the blue work shirts traditionally worn in such jobs). Recent figures indicate that civilian government employees include 350,000 secretaries and

clerks, 192,000 letter carriers, 151,000 engineers, 88,000 scientists, 8000 doctors, 5000 telephone operators, 3000 photographers, 2300 veterinarians, and 461 chaplains. In addition, there are 54,000 manual laborers, 32,000 aircraft workers, 18,000 plumbers, and 11,000 painters and paperhangers.

Who They Are

What kinds of people actually have these government jobs? Because the jobs vary so much, the qualities of their holders vary, too. Table 9.3 describes the various categories of these civilian jobs. Surveys by the Census Bureau (the same agency that counts you and asks various questions about you and every other citizen every decade) reveal that "typical bureaucratic executives" come from a middle-class background, are now more than 40 years old, have a college degree, and have worked their way up from the bottom to near the top of their bureau over some 20 years or so. They are also likely to be male. And they are more likely to be white than black or of Spanish-speaking heritage.

Generally speaking, there is less discrimination against women and minorities within the government than outside it, but the many decades of past discrimination have not been overcome at the higher levels because promotion to them requires long service at lower levels. Thus, at the lower levels some 80 percent of all employees are women while at the top level only 3.4 percent are women. One recent study found that women are underrepresented in all jobs paying $18,000 or more. The same study showed blacks underrepresented in all jobs at $15,000 or above and Hispanic men underrepresented in all white-collar jobs.[19] Another study found that 20 percent of the white and Asian-American men in the federal government are supervisors versus 10 percent of black and Hispanic men and less than 7 percent of white women, 5 percent of black women, and 3 percent of Hispanic women.[20]

[18]See David L. Altheide and John M. Johnson, *Bureaucratic Propaganda* (Boston: Allyn & Bacon, 1980), and "The Great American Bureaucratic Propaganda Machine," *U.S. News & World Report*, August 27, 1979, pp. 43–47.

[19]See "Washington Problem: Bias in Own Ranks," *U.S. News & World Report*, May 14, 1979, pp. 74–75.

[20]Gregory B. Lewis, "Race, Sex, and Supervisory Authority in Federal White-Collar Employment," *Public Administration Review*, January–February 1986, pp. 25–29.

TABLE 9.3

Major Categories of Federal Civilian Employees

LEVEL	HOW THEY ARE APPOINTED	HOW THEY ARE RECRUITED	THEIR TYPICAL CHARACTERISTICS	THEIR MAJOR TASKS
Top management	Politically	From political and occasionally civil service ranks; loyalty to administration usually important	Short-term service; relatively unrestricted by red tape; much and varied experience, but not always in similar jobs	Developing and implementing president's program; long-range planning; protection of the agency
Middle management	By competition	Examinations testing administrative competence	Career ambitions; devotion to procedural rules; sometimes hostile to both politically appointed agency head and Congress	Oversee daily operations of the agency
Professional and technical staff	By competition	By examination or by selection from lists of licensed professionals	Devoted to professional work; often hostile to and ignorant of politics; oriented more toward professional peers than toward agency	Technical and professional tasks, such as those of the lawyer, engineer, and accountant
Clerical, manual, and routine worker staff	By competition	Examinations testing relevant skills or straight hiring	Low skill levels, low aspirations; see government work as a "a job"	Routine work, but tasks essential to getting agency's work done

Source: Adapted, expanded, and updated from Charles Adrian and Charles Press, *The American Political Process* (New York: McGraw-Hill, 1965), p. 528.

THE FUNCTIONS OF BUREAUCRATS

Assuring Continuity

The primary function of the bureaucracy is to assure continuity in government. Presidents come and go, and Congress changes somewhat from session to session, but the bureaucracy carries on. This leads some to refer to the bureaucracy as "the permanent government" in contrast to "the presidential government," which is always temporary. Of course, there is some change in bureaucratic personnel from year to year (about 600,000 new faces per year, as we noted earlier). But as we have seen, the essence of bureaucracy is the *office* or the *role* rather than personality, so that at least in theory, this turnover should not matter; anyone with the appropriate training can take another's place. The responsibilities are set out by law, and the authority of the individual derives from his or her role in the bureau rather than from personal qualities.

In practice, however, things do not go quite this smoothly. Inevitably, the performance of individuals will be influenced in various ways by the personal relations they have with their superiors and with their subordinates. Still, in general, the continuity provided by the persistence of bureaucratic roles in the government does make the government work.

This can be seen most clearly at four critical times. The first is during a sustained major crisis for the system, such as Watergate. The second is at the beginning of a new administration, when new political appointees are still learning the ropes—generally from the senior bureaucrats in the agency they are to run. The third is at the end of the term of lame duck or retiring presidents whose power is waning, perhaps along with their interest in governing, and whose chief assistants are often actively job hunting. The fourth is toward the end of the term of presidents seeking reelection, when except for demanding flashy new developments, such presidents and their chief assistants are too preoccupied with electoral politics to run things. But because, as we saw in Chapter 8, a president is *always* too preoccupied with various other roles to be a full-time chief executive, the bureaucracy's role is always vital.

Berry's World

"Think of it! Presidents come and go, but WE go on FOREVER!"

(© 1976 by NEA, Inc.)

Implementing Decisions

Providing continuity such as this in a political system is only part of the bureaucracy's responsibility. Another vital component is *execution* or *implementation of decisions* made by superiors. In our system, important policy decisions are supposed to be made by the political appointees at the top of the executive-branch hierarchy. These decisions may concern, for example, the type of federal aid to education to propose to Congress, or whether to seek a further strategic arms limitation agreement with the Soviet Union, or what position to take on the question of a constitutional amendment to outlaw abortion.

Yet if we trace actual policy decisions from the highest levels, where they emerge as written proposals, through the various stages by which they are converted into governmental actions, we discover that neither the president nor the secretary of health and human services nor the secretary of state actually carries out a policy decision—or even

turns it into legislative form for submission to Congress. Nor do they write the rules and regulations that actually tell people what to do. Nor do they usually publicize policy to foster popular support or even see that their subordinates do what they're told. All these various activities, which convert a policy decision into a program of action and then carry it out, are necessarily the responsibilities of the members of the bureaucracy. (We will see all this in greater detail in Perspective 5.)

Making Policy

Even though policy is supposed to be made by the presidential government of political appointees, the "permanent government" plays a major role in this area. This key role begins when a new administration arrives—inevitably disorganized and understaffed as well as inexperienced. At this point, the bureaucracy fills the gap.[21] Indeed, there are enormous limitations on the ability of a new administration to have a real impact on policy in terms of budget and personnel. The box titled "Welcome to Washington, Reagan Man," written by a long-time high-level bureaucrat, explains why this is true. It was written to counsel high-level bureaucrats appointed by the Reagan administration in 1981. The picture it paints of the complexity of trying to change policy and programs in a new administration is very revealing, and the problems will be much the same for any new arrival.

Providing Information

Despite all these problems, not only a new but also an established administration must depend primarily on the bureaucracy for *information* about problems and for proposals concerning programs. As we have seen over and over again, in politics information is power. Nowhere is this clearer or more important than in the bureaucracy. As we shall see next, bureaucrats have ways of using their information to convert proposals into policy—even policy that deviates from the wishes of the political appointees who are, in theory, their bosses, or from the wishes of Congress.

---

[21]See Hugh Heclo, *A Government of Strangers* (Washington, DC: Brookings Institution, 1977), pp. 10–13.

Welcome to Washington, Reagan Man

Congratulations on your nomination to head an important federal agency. Supposedly you are about to manage hundreds or thousands of employees and millions or billions of dollars.

After surviving the confirmation process and taking office, you will want to review your budget for fiscal 1981. Alas, it is fixed; you have practically no authority to reprogram funds. If you want any changes, even changes developed in conversation with President Reagan himself, you must get permission from one of the four agencies that are the central regulatory mechanisms of the federal government.

Central agency No. 1 is the Office of Management and Budget. OMB staffers—Washington pros call them micromanagers—often try to prove their mettle by nickel-and-diming your budget until it meets their notions of what it should look like. . . .

Now suppose that you propose changes in the 1981 budget, and that they emerge in recognizable form from OMB. You're home free? Hardly. The gauntlet of congressional committees and subcommittees remains to be run.

Each member of each committee and subcommittee serves a different constituency and therefore is sharpening a different ax—but most of the axes will be aimed at your programs. Moreover, each committee and subcommittee has its own staff, whose members mean to micromanage as much as OMB staffers. . . .

Your current agency budget is cast in concrete, so you turn to next year's budget to discover that you're too late again. Fiscal 1982 has already gone to Congress, which means that, come February, you're going to have to defend a budget prepared by your predecessor.

In order to amend the 1982 budget, you will again have to face the committees and subcommittees. . . .

After resolving budget issues, you turn to the future. What plans does your agency have, you wonder. For an answer, you search out the members of your agency's long-range-analysis division. When you figure out who they are . . . you realize that you'll be long gone before any planning efforts reach fruition.

Personnel, you think. Maybe there's a hope in personnel . . . but be careful. Choosing whom to get rid of will soak up time just when you should be focusing on policy direction. And senior civil servants, once on the outside, can make a lot of legal and political trouble for you.

Dealing with personnel will put you in contact with central regulatory agency No. 2, the Office of Personnel Management, which has formida-ble powers of resistance. So do your Equal Employment Opportunity director, your Affirmative Action officer, your Minority Affairs officer, and your Federal Women's Program action official. . . .

You'll also contend with central agency No. 3, the General Services Administration, which allocates office space, maintains buildings, and provides word-processing equipment. . . .

About the only thing the General Services Administration is not concerned with, it seems, is services. Many federal buildings are dirty. Furniture is often old and worn. Poor security is a constant worry. The executive time wasted in negotiations with GSA over such problems is incalculable.

Finally, you'll want to get ready to deal with central agency No. 4, the General Accounting Office. In all probability, a GAO auditor will be situated within your agency. So while congressional and OMB staffers are micromanaging your agency, a GAO employee, also responsible to Congress, will be independently reviewing the whole process. . . .

. . . Never forget that an adversary relationship will always exist between you and the Washington press. . . . The best measure of your success with the press will be no press. For every column inch of coverage you receive, your standing with the White House will go down. In the President's eyes, the press is his press. You are on his team, and team players need no press.

The White House staff presents the toughest challenge, and another adversary relationship. Dealing with it will test your survival instincts to the utmost. . . .

Naturally, White House staff members think you work for them. In your judgment, of course, you are working for the President. . . . The power of the White House staff increases each day. The President's men have greater access to information on broad issues and goals, while you are bogged down with bureaucratic trivia. And don't forget: they are keeping book on your mistakes.

In short, you are about to become a full-time budget examiner, personnel analyst, and EEO adjudicator. You are not really going to be a manager. Federal executives have long since been deprived of the time to think through problems, plan, give policy direction, and control their agencies. . . .

From William G. McDonald, "Welcome to Washington, Reagan Man," *Fortune*, December 15, 1980, pp. 100–104. McDonald was executive director of the Federal Energy Regulatory Commission when he wrote this.

THE POWER
OF THE BUREAUCRATS

The absolutely vital and unavoidable bureaucratic responsibility for implementation gives the bureaucracy its greatest political power—as every president ultimately learns.

Bureaucratic Power and the President

Harry Truman always kept a sign on his desk that read, "The buck stops here." This slogan implied that Truman, as president, couldn't delegate responsibility any further and couldn't refuse to make difficult decisions. It also implied that his decisions were the ultimate decisions—the ones that determined exactly what would be done. But Truman learned early in his presidency that this was not the case: He confronted a bureaucracy already grown to some two million people—a scale well beyond the capacity of a president to control effectively. At one point, he remarked to NBC correspondent David Brinkley: "I thought I was the president, but when it comes to these bureaucracies I can't make 'em do a damn thing."[22]

In 1952, as Truman contemplated turning the White House over to General Eisenhower, he mused to his White House assistant Richard Neustadt: "He'll sit here and he'll say, 'Do this! Do that!' *And nothing will happen.* Poor Ike—it won't be a bit like the Army. He'll find it very frustrating."[23]

Truman's hunch—derived from his own seven years' experience—was prophetic. After six years of Eisenhower's presidency, an aide to the former general remarked: "The President still feels that when he's decided something that ought to be the end of it . . . and when it bounces back undone or done wrong, he tends to react with shocked surprise."[24]

Not long after he took office, John Kennedy was asked what he considered to be the most important thing he had learned in his presidency. His reply: the difficulty of getting things done. Subsequently, he was quoted as remarking to someone who made

President Harry S Truman at his desk. (The Harry S Truman Library)

a policy suggestion to him: "Well, I agree with you, but I'm not sure the government will."[25] Even Lyndon Johnson, a consummate politician with many years of experience in Washington politics when he took office and operator of the biggest battery of telephones in White House history, had such grave difficulties getting satisfactory results from the bureaucracy as our involvement in Vietnam deepened that he became more and more withdrawn and isolated.

But perhaps the clearest and the most conclusive instance of a recalcitrant bureaucracy was the one that resisted Richard Nixon. Nixon took office in 1969 intending to lead the country in directions very different from those taken by his presidential predecessors. In foreign affairs, he sought to improve relations with the Russians while at the same time opening relations with their neighboring adversary, the People's Republic of China. Yet he and Secretary of State Henry Kissinger concluded that they could not trust the State Department bureaucracy to develop these sensitive projects—or even to know of Kissinger's first China visit in advance. Such secrecy characterized foreign affairs in the Nixon-Kissinger years.

Such protective secrecy is impossible in domestic affairs. Here Nixon also sought to turn governmental policy around on a wide range of matters, including the use of busing for school integration and the War on Poverty. He attempted to disman-

[22]Quoted by David Brinkley on the public television program "Thirty Minutes with . . . ," July 13, 1971.

[23]Quoted in Richard Neustadt, *Presidential Power*, 2d ed. (New York: Wiley, 1976), p. 77.

[24]Ibid.

[25]Quoted in Roger Hilsman, *The Politics of Policy Making in Defense and Foreign Policy* (New York: Harper & Row, 1971), p. 1.

tle the Office of Economic Opportunity (OEO—the bureaucracy created to conduct that war). But everywhere he turned, he met opposition—in the very bureaucracy he was attempting to transform as well as in Congress. Bureaucrats and senators even went to court in 1973 to block the abolition of OEO.

One day he announced that he was unalterably opposed to "forced busing." The next day his own Justice Department, headed by his longtime business colleague and political crony Attorney General John Mitchell, filed suit in Austin, Texas, to force busing for school integration. In several speeches in 1971, he announced what he called a new American Revolution—a proposed reorganization of much of the bureaucracy into four superagencies. But people barely noticed, and Congress greeted the proposal with total lack of interest, refusing even to hold hearings on it. Nixon set up the largest White House staff in history to act as a kind of "counterbureaucracy." But by the end of his first term, he was convinced that his counterbureaucracy, headed by Haldeman and Ehrlichman, had itself become too bureaucratic.[26]

Meanwhile, programs that he and his aides were developing were continually "leaked" to the press in ways that enabled the opposition to unite and vitiate them, often before they were fully developed. The frustration and bitter resentment that these experiences generated in Nixon and in his close aides led eventually to the establishment of the secret task force called "the plumbers" that was assigned to stop "leaks." But gradually the assignments of the "plumbers" expanded to include more and more of the "dirty tricks"—electronic bugging, illegal break-ins into private homes and offices, and so on—that figured so prominently in Watergate.

This drastic reaction to the frustration of his plans by the bureaucracy in alliance with his adversaries outside government led ultimately to Nixon's downfall. But although many have been inclined to attribute his reaction to his character, it is particularly important to recognize and understand its origins, which are more complex. Partly to blame was the incessant and debilitating bureaucratic resistance to the Nixon White House.

This raises an important question: Why was this resistance so great—so much stronger during the Nixon years than during those of his predecessors? To find the answer, we must go back to the years of the great bursts of hiring in the federal bureaucracy. Apart from the temporary increases during wartime, these large and permanent increases have come during the terms of Democratic presidents Franklin Roosevelt, John Kennedy, and Lyndon Johnson. Republican President Eisenhower sought to restrain, if not actually reverse, that expansion. The result of this pattern of expansion was that in Nixon's time, most of the senior civil servants—those who actually run most segments of the bureaucracy under the supervision of political appointees—were people who had joined the government in the years of FDR's New Deal. They were remnants of an era characterized by an activist government dedicated to social reform and government intervention in the economy on the side of labor and consumers. These officials were unlikely to be sympathetic to the Nixon effort to cut or even eliminate many of those social-reform programs—especially when their own responsibilities might thereby be curtailed. At the same time, most of the newer and younger bureaucrats had arrived during the Kennedy-Johnson years—again, years of an activist government dedicated to new program innovations.[27] They, too, tended to be unsympathetic to Nixon's efforts at retrenchment.

Thus, when Nixon took office, he confronted a gigantic and largely hostile bureaucracy that was led by people with considerable experience in bureaucratic politics. They were, in other words, experts at defending the interests of their own agencies, personnel, and programs not only against other bureaucrats but also against political superiors. They did so in order to get their own way on a matter of policy or to get control over a program that would mean more jobs or a bigger budget for the winning agency. The importance of such success is that it makes it possible for them to be responsive to the interest groups, clientele groups, and congressional committees with which they regularly deal and on which they depend for their budgets and for political support.

---

[26]Garnett D. Horner, "Nixon Looks Ahead: 'A New Feeling of Responsibility . . . Of Self-Discipline,'" *Washington Star-News*, September 9, 1972. See also Richard P. Nathan, *The Plot That Failed: Nixon and the Administrative Presidency* (New York: Wiley, 1975).

[27]See Joel D. Aberbach and Bert A. Rockman, "Clashing Beliefs within the Executive Branch," *American Political Science Review* 70 (June 1976), 456–68; and Allen H. Barton, "Consensus and Conflict among American Leaders," *Public Opinion Quarterly* 38 (Winter 1974–1975), 507–30.

It is, therefore, hardly surprising that the bureaucracy was able to defy presidential direction so vigorously—and with virtual impunity—when Richard Nixon and his White House staff tried to actually run the government like an efficient business rather than the political organization it is. When Gerald Ford, who was even more conservative than his predecessor, took office, he too faced the same bureaucratic resistance when he tried to cut back on staff and programs. So did Jimmy Carter. So did Ronald Reagan. The likelihood is that any president who is bent on bureaucratic reform will face the same strong recalcitrance; for the bureaucracy is now predominantly activist in disposition.

Thus, the president will generally be limited to using traditional tools: appointments and firings, orders, and a budgetary process that requires approval of new programs and oversight of continuing ones. But the chief executive's success is likely to be limited in part by the fact that the bureaucracy has become so politicized, while as we saw in the last chapter, politicians have become more bureaucratized.[28]

Bureaucratic maneuvering, like the bureaucratic infighting that occurs over a particular policy decision, may appear insignificant in comparison to the substance of the policy being proposed or implemented. But *bureaucratic politicking may be more important* in determining the nature and the success or failure of a program *than the president's decision or congressional legislation*. This is especially true of decisions and legislation on complex matters, which must inevitably leave the "fleshing out" of programs to the bureaucracy. If we are to understand how American politics really works, we must understand the nature and roots of bureaucratic power.

Power Struggles among Bureaucrats

This sort of struggle is made possible by the fact that most government programs do not fall squarely within the recognized realm of one single bureau. One revealing example of the resultant bureaucratic infighting that has become traditional is interservice rivalry among the army, the navy, and the air force. When a new type of weapons system is being developed, the various branches of the military often compete in its development and then compete for the responsibility of deploying it. For example, when missiles were first developed, the army claimed that it should have responsibility for them because they were based on land and were, in a sense, merely modified artillery pieces. The air force also claimed them because they would fly through the air when launched against a target. The air force eventually won that struggle with the army, but meanwhile the navy was developing its own missiles to be launched from submarines at sea: the Polaris program, which eventually became the major element of American defenses alongside the air force's land-based Minuteman.

Such competition among the armed services is often supported or rationalized on the grounds that competition encourages innovation and, therefore, improves the quality of military defense. But competition is also very expensive because it requires so much duplication. And when the Defense Department tried to cut down on costly duplication by encouraging more coordination and standardization to limit overlap and bureaucratic quarrels, that only caused further problems by encouraging the three services to unite and cooperate—against their superior, the secretary of defense.

Problems of competition and coordination can, of course, be found throughout government. In the years following riots in major American cities like Los Angeles, Detroit, and Washington, the federal government intensified its efforts to cope with problems of unemployment, poor housing, law enforcement, public schools, hunger, and so on, in the cities. But because these problems were scattered throughout the Department of Health, Education and Welfare (HEW), the Justice Department, the Labor Department, and other departments, they could not be well coordinated, nor could duplication be avoided. After his sweeping victory in 1964, President Johnson proposed to bring some of these programs together by centralizing them in a new Department of Housing and Urban Development (HUD), which was done when Congress passed the necessary legislation. Much the same thing happened two years later with the establishment of the Department of Transportation. Then in the Carter years, the same

[28]For an analysis of this phenomenon and its significance, see Joel D. Aberbach, Robert D. Putnam, and Bert A. Rockman, *Bureaucrats and Politicians in Western Democracies* (Cambridge, MA: Harvard Univ. Press, 1981).

sort of process produced the Department of Energy and later the Department of Education.

While such efforts at centralization of responsibility can increase coordination and control, they usually result in a bigger bureaucracy. Further, centralization never succeeds in avoiding the struggles at the lower levels between various agencies, each seeking more programs and a bigger share of the budget. This larger share is necessarily at the expense of others, since programs and funds are always more limited than desires. The unending competition for scarce resources is usually fought out finally in Congress.

Bureaucratic Power and Congress

From what we have seen thus far, it may appear that only the president has trouble with the bureaucracy. But Congress, too, is in constant interaction with it. After all, when Congress passes a law, it is the bureaucracy that must implement it. When Congress passes the budget, it is the bureaucracy that spends the money. Because it passes laws, passes the budget, and holds investigations into, and hearings on, the operations on the bureaucracy, Congress does exercise some control. In addition, members try to influence decisions on key presidential appointments. They also contact bureaucrats directly on matters of special concern to them. Further, they write great detail into some legislation to limit bureaucratic discretion. (We will explore these processes in greater detail in the next chapter.)

Congress continually tries to impose its political will—its image of reality—on the bureaucracy, just as the president does; but often this doesn't work very well. Take the case of the Airline Deregulation Act of 1978. This law gave airlines freedom to decide where they would fly and what prices they would charge for tickets. Until that time, the bureaucracy—the Civil Aeronautics Board and the Federal Aviation Administration—closely regulated the airlines. Deregulation meant new competition, and that in turn meant that some less efficient airlines would shrink or go broke. Therefore, Congress included in the act provisions to protect the jobs of laid-off airline pilots and workers and to grant them special unemployment benefits. The law gave the Labor Department six

months to draw up the necessary regulations to implement these provisions.

That was in October 1978. By 1984 several airlines had gone bankrupt, and most others had shrunk; over 5000 pilots had been laid off, and many more flight attendants had lost their jobs. The law had been intended to help them. But by 1984 the Labor Department hadn't yet written the regulations to implement the law. Why? First, the Carter administration was hesitant to do anything just before the 1980 election. Then, the big airlines opposed the provision forcing them to rehire laid-off pilots before they could hire new, cheaper pilots; and they told this to the executive branch. Finally, the Reagan administration came into office, opposed to new regulations in general and to provisions favoring labor in particular. Congress, reflecting the views of labor, protested the Labor Department's inaction. But still nothing happened. When the Labor Department finally drafted proposed regulations, the Office of Management and Budget vetoed them on the grounds that the program would be too expensive. The conclusion of the person in charge of drafting the regulations was, "Important things have to have approval at so many levels. You've got to satisfy a lot of people. Everyone has to be heard. The way things work in government is, generally, slowly."[29]

Congress found the bureaucracy unresponsive—but bureaucrats found themselves getting contradictory advice from interest groups and changing orders from two administrations, in addition to legal instructions from Congress. The result was that nothing happened, and most people blamed the bureaucracy.

Such conflicts are common. They occur most often over budgetary matters. The budgetary process is a major focus of bureaucratic politicking, as we saw in Perspective 3. In theory, a bureau submits its budget request each year through its department to the central budget bureau in the executive branch (now called the Office of Management and Budget). The OMB modifies it so that it complies with the priorities of the president and the overall size of the budget the president wants to submit to Congress. But the Con-

---

[29]See Michael Wines, "Regulation Writing in Washington—Making Days Stretch into Years," *National Journal*, November 13, 1982, pp. 1937–40.

gress need not follow the wishes of the president. As a result, bureaus that have long maintained close ties with the congressional committees having jurisdiction over their activities sometimes find themselves getting more money from Congress than the president has requested.

Another strategy that may be used by a bureau to increase its budget is to appeal to the special interests its activities benefit. These interests, or "clientele groups," then lobby the Congress to increase the appropriation for the bureau. For example, the agency of HUD responsible for government-guaranteed home mortgages may encourage real estate groups and home builders to ask Congress to increase the funds made available for the program.

The "Subgovernments"

Over the years, strategic moves such as those discussed above often become routinized. Career bureau chiefs, the lobbyists for concerned special-interest groups, and the members of Congress presiding over the concerned committees or subcommittees in some cases meet regularly to decide important questions about programs and budgets—often without even consulting the president or presidential assistants. These common arrangements are often called **subgovernments** because they are able effectively to decide major questions of policy.[30] Another term for them that reflects their strength is **iron triangles**. They provide opportunities for bureaus that are unable to get satisfaction through infighting within the executive branch to achieve their objectives in another way. Subgovernments are facilitated by the fact that certain congressional chairpersons, senior bureaucrats, and lobbyists tend to hold office for long periods of time—much longer than presidents. Therefore, they are able to establish and maintain such cooperative relationships comfortably. The subgovernment phenomenon was first found in

such policy areas as agriculture, water, and public works, where the major active figures have tended to outlast both presidents and specific issues. The box on subgovernments describes the operation of the phenomenon as it has characterized these types of policy making. But not all policy making is of this type. Indeed, subgovernments may actually be less important now than they were a decade ago. The reason for this change has been the rise of what one expert calls issue networks.

Issue Networks

Government is becoming more and more specialized as the issues it must deal with become more complex and change more rapidly. In the past, "agriculture" was thought of primarily as "the farm problem." It was a problem of guaranteeing stable incomes to farmers facing uncertain weather and changing interest rates on the money they had to borrow between planting time and the harvest. Coping with this problem was the continuing responsibility of farm lobbyists, the Agriculture Department, and the congressional agriculture committees and their subcommittees. Standard policies developed and were maintained. Today the problem of agriculture is much greater. It involves using food as a lever against foreign countries, as in the grain embargo placed on the Soviet Union after it invaded Afghanistan. It also involves coping with the use of oil as a weapon against the United States by other foreign countries because oil powers farm machinery and is used in making fertilizer and pesticides. What was once simply called farm policy now involves not only foreign policy but also the multibillion-dollar food stamp welfare program and many other human-service programs. These and other aspects of "the farm problem" require more and more expert opinion. In the past, it was agricultural experts who were most involved. Now it is also energy experts, foreign policy experts, social-service experts, and many others. Further, welfare policy, health policy, and energy policy, among other concerns, involve "webs of influence" exercised by many different experts or specialists, in and out of government. Hugh Heclo, who has studied this shift closely, calls these new systems *issue networks*. He describes the differences between these groups and subgovernments this way:

[30]See Douglass Cater, *Power in Washington* (New York: Random House, 1964), and J. Leiper Freeman, *The Political Process* (New York: Random House, 1965). See also, for a more detailed study, Randall Ripley and Grace Franklin, *Congress, the Bureaucracy, and Public Policy*, rev. ed. (Homewood, IL: Dorsey, 1980). And for a survey of research, see Keith E. Hamm, "Patterns of Influence Among Committees, Agencies, and Interest Groups," *Legislative Studies Quarterly* 8 (1983), 379–425.

Subgovernments and the Triple Alliance

Career officials have their own policies to promote. These may place them in conflict with the administration and its political executives. . . . [These officials] are likely to be incrementalists, interested in preserving agency routines and standard operating procedures, and working within the repertoire of programs and technique they have developed over the years. They seek to preserve the mission of their agency, to serve its constituencies, and to maintain control and jurisdiction over its policy domain.

Congressional committee leaders similarly have spent many years working up the seniority ladder. Like the careerists, they view themselves as experts. . . . Both careerists and legislators regard government service as their career; by contrast, many political executives, from business, law, and academia, regard service as temporary. Both lawmakers and careerists have similar educational and social backgrounds: both think similarly about public issues and use similar methods of analysis and conceptualization. No significant differences in liberalism and conservatism are apparent between the two groups. Both work closely with lobbyists representing interest groups that benefit from programs. A resultant "triple alliance" of careerists, legislators, and lobbyists engages in transactions that directly affect the way programs are run:

1. Bureau-interest group: Interest groups want to write guidelines for programs, gain formal access to officials by instituting advisory committees, and win formal or informal vetoes over agency decisions. They expect to staff some noncareer positions at the top levels of the bureaus. Careerists expect interest groups that benefit from their programs to testify favorably at congressional committee hearings and to lobby at the department level for additional funds for the program.

2. Bureau-committee: Careerists want statutory language giving them maximum authority and discretion, expanding their jurisdiction, and funding more missions. They want better facilities, more personnel, and "grade-creep" (promotions for career personnel and more positions allocated to high civil service categories). Committee members want special treatment for their constituencies and for interest groups. They want to influence the distribution of goods, services, patronage, and contracts.

3. Committee-group: Committee members want campaign contributions, help in their election campaigns, and honoraria for speeches. They rely on expertise of lobbyists in writing laws. Interest groups expect members of committees to provide them with formal and informal access to the bureaus and funds for programs that benefit them. They expect committee members to help them win the nomination of group members by the president to the department level.

The president must confront this triple alliance (sometimes referred to as the "permanent government" or "subgovernment") when he attempts to institute a chain of command from the departmental to the bureau level.

From *The American Presidency* by Richard Pious. © 1979 by Richard M. Pious. Published by Basic Books, Inc., New York. Reprinted by permission.

The notion of iron triangles and subgovernments presumes small circles of participants who have succeeded in becoming largely autonomous. Issue networks, on the other hand, comprise a large number of participants with quite variable degrees of mutual commitment or of dependence on others in their environment; in fact it is almost impossible to say where a network leaves off and its environment begins. Iron triangles and subgovernments suggest a stable set of participants coalesced to control fairly narrow public programs which are in the direct economic interest of each party to the alliance. Issue networks are almost the reverse image in each respect. Participants move in and out of the networks constantly. Rather than groups united in dominance over a program, no one, as far as one can tell, is in control of the policies and issues. Any direct material interest is often secondary to intellectual or emotional commitment.[31]

The Sources of Bureaucratic Power

Modern bureaucracy has been developed to make administration in a complex society more efficient, just as the assembly line was developed to make

---

[31]Hugh Heclo, "Issue Networks and the Executive Establishment," in *The New American Political System*, ed. Anthony King (Washington, DC: American Enterprise Institute, 1978), p. 102.

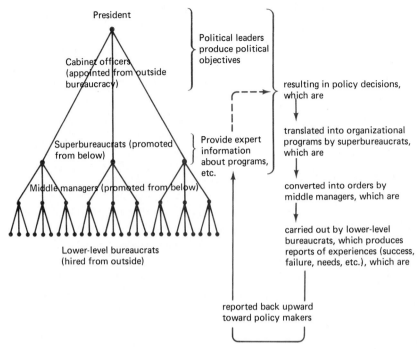

FIGURE 9.1
The Stages of Bureaucratic Activity.

production of automobiles more efficient. On an assembly line, each worker puts one part on the auto as it moves down the line. If just one worker should fail or refuse to do so, the car is incomplete and may not even run at all. The same thing holds true for a bureaucracy. If one bureaucrat withholds specialized expert knowledge or provides the wrong "knowledge," the policy developed may prove unworkable or even dangerous. Similarly, if a bureaucrat fails to pass on orders to his or her subordinate, some part of the required action will not occur, and as a result, the entire program may break down or fail.

In a sense, then, we can think of a bureaucracy as an assembly line of information. Specialized expert information about a situation (which is generally called expertise) goes up to decision makers, and fragmented information about a decision (orders) goes back down to the bureaucratic organizations and people who carry out the decision.[32]

[32]Karl Deutsch, *The Nerves of Government* (New York: Free Press, 1963), p. 75.

This way of viewing a bureaucracy makes it easier to understand how powerful bureaucrats can be. If they fulfill their responsibilities completely, both up and down the assembly line of information, then policies have a chance of working. But if they are either inefficient or uncooperative, they can delay, torpedo, or distort the decision being made or its eventual implementation. Figure 9.1 illustrates compactly and somewhat abstractly the stages of bureaucratic activity, indicating where problems are most likely to arise. The diagram indicates that policy making and implementation depend on bureaucrats for supplying accurate information upward as well as for passing orders downward and executing orders effectively.

Many instances of distorted information or diversionary orders have been uncovered by journalists and scholars studying bureaucratic politics. These studies and their own experience led two former bureaucrats, Morton H. Halperin and Leslie H. Gelb, to develop "the bureaucrat's ten commandments," a set of tongue-in-cheek rules assertedly designed to enable the bureaucrat to survive in his or her job and achieve success in shaping policy.[33] Included among them are such rules as:

- "Say what will convince, not what you believe."
- "Veto other options" leaving your own the sole survivor.
- "Predict dire consequences" if your option is not chosen.
- "Argue timing, not substance" to keep others from having a chance to question the basic proposal you are supporting.
- "Leak what you don't like" to enable its various opponents to unite in attacking it with forewarning.
- "Ignore orders you don't like."

These "rules" for action in bureaucratic politicking emphasize the importance of information—both expertise offered and orders passed on. They reveal something of the leverage that bureaucrats can exercise against others who must depend on them for information, and they suggest ways in which bureaucrats may struggle among themselves for power to shape policy and practice.

THE IMPACTS OF BUREAUCRATIC POLITICS

Effects on the Government

Experts often criticize bureaucratic politicking. But would we be better off if our government were so highly centralized with instructions from the top down that it never received proposals and objections from the bottom up? Or does our system, which combines proposals from top and bottom, have particular advantages? Both our capitalist economy and our democratic political system are founded on the principle that competition is healthy, both because it provides real alternatives and because it leads to better—usually more efficient—decisions. We might, therefore, be inclined to conclude that bureaucratic competition, too, should be beneficial. But before we settle on that general conclusion, we should recall the actual costs of this competition not so much in dollar terms as

in terms of its actual effect on particular policies. And we should also assess the effects on the government itself.

We know that the bureaucracy and its politicking are partly responsible for a larger government with a larger budget than there would be if the structure were more centralized. But centralization would make the government inevitably less attentive and less responsive to the population at large and to the interest groups concerned with particular policies and programs. Indeed, if we want our government to develop active programs in such wide-ranging areas as national defense, consumer protection, antitrust activities, insuring our bank accounts, agricultural development, and pollution controls, we cannot escape big bureaucracy. And as long as we have big bureaus dealing with so many different—yet often overlapping—concerns organized into a governmental structure, no matter what that particular structure is, we will have bureaucratic politicking to accompany bureaucratic administration.

In other words, the bureaucracy—the very same bureaucracy that so often infuriates us with its costs, red tape, and inefficiency—makes government of the sort we demand possible in a large, complex, specialized society like our own.[34]

Effects on Individuals

What about bureaucracy's effects on individuals, on the citizens who pay the taxes that pay the salaries, support the offices, and finance the programs of the bureaucracy? What is bureaucracy's actual effect on citizens, and must it stimulate in them such generally negative reactions?

Many people in business, as we shall see in more detail in Chapter 15, have strongly objected to certain aspects of inspection and regulation of business by federal bureaucrats. They have also complained about the large cost in time and money of filling out forms for those bureaucrats. At the other extreme, the poor who must confront the welfare bureaucracy—which is still largely state and local rather than federal—often voice comparable objections. They resent being shunted from place to

---

[33]Leslie H. Gelb and Morton H. Halperin, "The Bureaucrat's Ten Commandments," *Harper's*, June 1972, pp. 28–29. See also, for a more serious study, Heclo, *A Government of Strangers: Executive Politics in Washington*. For a different set of rules about bureaucratic behavior, see Downs, *Inside Bureaucracy*, p. 262. For official guidance, see two publications of the Office of Personnel Management: *Manager's Handbook* (1980) and *Federal Manager's Guide to Washington* (1981).

[34]See Krislov and Rosenbloom, *Representative Bureaucracy and the American Political System*, for a study of how bureaucracy can and does achieve representation by personnel, by organization, through accountability and direction, and through interaction with the public.

place, office to office, person to person, and being forced to face frequent interviews with case-workers who, frequently overloaded and perhaps underpaid, are sometimes inconsiderate to clients.

Most of the rest of us, however, rarely meet federal bureaucrats. Therefore, our reservations about the bureaucracy are more likely concerned with deteriorating mail service and escalating tax rates than with unresponsive small individual cogs in the large bureaucratic machine.

Nevertheless, experts are not quite sure about the actual impact of bureaucracy on citizens, for few studies have yet been done on the actual bureaucratic encounters of various individuals.

To fill this important gap in our knowledge, the Institute for Social Research at the University of Michigan studied citizens' encounters with bureaucracies at all levels of government. The study discovered that fully one-third of those having relevant problems never even sought bureaucratic assistance, despite the fact that most of these individuals said they knew such aid was available. Of those who did seek bureaucratic help, about two-thirds reported that they were satisfied with the way the office handled their problem, almost half termed themselves very satisfied, and only 14 percent were very dissatisfied. This degree of satisfaction is far from ideal, for we might hope that in a service agency, at least 90 percent of clients would be satisfied. But a two-thirds satisfaction level refutes the common assumption that virtually everyone is dissatisfied with the bureaucracy.

Furthermore, the study called into question the common assumption that citizens consider bureaucrats to be disinterested professionals, exploitive politicians, or representatives of an antagonistic race or class. For in answer to the question, "Are the people in the office pretty much people like you?" only 17 percent said no.

Yet this same random sample of the American population also reaffirmed a number of the conventional negative attitudes toward bureaucracy and bureaucrats. For example, 58 percent agreed with the statement that "the people who gain the most from government offices are the officials who run the agencies." Sixty-two percent believed that "people in the government waste a lot of money we pay in taxes," while another 31 percent believed they waste "some of it." Forty-five percent believed that "quite a few of the people running the government don't seem to know what they are doing."

Finally, 77 percent agreed that "there are too many government offices doing the same thing."

This study seems to reveal a contradiction in the beliefs of this sample of the American population. They have one set of beliefs about the bureaucracy in general—beliefs that are negative and even hostile. But the 57 percent of the survey who have had experience with the bureaucracy have another set of memories and beliefs about their own particular experiences. They are largely positive about their satisfaction and their impressions of the real bureaucrats they met.

It may be that the common popular expressions of unhappiness with bureaucracy in general are really indications of deeper discontent. This extends to such matters as the unfairness of taxation in America or the inability or refusal of the government in Washington to legislate and administer solutions to the serious problems that confront many Americans in everyday life in this country—problems such as health, education, justice, housing, and consumer protection.[35]

CAN BUREAUCRACY BE IMPROVED?

We have already seen how the development of our federal bureaucracy has paralleled the development of our society, our economy, and our government. Our bureaucracy was supposed to improve governmental efficiency in such an increasingly complex world by standardizing and rationalizing the conduct of governmental operations. But perhaps we have paid too high a price in the alienation of our citizens and in the dehumanization of our bureaucratic employees in order to gain this greater efficiency. Or perhaps the government has become so big and complex that no bureaucracy can function efficiently and humanely.[36]

The historical alternative to bureaucracy—a system of volunteer citizen-administrators—is now dying out even in local politics. Everywhere governments are becoming bureaucratized. They are staffed by professional bureaucrats who tend to

---

[35]Daniel Katz, Barbara A. Gutek, Robert L. Kahn, and Eugenia Barton, *Bureaucratic Encounters: A Pilot Study in the Evaluation of Government Services* (Ann Arbor, MI: Institute for Social Research, 1975). For summaries of other surveys with generally similar findings, see Charles T. Goodsell, *The Case for Bureaucracy*, 2d ed. (Chatham, NJ: Chatham House, 1985), chap. 2.

[36]For studies of how to improve bureaucracies, see Carol H. Weiss and Allen H. Barton, eds., *Making Bureaucracies Work* (Beverly Hills, CA: Sage, 1980).

specialize in their responsibilities because the matters to be dealt with have become so complex and because successful management (and hence bureaucratic careers) depends upon the efficient performance of these difficult tasks.

Contract and Reprivatization

One of the most common complaints about bureaucrats is that they are addicted to established practices, even when these practices have become inefficient as the government or the population being governed has grown and changed. In an effort to overcome this inherent conservatism of bureaucracy, some governments have contracted with private business organizations to perform certain services. Some cities, for example, have contracted out garbage collection; others have arranged for private organizations or county governments to furnish virtually all services.[37] There is increasing suggestion that mail and parcel delivery nationally should also be turned over to private business. The hope is that the private organizations will be more flexible because they will have to show good results in order to retain the contract. Such decentralization to private organization—**reprivatization**, as it is often called—may result in an improvement for certain services in the short run. But eventually, private organizations, too, will tend to become bureaucratized if their tasks are large. Some experts, therefore, doubt that this private alternative to bureaucracy is generally very promising. Further, even though both the Carter and Reagan administrations favored more contracting out, not much has actually occurred.

Sunset Laws

Disappointment with the results of efforts at bureaucratic reform and decentralization has led more and more governmental units to experiment instead with what are called **sunset laws**. A sunset law requires that an existing program or agency be reviewed for its effectiveness regularly. If it passes that review, it is extended; if not, the program is terminated or the agency abolished or reorganized.

The sun, in other words, automatically sets on any program or agency that is not purposely extended after a fixed period of time.

This idea is by no means new. A similar policy was suggested when President Franklin Roosevelt was beginning the creation of the many New Deal programs and bureaus to get America out of the Depression. The proposal was not adopted. Indeed, four decades passed before it was revived in 1976 by the state of Colorado, which adopted legislation prescribing a six-year life for state regulatory boards and commissions. Coming at a time of great dissatisfaction with bureaucracy, the Colorado law proved quite contagious. Within a few years, 28 states had adopted some type of sunset law. Sunset legislation has even been proposed at the federal level.

Research conducted in 1976 by Common Cause, the "citizen lobby" group in Washington, revealed that in the previous 15 years, 236 new federal departments, agencies, and bureaus had been created, while only 21 had been abolished.[38] Another study, by Herbert Kaufman, found that 148 of the 175 agencies alive in 1923 were still functioning 50 years later. And this study didn't even count the various agencies in the massive Defense Department and Post Office. Furthermore, Kaufman found another 246 new agencies created to work in the same areas in those 50 years.[39]

Times change, and so do public needs—but because bureaucracies tend to be inflexible and often unresponsive to new demands, the first inclination of both presidents and Congress is to create a new bureau to meet a new problem or need rather than attempt to remake an old one. At the same time, the established clientele of an old bureau, in league with the bureau's employees, is generally strong enough to prevent the abolition of a bureau whose time has come and gone. And sometimes inactive bureaus just seem to escape people's attention. A few years ago, a bureaucrat named Jubal Hale called the media's attention to the Federal Metal and Non-Metallic Safety Board of Review. It had

---

[37]See Gary N. Miller, *Cities by Contract* (Cambridge, MA: MIT Press, 1981).

[38]*Sunset: A Common Cause Proposal for Accountable Government* (Washington, DC: Common Cause, 1976).
[39]See Herbert Kaufman, *Are Government Organizations Immortal?* (Washington, DC: Brookings Institution, 1976). *The Government Manual* nonetheless lists, on 103 pages of the 1980–81 edition, well over a thousand "executive agencies and functions of the federal government abolished, transferred or terminated" since 1933.

been created four years earlier by the Congress, and Hale had been appointed its director. But it had never been given any cases to review. So Hale simply spent his days reading and listening to Beethoven records in his office until, at his suggestion, the agency was finally abolished.[40]

Legal provisions for automatic periodic scrutiny of existing agencies and for abolition of those not then specifically extended by new legislation offer some hope of getting greater control over the growth of bureaucracy. They might even help to reduce that growth somewhat, both by putting moribund bureaus to death and by stimulating bureaus that wish to live to a ripe old age to be more responsive to new needs and problems.

Sunset legislation is, of course, intended primarily to cope with the problem of bureaucratic growth and stagnation rather than that of unresponsiveness. True, a new or renewed agency may be more likely to respond to the needs and wishes of the public at large than an old entrenched agency. But citizens often complain of bureaucratic red tape and delay. A different device has been developed to cope with this problem: the ombudsman.

Ombudsmen, or Citizen Advocates

An **ombudsman** is an individual whose office serves as a channel through which a citizen can express his or her grievances over the operation of a bureau or the action of a bureaucrat and seek whatever redress is appropriate. The term itself is Swedish, the first such individual having been appointed by the Swedish Parliament in 1809 to provide a way for citizens to complain effectively about mistakes, abuses, or neglect in their experience with the king's bureaucracy. In the 1960s a number of American states and cities appointed ombudsmen. By 1977, 17 states and 36 cities had them. Recently, some universities and colleges have appointed ombudsmen to help students cope with recalcitrant administrators and faculty. Although federal bureaus have not yet appointed ombudsmen (or citizen advocates, as they are now often called in America), a federal law now requires all states to have ombudsmen programs to keep a watch on nursing homes that get Medicare or Medicaid money. The trend is probably irresistible and should significantly improve the efforts of individual citizens to seek redress.

Until now, individuals have been dependent for assistance primarily upon their members of Congress. However, although a congressional inquiry can be very powerful, members of Congress have virtually no authority to deal with most problems brought to their attention by constituents. In any case, they are both too busy and too removed from the bureaus in question to be able to act effectively on them enough of the time, even though they consider such "casework" a valuable political resource. In any event, should more than the present small percentage of constituents start to depend on their members of Congress for such aid, massive increases in staff would be required.

Whistle Blowers

We should remember that some of the complaints made about the bureaucracy have come from bureaucrats themselves. The Code of Ethics for Government Service declares that "Any Person in Government Service Should: Put loyalty to the highest moral principles and to country above loyalty to persons, party, or government department. . . . [and] Expose corruption wherever discovered." Persons who do so are now commonly called *whistle blowers*, because they "blow the whistle" on government crime or misconduct.

In 1970 A. Ernest Fitzgerald, a Pentagon financial analyst, exposed a $2 billion cost overrun in the production of the Lockheed C5A cargo plane that both Lockheed and the air force were trying to conceal. For his trouble, he was fired. It was later revealed that President Nixon had himself ordered the firing. After a four-year fight, including several trips to federal court, Fitzgerald was reinstated with back pay. However, he was not given the same sort of duties he had had previously.[41]

To protect whistle blowers, or at least to see that they receive better treatment than Fitzgerald did, the Carter Civil Service Reform Act of 1978 established the Merit Systems Protection Board mentioned earlier in this chapter. Since its creation,

---

[40]Donald Lambro, "The Five Worst Government Agencies," *Washingtonian*, November 1976, pp. 162–64.

[41]See Kenneth Bredemeier, "Tapes Show Nixon Role in Firing of Ernest Fitzgerald," *Washington Post*, March 7, 1979.

Ernest Fitzgerald, a civilian cost expert who blew the whistle on skyrocketing costs of the C5A cargo plane, in his office at the Pentagon on the last day of his job with the Air Force. (UPI/Bettmann Newsphotos)

however, both bureaucrats and outsiders have claimed that few of the hundreds of bureaucrats who have complained to the board of mistreatment have received protection.[42]

More successful has been a toll-free hotline to Congress's investigative arm, the General Accounting Office, that citizens in and out of government can use to inform anonymously on bureaucratic fraud and waste. This line, whose number is 800-424–5454, was set up in 1979 and receives some 15,000 allegations of wrongdoing a year. Forty percent of the calls are followed up, and many result in saving the government money or in retrieving stolen property.

At this point, in the words of a lawyer who has represented whistle blowers for the American Civil Liberties Union, "whistle blowing is lonely, unrewarded, and fraught with peril. It entails a substantial risk of retaliation which is difficult and expensive to challenge."[43]

[42]The best protection available seems to be the before-and-after counseling and the publicity for their cases provided by the Government Accountability Project, a division of the Institute for Policy Studies, 1901 Q Street NW, Washington, DC 20009. The GAP has also published *A Whistleblower's Guide to the Federal Bureaucracy* and sponsors an annual conference of whistle blowers in Washington.

[43]Peter Raven-Hansen, "Dos and Dont's for Whistleblowers: Planning for Trouble," *Technology Review*, May 1980, p. 44. See also, for an examination of instances of whistle blowing in the private sector, Alan F. Westin, ed., *Whistle Blowing* (New York: McGraw-Hill, 1980). And see David Ewing's study of employee rights, *Do It My Way or You're Fired!: Employee Rights and the Changing Role of Management Prerogatives* (New York: Wiley, 1983).

Programs to improve the performance of the bureaucracy, both for citizens and for bureaucrats, have had at best mixed success thus far. But if bureaucracy is to survive and overcome the erosion of public support, it must not only respond satisfactorily to grievances but it must also increasingly anticipate and avert difficulties. Perhaps the clearest cases of such grievances—and the strongest cases for sustaining an effective bureaucracy—concern the independent agencies, which together with the cabinet departments and the Executive Office of the President make up most of the federal bureaucracy. They affect every citizen's life in important ways every day, just as they affect every business. And the question of bureaucratic responsiveness takes on a special and complex meaning in the case of these agencies.

THE CHALLENGE OF THE INDEPENDENT AGENCIES

Few Americans could even name an independent federal government agency, let alone describe its functions and powers. And yet, as we saw at the opening of this chapter, virtually every aspect of our lives is seriously affected by the activities of these agencies.

The range of activities policed, encouraged, or conducted by specialized federal governmental agencies is staggering, as the agency titles listed at the bottom of Figure P1.2 in Perspective 1 suggest. At last count, the government listed some 58 independent agencies and government corporations and five quasi-official agencies. In addition, there are 77 boards, committees, and commissions, including such groups as the California Debris Commission, the Arthritis Coordinating Committee, and the Trade Policy Committee. The *boards and commissions* are generally advisory panels that meet occasionally in order to coordinate governmental programs and to advise governmental agencies on the problem each is concerned with. The *quasi-official agencies* are involved in fostering scientific research and charity operations, run national museums, and supervise most passenger services on railroads. In terms of their importance in the government, *independent agencies* are most significant. Included among them are seven major regulatory commissions and about 20 governmental corporations.

Independent Regulatory Commissions

The independent regulatory commissions (IRCs) generally set rates for such things as rail fares and freight charges or grant licenses to radio and television stations and banks. Some, such as the Federal Trade Commission and the Interstate Commerce Commission, are primarily concerned with regulation of the economy. We shall examine their activities in Chapter 15. The Federal Communications Commission, which regulates television and radio, has already been examined in Chapter 7. In a similar fashion, we shall encounter other independent agencies throughout the book.

All such agencies regulate a type of commercial activity or a sector of the economy. Often the objective is to protect "free enterprise" from its own abuses as much as to protect the consumer from business abuses. Thus, for example, the Securities and Exchange Commission, established in 1934, regulates aspects of the issuing of stock by business and the trading of such stock on the various exchanges.

The Nature of Their "Independence"

Because the regulation itself could also be abusive, the IRCs were designed to be free from politics as we usually think of it. For most such IRCs, the president appoints five commissioners with Senate approval. Their terms last for five to seven years and are staggered, so that at any time the commission will likely include appointees of various presidents.

These IRCs make rules for the organizations and activities they regulate similar to the way in which Congress makes laws. These rules are generally referred to as **administrative law** because they are made administratively rather than by congressional legislation. Still, these rules have the force of law because Congress so specified when it established each IRC. Thus, the IRCs have what is sometimes called a quasi-legislative function.

They also have a quasi-judicial function, for they are empowered to hear and resolve disputes among parties that fall under their regulatory power, and their resolutions have the same judicial status as the decisions of courts.

In these various ways, the IRCs are different from cabinet departments, which are directly under the president's control, at least in theory. And because they have legislative and judicial as well as executive powers and functions, they are sometimes referred to as the fourth branch of government.[44]

The Politics of the IRCs

These combined responsibilities were supposed to insulate the IRCs from politics. Instead, however, they have tended to intensify and make more complex the politics surrounding them. This has been even truer in recent years, for two reasons. The first is the attitude of the Reagan administration and Congress's responses to it.

When President Nixon created the Office of Management and Budget (OMB) in 1970, Congress responded by requiring that some IRCs submit their budgets directly to Congress so that Congress could see what the IRCs wanted before the president's political will was imposed on their budget requests by the OMB. By 1984 ten IRCs were required to give their budgets to Congress unchanged by OMB. Another eight, however, could submit budgets to Congress and to OMB for its changes at the same time. Thus, Congress could decide whether to accept the OMB's (and the president's) recommendations or not.

The same process used to apply to IRC regulations. But in 1981 President Reagan issued Executive Order 12291 asking IRCs to submit all proposed regulations to OMB for clearance, in terms of whether their benefits would be worth their likely costs. The agencies resisted at first, but once Reagan appointees became voting majorities, they agreed. Thus, their independence from the president has been lessening.[45]

A second factor in the growing complexity of IRC policies emerged in the 1970s. Some agencies have become less subject to "clientelism" and more responsive to citizen concerns and citizen involvement.

---

[44]For a thoughtful analysis of the administrative process, see James O. Freedman, *Crises and Legitimacy: The Administrative Process and American Government* (New York: Cambridge Univ. Press, 1978).

[45]See Ronald D. Brownstein, "Above Politics?" *National Journal*, June 18, 1983, p. 1291.

The Question of Citizen Participation

The expanding citizen role is especially important because it has begun to open up the regulatory process to the desires and needs of consumers as never before. This has brought about the involvement of more and more different types of citizens in politics: lawyers, activists, and complainers. Such citizen participation is clearest in the newest (and most flexible) agency, the EPA. Recent environmental politicking has given citizens and environmental lawyers opportunities to act as "citizen lobbies" in Congress. In addition, recent legislation and certain favorable court rulings have encouraged citizen suits against economic interests and against recalcitrant officials of federal, state, and local governments. Another consequence has been actions before the EPA and, experimentally, before other IRCs.

The changing and expanding nature of citizen participation in policy making and governmental action will concern us further in coming chapters. We must note, however, that the spread and success of such activism have begun to change the common answer to the most important question about the regulatory commissions—Whom or what do they really serve?—by opening them up to greater influence by public-opinion and citizen-action groups and to greater scrutiny by the media. We may yet see the day when such openness makes the regulatory agencies, which affect so much of our daily lives, among the more responsive elements of the federal bureaucracy. The question, as we might put it, is, Who will regulate the regulators?—and, for that matter, the rest of the bureaucracy. That question is of growing concern not only in Congress but in the courts as well. We shall examine both aspects in the next two chapters.

SUMMARY

All presidential candidates criticize the bureaucracy, and all presidents have trouble controlling it. Many citizens criticize it too and claim to have difficulty getting what they want from it. The federal bureaucracy consists of some 3 million Americans, who affect most aspects of our daily lives by the rules and regulations they write and enforce.

A bureaucracy has three key features: hierarchy, specialization of roles, and authority based in the law. It tends to conflict with democracy, which stresses equality, freedom, and citizen involvement.

Bureaucracy in the United States has developed as the government has expanded. In the Jackson era, the spoils system was developed to increase presidential control. In the 1880s the merit, or civil service, system was developed to protect bureaucrats from political pressure. Today many people feel the president needs more leverage. Carter's Civil Service Reform Act of 1978 reorganized the personnel system to improve management and protect whistle blowers, but the act hasn't worked well in the Reagan years. Nor has structural reform—reorganizing bureaus to make them more efficient. Vested interests inside and outside existing bureaus usually prevent such reform.

Federal bureaucrats are much like other Americans, although they are more likely to be white, male, middle-class, and middle-aged. They also tend to have more job security because it is very difficult to fire federal bureaucrats.

The major functions of bureaucrats are assuring continuity, implementing decisions, making policy, and providing information. Their power in relation to the president and the Congress derives primarily from the use of information, which they may hoard or leak, and from their ability to obstruct or facilitate desired programs. Bureaucratic politics—struggles between agencies for control of programs and for bigger budgets—is very common and often affects what government does. While bureaucracy often upsets citizens, most of those who actually deal directly with it report some satisfaction. Still, efforts to reform bureaucracy continue. They include contracting out services, or reprivatization; sunset laws; the use of ombudsmen; and whistle blowing.

The independent regulatory commissions, a special segment of the bureaucracy, are somewhat independent of Congress and the president and regulate many aspects of life. In recent years, citizens have gained a greater role in many of their activities. But the Reagan administration has also lessened their independence somewhat. Thus, once again—with the IRCs as with the rest of the bureaucracy—the question remains: Who should control the bureaucracy?

Suggestions for Further Reading and Study

Basic questions on the relations between democracy and bureaucracy are raised in F. C. Mosher, *Democracy and the Public Service* (New York: Oxford Univ. Press, 1968); Emmette S. Redford, *Democracy in the Administrative State* (New York: Oxford Univ. Press, 1969); John A.Rohr, *To Run a Constitution: The Legitimacy of the Administrative State* (Lawrence: Univ. Press of Kansas, 1986); and John P. Burke, *Bureaucratic Responsibility* (Baltimore: Johns Hopkins Univ. Press, 1986). On the politics of bureaucracy, see Francis E. Rourke, *Bureaucracy, Politics, and Public Policy*, 2d ed. (Boston: Little, Brown, 1986); Richard Neustadt, *Presidential Power*, 4th ed. (New York: Wiley, 1976); Hugh Heclo, *A Government of Strangers: Executive Politics in Washington* (Washington, DC: Brookings Institution, 1977); Morton H. Halperin, *Bureaucratic Politics and Foreign Policy* (Washington, DC: Brookings Institution, 1974); Richard P. Nathan, *The Plot That Failed* (New York: Wiley,

1975); and Harold Seidman, *Politics, Position, and Power: The Dynamics of Federal Organization*, 2d ed. (New York: Oxford Univ. Press, 1975), by a high-level bureaucrat. On reforms, see Carol H. Weiss and Allen H. Barton, eds., *Making Bureaucracies Work* (Beverly Hills, CA: Sage, 1980).

Among studies concentrating more on the interplay of agencies and public policy implications are Randall Ripley and Grace Franklin, *Congress, the Bureaucracy, and Public Policy*, rev. ed. (Homewood, IL: Dorsey, 1980); and Lawrence C. Dodd and Richard L. Schott, *Congress and the Administrative State* (New York: Wiley, 1979).

For continuing coverage of what it calls the culture of bureaucracy, see the many articles in *Washington Monthly*, or the collection of pieces from it edited by Charles Peters and Michael Nelson, *The Culture of Bureaucracy* (New York: Holt, Rinehart & Winston, 1979).

10

CONGRESS

Congress was established as the first branch of our government, in Article I of the Constitution—even before the presidency. It was empowered to make laws, levy taxes, decide how money can be spent, and propose amendments to the Constitution. The founders clearly thought of Congress as the primary policy-making body in the national government. It was to decide what should be done; and the president's executive branch was to execute, or implement, the will of Congress as expressed in legislation.

In general, throughout most of our history, these expectations have not been fulfilled. However, Congress sometimes does take the initiative and make policy. In so doing, it usually pays heed to a wide range of special interests that attempt to influence its decisions. It must also follow a complex procedure. The essence of this legislative process, as it is called, is found in the Constitution's specification that to become law, a bill must be passed in identical form by both houses of Congress. Over two centuries, each house of Congress has made and remade a complex set of rules by which it proposes, considers, and votes upon bills, as potential laws are called. Each house also has developed informal, but very important, customs or norms of behavior that members are supposed to observe during the process.

Much of the success, as well as much of the limitation, of Congress's role in American politics can be traced to these powers, rules, and practices. To understand Congress, we must first understand the legislative process. The best way to achieve that goal is to first examine the congressional history of an important bill: the National Environmental Policy Act of 1969.

THE BIRTH OF THE NATIONAL ENVIRONMENTAL POLICY ACT

The Growth of Environmental Concern

A series of ecological disasters occurred in the late 1960s: oil spills from large tankers; an oil-well blow-out off the Santa Barbara, California, beaches; fires on the polluted water of ship channels; large-scale deaths of fish on the coasts because of the dumping of chemical and human wastes; and other, similar incidents. Meanwhile, air pollution from autos and industry was worsening in most parts of the country, and studies were showing that this threatened people's health.[1] By 1969 when the Santa Barbara oil spill occurred, public sentiment for environmental protection had created support for legislation.[2] What happened then reveals much about the politics of legislation in American government—things that are as true today as they were then.[3]

A Bill Is Introduced in the House

To become a law, a bill must be passed in identical form by both the House of Representatives and the Senate and signed by the president. But before either house of Congress will vote on a bill, one of its committees must consider the bill and recommend its adoption. Getting a bill passed is, therefore, likely to involve complex strategy (see Table 10.1 and Figure 10.1). Although there were then more than 300 committees and subcommittees in Congress, in 1969 no committee in either house had as its primary responsibility developing environmental legislation. In the House, the Interior Committee, which deals with natural resources, was chaired by Wayne Aspinall (Democrat of Colorado). Aspinall was known as a friend of commercial developers of natural resources and as an enemy of strong environmental protection. He often used his power as committee chairperson to kill en-

vironmental-protection bills referred to his committee by the House for consideration.

Supporters of environmental protection hoped that the Merchant Marine and Fisheries Committee, because it dealt with fish, would be more sympathetic to environmental protection. Its subcommittee on Fisheries and Wildlife Conservation was controlled by supporters of environmental protection. Its chairperson, John Dingell (Democrat of Michigan), drafted a bill creating a Council on Environmental Quality (CEQ), which was intended to advise the president and report to the public on environmental concerns. But Dingell's committee had jurisdiction only over fish and wildlife. Therefore, his bill had to be attached as an amendment to the Fish and Wildlife Coordination Act, which his subcommittee was already considering. Had it simply been submitted to the House as a regular bill, it would have been referred to Aspinall's Interior Committee, the logical place for such a bill. It is likely that Aspinall would have killed it—as he had a similar bill submitted by Dingell the previous year.

Differing Bills Are Introduced in the Senate

At the same time, in the Senate, two somewhat similar bills were introduced. Senator Henry Jackson (Democrat of Washington) introduced a bill calling for creation of a Council on Environmental Quality—a bill rather like Dingell's House bill. Because Jackson was chairperson of the Senate Interior Committee (the counterpart of Aspinall's House committee), he could simply introduce the bill in the normal fashion, knowing it would be referred to his committee for consideration. Jackson conducted hearings on the bill during April. In June his committee approved, or "reported out," his bill, for consideration by the Senate as a whole. It had two major provisions. First, it established a CEQ; and second, it required that all government agencies prepare an Environmental Impact Statement (EIS) for each new program or action they undertook. This EIS was supposed to describe the effects the program would be likely to have on the environment.[4] It would thus enable people to eval-

---

[1] We shall examine some of these policy problems in more detail in chap. 18.

[2] See the NORC polls reported in Ben Wattenberg, *The Real America* (New York: Capricorn, 1976), pp. 226–27.

[3] The following account owes much to Richard A. Liroff, *A National Policy for the Environment* (Bloomington: Indiana Univ. Press, 1976); and Austin H. Kiplinger, *Washington Now* (New York: Harper & Row, 1975).

[4] For a study of the EIS, see Joseph Lee Rodgers, *Environmental Impact Assessment, Growth Management, and the Comprehensive Plan* (Cambridge, MA: Ballinger, 1976).

TABLE 10.1

How a Bill Actually Becomes a Law—and What Happens Then

1. The president proposes a bill to the Congress after it is developed and drafted (written in legal language) by an agency in the executive branch. The bill is then introduced in the House by a friendly representative, where it is given a number and referred to the committee that has jurisdiction over (or responsibility for) that area of legislation. The same thing happens in the Senate.

1a. Or the bill is conceived by a senator or representative, perhaps at the urging of constituents or of an interest group. The bill is drafted by the member's own staff and the legislative counsel and introduced by him or her. The bill is given a number and referred to a committee, as above. The same is done by a friendly member of the other house.

2. The committee staff, generally under the guidance of the chairperson, studies the bill, gets the opinion of the Office of Management and Budget in the executive branch on it, and reports to the committee chairperson on its contents and likely impact.

3. The committee chairperson refers the bill to a subcommittee, which may hold a hearing to allow interested parties to comment on it. These parties may include officials from the executive branch with responsibilities in the area the bill involves, interested members of Congress, representatives of interest groups, and even individual citizens.

4. The subcommittee then meets to mark up the bill (go over it line by line). It usually tries to rewrite it in a way that will maximize support for it through bargaining with supporters and opponents. At this point, a subcommittee sometimes will adopt as an amendment a bill that really should be a separate bill. This is done because the bill would not be reported out of the committee to which it would be referred or would not be passed by the whole House or Senate if it were not a part of a more popular measure.

5. If the subcommittee passes the bill with strong support, the committee as a whole will probably pass it without much debate. The committee staff then prepares a report on the bill, explaining it for the record.

6. If the bill is at all controversial, it must be scheduled for debate on the floor of the Senate or the House. In the Senate, scheduling is done by the majority leader (the head of the party with a majority in the Senate), in consultation with the minority leadership and even perhaps with the White House. In the House, for the bill to get any further, the Rules Committee must grant a rule for the bill. This is a set of specifications stating whether amendments will be allowed on the floor and how much time will be allowed for debate. The Speaker of the House and the majority leader then schedule it for debate, usually in consultation.

7. The Senate or the House then debates the bill and votes on it. Amendments are often proposed and sometimes adopted at this stage.

8. A bill passed by one house is then sent to the other house for its consideration because both houses must pass any bill before it can become law. The other house can either accept the bill as passed by the first house or refer it to the same procedures outlined above before deciding.

9. If each house produces a somewhat different bill on the same subject, a conference committee must meet and agree upon a compromise version. The conference committee, appointed by the leadership, usually includes representatives of the committees that originally passed the bill plus other interested members from each house.

10. Once the conference committee agrees on a compromise version, each house must accept the compromise exactly by voting favorably on it.

11. The bill then goes to the president, who may sign it—in which case it becomes a law—or veto it. If it is vetoed, the bill does not become law; instead, the president returns it to the Congress with a message giving reasons for the veto. The bill dies—unless it is then repassed by a two-thirds majority vote in each house; if this happens, the veto is overridden, and the bill becomes law without the president's signature.

12. Once a bill becomes law, it must be implemented, or put into effect. Executing the law is the responsibility of the executive branch. Often a department will announce a new policy or issue new regulations to implement the law. It does this by having the new policy or regulations printed in full in the *Federal Register*, a daily publication which lists all such official documents. Sometimes the president will issue an executive order to make changes believed to be necessary or desirable to implement the bill. From these actions, lower-level bureaucrats get their instructions on how to act.

13. Sometimes, however, a party (a company, an agency, or an individual) affected by the law dislikes either the law or the way it is being applied. This party may go to court to challenge the legality of the government's interpretation of the law or even the law's constitutionality. If so, the court rules on the case. This ruling may sometimes be appealed to a higher court. This appeal route may lead all the way to the Supreme Court.

uate the program in terms of its likely environmental effects.

Senator Edmund Muskie (Democrat of Maine), also a longstanding environmentalist, feared that the Jackson bill would not be effective without an agency to enforce it. Therefore, on June 12 he introduced a bill that would create an Office of Environmental Quality, with enforcement powers. He located it in the Executive Office of the President, which, as we saw in Chapter 8, contains agencies that assist the president. But Muskie couldn't simply introduce this proposal as a separate bill. If he did so, it would be referred to Senator Jackson's Interior Committee, which was naturally more interested in its chairperson's own bill. Instead, Muskie introduced his bill as an amendment to a bill on control of water pollution, which was being considered by the Public Works Committee's Subcommittee on Air and Water Pollution—which he chaired.

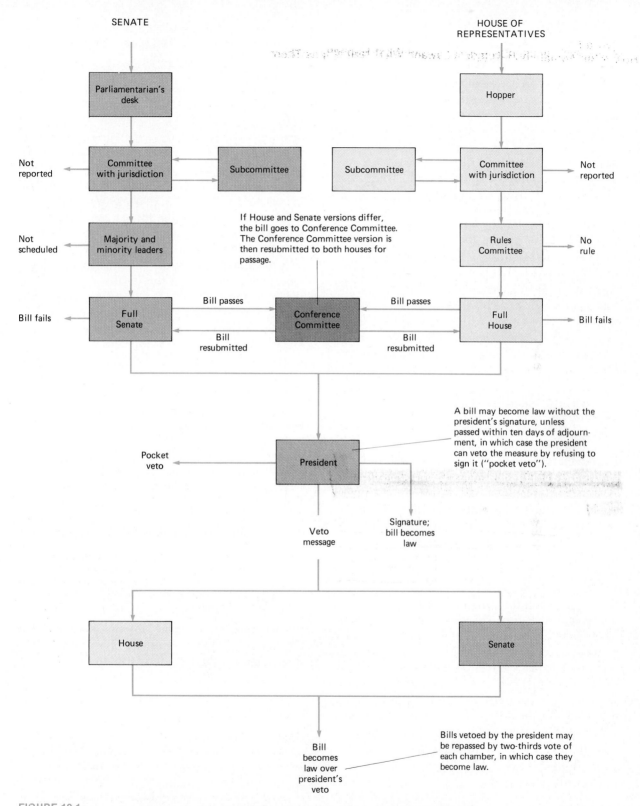

SENATE

HOUSE OF
REPRESENTATIVES

Parliamentarian's
desk

Hopper

Not
reported

Committee
with jurisdiction

Subcommittee

Subcommittee

Committee
with jurisdiction

Not
reported

Not
scheduled

Majority and
minority leaders

If House and Senate versions differ,
the bill goes to Conference Committee.
The Conference Committee version is
then resubmitted to both houses for
passage.

Rules
Committee

No
rule

Bill fails

Full
Senate

Bill passes

Conference
Committee

Bill passes

Full
House

Bill fails

Bill
resubmitted

Bill
resubmitted

A bill may become law without the
president's signature, unless
passed within ten days of adjournment, in which case the president
can veto the measure by refusing to
sign it ("pocket veto").

Pocket
veto

President

Veto
message

Signature;
bill becomes
law

House

Senate

Bill
becomes
law over
president's
veto

Bills vetoed by the president may
be repassed by two-thirds vote of
each chamber, in which case they
become law.

FIGURE 10.1
How a Bill Becomes Law. These are the basic steps of the most typical route. Table
10.1 summarizes the actual stages in greater detail.
Source: Richard Pious, *American Politics and Government* (New York: McGraw-Hill, 1986), p. 390.

307

The Senate Passes
a Strong Compromise Bill

The existence of two somewhat comparable bills in different Senate committees created something of a problem. Both Jackson and Muskie wanted to be known as the "father" of the first major environmental-protection legislation. Ultimately, despite strong egos, Jackson and Muskie were able to reach a compromise. Jackson's bill, which was numbered S. (for Senate) 1075, became the National Environmental Policy Act (NEPA). Finally passed by the Senate on October 8, 1969, in a form strengthened by Muskie amendments, it created the Council on Environmental Quality in the Executive Office of the President. Muskie's bill, S. 2391, eventually passed the Senate in April 1970 as the Environmental Quality Improvement Act. It established a new agency, with more staff designed to assist the CEQ. This agency was called the Office of Environmental Quality and was located in the Department of Housing and Urban Development.

The House Passes a Weak Bill

Before these bills could become law, however, there were more obstacles to overcome. The House of Representatives also had to approve the bills. In the House, once a bill is passed by a committee, it must be scheduled for consideration by the whole House. That requires getting a "rule" from the powerful House Rules Committee. This committee polices the "traffic" of bills going to the House floor by stating how much floor debate will be allowed on each and whether amendments will be allowed. Representative Aspinall, who had been the victim of Dingell's "end run" on the House CEQ bill, was unhappy. But having friends on the House Rules Committee, he was able to force Dingell to accept an amendment that crippled the bill. The amendment stated that the bill would not alter any existing responsibilities of existing agencies. Thus, when the bill passed the House, it passed by an overwhelming majority—but it was only a pale shadow of its former self.

Both Senate and House Pass
a Compromise Bill

Dingell was willing to settle for a very weak bill rather than no bill at all because he hoped that something could be worked out in a conference committee. When the House and Senate pass different bills on the same subject, a conference committee is appointed to try to iron out the differences. This is so that each house can then pass the same compromise bill, as is required for a bill to become law. Conference committee members are appointed by the leaders of the House and Senate from among those most involved in preparing and passing the legislation. In this case, the conference committee included Jackson and Dingell, who had introduced the bills being "harmonized." But it also included Aspinall because his committee normally had jurisdiction over environmental questions. In the conference committee the supporters of a strong bill prevailed and struck the crippling House amendments forced on the bill by Aspinall from the final text. The final version, therefore, was much like the Senate bill developed by Jackson, with one exception: The Jackson bill's assertion that every citizen has a "right" to a clean environment was dropped as part of the compromise. The compromise legislation passed Congress with strong support, and President Nixon signed this National Environmental Policy Act on January 1, 1970.[5] He too, like Dingell and Jackson and Muskie, wanted to be seen by the public as a protector of the environment.

WHAT IS CONGRESS?

The story is often told in Washington of the tourist who approached a U.S. Capitol guide and said: "I've seen the House, and I've seen the Senate, but where do I find Congress?" Such a joke can be told only because, according to one recent survey, 8 percent of the American people believe Congress is just the Senate, 6 percent believe Congress is just the House of Representatives, and fully 20 percent believe that Congress consists of the Senate, the House, and the Supreme Court.[6]

---

[5]The act established the Council on Environmental Quality to advise the president and coordinate policy and to report regularly to the American people on the state of the environment. At the time NEPA was passed, responsibility for environmental matters was scattered throughout various existing departments and agencies. Nixon, as we saw in the last chapter, generally favored governmental reorganization. Thus, he soon issued an executive order combining 15 units from various departments and agencies into the Environmental Protection Agency (EPA). We will examine the impact of the CEQ and the EPA in chap. 18.

[6]Don Radler, *How Congress Works* (New York: Signet, 1976), p. xii.

How We Got the Congress We Have

Article I, Section 1, of the Constitution says: "All legislative powers herein granted shall be vested in a Congress of the United States, which shall consist of a Senate and House of Representatives."

The decision to establish a **bicameral** (*bi*, "two," and *camera*, "chamber") Congress was agreed upon early in the constitutional debates. In part, it was a compromise between representatives of larger and smaller states, as we saw in Chapter 1. But there was another reason for it as well. Virtually everyone wanted some check upon a popularly elected assembly that might act too hastily and might move against the interests of the well-to-do bankers and business people in favor of the interests of the more numerous farmers.

The House was to represent the people as a whole—the will of the majority—by having its members apportioned by population.[7] The question of just which people would actually be allowed to vote was left essentially to the states. And in fact, neither blacks nor women—nor even those not owning property—were allowed to vote in most states, as we saw in Chapter 3.

The Senate was supposed to protect minority interests. But which minority? The rich, the bankers, the business leaders? That would be difficult to justify; and it might be difficult to get the people of the states to ratify, or agree to, a Constitution calling for that. Therefore, the solution agreed upon was to have the Senate represent the states rather than the people. Each state was to have two senators regardless of its population. This would protect the interests of small states by giving them the same representation as the large ones. Senators would be elected by state legislatures, instead of by the people. In this way, they could check the dangers of uncontrolled popular government, for each body would have to approve all legislation before it became law. In addition, senators would serve for six years, which would exceed both the two-year House term and the four-year presidential term. This provision was intended to insulate senators from presidential pressures and from the need to be reelected frequently.

---

[7]As this system evolved, House members were elected from single-member districts. This is now provided for by law. In certain cases, however, such as failure of a state to reapportion districts legally after a new census, all members from a state may be elected at large (by the whole state population).

The west front of the Capitol building undergoing reconstruction. (S. L. Alexander/UNIPHOTO)

Congress shares power with the executive. For a bill to become law, Congress must pass it, and the president must sign it, as we saw in the case of NEPA. Each branch of government also has checks upon the other. The president can veto a bill. But if both houses of Congress then pass the bill once again, this time by a two-thirds majority, it becomes law anyway. Furthermore, as we saw in Chapter 8, major presidential appointments and all treaties must be approved by the Senate.

These checks and balances are only part of the story. The actual operation and effectiveness of Congress depend especially on two further features: the powers of Congress and the rules by which Congress operates. The Constitution enumerates the powers. It also provides that "each house may determine the rules of its proceedings." We shall see shortly how important the "self-government" of each house has been.

The Powers of Congress

The Constitution specifies rather precisely the powers of Congress in Article I, Section 8. Some of them are specific to the time of the founding: the power "to define and punish piracies and felonies committed on the high seas," for example. But most remain important to this day.

"The Congress shall have Power," Section 8 begins, "to lay and collect taxes [and] duties [on imported goods], . . . to borrow money, . . . to regulate commerce with foreign nations, and among the several states. . . . " The same section gives Congress the power to establish uniform rules of naturalization (by which foreigners may become American citizens) and uniform bankruptcy laws, to coin money and regulate its value, to provide for the punishment of counterfeiting, to establish post offices, to enact patent and copyright laws, and to create lower federal courts under the Supreme Court. Then come the major foreign-affairs powers: to declare war and to provide for armed forces. Finally, Congress is granted the power to govern the federal city, which we call the District of Columbia, or Washington, DC.

The American experience has shown the most important of these enumerated powers to be the power to tax, the power to regulate commerce, and the power to ratify treaties.[8] Elsewhere in the Constitution Congress is given the power to impeach and remove from office officials guilty of "treason, bribery, or other high crimes and misdemeanors." Congress also has the power to admit new states to the Union and to initiate constitutional amendments, which must then be ratified in the states. But in a sense, the most important power is that contained in the last clause of Article I, Section 8: the power "to make all Laws which shall be necessary and proper for carrying into execution the foregoing powers, and all other powers vested by this constitution in the government of the United States, or in any department or officer thereof." This "necessary and proper" clause, as it is often called, is a kind of blank check. It has been used as such time and time again by the Congress; in the process, it has been stretched so much that it is also called the elastic clause.[9]

Powers, of course, become significant when they are exercised. We saw in Chapter 8 that the powers of the presidency have been enhanced beyond what

the Constitution provided by presidential actions and by law. Congress, on the other hand, has often chosen not to exercise all the powers granted to it. It often delegates some powers to the executive branch. The exercise of power by Congress depends in part on the procedures Congress adopts to govern itself. However, it depends even more on the members of Congress: who they are and what they actually want to do.

MEMBERS OF CONGRESS

Their Number

In the early years of our nation, some distinguished participants in the founding of the Republic served in the Congress. By the 1820s some observers found the Senate full of statesmen and the House peopled by ordinary citizens. Over the years, as more states were admitted to the Union, the number of senators grew from the original 22 to the present 100, reached when Alaska and Hawaii were admitted in 1959. The House, too, grew with the population, from an original 59; in 1929 the Reapportionment Act made the total number permanently 435 and required that these seats be reapportioned among the states every time there is a new census. (The House membership by state, based on the 1980 census, is shown in Figure 10.2.)

Their Districts

Actual apportionment has been left to the state legislatures, which decide where district lines are drawn, or which voters will vote together to select a representative. Over the years, districts were often malapportioned, protecting incumbents or dominant parties by creating districts that were unequal in numbers of voters or strangely shaped in terms of territory. This is often called gerrymandering, in "honor" of Elbridge Gerry (governor of Massachusetts in 1812, when the state legislature carved up Essex County in a way that favored his party, making a district that looked like a salamander). In *Baker* v. *Carr* (1962) the Supreme Court held that the Tennessee state legislature's malapportionment violated the constitutional requirement of equal protection. Finally, in 1964 it ruled in *Wesberry* v. *Sanders* that congressional

---

[8]The Senate is given the power to give its "advice and consent" to any treaty (Article II, Section 2).

[9]For a useful discussion of congressional powers and their development, see Congressional Quarterly, *Origins and Development of Congress* (Washington, DC: CQ Press, 1976), esp. chap. 5, and the same organization's *Powers of Congress* (Washington, DC: CQ Press, 1976).

FIGURE 10.2
Current State Representatives in the House of Representatives.

Note: In addition, the District of Columbia, Puerto Rico, and the Virgin Islands each have a nonvoting representative in the House.

districts must have equal population. The long-standing tendency of state legislatures to apportion in ways that overrepresented rural voters and underrepresented city voters began to be corrected.

Their Perquisites

If you were a member of Congress, you would have an annual salary of over $89,500. You would have a free office in Washington and at least one free office in your home state or district. You would get cut rates at the Capitol barbershop or beauty parlor and at a private congressional restaurant. Parking at the Capitol, which is almost impossible for ordinary citizens, would be free; and if you nonetheless parked illegally, you would not get a ticket. You would be entitled to 40 or more free trips a year back to your home to see your constituents. You would get up to $6500 a year to buy stationery, and you would have the privilege of mailing newsletters and other official letters and documents free of charge. You would have a budget ranging from $352,536 to $1,247,879 to hire office staff, depending on the size of your district or state. If you got sick, you would have free care in the Capitol

medical clinic, and if you wanted exercise, the Capitol gym and swimming pool would be yours to use. When vacation time came around and Congress was not in session, you could take a free "fact-finding" trip abroad to study something relevant, or not quite so relevant, to your congressional work, such as the Paris Air Show or NATO meetings in Brussels.

Sounds like a pretty good life, doesn't it? And yet most members of Congress can't live on their salaries and benefits and have to dip into savings or rely on outside income to make ends meet. Fortunately, most of them have savings—at last count there were 22 representatives and 25 senators who admitted to being millionaires. Also, many more own stocks and bonds that provide substantial extra income. Those who do not, and so are more like typical Americans, have to make special adjustments to maintain two homes, pay high taxes, entertain constituents, and often pay off leftover campaign debts. But even the latter differ from the rest of the population in very many other ways. For while Congress represents the people in political terms, it is not very representative in economic, racial, sexual, educational, or religious terms.

Their Characteristics

A study of the 100th Congress, whose period of service runs from 1987 to 1989, revealed that the average age of House members was 51 while that of senators was 54. The average American is just under 29 years of age. In terms of sex and race, members of Congress are even less typical of the population at large. In 1987 there were two elected women in the Senate and only 23 in the House. Racial and ethnic minorities totaled only 5 percent of the House (23 blacks, 14 Hispanics, and 2 of Oriental descent) and 3 percent of the Senate (all of Oriental descent). Such minorities make up about 20 percent of the population. Only 3 percent of senators and 9 percent of members of the House lack a college degree, and 79 percent of senators and 64 percent of representatives have advanced graduate degress. Forty-five percent of the representatives and 59 percent of the senators are lawyers by profession. In terms of religious preference, Catholics are but 27 percent of the House and 12 percent of the Senate; 72 percent of the Senate and 55 percent of the House are Protestants, although Protestants are about half of the population. Jews account for 6 percent in each house, but less than 3 percent in the population.[10]

These statistics indicate that members of Congress are not very typical of the American population. The underrepresentation of women and minorities may make it difficult for Congress to fully understand and respond to the problems of these groups. But in general, these statistics tell us relatively little about how Congress is likely to act; members often vote in ways not predictable from their social and economic characteristics.

WHAT MEMBERS OF CONGRESS DO

Images of laws and lawyers may conjure up the wrong notions of what a member of Congress does, just as the long list of privileges may suggest more comfort than is usual. The best way—perhaps the only way—to understand what the life of a member of Congress is like is to follow one through a typical day. This is what we shall do in the box entitled "A Day in the Life of Senator Bill Bradley."

Speaker of the House Jim Wright, Democrat of Texas. (UPI/Bettmann Newsphotos)

"Casework" for Constituents

Most members of Congress report that a very large part of their time goes to personalized work for constituents—casework as it is called. Studies find that about a quarter of a member's time and half to two-thirds of his or her staff's time is so committed.[11] We still call members of Congress legislators, a term derived from the Latin word *leges*, or "laws." But Representative Jim Wright, Democrat and current Speaker of the House, complained in his book *You and Your Congressman:* "I came here to write laws and what do I do? I send out baby books to young mothers, listen to every maladjusted kid who wants out of the service . . . and give tours of the Capitol to visitors who are just as worn out as I am."[12] One former senator

[10]David Rapp, "Characteristics of Congress," *CQ Weekly Report*, Nov. 8, 1986, pp. 2861–63.

[11]See Roger Davidson, *The Role of the Congressman* (New York: Pegasus, 1969), and Bruce Cain, John Ferejohn, and Morris Fiorina, "Constituency Service in the United States and Great Britain," in *Congress Reconsidered*, 3d ed., ed. Lawrence C. Dodd and Bruce Oppenheimer. (Washington: CQ Press, 1985), chap. 5.

[12]Quoted in the Ralph Nader Congress Project's study by Mark Green et al., *Who Runs Congress?* (New York: Bantam, 1972), pp. 203–4. See also Stephen E. Frantzich, *Write Your Congressman: Constituent Communications and Representation* (New York: Praeger, 1986).

A Day in the Life of Senator Bill Bradley

On some days, a senator spends relatively little time on the Senate floor, as the schedule of Senator Bill Bradley's activities on July 28, 1981 reveals. That day, the Senate went into session earlier than usual, at 8:15 A.M., so that it could finish its consideration of President Ronald Reagan's proposed tax bill and start a recess ("working holiday") in August that would last until just after Labor Day.

Bradley's workday began with phone calls and conferences with staff aides to discuss the day's schedule and the positions he would be taking in committee meetings that day.

Because the Senate was debating the Reagan tax bill, Bradley had to interrupt his other activities from time to time during the day to go to the Senate floor to vote.

Bradley had been selected by the Democratic party leadership to appear on national network television the night before and respond immediately after an economic address by the president. But he was not deeply involved in floor debate on this day and was free to participate actively in committee meetings.

Like all other senators, Bradley is a member of two standing committees. Those he selected from the vacancies available when he first won election to the Senate in 1978 were the Finance Committee and the Energy and Natural Resources Committee.

On the day we are following, Bradley wanted to attend two meetings scheduled at the same time. The Finance Subcommittee on International Trade, on which he serves, was hearing

8:00 A.M.—Senator Bradley arrives at his office. (Alessandra Lippucci)

8:30 A.M.—Bradley discusses day's schedule with aide and visiting political scientist David V. Edwards. (Alessandra Lippucci)

Senator Bradley's Schedule, Tuesday, July 28, 1981

8:00 A.M.	Arrival at the office	1:30	Vote on Senate floor on tax bill
8:30	Discuss day's schedule with aide and visiting political scientist David V. Edwards	2:00	Interview with reporter from *Congressional Insight* newsletter in room off Senate floor
9:00	Vote on Senate floor on tax bill	3:00	Joint press conference with other Democratic senators on President Reagan's Social Security proposals
9:30	Meeting with Legislative Assistant on Energy to discuss upcoming hearing		
10:00	Finance Subcommittee on International Trade meeting to hear testimony on situation in Poland by Secretary of State Alexander Haig	4:00	Meeting with administrative assistant
		4:30	Office work: correspondence and phone calls
10:30	Energy and Natural Resources Committee meeting to consider bill to authorize president to allocate petroleum supplies during a serious supply shortage	5:15	Meeting with legislative assistant to discuss Clean Air Act
		5:45	Reception for the American Textile Manufacturers Institute
11:00	Vote on Senate floor on tax bill	7:00	Reception for Representative Florio, Democratic candidate for governor of New Jersey
12:00	Photo of Bradley with a Senate page outside office		
12:30 P.M.	Democratic Conference Committee luncheon	7:30–9	Office work
		9:00	Home

8:45 A.M.—Bradley receives an unscheduled phone call from his daughter wishing him a happy 38th birthday. (Alessandra Lippucci)

9:00 A.M.—Bradley rides the subway to the Senate floor for a vote. (Stan Wakefield)

testimony from Secretary of State Alexander Haig on the tense situation in Poland. The Energy and Natural Resources Committee was considering a bill to give the president authority to allocate gasoline and other petroleum products among various regions of the country when

9:15 A.M.—While returning from Senate floor, Bradley talks with a lobbyist. (Stan Wakefield)

supplies were unusually short—a topic of special interest to Bradley and to his state, New Jersey, because it is not an energy producer. Bradley decided to alternate between the two meetings, as members of Congress often do.

Bradley is also a member of the Senate Special Committee on Aging. As a "special committee," it can report its findings and recommendations to the Senate, but it cannot report legislation. Thus it is less important than the other two committees Bradley serves on. It was not meeting that day.

In addition to committee meetings and floor action, a senator has numerous other daily responsibilities. Among them is the need to explain his views on public issues to the media. During the day, Bradley was interviewed at the Capitol by a reporter for a special newsletter on Congress, and he spoke by telephone with reporters for a radio station in his home state for a New York City paper.

As he hurries to and from the votes on the floor, he confers with other senators and listens to representatives of various interest groups seeking his support for their favored legislation.

10:00 A.M.—At hearing of Finance Subcommittee on International Trade, Bradley questions Secretary of State Alexander Haig. (Stan Wakefield)

10:30 A.M.—Bradley makes statement at meeting of Energy and Natural Resources Committee. (Alessandra Lippucci)

12:00 noon—Bradley listens on elevator on the way to a special luncheon meeting. (Alessandra Lippucci)

2:00 P.M.—Bradley explains his position to a reporter for a Washington newsletter in a room off the Senate chamber. (Alessandra Lippucci)

This "life on the run" may not be as hectic as that Bradley lived in the National Basketball Association as a star player with the New York Knicks from 1967 to 1977. (You can read about that life in Bradley's autobiographical account, *Life on the Run*.) But it never seems to let up. Between meetings Bradley takes care of mail, answers phone messages, and makes plans with his staff for activities scheduled in his home state of New Jersey during the upcoming recess.

Meanwhile, the members of Bradley's staff in Washington and New Jersey are working as usual—doing research, receiving phone calls and letters from constituents who express views on policy questions, and doing casework to help New Jersey residents cope with the federal bureaucracy.

No day in the life of a senator or a representative is entirely typical—except perhaps in its unexpected challenges. This day there was a last-minute decision by the Democratic party leadership in the Senate to hold a press conference to denounce remarks on Social Security that the president had made in his nationwide television address the night before. Attending

this press conference further extended Bradley's day.

When we finally left him that day at dinner time, he was still at work at his desk, likely to stay there until 9:00 P.M.—although at last no longer on the run.

2:55 P.M.—Bradley makes final check of his notes as Democratic senators gather for press conference. (Alessandra Lippucci)

3:00 P.M.—Bradley and other Democratic senators hold press conference to attack Reagan's Social Security proposals. (Alessandra Lippucci)

4:00 P.M.—A final meeting with his administrative assistant is interrupted by a telephone call. (Stan Wakefield)

315

kept a tally and once reported that his office received an average of 275 phone calls a day, had 6000 visitors a year, and got 45,938 letters (which it responded to with 50,678 letters!) in one year. Indeed, in an average year, members of Congress mail about half a billion letters marked "official business" to the American people—an average of five to each household in the country.

Individual members of Congress relate in varying ways to large numbers of their constituents. Casework such as we have just described is one way. But despite Representative Wright's remark, it is only a part—and a relatively small part—of the life of most legislators. Table 10.2 lists the breakdown of average time expenditures per day reported by members. Congress does serve as the major route for citizen complaints about government. But it also makes laws—lots of them. When it does this—as it does most days of the week—its members are also relating to their constituents, but in very different—and controversial—ways.

Legislating for Constituents

Legislators disagree about the proper way to relate to the views of their constituents. The most common conception of the role of a legislator is that of trustee. This concept is generally traced to the British writer and politician Edmund Burke, who told his constituents after they elected him to the House of Commons (the British equivalent of our House of Representatives) in 1774:

> Certainly, gentlemen, it ought to be the happiness and the glory of a representative, to live in the strictest union, the closest correspondence, and the most unreserved communication with his constituents. Their wishes ought to have great weight with him, their opinions high respect, their business unremitted attention. . . . But his unbiased opinion, his mature judgment, his enlightened conscience, he ought not to sacrifice to you, to any man, or to any set of men living. . . . Your representative owes you, not his industry only, but his judgment, and he betrays, instead of serving you, if he sacrifices it to your opinion.

TABLE 10.2
The Typical Representative's Average Day

ACTIVITY	AVERAGE AMOUNT OF TIME SPENT ON ACTIVITY	TOTALS
In the House chamber		2 hours, 53 minutes
In committee/subcommittee work		1 hour, 24 minutes
Hearings	26 minutes	
Business	9 minutes	
Markups	42 minutes	
Other	7 minutes	
In his/her office		3 hours, 19 minutes
With constituents	17 minutes	
With organized groups	9 minutes	
With others	20 minutes	
With staff aides	53 minutes	
With other representatives	5 minutes	
Answering mail	46 minutes	
Preparing legislation, speeches	12 minutes	
Reading	11 minutes	
On telephone	26 minutes	
In other Washington locations		2 hours, 02 minutes
With constituents at Capitol	9 minutes	
At events	33 minutes	
With leadership	3 minutes	
With other representatives	11 minutes	
With informal groups	8 minutes	
In party meetings	5 minutes	
Personal time	28 minutes	
Other	25 minutes	
Other		1 hour, 40 minutes
Total		11 hours, 18 minutes

Source: U.S. House of Representatives, Commission on Administrative Review, *Administrative Reorganization and Legislative Management* (95th Congress, 1st session, 1977, H. Doc. 95-232), pp. 18–19.

Edmund Burke. (Culver Pictures)

Scholars who have studied the behavior—not just the public statements—of members of Congress have developed a third category: politico. The politico is someone concerned primarily with re-election or personal advancement. This individual will vary his or her views depending on the circumstances and rewards. Many think that most members of Congress act, in fact, as politicos.

Relating to Constituents: "Home Style"

Research by Richard Fenno suggests that the above-named categories are too general. Fenno traveled with a wide variety of representatives in their districts, studying what he came to call their home style. The three components of home style are (1) the representative's allocation of resources—his or hers and those of the staff, (2) the representative's "presentation of self" to constituents, and (3) the representative's explanation of his or her Washington activity to those in the district. Each person does each of these tasks somewhat differently, Fenno found. Even more interesting, representatives tend to divide the constituency into four different groups, and they treat each group differently. The largest group is the district as a whole, or the *geographic constituency*. More important to most members is the second, smaller group: the *re-election constituency*—those citizens the member believes have voted or will vote for him or her. Smaller still is what Fenno calls the *primary constituency*—the strongest supporters, those who determine election results. Finally, there is the smallest group—the handful of close advisors, longtime friends, and emotional supporters who make up the *personal constituency*. Interestingly, Fenno concluded: "The House members I observed give the same explanations for their Washington activity before people who disagree with them as before people who agree with them—before nonsupporters as well as supporters, from one end to the other in the most segmented of districts."[16]

According to this view, the representative is a free agent. Studies have shown that in most legislative bodies, a majority of representatives view their role in these terms.[13] But there is another role concept, less commonly held by legislators but more commonly held by constituents: that of the representative as a delegate or agent of the voters who elected him or her. This view is common in the House but less so in the Senate.[14] As one representative told Lewis Dexter:

> I'm here to represent my district. . . . This is part of my actual belief as to the function of a congressman. . . . What is good for the majority of districts is good for the country. What snarls up the system is these so-called statesmen—congressmen who vote for what they think is the country's interest. . . . Let the senators do that. . . . They're paid to be statesmen; we aren't.[15]

[13]See John C. Wahlke, Heinz Eulau, William Buchanan, and Leroy C. Ferguson, *The Legislative System* (New York: Wiley, 1962).

[14]For the results of a study, see Davidson, *The Role of the Congressman*, p. 117. Davidson found that in a group of 87 representatives, 46 percent were "politicos," 28 percent were "trustees," and 23 percent were "delegates."

[15]Lewis A. Dexter, "The Representative and His District," in *New Perspectives on the House of Representatives*, ed. Robert L. Peabody and Nelson W. Polsby (Chicago: Rand McNally, 1963), p. 6.

[16]Richard F. Fenno, Jr., "U.S. House Members in Their Constituencies: An Exploration," *American Political Science Review* 71, no. 3 (September 1977), 913. For a more detailed presentation, see his subsequent book, *Home Style: House Members in Their Districts* (Boston: Little, Brown, 1978). See also Glenn Parker, *Homeward Bound: Explaining Changes in Congressional Behavior* (Pittsburgh: Univ. of Pittsburgh Press, 1986).

Representing the People in Theory

Just what do we mean when we say that Congress does, or should, represent the people? One view, often called the *authorization* concept, emphasizes elections. The people authorize certain individuals—members of Congress—to represent them by electing them to serve.

Others argue that the essence of representation is *accountability*—the fact that representatives must stand trial for their behavior in elections by which they can be supported or validated by reelection or rejected by defeat.

Still others suggest that the essence of representation is *similarity*—the similarity, sameness, likeness, or resemblance of the representative and those being represented. This is what we mean when we speak of a photograph or a painting as being "a good representation" of its subject. In a political representative, this similarity may be in background, attitudes, or behavior.

There is another, more difficult view. It holds that representation is *symbolization*—that the representative is a symbol standing for what he or she represents. We know this best in our flag, which represents or symbolizes our nation. Indeed, we even "pledge allegiance *to the flag* of the United States of America, *and to the Republic for which it stands*. . . . " Notice, we do not simply say "I pledge allegiance to the Republic for which the flag stands." We may view presidents in the same way, as symbols of the people as well as of the country, not only when they go abroad to represent us externally to other nations and peoples but also when they speak to us at home as our government.

But something is missing from all four of these concepts of representation—something that most Americans seem to feel is important. That something is *responsiveness*—a tendency to solicit, understand, and take account of the views of constituents. As Hanna Pitkin remarked after surveying these other concepts of representation:

> It seems to me that we show a government to be representative not by demonstrating its control over its subjects but just the reverse, by demonstrating that its subjects have control over what it does. Every government's actions are attributed to its subjects formally, legally. But in a representative government this attribution has substantive content: the people really do act through their government, and are not merely passive recipients of its actions. . . . For in a representative government the governed must be capable of action and judgment, capable of initiating government activity, so that the government may be conceived as responding to them.[17]

Representing the People in Practice

Which of these concepts of representation is relevant to the way our Congress represents us, the people? The concept of *representation as authorization by election* seems of limited relevance in our system, where barely a majority of those eligible vote for president, and even fewer vote in congressional elections.

The concept of *representation as accountability by reelection* suffers, too; study after study shows that voters are largely ignorant of the positions taken by incumbents. In addition, there seem to be significant built-in advantages to incumbency in elections—ranging from free mailing privileges to greater visibility in the media—that limit the power of the discontented to oust the occupant.

The concept of *representation as similarity between elected and electors* seems not to apply well; as we saw above, our members of Congress are very unlike the electorate in age, sex, race, religion, wealth, and previous occupation.

What of the concept of *representation as symbolization?* Our legislators may fare better as symbols. It is significant that studies report that people look negatively upon Congress and yet have generally positive assessments of their own individual senators and representatives. The member of Congress may be able to symbolize the government as a whole in much the same way that the president, or even the flag, does.[18]

We are left nonetheless with our fifth concept: *representation as responsiveness.*[19] On this we have much more information. Studies we shall examine below conclude that representatives often do seem to vote in accordance with their images of what their constituents want. But there is ample evidence that these images are often inaccurate and generally somewhat foggy. As one pioneering study concluded: "Busyness blocked effective communication of constituents' views to their congressmen.

---

[17]Hanna Pitkin, *The Concept of Representation* (Berkely: Univ. of California Press, 1967), p. 235.

[18]In *Congress in Change: Evolution and Reform*, ed. Norman J. Ornstein (New York: Praeger, 1975), p. 286.

[19]Some scholars further distinguish among categories or types of responsiveness: service (to individual constituents), allocation (to the district as a whole), policy, and symbolic. See Heinz Eulau and Paul Karps, "The Puzzle of Representation," *Legislative Studies Quarterly* 2 (1976), 233–54.

A congressman can seldom readily inform himself as to how his constituents feel about any issue. A sense of acting in the dark about public opinion plagued many of the legislators we interviewed."[20] These researchers concluded: "A congressman very largely gets back what he puts out. . . . He controls what he hears both by his attention and by his attitudes. He makes the world to which he thinks he is responding."[21] To the extent that this is true, the representative plays much the same role as the president and other political figures in shaping political images in the minds of the public—a role we examined in our discussion of participation in Chapter 3.

It may be, then, that as our system operates, the representative actually functions less as someone who responds to constituency input or The Will of the People and more as someone who generates support for the existing system in the minds of the public by serving as a symbol of responsiveness.[22]

Upon closer reflection, this situation is not surprising. A large percentage of a representative's constituents will have voted for the opponent, and a majority will not belong to the representative's party. Furthermore, public opinion on a given question will likely be seriously split, even within a given district. Thus, the most a member can do on a given issue is reflect the majority sentiment in the district, assuming he or she knows what it is. In some cases, this may not be too difficult. Some districts are remarkably homogeneous. For example, residents of Maryland's Washington suburban district have about ten times the family income of residents of the Bronx in New York City. But such homogeneous extremes are unusual. Most members have districts that are much more diverse.[23] This makes it harder for members who want to represent their districts to know how to do so.

Observers and members alike also often point out that developments in the environment in which Congress operates make representation of any sort very difficult. Among them are the decline of parties; the fragmentation of the electorate into small, diverse special-interest groups; the fact that congressional districts rarely coincide with the communities that do exist (an unfortunate byproduct of *Baker* v. *Carr*); a growing selfishness among many voters; the rules governing (or misgoverning) campaign finance; the trend toward early, voluntary retirement from Congress; and what Dennis Hale speaks of as the "fear" that grips more and more members of Congress as they confront their constituents.[24]

While this picture is perhaps too gloomy, there is no doubt that the job of a representative is more demanding than ever. Experts have reached several different conclusions regarding these limits on representatives' responsiveness.[25] Fenno suggests "the possibility that constituents may want good access as much as good policy from their representative. They may want 'a good man' or 'a good woman' whom they judge on the basis of home style and whom they trust to be a good representative in terms of policy."[26]

A different approach argues that it is the *Congress as a whole* that should be assessed in terms of its representation of *American public opinion as a whole*. This concept of "collective representation" can be used in comparing congressional votes to public opinion on major issues.[27] One such study found that

> however it happened—by recruitment, campaigning, election, adjustment of opinions because of representational roll commitments, or whatever—Congress was reasonably representative of the nationwide public on major issues, a finding that might surprise the cynics who assert that our political system does not reflect the will of the people.[28]

[20]Raymond Bauer, Ithiel de Sola Pool, and Lewis Dexter, *American Business and Public Policy* (New York: Atherton, 1963), p. 413. See also John Kingdon, *Congressmen's Voting Decisions*, 2d ed. (New York: Harper & Row, 1981).

[21]Bauer et al., *American Business and Public Policy*, pp. 420–21.

[22]John C. Wahlke, a close observer of legislative politics, has suggested something like this. See his article "Policy Demands and System Support: The Role of the Represented," in *Modern Parliaments: Change or Decline?* ed. Gerhard Loewenberg (Chicago: Aldine-Atherton, 1971), pp. 141–71. My tracing of these arguments owes much to an unpublished manuscript by Jack D. Jacobs on the concept of representation in American politics.

[23]You can find out what your own district is like by checking the volume for your state issued after the 1980 census by the Census Bureau. Or, for a capsule description, look up your congressional district in the *Almanac of American Politics*, published every two years by National Journal, or *Politics in America: Members of Congress in Washington and At Home*, published every two years by Congressional Quarterly.

[24]Dennis Hale, Introduction to *The U.S. Congress*, ed. D. Hale (New Brunswick, NJ: Transaction, 1983), p. xxvi.

[25]For a comprehensive survey, see Malcolm E. Jewell, "Legislator-Constituency Relations and the Representative Process," *Legislative Studies Quarterly* 8 no. 3 (August 1983), 303–37.

[26]Fenno, "House Members in Their Constituencies" p. 915.

[27]See Robert Weissberg, "Collective vs. Dyadic Representation in Congress," *American Political Science Review* 72, no. 2 (June 1978), 535–47.

[28]Charles H. Backstrom, "Congress and the Public: How Representative of the One Is the Other?" *American Politics Quarterly* 5, no. 4 (October 1977), 411–35. The study actually found that in the 92nd Congress, elected in 1970, the House averaged 11 percentage points and the Senate 20 percentage points less conservative than the public across six issues.

If this is true, it may explain why there is such great citizen apathy toward legislative elections and why citizens are generally willing to tolerate unresponsive legislators in their districts, as Robert Weissberg suggests.[29]

In any case, our representatives still must face their constituents and stand for reelection from time to time; and in between they must legislate. Large, almost philosophical questions of how to "represent the people" may rarely arise in daily legislation. But critical questions of how to vote certainly do. We have already seen something of what a day in the life of a member of Congress is like in practical terms. We shall now approach the subject from the other direction, to see what a day in the life of Congress is like.

WHAT DOES CONGRESS DO?

If we wish to know what Congress actually does, we might think that a sensible place to look would be the *Congressional Record*. This official daily publication, which describes itself as containing "proceedings and debates of the Congress," has been published every day Congress was in session since 1872. A glance at it suggests that it prints every word every member says on the floor of either house, for it averages perhaps 250 pages of small print a day.

On October 18, 1972, the Congressional Record reports, Representative Hale Boggs (Democrat of Louisiana) addressed the House. "In the next few minutes," he is quoted as saying, "I would like to note for members the great amount of significant legislation enacted during the session." After doing so, according to the report, he wished every representative a Merry Christmas and a Happy New Year.

Observers might disagree about the impressiveness of the record of that session of Congress. But no one could fault the sentiments, coming as they did as the Congress was about to adjourn. However, any follower of Congress, or any reader of the daily paper, would question the report that Hale Boggs had addressed the House that day. For Hale Boggs had been killed in an airplane crash in Alaska two days earlier.

[29]Weissberg, "Collective vs. Dyadic Representation in Congress," p. 547.

The Activities of Congress

Bizarre reports such as the one above may occur because Congress has developed a way of allowing members to record not what they actually said but what they would have said had they been present and had there been time. Members are so busy with other important tasks that they cannot always—or often—be present. Indeed, at any given time, unless an important vote is actually being taken, it is unlikely that there will be more than a handful of members "on the floor." Nor is there often enough time. If each of the 435 representatives spoke only once for only one minute, a debate would take more than seven hours! In the session Representative Boggs was "addressing," 17,230 bills were introduced in the House, 954 were reported out of committee for floor debate, and 858 were passed. (In the Senate 4133 bills were introduced, 930 were reported out of committee, and 927 were passed.) If the House were in continuous round-the-clock session seven days a week for two years, there would be barely enough time for each representative to speak for one minute on each bill. Table 10.3 shows the number of bills and laws dealt with by the Ninety-ninth Congress in its two-year term.

The workload of Congress—and therefore of every member—is staggering, even if we omit the constituency services and consider only the legislation. It should be clear that it is virtually impossible to have actual debate on a proposed bill on the floor—debate that might change someone's mind or even just inform that person of what the

TABLE 10.3

Congressional Workload, Ninety-ninth Congress, January 1985 to October 1986

	SENATE	HOUSE
Days in session	313	218
Time in session	2519	1,894
Measures introduced and referred to committee	4080	11,602
Measures reported out of committee for action	1023	837
Measures passed[a]	1327	1,368
Bills vetoed[b]	1	6
Vetoes overridden	2	2

[a]For the most part, the same measures are included in House and Senate totals.

[b]Indicates in which house the vetoed bill originated.

Source: Congressional Record, December 20, 1985 and October 18, 1986.

ACTION UNIT 10.1

How to Find Out What's Going On in Congress

It is easy to find out the current status of any bill in Congress, or even whether or not a bill has been introduced in the current session—or any session back to 1974—on a particular subject. Just call the Legislative Status Office, 202-225-1772, or write to it at Washington, DC 20515. Its computer can produce a free printout overnight.

To find out whether a bill that has been passed by Congress has been signed or vetoed by the president, call 202-456-2226.

To learn what the current legislative program is, call 202-225-7400 for the House, or 202-224-8601 for the Senate. Both parties prepare tapes providing running accounts of proceedings on the floors of both houses. To listen to these "cloakroom tapes," call these numbers:

- Senate Democratic: 202-224-8541
- Senate Republican: 202-224-8601
- House Democratic: 202-225-7400
- House Republican: 202-225-7430

You can also get information or help from your own senators or representative. To speak to their offices, call the Capitol Hill switchboard, 202-224-3121, and ask for them by name.

If you want to know who's in Congress, or who your representative and senators are, you can consult the *Congressional Directory*, published each year by the government and available either in most libraries or from the Government Printing Office, Washington, DC 20402, in paperback. It includes biographies of all members, maps of their districts, lists of committees, their members and staffs, as well as lists of government departments, agencies, and courts. To learn more about your members' views and the politics of their districts, take a look at the *Almanac of American Politics,* edited by Michael Barone et al. and published every two years as a paperback by *National Journal.* The newest resource to summarize and evaluate the performance of all members of Congress and to describe each district is *Politics in America: Members of Congress in Washington and at Home* (Washington, DC: Congressional Quarterly Press), also published every two years. And for a wide range of statistical data, see *Vital Statistics on Congress,* published every two years in paperback in Washington, DC, by American Enterprise Institute.

You could follow what happens in Congress by subscribing to the official *Congressional Record.* But you'll understand more if you read instead the *Weekly Report* published by a private Washington research organization called Congressional Quarterly (CQ). This report covers all important happenings in Congress, as well as many developments in the executive and judicial branches. Most academic libraries subscribe to the CQ *Weekly Report.* You can, too, as a student, for $90 per year, from CQ, 1414 22nd Street NW, Washington, DC 20037. Another useful weekly source is *National Journal,* which concentrates on the executive branch but includes helpful coverage of Congress. It, too, is available in most academic libraries, and it may be obtained at the special academic rate of $78 a year from Government Research Corp., 1730 M Street NW, Washington, DC 20036.

Finally, if you live in an area wired for cable, you can probably watch the House of Representatives and the Senate live every day they are in session over the C-SPAN networks, which also carry other interesting public-affairs programming when the House is not in session.

bill says (bills are almost always too long to read conveniently), let alone what it will really do.

This means that members of Congress are generally dependent on their staffs for assistance—and often for instruction—on how to vote. But even more, it means that the Congress itself is dependent upon its committees for the real work. In turn, the committees are dependent on their staffs of professionals for preparing legislation for committee consideration, arranging committee hearings, and doing background research. There are now over 30,000 people working as congressional staff. The best account of a day in the life of Congress is therefore likely to be found in its *Daily Digest*, which lists the day's schedule of floor action and committee meetings. Action Unit 10.1 shows how to find out what's going on in Congress.

Given how many things members of Congress have to do, we could be excused for wondering how legislation ever gets passed. In a sense, the obstacles are doubled by the fact that both houses of Congress must pass each bill in identical form before it can become law. And if they don't agree, they have to appoint members to serve on a conference committee to iron out the differences or construct a mutually acceptable compromise.

The Functions of Congress

If we look deeper, we find that the challenge is even greater. For Congress has three basic functions on most topics: making policy, providing funds, and oversight (checking how programs are carried out).

Policy Making

The first function of Congress is to *develop and approve policy* on a question or topic—usually by passing a bill establishing a government agency or instructing an existing agency to take on a new task or program. Once such an agency or program is set up, it may carry on for many years without further long-term congressional policy making.

Funding

Second, Congress must provide the funds necessary to carry out its policy instructions. Funding is done in three major stages, as we saw in Perspective 3. First, Congress passes a "budget resolution" early each year that sets targets for spending in all areas of government activity. Second, Congress *authorizes expenditure* of a certain specified sum for a program or agency over the coming year. This decision is made first in a committee specializing in the subject. The whole House and the whole Senate must then approve the authorization bill. The third stage of funding is the *appropriations* phase. Appropriations bills originate in the House Appropriations Committee and, after passage by the whole House, go to the Senate for approval or modification. Of course, if the Senate makes changes—as it always does—a conference committee must develop a compromise, which then must be passed in identical form by both houses.

Oversight

Once money has been both authorized and appropriated, and the president has signed both bills, the proper agency or program in the executive branch may spend the money. But that doesn't end the role of Congress. The third major legislative responsibility of Congress is to keep an eye on how well the various parts of the executive branch are fulfilling their responsibilities to carry out the laws, and how effectively they are spending their appropriations. This function is generally called **congressional oversight**, and we shall examine it later in this chapter.[30]

Policy making, funding, and oversight are very large responsibilities. They must be done by the Congress on each of hundreds of problems, from national energy policy to day care, from foreign affairs and military policy to relations with cities, from space exploration to urban housing. With so many concerns on which they must act and vote, members of Congress inevitably tend to specialize on one or two problems. Yet matters are so complex that they still need massive help. As a result, the major responsibility falls to the committees.

THE STRUCTURE OF CONGRESS

The Committee and Subcommittee System

A century ago a young political scientist named Woodrow Wilson wrote a book on Congress. As president he would later be accused of failing to understand the powers and privileges of Congress. But when he wrote *Congressional Government*, he understood perfectly.

"The House sits," he wrote,

> not for serious discussion, but to sanction the conclusions of its committees as rapidly as possible. It legislates in its committee rooms, not by the determination of majorities, but by the resolutions of specially commissioned minorities; so it is not far from the truth to say that Congress in session is Congress on public exhibition, whilst Congress in its committee rooms is Congress at work.[31]

It wasn't always that way. Both houses got along fine without standing (permanent) committees in the early years of the Republic. The House began slowly to establish them from 1795 on, and the Senate began to follow suit in 1816. By the time Wilson wrote, in 1885 there were some 60 in the House and 70 in the Senate. And it was not until the Legislative Reorganization Act of 1946 that the number went from over 100 in each house to 19 in the House and 15 in the Senate. But the result of the pruning of committees has been a multiplication of subcommittees (145 in the House and 111 in the Senate); and it is probably fair to say that

---

[30]See Marcus E. Ethridge, *Legislative Participation in Implementation* (New York: Praeger, 1985).
[31]Quoted in Warren Weaver, *Both Your Houses* (New York: Praeger, 1972), p. 60.

TABLE 10.4
House and Senate Committees, 100th Congress

HOUSE COMMITTEES	SENATE COMMITTEES
The major committees	The major committees
Appropriations: Handles all appropriations bills, which fund about half of all government agencies.	Appropriations: Handles all appropriations bills, which fund about half of all governmental agencies.
Armed Services: Handles all bills involving the military.	Armed Services: Handles all bills involving the military.
Budget: Reports resolutions that set taxing and spending target figures for the federal budget.	Budget: Reports resolutions that set taxing and spending target figures for the federal budget.
Foreign Affairs: Handles foreign policy programs and issues.	Finance: Handles revenue measures and funding for programs that do not require appropriations.
Rules: Grants each bill reported to the floor a "rule" specifying the procedures for debate. It is controlled by the majority leadership.	Foreign Relations: Has jurisdiction over treaties, nominations of ambassadors and important national security officials and handles foreign policy programs and issues.
Ways and Means: Handles all revenue measures and funding for programs that do not require appropriations.	Other important committees
Other important committees	Agriculture, Nutrition and Forestry
Agriculture	Banking, Housing and Urban Affairs
Banking, Finance, and Urban Affairs	Commerce, Science and Transportation
Education and Labor	Energy and Natural Resources
Energy and Commerce	Environment and Public Works
Government Operations	Judiciary
Interior and Insular Affairs	Labor and Human Resources
Judiciary	Minor committees
Merchant Marine and Fisheries	Governmental Affairs
Public Works and Transportation	Rules and Administration
Science, Space, and Technology	Small Business
Minor committees	Veterans' Affairs
District of Columbia	Select committees
House Administration	On Ethics
Post Office and Civil Service	On Intelligence
Small Business	Special Committee on Aging
Standards of Official Conduct	
Veterans' Affairs	
Select committees	**JOINT COMMITTEES**
On Aging	
On Children, Youth and Families	Economics
On Hunger	Library
On Intelligence	Printing
On Narcotics Abuse and Control	Taxation

what Wilson saw happening in committees now happens instead in subcommittees. Table 10.4 lists House and Senate committees. The abundance of subcommittees to these committees reveals the extent of the multiplication, even after the further Senate reorganization and pruning in 1977. In addition, the Speaker of the House occasionally appoints "select committees" to deal with special concerns.[32]

There is evidence that subcommittees are now sometimes more powerful than committees themselves. In 1977, for example, two veteran House members passed up the opportunity to head a standing committee (Merchant Marine and Fisheries) in order to keep their places as chairpersons of subcommittees of another more important committee (Interstate and Foreign Commerce).[33]

Members of Congress are so busy, and the congressional agendas are so long, that committees and subcommittees gain more and more responsibility—and more and more power.[34] One study of the Senate revealed that if 60 to 80 percent of a committee voted for a provision, that provision

---

[32]See Steven S. Smith and Christopher J. Deering, *Committees in Congress* (Washington: CQ Press, 1984), and *National Journal*, May 16, 1987, a special issue on "The Hill People."

[33]Michael J. Malbin, "Subcommittee Musical Chairs," *National Journal*, March 5, 1977, p. 360.

[34]See Roger H. Davidson, "Subcommittee Government: New Channels for Policy Making," in *The New Congress*, ed. Thomas E. Mann and Norman J. Ornstein (Washington, DC: American Enterprise Institute, 1981), chap. 4.

would be passed on the floor of the whole Senate 90 percent of the time. If more than 80 percent of committee members supported it, its passage by the Senate was a certainty.[35] This suggests the extent to which members depend on the judgment of their committees and thus reveals something of the power of committees in general.

But some committees are more powerful than others. As we have already seen, the appropriations committees control the purse strings and, therefore, have greater power than other committees. And because money bills originate in the House, the House Appropriations Committee is more important than the corresponding committee in the Senate. Each house also has a committee that has jurisdiction over tax and other revenue bills: the House Ways and Means Committee and the Senate Finance Committee. Every American knows the importance of taxes, so the importance of the tax committees is not surprising. The two Budget Committees, created in 1974, round out the list of financial committees.

Informal Groups

Committees are not the only important groups in Congress. In the past several decades, state and city delegations, regional groupings, programmatic groups, and special-interest caucuses have all come to play important roles in the legislative process. These groups serve several important functions for their members. They provide information; and they may offer leadership where relevant legislative issues are being considered in committee or on the floor.[36]

State and City Delegations

When issues of special concern to a city or a state arise, the members of the House from that unit, regardless of party, may unite to influence the outcome. They may also join together to support a member of their delegation in his or her quest for a committee position. The cohesiveness of state delegations varies, however. One California journalist

in Washington recently wrote: "One out of every ten members of Congress is from California. That should be good news for all of us. But the delegation is much less powerful than its sheer numbers would indicate. The 43 Congressmen can't agree to disagree long enough to figure out what's best for the folks back home."[37] On the other hand, a senior House Democrat remarked of the members of the Texas delegation: "They have good cohesion. They think as a republic. There's a strong kind of identity. Texans have a self-image of loyalty and devotion to Texas."[38]

Regional Groupings

We noted the activities of the Northeast-Midwest Congressional Coalition in our discussion of the Snowbelt in Chapter 2. Among others are the Congressional Rural Caucus and the New England Congressional Caucus.

Programmatic Groups

Some groups are united by interest in particular policy questions. The first informal group organized was the Democratic Study Group. It was founded in 1959 by liberal Democrats after they had made electoral gains. Its purpose has been to help liberals with research and organization. In 1972 conservative Democrats founded the Democratic Research Organization as a counter to the DSG. The next year, conservative Republicans created the Republican Study Committee. Liberal Republicans, who are few in the House, have had a small organization, the Wednesday Group, since 1963.

Special-Interest Caucuses

A caucus is a group of members with a common interest. There has been a Congressional Black Caucus in the House since 1971 and a Hispanic Caucus since 1976. There is also a caucus on women's issues, which has 100 members, including 22 women. In recent years special-interest caucuses have sprung up like mushrooms after a storm. In fact, there is even a Mushroom Caucus formed sev-

[35]Donald Matthews, *U.S. Senators and Their World* (New York: Vintage, 1964).

[36]See Arthur G. Stevens, Jr., Daniel P. Mulhollan, and Paul S. Rundquist, "Congressional Structure and Representation: The Role of Informal Groups" (paper delivered at the 1980 annual meeting of the American Political Science Association, Washington, DC, August 1980).

[37]George L. Baker, "Our Men in Washington," *New West*, October 20, 1980, p. 52. California now has 45 House members following the 1980 reapportionment.

[38]Quoted by Irwin B. Arieff, "State Delegations Strive to Protect Their Interests through Concerted Effort," *Congressional Quarterly Weekly Report*, August 2, 1980, p. 2189.

eral years ago to seek protection for the American mushroom growers against imports of Asian mushrooms—and it has 61 members! Other caucuses are concerned with matters such as steel, shipyards, textiles, ports, solar energy, and tourism.[39]

The "Conservative Coalition"

Some experts also refer to a "conservative coalition" made up of Republicans and southern Democrats who tend to vote together against northern Democrats. Such a voting pattern has long been found on such issues as balancing the budget, limiting federal regulation of business, and shifting federal spending from social programs to defense. Indeed, some trace its origin to 1937. In earlier times, it operated to prevent passage of civil-rights laws. The conservative coalition is less organized than most of the other informal groups: It has no staff and office, while the DSG—the largest—has a paid staff of 20. But it has been very effective in reducing the ability of the Democratic party to function as a governing party even when the party has had congressional majorities. Indeed, as David Brady and Charles Bullock have argued, it might be said that "the conservative voting alliance's early and continued success helped to make congressional government coalition government."[40]

Rules in the House and the Senate

Certain differences in the power of committees and informal groupings derive from differences in the ways the two houses operate. Because the House has 435 members, the time allowed for debate must be limited. In practice, this is done by the House Rules Committee. The Rules Committee is extremely powerful; it decides which of the bills "reported out" (approved) by committees will be scheduled for consideration by the House as a whole, whether amendments will be allowed on the floor, and how much debate will be permitted. This decision by the committee is called **granting a rule.** The "rule" is the statement of terms on which the bill may be considered by the House. The Rules Committee has usually acted as an arm of the leadership—one reason why it has long been powerful. For many years, its members were mostly Republicans and southern Democrats, and its influence was very conservative. In recent years its ability to kill bills has been limited somewhat by changes in its membership and in House procedures. Still, it continues to be a very powerful committee.

The Senate, with only 100 members and a tradition of unlimited debate, operates quite differently in these matters. The majority leader—the elected head of the party that has a majority in the Senate—determines the scheduling of bills; and Rule 22 of the Senate allows unlimited debate unless cloture is voted. **Cloture,** or closing of debate on a given bill, can be forced only if (1) 16 senators sign a petition requesting it, (2) two days pass, and then (3) three-fifths of the senators present vote for cloture. If all this occurs, then no senator may speak for more than one additional hour on the bill before a vote must be taken.

The importance of the cloture rule is that it is the only way of preventing a small group of senators from killing a bill by talking it to death. Even a single senator can **filibuster**[41] a bill by talking nonstop for several days. With the help of a few colleagues, he or she can delay proceedings so long that others give up and agree to let the bill die so that the Senate can get on with bills the senators are more interested in. This is how southern senators long prevented passage of civil-rights legislation. Ultimately, the cloture rule was eased in the 1960s. This variation in limits on debate is but one of the important differences between the Senate and the House. Generally, it is from the Senate rather than the House that presidential candidates come. While representatives often try to "advance" to the Senate when an opportunity arises, there is no known case of a senator seeking to switch to the House. Table 10.5 summarizes important differences between the two houses of Congress.

---

[39]See Ward Sinclair, "Got a Cause? Get a Caucus," *Washington Post*, October 7, 1979.

[40]David W. Brady and Charles S. Bullock III, "Coalition Politics in the House of Representatives," in *Congress Reconsidered*, 2d ed., ed. Lawrence C. Dodd and Bruce I. Oppenheimer (Washington, DC: CQ Press, 1981), p. 202. For an account of the coalition's recent success, see "Conservative Alliance Votes Less Often, More Effectively," *Congressional Quarterly Weekly Report*, January 10, 1981, pp. 84–86.

[41]No one knows how this term, which originally meant a "pirate," came to be applied to a political speech. Perhaps it is because the speaker hijacks or seizes the debate, or commandeers the body, by this intrusion. For a less venturesome discussion of the term, see William Safire, *The New Language of Politics* (New York: Random House, 1968), p. 143.

TABLE 10.5
Important Differences between the House and the Senate

HOUSE		SENATE
Initiates all revenue bills	Special constitu-tional powers	Must give "advice and consent" to treaties
Must pass all articles of impeachment		Must approve many presidential appointments
		Must try impeached officials
Larger (435 voting, 3 observers)	Structure	Smaller (100)
More hierarchically organized		Less hierarchically organized
Power less evenly distributed		Power more evenly distributed
Shorter term (two years), all elected at once		Longer term (six years), one-third elected every two years
Nongermane amendments allowed		Broader, more diverse constituencies (states)
Centralized in practice	Leadership	Less centralized in practice
Major officers:		Major officers:
Speaker of the House		Vice-president
Majority leader		President pro tempore
Majority whip		Majority leader
Minority leader		Majority whip
Minority whip		Minority leader
		Minority whip
More committees	Committee procedures	Fewer committees
Bills are introduced into "the hopper"		Bills may be introduced from the floor
Speaker refers bills; challenge very difficult		Referral decisions may be appealed from the floor
Speaker may create ad hoc committees		No ad hoc committees may be created
Committees almost always consider legislation first		Committee consideration of legislation may be bypassed
Committees are more important than floor for decision		Floor action is as important as committees for decision
Generally controlled by majority party leader and Rules Committee	Scheduling	Generally mutually agreed by majority and minority leaders
Only key members consulted		Major efforts are made to accommodate senators' scheduling requests
Elaborate systems of "calendars" and special days for calling up measures		Scheduling is by informal consultation
Voting by voice, standing, roll call, and teller		No teller votes
More rigid	Debate rules	More flexible
Seniority more important in determining power of members		Seniority less important in determining power of members
Debate limits determined by Rules Committee (usually one hour)		Debate limits rare; if any, set by full Senate via unanimous consent or cloture
Amendment rules determined by Rules Committee		Amendments controlled by full Senate
Nongermane amendments prohibited on floor		Nongermane amendments allowed
Acts more quickly	Other characteristics	Acts more slowly
Usually less dominant in conference committees		Usually more dominant in conference committees
Impersonal		Personal
Less prestige		More prestige
Less media coverage of members		More media coverage of members
More member specialization with fewer committee assignments		Less member specialization with more committee assignments
Lower turnover in membership		Higher turnover in membership

Rivalry between the House and Senate

Not surprisingly, there tends to be strong rivalry between the two houses. This rivalry may well be an outgrowth of their different functions. The Senate, as we have seen, has more foreign policy re-sponsibilities because it must ratify treaties and confirm or reject presidential appointments. These responsibilities tend to make it more sympathetic to the presidential perspective. The House, on the other hand—with special revenue responsibilities and with smaller districts in which members face

TABLE 10.6
Important Recent Changes in Congress

1970–present	Many caucuses and other informal groups created (see Table 10.5.)
1971–1972	Office of Technology Assessment created
	Computers introduced
	House Republicans weaken automatic seniority norm
1973–1974	House opens most committee sessions to public
	War Powers Act passed (see Chapter 19)
	Budget and Impoundment Control Act passed (see Perspective 3)
	Budget Committee established
	Congressional Budget Office created
	House Democrats weaken automatic seniority norm
	House subcommittees strengthened
1975–1976	Senate reduces filibuster cloture requirement
	Senate opens most committee sessions to public
	Conference committee sessions opened to public
1977–1978	Senate and House adopt new ethics rules to guide conduct of members
	Senate revises committee system

elections every two years—is bound to identify more closely with the taxpayers. This situation is often to be reflected in more conservatism in the House as a whole.

The policy impact of these differences must constantly be reconciled in the conference committees that iron out serious differences in perhaps 10 percent of all congressional bills.[42] They may also be moderated somewhat by the effects of party membership on legislative behavior.

THE PROCESS OF THE CONGRESS

No organization can function without structure. The houses of Congress depend most heavily on the committee system and the rules to provide the framework within which they actually conduct the nation's and their own business. However, understanding the structure is not enough. We must also understand the process—the ways in which committees and rules are used by the leaders and the members to make laws. Therefore, we now look at the roles of party, leaders, rules, norms of behavior, and strategies in shaping the actual conduct of the legislative process in Congress.[43] We shall find that the process, like the structure, has undergone important changes in recent sessions. Table 10.6 summarizes the more important of these changes.

The Role of Party

The Democrats have had a majority in the House continuously since 1955 and had a majority in the Senate from 1955 through 1980 and again starting in 1987. Indeed, as Figure 10.3 shows, in the last half century, the Republicans have controlled the House and the Senate together only in 1947–1948 and 1953–1954. We might expect that when the same party controls both houses, there is greater cooperation between them. After all, on the face of it, the most important division of Congress is not into committees but into parties.[44] Seating on the floor of each house is arranged by party, with Democrats on one side, Republicans on the other, and the occasional independent located in between.

The Party Caucus

Party is especially important in determining leadership of each house. Each party has its own party caucus in each house. The caucus is a meeting of all party members. (The name comes from an old American Indian term for elder or counselor.) The caucus decides on candidates or policy positions, and these decisions are then "counsel," or advice, to members on how to vote in the body as a whole. This caucus is extremely important at the beginning of each two-year session of Congress, when newly elected members arrive and nominations for

---

[42]The figure is Warren Weaver's, from his book *Both Your Houses*, p. 131.
[43]See Walter Oleszek, *Congressional Procedures and the Policy Process* (Washington: CQ Press, 1980).

[44]For recent studies, see *Congress Reconsidered*, 3d ed., ed. Dodd and Oppenheimer; and Barbara Sinclair, *Majority Leadership in the U.S. House* (Baltimore: Johns Hopkins Univ. Press, 1983).

President	Senate		Congress	House of Representatives	
	35	60	1933–73rd	117	310
	25	69	1935–74th	103	319
Roosevelt	16	78	1937–75th	89	331
	23	69	1939–76th	164	261
	28	66	1941–77th	162	268
	37	58	1943–78th	208	218
	38	56	1945–79th	190	242
Truman	51	45	1947–80th	246	188
	42	54	1949–81st	171	262
	47	49	1951–82nd	199	234
	48	47	1953–83rd	221	213
Eisenhower	47	49	1955–84th	203	232
	47	49	1957–85th	200	233
	34	64	1959–86th	153	283
Kennedy–Johnson	35	65	1961–87th	175	262
	34	66	1963–88th	176	258
Johnson	32	68	1965–89th	140	295
	38	64	1967–90th	187	248
Nixon	42	58	1969–91st	192	243
	44	54	1971–92nd	180	255
Nixon–Ford	43	57	1973–93rd	192	243
Ford	38	61	1975–94th	145	290
Carter	38	61	1977–95th	142	293
	41	58	1979–96th	159	276
	53	46	1981–97th	191	242
Reagan	55	45	1983–98th	166	269
	53	47	1985–99th	182	253
	45	55	1987–100th	176	259

Republican   Democratic

FIGURE 10.3

Party Strength in Congress. In the years shown in color, both houses of Congress were controlled by the party in opposition to the president. (Independents not shown.)

officers are made and voted upon. The Democratic caucus in the House also selects possible committee chairs when the Democrats control the House.

The Party Leadership

Each party caucus in the Senate chooses candidates for *party leader* and for **whip** (the person who, with deputy whips, is responsible for rounding up, or whipping into line, party members when a vote is coming). It also elects a policy committee to discuss party positions on legislation, and a committee (the Steering Committee for the Democrats, the Committee on Committees for the Republicans) that then appoints party members to the various standing committees of the Senate.

In the Senate, the party leader of the majority party (almost always the Democrats in the past 50 years) becomes the effective leader of the Senate. The Constitution provides that the vice-president of the United States will serve as the president of the Senate, but in fact the vice-president is rarely there to preside unless a close vote on an important bill is anticipated, on which the vice-president could cast the deciding vote in the event of a tie. The Constitution also created the office of president pro tempore (Latin for "for the time being") to preside in the vice-president's absence. In practice, though, that post has generally gone as an honor to the longest-serving senator, who usually is not interested in the unexciting job of presiding. As a result, the task of presiding is passed around among senators—particularly "junior" senators (those who have served least long).

The situation in the House is somewhat different. The Speaker of the House is necessarily powerful, for he or she presides over sessions, decides who will be recognized to speak, and appoints members of "*select*" (as distinct from "standing") committees to conduct special investigations. The Speaker is elected by the House as a whole but invariably is the candidate chosen by the majority party in its caucus.[45] Nonetheless, the majority party also has a majority leader and a majority whip, just as the minority has a minority leader and a minority whip. Throughout our history, the actual power of the Speaker has varied. At present that power is somewhat limited by recent Democratic reforms, which we shall discuss shortly. Nonetheless, Thomas P. O'Neill, who became the House Speaker in the Ninety-fifth Congress and served until his retirement in 1986, gained power and influence in Congress with the arrival of a Democratic president and remained powerful once a Republican president took office.

The Role of Leadership

"You know, you ask me what are my powers and my authority around here," O'Neill once said to Michael Malbin.

The power to recognize on the floor; little odds and ends—like men get pride out of the prestige of han-

[45]See Garrison Nelson, "Partisan Patterns of House Leadership Change, 1789–1977," *American Political Science Review* 71 (September 1977) 918–39.

Thomas P. O'Neill, speaker of the House from 1976 to 1986. (Alex Webb/Magnum Photos)

dling the Committee of the Whole, being named the Speaker for the day; those little trips that come along—like those trips to China, trips to Russia, things of that nature; or other ad hoc committees or special committees, which I have assignments to; plus the fact that there is a certain aura and respect that goes with the Speaker's office. He does have the power to be able to pick up the telephone and call people. And Members oftentimes like to bring their loyal political leaders or a couple of mayors. And oftentimes they have problems from their area and they need aid and assistance, either legislative-wise or administrative-wise. We're happy to try to open the door for them, having been in the town for so many years and knowing so many people. We do know where a lot of bodies are and we do know how to advise people. And I have an open-door policy. Rare is the occasion when a man has a personal fund-raiser or [is] being personally honored that I don't show up at it. I've made more public appearances and visited areas if they believe I can help them. I'm always accessible. These are part of the duties and the obligations of the Speaker, and it shows the warm hand of friendship. So that's what it's all about.[46]

Speaker O'Neill refers to "little things you can do for people." But the effectiveness of a Speaker depends on much more. A senior Democratic representative who several times tried and failed to win a leadership role, Richard Bolling (Democrat

of Missouri), long watched the techniques of Sam Rayburn (Democrat of Texas)—Speaker whenever the Democrats controlled the House from 1940 to 1961 and generally conceded to be the most effective Speaker in modern history. Bolling later wrote, in a book lamenting the requisites of leadership:

> To maintain personal influence the Speaker is forced to engage in a savage political scramble involving sectional interests, local claims and personal advancements, all of which are more fondly regarded by the inner circle of the House [of which the Speaker has long been a member] than party loyalties or vital national issues. All too often, wise and just legislation becomes a subordinate issue and frequently a total casualty.[47]

Rayburn developed and practiced his varied leadership skills with a group of trusted colleagues. One of them was Lyndon Johnson, who moved on to the Senate, where he became known for his own brand of leadership, often called The Treatment. Historian Arthur Schlesinger, for a time an LBJ aide, later conveyed Johnson's own description of his technique as Senate majority leader:

> The Treatment began immediately: a brilliant, capsule characterization of every Democratic Senator, his strengths and failings, where he fit into the political spectrum; how far he could be pushed, how far pulled; his hates, his loves. And who must oversee all these prima donnas, put them to work, knit them together, know when to tickle this one's vanity, inquire of that one's health, remember this one's five o'clock nip of Scotch, that one's nagging wife? Who must find the hidden legislative path between the South and the North, the public power men and the private power men, the farmers' men and the unions' men, the bomber-boys and the peace-lovers, the eggheads and the fatheads?[48]

Such roles fall generally to the leadership. Some leaders welcome the opportunities, while others resist them. Leaders differ in personality. But to be effective, all must have one key quality: knowledge of—and willingness to use—the rules. Robert C. Byrd (Democrat of West Virginia), served as ma-

[46]Michael J. Malbin, "House Democrats Are Playing with a Strong Leadership Lineup," *National Journal*, June 18, 1977, p. 942.

[47]Richard Bolling, *House Out of Order*, quoted in Weaver, *Both Your Houses*, p. 156. For an interesting collection of articles, see Frank Mackaman, *Understanding Congressional Leadership* (Washington, DC: CQ Press, 1981). And for a survey of eight speakers from Henry Clay to Sam Rayburn, see Richard Cheney (currently a Republican representative) and Lynne Cheney, *Kings of the Hill* (New York: Continuum, 1983).

[48]Quoted in Rowland Evans and Robert Novak, *Lyndon B. Johnson: The Exercise of Power* (New York: New American Library, 1966), pp. 104–5. For more accounts see Merle Miller, *Lyndon: An Oral Biography* (New York: Putnam, 1980), chap. 2. Robert A. Caro, *The Years of Lyndon Johnson: The Path to Power* (New York: Knopf, 1982), discusses Rayburn's style.

jority leader from 1977 until the Republicans gained control of the Senate in 1981 and then again when the Democrats recaptured it in 1987. He once described his role this way:

> The Senate is a forest. There are ninety-nine animals. They're all lions. There's a waterhole in the forest. I'm the waterhole. I don't have power but I have knowledge of the rules. I have knowledge of the precedents. I have knowledge of the schedule. So I'm in a position to do things for others.[49]

The Role of the Rules

Not all rules are readily usable by the leadership in the way that procedural rules are.[50] We have already examined the rules for selection of the leadership itself. Historically, the most important rule in Congress, according to most observers, has been another organizational rule, the seniority system.

The Seniority System

The term *seniority* comes from the same Latin root, meaning "old," as do *senior*, *senile*, and even *senate*. The **seniority system** provides that whoever has served longest gets first choice of whatever is to be chosen. This has important consequences in Congress, especially as regards the selection of committee chairpersons and choice of committee assignments or memberships. According to the seniority rule, the chairperson of a committee is always that committee member from the majority party who has served longest on that committee. And when a committee slot opens up through death, retirement, or defeat, the member of Congress with the longest consecutive service in the Congress has the option of trading a present committee post (perhaps on a less important committee) for the newly available slot.

Because southern members of Congress traditionally came from "safe districts" and were reelected usually without opposition, they rapidly gained seniority. The result was that as long as the

Democrats controlled Congress, southern conservative Democrats controlled committee leadership. In recent years, two things have happened to change this situation. First, some northern liberal Democratic members of Congress have developed safe seats and gained seniority, while Republicans in the South have begun to contest previously safe Democratic seats. Second, both parties have begun to move away from an automatic seniority rule.

In 1971 House Republicans decided to vote by secret ballot for "ranking" minority committee members (the people who would become chairpersons if the Republicans should gain control of the House). Then in January 1973 House Democrats, too, decided to vote. The results were identical to the seniority lists that year. But in 1975, with the influx of new, generally liberal Democratic members, the caucus voted to replace three old senior southern chairpersons. In 1979 it moved three more junior members into important subcommittee chairs. Meanwhile, the Senate Democratic members had also changed their rules to allow voting for chairpersons. Thus far, the changes have been minor. But the rule has been broken, and further change seems likely. Meanwhile, more rapid turnover in membership has lessened the significance of the seniority system.[51]

Procedural Rules

The rules of any body are subject to change, as they are to interpretation. For an organization—or more accurately two organizations, the House and the Senate—run personally, the Congress is remarkably influenced by its procedural rules.[52] "The general impact of the rules in both the House and the Senate is the same," Randall Ripley writes. "The rules protect the power and prerogatives of the standing committees of the House and the Senate by making it very difficult for a bill that does not have committee approval to come to either floor and by making it very difficult to amend bills reported from committee."[53]

This is particularly true in the House, where the Rules Committee is so important. The net effect, as Ripley demonstrates, is that there are multiple

---

[49]Quoted in Laurence Leamer, "Changing," *Washingtonian*, May 1977, p. 127. For an account of the leadership style of Byrd's successor, Republican Howard Baker, see James A. Miller, *Running in Place* (New York: Simon & Schuster, 1986). Baker retired after two years and was succeeded by Robert Dole, who gave way to Byrd again when Democrats recaptured the Senate in 1986.

[50]For a helpful survey of the evolution of the rules and reform efforts, see Norman J. Ornstein, "The Open Congress Meets the President," in *Both Ends of the Avenue*, ed. Anthony King (Washington, DC: American Enterprise Institute, 1983), chap. 7.

[51]See Albert D. Cover, "Seniority in the House: Patterns and Projections," *American Politics Quarterly* 12 (October 1983), 429–40.

[52]For the text of these rules, see Frank Cummings, *Capitol Hill Manual* (Washington, DC: Bureau of National Affairs, 1976), pp. 135–91 (for the standing rules of the Senate) and pp. 192–232 (for the House rules).

[53]Randall Ripley, *Congress: Process and Policy*, 2d ed. (New York: Norton, 1978), pp. 138–39.

"veto points" at which any bill can be delayed or defeated by opponents if they are strong enough. Almost any proposed law must be approved by a House subcommittee, a House committee, the House Rules Committee, the entire House, a Senate subcommittee, a Senate committee, the entire Senate, a conference committee, the entire House and Senate again, and then the president.

To be approved at so many different stages, a major bill must have broad support to begin with. But even that is not likely to be enough. It must also, in most cases, benefit from bargaining, coalition building, and logrolling (or vote trading: I'll support a bill you want if you'll support one I want) among members. We saw these things happening in the case study of NEPA earlier in this chapter. We would find the same thing in studying any important legislation.[54]

"Congressional rules serve many functions," Walter Oleszek writes,

> —they promote stability, divide responsibilities, minimize conflict in daily decisionmaking, legitimize decisions, and distribute power. Paradoxically, because the rules do distribute power, they create tensions between those whose influential positions are protected by the rules and those who have limited influence.[55]

One way in which such tensions have been moderated has been relaxation of seniority rules to allow more recent arrivals more of a role. Another moderating force is the longstanding but always evolving set of informal "norms" that generally govern the conduct of members of Congress.

The Role of Norms, or "the Rules of the Legislative Game"

"There are unwritten rules of behavior, which we have called folkways, in the Senate," Donald Matthews wrote in a pioneering study in 1960.

> These rules are normative, that is, they define how a senator ought to behave. Nonconformity is met with moral condemnation, while senators who conform to the folkways are rewarded with high esteem by their

colleagues. Partly because of this fact, they tend to be the most influential and effective members of the Senate.[56]

"Should the new legislator wish to be heard," George Washington wrote in 1787, "the way to command the attention of the House is to speak seldom, but to important subjects. . . ."[57] Almost 200 years later, newly elected Senator Joseph Clark, while having lunch with Senator Hubert Humphrey, asked Humphrey to tell him how he should behave when he got to the Senate. "In essence he said, 'Keep your mouth shut and your eyes open. It's a friendly, courteous place. You will have no trouble getting along. . . . Don't let your ideology embitter your personal relationships. It won't if you behave with maturity. . . . And above all keep your mouth shut for awhile.'"[58]

In recent years such "rules" have been relaxed, and junior members of Congress now take more active roles than they used to. But there persists a general set of "rules of the game" by which legislators often find it convenient to operate. Perhaps the best general summary of the traditional rules is former Speaker Sam Rayburn's axiom, "If you want to *get* along, *go* along."[59]

Until the 1960s, the norms dictated that a senator was to be a legislator first—and a public personality only if that followed from the conduct of legislative responsibilities. They called for issue specialization, courtesy, and compromise, and a time of apprenticeship for new members. The result, in the view of admirers and critics alike, was a conservative style of decision making that seemed to produce conservative policy outcomes.[60] From the late 1950s on, more and more liberals were elected to the Senate. They found the folkways oppressive and gradually rejected most of them.[61]

[54]For a fascinating case study by a *Washington Post* journalist who covered the entire "career" of a bill in the 95th Congress to charge users of the nation's inland waterways a fee to help maintain them, see T. R. Reid, *Congressional Odyssey: The Saga of a Senate Bill* (San Francisco: Freeman, 1980). And for case studies in the House, see Sinclair, *Majority Leadership in the U.S. House.*

[55]Walter J. Oleszek, *Congressional Procedures and the Policy Process* (Washington, DC: CQ Press, 1978), p. 215.

[56]Matthews, *U.S. Senators and Their World*, p. 116.

[57]J. A. Carroll and M. W. Ashworth, *George Washington*, vol. 7 (New York: Scribner, 1957), p. 591. (vols. 1–6 by Douglas S. Freeman.)

[58]Joseph S. Clark, *Congress: The Sapless Branch* (New York: Harper & Row, 1964), p. 2.

[59]Quoted in Davidson, *The Role of the Congressman*, p. 180, but widely heard on Capitol Hill as elsewhere in America.

[60]See Matthews, *U.S. Senators and Their World*, and William S. White, *Citadel: The Story of the U.S. Senate* (New York: Harper, 1956).

[61]Ross K. Baker, a political scientist who worked as a senator's aide for some years, argues that the place of enfeebled norms and folkways was taken in large part by what he calls "institutional kinship"—"a structure of private understandings among individual senators" which involves "the ability of each senator to define for himself those qualities he prizes in a colleague, rather than have them defined for him by collective agreement on what constitutes the 'good Senator' or 'Senate type.' Each senator is thus free to set his own standards and enforce them unilaterally. It is a form of pact which stipulates that adherence will produce mutual benefits and breaches will bring about common grief." See Baker, *Friend and Foe in the U.S. Senate* (New York: Free Press, 1980), p. 41.

Many of the newer senators had presidential ambitions and became generalists seeking publicity rather than specialist "workhorses." But a careful study of this "new Senate" by Michael Foley found that senators increasingly reacted against the expansion of presidential power at the expense of senatorial prerogative. The result was a renewed appreciation of the value of many of the old norms, not as binding but as desirable when not oppressive.

> Given the increasingly atomized structure of the institution, the proliferation of individual power points, the innumerable opportunities for individual objection, and political aspirations and appetites of the members themselves, any concerted legislative action could only be achieved through the medium of mutual accommodation.[62]

The norm of *mutual accommodation* remains strong in both houses of Congress.[63]

The late Senator Sam Ervin (Democrat of North Carolina), who gained fame as chairperson of the Watergate Committee, expressed it well in a description of his relations with Senator Milton Young (Republican of North Dakota): "I got to know Milt Young very well. And I told Milt, 'Milt, I would just like you to tell me how to vote about wheat and sugarbeets and things like that, if you will just help me out on tobacco and things like that'"[64]

Another norm that remains strong in both houses is institutional loyalty. In practice, this means that members should refrain from criticizing their own institution or its members. The one exception—and it has become an enormous one—is in reelection campaigns. In this study of home style, Fenno found a surprising consistency in one thing:

> Individual members do not take responsibility for the performance of Congress; rather each portrays himself as a fighter against its manifest shortcomings. Their willingness, at some point, to stand and defend their votes contrasts sharply with their disposition to run and hide when a defense of Congress is called for. Congress is not "we"; it is "they." And members of Congress *run* for Congress by running *against* Congress.[65]

The other common norms, specialization and seniority plus apprenticeship, are changing in both houses and are somewhat different in each. *Specialization* is still generally expected in the House, where members have only a few subcommittee assignments, but it is becoming less binding as more members aspire to the presidency. In the Senate, specialization is generally considered a wise way to be effective in lawmaking. But senators are also expected to contribute to developing a national policy agenda, and so they cannot be too narrow.

We have already noted the increasing limitations on seniority as a norm in both houses. *Apprenticeship*—the norm that junior members should learn from their elders for a time before speaking out and becoming active in lawmaking—is a related norm. It has fared even worse. It is virtually dead in the Senate and very weak in the House.

A major reason for the change in norms in both houses has been the turnover in personnel. Barbara Sinclair has explained the situation in the House this way:

> Socialized to politics during the turbulent 1960s, entering the House in a period of challenge to the power structure, and, in the case of many of the large '74 Democratic class, elected from previously Republican districts, the freshmen of the 1970s were unwilling to wait to make their mark. Both personal inclinations and political necessity dictated a high level of activity and full participation at the committee and floor stage immediately. Rules changes which lessened the control of seniority leaders and augmented the staff resources of junior members make such activity possible. Thus norms of apprenticeship and of deference to senior members, already weakened during the 1960s, were given a final blow.[66]

A related casualty has been the norm of *reciprocity* among committees. This norm held that each committee should be presumed to have done its homework on its own bills, so members should "go with the committee on the floor." Now, because of better member staff work and more concern with "making a public record" by legislating, more and more members seek to "legislate on the floor."

Thus, some norms—especially those of mutual

[62]Michael Foley, *The New Senate: Liberal Influence on a Conservative Institution* 1959–1972 (New Haven, CT: Yale Univ. Press, 1980), p. 258.

[63]For a survey of prevailing norms, see Ripley, *Congress*, pp. 121–32.

[64]Quoted in Ripley, *Congress*, p. 125.

[65]Fenno, "House Members in Their Constituencies," p. 914.

[66]Barbara Sinclair, "The Speaker's Task Force as a Leadership Strategy for Coping with the Post-Reform House" (paper delivered at the 1980 annual meeting of the American Political Science Association, Washington, DC, August 1980), p. 3. See also her book *Majority Leadership in the U.S. House*.

accommodation and institutional loyalty—have survived in good shape. Others—specialization and reciprocity—are less powerful now but persist. Seniority is even weaker, and apprenticeship is virtually dead.

But do changes in norms affect the way Congress operates? Michael Foley argues that this question should instead be asked about individual members. Experts find that, in general, the most effective members of Congress are those who still observe the norms of accommodation and reciprocity along with institutional loyalty. Those in the House also observe the norm of specialization. But the most important thing to recognize is that there is now much tolerance of deviation from these norms. As the late Philip Hart, one of the leaders of Senate reform, once put it: "We are all constructively free-wheeling individuals."[67]

INFLUENCES ON CONGRESSIONAL CAREER BEHAVIOR

We have already discussed differing conceptions of the proper role of a legislator—trustee, delegate, and politico—and the more general question of how Congress should represent the people. One's image of how one should behave as a representative is bound to have a general influence on one's conduct. In addition, the conduct of members of Congress will be influenced by their own personal objectives.

Objectives of Members of Congress

Good Public Policy

If we thought about it in the abstract or listened only to the rhetoric of our representatives, we might conclude that the objective of a member of Congress is to discover *the common good* of the country, the state, or the legislative district and then make good public policy so as to achieve it. This action would presumably include developing, supporting, and voting for good legislation. Some politicians may indeed believe that discovering the common good and then making good public policy

is, indeed, their major objective and may act accordingly. But, these days anyway, most observers are more skeptical about the motives of public officials, and few would believe this attitude to be true of them.

Personal Gain

A possible alternative to this selfless pursuit of the common good is seeking *personal gain* or special benefits for oneself. Members of Congress have long been subject to criticism for *conflict of interest*. This term refers to a situation in which someone acts in his or her role as an official in a way that benefits that person as an individual. In other words, one's own personal interest is in conflict with the public interest. In other bodies, such as the courts, officials will usually remove themselves from a case if it involves, for example, a company in which they own stock and so could benefit from their own decision. Members of Congress, however, have never been known to disqualify themselves from voting on legislation in which they have personal financial interests. Nor have they been known to sell their stocks before serving to prevent such situations from arising. In fact, quite the opposite has often been true. Drew Pearson and Jack Anderson some years ago wrote a massive book called *The Case Against Congress*, documenting case after case of apparent conflict of interest.[68] On most issues, however, most representatives have no personal material interest.

Reelection

The third factor often cited is what political scientist David Mayhew calls the electoral connection. Mayhew argues that members of Congress act as "single-minded seekers of reelection." Virtually everything they do, he argues, can be understood best as motivated by the wish to guarantee their own victory in the next election. According to Mayhew, there are really only two things a polit-

---

[67]Quoted in Foley, *New Senate*, p. 258.

[68]Drew Pearson and Jack Anderson, *The Case Against Congress* (New York: Simon & Schuster, 1968). When Susan Welch and John G. Peters studied congressional roll-call votes and personal financial interests as revealed in financial-disclosure statements, they found some evidence of conflict-of-interest voting. When they considered the interests of the members' constituencies, however, they found that these adequately explained the voting. See their paper "Private Interests and Public Interests." presented at the 1980 annual meeting of the American Political Science Association.

ical figure in Congress can do that can be converted into votes: credit claiming and position taking. *Credit claiming* involves doing something that can be cited as a personal accomplishment in office. *Position taking* is stating popular views on issues of public concern. According to Mayhew, the daily chores of Congress, especially legislating, are done *despite* the fact that voters rarely pay attention to them. Voters rarely hold members of Congress responsible for their votes. Indeed, as we noted earlier, voters rarely know how their representatives voted on particular issues.[69]

Higher Office

There is, however, another theory that takes issue with, or at least qualifies, this reelection theory. We met it in Chapter 3 when we considered participation. It is "ambition theory," and it argues that some politicians are not so much interested in being reelected to their present positions as they are in laying the groundwork for election to higher office. This objective is not necessarily a bad one, according to Joseph Schlesinger:

> If anyone is going to search for solutions, it is the man whose career depends on finding solutions. The politican with static ambitions is far more likely to be driven by immediate pressures, whether it be the pressure of opinion, party, or special interest groups. . . .[70]

Constituency Service

Doing favors for your constituents is often a good way to advance your career prospects, especially if you help constituents who have political influence. But both ambitious and stodgy members of Congress are likely to get satisfaction in helping those from their states or districts. So constituent interests may also be a factor in influencing decisions—especially those of members of the House, who are closer to their populations than are senators.

Power in Congress—and in Washington

A final factor in shaping the decisions of some members of Congress is the desire for personal power in Congress—and perhaps in government generally. Some members appear from the outside to be without ambition but in fact have considerable power within the Congress. They spend their time and energy not in seeking national publicity, as the more outwardly or upwardly ambitious do, but rather in studying and using the rules and procedures of the House or Senate to make their influence felt, not seen, in the outcomes.

INFLUENCES ON CONGRESSIONAL VOTING BEHAVIOR

Many factors may influence how a member of Congress votes on a given bill.[71] The general factors we have just examined sometimes play a role. Also important may be his or her perception of the wishes of the president or of the congressional leadership. In general, members tend to vote with the majority of their party about two-thirds of the time. Also important may be influential interest groups or individuals such as campaign-fund contributors. But we should not conclude from this that a legislator ignores the merits of the bill in question.

The point, rather, is that patterns often do emerge in voting behavior. These patterns make it possible for us as outside observers to generalize about factors that influence voting, although members of Congress may not be conscious of the influences we uncover. Research in this area is still in its early stages, and so our conclusions must be tentative.

Cue Giving and Cue Taking

There are very many votes, and members have very little information about most of them. For this reason, members seem to rely heavily on *cues* from other members to help them decide how to vote much of the time. The cue-givers tend to be those known as experts on the topic or known to be knowledgeable about the views of important officials or interest groups.

A study on House voting by John Kingdon attempted to determine the influences on members' votes not only of constituency but also of House colleagues, interest groups, their party leaders, the Nixon administration, and their own staff. The re-

[69]See David R. Mayhew, *Congress: The Electoral Connection* (New Haven, CT: Yale Univ. Press, 1974).

[70]Joseph Schlesinger, *Ambition and Politics* (Chicago: Rand McNally, 1966), p. 209.

[71]See Roger H. Davidson and Walter J. Oleszek, *Congress and Its Members*, 2d ed. (Washington: CQ Press, 1985), chap. 14.

search found that no one factor was dominant enough to be called *the* major influence. Instead, Kingdon concluded that members of the House use a kind of "consensus model" of decision making in which they *"take their cues,"* as some would say, from various individuals and groups.[72]

When House members begin to consider how to vote on a bill or amendment, Kingdon found, their first question is, "Is it controversial?" If there is no disagreement among fellow representatives, interest groups, party leaders, the administration, and their own staff, representatives "vote with the herd." But if there is some conflict in their total environment, representatives must then decide whether the source of the conflict is important for them. A Republican, for example, might worry about the Reagan administration's views, while a Democrat wouldn't. A Democrat, on the other hand, might well worry about organized labor, while a Republican wouldn't. In other words, at this second step the question is whether there is conflict in what Kingdon calls the field of forces that would likely affect the representative's own decision. Usually there isn't; and if that's the case, he or she votes with that field. If there is conflict among those important forces, the member then proceeds to the third step, which is to see how many actors in the field of forces are disagreeing with the rest. If only one, he or she is likely to vote against that one actor. If there are two, the member is quite likely to vote against that pair. But if there are more than two forces out of line, the representative faces a major, difficult choice where such informal, perhaps nonconscious "cue-taking" decision rules are not helpful, and the decision must be made on other grounds. However, this is rare: It happened in only 14 of 222 controversial voting decisions Kingdon studied.[73]

There is some evidence that members of Congress tend to vote consistently on a given type of issue until circumstances change drastically.[74] In an effort to find patterns of causation within voting, some scholars have divided voting situations into categories to see whether patterns emerge. David Kozak interviewed representatives and found five different patterns for five different types of vote. He found that on "nonvisible votes," which don't matter to constituents or interest groups, decisions are usually by consensus. On complicated questions, members tend to take cues from other members. On routine votes, such as recurring authorization and appropriations bills, members usually vote in terms of their own ideologies or ongoing policy positions. The votes most relevant to members are those involving federal grants to their districts. On such bills, they tend either to take cues from their own staff people who have studied the program, or they vote as their constituency has requested. Kozak calls the final type of bill "hot votes"—controversial topics that are very visible. On such bills, there is no most common way of deciding. Some use campaign promises, others use their own ideology, and still others refer to constituency interests.[75]

Policy Areas

Another way of analyzing voting is by looking at policy areas. Perhaps the most interesting instance of such an approach is Aage Clausen's study of Senate and House voting decisions. Clausen focused on the policy issues involved, instead of on the decision process itself. He divided votes into five policy areas: civil liberties, international involvement (such as foreign aid and trade), agricultural assistance (such as farm subsidies), social welfare, and government management (including government regulation of the economy, conservation, balancing the budget, and so on). Clausen then examined the policy positions taken by individual members of Congress in a 12-year period and looked for pat-

[72]The term *cue taking* comes from a study by Donald R. Matthews and James A. Stimson, *Yeas and Nays: Normal Decision-Making in the U.S. House of Representatives* (New York: Wiley, 1975). Their 1969 study found considerable support for the following hypothesis: "When a member is confronted with the necessity of casting a roll-call vote on a complex issue about which he knows very little, he searches for cues provided by trusted colleagues who—because of their formal position in the legislature or policy specialization—have more information than he does and with whom he would probably agree if he had the time and information to make an independent decision. Cue-givers need not be individuals. When overwhelming majorities of groups that the member respects and trusts—the whole House, the members of his party or state delegation, for example—vote the same way, the member is likely to accept their collective judgment as his own" (p. 45).

[73]John W. Kingdon, *Congressmen's Voting Decisions* (New York: Harper & Row, 1973), esp. chap. 10. His study was done in 1969. A second edition, slightly revised, was published in 1981.

[74]See Herbert B. Asher and Herbert F. Weisberg, "Voting Change in Congress: Some Dynamic Perspectives on an Evolutionary Process," *American Journal of Political Science* 22 (May 1978), 391–425.

[75]See Kozak, "Decision Settings in Congress," in Congress and Public Policy, ed. David C. Kozak and J. D. Macartney (Homewood, IL.: Dorsey, 1982); and "Decision-Making on Roll-Call Votes in the House of Representatives," *Congress and the Presidency* 9 (Autumn 1982), 51–78.

terns of influence upon them by three major factors: party, constituency, and the president.

Clausen found that *government management issues* are most influenced by *party*. Democrats tend to favor government intervention in economic affairs, while Republicans tend to oppose it. The voters—the constituents—have no real role, according to Clausen, because policy alternatives are complex and often unpredictable. Indeed, the voter can't even have an opinion on alternatives being considered. All he or she can do is complain when economic conditions worsen. *Agricultural assistance* and *social-welfare issues* are influenced by both *party* and *constituency*. *Civil-liberties* issues are influenced exclusively by *constituency*, with northerners supporting and southerners opposing civil-rights laws. *International-involvement issues* are dominated by the *president*, but constituency is also an important consideration.

One of Clausen's general conclusions was that "the differences in the policy positions of congressmen elected from the same state and party are minimal on the four domestic policy dimensions, while remaining substantial on the international involvement dimension."[76]

This conclusion may be less true today, according to a more recent but less extensive study. Taking a different approach, this examination of voting by all senators and representatives in 1975 found what appeared to be a generation gap in Congress. Those first elected after Vietnam, the environmental movement, and "good government" public-interest lobbying voted quite differently from more senior members.

Junior northern Democrats are more liberal than their senior counterparts on environmental policy, defense spending, and congressional and campaign-reform questions, the study concluded, but all northern Democrats vote about the same on economic and public-welfare issues. Junior southern Democrats and northern Republicans, on the other hand, are more liberal than their more senior colleagues on economic, public-welfare, and defense-spending issues, but both groups tend to vote with their seniors when there is a conflict between energy development and the environment.

Seniority is not a significant factor in the way southern Republicans vote.

These rules appear to suggest that geography and age are the major determinants of voting. But the study reached a somewhat different conclusion:

> The differences that show up . . . are less a product of age or tenure than a reflection of the issues that were important when a Member first was elected. Thus new Members tend to reflect new issues, while veterans echo the issues that predominated when they first came to Congress. Voting by seniority, therefore, is less a cause of differences than the result of existing differences.[77]

Presidential Support

Voting may, however, be influenced by the position taken by the president. Ronald Reagan won major budgetary battles in Congress in his first two years. He did so with great support from Republicans who had previously opposed the large spending cuts and tax cuts he sought. This surprised observers who had downplayed the influence of the president on voting, even by members of the chief executive's own party. A study of key votes in Congress during the Johnson and Nixon years, however, suggests that perhaps Reagan's success should not surprise us. It found that

> when a president is responsible for a policy area—for example, foreign affairs or management of the economy—the members of the president's party frequently change their policy positions in order to provide their president with the tools he needs to meet these responsibilities.[78]

To win in the House, which was controlled by the Democrats, Reagan also needed some Democratic support. He got it from conservative Democrats, mainly from the South, who came to be called Boll Weevils.

Where do these varying studies leave us? With certain disagreements needing further study, but nonetheless with a better sense of the relevance of such influences on voting behavior as legislative

---

[76]Aage R. Clausen, *How Congressmen Decide: A Policy Focus* (New York: St. Martin's Press. 1973), p. 231. Clausen studied the period from 1953 to 1964.

[77]Michael Malbin, "Times Change, But Congressmen Still Vote the Way They Used To," *National Journal*, March 20, 1976, pp. 370–74.

[78]Anita Pritchard, "Presidents Do Influence Voting in the U.S. Congress: New Definitions and Measurements," *Legislative Studies Quarterly* 8 (November 1983), 691–711.

President Reagan meets with Congressional leaders at the White House. (UPI/ Bettmann Newsphotos)

practices, party, constituents, interest groups, presidential leadership, and individual judgment.

We should recognize that these studies are all based on interviews and roll-call voting. And we must be careful not to jump to conclusions about the significance of results based on studies of voting records alone, for voting records may be misleading accounts of what our representatives actually do and really support (see Action Unit 10.2).

Nonetheless, these findings do advance our understanding of how and why members of Congress act as they do, especially if we bear in mind a conclusion Clausen urges upon us:

> The individual members of Congress, when seen behind the trappings of office, are persons of few extraordinary endowments. The congressman is not a political virtuoso constantly performing political maneuvers of great complexity with an unerringly delicate sense of political balance. Members of Congress are best understood as typical participants in the politically activist segment of our citizenry, with no special calling to the ministry of policymaking. Their decisions result from a blend of prejudice, reason, and practicality. These decisions are sometimes based upon much information and at other times upon little; they are sometimes the product of political necessity and at other times the result of unencumbered judgment.[79]

---

[79]Clausen, *How Congressmen Decide*, p. viii.

HOW MEMBERS OF CONGRESS GET ELECTED—AND REELECTED

Our study of roles and voting has emphasized concern with reelection as a major influence on behavior. If members really are so concerned, we might expect that reelection would be generally difficult to achieve. However, just the opposite is true.

The Incumbency Effect and the Vanishing "Marginals"

In virtually every election, 90 percent or more of the incumbents seeking reelection to Congress succeed. In 1986 only eight members of the House who ran for reelection and seven senators were defeated in November. The record in the Senate in percentage terms is almost always worse than that in the House. Nonetheless, the general pattern is that incumbents win. Experts call this the incumbency effect.

If a House district tends to have close elections—one in which the winner receives less than 55 percent—experts call it a marginal district. In recent decades, the number of marginal, or close, districts has been declining. Thirty years ago about one-

ACTION UNIT 10.2

How to Find and Interpret Congressional Voting Records

All "record" or "roll-call" votes on the floor of either house on bills and amendments are printed in the *Congressional Record.* You can find the *Congressional Record* in most large libraries. You can also purchase individual copies for particular days at $1 each or subscribe for $218 per year, from the Superintendent of Documents, Government Printing Office, Washington, DC 20401. Congressional Quarterly's *Weekly Report* (which we discuss in the bibliography at the end of the chapter) is available in many libraries and prints records of all important votes. Some newspapers, such as the *New York Times* and the *Washington Post,* print the breakdown of votes on major topics. And many local papers will print weekly summaries of how local representatives and senators voted on key issues.

Nevertheless, unless you've been following a certain issue and know just what was being voted on, this is not likely to tell you very much. Members of Congress may vote with public opinion in their constituency on final passage of a bill but may have voted against this public opinion in committee or during the amending process. Members may also change their vote once voting is completed. For example, members who voted with the party and against the interests of their district and who then discover their vote was not crucial may have their vote changed. Such representatives get credit in public for voting with their constituency, when in fact they voted against the constituency the first time around.

To examine key votes—usually on amendments before final passage—you really need studies prepared by interest groups. By a recent count, 60 organizations prepare such lists after each session of Congress, rating the members by whether they vote as the groups believe they should. Among the major rating groups—to which you can write for their latest set of ratings—are the following, each identified by its special interest or political preference: AFL-CIO Committee on Political Education (COPE), 815 16th St. NW, Washington, DC 20006; American Conservative Union, 422 1st St. SE, Washington, DC 20003; American Farm Bureau Federation, 425 13th St. NW, Washington, DC 20004; Americans for Democratic Action, 1424 16th St. NW, Washington, DC 20036; Consumer Federation of America, 1012 14th St. NW, Washington, DC 20005; Environmental Action, 1346 Connecticut Ave. NW, Washington, DC 20036; League of Women Voters, 1730 M St. NW, Washington, DC 20036; National Associated Businessmen, Inc., 1000 Connecticut Ave. NW, Washington, DC, 20036; National Council of Senior Citizens, 1511 K St. NW, Washington, DC 20005; Women's Lobby, Inc., 1345 G St. SE, Washington, DC 20003. For background on the rating systems, see Bill Keller, "Congressional Rating Game Is Hard to Win," *Congressional Quarterly Weekly Report,* March 21, 1981, pp. 507–12.

---

quarter were marginal. In 1986 three-quarters of all incumbents who ran won with vote totals of 60 percent or better. Thus, most districts seem to be becoming less and less competitive.

The Advantages of Incumbency

Experts are not sure what explains the incumbency effect,[80] but various possibilities have been suggested. First, incumbents are likely to have better name recognition among voters than their less well known adversaries. Some of the reasons for this are

evident in Table 10.7. They have campaigned before. They visit their districts regularly, and they send newsletters to voters and appear in the media often. These activities are likely to be especially true of those first elected recently, who—as we have already seen—tend to serve vigorously. A survey taken during the 1978 elections found that 92 percent of the voters recognized and could rate the incumbent in their House race, while only 44 percent could do so for the challenger. Thus, name recognition does seem to be an advantage for the incumbent.[81]

On the other hand, if times are bad, voters may blame incumbents and seek to "throw the rascals

---

[80]For a survey of research, see Richard S. Beth, "'Incumbency Advantage' and Incumbency Resources," *Congress and the Presidency* 9 (Winter 1981–1982), 119–36.

[81]Barbara Hinckley, "The American Voter in Congressional Elections," *American Political Science Review* 74 (September 1980), 641–50.

TABLE 10.7
Americans and their Congress

SURVEY ITEM	PERCENTAGE
"Very" or "fairly" interested in the activities of Congress	58
Can recall representative's name	50
Comments postively about representative's activities or stands	54
Read newspaper story or heard television story about representative	68
Received mail from representative	66
Sent letter or telegram, or signed petition, to representative	29
Met representative or heard representative speak at a public meeting	26
Respondent or family members requested assistance from member of Congress or staff	15
Contributed financially to candidate	11
Personally visited representative	8
Campaigned for congressional candidate	7
Own representative "excellent" or "pretty good"	40
Same as or better than other representative	63
Congress "excellent" or "pretty good"	22

Note: Percentages are of Americans reporting having these attitudes toward and experiences of Congress or their own representatives.

Source: Based upon interviews in January 1977 with 1510 respondents, conducted by Louis Harris Survey for the U.S. House of Representatives' Commission on Administrative Review.

out." Or they may hold their bad opinion of Congress against the incumbent. Interestingly, however, studies find that there is little negative perception of any congressional candidates for either house, whether they be incumbents or challengers.[82]

It appears, then, that a record of servicing the constituency may be the biggest advantage of incumbency. One part of such service is casework. The other part is getting for the district public works projects, federal grants, and government contracts, which together are known as the pork barrel.[83]

In the words of Morris Fiorina,

Even committee chairmen have a difficult time claiming credit for a piece of major legislation, let alone a rank-and-file congressman. Ah, but casework, and the pork-barrel. In dealing with the bureaucracy, the congressman is not merely one vote in 435. Rather he is a nonpartisan power, someone whose phone calls snap an office to attention. He is not kept on hold. The constituent who receives aid believes that his congressman and his congressman alone got results. Similarly, congressmen find it easy to claim credit for federal projects awarded in their

districts. The congressman may have instigated the project in the first place, issued regular progress reports, and ultimately announced the award through his office. Maybe he can't claim credit for the 1965 Voting Rights Act, but he can take credit for Littletown's spanking new sewage treatment plant.[84]

But this is not the whole story. After studying survey data, Thomas Mann and Raymond Wolfinger emphasize the importance of the typical absence of a serious challenger in most districts as a major factor in the incumbent's success. They found impressive reason to believe that "most elections to the House are won for lack of a contest.[85] Indeed, in 1986, 25 percent of the Democratic victors and 17 percent of the Republican winners had no opponent at all.[86]

The situation is quite different in the Senate, where the incumbency effect is much smaller.[87] Alan Abramowitz compared 1978 Senate and House races to explain the greater difficulty Senate incumbents have. He found Senate challengers have greater visibility than those in House races, which could be an advantage if people made their

[82]Hinckley, "American Voter in Congressional Elections."

[83]This term is derived from the practice common before the days of refrigeration and chemical preservatives of preserving meat or fish in a barrel of pork fat. When times were bad or in winter, one went "to the pork barrel" for food. That's approximately what members of Congress do too, going to the national treasury for funds for local projects. These funds have come to be called pork for short. See John Ferejohn, *Pork Barrel Politics* (Stanford, CA: Stanford Univ. Press, 1974).

[84]Morris Fiorina, *Congress: Keystone of the Washington Establishment* (New Haven, CT: Yale Univ. Press, 1977), pp. 44–45.

[85]Thomas E. Mann and Raymond E. Wolfinger, "Candidates and Parties in Congressional Elections," *American Political Science Review* 74 (September 1980), 631.

[86]James R. Dickenson, "America's House of Lords," *Washington Post National Weekly Edition*, December 8,1986, p. 25.

[87]See Peter Tuckel, "Length of Incumbency and the Reelection Chances of U.S. Senators," *Legislative Studies Quarterly* 8 (May 1983), 283–88.

decisions on senators the way they seem to on House candidates. However, it turns out that they do not. Voters tend to use party and ideology as criteria to judge Senate candidates but not House candidates.[88] Such criteria tend to operate against incumbents in times of difficulty. This does not mean that incumbents, even in the Senate, are doomed, however. Another critical factor in determing election outcomes is money.

Money in Congressional Elections

It is no surprise that money matters in campaigns. In 1980 the average cost of defeating an incumbent in the House was $325,000, and in the Senate, $1,318,000. In 1982 and again in 1986 these costs were slightly less—because Democrats, who usually have less to spend, were defeating Republican incumbents. Gary Jacobson studied patterns of campaign spending in recent elections. He found that campaign expenditures by nonincumbents have a substantial impact on their share of the vote, whereas expenditures by incumbents have little effect. But the situation is more complicated than this suggests. "Incumbents who appear vulnerable inspire effective, well-financed challenges; most do not, however, and the great majority of challengers remain severely underfinanced."[89]

Most successful challengers in House elections outspend the incumbents they fight. In the Senate, however, most defeated incumbents outspend their challengers. The moral, according to the *National Journal:* "If you want to run against a Senator, you can count on the news media to provide you with the attention you will need. But if you're running for the House, you had better be prepared to outspend the incumbent in order to get your message across to the public."[90]

"It is not popular appeal, but rather anticipated capacity for winning popular support, that fills campaign coffers." Jacobson concluded.[91] Why do people—and to greater extent the political action committees (PACs) of special interests—contribute primarily to likely winners? They want to have been on the winning side before it won. Then they can say they have been a supporter when they go to a representative to seek support on some issue of public policy.

CONGRESS AND PUBLIC POLICY

Despite recent reforms many observers still believe that Congress is too weak to make a major contribution to the formulation of public policy. The president proposes and Congress disposes, they often say.

Some have argued that the problem is the rules and procedures—and that reforms Congress has recently made could bring about a great improvement. However, only time will tell.[92] Others argue that the basic problem is the people in Congress, many of whom do not wish to do more. However, in recent years many more spirited members have been elected and then reelected.

There is also a third position on the policy impact of Congress. "Congress is powerful," Gary Orfield has written, "and it has regularly exercised considerable power in the shaping of domestic policy." Orfield dismisses "the perception of Congress as an obstacle to progressive social policy proposed by the President." He cites the constructive and innovative role of Congress on voting rights, federal aid to education, and school desegregation, and its initiation of public jobs legislation.[93] Others point out that the Senate has played a major innovative role in such programs as Medicare, pension reform, votes for 18-year-olds, political campaign reform, pollution control, reduction of America's role in Vietnam, and minimum-wage increases.

Orfield concludes:

[88]Alan Abramowitz, "A Comparison of Voting for U.S. Senator and Representative in 1978," *American Political Science Review* 74 (September 1980), 633–50.

[89]Gary Jacobson, *Money in Congressional Elections* (New Haven, CT: Yale Univ. Press, 1980), pp. xvi–xvii. See also his "Parties and PACs in Congressional Elections," in *Congress Reconsidered*, 3d. ed., ed. Dodd and Oppenheimer, chap. 6.

[90]"Big Spenders Did Better in the House Than in the Senate," *National Journal*, March 7, 1981, p. 379.

[91]Jacobson, *Money in Congressional Elections*, p. xvii.

[92]For a variety of studies, and some speculation, see *Congress Reconsidered*, 2d and 3d eds. ed. Dodd and Oppenheimer; and Ornstein, *Congress in Change*.

[93]Gary Orfield, *Congressional Power: Congress and Social Change* (New York: Harcourt Brace Jovanovich, 1975), p. iv.

It is vital to realize . . . that the making of national domestic policy takes place in a context of genuinely divided power, and that the Congress as well as the President possesses both the ability to initiate and the power to veto major policy changes. The system works well when there is a clear consensus in the country, or clear control of both branches by the dominant wing of either party. Usually these conditions are not present and the system is biased either toward compromise and incremental change, or toward confrontation and interaction.[94]

It is essential to remember that Congress is but one of three coequal branches of our government. This suggests that its record should be compared to those achieved by the president and bureaucracy, on the one hand, and the courts on the other. But it also suggests that to get an accurate picture of the record of Congress, we must look also at the relations Congress has with these other branches—especially the president and the bureaucracy.

Congress and the President

It is obvious that Congress and the president need each other. Neither can develop a program or solve a major national problem without support from the other. But each is chosen by different constituencies, usually at different times. Thus, relations between the branches are always somewhat strained.

In recent decades, Congress has generally sought to convert the separation of powers into more of a sharing of powers.[95] It has asked for more consultation in advance on treaty making abroad and policy making at home. A major weapon in this effort has been the legislative veto.

The Case of the Legislative Veto

In 1932 Congress began to insert in some bills a legislative veto.[96] It provides that once an agency develops a program, it must submit the program to Congress (the two-house veto) or to a congressional committee (the committee veto) or to the entire House or Senate (the one-house veto) for possible rejection. By 1983 Congress had built one or another type of legislative veto into over 200 major laws. The War Powers Act, for example, has a two-house veto provision. The Trade Act of 1974 (which we will encounter in Perspective 5) has a one-house veto. And the amendments to the National Traffic and Motor Vehicle Safety Act of 1966 have a committee-veto provision. Congress rarely exercised this veto power. A study of all such instances since 1932 found a total of only 81 such executive actions reversed by Congress.[97]

It has long been clear that such provisions exceed the intentions of the founders. Presidents have claimed that the legislative veto obstructs the exercise of their responsibility to carry out laws. In June 1983 the Supreme Court agreed. It ruled by a vote of 7 to 2 in *Immigration and Naturalization Service* v. *Chadha* that the legislative veto is unconstitutional. When Congress delegates the authority to issue regulations or make decisions, the majority opinion of the court said, it "must abide by its delegation of authority until that delegation is legislatively altered or revoked." Congress, fearing loss of a major control over the executive branch and hoping that later Supreme Court rulings might limit this decision, has continued to insert legislative vetoes in some critical bills.[98]

The Continuing Quest for Shared Administration

The quest for shared administration can be seen as a response to the growth of executive initiation of legislation. Some 80 percent of bills passed by Congress now originate, in some form, in the executive branch, which after all has primary responsibility for national concerns, just as the Congress has a more regional and local focus.[99] And if most bills originate in the executive branch, *all comprehen-*

[94]Orfield, *Congressional Power*, p. 325.

[95]For an account of the evolution of congressional-presidential relations, see Lawrence C. Dodd, "Cycles of Congressional Power," *Society* 16 (November–December 1978), 65–68.

[96]See Robert G. Dixon, Jr., "Congress, Shared Administration, and Executive Privilege," In *Congress against the President*, ed. Harvey C. Mansfield, Sr. (New York: Praeger, 1975), pp. 125–40.

[97]See "Using Its Legislative Veto Power," *National Journal*, January 13, 1979, p. 48.

[98]See Joseph Cooper, "The Legislative Veto in the 1980s," in *Congress Reconsidered*, 3d., ed. Dodd and Oppenheimer, chap. 16.

[99]The figure is from Ira Katznelson and Mark Kesselman, *The Politics of Power* (New York: Harcourt Brace Jovanovich, 1975), p. 288. It refers only to public bills.

sive policies do too. Congressional committees have jurisdictions so limited and so jealously guarded that Congress cannot coordinate military and political foreign policy programs, or fiscal and monetary policy, for example. Except in the area of the budget, remarks James Sundquist, a sympathetic critic,

> there remains no regular institutional structure in either house to deal effectively with matters that cut across the jurisdiction of two or more committees. . . . Congress still has no way of setting an agenda, or priorities, for its own activities, no way of ensuring consistency and completeness in its consideration of the country's problems.[100]

Congress and the Bureaucracy

Relations between Congress and the president may change when the presidency changes hands. Relations between Congress and the bureaucracy tend to be much more stable. Contact between the two occurs formally over budgets, appointment of high-level officials, decisions about where to locate projects, and occasional decisions to establish, reorganize, or abolish programs or agencies.[101] Contact also occurs much more frequently and less formally between bureaucrats and congressional staffers who are doing casework to cope with the needs of constituents. But there are two other major points of contact between Congress and the bureaucracy. The first is exercise of the formal congressional responsibility of oversight. The second is the use of "subgovernments," which consist of members of Congress, bureaucrats, and lobbyists, to develop policy in a given area. We have examined this practice in Chapter 9.[102]

Congressional oversight is extremely important because it is the only regular way for Congress—and thus the people—to get information on how well the bureaucracy is doing its job. As we saw in Chapter 9, there are many forces that operate against good bureaucratic performance. Congress has long realized this. Therefore, when it reorganized itself in 1946, it directed each committee to exercise continuous watchfulness over the execution of laws by the administrative agencies.

The chief instrument of actual congressional oversight is the investigation—research and often hearings, in which bureaucrats testify about their past activities and future plans. Some regular oversight is performed by the General Accounting Office (GAO), an instrument of Congress that audits expenditures and increasingly evaluates operations of agencies.

Many laws require that agencies report regularly to Congress on their activities. Some of these reports deal with enforcement of the laws. Others concern spending plans. Still others describe policy failures and the steps being taken to correct them. In 1983 the House produced a report listing some 3000 such required reports. Then the GAO produced a report uncovering several thousand other required reports. The trouble with such required reports is that they are hard to find and still harder to read. Investigations get more attention and sometimes unearth more information. But investigations are difficult to organize and costly in terms of both money and the time of members. Thus, Congress has shown little interest in expanded oversight responsibilities. Nor do most observers believe it handles its present efforts particularly well—with occasional exceptions, such as Watergate.[103]

Certain things tend to encourage more oversight. One is control of one or both houses of Congress by the party not holding the White House. Another is the wish to protect certain agencies—as when Reagan began major budget cutting. Others include scandals and casework needs. But more oversight is not necessarily better oversight. Improved oversight is most likely to come with election of more skeptical new members, increase in program evaluation, and a general scarcity of resources.[104] All three of these conditions have per-

[100]James L. Sundquist, "Congress and the President: Enemies or Partners?" in *Congress Reconsidered*, 1st ed., ed. Dodd and Oppenheimer (New York: Praeger, 1977), p. 240.

[101]For a study of the influence each has over the other, see R. Douglas Arnold, *Congress and the Bureaucracy* (New Haven, CT: Yale Univ. Press, 1979). This study supports the notion that bureaucrats carefully tailor their decisions about allocation of programs and funds to fit each program's situation in Congress.

[102]For a survey of research, see Keith E. Hamm, "Patterns of Influence among Committees, Agencies, and Interest Groups," *Legislative Studies Quarterly* 8 (August 1983), 379–426.

[103]The most comprehensive study of oversight is Morris S. Ogul, *Congress Oversees the Bureaucracy* (Pittsburgh: Univ. of Pittsburgh Press, 1976).

[104]See Joel Aberbach, "Changes in Congressional Oversight," *American Behavioral Scientist* 22 (May–June 1979), 495–502.

sisted since the 1980 election. For these reasons, we may anticipate—but not count on—improvements in congressional oversight.

Reform and Renewal

There have been many efforts at congressional reform and renewal in recent years, as we have seen. But what has been done to make Congress more democratic and open (such as less power for committees and more open meetings) has often come at the expense of efficiency. Congress now spends more time than ever in committee meetings, not just because the issues are more complex but also partly because chairpersons are less able to run things dictatorially and partly because so many meetings are open to the press—which encourages more vocal participation.

It is already clear that reform is not necessarily conducive to efficiency—nor to a more responsive Congress. Many reformers have argued for abolition, rather than just moderation, of the seniority system for selecting committee leadership. But no one has come up with an alternative principle that would not cost much more time and energy in battles for leadership—time and energy that would be diverted from efforts to improve public policy. Others have argued for longer terms for representatives, who now have to begin worrying about reelection the moment they win a two-year term and so have less time to ponder policy problems. But it is this very obsession with reelection that makes representatives as responsive to the public—and to public problems—as they are.

There have recently been renewed efforts to publicize, if not to control, the influence of special interests on Congress. Interest groups exist in large part to operate upon or influence indirectly the legislative process. We examined in Chapter 5 the ways and means they use to do so. Those ways and means at the federal level have been somewhat limited by the 1946 "regulation of lobbying" act. But because that act requires the registration only of organizations and people whose "principal purpose" is lobbying, many have not registered. Some of the corruption surrounding Watergate involved lobbyists making illegal campaign contributions or other gifts to members of Congress. That embarrassment stimulated efforts for further regulation.

But little real progress has yet been made, despite the fact that some members of Congress have pleaded guilty to, or been convicted of, corruption in cases such as Abscam in the past decade.[105]

CONGRESS AND US

Limitations on lobbying will affect not only the business and labor interest groups but also the so-called public-interest groups such as those Ralph Nader has organized. That is why Nader has joined the stronger special interests in opposing stricter lobby-control laws. The result of these efforts—and failures—at reform is a Congress that continues to be, as we saw early in this chapter, not very representative of the people at large, who are neither organized nor powerful.

Still, it may well be true, as Gary Orfield has argued, that

> recent Congresses have rather accurately reflected the values and the confusion of the the public in dealing with the major issues of social change. . . . Most of the time, we have the Congress we really want and the Congress we deserve. We send the same members back to Washington time after time. Congress is inherently neither liberal nor conservative. Its political tendencies change with the times, with political circumstances, with the delayed responses of the seniority system, and with tides of public opinion.[106]

Those "tides of public opinion," after all, are—or at least could be—generated by waves of letters, telegrams, phone calls, and visits to members of Congress by concerned and informed citizens. As Action Unit 10.3 suggests, there are ways of making sure your messages and your visits have maximal impact upon your legislators. Only if you and your friends and neighbors—and many others like and unlike you—do so, are your "representatives" likely to become *your representatives*. And only if they do, will it be possible for the Congress to become, as the founders intended, the representative branch—the first branch—of our government.

---

[105]Abscam was a large undercover investigation by the Justice Department of political corruption in four states. It ended in May 1981 with the conviction of 16 persons, including 6 members of Congress. It sought to catch corrupt officials by creating criminal opportunities and prosecuting those who "took the bait." Officers posed as Arab sheiks seeking help with immigration and investment opportunities and offering bribes to members of Congress and other officials.

[106]Orfield, *Congressional Power*, pp. 9–10.

How to Communicate Effectively with Your Members of Congress

Most members of Congress are so busy, as we've seen in this chapter, that they can't possibly read all their mail—incoming or outgoing. However, you can take certain steps to make it more likely that the member of Congress to whom you write will see your letter. If your letter asks a question that cannot be answered by a form letter, someone will have to answer your letter personally. If you are an expert on the matter your letter discusses or have otherwise written a particularly analytical letter with well-thought-out arguments, it is likely that the staff member who opens the letter will set it aside for the member of Congress to read personally. But the best way to assure that the member will read your letter is to refer to any personal contact you might have had with him or her or with his or her family, friends, or staff.

The following are some helpful hints prepared by Representative Morris K. Udall (Democrat of Arizona) for the League of Women Voters: (1) Be sure your letter is addressed properly: to Senator——————— or Representative———————, at the U.S. Senate or the U.S. House of Representatives, Washington, DC 20515 (House) or 20510 (Senate). (2) If the subject of your letter is a bill or issue, mention it in the first paragraph. (3) Write as soon as possible; don't wait until a bill has been passed. (4) Keep your letter as brief as possible. (5) Give your reasons for taking a stand. Be specific and constructive. (6) Don't make threats or berate your representatives. (7) Say "well done" when it's deserved.

You can also contact your member of Congress by phone, telegram, or personal visit.

Phone calls can be made simply by dialing (202) 224-3121, the number for both the House and Senate, and then asking for the member's office. When the receptionist answers, give your name and ask for the legislator by name. If he or she is not in or is busy, ask to speak with the "legislative assistant" who handles the subject you're concerned about. He or she talks almost every day with the legislator and helps develop his or her positions on issues, and so your views are quite likely to be noted.

Communicating by telegram is more expensive than by letter but also possibly more impressive. You can send a "Personal Opinion Message" of 20 words or less to a member of Congress or the president for only $4.45; it will be delivered within 24 hours. Or you can send a Mailgram of up to 50 words, which looks like a telegram but is delivered with the next day's mail, for $4.95. Call Western Union at the number listed in your phone book for more information or to send your message.

If you can get to Washington, you may be able to visit your legislator personally there. Write or phone for an appointment before you go. A better bet, however, is to visit your legislator when he or she is in the district—most weekends, most holidays, and during congressional recesses. You'll find a listing in the phone book under "U.S. Government" for your legislator's local or district office. This office is always staffed by one or more assistants who will be happy to hear your views as well as to arrange appointments in the home district.

The most likely way to get to see your legislator, however, is to invite him or her to speak to a group, even one you set up just for the occasion. Most legislators are especially interested in speaking to student groups. At such a meeting, you will usually get to express your views, too. Representative Udall's guidelines for letter writing apply here also: be brief; give your arguments for taking a stand; be specific and constructive; don't make threats; and give the legislator a pat on the back if deserved. After the visit write a letter of thanks and restate your views. If the legislator does what you urged, write again to say "well done."

Positive contacts with your legislator—whether by mail, phone, or personal visit—will make it easier for you to have access the next time an issue that concerns you arises. And if you find yourself in general agreement with your legislator, volunteering to help in the local office or in the next campaign can be an excellent way to strengthen your access and even your influence. It is also a fascinating way to learn more about politics from the inside.

For detailed information see George Alderson and Everett Sentman, *How You Can Influence Congress: The Complete Handbook for the Citizen Lobbyist* (New York: Dutton paperback, 1979).

SUMMARY

Congress, the "first branch" of government, was established by Article I of the Constitution. It is bicameral, with the House of Representatives composed of members from 435 districts, and the Senate consisting of two representatives from each of the 50 states. Congress shares power with the president. To become law, a bill must be passed in identical form by both houses and signed by the president. If the president vetoes a bill, a two-thirds vote by each house can override that veto. Other powers of Congress are enumerated in Article I, Section 8.

Members of Congress do "casework" for constituents and legislate as trustees, delegates, or politicos. There are five major concepts describing the way they may represent the people: authorization, accountability, similarity, symbolization, and responsiveness. Representation, in practice, is difficult and complicated.

The major functions of Congress include policy making, funding (budget resolution, authorization, and appropriations), and oversight. It carries out these responsibilities via committees and subcommittees. Outcomes are affected by many factors, including caucuses and other informal groups of members; procedural rules; rivalry between the House and the Senate; the role of party and leadership; and norms, or "rules of the game," such as seniority.

Members have various objectives—among them good public policy, personal gain, reelection, attaining higher office, serving constituents, and having power in Congress and in Washington. We may be able to account for their voting behavior by these objectives and by cue taking, as well as by their interests in particular policies and the position of the president.

To understand congressional elections, we must study the advantages of incumbency, the disappearance of marginal districts, and the major role of money, especially when a challenger seeks to unseat a representative.

Congress plays an important role in influencing public policy, even though it rarely initiates policy. In so doing, it has many, often conflictual, interactions with the president and the bureaucracy. It has long sought to use the legislative veto to control enforcement of the laws it passes, but the Supreme Court in 1983 ruled that device unconstitutional. It thus seeks other ways to share administrative responsibility, including especially "oversight."

Everything Congress does has become more complex with reforms of the past several decades that have democratized and decentralized its operation. One result is that we as citizens—or as special interests—can have more of a role in influencing what Congress does. But doing so requires special knowledge and resources.

Suggestions for Further Reading and Study

For accounts of how Congress works, its powers and politics, see the third edition of CQ's *Guide to Congress*, over a thousand pages of facts and analysis published in 1982. CQ also publishes a wide range of other books on Congress, including an annual *Almanac*, along with a weekly newsletter, *Congressional Insight*.

Several members of Congress have written interesting books, using their own experience to analyze the institution and in some cases suggest reforms. These five are well worth reading: Richard Bolling, *House Out of Order* (New York: Dutton, 1965); Paul H. Douglas, *In the Fullness of Time* (New York: Harcourt Brace Jovanovich, 1971); Donald Riegel, *O Congress* (New York: Popular Library, 1976); Clem Miller, *Member of the House* (New York: Scribner, 1962), a collection of very thoughtful and revealing letters to constituents; and Donald G. Tacheron and Morris K. Udall, *The Job of the Congressman*, 2d ed. (Indianapolis: Bobbs-Merrill, 1970).

The scholarly literature on Congress by now is immense. Much of it appears in academic journals that we cannot detail here. Many of the scholarly books are cited in this chapter's footnotes. For helpful general studies, see Lawrence C. Dodd and Bruce I. Oppenheimer, *Congress Reconsidered*, 3d ed. (Washington: CQ Press, 1985); Thomas E. Mann and Norman J. Ornstein, eds., *The New Congress* (Washington, DC: American Enterprise Institute, 1981); Philip Brenner, *The Limits and Possibilities of Congress* (New York: St. Martin's Press, 1983); Barbara Hinckley, *Stability and Change in Congress*, 3d ed. (New York: Harper & Row, 1983); Charles O. Jones, *The U.S. Congress: People, Place, and Policy* (Homewood, IL.: Dorsey, 1982); David C. Kozak and John D. Macartney, *Congress and Public Policy* (Homewood, IL: Dorsey, 1982); and Roger H. Davidson and Walter J. Oleszek, *Congress and Its Members*, 2d ed. (Washington: CQ Press, 1985).

11

THE SUPREME COURT AND THE LEGAL SYSTEM

We encounter the law every day in countless ways: There are laws concerning work and play, what we can do in school, what we can't do at home, and so on. These law are occasionally enforced by the police, but most often we simply decide to obey—or disobey—the law. Disobeying the law or charging someone else—or the government—with disobeying it may bring us to court.

To understand the law, the courts, and the legal system, we shall first look at our Supreme Court in action. This look will illustrate for us what the Court is, what its justices do, how they make up their minds, and how the Court interacts with other institutions in the judicial, executive, and legislative branches. Then we'll examine our court system and the problems of law and order in America today. ∎

A block from the Capitol stands a square marble palace. Atop the 32 marble columns in front is carved in stone the phrase "Equal Justice Under Law." You climb 53 steps to reach the Great Hall and walk through a pair of massive bronze doors. A sign on a pedestal says simply "SILENCE." Before you is an electronic inspection station like those now used at airports to detect concealed weapons. Once you pass inspection, you enter the courtroom of the Supreme Court of the United States.

The Constitution provides in Article III that "the judicial power of the United States, shall be vested in one supreme Court, and in such inferior Courts as the Congress may from time to time ordain and establish. The Judges, both of the supreme and inferior Courts, shall hold their offices during good Behaviour. . . . " Their terms, therefore, are for life, or until they retire, resign, or are impeached and removed for bad conduct. According to the Constitution (Article II, Section 2), the president "shall nominate, and by and with the Advice and Consent of the Senate, shall appoint . . . Judges of the supreme court. . . . " Originally, in 1789, Congress provided for a chief justice and five associate justices. In 1807 it increased the size by one, in 1837 by two more, and in 1863 by one more, bringing the total to ten. In 1869 the number was changed

to nine, where it has stayed since, despite occasional efforts to change it.[1] Until President Reagan appointed Sandra Day O'Connor in 1981, no woman had ever served as a Supreme Court justice.

The nine justices of the Supreme Court are charged with interpreting the Constitution for the rest of our government and applying it in particular cases that come before it. Those cases are argued in a monumental courtroom. Its ceiling is 44 feet high. Its walls are topped with marble figures of lawgivers, sages, and other symbols of the power of government and the majesty of the law.

At the front of the courtroom is a long bench with nine high-backed, padded chairs, each of different design. As a visitor, you sit facing them in benches like church pews. The marshal raps a gavel, commands "All rise!" and pronounces the traditional cry, "*Oyez! Oyez! Oyez!*" ("Hear ye! Hear ye! Hear ye!"), announcing the appearance of "The honorable, the chief justice and the associate justices of the Supreme Court of the United States."

On a typical day, the nine justices in flowing black robes enter quickly and silently in groups of three through each of three dark-red-curtained doorways and take their seats at the bench. The marshal continues: "All persons having business before the honorable, the Supreme Court of the United States are admonished to draw near and give their attention, for the Court is now sitting. God save the United States and this Honorable Court." On a typical day, most Mondays through Wednesdays for nine months a year, within seconds come the words "Counsel, you may proceed whenever you are ready," and the Court begins "oral argument" sessions of an hour per case on 4 of the 200 or so cases it is hearing—out of the 5000 it considers and the 450 it decides—in that year's term.

Just after 10 A.M. Monday, July 8, 1974, eight justices appeared in the courtroom from behind the burgundy drapes.[2] The procedure was the same as

---

[1]The most famous of these was President Franklin D. Roosevelt's effort to expand it to 15 in the 1930s to stop it from ruling his New Deal legislation unconstitutional. Roosevelt failed in his effort to get Congress to change the size of the Court—"court packing," opponents called it. But shortly after the threat was made, the Court began to find the legislation constitutional—a change that is often referred to as "the switch in time that saved nine."

[2]There were only eight because Justice William Rehnquist, who had been appointed by President Nixon, had previously worked for the president in the Justice Department on the early stages of the very case the Court was hearing. He therefore disqualified himself from the case.

always, but it was clearly not an ordinary session of the Court. The courtroom was packed, and people had started gathering the day before to wait in line for the limited number of places. "You may proceed whenever you are ready," said Chief Justice Warren Burger. At that point began one of the most momentous and important Supreme Court cases in American history, *U.S.* v. *Nixon*, commonly referred to as the Watergate tapes case.

THE SUPREME COURT IN ACTION: THE WATERGATE TAPES CASE

The Supreme Court, the Constitution, and Watergate

By the summer of 1974, the investigation of the Watergate affair, which we considered in Chapter 8, had broken wide open. The Special Senate Watergate Committee had held hearings the previous summer. It had subpoenaed certain presidential records and tapes of White House conversations. A **subpoena** action is serious because it can involve legal punishment for refusal to comply. The term itself comes from the Latin words *sub* ("under") and *poena* ("punishment"). In this case, the president was being required to provide these materials, with the threat of (unspecified) punishment if he refused.

President Nixon had indeed refused to comply with the request, on grounds of executive privilege. As we noted in Chapter 8, *executive privilege* refers to the asserted privilege of the executive, the president, to refuse to testify before Congress and to refuse to allow presidential assistants to testify in cases in which the president believes that the independence of the executive branch would be eroded or compromised. The practice has long been recognized as an important protection for the separation of powers between the branches.

What has not been recognized or accepted is *how far* executive privilege extends and *who decides* whether a claim to it is too great. These two questions became the heart of the legal dispute that reached the Supreme Court in the summer of 1974.

The Question of the Separation of Powers

After refusing to let the Senate committee have the tapes, the president then refused to give them to the special Watergate prosecutor, Harvard law professor Archibald Cox, whom he had appointed to investigate criminal wrongdoing in the matter. Defending this decision, the president, through his lawyers, argued in court:

> In the exercise of his discretion to claim executive privilege the President is answerable to the nation but not to the courts. The courts, a co-equal but not a superior branch of government, are not free to probe the mental processes and the private confidences of the President and his advisors. To do so would be a clear violation of the constitutional separation of powers. Under that doctrine the judicial branch lacks power to compel the President to produce information that he has determined it is not in the public interest to disclose.

Special Prosecutor Cox responded that

> the grand jury is seeking evidence of criminal conduct that the [president] happens to have in his custody. . . . All the Court is asked to do is hold that the president is bound by legal duties in appropriate cases just as other citizens—in this case, by the duty to supply documentary evidence of crime.

For his trouble—or his refusal to accept Nixon's claim that only the president could decide what information to release—Cox was fired. Gone with him were Attorney General Elliott Richardson,

Watergate Special Prosecutor Archibald Cox speaks to the media. (UPI/Bettmann Newsphotos)

The second Special Watergate Prosecutor, Leon Jaworski, was appointed after Nixon fired Archibald Cox. (UPI/Bettmann Newsphotos)

who resigned rather than fire Cox, and Deputy Attorney General William Ruckelshaus, who was fired for the same refusal. But the event, on November 2, 1973, which became known as the Saturday Night Massacre, backfired on Nixon. It created such public outcry that Nixon was forced to release the subpoenaed tapes and appoint a new, truly independent special Watergate prosecutor, Houston lawyer Leon Jaworski, who carried on the investigation just as Cox had done. The tapes released included one with a crucial and mysterious 18-minute gap, which generated more suspicion of the president's own role in the Watergate affair and its cover-up.

The Watergate Grand Jury

Jaworski then presented evidence to a special Watergate grand jury. A **grand jury** is a group of citizens asked to decide whether there is enough evidence to merit a trial in a given case.[3] This grand jury—on March 1, 1974—found that indeed there was. It indicted ("charged") seven of Nixon's high-ranking aides for conspiracy to defraud the United

---

[3]A grand jury is distinguished from what we normally call a jury. The latter is historically called a petit jury, or small jury, and is selected to hear only one case. The grand jury, which may sit for several months, evaluates evidence to decide whether it is sufficient to hold trials in a number of cases. It indicts but does not convict.

States and for "obstruction of justice." And, we later learned, it named Nixon himself secretly as an "unindicted co-conspirator." This meant that there was already enough evidence to prosecute Nixon in the minds of the grand jury members. But the fact that he was president meant, the grand jury believed, that he could not be subjected to criminal prosecution while in office and so would have to be impeached in Congress rather than tried in court.

The Case Reaches the Supreme Court

From there Jaworski and his staff moved fast. On April 16 he asked the district court to subpoena 64 more tapes. On April 30 Nixon released edited transcripts of 43 conversations to the House Impeachment Committee, which was then investigating Nixon on its own. But Nixon's lawyers went to court to get the tape subpoena *quashed*, or nullified. And the Supreme Court agreed to hear the case, with extraordinary rapidity, on July 8.

In his brief, or written argument, to the Court, Nixon's new lawyer, Boston attorney James D. St. Clair, argued:

> At its core, this is a case that turns on the separation of powers. All other considerations are secondary, because preserving the integrity of the separation of powers is vital to the preservation of our Constitution as a living body of fundamental law. If the arguments of the Special Prosecutor were to prevail, the constitutional balance would be altered in ways that no one alive today could predict or measure.

For a highly unusual three hours, the oral argument of this extraordinary case went on as the opposing lawyers made arguments to the justices and answered questions from them. Jaworski summarized:

> Now . . . the President may be right in how he reads the Constitution, but he may also be wrong. And if he is wrong, who is there to tell him so? And if there is no one, then the President, of course, is free to pursue his course of erroneous interpretations. What then becomes of our constitutional form of government? . . . In our view, this nation's constitutional form of government is in serious jeopardy if the President, any President, is to say that the Constitution means what he says it does, and that there is no one, not even the Supreme Court, to tell him otherwise.

"The President is not above the law," St. Clair concluded. "Nor does he contend that he is. What he does contend is that as President the law can be

applied to him in only one way, and that is by impeachment, not by naming him as a co-conspirator in a grand jury indictment, not by indictment or any other way."

The Watergate Decision

Fifteen days later long lines began to form on those 53 steps at the front of the Supreme Court building. People were coming a whole day and a night early to guarantee they'd get a place the following day for the next announced session of the Court. The subject, as usual, had not been announced in advance. But everyone assumed that it would be the historic resolution of the Watergate case. Shortly after 11 A.M. on Wednesday, July 24, 1974, Chief Justice Warren Burger, Nixon's own choice for chief justice, delivered the opinion of the Court.

The lengthy, careful examination of the various aspects of the case included two especially important assertions. One explained the conclusion that the subpoena must be observed, and the tapes surrendered:

> We conclude that when the ground for asserting privilege as to subpoenaed materials sought for use in a criminal trial is based only on the generalized interest in confidentiality it cannot prevail over the fundamental demands of due process of law in the fair administration of criminal justice. The generalized assertion of privilege must yield to the demonstrated, specific need for evidence in a pending criminal trial.

Earlier in the opinion, however, the Court answered Nixon's assertion in more general, almost philosophical terms:

> In the performance of assigned constitutional duties each branch of the Government must initially interpret the Constitution, and the interpretation of its powers by any branch is due great respect from the others. The President's counsel, as we have noted, reads the Constitution as providing an absolute privilege of confidentiality for all Presidential communications. Many decisions of this Court, however, have unequivocally reaffirmed the holding of *Marbury* v. *Madison* (1803), that "it is emphatically the province and duty of the judicial department to say what the law is." . . .
>
> Our system of government "requires that federal courts on occasion interpret the Constitution in a manner at variance with the construction given the document by another branch." *Powell* v. *McCormack*. And in *Baker* v. *Carr* . . . the Court stated: "Deciding whether a matter has in any measure been committed by the Constitution to another branch of government, or whether the action of that branch exceeds whatever authority has been committed, is itself a delicate exercise in constitutional interpretation, and is a responsibility of this Court as ultimate interpreter of the Constitution." Notwithstanding the deference each branch must accord the others, the "judicial power of the United States" vested in the federal courts by Art. III sect. I of the Constitution can no more be shared with the Executive Branch than the Chief Executive, for example, can share with the Judiciary the veto power, or the Congress share with the Judiciary the power to override a presidential veto. Any other conclusion would be contrary to the basic concept of separation of powers and the checks and balances that flow from the scheme of a tripartite government.

The decision was unanimous. Because Supreme Court deliberations are always held in utmost secrecy with none but the justices present, we normally would know little or nothing of how it had been reached. In this case, however, we now have a very detailed account of the struggles among the justices that preceded the agreement. That account was pieced together by Bob Woodward, who had earlier helped to break the Watergate story with Carl Bernstein,[4] and Scott Armstrong, who had been an investigator for the Senate Watergate Committee. To get their information on this and various other cases decided by the Court over a seven-year period, they had to rely primarily on interviews with the young lawyers—called clerks—who worked with the justices.[5]

In this case, the eight justices met "in conference" the morning after they heard oral argument to vote on the case. They all agreed at once that the case was of sufficient constitutional significance that it should indeed be appealed to the Supreme Court. This was only a technical question. But had the Court decided otherwise, it could have

---

[4]Their adventures in doing so are described in their book *All the President's Men* (New York: Simon & Schuster, 1974) and portrayed in the movie of the same name. Their account of the end of the Nixon administration, including an early, brief effort at describing how the Court reached this decision, is in their book *The Final Days* (New York: Simon & Schuster, 1976)—see esp. p. 262.

[5]Bob Woodward and Scott Armstrong, *The Brethren: Inside the Supreme Court* (New York: Simon & Schuster, 1979). Their fascinating account has proved highly controversial. Few question the basic accuracy of the picture it paints, but many argue that its portrayal of the justices is unfortunate in "demystifying" this most important body. "The justices are shown scheming, flattering, and lobbying to obtain majorities for their own opinions, jockeying to insert their language into somebody else's opinion. Some of them are insecure, most are egotistical, and all are extremely concerned with individual and collective images. They bend principles, read the election returns, and gauge the political consequences of their actions," as Robert Kaus has summarized the picture. See Kaus, "They Were Wrong About the Brethren," *Washington Monthly*, March 1981, pp. 32–40. The article offers an interesting survey of the reaction to the book in the course of a favorable assessment.

thrown the case out.[6] They also agreed that the judiciary's specific need for 64 tapes for a criminal trial outweighed the president's claim to executive privilege—although they also agreed that some form of executive privilege did and should exist. These agreements meant that Nixon had already effectively lost the case, even though there remained other disagreements.[7]

However, it wasn't clear that losing the case would affect Nixon's behavior. In the oral argument, St. Clair had implied that Nixon might ignore the decision: "This case is being submitted to this Court for its guidance and judgment with respect to the law. . . . The President, on the other hand, has his obligation under the Constitution."

Therefore, several justices thought it especially important that the decision be unanimous. They saw the need for a single court opinion presenting the reasons for the decision in such a tightly argued fashion that there was no "air," as Nixon referred to it—no room for maneuver by which he might in practical effect accept the decision while refusing to abide by it.

Because of this concern for unanimity and because there were important differences among the justices, it took 15 days of negotiation before agreement was reached. These days were filled with memo writing, informal meetings, and drafts of proposed parts of the opinion written by one justice and circulated for comments to the others. In the course of these 15 days, tempers flared and justices plotted. Coalitions formed and dissolved. Drafts came and drafts went. Finally, on July 23, the justices gathered at 1:30 P.M. for what all hoped would be the final conference. According to Woodward and Armstrong:

> The tension was more pronounced than ever. Various pieces of the opinion draft had been okayed, but this was really their first look at the whole. It was now virtually impossible to trace the turns and twists the opinion had taken: ideas articulated by Douglas and Powell, modified by Brennan, quickly sketched by the

Chief; a section substituted by White; a footnote dropped by Marshall; Blackmun's facts embroidered over the Chief's; Stewart's constant tinkering and his ultimatum. Still hanging over them all was the possibility that the President of the United States might ignore them.[8]

After some final maneuvering by several justices, some four hours later the final vote was taken. It was 8 to 0, a unanimous opinion.[9]

When the decision was announced the next morning, Nixon's chief of staff, Alexander Haig, telephoned him with the news. Nixon guessed that the decision had been unanimous. Haig informed him that "there is no air in it at all."

"None at all?" Nixon asked.

"It's tight as a drum" was Haig's reply.[10]

As a result, Nixon decided he had to surrender the tapes. Those tapes revealed that Nixon's claim of executive privilege was itself a part of the very cover-up Nixon had denied even knowing about. The evidence was so damaging that the last vestiges of political support for Nixon evaporated: 16 days later he became the first American president to resign.

The courts were not solely responsible for removing Nixon from office. But they played an essential role—the role the courts are meant to serve in the realm of constitutional law: that of interpreting and applying the law. In the case of *U.S. v. Nixon* (418 U.S. 683, 94 S. Ct. 3090, 1974)—or, as it might in effect have been called, *The Nation v. Its Leader*—the Nation was the ultimate victor. However, the American legal system was, in a sense, the immediate victor. To understand this aspect of the case, we must know more about both the law and our legal system.

WHAT THE LAW IS

Our courts are supposed to interpret and apply the law. As the case of *U.S. v. Nixon* shows, this sounds easier to do than it usually is. Underlying many of the disputes about *what the law is* in a particular

---

[6]In this instance, the Court had agreed to hear the case directly, without waiting for a lower appeals court to hear it because the justices had decided it was extraordinarily urgent that Nixon's claim to executive privilege be resolved before the impeachment proceedings in Congress were concluded. Deciding to hear such a case early—to grant expedited review—requires the votes of at least five justices. Only four votes are required when the Court normally accepts a case on appeal by "granting cert"—writing a writ of certiorari. The vote in this case was 6 to 2.

[7]The major dispute at this point was over whether the president should be treated just like any other citizen, or whether he should be entitled to use a higher standard to withhold evidence because of national security or some other special presidential claim.

[8]Woodward and Armstrong, *The Brethren*, p. 344. The entire 15-day ordeal is chronicled in fascinating detail on pp. 308–46.

[9]Leon Friedman, ed., *United States v. Nixon: The President before the Supreme Court* (New York: Chelsea House, 1974), reprints all the briefs and oral arguments in the case and the full texts of all opinions from the district court, the appeals court, and the Supreme Court.

[10]See Richard Nixon, *RN: The Memoirs of Richard Nixon* (New York: Grosset & Dunlap, 1978), pp. 1051–52.

A headnote which precedes the Court's report of a case and summarizes the principles of law as established in that case.

Page number on which the case begins.

Page number in **U.S. Reports**

Syllabus

UNITED STATES *v.* NIXON, PRESIDENT OF THE UNITED STATES, ET AL.

The official title of the case.

"Certiorari" means "to be informed of" in Latin; indicates that the Court sent a message to the lower court informing it to send up the materials on the case because the Supreme Court has decided to review it "on appeal."

CERTIORARI BEFORE JUDGMENT TO THE UNITED STATES COURT OF APPEALS FOR THE DISTRICT OF COLUMBIA CIRCUIT

The number of this case in the October 1973 session of the court.

No. 73-1766. Argued July 8, 1974—Decided July 24, 1974*

Following indictment alleging violation of federal statutes by certain staff members of the White House and political supporters of the President, the Special Prosecutor filed a motion under Fed. Rule Crim. Proc. 17 (c) for a subpoena *duces tecum* for the production before trial of certain tapes and documents relating to precisely identified conversations and meetings between the President and others. The President, claiming executive privilege, filed a motion to quash the subpoena. The District Court, after treating the subpoenaed material as presumptively privileged, concluded that the Special Prosecutor had made a sufficient showing to rebut the presumption and that the requirements of Rule 17 (c) had been satisfied. The court thereafter issued an order for an *in camera* examination of the subpoenaed material, having rejected the President's contentions (a) that the dispute between him and the Special Prosecutor was nonjusticiable as an "intra-executive" conflict and (b) that the judiciary lacked authority to review the President's assertion of executive privilege. The court stayed its order pending appellate review, which the President then sought in the Court of Appeals. The Special Prosecutor then filed in this Court a petition for a writ of certiorari before judgment (No. 73-1766) and the President filed a cross-petition for such a writ challenging the grand-jury action (No. 73-1834). The Court granted both petitions. *Held:*

The Court summarizes the development of the case up to the point it reached the Court.

The District Court reached its decision, but suspended it to allow the President to appeal it to a higher court.

A statement of a decision by the Supreme Court to hear the case before the lower court to which it had been appealed decided it.

The Court states that it agreed to hear the case.

The Court summarizes its finding.

Citation of a part of the **U.S. Code** by volume and section that applies to this case.

1. The District Court's order was appealable as a "final" order under 28 U.S.C. §1291, was therefore properly "in" the Court of Appeals, 28 U.S.C. §1254, when the petition for certiorari before judgment was filed in this Court, and is now properly before this Court for review. Although such an order is normally not final and subject to appeal, an exception is made in a "limited class of cases where denial of immediate review would render impossible any review whatsoever of an individual's claims," *United States* v. *Ryan,* 402 U.S. 530, 533. Such an exception is proper in the unique circumstances of this case where it would be inappropriate to subject the President to the procedure of securing review by resisting the order and inappropriate to require that the District Court proceed by a traditional contempt citation in order to provide appellate review. Pp. 690-692.

The Court quotes its decision in a previous case.

Page numbers in **U.S. Reports** on which text of decision appears.

Volume number of **U.S. Reports** in which cited case appears.

2. The dispute between the Special Prosecutor and the President presents a justiciable controversy. Pp. 692-697.
(a) The mere assertion of an "intra-branch dispute," without more, does not defeat federal jurisdiction. *United States* v. *ICC,* 337 U.S. 426. P. 693.
(b) The Attorney General by regulation has conferred upon

The Court cites a previous case it believes relevant.

186, 211. Absent a claim of need to protect military, diplomatic, or sensitive national security secrets, the confidentiality of Presidential communications is not signi-

and that such material be returned under seal to its lawful custodian. Until released to the Special Prosecutor no *in camera* material is to be released to anyone. Pp. 714-716.

Location of the original decision on the case by the District Court.

No. 73-1766, 377 F. Supp. 1326, affirmed; No. 73-1834, certiorari dismissed as improvidently granted.

The Court agrees with (affirms) the decision of the lower court.

The Court dismisses Nixon's countercase.

The decision—and the written opinion—were unanimous.

BURGER, C. J. delivered the opinion of the Court, in which all Members joined except REHNQUIST, J., who took no part in the consideration or decision of the cases.

One justice removed himself from the case.

(The actual text of the Supreme Court's opinion follows.)

Indicates both cases were combined by the Court for its consideration.

*Together with No. 73-1834, *Nixon, President of the United States* v. *United States,* also on certiorari before judgment to the same court.

684 OCTOBER TERM, 1973

Syllabus 418 U.S.

Volume number of **U.S. Reports**, the official series in which all decisions and opinions are printed.

FIGURE 11.1

Excerpts from the Supreme Court's Summary of Its Action on the Watergate Tape Case.

case is a more general dispute over *what law is.* Philosophers have been debating this question for thousands of years, offering abstract definitions of law. Generally, dictionaries define law as "a uniform system of rules to govern or prescribe certain behavior for everyone living within a given area or legal jurisdiction."[11] But an abstract definition doesn't help us much in understanding what law really is. For that we need to put some historical flesh on these eternal bones.

Any society, to be and remain a society, requires predictable, common behavior by its members. In traditional societies—those we often call primitive or underdeveloped because they have not been transformed by industrialization—this social control is generally maintained by custom. People grow up living as their parents did; expectations don't change much, and so behavior is quite consistent. If someone deviates, everyone recognizes it. "Punishment" for deviance often takes the form of more intense efforts to integrate the deviant into the society rather than exiling or imprisoning him or her. We sometimes refer to these accepted rules of conduct as **customary law.**

Customary law works well as long as society is stable and as long as outside influences such as colonization or even trade are limited. But in a world of rapid social change, with growing commerce and industry, social stability tends to break down and customary law becomes less effective. However, no society can long survive without law. It is impossible in a complex and changing world to depend on actual police power for social control. There are never enough police officers around to observe and channel every person's every action. It is essential for society to move toward voluntary compliance. But in order to comply voluntarily, people must know the rules and believe them somehow deserving of acceptance. There must, in other words, be law.

We might think of law as "paper power," replacing the "gun power" and "police power" that keep whatever order there is where law does not exist or has broken down. But we shouldn't be fooled into thinking that paper power is weaker than gun power or police power. Quite the contrary. In the cases of both law and money, mere pieces of paper affect people's behavior because people believe that the paper *means* something in the society. The people accept the society—which stands behind the paper—and so they accept the paper itself as real money and real law. In other words, the eixstence of paper power is an indication of the strength and stability of the society, whereas reliance on gun power is a sign of weakness.

This law and the legal system that develops and interprets it operate in a changing environment. The legal system must therefore develop ways of maintaining the law while changing it so that people will continue to accept it. Every society thus faces a dual problem: first, to maintain law and order; and second, to remain flexible enough to alter that law and order in the face of new challenges to the society. The legal dimension of the problem has two aspects. The first is to find ways to change the law enough so that people will continue to accept it as fair, appropriate, binding, or legitimate in changing circumstances. The second is to avoid changing it so much that people begin to see the law as nothing more than the momentary whims of the people, or of the ruling power, in which case they may lose respect for the law as an institution. Laws that change too quickly may threaten the legal system every bit as much as laws that do not change quickly enough.

Indeed, even when the old bases for customary law and equity have disappeared, beliefs still linger in the minds of the people. Today, for example, "gay (homosexual) rights" activists and proabortion groups are vehemently opposed by many who continue to believe these activists are violating "the laws of God" or "the laws of nature," even where "the laws of man"—as our legislatures have passed them and our courts have interpreted them—no longer support this position. And these opponents attack the law that deviates from traditional standards and attempt to restore it to its previous condition.

There is another way in which rapid change in the law may threaten the legal system. As society becomes more complex, the law itself becomes more complex and extensive. It thus becomes *harder* for citizens—and even for enforcement officials and lawyers—*to know what the law actually is* on a given subject. If you don't know what the law is, you may well have trouble obeying it. But your responsibility to do so remains just the same.

---

[11]For philosophical discussions on the nature of law, see M. P. Golding, ed., *The Nature of Law* (New York: Random House, 1966). And for a particularly stimulating study, see H. L. A. Hart, *The Concept of Law* (New York: Oxford Univ. Press, 1961).

WHERE THE COURTS GET THE LAW TO INTERPRET

The courts, it is said, interpret the law. But where do they find the law they interpret? The major source—or at least the most basic source—is the Constitution, which is the highest law of the land. But the Constitution is a very brief document. Its 7500 words couldn't possibly cover adequately most of the cases that come before the courts. The people who wrote it intended it to provide a detailed statement of the structure or machinery of national government along with general guidelines for its operation. The specific rules were to come primarily from five other sources: statutory law, common law, equity, administrative law, and judicial interpretation of the Constitution.

Constitutional Law

The Supreme Court's most significant concern is with constitutional law. The case we've just looked at demonstrates that this term refers to much more than just the words in the Constitution. The opinions we quoted from above deal with terms, such as *executive privilege*, that do not appear anywhere in the Constitution. And the Court's deliberations make constant reference to previous decisions and the language used in those opinions. This is all included in what we mean by constitutional law. It is law invoking the interpretation and application of the Constitution. It is concerned primarily with describing the extent and limits of governmental power and the rights of individuals, as set forth in the United States Constitution.[12]

Statutory Law

Most court cases are not concerned with constitutional law. Rather, they involve what we call **statutory law**—law made by statutes; in other words, legislation. Such statutory law covers a wide range of subjects because governments make laws on a wide range of topics. At the federal level, it is law made by Congress. At the state level, it is law made by state legislatures. At the local level, it is law made by county governing bodies, city councils, and other such groups.

Criminal Law versus Civil Law

Another distinction is often made between two types of statutory law. **Criminal law** defines crimes against the public order. It consists of cases in which the government sues because of actions violating laws protecting the health, safety, and morals of the community.

Laws applying to relations between individuals are categorized as **civil law.** One branch of civil law concerns contracts—disputes coming out of voluntary actions. Another branch concerns torts—wrongs or disputes arising out of obligations inherent in social life. Examples of torts are slander and negligence.

Common Law

But even though it often seems that there are laws concerning virtually everything, in fact much of the time judges still apply what we call **common law.** Common law is customary law or precedent—the way things have traditionally been done. It is judge-made law, in that it is based on the totality of decisions made by judges in past cases decided in past years. In fact, common law can be traced back to 12th-century England, where judges began to travel around the country deciding cases in terms of local customs—the practices of the common people. The decisions were generally intended to repair damages once they were done, rather than to prevent damages from occurring. When the English came to America, they brought their common law with them. When America gained its independence, it kept its common-law heritage, so that there was law to be applied on all sorts of subjects even before there was a Congress to begin passing statutes. But the law to be applied had to be selected from precedents by a judge, for it had not been passed by a legislature.

Stare Decisis

The fundamental principle of common law is the continuity of precedent, or previous court decisions. This principle is reflected in the maxim *stare decisis*, a Latin term meaning "let the decision stand." But of course each region has its own unique experience and its own history of judges'

---

[12]The U.S. Constitution is "the supreme law of the land." Each of the 50 states also has a state constitution and a state supreme court to interpret it.

decisions; thus, the common law differs from state to state. (The exception is Louisiana, which because of its French heritage has a legal system based on a "civil code" of statutory law.) As a result, in the United States we have 49 somewhat different state common-law systems.

Equity

Another component of our legal system is **equity.** Equity, in everyday usage another term for fairness, provides guidance to judges where the common law does not apply. Common law, as we said above, usually applies after the fact, to correct matters once damage is done. Equity law was developed to allow judges to order that something not be done—in order to prevent damage—or to order that something be done—in order to avert damage. Equity is applied where waiting until the law is broken would not be advisable.

Administrative Law

So far we have been examining forms of law developed by legislation and judicial decision. We have not yet mentioned the fastest-growing type of law: **administrative law.** We noted in Chapter 9 that bureaucratic agencies have developed their own ways of making regulations that are as binding on us as if they were laws passed by Congress. Indeed, in an indirect sense they are laws passed by Congress because Congress often grants such agencies the power to issue binding regulations. Congress also allows or instructs these agencies to establish their own internal court systems to review compliance with their regulations and to hear complaints about them. Citizens or businesses unhappy with an administrative ruling may appeal the decision to the regular federal court system, where the courts will generally compare the ruling with the terms of the original statute establishing the agency.[13]

These, then, are the major types of law that are likely to affect us as citizens.[14]

---

[13]See Martin Shapiro, *The Supreme Court and Administrative Agencies* (New York: Free Press, 1968).

[14]We have not considered several others. Admiralty and maritime law is federal law concerning shipping on rivers and on the high seas. International law is the law of custom, treaty, and agreement among nation-states.

THE COURTS WE HAVE

Providing legal protection—to the accused, to the police themselves, and to us as ordinary citizens—is the job of our courts. We normally think of the Supreme Court as our chief protector, followed by the "lower" federal courts. But of the ten million court cases heard annually, less than 2 percent are heard in federal courts. The rest take place in state and local courts. This is because the Constitution reserves general police powers to the states. Therefore, such crimes as murder, robbery, assault, and rape are normally state offenses rather than federal crimes. Congress determines federal offenses by passing bills outlawing certain things. The list of federal offenses now includes, among other specific prohibitions:

- Offenses against the U.S. government or its property
- Offenses against U.S. government employees while they are on duty
- Offenses by U.S. government employees while they are on duty
- Offenses that involve crossing state lines (and so would involve two different state legal systems)
- Offenses that involve interference with interstate commerce
- Offenses occurring in federal territories or on federal reservations
- Offenses occurring on the high seas
- Offenses against federally insured institutions

Cases that concern constitutional questions such as freedom of speech or of assembly are also tried by federal courts.

The State and Local Courts

The individual state court systems vary greatly. Their general structure is relatively common, however. At the bottom are local courts of limited jurisdiction, such as justices of the peace, police courts, traffic courts, family courts, small-claims courts, juvenile courts, and so on. These courts handle minor cases. Next come the general trial courts, which handle major offenses against state laws. These courts have various names in various states: district, circuit, common pleas, or superior courts. Some states then have an intermediate or appellate court to hear appeals based on points of law after the facts have been determined and the

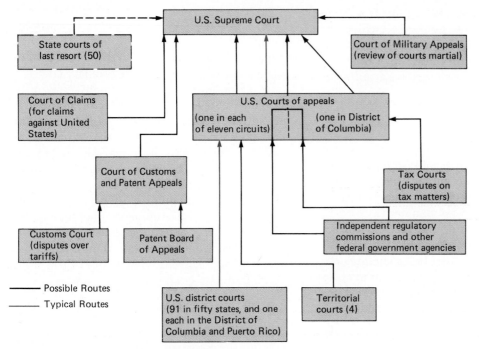

FIGURE 11.2
The Court System of the United States.

case has been tried and decided by the lower court. At the top in all states is the state court of last resort, usually called the supreme court, which is the final interpreter of the state constitution and laws and which hears appeals of decisions from lower courts. Cases can go from the state court of last resort to the U.S. Supreme Court if a federal question is involved and if the Supreme Court agrees to review the case.

The Federal Courts

Most federal cases originate in federal district courts (see Figure 11.2). There are 91 such districts: one or more for each state and one each for the District of Columbia and Puerto Rico. In addition, the Virgin Islands, the Canal Zone, the Mariana Islands, and Guam each have a territorial court. Each district has a group of federal judges, the number related to the number of cases it generally gets. There are some 507 district judges in all.

A party that loses a case in a district court may attempt to appeal that decision to a higher court. There are 12 such U.S. courts of appeals, each of which is called a circuit. The appeals courts—with

132 judges in all—hear perhaps 5000 cases a year. A loser in an appeals court may then ask the Supreme Court to hear the case, and many do so. These appeals from lower courts are the bulk of the 5000 cases submitted to the Supreme Court each year.[15] Appeals are supposed to be made in cases that involve questions of law and constitutionality rather than simply to examine new evidence. If an appellate court agrees to hear a case on appeal, it issues a **writ of certiorari**, which is an order to the lower court to send up the records of the case for review.[16] By the unwritten "rule of four," observed for some 50 years now by the Supreme Court, any four Supreme Court justices can agree to *grant cert*, as it is called, and the Court will then review the case, either hearing oral argument on it or deciding it without oral argument.

There are, in general, four types of cases which may finally reach the Supreme Court on appeal:

---

[15]See Doris Marie Provine, *Case Selection in the U.S. Supreme Court* (Chicago: Univ. of Chicago Press, 1980).

[16]There are also several categories of cases in which appeal is a "right." One whose claim under federal law is rejected by the highest state court or whose claim that a state law violates the federal Constitution is rejected in the highest state court has such a right of appeal. Appeal is also a matter of right when a lower federal court declares a state law unconstitutional or generally when a lower federal court finds an act of Congress invalid. The Court takes such cases on a *writ of appeal*.

- A case involving a private individual or a corporation and a government agency disputing the meaning of a federal law being applied by the agency to the private party.
- A case involving two parties who are disputing the meaning of a federal law and a federal agency's enforcement of it.
- A federal *or state* criminal prosecution in which the defendant being prosecuted claims that the law being enforced violates the Constitution or that the way he or she was arrested, investigated, tried, or sentenced violated his or her federal constitutional rights.
- A suit asking the court to order a public official either to stop doing something prohibited by the Constitution (called an **injunction**) or to do something required by the Constitution. However, the only individual with "standing to sue" (that is, with a position entitling him or her to go to court) in these instances is one who can show that he or she has been personally harmed by the administration of the law in question. One generally shows this by violating the law and being punished for the violation.

The Supreme Court also gets some cases on original jurisdiction—as the first and only court to hear them. These are cases involving disputes between two states, disputes between a state and the federal government, and cases involving ambassadors, consuls, or other public ministers. Figure 11.3 indicates the routes cases may take to the Supreme Court.

WHO SERVES ON OUR COURTS

Supreme Court Justices

Through its 200-year history, only 107 men and 1 woman have served as Supreme Court justices. Because tenure is for life or until retirement—or, in rare cases, resignation—justices generally serve for a long time. Because all federal judges are lawyers by profession, justices are inevitably an elite group. But they are much less representative of the population than are lawyers as a whole. Through 1986 all justices but one had been men, and all but one (Thurgood Marshall) had been white. Indeed, about 90 percent have been of British ethnic origin, and over 85 percent have been Protestant. In recent times, it has been customary to have a Catholic and a Jew on the Court. But President Nixon declined to refill the "Jewish seat" with a Jew, and so that token variety disappeared. The result is that the typical justice has been a white, male, Prot-

FIGURE 11.3
How Cases Get to the Supreme Court.

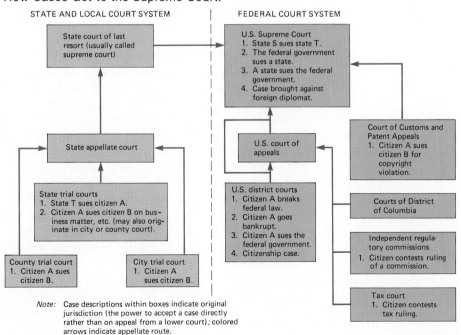

Note: Case descriptions within boxes indicate original jurisdiction (the power to accept a case directly rather than on appeal from a lower court); colored arrows indicate appellate route.

TABLE 11.1
Supreme Court Justices

NAME	YEAR OF BIRTH	STATE OF RESIDENCE	LAW SCHOOL ATTENDED	POSITION WHEN APPOINTED	PREVIOUS YEARS AS A JUDGE	PRESIDENT WHO APPOINTED	YEAR APPOINTED
William H. Rehnquist, Chief Justice	1924	Arizona	Stanford	Assistant Attorney General	0	Nixon (to court) Reagan (to Chief Justice)	1972 1986
William J. Brennan, Jr.	1906	New Jersey	Harvard	State Supreme Court	7	Eisenhower	1956
Byron R. White	1918	Colorado	Yale	Deputy Attorney General	0	Kennedy	1962
Thurgood Marshall	1908	Maryland	Howard	U.S. Solicitor General	4	Johnson	1967
Harry A. Blackmun	1908	Minnesota	Harvard	U.S. Court of Appeals	11	Nixon	1970
Lewis F. Powell, Jr.	1907	Virginia	Washington and Lee	Private practice of law	0	Nixon	1972
John Paul Stevens	1916	Illinois	Chicago	U.S. Court of Appeals	5	Ford	1975
Sandra Day O'Connor	1930	Arizona	Stanford	Arizona Court of Appeals	8	Reagan	1981
Antonin Scalia	1936	Washington, D.C.	Harvard	U.S. Court of Appeals	4	Reagan	1986

estant Anglo-Saxon, from an upper-class or an upper-middle-class urban family, with a law degree and a career including previous public service and often political activity as well.[17] Table 11.1 summarizes personal characteristics of the current court justices.

Other Federal Judges— and Senatorial Courtesy

Federal judges in lower courts have generally been slightly less atypical of the population—although they are still usually WASP males—and much less distinguished. The primary reason is the custom called senatorial courtesy. According to this practice, the president is expected to consult with the senators from the state to which a district judge is to be appointed. If a senator and the president are of the same political party, the senator is allowed to have an absolute veto over the choice. If both senators are from the same party as the president, the senior senator has the veto power. The result, not surprisingly, has been the tendency to appoint political friends of senators—appointees who may have better political than legal qualifications. All this is made possible by the fact that the Senate as a whole must approve these appointments, and it defers to the judgment of the relevant member.

Legal qualifications of possible and actual nominees are usually assessed by the Committee on the Federal Judiciary of the American Bar Association (the major professional association of lawyers in America). Some critics believe the ABA's standards of adequacy are too lax. But they have at least made it more difficult for a president to appoint political hacks who are officially rated incompetent by the lawyers who would be practicing before them.[18]

[17]For details on judicial recruitment, as the selection of justices is called, see John R. Schmidhauser, *The Supreme Court: Its Politics, Personalities, and Procedures* (New York: Holt, Rinehart & Winston, 1960), and Henry J. Abraham, *Justices and Presidents* (New York: Oxford Univ. Press, 1974).

[18]See Harold W. Chase, *Federal Judges: The Appointing Process* (Minneapolis: Univ. of Minnesota Press, 1972), and Joel B. Grossman, *Lawyers and Judges: The ABA and the Politics of Judicial Selection* (New York: Wiley, 1965).

The members of the Supreme Court in a photo taken just before Justice Lewis Powell announced his retirement in the summer of 1987. (Left to right) Standing: Sandra Day O'Conner, Lewis F. Powell, Jr., John Paul Stevens, and Antonin Scalia; seated: Thurgood Marshall, William J. Brennan, Jr., William H. Rehnquist (Chief Justice), Bryon R. White, and Harry A. Blackmun. (UPI/Bettmann Newsphotos)

In his presidential campaign, Jimmy Carter pledged to reduce the politics in the selection of federal judges and to select more women and minorities for these posts on the federal bench. He had a special opportunity to do so because Congress created 152 new federal judgeships, an increase of 29 percent, shortly after he took office. All told, Carter's 262 appointments drastically changed the makeup of the federal bench. Neither Nixon nor Ford had appointed any women or minorities to the U.S. Court of Appeals; Carter chose 11 women, 9 blacks, and 2 Hispanics among his 56 appointees to that court. At the district-court level, Nixon and Ford had appointed several members of each group; Carter picked 29 women, 29 blacks, and 14 Hispanics among his 206 appointments.[19]

Experts expect these appointments to change the functioning of the courts over time somewhat. As Althea T. L. Simmons of the NAACP remarked: "I think it's going to have a long-range effect. You're going to have persons on the bench who can bring an additional kind of sensitivity to those groups who have not been represented in the past in large measure."[20] But even now, women make up less than 7 percent of the federal bench, although 45,000 women practice law.

President Reagan kept his campaign pledge to appoint a woman to one of the first Supreme Court vacancies. But his platform called for appointing judges who believed in "the decentralization of the federal government" and "who respect the traditional family values and the sanctity of innocent human life." During Reagan's presidency, Congress increased the number of judges by another 12 percent. He appointed few women and very few blacks and Hispanics. Selections were made in a very deliberate manner. The assistant attorney general who handled the nomination process, Stephen J. Markman, described its purpose as

---

[19]In fact, these figures overstate the totals slightly because 1 of the 9 black appeals judges was a woman, and 6 of the 29 black and 1 of the Hispanic district judges were women.

[20]Quoted in Nadine Cohodas, "Carter's Efforts to Diversify the Bench . . . Leave Reagan a Tough Act to Follow," *CQ Weekly Report*, February 14, 1981, p. 301.

Matthew Brady took the first photograph of the Supreme Court in 1869. (National Archives and Records Service)

to ascertain the approach to jurisprudence that will be taken by our appointees—an understanding of the limited judicial role, a proper sense of deference to the representative branches of government, a respect for . . . federalism and separation of powers, and a commitment to interpreting the Constitution consistent with the intended meaning of its drafters."[21]

Because of retirements and new judgeships, Reagan appointed over 300 new judges. This promises to have a major impact on court decisions quite different from that of the Carter appointees because the Reagan selection criteria have been based in political philosophy.

THE LIFE OF A SUPREME COURT JUSTICE

Once selected and confirmed by the Senate, the life of a judge is one of prestige but rarely one of leisure. Lower court judges are, by common observation, seriously overworked. Supreme Court justices now work in "the great marble palace," as it is often called; are paid $110,000 a year; and have assistants to help with everything from looking up the laws to keeping in good physical shape.[22] But they too are extremely busy. The Court began life in 1789 in a commercial building in New York City, eventually moved to the Old City Hall in Philadelphia, and finally spent 75 years in spare rooms of the U.S. Senate. Only in 1935 did it move to its present palatial quarters.

All justices have their "chambers"—four private offices, for themselves, their three or four law clerks (recent graduates of top law schools), and two secretaries—clustered near the courtroom. Justices are very secretive about their activities, but we have recently learned something of what their working lives are like. They generally spend 4 hours each of three days every two weeks (a total of 24 hours a month) hearing oral argument on a total of 24 cases per month in Court. They have secret conferences

[21]Quoted in Nadine Cohodas, "Reagan Leaving Conservative Mark on Courts," *CQ Weekly Report*, November 1, 1986, p. 2729.

[22]Some law clerks exercise with their justices in the Supreme Court gym.

Former Justice Potter Stewart. (AP/Wide World Photos)

on Wednesday afternoon and all day Friday of the weeks they hear oral argument. At these meetings, they debate and vote on cases. Some of the justices occasionally eat lunch together in their private dining room. But "for the most part," Justice Lewis F. Powell, Jr., told an American Bar Association convention in 1976, "perhaps 90 percent of the time, we function as nine small, independent law firms," meeting as a group only for the oral argument sessions and the conferences. The justices, he reported, communicate with each other mostly in writing. "Indeed, a Justice may go through an entire term without being once in the chambers of all the other eight members of the court." The Court, he concluded, is not at all the collegial body he expected to find it, despite the homogeneity of background of its members. Rather, it is "one of the last citadels of jealously preserved individualism."[23] (For a more detailed account by Justice Potter Stewart, who retired in July 1981 after 24 years of service, see the box entitled "Inside the Supreme Court."[24])

[23]John P. MacKenzie, "Powell Calls Court Criticism 'Alarmist,'" *Washington Post*, August 12, 1976, p. A28.

[24]For interesting, detailed accounts, unprecedented from sitting justices, see John A. Jenkins, "A Candid Talk with Justice Blackmun," *New York Times Magazine*, February 20, 1983, p. 20; and Jeffrey T. Leeds, "A Life on the Court," a conversation with Justice Brennan, *New York Times Magazine*, October 5, 1986, p. 25.

HOW JUDGES DECIDE

Despite this "jealously preserved individualism," the Court must reach its decisions collectively. To the extent that our account of *U.S.* v. *Nixon* is indicative, this process in critical cases is rarely harmonious—even when the justices are in general agreement. Except for the rare insider account of the sort in *The Brethren*, we have little to go on in understanding how judges make up their minds. However, justices occasionally speak to that question.

Many years ago, a decade before he was appointed to the Supreme Court, Appeals Court Judge Benjamin Cardozo gave what is probably still as good a characterization of judicial decision making as we have:

> My analysis of the judicial process comes then to this, and little more: logic, and history, and custom, and utility, and the accepted standards of right conduct, are the forces which singly or in combination shape the progress of the law. Which of these forces shall dominate in any case must depend largely upon the comparative importance or value of the social interest that will thereby be promoted or impaired. . . . If you ask how [the judge] is to know when one interest outweighs another, I can only answer that he must get his knowledge just as the legislator gets it; from experience and study and reflection; in brief, from life itself.[25]

Scholars have attempted to be more systematic in explaining judges' decisions. They generally focus their analyses on four factors. The first is *the state of the law* that is applicable in the case—and laws usually need interpretation. Thus, justices may attempt to discover **legislative intent**—what Congress meant to do when it wrote the law. They may study hearings and reports and the *Congressional Record* to discover this, but it often remains unclear. Another aspect of the state of the law is precedent: the Court's previous decisions. Only on rare occasions (one study found an average of four cases a year) does the Court overturn one of its previous decisions.[26]

In general, then, the state of the law will tend to limit or channel the justices' decisions, but it may not determine them.

[25]Benjamin N. Cardozo, The Nature of the Judicial Press (New Haven, CT: Yale Univ. Press, 1921), pp. 112–13.

[26]Congressional Research Service, *The Constitution of the United States of America: Analysis and Interpretation* (Washington, DC: GPO, 1981).

Inside the Supreme Court

Each Justice receives copies of every certiorari petition (a request to the Court to hear a case) and response. Each Justice, without consultation with his colleagues, reaches his own tentative conclusion whether the petition should be granted or denied. The first consultation comes at the Court conference at which the case is listed for discussion on the agenda. We sit in conference almost every Friday during the term. Those conferences begin at 9:30 and continue through the day, except for a half-hour recess for lunch. Only the Justices are present. There are no law clerks, no stenographers, no secretaries, no pages—just the nine of us. The conferences are held in an oak-paneled room with one wall lined with books from floor to ceiling. Over the mantel of the marble fireplace at one end hangs the only picture—a portrait of Chief Justice John Marshall. In the middle of the room stands a rectangular table, large enough for the nine of us. Upon entering, each of us shakes hands with his colleagues. This handshake tradition originated many years ago. It is a symbol that harmony of aims, if not of views, is the Court's guiding principle. Each of us has his own copy of the agenda of the cases to be considered, and each has done his homework and noted on his copy his tentative view in every case as to whether review on the merits should be granted or denied.

The Chief Justice begins the discussion of each case. Then discussion proceeds down the line by seniority until each Justice has spoken. Voting goes the other way, if there is any need for a formal vote following the discussion. When any case receives four votes for review, certiorari is granted, and that case is then transferred to the Argument List. This "Rule of 4" is not written down anywhere, but it is an absolutely inflexible rule.

Oral argument ordinarily takes place about four months after the petition for certiorari is granted. Each party used to be allowed one hour for argument, but in recent years we have limited oral argument to half an hour a side in almost all cases. Counsel submit their briefs and record in sufficient time for the distribution of one set to each Justice two or three weeks before the argument. We follow a schedule of two weeks of argument, followed by two weeks of recess for opinion writing and the study of petitions for review. The Friday conference discussion of the dozen or so cases that have been argued that week follows the same procedure described for the discussion of certiorari petitions, but, of course, the discussion of an argued case is generally much more extended. Not until the discussion is completed and a vote is taken is the opinion assigned. The senior member of the majority designates one of his colleagues or sometimes himself to write the opinion of the Court. This means that the Chief Justice assigns the opinions in those cases in which he has voted with the majority, and the senior associate Justice in the majority assigns the opinions in all other cases. The dissenters agree among themselves who will write the dissenting opinion. But each Justice is free to write his own individual opinion, concurring or dissenting.

The writing of an opinion is not easy work. It always takes weeks, sometimes months. When the author of an opinion for the Court has completed his work, he sends a printed copy to each member, those in dissent as well as in the majority. Often some of those who voted with him at the conference will say that they want to reserve final judgment pending circulation of the dissent. It is a common experience that drafts of dissenting opinions change votes, even enough votes to become the majority. Before everyone has finally made up his mind, a constant interchange goes on while we work out the final form of the Court opinion. There was one case this past term in which I circulated 10 printed drafts before one was finally approved as the opinion of the Court. The point is that each Justice, unless he disqualifies himself in a particular case, passes on every piece of business. The Court does not function by means of committees or panels. The process can be a lonely, troubling experience for fallible human beings conscious that their best may not be adequate to the challenge. A Justice does not forget how much may depend on his decision. He knows that it may affect the course of important social, economic and political currents.

From Potter Stewart, "Inside the Supreme Court," the *New York Times,* October 1, 1979. This is a portion of an address to the Cincinnati Bar Association. It draws upon an article written by his colleague, William J. Brennan, Jr., which appeared in 1963 in the *New York Times Magazine.* © 1979 by The New York Times Company. Reprinted by permission.

The Court operates in *a political environment:* This is the second influence on justices' decisions. Justices, like other political figures, are aware of public opinion and of the interests and concerns of other political actors in the executive and legislative branches. Presidents, after all, appoint all federal judges, and the Senate must confirm these appointments. Congress creates all courts other than the Supreme Court, and it sets the number and salaries of all judges. In addition, Congress occasion-

The Supreme Court's conference room. (Yoichi R. Okamoto/Photo Researchers)

ally threatens to pass laws removing certain areas (such as abortion or school prayer) from the Supreme Court's jurisdiction—which would prevent the Court from accepting cases in those areas. Experts disagree as to whether Congress has the power to do this, but we won't know for sure unless and until Congress tries it.[27] In addition, special-interest groups may bring suit or file amicus curiae briefs on cases before the courts.[28]

This brings us to the third—and, most experts agree, the most important—factor: *the values and policy preferences of the judges.* At any given time, some justices seem more liberal, others more conservative. One study found that most issues before the Court have fallen into one of three categories: freedom or civil liberties, equality or discrimination, and government regulation of the economy. In each area, justices have tended to divide along liberal-conservative lines. The same justices have tended to vote together from one case to the next in each area.[29] Some justices do change their orientations over time, but the big changes in the

Court come when one justice dies or retires and another joins the Court.

The final influence on decision making is the *interaction among the justices.* In general, justices have sought to reach agreement before finally deciding a case, and to keep concurring opinions (opinions written by justices who agree with the decision but not with the grounds for it expressed in the Court's majority opinion) to a minimum, so that not only the decision but also the *reasoning* of the Court will be clear. But in recent years, there have been more and more concurring opinions, and many of them have contained openly critical statements about other justices' arguments. Thus, justices seem to influence each other, positively and negatively, more now than in the past.

WHAT JUDGES AND COURTS DO

Constitutional Powers

We must still ask, however, what roles Supreme Court justices play in our legal system and what functions the legal system has in our society. The brief passage on judicial power in the Constitution says only that "the judicial power shall extend to all cases, in law and equity, arising under this Constitution, the laws of the United States, and Treaties made, or which shall be made, under their authority. . . . " This language tells us which cases

---

[27]See Nadine Cohodas, "Members Move to Rein in Supreme Court," *Congressional Quarterly Weekly Report*, May 30, 1981, pp. 947–51, for a discussion.

[28]See Stephen L. Wasby, "Interest Groups in Court: Race Relations Litigation," in *Interest Group Politics*, ed. Allan J. Cigler and Burdett A. Loomis (Washington, DC: CQ Press, 1983), chap. 11, and Aryeh Neier, *Only Judgment: The Limits of Litigation in Social Change* (Middletown, CT: Wesleyan Univ. Press, 1983).

[29]See David W. Rohde and Harold J. Spaeth, *Supeme Court Decision Making* (San Francisco: Freeman, 1976).

the federal courts can handle. But it says nothing of how the judicial power will conduct itself.

Judicial Decision

Our system is called an adversary system of justice because, in most cases, each party to a dispute is represented by a lawyer who argues that side as strongly as he or she can. The judge and/or jury then decides which party has the better case, given the existing law, and decides the case in favor of that party.[30]

Judicial "Lawmaking"

The judge is supposed to be a neutral observer applying the law to a case. But in fact, inevitably, he or she has to interpret the law—figure out what it really means or what it really implies about the particular case. And this role of interpretation—of applying general laws to specific cases—inevitably requires that *judges make law*. The laws and the Constitution are full of general terms such as *reasonable care, due process, adequate notice*, and *unreasonable search and seizure*. In deciding what these terms mean, judges extend them to cover cases they did not previously cover—perhaps because situations did not exist when the words were first written. This is what is meant by the term *judge-made law*.

The role of the Supreme Court here is special because it is the highest court in the land. In the famous words of the late Justice Robert H. Jackson: "We are not final because we are infallible, but we are infallible only because we are final."[31] The Supreme Court, as the court of last resort, can overrule a decision by a lower court. But the only thing that can overrule a Supreme Court decision is another Supreme Court decision or a constitutional amendment.[32] In the words of Justice Byron R. White: "This Court has overruled itself more

than 150 times since 1789: Justices will change their minds, and new Justices do come along; they renew the Court."[33]

Judicial Review

The Practice

Not surprisingly, justices are more apt to overrule others than they are to overrule themselves. Judges sometimes find that certain behavior conflicts with the stipulations of the Constitution. In the case of *U.S.* v. *Nixon*, for example, the president's claim to executive privilege was found consistent with the constitutional provision of separation of powers but insufficiently strong to overcome the demands of due process for a fair trial in the Watergate prosecutions. Similarly, in the Pentagon Papers case, the government's efforts to suppress the publication of news articles about a secret government study of American involvement in Vietnam were found inconsistent with the right to freedom of the press.

More significant, perhaps, but less common are the instances in which the judges interpreting a law conclude that the law itself conflicts with the terms of the Constitution, which is the highest law of the land. In its 200-year history, the Supreme Court has declared just over 100 federal laws—or parts thereof—unconstitutional. The Court may also declare state and local legislation unconstitutional. The latter happens more frequently, in large part because there are 50 different states, 3000 counties, and 35,000 cities passing laws that may conflict with the federal Constitution. In 200 years there have been just over 1000 such cases.[34]

The Case of Marbury v. Madison

The Constitution does not explicitly give the Supreme Court the power to decide that a law or an act is unconstitutional. That power was "read into" the Constitution by the Court when it decided the landmark case of *Marbury* v. *Madison* in 1803.[35] On the day before he left office, after being defeated by Thomas Jefferson in 1800, Federalist

---

[30]Other systems work quite differently. In much of Europe, for example, the judge acts as the inquiring lawyer as well as the decider. And in China, courts may in a sense decide that both parties are somewhat right and hand down two decisions, one for each party, so that there need not be a winner and a loser, as in our system.

[31]In his concurring opinion in *Brown* v. *Allen*, 334 U.S. 433 (1953), at 540.

[32]Of course, should the Supreme Court rule that a particular action is contrary to a law, Congress may change the law to make the action legal in the future.

[33]Quoted in Richard L. Williams, "Justices Run 'Nine Little Law Firms,'" *Smithsonian*, January 1977, p. 90.

[34]For details on both categories, see Congressional Research Service, *The Constitution of the United States of America*.

[35]*Marbury* v. *Madison* was the first instance of a federal law being declared unconstitutional, but several state statutes had been declared unconstitutional before 1803.

President John Adams appointed some political friends to be judges. One of them, William Marbury, was given a five-year appointment as a justice of the peace for Washington, DC. But Adams's secretary of state, John Marshall, forgot to deliver to Marbury the certificate (or "commission," as it was called) declaring him a judge. When Jefferson took office the next day, his secretary of state, James Madison, refused to deliver the commission to Marbury. Congress had stated in the Judiciary Act of 1789 that one could ask the Supreme Court directly for a **writ of mandamus** (Latin for "we command"). Such a writ orders a government official or court to perform duties required of it by law. Marbury therefore asked the Supreme Court for a writ requiring Madison to give him his commission so that he could serve as a justice of the peace.

John Marshall, who had forgotten to deliver the commission to Marbury, had by then taken up his appointment as chief justice. He and the rest of the Court agreed that Marbury had a legal right to his commisssion. But the Court refused to issue the writ of mandamus. It ruled instead that Article III of the Constitution did not give it the power to do so when defining the Court's original jurisdiction (the power to accept a case directly rather than on appeal from a lower court). The Judiciary Act of 1789 was thus, it said, an unconstitutional attempt to enlarge the power of the Court. The Court defended this decision by stating:

> The particular phraseology of the Constitution of the United States confirms and strengthens the principle, supposed to be essential to all written constitutions, that a law repugnant to the constitution is void, and that courts, as well as other departments, are bound by that instrument.[36]

The Doctrine

Marbury v. *Madison* was the first time the Court declared a federal law unconstitutional—and the last time it did so for another 54 years. **Judicial review**, as it came to be called, remained a controversial doctrine. Jefferson and many others continued to argue that all three branches of government were coequal, and so each had to be the final judge of the constitutionality of its own acts. If differ-

ences arose, they argued, those disputes should be resolved through the political process—by such clearly constitutional devices as impeachment or elections. This was basically the same argument President Nixon and his lawyers made 170 years later concerning the Watergate tapes, as we saw earlier in this chapter. But others have pointed to various statements during the drafting of the Constitution and again during the debates over its ratification by the states in which the power of judicial review was ascribed to the judicial branch.[37]

The doctrine of judicial review has survived the objections of Jefferson and Nixon and many in between. It remains the basis for an important part of the power of the courts. This power to review the actions of individuals and agencies or the laws of Congress, of states, or of localities may be exercised by a judge or a court at any level of the federal system. But it is most effective when done by the Supreme Court, from whose decision there is no further legal appeal.

Still, the Court, with good reason, employs the power with great restraint. For, as James Bradley Thayer remarked, the exercise of the power of judicial review,

> even when unavoidable, is always attended with a serious evil, namely that the correction of legislative mistakes comes from the outside, and the people thus lose the political experience, and the moral education and stimulus, that comes from fighting the question out in the ordinary way, and correcting their own errors.[38]

Judicial Opinions

All it takes to get a Supreme Court decision is a majority of the justices voting the same way on the question of whether to affirm (sustain) or to reverse (overturn) a decision by a lower court. But voting is not all the justices do. And often in the longer run, the actual vote proves to be less important than the opinions the judges write to explain their reasoning.

If a case is clear to the justices, or if it seems relatively insignificant as they decide it, there may be no opinions, only a vote. If the Court's decision

---

[36]For an account of this interesting case, including its political context, which we cannot summarize here, see Donald O. Dewey, *Marshall versus Jefferson: The Political Background of Marbury v. Madison* (New York: Knopf, 1970), or Charles Warren, *The Supreme Court in U.S. History,* vol. 2 (Boston: Little, Brown, 1926), pp. 169–316.

[37]See, for example, Raoul Berger, *Congress v. the Supreme Court* (Cambridge, MA: Harvard Univ. Press, 1969), pp. 8–285. For a stimulating recent analysis, see John Hart Ely, *Democracy and Distrust: A Theory of Judicial Review* (Cambridge, MA: Harvard Univ. Press, 1980).

[38]James Bradley Thayer, *John Marshall* (Boston: Houghton Mifflin, 1901), p. 106.

is unanimous, there may be but one opinion—as in *U.S.* v. *Nixon*. In a case of considerable difference, there may even be nine different opinions. When opinions are written, there are usually both a **majority opinion**, expressing the views of the majority of the Court, and one or more **dissenting opinions**, by those voting the other way. In addition, if someone voting with the majority disagrees on the grounds for the decision or on the route to the conclusion, that justice may write a **concurring opinion** instead of signing the majority opinion. (See the box by Justice Potter Stewart [p. 362] on how the decision is reached as to who will write the majority opinion.)

Writing these opinions is hard work. Writing them so that a number of independent-minded justices can agree on them and will sign them is particularly demanding. In a typical year, the Court will decide close to 200 cases; in some 150 of them there will be around 400 written opinions when concurring and dissenting opinions are added in.[39] Still, the majority opinion is the primary means by which the Court makes and communicates policy.

The Audiences for Court Opinions

To whom does the Court communicate? There are various audiences. The first, obviously, is *the two parties to the case*. The opinion explains and justifies the decision to them. Second is *the lower courts in which the case originated* and whose decision the Court has either affirmed or reversed. The opinion further instructs these lower courts as to how the Supreme Court viewed the case and why it decided as it did.

But the opinion is also directed to *other citizens, administrators, and lawyers with similar cases, and to other lower courts*. To all of these, it offers guidelines on how to interpret the law so as to avoid having a case end up in the Supreme Court, or to know when to appeal it to the Court. In addition, the opinion may be directed at *public officials, lawyers, and even Congress*. Sometimes it invites submission of further cases, as when it says: "Nothing in this opinion should be taken to apply to a case in which. . . . " Other times it may suggest legislation: "in the absence of action by the Congress, we. . . . "

Opinions are also sometimes directed to lower-level *officials whose behavior the Court wishes to change*. The most common instances of this type of opinion direction are decisions on criminal procedure designed to change the behavior of police. The Court in the years under Chief Justice Earl Warren (1953–1969) issued a number of decisions reversing traditional police behavior. For example, *Mapp* v. *Ohio* held that evidence improperly seized (for example, without a search warrant) could not be admitted at state trials. And *Miranda* v. *Arizona* held that no confession would be admissible unless the person arrested had been informed of his or her rights before confessing and had been warned that whatever he or she said could be used against him or her.

But how does the message from the Court, expressed in the majority opinion, get to the police officer? Certainly no officers read Court opinions as a matter of course. In large police forces, special instruction is often given by superiors. But for most officers, television and newspapers—which rarely give literal quotations from opinions—tend to be the major sources. Clearly, much improvement in communication is needed here.[40]

There is another major audience for Supreme Court opinions that should not be overlooked: *the Court and its justices*. Many assertions in dissenting opinions are pointed directly at assertions by fellow justices. "I disagree with Brother So-and-so on . . . " they may say. But it often goes deeper or further than that. Justice Felix Frankfurter once wrote to Justice Frank Murphy about a dissenting opinion:

> This is a protest opinion—a protest at the Bar of the future—but also an effort to make the brethren realize what is at stake. Moreover, a powerful dissent . . . is bound to have an effect on the lower courts as well as on the officers of the law. . . . And so in order to impress our own brethren, the lower courts, and enforcement officers, it seems to me vital to make the dissent an impressive document.[41]

Charles Evans Hughes (who served as a justice from 1910 to 1916 and as chief justice from 1930 to 1941) commented in 1928 that "a dissent in a court of last resort is an appeal to the brooding spirit of the law, to the intelligence of a future day when a later decision may possibly correct the er-

[39]In the 1982–1983 term it decided 183 cases, 151 of them with written opinions.

[40]See Stephen L. Wasby, *Small Town Police and the Supreme Court: Hearing the Word* (Lexington, MA: Lexington Books, 1976), esp. chaps. 2, 8.

[41]Quoted in Daniel M. Berman, *It Is So Ordered: The Supreme Court Rules on School Segregation* (New York: Norton, 1966), pp. 60–61.

ror into which that dissenting judge believes the court to have been betrayed."[42]

Principles of Judicial Restraint and Practices of Judicial Activism

As we have seen, the first stage in judicial behavior is the decision as to whether even to take up a case—and the Court in most cases decides not to decide at all. But once a case is chosen as being important enough to merit the sustained attention of a very busy Court, there are certain guiding principles which tend to restrain the Court and its justices.

Archibald Cox, whom we met earlier as special Watergate prosecutor, once wrote of the principles of restraint that seemed to guide the Court under the leadership of Chief Justice Warren:

> First, the courts should avoid constitutional issues wherever possible. Such issues should be decided only when raised in ordinary litigation by one who could show that his own constitutional rights were violated and who could not prevail without a constitutional decision.
> Second, the courts should not invalidate laws unless they were inconsistent with some specific constitutional prohibition.
> Third, wherever there was room for rational difference of opinion upon a question of fact or upon the relative importance of different facts or conflicting interest . . . the doctrines of federalism and separation of powers would require the Court to uphold the legislation.[43]

The fact that such principles of restraint can be seen to have guided the Warren Court is significant, for that period (1953–1959) is generally thought of as the Court's most activist one. **Judicial activism** is the doctrine that advocates an active role for the Supreme Court in enforcing the Constitution and in using judicial review.

The doctrine of **judicial restraint** argues that the Court should be very hesitant to use judicial review or otherwise to intervene in the political process.[44]

Limitations on the Supreme Court

Even if the Court inclines toward activism, there are factors that tend to set a limit on how far it can go. Among the most important are the following.

The Constitution

The Constitution sets the outer limits by guaranteeing certain rights and prohibiting certain governmental activities. We'll examine both of these in Chapter 12.

Precedents

Past decisions, or precedents, usually serve as general guidelines for current decisions. The principle of *stare decisis*, described above, has great weight with justices.

The Doctrine of Political Questions

This doctrine is often used by the Court to decline to rule on controversial issues that go to the heart of the operation of the government and to the proper sphere of the executive or legislative branches. The courts have used the **doctrine of political questions** to refuse to rule on various cases involving international law. They have also used it to avoid ruling on the validity of ratifications of constitutional amendments. Further, they refused to rule on the constitutionality of laws concerning legislative apportionment—on grounds that apportionment, too, was a political question—until the famous *Baker* v. *Carr* decision in 1962, which we examined earlier.[45]

Legal experts who have tried to find or develop a consistent definition of "political questions" as used by the courts have failed. In the words of one commentator:

> The term "political questions" is a magical formula which has the practical result of relieving a court of the necessity of thinking further about a particular problem. It is a device for transferring the responsibility for decision of questions to another branch of

[42]Quoted in Henry J. Abraham, *The Judicial Process*, 2d ed. (New York: Oxford Univ. Press, 1968), p. 182.

[43]Archibald Cox, *The Warren Court* (Cambridge, MA: Harvard Univ. Press, 1968), pp. 3–4. For a detailed account of the maxims of judicial self-restraint that generally guide the Court, see Henry J. Abraham, *The Judicial Process*, 4th ed. (New York: Oxford Univ. Press, 1980), pp. 373–97.

[44]For an argument in favor of a more limited practice of judicial review based on constitutional interpretation, see Ralph K. Winter, Jr., "The Growth of Judicial Power," in *The Judiciary in a Democratic Society*, ed. Leonard J. Theberge (Lexington, MA: Lexington Books, 1979), chap. 2.

[45]When asked to rule on the constitutionality of the Vietnam War, which had not been formally declared by Congress, the Supreme Court termed the case "nonjusticiable." We may presume that it reached this conclusion because the power to make the kind of decision involved has been constitutionally delegated to one of the two "political" (as distinguished from "judicial") branches of the government. This would make it a "political question" in the view of the Court. For an account of these Vietnam cases, see Leon Friedman and Burt Neuborne, *Unquestioning Obedience to the President* (New York: Norton, 1972).

the government; it may sometimes operate to leave a problem in mid-air so that no branch decides it.[46]

Inability to Enforce Its Own Decisions

Lack of enforcement power, a factor in the resort to the doctrine of political questions, also limits what the Court will dare to attempt. The judiciary in general and the Supreme Court in particular operate in dangerous areas of conflict. There is conflict between levels of government: federal, state, and local. There is conflict between government action and the Constitution; and there is conflict between the branches of the federal government over the requirements of the Constitution. The Supreme Court is supposed to resolve such conflicts. But once a ruling is made, something must be done to enforce the resolution on the parties to the conflict. The Supreme Court consists of 9 justices and a staff of some 300—including law clerks assisting the justices, police officers protecting them, and other aides from cooks to a cabinetmaker. Thus, the Court itself cannot possibly attempt to enforce—or even to oversee the enforcement of—its decisions. The task of enforcement must therefore fall primarily to the executive branch; and the task of oversight, to the lower courts. Consequently, the Court tends to be very cautious about what and how much it decides. But it still regularly accepts and decides cases of great import.

The Necessity for Public Acceptance

Public acceptance of its decisions is recognized by judges as an ultimate requirement, largely because of the inability to enforce its own rulings. As Archibald Cox has written: "The most important quality of law in a free society is the power to command acceptance and support from the community so as to render force unnecessary, or necessary only upon a small scale against a few recalcitrants."[47] Studies show that Court decisions do tend to gain public acceptance, even on most controversial questions, as time passes.[48] But for this pub-

lic acceptance to be possible, the Court must not get too far in front of public attitudes. Judges at all levels seem generally to recognize this.

Ultimate Limitations

If the Court does get too far ahead of public opinion, it can be overruled by constitutional amendment—as opponents of the abortion decision in *Roe v. Wade* (to be discussed in Chapter 12) have sought in recent years. Second, its members can be impeached and removed from office—as conservative opponents of former Chief Justice Warren sought unsuccessfully to do. And third, the Court can be "packed"—expanded in size by the addition of new members likely to vote to overrule the dominant decision—as FDR sought to do in the 1930s when the Court was ruling his New Deal economic legislation unconstitutional.

If all these factors are important limitations—actual or potential—on the Supreme Court's power, how does the Court manage to be effective? To get a sense of what the Court can do and how it may be successful, we need to look at this body as a political institution making policy.

THE SUPREME COURT AS A POLITICAL INSTITUTION

The Court is a political institution, one of the three branches of the federal government and—with the presidency, the bureaucracy, and Congress—one of the four major decision makers. When the Court refuses to rule on a question on the grounds that it is a "political question" that should be left to the "political branches," it is even then making a political decision.

The notion that the executive and the legislative branches are the political branches, "is an interesting one," Philippa Strum has observed,

> primarily because it reflects a desire on the part of both rulers and ruled to ignore the actual function of the judiciary under a system of separation of powers and judicial review. The interpretative power of the courts serves as a methodology by which a supposedly neutral third force can arbitrate between the government and its citizens when a difference of purpose or of understanding arises between them. . . . Popular belief in an independent judiciary enables the courts to place a final stamp of legitimacy upon all governmental acts, including those which might otherwise

[46]Philippa Strum, *The Supreme Court and "Political Questions": A Study in Judicial Evasion* (Birmingham: Univ. of Alabama Press, 1974), pp. 144, 145.

[47]Archibald Cox, *The Role of the Supreme Court in American Government* (New York: Oxford Univ. Press, 1977), p. 103.

[48]For a summary of the results of such studies, see Martin Shapiro, "The Supreme Court: From Warren to Burger," in *The New American Political System*, ed. Anthony King (Washington, DC: American Enterprise Institute, 1978).

come under direct attack in the form of disobedience."[49]

In other words, the Supreme Court is also *more* than a political institution on a par with the other two branches. Granted, it has no enforcement powers of its own, and it manifests a strong respect for tradition and hence a great tendency toward conserving existing arrangements and practices. Still, the power of the Court should not be understated—least of all when it has that very tradition and almost 200 years of recognition behind it.

That tradition serves to legitimize not only the Court's decisions but also the actions by the other federal branches and by the states that the Court chooses not to challenge.[50] The existence—and the activism—of the Court help preserve respect for law and for government. But, in Strum's words, it also "absolves the citizen from what might otherwise be the uncomfortable necessity of participating in an unending re-examination of political actions and assumptions."[51]

Nevertheless, if the Court goes too far in adapting the law and the institutions, it runs the grave risk of sacrificing its own legitimacy in the minds of the people. In the same way, it may also—as Archibald Cox has warned—encourage

> excessive reliance upon courts instead of self-government through democratic processes [which] may deaden a people's sense of moral and political responsibility for their own future, especially in matters of liberty, and may stunt the growth of political capacity that results from the exercise of the ultimate power of decision.[52]

Thus far, this double fear seems unwarranted. The Court is held in higher esteem than its partner branches, largely, it appears, because the public has appreciated its greater activism.

THE WARREN COURT, THE BURGER COURT —AND THE REHNQUIST COURT?

The Court's greater activism was first found in the years of the Warren Court. Chief Justice Earl Warren was appointed by President Eisenhower and presided for 16 years.[53] He regarded the Court's legislative reapportionment decisions (which we discussed earlier), effectively opening the political process to many people, as the most important decisions of his tenure. But he also singled out decisions on public-school integration and on the right of an accused to have a lawyer as being extremely important.[54] These two areas represent the major controversial emphases of the Warren Court. Warren and the "liberal" majority on the Court in most of these years were, in the words of Archibald Cox, "influenced by an extremely self-conscious sense of judicial responsibility for minorities, for the oppressed, for the open and egalitarian operation of the political system, and for a variety of 'rights' not adequately represented in the political process."[55] As a result, they made decisions and issued opinions that greatly expanded civil rights and civil liberties.

One set of decisions extended civil rights of blacks by outlawing segregation in public schools (*Brown v. Board of Education*, 1954, followed by numerous other cases), racial gerrymandering (*Gomillion v. Lightfoot*, 1960), poll taxes (*Harper v. Virginia*, 1966), and laws prohibiting racially mixed marriages (*Loving v. Virginia*, 1967).

Another set of decisions increased the civil liberties of the accused in state and local criminal proceedings under the Fourth Amendment (against illegal searches and seizures—*Mapp v. Ohio*, 1961); the Fifth Amendment (against self-incrimination—*Malloy v. Hogan*, 1964); the Sixth Amendment (the right to counsel—*Gideon v. Wainwright*, 1963—and also to speedy trial and to trial by jury, among others); and the Eighth Amendment (the prohibition against cruel and unusual punishment—*Robinson v. California*, 1962).

Some of these new or strengthened limitations on government power have since been redefined or limited by what has come to be called the Burger Court. Once Burger replaced Warren in 1969, he and other Nixon, Ford, and Reagan appointees

---

[49]Strum, *Supreme Court*, p. 2.

[50]This argument is made by Philip Kurland. For example, see his book *Politics, the Constitution, and the Warren Court* (Chicago: Univ. of Chicago Press, 1970).

[51]Strum, *Supreme Court*, p. 3.

[52]Cox, *Role of the Supreme Court*, p. 103.

[53]For a fascinating account of Warren and "his Court," based on interviews, private papers, and authenticated reports from the justices' secret judical conferences, see Bernard Schwartz, *Super Chief: Earl Warren and His Supreme Court—A Judicial Biography* (New York: New York Univ. Press, 1983), or a more popular version Schwartz prepared with Stephan Lesher, *Inside the Warren Court* (Garden City, NY: Doubleday, 1983).

[54]See Congressional Quarterly, *CQ Almanac 1968* (Washington, DC: CQ Press, 1968), p. 539.

[55]Cox, *Role of the Supreme Court*, p. 36.

Former Chief Justice Warren, then Chief Justice Burger, and Justice Blackmun. (UPI/Bettmann Newsphotos)

Lawyers who led the fight to abolish segregation in the public schools congratulate one another as they leave the Court after the decision in 1954 that declared segregation unconstitutional. Left to right are George E. C. Hayes, Thurgood Marshall (who later became the only black yet to serve as a Supreme Court Justice), and James M. Nabrit. (AP/Wide World Photos)

changed the Court's political complexion. The Warren Court was increasingly criticized for being too protective of the rights of alleged criminals at the expense of the rights of the victims. It was also criticized for being too sensitive to the needs of the poor and powerless. Perhaps in reaction to these criticisms, decisions of the Burger Court made it more difficult for the underprivileged to get relief in court.

The Burger Court in general was more supportive of the legal position of women, however. (We shall discuss its abortion ruling, *Roe* v. *Wade*, in Chapter 12.) The Burger Court rejected the traditional argument that sex discrimination is tolerable as long as it is "reasonable." Instead, the Burger Court held that distinctions based on gender can be constitutional only if they establish "important" government objectives and if they further

those objectives in "substantial," not merely "reasonable," ways. In addition, the Burger Court ruled that laws that grant women special compensatory treatment for past economic discrimination are constitutional. But it also ruled that a woman on pregnancy leave is not eligible for temporary disability or sick-pay benefits—a ruling deplored by women's groups.

In its early years, many activists feared that the Burger Court would prove disastrous to the gains in civil liberties and civil rights under the Warren Court. But one law professor concluded, in a view many share:

> The Burger Court appears conservative only when compared with its predecessor. Otherwise, it has been more responsive to individual rights and liberties than any Supreme Court in the nation's history. Landmark decisions restricting capital punishment, protecting reproductive freedom, expanding constitutional remedies for individuals and upholding affirmative action to redress discrimination have all come after 1970.[56]

Many of these critical decisions, however, were by close votes. By most reckonings, the Court now contains two liberals (Justices Brennan and Marshall), four conservatives (Chief Justice Rehnquist, and Justices Powell, O'Connor, and Scalia), and three centrists (Justices White, Blackmun, and Stevens). Table 11.1, which describes the justices, reveals that four are now well into their seventies and so are likely to leave the Court in the next few years. If this happens, it will give whoever is presi-

[56]Stephen Gillers, "The Warren Court—It Still Lives," *The Nation*, September 17, 1983, p. 209. See also Vincent Blasi, ed., *The Burger Court: The Counter-Revolution That Wasn't* (New Haven, CT: Yale Univ. Press, 1983).

dent a unique opportunity to attempt to shape the orientation of the Court for years—and perhaps even decades—to come. It is difficult to predict just how appointees will vote over the years, of course. And, as we have noted, the Court is a political institution and so tends to respond eventually to major political forces. How strong—and how rapid—such responses are will depend on who is sitting on the Court.[57]

With Chief Justice Burger's retirement and Justice Rehnquist's accession to the leadership of the Court in 1986, observers have differed over whether the Court would likely become more conservative or self-restrained. Rehnquist had tended to dissent from majority positions in the Burger years—so much so that his law clerks called him the Lone Ranger. But as often as not, his own views favor a strong state instead of individual liberties.

In a lecture in 1980, he sought to debunk the idea that the Constitution is a guarantee of individual liberties against the government. Rather, he argued, the purpose of the Constitution was to establish a government "to have direct authority over the individual citizen."[58] This view can be a recipe for cutbacks in the sorts of civil liberties that the Warren Court instituted and the Burger Court consolidated. But only time will tell whether Rehnquist is able to lead "the Brethren" in his preferred position—and whether he sees things the same in the chief justice's seat as he did before his elevation. Thus, we won't know for some time whether we have a Rehnquist Court.

Time and again under Burger, as well as under Warren, the Court took major action in the interest of minorities and outsiders. Martin Shapiro has singled out the Court's decisions in the last 30 years concerning school desegregation, reapportionment, criminal-justice reform, obscenity law, and birth control and abortion as its major policy-making achievements.[59] Many of the pioneering decisions of the Supreme Court in recent decades have expanded the rights of the accused in criminal cases. This has occurred in a period during which the increase and spread of crime have made it a threat to every American.

Chief Justice Rehnquist dons his judicial robe. (Ken Regan/Camera 5)

LAW, DISORDER, AND JUSTICE IN AMERICA

Law and Order and Us

If you are an American citizen, the odds of your being murdered at some point in your life are 1 in 153. If you are male, it's 1 in 100; if female, 1 in 323. If you are white, it's 1 in 240; nonwhite, 1 in 47, and if a nonwhite male, 1 in 28.[60] A murder is committed somewhere in America every 23 minutes, day and night, on the average. There is a violent crime (murder, forcible rape, robbery, or assault with intent to kill) every 31 seconds. Forcible rape occurs once every 6 minutes, robbery once every 58 seconds, and auto theft once every 28 seconds.[61]

But you don't have to be out on the streets to experience violence or even to be murdered. Two places we all frequent are even more dangerous than the streets: the home and the school.

A quarter of all murders occur within the family—half of these, husband or wife killings. It is estimated that over half of all married women suffer physical abuse at the hands—or weapons—of their husbands: That means 28 million wives. And

[57]For an interesting analysis of voting patterns in the 1982–1983 term, see Elder Witt, "Justice White: The Man in the Middle," *Congressional Quarterly Weekly Report*, July 16, 1983, p. 1457.

[58]See Sidney Blumenthal, "How Rehnquist Came Down in Hobbes v. Locke," *Washington Post National Weekly Edition*, October 6, 1986.

[59]Shapiro, "The Supreme Court: From Warren to Burger," pp. 180–81.

[60]These figures come from an FBI report, *Crime in the United States*, appendix 5: "Probability of Lifetime Murder Victimization" (Washington: GPO, 1986).

[61]Federal Bureau of Investigation, *Uniform Crime Report, 1982* (Washington, DC: GPO, 1982).

in many states the wife still has no legal recourse in such cases other than filing a criminal complaint against her husband. Only 2 percent of the men who beat up their female living partners are ever prosecuted. Sex crimes are also commonly committed in the home and rarely prosecuted in the courts. In most states, a man cannot be charged with rape of a woman if she is his wife, no matter what the circumstances.

Even more stunning, it is estimated that 7 or 8 million children are physically abused by their parents every year. And some experts believe that as many as a million of these are victims of incest—sexual relations between a parent and child. Indeed, some claim that one in every four women in America has been involved in incest or otherwise sexually molested. There are, of course, no exact figures because few such acts are reported to police or other authorities. But there is growing agreement among experts that figures such as these express the scale of family violence today. Experts also agree that about 50 million people suffer physical harm from another family member every year. That's about one in four Americans.

School, too, seems just as bad. A congressional subcommittee investigating violence in the public schools in the 1970s found that about 10,000 rapes occur every year in schools—many of them rapes of female teachers.

The highest proportion of arrests for murder, forcible rape, robbery, and aggravated assault in recent years has been of 18-year-olds. For burglary and auto theft, 16-year-olds have the highest arrest percentage. Most of them are males: 90 percent of those arrested for violent crimes and 80 percent of those for property crimes. Female crime is increasing but seems unlikely ever to equal male crime.

Serious crime has been steadily on the increase in America since 1960, rising to almost 35 million offenses in 1985. This means that your odds of being a victim of a serious crime in a given year are better than one in seven. This steady growth in crime has produced support for harsher anticrime measures and for "law and order" political campaigns. Yet even though there are now over 100 million handguns in circulation in the United States, conservative opposition has prevented handgun-control legislation from being passed in Congress.

Law and Order and White-Collar America

"Today it is comparatively safe to break the law," proclaimed Richard Nixon in his victorious 1968 presidential campaign. "Today all across the land guilty men walk free from hundreds of courtrooms. Something has gone terribly wrong in America." Nixon's remark took on a certain ironic cast five years later, when his own selection as vice-president, Spiro Agnew, famous for his own "law and order" rhetoric, walked free from a federal courtroom after pleading no defense against serious corruption charges. Only a year later, Nixon himself was revealed by his own White House tapes to be guilty of covering up criminal deeds by his closest aides—which is itself a crime—and had to resign in disgrace. But Nixon was saved even from having to enter a courtroom by a presidential pardon from the successor he had picked, Gerald Ford. Many Nixon aides, however, including Attorney General John Mitchell and presidential assistants Bob Haldeman and John Ehrlichman, did go to prison—if only briefly—for their own lawbreaking. But a number of others, including Attorney General Richard Kleindienst, who in effect lied under oath to a congressional committee, and many business leaders who admitted giving funds illegally to the Nixon campaign, "walked free from courtrooms" with only a rebuke or a small fine.

Watergate crimes and political corruption such as this are called white-collar crime—or "crime in the suites" instead of "crime in the streets." White-collar crime, too, has been on the rise. More than 11,000 cases a year of bank embezzlement and consumer-related fraud are now recorded by the government, for example. And at least 1000 federal, state, and local officials were convicted on federal corruption charges in the years from 1970 to 1975,[62] and the rate has risen since then.

But few of these white-collar criminals went to jail for their corruption. Few white-collar criminals ever do, even though their crimes are estimated to cost the nation between $40 billion a year (the Chamber of Commerce estimate) and $200 billion a year (the late Senator Philip Hart's esti-

---

[62]Marianne Means, "A Basic Right to Know," *Austin American-Statesman*, August 19, 1976.

mate). Included in the chamber figure are $21.7 billion in robbery, shoplifting, employee theft, arson, and so on; $7 billion in bribery, kickbacks, and payoffs; $6 billion in fraud; and $5 billion in the cost of anticrime measures taken to try to prevent these losses. Hart's estimate includes the fraud, extortion, bribery, and theft that rob the government, and so the taxpayers, of many millions more. In addition, narcotics crime is estimated to generate some $70 billion a year. Whatever the total, it is clearly far higher than the cost of blue-collar, or "T-shirt," crime.[63]

Law Enforcement in America

Nonetheless, the jails and prisons are full to overflowing—some 490,000 inmates in federal and state prisons and about half as many in local jails by 1985, with the number rising at about 10 percent per year. Further, three times as many are out on probation or parole after being convicted of serious crimes. The median sentence served for murder is less than 6 years, while the median term served by all inmates is only 16 months, according to the U.S. Bureau of Justice Statistics. And although only 23 percent of our population is between the ages of 17 and 29, over half of the prison population is of that age.

There is ample evidence that the jails would be even fuller were our law-enforcement system more efficient. It is not so much a matter of lenient judges—as Nixon, Agnew, and others have argued—although it is true that many offenses are committed by repeaters. Instead, the major enforcement problem is the fact that most crimes are never even solved. In one study of criminal behavior by adults, people were asked which of 49 offenses other than traffic violations they had committed without being caught. Ninety-nine percent of the people admitted they had committed one or more offenses for which they might have received jail or prison sentences had they been caught. Among the males, 26 percent admitted auto theft, 17 percent burglary, and 13 percent grand larceny.

"MY CLIENT PLEADS NO MORE GUILTY THAN EVERYONE ELSE, YOUR HONOR."

(*Dunagin's People* by Ralph Dunagin. © 1980 Field Enterprises, Inc. Courtesy of News America Syndicate.)

Some 64 percent of the males and 29 percent of the females admitted to committing at least one felony for which they had not been caught.[64]

The fact is that only about a third of all serious crimes (murder, forcible rape, robbery, aggravated assault, burglary, larceny over $50, and auto theft) are ever even reported to the police by the victims. Of all serious crimes reported, in only 19 percent of the cases is a suspect ever arrested, although the figure can go as high as 78 percent for murder. Only about half of all suspects arrested are ever convicted. And only about a quarter of those convicted actually ever do time for their crime.

The odds are, then, that you, like most Americans, have done something criminal but were most likely not even apprehended, let alone jailed. Yet you probably do not think of yourself as a criminal. One reason may be that you were not apprehended. Another may be that you do not believe that what you did was really criminal, even though it was against the law—whether it was taking drugs, dodging the draft during the Vietnam War,

[63]See "A $40 Billion Crime Wave Swamps American Business," *U.S. News & World Report*, February 21, 1977, pp. 47–48; and "How People Cheat Uncle Sam Out of Billions," *U.S. News & World Report*, July 11, 1977, pp. 16–19.

[64]Reported in *The Challenge of Crime in a Free Society: A Report by the President's Commission on Law Enforcement and Administration of Justice* (Washington, DC.: GPO, 1968).

gambling, taking a payoff in a business venture, or cheating on your income tax. If you fall into this category, you have lots of company, and you probably know it. And this very fact tends effectively to change the definition of crime in our society.

The Social Objective of the System

Underlying this "politics of crime" is the deeper political question of what our basic social objective is. For some, the basic objective is *order*. They tend to define crime broadly, with emphasis on protecting property.

For others, the primary objective is *justice*. For thousands of years philosophers have debated the meaning of this word, and they continue to debate today. The preamble to our Constitution asserts that our government is created to "establish justice"—but it nowhere says what justice is. Most of us have a general sense that the concept as a goal refers to some sort of fairness or equality of treatment, as is implied by the words "Equal Justice Under Law" inscribed over the entrance to the Supreme Court. But beyond that, it is hard to find much agreement. Still, we can say that in general, those who emphasize justice as the objective of society tend to favor protection of life over protection of property.[65]

Still others would emphasize as the prime objective of the social order *the legitimacy of the system*. For them, what is important is public acceptance of the existing order and its institutions as being worthy or correct.[66] Accordingly, obedience to the law tends to become more important to them than exactly what the law is. If the law is generally obeyed, the system will tend to appear legitimate. It will thus be more likely to survive, and so will its rulers, who tend to be the strongest supporters of this concept.

Concepts of Punishment

Along with differing concepts of social objectives go differing concepts of proper punishment. In general, those seeking order think of punishment in terms of *deterrence*. Those emphasizing justice usually see punishment as treatment of the criminal to restore him or her to a proper social role. Those emphasizing legitimation of the system tend to think in terms of retribution, to pay back an offender and thereby demonstrate to all that the law was both right and effective. Many supporters of capital punishment justify it as retribution, although some claim it should be justified in terms of deterrence.

The biggest blow to the seekers of legitimacy is governmental crime. For when the government itself or one of its officials breaks the law, it tends to call its own legitimacy into question.[67] And because the offending officials are rarely punished severely, the public's sense of satisfaction with the justice system is threatened.

The biggest problem to seekers of order through deterrence is what experts call recidivism—the tendency of offenders to become repeaters. By becoming repeaters, criminals demonstrate the failure of the deterrence model of punishment. We might expect that anyone knowing that only 1.5 percent of all committers of crimes ever do time would be unlikely to be deterred by our justice system. It appears that even those who are caught and punished often become repeaters. FBI statistics report that 67 percent of those who serve time or are pardoned for a serious offense are arrested again for a serious offense within three years. And of those paroled (released early under the supervision of a law officer), 64 percent are again arrested within three years.[68]

Experience thus suggests that punishment neither deters nor rehabilitates. A prison term is rare even for serious offenders, and the average criminal in prison spends only 17 months behind bars before being released.[69] Furthermore, many convicted offenders are released early or are never even sentenced to prison because our prisons are grossly overcrowded. And white-collar criminals, if they go to prison at all—which is rare—usually go to

---

[65]For a prominent discussion of concepts of justice and recommendation of the concept of "justice as fairness," see John Rawls, *A Theory of Justice* (Cambridge: MA: Harvard Univ. Press, 1971).

[66]See the discussion of legitimacy in Perspective 1.

[67]See Jethro Lieberman, *How the Government Breaks the Law* (Baltimore: Penguin, 1973), for an appalling survey. And for a more recent study of abuses by intelligence agencies, see David Wise, *The American Police State* (New York: Random House, 1976).

[68]*Crime in the U.S.—Uniform Crime Reports.* For an account of another study, which found a recidivism rate of only 23 percent in the 1970s (versus 33 percent in the 1960s), see Selwyn Rabb, "U.S. Study Finds Recidivism Rate of Convicts Lower Than Expected," *New York Times,* November 7, 1976.

[69]This figure is from the National Council on Crime and Delinquency. See Patrick Oster, "U.S. Criminal Justice Is Story of Attrition," *Chicago Sun-Times,* April 24, 1977.

"gentlemen's prison farms" that are unlikely to deter or rehabilitate—or to offer the retribution that might increase public confidence in the legitimacy of our system.

Soft treatment seems common also when occasionally a kingpin of organized crime is convicted of tax evasion or racketeering. Such crimes usually draw sentences of no more than two years—sentences that are often suspended. Yet these are people who preside over an empire that plays a major role in corrupting public officials and who net perhaps $25 billion in illegal, untaxed profits each year on gambling, drugs, prostitution, pornography, and loansharking.[70]

Proposals and Prospects

We have only skimmed the surface of the problems of our justice system today. Some of the problems may decline with the birthrate, for most violent crimes are committed by the young, and the country's teenage population started to shrink in 1977. If we make progress in controlling the drug problem, that too will cut crime because much burglary is committed to finance drug habits. Further, if times are good economically, the crime rate should drop, for much crime is committed by people without jobs or economic prospects.

If judges do indeed deal more harshly with criminals, that may postpone their return to the streets, at the least. If we have *more judges*, so that we can have faster trials, that too may help. So would any ways of making punishment more certain.

Some argue that more severe sentences, including even widespread use of the death penalty, would increase the deterrence of crime. Most research evidence does not confirm this argument. In the words of several experts: "Those studies which do attempt to separate the effects of severity and certainty . . . indicate that certainty rather than severity of legal sanctions is the primary deterrent factor."[71]

But all these measures still leave untouched the problem of reforming our prisons so that they rehabilitate prisoners. Ninety-five percent of those in prison will sooner or later be released back into society. Today they are rarely well prepared for that return. As one group of critics has pointed out:

> While we cannot predict those who will be dangerous to society, we can predict some of the responses by those who are subjected to the brutalizing environment of prisons. Resentment, rage and hostility on the part of both keeper and kept, are the punitive dividends society reaps as a result of caging. . . . the punishment of prison damages persons, and consequently, creates more danger to society. . . . The negative effects of caging reach beyond prison walls, allowing citizens a false sense of safety. Prisons, by their very existence, exonerate communities from the responsibilities of providing the necessary human services which might effectively reduce "crime."[72]

Some argue for more prisons, some for better prisons, some for no prisons at all. Some argue for more judges, some for harsher judges. Some argue for retribution, others for rehabilitation, and others for restitution (by which a convict repays his or her victim for the damage done, rather than just doing time). Experts disagree as widely as ordinary citizens on the question of how to improve what everyone recognizes as an inadequate and dangerous system.

But, as Jerome Skolnick, a professor of criminology at the University of California, Berkeley, reminds us:

> There are no easy prescriptions for crime in America. It has become an intrinsic part of life in this country as a result of fundamental contradictions of American society. We maintain an egalitarian ideology amidst a history of slavery and contemporary unemployment. We say we are against organized crime, but millions of us enjoy and consume its goods and services—drugs, gambling, prostitution, pornography. We demand heavier punishment—longer prison terms—yet fail to appreciate the social and economic costs of prisons. We support the Constitution and its protection of individual liberties—yet criticize judges who insist the police conduct themselves in accord with [it].[73]

---

[70]Jack Anderson, "The Shadow of the Mafia over Our Government," *Parade*, August 7, 1977.

[71]Richard Salem and William Bowers, "Severity of Formal Sanctions as a Deterrent to Deviant Behavior," *Law and Society Review* 5 (August 1970), 21. The most comprehensive study of the alleged deterrent effect of capital punishment has concluded that there is none. See Hans Zeisel, "The Deterrent Effect of the Death Penalty: Facts v. Faiths," in *Supreme Court Review 1976*, ed. Philip B. Kurland (Chicago: Univ. of Chicago Press, 1977), pp. 317–43.

[72]Fay Honey Knopp et al., *Instead of Prisons: A Handbook for Abolitionists* (Syracuse, NY: Prison Research Education Project, 1976), p. 41. The National Center on Institutions and Alternatives also argues against imprisonment for all but dangerous or hardened criminals.

[73]Jerome H. Skolnick, "The Frustrations of Having No Easy Solutions for the Complicated Problems of Crime in America," *Washington Post*, September 15, 1977.

We turn to our legal system to protect us from the crime and the criminals that increasingly stalk our everyday lives. Most of us favor a stronger legal system when it comes to issues of law and order. Yet the greatest impacts of our legal system on our everyday lives are not likely to come in crime fighting. Rather, they are likely to come, as they long have, in the protection and advancement of our civil liberties and our civil rights. It is to this topic that we now turn our attention.

SUMMARY

The function of our court system is to apply the law. It does this by interpreting it. This law has five basic sources: the Constitution, statutes (criminal or civil), common law, equity, and administrative law.

Our system is composed of local courts, state courts, and federal courts. The lowest federal court is the district court, of which there are 91. A person who loses a case there may appeal to one of the 12 appeals courts. From there he or she may be able to go to the Supreme Court—but only if the Court decides to make that case one of the 200 or so cases (out of 5000 requests) that it will hear in its annual term. If so, it issues a writ of certiorari. In general, the Court hears only four types of cases on appeal: those involving a private individual or corporation and a government agency disputing the meaning of a federal law; those between two private parties disputing the meaning of a federal law; a federal or state criminal prosecution in which the defendant claims that the law or his or her treatment violates the Constitution; and a suit asking the Court to order a public official to stop doing something unconstitutional or to start doing something required by the Constitution. The Court hears cases involving disputes between two states or between a state and the federal government, under its original jurisdiction.

Supreme Court justices are a very atypical group. In almost 200 years just over 100 have served, and in that group there have been only one black and one woman. Justices and other federal judges are appointed by the president and confirmed by the Senate. A custom called senatorial courtesy allows the senior senator from the president's own party to have a veto over appointments to federal courts within his or her state. President Carter made a major effort to appoint women, blacks, and Hispanics to the federal bench, but President Reagan has returned to the usual pattern of appointing white males, primarily because he has used political philosophy as the major test for selection.

Supreme Court deliberations and voting are secret, so we know relatively little about how decisions are made. Justices seem to be influenced most by their own values and policy preferences, but their use of these is limited by the state of the law and by the political environment. Interaction among the justices is the fourth factor.

Although judges are meant to interpet the law, there is little doubt that in practice they often *make* law or make policy in the course of this interpretation. Their greatest power derives from the practice of judicial review, established in the case of *Marbury* v. *Madison* (1803).

The Court reaches a decision by vote but also often issues written opinions—a majority opinion and sometimes also one or more concurring opinions and dissenting opinions. These opinions are in fact addressed not only to the parties involved, the lower courts, and citizens, administrators, and lawyers with similar concerns but also sometimes to Congress as well as to the justices of the future, who will be looking for precedents.

Because judges do make policy, there is a running debate between advocates of judicial activism and of judicial restraint. In fact, the Court uses principles of self-restraint to limit the cases it accepts and to decide these cases on narrow grounds. Its decisions are limited not only by the Constitution and precedents but also by the doctrine of political questions. Further, it cannot enforce its own decisions and so must depend on public acceptance and the efforts of the executive branch. Still, both the Warren Court and the Burger Court have proved to be activist in their orientation. One area in which this has been manifest is in the rights of the accused.

Crime is a major problem—both violent and white-collar crime. Law enforcement is often of limited effectiveness, in part because of disagreements over the objectives of the justice system and in particular over the issue of punishment. Consensus on these matters is still lacking, and the crime rate remains at a very high level.

Suggestions for Further Reading and Study

There is no substitute for seeing the Supreme Court in action. If you have a chance to get to Washington, try to attend a Court session, morning or afternoon, Monday through Friday, October through June. Arrive an hour before the beginning and, once at the Court building, join the line for those wishing to see the entire session rather than that allowing a mere five-minute tourist visit. To find out what is being discussed, look in the morning's *Washington Post* for a schedule, or call the clerk of Court at 393-1640. You can also visit other federal and state courts nearer your home or school as well as local courts.

There are various ways to follow the Supreme Court from afar. All Court decisions and opinions appear in volumes of *U.S. Reports*, published by the government, and in two more elaborate, annotated versions published privately: *United States Supreme Court Reports, Lawyers' Edition*, and *Supreme Court Reporter*. Any academic library will have *U.S. Reports* and probably the preliminary pamphlets containing decisions and opinions that are produced between volumes. Some will also have one of the more elaborate weekly services, *United States Law Week* and *U.S. Supreme Court Bulletin*. For analyses of major cases and related topics, see Leonard W. Levy, Kenneth L. Karst, and Dennis J. Mahoney, *Encyclopedia of the American Constitution*, 4 vols. (New York: Macmillan, 1986).

For detailed accounts of individual cases, which offer a more comprehensive understanding of how the courts work, see Richard Kluger, *Simple Justice* (New York: Vintage, 1976), on *Brown* v. *Board;* Alan F. Westin, *Anatomy of a Constitutional Law Case* (New York: Macmillan, 1956), on the "steel seizure case," more formally known as *Youngstown Sheet & Tube Co.* v. *Sawyer;* and Anthony Lewis, *Gideon's Trumpet* (New York: Vintage, 1964), on *Gideon* v. *Wainwright*.

There are several good books by judges: Benjamin N. Cardozo, *The Nature of the Judicial Process* (New Haven, CT: Yale Univ. Press, 1921); and Robert H. Jackson, *The Supreme Court in the American System of Government* (Cambridge, MA: Harvard Univ. Press, 1955). Bob Woodward and Scott Armstrong's fascinating study of the Supreme Court, *The Brethren* (New York: Simon & Schuster, 1980), discussed in this chapter, is based primarily on interviews with the justices' clerks. One clerk has written his own book: J. Harvie Wilkinson III, *Serving Justice: A Supreme Court Clerk's View* (New York: Charterhouse, 1974).

Among the many helpful studies by outsiders are Henry J. Abraham, *The Judicial Process*, 4th ed. (New York: Oxford Univ. Press, 1980), which includes helpful material on federal and state systems as well as those of other countries; Lawrence Baum, *The Supreme Court* (Washington, DC: CQ Press, 1981); Lawrence H. Tribe, *God Save This Honorable Court* (New York: Random House, 1985); and David M. O'Brien, *Storm Center: The Supreme Court in American Politics* (New York: Norton, 1986).

Finally, if there is something you want to know about the Supreme Court that you can't easily find elsewhere, your best bet is *Congressional Quarterly's Guide to the U.S. Supreme Court*, a mammoth and comprehensive book of over a thousand pages, published in 1979, or Stephen P. Elliott, ed., *A Reference Guide to the U.S. Supreme Court* (New York: Facts on File, 1986).

Perspective

THE POLITICS OF EDUCATION:
The Rights of Children of Illegal Aliens

In 1975 the Texas legislature passed a law stating that Texas school districts could not get state funds to help finance the teaching of the children of illegal aliens. Millions of Mexican citizens cross the border into Texas to pick crops or to work as manual laborers. Some come in legally, with "green cards," which entitle them to work. Others slip across the 2000-mile-long U.S.-Mexican border out of sight of the federal Immigration and Naturalization Service (INS) police. Some of them come as families and settle in Texas towns and cities. If their children are born in Texas, the children become American citizens, even if their parents are not. As such, they are entitled to free public schooling. But if the children were born in Mexico or some other country, they are aliens—foreigners. A 1975 amendment to the Texas Education Code declared that local school districts could either bar these children or charge them tuition.

The Tyler, Texas, school district decided to charge $1000 per child per year. At that time there were about 40 Mexican children among its 16,000 students. All of those children were from poor families, and so they had no choice but to drop out of school. The Mexican-American Legal Defense and Education Fund (MALDEF) filed suit in the name of 16 of those children. It claimed that the Texas law violated the Fourteenth Amendment to the Constitution.

The Fourteenth Amendment declares that "no State . . . shall . . . deny to any person within its jurisdiction the equal protection of the laws." Lawyers for the children argued that Texas welcomes illegal aliens because they are a source of cheap labor. While they are in Texas, many of them pay taxes on their income, and all pay state and city sales taxes on most everything they buy besides food. Schools are now financed primarily by local property taxes, as we'll see in more detail later on. Anyone who owns property in the state pays those taxes. Anyone who rents pays them indirectly through the owner of the rental property, who includes the taxes in the rent. Thus, most aliens are paying toward the costs of schools like any other

An early American school in the colonial period. (The Bettmann Archive)

resident, whether or not they have children in school.[1]

The state of Texas opposed the MALDEF suit, arguing that any person who is in the state illegally is technically not within the state's jurisdiction. If that is true, the Fourteenth Amendment does not apply. Further, the state argued that these children are in the state as a result of the failure of the INS to enforce the immigration laws. Thus, said Texas, if the children are to be educated, federal funds should pay the costs rather than state and local funds.

The case, which became known as *Plyler* v. *Doe*, caused great controversy in Texas and great interest in other states with large immigrant populations, such as California, Colorado, and New York. It raised once again many longstanding political questions. Are all people entitled to an education? How should public education be financed? And what are the rights of aliens—especially of children

of illegal aliens, who are brought into the country by their parents rather than coming on their own? To see how our political system has answered these questions, we must first look at how our educational system has developed.

THE DEVELOPMENT OF AMERICAN EDUCATION

The first laws concerning education in America were the Massachusetts Bay Colony Act of 1642 and the Old Deluder Satan Act of 1647. These laws, passed by the ancestor of the state of Massachusetts, required that local communities establish schools. Those schools were to teach the Bible so that the "Old Deluder," Satan, would not be able to fool and corrupt the children of the colony. Under the Articles of Confederation, the Continental Congress in 1787 declared that "religion, morality, and knowledge, being necessary to good government and the happiness of mankind, schools and the means of education shall be forever encour-

---

[1]A recent study found that revenues from taxes paid by illegal aliens do exceed the states' cost of providing public services to them.

aged." To do so, it set aside some money from the sale of public lands in the Northwest to create local schools.

Principles Concerning Access

Since that time, however, education has been primarily the responsibility of the states. They, in turn, have delegated control over schools and the responsibility for financing them to localities. In the early years, schools generally charged the parents for their children's education. In other words, the principle of *ability to pay* determined who got formal education.

Gradually, a movement for statewide systems of free (because tax-supported), non–church–run schools spread. Ability to pay was giving way to the principle of *democracy*, or opportunity for all—except in most cases for minorities and in some cases for women. Public colleges and universities were also being established. They received their biggest impetus from passage of the Morrill Act in 1862 (formally called the Land Grant College Act), which gave federal land to states for creating colleges specializing in agriculture and home economics.

In the early 20th century, states increasingly passed laws making attendance at school compulsory up to a certain age. But they allowed parents to send their children to private schools (almost all of them church related, many of them Catholic) if they preferred. Thus, the principle of *freedom of choice* was applied within the broader principle of *compulsory education.*

Nevertheless, the old principle of ability to pay had not disappeared from American education. It had only moved into private schools and higher education. However, American business and American education needed more well-trained people than this criterion allowed into our better schools. Therefore, scholarships to bright but needy students became more common. The principle here was merit. And until community colleges spread in the 1950s and 1960s, merit seemed to be replacing not only wealth but also democracy or equality of opportunity in determining who could and would get higher education.

Federal scholarships began with the GI Bill of Rights (passed in 1944, later renewed for the Ko-

rean and Vietnam War veterans). In Chapter 5, we examined the six major programs that have since been developed. (See Table 5.1.) These programs offered the chance to obtain a higher education to those who might not be able to earn scholarships on merit.

At the same time, however, the application of the principle of merit was itself being qualified, or limited, in higher education by the principle of *affirmative action.* Court decisions in the 1950s began to open up equal educational opportunities, in a legal sense, to blacks. But where the Court called for "all deliberate speed" in desegregation, school officials dragged their heels. The Civil Rights Act of 1964 not only called for desegregation of public higher education but also prohibited discrimination wherever federal funds were involved (which by then applied to all of higher education).

In 1965, as the concept of affirmative action was being developed, the Higher Education Act—the first major commitment to federal aid—provided for compensatory services to those deprived of adequate preparation. Further moves in that direction were made in the Education Amendments of 1972. But it became increasingly clear that simply providing equal opportunity and compensatory services would not bring about desired increases in minority enrollments. The consequence at the lower levels of public schools was busing for integration. At the higher levels programs of affirmative action were designed to guarantee special treatment for minority—and female—youths interested in further education. We shall consider these developments in more detail here in Part 4.

Principles Concerning Substance

Thomas Jefferson favored mass public education to create wise citizens and widen their opportunities to develop their talents. Andrew Jackson opposed the elitism then characteristic of education and society by arguing for "common schools." Education may serve to select and train elite leaders, of course, but its main function is to socialize people into being good workers in the economy and good citizens in the polity.

However, economist Samuel Bowles points out that

the history of United States education provides little support for the view that schools have been vehicles for the equalization of economic status or opportunity. Nor are they today. The proliferation of special programs for the equalization of educational opportunity has had precious little impact on the structure of education, and even less on the structure of income and opportunity in the economy.[2]

By this reckoning, our schools have been largely successful in economic socialization, although at the expense of equal economic opportunity. The notion that the schools should contribute to economic reform is not commonly held by educators any more than is the notion that schools should contribute toward political reform. Instead, the common view is that schools exist, and should function, to train people to understand and appreciate their economic and political system.

Practices Concerning Access

The influence of education, whatever its strength, has reached different population groups differently. In the past decade, according to the Census Bureau, 80 million people—40 percent of the population—attended elementary or secondary school for at least a year. Yet the educational achievement of various population groups is still very different.

Schooling

College attendance is still very much affected by the economic level of the family, regardless of race or ability. About 54 percent of those with family incomes of $15,000 and over go to college, while only about 13 percent of those from families with incomes under $3000 do so.[3]

Another governmental study found that not only family income but also the father's educational level has a marked effect on a child's likelihood of attending college, again regardless of race or ability. For example, in the same income bracket, a child of a college graduate is much more likely to attend college than the child of a nongraduate.[4] Thus, high income may overcome lack of family educational background, but low income usually means no college, even for the child of a college graduate.

As the cost of higher education skyrockets, the impact will most likely increase. However you are managing your own college education, you're likely to find paying for the education of your children a real challenge. In the 1980s the average total cost of a year at a private college was over $9000, and that at a state school over $4500. These costs have been increasing at a rate of about 7 percent a year. This means that if you have a child in the next few years, putting him or her through college is likely to cost over $50,000 at a state school or up to $200,000 at a private school. And that doesn't even include any graduate education. To provide for four years of state school education for a child born today, you'd have to start immediately putting more than $1500 in a savings account every year for 18 years. How many Americans will be able to do anything like this? The likely result, unless drastic steps are taken, will again be that receiving an education will depend on one's ability to pay.

Illiteracy

It might help also to look at the opposite extreme. In 1969 the U.S. Census found that 1 percent of all Americans 14 or older—1,400,000 people—were totally unable to read and write in any language. A 1970 Harris Poll of Americans 16 or older found that 8 percent couldn't read and write well enough to fill out a driver's license application, and 11 percent were unable to complete a simple bank account application.[5]

The figure has been growing every year. Current studies, summarized in Table P4.1, show that many Americans have real trouble just coping with everyday chores. They find that about one in five is "functionally illiterate" in this sense, and only 46 percent are proficient in coping with daily tasks.

---

[2]Samuel Bowles, "Educational Reforms under Fire," *New York Times*, July 26, 1976. Bowles believes that educational reform is impossible without economic reform: participatory workers' control and democratic socialism. The argument is developed in two books by Bowles and Herbert Gintis: *Schooling in Capitalist America* (New York: Basic Books, 1976); and *Democracy and Capitalism: Property, Community, and the Contradictions of Modern Social Thought* (New York: Basic Books, 1986).

[3]Census Bureau, *Social and Economic Characteristics of Students: October 1973*, series P–20, no. 272 (Washington, DC: GPO, 1974), pp. 43–44.

[4]Census Bureau, *School Enrollment of Young Adults and Their Fathers: October 1960*, series P–20, no. 110 (Washington, DC: GPO, 1961), p. 15.

[5]"Why 1.4 Million Americans Can't Read and Write," *U.S. News & World Report*, August 19, 1974, pp. 37–40. Herman Wong, "Illiteracy: Fear and Shame: 1 Out of 5 Adults May Not Be Able to Read This," *Austin American-Statesman*, November 15, 1976.

A bilingual class in elementary school. (Bohdan Hrynewych/Stock, Boston)

TABLE P4.1
The Extent of Functional Illiteracy
in the United States

EVERYDAY CHORE	PERCENT FUNCTIONALLY ILLITERATE	PERCENT PROFICIENT
Getting and keeping a satisfactory job	19.1	49.0
Managing family budget	29.4	37.6
Awareness of rights	25.8	48.0
Ability to maintain good health	21.3	48.3
Ability to use community resources	22.6	51.4
Reading	21.7	46.1
Problem solving	28.0	48.5
Computation	32.9	40.8
Writing	16.4	58.1
Overall competence	19.1	46.3

Compiled at the Adult Performance Level Project at the University of Texas. Figures are based on the entire U.S. population in 1983.

As educator Jonathan Kozol recently summarized the situation, today 60 million Americans can read neither the Constitution nor the Bible—nor can they read daily newspapers, which are written at a tenth-grade level.[6] In addition, as another expert asserts, "The educational system is adding one million functional illiterates to the poor each year either by dropouts or graduates unable to pass minimal competency tests."[7]

Bilingual Education

In addition, some 2,500,000 American children have difficulty with English because Spanish, Eskimo, or one of 40 other languages is their native tongue. They need bilingual education—teaching in two languages. But until 1967, when Congress passed the Bilingual Education Act, no concerted efforts were made to help them. And until 1974, when the Supreme Court ruled that San Francisco schools were violating the civil rights of Chinese-speaking students by not offering bilingual teaching, little energy was shown. All but eight states have bilingual education programs. The city of Chicago offers public school classes taught in 17 languages—5 more than even New York City. Such programs have been encouraged with federal funds—$140 million in 1986—and enforced where necessary in some 500 school districts in the United

[6]Jonathan Kozol, *Illiterate America* (Garden City, NY: Doubleday, 1985).

[7]Jim Cates of the Adult Performance Level Project at the University of Texas, quoted in Rhonda Cook, "Widespread 'Functional Illiteracy' Gaining Stranglehold on Society," *Austin American-Statesman*, November 6, 1983.

States. Still, these programs reach only 210,000 students—perhaps a tenth of those who could benefit from them. They have also become increasingly controversial. Even Education Secretary William Bennett, who oversees the programs, has attacked them, charging that "after $1.7 billion of federal funding, we have no evidence that the children we have sought to help . . . have benefited."[8] Yet experts have found that children who learn two languages are more imaginative, better with abstract notions, and more flexible in their thinking.[9] Others are arguing that bilingual programs are wasteful and "keep immigrant groups in a linguistic and economic ghetto." They have established groups called English First and U.S. English to lobby Congress to pass a constitutional amendment making English the official language of the United States. In any event, bilingual programs seem likely to become all the more common as the children of aliens enter schools in greater numbers.

POLITICS IN EDUCATION

The classifying of bilingual education as a civil right of non–English-speaking Americans marks yet another expansion of our rights. So does the adoption by the federal government of "right-to-read" programs to overcome illiteracy. But as we have seen again and again, getting something declared a right and getting that right actively and successfully provided to citizens can be very different things—and very political things.

The Politics of School Control

Politics in education operates at every level, as different forces, groups, and individuals seek to control or influence educational policy and practice. There are 16,000 local school systems in America today. Each has political conflicts among parents, teachers, administrators, and the school board—and occasionally, where they're given a role, students too.

Parents have often complained, sometimes with success, about the content of courses (especially on

sex and evolution) and of textbooks and about the school library.[10] But generally their powers are limited.[11]

Recent court decisions, some of which we'll examine in Chapter 12, have opened up the field of parent and student rights. Because it is a new area it is still growing and being shaped by court decisions and by federal and state laws. As of now, major rights include the following:[12]

- The right to appeal a school policy or decision that prevents a student from expressing controversial views so long as they are not obscene, slanderous, or libelous and so long as they do not cause serious disruption—recognized by all states
- The right to take action against a school official if a student is disciplined with "excessive or unreasonable" physical force—recognized by all states
- The right to appeal suspension from school—recognized by all states
- The right to be excused from studying subjects parents object to on religious, moral, or other reasonable grounds—recognized by Alaska, Arizona, Colorado, Delaware, Florida, Idaho, Illinois, Indiana, Iowa, Louisiana, Maryland, Michigan, Nevada, New Hampshire, New York, North Carolina, Ohio, Pennsylvania, Vermont, West Virginia, and Wisconsin

Teachers' unions have recently become very strong in many large cities, especially in the North. They are now playing bigger roles not only in curriculum and salaries but also in school budgets as a whole. In longtime observer Fred Hechinger's view, the new teacher militance derives from "the unconscionable past exploitation of teachers as underpaid servants and second-class citizens—a system in which teachers and children were equally the victims." But since unionization, he argues, "the harsh fact [is] that the children's interests occupy a low place on the scale of the establishment's priorities and self-interest."[13] How true this is of

[8]"Educating the Melting Pot," *U.S. News & World Report*, March 31, 1986, pp. 20–21.

[9]See Kenji Hakuta, *The Mirror of Language* (New York: Basic Books, 1986).

[10]See Dorothy Nelkin, *Science Textbook Controversies and the Politics of Equal Time* (Cambridge, MA: MIT Press, 1977).

[11]See Tyll van Geel, *Authority to Control the School Program* (Lexington, MA: Lexington Books, 1976).

[12]These and other rights of parents and students are summarized in several publications by the National Committee for Citizens in Education, founded in 1973, at 10840 Little Patuxent Parkway, Suite 301, Columbia, MD 21044. It has a 24-hour toll-free phone hotline: (800) NETWORK, which you can call to report problems, get advice on school-related problems, or get a free copy of its Parent Rights Card. It also publishes a newsletter, *Network*, for members and a book by David Schimmel and Louis Fisher, *The Rights of Parents in the Education of Their Children* (1977). It has some 300 local affiliate organizations across the country.

[13]Fred M. Hechinger, "An Exploded Myth," *New York Times*, February 17, 1976.

individual districts is beside the point. What is important to recognize is that old concerns about curriculum and method now are often decided in larger arenas where political power predominates. And teachers, like administrators, are becoming more organized and more powerful. The National Education Association—with some 1,800,000 teacher members and an average of 6000 members in each congressional district—and the American Federation of Teachers—a growing union affiliated with the AFL-CIO—together represent all but about 100,000 of the nation's 2,000,000 elementary and secondary school teachers. When they cooperate, they are a very powerful lobby at all levels from the school district to the national level. It was their efforts that resulted in the establishment of the Department of Education during the Carter administration—and that resisted the Reagan administrations's efforts to fulfill a campaign pledge to abolish it.[14] They have also been important forces in state efforts to reform the public education, which we discussed in Chapter 2.

The Politics of School Finance

Educators have also been meeting resistance from another growing group: taxpayers opposing increased school taxes on their property. At the same time, school property taxes are under attack from another direction: citizens claiming that equality of educational opportunity is denied to many because rich school districts get more tax revenue to spend on their schools than poor districts do.

In one case Demetrio Rodriguez, a Mexican-American laborer, was concerned about the quality of the education his three children were able to get in the poor San Antonio neighborhood the family lived in. Their school district couldn't raise as much money by taxing its less valuable homes and other property as could other districts with more valuable property. Rodriguez sued in 1968 to get the property tax declared unconstitutional as a means of financing schools. He argued that it violated the constitutional right to equal protection. His lawyers contended that even though education is not mentioned in the Constitution, it is so fundamental to other guaranteed rights, such as voting, that it should be protected.

Demetrio Rodriguez of San Antonio, Texas, chief plaintiff in the Texas public school financing case that came before the U.S. Supreme Court. (AP/Wide World Photos)

In 1973 the Burger Court majority disagreed. By a five-to-four vote the Court rejected Rodriguez's claim that education is a right guaranteed by the Constitution in *San Antonio Independent School District* v. *Rodriguez*. That left the question once again to the states. The states, which provide about 40 percent of all funds for schools (compared to 50 percent local funds and 10 percent federal) have constitutional responsibility for education. But state legislatures are frequently insensitive to the needs of the poor and minorities. And so, as Rodriguez himself commented: "The poor people have lost again."

Since the *Rodriguez* decision, some states have made progress toward equalizing the quality of public education among the rich and the poor, notably California and New Jersey, because of state supreme court rulings based on state constitutions.

Meanwhile, more has been learned about who really pays for public higher education. State colleges and universities get 17 percent of their reve-

---
[14]See Stephen Chapman, "The Teachers' Coup," *New Republic*, October 11, 1980, pp. 9–11.

President Johnson signs the Higher Education Act of 1965 at the old one-room country school he once attended in Johnson City, Texas. (UPI/Bettmann Newsphotos)

nue from tuition and almost all the rest from state taxes. The Carnegie Corporation made a comprehensive study of higher-education finance. It concluded, in the words of chairperson Clark Kerr:

> You could say that low tuition for the middle class, which can afford to pay more, is a subsidy of the middle class, at the expense of the high-income groups who pay much more in taxes, and particularly at the expense of the low-income groups whose kids can't afford to go to college.[15]

The Politics of Federal Aid

Of course, as the federal government's role in education grows, the federal politics of education increases. In the Johnson years, 60 education-related bills became law, and government spending on schools shot up from $2.3 billion in 1963 to almost $11 billion in 1968.[16] Johnson was responsible for

many major innovations, such as new school desegregation guidelines, extension of integration requirements to northern schools, and large grants of federal aid to disadvantaged areas. Included also were education "laboratories" to test innovations, student loans for college students, work-study programs, and Head Start and Follow Through programs to give special preschool training to the disadvantaged to prepare them for public school.[17]

However, after continuing growth under later presidents, the Reagan administration managed to slow the rate of increase in federal spending on education, even though it couldn't achieve major cuts or abolish the Department of Education created under Carter.

It should be clear, then, that political struggles over education occur at every level of our political system. This is particularly true when the principle of access to education is at stake, as we can see by returning to the case of the children of illegal aliens.

---

[15]Quoted in Iver Peterson, "Carnegie Panel Bids Middle Class Pay Bigger Share of College Cost," *New York Times*, July 13, 1973. The Carnegie study is entitled *Higher Education: Who Pays? Who Benefits? Who Should Pay?* (New York: McGraw-Hill, 1973).

[16]These figures are from the National Center for Education Statistics. HEW counts rather differently and arrives at significantly lower totals.

[17]For interesting studies of many of these and other programs, see Joel Spring, *The Sorting Machine* (New York: McKay, 1976); and Norman C. Thomas, *Education In National Politics* (New York: McKay, 1975).

ALIENS AND EDUCATION

The Rights of Aliens

The Constitution gives Congress the authority to decide who may enter the country and who may be expelled. The Immigration and Nationality Act of 1952, as amended, now lists 33 grounds for excluding aliens, including poverty, prostitution, and polygamy. Under the laws Congress has passed, some 50 million immigrants from all over the world have settled in the United States. Some of them became citizens through the process of naturalization (see Chapter 12). All children born in the United States become citizens automatically, whether or not their parents are citizens.[18]

The Constitution, and especially the Bill of Rights, contains many protections for the rights of individuals. These rights and liberties are granted *to persons, not to citizens.* Until recently Congress and state legislatures sometimes passed laws distinguishing between citizens and aliens in terms of their rights and privileges.

In 1971 the Supreme Court issued a landmark decision in the case of *Graham* v. *Richardson.* Arizona had restricted certain welfare benefits to citizens and to aliens who had lived in the United States for at least 15 years. The Court ruled against Arizona, declaring in a unanimous opinion that "classifications based on alienage, like those based on nationality or race, are inherently suspect and subject to close judicial scrutiny. Aliens as a class are a prime example of a 'discrete and insular' minority . . . for whom such heightened judicial solicitude is appropriate."[19] What this meant in practical terms was that any discrimination against aliens would require demonstration of a compelling governmental interest if such discrimination were to be constitutional.[20]

The Question of the Right to Education

Since the *Graham* decision the Court has been carving out certain areas in which distinctions between citizens and aliens can be made. One is the question of the right to hold public office, and another is the right to vote.[21] In *Plyler* v. *Doe,* which we discussed at the beginning of this perspective, the question was the right to education. When the Tyler, Texas, school board tried to charge the children of illegal aliens for their education, the Mexican-American Legal Defense and Education Fund (MALDEF) filed suit on behalf of some of these children. In opposing this suit, the state of Texas was hoping to get the courts to permit a distinction between citizens and illegal aliens in the area of free public education. Those efforts did not fare well in the courts. The Supreme Court ruled in *Rodriguez* that education is not a right. But since *Brown* v. *Board of Education* in 1953, the Court has consistently held that when the group excluded from education is a racial minority, this exclusion violates a most fundamental national policy as well as the rights of individuals. Thus, in 1982 the Court ruled in *Plyler* v. *Doe* that the children of illegal aliens do have a right to free public education.

The Practical Problems

Decisions such as *Plyler* v. *Doe* are usually strictly on legal grounds. They almost always raise practical problems. In the case of *Plyler* v. *Doe*, there was uncertainty as to how many children of illegal aliens would require or request schooling. The state estimated 110,000. In fact, some 11,000 registered in the first year after the Court ruling. But that number rose to 30,000 by 1984 and could go much higher, now that the more general question of the legal status of "undocumented" aliens has finally been resolved in a way that grants them resident status. This question of status is really a part of the broader matter of United States policy toward refugees and aliens.

ALIENS AND REFUGEES: THE BROADER QUESTION

Refugees—people seeking refuge from wars, natural disasters, persecution, or other such disruptions—are a phenomenon as old as the problems

---

[18]The one exception to this is children of foreign diplomats because diplomats are not under U.S. jurisdiction.

[19]*Graham* v. *Richardson*, 403 U.S. 365 (1971), p. 372.

[20]See David Carliner, *The Rights of Aliens, An American Civil Liberties Union Handbook* (New York: Avon, 1977).

[21]See, for example, *Skafte* v. *Rorex*, 430 U.S. 961 (1977); *Dunn* v. *Blumstein*, 405 U.S. 330 (1972); *Sugarman* v. *Dougall*, 413 U.S. 634 (1973). For a study of Court decisions, see Elizabeth Hull, *Without Justice for All: The Constitutional Rights of Aliens* (Westport, CT: Greenwood, 1985).

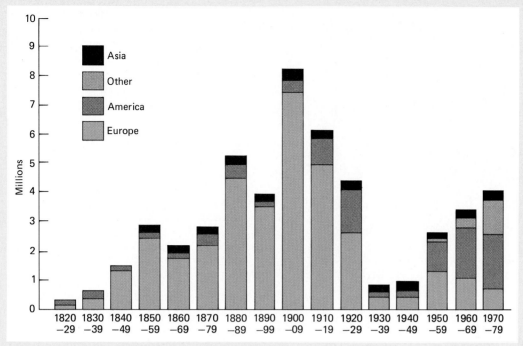

FIGURE P4.1

Immigrants by Continent of Origin and Decade, 1820 to 1979.

Source: Chart prepared by U.S. Bureau of Census.

themselves. Today the phenomenon has reached new heights: some 15 million refugees in recent years worldwide, according to the U.S. State Department. Since 1981 the United States has received over half a million. The 1987 quota was set by the Reagan administration at 70,000.[22]

Other people seek to enter the United States to take advantage of the greater economic opportunities found in this country. A recent study by the International Labor Organization estimates that developing countries will have to create some 600 million to 700 million new jobs in the next two decades simply to avoid worse unemployment than they already face. A similar study for Latin America by the Inter-American Development Bank found a need for 4 million jobs each year in that area of the world alone. Even now the flow of workers toward the United States is growing. The Immigration and Nationality Act as amended in 1976 allows only 290,000 legal immigrants for residence a year plus special cases for immediate relatives of U.S. citizens, bringing the actual total to 400,000.[23] In addition, some 10 million foreigners—tourists, business visitors, students, and so on—enter the country legally. Others come illegally, especially from Mexico and from countries farther south. No one knows how many of these come each year—or how many are already here. The Census Bureau estimates the present total at 3.5 million, but some experts think the actual total may be more like 12 million.

Illegal immigration has recently been at the rate of about a million a year, according to most estimates. Another 1.5 million are caught and deported by the INS each year. Most agree this has been a serious problem, notably for services such as education and welfare but also for some Americans who may lose jobs to foreigners willing to work for less. Others argue, however, that the immigrants' net effect is to create jobs by increasing demand for labor and consumer goods.[24]

[22]For a study of U.S. policy, see Gil Loescher and John A. Scanlan, *Calculated Kindness: Refugees and America's Half-Open Door, 1945 to the Present* (New York: Free Press, 1986).

[23]See Neil R. Peirce and Roger F. Fillion, "Should the U.S. Open Its Doors to the Foreigners Wanting to Come In?" *National Journal*, March 7, 1981, pp. 390–93.

[24]For a survey of recent studies, see "Reform of Immigration Laws Only Adds Fuel to the Debate," *Insight*, December 15, 1986, pp. 40–43.

The frontier grill separating the United States and Mexico at San Diego, California. (Alex Webb/Magnum Photos)

A New Immigration Law

Experts have long disagreed on how the problem should be approached.[25] Some have called for the strengthening of the Immigration and Naturalization Service, which has to police the 2000-mile border with Mexico and inspect almost 300 million entrants to the country each year with a staff of just over 10,000.[26] Others have proposed an identity-card system for all people—citizens and legal aliens alike—who are entitled to work, with requirements that employers check these cards. Civil libertarians oppose identity cards. Still others have called for a law prohibiting the hiring of illegal aliens and punishing employers who do hire them. Employers have said this would be unfair to them. They argue that most of the jobs the aliens do are unwanted even by unemployed citizens or wouldn't be worth paying the minimum wage for.

Because experts and vested interests as well disagreed over how to solve the problem of uncontrolled illegal immigration, Congress tried without success for five years to pass a new law. Finally, in

October 1986, it succeeded. Sponsored by Senator Alan Simpson (Republican of Wyoming) and Rep. Peter Rodino (Democrat of New Jersey), the Immigration Reform and Control Act of 1986 was built around a compromise on the issue of farm labor. Its major provisions include:

- An amnesty program giving legal status to illegal aliens who can prove they have lived in the U.S. since January 1, 1982
- A seven-year program of temporary resident status for up to 350,000 illegal farm workers who can prove they worked on U.S. farms in 1985 and 1986
- Fines, and in repeat cases jail terms, for employers who knowingly hire illegal aliens
- Provision for protection of the rights of legal immigrants and others against discrimination in hiring on suspicion of being illegal aliens

Observers were surprised by the sudden passage of the bill but attributed it to a growing belief that the problem had become urgent and a realization that there was no ideal solution. Still, many believe that the terms of the law—especially the amnesty and employer sanctions—are impossible to enforce effectively. They therefore doubt that the problem has been solved.

In any event, little is known for certain about the actual impact of refugees and aliens on Americans. A recent study found that on the average, refugee families earn as much as native families by the time they've been in the United States for six years. It also found that such families on average pay more money in taxes than they receive in welfare and other services.[27]

Popular Attitudes

Despite these findings, popular attitudes toward immigrants seem to be hardening. Polls taken before Congress acted were showing a majority of Americans favoring a decrease in immigration. It is not clear how to interpret this backlash. Some say it manifests racist attitudes and reflects the fact that half of the U.S. population growth is now attributable to Spanish-speaking immigrants. Others agree with John Roche, who has written that

[25]For a comprehensive yet concise survey of the problem and proposed solutions, see Michael S. Teitelbaum, "Right versus Right: Immigration and Refugee Policy in the U.S.," *Foreign Affairs* 58 (Fall 1980), 21–59.

[26]One reporter found the INS "shot through with nepotism, incompetence, corruption, and brutality. . . . suffocating beneath a mountain of paperwork, its harassed staff badly demoralized." See John Crewdson, *The Tarnished Door: The New Immigrants and the Transformation of America* (New York: Times Books, 1983).

[27]The study was conducted for the Select Committee on Immigration and Refugee Policy. See "Refugees: Stung by a Backlash," *U.S. News & World Report*, October 13, 1980, pp. 60–64.

President Reagan signs the Immigration Reform and Control Act of 1986. (UPI/Bettmann Newsphotos)

disputes over current national policy have few racial overtones. No one seriously objects to the 20,000 Mexicans or Jamaicans who can legally immigrate. On the contrary, the objections are founded on concern for the quality of American life, and the closely related thrust for zero population growth.[28]

"Our uneasiness with the current wave of newcomers reflects our uncertainty," writes one who came to the United States as a refugee in 1956.

Have we reached the point of losing those qualities that made this country different from Old World nations? Whether one considers the productivity of the American worker, the passivity in the face of the energy crisis, or the choice the electorate is likely to have. . . . America looks like a declining civilization. . . . But to be American is to be rashly innovative and to refuse to defer to complexity. We need the refugees's vigor and ambition. They remind us, those who are no longer refugees, that restlessness is valuable human capital and that the U.S. is still the frontier of possibilities.[29]

It remains to be seen, however, just how quickly the United States will actively extend to its latest immigrants the rights and liberties of all Americans, starting with that fundamental concern: education. In Chapters 12, 13, and 14, we shall examine these rights and liberties and the extent to which they now extend to minorities and to "outsiders" such as women, the young, the elderly, and the handicapped.

"Well, here they come . . . Illegal aliens!" (Reprinted by permission of Tribune Media Services, Inc.)

[28]John P. Roche. "Immigration and Nationality: A Historical Overview of U.S. Policy," in *Ethnic Resurgence in Modern Democratic States*, ed. Uri Raànan (New York: Pergamon Press, 1980), p. 75.

[29]Charles Fenyvesi, "Immigration Anxiety," *New Republic*, June 14, 1980, p. 20.

12

THE POLITICS OF LIBERTY:
Civil Liberties, Civil Rights, and Human Rights

Arrested for passing out political campaign leaflets in a city square? Incarcerated in a concentration camp because of your religious heritage? Jailed for reading a radical political book? Or for belonging to an unpopular political party? Exiled for unsuccessfully trying to run for political office? Suddenly missing without trace, without one's loved ones being notified, without the opportunity to consult a lawyer?

It's likely you don't even know anyone to whom any of these things has happened, unless you know a Jewish survivor from Nazi Germany or an exile from a Communist country or an escapee from a dictatorship in Latin America, Africa, or Asia.

Political persecution is rare in the countries of the Western world that we call democratic. But it wasn't always that way. And there are still groups, even in our own country, that sometimes experience

treatment somewhat resembling political persecution. For example, over the years, various socialist parties and organizations have claimed such mistreatment. And for many years American citizens lost jobs and even served jail terms for belonging to the Communist party.

Infringements of such civil liberties as freedom of religion and freedom of speech were major factors in the decision of Europeans to colonize America hundreds of years ago. Today some immigrants come for the same reason. However, as we have just seen in Perspective 4, aliens and refugees have not always received the benefits of these civil liberties once they arrived. Nor have American citizens. In this chapter, we'll learn what our rights are as individuals (civil liberties), as members of groups (civil rights), and as human beings (human rights), and how we got these rights. ■

LIBERTIES AND RIGHTS

People making claims to new opportunities or new forms of treatment tend to call these objectives liberties or rights. Those opposing them are as likely to refer to the claims as special privileges or reverse discrimination.

The terms *liberties* and *rights* tend to carry with them a claim to legitimacy, in our way of thinking. When we can find the claims upheld by the language of the Declaration of Independence or the Constitution—freedom of speech or freedom of religion, for example—we may well agree at once. But when someone claims a right nowhere mentioned in the Constitution or even in legislation—such as the right to abort an unborn fetus or the right to privacy—we need to know how to determine whether or not it is indeed a right. We must therefore be certain just what we mean by rights and liberties, and we must know where they come from and to whom they apply.

Civil Liberties as Freedom from the State

"Of all the loose terms in the world, liberty is the most indefinite," wrote the British philosopher and politician Edmund Burke in 1789. He was contemplating the American and French revolutions, which were grounded in appeals to liberty as a "natural right of man." The American Constitution of 1787 guaranteed the right to personal liberty in absence of demonstrated cause for imprisonment, as it assured the right to a jury trial. But Jefferson wrote to Madison the same year that "a bill of rights is what the people are entitled to against every government on earth." And it was the Bill of Rights—the first ten amendments to the Constitution, adopted in 1791—that provided the basis for the civil liberties we now, perhaps, take for granted.

The very notion of civil liberties makes sense only in a society governed by law. A human being may have a "natural right" to freedom, but as the French philosopher Jean-Jacques Rousseau observed in a famous passage written in 1762: "Man is born free, but everywhere he is in chains." Government is established, in the view generally held by the founders, to preserve people's rights to life, liberty, and property from the chaos, violence, and theft characteristic of *anarchy*—the absence of government. But government uncontrolled may become a *tyranny*. And a tyranny may prevent individuals from enjoying these rights every bit as much as does a state of anarchy. For this reason, government's power to interfere with individual liberty must be restricted, the founders believed.

Government, in other words, does not provide liberty. It provides or fosters only the conditions of legal order in which liberty can be exercised by individuals doing as they wish, so long as they do not interfere with the liberty of others. But if the government gets too strong, it becomes the chief threat to the achievement and exercise of liberty. Therefore, government's powers must be limited. That is why we have a Bill of Rights. It protects citizens' liberties against arbitrary governmental demands, unfair legal processes, and especially political interference with the individual exercise of the rights to speak freely, to assemble, to worship, and to publish. In the form in which they appear in the Bill of Rights, the legal guarantees that establish our **civil liberties** assert *negative governmental duties* or prohibitions. In doing so, they also imply *positive individual liberties.* But these civil liberties take on significance only as they are actually exercised by individuals and then only if the government abides by the constitutional limitations and does not interfere.

This concept holds that civil liberties provide and guarantee freedom from the state. It was adopted in an era of optimism about one's ability to fulfill oneself if left alone. Slavery and its aftermath of discrimination made it clear that such "negative" civil liberties were not enough to guarantee equal citizen participation in political and economic life. Thus, Americans became less optimistic about a human being's ability to be free individually; and at the same time, they grew more optimistic about government's ability to help achieve or restore equality among all people. The emphasis in politics gradually shifted from civil liberties (prohibitions against state interference in public life) to **civil rights** (regulations permitting state interference to guarantee rights of full political participation to groups that had been excluded by law or custom or conditions of poverty).

Civil Rights as the Opportunity to Take Part in the State

Civil rights, then, allow the individual the *freedom or opportunity to take part in the state*. The trend toward democratization that arose in the last century and continues to the present is thus usually referred to as a civil-rights movement. Such rights are guaranteed not just to individuals, as is generally the case with civil liberties, but to members of a group previously excluded from these rights and privileges. The civil-rights laws, for example, gave the federal government power to supervise elections in the South so that it could guarantee to blacks the right to vote.

The expansion of liberties and rights has not stopped there. Instead, there has been a growing movement to grant or guarantee what are often called **positive rights.** These are rights to basic human needs that are not otherwise attainable in a society with large-scale inequality. Among the positive rights increasingly sought are the right to a job or to economic opportunity and security, the right to health and medical care, the right to retire in old age with a pension, and the right to an education. In earlier eras, characterized by greater individualism and self-sufficiency and less industrialization and urbanization, these concerns were generally thought to be the individual's—and his or her family's—own responsibility. Increasingly they have come to be seen as beyond most individuals' ability to attain without *positive governmental assistance.*[1]

The argument for such assistance is based on what may be a return to the old concept of "the rights of man." But today, in an interdependent world linked by mass communications, these rights are more and more conceived of as **human rights.** They are, in other words, rights to which all individuals, wherever they live and under whatever sort of government they live, should be entitled, simply by virtue of being human beings.

The concept of human rights can be traced back to the beliefs of the founders that "all men are endowed by their Creator with certain unalienable rights [to] life, liberty, and the pursuit of happiness." In the United States today human rights take the form primarily of economic and social rights: the right to a job, to earn a livelihood; the right to an education; the right to medical care; the right to a sufficient retirement income. Around the world these rights are increasingly sought by citizens of various countries appealing to the Universal Declaration of Human Rights passed by the United Nations in 1948. We can understand them better, even in their global context, if we first examine them more specifically in their American context, where they continue to pose policy questions for American politics.

WHAT ARE YOUR RIGHTS AS AN AMERICAN CITIZEN?

From Natural Rights to Civil Liberties

The Declaration of Independence asserted that all men had "unalienable rights"—rights they could not lose, renounce, or have taken from them. Among these were included "life, liberty, and the pursuit of happiness." However, this formulation is too general to guide the government. For more specific guidance we turn to the Constitution, which includes guarantees of seven *civil liberties*, as we generally call them.

- Habeas corpus (Article I, Section 9, Clause 2). This Latin term means "you may have the body." It guarantees that someone who has been imprisoned can ask a federal court for a **writ of habeas corpus.** If the court finds that the imprisonment violates the Constitution or the laws of the United States, it issues such a writ and the prisoner must be released.
- Bill of attainder (Article I, Section 9, Clause 3, and Section 10, Clause 1). A **bill of attainder** is a special law passed to declare that some person or group has committed a crime and to impose punishment. The Constitution prohibits such bills because under our system of separation of powers, only a court can try a person or impose punishment.
- Ex post facto laws (Article I, Section 9, Clause 3, and Section 10, Clause 1). **Ex post facto** is Latin for "after the fact" or "after the deed." An **ex post facto law** declares something a crime only after it has been done. The Constitution prohibits such laws.
- Trial by jury (Article III, Section 2, Clause 3). The Constitution provides that all federal crimes must be tried in front of a jury—a group of fellow citizens, instead of just a judge—except for impeach-

---

[1]For a helpful discussion of these types of rights and their development, see Richard P. Claude, "The Classical Model of Human Rights Development," in *Comparative Human Rights*, ed. Richard P. Claude (Baltimore: Johns Hopkins Univ. Press, 1976), chap. 1.

ment of an official, which involves a trial by the United States Senate. The courts have held that the provision need not hold for petty offenses (small crimes) nor when a defendant waives the right to a jury.

■ Trial location (Article III, Section 2, Clause 3). Trials must be held in the state where the crime has been committed.

■ Treason (Article III, Section 3). Treason is the only crime defined by the Constitution. "Treason against the United States," it says, "shall consist in levying war against them [the United States], or in adhering to their enemies, giving them aid and comfort." But the Constitution thereby protects people who express unpopular views from being prosecuted as traitors and goes on to require "the testimony of two witnesses to the same overt Act" or "confession in open court" for conviction of treason.

■ Religious tests (Article VI, Clause 3). The prohibition of religious tests or vows about one's religious beliefs for those who want to serve their country protects citizens from religious discrimination in federal jobs.

These seven civil liberties offer important protection to citizens. But as we saw in Chapter 1, when the Constitution was being debated, many feared that these liberties were not sufficient. As a result, 12 amendments to the Constitution were passed by the House and Senate and submitted to the states for ratification. Of the 12 amendments, 10 were quickly ratified. Two were never ratified.

The Bill of Rights

The ten constitutional amendments ratified by the states eventually became known as the **Bill of Rights.** The First Amendment provides for freedom of religion, freedom of speech, freedom of the press, and freedom to assemble peaceably and protest to the government. This amendment has been the cornerstone of the liberty of ordinary Americans in everyday life. It has also caused the greatest debates about the real—and the ideal—extent of the liberties of Americans. To understand its import, we must examine the ways in which its major provisions have been interpreted.

Freedom of Speech

"Congress shall make no law . . . abridging the freedom of speech," says the First Amendment. That language seems clear enough. But in fact,

"Oh, yeah? Well, I just happen to have a copy of the Bill of Rights with me." (Drawing by Charles Barsotti; © 1981 The New Yorker Magazine)

Congress has made laws prohibiting certain forms or types of speech. The first major instance occurred just seven years after the First Amendment was ratified. The Sedition Act of 1798 made it a crime to write, utter, or publish "any false, scandalous, and malicious writing" against the president, the Congress, or the government "with the intent to defame [the government or] excite against it the hatred of the people." The Sedition Act expired in three years, and convictions under it were never reviewed by the Supreme Court. However, there was much opposition to it, and the Federalist party, which sponsored the act, lost the next election.

The Sedition Act was passed in a time of troubles in foreign relations. Since then, other limits on free speech have been passed by Congress in similar situations: during World War I, World War II, and the cold-war era of the 1950s. Gradually, the Supreme Court has set limits on such laws restricting free speech, but it has also set limits on free speech itself.

In setting forth what is and what is not *protected* exercise of First Amendment freedoms, the Court has had to define what it considers to be speech. The first and most obvious type is called *pure speech*—the peaceful expression of ideas to a voluntary audience. This type is generally protected by the First Amendment. The second type, sometimes called *speech plus*, is verbal expression combined with some sort of action, such as marching or picketing. The Court has ruled that such speech plus is in general protected only if it does not obstruct traffic or endanger the public safety. The third type is *symbolic speech*—using symbols such as wearing armbands in protest to express an opinion. Here the Court has been selective. For example, when people burned their draft registration cards in protest against the Vietnam War, the Court held that this was an illegal act rather than expression of an idea. But when students in Des Moines wore black armbands to school to protest the same war and were subsequently suspended, the Court classified this act differently. The wearing of an armband is an act of symbolic speech, the Court said in *Tinker* v. *Des Moines School District* (1969). It overturned the suspensions, asserting that students do not "shed their constitutional rights to freedom of speech or expression at the schoolhouse gate." Thus, not only content but also locale of speech may be important.

Generally speaking, political speech has been granted protection, whereas advertising, obscenity, libel, and slander have not. However, the Court has had to decide how to classify specific instances. Is it libelous to attack a public official unjustly? This, the Court has said, is protected political speech. Yet unjustly attacking a private citizen can be another matter.

Classification is not sufficient, however. The Court also needs general principles for interpreting the prohibition. Three major principles have been used to interpret the right to free speech. As early as 1919, in *Schencky* v. *U.S.*, Justice Oliver Wendell Holmes stated the **clear and present danger** test. Falsely shouting "Fire!" in a crowded theater is the example most often used to illustrate this test,

although the case the Court was considering concerned urging men to resist the draft in World War I. The Court held that urging draft resistance could not be considered a protected activity in wartime because it posed a clear and present danger to the state.

Other justices have taken the *absolutist position*, saying that "no law . . . abridging the freedom of speech" means "no law," and so all speech of whatever sort should be protected. Justices Hugo L. Black (served 1937–1971) and William O. Douglas (served 1939–1975) favored this position, but their views were not accepted by the Court majority.

A more common view is that the right of free expression occupies a *preferred position*. As such, although it is not absolute, it is higher than other constitutional rights, such as the right to property, because it is more fundamental. Thus, any law that restricts free expression will be viewed skeptically by the Court.

Freedom of the Press

The preferred-position doctrine is generally applied not only to speech but also to the other activities covered by the First Amendment—especially religion and the press. Deciding how any general test is to be applied to these other activities is hard, however, for these too require definition and interpretation.

When the drafters wrote the First Amendment, the term *press* referred to newspapers, books, and magazines—all of which were printed by *presses*. Today we refer to all these as media of communication. But we use the same term or category to cover TV, radio, and films. Are they too to be protected? All convey information, after all; and all can, and sometimes do, convey political views. But the Court has held that the broadcast media—TV and radio—use the public airwaves and are granted that *privilege* by the government, which regulates who can broadcast where and on what wavelengths, as we've seen in Chapter 7. The Court has ruled that because this grant of airwave frequencies is a privilege, expression over them is *not a right* but instead is governed by federal laws.

Does this mean that newspapers and books can publish anything they wish? Not if it is deemed obscene or libelous of a private citizen or if it would deny a fair trial to a person accused of a crime by biasing potential jurors. In general, however, the

Mary Beth Tinker and her brother John and the black arm bands they wore to school to protest the Vietnam war. The Supreme Court upheld their right to wear the arm bands as an instance of symbolic speech. (UPI/Bettmann Newsphotos)

Court has used the doctrine of **no prior restraint** (that is, no prior censorship), which holds that the press cannot be *prevented* from publishing something but instead can be punished afterward if it publishes something illegal. The Court argues that if censorship were permitted, government officials could prevent the publication of almost anything they didn't like simply by arguing that it might be damaging. Thus, press freedom is protected while press responsibility is fostered.

Freedom of Religion

The early colonists came to the New World in large part to escape from laws limiting their religious activities and beliefs. Not surprisingly, therefore, the First Amendment prevents Congress from "establishing" an official religion. The Court has held that this provision also prohibits religious instruction, Bible readings, and prayers in public schools. But it has allowed state and federal aid for nonreligious purposes to church-related schools, and it ruled in 1980 that Christmas celebrations, although they are clearly Christian, can be conducted in public schools. And of course our paper money and coins carry the motto "In God We Trust," and the military services have religious chaplains representing the larger denominations. Thus, the separation of church and state need not be total, according to the Court, but it must be sufficient to prevent the imposition of religious views on citizens.

The First Amendment also bars Congress from "prohibiting the free exercise" of any religion. When we think of religion in the United States, most of us tend to think only of Catholicism, the major Protestant denominations, and Judaism. But a survey by a Methodist minister completed in 1980 found almost 1200 different religious denominations in America, each with its own distinctive beliefs and practices.[2] Clearly, the First Amendment prevents Congress from outlawing a religion. But what about certain religious practices that are normally against the law? Some Navaho Indians have long used peyote, an illegal drug, in their religious services. Is that illegal? The Court has said no. And what about civil practices that violate a religion's views? Jehovah's Witnesses are prohibited by their

This city-sponsored nativity scene in Pawtucket, RI, was ruled constitutional by the Supreme Court. (Bryce Flynn/Picture Group)

beliefs from worshiping "graven images," and they consider saluting the American flag a violation of this prohibition. The Court has ruled on free speech grounds that a Jehovah's Witness cannot be forced to salute the flag. However, Jehovah's Witnesses also object to blood transfusions because they believe these violate the biblical prohibition against "eating blood." When parents have invoked such beliefs to prevent needed transfusions for their children, the courts have overruled the claim to free exercise of these religious beliefs because human life was at stake.

Such decisions can be seen either as preventing Congress from in effect outlawing certain religions or as actually supporting particular religions. The former view is the traditional one. However, various recent decisions suggest that the Supreme Court is moving toward the latter position. In 1983 the Court upheld by a vote of five to four the granting by Minnesota of a state income tax deduction for tuition, transportation, and textbooks for children attending private schools. It also upheld by a vote of six to three the practice of opening legislative sessions with prayer. In 1984 it made its rationale explicit. It ruled, by a vote of five to four, that city officials in Pawtucket, Rhode Island, did not violate the First Amendment by sponsoring a Christmas Nativity scene. The Reagan administration had asked the Court "to make sure that the hand of government does not suppress this vital freedom" of religion.[3]

---

[2]The survey was conducted by J. Gordon Melton. See "Pastor Catalogues 1,200 U.S. Religions," *New York Times*, March 16, 1980.

[3]The statement was made by Attorney General William French Smith. The case in question was *Lynch* v. *Donnelly*.

How to Get—and How to Lose—American Citizenship

It's likely you're an American citizen. If you were born in the United States, regardless of who your parents were or of whether they were American citizens, you are an American citizen. (There are a few unlikely exceptions: If you were born of a foreign king, queen, or diplomat or on a foreign public ship while it was in American waters or of an enemy occupying the United States, you would not be an American citizen.) Indeed, if you were born on an airplane while it was flying over the United States, you're a citizen. You're also a citizen if you were born abroad of an American parent.

You don't have to remain an American citizen. You may renounce your citizenship simply by declaring that you no longer wish to be a citizen. The official term for this voluntary expatriation (from *ex,* "out of," and *patria,* the "fatherland" or "country"—you put yourself "out of the country").

If you were born in the United States or had an American parent, you are called a natural-born citizen. If you weren't born in the United States and didn't have an American parent, you are called an alien (a term derived from the Latin word for *other).* As an alien, you may still be able to become a naturalized citizen. Sometimes Congress "blankets in" a whole group, as it did for Native American Indians in 1924. More often an individual applies for citizenship.

To become a naturalized citizen, you must meet certain qualifications. You must show that you entered the country legally. You must have "good moral character." you must be able to read, write, speak, and understand English. You must pass a test showing that you know the history, principles, and form of American government, and you must pledge allegiance. You must renounce any titles of nobility, such as lord or prince, which you may hold in your previous country of citizenship. You will not be granted citizenship if you are a polygamist, a draft evader or a deserter from the armed forces, an anarchist, or a member of a Communist party.

To become a citizen, you normally must file a petition with the government. To be allowed to do so, you must be 18 or older and must have lived in the United States for five consecutive years. The Immigration and Naturalization Service then investigates you and holds a preliminary hearing on your application. If you get that far—and most applicants do—a federal or state court judge holds a final hearing (which is usu-

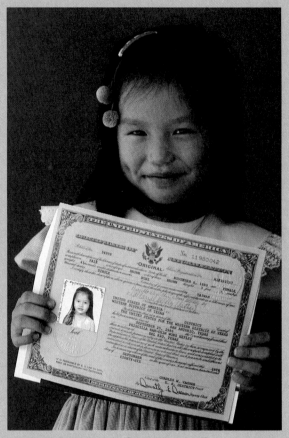

A new U.S. citizen in San Antonio, Texas. (Daemm-rich/UNIPHOTO)

ally a mere formality) and then administers an oath and issues a certificate of naturalization.

A naturalized citizen has all the rights of a natural-born citizen except that he or she is not eligible to be president or vice-president. In addition, naturalized citizenship can be canceled or revoked if it is found that someone lied when applying for it.

Until the 1960s the federal government could revoke your citizenship if you deserted from the armed forces in wartime or voted in an election of another country. In a landmark case, *Afroyim v. Rusk* (1967), the Supreme Court finally forbade revocation of citizenship altogether, on grounds that such action violated the Fourteenth Amendment.

The issue of school prayer has also been controversial. More than two decades ago the Court ruled that organized oral prayer in public school classrooms was unconstitutional. Still, the practice has continued in many schools across the country. These prayers are almost always Christian. Non-Christians, leaders of most Christian faiths, and civil libertarians have all fought these practices in the courts. But the polls have shown that about four-fifths of the public support such prayer. Some 200 proposed constitutional amendments allowing school prayer have been introduced in Congress, and Ronald Reagan supported such an amendment before and after his election in 1980. Still, Congress has refused to pass such an amendment.

These and similar conflicts, which arise frequently, remind us that freedom of religion (like other First Amendment freedoms) is more complicated than it appears, requiring constant interpretation by the courts.

The Other Provisions

Interpretation is essential as regards the other provisions of the Bill of Rights as well. The Second and Third Amendments protect the right to keep and bear arms and prohibit forced quartering of soldiers in private homes. These arose out of special colonial concerns and have had little practical significance in American constitutional history since that time. But the right to keep and bear arms is still cited by opponents of gun control in support of their position.

The next five amendments provide special protection for those involved in the justice system and have been subject to considerable interpretation by the courts over the years. Among their major provisions are the following:

- The government may not search a person or his or her home or seize that person's personal possessions unless it has good reason (**probable cause**) to believe a crime has been committed and/or it obtains a **search warrant**—Fourth Amendment.
- A person cannot be tried a second time for the same crime if he or she has once been acquitted (**double jeopardy**)—Fifth Amendment.
- The government cannot compel someone to testify against himself or herself (**self-incrimination**)—Fifth Amendment.
- "Nor shall any person . . . be deprived of life, liberty, or property, without **due process of**

law"—Fifth Amendment. This clause gives us protection against arbitrary or unfair procedures in judicial or administrative proceedings and against laws that could affect our personal or property rights.
- An owner must be justly compensated by the government if his or her private property is taken for public use—Fifth Amendment.
- Someone being criminally prosecuted is entitled to a fair trial—one that is speedy, public, and with a jury; one in which the defendant is informed of the charges against him or her, is allowed to cross-examine any witnesses against him or her, has the power to force favorable witnesses to testify for him or her, and has the right to be represented by a lawyer—Sixth Amendment.
- The government may not require excessive bail (the money the accused has to put up to obtain release while awaiting trial) or impose excessive fines or "cruel and unusual punishment"—Eighth Amendment.

Perhaps the most controversial civil-liberties question raised by these amendments has concerned the death penalty, which many opponents have termed cruel and unusual punishment. In 1972 the Supreme Court ruled that laws providing for capital punishment, as it is called,[4] were unconstitutional. Without specific legislative guidelines, said the Court in *Furman* v. *Georgia*, the penalty was imposed in arbitrary ways. It was, in fact, more often imposed on the poor and the black than on others who had been convicted of the same crimes. Many states then rewrote their laws; and in 1976 the Court recognized as constitutional new death-penalty laws passed by the states of Georgia, Florida, and Texas. Since 1977 occasional executions have been carried out in various states. But there are still over a thousand prisoners awaiting execution "on death row." The Supreme Court has not yet stated its criteria of interpretation clearly enough to limit complicated legal maneuvering by defense attorneys and the states whenever a scheduled execution date approaches. People on both sides of the issue are still attempting to interpret the Supreme Court's ongoing interpretation of the Eighth Amendment.[5]

---

[4]From the Latin word *caput*, which means "head"—the traditional means of executing criminals was decapitation.

[5]For an analysis, see William J. Bowers, Glenn L. Pierce, and John F. McDevitt, *Legal Homicide: Death as Punishment in America, 1864–1982* (Boston: Northeastern Univ. Press, 1984).

TABLE 12.1
Major Stages of the Nationalization of the Bill of Rights

YEAR	ISSUE	AMENDMENT INVOLVED	COURT CASE
1925	Freedom of speech	I	*Gitlow* v. *New York*
1931	Freedom of the press	I	*Near* v. *Minnesota*
1932	Right to a lawyer in death-penalty cases	VI	*Powell* v. *Alabama*
1934	Free exercise of religion	I	*Hamilton* v. *Regents of the University of California*
1937	Freedom of assembly and right to petition	I	*De Jonge* v. *Oregon*
1947	Separation of church and state	I	*Everson* v. *Board of Education of Ewing Township, N.J.*
1948	Right to a public trial	VI	In re *Oliver*
1961	No unreasonable searches and seizures— the exclusionary rule for evidence	IV	*Mapp* v. *Ohio*
1962	No cruel and unusual punishment	VIII	*Robinson* v. *California*
1963	Right to a lawyer in all criminal cases	VI	*Gideon* v. *Wainwright*
1964	No compulsory self-incrimination	V	*Mallory* v. *Hogan*
1965	Right of privacy	I	*Griswold* v. *Connecticut*
1966	Right to an impartial jury	VI	*Parker* v. *Gladden*
1967	Right to a speedy trial	VI	*Klopfer* v. *North Carolina*
1969	No double jeopardy	V	*Colgrove* v. *Battin*

The "Nationalization" of the Bill of Rights

Later amendments have further extended and strengthened our rights as American citizens. The Thirteenth Amendment outlawed slavery. The Fourteenth Amendment extended citizenship rights automatically to "all persons born or naturalized in the United States," but its most important effect is to extend to the states the limitations imposed on the federal government by the Bill of Rights:

> No State shall make or enforce any law which shall abridge the privileges or immunities of citizens of the United States; nor shall any state deprive any person of life, liberty, or property, without due process of law; nor deny to any person within its jurisdiction the equal protection of the laws.

Ratified in 1868, the Fourteenth Amendment has been more and more actively and extensively interpreted by the Supreme Court since 1925. This process is sometimes referred to as the nationalization of the Bill of Rights.[6] Major aspects of the process of nationalization have included the out-

lawing of private acts of discrimination when these are enforced by a state and the outlawing of unequal apportionment of state legislatures as contrary to the equal protection clause. Table 12.1 lists the major stages in this process.

The Fifteenth, Nineteenth, Twenty-fourth, and Twenty-sixth Amendments extended the right to vote, as we saw in earlier chapters. The Equal Rights Amendment (ERA), which was submitted to the states for ratification in 1972, was designed to abolish unfair and unreasonable discrimination against women by the laws of the federal and state governments. It was not ratified by the required three-fourths of the state legislatures before its seven-year deadline nor during a three-year extension voted by Congress. (We'll learn more about the politics of the ERA in Chapter 14.) In 1978 Congress passed and submitted to the states another amendment, proposing that the District of Columbia be treated as a state for purposes of congressional representation and election of the president and vice-president. State legislatures were generally slower to ratify this amendment than they were to endorse the ERA.

The extension of rights to particular groups of citizens (such as blacks or women or residents of the District of Columbia) is generally termed civil

---

[6]Reagan administration Attorney General Edwin Meese 3d has argued that this process violates states' rights and that states should not be bound by the guarantees of freedom in the federal Bill of Rights. Virtually no legal scholars or jurists agree with this position.

rights or special rights to distinguish them from the general rights or civil liberties we have been discussing.

What Determines Which Liberties and Rights We Have?

Lists of our liberties and rights such as the one we have been developing here may seem to imply that rights and liberties are made by constitutions and amendments. But in the words of Jay Sigler:

> No one can say with finality just which rights Americans do possess. The Constitution and several important amendments to that document provide the best guide, but ambiguity shrouds the significance of almost every important phrase. Courts, legislators, presidents and governors must define our rights for us, and even though they often refer to constitutional language, the terms almost always require interpretation.[7]

American citizens have demanded more and greater liberties, and excluded groups have demanded the rights others have had. Both the courts and the legislatures have continued to interpret and expand the dominant conceptions of rights and liberties. In the era of the so-called Warren Court, in the 1960s, both civil rights (for blacks) and civil liberties (especially for accused criminals) were expanded. The Burger Court then reacted against these expansions in some areas, emphasizing "society's rights" instead of "criminals' rights." This apparent shift, which we discussed in Chapter 11, reflects the constant tension between order and liberty. On balance, however, the history of America has been one of expanding liberties.

Major Claims to New Liberties and Rights

The Right to Know

In recent years, one important dispute has been over "the right to know." Over the years, as we have noted in previous chapters, the government has refused to disclose certain information on the grounds of executive privilege. It has also, since 1917, developed a *security classification system* to limit access to information deemed vital to na-

tional security to those who have "a need to know." No government likes leaks of its private deliberations and decisions or of its policy proposals. Sometimes such leaks are thought to damage the national interest, and often they make policy more difficult to decide by stimulating opposition in advance. Also, no government likes leaks of its mistakes and its purely political calculations. Governments try to keep secret not only information vital to national security but also the things that would embarrass it or otherwise help its political adversaries.[8] Therefore, many government documents are classified as "confidential," "secret," or "top secret." Still, both opponents of the government and ordinary citizens need to know as much as possible about the government's thoughts and actions in order to assess its judgment and competence. Those outside the government have often accused it of being unnecessarily secretive, often protecting itself instead of the national interest.

Partially in response to this criticism, Congress in 1966 passed the **Freedom of Information Act (FOIA)**. Its purpose was to make information maintained by the executive branch more available to the public. It provides that access and disclosure rather than secrecy must be the prevailing policy. However, it lists nine different categories of information that are excluded from its terms, including matters officials assert to involve national security and documents involved in policy making. Thus, it does not really grant full access of the kind many outsiders have sought.

Nonetheless, the Reagan administration was alarmed by the trend toward declassification, and in April 1982 Reagan signed an executive order to reverse it. The order abolished the rule set by Nixon and expanded by Carter, which said that classified documents should be reviewed after 6 years and again after 20 years, for the purpose of releasing them unless national security is at risk. Reagan's order also expanded the range of materials that could be classified—on the general grounds of national security—although it left at 7000 the number of officials who could classify materials. Many outside government, including historians concerned about access to research materials, saw this as an ominous reversal of a 30-year trend toward more openness.

---

[7]Jay A. Sigler, *American Rights Policies* (Homewood, IL: Dorsey, 1975), p. 1.

[8]See David Wise, *The Politics of Lying* (New York: Random House, 1973).

The Right to Privacy

One of the items exempted from the FOIA is personal, medical, and similar files, if their release would be a clearly unwarranted invasion of personal privacy. The importance of this provision lies in the fact that the government collects enormous amounts of data on us and on the country. In so doing, it has two basic purposes. The first is to conduct its specific responsibilities. The Internal Revenue Service, for example, collects information as part of its task of collecting taxes. The second is to have general-purpose statistics for use by the government and the public in analyzing social and economic factors affecting the nation. General-purpose information is gathered by four agencies: the Census Bureau, the Bureau of Labor Statistics, the Statistical Reporting Service of the Agriculture Department, and the National Center for Health Statistics in the Department of Health and Human Services.

As a result of all this data collection, the government knows a lot about virtually everyone in the country—including most businesses and organizations, as Action Unit 12.2 reports. At this point, much of this information is decentralized—some held in one agency's files, some in other agencies' files. In fact, a recent government study reported that the executive branch maintains 6723 record systems, containing more than 3.8 billion records on individuals—an average of 17 different records for every American man, woman, and child.[9] Because this system is inefficient there are strong pressures to pool all information in a giant data bank, where it would all be computerized for instant access. If that happens, any government agency might be able to learn everything about you at the push of a few buttons.

In the past federal, state, and local governments have secretly gathered, stored, and occasionally used publicly or privately information—or *intelligence*—about the political views and activities of many American citizens.[10] Sometimes this information has even concerned a person's social and sexual activities. Debate over the extent to which such covert domestic surveillance should be allowed continues despite the growing recognition of a right to privacy.[11]

In the face of claims that the government needs many types of information on each of us, who will protect our privacy? Do we actually have a right to be let alone or a right to privacy? Until recently the courts have not thought so. In *Olmstead* v. *U.S.* (1927), the Supreme Court upheld the tapping of telephones as a legal source of information on bootleggers during Prohibition. But in a dissent in that case, Justice Louis Brandeis argued that the founders had granted citizens "the right to be left alone—the most comprehensive of rights and the right most valued by civilized men."

It was not until 1965, however, in *Griswold* v. *Connecticut*, that the Court found privacy a right peripherally protected by the First Amendment. This decision overthrew a Connecticut law prohibiting the sale or distribution of contraceptives, and so has become known as the birth-control case. In his majority opinion, Justice William O. Douglas found the right to privacy a constitutional right formulated by the specific guarantees of the First, Third, Fourth, Fifth, and Ninth Amendments, which, the Court said, "have penumbras, formed by emanations from those guarantees that help give them life and substance." The Court concluded that "various guarantees create zones for privacy." The citing of the Ninth Amendment was especially significant, for it suggested, in the words of a concurring opinion, that the framers intended it "as a declaration, should the need for it arise, that the people had other rights than those enumerated in the first eight amendments."

Soon thereafter the Burger Court extended the doctrine of the right to privacy even further, using it as the basis for overturning a Texas law prohibiting abortion. In *Roe* v. *Wade* (1973), which we shall examine in more detail in the next section, the Court declared privacy a "fundamental right"—but one subject to limitation when it conflicted with a "compelling state interest."

Nevertheless, specifying the the extent of the right to privacy has been left to Congress. The Privacy Act of 1974 was the first law to regulate the

---

[9]Office of Management and Budget, *Federal Personal Data Systems Subject to the Privacy Act of 1974* (Washington, DC: GPO, 1975), p. 3.

[10]See Frank J. Donner, *The Age of Surveillance: The Aims and Methods of America's Political Intelligence System* (New York: Knopf, 1980).

[11]Richard E. Morgan, *Domestic Intelligence: Monitoring Dissent in America* (Austin: Univ. of Texas Press, 1980), pp. 10, 12.

ACTION UNIT 12.2

How to Get Access to What the Government Knows About You

Under the Privacy Act of 1974, you as a citizen have the right to get copies of personal records collected by federal agencies and to correct any inaccuracies in those records.

If you want to find out what personal records the federal government maintains on you, here's what you need to do:

1. Select the agency whose files you wish to examine, such as the FBI (for criminal activity or political activity—9th and Pennsylvania Ave. NW, Washington, DC 20535); the Veterans Administration (Vermont Ave. NW, Washington, DC 20420); the State Department (for activities abroad—Department of State, Washington, DC 20520); the Department of Education (for student loans—200 Independence Ave. SW, Washington, DC 20201); or the CIA (for who-knows-what—Central Intelligence Agency, Washington, DC 20505). You'll find other agencies and their addresses in the *United States Government Manual* in your library.

2. Write a letter to the "Privacy Act Officer" of that agency in Washington (or elsewhere, if it is a local office you wish to ask). Your letter should read something like this:

Dear Privacy Act Officer:

In accordance with the Privacy Act of 1974, 5 U.S. Code 522a, I hereby request a copy of [describe as accurately and specifically as possible the records you want, and provide all the relevant information you have concerning them].

If there are any fees for copying the records I am requesting, please inform me before you fill the request. [Or: please supply the records without informing me if the fees do not exceed $_____.]

If all or any part of this request is denied, please cite the specific exemption(s) that you think justifies your refusal to release the information. Also, please inform me of your agency's appeal procedure.

In order to expedite consideration of my request, I am enclosing a copy of [some document of identification].

Thank you for your prompt attention to this matter.

Sincerely,
[Your name, address, city, state, zip, and social security number]

3. Include proof of your identity, such as a copy of an official document containing your name, address, and signature, or a copy of your signature notarized by a notary public, and your social security number.

4. Be prepared to pay a fee of about 10 cents per page of the file; the agencies can charge this copying fee but cannot charge for their time in searching.

5. Expect a response within 10 working days of receipt of the request, and the files within 30 working days, as the law provides. If you do not receive an answer, write again inquiring why.

6. If your request is denied, you may appeal the denial to the head of the agency, or even to the courts, where, if you win, the government must pay your attorney's fees as long as they are reasonable.

7. If you find erroneous information in a file, you may write requesting that your records be amended.

For further guidance on special exceptions to the law, on appeal procedures, and on going to court, as well as information on using the Freedom of Information Act as amended in 1974 to get other types of government documents, write your member of Congress for a free copy of the Government Operations Committee report, *A Citizen's Guide on How to Use the Freedom of Information Act and the Privacy Act in Requesting Government Documents.* You can also get help from the American Civil Liberties Union, 22 East 40th St., New York, NY 10016, or from any of its regional offices. And if you wish further information on the FOIA, write for a free booklet to the Center for National Security Studies, 122 Maryland Ave. NW, Washington, DC 20002. Finally, for the most comprehensive guide, see James T. O'Reilly, *Federal Information Disclosure* (New York: Shepard's Inc./McGraw-Hill, 1977), available in law libraries.

use of personal information records by the federal government. It gives citizens the right to see and copy most records about themselves stored by federal agencies. It also gives citizens the right to challenge and correct any inaccurate information in federal files, as described in Action Unit 12.2. The act also established the Privacy Protection Study Commission, which has since found a wide range of abuses. Medical records are obtained by employers and insurance investigators, to be used against people. Tax returns have been used by various government agencies with such ease that the IRS has been called a national lending library. Private investigators dredge up malicious gossip and put it in company files without checking it.[12]

Protecting privacy is now becoming much more difficult—some would say impossible—because of new technology. The 1968 Omnibus Crime Control and Safe Streets Act allows government agents to use wiretaps, provided they first get a warrant from a judge. In fact, such requests for warrants are rarely denied. In one recent year, for example, all 578 federal and state requests were granted.

Still, the law doesn't even cover most new and effective technologies. For example, we now have the "bumper beeper"—an electronic tracking device attached to car bumpers that reports a car's location at all times. Also effective is the "pen register"—a device that will record the numbers dialed from a telephone. Another such device is the "parabolic microphone"—the dish-shaped device used by television crews at football games to pick up quarterbacks' signals—which will pick up conversations at great distances. Finally—and most significant of all—are computer telecommunications intercepts.

It is clear that while federal law both limits government snooping and prohibits private electronic surveillance, these practices continue to be used. Indeed, bugging devices can be bought openly for as little as $35 each.

The right to privacy is but one of a long line of civil liberties that American citizens have sought for themselves and that the American political system has, gradually, moved to protect or guarantee. Like all civil liberties, its nature and extent are far from clear—as its value to society is often far from clear to citizens at large and officials.

The Right to Life versus the Right to Control One's Own Body: The Case of Abortion

Similar uncertainty and even greater argument are raised by the subject of abortion. As is the case with most such disputes, there are claims to rights on both sides. Opponents of abortion have claimed that the unborn fetus has a right to life that the law must protect because the fetus is defenseless. Their adversaries claim to be defending the right of a woman to control her own body, and so they argue for freedom of choice. They assert that the woman should be free to choose whether or not to bear a child.

Until January 22, 1973, 31 states had laws making performance of an abortion a criminal offense, and 15 others had laws severely limiting the legality of abortion. But on that day, when the Supreme Court issued its ruling in the case of *Roe* v. *Wade*, those laws suddenly became unconstitutional, and abortion suddenly became legal. The case was brought by "Jane Roe"—a pseudonym adopted to protect the woman. Jane Roe was a pregnant, single Texas woman who challenged a Texas state law that outlawed all abortions except those essential to save the life of the mother. Roe argued that this law violated her rights under the Constitution.

The Fourteenth Amendment asserts that no state can "deprive any person of life, liberty, or property . . . nor deny to any person within its jurisdiction the equal protection of the laws." The state of Texas argued that the fetus is a "person" and so is entitled to protection by state laws preventing abortion. The Supreme Court studied this argument and concluded that "the use of the word 'person,' as used in the Fourteenth Amendment, does not include the unborn." Thus, the fetus was not automatically protected by the Fourteenth Amendment. But this didn't mean it still might not be protected by some other provisions of the Constitution.

Texas also argued that life begins at conception and is present throughout pregnancy, even if the fetus is not yet "a person," and so the fetus—as "life"—is entitled to protection. Lawyers had debated this question vigorously on both sides. In its decision, the Supreme Court noted that experts disagreed strongly about this matter, and concluded: "We need not resolve the difficult question of when

---

[12]For a study of the difficulties in implementing the FOIA and the Privacy Act, see David M. O'Brien, *Privacy, Law, and Public Policy* (New York: Praeger, 1979).

(Martin A. Levick/Black Star)

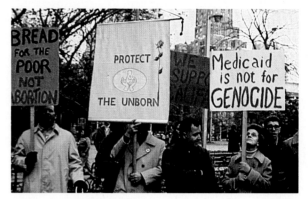

(Martin A. Levick/Black Star)

life begins. When those trained in the respective disciplines of medicine, philosophy, and theology are unable to arrive at any consensus, the judiciary . . . is not in a position to speculate as to the answer."

In the face of such disagreement among nonlegal authorities, the Court avoided deciding the question of when life begins. Instead, it invoked its legal authority to decide the case at issue. Doing so, it upheld Roe's claim that her right to privacy entitled her to an abortion. "The right to privacy," the Court said, "is broad enough to encompass a woman's decision whether or not to terminate her pregnancy."

This right to privacy, which is not even mentioned in the Constitution, is not, the Court asserted, an absolute right. Instead, "a State may properly assert important interests in safeguarding health [of the mother], in maintaining medical standards [by regulating how and by whom abortions are performed], and in protecting potential life."

Whatever the unresolved disputes among the various types of experts over when life begins, the Court could not deny that at some stage the fetus reaches "the point of viability"—the point at which, if the fetus were removed from the mother's womb, it could survive as a premature baby with intensive hospital care. Nor did the Court deny that the health of the mother was a legitimate matter for the state to be concerned about.

Thus, the Court had to balance the mother's right to have an abortion and the state's right to legislate to protect the mother and the fetus. "In assessing the State's interest," the Court declared, "recognition may be given to the less rigid claim that as long as at least *potential* life is involved, the state may assert interests beyond the protection of the pregnant woman alone."

There were, in other words, three rights at issue: the mother's privacy, as protected by the Constitution (according to the Court's interpretation of that document); the mother's health, as protected by state laws; and the fetus's life, as protected by state laws.

The Court's decision was an intricate balancing of these three claims.[13] By a vote of seven to two it decided:

■ For the first three months after conception, the state cannot limit abortions except to require that they be performed by doctors. This conclusion recognized the woman's right to privacy.

---

[13]For a fascinating account of the Court's debate and decision, based on interviews with the justices' law clerks, see Bob Woodward and Scott Armstrong, *The Brethren* (New York: Simon & Schuster, 1979). And for an equally fascinating account of how the abortion debate has evolved in the American public, see Kristin Luker, *Abortion and the Politics of Motherhood* (Berkeley: Univ. of California Press, 1984).

- For approximately the second three months, the state can specify the conditions under which abortions may be performed, in order to safeguard the health of the mother.
- For the final three months, the state may, if it chooses, regulate, and even outlaw, abortion, in order to protect the "viable" fetus, except for cases in which the health of the mother is in question.

Polls have long shown majority support for reproductive freedom, as the right to abortion is increasingly called. Still, there has always been strong opposition to it in Congress. Starting in 1977, Congress banned federal funding of abortion through Medicaid (the federal-state program that helps pay medical bills of welfare recipients and some other poor families) except when the life of the mother is at stake. The vehicle was an appropriations amendment sponsored by Representative Henry J. Hyde (Republican of Illinois). The Supreme Court upheld the constitutionality of this legislation in June 1980.

Opponents of abortion have also pressed for a constitutional amendment to let states and Congress enact new antiabortion laws, but they have been unsuccessful thus far. Meanwhile, the Supreme Court has reaffirmed *Roe* v. *Wade* in various subsequent cases despite the Reagan administration's opposition. And legal abortions continue to be performed at a rate of about 1,500,000 a year. Clearly, no court decision will end political disputes between the advocates of "the right to reproductive freedom" and the advocates of "the right to life" of the fetus.

Some Novel Claims to New Liberties and Rights

The right to know and the right to privacy—along with the right to exercise control over one's own body, or the right to life of the fetus—are but a few of the claims now being made in the struggle over the politics of liberty. Among others gaining more support are the right to travel, the right to die with dignity, and the right to breathe clean and healthy air instead of other people's cigarette smoke. Many now even argue that we should recognize the rights of animals, and some even assert the right of the environment.

The Right to Travel

In the years after World War II, the U.S. government declared about a dozen Communist countries off limits to Americans. Those few Americans who went anyway had their passports seized when they returned and were thereby banned from leaving the country again. But in 1958, in *Kent* v. *Dulles*, the Supreme Court declared that "the right to travel is a part of the 'liberty' of which the citizen cannot be deprived without due process of law under the Fifth Amendment."

In recent years, three presidential actions raised once again the question of whether Americans have a right to unrestricted travel. First, when the Soviet Union invaded neighboring Afghanistan in December 1979, President Carter announced that the United States would boycott the 1980 Olympics scheduled for Moscow that summer. To enforce his declaration on the American people and especially the athletes, he threatened legal sanctions against the U.S. Olympic Committee (the private organization that sponsors American Olympic participation) and any individual athletes who attempted to compete. Second, when a dozen American citizens led by former Attorney General Ramsey Clark went to a conference in Iran in an attempt to help gain release of the American hostages being held by the Iranian revolutionaries, Carter declared that he was inclined to prosecute them for violating his stated prohibition on American travel to Iran. Then Treasury Secretary Donald Regan in 1982 banned travel to Cuba by making it illegal to spend American money there. The expressed hope was to put pressure on Cuba not to support revolutionaries in other South American countries. A federal appeals court in Boston ruled the action unconstitutional in 1983, so the Reagan administration appealed to the Supreme Court, which in 1984 heard the case, *Regan* v. *Wald*, and upheld the administration.

Did the president have the power legally to ban travel in these three instances? In 1978 Congress had passed and Carter had signed a new law limiting the president's authority to restrict travel. Such restrictions were to be limited to countries "with which the U.S. is at war, where armed hostilities are in progress, or where there is imminent danger to the public health or the physical safety of U.S. travelers." By this reckoning, the ban on travel to the Moscow Olympics was illegal, but the ban on travel to Iran could be justified. However, the Supreme Court in 1967 had ruled unanimously that "area restrictions on the use of an otherwise valid passport are not criminally enforceable"; so although such travel could be banned, no punishment could be imposed. It would therefore appear that the right to travel is slowly becoming recognized as a civil liberty of American citizens.

However, limits may be imposed on specific individuals. In 1982 the Court ruled that the executive branch has broad legal and constitutional authority to revoke passports on national security grounds. The case was brought by Philip Agee, a former CIA agent, after the State Department stripped him of his passport. Agee had proposed that the United States resolve the Iranian hostage crisis by trading CIA files on Iran for the hostages. Before that he had written a book revealing CIA secrets. Chief Justice Burger wrote the opinion for the majority. He noted that while Congress had not authorized such passport seizures, it had for decades tacitly allowed the executive branch broad discretion in regulating citizens' foreign travel.[14]

The Right to Die

Still highly controversial are claims that someone incurably ill should have the right to request to be allowed to die without medical treatment that artificially prolongs life ("death with dignity"). Some even claim that one should be allowed to request and receive medicine that would end one's life in such a case. And recently groups have emerged that argue that one should have a right to commit suicide if one so chooses. Euthanasia, or "mercy killing," and suicide are both illegal now. Being allowed to die with dignity may not be illegal, but it is still widely disapproved. Nonetheless, the claims to such rights are growing.

Such claims will certainly generate great protests and strong arguments. But then, so did earlier claims to the right to privacy and so do present claims to the right to control one's own body via abortion. Public opinion has been uneven and governmental leadership has been sporadic on the extension of such civil liberties. But when the government has recognized such a thing as free speech

---

[14]The case was *Haig* v. *Agee* (1981).

or privacy as a right, it has generally extended the right, as it defined it, to all citizens. That is why such civil liberties are often referred to as *general rights*. The situation is very different, however, in the cases of other rights that we may think at least as important, such as the right to vote. The uneven extension of such civil rights makes them better understood as *special rights*, or rights belonging to or granted to particular groups.

WHAT ARE YOUR RIGHTS AS A MEMBER OF A GROUP?

From Civil Liberties to Civil Rights

The United States, as we have seen, was created to be a republic but not necessarily a democracy. The government was supposed to be responsive to the needs of citizens but not necessarily directly responsible to them. The political history of America since those early years has been the history of the extension of the opportunity to participate in politics to more and different groups of people. These rights to participate in politics are the heart of what we usually refer to as civil rights. They are *special* rather than *general* rights because historically they have been extended to some groups—and at the same time, by implication, denied to other groups.

There are five major components or stages to civil rights as they have developed in America.

The most fundamental is the act of *voting*. We traced the extension of the right to vote in Chapter 3.

The second is protection of the right to vote through development of the *secret ballot* and of laws against vote buying, electoral tampering, and fraud in general.

Third is the effort to *equalize the weight of each person's vote*, in terms of its impact on an election, by abolishing malapportionment and geographical discrimination.

Fourth is efforts to establish and protect all groups' rights or opportunities to *nominate* candidates. These rights can be fostered by lowering economic barriers such as fees that must be paid by candidates when they file for office and also by rules that open party conventions to various minorities, such as those recently adopted by the Democratic party.

TABLE 12.2

Major Provisions of Recent Civil Rights Laws

Civil Rights Act of 1957	Made attempting to prevent someone from voting a federal crime; established the Civil Rights Commission.
Civil Rights Act of 1960	Strengthened prohibitions against obstructing voting; empowered the federal government to appoint special registrars to register black voters in the South.
Civil Rights Act of 1964	Forbade discrimination in employment on grounds of race, color, religion, sex, or national origin (later extended to include age and handicapped status) and created the Equal Employment Opportunity Commission to enforce these prohibitions; barred discrimination in public accommodations such as motels, service stations, restaurants, theaters, buses, and trains; empowered the federal government to sue to integrate public schools and authorized the withholding of federal aid from segregated schools; made a sixth-grade education in the English language a presumption of literacy.
Voting Rights Act of 1965	Strengthened the powers of federal voting registrars or examiners in the South; permitted the outlawing of discriminatory literacy tests.
Civil Rights Act of 1968	Outlawed racial and religious discrimination in selling and renting housing; prohibited interfering with the legal activities of civil-rights activists.
Voting Rights Act Amendments of 1970	Extended the provisions of the 1965 act for another five years and expanded them to cover areas of the North as well as the South.
Voting Rights Act Amendments of 1975	Extended the provisions of the 1965 act until 1982 and broadened the provisions to cover language minorities such as the Spanish-speaking and Native Americans.
Voting Rights Act Amendments of 1982	Extended the provisions another 25 years.

The fifth and present stage in democratization is *increasing the public's control over public policy* between elections. This is generally attempted through regulations on lobbying and political contributions that are designed to equalize public influence.[15]

Still another stage, to which we have not yet progressed, is *expanding government service* to include the whole population. Should we eventually decide to attempt this, the logical way would be by drawing lots for political offices. Each would have a short term, so that roles could rotate among any and all members of society, rather in the way that jury service now does.

We still think first of blacks when the topic of civil rights is raised. Government action toward equal rights for blacks has moved through three major phases. The first, which lasted from the Civil War through the end of World War II, can be called the laissez-faire approach of *inaction*. The second, or *conciliation*, period emphasized creating situations where the races were brought together informally. This was accomplished by laws against discrimination and mechanisms for receiv-

ing complaints concerning violation of those laws, but without government enforcement or litigation power.

The third and present phase can be termed that of *positive action*. It involves both empowering this existing machinery to take action to compel compliance and requiring past offenders to demonstrate that they are in fact remedying failures before the government does any further business with them. Recent civil-rights laws are summarized in Table 12.2.

From Equal Opportunity to Affirmative Action

No one doubts that there has been severe discrimination against blacks and other minorities throughout American history. No one denies that discrimination persists to this day, denying many Americans not just equality but in many instances even a fair chance. Increasingly people are recognizing that women too—although they are actually the majority—have been subject to discrimination that is in some ways quite similar to, and in others quite different from, that experienced by minorities.

---

[15]For a discussion of these five stages, see Stein Rokkan, *Citizens, Elections, Parties* (New York: McKay, 1970), pp. 147–68.

The major disputes arise when programs are proposed to cope with continuing discrimination and its lingering effects. During the 1960s efforts were made at conciliation: increased racial contact, desegregation, and then programs for active integration of public facilities, coupled with the positive extension of voting rights to blacks. But the conciliatory approach did not produce equality. Resistance was too great, especially in housing, employment, and economic opportunity in general.

The federal government began to legislate programs of **equal employment opportunity** (EEO). Such programs require that personnel practices of employers guarantee the same opportunities to all individuals, whatever their race, color, religion, national origin, sex, or handicap. In other words, such EEO programs require nondiscrimination. But experience soon showed that this was not enough either. If minorities had less or inferior education because they had experienced discrimination in school, they would be excluded from good jobs because of their training rather than their race. This might not seem to be job discrimination, but the effect would be the same: continued inequality.

Consequently, a new strategy was developed to put teeth into the EEO laws. That new program, first initiated in Executive Order 11246 issued in 1965 by President Johnson, came to be called **affirmative action** (AA). This term refers to positive action taken specifically to overcome the results of past discrimination. In terms of jobs, it requires an employer to follow government guidelines to ensure that its workers include sufficient representatives of groups previously excluded. The employer may have to recruit, select, train, and then promote minorities, women, or other victims of past discrimination—or members of groups that have been subject to such discrimination, even if the individuals recruited and promoted had not themselves been victimized. Federal law now requires that written AA employment plans be developed by companies that have large federal government contracts and by labor unions that have been found to discriminate against minorities or women.

The reaction to such AA programs in some quarters has been hostile. Some have said that AA programs are actually instances of **reverse discrimination,** penalizing whites and males who are themselves innocent for the sins of earlier genera-

tions. Such reactions have been particularly strong in the cases of programs designed to increase minority enrollment in colleges and universities.

The Bakke Case

At age 32 Allan Bakke, a Vietnam veteran and an engineer, applied for admission to medical school. He was turned down in 1973 and again in 1974 by 11 different medical schools, including his alma mater, the University of Minnesota, and a nearby state school, the University of California at Davis.

Bakke had a good record. In fact, he learned that his academic record was better than that of some of those whom U.C. Davis admitted. The only explanation, it seemed to him, was that those admitted were black, Mexican-American, Asian-American, or Native American Indian, while he was white.

Bakke sued U.C. Davis, alleging that it had discriminated against him solely on grounds of race—because he was white. Davis Medical School had a policy at that time of admitting 100 students a year. But it held 16 places of the 100 for "disadvantaged students," which in practice meant members of minority groups.

Allan Bakke. (UPI/Bettmann Newsphotos)

Davis admitted using race as one criterion for admission, arguing that the people of California would benefit if more minority students became doctors. Many of these new doctors would practice in ghettos, improving the health care of minorities and the poor generally, it said. Thus, the policy of holding places for minority students was part of affirmative action.

Was Bakke therefore a victim of racial discrimination, or was he merely the unfortunate victim of a policy adopted at government urging?

The debate was left to the courts to decide. Allan Bakke filed his suit seeking admission to the U.C. Davis Medical School in California trial court in 1974, alleging that his exclusion violated his rights under the Fourteenth Amendment, which says that "no state shall . . . deny to any person within its jurisdiction the equal protection of the laws." The court agreed. The university then appealed to the California Supreme Court. It, too, supported Bakke. The university decided to appeal to the Supreme Court. The Court heard the case of *Regents of the University of California* v. *Bakke* in October 1977.

Various organizations with interests in the general principles involved filed **amicus curiae** ("friend of the court") briefs on it. Such briefs are really arguments to the court recommending a particular decision or way of reasoning about it. The lineup was interesting. Among the briefs supporting the university were those from other colleges and universities, minority students, some unions, and civil-rights groups. Supporting Bakke were the American Federation of Teachers, the Chamber of Commerce, Jewish groups, and some other ethnic groups. The ethnic groups believed their members often were victims of such quotas. But the *amicus curiae* brief everyone was waiting for was that from the U.S. government. After much internal debate, Carter and the Justice Department decided to strongly support affirmative action and avoid the question of quotas, recommending that the Court return the case to the California court for further consideration, rejecting Bakke's claim to be admitted.

On June 28, 1978, the Supreme Court handed down its long-awaited decision. It tried to placate both sides. First, the Court affirmed the constitutionality of college admissions programs that give special consideration to members of minority groups in an effort to remedy past discrimination. Second, it ruled that Bakke must be admitted to

A demonstration against the legal claims of Allan Bakke. (Eric Stein/Black Star)

the U.C. Davis Medical School because its admissions policy used race as the sole criterion for the 16 positions it held open for minority applicants. The Court's position was that race could be one of many criteria for admission but not the only one. Thus, the Court upheld the constitutionality of affirmative-action programs.[16] Allan Bakke finished medical school and became a doctor in 1986.

The Weber Case

The Supreme Court decision in *Bakke* left experts wondering about the legal status of affirmative-action programs. But they didn't have to wait long, for in less than six months the Court agreed to hear another important case: *United Steelworkers* v. *Weber.* Under the AA program some 11,000 contractors with 28 million workers were then required to prepare written AA plans. Another 175,000 major companies already had voluntary AA programs. Such plans included setting goals and timetables for areas where minorities and women were "underutilized" in any job group. One such contractor was Kaiser Aluminum and Chemical Corp. Together with the United Steelworkers union, Kaiser set up a special training program in 1947 to increase the number of minority workers in each craft job. Candidates for training were to be selected by seniority, but one black was to be selected for every white selected in order to correct the existing imbalance in craft jobs.

Brian F. Weber was a white employee in Kaiser's plant in Gramercy, Louisiana. Because of the AA program he was passed over in favor of blacks with less seniority. He sued his union, complaining that his rights had been violated. The lower courts agreed with him. But on June 27, 1979, the Supreme Court rejected his claim, upholding the legality of the special AA training program. The Court, by a vote of five to two, declared that the law "does not condemn all private, voluntary, race-conscious affirmative-action plans" and found that racial quotas are consistent with the intent of the Civil Rights Act of 1964. In reaching its decision in *Weber*, the Court was interpreting statutes. It thus avoided a technical conflict with *Bakke*, which was decided on constitutional rather than statutory grounds.

Brian Webber. (UPI/Bettmann Newsphotos)

The Fullilove Case

The Court then agreed to hear yet another AA case, *Fullilove* v. *Klutznick.* In this case, New York contractors challenged the constitutionality of a law passed by Congress requiring that 10 percent of federal grants for local public works projects (such as highways) be set aside for minority businesses, even if they are not the lowest bidders, as long as they are controlled by "Negroes, Spanish-speaking, Orientals, Indians, Eskimos, or Aleuts." On July 3, 1980, the Court upheld this law by a vote of six to three. In his majority opinion, Chief Justice Burger wrote that the constitutional power to provide for the "general welfare" gives Congress "latitude" to allocate special rights to racial or ethnic minority groups in order "to achieve the goal of equality of economic opportunity."

Thus, efforts to cope with racial discrimination moved from passive conciliation to positive affirmation action. Their original focus was on segregation in public accommodations such as lunch counters, theaters, and motels (Title II of the 1964 Civil Rights Act). Efforts shifted to school segregation (Title VI) later in the 1960s. But by the 1970s the focus had shifted once again, this time to employment (Title VII). By the late 1970s the Equal Employment Opportunity Commission was receiving over 85,000 job discrimination com-

---

[16]See Allan P. Sindler, *Bakke, DeFunis, and Minority Admissions: The Quest for Equal Opportunity* (New York: Longman, 1978).

Two Cheers for Affirmative Action

The case for affirmative action has weaknesses too, but they are not those alleged by its enemies. They are rooted, rather, in the inadequacy of the ideals to which affirmative action is forced to appeal. As currently defined, equal opportunity, because of its internal contradictions, ends up setting the rules for a white man's game. A successful affirmative-action program would involve nonwhites in the game on an equal footing. The trouble is that, to contest the unfairness of the game's rules, one must act as if it were a fair game. Minorities have no alternative; it is the only game in town. But the trouble remains: The more fair the rules are made to seem, the more legitimate and defensible the game appears.

The system in which equal opportunity now operates has been labeled a *meritocracy.* The term describes a technocratic and bureaucratic social order in which individuals occupy places in a hierarchy of income, status, and power that they have earned exclusively on the basis of their demonstrated individual abilities. . . . Without effective affirmative-action programs, meritocracy functions as a color-blind defense of the advantages of white elites. But, purified of its hidden racial bias, meritocracy would function as a defense of the advantages of integrated elites against the integrated poor and powerless. Affirmative action is not a populist conspiracy against the rule of merit. It would integrate the "elite of merit," nothing more. If we are to have an elite of merit, there is no alternative to integrating it. To refuse to take the necessary steps to do so is to insure its collapse. That, finally, is why I am uneasy about such programs. There is no chance that we might be ruled by a racially exclusive meritocracy, but a good chance that an integrated meritocracy might prevail. And the very process of integrating the meritocracy may facilitate its triumph. We need a nobler, more humane goal than an integrated meritocracy, drawn from the ranks of an integrated, anxious, climbing middle class that is blind to the plight of an integrated underclass of hopeless losers. For that nobler goal I reserve my third cheer.

From John C. Livingston, *Fair Game? Inequality and Affirmative Action* (San Francisco: Freeman, 1980), pp. 17–18.

plaints a year from minorities and women. Affirmative action remains a very controversial tool. Even some of its supporters have reservations about it, as the quotation from John C. Livingston in the box entitled "Two Cheers for Affirmative Action" reveals.

But the reservations of the Reagan administration were far greater. It took office firmly opposed to any use of quotas to undo the wrongs of previous discrimination in schools and jobs. It argued that such quotas discriminate against others, such as whites or males. It also favored voluntary action over government action. It frequently advised the courts to overturn decisions such as *Weber* that it saw as discriminatory.

In 1986 the Supreme Court issued decisions in three important AA cases that indicated that "race-conscious" plans such as numerical goals and timetables for hiring or promoting minorities instead of better qualified or longer-serving whites are constitutional.[17] That is true, the Court said, even if those so favored were not themselves victims of discrimination but only members of an ethnic group that as a class had suffered. However, the Court ruled against such AA in layoffs or firings that would force innocent whites to lose existing property interests (their jobs). These decisions directly contradicted the argument by the Reagan administration Justice Department and Attorney General Edwin Meese 3d that any discrimination in terms of race is unconstitutional.

(United Features Syndicate. © 1984 Dayton Daily News)

---

[17]The cases were *Wygant* v. *Board of Education; Local 28, Sheet Metal Workers* v. *EEOC;* and *Local 93, Firefighters* v. *Cleveland.*

The "Popularization" of the Bill of Rights

Controversial as affirmative-action programs remain, more and more requests for such programs are filed—not just by blacks and other ethnic minorities but also by women, by the handicapped, and by others who find themselves (or at least believe themselves to be) victims of discrimination. We have already seen the three phases that characterized efforts to overcome racial discrimination—inaction, conciliation, and positive action—manifest, in a briefer period, in efforts to combat sex discrimination. We may also soon see them in the struggle against discrimination based on age—the very young and the elderly—or on physical handicap or even on status as previous mental patients. In the next two chapters, we'll look at these and other groups to discover their conditions and the government policies designed to improve their conditions. In each case, their civil rights, or opportunity to participate in politics specifically and in social life more generally, are at issue.

We saw the "nationalization" of the Bill of Rights in the movements to increase civil liberties so that they covered state actions as well as federal actions. In a similar sense, we see the "popularization" of the Bill of Rights in the movements to extend participation, or civil rights, to all segments of the population. Now, as we look at human rights, we shall see what might be called the internationalization of the Bill of Rights.

WHAT ARE YOUR RIGHTS AS A HUMAN BEING?

The Development of the Idea of Human Rights

In earlier eras, citizens were expected to be self-sufficient, depending on themselves or on their families for their own welfare. As industrialization spread and mobility increased, families separated and people in need had to depend on private charity in times of unemployment, sickness, and old age. As labor unions grew in strength and political parties appealed to broader segments of the population for support, government became the focus of more and broader demands for aid. The result was the emergence of new ideas about rights—positive rights to health, education, welfare, jobs, pensions, and so on. The major proponents of these ideas were the socialist and Communist countries of the world. Capitalist countries like the United States followed with reluctance. They hesitated to abandon the belief in self-reliance and the economic incentive to hard work which that belief supposedly fostered.

Human Rights in the International Political System

In 1947, shortly after it was created, the United Nations established the Commission on Human Rights. It was led by Eleanor Roosevelt, widow of the late American president Franklin D. Roosevelt. That body of international representatives drafted the Universal Declaration of Human Rights. This was the first effort to set common standards of achievement in human rights for all peoples. It was passed unanimously by the United Nations on December 10, 1948.

In later years the United Nations drafted the International Convention on the Elimination of All Forms of Racial Discrimination (1965), the International Covenant on Economic, Social, and Cultural Rights (1966), and the International Covenant on Civil and Political Rights (1966). These documents—which have never been ratified by the United States—try to specify and implement the general rights outlined in the declaration.

In recent years nongovernmental efforts to develop support for human rights have increased. In 1979 the International Institute of Human Rights, first organized in Europe a decade earlier, held a conference with participants from around the world. It took note of both the "first generation" of human rights—civil and political—and the "second generation"—social, economic, and cultural. Building upon them, it called for recognition of a "third generation" that would include the rights to peace, to development, and to protection against threats to the common heritage of humankind, such as pollution. But although the delegates, acting as private citizens, agreed on this list, they disagreed on other important questions, such as whether a person has a right to refuse military service if such service constitutes a threat to peace.[18]

---

[18]See Henry Giniger, "International Group Urges Peace as a Human Right," *New York Times*, August 27, 1979.

Human Rights in the American Political System

Such controversy over human rights is not confined to international gatherings. It appears regularly in American politics as well. It became an issue at the outset of both the Carter and the Reagan administrations.

As president, Carter made human rights an issue in world affairs and an objective of American foreign policy. He spoke out in defense of political prisoners in other countries, appointed the first assistant secretary of state for human rights and humanitarian affairs, and pledged to use American influence—and American foreign aid—to attempt to strengthen human rights around the world. In practice, this was easier to pronounce than to execute, for there was much opposition to the new emphasis.

It is difficult to find people who say they support torture and imprisonment of political critics. But it is easy to find people who oppose emphasis on human rights in American foreign policy. Some critics say that we must support dictators because they are the strongest opponents of communism. Others say we should seek détente with the USSR and so should not upset the Russians by criticizing their handling of Jews and dissidents. Still others say we should improve the human rights of our own citizens before trying to improve those of foreigners. Yet others claim we should mind our own business instead of meddling in the internal affairs of other countries, whatever their politics. And some human-rights activists fear that *governmental* pressure for global human rights will "politicize" what they try to keep a "humanitarian" rather than a political issue, and so will set back progress in the long run.

All these views are well represented among experts on American foreign policy, and this has made any emphasis on human rights very controversial domestically. There has also been international controversy. Much of it seems traceable to varying concepts of human rights. As Denis Goulet, an expert on political and economic development, has written:

> Different approaches to human rights are observable across ideological borders. Socialist regimes, the older as well as the more experimental recent ones, emphasize economic and social rights, at least of oppressed masses, while often downplaying political and

civil rights. Conversely, liberal democracies tend to err in the opposite direction, placing great weight on politico-civil rights while relegating economic rights to a secondary position.[19]

After his victory, Ronald Reagan remarked: "I think that all of us in this country are dedicated to the belief in human rights." He added, however, that it wasn't "practical" to defend human rights by "turning away from countries that are basically friendly to us because of some disagreement on some facet of human rights" because such countries might then lose all human rights if worse regimes came to power.

In practice, the Reagan administration has not been noted for its active support of human rights in right-wing dictatorships such as El Salvador and Guatemala (although it continued to advocate them for left-wing revolutionary regimes such as Nicaragua and Cuba).[20]

The "Internationalization" of the Bill of Rights

So the dispute over what policy the United States should have on human rights continued in the Reagan administration just as it did under Carter. Similarly, the dispute over which rights people do have and should have—over which rights are indeed "human rights"—continues to this day inside the United States as it does within the world community. Because mass communications are now worldwide the different conceptions of human rights penetrate the borders of the Soviet Union, of Uganda, of Chile—and of the United States. The result is the "internationalization" of the Bill of Rights, in a double sense. Other countries come to take more seriously the political liberties emphasized in our Bill of Rights as well as the civil rights that have been the more recent focus of Supreme Court decisions. At the same time, other countries' emphases on social and economic rights become more contagious or influential in the United States, leading to a greater acceptance of such needs as education, health, housing, and welfare as legitimate human rights of the American people. Our

---

[19]Denis Goulet, "Thinking About Human Rights," *Christianity and Crisis*, May 16, 1977, p. 100.

[20]For a comprehensive survey of the debate over human rights, see Robert C. Johansen, "Human Rights in the 1980s: Revolutionary Growth or Unanticipated Erosion?" *World Politics* 25 (January 1983), 286–314.

courts have not yet found a basis for most of these human rights in the Bill of Rights. But some observers believe it will only be a matter of time before they do. If that occurs, it will be at least in part an instance of attitudes from abroad influencing, or "internationalizing," our own concepts underlying our Bill of Rights. Organizations participating in this process are described in Action Unit 12.3.

RIGHTS, DUTIES, AND OPPORTUNITIES

Who Preserves and Protects Your Rights?

It is often said that governments are established to maintain order and protect citizens from both external and internal threats. If that is so, we would expect our government to value and defend the rights it guarantees its citizens in the Constitution and the laws. Clearly, many Americans have suffered deprivation of their rights throughout our history—sometimes by the government itself. Political activists have sometimes been prevented from speaking. Minorities and women have often suffered discrimination. Aliens have been excluded from our educational system.

Still, the Supreme Court has reached many decisions important in advancing the rights of dissenters, minorities, and women. Presidents have issued executive orders creating and expanding the affirmative-action programs so vital to increased economic opportunities. Congress has passed many civil-rights laws outlawing discrimination—and it has provided for enforcement of these laws.

Neither the Constitution nor the law enforces itself. Government is required to mobilize the resources—police, inspectors, bureaucrats, and others—required to change patterns of discrimination. Government rarely decides to act, however, unless citizens demand that their liberties be protected and their rights enforced. In the next two chapters, we will encounter many examples of groups of citizens organizing to make such demands on the political system. However, such demands may not receive a favorable response if there is not sufficient public support. Generally speaking, support for civil liberties has increased dramatically in the past several decades. Much the same is true for the civil rights of blacks. Still, it may be one thing for cit-

izens to endorse civil liberties or civil rights in the abstract and quite another to support them in concrete situations, where, for example, one person's affirmative action is another person's reverse discrimination. Decisions and policy on such questions most often involve not just one right but rather two rights in conflict. We therefore have the politics of liberty as we do the politics of other public questions. Such debates are not the only struggles over the citizen's relations to his or her government, however.

Rights and Duties

The American government expects its citizens to obey the law. In other words, our leaders expect us to follow. Indeed, they believe we have a *duty* to obey the law as it is passed by Congress, implemented by the executive, and interpreted and assessed by the courts.

For thousands of years philosophers have debated the nature and extent of *political obligation*—the duties of citizens.[21] There is a major dispute over whether citizens are obliged to obey an unjust law. This often raises the problem of civil disobedience. Some argue that if we have rights, the government cannot or should not order us to do something that violates these rights: If it does, we should refuse. Others say that rights make sense and have value only if the state exists and functions well. This means, they say, that we must obey the state and support the laws even if it means sacrificing some of our rights. It is an argument often made to defend the claim that citizens should risk their lives to defend the state. Without the state, according to this viewpoint, there would be no actual or effective rights.

If philosophers have been unable to resolve these disputes after thousands of years, we certainly won't be able to solve them in several paragraphs. What we can do is note that in practice our courts do tend to uphold obedience to the law as our duty as citizens. "Rights imply duties," as the saying goes. The courts also tend to set limits on the exercise of our rights. For example, we may recall

---

[21]For interesting recent examples and analyses of the debate, see Eugene V. Rostow, ed., *Is Law Dead?* (New York: Simon & Schuster, 1971), and Burton Zwiebach, *Civility and Disobedience* (New York: Cambridge Univ. Press, 1975).

ACTION UNIT 12.3

How to Organize to Support Human Rights

If you wish to learn more about struggles for human rights at home and around the world, a good way to start is by writing to one or more of the organizations active in the field for information on their programs.

The foremost organization in the field is **Amnesty International** (U.S. branch, 2112 Broadway, New York, NY 10023). It was founded in 1961 by British lawyer Peter Benenson to fight to obtain release of political prisoners around the world. In 1977 it won the Nobel Peace Prize for "defending human dignity against violence and subjugation." It has become a worldwide network of over 200,000 people with branches in 44 countries and more than 100 researchers who compile the latest information on torture and state-supported abuses of human rights. It concentrates on the cases of prisoners who have neither committed nor advocated violence but have been jailed for their political, racial, or religious beliefs. It estimates that there are over 250,000 such "prisoners of conscience" in 90 countries around the world, and it attempts to win their freedom—and to oppose torture and the death penalty—by publicity, lobbying, legal aid, and letter writing focused on the cases of specific individuals.

Operating in the American political sphere is the **Coalition for a New Foreign and Military Policy** (712 G St. SE, Washington, DC 20003), which unites three dozen national religious, peace, labor, professional, and social-action organizations. It seeks to develop support for a noninterventionist, humanitarian U.S. policy. Its Human Rights Working Group monitors human-rights legislation in Congress and lobbies on Capitol Hill. It will put you on its mailing list to receive background information on human rights and notice of relevant legislation in Congress.

Other organizations engaged in human-rights activities include the **International League for Human Rights** (236 E. 46th St., New York, NY 10017), which concentrates its efforts at the United Nations; **The International Federation of the Rights of Man** (27 rue Jean-Dolent, 75014 Paris, France); and the **International Commission of Jurists,** (109 Route de Chêne, P.O. Box 47, 1224 Chêne-Bougeries, Geneva, Switzerland), a group of 38 eminent international lawyers that regularly reports on the human-rights situation in various countries.

The Human Rights Internet (1338 G St., SE, Washington, DC 20003) publishes an annual *Human Rights Directory*, which lists hundreds of U.S.-based organizations engaged in work on international human rights, as well as a comprehensive newsletter issued nine times a year.

With the help of such organizations, you can organize special meetings devoted to human rights and develop a group to lobby your representative and senators on relevant legislation by mail and visits. The coalition for a New Foreign and Military Policy can provide you with needed materials, from leaflets to films. Or you can organize a local chapter of Amnesty International U.S.A. and take on the cause of specific "prisoners of conscience" in various Eastern and Western countries.

Justice Oliver Wendell Holmes's assertion that the right of free speech does not extend to falsely yelling "Fire!" in a crowded theater and causing a panic.

If society and government limit rights in order to preserve themselves, then the burden of defending, preserving, and extending rights often falls to individual citizens, lawyers, and activist groups. In America these groups abound. And they are paying growing attention to such new rights or claims to rights as the right to travel and the rights of animals and of the environment.[22]

---
[22]For a discussion of some of these claims, see Sigler, *American Rights Policies*, chap. 15.

Rights and Opportunities

Many believe that the law and our legal institutions do indeed provide opportunities for extending and strengthening human rights. But Stuart Scheingold warns against too much confidence:

> At all points, law and politics are inextricably intertwined and in this combination politics is the senior partner. Laws are delivered to us by the dominant political coalition as are the judges and other officials responsible for interpretation and implementation. As a consequence our rights are always at risk in the political arena and therefore provide very little independent leverage.

Because of this, Scheingold argues, "rights are no more than a political resource which can be deployed, primarily through litigation, to spark hopes and indignation." Nonetheless, "rights can contribute to political activation and mobilization, thus planting and nurturing the seeds of mobilization," and "there is evidence to indicate that legal tactics can be useful. The civil rights experience provides the clearest demonstration that legal tactics—even with reluctant legal leaders—can release energies capable of initiating and nurturing a political movement."[23]

We turn in the next chapter to an examination of the civil-rights movement in America. What we learn there should make us better able to assess the views of optimists and pessimists alike on the question of rights and liberties. And it should give us a firmer basis for considering, in Chapter 14, the claims of others still largely excluded from American politics: especially, women, the young, and the elderly.

SUMMARY

Civil liberties offer us as individual citizens freedom from the state. Civil rights offer us as members of a group (such as blacks or women) the opportunity to take part in the state—for example, by voting. Human rights is a controversial term. In the United States, it generally means economic and social rights, such as the right to a job, to an education, and to medical care. When American leaders speak of human rights in other countries, however, they generally mean what we call civil liberties.

Our civil liberties derive from the concept of natural rights. The Constitution as it was originally drafted guarantees us seven civil liberties, but the most important ones are those in the Bill of Rights. Among these are the First Amendment freedoms (especially speech, press, and religion) and the rights of the accused in the justice system (concerning such issues as unreasonable search and seizure, double jeopardy, self-incrimination, due process, and fair trial). All these rights have been controversial at various points in American history, and most of them are still being interpreted by the Supreme Court.

The Fourteenth Amendment, which prevents the states from depriving us of our rights, is the vehicle by which the Court has extended the protections in the Constitution to cover state action. This process has been called the nationalization of the Bill of Rights.

This "nationalization of the Bill of Rights" is an example of the way in which the courts along with other parts of government determine, by interpretation, which liberties and rights we have. We may get new liberties and rights when groups demand them politically. For example, demands to know what government does behind closed doors or what it keeps in its secret records eventually produced the Freedom of Information Act (1966). The government has also come to recognize a right to privacy, and the Court has used it as the basis for declaring the right to abortion in *Roe* v. *Wade.* New technology makes protecting the right to privacy increasingly difficult. Still at issue are the right to travel freely and the right to die with dignity, among others.

The major civil right is the right to vote. It has been strengthened since 1957 through the passage of civil-rights acts. Racial discrimination in employment has been fought through the development of affirmative-action programs that provide for quotas for hiring minorities or women. The Reagan administration has called these programs examples of reverse discrimination, but the Supreme Court has supported them—for example, in the *Weber* and *Fullilove* cases. We call the process of extending participation to various segments of the population the popularization of the Bill of Rights.

The issue of human rights has been very controversial, especially since the Carter administration emphasized such rights in American foreign policy. This campaign, which the Reagan administration curtailed, can be called the internationalization of the Bill of Rights.

Rights are of no value if they are not enforced. That is the duty of the government. But citizens have duties to obey the government, for rights imply duties. Thus, all elements of the nation are involved in the politics of rights.

[23]Stuart A. Scheingold, *The Politics of Rights: Lawyers, Public Policy, and Political Change* (New Haven, CT: Yale Univ. Press, 1974), pp. 203–211.

As a general introduction to civil liberties and civil rights in their judicial context, Henry J. Abraham, *Freedom and the Court: Civil Rights and Liberties in the United States* (New York: Oxford Univ. Press, 1977), provides a useful discussion of the development of the Bill of Rights. See also Jonathan Casper, *The Politics of Civil Liberties* (New York: Harper & Row, 1972); Nat Hentoff, *The First Freedom: The Tumultuous History of Free Speech in America* (New York: Delacorte, 1980); Andrea Bonnicksen, *Civil Rights and Liberties: Principles of Interpretation* (Palo Alto, CA: Mayfield, 1982); and John Brigham, *Civil Liberties and American Democracy* (Washington, DC: CQ Press, 1984). For a comprehensive discussion of rights, see Norman Dorsen, ed., *Our Endangered Rights* (New York: Pantheon, 1984); Ellis Sandoz, *Conceived in Liberty: American Individual Rights Today* (North Scituate, MA: Duxbury, 1978); and Jay A. Sigler, *American Rights Policies* (Homewood, IL: Dorsey, 1975).

The field of human rights is still developing. But see Vernon Van Dyke's pioneering book *Human Rights, the United States and World Community* (New York: Oxford Univ. Press, 1970), and the collection of studies edited by Richard P. Claude, *Comparative Human Rights* (Baltimore: Johns Hopkins Univ. Press, 1976). See also Louis Henkin, *The Rights of Man Today* (Boulder, CO: Westview, 1978); Ved P. Nanda, James R. Scarritt, and George W. Shepherd, Jr., eds., *Global Human Rights* (Boulder, CO: Westview, 1981); and Jorge I. Dominguez, Nigel S. Rodley, Bryce Wood, and Richard Falk, *Enhancing Global Human Rights* (New York: McGraw-Hill, 1979).

13

MINORITIES IN MAJORITY POLITICS: Blacks, Hispanics, Native Americans, and Asian-Americans

Does anyone in your family speak a non-English language that is native to his or her country of origin? Do you think of yourself as being of a national origin other than American? Are you much interested in the history and culture of people with that national origin?

If you answered yes to any of these questions, you are probably conscious of being a member of a minority group. But whether or not this consciousness exists, you are bound together with others by ties of common national origin, race, and religion—and perhaps by language as well. Your background may be "mixed" in these aspects, as it is for more and more Americans because of intermarriage. Even so, you are—at least predominantly—a member of one such ethnic group.

However, it is most likely that you're a white Protestant, although the chances are just slightly better than even, for by now only 55 percent of the American population are white Protestants.

Why does this matter? If you're white, you may not have had experiences in which you thought your race affected how you were treated. If you're not white, however, you can probably point to countless cases where you're sure it did. In this chapter, we'll see how race or ethnic status affects the lives of Americans and American politics. We'll also see how different ethnic groups are affected differently. And we'll see how ethnic groups are affecting American politics. ■

417

THE MAKING OF MINORITIES IN AMERICA

The Current Situation

Two hundred years ago about half the population of the new United States was of English origin. In the 1800s heavy immigration of Europeans seeking work in American farms and factories changed that. But enough of those Europeans were Protestants—and white—so that white Protestants are still holding on to a 55 percent majority. Another 25 percent of the population are Catholic, 10 percent are black Protestant, and about 10 percent are Jewish or atheist or "other." Thus, we can speak of Catholics, Jews, and black Protestants as minorities in America today and be correct. But we rarely do so. Instead, we tend to reserve the term *minority* for what we now usually call racial or ethnic minorities.

Skin color is still the strongest distinction, and it often organizes life for Americans—especially for the 27 million blacks, 17 million Mexican Americans, 5 million Asian Americans (Chinese Americans, Japanese Americans, Vietnamese Americans, and others), 3 million Puerto Ricans, 1.4 million Native Americans, and 1 million Cuban Americans.

This leaves some 185 million Americans of European descent. However, certain ethnic consciousness still persists among many of those. In varying degrees, perhaps 34 million people claim a British heritage; 29 million a German heritage; 18 million an Irish heritage; 10 million an Italian heritage; 7 million a Scandinavian heritage; and 5 million a Cajun, French, or French-Canadian heritage. More than 6 million people are aware of their roots as descendants of Jews from eastern and southern Europe; another 16 million as descendants of eastern European Roman Catholics; and perhaps 4 million as children of Orthodox (Catholic) immigrants from eastern and southern Europe. In a total population of 242 million people, the United States may have more than 180 million people who are at least aware of their racial and nationality backgrounds.[1]

[1]James Stuart Olson, *The Ethnic Dimension in American History* (New York: St. Martin's Press, 1979), p. 436.

The Historical Development

In America Protestants from England were the first majority. They imported people with black skins from Africa as slaves to do hard labor. They also encountered people with reddish-brown skins who were already living here when they arrived. Farther west and south, they eventually ran into tan-skinned people from Mexico, and on islands due south they found other tan-skinned peoples whose leaders, at least, spoke Spanish. The reddish-brown peoples were generally obstacles to the move westward and to economic development because they thought they had a claim on the use of the land. The tans also were obstacles in many cases, but they were workers, too, as were the Europeans who came in large numbers in the nineteenth century.

All these other groups became "minorities" because there was a "majority" with the will and the power to dominate. The black slaves, who were kidnapped or bought from many different tribes throughout west Africa with many different cultures and who spoke many different languages, were lumped together by the white, Anglo-Saxon Protestants (WASPs) as *Africans* or *slaves* or *Negroes* or *blacks*. All these terms were applied collectively to people who didn't think of themselves as having anything in common but their "involuntary servitude" (the legal term the dominant have often used instead of the word *slavery*).

The reddish-brown natives, who came from many hundreds of different tribes, again with vastly different languages and cultures, the colonizers chose to bunch together as "Indians" (because the early explorers thought they'd landed in India) or as "redmen" or, as we now say, "Native Americans."

The tan or brown people of southern origins, already colonized by Spaniards and so somewhat homogenized linguistically, we have come to call Mexican Americans, or Chicanos, and Puerto Ricans. When we lump them together further and add Cuban Americans, we generally say Hispanics or Spanish-speaking or Spanish-surname, for obvious reasons.

Even the whites from Central Europe—some of whom are Protestant—we have long referred to as Germans, Czechs, Slavs, Croatians, Poles, Italians, and so on.

We can see, then, that the peoples who live in the United States have vastly varying national, cultural, linguistic, and religious origins. But they often find themselves lumped together rather indiscriminately by WASPs, by the federal government, by real estate agents selling houses, by politicians, by professors, by authors, and by other ordinary citizens.

In discovering—or, more accurately, making—a minority group, we generally look first for identifiable qualities such as skin color, eye shape and color, specific language, or accent. We also generally find, whether we look for them or not, less power and worse treatment than is the case with the majority. And finally, these days at least, we shall probably find awareness on the part of the members that they belong to a minority group.

The Human Consequences of Minority Status

There are various ways of studying and describing the effects of minority status (or, for that matter, majority status) on people. Three are particularly important for our purposes.

The first focuses largely on *material effects*. The major aspects are income, occupation, education, political power, and life chance (or one's opportunity to advance or improve one's standing throughout one's life).

The second focuses on the *organizational effects and responses* that follow from minority status. What sorts of associations or relations—especially political—do members form as a result of their material position in society? What religious, educational, or voluntary associations, for example, do they create? What are the goals and strategies of these organizations? How do they interact with dominant organizations?

The third important aspect, *consciousness*, refers to the individual's awareness of reality—especially regarding the psychological effects the social structure and organizations (points one and two above) have on the way the individual thinks, acts, and interacts. Members of minority groups often suffer from what we might call dominated consciousness—a situation in which their images of reality, indluding their images of themselves and of their possibilities, are imposed on them by the dominant culture, or the majority.

To get a better sense of the present situation and the prospects for each large minority group, we need to look more closely at each of these aspects and at the roles and responses of the political system. First, we'll compare the material status of all the groups; then we'll examine each group's organizational status and the system's response to it. Finally, we'll consider consciousness more generally.

THE STATUS OF MINORITIES

Blacks now constitute about 12 percent of the population. Mexican Americans are about 6.4 percent, and Puerto Ricans account for about 1 percent. Asian Americans make up over 2 percent, while Native Americans, or Indians, total just over half a percent. That is the breakdown according to official Census Bureau figures. But those figures do not include illegal aliens. Some observers believe there are as many as eight million Mexican citizens illegally in the country doing farm and domestic work—as large a number as that of the Mexican Americans who are legally here. Excluding illegal aliens, then, just over 20 percent of our population, or one in five Americans, is a member of one or another of these large minority groups.

Economic Status

But these same minorities who make up 20 percent of the population are about 35 percent of the poor and 40 percent of those on welfare. Table 13.1 shows more specifically the economic status of each group, comparing it to the status of whites. It reveals that about 28 percent of blacks are below the poverty line. Even worse off are Puerto Ricans, 32 percent of whom are poor. When whites are compared to the minorities, we learn that the poverty rate among whites is only about one-third of what is is among minorities. And the per capita income of the minorities is about half that of whites, excepting Asian Americans. The figures for *adjusted average earnings* are especially revealing of discrimination, for they show averages that compare people with the same jobs, education, age, location, and amount of work. Notice that whites fare better than any other ethnic group, even when otherwise similar individuals and situations are compared.

Other figures show that in the years 1960–1976, black family income doubled. This gave blacks an

TABLE 13.1
Economic Status of Minorities

	BLACKS	MEXICAN AMERICANS	PUERTO RICANS	NATIVE AMERICANS	JAPANESE AMERICANS	CHINESE AMERICANS	WHITES
Median household per capita income as a percentage of that of whites[a]	52	49	50	57	141	89	100
Percentage of persons in poverty	28	24	32	26	7	17	9
Number of times more likely to be in poverty than whites	3.1	2.7	3.6	2.9	0.8	1.9	1
Adjusted average earnings for those with earnings[b] Males—as a percentage of earnings of white males	85	82	98	92	88	77	100
Females—as a percentage of earnings of white males	61	48	57	54	58	70	57

[a]Household per capita income is the income of each individual living alone and the equal share of each member of a family's total income. *Median* means that half of all people in the group are above this figure and half are below.

[b]Adjusted average earnings are earnings for those with the same occupational prestige, age, education, weeks worked, hours worked, and state of residence. Thus, these figures are indicators of discrimination based on ethnicity and, in the case of females, on sex, too.

Note: These percentages are based on statistics from 1975. The federal government has not recalculated them for all minority groups since then. There is no reason to think that the status of minority groups has improved significantly since then relative to that of whites. It may have worsened.

Source: Civil Rights Commission, *Social Indicators of Equality for Minorities and Women* (1978).

improved income ratio in relation to whites: In 1960 blacks made an average of only 52 percent of what whites made; by 1976 the figure was 62 percent. Since then, however, it has been dropping, and in 1982 it hit 55 percent, according to the Census Bureau.[2] For those of Spanish origin, the figure was 66 percent in 1982.

These income figures change slightly from year to year. In hard times, for example, minorities get significantly worse off in absolute terms as well as relative to whites. But the general pattern as outlined here persists over the years.

The situation in terms of *wealth*—savings and owned property such as stocks and bonds, houses, and cars—is even less favorable to minorities. The Census Bureau in 1986 released a study of the median wealth of each group. That's the middle level, with half owning more and half less. It found the median wealth for white households is $39,135, while for Hispanics it is only $4,913 and for blacks, only $3,397.[3]

---

[2]*Statistical Abstract of the U.S. 1984* (Washington, DC: GPO, 1984), p. 463.

[3]Census Bureau, *Household Wealth and Asset Ownership: 1984,* Current Population Reports series P070, no. 7, July 1986.

Employment Status

Figures on the sorts of jobs minorities tend to have help account for their relatively lower incomes and net wealth. As Table 13.2 shows, unemployment is higher, laborers' jobs are more common, and the percent of males working full time is lower for minorities. In general, blacks have the worst-paying jobs of any minority, but Native Americans have the highest unemployment rates. In times of increased economic difficulties, the employment situation worsens for all groups—but for minorities more than for whites, and most of all for black teenagers. In 1986, for example, the unemployment rate for all white males averaged 4.3 percent, while for black males it was 9.3 percent. For white teenagers (age 16 to 19) the figure was 16 percent, while for black teenagers it was 45 percent.

Educational Status

In measuring education, the Census Bureau looks at those age 25 and older because they are likely to have finished their schooling. Table 13.3 shows the

TABLE 13.2
Employment Status of Minorities

	BLACKS	MEXICAN AMERICANS	PUERTO RICANS	NATIVE AMERICANS	WHITES
Percentage of workers in service and laborer occupations					
Males	36	33	27	29	15
Females	44	32	16	36	19
Percentage unemployed					
Males	6.3	6.1	5.6	11.6	3.6
Females	7.7	8.9	8.7	10.2	6.8
Percentage of males working	70	74	76	63	77
Percentage of males working the full year	58	59	62	50	68

Source: Data from 1970 census.

percentages of those who have gotten a high school diploma and the percentages of those who never even finished eighth grade. Here, presumably largely because of the special difficulties of schooling for people whose native language is likely to be Spanish, blacks and Native Americans fare better than Hispanics—but again far worse than whites. The figures on younger (age 20 to 24) males and females who have finished high school do reveal major improvements for all minorities, but they also reveal that whites still are more likely to finish. The table also shows the percentages of males and of females who have had four years of college and reveals further large differences there.

Geographical Concentration

One indicator of the degree of integration of minorities into the dominant society is their geographical concentration. Almost 90 percent of all Chicanos live in five states: California, Texas, Arizona, Colorado, and New Mexico. Fully 75 percent of all Puerto Ricans live in New York and New Jersey—indeed, 60 percent live in New York City. Some 60 percent of all Native Americans live on or near official reservations.

The situation of blacks is a bit more complex. Fifty-three percent still live in the South, although only 28 percent of whites live there. Twenty-eight

TABLE 13.3
Educational Status of Minorities

	BLACKS	MEXICAN AMERICANS	PUERTO RICANS	NATIVE AMERICANS	WHITES
Percentage of persons age 25 and older with a high school diploma	31	24	23	33	58
Percentage of persons age 25 and older with less than 8 years of schooling	44	59	54	44	27
Percentage of persons age 20–24 with a high school diploma					
Males	74	64	68	70	87
Females	74	58	60	58	86
Percentage of persons age 25–29 with at least 4 years of college					
Males	11	11	6	8	34
Females	11	5	4	4	22

Source: Data from 1970 census and from Civil Rights Commission, *Social Indicators of Equality for Minorities and Women* (1978). A similar study using 1980 census data has not been made.

percent live in the ten largest cities of the nation—versus only 9 percent of whites. Location becomes even more interesting when we focus on the dominant white Protestant majority. About 65 percent of this group live in localities of less than 100,000 people, and only 25 percent reside in areas of 250,000 or more.

We can see, then, that in broad terms *America is still largely a nation of ethnic concentrations*. And when we look at neighborhoods, we find high degrees of residential segregation by ethnicity.

Figures such as these on material status can reveal the broad contours of the social structures within which our minority groups find themselves and the economic conditions with which they must struggle. But they tell us very little about the struggles. To understand the life circumstances and prospects of minorities more fully, we must also examine their organizational status and its relation to the dominant—especially political—structures.

BLACKS IN AMERICAN POLITICS

Black Challenges to the American Political System

The first Africans to arrive in the colonies were 20 slaves sold to Virginia settlers in 1619, a year before the landing of the *Mayflower*. By the time of the American Revolution, blacks made up about 20 percent of the population—all but 60,000 of them slaves. The arrival of waves of European immigrants once the slave trade was ended slowly halved their percentage in the population but did little to improve their status. From time to time, there were slave uprisings, and there also developed a strong antislavery movement in the North, much of it led by women. By 1860, when the Civil War broke out, there were about half a million blacks in America who were free in legal terms. But they were rarely free in practical political and economic terms.[4]

The Civil War and the Thirteenth Amendment abolished slavery in America. But when the war ended, whites in the southern states passed a series

of harsh laws to keep blacks in virtual slavery. These Black Codes, as they were called, led Congress to impose Reconstruction on the southern states in an effort to relieve the misery of blacks and perhaps to further punish southern whites for their revolt. But when the North and the Congress ceased trying to control the South, whites took control again and passed harsh segregation laws. And while blacks had been granted the right to vote under the Fifteenth Amendment (1870), terrorist activities by the Ku Klux Klan and other white groups, plus the restrictive laws we discussed in Chapter 3, prevented most from ever exercising it.

Brown v. Board of Education

Legal challenges to segregation were pressed from time to time. But in 1896, in *Plessy* v. *Ferguson*, the Supreme Court ruled that laws providing separate public facilities for blacks were constitutional so long as the facilities were equal. Not until *Brown* v. *Board of Education of Topeka*, more than half a century later, did the legal move toward integration resume. In that case, the Court overturned

Mrs. Linda Brown Smith at home in Topeka, Kansas, with her two children. She was the 9-year-old student whose father's suit against the local school board led to the Supreme Court's ruling on *Brown* v. *Board of Education of Topeka*, which outlawed "separate but equal" school systems. Mrs. Smith's children attend an integrated school a block away from home. (AP/Wide World Photos)

---

[4]For an interesting account of pre-Civil War "free persons of color," the slaves freed by the Civil War, and the black immigrants from the Western Hemisphere, see Thomas Sowell, "Three Black Histories," in *Essays and Data on American Ethnic Groups*, ed. Sowell (Washington, DC: Urban Institute, 1978), pp. 7–64.

the *Plessy* decision. Linda Carol Brown, a black girl living in Topeka, Kansas, had been prevented from attending a school four blocks from her house because it was a school for whites only. Instead, the school officials ordered her to attend an all-black school 21 blocks away. Her father sued to get her admitted to her neighborhood school. Lower courts ruled against the Browns, holding that the separate, segregated schools were substantially equal in quality and so were legal. The opinion in the Supreme Court's unanimous decision was written by Chief Justice Earl Warren. It held that "in the field of public education the doctrine of 'separate but equal' has no place [because] separate educational facilities are inherently unequal." The reason for this conclusion was the Court's view that racial segregation in education "has a detrimental effect upon the colored children" in that it creates "a feeling of inferiority as to their status in the community" that may "affect their hearts and minds in a way unlikely ever to be undone." Thus, Brown was protected from the harm of segregation by the Fourteenth Amendment's guarantee of "equal protection of the laws."[5]

The next year, in a follow-up case to implement this decision, the Court declared that local school systems should develop their own plans for desegregation "with all deliberate speed."[6] However, few schools went ahead with any speed at all, and in the South a policy of "massive resistance" to any change developed. Eventually, after federal troops were used to protect students integrating schools in Little Rock in 1957, token integration turned into more substantial progress. By 1970 only 14 percent of southern blacks attended all-black schools, and 39 percent attended largely white schools.

Busing

Such school integration was still limited by segregation in housing, however, wherever children went to neighborhood schools. This was true in the North even more than in the South, for in the South many students had always taken buses to school. Because residential segregation perpetuated school segregation, courts increasingly ordered that school districts transport students of one race from one neighborhood to another so that they could attend a school whose students were primarily of another race. The controversy over this practice, called **busing**, continues to this day. Busing is popular with few people. However, the only alternative to it as a means of ending some school segregation would be laws to end residential segregation by integrating neighborhoods. That would probably be even less popular, even though surveys show that a growing percentage of Americans (now over 90 percent versus 57 percent in 1964) believe that "blacks have a right to live wherever they can afford to, just like anybody else."[7]

Although there has as yet been little progress toward integrated housing in most of the United States, the past 20 years have seen important efforts to expand the political and economic rights of blacks in education, access to public accommodations such as restaurants and hotels, employment, and voting as well as other aspects of political participation.

Participation

In 1964 only 41 percent of adult blacks in the South reported ever having voted.[8] In 1960 the black registration in the South was only 29 percent. By 1972 it was up to 64 percent, primarily because the 1965 Voting Rights Act brought federal intervention to protect and encourage black southern voters. In recent years, as we saw in Chapter 3, voting has fallen off among blacks and whites alike, but turnout of blacks in the South increased to 48 percent. In 1984 about 67 percent of the 18 million eligible blacks nationwide were registered, and about 56 percent voted—a gap of about four points in comparison to the total national figure. Twenty-seven states now have over 100,000 blacks of voting age. Black turnout in the 1984 election increased from 8 percent of the voters in 1980 to 12 percent.

Representation

The increase in the number of black voters in the past 15 years or so has brought with it an increase in the numbers of black elected officials, as Table 13.4 shows. Indeed, including Atlanta, Birming-

[5]*Brown* v. *Board of Education of Topeka*, 347 U.S. 483 (1954). For a fascinating, detailed study of this case, see Richard Kluger, *Simple Justice* (New York: Knopf, 1976).

[6]*Brown* v. *Board of Education of Topeka*, 349 U.S. 294 (1955).

[7]Philip Converse et al., *American Social Attitudes Data Sourcebook 1947–1978* (Cambridge, MA: Harvard Univ. Press, 1980), p. 65, and CBS News/*New York Times* survey, February 1978.

[8]Donald R. Matthews and James Prothro, *Negroes and the New Southern Politics* (New York: Harcourt Brace Jovanovich, 1966), p. 44.

TABLE 13.4
Black Elected Officials

	1964	1968	1970	1972	1974	1978	1980	1982	1984	1986
U.S. total	103	1125	1860	2625	2991	4503	4912	5160	5700	6424
House of Representatives										
United States	5	9	13	15	16	17	17	18	21	20
From South	0	0	2	4	4	2	3	4	4	4
Senate										
United States	0	1	1	1	1	1	0	0	0	0
From South	0	0	0	0	0	0	0	0	0	0
State legislatures										
United States	94	172	198	238	239	307	317	336	389	400
In South	16	53	70	90	90	*	128	161	202	214
Mayors										
United States	*	29	81	83	108	170	182	223	255	289
In South	*	17	47	49	63	*	120	153	173	199
Local										
United States	*	914	1567	2288	2627	1989	2174	2451	2735	2823
In South	*	468	763	1242	1452	*	*	1523	1653	1937

*Not tabulated.

Source: The Social and Economic Status of the Black Population in the U.S., 1974 (Washington, DC: Census Bureau, 1974); *National Roster of Black Elected Officials,* vol. 12, 1982 (Washington, DC: Joint Center for Political Studies, 1981); *Black Elected Officials: A National Roster,* 1986 (Washington, DC: Joint Center for Political Studies, 1986).

ham, Charlotte, Chicago, Detroit, Los Angeles, Newark, New Orleans, Philadelphia, Richmond, Spokane, and Washington, DC, 20 large American cities now have black mayors. But it is important to note that the 21 black representatives are but 5 percent, and the 380 state legislators about 5 percent, of the total elected. And although the total number of black elected officials increased to over 5000 in the 1982 elections, the total is still less than 3 percent of America's elective offices. Thus, blacks are still far from being proportionally represented in electoral politics. Furthermore, with few exceptions, most black elected officials have come from largely black districts. By now most of the largely black districts already have black representatives. This means that the opportunities for further gains will be quite limited unless and until largely white districts start electing blacks.

Administration

Another important sign of progress is the percentage of blacks in high-level government posts. Looking at the top six slots of each section of the federal bureaucracy, we find that in the decade from 1962 to 1972, the number of blacks increased by 8000, or 600 percent. But remembering our discoveries in Chapter 9 about how many bureaucrats there

are, we'll not be surprised that these gains brought the total percentage of blacks in high posts up to only 3 percent. The total of blacks in all federal jobs is now about 15 percent—but that only reveals how concentrated they are toward the lower end of the salary and skill spectrum.

The situation of blacks in the private sector is generally even worse. In business, blacks now hold but 2 percent of high-level posts. Among local police, the figure is up to 7 percent; for state police, 2.3 percent; for lawyers, 1.3 percent; for state and local judges, 2.3 percent; for local union officials, 5.7 percent; and for military officers, 2.2 percent.[9]

Organizations

Much of what progress there has been can be attributed to a series of black organizations. Throughout this century, these groups have attempted both to mobilize blacks so as to increase their power and to pressure public and private organizations to make concessions to blacks. But their ancestry reaches much further back in American political history.

---

[9]These figures, the latest available, are for 1972. See Sar Levitan et al., *Minorities in the U.S.* (Washington, DC: Public Affairs Press, 1975), p. 32. For an account of black progress in private enterprise, see Gary Puckrein, "Moving Up," *Wilson Quarterly*, Spring 1974, pp. 74–87.

As early as the 1790s, small groups of free blacks petitioned state legislatures to grant them the right to vote. Later, similar groups asked Congress to grant that right and to abolish slavery. During Reconstruction blacks participated actively in the elective political process. But when that opportunity was foreclosed, they returned to group activity.[10]

The first major organization with the power to last was the National Association for the Advancement of Colored People (NAACP). It was founded in New York in 1909 by a group of white and black activists. It has continued to seek equality for blacks, largely through the use of the law and through legal reform. Perhaps its greatest success was the Supreme Court ruling against "separate but equal" schools in *Brown* v. *Board of Education of Topeka.*

In 1911 whites concerned about the plight of blacks in large cities organized the Urban League, seeking housing and jobs for urban blacks. It remained conservative—but often effective—until 1961, when in the midst of the civil-rights movement, Whitney Young's leadership made it a more activist organization.

The first of the modern protest organizations was the Congress of Racial Equality (CORE). It was organized in 1942 to conduct nonviolent protests against segregation in Chicago. It became prominent nationally only in 1961, when under James Farmer's leadership, it organized "freedom rides" in which blacks and whites rode buses south to protest segregation in bus travel. As a result of these freedom rides, the Interstate Commerce Commission finally issued regulations banning segregation on buses and in terminals.

On December 1, 1955, a black seamstress named Rosa Parks took a seat in the "whites only" front section of a public bus in Montgomery, Alabama. When ordered to leave it so that a white man could sit there, she refused. The police arrested her, and in response the black community organized a bus boycott, walking everywhere instead of riding in "the back of the bus." The nonviolent boycott, under the leadership of Rev. Martin Luther King, Jr., and a coalition of church groups called the Southern Christian Leadership Conference (SCLC), lasted over a year. Then in December 1956 the Su-

Mrs. Rosa Parks sits in the front of a city bus on December 21, 1956, as a Supreme Court ruling that banned segregation on the city's public transit vehicles took effect. Mrs. Parks's arrest on December 1, 1955, for sitting up front among white passengers touched off the black boycott against the city's bus lines. (UPI/Bettmann Newsphotos)

preme Court outlawed segregation on public buses.[11]

The following years brought court orders requiring integration of various colleges and public schools in the South. Time and again students, parents, and outside agitators demonstrated and rioted against those blacks who sought to enter all-white schools. State legislatures adopted a policy called massive resistance, passing law after law to shore up segregation. A hundred southern members of Congress signed the Southern Manifesto opposing the Court decision on school integration as unconstitutional and vowing to use all lawful means to reverse it.

These were difficult times in America. Ugly attitudes surfaced, and vicious behavior flared up. But through it all, more and more courageous blacks in the South and some courageous southern whites demonstrated both personal strength and deep commitment to the values of racial brotherhood, nonviolent direct action for social change, and democracy.

These courageous southerners were joined by increasing numbers of concerned northerners. Out of this, in 1960, grew the Student Nonviolent Coordinating Committee (SNCC), the most radical of

---

[10]See Hanes Walton, Jr., *Black Political Parties: An Historical and Political Analysis* (New York: Free Press, 1972).

[11]For the story of the boycott and the philosophy underlying it, see Martin Luther King, Jr., *Stride Toward Freedom* (New York: Harper, 1958).

Rev. Martin Luther King. (UPI/Bettmann Newsphotos)

the civil-rights protest groups. Led by Stokely Carmichael, it organized "sit-in" demonstrations in which black and white students would sit at lunch counters in dime stores and other public places waiting to be served. Stores refused to serve them, local whites beat them up, and local police arrested them. But SNCC organized national boycotts of chains that refused to serve lunch to blacks in the South—and eventually the campaign succeeded.

The Civil-Rights Movement

From buses and lunch counters the civil-rights movement, as it came to be called, spread to public libraries, swimming pools, public parks, and vot-

A march on Washington by a coalition of civil rights groups in 1963. (Steve Schapiro/Black Star)

ing booths. Finally, after President John Kennedy was assassinated, southerner Lyndon Johnson managed to get the Civil Rights Act of 1964 through Congress. This act outlawed segregation in public accommodations and facilities, in federally funded projects, and in unions. It also strengthened the federal government's hand in protecting the right to vote and integrating public schools. (See p. 406 for a summary of recent civil-rights laws.)

With the passage of the Voting Rights Act of 1965, the civil-rights movement began to dissipate. *Legal barriers* to blacks had been largely removed. *Economic barriers*, however, were as strong as ever, for most blacks remained poor. And *mental barriers*—attitudes that obstructed progress—in both blacks and whites were still present. The result was a shift among activist blacks toward what came to be called black nationalism.

The Black Power Movement

Black Muslims led by Malcolm X had begun arguing that blacks should seek to improve their own situation without depending on whites. Malcolm X was assassinated, but the black nationalist movement continued to grow. Finally, in 1965 Stokely Carmichael coined the term *Black Power* as a goal for the movement. At this point, the movement split and diversified. Black Panthers and others emphasized armed self-defense and threatened to resort to violence if necessary to gain full equality. Martin Luther King increasingly emphasized the problems of poverty and the connections between American racism, black poverty, and the war in Vietnam. While leading a "Poor People's March" to Washington in April 1968, King was assassinated in Memphis. One of his followers, Rev. Jesse Jackson, then organized "Operation Bread Basket" in Chicago, which increasingly emphasized economic self-help for blacks. Still others placed their emphasis on Black Power—on building cultural and political strength in cities such as Newark, Gary, Cleveland, and Detroit, all of which soon had black mayors.

The Recent Period

Since the early days of Black Power, times have been difficult for blacks and whites alike. The Vietnam War distracted the attention of both activists and government from race and poverty and

The civil rights march at Selma, Alabama. (© James Karalas, DPI)

focused it on foreign affairs. In the Nixon years, the worst recession since the 1930s hit blacks much harder than whites and substantially set back their economic progress. Urban riots in the mid-1960s left black ghettos charred and scarred down to this day in some cities. A drug problem that now affects the children of the white middle class has devastated sections of black ghettos. The urban crime

Black Nationalist leader Malcolm X. (UPI/Bettmann Newsphotos)

that whites now fear so much is much more than a fear to most urban blacks.

These facts indicate the depth of the continuing problem. But they do not reveal the breadth of the progress that has been made through governmental programs and self-help actions alike.

Responses of the American Political System to Blacks

The black quest for equality has been fought first and foremost in the courts. The Supreme Court eventually did rule segregation unconstitutional in schools, buses, and elsewhere. But as Milton Morris suggests: "What the Court has been doing on behalf of blacks—or more precisely its greatest willingness in recent years to extend basic constitutional protection to blacks—is merely an undoing of the formidable obstacles to black advancement which it helped to erect."[12]

Blacks have tended increasingly to look toward the presidency and its bureaucracy for progress, first in proposing and backing legislation and then in implementing it. In their pronouncements, Democratic presidents have been increasingly sympathetic to black concerns. Republicans Nixon, Ford, and Reagan have been less so. But no president has yet developed a prominent and effective mechanism in the White House policy machinery with the clear responsibility for civil rights.

[12]Milton Morris, *The Politics of Black America* (New York: Harper & Row, 1975), p. 249.

President Johnson signs the Voting Rights Act of 1965 in the Capitol rotunda. (UPI/Bettmann Newsphotos)

The mule train of the Poor People's Campaign, made up of eleven wagons, approaches Washington in 1968. (UPI/Bettmann Newsphotos)

In 1971 the 13 black representatives in Congress organized the Congressional Black Caucus (CBC) to attempt to develop and present in Congress and to the president unified sets of policy proposals. It has provided a focus for black citizens around the country as well as for the media. But it has not yet been able to develop the leadership role once hoped for.[13] However, this may gradually change. The senior members of the Black Caucus came of age during the civil-rights struggle and represent districts with black majorities. Younger members increasingly come from mixed districts and have a different orientation. As Representative William H. Gray III (Democrat of Pennsylvania) remarked: "We have a group of new members whose strategies were shaped in the post-civil rights movement—who use leverage within the system. We see ourselves not as civil rights leaders, but as legislators. By the time we came along, the pioneers had made it possible for us to be technicians."[14]

Milton Morris, surveying the political system's response to blacks, reached several important general conclusions: (1) Federalism has allowed the states to sustain black subordination for many dec-ades, and the separation of powers has complicated efforts at change that require action by all three branches. (2) Most governmental responses have been incremental rather than comprehensive, even though both the problems and the needed measures had long been clear. For example, it took five separate major civil-rights laws from 1957 on to achieve a barely adequate program. (3) "Finally, governmental responses to demands by blacks for change in the pattern of race relations have not been systematic and carefully planned, so that change is often hampered by administrative inefficiency, disorganization, and even deliberate bungling."[15]

Many blacks had high hopes for the Carter administration; they believed that Carter as a southerner understood their problems and was genuinely committed to improving their situation. Carter did appoint more blacks to federal posts than had any of his predecessors. But his financial conservatism, coupled with declining congressional interest in passing new civil-rights laws, disappointed black hopes. The election of Ronald Reagan and the accompanying conservative swing in Congress dealt further blows to black expectations. Reagan's election represented a move away from the sort of interventionist government that has been responsible for most of the gains blacks have attained in education and jobs. As a consequence, blacks are having to depend more on their own organizations for help in improving their situation—as are other minorities and activist groups.

---

[13]See Marguerite Ross Barnett, "A Historical Look at the CBC," *Focus*, August–September 1977, pp. 3–4.

[14]Quoted in Alan Ehrenhalt, "New Black Leaders Emerging in Congress," *Congressional Quarterly Weekly Report*, August 6, 1983, p. 1643.

[15]Morris, *The Politics of Black America*, p. 245.

HISPANICS IN AMERICAN POLITICS

Hispanics as a group represent 6.4 percent of the American population, but they vary widely in their national origin as well as in their economic status. Some 60 percent are Mexican Americans, concentrated in the Southwest but increasingly also in the Middle West. Another 14 percent are Puerto Ricans, who live mostly in the New York metropolitan area. Six percent are Cubans, who live mainly in southern Florida. Table 13.5 depicts this geographical concentration. The remaining 20 percent are recent immigrants from Central and South America.

The Mexican-American Experience

Whereas blacks were brought to this country by slave traders, the ancestors of the people of mixed Native-American and Spanish ancestry—whom we now call Mexican Americans or Chicanos—were here in small numbers before the early colonists, or Anglos (as whites are called in the Southwest), arrived.

Early in the last century, Mexico formally possessed much of the Southwest and California. But by 1853 the United States had added the present states of Texas and New Mexico, along with parts of Colorado, Arizona, Utah, Nevada, and California, by a combination of war, treaty, and purchase. In the century since, Mexican citizens have continued to immigrate to the United States, sometimes fleeing Mexican politics, other times seeking better jobs. Some of those already here have moved

TABLE 13.5
Potential Hispanic Voting Power

California	1,501,000	8.7%
Texas	1,414,000	14.2%
New York	811,000	6.3%
Florida	313,000	4.2%
New Mexico	286,000	32.3%
New Jersey	242,000	4.5%
Arizona	222,000	11.5%
Colorado	196,000	9.4%
Illinois	189,000	2.3%
Michigan	74,000	1.1%

The table shows the number of Hispanic citizens of voting age and their percentage in each of the ten states with the greatest number of Hispanics.
Source: Southwest Voter Registration Education Project.

to northern states. Only in the Southwest, however, have their numbers been large enough for them to play significant political roles as a distinct minority group.

The Puerto Rican Experience

The United States took control of Puerto Rico after the U.S. victory in the Spanish-American War in 1898. The Spanish had ruled the island southeast of the American mainland for 400 years after "discovering" it early in the 16th century. At that time the island was inhabited by "Indians" who were relatively peaceful and who thus tended to assimilate the Spanish culture. The result was a population of mixed Spanish and "Indian" origins, with the addition of some black slaves brought in to work on sugar plantations. But everyone spoke Spanish.

The United States controlled Puerto Rico as a colony for 50 years. The population was granted American citizenship by the Jones Act of 1917 and was allowed to elect its own governor starting in 1947. But not until 1950 was it allowed to draft its own constitution and create a new government. On July 25, 1952, Puerto Rico became an American *commonwealth*, having besides common citizenship and common military defense, a common market (free trade between the island and the mainland) and a common currency (the American dollar). Since then, Puerto Ricans have debated whether to retain commonwealth status, to seek full independence, or to seek to become the 51st state.

Independence would give Puerto Rico greater control over its economy—especially over newly discovered oil, now largely owned by Americans from the mainland—and its politics. But it would also put an end to the large sums of economic aid, welfare payments, and so on, that now flow from Washington to the people of Puerto Rico. Statehood would limit the control Puerto Ricans would have over their own affairs. Thus, the issue of the island's future is clouded by disagreement and uncertainty.

At the same time, the question of the prospects of the island's 3,380,000 citizens is clouded by the large migration flows to and from the mainland. Because Puerto Ricans are American citizens migration is easy, and there are now 1,800,000 Puerto

Ricans on the mainland. Because they are Spanish-speaking and generally have less formal training than mainland Americans, adjustment and economic success are hard to achieve. The result is that many Puerto Ricans come to the mainland for a time and then return to the island. Because most Puerto Rican families in America are first- or second-generation arrivals (migrants themselves or children of island-born parents), their progress in education, occupation, and income has thus far been limited.

The Cuban-American Experience

The third important component of the Hispanic minority is made up of immigrants from Cuba. While this group also has Spanish as its native tongue, its similarities with the other Hispanics stop there. Both Chicanos and Puerto Ricans have come to the United States primarily as poor people seeking economic opportunity. Cuban Americans, by contrast, are mostly middle-class, and many are professionals. They have come to the United States in large numbers in the years since Fidel Castro expelled dictator Fulgencio Battista in 1959. Declaring himself a Communist after gaining power, Castro began socialist reforms such as land distribution and nationalization. The United States responded with economic sanctions, and much of the Cuban middle class chose to settle in Florida. There the Cubans have become economically established. Many own their own businesses, especially in the Miami area, where they constitute one-third of the population. All told, there are about 700,000 Cubans living in the states, and the Cuban-American population now totals just over a million.

Because they have been largely middle-class in origin, Cubans have not made many economic demands on the American political system. Instead, their demands have been political: that the United States should overthrow Castro so that they can return home. In recent years, more of those leaving Cuba for America have been working-class in status. In addition, some have been black rather than white. These black Cubans—about 5 percent of the new arrivals—have experienced racial discrimination even in white Cuban neighborhoods in Miami, and most have moved to northeastern states. Also, more Cubans have become naturalized citizens in recent years; but few register to

vote, and fewer still actually do vote. Thus, except in Miami, Cuban Americans have yet to become important factors or actors in American politics.

Hispanic Political Participation

Until recently, Hispanics did not exercise much political power. Even today only 59 percent are old enough to vote, and about one-third are resident aliens or illegal aliens ineligible to vote. This leaves a third of the Hispanic population eligible. Half of this group—3.4 million—were registered in 1980. To increase their influence in politics, Hispanics established the Southwest Voter Registration Education Project, which seeks to register millions of new Hispanic voters.

Representation

Historically, Hispanics have had little clout at the national level, for two reasons. First, their voting participation has been low. Second, most of those elected to office have become well integrated into the dominant political and economic system. When in December 1976 a Hispanic Caucus was formed in the House, it had only five members: a Puerto Rican from New York City, the resident commissioner from Puerto Rico, two Texas Chicanos, and a California Chicano. That membership remained constant through the 1980 election. In 1982, however, five new members were elected. The membership is now nine plus the nonvoting delegates from Puerto Rico and the Virgin Islands. Its political orientation is almost the opposite of that of the Black Caucus, which we examined above. The senior Hispanics are accustomed to traditional behind-the-scenes vote-trading politics, while the new members tend to use the news media to get attention for national Hispanic concerns.[16]

Politically, Chicanos have done better in recent years in states and cities where they have large population blocs. Two major cities have Chicano mayors. San Antonio, where Chicanos make up 54 percent of the population, has Henry Cisneros. Denver, despite having only an 18 percent Hispanic population, has Federico Pena.

Miami had a Puerto Rican mayor, Maurice Ferre, for 11 years. Because they are American cit-

---

[16] See Dan Fagin, "The Congressional Hispanic Caucus," *National Journal*, January 19, 1983, p. 2413.

Mayor Henry Cisneros of San Antonio. (Dennis Brack/ Black Star)

izens by birth, Puerto Ricans can vote in American elections as soon as they establish residency on the mainland, while immigrants must first achieve citizenship. But Puerto Ricans are still small minorities in most communities where they settle, so they tend to lack political clout.

In New York City Puerto Ricans are concentrated in several *barrios* (neighborhoods) and constitute at least 10 percent of the city's population. Fewer than 35 percent are registered to vote, and so they have elected only several city council members and one member of Congress. Further, in the city bureaucracy only 1 percent of agency heads and 3 percent of administrators are Puerto Rican.

The roles of Hispanics in government at lower levels are still far below their percentage of the population. Because of their regional concentration Chicanos do somewhat better in state legislatures, where they have elected about 100 members in five states. But their percentage representation never equals their population percentage. For example, they make up 19 percent of the Texas population but only 6 percent of the legislature; in California they constitute 16 percent of the population but only 4 percent of the legislature. They are generally underrepresented in bureaucratic positions at both state and national levels. As president, Jimmy Carter appointed Hispanics to one in every ten posts he filled—more than any previous president. Yet none of these was

cabinet level, nor were any of the Reagan appointees. And overall, Hispanics continue to hold less than 4 percent of federal bureaucratic jobs.

The Hispanic birthrate is 50 percent higher than that of the rest of the population. Thus, we can expect increasing political power for this group and more Hispanic officials at all levels—but only when registration and turnout are increased and sustained over a series of elections.

Organizations

In the short run, then, Hispanics will probably continue to rely on their own nongovernmental organizations for support. This has, in fact, always been the pattern. Historically, Mexican Americans relied on their Catholic churches and on local community organizations called *mutualistas* for assistance. Once large-scale migration to the United States began (after World War I and the Mexican Revolution), other organizations were formed. The League of United Latin American Citizens (LULAC) was born in Corpus Christi, Texas, in 1929 and spread throughout the Southwest. LULAC began as an organization to facilitate assimilation of Mexican Americans into the Anglo culture. Its official language is English. With the experience of segregation and discrimination in World War II, it took to the courts—like its black counterpart, the NAACP—in often successful efforts at the state level to remove discriminatory barriers in education, employment, and public facilities. In these efforts it was often joined by the G.I. Forum, a Mexican-American veterans' group especially active in the 1950s and 1960s. The G.I. Forum was founded after private cemeteries and mortuaries in Texas refused to handle the body of a Mexican-American soldier—discrimination rather typical of what Mexican Americans have faced.

In these postwar years another group, the Community Service Organization (CSO), created in Los Angeles in 1947, emphasized voter registration and political action in the style of Saul Alinsky, whom we discussed in Chapter 3. Many current Mexican-American leaders, such as Representative Edward Roybal and migrant-farm-labor-organizer Cesar Chavez, were active in the CSO.

The movement toward greater political action gained strength in the 1960s. The Mexican-American Political Association (MAPA) in California and the Political Association of Spanish-Speaking Or-

Cesar Chavez. (UPI/Bettmann Newsphotos)

ganizations (PASO) in Texas worked in local politics with some success.

These organizations all focused on legal and political equality, leaving aside the social and economic inequalities that were then believed to be "nonpolitical." But the growth and success of the black civil-rights movement suggested a broader perspective. So did the Black Power movement's emphasis on separatism instead of assimilation. And finally, so did the pledges of aid that blacks received after the big-city riots—more aid than Mexican-Americans had ever gotten in all their years of peaceful protest and efforts at assimilation.

The result was a new militancy among Mexican Americans. Cesar Chavez began organizing farm workers in Delano, California, in 1962. Reis Tijerina began a movement in New Mexico to regain lands lost in the Anglo conquest, even appealing to the Mexican government for support and then occupying certain forests until expelled by troops. In Denver Rodolfo "Corky" Gonzalez founded La Crusada Para La Justicia ("Crusade for Justice"), which protested police brutality and opposed the Vietnam War. In 1967 new militant groups were formed: the Mexican-American Youth Organization (MAYO), the United Mexican-American Students (UMAS), and the Brown Berets. It was at this point that the outlines of a new ideology began to emerge. The militants generally preferred to be called Chicanos—a term whose origins are not certain but that once referred to lower-class Mexican Americans.[17] More and more, the emphasis was on self-determination with preservation of the native culture—*chicanismo*—rather than on assimilation.

The major vehicle for this movement soon became La Raza Unida party. A Chicano political party, it was founded in Crystal City, Texas, in 1969 by Jose Angel Gutierrez, a MAYO organizer. Chicanos often refer to themselves as *la raza* ("the race"), so the party's name translates to "the united race." Gutierrez's group had organized a school boycott to make the schools more reflective of the Mexican-American majority and elect a Chicano majority to the school board. This was followed by victories in other city and county elections after extensive voter-registration work.[18] From Crystal City the party spread elsewhere, even running candidates for governor of Texas in several elections and establishing itself in California, Colorado, New Mexico, and Arizona. But in subsequent years, it failed to extend its elective political base beyond south Texas.

Chicano political organizing—covering labor, community, and political party—is still in its early stages. Already it has made major progress in the agricultural fields of California, in the *barrios* of San Antonio, and in the elections of south Texas. Its prospects are potentially as great as the large Mexican-American populations of the five southwestern states—but so too are the difficulties.[19]

Meanwhile, elected Mexican-American officials are working within the political system—as is the Mexican-American Legal Defense and Education Fund (MALDEF) that we encountered in Perspective 4.

Most Puerto Rican organizing thus far has been of a nonpolitical, community-service sort, such as that offered by Aspira clubs, which provide bilingual teaching and educational counseling. In big cities, political machines try to control political or-

---

[17]The most commonly accepted view is that it derives from the way rural native Americans of Mexico pronounced *Méjicano* "Meh-chee-cano."

[18]For an account of the Crystal City incident, see John Shockley, *Chicano Revolt in a Texas Town* (Notre Dame, IN: Univ. of Notre Dame Press, 1974). For a study of popular attitudes and their formation in Crystal City, see Herbert Hirsch and Armando Gutierrez, *Learning to Be Militant: Ethnic Identity and the Development of Political Militance in a Chicano Community* (San Francisco: R & E Research Associates, 1977).

[19]For helpful accounts of Mexican-American politics, beyond those already cited, see F. Chris Garcia and Rudolph O. de la Garza, *The Chicano Political Experience* (North Scituate, MA: Duxbury, 1977); Armando Rendon, *Chicano Manifesto* (New York: Macmillan, 1971); and F. Chris Garcia, *La Causa Politica* (Notre Dame, IN: Univ. of Notre Dame Press, 1974).

ganizations, of course, and so maintaining a non-political posture probably helps the organizations to aid "mainland islanders" (as they are often called). But at the same time, nonpolitical action limits the extent to which Puerto Ricans can develop the only kind of political strength that will force a city to take note of them politically: effective organization that can turn out votes. Even sporadic terrorist bombing, mostly in New York City—for which responsibility has been claimed by the Armed Forces of National Liberation (Fuerzas Armadas de Liberacion Nacional, FALN)—seeking independence for the island, has had little impact.

Responses of the American Political System to Hispanics

The federal government's responses to Hispanics continue to be limited and at best are mostly symbolic. President Johnson established a Cabinet Committee for Spanish-Speaking People, which his successors continued. President Nixon created greater job opportunities in government. Special efforts by the Carter administration raised the number of Hispanics to over 4 percent, but these groups are about twice that proportion of the population.

The political system's response to the needs and desires of Puerto Rican Americans in particular has been more complicated because of the special status of Puerto Rico; but it has still been quite limited. Antipoverty and job-opportunity programs have been made available to "mainland islanders" in the same way they are to other impoverished groups, but there have been few special federal programs directed to them. Nor are there likely to be until Puerto Ricans in America develop more political muscle.[20] Meanwhile, in 1979 the U.S. Congress passed a resolution formally supporting the right of Puerto Rico to determine its own political status. The dispute over statehood has since become a growing issue in Puerto Rican politics, but no strong consensus has yet emerged.[21]

In general, federal responses reflect the limited political clout in Washington thus far achieved by Spanish-surnamed Americans. But even this seems to be changing. Hispanics are now represented in Washington by the National Council of La Raza, along with MALDEF and LULAC. Many in these groups believe that large-scale immigration plus a high birthrate will soon make Spanish-speaking citizens the largest minority group in America. That should change American politics nationally as well as regionally. But how much impact it will have will depend especially on the degree of cooperation between Chicanos and Cubans and Puerto Ricans—something that has yet to develop to any great extent.

NATIVE AMERICANS IN AMERICAN POLITICS

Native-American Challenges to the American Political System

Native Americans' cars and pickup trucks often carry a bumper sticker saying "America: Love it . . . Or Give It Back To Us." That slogan capsulizes half the story of our relations with the descendants of the peoples who inhabited the continent from the North Slope in Alaska to the southern tip of South America for perhaps 30,000 years. When Europeans "discovered" America, there were already tens of millions of people living there, with about one-ninth of them in what we call the United States. By 1900 the number left in the United States had shrunk to a mere 245,000, the result of diseases brought from Europe by the white settlers, starvation resulting from seizure of Native American's farmlands, and extermination by American settlers and cavalry in the "Indian Wars."[22]

Today the number is rising again, for their birthrate is about double that of Americans as a whole. The Census Bureau in 1980 counted 1,418,195 people who identify themselves as "Indians," Eskimos, or Aleuts when asked. They are most heavily concentrated in Arizona, Oklahoma, New Mexico, and California.

[20]For discussions on the status and prospects of Puerto Rican Americans, see James Jennings and Monte Rivera, eds., *Puerto Rican Politics in Urban America* (Westport, CT: Greenwood, 1984).

[21]For a description of the current federal-commonwealth relation and outlines of the possible consequences of the three choices for Puerto Rican residents, see the General Accounting Office's Report to Congress: *Puerto Rico's Political Future* (Washington, DC: GAO, 1981).

[22]See Henry F. Dobyns, *Their Number Become Thinned: Native American Population Dynamics in Eastern North America* (Knoxville: Univ. of Tennessee Press, 1983).

TABLE 13.6
Major Native-American Indian Tribes

TRIBE	MEMBERSHIP
Navajo	97,000
Cherokee	66,000
Sioux	48,000
Chippewa	42,000
Pueblo	31,000
Lumbee	28,000
Choctaw	24,000
Apache	23,000
Iroquois	22,000

Source: Census Bureau.

Experts have distinguished 481 different Indian tribal groups, which at one time spoke some 300 different languages—50 of which are still in use. Of these groups, 267 have had special reservations—pieces of land "reserved" for use by the tribes, held "in trust" for them and supervised by the Bureau of Indian Affairs in Washington. By 1980 the number of recognized Indian groups had declined to 173. The tribal reservations remaining total about 53 million acres, or just about 2 percent of the total land area of the United States. Most of the reservations are in the West, and 77 percent of all Native Americans live west of the Mississippi. Furthermore, about half now belong to nine basic tribes, as Table 13.6 reports. The 827,000 who are "urban Indians" are concentrated in a dozen cities.

Responses of the American Political System to Native Americans

The situation was very different during the Revolutionary War.[23] In 1778 the United States, still without a Constitution, signed a treaty with the Delaware Indians that envisaged the formation of an Indian "state whereof the Delaware Nation shall be the head and have a representative in Congress." Had such a possibility come to pass, the fate of the Indians in America might have been very different. In wartime Indian strength was valued. But once peace was achieved, Indian lands were coveted.

In 1787 the Continental Congress passed the Northwest Ordinance concerning the development of the Northwest Territory, then possessed by Indians. It contained this pledge:

> The utmost good faith shall always be observed toward the Indians; their lands and property shall never be taken from them without their consent; and in their property, rights, and liberty, they shall never be invaded or distributed, unless in just and lawful wars authorized by Congress.[24]

The succeeding 200 years have been a record of the violation of these promises. In these two centuries, federal policy has vacillated between the conflicting aims of separation and assimilation. But until very recently, Indian self-determination has never been a course acceptable to Washington.

One Hundred Years of War

The Constitution (1789) gave the federal government power to negotiate treaties with "the Indian nations." Indians were then viewed as foreign nations, and so in 1824, when a Bureau of Indian Affairs (BIA) was first established, it was located within the Department of War.

White settlers then wanted more land, and the new state of Georgia claimed jurisdiction over Cherokee Indian lands within the borders that had been recognized by federal treaty. The Supreme Court, in *Worcester* v. *Georgia*, ruled that

> the Cherokee nation, then, is a distinct community occupying its own territory, with boundaries accurately described, in which the laws of Georgia can have no force, and which the citizens of Georgia have no right to enter, but with the consent of the Cherokees themselves, or in conformity with treaties, and with the acts of Congress.

Court decisions are supposed to be enforced by the president. But the president then was Andrew Jackson, the famous Indian fighter. He is reported to have remarked: "That's Marshall's decision; let him enforce it."

Meanwhile, in 1830 Congress had passed the Indian Removal Act, instructing the BIA to relocate all Indians west of the Mississippi River—but only with their consent. Those Indians who refused consent were forced to move by the military. Subsequently, in 1849 legislation transferred the BIA to the Interior Department—the very agency trying

---

[23]For an account of the history of U.S. policy, see Francis Paul Prucha, *The Great Father: The U.S. and the American Indians*, 2 vols. (Lincoln: Univ. of Nebraska Press, 1984); see also Vine Deloria, Jr., ed., *American Indian Policy in the Twentieth Century* (Norman: Univ. of Oklahoma Press, 1986).

[24]Quoted in D'Arcy McNickle, *The Indian Tribes of the U.S.* (London: Oxford Univ. Press, 1961), p. 30.

to free Indian lands for white settlers. The result, not surprisingly, was continued military defeats and removal of Indians farther and farther westward, away from their ancestral homelands to virtually worthless, often unfarmable land—the reservations Indians still occupy today.

In 1871 Congress decided that Indians were no longer to be viewed as nations, or sovereign political units. Instead, they were to be assimilated into the mainstream of the United States by becoming farmers. Each family was allocated 40 to 160 acres within the reservation by the General Allotment Act (or Dawes Act) of 1887. All leftover land was then sold by the federal government to white settlers. Thus were the reservations further whittled down—from 138 million acres to only 47 million by 1934. Tribes that resisted "allotment" were "terminated" immediately: Their reservations were abolished, and they had to fend for themselves in American society.[25] Since then, some reservation lands have been restored.

Fifty Years of Accommodation

The last military battle with Indians was fought in 1890—the famed Wounded Knee Massacre.[26] When thousands of Indians volunteered to serve in the army in World War I, Congress responded by granting Indians citizenship—and so the right to vote—in 1924. But this right in law did not become fully a right in practice until 1948, when the Supreme Court struck down clauses in the constitutions of Arizona and New Mexico forbidding Indians from voting.

By the Indian Reorganization Act of 1934, Congress granted Indian tribes the right to develop their own constitutions, to administer justice (subject to Congress's limitation), and to determine tribal membership. And that same year the Johnson-O'Malley Act laid the groundwork for what we might call foreign aid to Indian tribes: educational, medical, and other services to be paid for by Washington but provided by states and later by private groups. This marked the high point of Indian-federal relations.

---

[25]For a discussion of this and other important aspects of Indian history, see Curtis E. Jackson and Marcia J. Galli, *A History of the Bureau of Indian Affairs and Its Activities among Indians* (San Francisco: R & E Research Associates, 1977).

[26]See Dee Brown, *Bury My Heart at Wounded Knee* (New York: Holt, Rinehart & Winston, 1970).

The Growth of Indian Organizations

In the 20th century Indians made new efforts to organize in order to make their views felt. In 1911 the Society of American Indians (SAI) was formed with the twin objectives of "pan-Indianism" (uniting all Indians) and "assimilation" (adopting the culture and lifestyle of the non-Indian majority). But pan-Indianism did not gain real strength until the 1944 founding of the National Congress of American Indians (NCAI) by returning World War II veterans no longer willing to accept discrimination and inequality. The NCAI was active in lobbying the government and litigating in the courts.

When the Eisenhower administration sought to "terminate" federal aid to tribes, the NCAI led the opposition. Still, the BIA continued to try to relocate Indians from the economically depressed reservations to urban areas where jobs and training opportunities were greater. This policy of encouraging assimilation met with growing resistance. Leaders of that resistance were militant young Indians who formed the National Indian Youth Council (NIYC) in the early 1960s.

This new militance resulted in a series of direct action projects. One was the temporary occupation of Alcatraz island, an abandoned federal prison, by a group of "Indians of All Tribes" in 1969. Another was the occupation of Wounded Knee, South Dakota, in 1973 by 200 members of another activist group, the American Indian Movement (AIM), which had been founded in 1968 and now has chapters throughout the Midwest.

Another action that received major media attention was a march on Washington in the fall of 1972, conducted by AIM, NAIC, NIYC, and other national Indian organizations. Earlier, President Nixon had declared a "New Trail" for the American Indian. In a message to Congress on July 8, 1970, he asserted that "American Indians have been oppressed and brutalized, deprived of their ancestral lands, and denied the opportunity to control their own destiny." He declared that "it is long past time that the Indian policies of the federal government began to recognize and build upon the capacities and insights of the Indian people." Shortly thereafter, certain ancestral lands were restored to their tribal owners, and the BIA was reorganized to give Indians more of a role in it. But Congress resisted most of Nixon's proposals, and the BIA did not become more responsive. And so the Indian groups called their 1972 march on Washington the

A protest by American Indians in Arizona. (Paul Fusco/Magnum Photos)

Trail of Broken Promises. When their four-mile-long caravan arrived, it occupied the BIA for six days. During the occupation, they destroyed some property and seized some records. They and columnist Jack Anderson, to whom they showed some of the records, found a history of mishandling of Indian affairs by the BIA.[27]

As one important outcome of the reports about these documents. Congress established an American Indian Policy Review Commission. It concluded in 1977 that the BIA had mishandled Indian money, neglected Indian safety, and failed to protect Indian property rights. The report also called for abolition of the BIA and its replacement by a Department of Indian Affairs independent of the Interior Department.[28]

When the Carter administration came to power, it faced a changed situation. Tribes in many states were making new claims on land taken from them illegally by white settlers over 100 years ago, and the government was recognizing the legal validity of some claims. At the same time, 22 tribes whose lands contain oil and coal reserves set up a Council of Energy Resource Tribes (CERT) patterned on the Organization of Petroleum Exporting Countries (OPEC), in order to gain advantages in leasing their lands to oil and coal companies.

Carter attempted to increase the role of Native Americans in government, selecting a Blackfoot as his assistant secretary of the interior for Indian affairs. The man chosen to head the BIA was a Chippewa. In addition, the administration supported various tribes' claims to tribal lands and trust funds. Since then, more and more claims to ancestral water rights and fishing rights have been raised in courts by militant tribes. They have been supported by a nonprofit law firm, the Native-American Rights Fund. The Reagan administration cut federal spending for Native Americans by about a billion dollars a year, to $2.5 billion. It also gave the tribes control of about a third of the programs formerly administered by the Bureau of Indian Affairs. And it called on the Indians to develop partnerships with private corporations instead of with Washington. Indian reaction to these developments has not been favorable. In the words of William A. Means of the International Indian Treaty Council, the Reagan plan "will merely shift economic dependency from the Federal bureaucracy to corporate boards, and they will withdraw their support when they have exhausted the resources on the Indian lands."[29]

The Native Americans face opposition in the West as well as obstacles in Washington.[30] Many observers would agree with the analysis of anthropologist Jeanne Guillemin, who has concluded:

> Planning for a future with a reasonable balance of economic activity, education, and social programs can be done only by assessing the potential of each tribe (with its cultural, demographic, and regional variations) and with an eye to non-Indian relations at the local and state level. . . . The frequent suggestion to establish an independent Office of Indian Affairs, complete with a cabinet post, has never made more sense than now.[31]

[27]The story is told briefly in Joseph Stauss, Bruce A. Chadwick, and Howard M. Bahr, "Indian Americans: The First Is Last," in *The Minority Report*, ed. Anthony G. Dworkin et al. (New York: Praeger, 1976), pp. 221–53.

[28]See the *Final Report to the American Indian Policy Review Commission* (Washington, DC: GPO, 1976).

[29]See Brian W. Dippie, *The Vanishing American: White Attitudes and U.S. Indian Policy* (Middletown, CT: Wesleyan Univ. Press, 1982).

[30]Iver Peterson, "Bringing Decentralization to the Reservation," *New York Times*, October 30, 1983.

[31]Jeanne Guillemin, "Federal Policies and Indian Politics," *Society*, May–June 1980, p. 34.

Still, there are disagreements among Indians over the wisdom of such efforts at modernization. On one side are the militants; on the other are the traditionalists, or nationalists, as they are sometimes called. According to Vine Deloria, Jr.:

> Most Indians are nationalists. That is, they are primarily concerned with the development and continuance of the tribe. As nationalists, Indians could not, for the most part, care less what the rest of the Society does. . . . Militants, on the other hand, are reactionists. They understand the white society and they progress by reacting against it.[32]

This highlights an important distinction made by Frances Svensson, herself an Indian, that helps explain the differences between Indians and other minorities, and so the difficulties of coalition building.

> Where the Black goal has seemed to be equal participation in the benefits and privileges of American society, the fundamental Indian objective is best summed up as the right not to have to participate and still maintain an autonomous Indian identity, legally rooted in the historic treaty relationship and the traditional land base.[33]

"Indian tribes need greater political power to act," asserts Indian leader Mel Thom. "This country respects power and is based on the power system. If Indian communities and Indian tribes do not have political power we will never be able to hang on to what we have now."[34]

The power Indians have today derives primarily from their right to vote in federal and state elections. This right carries with it the duties to pay federal taxes and do military service when called upon. The tribes themselves, however, have no powers as such. Some have argued that because tribes are small and scattered the right to vote will not become a political power for Indians until the tribes are separately represented in the federal government. Representation could be achieved via statehood, but that would be impractical and politically unacceptable because the tribes are so small.

The alternative, some say, is what has been called treaty federalism, which advocates have described as "a procedure . . . for the creative establishment of governments in circumstances where conventional statehood would be economically, socially or politically inappropriate, but where both sovereignties recognize the expediency of permanent union." Such an approach would require both consent of the tribal peoples by treaty and the approval of two-thirds of the Senate. Its terms, suggest advocates, should include:

- Clarification of the reserved territorial powers of the tribes and of the tribes' authority to delegate additional powers to Congress, along the model of the states
- Reservation to the tribes of the power of naturalization, or determining tribal citizenship
- Voting representation of Tribal Caucuses in the U.S. Congress
- Elimination of Indian voting rights in state elections and of state powers over reservations within their borders.[35]

Some Native-American activists are coming to favor novel political solutions such as this. Others, being traditionalists, differ. In the words of one older Indian:

> As Indians we will never have the efficient organization that gains great concessions from society in the marketplace. We will never have a powerful lobby or be a smashing political force. But we will have the intangible unity which has carried us through four centuries of persecution. We are a people unified by our humanity—not a pressure group unified for conquest. And from our greater strength we shall wear down the white man and finally outlast him. . . . We shall endure.[36]

ASIAN-AMERICANS IN AMERICAN POLITICS

Because they are generally better off materially than the groups we have thus far examined, we rarely think of groups of Asian origin as minorities. Yet peoples from China, Japan, and more recently

---

[32]Vine Deloria, ed., *Custer Died for Your Sins* (New York: Macmillan, 1969), p. 237.

[33]Frances Svensson, *The Ethnics in American Politics: American Indians* (Minneapolis: Burgess, 1973), p. 39. This short book contains an excellent introduction to American Indians in politics. For a more general study, see Murray L. Wax, *Indian Americans: Unity and Diversity* (Englewood Cliffs, NJ: Prentice-Hall, 1971).

[34]Mel Thom, quoted in Alvin M. Josephy, Jr., *Red Power* (New York: American Heritage Press, 1971), p. 68.

[35]This proposal is made in Russel Lawrence Barsh and James Youngblood Henderson, *The Road: Indian Tribes and Political Liberty* (Berkeley: Univ. of California Press, 1980), pp. 275, 280–81.

[36]Quoted in Virginia Armstrong, *I Have Spoken* (Chicago: Swallow, 1971), pp. 162–63. For a manifesto by activist Russell Means and AIM, see "Fighting Words on the Future of the Earth," *Mother Jones*, December 1980, pp. 24–38.

TABLE 13.7
Asian-American Population, 1985

	NUMBER	PERCENT
Chinese	1,079,400	21.0
Filipino	1,051,600	20.4
Japanese	766,300	14.9
Vietnamese	634,200	12.3
Korean	542,400	10.5
Asian Indian	525,600	10.2
Laotian	218,400	4.2
Kampuchean	160,800	3.1
All other	169,200	3.3
TOTAL	5,147,900	100.0

Source: Population Bulletin 40 (October 1985), 5.

Indochina (Vietnam, Laos, and Kampuchea), the Philippines, and Korea, have experienced prejudice, discrimination, and exploitation often comparable to that faced by the others.[37]

The first large group of Chinese came to the United States in the mid-1800s to prospect for gold or to work in factories or to build the railroads in the West. Japanese came to do this work after Congress passed the Chinese Exclusion Act in 1882. Filipinos came to work in factories and fields and later hospitals earlier in this century, following America's defeat of their colonial master, Spain, in 1898 and suppression of a guerrilla nationalist movement in the Philippine Islands.

Prejudice became widespread. Chinese immigration was banned in the 1880s. When the San Francisco earthquake destroyed schools in 1906, the board of education forced Japanese-American students to attend makeshift segregated schools so that white children could have their buildings. Because President Theodore Roosevelt couldn't intervene in California affairs he worked out a "gentlemen's agreement" with Japan to limit immigration.

Japanese already in the United States were buying land to farm, thus removing themselves from a shrinking labor force. So California passed the Alien Land Act in 1913, prohibiting noncitizens from buying land. Because federal law prohibited Asians from becoming naturalized citizens this law prevented Japanese Americans from owning land. As a result, most Japanese Americans became self-employed.

In 1941 Japan bombed the American naval base in Pearl Harbor, Hawaii, and then won victories in Asian island battles. Fear and hatred of all Japanese intensified. Finally, on February 19, 1942, President Franklin Roosevelt signed Executive Order 9066 calling for all Japanese Americans living in California, Oregon, Washington, and southern Arizona to be relocated to concentration camps in California, Arkansas, Idaho, Wyoming, Colorado, Utah, and Arizona. By November 1942 all 110,000 Japanese Americans had been removed after having to dispose of their property at prices below the going rate. Some were allowed to join segregated army units fighting in Europe (but not in Asia), and others were allowed to work on the farms, but most lived penal lives in the camps. Finally, on December 18, 1944, the Supreme Court ruled unanimously that the government had no legal authority to incarcerate loyal, law-abiding citizens, even if they were of Japanese ancestry, and over the next 12 months the camps were closed and the prisoners freed.[38]

Despite these appalling setbacks, Japanese Americans have managed to attain the highest median number of years of education of any ethnic group in America, including whites. The Japanese median family income is higher than that of whites as well. Still, the Japanese, especially those who live on the West Coast, continue to suffer discrimination.

Since Congress eliminated immigration quotas (which had specified the number of immigrants allowed from each country or region each year) in 1965, there has been growing Chinese migration to the United States. Many who have come have been poor, and the result has been greater poverty and social conflict in the "Chinatown" ghettos in which most Chinese Americans live.

The most difficult situation, in some ways, has been that of the Indochinese refugees who have come to America since the Vietnam War ended in 1975. These war refugees arrived with little preparation for the changes they would face, although many had education, training, or experience that promised to help them adjust. Indeed, about two-thirds have come from white-collar backgrounds. In the past decade, over a million Indochinese war refugees have arrived in the United States, most of them from Vietnam.

Recent studies of the progress of Vietnamese immigrants are encouraging. The most comprehen-

---

[37]See Robert W. Gardner et al., "Asian Americans: Growth, Change, and Diversity," *Population Bulletin* 40 (October 1985).

[38]See Allen R. Bosworth, *America's Concentration Camps* (New York: Norton, 1967).

Vietnamese boat people. (© Magnus Bartlett, Asia Pix/Woodfin Camp & Associates)

sive of these found most—95 percent of males and 93 percent of females—employed, although generally at a lower-level job than their previous training would have called for. Family income has increased to the point where fewer than one-third of all households are receiving public assistance ("welfare") of any sort. There are three reasons for this. First, most refugees arrived as families rather than as isolated individuals, and so each family has several income earners. Second, 99 percent of the refugee families have been "sponsored" by American families or church groups, and so they have had access to private help when they needed it. Third, Vietnamese families seem to be relocating in large cities where they can create ethnic enclaves that offer mutual physical and emotional support.

Refugees continue to arrive, although at a much slower rate, and most of the later arrivals are "boat people"—those who fled without possessions on small craft in desperation—many of whom are less skilled than their predecessors. Thus, the challenge of Vietnamese refugees to the American system is far from over.[39] It is also possible that prejudice

---

[39]See Darrell Montero, *Vietnamese Americans: Patterns of Resettlement and Socioeconomic Adaptation in the U.S.* (Boulder, CO: Westview, 1979).

and discrimination born of resentment may set in among other Americans once the Vietnamese become well established and are seen as economic threats rather than as useful labor. This has been the pattern with other immigrant minorities.

MINORITY-MAJORITY RELATIONS

Governmental Approaches to Solving the Problems of Minorities

Both dominant elements and the subordinate peoples in society view the problem posed by minorities differently at different times. This means that beliefs about what the appropriate remedies are also vary through time. Let us look, for example, at the situation of blacks.

Emancipation

When the problem was seen as *slavery*, the solution was **emancipation** by destroying slavery or the society that sustained it. The Civil War did accomplish that, but of course race relations did not really improve very much as a result.

Abolishing Legal Segregation

People then concluded that the problem was **discrimination**—a set of *residual practices* based on race, left over from slavery. The way to solve that problem, it appeared, was to change those practices. The legal practices were declared unconstitutional by the Supreme Court or were changed by new laws. At that point, it was believed that *abolishing legal segregation* would result in desegregation.

Education

But that approach was not sufficient either, although it certainly improved the conditions of many blacks in the South. Perhaps, then, the problem was not so much residual practices of discrimination but rather *residual attitudes* of discrimination—or **prejudice**. This suggested that what was needed was *more education about race and about prejudice*, with two important goals. The first was to show people that their beliefs about the inferiority of blacks were unfounded: that there was no factual basis for discrimination because blackness was only "skin deep," or perhaps only "culture deep." Coupled with this was emphasis on the desirability of an unprejudiced, integrated society in which brotherhood replaced hostility.

Integration

However, experience showed that even this effort was not enough. The next stage in the struggle to solve our racial problems involved efforts to increase actual contact between whites and blacks of the same social status, occupation, income, or whatever. The theory behind this approach relied on the fact that forced contact in the military between the races engaged in common tasks with the same rank had usually overcome prejudice. But the question was how to bring about such contact among people so prejudiced that they resisted it. The answer was *a shift in emphasis from* **desegregation** (removing barriers to contact) *to* **integration** (bringing people together).

Compulsion

There are two basic approaches to achieving integration: compulsion and incentives. Both have been tried, for example, in public schools. The *compulsion approach* simply decrees that the races will be joined in the same school, perhaps by consolidation of white and black schools, or perhaps by busing of students. This approach, widely used, has achieved some success, but much turmoil and apparent hardening of attitudes, especially in big cities such as Boston, have accompanied it.

Incentives

The *incentive approach* has generally worked better where it has been tried. One approach is simply letting students transfer to a better school. This usually involves blacks transferring to a predominantly white school because white schools have usually been better than black schools. In such cases, the incentive of attending a better school draws blacks to the white school and also keeps whites there. In recent years, however, a more active effort has been tried: development of "magnet schools." Magnet schools are special schools developed with special strengths, such as emphasis on science or on the performing arts. They attract students of all races from a whole region by their special programs. Magnet schools seem to be more successful at fostering integration than other efforts. The drawback is that they are expensive to run and only work to integrate students who are especially interested in good education—something many students of all races do not now seem to be.

Affirmative Action

To cope with situations where such incentives to participants were not available, other approaches had to be found. This led to the next stage: *a movement from providing equal opportunity to requiring affirmative action* to achieve integration (an approach we discussed earlier)—which some saw as itself a form of racism.

Racism

Racism is the belief that a person's race should be used as a criterion to determine how he or she is treated, implying that some races are or should be treated better than other races. Racism has been a characteristic of the views of many citizens throughout American history. We call this attitude **personal racism**.

Personal Racism

In a sense, the civil-rights movement of the early 1960s was based on the assumption that racial problems were problems of individual attitudes. Racially prejudiced people—people who feared strangeness, difference, or foreignness—were generally thought of as misinformed or even mentally sick. Efforts were made to correct that misinformation or treat that sickness by achieving education and contact.

Institutional Racism

But the civil-rights movement died in part because even when there were more contact and less prejudice, the problems of minorities were not solved. This led more and more observers and activists to conclude that the problem was deeper than attitudes—that it was more than just personal. Instead, many came to believe, the United States suffered not just from personal racism but also from **institutional racism**. According to this view, whatever people's views may be, our institutions set contexts within which some people are kept poor and powerless by being denied real opportunities for education, good jobs, good housing, and political roles.

Our economic system, for example, is based on capitalist competition. Those with money have economic power. Those with good educations and good connections do best at earning money. People who are born into well-off families have an easier time getting these advantages. So the system, through its institutions, tends to perpetuate the same economic classes in power.

Furthermore, political power tends to depend on economic power. If you are poor, you can't take time off from your work to run for office, nor can you contribute money to someone's campaign to get him or her to do you favors. In addition, the system tends to set *economic prerequisites* to participation, such as poll taxes for voting (now outlawed) or high costs for good housing or the ability to take time off from work to serve on juries. This kind of pattern tends to perpetuate unequal opportunity *regardless of people's attitudes* about race. This suggests that changing the status and prospects of

minorities will require *changing the economic and political system*. Simply changing people's attitudes won't be enough.[40]

Problems of Consciousness

The attitudes and deeper beliefs of people are still important, however, and may even hold the key to the next stage of progress for minorities. But the attitudes that are most important may be those not of the prejudiced dominant people but rather of the dominated minorities.

Discrimination and domination tend to make the victims feel inadequate, unequal, and incompetent. The victims tend to grow up believing they are less valuable and less able to act effectively in society. Until recently, the major resistance to domination has been occasional revolts and riots, strikes and boycotts, and traditions of ethnic humor and culture. In recent years, however, groups dominated economically, socially, and politically have been working to combat their situation at the level of consciousness as well.

Leaders have been much more actively emphasizing the *strengths* of the minority cultures, their *values*, and the *prospect of power*: black power, brown power, red power, and yellow power. These efforts seem to have developed greater ethnic pride in many members of the minority groups we have examined. This pride has contributed to a greater sense of efficacy, or ability to operate effectively in society, even while the society remains racist in many ways. One result is higher hopes among many young people—hopes that motivate greater efforts.

Peoplehood is the name historian Page Smith gives to this new sense of self and possibilities. "Peoplehood," he writes,

> is a particular kind of self-definition whereby masses or wards of the public seek to achieve an identity and a power of their own. . . . the definition always comes out of the mass; it can never come from outside, from well-intentioned liberals, benefactors, reformers, philosophers, psychologists, sociologists.

---

[40]For a presentation of various aspects of institutional racism, see Charles Bullock and Harrell Rodgers, *Racial Equality in America* (Santa Monica, CA: Goodyear, 1975). See also Joe R. Feagin, "Indirect Institutional Discrimination," *American Politics Quarterly* 5 (April 1977), 177–99, and his book *Racial and Ethnic Relations* (Englewood Cliffs, NJ: Prentice-Hall, 1978).

Smith goes on to point out that

> the dependent group in the process of defining itself, of creating itself, of speaking itself into life, draws on remarkable new sources of energy and releases these into the world. . . . They become electrified, plugged in, almost literally, to history. They sense that they, too, can make history.[41]

This new sense of power and the new hopes that go with it give strength to activists. But they also create hopes that increase the risk of disillusionment should the dominant society be unresponsive or inflexible. This uncertainty about prospects makes it all the more important for the ethnic groups to be as clear as possible about their choice among various possible objectives.

American Goals and Minority Groups

Paternalism

Historically, American society seems to have had **paternalism** as its goal in handling minority groups. This term, derived from *pater*, the Latin word for "father," refers to maintaining dominance over another while deciding what is best for the one dominated.

Recently, some observers have argued that America has used a special variant of paternalism called domestic colonialism, or **internal colonialism**, treating blacks, Hispanics, Native American Indians, and Asian Americans as if they were a colony. There are four major characteristics of internal colonialism as it is usually described.

- Forced entry of subordinates into the world of the dominant—by slavery for blacks and conquest for Chicanos and Native Americans
- Forced transformation of the culture of the minority group—by requiring the use of English and prohibiting the use of native languages, for example
- Management and manipulation of economic and political affairs of the dominated by the dominant—such as white ownership of stores in the black ghettos or white officials running the Bureau of Indian Affairs
- Racist attitudes held by the dominant and imposed where possible on the minorities so that they believe they are basically inferior[42]

---

[41]Page Smith, "From Masses to Peoplehood," *Historical Reflections* 1 (June 1974), 134–35.

[42]For one of many recent discussions on internal colonialism, see Harry H. L. Kitano, *Race Relations*, 2d ed. (Englewood Cliffs, NJ: Prentice-Hall, 1980).

Divide and Conquer

A second strategy has been *divide and conquer*—setting one minority group against another to prevent them from uniting to achieve greater power. This strategy has been especially common where the government has been distributing resources such as aid money or business contracts. When blacks struggle with Chicanos for antipoverty funds, for example, the government gains power. It has, understandably, been very difficult thus far for minority groups that have little in common besides their subordinate status to form coalitions.

Anglo Conformity

The longer-term goal of U.S. society in its handling of minorities appears to be the creation of *Anglo conformity*. This term refers to desires and requirements that minorities adopt the attitudes, lifestyles, and culture of the dominant Anglo society. In ethnic terms, it is often called *acculturation* and *assimilation*.

The Melting Pot

At the same time, there has long been an American ideology of the melting pot. This view holds that America is a mixture of many different nationalities and that the people's strengths come from a combination of the special qualities of different minorities, all "melted down" into a new "American" culture.

This view sounds appealing, and for decades it was widely accepted. But then leaders of various minorities began to argue that it was not happening in fact. In the angry words of one Chicano militant:

> The United States has been anything but a melting pot, because the gringo has purposely segregated, and relegated the non-Anglo to an inferior and degraded status. Melting pot has meant surrender of one's past and culture to something euphemistically called American society or culture. The melting pot worked only for immigrants with a white skin who came to America.[43]

By now, it is hard to find a supporter of the melting-pot approach. Even the immigrants with white skin—the Italians, the Irish, the Germans, the Greeks, the Poles—are reemphasizing their

---

[43]Rendon, *Chicago Manifesto*, p. 107.

ethnic roots and cultures. But the strongest opposition to the melting-pot image comes from the most "unmeltable" ethnics, the "people of color." As Earl Shorris has written of the Native American: "Conquered and loved, butchered and smothered, the Indian staggers into the battle for a pluralistic society; he has seen death in the melting pot."[44] In short, the melting pot has turned out to be a "pressure cooker."[45]

Cultural Pluralism

And so, most ethnic groups have "staggered"—or charged—into the battle for a pluralistic American society. But **cultural pluralism**—in which each individual culture survives and flourishes within a broader framework—can take various forms: (1) One image now much in favor is that of *the symphony orchestra*. In such a society, every group plays a different instrument, but all are playing their own part in a larger piece. This image raises two unanswered questions: Who will conduct the orchestra? And who will compose the symphony? Many of the more militant and younger ethnic leaders fear the answer in both cases will be Anglos. And they also suspect that if they don't play it the way the Anglos write it and conduct it, they'll be thrown out of the orchestra. (2) So some favor a second image or objective, which might be that of *a jazz combo*. There would still be a piece to be played, and the performers would have to cooperate and support each other. But each would also be able to improvise from time to time, and the piece would be somewhat different every time it's played. (3) The more extreme image, just short of total separatism (which few now favor), could be termed *separate but equal recitals*, taking place, to stretch the metaphor, in the same recital hall.

Perhaps no one is now certain which of these ultimate objectives is the most desirable. Perhaps few sense just what would be required to achieve any of them. But several important points are clear even now. First, each of us must be more open to other cultures and more supportive of their efforts at self-determination. Second, our government must be supportive—especially with funds for development—without insisting on shaping and dominating the activities of our various cultures. And third, the members of each subgroup must continue to explore and experiment and try to develop greater agreement among themselves. Ultimately, each group would then be likely to develop its own variation of the principle of self-determination.

SUMMARY

The United States population majority has long been white Protestant, but immigration from Catholic Europe, the importation of black slaves, and then immigration from Central and South America have reduced white Protestants to about 55 percent.

Racial and ethnic minorities have long played important economic roles in the United States, and now increasingly they are playing major political roles as well. Research reported in this chapter summarizes their weaker economic, employment, and educational status.

Blacks were the first group to become politically active, seeking, and ultimately getting, such civil rights as desegregated schools and the right to vote through passage of a series of civil-rights acts from 1965 through 1984. They now play important, though still limited, roles in politics as voters, candidates, and administrators. Hispanics—especially Mexican Americans, Puerto Ricans, and Cuban Americans—have increased in number and become more active politically in recent years. Mexican Americans, or Chicanos, as they are sometimes called, are most concentrated in the Southwest. Puerto Ricans, who are U.S. citizens, although Puerto Rico is a commonwealth rather than a state, are concentrated in the metropolitan New York area. Cuban Americans are strongest in southern Florida. Recent efforts to register more Hispanics have resulted in election of Hispanic mayors in Denver, San Antonio, and Miami, but political participation by Hispanics is still quite limited.

Native Americans, or Indians, as they are usually called, were here before the European colo-

[44]Earl Shorris, *The Death of the Great Spirit* (New York: New American Library, 1972), p. 61.

[45]John W. Berry, "Acculturation as Varieties of Adaptation," in *Acculturation: Theory, Models and Some New Findings*, ed. Amado M. Padilla (Boulder, CO: Westview, 1980), p. 15.

nists. Their history as a people since the American Revolution is often described as 100 years of war followed by 50 years of accommodation. They were granted American citizenship, and hence the right to vote, in 1924. However, most of them have lived on reservations and so not participated actively in traditional politics. Activists are attempting to change this now.

Chinese Americans have been in America since the middle of the last century. Japanese Americans came at its end. Indochinese arrived after the Vietnam War. In general, Asian Americans have been more prosperous than other minorities, but they have not been especially active in politics.

Governmental approaches to solving the problems of minorities have passed through various stages. For example, in the case of blacks, the stages have been: emancipation, abolishing legal segregation, education, integration, compulsion, incentives, and affirmative action. The underlying obstacles have been both personal racism and institutional racism. Part of the problem has been the diversity of goals, from paternalism or internal colonialism through divide and conquer to Anglo conformity and then the melting pot. The current goal is best expressed as cultural pluralism. The United States and its various ethnic and racial minorities still have a long way to go, but progress has been and is increasingly being made.

Suggestions for Further Reading and Study

A recent book containing accounts of over 100 ethnic groups in American is the *Harvard Encyclopedia of American Ethnic Groups* (Cambridge, MA: Harvard Univ. Press, 1980), ed. Stephen Thernstrom. For a shorter survey with helpful theoretical analysis, see Joseph Hraba, *American Ethnicity* (Itasca, IL: Peacock, 1979). Among the most interesting historical surveys are Ronald T. Takaki, *Iron Cages: Race and Culture in 19th-Century America* (New York: Knopf, 1979), and James Stuart Olson, *The Ethnic Dimension in American History* (New York: St. Martin's Press, 1979). A collection of interesting essays on seven different ethnic groups is John Higham, ed., *Ethnic Leadership in America* (Baltimore: Johns Hopkins Univ. Press paperback, 1978). A guide, in question-and-answer format, to *The Rights of Racial Minorities* in voting, employment, education, housing, and public accommodation is edited by E. Richard Larson and Laughlin McDonald for the American Civil Liberties Union (New York: Avon paperback, 1980).

The footnotes scattered throughout the chapter will lead you to helpful books on each of the minority groups discussed. For an analysis of WASPs, see Charles H. Anderson, *White Protestant Americans* (Englewood Cliffs, NJ: Prentice-Hall paperback, 1970). A helpful treatment of race relations generally is Michael Banton, *Race Relations* (New York: Basic Books, 1967).

14

OUTSIDERS IN INSIDER POLITICS:
Women, the Young,
the Elderly, and Others

The largest "minority group" in America is the majority: the 51.3 percent of the population that is female. Women in our country are the most underrepresented group in our political and economic systems. But they are not the least active group in American politics. That distinction goes instead to the young, who are barred not only from serving in national office until they are 25 but also from voting for candidates for any office until they are 18. The distinction of being the least visible element in our population, on the other hand, falls to the 11 percent of the American people who are over the age of 65.

All of these groups, and others as well, are outsiders in our political system. But each presents challenges to the system, and each is the subject of special policies. ■

OUTSIDERS AND POLITICS

Women, the young, and the elderly—along with the handicapped, the mentally ill, and the homosexual—are the outsiders in American politics. The members of racial and ethnic minorities, so long excluded from most of the benefits of American life and from the ability to shape those benefits, are at last being inducted into politics. But most of those being so inducted are male, middle-aged, and of sound mind and body. For American politics is still in general off limits to women, to the young, to the elderly, and to those having unusual physical, mental, or sexual characteristics. By examining each of these still-excluded groups to determine its size, interests, activities, and the way in which our political system responds to it, we may better understand what seem likely to become the next great waves of unrest and activism in America: the campaigns of the outsiders to tear down the walls that bar them from full, active, and profitable roles in American politics.

Political Power and Outsiders

Politics, as we have seen time and again, is made up of actions by individuals who run for office, work in campaigns, vote, lobby, make policy, and execute policy. Most of this political activity is undertaken by individuals organized into groups. Most groups in politics are organized around a candidate, as is a political party in a campaign, or around an issue, as is the anti-gun-control lobby. But when one segment of the population is not represented in politics or is generally not listened to, eventually it will tend to organize simply to gain a fairer share of political power. The prospect that a group such as blacks, who are about 13 percent of the population, might begin to vote actively as a bloc and to lobby for the same general goals almost regardless of their wealth or social position was enough to bring about major new legislation. The same thing may increasingly occur with groups such as the elderly or the handicapped, for example, each of which is a sizable, distinct minority.

The prospect of the same sort of political solidarity among women, or even just among a substantial percentage of women, should be enough to bring massive changes in American politics. Why,

then, did so fundamental a quest as that for ratification of the Equal Rights Amendment (ERA) intended to prevent discrimination against women run into such staunch resistance?

The Politics of Advocacy

The first, most striking point is that outsiders must advocate their positions to insiders—to those who control politics. In the case of ERA, activist women and their male supporters had to convince the male-dominated Congress to pass, and thereby propose, the amendment and then had to convince two-thirds of the state legislatures, also dominated by males, to ratify it. As it happened, they were not able to convince enough state legislatures.

Second, and probably more significant ultimately, active outsiders who want "in" must convince the other members of their social group to support their cause. In the instance of ERA, supporters had to advocate their case to unconvinced and even fearful women. With relative unity, they would have been a political force difficult to resist, even for the most male-chauvinist state legislators. But without it, their case became much weaker.

WOMEN IN AMERICAN POLITICS

The Status of Women

Women have always been called the second sex, and outside the home at least they have been treated as such. Neither in politics nor in economic life have they had anything approaching equality with men. There have always been some who have opposed this second-class status, and many who have resented it. But until recently, they have been opposed both by men and by the institutions men dominated. In recent years, this has begun to change.

The contemporary women's movement is most often said to have begun with publication of Betty Friedan's book *The Feminine Mystique* in 1965. Several years later, the first of the new national activist groups, the National Organization for Women (NOW), was founded. In 1970 NOW members climbed the Statue of Liberty and unfurled a banner saying, "Women of the World, Unite!" Thus began a decade that was to see enormous changes in the status of women.

(Dino Pellegrino/Black Star)

Today women have almost attained equality in education. However, they are held back in the societal roles they play by a combination of their own attitudes and men's attitudes. Neither women nor men, on the average, yet believe that women can and should do every job men do, and neither yet believe that women should be paid what men are paid for the same job. More women are working than ever before—twice as many as in 1950. The percentage of women who work has risen from 34 percent in 1950 to 55 percent today, while that of men working has declined from 86 percent to 77 percent. Yet these women are being paid less, relative to men, than was true before. Today women make, on average, only 64 percent of what men make.[1] All this despite some 20 years of an active and growing "women's movement." This is not to say there's been no real improvement during these years. In 1950 only 66 women for every 100 men

received four-year college degrees. By 1980 women starting work were more likely than men to be college graduates. Similarly, in 1950 only 10 percent of all Ph.D.s were women; now the figure is almost double that. And women now get 40 percent of all business degrees awarded.[2]

Equality in educational level, however, is not reflected in income. Women between the ages of 30 and 44 make an average of $3000 a year less than men in the same age group with similar education and careers. Further, women who have finished four years of college generally make less than men who have finished only eighth grade. Table 14.1 compares the earnings of men and women for various types of jobs.

Several basic points should be made about women's income. First, women are still paid less than men. But second, this fact is all the more important because so many more women are working now than previously. Of every 100 jobs in the U.S. economy, 43 are now held by women. And that percentage is rising because women are now getting about 55 percent of the 3.3 million new jobs the economy is creating each year. As of 1986 there were about 52 million women in the work force—55 percent of all women. Over 13 million of them were single, widowed, or divorced and so could not depend on a man for support. About 70 percent of the female work force are married.

In 1963 the Equal Pay Act made it illegal to discriminate against women by paying them less than men because of their gender. Yet all the figures show that this pattern continues. Why? The Labor Department has attempted to explain such earnings gaps this way:

> Historical patterns concerning "men's jobs" and "women's jobs" still persist. . . . Such sex stereotyping still seems to restrict or discourage women from entering many higher paying, traditionally male occupations. . . . Although women are as well educated as their male counterparts in terms of median years of schooling, there are differences in the kinds of education, training, and counseling they receive, which directs them into traditional and low-paying jobs.[3]

The percentage of women in professional and managerial jobs has risen from 33 percent in 1972 to 41 percent. But even so, only 22 percent of all

---

[1]Cynthia Taeuber and Victor Valdiser, *Women in the American Economy* (Washington, DC: Census Bureau, 1987).

[2]David E. Bloom, "Women and Work," *American Demographics*, September 1986, pp. 25–30.

[3]Department of Labor, "The Earnings Gap between Men and Women" (Washington, DC: Department of Labor, 1976).

TABLE 14.1

Earnings of Women and Men for Full-Time Work, by Occupation

OCCUPATIONAL GROUP	MEDIAN ANNUAL WAGE OR SALARY INCOME[a]		RATIO OF WOMEN'S MEDIAN ANNUAL INCOME TO MEN'S	RATIO OF WOMEN TO MEN IN THIS TYPE OF EMPLOYMENT
	Women	Men		
Professional and technical workers	11,995	18,224	0.66	0.55
Managers and administrators	9,799	18,086	0.54	0.24
Sales workers	6,825	16,067	0.42	0.34
Clerical workers	8,601	13,966	0.62	3.11
Crafts workers	8,902	14,517	0.61	0.04
Machine operators (including transport)	7,350	12,612	0.58	0.38
Service workers (except private household)	6,330	10,338	0.61	0.86
Private household workers	2,714	—[b]	—	—
Nonfarm laborers	7,441	10,824	0.69	0.09
Totals	8,618	14,626	0.59	0.49

[a]Median income is the middle income; half of all workers in this occupation earn more than this and half earn less. The figures include all full-time workers, year round, age 14 and over.

[b]There are less than 75,000 men employed here, so the figures are not calculated.

Source: Adapted from Census Bureau, *A Statistical Portrait of Women in the United States: 1978* (Washington, DC: GPO, 1980), p. 76. These are the latest such figures available.

working women are now professionals or managers. The leading occupations for women continue to be secretary, elementary-school teacher, bookkeeper, cashier, and store clerk, according to the Census Bureau.[4]

In our society, work is defined as labor for which one is paid. This has meant that women have received neither income nor credit for their work in the home. Today it is common for women to work outside the home and continue to play the role of wife and mother inside the home. The result, according to Cynthia Lloyd and Beth Niemi, is this:

> Men's behavior has been changing as well, but by no means as rapidly or as radically as women's. This lack of complementary change has created strains and stresses both at home and on the job. Traditional functions must still be performed, but they are by no means equally shared. As a result, most working women are in fact moonlighting, holding down one job during the day and another in the evening, in order to sustain the physical, financial, and emotional health of the household.[5]

About 8.5 million families (about 15 percent of all families) are headed by women. These women are forced to assume burdens even greater than those borne by working wives, who at least have husbands to share the load at home. The median income of women working full time is $15,600—versus a $24,004 median income for men.[6] And this is true even though 1.4 million women moonlight "officially"—that is, hold down more than one paying job.[7]

Whether they are married, widowed, separated, or divorced, women continue to work outside the home in greater numbers. It is estimated that by 1990 only a quarter of all American wives will stay home to care for children. Today the figure is about one-third. Indeed, almost half the mothers with children under the age of one year are now in the work force, as are 60 percent of those whose youngest child is three to five years old.[8]

All these changes in work patterns—at home as well as on the job—will put new pressures on the economic and political systems. They have already caused big changes in attitudes.

[4]UPI dispatch, "Census Report Finds Women Still in Traditional Jobs," *New York Times*, November 20, 1985.

[5]Cynthia Lloyd and Beth Niemi, *The Economics of Sex Differentials* (New York: Columbia Univ. Press, 1979), p. 315.

[6]These Census Bureau figures are for 1984, the latest year available.

[7]See Nadine Brozan, "Women Now Hold 30 Percent of 2nd Jobs," *New York Times*, June 24, 1980.

[8]Ellen Goodman, "Pregnant Workers Need Both Equal and Special Treatment," *Austin American-Statesman*, April 12, 1984.

Feminist Gloria Steinem. (Mark Klamkin/Black Star)

Attitudes toward Women

The United States, like the rest of the world, is still beset by sexism—"the range of attitudes, beliefs, practices, policies, laws, and behaviors discriminating against women (or against men) on the basis of their gender."[9] These attitudes are nothing new. Indeed, they have lessened somewhat over the years. Today, many women and growing numbers of men would agree with Dr. Joyce Brothers's assertion that "no one should be denied equal rights because of the shape of her skin."[10]

Public attitudes have indeed changed. As she surveyed the recent past, Gloria Steinem reminded readers of *Ms.* magazine that

> . . . every major issue raised by the Women's Movement now has majority support in national public opinion polls: from the supposedly "easy" ones like equal pay, women in political office, and equal access to education to the supposedly "controversial" ones like the Equal Rights Amendment, a woman's right

to choose abortion and "would-you-work-for-a-women?" That represents a major change from the early '70s when most such issues were supported by only a minority; and an even bigger change from the '60s, when they weren't included in public opinion polls at all.[11]

Nonetheless, there remain big differences in attitudes, not only between women and men, but also among women. Such differences are hardly a recent development.

Women's Objectives in Politics

Women were active in the antislavery movement early in the last century, and in a sense, the origins of the women's rights movement might be traced to their experience in that campaign. In 1840 there was a World Antislavery Convention in London. The American women delegates were refused admission because of their sex. When the American men then refused to participate, a compromise was reached: The women were allowed to sit in the balcony—but with a curtain drawn in front of them so that they wouldn't distract the men by their presence.[12]

The outrage of women at this treatment by supposedly enlightened men led eventually to the calling of a Women's Rights Convention at Seneca Falls, New York, in 1848. It issued the Women's Declaration of Independence, modeled on the American declaration and drafted by activist Elizabeth Cady Stanton. The declaration said in part:

> We hold these truths to be self-evident: that all men and women are created equal. . . . The history of mankind is a history of repeated injuries and usurpation on the part of man toward woman, having in direct object the establishment of absolute tyranny over her. . . . He has endeavored in every way that he could, to destroy woman's confidence in her own powers, to lessen her self-respect and to make her willing to live a dependent and abject life.

Stanton and some others insisted then that women had "a sacred right to the elective franchise." But the question of the right to vote split the movement at that time. For some time thereafter, most active efforts were directed at self-help

---

[9]Constantina Safilios-Rothschild, *Women and Social Policy* (Englewood Cliffs, NJ: Prentice-Hall, 1974), p. 1.

[10]*Washington Post*, March 6, 1971.

[11]Gloria Steinem, "The Decade of Women," *Ms.*, December 1979, p. 71.

[12]Page Smith, "From Masses to Peoplehood," *Historical Reflections* 1 (1974), 118.

Elizabeth Cady Stanton. (National Portrait Gallery, Smithsonian Institution)

through trade union organization and negotiation with employers. But at this time, as we shall see in more detail in Chapter 15, even men had difficulty organizing unions, and little was gained by women using this approach.

Legal Protection

As a result, women turned to governments for protection. Constitutional interpretation at that time reserved to the states the power to police business and private property in the interest of health, welfare, and safety. Therefore, appeals were made to the states. The leading organization at the time was the Women's Christian Temperance Union (WCTU). Its name, however, is misleading, for it campaigned not only against alcoholic beverages but also for city sanitation, child-labor laws, abolition of prostitution, improved working conditions, and many other progressive causes. The WCTU was very well organized. It had some 40 departments and perhaps 10,000 local "unions," or branches. It succeeded in getting a variety of laws passed that protected women, particularly in the

work place. But because the laws did not apply to men also, men were able to get and keep the riskier, more demanding jobs—so to women were left the jobs with the lowest pay and with the least prospects of advancement.[13]

Legal Equality

When it became clear that such protective legislation was not enough, women began to seek laws designed to achieve equality. Such laws have been the focus of what is now usually called the women's liberation movement (WLM) in its political manifestations. The WLM can trace its origins back at least as far as the early years of this century, as the description of presently active women's political groups in Action Unit 14.1 reveals. Two organizations have been particularly prominent in recent efforts to achieve equality through law: the National Organization for Women (NOW) and the National Women's Political Caucus (NWPC). We shall examine them and their efforts shortly.

The Equal Rights Amendment

In recent years, much attention and many resources have been devoted to ratification of the ERA. The ERA asserts simply: "Equality of rights under the law shall not be denied or abridged by the United States or by any state on account of sex." Congress submitted the ERA to the states for ratification in 1972. Within a year, 30 state legislatures had ratified it. Because the approval of only 8 more states was required, and because Congress had provided 7 years for the process, most thought the amendment would be easily adopted. But by then opponents were organizing.

The basic function of an ERA is to shift the burden of proof onto those who wish to discriminate so that they must show that they are not behaving illegally. Without ERA anyone claiming to face discrimination must challenge it in local, state, or federal court, using existing laws against discrimination. There are still more than 800 sections of the U.S. Code that make sexual distinctions. There are thousands more such laws at lower levels. Even

---

[13]The WCTU is active to this day, claiming some 250,000 members and 4500 local unions, and fighting the abuse of alcohol while *opposing* the ERA.

How to Contact Women's Political Organizations

American Association of University Women (2401 Virginia Ave. NW, Washington, DC 20037), one of the oldest women's organizations, sponsors various political and education projects and has local chapters throughout the country.

American Civil Liberties Union Women's Rights Project (22 E. 40th St., New York, NY 10016) has programs for litigation of sex-discrimination projects and lobbies Congress.

Black Women's Agenda (2018 16th St. NW, Washington, DC 20009) works for equity in education, employment, housing, and politics.

Center for the American Woman and Politics, Eagleton Institute of Politics (Rutgers University, New Brunswick, NJ 08901), a nonpartisan research and educational center, sponsors programs to increase knowledge about American women's participation in government and politics.

Center for Women's Policy Studies (2000 P St. NW, Washington, DC 20036) runs many programs of research and education on policy issues of concern to women and publishes the *Yearbook in Women's Policy Studies*.

Eagle Forum (Box 618, Alton, IL 62002), founded by Phyllis Schlafly, a leader in the campaign against the ERA.

League of Women Voters (1730 M St. NW, Washington, DC 20036) consists of women and men interested in nonpartisan political action and study and works to increase participation and to provide information on candidates, platforms, registration, and balloting; also has state and local branches throughout the country, listed in the telephone book, which publish booklets on how state and local governments work and how women can be politically effective.

Mexican American Women's National Association (1201 16th St. NW, Washington, DC 20036) seeks to advance the status of women of Mexican descent through leadership development.

National Organization for Women (1401 New York Av. NW, Washington, DC 20005), which consists of women and men interested in civil rights for women, acts through political, educational, and legal means to improve the condition of women.

National Women's Law Center (1616 P St. NW, Washington, DC 20036) provides free legal services for individual women and women's organizations in their area of employment.

National Women's Educational Fund (624 9th St. NW, Washington, DC 20001) offers technical training to prepare women for party and political office.

National Women's Political Caucus (1725 K St. NW, Washington, DC 20005) is composed of organizations and persons interested in greater involvement of women in politics; it runs workshops on practical politics for potential candidates and publishes educational materials as well as a newsletter.

Washington Institute for Women in Politics (Mount Vernon College, 2100 Foxhall Rd., Washington, DC 20007) develops work-study programs for students, provides on-the-job training for women interested in public service, and runs conferences and workshops.

Wider Opportunities for Women (1325 G St. NW, Washington, DC 20005) seeks to provide equal access to jobs, career guidance, education, and training to women.

Women's Campaign Fund (815 15th St. NW, Washington, DC 20005) is a nonprofit fund-raising group that seeks to raise campaign money for outstanding women candidates for elective office at the federal or state level.

Women's Equity Action League (1250 Eye St. NW, Washington, DC 20005) consists of individuals seeking to promote full enforcement of antidiscrimination laws as well as abortion rights and the ERA.

Women's International League for Peace and Freedom (1213 Race St., Philadelphia, PA 19107) since 1915 has campaigned for peace, freedom, justice, education, and international action, using the slogan "A woman's place is in the world."

Women's Legal Defense Fund (2000 P St. NW, Washington, DC 20036) is composed of lawyers and interested citizens; it provides free legal assistance in sex discrimination cases and publishes educational materials on employment discrimination, on credit problems of women, and for married women who retain their premarriage names.

Sources: Literature provided by various organizations: Congressional Quarterly's *Washington Information Directory*; Phyllis Butler and Dorothy Gray, *Everywoman's Guide to Political Awareness* (Millbrae, CA: Les Femmes Publishers, 1976); and Women's Action Alliance, *Women's Action Almanac* (New York: Morrow, 1979).

(Owen Franken/Sygma)

(Rick Friedman/Black Star)

without ERA these laws may be challenged in federal court—the Fourteenth Amendment says that no state may "deny to any person within its jurisdiction the equal protection of the laws." Furthermore, 17 states have ERAs in their own constitutions. But such legal processes are very slow and costly. The ERA would make it easier to win such challenges and would end the practice of placing sexual distinctions in new laws and regulations.

These arguments are less striking than the fears instigated by ERA opponents that the ERA would lead to women in combat, to homosexual marriages, and to coed toilets. As a consequence, only five more states ratified before the original deadline was reached. Furthermore, some states then tried to rescind, or take back, their ratification. (Legal experts argued that such a move was unconstitutional.[14]) Finally, Congress voted to extend the deadline until June 30, 1982. But resistance continued, culminating in the Republican party's decision to omit support of the ERA from its platform in 1980. The new deadline passed with the ERA still three states short of the number required for ratification.[15] The ERA has since been reintroduced in Congress but has failed to get the necessary two-thirds vote.

Abortion

Despite the Supreme Court decision in *Roe* v. *Wade* (1973) legalizing abortion under certain conditions (see Chapter 12), opponents still seek to outlaw

abortion. Because the Court's decision was made on *constitutional* grounds the only way it can be overturned is by a constitutional amendment. Nineteen states have called for a special constitutional convention to propose an antiabortion amendment. Such a procedure is the alternative to congressional passage of an amendment for submission to the states, as we saw in Chapter 1. Following the 1980 election, opponents of abortion introduced in Congress what they call a human life amendment, to guarantee a fetus's right to life from the moment of fertilization. However, they have not been able to pass it. Meanwhile, opponents of abortion in Congress have continued to attach a rider called the Hyde Amendment to appropriations bills. This rider prohibits the spending of federal funds to pay for abortions. This cluster of abortion issues promises to remain controversial.

Work of Comparable Worth

While the pattern of "ghettoized opportunities" may explain the wage and salary differential between men and women, it also suggests that the old formula "equal pay for equal work" will never overcome the income gap. Most women are not doing the same work as men, as Table 14.1 clearly shows. What then is needed? Activists now call for *equal pay for work of comparable worth*. They argue that jobs should be evaluated in terms of the skills they demand and the responsibilities they impose. If two jobs do require similar skills and responsibilities, then the jobs are of equal value or involve comparable work. Thus, persons holding the two jobs should be paid equally, even though the jobs themselves are different.

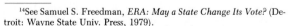

[14]See Samuel S. Freedman, *ERA: May a State Change Its Vote?* (Detroit: Wayne State Univ. Press, 1979).

[15]For interesting explanations, see Jane J. Mansbridge, *Why We Lost the ERA* (Chicago: Univ. of Chicago Press, 1986); and Mary Frances Berry, *Why ERA Failed*, (Bloomington: Indiana Univ. Press, 1986).

Washington County, Oregon, called women prison guards matrons and paid them 30 percent less than it paid men prison guards, whom it called deputy sheriffs. The women sued, and in 1981 the Supreme Court held that the suit could be pressed. That decision opened the legal door to other comparable-worth cases. Meanwhile, the state of Washington was being sued by women who found that while it valued the skills of different jobs equally, it paid women less than men for doing equally skilled jobs. For example, it equated electricians and special secretaries in terms of skills but paid the secretaries almost $600 a month less. In December 1983 a federal court in Seattle ordered the state of Washington to spend almost a billion dollars to correct such inequities between its male and female employees. Over 100 states and cities have since reviewed their pay structures, and many have started raising the pay of certain jobs held primarily by women.

The Reagan administration's response has been to oppose comparable worth on grounds that, in the words of Civil Rights Commission chair Clarence Pendleton, it "is preferential treatment, just like [racial] quotas." His fellow commissioner Morris B. Abram has even argued that

> The attempt to write comparable worth into Federal laws marks a reversal of the civil rights revolution. Comparable worth moves from the assertion of civil and political equality, which we all support, to economic and social equality, which many of us do not support. Guaranteed economic and social equality have never been part of the heritage of a free country because they ultimately impinge on freedom, by making government the arbiter of the rewards of human effort.[16]

In general, the marketplace does not reflect equal value in terms of skills, effort, and responsibility—at least not in jobs that are predominantly held by women. As Helen Remick of the University of Washington (Seattle) points out: "Many systems evaluate responsibility for money but not for people. This hurts women because they tend to have jobs where they're responsible for people, like nurses and teachers."[17] The Equal Employment Opportunity Commission (EEOC) decided in 1980 to take action to change job-valuation practices that discriminate in this way. "For the average woman who works—who is increasingly the average woman—I do believe this is the issue of the 1980s." said EEOC head Eleanor Holmes Norton. A Chicago-based group called Women Employed has been filing lawsuits to force the wage-gap issue toward the Supreme Court. On their side, employers are resisting strongly. Their specialized interest group, the Equal Employment Advisory Council (EEAC), has a budget of over a million dollars a year and spends much of that opposing such proposals in the courts. The Business Roundtable argues that adoption of a comparable-worth policy could result in "a complete restructuring of the U.S. economy, costing billions of dollars." And another interest group, the National Public Employer Labor Relations Association, estimates that the cost to state and local governments alone could be $15 billion a year in increased wages to women.[18] This estimate gives us an indication of the scale of what many see as salary and wage discrimination against women today.

Sexual Harassment

Another growing issue is sexual harassment on the job—touching, jokes, lewd comments, and demands for sexual favors in return for raises or promotions or just to retain one's job. Surveys find that 60 to 75 percent of working women report such experiences. The EEOC started counting such reports in 1981. In the first five years, reported incidents increased by 50 percent. In 1986 the Supreme Court ruled that workers can sue their employers for sex discrimination on the grounds that sexual harassment by supervisors creates a hostile job environment, even if loss of a job or promotion is not involved.[19]

Other Issues

Comparable worth and sexual harassment are but two of the women's issues of the 1980s. Others include the following:

■ Eliminating *barriers to equity* in publicly funded educational, employment, and training programs

---

[16]Abram, "Against 'Comparable Worth'", *New York Times*, Nov. 4, 1985.

[17]Quoted in James W. Singer, "Undervalued Jobs—What's a Woman (and the Government) to Do?" *National Journal*, May 24, 1980, p. 862.

[18]See Singer, "Undervalued Jobs." See also "A Business Group Fights 'Comparable Worth,'" *Business Week*, November 10, 1980, pp. 100–105; and Leslie Bennetts, "The Equal Pay Issue: Focusing on 'Comparable Worth,'" *New York Times*, October 26, 1979.

[19]*Meritor Savings Bank v. Vinson* (1986).

- Promoting *healthy, safe working conditions*, especially for clerical workers, whose jobs rank second highest in numbers of victims of stress-related diseases, and for the 20 million workers whose jobs involve exposure to materials that could possibly cause genetic damage
- Providing *day care* for children, the elderly, and handicapped dependents of working women (only 1.6 million licensed day-care slots are now available for 6.9 million children under age six with working mothers)
- Requiring adequate *job benefits*, such as paid maternity leave, health care, health insurance, and pensions (only 20 percent of women in the private labor force are now covered by pensions)

These issues have been supported by members of the Congressional Caucus for Women's Issues, which includes 15 of the 23 women in Congress—and 81 men. They are among those that were drawn up into a "platform" by the National Commission on Working Women (NCWW) in cooperation with the Coalition of Labor Union Women, the Displaced Homemakers Network, and Wider Opportunities for Women. Many other groups have also emerged recently to represent women. (See Action Unit 14.1.) Yet, as with any social group, there remain grounds for wondering to what extent any particular group really represents women as a whole. It is impossible to speak with certainty of what women want or what women believe because the more than 100 million women in this country hold quite varying views.[20]

Despite the wide variations in women's views, however, certain important trends in opinion can be discerned. Carol A. Whitehurst suggests the breadth and depth of concerns motivating the women's movement and the differences among women over these issues:

> One group sees the root cause of oppression in economic exploitation, and suggests that women's liberation is part of a worldwide struggle of all exploited people against more powerful classes. . . . Another group within the movement is less interested in the economic basis of oppression than in the power struggle between men and women; it sees the oppressor not as the capitalist system but as men. . . .
>
> Depending on which branch of the movement she identifies with, a woman may feel that other women

are selling out or being bought off with token changes, or dividing women by rejecting those who are happy in traditional roles. Some feel the women's movement is only a fad which takes attention away from the more pressing problems of black liberation.[21]

Whitehurst nonetheless finds a common core to the movement: belief in the existence of sexism and in the necessity of changes to free people from oppression and create new opportunities.

Women's Organizations in Politics

Whatever the agreement on the general issues, disagreement is common on many specific questions, as we have already seen. This creates opportunities for many special-interest political-action groups. Some of the more prominent and long-lived ones are described in Action Unit 14.1.

The National Organization for Women (NOW) was founded in 1966 and has headquarters in Chicago. Its membership reached 250,000 in 1983, but by 1986 it was 150,000, mostly white and middle-class. Its concerns have been such issues as passage of the ERA and improvement in the job opportunities and pay of working women. In the past decade, in an effort to broaden its base and meet criticism, it has also taken up concerns of housewives, such as obtaining job training for divorced or widowed homemakers and establishing a "homemakers' bill of rights" giving each partner in a household legal right to equal portions of household income.

Lobbying is done by NOW and by other groups such as the Women's Lobby in Washington. But the practical, political arm of the women's movement is the National Women's Political Caucus, an umbrella group of 300 state and local caucuses with 77,000 members. It was founded in 1971 by such activists as Rep. Bella Abzug, black organizer Fannie Loù Hamer, author Betty Friedan, and journalist Gloria Steinem. At the founding meeting, Steinem declared:

> We don't want to elect female Uncle Toms who are themselves imitating men, and who, once in power, only serve to keep their sisters down. But we do want to take our rightful position as 50 percent of every elected and appointed body in this country. No one

---

[20]This has always been true, of course. See Judith A. Sabrosky, *From Rationality to Liberation: The Evolution of Feminist Ideology* (Westport, CT: Greenwood, 1979); and Sheila M. Rothman, *Woman's Proper Place: A History of Changing Ideals and Practices, 1870 to the Present* (New York: Basic Books, 1978).

[21]Carol A. Whitehurst, *Women in America: The Oppressed Majority* (Santa Monica, CA: Goodyear, 1977), p. 145.

gives political power. It must be taken. And we will take it.[22]

Since then, NWPC has run technical workshops on electoral politics at its biennial conventions, proposed women as nominees for governmental jobs, lobbied political parties for greater female representation, and lobbied candidates and Congress for more support of women's issues and passage of ERA.

Women's Roles in Politics

Voting

The voting turnout for women has increased to the point where it is now about equal to that of white men, except in the South, where more traditional attitudes keep some women from voting. But even on issues of women's rights, there has been no significant difference between men's and women's votes. However, starting in 1982 there appeared to be a growing gender gap in voting. In that year's congressional elections, exit polls found that women voted for Democrats more than men did. The difference was only about 4 percent—not enough to be the margin of victory in most races but enough to cause some Republican politicians to question the Reagan administration's attitudes on women's issues such as the ERA, abortion, and equal pay. Opinion polls since then have shown this gender gap widening.[23]

Representing

The American Congress is still effectively a male club. Never in history have there been more than two female senators at the same time—the number after the 1986 elections. In the House there were 24 women in 1987—an all-time record but still a mere 5 percent of the total. The numbers haven't changed much over the past several decades; there were 16 congresswomen and one female senator in 1955. And of the 9699 House members who have served since the founding, only 90 have been women.[24] And no woman has yet held any important leadership post in either house.

Members of a women's political action committee help women voters to register in June 1984. (NYT Pictures)

Would the presence of more women in Congress affect policy outcomes? No one can say for sure. But a study of the voting records of the 19 women in the House in 1975 found that a majority of women in both parties had voting records that were more liberal than those of their party leaders.[25] A study of women holding offices in state and local government in 1983 found the same thing. "Women elected and appointed officials' positions on issues ranging from federal regulation and the death penalty to the ERA and a constitutional amendment prohibiting abortion were consistently more liberal than men within the same office."[26] More generally, Harvard psychologist Carol Gilligan argues that because of their early experiences women tend to develop a moral view that is different from that of men. Women tend to stress interdependence and "an ethic of care," while men emphasize independence and "an ethic of rights," she has found in her studies.[27] If this different view were to influence the votes of an expanded women's group in Congress, policy outcomes might indeed be quite different.

Women have gained strength at the state and local levels in recent elections. By 1987 there were 1157 female state legislators—15 percent, or triple

---

[22]Quoted by Tim O'Brien, "Women Organize—For More Power," *Washington Post*, July 11, 1971.

[23]For the most comprehensive study yet of women's political attitudes, see the report of a Louis Harris survey, "How Women Live, Vote, Think. . .," *Ms.*, July 1984, pp. 51–66.

[24]Dena Kaye, "The Woman Politician 1980," *Town & Country*, October 1980, p. 181.

[25]Clayton Fritchey, "The Women's Caucus," *Washington Post*, April 24, 1976.

[26]The study was done by the Center for the American Woman and Politics, Rutgers University, and released in December 1983.

[27]Carol F. Gilligan, *In a Different Voice: Psychological Theory and Women's Development* (Cambridge: Harvard Univ. Press, 1982).

the number elected in 1970. But women held only 7 of the 279 top legislative leadership positions. Women also serve as mayors of 83 cities with populations of 30,000 or more—up from 7 in 1971. But that's only a rate of 10 percent, and only 4 of the 100 largest cities (Houston, Sacramento, San Francisco, and Toledo) have women mayors, while only 2 of the 50 states have women governors.[28]

There is good evidence that the American people are ready to support more women in politics. Gallup Polls show that 70 percent believe that the nation would be governed as well or better if more women held political office. And some 80 percent say that they'd vote for a women for president—up from 66 percent in 1973, and only 31 percent in 1937. Almost 37 million did vote for Geraldine Ferraro for vice-president in 1984. But women still occupy only 5 percent of all elective offices. This underrepresentation extends even to local school boards, of whose members only 13 percent are women.

Administering

Today the percentage of women in managerial posts in the government bureaucracy is 25 percent.[29] Reagan, like Carter, appointed three women to major cabinet posts. In 1969 President Nixon had declared that "a woman can and should be able to do any political job that a man can do." But he never appointed a woman to the cabinet or to the Supreme Court. His successor, Gerald Ford, did appoint a women to his cabinet. But when he was urged by many, including his wife, to appoint a woman to the Court, he found it impossible to find a "qualified" woman. That decision reminded some of Abigail Adams's plea to her husband, John Adams, to "Remember the Ladies" while drafting the Constitution. John Adams's response was: "I cannot but laugh. . . . We know better than to repeal our Masculine systems." And when Betty Ford stated her support for abortion, President Ford criticized the Supreme Court decision making it constitutional. So Letty Cottin Pogrebin, a feminist activist, wrote:

> Thanks to Abigail Adams and Betty Ford, we have learned that we cannot marry power; we must have

it ourselves. . . . Asking men to Remember the Ladies just won't do. We must speak for ourselves, fight for ourselves, invent our own futures. In the nation's third century, let us celebrate the Bicentennial in the only way that makes sense. By using our vote, our voice and our rage to plot the next and deepest American Revolution—the one that frees the real silent majority: womankind.[30]

Responses of the American Political System to Women

The women's movement has already achieved passage of important legislation. In 1963 Congress passed the Equal Pay Act, which extended protection to some—but far from all—women workers. In 1964 opponents of the Civil Rights Act added wording to the bill that made women another group to be protected. They did so in order to increase opposition to the bill, which was intended to help blacks. But favorable public reaction to the inclusion of women instead helped the bill pass. Since then, Title VII, as that part of the act was termed, has become a major part of the legal fight against sex discrimination.

An amendment to the Equal Pay Act passed in 1972 extended its coverage to the professions. Subsequent executive orders by presidents have banned job discrimination against women and minorities in the federal government and by federal contractors. Nonetheless, studies of government salaries still show considerable inequality.[31]

Most of the progress being made in women's rights is being made in the Supreme Court. It hasn't always been that way. In 1948 the court upheld a law that prohibited a woman from being a bartender unless she was the wife or daughter of a male bar owner. This ruling meant that a women could be a bartender if her father owned the bar but not if he died and her mother became the owner. It meant that a women could tend bar in a tavern owned by her husband but not in one owned by her brother—or by herself. It meant that a woman could be a waitress in a bar but not a bartender.

None of this bothered the Court in 1948. But in 1976, just 28 years to the day after the original de-

---

[28]See Doml Bonafede, "Still a Long Way to Go," *National Journal*, Sept. 13, 1986, pp. 2175–2179.

[29]The figures are from a 1984 Census Bureau analysis. See "Women Increase Roles in Management, Study Says," *Austin American-Statesman*, April 11, 1984.

[30]Letty Cottin Pogrebin, "Sexism Rampant," *New York Times*, March 19, 1976.

[31]Mike Causey, "Men Top U.S. Pay Scales," *Washington Post*, December 29, 1976.

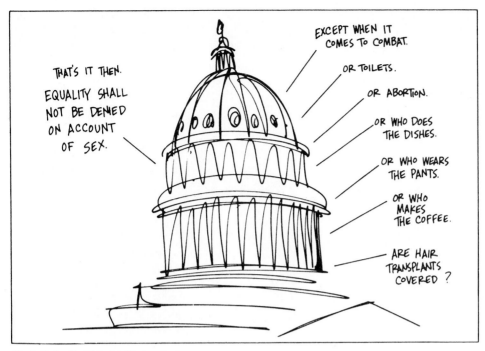

(By Auth for the Philadelphia Inquirer)

cision, the Court changed its mind. It held unconstitutional an Oklahoma law which prohibited the sale of 3.2 percent alcohol beer to men under the age of 21 and to women under the age of 18. It held that this discrimination—against young men—was unconstitutional because it was not "substantially related to important governmental objectives." In other words, sex discrimination is legal only if it involves a matter of important governmental objectives.[32]

Many of the laws now felt to be most discriminatory were introduced to protect women. These included statutes concerning maximum daily or weekly working hours for women, as well as exclusion from occupations such as mining and bartending and from those requiring the lifting of heavy objects. In 1973 the Supreme Court asserted that "statutory distinctions between the sexes often have the effect of invidiously relegating the entire class of females to inferior legal status without regard to the actual capabilities of its individual members." Sex discrimination, it pointed out, "was rationalized by an attitude of 'romantic paternalism' which, in practical effect, put women, not on a pedestal, but in a cage."[33]

Still, in 1976 the Court ruled that bias in health insurance plans against pregnant workers was not sex discrimination. Then in 1977 it ruled against sick-leave pay for pregnancy. Such rulings reveal, as Susan Moller Okin has written, that "the judiciary, assuming the inevitability of the traditional structure of the family, has been far readier to refer to women's role or women's function than to acknowledge the importance of women's potential and their rights."[34] However, in 1987 the Court upheld a California law that grants pregnant women four months of unpaid maternity leave and guarantees them their old jobs back. Some saw this as a promising change in the Court's attitude.

Sometimes unsupportive attitudes in the judiciary are overcome in Congress. In 1978, for example, Congress passed a new pregnancy-disability law that in effect overturned the 1976 Court decision on pregnancy insurance. The new law, among other things, also made it illegal for an employer to refuse to hire or promote a woman because she is pregnant, to fire a worker who becomes pregnant, or to force a women to take maternity leave if she is able to continue to work.

In recent years Congress has passed laws guar-

---

[32]For an account of this case, see the editorial "Equal Rights: Still a Way to Go," *Washington Post*, December 27, 1976.
[33]*Frontiero* v. *Richardson*, 411 U.S. 677 (1973).

[34]Susan Moller Okin, *Women in Western Political Thought* (Princeton, NJ: Princeton Univ. Press, 1979), p. 273.

anteeing to women the right to get credit, the right to participate equally in school sports, the right to pensions, the right to tax deductions for child-care expenses, and the right to attend military academies. But the women's political agenda described above indicates that there is still a long way to go.

The Outlook

"An assessment of the entire array of government policies and programs to date," write Lloyd and Niemi,

> . . . suggests that, if anything, the government has reinforced traditional sex roles in the labor market rather than serving as an impetus for change.
> . . . it is only possible for the government to provide the impetus for further change if it commits substantial resources to the effort, both in terms of dollars and of talent, so that those who discriminate will find the cost of its continuation prohibitively expensive.[35]

Such an evolution in government policy will come only as a response to continued pressure from the women's movement. How might such pressure be developed? One possibility is through coalition politics. In the future, says Betty Friedan, "women will work closely with labor and civil rights groups on the burning issues of employment and health. Women in a certain sense will be the key to a new political alliance, to a human rights alliance."[36]

But others disagree. "Feminist activists have outlined a plethora of diverse programs and short-term goals," writes Judith Sabrosky.

> They are waging too many feminist battles on too many fronts without sufficient numbers, morale, or material. The source of this diversity lies primarily in the feminists' alignment with movements and causes extraneous to feminism. While the purpose of these alliances was to create allies and bolster numbers of supporters and subsequent political influence, the effect has been a female backlash. Other, less vocal supporters (the female silent majority), whose support is vital for the achievement of particularly long-term feminist goals, have been alienated.[37]

Many women now argue that the next emphasis for the movement should be on improving "family support systems" such as prenatal care, maternity or parenting leave, child care, and early-childhood

Betty Friedan. (Mark Peters/Black Star)

education programs. Women continue to bear most of the burden of raising children. Such programs would help to support child rearing while mothers combine it with a career—something financially necessary for, and often desired by, more and more women. Twenty percent of all children today live in single-parent households, most of them headed by women. The double burden of children and career in itself discriminates against both mothers and their children. Yet the U.S. lags behind many countries in providing such family support services. Indeed, 117 countries require that women be allowed to take leave from work to bear a child and return to the same job afterward. But not the United States.[38] Until American women get relief such as this job-protected parenting leave and child care, they will as a group continue to fare badly in the labor force. And if the women's movement does not emphasize these issues in coming years, many believe it will become increasingly irrelevant to most American women.

The movement has, of course, had very considerable success, as we have seen. In Sabrosky's words, "Woman has travelled a long road to come close to equality. More and more women control

[35]Lloyd and Niemi, *Economics of Sex Differentials*, pp. 307–8.

[36]Quoted in Judy Mann, "Friedan Much the Same: Society Is Changing," *Washington Post*, November 24, 1978.

[37]Sabrosky, *From Rationality to Liberation*, pp. 161–62.

[38]See Sylvia Ann Hewlett, *A Lesser Life: The Myth of Women's Liberation in America* (New York: Morrow, 1986).

their own lives, have a sense of who they are, and determine their own destinies."[39]

It will be up to women to decide the best course for the coming efforts to achieve real equality. What that course will be is not yet clear. What does seem clear is that the decision will be a political one—a struggle over claims to authority made by activists and scholars, by radicals and conservatives, by government officials and citizens, but perhaps most of all by women and by men.

THE YOUNG IN AMERICAN POLITICS

Those under the age of 18 constitute the single largest "group" in America. Yet—with a few exceptions—these 80 million citizens are still legally denied the right to vote. Nevertheless children have a large and growing interest in public policy—not just on issues of war and peace but also on education, health, welfare, and discrimination. Just when is a child mature enough to vote and to influence public policy? Does a child have rights?

The Rights of Children

As recently as 1967 children had no rights at all. Until that time the Bill of Rights was thought to apply only to adults. In that year the Supreme Court decided a case called *In re Gault*, brought by the father of one Gerald Gault, seeking his release from an industrial school. Gault had been sentenced in juvenile court to six years in the school for making an obscene phone call. He did not have a lawyer, his parents were not allowed to see the complaint against him, he was not allowed to cross-examine the person who complained, and he was prohibited from appealing by Arizona law. Had he been over 18, the maximum Arizona sentence for making an obscene phone call would have been a fine of $5 to $50 or two months in jail, and he would have been entitled to the above rights, as well as others contained in the Arizona and U.S. constitutions.

The Supreme Court considered the case and decided, for the first time in history, that "it would be extraordinary if our Constitution did not re-quire the procedural regularity and the exercise of care implied in the phrase 'due process.' Under our Constitution, the condition of being a boy does not justify a kangaroo court," one that pays no attention to fair rules or procedures. This decision granted children new rights—some, but not all, of the rights guaranteed by the Bill of Rights.

The Bill of Rights uses language such as "no person" and "the accused" that might seem to be universal. But according to the courts, children still don't have rights to bail or trial by jury, for example.[40] And in 1979 the Court upheld the constitutionality of state laws that allow parents to commit their minor children to state mental institutions without first granting the child a hearing. It argued that parents generally act in the best interests of their children, and so no hearing should be necessary even though some parents may at times be acting otherwise.

Children and the Political System

The federal government has a long but slowly growing history of involvement in the issue of children's rights.[41] The first White House conference on children occurred in 1909. Three years later the Children's Bureau was set up to study and report on the welfare of children. When Congress in the 1920s passed several bills outlawing child labor, the Supreme Court declared them unconstitutional overextensions of federal power. Congress then passed a proposed constitutional amendment granting it the "power to limit, regulate, and prohibit the labor of persons under eighteen years of age," but only 28 of the 38 required states ratified it. Eventually, the Court sustained child labor laws passed in 1937. But until 1958 private Catholic charities in big cities, which got public money for their child welfare programs, were sufficiently strong to force the government to limit other federal programs to rural children. It was only in the Johnson and Nixon years that federal programs for children grew by leaps and bounds, with programs such as limited day care and Head Start, and a new Office of Child Development in the Department of Health, Education, and Welfare.

---

[39]Sabrosky, *From Rationality to Liberation*, p. 162.

[40]See Hillary Rodman, "Children's Rights: A Legal Perspective," in *Children's Rights: Contemporary Perspectives*, ed. Patricia A. Vardin and Ilene N. Brody (New York: Teachers College Press, 1979).

[41]See Gerald Grant, "Children's Rights and Adult Confusions," *Public Interest*, Fall 1982, pp. 83–99.

The Lobbyists for Children

In the development of such programs, the interests of children are lobbied for by various groups. The oldest is the Child Welfare League of America (CWLA), founded in 1920 as a league of voluntary organizations and today the most conservative child lobby. At the other end of the action spectrum is the Children's Defense Fund (CDF), a nonprofit organization of lawyers, researchers, and lobbyists, supported by foundations. CDF is dedicated to long-range advocacy for children, with six major areas of concern:

■ The right to education for children excluded from school

■ Elimination of classification and labeling of children (as retarded, for example)

■ The right to treatment and education for children in special institutions

■ The proper care and treatment of children by juvenile systems

■ The right to adequate medical care and the delivery of health services for children

■ The use and abuse of children as subjects for medical and drug research[42]

In the Reagan years the combination of severe economic recession and major cutbacks in federal programs hit children especially hard. Early in 1984 the Children's Defense Fund issued a new study which reported that (1) 3000 children fell into poverty with their parents every day between 1979 and 1982; (2) over 13 million children now lived in poverty—including one in every two black children and two in every five Hispanic children, as well as millions of whites; (3) infant death rates were again increasing in 11 states, so that babies born in Panama, Guyana, and Cuba now have a better chance of living until the age of one year than those born in some parts of the United States; and (4) as a result of Reagan's cuts of $10 billion a year in federal health, nutrition, education, childcare, and family-support programs, only 52 out of every 100 poor children received any welfare payments, and these averaged only $24.32 per week.[43] This situation has not improved significantly since 1984, as we shall see when we study poverty in Chapter 16.

Children's Needs and Rights

If anything, the needs of children seem to be growing from year to year, even when there is no economic recession. Two million children run away from home every year. Suicide is the third leading cause of death for those between the ages of 15 and 24. Reports of child abuse and neglect now total more than a million every year. The juvenile crime rate is higher than that of any other age group and is growing faster than the juvenile population. The rate of childbirth out of wedlock has doubled in the last 30 years. These signs indicate that there will be plenty of issues to be studied and programs to be supported by organizations like the CDF.

Many issues raise questions of children's rights directly. There is still a major dispute over whether children should have the right to medical care, including contraception and abortion, without their parents' consent. Similarly, it is unclear whether children have a right to decide which parent gets custody of them when the parents divorce. Does a child have a right to keep whatever money he or she earns working? Should children be able to sue their parents for neglect?

The questions of the rights of young people seem almost endless. Few of them have yet found their way into legislation or adjudication in court.[44] The states or the federal government already try to protect children from abuses such as child labor, exploitation, incest, physical brutality from parents, drugs and alcohol, pornography, rape, and other problems. But what about hitchhiking, for example? And what about the questions involving the rights of students in school?

By the same token, some question the advisability of welfare-oriented actions governments undertake for children while others term such actions grossly inadequate. One expert's conclusion is that "the children's policy most feasible—and most desirable—is one targeted on poor children, handicapped children, and children whose parents cannot provide them a start equal to that provided most children."[45] But others note Reginald Lourie's warning that "there is serious thinking among some of the future-oriented child development research people that maybe we can't trust the family alone

---

[42]For an account of children's lobbies and the politics of government programs, see Gilbert Y. Steiner, *The Children's Cause* (Washington, DC: Brookings, 1976), p. 255.

[43]The CDF report is entitled "America's Children in Poverty." See Carl T. Rowan, "Do Only the Unborn Matter?" *Washington Post*, February 7, 1984.

[44]For a status report see the paperback volume edited by Alan Sussman for the American Civil Liberties Union, *The Rights of Young People* (New York: Avon, 1977).

[45]Steiner, *Children's Cause*, p. 255.

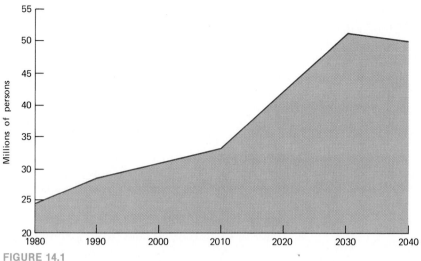

U.S. Census Bureau's Projection of Growth of the U.S. Population Age 65 and over, 1980–2040.

to prepare young children for this new kind of world which is emerging."[46] So children and politics seem certain to be linked more and more in coming years.

THE ELDERLY IN AMERICAN POLITICS

Today more than one in every nine Americans is 65 years of age or older. But by the time you're that old—if you're a typical college student—one in every five Americans will be old. In large measure, the elderly are supported by governmental services paid for by taxes that are paid by those still working. In 1955 there were seven people working and paying taxes for every retired person. In 1969 there was one retiree for every four workers. In 1974 there were three workers for every retiree. Now, every day in America 4950 people celebrate their 65th birthday, while 3300 people over age 64 die. Because the death rate in America is at an all-time low there are 1650 more elderly Americans every day. Therefore, by the next century—about a dozen years off—there will be only two workers for each person retired. In 1900 those over 65 made up only 4 percent of the U.S. population. By 1920 the figure had risen to 4.6 percent; by 1940, to 6.8 percent; by 1960, to 9.2 percent; it is now over 12 percent. According to some projections, those over 65

will make up over 20 percent of the American population by the year 2000. Figure 14.1 projects the growth of the U.S. population age 65 and older.

The Status of the Elderly

Many of these elderly are poor. Some 12.4 percent—3.3 million—are below the poverty line now, as compared to 30 percent in 1961, before Medicare and increased Social Security were introduced. Not all of the poor get help, although polls show that 80 to 90 percent of the American people believe that society should support the aged because they have earned such support by working all their lives.

The Problems of the Elderly

The biggest problem of our aged today is *economic security*. Our senior citizens have to live on relatively fixed incomes when inflation occurs, so their limited dollars buy less and less. One reason for this problem of economic security is the rapidly rising cost of health care. Even with Medicare, the average older American spends over $1500 out of pocket for health care each year.[47]

---

[46]Quoted from 1971 congressional testimony in ibid. Steiner.

[47]Stephen M. Davidson and Theodore R. Marmor, *The Cost of Living Longer: National Health Insurance and the Elderly* (Lexington, MA: Lexington Books, 1980), p. 6.

The federal government now allocates one-quarter of its outlays to the elderly.[48] Yet over three-quarters of all federal income transfers to the elderly consist of retirement benefits to which the elderly have contributed, such as Social Security. Certain parts of the Social Security system are in frequent financial trouble, and those approaching old age wonder how much they will be able to expect from it. Reform of the program continues to be a hot political issue.[49] Nonetheless, it is still true that "analysis of the income sources of elderly households shows that the elderly are largely supporting themselves through earnings, asset income, and benefits from retirement and pension plans to which they have contributed."[50]

A second growing problem for the elderly living in big cities is *physical security*. The rapid rise of crime takes its highest toll among the elderly, who are least able to escape or to defend themselves against hoodlums and con artists.

Finding ways to live *a meaningful life* after retirement is a third major concern. In 1900 some 68 percent of all men over 65 were still working. By 1960 that figure had dropped to 30 percent. Since then, with the spread of mandatory-retirement rules, the figure is down to 25 percent. In fact, the average retirement age continues to drop and is now approaching 60. Indeed, less than 75 percent of all men from 60 to 64 years of age are now working. Early and mandatory retirement are problems in our society not only because they often increase the ranks of the poor but also because we tend to view retirement as withdrawing from something rather than as an achievement. As a result, many people miss their work once it is behind them.

In June 1976 the Supreme Court, by a vote of eight to one, upheld a Massachusetts law requiring police to retire at age 50, regardless of their health. It argued that states are justified in assuming that the ability to perform official duties decreases with age and so in forcing early retirement. In the Court's view, drawing a line at age 50—unlike using race or religion as a criterion—"cannot be said to discriminate only against the elderly. . . . In-stead, it marks the stage that each of us will reach if we live out our life span." In fact, all the judges on the Court had already reached and passed that stage—and were still working. The youngest justice was then 51, and the average age of the justices was 63. But all of them were protected by the Constitution against forced retirement at any age except for bad behavior.

The following year, however, Congress passed a law extending the Age Discrimination in Employment Act so that it would prohibit mandatory retirement until age 70 for both federal workers and workers in private industry. This action followed passage of similar laws by a number of states from Maine to California. An end to mandatory retirement before 70 will please the many active employees who don't want to quit working as they approach 65. But it also makes it more difficult for the young and minorities to get jobs because fewer new jobs are being opened up by retirement. Indeed, this is a case where ending discrimination against one group automatically brings increased discrimination, practically speaking, against others.

Of course, continued work is not the only way for the elderly to maintain or increase their feelings that life has meaning. Continuing or adult education is another option—and one increasingly being tailored to the needs and interests of the aged.

For those who no longer like their jobs, early retirement may open up new possibilities—if they have adequate pensions. But fewer than half of all retirees now have pensions, and so the rest must live on Social Security alone—if they have that. Thus, early retirement may not be an option for most, unless and until the benefits available to the elderly are improved—something that becomes less likely when the financial difficulties of Social Security and Medicare mount.

What the Elderly Do Politically

Voting

Today one in every six voters is over the age of 65. It is commonly believed that as people age, they lose their interest in politics and vote less. It is generally true that those who are old now vote less than those who are middle-aged. But we find generally that the better educated people are, the more they vote. We also find that historically women have

[48]See Cheryl G. Swanson and Allan J. Cigler, "Senior Power and Public Policy" (Paper delivered at the Annual Meeting of the Southwest Social Science Association, 1979), p. 4.

[49]For a fascinating account of the politics behind the most recent reform of the Social Security system, see Paul Light, *Artful Work* (New York: Random House, 1985).

[50]W. Kip Viscusi, *Welfare of the Elderly* (New York: Wiley, 1979), p. 93.

voted less than men. The majority of the present elderly are less well educated, and the majority are women. So experts now believe that the fact that those presently elderly vote less is a reflection of these longstanding tendencies. In other words, those elderly who don't vote now didn't vote when they were younger either. Indeed, research shows that interest in politics actually grows as people get older. The aging seem to engage in all but the most strenuous types of political activity, such as canvassing.[51]

Serving

We still know relatively little about officeholding among the elderly except for those at the national level, where it's easy to count. The elderly are quite overrepresented in the Senate and House in comparison to their percentage in the population. This overrepresentation might suggest that the elderly would be well taken care of. But experience suggests, to the contrary, that the elderly in Congress rarely show special concern for the elderly in the rest of the population.

Administering

Until 1977 federal law prohibited people over the age of 70 from continuing to serve in the bureaucracy but not in appointive posts—for example, as justices of the Supreme Court or as ambassadors—or in elective posts. In 1977, as we noted earlier, Congress removed the provision for mandatory retirement at age 70, but the effect of this new law has not yet been widely felt.

The Elderly's Challenges to the American Political System

Groups supporting the elderly first became prominent during the Great Depression of the 1930s. A major reason, besides the troubled economic times, was the fact that the Social Security Act of 1935 provided for government payments to citizens who reached old age. This made it possible for the aged to live alone even after retirement, where previously they generally had to live with their children when they could no longer support themselves.

Maggie Khun, founder and leader of the Gray Panthers. (Dennis Brack/Black Star)

Further, the precedent of Social Security drew more attention to pensions generally, which were in most cases still inadequate to support the few elderly lucky enough to have them.

Interest Groups

Today there are three major groups representing the interests of the elderly.[52] The oldest, dating from 1921, is the 200,000-member National Association of Retired Federal Employees (NARFE). The largest is the combination of the National Retired Teachers Association (NRTA), established in 1947, and the American Association of Retired Persons (AARP), founded in 1958. The NRTA, a more specialized group, includes half a million retired teachers. The AARP is made up of 11.5 million people age 55 or older. The two groups have the same staff and devote most of their attention to providing services to members such as insurance, travel programs, and tax assistance.

---

[51]See Norval Glenn and M. Grimes, "Aging, Voting, and Political Interest," *American Sociological Review* 33 (1968), 563–75.

[52]See Henry J. Pratt, *The Gray Lobby* (Chicago: Univ. of Chicago Press, 1976); and Robert Butler, *Why Survive? Growing Old in America* (New York: Harper & Row, 1975), esp. pp. 343–49.

The most politically active of the three groups is the National Council of Senior Citizens. This group grew out of the 1960 Senior Citizens for Kennedy groups and was established to fight for passage of Medicare. It consists of about 3500 local clubs and 23 state affiliates, many of whose members come from organized labor. It keeps its members informed of important votes coming up in Congress so that they can lobby effectively.

The liberal and labor-oriented political stance of the NCSC encouraged the founding in 1975 of the more conservative National Alliance of Senior Citizens with some 20,000 members, free from labor influence but still without much political clout.

Other somewhat specialized groups have also been founded recently. In 1970 the National Center on Black Aged was established to represent its 2 million aged black members. And then in 1975 the Asociacion Nacional Pro Personas Mayores was founded in Los Angeles to do the same thing for Spanish-speaking elderly.

But perhaps the most interesting of the special groups is the Gray Panthers, founded in Philadelphia in 1970 to combat "ageism" abuses through direct action. The Gray Panthers was founded with the motto "age and youth in action," and the group includes 50,000 young members as well as older members in its 15 chapters in various cities.

Lobbying

How important these organizations are in influencing legislation is far from clear. So far, the evidence suggests that there is not an "aged vote" as such, and politicians are aware of that. Nonetheless, there are occasional instances where interest groups for the aged play important roles. But up to now, the organizations have tended to represent only the middle-class aged and those with trade union connections. The large numbers of elderly who are poor still lack adequate representation. Nevertheless, many government programs on the aged have been intended to help them.

Responses of the American Political System to the Elderly

Social Security was the first major federal program directly addressing the needs of the aged. Since 1935 the United States has moved closer and closer to becoming a **welfare state** in which the govern-ment meets the various human needs of its citizens. More and more it appears that the "welfare state is fundamentally focused on the aged."[53]

Today, some government programs are *direct income maintenance* programs. Social Security and related programs are the strongest examples. Others involve *indirect income maintenance* through food stamps, for example, which free up some income for other uses by providing food free or at a discount. Others involve *health care*: Medicare and Medicaid. Still others provide *social services* such as nutrition and legal services programs. And still others are *regulatory actions*, such as controls over nursing homes.

The proliferation of federal programs has several important causes. It is, of course, true that the proportion of old people in the population is growing. But as we have seen, the aged themselves have had a rather limited role in the passage of new laws. Organized labor has been a major factor. But also important is the fact that the Social Security program legitimized aid to the aged and created large bureaucracies with vested interests in more such programs. At the same time, it encouraged the organization of professionals dealing with the aged outside the government into strong groups, such as the American Public Welfare Association (of state and local welfare officials), the National Association of Social Workers, and the National Conference of Social Workers.

The 48 major federal programs directed specifically at the elderly make important contributions.[54] But where they are confined to the elderly, they miss much of the problem; for many of these needs—housing, income, health care—arise long before one turns 65. Thus, better screening and preventive health care in middle age could improve the welfare of the future elderly.[55] In any event, there are signs that the elderly themselves may be taking a more active role helping themselves and each other to meet their special needs.[56] It remains for us as a society to decide what rights the elderly do have and should have, above and beyond those owed to all citizens. In doing so, we would be wise to listen more closely than before to

[53]Harold Wilensky, *The Welfare State and Equality* (Berkeley: Univ. of California Press, 1975), p. 27.
[54]See Beth J. Soldo, "America's Elderly in the 1980s," *Population Bulletin*, November 1980.
[55]Viscusi, *Welfare of the Elderly*, p. 233.
[56]See Beth B. Hess, "Self-Help among the Aged," *Social Policy* (November–December 1976), 55–62.

the beliefs of the elderly themselves. As time passes, our elderly will inevitably become better educated, more socially skilled, and more affluent and will be in better physical health. Because they also, as elderly, will have high levels of political activity, they may become a powerful force for social change.[57]

But how will political action by the elderly, should it come in greater force, relate to the needs of other groups in society? Will the elderly be fighting for scarce resources against minorities, women, the young, and the handicapped? Or will the fact that so many of the elderly are also members of others of these groups lead them to take a broader view of the continuing, developing needs and desires of Americans? To a large extent, these decisions may well come to lie in our hands—not because we will make them for the elderly, but rather because we will be the elderly.

THE OTHER OUTSIDERS

The outsiders we've been studying—women, the young, and the elderly—are the most prominent groups commonly excluded from, or limited in, participation in politics. But they are hardly the only ones.

Homosexuals

There are such social—and political—stigmas attached to homosexuality that relatively few males (homosexuals) or females (lesbians) now "come out," or admit publicly their sexual preferences. Most experts seem in agreement, however, that 10 percent or more of the U.S. population is homosexual, or "gay"—the term most commonly preferred by homosexuals today. There are raging disputes among psychologists, clergy, and other professionals as to the causes of homosexuality and its "naturalness." As a result, there is a patchwork of laws concerning gays around the country. Until recently, homosexuality was against the law in every state. Since 1960 23 states have eliminated antigay laws. A Louis Harris survey in 1978 found that 70 percent of Americans believe that homo-

sexual relations between consenting adults in private should not be illegal. A Gallup Poll in 1983 found that 65 percent believe that homosexuals should have equal rights in job opportunities. Yet laws making homosexual conduct a crime do persist in many states and cities.

In 1986 a bitterly divided Supreme Court ruled five to four that the Constitution does not protect homosexual relations between consenting adults, even in the privacy of their own homes. The decision, in *Bowers* v. *Hardwick*, was seen as an interruption of the Court's extension of the right of privacy to areas of sexual conduct, which we examined in Chapter 12. It was a serious blow to the efforts of gay activists to gain legal sanction for homosexuality.

But one consequence was that the National Gay and Lesbian Task Force, the major gay lobbying group in Washington, received an outpouring of contributions from people aghast at the decision.

A gay and lesbian voter registration campaign.
(Charles Steiner/Sygma)

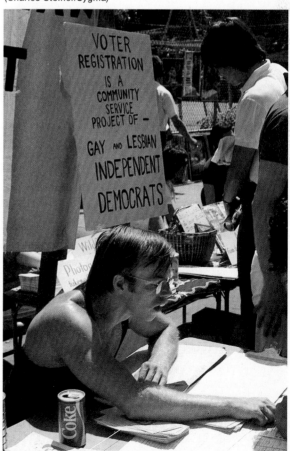

[57]This argument is developed in B. Neugarten, "Age Groups in American Society and the Rise of the Young-Old," *Annals of the American Academy of Political and Social Science* 415 (1974), 187–98.

The Human Rights Campaign Fund, a gay political action committee, raised more than $1.5 million to give to sympathetic candidates in the 1986 congressional elections—twice what it raised for the 1984 elections.[58]

The biggest issue for gays—and a rapidly growing concern for everyone—is Acquired Immune Deficiency Syndrome (AIDS). This viral disease cripples the immune system—the body's way of defending itself against illness. It thus virtually guarantees that someone who has it will die of whatever serious illness he or she contracts, such as pneumonia. The disease is spread primarily by sexual relations or blood transfusions, according to experts on it. Two-thirds of those who have it are homosexuals, but the other third are heterosexuals. The disease is spreading fast, with no cure in sight and no preventive vaccine available.

By 1987, 220 Americans were dying of AIDS every week, and 374 more, 28 of them heterosexuals, were being infected by it each week. As of 1986, 29,000 Americans had contracted AIDS. By 1991 estimates that many believe are too conservative are that 270,000 Americans will have it, and 179,000 of them will have died. The government's Centers for Disease Control estimate that 1.5 million Americans now carry the virus even though they show no symptoms. Thus the disease shows all the signs of becoming a real epidemic. Yet the government has not organized a major attack upon it. Many believe that this is because the disease has been seen as a problem of homosexuals. Each year since 1984 the White House has requested less money for research and education than the Public Health Service wanted. Each year Congress has appropriated much more. The 1987 total of $411 million doubled the Reagan request. But disease specialists say this is woefully inadequate.

The public is still not well informed about the disease, but many people fear that as information spreads, so will discrimination against those who have AIDS—and even those who *might* have it.[59] The major victims of such discrimination now are homosexuals. It already occurs in such areas as housing, insurance, employment, child custody, and health care. Such discrimination is understandable, given the incomplete state of expert knowledge and the massive public ignorance about the disease. The Justice Department in 1986 stated that federal laws protecting the handicapped from discrimination did not prohibit discrimination against AIDS victims. It said that employers could legally fire AIDS victims because of a "fear of contagion whether reasonable or not." Many states rejected this Justice Department opinion. A quarter of the states have adopted policies specifically barring such discrimination. Most other states have more general laws that should protect AIDS victims from discrimination. But many victims of discrimination—losing jobs and health insurance—are reluctant to sue for fear that a prolonged court case will kill them faster and that they will be dead before the case is decided. Thus, some AIDS-discrimination sufferers have taken their cases to the courts seeking a ruling that AIDS is indeed a physical handicap.[60]

In March 1987 the Supreme Court ruled that an individual who was physically impaired by a contagious disease could be classified as handicapped and therefore could not be fired simply because he or she was ill. The disease in question was tuberculosis, which is more easily transmitted than AIDS. Thus observers concluded that the Court would ultimately extend such protection to AIDS victims. But only time will tell how far such protection will be extended. And until a cure for AIDS is found, such legal protection will be little comfort for the disease's victims.

The Mentally Handicapped

Another large group facing discrimination and exclusion is present and former mental patients, or the *mentally handicapped* (as they are increasingly called). No one really knows how many mentally handicapped there are in America. But we do know that one in every ten Americans spends time in a mental institution at some time in his or her life. And according to an estimate by the President's Commission on Mental Health, almost 15 percent of the American people are in need of mental health

[58]Lisa Leff, "After the Supreme Court Defeat, a Resurgence of Gay Power," *Washington Post National Weekly Edition*, Sept. 8, 1986.

[59]See "AIDS: At the Dawn of Fear," *U.S. News & World Report*, January 12, 1987, pp. 60–70.

[60]Sandra G. Boodman, "As AIDS Spreads, So Does Discrimination," *Washington Post National Weekly Edition*, Dec. 8, 1986.

services for problems ranging from serious mental disturbances to alcohol and drug problems, juvenile delinquency, and anxiety.[61] And this figure does not include the 6,400,000 mentally retarded people in America today—1,057,000 of them children.

The problems of the mentally handicapped vary considerably, and so therefore do their needs. So, unfortunately, does the public's willingness to accept former mental patients who can live outside institutions.[62] The result has been government regulations requiring any company having government contracts in excess of $2500 to take affirmative action to employ the mentally and physically handicapped. The government itself also has new programs to hire the handicapped. Further, it funds special programs to train the retarded. In recent years many states and some cities have passed laws recognizing the rights of the handicapped. In addition, private organizations such as the Mental Health Law Project file suits to expand the recognized rights of these people. There are also "mental patient liberation" groups scattered about the country, devoted to giving mutual support to former patients and to defending their rights.

The Physically Handicapped

According to a 1986 Census Bureau study, one in five American adults suffers from some type of physical disability, and many suffer from more than one.[63] These physically handicapped face special problems. Barriers such as curbs, stairways, counters, and so on, make mobility difficult. But most of the handicapped would argue that the most difficult barriers to overcome are social: the unwillingness of most nonhandicapped people to relate openly and comfortably with those who, for example, have lost limbs, cannot speak, or are deaf or blind. However, some progress is being made with private and governmental help, toward equal opportunity for the handicapped. Such progress builds on Public Law 94–142, the Education for

TABLE 14.2

Number of Handicapped American Children and Teenagers

	NUMBER AFFECTED
Speech impaired	2,293,000
Mentally retarded	1,507,000
Learning disabilities	1,966,000
Emotionally disturbed	1,310,000
Crippled and other health impaired	328,000
Deaf	49,000
Hard of hearing	328,000
Visually handicapped	66,000
Deaf-blind and other multihandicapped	40,000

Source: National Advisory Committee on the Handicapped, *Annual Report,* 1976.

All Handicapped Children Act passed by Congress in 1975 and often referred to as the Bill of Rights for the Handicapped. This law guarantees for all handicapped children an appropriate education, something formerly available to only half of such children. Table 14.2 shows the number of handicapped children and teenagers according to type of handicap.[64]

The handicapped have always had a difficult time receiving attention, let alone assistance. On April 6, 1977, groups belonging to the American Coalition of Citizens with Disabilities (ACCD) occupied various Washington offices of the Department of Health, Education, and Welfare, including that of the secretary himself. HEW still had not issued the regulations required to implement the Rehabilitation Act of 1973. Twenty-two days after the "wheel-in" began, the regulations were issued, and the process was begun.[65]

The act had been vetoed twice by then President Nixon on financial grounds before it was finally approved. Section 504 required that handicapped people have equal access to all federally financed programs. Later amendments in 1978 resulted in establishment of the Architectural and Transportation Barriers Compliance Board. Among the people President Carter appointed to its 11 slots

[61]"Estimated Mental Illness Increases," National Association of Social Workers, *News*, October 1977, p. 7.
[62]See Joseph Halpern et al., *The Myth of Deinstitutionalization: Policies for the Mentally Disabled* (Boulder, CO: Westview, 1980).
[63]Census Bureau, *Disability, Functional Limitation and Health Insurance Coverage: 1984–85* (Washington, DC: GPO, 1986).

[64]See John Gliedman and William Roth, *The Unexpected Minority: Handicapped Children in America* (New York: Harcourt Brace Jovanovich, 1980), a report of a comprehensive study sponsored by the Carnegie Council on Children.
[65]See James Haskins, *The Quiet Revolution: The Struggle for the Rights of Disabled Americans* (New York: Crowell, 1979).

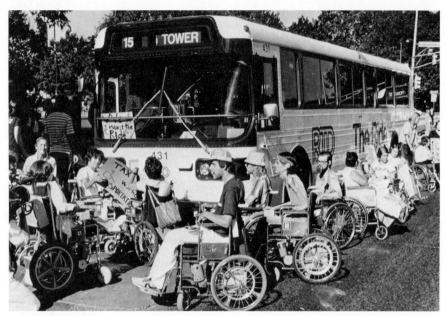

A protest by Denver's Disabled Citizens against the inaccessibility of public transportation for wheelchair disables. (UPI/Bettmann Newsphotos)

were six in wheelchairs, one blind person, and two with hearing problems. The board's staff also included many with handicaps, including even Bobby Van Etten, the three-foot, two-inch president of Little People of America. Not surprisingly, the board proved very militant in issuing regulations for ramps, elevators, toilets, and so on, in all federal buildings just before Carter left office.[66]

In the Reagan years, a backlash developed over the enormous cost of special provisions for the physically handicapped. The greatest problem thus far has been with mass transit. Experts estimated that complying with the rules there could cost an extra $7 billion over 30 years. Schools, too, have found the rules very expensive. Many now wonder whether society can afford such broad recognition of the rights of the disabled.[67] The Reagan administration therefore took steps to rescind many of the

advances achieved in the Carter years. And the Supreme Court ruled that Section 504 did not require "affirmative action" by recipients of federal grants.

Other Outsiders

The list of outsiders can be extended further—to soldiers, to veterans, to prisoners, and even to dwarfs and fat people. Like those whose problems we have been examining here—women, the young, and the elderly—such outsiders confront a world and a political system designed and run by people who may neither know nor care about their special needs and desires. But as our account has shown, outsiders, like minorities, are increasingly challenging our political system. Sometimes they do so by opposing the insiders who run it; at other times they do so by posing policy problems for the system to resolve. In Part 5 we shall examine how the government and the interests interact to produce public policy. We shall also consider major policy problems involving the economy, poverty and property, the cities, energy and the environment, and foreign affairs.

---

[66]See Timothy B. Clark, "Here's One 'Midnight Regulation' That's Slipped through Reagan's Net," *National Journal*, February 7, 1981, pp. 221–24.

[67]See Harrison Donnelly, "Equality for the Handicapped: Can the Nation Afford It?" *Congressional Quarterly*, May 31, 1980, pp. 1505–09.

SUMMARY

Women have virtually attained equality in education, but they are still paid less than men at work, despite the Equal Pay Act of 1963. Many have advocated the Equal Rights Amendment to help women by shifting the burden of proof of discrimination onto those who discriminate. However, the ERA has not been ratified—falling three states short of ratification in 1982. Other women's issues on which progress has been made include abortion and equal pay for work of comparable worth. The women's political agenda also now includes such issues as working conditions, sexual harassment, day care, and job benefits. To seek these objectives, women have organized politically. The major groups active today include the National Organization for Women and the National Women's Political Caucus.

Women's voting turnout is now about equal to that of white men, but there is a gender gap, in that women are more likely to vote Democratic than are men—a tendency that emerged during the Reagan administration. But women still hold only 4 percent of all governorships, 5 percent of the seats in Congress, and 13 percent of seats in state legislatures. They make up about 25 percent of the federal bureaucracy but hold only a few cabinet posts. Today, there is one woman on the Supreme Court (the first ever appointed). Thus, women still have a long way to go to reach political equality.

The young are the largest group fully excluded from politics, for they can neither vote nor serve in government. Until recently, children had no rights at all. Gradually, the courts are extending certain protections of the Bill of Rights to children. Their interests are supported politically by groups such as the Children's Defense Fund, but their claims are still controversial.

A growing percentage of all Americans are elderly, and the trend is increasing. Many of the elderly are poor, trying to live in retirement on relatively fixed incomes in a time of inflation. Until recently, the elderly were not very active in politics, but that is now changing. Many public officials are above retirement age. The elderly now have their own interest groups, which lobby with increasing effectiveness in Washington. There are now 48 major federal programs directed specifically at the elderly, but many of the latter's problems begin before they become old, so the programs do not suffice.

Among other outsiders seeking greater roles in politics or more benefits from politics are homosexuals, the mentally handicapped, the physically handicapped, and groups such as veterans and prisoners.

Suggestions for Further Reading and Study

The chapter footnotes in each section have already pointed to many useful works, but several others should be mentioned. On women's history, see Eleanor Flexner, *Century of Struggle: The Women's Rights Movement in the United States* (Cambridge, MA: Harvard Univ. Press, 1959). For philosophy, see Mary Anne Warren, *The Nature of Women: An Encyclopedia and Guide to the Literature* (Inverness, CA: Edgepress, 1980). For policy, see Jessie Bernard, *Women and the Public Interest: An Essay on Policy and Protest* (Chicago: Aldine-Atherton, 1971); and Dorothy Jongeword and Dru Scott, *Affirmative Action for Women: A Practical Guide* (Reading, MA: Addison-Wesley, 1973). And for further guidance to the movement or the literature, see Phyllis Butler and Dorothy Gray, *Everywoman's Guide to Political Aware-* *ness* (Millbrae, CA: Les Femmes Publishers, 1976); and the *Women's Action Almanac*, produced by the Women's Action Alliance (New York: Morrow, 1979).

On children, see Richard Farson, *Birthrights* (New York: Macmillan, 1974). See also Patricia A. Vardin and Ilene N. Brody, eds., *Children's Rights: Contemporary Perspectives* (New York: Teachers College Press, 1979).

The most accessible comprehensive introduction to the elderly is Robert N. Butler, *Why Survive? Being Old in America* (New York: Harper & Row, 1975). But for comprehensive treatment in depth of a wide range of more specialized topics, there is no substitute for Robert H. Binstock and Ethel Shanas, eds., *Handbook of Aging and the Social Sciences* (New York: Van Nostrand Reinhold, 1976).

Perspective

THE POLITICS OF POLICY MAKING: The Case of Shoe Imports

Take a look at the shoes you're wearing. Where were they made? More likely than not, they were made in a foreign country. If they were either very cheap or very expensive, the odds are overwhelming that they were foreign made. By buying them, you became a part of—part of the cause of—a major policy problem for the United States government.

That problem is, how many foreign-made shoes should be allowed into the country? Imported shoes are cheaper than home-made footwear, and American shoe factories have trouble competing with them. Thus, more shoe imports mean more American shoe factories shut down—and more workers jobless. But fewer shoe imports mean higher prices on shoes for American consumers. Shoe imports have thus been a problem for every president from Ford through Carter to Reagan. We'll find out how—and what each did about it—in this perspective.

In studying the case of shoe-import policy, we will also be learning how our government makes

policy. Which actors get involved? How do they decide what to do? What determines which interest groups succeed in getting their way? Government makes policy every day, and it is important to know how the policy process works in order to understand the politics of the various policies we'll be studying in this concluding part of the book.

THE POLITICS OF SHOES

When Ronald Reagan took office, he faced runaway inflation, sky-high interest rates, endless conflict in the Middle East—and shoe problems. When Jimmy Carter took office, he faced a chronic recession, high unemployment, rocky relations with the Soviet Union—and shoe problems.

The policy each president adopts on shoe imports affects the choice of shoes available in your stores and the prices you have to pay, whether or not the shoes you buy are imported. That policy also affects the cost of living for all of us, the jobs of thousands of Americans, the profits (or losses) of many businesses, and our nation's relations with other countries. Examining the politics behind the development of that policy will tell us much about the process of policy making in America.

On January 6, 1977, just two weeks before President Carter took office, the United States International Trade Commission recommended a *tariff-rate quota* on shoes. By doing so, it presented Carter with one of his first difficult policy decisions. To understand what was at issue, and what was at stake, we must first look more broadly at the place of the shoe industry in America's economy and in the world economy as well.

The Shoe Industry in America

Like all countries, the United States has long had its own shoe industry. Until recently, the factories—concentrated in Massachusetts, Ohio, Wisconsin, Maryland, and Pennsylvania—made most of the shoes Americans wore. In the early 1960s they employed almost 250,000 people, who made over 600 million pairs of shoes a year, more than three pairs for every American each year.

Shoemaking is what is called a labor-intensive, low-skill business. The major ingredient is labor, with a low level of skills, rather than capital (money, to buy expensive modern equipment). Because of this, shoemaking is an easy business for a less developed country to enter, for such a country has plenty of unskilled labor but little capital to invest in machinery.

In the 1960s this is just what happened. In the United States the cost of making shoes was increasing, for several reasons. American factories did not modernize by developing and buying new, more efficient equipment. At the same time, labor costs were increasing in three ways. First, wages were rising. Second, employers had to contribute more and more to Social Security and pension plans for many workers. And third, employers were also required by our government to improve the working conditions in their factories.

The result was that shoes could be made much more cheaply in a country like Italy. So American businesses began importing more and more shoes from Italy and other countries to sell here to Americans. To import them, they had to pay *duty*—a tax that is a percentage of a product's value—to the

government. This duty, or tariff, as it is also called, is imposed in part to raise revenue. Indeed, before the income tax was imposed, such tariffs were the chief source of income for the federal government. But duties have another function: to protect domestic industry from foreign competition by raising the price of imported goods.

In earlier years, America had high tariff barriers—a policy often referred to as **protectionism.** In recent decades, efforts have been made by many countries to lower tariffs on most goods and move toward *free trade.* Ninety-eight countries do this by getting together and negotiating under what is called the General Agreement on Tariffs and Trade (GATT).

By the 1970s the American tariff on shoes was only 10 percent of their value. This meant that it would pay for a business to import shoes if their cost abroad was so low that they could still be sold more cheaply than shoes made here, even after the 10 percent tariff and the cost of shipping were added.

As American wages rose, this price advantage became even greater. By 1976 wages for shoemakers averaged $3.25 an hour in America but only $1.79 in Italy, for example. In 1963 we imported only 14 percent of our shoes. By 1975 the figure was 45 percent, and in 1977 it was more than 50 percent. As a result, some 70,000 American shoe workers lost their jobs over the years since 1968. And over a 15-year period, the number of American shoe factories dropped from 1000 to 350. Furthermore, the outlook was bleak. Other countries, where wages were even lower, were now exporting to the United States. Indeed, Taiwan and Korea alone sent 200 million pairs to the United States in 1976, and almost all sold for less than $10. Italy shipped 47 million pairs, Spain 39 million, and Brazil 27 million.

Shoes Enter American Politics

The Interests and the Imports

Among those who benefited from this increase in imported shoes were the *consumers*, who were spending a smaller percentage of their income on shoes (and other clothing) in the 1970s than they had in previous decades. Other major beneficiaries were the *shoe importers*, of course, and the *retail merchants*, who could sell more shoes because prices were lower. In addition, *shipping companies* benefited somewhat, as did the *foreign workers* employed to make shoes for the American market.

But others were badly hurt. Many American shoe manufacturing companies—especially the smaller ones—went out of business because they couldn't compete. And as a result, more and more American shoe workers lost their jobs—permanently.

The result was that the shoe industry and labor both appealed to the government for help. Industry was represented by the American Footwear Industries Association (one of those Washington lobbies we examined in Chapter 5). The workers were represented by such AFL-CIO unions as the United Shoe Workers of America (which represents 40,000 workers) and the Boot and Shoe Workers' Union (35,000).

Industries and unions that want protection from foreign competition go to the U.S. International Trade Commission (ITC). The ITC was created by Congress in 1916 as an independent agency. It was originally called the Tariff Commission. In 1970 the shoe interests asked it for aid. At that time, according to law, such protection could be granted only if imports were the "major" cause of an industry's distress and if there had recently been a tariff reduction. The six commissioners split three to three on the request, and no aid was granted.

The Trade Act of 1974

Both industry and labor were unhappy with the difficulty of getting protection from the old commission. At the same time, supporters of freer trade were unhappy with existing limits on the president's ability to negotiate away existing tariffs. They also opposed the fact that Congress could delay approving such tariff cuts.

The protectionists and the free-traders finally reached a compromise agreement in the Trade Act of 1974. That act gave the president the power to negotiate with other countries to reduce or eliminate many tariff barriers. It also gave Congress only 90 days to reject the president's proposals before they automatically took effect. Both provisions improved the prospects for freer trade. But in return for these concessions, the protectionists got a loosening of the criteria for protection against imports. All that need be shown now is that imports are "a substantial cause" of injury to a domestic

industry. The old Tariff Commission was renamed the International Trade Commission and was empowered to decide these cases.

The Shoe Interests and the Policy Makers

The ITC Recommendation

The shoe interests were powerful enough to get shoes mentioned specifically in the Trade Act as products deserving protection. Immediately after the act was passed, the industry appealed for aid. In 1976 the ITC recommended protection, but President Ford vetoed the suggestion for two main reasons. First, he considered it inflationary, for it would raise the cost of shoes for American consumers. Second, he feared it would cause unrest in Italy among leftist workers who would lose *their* jobs making shoes for America and might then threaten the conservative Italian government, which was an American ally.[1]

Then in 1977, as mentioned earlier, the ITC once again recommended protection: a tariff-rate quota. This meant that there would be a new 40 percent (instead of 10 percent) tariff rate on all shoes from a given country above the number imported from that country in 1974—the quota. The ITC estimated that this protection would increase production of shoes in America by 15 million pairs a year, increase jobs in the shoe industry by 5000, and cost consumers $190 million a year in higher shoe prices.

The Responses of the Shoe Interests outside Government

According to the law, Carter had 60 days to accept or reject the ITC proposal once it was formally submitted. Immediately he became subject to intense lobbying from various sides. The *shoe industry and labor* believed that the recommended protection was insufficient. They wanted an absolute quota that prohibited any country from shipping any more shoes than it had in 1974. Such a policy would result in more domestic shoe production, more jobs, and even higher prices to consumers.

---

[1] For a description of the policy making on this case in the Ford administration, see Roger B. Porter, *Presidential Decision Making: The Economic Policy Board* (New York: Cambridge Univ. Press, 1980), chap. 6. It is interesting to compare Porter's account with this account of the Carter administration's decision.

George Langstaff, president of the Footwear Industries of America, holds up a shoe during a Washington news conference in January 1984 and urges the International Trade Commission to put import quotas on shoes to save the United States shoe industry. (AP/Wide World Photos)

Industry and labor argued that if the United States did not protect its domestic shoe industry, the whole industry would soon go out of business. At that point, some predicted, the foreign producers and the importers would be able to raise prices as high as they wished, and the United States would have no alternative but to pay. Some even suggested that we might face an "organization of shoe exporting countries" like the oil cartel (Organization of Petroleum Exporting Countries). And still others raised the ominous prospect that were a war to break out and so interrupt trade, the United States might find itself virtually shoeless.

But there were powerful forces on the other side, too, resisting protection and favoring free trade. *Consumers*, who would have to foot the bill, were represented by the Consumer Federation of America (a citizen-interest-group federation of national, regional, state, and local consumer groups). They pointed out that protection would cut the supply of cheap shoes, which are purchased primarily by low-income Americans. They estimated it would raise the price of shoes anywhere from $2 to $10 or more a pair. *Shoe retailers*, who wanted cheaper shoes to sell, joined the opposition. They were led by the Volume Footwear Retailers of America, another trade association, which commissioned a

study that concluded that the quotas would cost American consumers a total of $500 million a year in higher shoe prices.

Also joining the opposition were those who believed in the principle of free trade, including *exporters*, whose business depended on freer trade. They feared that other countries would respond to American shoe protection by other types of protection directed at goods that America, the largest exporter of manufactured goods in the world, was then selling abroad.

The Responses of the Shoe Interests inside Government

The lobbying outside the government was matched by comparable debates within it.[2] As part of his introduction to the presidency, President Carter,

---

[2]We know an unusual amount about how the Carter administration made its decision on shoe imports. As part of his effort to reorganize the White House staff, Carter commissioned studies of how eight important decisions were made, emphasizing good and bad features of the decision process as it actually worked. One of them was the shoe-import case. Journalist David Broder of the *Washington Post* was given access to the report on this decision by the White House. He wrote about its contents in "The Case of the Missing Shoe-Import Option," *Washington Post*, July 23, 1977. Many of the details of the following account rely on this article, which as Broder wrote, gives one "a rare look at the way in which bureaucratic conflicts and sometimes sheer accidents can shape a major decision by the American government."

immediately after his inauguration, was given a series of "presidential review memoranda." PRM 7, given to Carter the day after he took office, concerned a wide range of international trade issues, one of which was shoe imports. Prepared by the National Security Council, which advises the president on foreign policy matters, PRM 7 spelled out the implications of the shoe-import decision Carter would soon have to make.

Meanwhile, other parts of the executive branch were also at work on the matter. The Trade Act of 1974 had established the post of *special representative for trade negotiations*, in the Executive Office of the President. The special representative was made responsible for supervising and coordinating the trade-agreement program. He or she was also to direct American participation in trade negotiations with other countries. The special representative is thus a very powerful individual, able to do favors for many important people in the business world as he or she negotiates. This official gets a salary of $66,000 a year plus offices in Washington and in Geneva (where most negotiations occur).

Because the special representative is so involved in trade questions it was natural for the occupant of the office to be involved in deciding the Amer-

Robert Strauss, special representative for trade negotiations. (Bruce Hoertel/Camera 5)

ican policy on shoe imports. There was only one problem: There was no special representative, no occupant of the office. The previous occupant, a Republican, had left with the Ford administration. The post was so important that the various special interests outside the government were lobbying hard to influence Carter's choice of a new appointee. So were other interests within the government, including especially the Departments of Labor, State, and Treasury. The lobbying was so intense that Carter did not make up his mind on a candidate for the post until a month after he took office.

But the lack of a special representative did not stop the permanent staff—the career, or civil service, officials, who continue to serve under any presidential appointee. Indeed, lack of a head official rarely if ever stops a bureaucracy from functioning, as we noted in Chapter 9. These career bureaucrats sent a memo on the case to the *Economic Policy Group* (EPG) on February 4. It listed five major options as regards United States policy on shoe imports.

The EPG, as its name indicates, was a group of officials formed to advise Carter on questions of economic policy, such as shoe-import restrictions. Cochaired by the secretary of the treasury and the head of the president's Council of Economic Advisors, it included the vice-president, the secretaries of commerce, labor, and state, the president's National Security Affairs advisor, the assistant to the president for domestic affairs, the director of the Office of Management and Budget, and the special representative for trade negotiations. The EPG scheduled a meeting for March 25 to discuss the issue.

Lobbying on the issue, inside the government as well as outside, continued through February and March. The *Department of Labor*, not surprisingly, supported the position of labor. Its new deputy undersecretary for international affairs, Howard Samuel, had just come to the government from the Amalgamated Clothing Workers Union—a union particularly concerned about large imports of textiles and apparel. The Department of Labor argued that workers needed protection—especially because those most likely to lose their jobs were women, minorities, old people, and young people. Also supporting the ITC's recommendation for tariff-rate quotas were the *Departments of Commerce and Agriculture, the Office of the Special*

Pres. Carter meets with his economic policy advisors. (James Percy/UNIPHOTO)

Representative for Trade Negotiations, and *the Office of Management and Budget*.

On the other side, opposing protection, were five agencies. The *White House Council on Wage and Price Stability* opposed the proposal because they felt it would be inflationary. So did the *Council of Economic Advisors*, a group of economists who advise the president on such questions. *The Department of State* opposed it because it preferred having the flexibility to offer trade concessions (such as lower tariffs) to other countries in return for their support on political and military questions. *The Treasury Department* also opposed the plan. It supported freer trade as a way of creating greater international economic harmony and stability. It also argued that in the long run, American business was hurt by protection, which, it said, coddled inefficiency at home and triggered responses of protection abroad, both resulting in economic slowdown. The *Department of Housing and Urban Development* also joined in the opposition, concerned as it was with the interests of consumers and particularly of the urban poor.

Options and Considerations

The Policy Options

Carter faced the conflicting interests portrayed in Figure P5.1. He had five major options, as they had been spelled out in the February 4 memo from

the Office of the Special Representative to the Economic Policy Group.

1. At the protectionist extreme, he could grant the request of labor and the shoe industry to set outright quotas limiting the number of shoes each country could export to the United States in any year. There seemed to be considerable support for such a position in Congress, too, where these interests had lobbied hard.
2. He could accept the recommendation of the ITC for tariff-rate quotas—something that would at least please, if not fully satisfy, labor and the shoe industry and perhaps the Congress as well.
3. He could reject the ITC recommendation and opt for the status quo: relatively free trade in shoes— a low 10 percent tariff with no quotas at all. This approach would please not only the Departments of Treasury and State but also the shoe-exporting countries and the American consumers and shoe retailers. However, it would infuriate labor, which would then pull out all the stops to get Congress to reverse the decision—a right that Congress had reserved for itself under the Trade Act. Other industries seeking comparable protection—among them steel, electronics, textiles, apparel, and sugar—would also lobby for reversal. They would, however, most likely be opposed by agricultural interests, who fear foreign reprisals against their food exports if America goes protectionist.
4. He could attempt to lessen the impact of shoe imports by increasing "trade adjustment assistance" to workers. This program provides job retraining as well as special payments—70 percent of earnings up to $190 a week for a year—to workers losing their jobs. But this program would never sat-

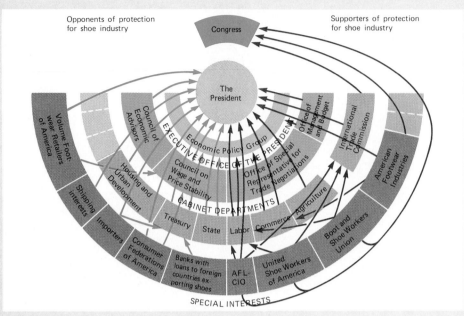

Opponents of protection for shoe industry

Supporters of protection for shoe industry

Congress

The President

EXECUTIVE OFFICE OF THE PRESIDENT

Council of Economic Advisors

Economic Policy Group

Office of Management and Budget

International Trade Commission

Housing and Urban Development

Council on Wage and Price Stability

Office of Special Representative for Trade Negotiations

CABINET DEPARTMENTS

Treasury   State   Labor   Commerce   Agriculture

American Footwear Industries

Volume Footwear Retailers of America

Shipping interests

Importers

Consumer Federations of America

Banks with loans to foreign countries exporting shoes

AFL-CIO

United Shoe Workers of America

Boot and Shoe Workers Union

SPECIAL INTERESTS

FIGURE P5.1
Conflicting Interests in the Shoe-Import Case.

isfy labor, which often refers to adjustment payments as burial payments or flowers on the grave. Labor has pointed out that the program makes no provision for job creation once people are retrained, so that they may well remain unemployed, especially if their closed factory is in a small town with few other job opportunities. Further, such adjustment assistance makes no provision for older workers who can no longer reenter the job market. In the words of an AFL-CIO lobbyist: "It sounds great if you're an economist, but it's pretty pitiful if you're a person. It's roughly an extra year of unemployment compensation for losing a job for the rest of your life."[3]

5. Carter could opt for an OMA—an orderly marketing agreement. An OMA is a "voluntary" agreement between the United States and an exporting country to limit the number of goods the country ships to the United States. It is voluntary in the sense that it is not imposed directly by the United States. But it would be accepted by an exporting country—if at all—only under the threat that higher tariffs or quotas would be the only alternative. And it might not satisfy any of the special interests.

Carter's Considerations

No one knew just what decision President Carter would make, but most observers expected that he would accept the ITC recommendation. During

the campaign he had said, in an address to the Foreign Policy Association: "There are many ways democracies can unite to help shape a more stable world order. We can work to lower trade barriers. . . ." But at the same time, he was sending a message to the Amalgamated Clothing and Textile Workers Union, saying: "You may be assured as president I would always keep a watchful eye out for your industry to insure that it was not unreasonably prejudiced by unrestrained foreign competition." The shoe manufacturers had raised $100,000 to lobby the Carter administration. They had also contributed small amounts, legally, to his campaign, after being rebuffed by Ford in 1976; and they claimed that their support in Ohio, Wisconsin, Maryland, and Pennsylvania had helped elect Carter.

Carter's decision on shoes was complicated by the fact that at the same time, the ITC was recommending similar relief for manufacturers of television sets and for sugar producers. Further, the case of textiles and apparel would come to a head shortly, for the existing OMA in that area would expire at the end of 1977, and both labor and industry wanted more relief from foreign competition.

One problem Carter faced was that any move to limit imports would stir fears in other countries that the United States was turning protectionist. These countries might retaliate by cutting their im-

[3]Quoted in Robert J. Samuelson, "Will the U.S. Trade Protectionism for Harmony Abroad?" *National Journal*, February 14, 1977, p. 278.

ports of U.S. goods, which would hurt other American businesses. It would also hurt labor, because one of every six American jobs in manufacturing now produces for the export market. Or other countries might simply default on repayment of American loans either from the government or from private banks. By 1977 developing countries had outstanding debts of about $250 billion—some $40 billion of it owed to American banks. If these countries cannot sell goods to the United States, they cannot earn the money required to pay off these debts as they come due. Default would disrupt—and might bankrupt—the major American banks. The consequence of that would be the collapse of the U.S. economy. Therefore, even American businesses and banks have a strong interest in allowing other countries to sell their shoes, textiles, and television sets in America.

Obviously, then, decisions on protectionist measures are basically no-win situations for an American president, in both domestic and international terms. Regardless of his decision, President Carter would have to carry on careful political negotiations with American interests at home and foreign interests abroad in order to carry it out.

The major figure in such foreign negotiating is the special representative for trade negotiations. The threatened business and labor interests wanted a sympathetic supporter of protection appointed to this post. The State and Treasury Departments wanted a free-trade advocate. Neither group got what it wanted. Instead, Carter picked a politician of sorts: Robert Strauss, who had just served as the Democratic party's national chairperson and chief fundraiser. Strauss was known as a good negotiator, able to bring business and labor together. President Carter obviously hoped he would be able to negotiate not only with domestic interests but with foreign interests as well. Perhaps Carter's choice as special trade representative should have foreshadowed his decision on the shoe question. But few read it that way.[4]

The actual process by which the final policy decision was reached was more complex than a simple compromise. It involved bureaucratic politicking of the sort we discussed in Chapter 9. But it

also involved bureaucratic mistakes of the sort no president likes but that a new president must expect occasionally.

Final Stages in the Policy-Making Process

Round One: The EPG

When the Economic Policy Group met as scheduled on Friday, March 25, it considered the five available options. Every agency represented favored adjustment assistance for the industries, communities, and workers affected by rising shoe imports. But as we noted above, Labor, Commerce, Agriculture, OMB, and the special representative for trade negotiations favored the ITC recommendation of tariff-rate quotas, while State, Treasury, HUD, and the Council of Economic Advisors opposed any further import relief.

After the meeting, Special Representative Strauss sent a memo to Carter summarizing the views of the EPG. In it he developed arguments for and against the major options that had been supported by one faction or the other: adjustment assistance, tariff-rate quotas, and no import relief at all. He did not even mention the orderly marketing agreement (OMA) option because it had not received support from either the protectionists or the free-traders in the EPG, in that it was something of a compromise.

Round Two: The EPG and Carter

President Carter was scheduled to meet with the EPG three days later (on Monday, March 28) to decide what policy to adopt. Normally, such a meeting would decide among the options that had been "staffed out" (studied by the staff of the EPG) and presented in Strauss's memo. But in such a meeting, the advice of the assistant to the president for domestic affairs—Stuart Eizenstat in this case—is also asked.

Unfortunately, the White House "paper flow" had been fouled up, and Eizenstat had not gotten a copy of Strauss's memo. He was therefore unable to comment on the several options as they had been presented there. However, he had previously studied the question on his own in terms of its domestic consequences and the attitudes of Congress; and he had been leaning toward the OMA option as a

[4]For an account of the politics of Strauss's selection that reveals many of the same political interests as were at work in the shoe-import case, see Robert G. Kaiser, "Politics of Trade Post," *Washington Post*, March 13, 1977.

compromise. So he raised that option anew, to the surprise of Carter, who had not been prepared for it by Strauss's memo.

Vice-President Mondale, a member of the EPG, had been unable to attend the Friday meeting, but one of Strauss's deputies had, by chance, sent him a different report on the session. In his memo, Strauss's aide again raised the OMA option, pointing out that it might be a good compromise, especially in view of congressional support for protection. As a former senator, Mondale saw the attraction of the OMA option. Thus, when Eizenstat raised it in the Monday meeting, Mondale gave it his support.

The result was that discussion shifted away from the two extremes of no protection and tariff-rate quotas toward the OMA option. Carter then instructed Strauss to prepare a new memo on the OMA option.

Round Three: Memos to Carter

Before Strauss could do so, Eizenstat gave Carter a new memo endorsing OMA. Carter returned it on Wednesday, March 30, with a penciled note saying he wished he had been given such advice prior to the Monday meeting. Later that afternoon Strauss's memo arrived. It, too, supported the OMA option.

On the same afternoon Carter was hit by a blizzard of memos on the subject. State sent one opposing OMAs as too protectionist and favoring voluntary self-restraint by Korea and Taiwan. Labor sent one attacking voluntary restraints as inadequate and terming OMAs only slightly better. In addition, an official in London making preparations for the upcoming international economic summit meeting sent in a memo. It favored voluntary restraints as the best policy for the United States to adopt in preparation for Carter's first major international economic conference.

Round Four: Carter Decides

Later that afternoon, Carter finally decided on the OMA option, with an expanded program of trade adjustment assistance to total $56 million over three years. Two days later, on April 1, he announced the decision as the new American policy on shoe imports.

Round Five: Strauss Implements

Even the compromises finally achieved were gambles unlikely to satisfy any of the interests most directly involved. In the case of shoe imports, Carter charged Strauss with the task of obtaining a voluntary curtailment in shoe imports to the United States from Taiwan and South Korea, which were chiefly responsible for the recent increases in imports. Taiwan agreed to cut its shipments to 122 million pairs in the first year, from 156 million in 1976. Korea agreed to reduce its shipments from 44 million to 33 million. The agreements were reached in less than two months. As a result, although none of the interests involved was wholly satisfied, Carter and Strauss had managed to achieve a compromise program on the shoe-import question.

Round Six: Congress Considers and Agrees

Nevertheless, announcement of a policy decision and negotiation of an OMA are not enough to make a policy final. As we noted earlier, Congress has 90 days after the president announces a decision in which to overturn the decision if it wishes to. This means that the politicking shifts to the Congress, where special interests of many sorts often have more access. In this case, by March 18 Carter had received letters from Congress, signed by 47 senators and 149 representatives, urging him to adopt the ITC's recommendations.

He had attempted to soften up the congressional opposition by sending Strauss, who was popular "on the Hill," to brief congressional leaders on the morning of April 1, as he was about to announce his decision. Strauss later described the session:

When I walked into [House Speaker Thomas P.] Tip O'Neill's office, after I had called him and asked him to assemble the 30–40 Congressmen and 15–20 Senators who were primarily interested in the shoe case, they all knew, of course, I was coming to say that we were going to reject the ITC decision and I said, "I want to tell you what the President is going to do today," and Tip said, "I know what he has done; he's sent the only fellow in town up here that could bring the message you are going to deliver and get out without getting lynched." Everybody laughed . . . but after everyone had had a chance to tell me how terrible the decision was, and what an operator he [Carter] was, how the Senate and House weren't going to stand for it—it took somebody to say, "Now wait a minute, all Bob's asking for is 60–90 days to work something out and he'll solve this thing if you give him 60–90 days. He's solved it before and that's the least we can do. There is plenty of time to kick him in the ass or override the President." And we did solve it.[5]

Whether Congress would finally go along with the OMA on shoes or would instead override the president depended in large part on how the special-interest groups reacted. After deliberation and after analyzing the agreements, the American Footwear Industries Association announced that it was a good start. The Volume Footwear Retailers of America, the stores, were unhappy. They commissioned yet another study—this one on the impact of the OMA on shoe prices. The study concluded that the OMA would raise the average price of shoes by almost 10 percent in the first 12 months. This meant it would cost American consumers $1 billion in the first year in higher prices. Furthermore, it would result in a "reduced range of choices" of shoes for low-income consumers.[6]

Indeed, the Volume Footwear Retailers were so unhappy with the decision that in June they filed suit in a federal court in Brooklyn, New York, seeking to block the OMAs with Taiwan and Korea. Such suits are usually dismissed—as this one eventually was. But these kinds of suits make actions by the government more difficult—and often suits are pressed by both sides. Indeed, the Trade Act of 1974 gives industries the right to appeal to the courts as well as to the Congress if their requests for government assistance are denied.

In this same period, the administration also reached a similar OMA with Japan limiting its export of television sets to the United States. These OMAs were *programs to deal with specific problems*. But as they increased in number, they contributed toward the construction of *a general policy* to deal with the problems caused by increased imports through voluntary agreements rather than through import quotas imposed by the United States.

On June 2 Treasury Secretary Michael Blumenthal, in his first press conference since he took office, made the emerging policy clearer. He defended the OMAs on television sets and shoes as necessary to avoid more drastic protectionist measures. He asserted that the Carter administration would continue to resist the extension of import quota restrictions to other industries as the ITC was recommending. He admitted that any restriction on imports was "a deviation from open trade principles" to which the United States still subscribed. But he announced that "we would like to see the spread [of OMAs] to other industries."[7]

Thus was the Carter administration's policy on trade and trade restrictions finally clarified. It had begun as responses to particular situations and eventually had become formalized in an announced intention to rely on OMAs. It was finally ratified or legitimated when Congress took no action to overturn the OMAs Strauss had negotiated.[8]

The Aftermath

The $56 million, three-year Revitalization Program provided funds for research to improve production and for loans to enable firms to modernize. Some successes were achieved with this help in the first half of the period. But then the price of leather hides skyrocketed because cattle farmers had faced high feed costs and so had slaughtered more cattle; therefore, they now had smaller herds to provide hides. Meanwhile, the dollar had become devalued, so that it was cheaper for foreign producers to buy American hides, thus reducing the available supply and increasing the price of hides in the United States. In 1978 over 60 percent of the hides produced in the United States were sold abroad. At the same time, U.S. tanneries, which treat the leather, faced higher costs because they use petroleum-based chemicals and because they must meet costly new environmental regulations. That raised prices of leather even more. The net result was even more difficulty for the American shoe industry—through no fault of its own.

[5]Interview, *National Journal*, July 9, 1977, p. 1077.

[6]Richard Lawrence, "Footwear Import Curbs Seen Costing Consumers $1 Billion," *Journal of Commerce*, May 25, 1977.

[7]Hobart Rowen, "U.S. to Resist Spread of Import Quota Curbs," *Washington Post*, June 3, 1977.

[8]Sources for this account of the politics of shoe imports, besides those cited above, include Nick Thimmesch, "The Shoe Tariff Controversy Is Giving Carter Tight Fits," *Chicago Tribune*, April 20, 1977; Philip Shabecoff, "Washington & Business: A Pragmatic Stance on Free Trade," *New York Times*, June 2, 1977; "Carter's Plan to Stem Imports," *U.S. News & World Report*, April 11, 1977, p. 94.

The OMAs did restrict shoe imports from Taiwan and Korea, but imports from other countries were unrestricted, and these imports soon more than filled the gap. Hong Kong shipped 22 million pairs to the United States in 1979, up from 6.6 million in 1976; Italy doubled its shipments to 97 million pairs; Brazil's shipments increased by one-quarter to 32 million; Singapore and the Philippines, both new shoe exporters to the United States, sent another 20 million. Thus, in 1979—despite the OMAs—shoe imports rose to 405 million pairs, up from 370 million pairs in 1976.

"If Washington were really concerned with the health of the shoe manufacturers," wrote a retail trade journal, "it would have offered effective trade restrictions, stabilized hide prices and quantities, and increased tax incentives in order that new capital could be generated. But . . . political forces will not permit such aggressive action. . . ."[9]

On October 23, 1980, the U.S. shoe industry asked the ITC to extend the import restraints for another three years. A study by the Federal Trade Commission had found that the shoe OMAs had cost $288 million in higher shoe prices, especially for the poor who depended on cheap shoes, and in lost customs revenue. The American Footwear Industries Association, however, claimed that the OMAs had had no inflationary impact. Instead, it argued, they had given the industry "a breather," in which to modernize. But, a spokesperson added, "we need more time."[10]

The Reagan Reversal

The Carter administration had successfully resisted the political and economic arguments—and pressures—for stronger protection. Developments outside the shoe industry itself, however, had made the limited curbs Carter imposed inadequate in stemming the tide of shoe imports. By requesting further controls in the fall of 1980, the shoe industry guaranteed that the Reagan administration, like the Ford and Carter administrations before it, would have to develop a shoe-import policy.

On April 9, 1981, the ITC recommended a two-year extension of the OMA on shoes with Taiwan, the largest shoe exporter to the United States, but an end to the OMA with Korea. The Reagan administration had negotiated limits on Japanese auto exports to protect Detroit, so many believed it would also agree to the proposed extension of the OMA on shoes. But the American shoe industry had not taken advantage of its four-year breather to retool to become more competitive.

Therefore, on June 30, 1981, President Reagan ordered an end to import quotas on shoes. He said the decision would lower retail shoe prices and strengthen the administration's commitment to free trade.

But there was also another, unspoken, reason for the decision. President Reagan was in the process of improving relations with the People's Republic of China—the Communist enemy of Taiwan. Letting Taiwan export more shoes to the United States would lessen the blow of this shift in American diplomacy. The PRC's adversary, Taiwan, had always been a close ally of the United States. Thus, foreign diplomatic concerns influenced Reagan's decision, just as they had affected Ford's decision on shoes five years earlier.

Then, on July 8, 1981 the Reagan administration sent to Congress a statement outlining U.S. trade policy. It declared the intention to steer away from the use of OMAs and trade adjustment assistance to protect industries hurt by imports. The Carter policy of limited protection—constructed out of programs of OMAs to benefit certain industries such as shoemaking and the production of television sets—was reversed. The new policy was to rely on market forces.

The result was that shoe imports surged, from 375 million pairs in 1981 to 480 million in 1982. Almost all the increase came from Korea and Taiwan. Jobs in the American shoe industry dropped from 143,000 in 1981 to 129,000 in 1982. But there was little the domestic footwear industry could do except try to modernize to compete more effectively. The Trade Act prohibited the industry from asking for relief again for a period of two years after any decision by the president on an ITC recommendation. In fact, parts of the industry did modernize, and their economic condition improved.[11]

[9]"Productivity and Export Grants: Fast Relief or Fizzle?" *Retailweek*, March 15, 1979, p. 63.

[10]"Shoe Industry Asks Trade Commission for Extended Import Limits," *National Journal*, November 1, 1980.

[11]See Robert M. Press, "Look for Shoes with U.S.-British-Japanese-Italian Label," *Christian Science Monitor*, April 15, 1983. See also Christopher Madison, "The Troubled U.S. Footwear Industry Is Kicking for Relief from Imports," *National Journal*, February 5, 1983, pp. 283–85.

But imports still climbed to 800 million pairs of shoes in 1983—65 percent of total sales—and the rest of the shoe industry and its unions still wanted help. They knew, however, that the best time to seek help was when a presidential election was near. Thus, the industry waited until January 1984 and then applied for curbs on all foreign footwear for a period of five years. The ITC would then have six months to investigate the proposal and make its recommendations for relief, and President Reagan would then have two months to decide what to do.

In June the ITC surprised everyone by ruling unanimously against protection. It pointed out that the industry as a whole was profitable. One of the reasons for this profitability has been that 12 of the largest domestic shoe producers also import 41 percent of the foreign shoes sold in America. Thus, the shoe industry has chosen to preserve itself by joining as well as fighting the foreign competition. And thus President Reagan was saved from having to make a difficult political decision in an election year.[12]

But only 11 months later, in June 1985, the ITC reversed itself again, recommending that the president impose shoe-import quotas. Imports were taking 77 percent of the U.S. shoe market, and the shoe manufacturers were complaining more loudly than ever. Two months later, Reagan announced his decision. Once again, he refused to protect shoes. He argued that shoe-import quotas would cost American consumers about $3 billion a year in higher prices. He also pointed out that restraints would hurt U.S. trade with countries such as Brazil, which would be less able to import American goods if they could not earn dollars by selling shoes to the United States. Once again, the issue of shoe-import limitations was settled—but for how long? Only time would tell, for by 1987 imports made up 84 percent of all shoes sold in the United States.

We shall now look more generally at policy making and the policy process and compare what we found happening in the case of shoe imports in the Carter administration with what usually happens, to see how typical that case really was.

[12]Stuart Auerbach, "ITC Rejects Quotas on Shoe Imports," *Washington Post*, June 7, 1984.

THE NATURE AND TYPES OF POLICY

The Nature of Policy

All of us are policy makers in our everyday lives. We constantly face decisions about what to do—whether to spend the afternoon going to classes or relaxing, whether to spend our limited funds on books or beer, whether to study one subject or another. Often we make these decisions on a momentary, individual-case, or ad hoc basis, especially if we think they aren't all that important. When something important is at stake—say, our future opportunity to qualify for a trade or to go to law school—we tend instead to adopt a *policy*, such as "study hardest in the courses that matter most for one's job prospects."

A **policy**, then is *a general principle concerning the pattern of activity,* or a general commitment to the pattern of activity, developed or *adopted for use in making particular decisions* about programs or actions.

We often speak of U.S. foreign policy. By this we mean the principle—or really collection of principles—concerning how our country will relate to other countries: who our allies are and how we treat them; who our enemies are and how we relate to them; what economic aid we give to other countries; how we respond to military threats, and so forth. The government uses its foreign policy in deciding how to act in particular cases or how to resolve specific dilemmas. We will examine American foreign policy in Chapter 19.

The *domestic policy* of the United States is really a large collection of policies on a wide range of subjects. Urban policy includes principles about federal aid for housing and job programs, for example—topics we shall examine in Chapter 17. Policies on minorities are designed to achieve equal opportunities for blacks, browns, and others—our focus in Part 4. Economic policy includes principles about how to deal with inflation, unemployment, monopolies, taxes, and other topics (Chapters 15 and 16). Human-resources policy covers health, education, and welfare. Natural-resources policy includes principles for dealing with pollution of various sorts and energy. Agricultural policy consists of principles about how to guarantee supplies of food to consumers while seeing that farmers get good incomes. Different observers would organize these various policies under different headings; and this list covers only the major topics that arise often in this book, leaving out such other subjects as space policy, medical research policy, and postal service policy.

Policy, Program, and Action

Once a policy is established, it must be implemented. Normally, that happens through a series of related actions designed to bring about a desired effect. We usually call this series of related actions a **program.** In the case of shoe imports, the Carter policy involved a program of achieving orderly marketing agreements and granting trade adjustment assistance to affected workers and their factories. So we often distinguish between individual actions, programs made up of such actions, and policies implemented by programs.

Types of Policy

Distributive Policy

Because there are so many important domestic policy areas it may be useful to divide the major ones into three categories, as Theodore Lowi has suggested.[13] The first category is *distributive* policies: those by which government tries to stimulate private activity that citizens or groups would not otherwise undertake. The major tool here is a **subsidy**—a grant of money or special privilege to, say, farmers to grow wheat or a shipping company to maintain its fleet or a railroad to keep up an unprofitable service.

Regulatory Policy

The second type is *regulatory* policies: those by which government sets conditions under which private enterprises operate. The regulatory agencies, such as the Environmental Protection Agency (which we will study in Chapter 18) and the Federal Communications Commission (Chapter 7), make rules or issue licenses to regulate a business or industry.

Redistributive Policy

The third category is *redistributive* policies: those in which the government acts in ways that benefit one group of people at the expense of another group. A policy of taxing the rich to pay welfare benefits to the poor is an example.

Just which policy makers are important in shaping policies tends to depend on the type of policy being made. For example, distributive policy is most often made by "subgovernments," as we discussed in Part 3—bureau officials, congressional subcommittee representatives, and lobbyists for the interests involved. Regulatory policy is often made by the process we discussed in Part 1 as "clientele" influence—the regulator-bureaucrats and the congressional figures responding to the needs and desires of those in the private sector who are supposed to be regulated. Redistributive policy, on the other hand, is generally made by the conventional political process as we normally think of it—the president and Congress responding to the influential groups or associations representing private-sector groups.[14]

While a wide range of actors may be involved in the policy-making process, we shall always find that some actors are more important than others, depending on the issues and the circumstances.

TYPICAL STAGES IN THE POLICY PROCESS

How do these actors get involved in policy making, and what happens when they do? It is possible to develop a model or outline of the stages of the policy process, and many scholars have done so.[15] These models have much in common, as does policy making on the various issues. To get a clearer idea as to the typical stages in the policy process, let us examine them in terms of shoe-import policy making.

---

[13]Theodore Lowi, "Distribution, Regulation, Redistribution: The Functions of Government," in *Public Policies and Their Politics,* ed. Randall B. Ripley (New York: Norton, 1966).

[14]These are the findings Randall B. Ripley and Grace A. Franklin reported in their book *Congress, the Bureaucracy, and Public Policy,* rev. ed. (Homewood, IL: Dorsey, 1980).

[15]For a survey of the field and the literature, see Charles O. Jones, *An Introduction to the Study of Public Policy,* 3rd ed. (Monterey, CA: Brooks/Cole, 1984); Randall B. Ripley, *Policy Analysis in Political Science* (Chicago: Nelson Hall, 1985); and Laurence E. Lynn, Jr., *Managing Public Policy* (Boston: Little, Brown, 1987).

Getting on the Agenda

The first stage in policy development is *getting on the agenda* in order to get a problem to government.[16] As we saw, both shoe manufacturers and labor unions got the problem of shoe imports on the agenda by submitting it to the International Trade Commission. The ITC is obliged by law to consider cases brought to it, just as the president is obliged by the same law to consider the ITC's recommendations.

Formulation of a Policy Proposal

Once a problem is on the agenda, a *policy proposal* must be *formulated*. This second stage typically involves (1) collecting information, (2) passing it to relevant actors, (3) developing alternative policies for consideration, (4) advocacy by supporters of various alternative policies before those who will decide, and (5) the decision or selection. In the case of shoe imports, the industry and unions (1) gathered information about the scale of imports, the closing of factories, and the loss of jobs and then (2) submitted it to the ITC, which did further research and gathering of data. The ITC then (3) developed various possibilities, such as higher tariffs, quotas, tariff-rate quotas, and doing nothing. It then (4) heard arguments by various interested parties and (5) decided to recommend tariff-rate quotas to the president.

Legislation or Pronouncement

The ITC's recommendation is only that: a recommendation. But that is as close as an advisory body can get to actually making policy. The law in this case requires that the president pronounce a policy decision and then that Congress decide whether to accept that policy pronouncement or legislate a different one. *Legislation* or *pronouncement* is the third stage of the policy process.

Often, before this third stage can occur, the actor responsible for it—the president in the case of imports—must go back and repeat the stages of

---

[16]See Paul C. Light, *The President's Agenda* (Baltimore: Johns Hopkins Univ. Press, 1982); and John W. Kingdon, *Agendas, Alternatives, and Public Policies* (Boston: Little, Brown, 1984).

policy formulation. The reason is that the president must consider all interests, domestic and foreign, while the ITC is responsible only for the interests of hurt industries and workers. Thus, Carter and his assistants had to develop and consider a broader group of alternatives, based on a broader range of information. He also heard more and different advocacy of various possibilities.

Carter finally weighed all the arguments and made his decision—his pronouncement—in favor of an OMA to be negotiated with foreign countries that exported shoes.

Legitimation

However, this decision was not enough to produce a final policy. Carter's pronouncement first needed *legitimation*—it needed to be made legitimate, or lawful, by congressional action. Policy must go through some sort of legitimation stage to become effective. Most policies cost money to implement: a subsidy to farmers, for example, or foreign aid to a developing country, or job-training grants to the unemployed. In such cases, Congress provides the legitimation by appropriating money for the program or activity—usually after a budgetary request by the executive branch.

In the case of Carter's decisions to seek an OMA on shoes, no money was required. Instead, what was needed was congressional acquiescence. Congress had to decide not to pass a law adopting the ITC recommendation. For the law gives Congress the power to override the president if the latter rejects an ITC recommendation.

In other cases, legitimation may be achieved by other means. Those affected by the decision may welcome the policy, for example. If they do so, it may gain a degree of legitimacy thereby. Or, if they challenge it, they may lose in court—which establishes the policy's legitimacy. Or public opinion may endorse the policy through polls. There is no one way in which a policy is legitimated. The key point is that people must come to believe the policy is legal, proper, or right.

Implementation

In the case of Carter's decision on shoe imports, Congress accepted the policy, at least as a temporary effort worth trying. This moved the matter on to the fifth stage in the policy process: *implementation*. In this case implementation required actually achieving an OMA with Taiwan and South Korea. And of course, once such an agreement was reached, the shoe-exporting countries themselves had to implement that agreement, which was a new policy for them: restraining their own shoe exports to the United States.[17]

Intergovernmental Cooperation

Most policy, then, requires a sixth stage: *intergovernmental cooperation*. In domestic affairs this usually means coordinating efforts of the federal government, state governments, and local governments—as in crime control. In foreign affairs the federal government has full responsibility. But it must sometimes coordinate activities with foreign countries.

Policy Adjudication

Once a policy has been implemented, a seventh stage may become necessary: *policy adjudication*, or settling disputes as to what the policy is, what it requires, and who is to conduct it. In the case of shoes, disputes might arise as to whether the term *shoes* includes slippers or rubbers or boots. The affected parties may try to negotiate a settlement, but if they fail to agree, they may have to turn to an outside arbiter.

Monitoring

Even then, the policy process is not complete. For the policy must be *monitored* to see what effects it is having. Monitors look especially for undesirable unintended effects. In the case of shoe imports, the questions to be monitored included whether the industry grew, whether more jobs developed, and by

how much prices to consumers rose—as well as how the policy affected our foreign relations and our other trade.

Evaluation

Once the policy effects are monitored, the policy can be *evaluated* to see whether it has succeeded or failed. But that determination can be made only in terms of particular objectives.[18] There may be dispute over which objectives should be used to test its effects and over who should do the evaluating.

Policy Modification

The tenth stage in the policy process is *policy modification*. If the policy fails or better ideas emerge, there is likely to be pressure to change the policy. In that event, the whole policy process may start over again.

Termination

The eleventh—and least common—stage is *policy termination*. Once a policy's objectives have been reached—and, if necessary, their maintenance assured—the policy should be ended. But policies, like the bureaus that implement them (as we saw in Chapter 9), seldom die. Only when the target is extremely weak, isolated, and without powerful political allies is termination likely. In the case of shoe-import OMAs, once the program was established, the interests sought to continue it; but with the advent of a new administration more committed to free trade, they failed. In general, however, the final stage is the least likely to occur, and policies tend to continue.[19]

From this survey and our references to the case of shoe imports, we have a better sense of the typical stages in the policy process. Not all policies go through all stages, we must remember. But policy making is complicated enough, especially in a

---

[17]Political scientists are increasingly studying policy implementation. Among the most interesting studies are Jeffrey L. Pressman and Aaron Wildavsky, *Implementation* (Berkeley: Univ. of California Press, 1973); Eugene Bardach, *The Implementation Game* (Cambridge, MA: MIT Press, 1977); Beryl A. Radin, *Implementation, Change, and the Federal Bureaucracy* (New York: Teachers College Press, 1977); Robert T. Nakamura and Frank Smallwood, *The Politics of Policy Implementation* (New York: St. Martin's Press, 1980); and George C. Edwards, III, *Implementing Public Policy* (Washington, DC: CQ Press, 1980).

[18]For a discussion of this point, see Eugene Meehan, *The Quality of Federal Policymaking: Programmed Failure in Public Housing* (Columbia, MO: Univ. of Missouri Press, 1979), esp. pp. 4–9.

[19]See Peter deLeon, "A Theory of Policy Termination," chap. 12 in *The Policy Cycle*, ed. Judith V. May and Aaron Wildavsky (Beverly Hills, CA: Sage, 1978).

country with active interest groups, and the world is complex enough that often we will find these stages in the process by which most policies are born, live, and eventually die.

Policies once developed may be effective or ineffective, and they may be consistent among themselves or contradictory with each other. They may be adopted or developed after careful study, or they may be selected haphazardly or without much thought. In the coming chapters we shall assess governmental policies in many of these ways.

COMMON TENDENCIES IN POLICY MAKING

Experts who have studied the making of public (that is, governmental) policy in America have uncovered certain common tendencies. These tendencies affect how well or how poorly policy works or indeed whether it can be made and implemented effectively at all.

1. *The interaction of special interests at every stage of policy making tends to produce compromise policies.* Different values produce conflicting demands, making it difficult to develop a strong, single-minded policy on almost anything important. In the case of shoe imports, the conflict among domestic interests (shoe manufacturers and workers versus traders, retail sellers, and consumers) and that between domestic interests (the ITC and the Department of Labor) and foreign interests (developing countries and their bank creditors) forced President Carter to settle upon a policy of some protection—a policy that was a compromise among these interests. In general, the watchword—the ultimate favorable comment about a policy—tends to be that it is "balanced."

2. *The policy compromise tends to result in "differential dissatisfaction" for almost everyone.* This simply means that all the interests will be dissatisfied to some extent, but some will likely be more unhappy than others. The shoe-import OMA displeased free-traders somewhat, but it displeased the hurt industries and workers even more.

3. *Policy once established tends to be maintained by bureaucratic inertia.* Once the government or a bureau starts doing something, it tends to keep doing it unless and until events force it to stop. The ITC started recommending aid for the shoe industry years earlier and kept doing so yearly. President Nixon, on the advice of his bureaucracy, rejected the suggestion; so then did President Ford; and so eventually did President Carter. In each case, Treasury and State continued to recommend rejection.

4. *Policy tends to be vitiated* (weakened, crippled, or terminated) *by a changing world.* The do-nothing policy on shoe imports was finally made inadequate by the massive new exports—200 million pairs of shoes a year—by Taiwan and South Korea, which weren't in the business a few years earlier.[20]

5. Changing policy consciously, in the absence of drastic new developments recognized by all, is very difficult. Instead, *policy is usually changed consciously by "incrementalism"*—by a series of small increments or "pieces" or "steps" that together constitute a larger change.[21] America's policy of freer trade rather than more tariffs and quotas became a policy of OMAs, not by a sudden decision so much as by a series of compromise programs to aid the shoe industry, the television-set industry, and others. These changes were sought by those in government who were especially sympathetic to hurt industries—or fearful of their political power.

6. Policy change by incrementalism may be conscious or unconscious, sought or not. But *the most common sort of policy change sometimes seems to be unconscious policy change by program change.* Small changes in programs dealing with the needs of hurt industries tended to result in a policy of seeking OMAs—perhaps to the surprise of governmental officials who were not consciously seeking to change America's previous policy.

7. *Many different issues are substantively interdependent.* The content of one policy on one issue will often affect the effectiveness of other policies. A policy of limiting shoe imports will limit the income of developing countries; they will therefore have trouble maintaining their economic growth; they will also have trouble repaying their loans from American banks. Thus, America's policy of limited protection will tend to interfere both with America's foreign policy of encouraging economic growth in poorer countries and with America's domestic policy of maintaining the soundness of its banking industry. On the other hand, if the United States denied protection, that policy would produce economic distress in some industries and put more people on welfare—contradicting America's policy of economic stability at home. This interdependence is true of most policies.

8. Just as *many issues and policies* are substantively interdependent, so they *are also inevitably fiscally interdependent.* Resources are always scarce in government. Most policies cost money. This means that different policies and programs struggle for

---

[20]For an interesting account of various ways in which policies fail, see Sam D. Sieber, *Fatal Remedies: The Ironies of Social Intervention* (New York: Plenum Press, 1981).

[21]This concept has been developed by Charles Lindblom. For an account see David Braybrooke and Lindblom, *A Strategy of Decision* (New York: Free Press, 1963). For Lindblom's current views see his *Policy-Making Process*, 2d ed. (Englewood Cliffs, NJ: Prentice-Hall, 1980).

money. That struggle occurs in what is called the *budgetary process*—the making of the federal budget by the executive branch and the passage of appropriations bills by the Congress.

The politics of the budgetary process can be harsh indeed, as we saw in Perspective 3. It concerns the distribution of scarce resources. But it also concerns questions of income—taxation—and the decision as to how much of a budgetary deficit, if any, there should be. Thus, struggles that seem to be about "fiscal responsibility" (balanced budgets) or "economic stimulation" (greater government spending) also involve questions of how big a budgetary "pie" there will be to slice up for the competing interests. So policy decisions on the budget and taxes and on programs are interdependent fiscally as well as substantively.

9. The result of all these tendencies is that *policy makers usually have less real control over policy making than we would expect* from looking at their apparent powers.

POWER IN POLICY MAKING

We should not be fooled by this conclusion into thinking that people and bureaus do not and cannot have power in policy making. There are two important sources of power in policy: political resources and information. Political resources involve the ability to deliver *votes*—in an election, in Congress, or sometimes in bureaucratic politicking. The importance of this is obvious.

The power of *information* is less obvious, perhaps. But after our study thus far, we should have a fair sense of how it works. The only way an official can operate effectively in a large organization like the government is by having accurate and useful information about what is happening, what is to be decided, who stands where on an issue, what is possible, and so on. Just as citizens must depend on experts for information about politics, so politicians must depend on experts for information about policy. The president would be lost without the "assembly lines of information" we discussed in earlier chapters. But so would the president's underlings. People with good information have power in government—often enough power to shape the policy alternatives that are considered and sometimes enough power to decide the outcome of those considerations by the ways they share information with others.

Again, we can see that *government is a matter of authority.* Those who take your information seriously give you authority to influence policy

decisions. Increasingly, as policy questions become more complex, the role of authority moves outside the normal channels of the bureaucracy. Instead, authority about political resources is held by political advisors; and authority on technical questions is gained and held by nongovernmental experts, who act as advisors or consultants.[22]

POLICY MAKING AND AMERICAN DEMOCRACY

"Knowledge will forever govern ignorance," wrote founder James Madison. "And a people who mean to be their own governors, must arm themselves with the power knowledge gives. A popular government without popular information or the means of acquiring it, is but a prologue to a farce or a tragedy or perhaps both."

1. The Constitutional Model

As we have seen, Madison believed the ideal form of government to be a republic, or representative government. In the *constitutional model*, which the founders developed, policy was to be primarily a legislative responsibility. The legislature was to represent the interests and opinions of the people. But the separation of powers and the checks and balances in the federal government were supposed to limit the national role in policy making by requiring consensus among different political interests before action could be taken.

2. The Interest-Group, or Pluralist, Model

But it wasn't long, in American politics, before the very thing the founders feared came to pass. Political parties emerged and were soon captured by special interests. As the world grew more complex, government became more bureaucratized. The specialization of bureaucracy within the government strengthened the specialization of interests outside it. The result was a new model of policy making: the *interest-group model*, which eventually became known as pluralism.

---

[22]For an interesting analysis with case studies, see Howard Margolis, *Technical Advice on Policy Issues* (Beverly Hills, CA: Sage, 1973). A guide based on firsthand experience is Guy Benveniste, *The Politics of Expertise* (Berkeley: Glendessary Press, 1972). And see also Hugh Heclo, "Issue Networks and the Executive Establishment," chap. 3 in *The New American Political System*, ed. Anthony King (Washington, DC: American Enterprise Institute, 1978).

As we noted in Chapter 5, according to pluralism, policy is the outcome of the interaction of groups, or special interests, none of which is powerful enough to prevail except in a coalition with others. Of course, the only groups able to participate are those that are organized and that are allowed to enter the political arena. Until recently, this requirement excluded minority groups and women.

3. *The Ruling-Elite Model*

It also excluded the poor and the inarticulate—immigrants, for example, who could not use the English language effectively. In general, these uninvolved and unorganized groups have been those most in need of governmental policies to improve their education, health, and welfare. But is their fate much different from that of the common person in terms of ability to influence policy? Many have thought not. They have seen policy as the product of small groups of skilled and informed individuals able to manipulate the instruments of power to their own advantage. Those seeing things this way use the *ruling-elite model* of policy mak-

ing, which we also discussed in Chapter 5. According to this view, elites have more in common with each other than they do with the groups from which they come or which they supposedly represent. Policy making thus becomes more a product of bargaining or trading and compromising among the privileged and the powerful.

4. *The Participatory Model*

There has been growing dissatisfaction with both the pluralist and elitist models, coupled with the widespread realization that the constitutional model did not apply for long, if indeed it ever did. One consequence has been disillusionment and despair—reflected in the falling rates of electoral participation. But another product has been a new or renewed concept of *participatory democracy*, grounded in the belief that people should gain greater control over the institutions that affect their lives. One implication of this is that the people should be actively involved in policy making. In coming chapters, we shall see just how far popular participation in policy making now extends.[23]

---

[23]For a more general discussion of participatory democracy, see the Epilogue to this book.

15

THE POLITICS OF PRODUCTION:
Capitalism and Democracy

We call our economic system capitalism. The term is supposed to mean that people are free to do what they want with their labor, with the goods they own, and with the money they have. If we think about it, however, we can see that our system is hardly like this. Government takes large slices from our incomes, whether we so wish or not. It tells us many things we can't do (such as breaking pledges we make in the form of contracts) and some we must do (such as saving for our retirement via Social Security). In other words, government increasingly makes the rules by which our economic system—and each of us as a member of it—operates. Why? Where does government get the authority to do this? Is its role legitimate?

In this chapter and the next, we'll learn answers to these questions by studying how our economy actually works given this governmental involvement and what it does to us and for us. Along the way, we'll learn how government tries to cope with a wide range of economic problems. Many of these problems have worsened in recent years: inflation, unemployment, poverty, competition for older American industries from more efficient overseas industries. The basic reason is that both the American economy and the whole global economy are undergoing a revolution. We'll learn what's causing this revolution and how it is transforming both American capitalism and our lives. And we'll learn what our government is doing—and not doing—to cope. ■

CAPITALISM

The Nature of Capitalism

The economic system that has developed in the United States is called **capitalism.** That term indicates that the system is based on "capital," or money that is invested in the production of goods and services to be consumed. In capitalism, the "means of production" (factories, machines, and land) are owned by individuals rather than by government. They are operated with the intent of making a profit for the owners. Actual operation is usually by managers and workers employed by the owners and paid salaries and wages for their work. They then use this money to purchase goods and services themselves, thereby creating a *demand* that the capitalist economy *supplies.* Thus, at the heart of capitalism, it is said, is "the law of supply and demand." Capitalism will tend to function so that supply equals demand.

The Principles of Capitalism

Through history, through boom and bust, most Americans have clung to beliefs about economics that qualify them as capitalists—or at least capitalist sympathizers. The central tenets of capitalism are five:

- *Capital*—wealth and any goods that can be converted into wealth—should be *owned by individuals* and disposed of as they wish.
- *Accumulation of capital* in private hands results in investment that *produces economic development* that benefits everyone.
- *Corporations* (groups of investors or owners) are the *most efficient* agents of capital accumulation (also called capital formation) and investment.
- *Profit* is the motive that makes investment possible and so *is essential and desirable.*
- The *"free market" where individuals and corporations compete is* the most *efficient* way to have economic decisions made through the operation of supply and demand.

These beliefs together constitute what might be called the culture of capitalism. It emphasizes private ownership, competition, and profit, arguing that these will result in two beneficial effects. First, people will get what they deserve, on the basis of

their work. And second, people will be able to exercise "consumer sovereignty"—they will decide what goods and services they are willing to pay for, and the "market system" will offer them so the companies can make profits. In a sense, people vote for goods and services with their dollars.

In recent decades, the principles of this basic capitalism have been challenged by socialists and Communists, who reject it entirely, and by today's liberals, who believe capitalism will work only with stronger governmental intervention. Socialists and Communists generally argue that the state, rather than individuals, should own the "means of production," so that inequality is avoided and wasteful competition replaced by planning and efficiency. Today's liberals, less willing to junk capitalism, argue instead for reforms. Government must regulate the economy, provide goods and services that private firms will not or cannot offer (everything from national defense to clean air), and develop long-term plans to see that human and social needs are met.

GOVERNMENT AND THE EVOLUTION OF AMERICAN CAPITALISM

The government has always had a role in American capitalism, but that role has changed drastically through our history. Its role has been important in the transformation of the typical American from a small, relatively self-sufficient rural farmer working his own land in 1780 to a wholly dependent urban factory worker selling his or her labor for a wage. In 1780 about 80 percent of the nonslave population (slaves constituted about one-fifth of the population) were self-employed and 20 percent worked for hourly wages or salaries. One hundred years later, only 37 percent were self-employed, and 62 percent were employed by others as workers. Today, another hundred years later, the self-employed are down to less than 10 percent, the wage and salary workers are 84 percent, and some 7 percent serve as managers or other supervisory officials.[1]

---

[1] See Michael Reich, "The Evolution of the U.S. Labor Force," in *The Capitalist System,* ed. Richard Edwards et al. (Englewood Cliffs, NJ: Prentice-Hall, 1972), p. 175, for more detailed statistics.

Laissez-Faire Capitalism

When the nation was founded, its economy was moving toward what we now call free-enterprise capitalism or laissez-faire capitalism. The term *free enterprise* means that anyone can set up a business if he or she can get the necessary capital (money) or can sell his or her own labor if he or she can find a job. The French term *laissez faire* is loosely translated "leave things alone." It implies no legal regulations—even those to prohibit disadvantageous types of activity, such as development of a monopoly (in which one company drives out all competition) or selling dangerous goods to an unsuspecting public.

The leading theorist and proponent of laissez-faire capitalism was a Scot named Adam Smith, whose great book *The Wealth of Nations* was published in 1776, the year of the Declaration of Independence. Smith argued in favor of free, unregulated enterprise in which every individual looked out only for his or her own selfish interests. He claimed that this would inevitably result in the most efficient production and distribution of goods and services—as if, in his words, there were an "invisible hand" at work constantly adjusting things for the better.

The United States developed as largely a laissez-faire capitalist country during its first century. The national government then had four major roles in the economy. The first was to *develop a common currency* for all states and citizens to use. Without a common currency, commerce would have been very complicated, and so development would have been slowed.

The second role was to *impose a tariff*—a fee charged on each item of a specified sort imported into the country from abroad. The tariff had two important functions. It produced the revenue to run the government, for there was then no income tax. It also served to protect fledgling industries producing goods here at home from competition by well-established industries abroad. That was because the tariff in effect raised the price of the imported good to the buyer.

The third role was to *sell public lands*, especially in frontier areas, to land speculators. These people wouldn't use the land themselves, as Jefferson had intended. Instead, in good capitalist fashion, they would sell it to anyone who could pay for it as a homestead. The fourth role was to *subsidize the construction of railroads* throughout the country to make trade and travel easier.

As these activities indicate, the United States was never really a fully laissez-faire capitalist economy. It became less so all the while. When the relatively free-enterprise capitalist era ended in the 1880s, America was an industrializing and an urbanizing nation. The country was dominated by powerful capitalist landowners, railroad owners, and industrialists who were behaving in ways that conclusively disproved Adam Smith's theory. There was grinding poverty in the cities, and child labor (young children working long hours in dangerous factories) was common everywhere. Furthermore, efforts to control these abuses failed because the vested interests were too strong politically as well as economically.

The Government and Business

The result was that Americans began to abandon free-enterprise capitalism in favor of government-regulated capitalism. The Congress began to pass laws establishing regulatory agencies to control railroads, industrial monopolies, food and drugs, and banks. The Interstate Commerce Act of 1887 set up an Interstate Commerce Commission (ICC) to regulate railroad rates and stabilize railroad revenues, to the benefit often of both businesses using the railroads for shipping and businesses running the railroads for profit.

The Sherman Antitrust Act of 1890 was the first in a series of acts designed to limit the ability of companies to merge into monopolies or to engage in unfair "restraint of trade or commerce" to cut down competition.[2] Then in 1914 came the Clayton Act, which extended antitrust controls. In the same year came the Federal Trade Commission Act, which was intended to oversee the business trading practices of corporations.

None of these regulatory agencies worked well. They all tended to be dominated by representatives of the business they were supposed to regulate. And the courts often ruled on cases in ways that limited

---

[2]The term *antitrust*, still generally used today to refer to antimonopoly programs, came from the practice of many companies combining to designate a group of men as "trustees" with control over the stock. The resulting arrangement, which gave these men complete control over all member companies, was called a trust. The most famous was the Standard Oil Trust that in 1879 controlled 40 different oil companies and thereby eliminated competition among them.

the agencies' power. But they nevertheless set the stage for further movement in recent years.

The Progressive Era is the name often given to the period 1900–1916 dominated by Teddy Roosevelt, who was president from 1901 to 1908. In it, the reformist focus was broadened to seek regulation of the exploitation of natural resources, as well as controls on trusts, and passage of the first legislation to improve the conditions of labor.

The Government and Labor

Working conditions for urban labor—primarily impoverished immigrants and their children—were poor throughout these decades: 10- or 12-hour workdays were typical, wages were too low to meet minimal human needs, factories were unsafe, and on-the-job accidents were commonplace.[3] Also, there were no disability payments for those hurt on the job and no retirement benefits for workers once they became too old to work. Efforts by workers to organize into local unions and to strike were always resisted by owners—frequently with violence and sometimes with the cooperation of local police. In 1894 the resistance even included federal troops in the famed Pullman strike in Chicago.

In the late 19th century, labor groups made efforts to gain strength through affiliation with other local unions in confederations like the National Labor Union and the Knights of Labor. Others joined socialist and anarchist organizations. The culmination of this effort at labor organizations was the expansion of the Federation of Organized Trades and Labor Unions, established in 1881, into the American Federation of Labor (AFL) in 1886.

At this point, the right of workers to organize was still not widely recognized, and the struggle to win that right was far from over. Courts had generally held that both labor organizations and business combinations were illegal, until businessmen were given the right to organize early in the 19th century. The Sherman Antitrust Act of 1890, designed to combat business monopolies, was then applied by the courts to unions, which were treated as illegal monopolies of workers. The Clayton Act of 1914 declared that human labor was not to be considered a commodity or article of commerce

---

[3]See Stephen B. Wood, *Constitutional Politics in the Progressive Era: Child Labor and the Law* (Chicago: Univ. of Chicago Press, 1968).

subject to such restrictions, but the courts continued to apply antitrust regulations to unions until 1942.

Meanwhile, in the 1930s, laws were passed protecting the right of labor to organize. The most important was the National Labor Relations Act (or Wagner Act) of 1935. Finally, in 1938, the Fair Labor Standards Act was passed. It set a minimum wage of 25¢ an hour and a maximum workweek of 44 hours, and it outlawed child labor. Subsequently, the Labor Management Act of 1947 (or Taft-Hartley Act) placed new regulations on union activities, and the Landrum-Griffin Act of 1959 curtailed the powers of union leaders over their members. Both laws represented efforts to adjust the balance between business and labor once again. Some then believed that the Wagner Act, intended to make unions able to compete effectively with big business, had gone too far, although labor vehemently disagreed.

In a sense, the most significant aspect of this collection of labor laws was its further expansion of the powers of the federal government to intervene in and police the economy. At the same time, that power was growing in its other two dimensions, the regulation of business and the development of the federal government's own economic activities.

Government Regulation of Business

The major regulatory steps in this period were creation of the Federal Trade Commission in 1914, the Federal Power Commission (FPC) in 1920 to regulate interstate electric power and natural gas, and the Federal Communications Commission (FCC) in 1934 to regulate radio, telephone, and television. In addition, following the collapse of the stock market in 1929, the Securities and Exchange Commission (SEC) was established in 1934 to regulate the issuance of securities (stocks) and the conduct of stock exchanges to protect investors from deceit and manipulation by companies or stock sellers.

Government as a Business

In the same period, the government was itself becoming more and more of a business in several important ways. First, the growth of the federal budget continued to increase. We can of course measure this growth in dollar terms—by the total cost of all government expenditures—as we did in Perspective 3. But it is more revealing to examine the total value of all goods and services produced and provided in the entire country (the **gross national product,** or **GNP**) and see what percentage of that total is purchased by the government. In 1930 the federal budget was only 3.6 percent of the GNP; in 1950 this figure had risen to 14 percent; in 1970, to 20 percent; since the 1970s it has been over 20 percent. This growth, by World War II, made the U.S. government by far the biggest customer for U.S. business and industry. Indeed, more than one out of every five dollars spent for goods or services in the United States today is spent by the U.S. government.

In addition, the federal government has itself gone further and further into *production of goods and services* for sale to the people. Its premier venture was the national postal system. Subsequently, the government has developed waterways and rivers and even gone into the electric power business, most extensively with the Tennessee Valley Authority (TVA), established in 1933. TVA not only provides power but also controls floods, manufactures minerals for fertilizers and explosives, and develops conservation and recreation programs for the states of Tennessee, North Carolina, Kentucky, Virginia, Mississippi, Georgia, and Alabama.

Government Fiscal and Monetary Policy

These regulatory, purchasing, and production powers of the federal government further increased its influence over the economic and social health of American business and labor. But the major contribution to government's capacity to influence if not control the economic situation in America came with the development of new ways of intervening in the economy generally.

There are two basic ways government can intervene. The first is through what is called **monetary policy.** Basically, monetary policy involves decisions about "how much money to print" or how much credit to create for banks to use in making loans to businesses and individuals. The second is **fiscal policy**—essentially, decisions about what

taxes to impose on whom and how much money to spend on what.

The origins of these capabilities lie in the Federal Reserve Act of 1913 and in the New Deal laws of the 1930s. The Federal Reserve Act established a national central bank to influence the behavior of other banks. The New Deal legislation during the Depression was designed to create new jobs and train workers, to raise farm prices to benefit farmers, and to establish the Social Security system to provide income for the elderly and the disabled.

The Changing Character of American Capitalism

The new government regulatory programs established from 1887 on were clear indications that even the subsidies (protective tariffs, land grants to railroads, cheap land sales to developers, and so on) in the mid-19th century were not enough to achieve and maintain economic stability and growth. The Great Depression convinced even the diehards that what was left of the free-enterprise capitalist system wouldn't work well enough, even with regulation. But even the pioneering federal programs of the New Deal were insufficient to end the Depression. Only World War II managed to do that—and then only with massive military spending, extensive governmental planning, price controls, and direct governmental production.

As a result, most economic experts had little faith in the conventional capitalist system. Instead, they generally believed we must rely upon an activist government to develop and sustain economic growth. But with economic growth came governmental growth, and with governmental growth came governmental influence extending to more and more spheres of human life. With the government having so much influence, economists and politicians came to believe that the economy could always be controlled by the use of monetary and fiscal policy—fine tuning, as this regular manipulation of the money supply, taxation, and government spending is often called.

Then came the severe and long-lasting recession of the early 1970s. Coming in a time of growing felt needs for more regulation to protect the environment and the consumer, it raised new doubts about the knowledge of economic experts, the effectiveness of governmental controls, and even the viability of American capitalism itself. It also brought fresh calls for greater intervention in the economy—calls that were echoed when recession struck again in 1980.

GOVERNMENT AND ECONOMIC POLICY

The Four Basic Functions of Economic Policy

Economic policy has four general functions. The first is commonly called *allocation*. This means deciding what social goods—such as military security, economic liberty, and environmental protection—to provide by allocating resources to them.

The second is *distribution*. This involves deciding how to adjust the distribution of wealth and income that various individuals or groups get or keep. Such adjustment is usually made through tax policy and various types of money transfer that we'll examine later.

The third is *stabilization*. This refers to the use of fiscal policy—especially the budget—to maintain a reasonable amount of consistency at acceptable levels in such things as prices and unemployment.

The fourth is *growth*. This involves fostering economic development so that there will be more resources to allocate, to distribute, and to use in stabilizing the economy and changing allocation and distribution policies.

That these are the four economic functions of government is generally agreed upon by everyone concerned with economic policy. But there the agreement ends. People disagree over *which* specific allocative goals (such as energy efficiency or environmental protection) should be sought. They disagree over *how* wealth and income should be

(By Toles for *The Buffalo News*. Reprinted by permission of Universal Press Syndicate.)

redistributed (through policies such as business subsidies or welfare payments). They disagree over *what* levels of inflation and unemployment are acceptable as stabilization targets. And they disagree over *how much* growth is desirable or safe.

Some of these disagreements are over goals or values: how people should live and what government should do to and for them. Other disputes arise out of disagreements over how the economy really works. Even the supposed experts, the economists, disagree sharply among themselves over this. Let's look briefly at both types of disagreements.

The Conflict over Goals: Efficiency and Equity

Throughout American history, there has been conflict over what the goal of the economic system should be. Early capitalist theory argued that the capitalist system was the most *efficient* way to organize production because it would allow supply to equal demand. It also argued that the mechanism of "the invisible hand" would adjust the distribution of this production in the best way. The outcome of efficiency, in short, would be *equity*, or fairness—at least in the sense that those who worked would receive what they deserved.

Experience rapidly proved that this theory was not true in practice. At the individual level, hard work did not necessarily produce an adequate income, and many people had to depend on private charity for necessities. At the industry level, the most efficient—and often the most unscrupulous—firms tended to drive out the competition and become monopolies. Then they could exploit consumers. Thus equity rarely resulted from efficiency, and the two goals were usually in conflict.

Economic Thinking versus Political Thinking

This conflict between efficiency and equity as the goal or goals of economic policy persists to this day. In the words of two businessmen who were high officials in both the Nixon and the Reagan administrations,

> the business and financial system marches to the drummer of efficiency. But not the political system. Most politicians will nod to efficiency, but it is usually little more than a nod. The drummer that the politician marches to is equity. When a problem comes up, economic thinking says, "What is the efficient way to solve it?" Political thinking says, "What is the equitable solution?" In any exercise in political economy, these two distinct patterns of thought are interacting, and the task at hand is to see how they can be meshed.[4]

The Conflict over How the System Works: Keynesianism, Monetarism, and Supply-Side Economics

Every administration attempts its own meshing on the basis of its own understanding of the way the system works. In general, Democratic presidents have tended to emphasize equity; and Republicans, efficiency. Still, what they have done has been relatively similar—until the Reagan administration, which has attempted a new approach.

Keynesianism

John Maynard Keynes (1883–1946) was a British economist whose work revolutionized economic theory and policy. In explaining the Great Depression of the 1930s, he focused on the demand for goods and services. He found that this demand was, not surprisingly, dependent on spending. Spending was dependent on employment. People couldn't demand goods and services if they didn't have jobs by which they earned money. Thus, he concluded that to end the Depression it would be necessary to have high employment, and the only actor able to foster this was government since business was in a depression. World War II, in which governments bought large quantities of military goods, produced just this outcome. It thus seemed to confirm **Keynesianism.**

Both citizens and government, in the decades since the Great Depression of the 1930s, have tended to think of economic policy in terms of consumption. In the language of capitalism, consumption is the demand for goods and services. According to the theory on which our system is based, when people demand, or seek, certain goods, the producers will supply them. This can be thought of as **demand-side economic theory.** In theory, if you want more production, you can stimulate demand. One way to do this is for the government to spend more money, by hiring the unemployed

[4]George P. Schultz and Kenneth W. Dam, *Economic Policy beyond the Headlines* (New York: Norton, 1977), p. 3.

or increasing the defense budget, for example. That is how government has usually tried to get the economy out of depression or recession. In recent years, however, the government has run large deficits (see Perspective 3). Even so, the economy has been stagnant, and inflation has resulted. Why?

Monetarism

One answer, called **monetarism** because it focuses on monetary policy or the supply of money, has been favored by many conservative economists, the most famous of whom is Milton Friedman. Monetarists believe that inflation is caused by the government's printing too much money. The result is "too much money chasing too few goods." When the government tries to cure inflation, it cuts back sharply on the rate at which it is increasing the money supply. The result is likely to be recession. To cure that, the government uses Keynesian demand stimulation, running a deficit and printing more money to pay for the extra goods and services it is buying. The result is more inflation. Most monetarists believe that the government should restrain its intervention in the economy, merely increasing the money supply at the rate at which economic production is growing. The result is supposed to be economic stability produced by the operation of the free-market mechanism of supply and demand.

Economist Milton Friedman, a prominent monetarist. (George Rose/Gamma-Liaison)

This sounds like a reasonable approach, and many experts came to believe it. The problem was that when it was tried in the Nixon-Ford years, it didn't work very well. The government was unable to balance its budget and unwilling to let unemployment be determined by free-market forces. The result tended to be continued inflation with a stagnant economy—a combination often called **stagflation.** Many thought the reason was that ours is an aging economy, with outmoded factories and too much unskilled labor. Thus, the economy is less productive than it used to be.

"Supply-Side" Economic Policy in the Reagan Administration

The Reagan administration took office arguing something different. Instead of focusing on the demand side of the equation, it looked on the supply side. "The source of the gifts of capitalism is the supply side of the economy," writes George Gilder in a book called *Wealth and Poverty* that has become a kind of economic bible to supply-siders.

> The problem of contemporary capitalism lies not chiefly in a deterioration of physical capital, but in a persistent subversion of the psychological means of production—the morale and inspiration of economic man—undermining the very conscience of capitalism: the awareness that one must give in order to get, supply in order to demand. . . . In economics, when demand is permitted to displace supply in the order of priorities, the result is a sluggish and uncreative economy, inflation, and a decline in productivity. Such disorders afflict both our politics and our economics today.[5]

Supply-side economists argue more specifically that the economy stagnates, even with deficit spending, because production or supply of goods is limited by high taxes and government regulations. Regulations make it too expensive to produce goods. For example, the antipollution equipment on a car adds some $700 to its price, and antipollution regulations on factories actually force some of them to shut down. High tax rates mean that it isn't worth the extra work for labor to produce more because most of the wage increase goes to Uncle Sam in taxes. In the same way, high corporate taxes dissuade companies from taking the risk of producing more goods or new products.

---

[5]George Gilder, *Wealth and Poverty* (New York: Basic Books, 1981), pp. 28–30.

Demonstrators hostile to Reagan administration economic policy demonstrate in Boston. (Michael Grecco/Stock, Boston)

entire program. However, the results of supply-side economic policy did not match its promises. Tax rates were cut by large percentages, but the first result was more consumption, not the expected saving. And instead of producing growth of the economy that would result in more tax revenue at the lower tax rates, it produced the largest budget deficits in history. Further, the massive increases in military spending kept interest rates high, which made it harder for people to buy homes and delayed general economic recovery.

Still, the economy did finally improve—as it always does eventually. By 1984 the inflation rate had been cut to less than half of the 11 percent that Reagan inherited. Unemployment was finally declining but only after surpassing 10 percent—the worst level since the Great Depression. The recovery was slow, however, and the major casualty was supply-side theory. By 1984 the Reagan economic policy was basically an unprecedented combination of traditional economic conservatism—fighting inflation—plus a Keynesian reliance on deficit spending to boost the economy. The pattern continued in Reagan's second term.[6] Only its tax cuts survived from the original novel supply-side policy.

The Case of Antitrust

One important change that began under Carter but was strengthened under Reagan was in antitrust rules. Mergers have long been banned if they lead to large concentration of productive capacity, or market share, as it is often called. The reason is that a large firm can control prices and quality and can keep new firms from entering an industry. The results are little or no competition, higher prices, and lower-quality goods for consumers. Today, however, firms in electronics, steel, autos, and so on, face more competition from foreign firms, many of which get subsidies from their governments. So the Reagan administration adopted a policy of encouraging mergers that would cut competition at home but make American firms more efficient in competing with foreign firms. The hope is that consumers will benefit, and the economy will become stronger.

According to **supply-side economic theory**, the lack of incentive for workers and businesses, coupled with obstacles in the form of regulations, creates a scarcity of goods. So we have higher prices—inflation, in other words. The solution, according to supply-siders, is to cut back on regulations and reduce taxes. As that happens, inflation will lessen. At the same time, the economy will grow, and so the *amount* of revenue the government gets in taxes will be large enough even though the tax *rates*, or percentages, have been cut. Government will get a smaller percentage of a much bigger total of business profit and worker income, and so the result will be about the same.

This theory was attractive to the Reagan administration—not least because nothing else the federal government had attempted was working. So Reagan took office seeking massive tax cuts for individuals and businesses and an end to much governmental regulation of business. He also sought large cutbacks in spending on social programs such as welfare and student loans but at the same time, even larger increases in military spending. Eventually, Congress agreed to virtually his

---

[6]See the polemical memoirs of Reagan's first budget chief, David Stockman, *The Triumph of Politics* (New York: Harper & Row, 1986); Herbert Stein, *Presidential Economics* (New York: Simon & Schuster, 1984), by Nixon's chief economist; and John L. Palmer, ed., *Perspectives on the Reagan Years* (Washington, DC: Urban Institute, 1986).

The Politics of Supply and Demand

Supply-side economics had been based on a belief that incentives for profit would be sufficient to motivate people and that market forces would solve social problems. But experience showed that, in the words of social scientist Charles Lindblom:

> A market is like a tool: designed to do certain jobs but unsuited for others. . . . In simplest and very rough form, the distinction between what markets can and cannot do is this: For organized social life, people need the help of others. In one set of circumstances, what they need from others they induce by benefits offered. In other circumstances, what they need will not willingly be provided and must be compelled. A market system can operate in the first set of circumstances, but not in the second. Its limitation is conspicuous when compared with an authority system. Although authority is not required in the first set of circumstances, it can be used for both.[7]

That, then, is why we have politics. Politics supplements economics in supplying things for which there are not economic incentives, such as regulation of monopolies and provision of welfare. The choice, then, is not between politics and economics. Instead, it is over what approach to use where markets can work, and over what type of politics to use where markets do not work well.

In the United States, the *political* choice has been democracy, although an imperfect democracy. The late Arthur Okun, chief economic advisor to President Johnson, once wrote a defense of our system in a book entitled *Equality and Efficiency—The Big Tradeoff:*

> By preserving our basic institutional framework, we can build on its capacity to adapt gradually—and that adaptability is one of its greatest virtues. . . . All things considered, capitalism and democracy, though polar opposites in some respects, really need each other—to put some rationality into equality and some humanity into efficiency.[8]

Major Policy Problems

Most Americans are well aware of major economic problems facing our system because these problems affect them or their acquaintances. These prob-

lems include inflation, unemployment, economic stagnation, pollution, and consumer protection.

Inflation

Inflation fluctuates but is often at a high rate, with both prices and incomes rising regularly but unevenly, as we shall see in the next chapter.

Unemployment

Unemployment continues at a high rate, well above what seems "acceptable" to policy makers, let alone to the individuals looking for work but unable to find it. It strikes members of minority groups, particularly the young ones, especially hard. Furthermore, unemployment tends to persist at high levels even when the economy recovers from recession, as recent experience reminds us. We shall discuss this problem further in the next chapter.

Stagnation

Stagnation in the rate of growth of the economy now recurs quite often. The term *stagnation* means that the economy is not producing more *goods* to meet the demands or needs of people (and so prices of the goods that are produced tend to rise). It also means that the economy is not producing new *jobs* for those seeking work. This point is especially important because the growth of our population is such that our economy must now produce about 72,000 new jobs every week. We will return to this problem in the next chapter.

Pollution

Waste and pollution continue to plague us, as we'll see in more detail in Chapter 18. Coping with them will require new and stronger government intervention in business and industry in coming years, which will further complicate economic activity.

Consumer Problems

Consumer problems have always been with us. But people have only recently come to believe the government should protect consumers. That, as we'll see in the next chapter, demands still more and deeper government involvement in the economy.

[7]Charles E. Lindblom, *Politics and Markets* (New York: Free Press, 1977), pp. 76, 89.

[8]Arthur Okun, *Equality and Efficiency—The Big Tradeoff* (Washington, DC: The Brookings Institution, 1975), p. 3.

Unemployed workers wait in line to seek jobs. (Andrew Sacks/Black Star)

Government Responses

The way government attempts to cope with such problems is by involving itself more actively in the economy. It may impose wage and price controls to attempt to control inflation, as President Nixon did in 1971 without much success. It may spend more money to create more jobs and lower the unemployment rate—but this approach risks new inflation. It may attempt to regulate pollution—but at the risk of raising prices and driving some firms out of business. It may impose new regulations to protect consumers—but at the cost of higher prices for goods and less efficiency in production. And so on.

We can already see at work here one of the tendencies of policy making that we discussed in Perspective 5: the interconnectedness of everything and the consequent interdependence of various policies intended to solve different problems. Economists are paid to try to develop policies to solve such problems, just as politicians are picked and paid to adopt the right ones. So far, neither the politicians nor their economists have been any too successful. Thus, it will come as no surprise that we cannot here propose policies that will promise such successes.

What we can do is survey the scope of government intervention and then raise briefly the issues that arise when the government intervenes. We can then look to the future to try to envisage possible new approaches that may emerge as political issues.

The government copes with capitalism's policy problems in two different ways. One is to promote the growth of the economy. This approach is supposed to relieve unemployment, lessen inflation, and overcome stagnation. The other way of coping is regulation. This may control pollution and protect consumers. It may also, however, contribute to economic growth indirectly by preventing monopoly or making more money available for business expansion. The box entitled "The Tools of Government Intervention" describes the 12 major ways in which the government can promote and regulate economic activity. Let's examine how it uses such tools in promoting and regulating growth.

Promoting Growth

Since the first railroads, the American government has been actively involved in promoting economic growth. Some of this promotion derives from the enormous spending by government. Beyond that,

The Tools of Government Intervention

The government has a wide range of powers to intervene and many instruments to succeed at it. The most important are these:

Imposing wage and price controls When given the authority by the Congress, the president can set limits to increases in wages and prices. Nixon was given this authority in 1970 and used it in 1971.

Rationing Given the authority, the president can also take the more drastic step of rationing, or apportioning, goods that may be in short supply—as he has done in wartime.

Regulating prices Government agencies set prices in certain activities such as rail rates (by the ICC) and the rate of interest on savings in banks (by the Federal Reserve).

Licensing, franchising, and issuing permits Government permission to operate, which automatically excludes those not given it, is used by the FCC for broadcasters and the Federal Reserve for bank charters.

Setting standards Various agencies set minimum health standards, grades for meat, eggs, and grain, and allowable levels of auto emissions, for instance.

Granting cash subsidies Bureaus may grant gifts of money or free services to businesses, farmers, or others to encourage them to do certain things. The CAB has long granted subsidies to small local and regional airlines; the Department of Agriculture pays a wide range of subsidies to farmers.

Granting tax subsidies The government grants various special tax breaks to businesses and individuals in efforts to affect their behavior. Busi-

ness has various "tax loopholes" to encourage it to invest in expansion. People buying their own homes are allowed to deduct the interest they pay on mortgages from their taxable income. In fact, the total of tax subsidies is now well over $225 billion a year, spread among many citizens and businesses. This means the government loses $225 billion it would otherwise collect each year.

Allocating resources directly Agencies sometimes may decide which people or which regions will get certain goods and services. For example, during periods of energy shortages the federal government decides how much gasoline and fuel oil must be provided to different parts of the country by the oil companies.

Promoting competition The FTC uses its powers to issue orders and decrees, and the Justice Department goes to court to sue, to break up monopolies, or stop monopolistic practices that restrain free trade. These are "antitrust" activities.

Taxing to regulate The government may impose special taxes to influence behavior. High excise, or "luxury," taxes on liquor and tobacco are examples.

Expropriating The government has the right of *eminent domain,* or superior power, to seize private property for public use. The Fifth Amendment requires that the owner of such seized property be given "just compensation."

Contracting The government can also influence behavior through its large-scale purchasing. It presently refuses to do business with firms that discriminate, for example.

---

the promotion of growth takes four major forms: subsidy, bailout, protectionist trade policy, and expansionist fiscal policy.

Subsidies

A **subsidy** is a gift of money—either a direct gift or a reduction in required payments. The federal government now spends $22.5 billion in direct subsidies to business and grants business another $70 billion in special tax deductions each year.[9] Subsidies

prevent market forces from operating, but they are very popular with their recipients, and often with politicians who think they win votes.

Bailouts

Another type of growth program sometimes used by government is the bailout. When an important economic entity is in deep trouble, the government may decide to step in and bail it out by guaranteeing loans made to it by banks and creditors. That's what happened to the aircraft company Lockheed and the auto company Chrysler as well as to the Continental Illinois bank in Chicago. It also happened to New York City. Such bailouts save jobs and protect creditors in the short run. How-

---

[9]See Philip Webre, *Federal Support of U.S. Business* (Washington, DC: Congressional Budget Office, 1984). It also gives similar credit and tax benefits to other Americans. Even you may be a recipient—for example, if you have one or more of the types of federal scholarship aid discussed in Chapter 5.

ever, they are usually granted to weak businesses or other entities that are no longer competitive. Thus, they may only delay the final reckoning, at which point paying off the defaulted loans could cost the taxpayers a lot of money.[10]

Expansionist Fiscal Policy

Fiscal policy, we saw earlier, concerns taxes and government spending. Favorable tax laws may help business grow. Decisions about the types and level of government spending can play a major role in such growth. This situation has been an issue in American politics because of the decline in the growth rate of the economy and in productivity. In the 1950s the American economy's output grew at an average rate of 3.9 percent per year. That meant more jobs, higher wages, and more profits—as well as more tax revenue for the government. In the 1960s the growth rate averaged 4.1 percent per year, but in the 1970s it dropped to a 2.9 percent per year average. Productivity—output per hour worked—increased at an annual rate of 3.2 percent from 1948 to 1968. But then, from 1968 to 1973 the rate fell to 1.9 percent, and from 1978 to 1980 it was a mere 0.7 percent.[11] In the last several years, however, it has been rising slightly once again. Low productivity means a lessened ability to compete in world markets by exporting and a lowered standard of living at home.

Protectionist Trade Policy

When industries have trouble competing in world markets, they usually ask government to protect them from foreign competition in the form of cheaper imports. The shoe industry, which we examined in Perspective 5, is not the only American industry that wants protection from foreign competition. Autos, steel, and textiles have recently sought and received protection from the Reagan administration in the form of orderly marketing agreements and import quotas. These limits have helped the domestic industries in the short run. However, they have had other consequences as well. For instance, in December 1983 the textile

Demonstrators favoring limitations on textile imports. (Werner Wolff/Black Star)

industry convinced President Reagan to impose 144 new quotas on textile imports from 36 countries, most of them Third World countries. One was the People's Republic of China—our former adversary.[12]

The result was twofold. First, China cut its imports of American goods, hurting the farmers and chemical producers who had been selling to China. In other words, one sector of the American economy (textiles) benefited at the expense of two others (farmers and chemicals). The second effect was even worse for the economy as a whole. Third World countries now owe the United States, other developed countries, and international lenders such as the World Bank hundreds of billions of dollars. They get dollars to make payments on these loans by exporting goods to developed countries. When the United States erects barriers to their goods, it prevents them from earning the funds they need to make payments. As a result, the banks that lent them money—including most major U.S. banks—make fewer profits. Indeed, some of them run the risk of bankruptcy. Furthermore, these countries then lack the money to buy any other U.S.-produced goods. So everybody suffers. Indeed, the Commerce Department estimates that every time U.S. exports decline by a billion dollars, 25,000 American workers lose their jobs.[13] So although import barriers may help some U.S. producers in

[10]See Walter Adams and James Brock, *The Bigness Complex: Industry, Labor, and Government in the American Economy* (New York: Pantheon, 1987).

[11]For an analysis, see Nake M. Kamrany and David M. Chereb, "Productivity Performance of the United States: Issues and Problems," in *Economic Issues of the Eighties*, ed. Kamrany and Richard H. Day (Baltimore: Johns Hopkins Univ. Press, 1979).

[12]The story of how this happened is fascinating but involved. See Christopher Madison, "Free Trade Transgressions," *National Journal*, January 7, 1984, p. 27.

[13]Everett G. Martin, "Latin Debt Crunch Hurting U.S. Firms," *Wall Street Journal*, May 8, 1984.

the short run, they damage the whole economy—and especially certain industries dependent on exporting—even more over time. This pattern then leads to pressure for more government intervention.

Competitiveness Policy

Protectionist policy rarely solves domestic economic problems of industries and usually causes new problems in relations with other countries. Thus, in recent years there has been growing support for "competitiveness" policies as an alternative. But experts still disagree over what should be included. Some argue for special tax incentives and subsidies for export industries. Others support more government funds for research and development in promising—usually high-tech—industries. Still others argue for greater government investment in public education as well as in programs to retrain workers to be more efficient or to move to more promising industries. This debate will continue as long as the U.S. has a deficit in its trade relations with other countries—in other words, imports more than it exports. By 1987 that trade deficit was at an all-time high and still climbing.

Reindustrialization versus Downsizing and Services

As this review suggests, everyone is now worried about America's economic future. It was a major issue in the 1980 and 1984 presidential campaigns and the subject of debate within the Reagan administration as well as among its critics. The problem is that there is no consensus on what to do.

Industrial Policy

Every nation has an **industrial policy.** It consists of the various governmental programs that affect the pace and direction of industrial change. These programs include tax laws, research-and-development grants, credit subsidies, and import restrictions. All such programs benefit some industries at the expense of others. At present, however, governmental policies toward particular industries tend to be inconsistent.[14]

Take the case of the domestic auto industry. It now benefits from import restrictions (on Japanese cars), and it previously benefited from federal loan guarantees (to Chrysler). On the other hand, it pays a high rate of corporate taxes (48 percent, as contrasted with 23 percent for retail stores). It has to meet federal fuel economy, antipollution, and safety standards. One 1986 study found that safety and pollution controls add $2,200 to the cost of each new auto.[15] Further, the government spends very little on automotive research (it pays 8 percent of the industry's costs, as compared to 70 percent of the aircraft industry's costs). The auto industry is still very important for the American economy. Indeed, one in every six American workers still owes his or her job directly or indirectly (in steel production or gasoline sales, for example) to autos. So government could decide to make its various policies more consistent in helping the auto industry—an example of a special industrial policy.

The Carter administration did adopt an industrial policy that involved the government in helping to shape industrial development. When the auto and steel industries faced strong competition from Japan, Carter created committees with representatives of business, labor, and government to devise common approaches. He also proposed special tax breaks for ailing businesses and for those investing in regions of the country suffering economically.

The Reagan administration abandoned both policies because they involved too much of a government role in specific industries. Still, it did approve cuts in regulation of the auto industry, and it convinced the Japanese to limit their exports of cars to the United States. It also cut business tax rates, as well as various costly government regulations. But many doubt that these steps will suffice.

They point to several problems. First, the United States has lost its technological edge in many areas, such as steels, synthetic fibers, many chemicals, and electronics, although it retains an edge in such high-technology areas as aircraft and computers. Second, some of our troubled industries, such as steel, are vital to national security in time of war. Third, government now requires business to take steps to protect the environment and to hire work-

---

[14]See Robert B. Reich, "An Industrial Policy of the Right," *Public Interest*, no. 73 (Fall 1983), 3–17. See also his book, *The Next American Frontier* (New York: Times Books, 1983).

[15]Robert W. Crandall et al., *Regulating the Automobile* (Washington, DC: Brookings, 1986). We shall discuss this problem further in Chap. 18.

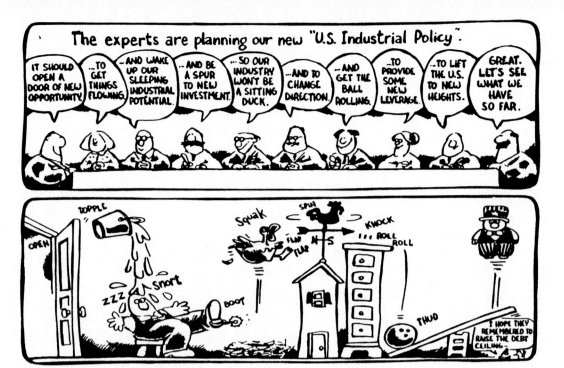

(By Toles for *The Buffalo News*. Reprinted by permission of Universal Press Syndicate.)

ers on the basis of affirmative-action criteria rather than actual productivity, and unions are insisting on more worker rights and "job enrichment." All of these factors may curtail productivity, desirable as they may be for the quality of life in America today and tomorrow.

Reindustrialization

Amitai Etzioni, a sociologist and public-policy specialist, argues that, given these problems, simply cutting taxes and red tape will not be enough.

> Congress will also have to enact specific measures to encourage corporations to pay out less in dividends and spend more on plant and equipment, encourage individuals to borrow less and save more, encourage youngsters to go into the coal mines rather than to college. In short, rebuilding America's industrial capacity cannot be achieved by a government policy that is merely passive. There are too many decades of neglect and misdirection to compensate for.[16]

The term Etzioni and some others have given to their proposals is **reindustrialization.** Calling for such a program in 1980, *Business Week* magazine declared that it

will require sweeping changes in basic institutions, in the framework for economic policymaking, and in the way the major actors on the economic scene—business, labor, government, and minorities—think about what they put into the economy and what they get out of it. From these changes must come a new *social contract* between these groups, based on a specific recognition of what each must contribute to accelerating economic growth and what each can expect to receive.

It also warned, however, that

> The great danger is that the U.S. political system will translate reindustrialization into some brand of "lemon socialism" whose main focus will be to save the lemons—obsolete jobs and companies that are going bankrupt because they are too inefficient to compete in world markets.[17]

Downsizing and the Service Economy

Others argue that planned reindustrialization is exactly the wrong way to improve things. They claim that the United States and the entire industrial world are undergoing a fundamental economic revolution. They often call it downsizing, referring to what has happened to cars and many other

---

[16]Amitai Etzioni, "Why U.S. Industry Needs Help," *Forbes*, August 18, 1980, pp. 120–21.

[17]"Revitalizing the U.S. Economy," *Business Week*, June 30, 1980, p. 56. See also Lester C. Thurow, *The Zero-Sum Solution: Building a World-Class American Economy* (New York: Simon & Schuster, 1985).

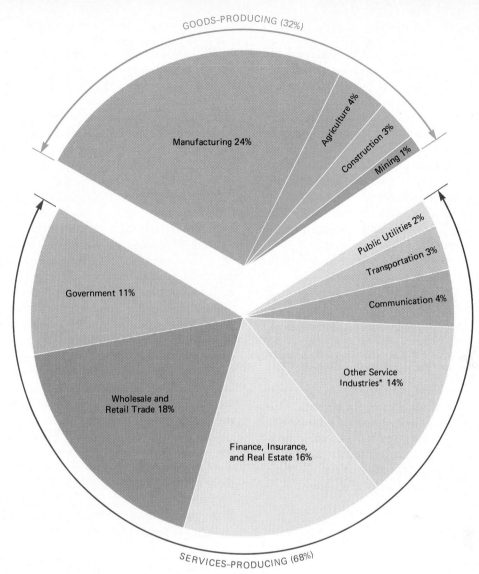

FIGURE 15.1
The New American Economy.
Source: Commerce Department figures for 1984 (percentages of gross national product).

products in recent years. Cars now weigh less, use fewer materials, and are more efficient. The same is true of houses. As *Forbes* magazine, a rival of *Business Week*, put it: "The simple fact is: A given standard of living no longer requires the same amount of iron and steel, labor, energy, rubber or glass it once did. So, lots of people get hurt."[18]

This change can be seen in the fact that for a decade now, manufacturing has employed some 25 million people. In that same period, employment in the service sector—banking, insurance, media, health, sales, government, and so forth—has in-

creased from 47 to 65 million.[19] Every recession reduces the number of manufacturing jobs, and they never return to previous levels. We are, in short, a "service economy." We have been that for some years and are becoming more so every day. Figure 15.1 depicts this new American economy. Because this revolution is bound to continue these analysts say government should give tax benefits to service businesses and help them increase their exports, just as it has always done for manufacturing industries.[20]

[18]James Cook, "The Molting of America," *Forbes*, November 27, 1982, p. 161.

[19]See Ronald K. Shelp, *Beyond Industrialization: Ascendancy of the Global Service Economy* (New York: Praeger, 1981).

[20]See James Cook, "You Mean We've Been Speaking Prose All These Years?" *Forbes*, April 11, 1983, pp. 142–49.

Many argue in addition that special benefits should also go to high-technology manufacturing industries such as computers, telecommunications, electronics, and biotechnology, which are also promising. The result would be an increasingly healthy economy, producing more jobs and higher standards of living for workers. But the "dislocations"—unemployment, job training, relocation— would be enormous, and many workers are not now willing to undergo them.

Still, whether workers and management adapt to it enthusiastically or not, a basic economic transformation is occurring.[21] As one Reagan Commerce Department official, D. Bruce Merrifield, summarizes it, in this global transition

> . . . we have incomparable advantages over every other country in the world. We have this advanced technology, . . . an incomparable industrial infrastructure, . . . an entrepreneurial culture, . . . the best capital-formation capability, the world's largest contiguous market, [and] a common language."[22]

But because innovation is risky and the prospects are uncertain, many Americans are hesitant. One result is more pressure for government intervention in the economy to protect weak firms. Such intervention is another form of regulation. To understand what it involves, we must survey the ways our government now regulates the economy.

Regulating Growth

Why Regulation?

Before we examine the major categories of regulation, we need to consider why we have regulation at all. It is important first to recognize that, as economist Lester Thurow reminds us, "all market economies depend upon a set of rules and regulations that define how property rights are acquired and the conditions under which these property rights can be exchanged."[23] Thurow points out that if your neighbor throws garbage onto your property, you have a right to protection

by the law, but if he or she burns it and pollutes the air, you have no such right—even though clean air is probably more vital to your existence than is clean space. This is an example of the way our regulations have developed historically. "The real question and the real debate revolves not around the virtues of the regulated versus the unregulated economy, but around the question of what constitutes a good set of regulations."[24]

That being true, it is not surprising that there are some dumb regulations on the books—or that some areas are overregulated. Regulations generally arise because the market mechanism fails to perform some task that people in general, or else powerful special interests, want performed. This is, for example, why we now have the Environmental Protection Agency. Business and industry could not or would not control their own pollution because that would have raised their costs. Thus, government had to intervene—in this case, in the public interest. The case of transportation is somewhat different. The ICC was set up when railroads were a natural monopoly, in order to protect consumers. When other forms of transport were developed, that argument no longer held. Competition was possible, and so an end to regulation would have made sense economically. Instead, these new forms of transport were also regulated. The result: less competition and higher prices for many consumers—but not for all.

Why do regulations survive? Thurow explains:

> The answer is simple—income security. Any long-standing set of regulations ends up raising the income of someone. And usually this someone includes some capitalists, some workers, and some consumers. When regulations are repealed, those individuals stand to suffer income losses.[25]

The Case of Economic "Fine Tuning" and the Federal Reserve

The regulation that affects you most is a type you never really see. It is the control over money. The government prints our bills and mints our coins, of course. But how does government decide how much money to make? That decision is made by the Federal Reserve Board in Washington. It is an independent agency made up of seven experts ap-

[21]For a fascinating and very unconventional analysis, see Hazel Henderson, *Politics for the Solar Age* (Garden City, NY: Doubleday, 1981). And for another stimulating economic analysis, see Harold T. Gross and Bernard E. Weinstein, "A Second Look at the Industrial Policy Debate," *Policy Studies Journal* 14 (March 1986), 389–401.

[22]Quoted in James Cook, "Two Economies: One Going Up, One Coming Down," *Forbes*, November 7, 1983, p. 58.

[23]Lester Thurow, *The Zero-Sum Society* (New York: Basic Books, 1980), p. 129.

[24]Ibid., p. 131.

[25]Ibid., pp. 132–33. See also Robert A. Leone, *Who Profits: Winners, Losers, and Government Regulation* (New York: Basic Books, 1986).

The Federal Reserve Board meeting in Washington.
(Dennis Brack/Black Star)

pointed to staggered terms of 14 years by the president with Senate agreement. The long terms are supposed to free the board to act on its best judgment free of political pressure. By controlling "the money supply" to our 14,836 banks and 3833 savings and loans, it can influence interest rates and the amount of credit available. The **Federal Reserve System** also serves as the clearinghouse for checks, so that a check you write on one bank to someone who deposits it in another bank gets sent back to your bank. The Fed, as it is called, until recently also had the power to set the rate of interest you got on a savings account. Related institutions also insure your checking and savings accounts.

These activities are often described as fine tuning the economy. They are supposed to make it possible to control inflation and influence the unemployment rate. In recent years, this regulation has been difficult to achieve, even when the Treasury Department's fiscal policy and the Fed's monetary policy have been coordinated. Still, government depends for the success of its economic policy on such regulation.

Conditions Fostering Regulation

Regulation may be supported for a variety of reasons. Many concern efficiency. Sometimes an activity is a **natural monopoly** such as a telephone system. If there were two phone companies in town competing, you'd have to have two phones if you wanted to be able to talk to people who had signed up with each one. To prevent this inefficiency, the town government picks one phone company and gives it monopoly power. But the government then regulates it because there is no competition to otherwise protect consumers or the public interest.

Some commodities, termed **public goods,** must be supplied to everyone if they are supplied to anyone, so it is difficult to get consumers to pay for them voluntarily. Consequently, government produces them and taxes people for providing them. Examples of such public goods include national defense, police, and public health programs.

Another reason for some government regulation is what are called *third-party effects*. Education, for example, is thought to benefit others besides the teacher and the one taught and so is often provided and regulated by government. The *absence of competition* is a rationale for some regulation—particularly antitrust moves against monopolies, which are not otherwise checked in the marketplace. *Inability to obtain information* is a situation that sometimes calls forth regulation. Consumers can't test the purity of drugs or meat, for example, and so the government does the job and then requires accurate labeling.

Some regulation is clearly intended to *change the distribution of income*. Special farm price supports or crop-size limitations, which guarantee a certain income to farmers, would fall in this category. Still other regulation comes about because *an interest with political power demands it*. The Interstate Commerce Commission falls in this category. So do tariff and quota provisions. And so do worker health and safety protection and the recent consumer protection regulation that we shall discuss in Chapter 16.[26]

The Extent of Regulation

Perhaps the best way to survey the scope and extent of government regulation is to examine Table 15.1. This table reveals something of the growth in both economic regulatory agencies (from 8 to 10) and social regulatory agencies (from 12 to 17) in the

---

[26]For a discussion of rationales, see George Daly and David W. Brady, "Federal Regulation of Economic Activity," in *Economic Regulatory Policies*, ed. James E. Anderson (Lexington, MA: Heath, 1976), chap. 14.

TABLE 15.1

The Extent of Major Government Intervention in the Economy

AGENCY AND DATE CREATED	NUMBER OF EMPLOYEES	BUDGET ($ MILLIONS)	FUNCTION
Antitrust Division of the Justice Department (1890)	704	45	Regulates all activity that could affect interstate commerce.
Civil Aeronautics Board (1940)	366	72	Regulates the airline industry.
Commodity Futures Trading Commission (1974)	550	24	Regulates futures trading on commodity exchanges.
Comptroller of the Currency (1863)	2,905	150	Charters and regulates national banks.
Consumer Product Safety Commission (1972)	542	35	Prepares regulations to reduce product-related injuries to consumers by mandating better design, labeling, and instruction sheets.
Corps of Engineers of the Defense Department (1824)	700	47	Concerned with construction along waterways and marshlands and dredging operations and mine dumping.
Economic Regulatory Administration of the Department of Energy (1977)	300	25	Regulates supply, pricing, and distribution of certain energy sources.
Environmental Protection Agency (1970)	8,669	1275	Develops and enforces standards for clean air and water. Controls pollution from pesticides, toxic substances, and noise. Approves state pollution abatement plans and rules on environmental impact statements.
Equal Employment Opportunity Commission (1964)	3,100	154	Investigates complaints of employment discrimination based on race, religion, and sex.
Federal Aviation Administration of the Department of Transportation (1958)	5,000	292	Regulates aircraft manufacturing through certification of airplane airworthiness. Also licenses pilots.
Federal Communications Commission (1934)	1,896	86	Regulates broadcasting and other communications and interstate telephone and telegraph service.
Federal Deposit Insurance Corporation (1933)	3,554	149	Shares regulatory powers with the states over state-chartered banks not in the Federal Reserve System and over mutual savings banks.
Federal Energy Regulatory Commission of the Department of Energy (1920)	1,701	93	Regulates interstate transmission and wholesale price of electric power, rates and routes of natural gas pipelines, and the wellhead price of gas for interstate shipment.
Federal Home Loan Bank Board (1932)	1,437	70	Charters and regulates federal savings and loan institutions, and insures deposits through a subsidiary.
Federal Maritime Commission (1936)	252	11	Regulates foreign and domestic ocean commerce.
Federal Reserve Board (1913)	26,000	15	Regulates state-chartered banks that are members of the Federal Reserve System and has jurisdiction over bank holding companies. Also sets money and credit policy.
Federal Trade Commission (1914)	1,131	60	Has broad powers to curb unfair trade practices, protect consumers, and maintain competition.

TABLE 15.1 Con't.

AGENCY AND DATE CREATED	NUMBER OF EMPLOYEES	BUDGET ($ MILLIONS)	FUNCTION
Food and Drug Administration of the Department of Health and Human Services (1931)	7,188	379	Responsible for the safety and efficacy of drugs and medical devices and the safety and purity of food. It also regulates labeling.
Interstate Commerce Commission (1887)	1,200	58	Regulates rates and routes of railroads, most truckers, and some waterway carriers.
Mine Safety and Health Administration of the Labor Department (1973)	3,184	149	Enforces all mine safety regulations, including air quality and equipment standards.
National Highway Traffic Safety Administration of the Department of Transportation (1970)	617	84	Regulates manufacturers of autos, trucks, buses, motorcycles, trailers, and tires.
National Labor Relations Board (1935)	3,213	133	Regulates labor practices of unions and companies and conducts representation elections.
Nuclear Regulatory Commission (1975)	3,235	467	Regulates civilian nuclear safety, which basically involves licensing atomic power plants.
Occupational Safety and Health Administration of the Labor Department (1971)	2,355	207	Responsible for regulating safety and health conditions in all workplaces—except those run by governments.
Securities and Exchange Commission (1934)	1,700	92	Regulates all publicly traded securities and the markets on which they are traded. Administers public disclosure laws and polices securities fraud.

Notes: Budget and employment figures are estimates for fiscal year 1984 from *1983 Report on Regulatory Budgets* (St. Louis: Center for the Study of American Business, 1983). *Date created* refers to origin of legislative authority, sometimes of a predecessor organization.

Source: Adapted and updated from *U.S. Government Manual, 1980–1981; Business Week,* April 4, 1977, pp. 52, 53, 56; *Federal Regulatory Directory, 1980–81* (Washington, DC: CQ Press, 1980); and *Directory of Federal Regulatory Agencies,* 3d ed. (St. Louis: Center for the Study of American Business, 1981).

early 1970s.[27] This was the period in which government began to respond actively to new demands for equal opportunities for minorities and women, for environmental protection, for consumer protection, and for job safety. As a result, spending by the economic regulatory agencies went from $166 million in 1970 to $428 million in 1975. That of the social agencies grew from $1.4 billion in 1970 to $4.3 billion in 1975. Since then, this growth has slowed, but costs have continued to rise.

[27]Actually, virtually every federal agency regulates to some extent. The General Accounting Office lists 116 regulatory agencies. For a detailed survey of regulation and a description of 15 major agencies, 17 other independent agencies, and 70 agencies belonging to cabinet departments, as well as 7 agencies involved in regulatory oversight and coordination, see the *Federal Regulatory Directory* published every year by Congressional Quarterly in Washington.

By 1975 the *Code of Federal Regulations,* which includes all the regulations developed by the federal government and currently in force, had grown to 72,200 pages in length. By 1983 it had reached 106,205 pages. The Reagan administration cut the *rate* of growth of regulation but was not able to shrink it.

The Cost of Intervention to Businesses and Citizens

There can be no doubt that these various types of government regulations are costly. The budgetary cost for government's role is put at over $3 billion a year. This covers the costs of issuing some 25,000 or more federal regulations every year and following up by inspection to see that they are observed.

The forms government regulation requires one firm to fill out. (John Marmaras/Woodfin Camp & Associates)

It also covers the distribution of over 5000 different federal reporting forms to business and the processing of responses by some 74,000 bureaucrats. And these figures do not include tax reports.

Once government issues regulations, business must abide by them. Filling out government forms is said to cost business some 130 million work-hours a year. And no one knows for certain how much it then costs business actually to do what the regulations require. General Motors estimates its "compliance cost" as $1.3 billion each year—costs passed on to consumers, of course, in the form of higher prices. And one study estimated the total cost of federal regulation in 1979 as $102.7 billion, or $461 for each American.[28]

The Benefits of Intervention to Citizens and Businesses

Regulation has protected citizens from poisoned food, deadly medicines, unsafe working conditions, and other serious threats. There can be no doubt that some regulation is inefficient, for safety rather than economic efficiency underlies some rules. Certainly some regulation results in special benefits such as subsidies for businesses, but other rules benefit consumers at business's expense. Regulation may limit technological innovation and diversity of products—but increase safety.

Conservatives and businesses tend to be very critical of regulation. Murray L. Weidenbaum, for several years one of Ronald Reagan's economic advisors, writes that

> no realistic evaluation of the overall practice of government regulation comfortably fits the notion of benign and wise officials making altogether sensible decisions in the society's greater interests. Instead we find waste, bias, stupidity, concentration on trivia, conflicts among the regulators and, worst of all, arbitrary and uncontrolled power.[29]

And yet when deregulation—freeing business from government regulation—is proposed, the affected industries often protest wildly. When President Ford proposed deregulating the airlines and the trucking industry, those special interests were fearful and outraged. Both benefited from regulation that protected them from competition. Both have been changed drastically by the subsequent deregulation.

[28]*Federal Regulatory Directory 1980–81* (Washington, DC: CQ Press, 1980), p. 45. The study was done by Murray Weidenbaum for a congressional committee.

[29]Murray L. Weidenbaum, "An Army of Regulators," *Houston Chronicle*, October 12, 1975.

The Problem of "Captured" Regulators

Some regulation limits competition automatically and purposely. Other regulation becomes limiting because the industry being regulated "captures" the regulating body. One reason for this development stems from the fact that each individual has but a small interest in regulatory policy, whereas the industry or business being regulated has a very large interest. The special interest therefore works harder to influence regulation favorably. Further, regulation of complex businesses requires special knowledge that is best—and perhaps often, *only*—had by people who have worked in the industry. One study by a House Commerce Subcommittee found that half of the 120 commissioners appointed to nine regulatory agencies came from the industries they were supposed to regulate. Where are their sympathies likely to lie?[30] Some observers, furthermore, assert that there is a kind of "life cycle" for regulatory agencies. They begin by regulating because they have been established as a result of political pressures for regulation. But over the years, they are "captured" by the industries they are supposed to regulate.[31]

Deregulation—The Great Reform Debate

The Carter Campaign

Shortly after taking office, President Jimmy Carter declared that one of his major goals was freeing the American people from

> the burden of overregulation. We must look, industry by industry, at what effect regulation has—whether it protects the public interest or whether it simply blunts the healthy forces of competition, inflates prices and discourages business innovation. Whenever it seems likely that the free market would better serve the public, we will eliminate governmental regulation.

The biggest steps taken in the Carter years involved efforts to deregulate various industries. First came airlines, which were, once Congress passed a Carter bill in 1978, allowed to select the routes they wished to fly and to alter their fares in most cases as they saw fit. Until then, the Civil Aeronautics Board (CAB) had allocated routes and set fares. The result of deregulation was cheaper fares, more competition on major routes, and a shift to smaller planes and commuter service on lesser routes. The airlines and their labor unions had generally opposed deregulation, and some companies suffered from the new competition, but overall most pronounce airline deregulation a success.

Then followed the railroad industry, which had been regulated by the ICC. In this case, the industry generally favored deregulation, but Congress balked, reflecting the interests of shippers—especially farmers and coal producers—who feared higher prices and lessened service. So the ICC began to deregulate rail freight by its own administrative orders.

The biggest battle of all came over trucking. Both Carter and Senator Edward Kennedy (Democrat of Massachusetts) proposed laws to end regulation of the 40 percent of trucking that is interstate. The trucking industry is a $70 billion a year business and includes 17,000 "common carriers" that have been regulated by the ICC. The industry also includes some 450,000 members of the Teamsters Union. Since 1935 the ICC has had responsibility for setting rates and allocating routes. Trucking companies have been allowed to get together into "regional rate bureaus" to set rates for ICC approval. Normally this would be illegal, monopolistic "restraint of trade." A special law passed in 1948 gave truckers immunity from antitrust legislation. Big trucking companies generally made 20 percent profit per year on their investment because of regulation, which kept out competition. Regulation was also very wasteful because rules required trucks to travel back from long-distance deliveries empty instead of carrying another cargo. Studies estimated that trucking regulation was costing consumers some $5 billion a year in excess shipping charges.

When deregulation was proposed, the American Trucking Associations, the industry's main lobbying group, joined with the Teamsters Union in trying to kill the plan. They also hired a big public relations firm to place ads saying that deregulation would do everything from cutting off service to small communities to raising the cost of Halloween candy. On the other side, the plan was favored by

---

[30]In addition, until Congress limited the practice in 1979, many regulators took jobs in the industries they regulated when they left government. This practice is often called the revolving door between business and government.

[31]See Marver Bernstein, *Regulating Business by Independent Commission* (Princeton, NJ: Princeton Univ. Press, 1955). But see also Martha Derthick and Paul J. Quirk, *The Politics of Deregulation* (Washington, DC: Brookings, 1985).

President Carter signing the bill deregulating the trucking industry at a ceremony in June 1980 in the Rose Garden. Standing behind the president are Senators Edward Kennedy and Howard Cannon. (AP/Wide World Photos)

the National Association of Manufacturers, the American Farm Bureau Federation, and the National Industrial Traffic League (which represents shippers). After a long and bitter struggle, the Motor Carrier Act of 1980 providing for major deregulation was passed in June and signed into law by President Carter.

Shortly thereafter, Congress passed another Carter-favored deregulation bill, this one to make moving easier. It loosened regulations on rates and services offered by moving companies and tightened rules protecting the consumer from fraud. In this case, both the industry and consumer groups favored the bill.

The Reagan War

The Carter administration was the first to make major strides in deregulation. The Reagan forces took up the campaign where Carter left off, but their objectives went much further. Reagan wished to use two criteria to assess all regulations, present and proposed. The first is that government inter-

vention is justifiable if—and only if—it produces benefits that outweigh the costs. The second is that the regulation must be the least expensive way of achieving the objective. Reagan quickly issued an executive order giving his Office of Management and Budget (OMB) the power to veto and make agencies rewrite new regulations and to order agencies to reexamine existing ones. Reagan also quickly slashed regulatory agency staffs and budgets by about 10 percent. The overall intent was to reduce the burden on business and industry in order to stimulate economic growth.

In its early phases, deregulation produced increased competition in trucking, railroads, airlines, and long-distance telephone. By 1987 airfares, adjusted for inflation, were down an average of 13 percent since 1978 saving consumers $2.5 billion annually, according to one estimate[32]); phone rates had fallen 9 percent since 1980; and trucking rates had decreased similarly. But at the same time, each industry had become more concentrated through bankruptcies, mergers, and purchases. For example, by 1987 the six largest airlines controlled 84 percent of the market versus 73 percent in 1978. Small competitors were disappearing in each industry. For example, Texas Air bought Continental, New York Air, Eastern, and People Express; TWA bought Ozark; and Northwest bought Republic. This led some observers to suspect that the decrease in competitors would lead eventually to effective cooperation in *raising* prices by the giant surviving firms no longer facing any real competition from new smaller entries.[33]

Reagan's efforts to deregulate in the area of environment and that of health and safety were immediately more controversial. A major scandal developed early over administration efforts to lessen regulation in the area of environmental protection (which we will discuss in Chapter 18). It resulted in the resignation of some two dozen officials in the EPA, including its head, Anne (Gorsuch) Burford.

The Reagan administration appeared then to sense that further efforts at deregulation might stimulate major opposition. In August 1983 it abolished the Task Force on Regulatory Relief headed by Vice-President George Bush. The task force declared that its work had been successfully com-

---

[32]See Steven Morrison et al., *The Economic Effects of Airline Deregulation* (Washington, DC: Brookings, 1986).
[33]See "Is Deregulation Working?" *Business Week*, December 22, 1986, pp. 50–55.

President Reagan with Treasury Secretary Donald Regan (left) and Budget Director David Stockman (right) in 1981 demonstrating their intention to chop off a large chunk of government regulations. (© Alon Reininger 1981/Contact Stock Images)

pleted. Staunch advocates of deregulation disagreed strongly. They attributed its demise to the fact that the 1984 election was imminent. As one White House aide remarked: "Deregulation doesn't have the same priority for us that it used to. The political dividends aren't very high."[34]

At this point, it is still unclear what the price of deregulation will turn out to be in terms of health, safety, and the environment. Surveys have consistently shown the American people to favor *more* regulation in such matters as drug safety, auto fuel economy, truth in advertising, and energy. The move toward deregulation is still in its early stages, and still responding to demands from business and industry rather than from the public.[35] It remains to be seen how the public will react to its consequences once they become clearer.

Other Proposed Reforms

Deregulation is not the only reform now seriously considered by experts on the relations between government and business. Also mentioned are proce-

dural reforms requiring regular reexamination of existing rules. Some people are calling for more government ownership of certain businesses.

Sunset and Sunshine Laws

A reform gaining increased favor is **sunset laws.** As we saw in Chapter 9, these laws provide that an agency is automatically abolished or self-destructs after a period of years (perhaps seven or ten) unless Congress passes a law extending it. The theory is that this abolition would occur before the agency had been captured and that it could then be replaced by a new, fresher, more public-interest-oriented agency if regulation were still desirable.

Other proposed reforms are designed to make regulators more responsive. One is to make their deliberations less legalistic and more social and economic in content, so that citizens could participate in and better understand their activities. Another calls for including consumer representatives on commissions or helping consumers to testify before them. And another, now partially in effect, called **sunshine laws,** requires that meetings be held in the open—in the sunshine—so that all can see what is happening.

Government Ownership—or Reprivatization

Some have even proposed government ownership of businesses and industries that need regulation. This type of ownership is virtually the case with many railroads now. But some railroads were near financial collapse when most of their passenger operations were largely taken over by Amtrak, a federal agency. And when later, control over certain freight operations was taken over by Conrail, another governmental body, it was also because of economic troubles. Healthy regulated industries seem unlikely to face strong pressures for government takeover. At the same time, the Reagan administration has sought to sell off some government owned businesses, such as Amtrak and Conrail. This is called **reprivatization.**

The Politics of Regulation

Some observers see such developments, coupled with the occasional capture of regulatory agencies by those regulated, as evidence of the further

---

[34]Quoted in "A Farewell to Deregulation," *Fortune,* September 19, 1983, p. 49.
[35]See Frederick C. Thayer, *Rebuilding America: The Case for Economic Regulation* (New York: Praeger, 1984); and Susan T. Tolchin and Martin Tolchin, *Dismantling America: The Rush to Deregulate* (Boston: Houghton Mifflin, 1983).

"blurring" of the original line between the public and the private. In Mark Nadel's view,

> through their considerable financial and organizational resources, corporations have attained superior access and leverage in the political system. Through a combination of inadequate legislation and their own efforts, giant corporations have been able to influence heavily and even, at times, to control the regulatory agencies that were supposed to hold the reins in the name of the wider public interest. Even more troublesome, . . . corporations themselves have been the promulgators of public policy—either in concert with government agencies or unilaterally.[36]

Thus, in a sense, government regulation of business is sometimes matched by what might be called business regulation of government. Some would say the same is true of labor because of its large-scale influence on campaigns and in Congress. And as will become clearer in Chapter 19, the role our government plays in influencing other governments is more and more matched by influence on the United States from other governments such as those of oil-exporting states. In addition, of course, business and labor influence each other, just as large American multinational corporations influence other governments which are trying to regulate them.

Much of this influence at all levels now occurs in a context of regulation. According to Michael Reagan,

> This is the regulatory pattern of the future: continued ad hoc adjustments between private market provisions of goods and services, and governmental intervention . . . to safeguard the citizen's person and pocketbook. . . . Such is the vital function of regulation in the American political economy.[37]

There are, in other words, major issues of economic and social policy still far from decided, far from agreed upon, within government and among the people. The politics of production, with which we have been concerned in this chapter, leaves much to be decided by the politics of scarcity. There is growing concern that many resources vital to our growth may be running out and that there may therefore be limits to production with which our system has not yet come to terms. Some even argue that our assumption that growth itself is necessary and desirable should be questioned. We'll return to these vital questions in our discussion of the politics of energy and environment in Chapter 18. In any case, the politics of production also leaves much to be decided by the politics of consumption. And consumption depends upon property—the distribution of income and wealth. So it is to the politics of property that we turn next.

SUMMARY

We call our economic system capitalism because it is based on capital, or money, invested in the production of goods and services. The means of production are owned by individuals or groups rather than by government. The system is supposed to operate in terms of the market forces of supply and demand. However, such laissez-faire capitalism has never existed in the United States. The government has always been involved in stimulating and regulating business and in regulating labor.

To control the economy, government uses monetary policy (determining the supply of money) and fiscal policy (decisions about taxes and spending). The twin goals of efficiency and equity are often in conflict. To increase economic efficiency, the Reagan administration introduced supply-side economics. This involved cutting taxes and cutting back on government regulation to stimulate work and production by encouraging savings. However, the large Reagan tax cuts did not result in the expected new savings; instead, the largest deficits in history were produced. Progress was made in controlling inflation but at the cost of greater unemployment.

Government has 12 basic tools with which to intervene in the economy, whether its purpose be efficiency or equity: wage and price controls, rationing, regulating prices, licensing, setting standards, cash subsidies, tax subsidies, resource allocation, antitrust, regulatory taxing, expropriating, and contracting. The major approaches currently used to stimulate growth are subsidies, bailouts, protectionist trade policy, and expansionist fiscal policy. There is now a major debate over the desirable in-

---

[36]Mark Nadel, *Corporations and Political Accountability* (Lexington, MA: Heath, 1976), p. 199. See esp. chap. 5.

[37]Michael D. Reagan, *Regulation: The Politics of Policy* (Boston: Little, Brown, 1987), p. 219.

dustrial policy—the combination of programs that affect the pace and direction of industrial change. Some favor policies to protect and assist weak "smokestack" industries (reindustrialization); others favor greater support of high-technology industries and services because these are the wave of the future.

Either approach involves increased regulation. Government regulates for various reasons, and regulation has both costs and benefits to consumers and to businesses. Regulators—especially the dozens of government agencies described in Table 15.1—tend to become "captured" by the interests they are supposed to regulate, which can lead to an increase in economic inefficiency. The Carter and Reagan administrations have sought deregulation in such areas as trucking, airlines, and environmental protection, but these efforts have proved politically controversial. Among other proposed reforms are sunset laws, sunshine laws, and government ownership of certain businesses. They too are all controversial.

Suggestions for Further Reading and Study

For background on the evolution of Western capitalist economies, see Barrington Moore, *The Social Origins of Democracy and Dictatorship* (Boston: Beacon, 1966); and Karl Polanyi, *The Great Transformation* (Boston: Beacon, 1957).

Books analyzing economic policy making are cited in chapter footnotes. For an argument that the problem is capitalism itself, see Paul A. Baran and Paul M. Sweezy, *Monopoly Capital: An Essay on the American Economy and Social Order* (Baltimore: Penguin, 1975); and for an argued cure, see Martin Carnoy and Derek Shearer, *Economic Democracy: The Challenge of the 1980s* (White Plains, NY: Sharpe, 1980). For a stimulating view by a practicing small-business man, see Paul Hawken, *The Next Economy* (New York: Holt, Rinehart & Winston, 1983). To keep up with current developments in the economy and government's role, the best sources are the major business periodicals, *Business Week*, *Fortune*, *Forbes*, and *Regulation*.

16

THE POLITICS OF PROPERTY:
The Rich, the Poor, and Those in the Middle

About 1 in every 240 Americans is now a millionaire—there were just over a million of them at the last count. But 1 in every 7 Americans lives in poverty, and studies suggest that many of these are malnourished or go to bed hungry every night. We cannot really understand the challenges confronting the American political system without taking note of the great distance between the rich and the poor in America—and the relatively large numbers of citizens who live at these extremes.

The United States is the richest large nation in the world, if we consider the total wealth of the country divided among the number of citizens. That wealth is now estimated at over $11.2 trillion, or $47,500 for every American. But of course that wealth is not really divided among the citizens with anything approaching equality. Indeed, roughly 25 percent of all wealth in America is held by 1 percent of American adults—a figure that has remained remarkably constant over the 150 years for which figures are available. And the richest 20 percent of the population hold 75 percent of the wealth, while the poorest 20 percent hold but 0.2 percent. So it is clear that the disparities between the extremes are massive. In this chapter, we'll learn why they are so great, what our government does to affect them, and the proposals some offer to change the distribution of wealth and income. ■

THE POOR IN AMERICA

In 1985 there were 33,064,000 Americans living below the official "poverty line," according to the Census Bureau.[1] This amounted to 14 percent of the entire American population. Who are they? Table 16.1 shows the breakdown and percentages.

The Census Bureau began keeping such statistics in 1959, determining the poverty line by calculating the cost of a basic nutritionally adequate diet for a family of four and then multiplying it by three because it found that families spend a third of their income on food. Any family whose income falls below that poverty line will be unable to live at minimal levels of nutrition, shelter, and health.[2]

This poverty line of $10,989 can be contrasted with the annual median (or middle) family income of $29,527.[3] Clearly the average family lives much better than the family at the margin. But a study of the "average wage earner" (a 38-year-old father of two who lives with his wife in a relatively comfortable home and drives a fairly new car) discovered that even he has trouble making ends meet on his income. He tends to spend about $500 more per year than he makes, and he hasn't enough savings in the bank to pay for his own funeral if he dies.[4] If this wage earner finds making ends meet so difficult, how much worse must it be for the really poor? That will depend to some extent on who and where they are.

The poor are found in every part of America today. Government studies show that poverty is greatest among two groups, as Table 16.1 indicates. One is the elderly, who generally have no jobs, are in poor health, and live on inadequate Social Security or welfare payments that are fixed. The other poor group is families that are black, Mexican American, or Native American Indian—especially those headed by women. Greater *percentages* of these groups—the old and the rural minorities—are poor. But because these groups are small percentages of the total American population, the largest *numbers* of the poor are white people and live in cities. In fact, about two-thirds of all poor people are white, and about 40 percent of all poor people live in central cities.

Consequently, if we were to try to locate a "typical" poor American, we would look among whites living in the central cities of America, and we would most likely settle upon an individual who moved his family into the city (perhaps Los Angeles, Chicago, or Detroit) from Oklahoma, for example, or the rural Deep South. But the poor are found in every area of the country. Southern states lead the nation in terms of the percentage of total population below the poverty line, followed by the Northeast, the Midwest, and finally the western states.

Another important point about the poor revealed by government statistics is the fact that about four out of every ten poor Americans are children under the age of 16, many of them living in families headed by a woman because the father is dead or gone.[5] Indeed, 23 percent of all children are poor. Emerging from poverty is difficult enough for a child in a typical household. It is much harder if the household is headed by a woman because women still face major job and wage discrimination and have a difficult time working while raising children. Moreover, that discrimination is compounded when the woman is black or Puerto Rican or Mexican American, as many poor mothers are. More than half of the children living in families headed by women are poor—eight times the percentage of poor children in families headed by men. Their prospects for escaping poverty are bleak.

Although there are more poor whites than poor blacks, the percentage of blacks who are poor is three times as great as the percentage of whites who are poor. More than one in every three blacks is below the poverty line, while only one in every eight whites is. Blacks are one-third of the poor, but because they are only one-eighth of the pop-

---

[1]Census Bureau, *Money Income and Poverty Status of Families and Persons in the U.S.: 1985* (Washington, DC: GPO, 1986, publication series P-60, no. 154). For a discussion of the concept, see Jan Drewnowski, "Poverty: Its Meaning and Measurement," *Development and Change* 8 (1977), 183–208.

[2]In 1986, for example, the Physicians Task Force on Hunger in America issued a report that concluded that up to 20 million Americans are chronically underfed and so are malnourished. They live in 24 states but are concentrated in 150 counties, primarily in the Mississippi Valley and in the Great Plains farm belt. See "Harvard Report Says Hunger Is Common in Rural Counties," *New York Times*, January 14, 1986.

[3]The poverty-line figure is for 1986. The median family income figure is for 1984. Thus, the actual disparity is even greater. (Both figures are for a family of four.)

[4]Harry Atkins, "Typical Wage Earner in the Red," *Boston Globe*, September 13, 1976.

[5]See Irwin Garfinkel and Sara S. McLanahan, *Single Mothers and Their Children: A New American Dilemma* (Washington, DC: Urban Institute, 1986).

(J. L. Atlan/Sygma)

ulation, blacks who are not poor are only one-twelfth of all those who are not poor. In other words, the common belief that most poor people are black is false; two-thirds of the poor are white. But it is true that a much higher percentage of black people than white people are poor.

Another common misconception is the belief that the poor are poor because they do not, or will not, work. In 1983, 17 percent of the heads of poor families worked full time all year long—as do many poor single individuals. Another 32 percent worked but less than year-round, full time. Only 10 percent of the heads of poor families did not work at all in 1983 because they could not find a job. In

TABLE 16.1
Who Are the Poor?

CATEGORY	NUMBER OF PEOPLE IN CATEGORY WHO ARE POOR	PERCENTAGE OF PEOPLE IN CATEGORY WHO ARE POOR
All Persons	33,064,000	14.0%
White	22,860,000	11.4
Black	8,926,000	31.3
Spanish origin[a]	5,236,000	29.0
65 years and over	3,456,000	12.6
Children under 15 years	11,110,000	21.5
In metropolitan areas	21,247,000	13.7
In central cities	12,696,000	19.9
Outside central cities	8,551,000	9.3
Outside metropolitan areas	13,152,000	17.8
Northeast	5,751,000	11.6
Midwest	8,191,000	13.9
South	12,921,000	16.0
West	6,201,000	13.0
All Families	7,223,000	11.4
Female householder, no husband present	3,474,000	34.0

[a]Persons of Spanish origin may be of any race.
Source: Census Bureau, *Current Population Reports,* series P-60 #154 (Washington, DC: GPO, 1986), p. 4.
Data are for March 1985, except for place of residence, 1983.

(UPI/Bettmann Newsphotos)

inheritances, and discrimination. The poor are in a vicious circle which is difficult to escape. What they need in order to move out of poverty they do not have and cannot afford to acquire [such as better education and training]. So they remain poor.[7]

But the problems and obstacles go deeper than this. In recent years, some sociologists have argued that the poor are poor and remain poor because they live in a "culture of poverty" that traps them in attitudes and experiences that are difficult to overcome. This assertion has stimulated much debate.[8] But whether or not the poor are trapped by attitudes and experiences, they are hurt by what some now call information poverty.[9] The lack of skills such as reading ability is exacerbated not only by poor education but also by the fact that often English is not their native language. In addition, the poor have health problems that they cannot afford to have corrected, some of which affect their hearing and eyesight and therefore make learning more difficult.[10] Furthermore, their backgrounds tend to make them inexperienced in such skills as budgeting and bargaining in purchasing, and so their economic plight may worsen.

The poor, in this sense, tend to live in an "information ghetto." They do receive information from outside via the media—but the media available to them tend to emphasize entertainment and fantasy rather than information useful for coping with real problems. Furthermore, the impact of their own group images, ideas, myths, and folklore will tend to be reinforced by limited personal contacts with people outside the ghetto.

Because the surrounding outside world is governed by a different culture of information—the set of images, ideas, myths, and folklore that are dominant and therefore determine the chances for success—people in the information ghetto are at a disadvantage mentally as well as physically. This mental domination and insulation help to explain why the poor may not know how to get help for such immediate physical problems as a shortage of food or an illness or rat bites—even though social service programs may exist in their neighborhood or city.

addition, one in every five poor families has two or more income earners and still remains below the poverty line.[6]

The point is that just working does not necessarily prevent poverty. If wages are not high enough, a family cannot escape poverty through work. Indeed, if a person worked full time for all 52 weeks of the year with no holidays at the 1986 federal minimum wage of $3.35 an hour, he or she would earn only $7396 before paying Social Security and other taxes due of $946. That would still be $3593 less than the poverty-line income for a family of four!

The Causes of Poverty

It is easy to describe the causes of poverty in economic terms. As two economists summarize the situation:

> The poor have small quantities and low qualities of resources. The market places a low value on the services they provide in the market [that is, the jobs they can do well]. The low productivity and, therefore, the low pay of the poor are due to the low levels of training and education, misfortune, relatively small

[6]Bureau of the Census, *Current Population Reports*, series P-60, no. 148 (Washington, DC: GPO, 1984).

[7]Richard H. Leftwich and Ansel M. Sharp, *Economics of Social Issues*, rev. ed. (Dallas: Business Publications, 1976), p. 221.

[8]For examples, see Eleanor B. Leacock, ed., *The Culture of Poverty: A Critique* (New York: Simon & Schuster, 1971).

[9]Thomas Childers, *The Information-Poor in America* (Metuchen, NJ: Scarecrow Press, 1975).

[10]For a survey of evidence from many studies, see Mary B. Sanger, *Welfare of the Poor* (New York: Academic Press, 1979).

Perhaps even more devastating to the life chances of the poor are their attitudes toward themselves and their future prospects. Because our culture tends to emphasize that people get what they deserve the poor tend to believe they are poor because in some way they deserve to be poor.[11] Furthermore, they tend to believe that the future holds little that will be different. Having such attitudes, they tend to participate less in politics than any other group, as we noted in Chapter 3.

THE RICH IN AMERICA

Who Are Today's Rich?

The percentage of poor in America has remained relatively constant in recent years, but the number of rich has skyrocketed, even in years of economic slowdown. In 1948 there were only 13,000 Americans who owned real estate, goods, stocks, and bonds worth a million dollars or more. In the next two decades, that number had increased almost ten times to 121,000. And by 1986 there were over a million millionaires in the United States, or about one in every 240 people. This amounts to one millionaire in every 100 households. What is more, these individuals together own over $500 billion worth of property, or 12 percent of all individually held property in America.[12]

Who are these American millionaires? Not much is known about their personal lives, for both scholars and the government tend to study the poor rather than the rich.[13] We do know that about one-third are 65 and older, while only 10 percent are under 40. And about half are women. However, although millionaires account for only about 0.4 percent of all Americans, those Americans with net worths of $100,000 or more total five million people, or more than 2 percent of the population.

Who Owns America?

Although 2 percent of the people own property worth $100,000 or more, 10 percent still own nothing or owe more than they own and so have a net indebtedness. *Ownership of property* (real estate, goods, stocks, bonds, and cash) is the most important measure of poverty and wealth in America. If we split the population in two, the bottom half owns only 3 percent of the privately held property, while the top half holds the other 97 percent—and 64 percent of that is owned by the richest 10 percent. Figure 16.1 gives more details.

A second important indicator of poverty and wealth is *annual income*. The top half receives 77 percent of all income, compared to 23 percent for the bottom half. The top 10 percent receives 29 percent, while the bottom 10 percent receives only 1 percent. Figure 16.2 shows income distribution by fifths of the population for various years since 1929, revealing how little the distribution has changed.

The importance of these figures on annual income is twofold. First, they reveal that many Americans have such small incomes that they have difficulty making ends meet, and so few can accumulate property or wealth. Second, the distribution is so unbalanced that in general the rich do indeed get richer while the poor tend to get poorer. Furthermore, what redistribution has occurred in recent years has favored whites over blacks and suburbanites over city dwellers. As a result, the problems of the center cities, where blacks and other poor people tend to be concentrated in urban ghettoes, continue to worsen year by year.

The Causes of Wealth

It may seem strange to speak of the causes of wealth as we do of the causes of poverty. Yet no one believes that wealth is somehow a natural state. About 20 percent of America's millionaires are born wealthy.[14] Research has shown that "one cause of the inequality of property and skills is the degree of privilege conferred by one's socioeconomic background and other parental influences."[15] One such

[11]See Jennifer L. Hochschild, "Redistributing Wealth: Positions, Payments, and Attitudes," in *Public Policy and Public Choice*, eds. Douglas W. Rae and Theodore J. Eismeier (Beverly Hills, CA: Sage, 1979).

[12]This figure is an estimate based on surveys conducted by U.S. Trust Co. of New York and *U.S. News & World Report*. See "Ordinary Millionaires," *U.S. News & World Report*, January 13, 1986, pp. 43–51. The largest percentage of millionaires is in Idaho, where one in every 38 citizens qualifies as one. The smallest is in Wyoming—one in every 3570.

[13]One exception is Ferdinand Lundberg, whose book *The Rich and the Super Rich* (New York: Lyle Stuart, 1968) was widely criticized for inaccuracies. Another exception (and a critic of Lundberg) is former Census Bureau official Herman P. Miller, whose book *Rich Man, Poor Man* (New York: Crowell, 1971) has a chapter devoted to the rich. Unfortunately, its data are so old now as to be virtually meaningless.

[14]"Ordinary Millionaires," p. 44.

[15]John A. Brittain, *The Inheritance of Economic Status* (Washington, DC: Brookings, 1977), p. 1. For a survey of studies on this subject, see p. 78.

The richest 10 percent of U.S. households (first decile)	each has on average money and goods worth	$585,900	which is	63.9 percent of the total household wealth held by all American people
The next richest 10 percent (second decile)	has on average	$136,000	which is	14.8 percent of the total household wealth held by all American people
The next richest 10 percent (third decile)	has on average	$ 80,100	which is	8.7 percent of the total household wealth held by all American people
The next richest 10 percent (fourth decile)	has on average	$ 53,000	which is	5.8 percent of the total household wealth held by all American people
The fifth decile	has on average	$ 35,400	which is	3.9 percent of the total household wealth held by all American people

HERE IS THE MIDPOINT: Half the people are above this and half below

The sixth decile	has on average	$ 20,700	which is	2.3 percent of the total household wealth held by all American people
The seventh decile	has on average	$ 8,600	which is	0.9 percent of the total household wealth held by all American people
The eighth decile	has on average	$ 1,500	which is	0.2 percent of the total household wealth held by all American people

The ninth decile has no wealth holdings, or net worth.

The poorest 10 percent owe, on average, $3,800 more than they own

FIGURE 16.1

The Distribution of Wealth by American Households. *Notes:* These averages are for 1983, the latest year available. Money and goods include savings and the value of stocks and bonds, homes, cars, stereos, etc., less outstanding debts.

Source: Adapted from data in Stephen J. Rose, *The American Profile Poster* (New York: Pantheon, 1986), p. 31.

FIGURE 16.2

Distribution of Family Income in the U.S. Population. (This chart shows how much of the total family income is received by each 20 percent of the population.)

Source: Data from *New York Times Magazine*, July 4, 1976, p. 102 and U.S. Census Bureau.

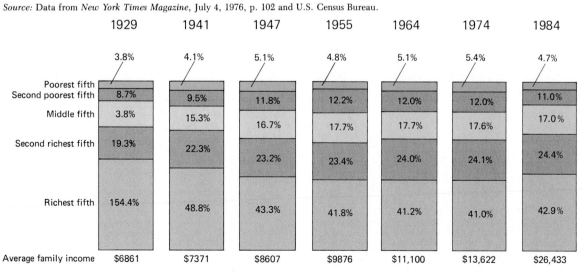

519

influence is educational advantage. Another is parental "pull" or connections (friends and acquaintances) that are helpful in getting jobs and making money. Also important is financial inheritance itself, although one study has found that actual estates are on average inherited when the heir is 38 years old and further that "the children of the rich in America tend to regress toward mean (average) incomes—and thereby prevent the increasing concentration of wealth."[16]

The other major factor in determining wealth is taxation. The federal income tax before the 1986 tax reform was supposed to be "progressive"—to tax those with larger incomes at higher rates. But there were so many loopholes or tax subsidies, as they are called, before tax reform, that much of the progressive effect was lost. Table 16.2 reports the "effective" rate of federal income taxes (the actual rate after allowed deductions) for each income group before reform. It reveals that those with incomes under $10,000 did indeed pay smaller percentages. But there was surprisingly little difference in the rate someone making $10,000 paid compared to that of someone making up to five times that much. Further, an income of $100,000 and an income of many millions of dollars were taxed at almost the identical rate in practice. (We won't have similar data on the actual effects of the new tax law for several years.)

State and local taxes, especially those on consumption, which we call sales taxes, tend to be "regressive"—to tax the poorest the most because everyone has to buy food, clothing, medical supplies, and so forth, but those taxed purchases are a bigger percentage of the income of the poor. When we add in all state and local taxes—on income and property as well as on consumption—the net effect is virtually to equalize almost everyone's burden at around 35 percent.[17] In fact, a 1987 study showed that families making over $500,000 a year paid a smaller share of their income in state and local taxes than those below the poverty line do.[18]

TABLE 16.2
Effective Federal Tax Rates on Income

INCOME RANGE	TAX RATE (%)
0– $3,000	0.5
$3,000– $4,999	1.7
$5,000– $9,999	5.1
$10,000– $14,999	8.6
$15,000– $19,999	10.5
$20,000– $24,999	11.8
$25,000– $49,999	13.9
$50,000– $99,999	22.2
$100,000–$499,999	31.0
$500,000–$999,999	32.8
Over $1,000,000	34.2
Average for all ranges	11.0

Source: Charles L. Schultze et al., *Setting National Priorities: The 1973 Budget* (Washington, DC: Brookings Institution, 1972), p. 434. Copyright © 1972 by the Brookings Institution.

These tax provisions—special subsidies and relatively constant tax rates—have made it easier for the rich to become richer, for they leave the rich with more after-tax income to use in making still more income. Our inheritance laws do the same.[19] The inheritance tax rate could have gone as high as 77 percent (on estates of over $10 million). But there have always been so many loopholes that the actual rate was about 0.2 percent even before rates were drastically lowered by the Reagan administration. Thus, most family fortunes can be passed on from one generation to the next largely intact.

THE WORKING MIDDLE CLASS— NEITHER RICH NOR POOR

Where the Typical American's Money Goes

These years, the average American taxpayer pays about 35 percent of his or her earnings in taxes—federal, state, and local. That means $1 of every $3 you earn is likely to go to the tax collectors. Viewed another way, if you work, you work for the tax collectors from January until early May, and after that your earnings are yours to spend on housing, food, clothing, and other items. Or viewed yet another way, in a typical eight-hour day, your first 2 hours and 40 minutes are spent working for the

[16]Stanley Lebergott, *The American Economy: Income, Wealth and Want* (Princeton, NJ: Princeton Univ. Press, 1976), pp. 176, 211.

[17]These matters are now widely discussed in the literature. See, for example, Miller, *Rich Man, Poor Man*, chap. 2, and Joseph Pechman and Benjamin Okner, *Who Bears the Tax Burden?* (Washington, DC: Brookings, 1974). See also Edgar K. Browning and William R. Johnson, *The Distribution of the Tax Burden* (Washington, DC: American Enterprise Institute, 1979), esp. chap. 4.

[18]Associated Press, "Study Shows State, Local Taxes Unfair to Poor," *Daily Texan*, January 15, 1987.

[19]See Lester Thurow, *Generating Inequality* (New York: Basic Books, 1975).

tax collectors. Then, if you're a typical American, you work another hour and 34 minutes to pay for your housing and an hour and 4 minutes to pay for food. After this comes 42 minutes for transportation, 36 minutes for medical care, 21 minutes for clothing, and 20 minutes for recreation. The last 43 minutes of the work day go for such things as personal items, education, savings, and so on.[20] It doesn't take much calculating, given figures like these, to see why the average American doesn't improve his or her financial situation much.

Is the Middle Class Disappearing?

Most Americans now call themselves middle class or working class, as Table 16.3 shows. Still, we can divide families in terms of income level. As Table 16.4 reports, 44 percent of all families have incomes ranging from $15,000 to $35,000. The median (or middle, with half earning more and half less) family income is now $29,527. These income levels have been achieved in large part by spouses going to work. Today, in more than half of all households with children, both parents hold paying jobs. Indeed, only 7 percent of households now fit the once-typical pattern of a working father, a homemaker mother, and two kids. But the limited opportunities for largely untrained women are such that the impact of the second income is usually quite small. And its impact on the status of the growing number of people living in families headed by women—about 11 million—is very severe. In the past decade, average household income adjusted for inflation has declined over 10 percent, and average wages have fallen by over 15 percent.

TABLE 16.4
Money Income of American Families, 1984

MONEY INCOME	PERCENTAGE OF FAMILIES	
Under $5,000	7.9	
$5,000– 9,999	13.2	33.3
$10,000–14,999	12.2	
$15,000–19,999	11.4	
$20,000–24,999	10.4	38.7
$25,000–34,999	16.9	
$35,000–49,999	15.3	
$50,000 and over	12.8	
Total number of families	86,789,000	
Median income	$22,415	
Poverty level	$10,609	

Note: Totals do not add to 100 percent because of rounding.
Source: Statistical Abstract of the United States 1986. p. 445.

Potentially even more significant for the economic status of middle-class households is the change in job opportunities. The traditional middle-income jobs in America are disappearing. Historically, these jobs were in manufacturing, and they paid on the average about three times the minimum wage. In the decade between 1958 and 1968, manufacturing added 4 million new jobs. In the next decade, 1968–1978, it added less than a million new jobs. And since then it has lost 3 million jobs. As we saw in the last chapter, our economy is undergoing a revolution. Service industries—from banking and computers to fast food—are replacing manufacturing.

The impact of this trend on incomes is severe. Some of the new service jobs (executives and computer programmers) are very high paying. But

TABLE 16.3
How Americans Identify Themselves

CLASS	1952	1978
Lower class	2.2%	0.0%
Working class	59.0	52.3
Middle class	35.5	46.9
Upper class	1.7	0.1
Other	1.5	0.6

Source: Robert J. Samuelson, "Blue Collar, White Collar," *National Journal,* April 2, 1983, p. 709.

[20]These figures, for 1984, were furnished by the Tax Foundation.

(By Gamble for the Florida Times-Union)

many of them (hamburger cooks and computer terminal typists) are very low paying. Thus, workers in the fastest-growing industries are earning an average of $5000 a year less than those in the declining industries. Indeed, 60 percent of the 8 million jobs created between 1979 and 1984 pay less than $7000 a year.[21] Most of the newer industries are not unionized; union membership among workers is now down to about 20 percent—the lowest level in almost 50 years.[22] The result is that between 1978 and 1983 about 13 percent of the middle portion of the middle class disappeared—10 percent of it heading toward poverty and only 3 percent gaining. Figure 16.3 shows this graphically.

These trends have been exacerbated by the recession of 1981–1982 and by the growing trade competition from countries with lower labor and manufacturing costs. Even the economic recovery that started in 1984 did not reverse them. Many experts believe they will continue and that their outcome may be the virtual disappearance of the middle class as we have known it in the United States.[23]

If the trend does prove lasting, it may have important political consequences. As economist Lester Thurow has written:

> It is a cause of concern for the American political democracy. What Karl Marx saw as an inevitable revolution was based on the assumption that the economy would eventually generate a bipolar income distribution composed of rich and poor. Once this bipolar situation existed, he said, the poor would revolt, destroy the rich, and establish communism. But Marx's predicted revolution did not occur because he did not foresee the rise of the middle class. The middle class had an interest in preserving capitalism and voted to alleviate the worse excesses of capitalism with social welfare programs. Their very presence gave the poor hope that they too could escape from poverty.[24]

[21]Jane Seaberry, "Been Up So Long It Looks Like Down To Me," *Washington Post National Weekly Edition*, January 19, 1987, p. 9. See also Timothy B. Clark, "Waging a New Debate," *National Journal*, Jan. 3, 1987.

[22]For a study of unions and their influence, see Richard B. Freeman and James L. Medoff, *What Do Unions Do?* (New York: Basic Books, 1984).

[23]See Bob Kuttner, "The Declining Middle," *Atlantic Monthly*, July 1983, pp. 60–72, on which this analysis is partly based; "Marketing: The New Priority," *Business Week*, November 21, 1983, pp. 96–106; and Bruce Steinberg, "The Mass Market Is Splitting Apart," *Fortune*, November 28, 1983, pp. 76–82. But for an argument that this conclusion is a misinterpretation of the evidence, see Robert J. Samuelson, "Middle-Class Media Myth," *National Journal*, December 31, 1983, pp. 2673–78, and "The Myth of the Vanishing Middle Class," *Business Week*, July 9, 1984, pp. 83–86.

[24]Lester C. Thurow, "The Disappearance of the Middle Class," *New York Times*, February 5, 1984.

If suddenly the middle class disappears, or cannot or will not support programs to combat poverty, American politics could change drastically.

POLICIES AND PROGRAMS TO COMBAT POVERTY

Until recently, aid to the poor was mostly the province of private charity and big-city "machines." The legislation and government programs affecting the poor often did more to control them (for example, restrictions on unionizing) than to help them meet their day-to-day needs, let alone help them escape poverty. Politicians, of course, had long talked of such improvements. In 1928 President Herbert Hoover had declared: "We shall soon, with the help of God, be in sight of a day when poverty will be banished in the nation." But Hoover instead found himself presiding over the coming of the Great Depression. Four years later there were 13 million unemployed, more than a quarter of the work force. It took Franklin Roosevelt's New Deal and World War II just to return America, almost 20 years later, to approximately the working conditions of 1928.

The keystone of the New Deal was legislation providing greater economic security for all Americans, rich as well as poor. The Social Security Act of 1935 established the system of contributions by workers into a *social security* fund called Old Age, Survivors, and Disability Insurance (OASDI) that paid pensions to the unemployed elderly. Similarly, a program of contributory *unemployment insurance* was established, which for the first time granted some of those losing jobs support payments while they looked for new jobs. Both programs, with certain modifications, persist to this day as the heart of the federal government's approach to the problems of the poor—but these programs are available to everyone, rich and poor alike. In fact, most federal economic programs affect both the rich and the poor, even if they were designed primarily to cope with poverty. There are five major categories of such programs:

- Welfare programs
- Employment and occupational safety and health programs
- Consumer-protection programs
- Inflation-control programs
- Tax-reform programs

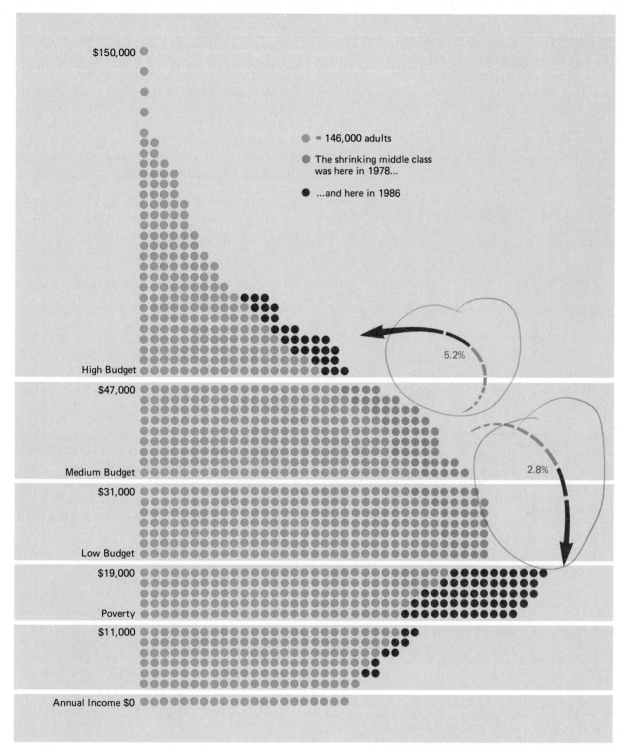

FIGURE 16.3

The Shrinking Middle Class, 1978–1986. (This chart shows that between 1978 and 1986 approximately 8 percent of the middle portion of the middle class [as defined by the Bureau of Labor Statistics] disappeared. Of this 8 percent, one-third rose into the upper-middle-class category, and two-thirds descended into the lower middle class. Furthermore, the number of people below the poverty line increased by 3 percent. This downward shift represents a significant change in the nature of the American social fabric. The chart, which is based on government statistics, was created by economist Stephen J. Rose and designed by Kathryn Shagas and Dennis Livingston.

Source: Stephen J. Rose, *The American Profile Poster* (New York: Pantheon, 1986) p. 10.

523

The last four can best be thought of as attempts to promote the general welfare. The first, which we call welfare, is intended to combat poverty. Let's look at each of the first four, since we looked at tax reform in Perspective One.

Welfare Programs

The Range of Welfare Programs

Many different welfare programs have been attempted or proposed over the years. In general, these fall into five major categories:

1. The *direct-income* programs attempt to increase the consumption of recipients by increasing their income. Foremost among these are the *social insurance* programs such as Social Security, unemployment insurance, and workers' compensation (which pays benefits to those injured on the job), and *public assistance* programs such as Aid to Families with Dependent Children. This group also includes proposals for a **guaranteed family income** or a **negative income tax** that would pay money directly to those poor who earn less than a minimum income.

2. The *direct services* programs provide needed services directly to those who can't afford them. The *food stamps* program, which grants coupons spendable only for food is one such program. Nearly one in every ten Americans receives food stamps. *Housing assistance* is another. The government subsidizes housing for about ten million families every year, at a cost of $9.9 billion. *Medicaid*, which provides federal funds to states to pay for some medical care for 22 million poor people, is yet another. Other such programs furnish day care, family-planning assistance, community legal services, and social casework services.

3. The *indirect services* programs provide services such as *education* or *manpower training* in job skills so that the poor can get better jobs.

4. The *indirect income* programs foster *economic development* of depressed areas to create jobs for the poor and *minimum wages* and *unionization* to improve the labor market.

5. The *community organizing* programs attempt to strengthen the political power of poor neighborhoods so that they can demand better treatment from local government and businesses.[25]

By now, more than one-third of all Americans, some poor but many far from poor, receive assis-

tance of some sort from one or more of these federal programs. These programs together cost well over $400 billion per year. The $400 billion total works out to almost one-fifth of all personal income in America and averages over $1000 per American, although the benefits are not spread evenly. Some of this aid is in Social Security payments and public assistance for the 32 million people who are blind, disabled, or elderly and for poor families with dependent children. But most Social Security, Medicare, unemployment, and veterans' benefits payments go to those who are not poor. And many other individuals, some far from poor, receive special government benefits. Figure 16.4 shows the various sources from which all families derive their incomes on the average and those from which the poor derive theirs.

The Extent of the Welfare System

Our concern at this point is with the part of this colossal spending that is intended to help the poor—the welfare system, as it is called. It is by now a massive system. It provides aid to about 25 million people at a cost of over $45 billion. Doing so requires some 350,000 employees, 4000 of whom are federal and the rest state and local officials. Most of these programs are administered by state and local governments but largely financed—and

FIGURE 16.4

Sources of Income for the Poor and for All Families. *Note:* These figures are percentages, based on U.S. Census Bureau figures for 1978.

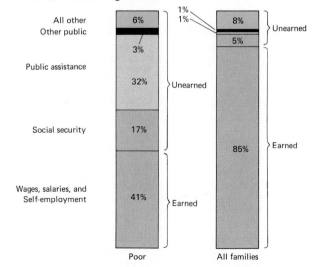

---

[25]For a summary of programs in these various categories, see Sar A. Levitan, *Programs in Aid of the Poor for the 1980s*, 4th ed. (Baltimore: Johns Hopkins Univ. Press, 1980).

controlled—by Washington. The sole exception is what is called general assistance, which is organized and financed by states and localities. One result of this decentralization of some programs is that welfare spending per individual varies considerably from state to state.

A more general result of this overlapping of responsibilities and funding is the complexity of the welfare system. Jimmy Carter, like most politicians, campaigned on a pledge to reform welfare. His secretary of health, education, and welfare, Joseph A. Califano, put the problem well:

> Given the vast resources this nation spends on income assistance, it is appalling that our programs are so poorly coordinated . . . , unfairly exclude millions from adequate aid, contain absurd incentives to break up families or discourage work . . . and are an administrative jungle, incomprehensible to legislators, administrators and the American people alike.

Califano should know, for the department he headed, HEW, shared with the Labor Department the primary responsibility for what we call our welfare system at the federal level.

Obviously, we cannot in this chapter solve a problem that is massive and complex enough to stymie our government. But we can clarify the objectives of the welfare program and the politics of the debate over welfare reform. With that accomplished, we should be able to examine the various programs, both those already attempted and those proposed, to see which seem most promising in terms of the objectives and most possible in terms of the politics.

The Objectives of the Welfare System

There is no agreement on just what the objectives of the welfare system are or should be. When the American people are asked whether they favor the welfare system, they say no. For example, one national survey found that 58 percent disapproved of "most government-sponsored welfare programs."[26] Included in that majority of disapprovers was even a majority of those who had received welfare! On the other hand, these same people favored food stamps for the poor by 81 to 13 percent, aid to poor families with dependent children, 81 to 13 percent, and health care for the poor, 82 to 13 percent. So the same people who oppose "welfare" over-whelmingly favor the three major welfare programs.

Perhaps these attitudes reflect the common uncertainty about just what welfare programs should seek to achieve. There seems general acceptance of the objective of improving the living conditions of the poor to a decent level. But what is a decent level? Even most of the poor in America are better off now than most citizens were in 1900, at least in certain respects. For example, in 1900 only 15 percent of all living quarters had flush toilets; now it is almost 99 percent. In 1900 only 3 percent had electricity, but by 1980, 99 percent did. In 1900 only 1 percent of all Americans had central heating, while now some 60 percent of the poor have it. The important point is that the poor are better off in *absolute* terms but remain worse off in *relative* terms. They suffer from what sociologists call **relative deprivation**—being deprived of something relative to what other people have.

Does this mean, then, that the American people, who favor overcoming various types of relative deprivation, support *equality* as a social goal? There have always been some liberals who advocate extensive equality—*an equal start* and *equal treatment under law*, of the sort we discussed in Chapters 13 and 14. Some go further to advocate virtual *equality of income*, and even *of possessions*. These are the socialists. Conservatives tend to support only so much equality as is necessary to preserve societal stability. If there were too much inequality, the result might be revolution in which the privileged would lose everything. This fear can be a powerful reason to support welfare programs. Indeed, some argue that a major function of such programs—and other government activities—has been to keep the working class quiet.[27]

Conservatives have also generally believed that *inequality* is functional for capitalism because it creates incentives for the poor to work harder, and it allows the system to give greater rewards to those who take risks or contribute specially. Conservatives thus tend to prefer efficiency and liberty to

---

[26]*New York Times*-CBS News Poll, July 1977, reported in the *New York Times*, August 3, 1977.

[27]For interesting discussions of some of these points, see Frances Fox Piven and Richard Cloward, *Regulating the Poor* (New York: Pantheon, 1971); Murray Edelman, *Politics as Symbolic Action* (Chicago: Markham, 1971); Philip Green, *The Pursuit of Inequality* (New York: Pantheon, 1981); and Douglas Rae, *Equalities* (Cambridge, MA: Harvard Univ. Press, 1981). And for an empirical study, see James R. Kluegel and Eliot R. Smith, *Beliefs about Inequality* (Hawthorne, NY: Aldine de Gruyter, 1986).

equality, while liberals prefer the reverse.[28] But public policy on the question of the welfare system rarely comes down to such basic attitudes because both poverty and welfare programs already exist and continue to grow. The question policy makers have to confront is how serious the present situation is.

The Definition of the Problem

There are basic differences in beliefs about the nature, causes, and cures of poverty that have important implications for the design of welfare programs.[29]

Is poverty basically caused by individual factors, such as effort, motivation, genetic inheritance, being old, and so forth? Or is it primarily caused by situational factors, such as growing up in a poor family, getting a bad education, seeking work in a time of high unemployment, facing racial or sexual discrimination, and so forth?

Those who consider poverty primarily a product of individual factors tend to hold the poor person responsible. They also tend to be pessimistic about the success of antipoverty programs. So they generally favor only as much welfare as is required to keep the population quiet.

Those who see poverty as primarily situational are more likely to support welfare programs. They may hope that such programs will change factors like poor job training or widespread unemployment. Or they may see welfare programs as "tiding over" the victim until the economy improves or discrimination lessens.

The situational view assumes that poverty can be temporary, if only conditions can be changed. The individual view, on the other hand, expects poverty to be lasting in the absence of character change or "lesson learning" by the poor. Which is closer to the truth? Until very recently, statistics seemed to show that most people who were poor stayed poor.[30]

A jobless woman uses food stamps to buy food.
(Mike Maple/Woodfin Camp Associates)

But a large-scale study of a representative sample of 5000 families from across the United States in the 1970s found that there are relatively few such "hard-core poor." This study, carried out at the University of Michigan, found that poverty is a temporary situation for most people. People may move into poverty when they get divorced or first leave the home of their parents. But they may also leave poverty by getting married, changing jobs, or getting more schooling. The fact is that while one of every seven or eight American families may be in poverty at any given time, *only about a quarter of these families are likely to stay in poverty for five years in a row.* Those who do are most likely to be families headed by uneducated blacks, but some have elderly, female, or disabled heads. On the other hand, the study found that *nearly one-third of all people fell below the poverty line for at least one of the ten years* over which the study had been conducted.[31]

But as William Ryan concludes from this study:

> The economic fate of most of us is not within our own control, but is, rather, intertwined with that of countless others. This means that at least seven out of ten families are economically vulnerable, with at least an even chance of spending some years of their lives in financial distress. It is not merely some vague minority called "the poor" who stand in economic peril; it is the majority of Americans.[32]

[28]For a discussion of the "functionalist theory of inequality" see Michael Best and William Connolly, *The Politicized Economy* (Lexington, MA: Heath, 1976), chap. 3; for a discussion of the conservative versus the liberal point of view, see Arthur M. Okun, *Equality and Efficiency: The Big Tradeoff* (Washington, DC: Brookings, 1975).

[29]See Lester M. Salamon, *Welfare: The Elusive Consensus: Where We Are, How We Got There, and What's Ahead* (New York: Praeger, 1978).

[30]Robert J. Lampman, *Ends and Means of Reducing Income Poverty* (Madison: Institute for Research on Poverty of the Univ. of Wisconsin, 1971), p. 62.

[31]The Panel Study on Income Dynamics, directed by James N. Morgan at the Univ. of Michigan. See Greg Duncan, *Years of Poverty, Years of Plenty* (Ann Arbor: Univ. of Michigan Institute for Social Research, 1984).

[32]William Ryan, "Most of Us Are Kept on a Short Leash," *New York Times*, July 10, 1977.

But though each of us may thus someday be affected by how the welfare system operates, few of us are actually involved in welfare reform. Nor are the interests of the majority of Americans of direct concern to those who are engaged in reshaping the program.

The Politics of Welfare Reform

Nobody admits to liking the welfare system the way it is.[33] But different groups mean different things by "welfare reform." To the public, reform means lower costs and less fraud. To welfare recipients, reform means better benefits. These two positions are already in conflict—but neither group plays much role in shaping programs. That responsibility is shared by the Department of Health and Human Services and the Department of Labor, which oversee the programs; by the Congress, which passes the laws creating and funding them; and by the huge "welfare bureaucracy" that has developed in state and local governments. State and local governments face the prospect of bankruptcy as welfare costs soar, and so they favor having Washington pay the shares they now pay. Many in Washington agree.

But what the government raises money and writes checks for, it also tries to control. State and local government welfare bureaucrats fear such control. The welfare bureaucracy now offers many places for politicians to put their friends and supporters in comfortable jobs. Employees and politicians are generally opposed to federal control of the welfare bureaucracy.

So the task of reformers in the White House and the cabinet departments is very difficult politically—as Presidents Johnson, Nixon, Carter, and Reagan all found out during their terms in office. They were always dealing with all these vested— and competing—interests while trying to bring order to, and make more effective and efficient, a wide range of programs costing billions of dollars every year.[34]

The War on Poverty and the Great Society

Many of these programs were established in the years of President Lyndon Johnson's Great Society. Under Johnson's "War on Poverty," federal aid to the poor almost doubled, from $7.7 billion in 1964 to $15 billion in 1968. Indeed, it kept rising in the Nixon-Ford years as well, to $18 billion in 1970, $27 billion in 1974, and about $40 billion in 1977. It is now over $60 billion. But public sentiment for these programs of cash support, employment and training, community and economic development, education, health, housing, food, and child care has been eroding year by year as Americans faced the unprecedented combination of inflation and recession under Nixon, Carter, and Reagan. Americans became more conscious of their own economic problems and less willing to help the even more impoverished poor.

Nonetheless, the War on Poverty was quite successful in lifting people out of poverty.[35] As Table 16.5 shows, the actual percentages of people in poverty, even today, are much lower than they would be without government benefits. For example, in 1982, at the depths of the recession, the official total of people living below the poverty level was 15 percent. Without these programs it would have been 24 percent. When food stamps and other noncash benefits are included, the percentage living in poverty in 1982 drops to 8.8.[36] The same trend was true in 1972, when the War on Poverty was at its height, as Table 16.5 also shows. But the War on Poverty has its critics as well—critics who argue that politics limited its success.[37]

First, it created tremendous conflicts within the government, for it established an Office of Economic Opportunity (OEO) to develop and administer programs that often overlapped and sometimes conflicted with existing programs in such departments as HEW, Labor, and Agriculture. The

---

[33]For an interesting analysis of the deep ambivalence in American culture, see Hugh Heclo, "General Welfare and Two American Political Traditions," *Political Science Quarterly 101* (1986), 179–96.

[34]For an interesting account of welfare-reform efforts during the Carter administration, see Joseph A. Califano, Jr., *Governing America: An Insider's Report from the White House and the Cabinet* (New York: Simon & Schuster, 1981). Califano had responsibility for welfare in Carter's cabinet until he was fired. See also the detailed account in Laurence E. Lynn, Jr., and David deF. Whitman, *The President as Policymaker: Jimmy Carter and Welfare Reform* (Philadelphia: Temple Univ. Press, 1981).

[35]See John E. Schwartz, *America's Hidden Success: A Reassessment of Twenty Years of Public Policy* (New York: Norton, 1983).

[36]For an analysis of this, see Charles A. Murray, "The Two Wars against Poverty: Economic Growth and the Great Society," *Public Interest* 69 (Fall 1982), 3–16, and also his book *Losing Ground* (New York: Basic Books, 1984).

[37]For varying assessments, see Sar A. Levitan and Robert Taggart, *The Promise of Greatness* (Cambridge, MA: Harvard Univ. Press, 1976), pp. 7–11; Theodore Caplow, *Toward Social Hope* (New York: Basic Books, 1975), p. 167; and Henry J. Aaron, *Politics and the Professors: The Great Society in Perspective* (Washington, DC: Brookings, 1978).

TABLE 16.5

The Percentage of Americans in Poverty

Year	OFFICIAL POVERTY RATE (BASED ON PERSONAL INCOME PLUS CASH BENEFITS FROM GOVERNMENT)[a]	POVERTY RATE (WITH FOOD STAMPS AND NONCASH BENEFITS COUNTED AS INCOME)[b]	ESTIMATED POVERTY RATE (WITHOUT ANY GOVERNMENT BENEFITS)[c]
1965	17.3%	12.1%	21.3%
1972	11.9	6.2	19.2
1976	11.8	6.7	21.0
1979	11.7	6.1	20.5
1982	15.0	8.8	24.0

[a]Census Bureau figure.
[b]Calculated by Timothy M. Smeeding, University of Utah; includes adjustments for underreporting and taxes.
[c]Calculated by Sheldon Danziger, University of Wisconsin.
Source: Washington Post, May 6, 1984.

result was endless bureaucratic politicking that only hindered efforts to help the poor.

This proliferation of overlapping programs also inevitably created confusion in the mind of an individual who wanted help. For example, a high school dropout in need of assistance might not know whether to go to the local branch of the Office of Education of HEW, the Office of Juvenile Delinquency of the Labor Department, the OEO's Neighborhood Youth Corps or Job Corps—or the local welfare bureaucracy.[38]

There were other problems that whatever the good reasons for them, in fact crippled the programs' effectiveness. Because local political and welfare bureaucracies were so often either corrupt or incompetent, officials in Washington decided to bypass them in designing and implementing the federal programs. The unfortunate but unsurprising result was that state and local officials often united to prevent such programs from succeeding or even to keep them out altogether.

Probably because they were more visible and easier to reach, the program increasingly concentrated on urban blacks, even though this group constituted a minority of the poor. The result was that other possible support for the program was missed, and when urban blacks became more militant and seemed ungrateful, public and congressional support for the programs virtually evaporated.

Nonetheless, the Johnson and Nixon administrations had enlarged income support programs and

added to them a wide range of devices that provided a "safety net" for the truly poor. But the United States suffered severe recessions in the mid-1970s and in 1981–1982. Most of the gains the War on Poverty had achieved for the poor disappeared.

The Reagan Administration

President Carter campaigned on a pledge to revamp welfare, but Congress would not go along. When he took office, President Reagan declared his objectives to be twofold: cutting federal spending on antipoverty and other social programs and returning responsibilities for such programs to the grassroots. His first budget, for fiscal 1982, as passed by Congress, produced the first absolute decline in federal aid in 25 years. In later years, Congress increased such spending slightly over Reagan's requests. At the same time, states took up much of the slack—and thereby gained much of the control. The result was that most welfare programs continued at a level less than would have been expected had Reagan not been president but more than Reagan wished.[39]

However, this pattern coincided with the worst recession in 40 years. The result was a drastic increase in those living below the poverty line. Furthermore, the one program the states did not pick up was income supplements for the working poor.

---

[38]For a discussion of this and other problems, see Ben Seligman, *Permanent Poverty: An American Syndrome* (Chicago: Quadrangle, 1970).

[39]See John Herbers, "States Finance Aid Programs Reduced by U.S., Study Finds," *New York Times,* June 10, 1984—a report of a three-year study by the Woodrow Wilson School of Princeton Univ.

Democratic senators eat the school lunch approved by the Department of Agriculture under President Reagan in order to dramatize charges that the meal is inadequate because, among other things, it substitutes ketchup for a vegetable. (David Burnett/Contact)

Reagan wanted the working poor removed from the welfare rolls, and he succeeded. The result was greater poverty for many who were trying to escape by working but couldn't earn enough to do so.

The Reagan administration argued that its budget cuts did not really hurt the poor more than anyone else. But the Congressional Budget Office, the nonpartisan research arm of Congress, found otherwise. Its reports showed that Reagan and Congress cut spending on human-resources programs, as they are called, to be 7 percent below the levels they would have reached under previous laws and patterns. That worked out to a loss of $1,340 in assistance for a family with an annual income of only $10,000. By contrast, a family with an income of $40,000 to $80,000 lost only $390. The reason was that programs specifically for the poor—"means-tested,"—were cut much more than programs available to all regardless of income, such as Social Security and veterans' benefits.

The Reagan administration justified such cuts on the grounds that they would lead to more economic growth, which would benefit most of the poor—especially female-headed households, 42 percent of which are poor, and adults 25 to 64 years old, 10 percent of whom are poor. These poor adults, it pointed out, make up 52 percent of the poor, and female-headed households are 33 percent. So greater economic growth should help 85 percent of the poor.[40] In fact, however, the savings on welfare programs were more than outweighed by massive increases in military spending. Such spending is not a very efficient way to increase economic growth.[41] Military-equipment contractors use highly skilled labor and materials (special metals and electronics) that are very expensive. So the number of people below the poverty line continued high even when the economy generally began to improve in late 1983.

So the problem of poverty is still very much with us and at a much higher level than usual when economic times are bad. This leads many to continue to support traditional antipoverty programs but to argue that we must also find ways to reduce basic, long-term poverty.

Further Programs for the Poor

Only about 10 percent of those on welfare are able-bodied males who could work if jobs were available. Thus, ending poverty will require more than economic growth and welfare payments. Experts argue that many other special programs will be essential. Some of these proposed programs are general, such as progress on birth control; programs of care for special needs of children, including health, special education, and day care; remedial education at the elementary and secondary levels; and progress toward an adequate guaranteed annual income for all Americans. Other proposed programs have immediate economic impacts and emphasize employment, such as further employment and training programs for employable poor; greater progress in equal employment opportunities for blacks, Hispanics, Native Americans, women, and the elderly; and increases in the level and coverage of the minimum wage. Still other programs concern protection of the health and safety of workers, protection of consumers, tax reform, and inflation control. In the rest of this chapter, we'll examine some of the most important—and most difficult—proposals designed to "promote the general welfare."

---

[40]Robert Pear, "Are There More of Those with Less?" *New York Times*, November 27, 1983.
[41]See Lloyd Dumas, *The Overburdened Economy* (Berkeley: Univ. of Calif. Press, 1986).

POLICIES AND PROGRAMS TO PROMOTE THE GENERAL WELFARE

Employment and Occupational Safety and Health Programs

In the colonial years, there was a shortage of labor in America, despite the fact that slaves constituted perhaps 20 percent of the population. It was with the great influx of immigrants seeking a better life in America some 100 years later that unemployment first became a sustained problem. The problem is now so great that even in good times, some seven or eight million Americans are consistently unable to find work. In an average year, one of every six Americans is jobless for some length of time, and the average length of unemployment is about eight months.[42] During the 1981–1983 recession, unemployment reached 10.7 percent, and 22 percent of all workers were jobless at some time in 1982. In 1983 only 78 percent of all men aged 16 or over worked at any time. Since then, the unemployment rate has declined somewhat.[43] Unemployment costs some $20 billion a year in various benefit programs, over and above its human costs. Simply bringing it down to 4 percent and absorbing workers displaced by new machines and people seeking their first jobs would require creation of an average of 72,000 new jobs every week for a decade.

The Quantity of Work

The government adopted the objective of full employment in 1946. Still, the first major effort to train workers and create jobs was the Manpower Development and Training Act (MDTA) of 1962. That act was funded with a mere $81 million in 1963. In the following 18 years, spending on jobs programs grew to around $11 billion a year. Total spending in that period was $75 billion. Most of this came under the Comprehensive Employment and Training Act (CETA), passed first under Nixon in 1973 and reauthorized under Carter in 1978. CETA was designed to train and employ mostly unskilled workers, largely in cities. It relied on some 500 contractors—both local government and private—to carry out this program, and so it was highly decentralized. The program became controversial because it cost an average of $28,000 to train one worker for a new job. As a result, CETA was one of the first targets of the Reagan administration budget cutters, who allowed it to end in 1982. Others, however, argued with the foremost expert on job programs, Eli Ginzberg, that

> the real choice that the American people face is not greater or lesser support for manpower programs in the future, but rather the basic decision as to whether or not they desire to affirm the nation's long-term commitment to a society built on work. In the event that they affirm this commitment, they have no option but to support the further elaboration of manpower policy and programming, which is a necessary if not sufficient condition for achieving this primary national goal.[44]

This thinking eventually led the Reagan administration to approve the Job Training Partnership Act. It replaced CETA in October 1983 with a program of vocational and on-the-job training, primarily for poor youths. With a budget only half the size of CETA's, it shifted attention from manufacturing to service-sector jobs such as health care, auto repair, and computers.

The Quality of Work

Jobs programs are aimed primarily at the poor and members of minority groups, people who have not been trained or educated for the sort of jobs increasingly available in our automating economy.[45] The fact that we need such programs reminds us that the United States continues to have a problem of the *quantity* of work. But at the same time, the

---

[42]The first figure is from the government's *Handbook of Labor Statistics*, which is published annually. The second comes from a study by economist George A. Akerlof reported in *Business Week*, March 30, 1980, p. 16.

[43]The government's official unemployment rate counts only those people not working at all and still actively seeking a job. Experts estimate that the rate would almost double if it included those who want to work but have given up looking plus those who work only part time but want full-time work. See "Is Government Masking Real Jobless Rate?" *New Age Journal*, March 1986, p. 10. But some economists believe the rate would be several points lower if those working in the illegal "underground economy" admitted this. See Don Hopey, "Researcher Questions Accuracy of Official U.S. Jobless Count," *Austin American-Statesman*, March 2, 1986.

[44]Eli Ginzberg, ed., *Employing the Unemployed* (New York: Basic Books, 1980), p. 193. See also Ginzberg's other book, *Good Jobs, Bad Jobs, No Jobs* (Cambridge, MA: Harvard Univ. Press, 1980). For a study that takes these arguments even further, see Samuel Bowles, David M. Gordon, and Thomas E. Weisskopf, *Beyond the Waste Land* (Garden City, NY: Doubleday, 1983).

[45]For a study of the politics of unemployment that attempts to explain why the unemployed do not unite to demand government aid, see Kay Lehman Schlozman and Sidney Verba, *Injury to Insult: Unemployment, Class, and Political Response* (Cambridge, MA: Harvard Univ. Press, 1980). And see Bryant Robey and Cheryl Russell, "A Portrait of the American Worker," *American Demographics*, March 1984, pp. 17–21.

"We've solved the 8% unemployment problem, Chief . . . We'll call it 92% employment!" (*Dunagin's People* by Ralph Dunagin. © 1979 Field Enterprises, Inc. Courtesy of News America Syndicate.)

movement for improved quality of work is gaining momentum. Workers still respond to questions of whether "you are satisfied or dissatisfied with the work you do" by saying "satisfied" in general. But when asked if they would work if money were not needed, 31 percent say no.

Furthermore, alcoholism, absenteeism, sabotage, and turnover—all marks of dissatisfaction—are increasing among American workers generally. As one government report put it:

> Significant numbers of American workers are dissatisfied with the quality of their working lives. Dull, repetitive, seemingly meaningless tasks, offering little challenge or autonomy, are causing discontent among workers at all occupational levels. This is not so much because work itself has greatly changed; indeed, one of the main problems is that work has not changed fast enough to keep up with the rapid and widescale changes in worker attitudes, aspirations, and values. A general increase in their educational and economic status has placed many American workers in a position where having an interesting job is now as important as having a job that pays well. Pay is still important: it must support an "adequate" standard of living and be perceived as equitable—but high pay alone will not lead to job (or life) satisfaction."[46]

Occupational Safety and Health

So some have no jobs while others have jobs they find unsatisfying. But in addition, many workers have jobs that are unsafe. Government reports estimate that some 14,500 workers die each year from on-the-job injuries. But another 100,000 die each year as a result of long-term exposure to conditions or materials that cause cancer, emphysema, and other fatal disorders. And a comprehensive study by the National Institute of Occupational Safety and Health in 1977 found that one out of every four Americans is exposed on the job to some substance thought to be capable of causing death or disease.[47] The Department of Labor reports that 1 in every 11 workers is injured or becomes ill on the job each year. The cost of these injuries totals over $16 billion each year, according to the National Safety Council.[48]

The Occupational Safety and Health Act passed by Congress in 1970 requires employers to see that the place of employment is "free from recognized hazards that are causing, or are likely to cause, death or serious physical harm to his employees" and gives employees the right to file complaints if they think there is a violation. Under the law, the Occupational Safety and Health Administration (OSHA) sets standards and inspects America's five million workplaces to see that the standards are observed. But thus far, enforcement has been difficult. First, OSHA has far too few inspectors—only about one for every 10,000 factories, or one for every 120,000 employees. Second, many of its inspectors still lack adequate training. Third, penalties for violations are so low that it can be cheaper for factories to pay occasional fines than to correct the violation. More generally, "OSHA has been relatively ineffective to date because the existing regulatory structure is simply not capable of addressing the millions of separate problems that constitute the occupational safety and health problem in the United States."[49]

Despite these limitations, the operations and the very existence of OSHA have been controversial from the beginning. Businesses have strongly ob-

[46]*Work in America, Report of a Special Task Force to the Secretary of Health, Education and Welfare* (Cambridge, MA: MIT Press, 1973), summary.

[47]See David Burnham, "1 in 4 Americans Exposed to Hazards on Job, Study Says," *New York Times*, October 3, 1977. See also James R. Michael, ed., *Working on the System* (New York: Basic Books, 1974), chap. 16.

[48]National Safety Council, *Accident Facts* (Chicago: NSC, 1975).

[49]Lawrence S. Bacow, *Bargaining for Job Safety and Health* (Cambridge, MA: MIT Press, 1981), p. 49.

jected to the costs of such regulation. One of the objectives of the Reagan administration has been deregulation. The Reagan approach has sought to balance the cost of regulation against the benefits.

At Reagan's urging, OSHA went on to limit regulation and inspection in one area after another. But in 1984, an estimated 5,400,000 workers suffered work-related illness or injury—an 11.7 percent increase over 1983. Some of this increase was attributable to the fact that workers worked more hours as the economy picked up. But most experts blamed cutbacks in regulation and inspection for much of it. In any case, the administration began to reverse its course. One reason was that as OSHA cut back regulations, states in which labor was politically strong passed their own regulations. Many of these regulations were stronger than those OSHA was abandoning, and all varied from state to state. As a result, large, nationally active corporations concluded that it was better to have one national standard than many different state rules. Thus, for example, OSHA in November 1983 decided to issue a "worker right-to-know" rule. It requires manufacturers to tell their workers about the health hazards of dangerous industrial chemicals they handle on the job. The cost to industry was estimated at $600 million—but it replaced 17 different laws in 17 states, so industry supported it.

Worker Democracy

Increasingly, advocates of the interests of workers go beyond physical working conditions to what is usually termed worker democracy. In some European countries, worker representatives now must be allowed to serve on the board of directors of an industrial firm. This has not yet happened in the United States, but unions are beginning to propose such codetermination, as it is called in Europe, and many observers believe it is inevitable.

Such a step, once it comes, may be only the first in a move toward further economic reform. Jeremy Rifkin, of the People's Business Commission (PBC), calls for a second American revolution to

> extend democratic principles to the economic institutions of our country. . . . A democratic economy is composed of firms controlled and managed by the people who work in them. Employees determine broad company policy and elect management on the principle of one person, one vote. In a self-managed firm all participants share in the net income of the

enterprise. The members jointly determine the income levels for different job tasks in the firm.[50]

Peter D. Hart Research Associates took a national poll in 1975 for the PBC in which those surveyed were given a choice of which type of economic system they would prefer to work in. The results were as follows:

- A system of companies "in which the stock is owned by outside investors who appoint their own management to run the company's operations" (our present capitalist system) was preferred by 20 percent of the population.
- A system of companies "in which the government owns the stock and appoints the management" (a form of *state socialism* or communism) was supported by only 8 percent.
- A system made up of companies "in which the stock is owned by the employees who appoint their own management to run the company's operations" was preferred by 66 percent.

Despite these preferences, 49 percent said there was little chance that such employee control of U.S. companies would come about within a decade. They are certainly right, especially given what we have learned about the distribution of wealth in America and about the political power such wealth gives to vested interests. But the 44 percent who believe there is "some" or "great" possibility of such "economic democracy" may well represent future political possibilities. In the meantime, we are likely to find growing movements for job enrichment to make work more meaningful, and for profit sharing with workers.

Furthermore, we are likely to see more and more companies owned in large part or entirely by their employees—as are United Parcel Service, Weirton Steel Corporation, the Chicago and North Western Railway, and America West Airlines. There are now hundreds of worker-owned companies and many thousands of companies whose employees own shares in them. Experience shows that workers tend to be more efficient and more committed when they become owners, and this fact alone may make employee stock ownership more common in years to come.[51]

---

[50]Rifkin, *Own Your Own Job: Economic Democracy for Working Americans* (New York: Bantam, 1977), pp. 28, 30. Subsequent references to the PBC survey come from this book (pp. 51–52).

[51]For a fascinating study, see Martin Carnoy and Derek Shearer, *Economic Democracy: The Challenge of the 1980s* (White Plains, NY: M. E. Sharpe, 1980).

Consumer-Protection Programs

Fully 74 percent of the American people told the Hart survey for PBC that they favored "a plan whereby consumers in local communities are represented on the boards of companies that operate in their local region." Why?

- Each year 20 million Americans are injured by products commonly found in the home, and more than 30,000 are killed, according to the United States Consumer Product Safety Commission. The dollar cost of these accidents in medical care, disability payments, and lost productivity is estimated at over $5.5 billion a year.
- On a typical day, the Consumer Product Safety Commission will receive some 300 calls about hazardous products on its toll-free hot line (the telephone number is 800-638-2772), with calls escalating to over 1000 a day when a "crisis" news story appears.
- Hundreds of calls a day come in to a comparable hot line for auto defects established by the National Highway Traffic Safety Administration. (You can reach it at 800-424-9393.) And the Center for Auto Safety in Washington, a Ralph Nader organization, receives some 12,000 such complaints a year. The center estimates that for every person who writes, there are another thousand with a similar problem.

These represent the *dangerous* consumer problems. But there is much more to consumer unhappiness. A study of 2400 urban households by Ralph Nader's Center for the Study of Responsive Law found that one of every four purchases by American consumers results in some problem. In addition, 10 to 17 percent of all expensive items such as TVs or cars are actually received broken. Also, consumers find the first repair job inadequate and have to get another in 26 percent of auto repairs, 19 percent of home repairs, and 13 percent of appliance repairs.

Consumer Sovereignty?

Why are things so bad? In theory, our capitalist system is supposed to be self-correcting. If consumers don't like what they buy, they stop buying it. Furthermore, the system is supposed to operate on the principle of **consumer sovereignty:** The consumer has the power to decide what he or she wants, and the business then produces it to sell. In fact, however, it doesn't work that way. Consumers may have free choice among whatever is produced. But no consumer can get a business to produce something he or she wants unless he or she can find others who want it too. And even then they must somehow get word to business about what they want. There is no regular way for consumers to pass that word because producers and suppliers control advertising, the usual information channel. All consumers can usually do is refuse to buy whatever is available—a sort of veto.

Consumer Protection

The growth of discontent has led the government to intervene to protect the interests of the consumer. The earliest stages of this intervention were the creation of the major regulatory agencies such as the Federal Trade Commission (1915) and the Food and Drug Administration (1931). Historically, they have tended to be more sympathetic to, and even under the dominance of, the businesses they are supposed to regulate. So recent years have seen the emergence of new legislation and new agencies. The Fair Packaging and Labeling Act was passed in 1966, followed by the Truth-in-Lending Act (designed to tell borrowers what credit really costs them in interest rates) in 1968. These were followed by the Public Health Smoking Act, which required warnings of health hazards on cigarette packages.

The Consumer Product Safety Act created the Consumer Product Safety Commission (CPSC) in 1972. The CPSC can set safety standards for many thousands of consumer products and can fine violating producers up to half a million dollars. Nonetheless, until the Carter administration came to power, it was known as a do-nothing agency. In its first five years, it was able to develop design standards only for architectural glass used in doors, windows, and walls; for matchbook covers; and for swimming-pool slides. In the Carter years, the CPSC developed priorities to concentrate on the most urgent matters. Among these were power lawn mowers (160,000 injuries a year), gas space heaters (8,700), children's playground equipment (229,000), and toys with sharp points and edges (179,000). The CPSC was also actively concerned with improving the safety of bicycles, aluminum electrical wire, cooking ranges and ovens, television sets, ladders, bathtubs and showers, power

How to Get Consumer Advice or Make a Consumer Complaint

There are two primary sources of consumer advice: the federal government and public-interest consumer organizations. The government can help in several ways. First, it tests many products before buying them, and you can now get copies of the results of its tests, as well as of other consumer-oriented government publications, by ordering them from *Consumer Information Catalog.* This free periodical is issued every three months by the General Services Administration's Consumer Information Center. You can get your copy at federal offices (such as Social Security offices or agricultural extension offices), at many libraries, or by writing to Consumer Information, Public Documents Distribution Center, Pueblo, CO 81009. Many of the 250 pamphlets each issue lists are free, and most others cost a dollar or less.

You can also get a free copy of the government's 100-page *Consumer's Resource Handbook,* which tells which offices offer which services and gives names and phone numbers. This guide is also available from the above address.

In addition, the government publishes *Consumer News,* a twice-a-month newsletter to report on government programs for consumers. It is sold by subscription at the same address.

There are also many private groups that offer consumer advice. Probably the best known is **Consumers Union** (256 Washington St., Mt. Vernon, NY 10550), which publishes the monthly *Consumer Reports* (available on newsstands and in libraries) rating product quality and economy. It also publishes a *Guide to Consumer Services* that deals with financial matters such as insurance and professional services such as doctors and dentists.

Another prominent consumer organization is the Ralph Nader public-interest conglomerate **Public Citizen** (2000 P St. NW, Washington, DC 20036). It includes the Health Research Group and various other projects. These groups regularly publish new consumer guides on various topics.

Other important sources of information for consumers are the following:

The Center for Science in the Public Interest (1501 16th St. NW, Washington, DC 20036) researches such issues as energy, environment, food, and nutrition.

The Chamber of Commerce of the United States, Consumer Affairs Section (1615 H St. NW, Washington, DC 20006) publishes general information about consumer issues and promotes consumer redress programs among businesses.

The Consumer Federation of America (1424 16th St. NW, Washington, DC 20036) is a federation of national, regional, state, and local consumer groups and other interested groups.

If you wish to create your own consumer group, you can get a free booklet entitled *Forming Consumer Organizations* from the Office of Consumer Affairs, Department of Health and Human Services, Washington, DC 20201.

All the information in the world may not avert misfortune. A useful general guide to where to complain in business and industry and in state and federal government is Joseph Rosenbloom's *Consumer Complaint Guide* (New York: Macmillan paperback, published annually.

Generally the best complaint route is: first, the merchant who sold you the product or performed the service; second, the manufacturer of the product; and third, government consumer agencies—either a state consumer agency in the state attorney general's office, or the Federal Trade Commission Consumer Product Safety Commission, or other agency in Washington, as appropriate.

The following are some rules for complaining effectively:

- Address your complaint to a specific individual, such as company director or head of an agency (names you can find in your public library or by calling the company or agency).
- Put your complaint in writing, rather than telephoning, so that you can keep a copy for future use if necessary.
- Be brief, clear, and unemotional, and type or write legibly.
- State what you have already done to try to solve the problem. Include copies of documentation such as a sales slip or warranty if you can, but always keep the originals.
- State just what you want the recipient to do.
- Identify yourself fully and state how and when you can be reached by a response.
- Follow up with an inquiry if you haven't received a response after several weeks.
- Write to government agencies and/or your representatives in the state capital or Washington if you are not satisfied with responses by a store, manufacturer, or other target.

To find out which federal government agency may be able to help you, write to Public Citizen at the address above or call your regional Federal Information Center (FIC) at the toll-free number listed under "U.S. Government" in your local phone book.

Referring to what he termed "the worst economic mess since the Great Depression," Ronald Reagan urged Americans to support his plans to avert "economic calamity," using coins and a dollar bill to dramatize his explanation to the television audience. (Dennis Brack/Black Star)

TABLE 16.6
Consumer Prices, 1965–1986

YEAR	PERCENT INCREASE IN CONSUMER PRICES
1965	1.7%
1966	2.9
1967	2.9
1968	4.2
1969	5.4
1970	5.9
1971	4.3
1972	3.3
1973	6.2
1974	11.0
1975	9.1
1976	5.8
1977	6.5
1978	7.7
1979	11.3
1980	13.5
1981	10.4
1982	6.1
1983	3.2
1984	4.3
1985	3.6
1986	1.1

Source: U.S. Bureau of Labor Statistics.

tools, and skiing equipment. Its activities were controversial, however. So the Reagan administration cut its budget drastically. Still, the CPSC, the FTC, the FDA, and the National Highway Traffic Safety Administration forced the recall in one recent year of 9 million autos, 100,000 coffee makers, and 72,000 cans of tomatoes, among other items. But surveys show that more than two out of three American consumers believe that even greater governmental regulation is needed to protect them.

Inflation-Control Programs

In simplest terms, as we've seen above, inflation refers to rises in the cost of goods and services. The government has developed a consumer price index (CPI) to measure the impact on an "average" family of four of the prices it must pay.[52] A few years ago the CPI was rising at very fast rates, as Table 16.6 reports. Recently, inflation has been tamed—but no one knows for how long.

One problem is that experts disagree on the underlying causes of inflation.[53] Increases in wages demanded by labor (often just to keep up with inflation) produce what economists call *cost-push* inflation. Increases in demand for goods by people with more money to spend produce *demand-pull* inflation. Higher government spending increases demand—especially if the government is running a deficit, as it now usually is. Higher energy prices increase costs of doing business and cause prices to rise. Traditionally, economists referred to a wage-price spiral as the cause of continuing inflation. Now, things seem much more complicated.

One important reason why inflation has not been brought under permanent control is that even the experts disagree about how to do this. The policies and programs frequently proposed—all of them controversial—include the following:

- Getting the Federal Reserve Board to slow down the rate of money growth (see Chapter 15)
- Charging user's fees for the many federal services that benefit only special interests, such as dredging of waterways and quality grading of food
- Slowing the growth of government benefits (as the Reagan administration has sought to do)

[52]Experts point out that this "average" family is no longer very typical in the United States. Thus the CPI does not necessarily reflect the actual impact of inflation on you or anyone else. If you want to figure out how inflation actually does affect you personally, see "Make a Budget for Your Inflation Rate," *Changing Times*, August 1980, pp. 21–25.

[53]See, for example, Robert M. Solow, "What We Know and Don't Know about Inflation," *Technology Review*, December–January 1979, pp. 30–46, and "The Intelligent Citizen's Guide to Inflation," *Public Interest*, Winter 1975, pp. 30–66.

- Reducing subsidies (see Chapter 15)
- Reducing regulation of business and industry (see Chapter 15)
- Stimulating greater energy production and/or conservation in order to limit price increases (see Chapter 18)
- Ending trade protectionism
- Imposing wage and price controls

Another reason for the failure to control inflation is the fact that some people benefit from inflation. Those who save their money lose because the interest they get is less than the inflation rate. Those who invest in real estate, gold, and silver generally profit. Some studies indicate that the big losers in inflation are the rich rather than the poor—at least when government transfer payments for the poor are maintained. Even here there is disagreement.

NEW APPROACHES, ATTITUDES, AND BEHAVIORS

Our survey only serves to emphasize once again the magnitude of the problem of promoting the general welfare in America—and the inadequacy of the efforts undertaken thus far. "Although the issue of social welfare continues to attract well-intentioned concern," writes Tom Joe of the University of Chicago's Center for the Study of Welfare Policy,

> this concern is not being effectively translated into the monetary, technical, and managerial capacity. . . . It is here that the challenge to the concerned humanitarian becomes manifest: to gather up and develop all the tools and opportunities available—fis-

cal, political, constitutional, legal, bureaucratic, organizational—and apply them to poverty, misery, and alienation.[54]

Hugh Heclo suggests that

> beyond this there will be a need for gradually building a sense of social solidarity—a sense that there are some things that we all owe to each other for our own good. . . . The democratic welfare state of the future . . . should help improve chances for individuals to make themselves happy, to find their own meaning, and to care whether others have a similar chance to do the same.[55]

After noting that it is not just the poor but the majority of Americans who are in economic peril, William Ryan contends that

> security and progress, then, cannot be gained by individual action, but only by simultaneous action of all who are intertwined together. . . . The somewhat paradoxical moral, is that tens of millions of individuals will remain vulnerable until they learn to function collectively—to act, together, to get, for each other, a bigger piece of the pie.[56]

Political sociologist Morris Janowitz draws a further lesson from the growing economic plight of the middle class:

> People have to take a more realistic view of how society operates. . . . if we're to have an effective government, we need a wide variety of grass-roots activity. That means that people must participate voluntarily in their community affairs—donate their time to serve on local boards and commissions, get involved in self-help activities. One big thing the middle class must learn is that life does not limit itself to the family. People have to be more involved in the community.[57]

It's to such local relations and their politics that we turn in the next chapter.

SUMMARY

There are great extremes of wealth and poverty in the United States. One in every 240 Americans is now a millionaire, but one in every 7 lives in poverty. A quarter of all wealth in America is held by 1 percent of adults, and three-quarters of the wealth is held by one-fifth of the people. The typical poor American is white and lives in a city—and is a child. However, three times as many blacks as whites are poor. Almost half the poor males work full time, and a fifth of the poor females. But working full time at the minimum wage still leaves

the head of a family of four $3593 below the poverty line in a year.

Poverty is caused by many factors. Chief among them are lack of skills and education, health prob-

[54]Tom Joe, "Sweeping the Poor under the Rug," *Humanist*, March–April 1977, p. 30. For Joe's account of the Reagan years, see Joe and Cheryl Rogers, *By the Few for the Few: The Reagan Welfare Legacy* (Lexington, MA: Lexington Books, 1985).

[55]Hugh Heclo, "A Question of Priorities," *Humanist*, March–April 1977, p. 24.

[56]Ryan, "Most of Us Are Kept on a Short Leash."

[57]Interview, *U.S. News & World Report*, May 2, 1977, p. 57.

lems, and feelings of low self-worth and power-lessness. The rich, on the other hand, are likely to have inherited wealth. They also benefit from the tax laws as well as educational advantages. In between is the middle class. It owns little, and much of it is getting poorer as manufacturing jobs are replaced by lower-paying service jobs in our economy.

Since the New Deal, the federal government has developed a wide range of programs to combat poverty. The chief program is welfare, which includes direct income programs, direct services programs (food stamps, housing assistance, Medicaid), indirect services (education and manpower training), indirect-income programs (minimum wage and unionization), and community organizing. Studies show that only about a quarter of the families in poverty are likely to stay there for five years in a row, and nearly a third of all people fall below the poverty line at least once in a decade. These antipoverty programs have been successful in keeping many people out of poverty who would otherwise be poor.

The Reagan administration, seeking greater economic growth and decentralization of power, convinced Congress to cut spending on these programs. Studies show that the poor have suffered seriously from these cuts. Poverty is once again at a high level, and experts are seeking new programs to try to cope with the causes of poverty as well as to improve the situations of the poor.

Other government programs are intended to promote the general welfare. Among these are employment programs (CETA and the new Job Training Partnership Act), and occupational safety and health (OSHA) programs. Other people advocate programs of worker democracy, including worker ownership of firms. The government runs various consumer-protection programs, especially through the Federal Trade Commission and the Consumer Product Safety Commission. Another approach to improving the economic situation of the population is controlling inflation—something at which government has been more successful recently.

Many experts believe that new approaches, attitudes, and behaviors will be required to solve our current economic problems.

Suggestions for Further Reading and Study

On poverty equality and welfare, in addition to works cited in the chapter footnotes, see Lester C. Thurow, *The Zero-Sum Society: Distribution and the Possibilities for Economic Change* (New York: Basic Books, 1980); Lars Osberg, *Economic Inequality in the United States* (Armonk, NY: Sharpe, 1984); and Benjamin I. Page, *Who Gets What from Government* (Berkeley: Univ. of California Press, 1983).

There is a large literature on the problems and possibilities of work. For accounts of what it's really like, see Studs Terkel, *Working* (New York: Random House, 1975). For a study of the relation between technological development and work organization, see Harry Braverman, *Labor and Monopoly Capital* (New York: Monthly Review Press, 1975). And on experiments with worker participation, see David Jenkins, *Job Power: Blue and White Collar Democracy* (New York: Penguin, 1974), and the collection of readings edited by Jaroslav Vanek, *Self-Management: Economic Liberation of Man* (New York: Penguin, 1975). See also Kenneth M. Dolbeare, *Democracy at Risk: The Politics of Economic Renewal*, rev. ed. (Chatham, NJ: Chatham House, 1986).

For a psychological analysis of the problems of consumption, see Tibor Scitovsky, *The Joyless Economy: An Inquiry into Human Satisfaction and Consumer Dissatisfaction* (New York: Oxford Univ. Press, 1976). On the consumer movement, see Robert N. Katz, ed., *Protecting the Consumer Interest: Private Initiative and Public Response* (Cambridge, MA: Ballinger, 1976).

17

THE POLITICS OF LOCAL RELATIONS:
Urban Policy

If you're like most Americans, you live in or near a city. If you're like most students, your college or university is located in a city. The United States is a nation of cities and city dwellers. It is cities that have made the kind of life most Americans desire—from jobs and leisure to cars and culture—possible and even necessary. But today most of our cities are having serious problems. They lack sufficient money to provide the services their citizens want. Their buildings and bridges are decaying, and their roads and transit systems are collapsing. Their air is polluted and their water quality is bad. Crime, too, is a serious problem. In this chapter, we'll find out why our cities have these problems and what role politics plays in creating—and solving—them. ■

URBAN AMERICA TODAY AND YESTERDAY

Everyone knows the problems of most of our big cities today: poverty, unemployment, inadequate housing, pollution, crime, and congestion. Few realize, however, that the cities are victims of their previous economic success, now held prisoner by their place in our federal system.

Today, three-quarters of all Americans live in one of our 277 metropolitan areas. (Table 17.1 summarizes where Americans now live.) In the 1970s these areas lost residents to rural areas, but in the 1980s the previous trend—movement to cities—has recurred, especially in the south and west. Even the centers of the larger cities are again gaining residents.

And yet, the problems of the cities are not getting better. The federal budget cutbacks of the Reagan era and the end to revenue sharing (see Chapter 2) have made most cities' situations even worse. How did things get to this point?

The Evolution of American Cities

Most of the problems our cities face today were faced by our cities in the last century too. Today's pollution comes from cars and factories. In the 1800s it came from horses and slaughterhouses. Disease at that time was rampant—smallpox, yellow fever, malaria, cholera, and typhoid—and it was often spread by unsanitary drinking water. Crime, too, was common: less mugging, but more pickpocketing and much murder. There were riots, too. The first race riot flared up in Philadelphia in

TABLE 17.1
Where Americans Live

SIZE OF CITY	PERCENT OF POPULATION
over 5 million	21
2.5–5 million	10.5
1–2.5 million	17
500,000–1 million	10
250,000–500,000	8.5
100,000–250,000	8
under 100,000	1
rural	24

Source: Figures for 1983 metropolitan areas from the Census Bureau.

1828, and ethnic battles were common. In short, the problems of our cities, bad as they are today, were generally worse a century ago.[1]

There were, however, important differences. To understand them, we must know more about the evolution of American cities and their present problems.

Frontier Development

The earliest American cities were, of course, seaports on the Atlantic Ocean. They conducted trade with Europe and between the colonies as well. As America developed, the frontier moved westward. In its wake it left new towns of traders, where goods were brought on their way to and from the coastal cities and Europe. The towns often grew to be cities as manufacturing developed locally.

The first great boost to the development of our cities came with the construction of railroads. By 1860 railroads extended from the east to Milwaukee, St. Louis, Memphis, and New Orleans, and soon they crisscrossed the country. Cities then grew up at railroad junctions. With the arrival of railroads, an area no longer needed to be self-sufficient in farming and manufacturing, for trade with other areas was much easier.

Immigration

Perhaps the greatest change in our cities is traceable to the arrival of new waves of immigrants from Europe. The first big waves reached America's eastern shores in the middle of the last century, before the Civil War. The immigrants came looking for work in the new factories or in the service trades such as shoemaking and baking. New waves then followed after the Civil War and on into the 20th century. By 1920 a majority of the American people lived in urban areas—a figure that would jump to 75 percent in the next half century.

These waves of immigrants had two major effects. One was to create ethnic neighborhoods, or ghettos, each populated by new arrivals from a given country. The other was the consequent flight of the natives to new neighborhoods as far from the city centers as local transportation—trains, buses, and eventually private cars—allowed.[2]

[1] See "Studies Find U.S. Cities Even Worse in the Past," *New York Times*, December 5, 1976. This article reports research by political scientist Charles Adrian.
[2] See Anselm L. Strauss, *Images of the American City* (New Brunswick, NJ: Transaction Books, 1976), esp. chap. 6.

(Ted Spiegel/Black Star)

(Alex Webb/Magnum Photos)

Migration

This same pattern of "invasion" and "flight" was repeated in the 20th century when rural blacks and whites headed from the South to the Northeast and the Midwest. The slum poverty that has resulted from these latest waves of migration into our cities is different from the slum poverty of previous decades. In earlier eras, most of this poverty was in a sense temporary—suffered by the first generation as it struggled to improve the fate of its children. Eventually, the family moved out of the slum neighborhood and often left behind the menial work it started out doing.

Discrimination and Poverty

Today, most of the migrants to the cities are black or Puerto Rican or Mexican-American or Oriental. All of these—but especially the blacks—suffer from discrimination that limits both their job opportunities and their possibilities. As a result, today's urban poverty tends to be passed on from one generation to the next.

We have discussed these problems of prejudice and poverty in previous chapters. For our present purpose we must take note of a second major difference between today's urban poverty and that existing in the past. Until recently, the city's poor were largely left to fend for themselves, with the help of local political machines (about which, more shortly) and charitable organizations such as churches. Thus, slum populations were not serious economic burdens for cities, nor did they demand much attention or many services from the city. Today, however, as poverty passes from one generation to the next, despair and resentment—and militance—increase, threatening law and order and commanding more and more city resources in the form of welfare payments, police and fire protection, and special programs.

Suburbanization

This pattern can be seen in Figure 17.1, which shows the population shifts in percentage terms between central-city, suburban, and nonmetropolitan (rural and small-town) areas. Between 1950 and 1980 the suburbs' share increased by 18 percent, whereas the cities lost 6 percent and the nonmetropolitan areas 12 percent. The suburbs were growing at the expense of both cities and rural areas.

This suburban shift may be one reason why relatively few Americans say that local government affects their lives personally. Even though people pay local taxes and get local services such as police and fire protection, polls show that fewer than half of the people think local government affects their lives "a great deal." Surveys also find that only a quarter of those interviewed have ever gone to their local government for help with some problem or have had any direct contact with local officials other than paying taxes and filling out forms.

Cities in the Federal System

The framers established a federal system to protect individual liberties. But, as we saw in Chapter 1, they disagreed about how this protection would be achieved.[3] Some shared Thomas Jefferson's view

---

[3]See Robert D. Thomas, "Cities as Partners in the Federal System," *Political Science Quarterly* 101 (1986), 49–64.

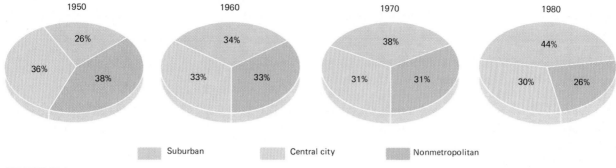

FIGURE 17.1
Percent of U.S. Population in Suburban Areas, Central Cities, and Nonmetropolitan
Areas, 1950–1980.
Source: Census Bureau data.

that individual liberties were best protected in small communities. Others agreed with James Madison that local communities might treat minority views badly and thus argued for including varied local communities in the state and nation so that the local interests would balance each other out there. The broader political bodies at the state and national levels would give views that were a minority locally a broader forum to which to appeal for support.

The system we have contains elements of both views. Cities are the building blocks of states and yet are politically powerful enough that their large groups of voters can influence what happens in Washington if they are not satisfied with their treatment at the local or state level. But our cities have changed drastically since the days of the founding.

THE UNDERLYING PROBLEM: THE TWIN POVERTIES OF THE CITIES

Some of America's communities are urban, but others are suburban, and many more are really rural. There are 17,000 towns in America today, as well as 18,000 cities, but only 500 of them have populations of 50,000 or more.[4] Do all these differing political units have problems in common? To a surprising extent, they do. Some of these problems are political, and some are economic. All involve power, and all have a common root in dependence on the states.

The Dependence of Cities on States

Cities are not mentioned in the Constitution. They therefore derive their authority from the states in which they are located. The classic formulation of this authority was made in 1872 by a state judge named John F. Dillon, in words that have become known as **Dillon's Rule.** This rule states that a city's powers are strictly limited to those expressly granted by the state, those necessarily implied by that grant of powers, and "those essential to the accomplishment of the declared objects and purposes" of the city.[5] This legal dependence has made cities subject to domination by their states and has left them open to exploitation by their political environment. In recent years, the greatest threat has come from suburbs.

Economic Poverty and Suburbanization

By 1970, for the first time, more people lived in the suburbs that ring America's large cities than lived in either the rural areas or the cities themselves. The movement to the suburbs continued through the 1970s, as we saw above. This trend seems to have been partly a *pushing* away of people by cities with racial problems, congestion, pollution, high housing costs, and so on. But it was also partly a *pulling*, or an attraction, of people to areas that offered more space for raising a family, more social homogeneity, more privacy, and so forth. What made it all possible, of course, was the

---

[4]The distinction between city and town varies from state to state and is defined by state law. In general, cities are larger and have more authority over budgetary matters and services than towns do.

[5]John F. Dillon, *Commentaries on the Law of Municipal Corporations,* 5th ed. (Boston: Little, Brown, 1911), Vol. I, p. 448.

development first of public transportation (especially commuter trains) and then the spread of the private automobile.

That helps explain how and why the suburbs came to challenge and threaten the cities they ringed. Most suburbanites continued to work in the big cities and often shopped and found entertainment there as well. This meant they benefited from a wide range of city services, from garbage collection to public concerts. But because they lived in suburbia they paid their property taxes to their suburban communities instead of to the cities. City services began to decline with city revenues. And when city services declined, businesses located in the cities, and so paying city taxes, began to follow their employees to the suburbs.

They left behind them large numbers of poor people, often unskilled and increasingly members of minority groups. As employment dropped, so did tax revenue. As a result, cities went further into debt and decay. (Table 17.2 shows the percentages of city revenues now derived from various sources.) But because they depended on the states for their political authority, there was often little cities could do to defend themselves. More and more, some argue, America's great cities have come to resemble the reservations on which Native American Indians have been isolated and kept from enjoying the full benefits of life in America.

The policies cities have followed have generally emphasized their own economic development.[6] The economic health of a city depends on having businesses that pay taxes and provide jobs. To attract such businesses, the city has needed to expand outward to new territory to incorporate or open up land for new factories and housing. But the "iron rim" of suburbs now surrounding most cities has prevented this expansion in recent decades. More recently, cities have instead offered lower tax rates as incentives to attract new businesses. But this approach has meant more demand for city services with lower tax revenues.

As a result, the cities have become more dependent on the federal government for financial aid. This federal aid has taken two forms. The one most often sought by cities has been support for the economic infrastructure, such as sewage-treatment

---

[6]See Roger Friedland, *Power and Crisis in the City: Corporations, Unions and Urban Policy* (London: Macmillan, 1982).

TABLE 17.2

The Sources of Urban Revenue

Property tax	37.2%
Other local taxes	25.7
User charges	6.5
Fees and miscellaneous	15.0
State aid	13.6
Federal aid	6.5

Source: Joint Economic Committee, U.S. Congress.

plants, highways, and mass transit. The other has been aid to the remaining residents, such as welfare and housing subsidies.

THE NATIONAL GOVERNMENT'S RESPONSE TO THE CITIES

The Kennedy-Johnson Era

Until the Kennedy administration took office in 1961, the only large federal programs for cities were urban renewal and public housing. President John F. Kennedy gained office on the strength of support in large urban areas. When Kennedy ran for president, there were only 44 grant-in-aid programs available to state and local governments. By the time Lyndon Johnson left office in 1969, there were almost 500. Most of these were products of Kennedy's New Frontier and Johnson's Great Society. They involved such programs as rent supplements for the poor, food stamps, teacher training, crime control, and other social-welfare measures. In the midst of all this new lawmaking, Congress in 1966 declared that "improving the quality of urban life is the most critical domestic problem facing the United States."

The Nixon-Ford Era Backlash

Many of these programs involved grants to special local districts set up to administer them or to private organizations. The intention was to make it more likely that funds would reach the needy instead of becoming "plums" for local politicians to distribute to their supporters. Not surprisingly, it made city and state officials mad. And when the antipoverty agencies began opposing and even attacking city governments and their policies, the politicians got even more furious. At the same time, the programs often lacked coordination, and local bureaucracy grew.

The result was a backlash led by local politicians, opponents of social legislation, and many Republican candidates. In 1968 Richard Nixon was elected president, and Republicans controlled 62 percent of the governorships. Under Nixon many of these social programs were canceled. Others were decentralized to state and local governments through the general revenue-sharing grants discussed in Chapter 2. In general, cities did not spend their revenue-sharing funds on social services. Instead, they emphasized transportation, environmental measures, and public safety.

In the Ford years, seven major federal urban and social programs that had survived were consolidated by the Community Development Act of 1974. In the words of two experts:

> By the Ford Administration, social and urban programs had become an entrenched part of the federal governmental apparatus. Whereas firm presidential leadership was required to create the programs of the 1960s, and they had come under attack under the Nixon Administration, by 1975 they were beyond the kind of attack launched in 1968. Even concerted presidential leadership could not dislodge them.[7]

The Carter Quest

Candidate Jimmy Carter proclaimed in the 1976 campaign:

> Our country has no urban policy or defined urban goals, and so we have floundered from one ineffective and uncoordinated program to another. . . . We need a coordinated urban policy from a federal government committed to develop a creative partnership with our cities.

The strong vote he pulled from the big cities, blacks, and labor suggested that he would indeed have support in such an effort.

Two months after he took office, he set up a special Urban and Regional Policy Group to (1) analyze urban problems, (2) review existing programs, (3) submit new proposals where needed, and (4) reorganize bureaucratic authority for urban pol-

icy.[8] The original instructions had been to "tilt" the policy toward the distressed large cities. During the year of deliberations, Carter became more concerned about the federal budget deficit and about his eroding political support in the suburbs. The result was new guidelines. The most important of these was that the new policy not require any new money. This meant no new programs unless old ones were ended. The second was a focus on neighborhoods. This meant less attention to the economic development of decaying center cities. The third was a strong role for the states. This meant more attention to smaller communities because state politics tends to overrepresent rural and suburban areas. The fourth was a strong role for the private sector. This meant less of a role for the federal agencies and for federal funds.

The proposals that emerged fared badly in Congress. The one exception was some tax credits for businesses hiring in urban areas. However, Carter did issue new executive orders for government agencies to locate their offices in central cities rather than in suburbs and to purchase their supplies and material from companies in areas with high unemployment. Even these measures, however, met with resistance from the agencies so ordered. In the two years between the order and Carter's departure, 230 offices moved back into central business areas across the nation. That's not many considering the many thousands of agency offices, but some—almost 90 percent—were already in central-city locations when the order was issued.

This new program stimulated effective resistance by the suburbs. That campaign was led by the Congressional Suburban Caucus, which consists of 55 House members. Other policies aimed at helping big cities have brought forth similar resistance. The result has been a continuing failure to develop a national urban policy. One expert concluded:

> Like so many other Carter initiatives, the urban policy was an attempt to please everyone that ended up pleasing no one. It tried with one stroke to satisfy the

---

[7]Dennis R. Judd and Francis N. Kopel, "The Search for National Urban Policy: From Kennedy to Carter," in *Nationalizing Government: Public Policies in America*, ed. Theodore J. Lowi and Alan Stone (Beverly Hills: Sage, 1978), p. 194.

[8]For an account of what happened, see previous editions of this book or Eric L. Stowe, "Defining a National Urban Policy: Bureaucratic Conflict and Shortfall," in *Urban Revitalization*, ed. Donald B. Rosenthal (Beverly Hills, CA: Sage, 1980); Harold L. Wolman and Astrid E. Merget, "The Presidency and Policy Formulation: President Carter and the Urban Policy," *Presidential Studies Quarterly* 10 (Summer 1980), 402–15; and Rochelle L. Stanfield, "Toward an Urban Policy with a Small-Town Accent," *Publius* 9 (Winter 1979), 31–43.

President Carter visits the rubble of abandoned apartment buildings on Charlotte Street in the south Bronx in 1977, promising renewal. (UPI/ Bettmann Newsphotos)

Ronald Reagan campaigns in the rubble of Charlotte Street in 1980. (AP/Wide World Photos)

traditional urban lobby—the big cities, blacks, labor, and Frostbelt states that made up the old Democratic constituency—and to curry favor with the rising new political forces in the small towns, suburbs and Sunbelt states. The result was a diffusion of resources at a time of scarcity when targeting was necessary. Carter had tried to bring consistency and coherency to a de facto urban policy that had been marked by conflict and inconsistency for half a century, but his policy caused greater confusion among urban officials who no longer knew "where they stood" with the administration, heightened tensions with Congress, and raised some problems for the working of the federal system.[9]

The Reagan Retreat

Ronald Reagan ran on a platform calling for the creation of **urban enterprise zones,** or special areas in distressed cities where taxes and regulatory controls on business and industries would be reduced.

[9]Stanfield, "Toward an Urban Policy," p. 31.

The argument was that these incentives would generate new economic life in otherwise dying cities. But little progress has been made on this idea because the Reagan administration chose to devote most of its energies to more general economic policy, as we have seen in previous chapters, rather than to the cities. The principle has been that improvement of the national economy should "trickle down" to the states and cities and to their residents. The administration did, however, finally succeed in abolishing federal revenue sharing in an effort to cut the federal budget deficit and rely on market forces. But, perhaps in part because big cities almost always vote Democratic, there was no effort to develop a Reagan urban policy.

THE NATURE OF URBAN POLITICS

Some have argued that the major obstacle to effective local government is money, but others say it is the types of politics found in many cities.

Charlotte Street once again, in June 1984, now the setting for a group of new "suburban" homes. (Jon Love, *New York Magazine*)

The Types of Politics

In the early days of the country, cities were run by a small elite elected by the mere 5 to 10 percent of the population (adult white male property owners) allowed to vote. This elite was referred to as the city fathers—a term that survives to this day, despite the growing percentage of women active in local electoral politics.

Two things happened to break the hold of this elite. First, cities kept growing on their fringes, and this small elite did little to maintain its political control over the new neighborhoods. Much the same thing is happening again today with the growth of suburbs outside the city limits. The second development—the rise of machine politics—was even more important.

Machine Politics

After about 1840 waves of European immigrants began to arrive to work in urban factories. These new arrivals needed help coping with poverty, scarcity of jobs, language problems, sometimes inadequate city services, and other matters. The existing elite was neither able nor willing to offer this help. The result was the development of what we call the **political machine**—a new organization in which each city block had its organizer, each neighborhood had its political club, each district or ward had its leader, and the whole machine had its "boss." In the traditional view, the machine served the people by offering its own "welfare" programs—such as free turkeys for the poor for the holidays, city jobs for the unemployed (or an introduction to a local businessperson anxious for machine-granted city contracts), a way to complain about poor city services, and so on. Politically, the machine served as a way of linking together the fragmented neighborhoods and ethnic groups into a strong political power base able to elect and reelect the mayor—or the boss.[10]

Such machines clearly do tend to deny the residents of the city a real democratic choice. Do the citizens go along because of the material incentives the machine offers? Some studies have emphasized the personal aspects of relations between the residents—usually immigrants—and the machine's precinct captains. The friendship and approval they find resembles what they knew in their village in the home country.[11]

---

[10]See, for example, the classic work by Harvey W. Zorbaugh, *The Gold Coast and the Slum: A Sociological Study of Chicago's Near North Side* (Chicago: Univ. of Chicago Press, 1929).

[11]See, for example, Edward Banfield and James Q. Wilson, *City Politics* (Cambridge, MA: Harvard Univ. Press, 1963). The classic study is Harold F. Gosnell, *Machine Politics: Chicago Model* (Chicago: Univ. of Chicago Press, 1937). The most recent is Dianne M. Pinderhughes, *Race and Ethnicity in Chicago Politics* (Urbana, IL: Univ. of Illinois Press, 1987).

Is it, then, personal affection or the exchange of material favors for votes that generally motivates machine supporters and so provides the "engine" for traditional city politics? It is clear that the employees of the machine get material rewards. The machine voters, though, may have more complex motives. (That is, after all, what we found in Chapter 3 as regards national voters.) Chicago is the city most famous for its machine. A recent study of Chicago politics concluded that voters who receive rewards from the machine are no more likely to be loyal to the patronage party, as it is called, than are those who don't get such rewards. Nor do supporters consider party regulars or officials *their* friends and supporters. Thus, neither image seems accurate, at least today. Instead, this study concludes, the machine leaders foster in the minds of supporters an image that they, the leaders, are concerned about local issues and are responsive to local people. In fact, however, the machine is often less concerned and more corrupt. It simply manages to conceal this fact from the voters while skillfully using the mass media, public ceremonies, and other traditional political devices to convince even thoughtful voters that the machine is morally and poltically upright.[12]

The years of the great machines, like the ones in New York City, Jersey City, Kansas City, and Philadelphia, are over now. And when Mayor Richard Daley of Chicago died in December 1976, he was widely called the last of the big-city bosses. Daley's success had been built on the uniting of the major ethnic groups in Chicago: the Irish, the Poles, and later the blacks. When he died, the remnants of the machine—or the organization, as Daley was always careful to call it—struggled over the succession. The deputy mayor was a black—a concession made by Daley to help sustain his coalition. One might have assumed that the deputy mayor would naturally succeed the mayor. But not in Daley's Chicago, where the blacks were by then always important—but never that important. Instead, the machine settled on a compromise candidate, Michael Bilandic, of Croatian ancestry. The reformers, hoping to beat the Daley machine at last, picked a black. But it was black votes that gave Bilandic the victory over the black candidate and a renegade Pole in the next Democratic primary.

Thus, the machine lurched on, weakened but still organized, and still able to defeat the reformers—until the 1979 election. At that point Jane Byrne, who had been fired as consumer-affairs officer by the mayor, turned against the organization and beat Bilandic. Once she became mayor, however, she and the machine got along well enough together that observers continued to speak of Chicago as a machine city.

Byrne's effort to cooperate with the machine led two candidates to oppose her in the 1983 mayoral primary. The new reform candidate was, ironically enough, Mayor Daley's son Richard M. Daley, then a state attorney. This time, however, black congressman Harold Washington surprised them both, winning the primary when blacks turned out in record numbers to vote for him. Washington then won a close and bitter general election by beating an unknown Republican businessman. Washington ran against the machine; and when he won, he declared that city employees would be judged on merit rather than by political favoritism. The remnants of the machine were outraged, and because they still had a majority on the city council, they were often able to resist Washington's initiatives. In 1987, Washington won reelection, easily defeating the leader of the opposition on the Council. As a result, he was able to consolidate his power as mayor for the first time. Nonetheless, Chicago's politics remain highly conflictual and very ethnic—if less machine dominated.

Reform Politics

Elsewhere things have been even worse for machine politics. The civil-rights movement of the early 1960s and the anti-Vietnam War movement of the late 1960s nurtured a new breed of "community power" activists and reformers who combined with older liberals to modernize politics in other cities. Reformers claimed that local government should involve administration rather than politics. Human services (police, fire, public health, and so forth) should be provided in efficient and honest fashion—without the payoffs, kickbacks, and graft that had long characterized machine politics. To achieve this shift from politics to administration, the reformers sought both to break up the system of centralized machine power and to establish strong administrative control over city government. Unfortunately, there was a serious conflict between these two objectives in prac-

---

[12]See Thomas M. Guterbock, *Machine Politics in Transition: Party and Community in Chicago* (Chicago: Univ. of Chicago Press, 1980).

Richard J. Daley (UPI/Bett-mann Newsphotos)

Michael Bilandic. (Steven M. Leonard, Click/Chicago)

Jane Byrne (Faverty/Liaison Agency)

Harold Washington (Steve Kagan/Gamma-Liaison)

tical terms. To prevent a machine monopoly of political power, reformers deliberately fragmented power, parceling it out to independent boards and commissions. But once this was done, there was not enough power left to achieve coherent administration control over the city government and its service delivery. As Douglas Yates remarked:

> Having divided power in the hope of taming it, there was no way to simultaneously achieve stronger and more coordinated public control of urban bureaucracies and service delivery. Rather the political order of reform added new political fragmentation to the existing administrative fragmentation in the city.[13]

Furthermore, some reformers began to point out that service delivery systems are essentially political agencies, disputing how human needs should be seen and what should be done to meet them.[14] Disputes over service delivery are, in other words, political disputes. By this analysis, the best—perhaps the only—way to improve the government is to improve politics.

THE POLITICS OF URBAN POLICY MAKING: POLITICIANS, INTERESTS, AND STRUCTURES

Politicians and Interests

Public officials like mayors and council members make policy decisions in urban politics. But how much power do they actually have? Political sci-

entists still debate this question. Some, as we have seen in earlier chapters, argue that public policy is the outcome of influences by organized groups (such as business, labor, or citizen activists) on politicians seeking to ensure their own reelection. In this view, politicians try to balance off special interests and tend to act as the final balance recommends.[15]

Others claim that political figures are most influenced not by such organizational interests but instead by their own ideologies—their beliefs about such things as race (black-white relationships), class (employer-employee relationships), and authority (citizen-official relationships). In urban politics, these ideological beliefs concern especially the role of citizen participation and the importance of rational, efficient administration.

David Greenstone and Paul Peterson studied the behavior of urban politicians in various cities. They found that *machine politicians* act according to the principle of balancing special interests, even when that tendency results in less popular participation or less efficient administration. *Conservative reformers*, like those described above, act to achieve greater efficiency rather than to play off the special interests against each other. *Liberal reformers*, by contrast, attempt to extend democratic participation.

Greenstone and Peterson found that both types of reformers are active in American city politics today. The importance of these findings should not be overlooked. The traditional argument—that

---

[13]Douglas Yates, "Service Delivery and the Urban Political Order," in *Improving Urban Management*, ed. Willis A. Hawley and David Rogers (Beverly Hills, CA: Sage, 1976), p. 160.

[14]See, for example, Richard Cloward and Frances Fox Piven, *The Politics of Turmoil* (New York: Pantheon, 1971).

[15]For applications of this view to urban politics, see Edward Banfield, *Political Influence* (New York: Free Press, 1961), a study of Chicago; and Robert Dahl, *Who Governs?* (New Haven, CT: Yale Univ. Press, 1961), a study of New Haven.

Pittsburgh city workers spread trash on a downtown street in preparation for a visit by civic leaders, who later swept the street to dramatize the start of an antilittering campaign. (AP/Wide World Photos)

politicians act according to the balance of interests and its implications for their reelection—suggests that actual citizen participation or sharing of power is not important because politicians will take citizens' interests into account. But if, in fact, politicians are willing to act *counter* to the balance of forces, and hence to their own electoral interests, then it is not enough for unrepresented groups such as blacks and the poor simply to vote. If they are to influence policy outcomes in cities, they must be deciders of policy themselves. They cannot rely on their potential electoral power to bring about politics and policies they support.[16]

"Street-Fighting Pluralism"

This tendency may be one reason why urban policy so often fails to meet, or even to recognize, the needs and interests of urban citizens. Another factor may be the frequency of what Yates calls street-fighting pluralism. He suggests that often

the new urban policy or "solution" is injected into a political and administrative system that is fragmented to the point of chaos. Further, there is no coherent administrative order to implement and control new policies. What exists instead is an extreme pluralism of political, administrative, and community interests . . . and in this context, the likely fate of the new policy initiative is that it will be ripped apart in the street fight between rival political interests.[17]

This situation is particularly characteristic of urban politics, according to Yates, for three important reasons. First, in most large cities politicians such as council members are underpaid and overworked and so pay little attention to citizen interests. Second, there are so many overlapping political jurisdictions (council member, state representative, state senator, national representative, and senator, among others) that it is rarely clear who should represent whom on what issues. Third, citizens disagree with each other as to what services should be sought and provided, and so they are often unable to unite to make demands.

The failure or inability of the various ethnic minorities among the urban poor to unite is a particularly potent example of the last point. One report found that despite antipoverty programs, inner-city neighborhoods had less success than other metropolitan areas in reducing poverty and maintaining stable families. Only a new willingness to cooperate on the part of racial and ethnic groups—who now see themselves in competition for scarce resources—may begin to change this.[18]

The Poverty of Urban Politics

But beneath this political weakness or urban peoples is the poverty of urban politics and government. This poverty has both political and economic aspects. The first is the generally *low quality of local politics*, which is often characterized by corruption, incompetence, administrative disorder, lack of party competition, and "street-fighting pluralism."

A *weak fiscal base* is a second flaw in urban government. Cities depend for their spendable revenue primarily on taxes. Most income comes from property taxes. Yet much property is not taxable, either because it is owned by some government or by nonprofit groups such as churches, colleges, or

[16]David Greenstone and Paul E. Peterson, *Race and Authority in Urban Politics* (New York: Russell Sage Foundation, 1973).

[17]Yates, "Service Delivery," p. 149.
[18]National Center for Urban Affairs, *Who's Left in the Neighborhood* (Washington, DC: NCUA, 1976).

hospitals or because its holders get special tax breaks. When the Reagan administration cut back on federal aid programs and then abolished revenue sharing, that worsened the cities' plight even more. A 1987 study by the National League of Cities found that half of all cities operated in the red in 1986. A third of all cities reported that they would not be able to maintain current services without raising taxes, while another third had already raised taxes in 1986.

The third major factor that weakens city government is *inability to exercise power beyond the city's rim*. Cities are surrounded by suburbs, counties, states, and the United States. Each of these units has powers over various aspects of the city's life. All are largely beyond the city's control. Thus, those dissatisfied with city politics increasingly are urged or driven to move outside or beyond the city for remedies.

Interests and Structures

Political Poverty and Suburbanization

We have already examined the economic impact on cities of the trend toward suburbanization. The suburbanization of America has complicated politics, too. Each local unit must have its own local government; but in addition, there must be new political units cutting across the city and suburban units to plan and coordinate such transurban services as education, transportation, water supply, pollution control, sewage, and police and fire protection. The result has been a proliferation of independent or semi-independent governing bodies with different but overlapping borders. The New York metropolitan area, for example, had by one count 1467 different governing bodies by the early 1960s (see Figure 17.2).[19] The creation of special districts has continued in recent years throughout the United States. Inevitably, however, reactions have set in against this practice.

Consolidation

In recent years, there have been growing efforts to consolidate at least the major planning functions of regions. The primary approach has been estab-

---

[19]See Robert C. Wood, *1400 Governments* (Cambridge, MA: Harvard Univ. Press, 1961); see also Wallace S. Sayre and Herbert Kaufman, *Governing New York City* (New York: Russell Sage Foundation, 1960).

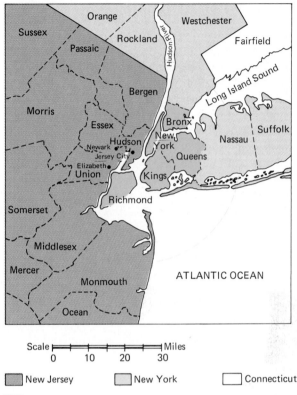

Scale 0 10 20 30 Miles

■ New Jersey   ■ New York   □ Connecticut

▨ New York City's five boroughs: Manhattan (New York County), Brooklyn (Kings County), Queens (Queens County), the Bronx (Bronx County), and Staten Island (Richmond County)

--- County borders (within each county are city governments, regional school districts, transportation authorities, planning authorities, and other subgovernments with overlapping jurisdictions)

Port of New York Authority (the authority operates airports, bridges, tunnels, many bus terminals, some rapid transit systems, and most marine facilities within circled region)

FIGURE 17.2
Overlapping Governments in the New York Metropolitan Area.

lishment of councils of governments (COGs) to integrate urban and suburban planning with financial inducements from the federal government. These COGs are supposed to review requests for federal grants from various local units, develop area priorities, and coordinate related activities among different units. But because they are voluntary they lack the power to impose their will on member units. As a result, some observers believe that, on balance, they only complicate matters.

Other programs, however, are fostering greater decentralization. Among these are movements for greater home rule and development of neighborhood councils for direct citizen participation.

Political Decentralization by Home Rule

Because cities derive their authority from the states, state legislatures must approve their system of government, as we have already seen. Normally the state offers a *city charter*, which is in effect the city's constitutions. But because it is granted by the state it can be changed by the state. The exception to this is the **home rule charter,** which is drafted by the city and cannot be changed by the state legislature. More than three-quarters of our large cities now have home rule charters. But even *they* cannot take action that exceeds the general grant of powers the particular state has made to its cities. Thus, matters like taxation and even education generally remain subject to state control.

The most interesting recent experiment in this direction took place in Montana in 1976. The new state constitution of 1972 provided that each community debate and decide on its own form of local government in 1975–1976 and every ten years thereafter. Any city wanting home rule could have it under a system of shared powers with the state government. This provision allows localities to make laws in any area not prohibited by the state constitution or the legislature. This system has been adopted by Illinois, Florida, Texas, Alaska, Pennsylvania, Massachusetts, Iowa, and South Dakota. It is likely to become more common as states recognize their inability to solve many local problems and cities rebel against state restrictions that hinder them from solving their own problems.

THE FUTURE OF OUR CITIES

Although there is growing favor for decentralization, there remains a strong desire in many quarters for a national urban policy, and there will always be an important—if changing—role for the federal government in our cities.

The Inescapable Urban Issues

Whatever the favorite policies of a particular administration, and whatever the successes and failures, key urban issues simply will not disappear,[20] certainly not the following:

[20]For a helpful survey, see Arthur P. Solomon, eds., *The Prospective City: Economic, Population, Energy, and Environmental Developments* (Cambridge, MA: MIT Press, 1980).

- The problem of rebuilding the cities' **infrastructure**—its four million miles of roads, 574,000 bridges, 2300 airports, 60,000 water and sewer systems, and its public transportation—which have been allowed to deteriorate for many years and will cost perhaps $1.1 trillion to rebuild[21]
- The problem of meeting the needs of poor residents of inner cities as young professionals and upper-middle-class suburbanites move into the city and revitalize it (a process known as **gentrification**)
- The problem of increasing the energy efficiency of the city while meeting needs for transportation and new housing
- The problem of balancing the needs for growth in facilities against the environmental costs of dense population
- The problem of preserving or altering constructively the older, distressed American cities
- The problem of financing increasingly expensive government and services in the face of growing resistance to increased taxes

If going to the local government for help in solving such problems has thus far largely failed, and if improving local politics has proved difficult, and if going beyond or outside the city to other governments has proved largely ineffective, that still leaves one important possibility: citizen participation.

Community Organization

When we examined political participation in Chapter 3, we found that it was low in most types of activity, including voting in local elections and lobbying in local politics. We also noted Saul Alinsky's efforts to organize the poor, politically excluded urban citizens into effective political action groups. It is citizen action groups that are now the most important opportunity for effective participation in urban affairs.[22] Many of those that are now active owe their inspiration to Alinsky.

One of them, not surprisingly, operates in Alinsky's hometown of Chicago: the Citizens Action Program (CAP), founded in 1970 to give citizens the power to force city government to respond to their needs. CAP is affiliated with the Midwest

[21]See "The Other Agenda," *Forbes*, May 21, 1984, pp. 58–62; and Gerald M. Boyd, "Big Fund Gap Cited in Works Needs," *New York Times*, February 25, 1984.

[22]See John H. Hutcheson, Jr., and Jann Shevin, eds., *Citizen Groups in Local Politics: A Bibliographic Review* (Santa Barbara, CA: Clio Books, 1976).

Academy, a school to train activists in the skills and strategies that make an effective organization. Similar organizations also exist in many other places, at the neighborhood as well as the city level. And many are growing. One is ACORN (the Association of Community Organizations for Reform Now), a loose confederation of groups that has branches in many states and cities.[23]

Local Self-Reliance Movements

Not every urban activist pays such attention to politics, however. Some concentrate on finding ways to solve local problems in the neighborhood without even depending on the broader economic system. For example, the Institute for Local Self-Reliance (ILSR) in Washington has developed ways of growing vegetables on rooftop gardens and raising fish in basements in the downtown areas of big cities so that residents needn't depend on others outside the community for good food.[24] It also has programs devoted to energy conservation. Others have undertaken urban homesteading: a program in which citizens rehabilitate rundown houses that they are given by the city and promise to occupy.

Citizen Advisory Groups

But there are still other types of urban citizen action besides neighborhood organization and local self-reliance. Increasingly, city charters are establishing Neighborhood Advisory Commissions (as they are called in New York City), elected from neighborhoods to advise city government.

National Associations of Neighborhood Groups

Furthermore, locally established citizen action groups like Chicago's CAP have united, forming the National Association of Neighborhoods (NAN) in 1975. This organization meets twice a year around the country to develop ways of offering mutual support. The NAN office offers help in organizing, fund raising, publicity, and even lobbying in Washington. Similar lobbying is done by other groups.

Former President Jimmy Carter at work as a volunteer for the Organization *Habitat,* building housing for the needy in Chicago. (Steve Leonard/Black Star)

From Citizens to Partnerships

In recent years, the federal government has stopped fostering such citizen participation. Many local governments too have deemphasized it. One reason is the fact that many of the citizen activists of the 1970s are now themselves city bureaucrats. Another reason is a growing concern for efficiency rather than equity in an era of limited resources. This has resulted in a focus on increasing productivity. Some cities are tying salaries to performance. Others are contracting out city services from garbage pickup to parking-fee collection, in arrangements called public-private partnerships. And others are increasing the user fees to anyone who makes use of special city services.[25] All over America, cities are experimenting.

The Urban Prospect

Are these changes grounds for optimism? Few would say so. After all, the problems of poverty and race in the large cities are still great, and they have not been helped by the budgetary cutbacks in federal, state, and local governments in the 1980s.

Still, urban expert Anthony Downs concluded recently:

[23]For an interesting collection of articles on organizing neighborhoods, see *Social Policy,* September–October 1979.

[24]For more detail, see Karl Hess and David Morris, *Neighborhood Power* (Boston: Beacon, 1975). Or see the interview with Hess in *Mother Earth News,* no. 37.

[25]See Neal R. Peirce & Robert Guskind, "Fewer Federal Dollars Spurring Cities to Improve Management and Trim Costs," *National Journal,* March 1, 1986, pp. 504–8.

I do not believe in pessimism. Instead I believe in continuing to try to improve conditions, no matter what the odds. The pursuit of that belief is what created this country, what brought it to adopt the concept of racial equality under law as its standard, and what will eventually make that concept a reality—perhaps in an America where minorities have become the majority. That is a hopeful conclusion, because hope is a great virtue. But hope is a virtue precisely when it goes beyond a purely rational response to the visible facts. Realism in assessing the situation, but hope surpassing realism when trying to influence policy and launch remedial actions: that is where the best future for America's large cities lies.[26]

SUMMARY

Our cities developed as the frontier moved westward and continued to grow as immigration increased. Today, many of them have large minority populations. Discrimination, poverty, and loss of tax base because of migration to the suburbs have caused major problems for the cities.

The federal government has attempted to cope with these problems in various ways. The Kennedy-Johnson approach focused on urban renewal and programs such as rent supplements, crime control, and other social-welfare programs. The Nixon-Ford years saw funding reforms in the form of revenue sharing. Carter attempted to create a comprehensive urban policy, but his efforts were unsuccessful for political reasons. Reagan emphasized other economic programs but never developed an urban policy.

Urban problems derive from the dependence of cities on their states (Dillon's Rule), from their economic poverty, and from their political weaknesses. The major types of urban governments are mayor-council charter, commission charter, and council-manager plan. The major types of politics involve "machines" and reformers. Urban policy making often suffers from conflicting citizen interests and sometimes from corruption, incompetence, administrative disorder, and a lack of party competition. It is also hampered by weak fiscal bases and the inability to exercise power beyond the city's rim.

Efforts to improve urban government include consolidation of the planning functions of regions via COGs and political decentralization by home rule.

Major urban issues persist—among them rebuilding the infrastructure, controlling gentrification, conserving energy, protecting the environment, and preserving the tax base.

A major hope for improvement in our cities is the growth of citizen participation. This participation is taking place through community organization, local self-reliance movements, citizen advisory groups, and national associations of neighborhood groups. Nonetheless, the future of our cities is unclear.

Suggestions for Further Reading and Study

Among the many interesting classic surveys of urban politics are Edward Banfield and James Q. Wilson, *City Politics* (Cambridge, MA: Harvard Univ. Press, 1963); Charles E. Gilbert, *Governing the Suburbs* (Bloomington: Indiana Univ. Press, 1967); and Robert C. Wood, *1400 Governments* (Garden City, NY: Anchor, 1964).

For helpful surveys of the major problems now facing the cities, see Katherine L. Bradbury, Anthony Downs, and Kenneth A. Small, *Urban Decline and the Future of American Cities* (Washington, DC: Brookings, 1982); Paul E. Peterson, ed., *The New Urban Reality* (Washington, DC: Brookings, 1985); and U.S. Conference of Mayors, *Rebuilding America's Cities* (Cambridge, MA: Ballinger, 1986).

If you're interested in looking at the politics of a major American city in more detail, there's no better place to look than Chicago, my hometown. You could start with Banfield's classic book *Political Influence* (New York: Free Press, 1961), and the other books cited in this chapter's footnotes. But perhaps the best thing to do is to focus on the life and works of the late Mayor Daley, on which there are now many interesting books, among them Mike Royko, *Boss: Richard J. Daley of Chicago* (New York: Dutton, 1971); Milton Rakove, *Don't Make No Waves, Don't Back No Losers* (Bloomington: Indiana Univ. Press, 1976); and *"We Don't Want Nobody Nobody Sent"* (Bloomington: Indiana Univ. Press, 1979).

---

[26]Downs, "The Future of Industrial Cities," in Paul E. Peterson, ed., *The New Urban Reality* (Washington, DC: Brookings, 1985), p. 294.

18

THE POLITICS OF ENERGY AND ENVIRONMENT

If you prove to be an average American, in your lifetime you will be responsible for consumption of 623 tons of coal, oil, and natural gas; 21,000 gallons of gasoline; 5.2 tons of plastics, rubber, and fibers; and 48 tons of wood, 51 tons of metal, and 19 tons of paper. These resources will be used to make 7 autos, 19,000 cans, and 19,250 bottles, which you will discard along with 823 tons of waste that those who make these goods will discard. The whole process will also produce 70 tons of air pollutants. In addition, you will eat 50 tons of food, and you will bathe. Indulging in those activities will consume 26 million gallons of water and 5 tons of fertilizer. The product of all that

will be 840 tons of agricultural wastes and 7 million gallons of polluted water.

The outcome of this—beyond whatever pleasure and pain you get from daily life and whatever you achieve—will be an enormous strain on the earth's resources. Where will all the resources come from? Where will all the garbage go? Until recently, no one gave much thought to these questions. But as population has grown and resources such as oil and food became expensive, scientists and politicians and citizens became concerned. And as pollution spread in our air, water, and land, many became alarmed. In this chapter, we'll see what happened and why. ■

Take a breath. It is almost certain that you just breathed polluted air. Not only if you're in a large city. Not only if you're near a factory or an oil refinery or a power plant churning out smoke. Not only if someone nearby is smoking a cigarette. The air you're breathing may seem clean, at least if you're in a rural area or at home. The fact is, however, that most Americans now breathe air that is harmful to their health most of the time.

Polluted air is air that contains one or more chemicals in high enough concentrations to harm you or animals or plants or materials. It may be carbon dioxide or carbon monoxide—from fires, cars, or cigarettes. It may be sulfur oxides from the burning of coal. It may be nitrogen oxides from fuel power plants or hydrocarbons from automobiles and furnaces. Or it may be dust, soot, oil, asbestos, lead, ammonia, radioactivity, or a wide range of other pollutants. These substances in the air we breathe may eventually worsen or even cause various human diseases such as bronchitis, emphysema, heart disease, and lung cancer. Many air pollutants also do serious damage to the places where we live, study, and work, as the box titled "What Air Pollution Does to Life in New York City" reports.

You breathe in some 30 pounds or 2000 gallons of air every day, whether it's clean or polluted.[1] You have no choice—other than death by suffocation. Do you have a right to breathe clean air—or at least air that won't make you ill? When the founders asserted the inalienable rights to life, liberty, and the pursuit of happiness, they were not thinking of clean air. But the air then had much less dangerous pollution because there were no internal-combustion engines, there was a much lower population density, and the Industrial Revolution had not yet taken place.

Not that there was no pollution. Before the American Revolution, the Massachusetts Bay Colony issued regulations to prevent pollution of the water in Boston Harbor. After the Revolution, local governments took on the responsibility of controlling water and air pollution. The problem was that a city downstream or downwind from a source of pollution outside its jurisdiction couldn't do anything to stop it. States, too, passed laws to control

water pollution in the 19th century once the connection between dirty water and contagious disease was clear. But the first state to pass and enforce air-pollution laws was Oregon—in 1952![2]

Air pollution did not become a major issue until the 1970s. Other forms of pollution received attention earlier. The Water Pollution Control Act of 1948 was the first result. It provided for research and federal technical assistance to the states, but this had little effect. The real importance of the act was that it legitimized federal action in the area of water pollution. The basis for this intervention was the Constitution's power to tax and spend for the general welfare.[3] The Air Pollution Control Act of 1955 was similarly limited to research and assistance to states and cities.

Enforcement remained with the states and cities, where polluters were politically powerful and generally prevented regulation. No one—and no agency—at the federal level was interested in enforcing pollution control. Meanwhile, the quality of the environment continued to deteriorate. Surveys began to show increased public concern.

Congress responded with the Clean Air Act of 1963. It had two new features. First, it authorized the secretary of health, education, and welfare to set air-quality standards. They were not binding, but they were standards, and so they enabled people to assess the quality of their own region's air. The act also authorized the HEW secretary to intervene in the pollution problems of a state if it could not properly handle them alone.

Two years later, the Motor Vehicle Control Act of 1965 extended concern from factories to autos. As a result, HEW began to set emissions standards for cars. The Air Quality Act of 1967 then required states to set clean air standards. But the environment became a political issue only after activists organized a national Earth Day on April 20, 1970—five months after Congress had passed the National Environmental Policy Act (NEPA), which we discussed in Chapter 10. NEPA established the Council on Environmental Quality (CEQ) in the White House to advise the president on environ-

---

[1]The figures on resource consumption in this chapter come from G. Tyler Miller, Jr., *Living in the Environment*, 2d ed. (Belmont, CA: Wadsworth, 1979), p. 7.

[2]See J. Clarence Davies III and Barbara Davies, *The Politics of Pollution* (Indianapolis: Bobbs-Merrill, 1975), p. 158. For Studies of early efforts to control air pollution, see Matthew A. Crenson, *The Un-Politics of Air Pollution* (Baltimore: Johns Hopkins Univ. Press, 1971), and Charles O. Jones, Clean Air: The Policies and Politics of Pollution Control (Pittsburgh: Univ. of Pittsburgh Press, 1975).

[3]See Frank P. Grad et al., *Environmental Control: Priorities, Policies, and the Law* (New York: Columbia Univ. Press, 1971), p. 50.

What Air Pollution Does to Life in New York City

The economic benefits of clean fuel regulations derive mainly from the damage dirty air does to metals, buildings, cloth, vegetation, and other materials. Most metals corrode faster, some of them (like nickel) nearly 100 times faster, in New York City air than in still-prestine regions. On a large scale, this means that bridges and elevated subways and highways age faster or must be repaired more often, or else the danger of collapse increases. On a small but just as economically harmful scale, air pollution damages low-voltage electrical contacts, relays, and switches. In may incapacitate semiconductors and miniaturized equipment. It requires large expenditures for cleaning or for using precious noncorroding metals like gold for the sensitive electronic equipment which is so abundant in Manhattan, the communications center of the nation.

More than $100 million in repainting alone is required in New York City every year because of the onslaught of air pollution. Cloth disinte-grates sooner and dyes fade faster in our sulfurous air, and curtains and clothing must be washed more frequently, adding a considerable expense to hotels and other businesses.

Pollution creeps through the windows and doors of our city's museums and erodes the varnish from paintings, blackens bronze objects, and tarnishes ancient jewelry. It damages paper and thereby destroys valuable records, necessitating expensive microfilming.

Airborne poisons destroy many of the city's remaining trees. Sulfur oxides deposited in the atmosphere by smoke-stacks travel hundreds of miles and are often then washed back to earth, causing an "acid rain" that has already damaged crops over wide areas of the Northeast and increased the acid levels in streams and lakes, killing many fish.

From Michael Gerrard, "The Economic Benefits of a Clean Environment," *Washington Post*, July 20, 1976.

---

mental issues. It also resulted in President Richard Nixon's creating the Environmental Protection Agency (EPA) out of 15 agencies scattered throughout the government.

THE POLITICS OF ENVIRONMENTAL PROTECTION

The Case of the Clean Air Act Amendments

Just after the NEPA was passed, and while the EPA was being established, Congress passed the Clean Air Act Amendments of 1970. These were designed to begin the process of establishing uniform federal and state air-quality standards. Eventually, programs were to include controls on motor-vehicle emissions and stationary-plant emissions (especially power plants that burn oil or coal) as well as controls on proposed uses for land, with the goal of reducing auto use and congestion in cities and thereby cutting pollution.

The primary power the EPA had was the power to withhold federal funds for all purposes from states and localities that refuse to develop and implement appropriate environmental regulations. Such power can be effective. But it is also time-

Coal being stripmined. (Lionel Delevingne/Stock, Boston)

Los Angeles in smog. (Maxtone-Graham/Gamma-Liaison)

consuming to use and subject to political pressures. So it was immediately apparent that other means had to be found to supplement it.

The Clean Air Act, as amended, was the first law to include special new powers. It gave the federal government the power to order an emergency halt to discharges that suddenly threatened public health or safety—say, because of stagnant air. The act also was written *to allow individual citizens to sue polluters* in court or even *to sue the head of the EPA* should he or she fail to perform his or her duty under it. It allowed the courts to make those being sued pay the legal fees of those who were suing. This provision opened the door to a new breed of activists: public-interest environmental lobbies and law firms.

The momentum of efforts to control pollution was soon interrupted by the energy crisis of 1973. Because of the Arab oil embargo of that fall there were calls for greater energy self-sufficiency for the United States. Greater self-sufficiency would require more burning of sulfur-laden, highly polluting coal, which is abundant in the United States, instead of imported oil. The increase in pollution such coal burning causes would not have been permissible without changes in the newly passed Clean Air Act Amendments. So the Nixon administration set about drafting more amendments to the act and thereby created a major dispute in the executive branch.

The White House—in particular, its chief economic agency, the Office of Management and Budget (OMB)—favored increasing the levels of air pollution allowable from coal-burning plants and auto emissions. It was joined in that position by two other parts of the Executive Office of the President. One was the Federal Energy Office (FEO), a special agency established in the December 1973 oil emergency. And the other was the president's Domestic Council (DC), a group of political advisors and policy makers very close to the president. On the other side, the EPA and the CEQ resisted the massive changes proposed, arguing that smaller changes would suffice. The ensuing struggle to develop an agreed-upon set of proposed amendments to submit to Congress was so virulent that in the end agreement could not be reached. Instead, two sets of proposals were submitted. One consisted of minor proposals agreed to by all segments of the executive branch. The other included the major changes favored by OMB, FEO, and DC but publicly opposed by the EPA and CEQ.

When the matter reached Congress, the lobbies were arrayed. On the side favoring relaxation of regulations were the affected industries, especially the coal industry and the electric power companies. On the other side were the environmentalists. (For a listing of major environmental lobby groups, see Action Unit 18.1.) The Senate favored only minimal relaxation, whereas the House supported greater relaxation. In conference committee, the Senate forces prevailed. So the final amendments, which became the Energy Supply and Environmental Coordination Act of 1974, were closer to those favored by the EPA and CEQ.[4]

On balance, it was a legislative victory for the environmental forces, including the government's two environmental agencies, despite strong lobbying and a widespread sense of national emergency. But it was not an unqualified victory, as the cases of autos and electric utilities indicate.

[4]For accounts of the struggle, see Alfred A. Marcus, *Promise and Performance: Choosing and Implementing an Environmental Policy* (Westport, CT: Greenwood, 1980), pp. 70–75 and chap. 5, and Jones, *Clean Air.*

ACTION UNIT 18.1

How to Contact Environmental Action Organizations

Among the environmental lobbyists now active in Washington and elsewhere are such old naturalist organizations as the **Sierra Club** (530 Bush St., San Francisco, CA 94108), founded in 1892 by mountaineers; the **National Audubon Society** (1130 5th Ave., New York, NY 10038), founded in 1905 by bird lovers; the **National Parks and Conservation Association** (1701 18th St. NW, Washington DC 20009), founded in 1919; the **Izaak Walton League of America** (1701 N. Fort Myer Dr., Arlington, VA 22209), founded in 1922 by fishermen; the **Wilderness Society** (1400 Eye St. NW, Washington, DC 20005), founded in 1935; and the **National Wildlife Federation** (1325 Massachusetts Ave. NW, Washington, DC 20036), founded in 1936. These older organizations have become more generalist in their concerns and more militant in their actions as well since the first environmental lobbying commenced in the 1950s.

They have also been joined by several dozen newer and even more activist groups. Both the **Environmental Defense Fund** (1616 P St. NW, Washington, DC 20036) and the **Natural Resources Defense Council** (1350 New York Ave. NW, Washington, DC 20005) wage legal battles. **Greenpeace U.S.A.** (1611 Connecticut Ave. NW, Washington, DC 20009), part of a worldwide coalition, specializes in direct action to obstruct polluters and protect nature and animal life.

Environmental Action (1525 New Hampshire Ave. NW, Washington, DC 20036), **Environmental Policy Institute** (218 D St. SE, Washington, DC 20003), **Solar Lobby** (1001 Connecticut Ave. NW, Washington, DC 20036), and **Friends of the Earth** (530 7th St. SE, Washington, DC 20003) lobby and conduct public education programs. The **League of Conservation Voters** (320 4th St. NE, Washington, DC 20002) has rated members of Congress on their environmental votes and drawn up lists of the twelve leading "enemies of the environment," the Dirty Dozen. Its campaigns to defeat these members of Congress have had a number of successes.

These citizen environmental lobbies have had occasional successes in Congress, such as stopping production of the supersonic transport because it would damage the environment and getting highway funds shifted to mass transit to cut auto pollution. But their major successes have come in the courts, where they have used NEPA to support and encourage EPA efforts to ban DDT and other dangerous pesticides, and to stop construction of new dams and nuclear power plants.

Another growing element of the envinronmental movement is international groups. The best known is the **World Wildlife Fund** (1255 23rd St. NW, Washington, DC 20037), which supports scientific research and conservation projects around the world with its national organizations in 23 countries.

They—and still more with similar interests, listed annually in *Congressional Quarterly's Washington Information Directory*—would welcome your support. Many offer memberships and provide information on environmental policy to citizens.

The Case of Autos

One side effect of autos is air pollution. Another is dependence on imported oil for the gasoline to run them. A third is deaths in highway accidents. The Clean Air Act attempted to cope with auto-exhaust pollution by requiring special equipment to lessen emissions. Unfortunately, studies showed that these devices reduced fuel efficiency by 7.5 percent. This meant that more oil would have to be imported. To reduce U.S. dependence on foreign oil—which at the time was running at 50 percent—Congress required that auto makers produce cars that got better mileage and passed a law setting a national speed limit of 55 mph. The result was that demand for gasoline dropped 2 percent (925 million barrels of oil a year), and highway deaths fell by 15 percent (4000 lives a year).

But to meet the energy-efficiency requirements, which decreased mileage, Detroit had to make cars smaller. A side effect of that was that cars offered less protection to occupants in accidents. One study estimated that this cost an extra 1400 lives a year and many additional serious injuries. To make cars safer in crashes, new safety protections such as side-door guard beams and energy-absorbing steering wheels have been required. These changes have added another 200 pounds to the weight of the average car—and so have meant less fuel efficiency. They have also made new cars up to $2000 more expensive. This rise in cost had led many people to keep their older cars longer. Those older cars are less safe, less fuel efficient, and more polluting. Other proposed changes, such as automatic seat-belts and airbags, could save lives at little cost in weight. However, they would increase the price of cars and decrease individual freedom of choice. Thus, the Reagan administration has consistently sought to postpone or cancel them, as have the automakers.[5] Finally, the Transportation Department's National Highway Traffic Safety Administration required that all cars have self-buckling seat-belts or automatically inflating air bags by 1989. But it promised to cancel this rule if enough states passed laws requiring use of seatbelts so that two-thirds of the population were covered. The purpose of the promise was to lessen the expense for car makers. Its side effect will be that the two-thirds required to use seatbelts will be safer (although perhaps not as safe as with automatic belts or airbags) while the other third will be less safe unless those people decide voluntarily to use seat-belts. So there are always tradeoffs between price, emissions, fuel economy, safety—and individual liberty.[6]

The Case of Electric Utilities

Much the same thing has occurred in the case of the utilities that provide our electricity. After the energy crises of 1973, Congress passed laws to encourage utilities to switch from burning natural gas and oil, which are quite clean, to coal, which pollutes. Many of the older plants had originally burned coal but had switched to oil in the early 1970s, when new pollution-control laws made oil a more appealing fuel.

The switch to coal became *economical* as the price of oil and gas skyrocketed. By 1980 burning oil to make electricity was three times as expensive as burning coal. The switch also had *foreign policy advantages*. The United States was importing almost half its oil by then but was exporting coal. The United States in fact has by far the world's largest coal reserves—one-third of all the known coal in the world. There's enough to last us cen-

turies. These factors make the switch to coal advantageous.

But the use of coal has its problems, too. The first is air pollution. Coal is very dirty to burn and its burning produces dangerous emissions, including harmful gases and irritating particles of solid materials, such as ash. There are two types of problems caused by these pollutants. Many of them cause heart and breathing problems for people. In addition, however, two of these pollutants, sulfur dioxide and nitrogen oxides, are now believed to cause **acid rain**. Rainfall in areas near coal-burning plants and for hundreds of miles downwind from them tends to be very acidic. This rain is often similar to lemon juice or stomach acid, as Figure 18.1 shows, and such rain is thought to damage plant and animal life. Acid rain has been protested most strongly by citizens and states and provinces in New England and Canada, which suffer from its effects but cannot control them because the sources are in states of the Midwest.

Efforts are now being made to limit the 30 million tons of sulfur dioxide and 25 million tons of nitrogen oxides pumped into the air by U.S. plants every year. Regulations by the EPA now require new power plants to install "scrubbers," which can trap up to 95 percent of the sulfur dioxide. But most plants are exempt from these rules because they were built before 1971.

Some suggest the better approach is to prevent the pollution before it happens. The sulfur dioxide comes from coal with a high sulfur content. Coal from the western United States has a low sulfur content. Thus, there would be less pollution if power plants in the East burned western coal. But

[5]Brock Yates, *The Decline and Fall of the American Automobile Industry* (New York: Empire Books, 1983).
[6]For an interesting study, see Robert W. Crandall, et al., *Regulating the Automobile* (Washington, DC: Brookings, 1986).

FIGURE 18.1

The Acidity of Acid Rain.

Note: Chemists measure the degree of acidity of a solution on a pH scale. The numbers on the scale in the drawing are pH numbers. Thus, distilled water has a pH of about 7. Each whole number increment indicates a tenfold difference. Some everyday compounds are displayed along the bottom of the scale; benchmarks of acid rain are shown along the top.

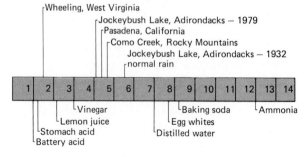

if they did so, the high-sulfur coal mines in the East would suffer, and miners there would lose their jobs. So there are strong political pressures against such otherwise obvious solutions.

The most striking example of this pressure is the Clean Air Act Amendments of 1977. They had the effect of *requiring scrubbers even when low-sulfur coal is burned*. This removes the advantage of burning low-sulfur coal, which is more expensive. The amendments also ban the importation of western coal in cases where it would threaten jobs in the mines of Ohio and Illinois. Why were such regulations imposed? The reason was lobbying by a coalition of environmentalists favoring scrubbers everywhere to get the maximum air cleanliness and high-sulfur-coal producers and mine workers' unions, combined with members of Congress representing the industrial East and Midwest. The end result is higher-cost energy and more pollution. In addition, using the pollution-control equipment increases a plant's own energy consumption by 5 to 10 percent, according to experts. So what began as efforts to clean the air has led to higher energy consumption, higher-cost energy, and more pollution than would have occurred had burning low-sulfur coal without scrubbers been allowed.[7] The Reagan administration chose further study rather than action on the problem while Congress remained deadlocked.[8]

Thus, once again we see how interconnected pollution and energy production are. If we carried our study of the case of coal further, we would have to consider issues such as mine safety and the environmental impact of surface mining. The Surface Mining Control and Reclamation Act of 1977 requires that mining companies restore strip-mined land to its original contours and replace its original vegetation while protecting its surface and ground water. By 1980, the Interior Department had produced 575 pages of interpretations of the law in the *Federal Register*. The Reagan administration, un-der its first secretary of the interior, James G. Watt, then sought to reverse this trend toward close watch over strip mining. It reduced the number of inspectors by half, closed regional offices, and rewrote regulations to weaken them.[9] It then moved to return authority to regulate strip mining back to the states. That is, after all, where the problems reside. But it is also where the big mining companies are strongest politically.

There is another, broader problem connected with the burning of all fossil fuels, especially coal. Any fossil (coal, oil, or gas) gives off carbon dioxide when burned. Coal produces more than other such fuels. Most experts believe that this increased carbon dioxide will absorb more heat from the sun and so will warm up the earth's atmosphere, turning the earth into a sort of greenhouse. If it does so, that warmer earth temperature may make the ice at the North and South Poles melt somewhat, which would raise ocean levels. This might flood many coastal lands—especially major port cities such as New York, London, and Hong Kong. If ocean levels rise three feet in the next 50 years, as the EPA now predicts, Boston, Baltimore, Norfolk, Charleston, Miami, and even Washington, D.C. will also be swamped. What can be done to prevent this **greenhouse effect**? Most experts believe that the only hope is a global campaign to reduce the chemical pollutants. Thus far, not even the United States has made much progress on this solution.[10]

The Case of Toxic Wastes

The U.S. population discards over 150 million tons of garbage a year. Industry creates more than 260 million metric tons of hazardous wastes a year—in addition to what it pumps into the air through smokestacks or into rivers and lakes.[11] Manufacturers claim to spend over $13 billion a year to control their pollution.[12] But this amount is far from adequate, as we've already seen. Experts know that *disposal* (in pits, deep wells, or at sea), the major current approach, causes more problems in later

[7]See Bruce A. Ackerman and William T. Hassler, *Clean Coal/Dirty Air: Or How the Clean Air Act Became a Multibillion-Dollar Bail-Out for High-Sulfur Coal Producers and What Should Be Done About It* (New Haven, CT: Yale Univ. Press, 1981), and Peter Navarro, "The Politics of Air Pollution," *Public Interest*, Spring 1980, pp. 36–44.

[8]For examination of the Reagan record, see Richard J. Tobin, "Revising the Clean Air Act: Legislative Failure and Administrative Success," in *Environmental Policy in the 1980s: Reagan's New Agenda*, ed. Norman J. Vig and Michael E. Kraft (Washington, DC: CQ Press, 1984), chap. 11. See also Rochelle L. Stanfield, "The Acid Rainmakers," *National Journal*, June 14, 1986, pp. 1500–1503, which discusses the debates among scientists as well as those among politicians.

[9]See Walter A. Rosenbaum, *Environmental Politics and Policy* (Washington, DC: CQ Press, 1985), chap. 7.

[10]See Rochelle L. Stanfield, "Attitudes about Ozone Are Changing," *National Journal*, November 1, 1986, p. 2638.

[11]Rochelle L. Stanfield, "Drowning in Waste," *National Journal*, May 10, 1986, pp. 1106–10.

[12]*Census Bureau Data User News*, September 1986, p. 6.

Fish killed by pollution. (Tom McHugh/Photo Researchers)

contamination of land and water. *Destruction*, usually by incineration, causes more air pollution. *Recycling*, or reusing, materials is better, although it tends to be more expensive than using new raw materials. More and more states and cities are developing recycling programs. For example, in 1987 New York began a program to reduce waste production by 50 percent over 10 years, and New Jersey announced a plan to recycle 25 percent of its waste.

Recycling cuts costs of disposal but is itself quite expensive. The ideal solution is waste *reduction* by not generating waste in the first place. But it often requires new research and new technology, both of which are also expensive. It's an unattractive option for U.S. firms competing with overseas firms in countries without environmental-protection programs.

In 1980 Congress created a **Superfund** (renewed in 1986) financed by fees from polluters to clean up major toxic waste dumps, but so far it has only amounted to a figurative drop out of the waste bucket.

Thus, the incentives are still to pollute now and worry (or let others worry) about the consequences later. In 1980 the EPA estimated that the United States would need 125 new sites for hazardous waste disposal. But in every case where it has tried to create such sites, local residents have objected that this violates their property rights. Consequently, no new waste sites have been created, and waste—including the most hazardous, nuclear waste—continues to mount in temporary storage. Of course, this kind of storage may be even more dangerous.

THE DEBATES ABOUT ENVIRONMENTAL PROTECTION

Such stalemates and the generally slow pace of environmental protection have led to serious splits, both in the government, and in the environmental movement.[13] The governmental disputes in the Reagan administration focus on the relative emphasis put on free-market economics—letting firms do what they wish in order to stimulate economic growth—and governmental regulation. When regulation is deemed necessary, the administration has preferred to use economic incentives (such as tax breaks for pollution reduction) rather than regulations requiring cutbacks in discharge of pollutants.

This approach is grounded in a belief that pollution cannot be avoided. The laws of conservation of matter and energy dictate that we cannot really get rid of anything. All we can do is change the form, nature, place, or timing of discharges. Government's only role, this view holds, is to step in when the market produces too much pollution and impose whatever minimal controls are essential.

However, the major environmental laws have been based on an assumption that pollution is bad—a wrong *in itself*. In this view, people have a *right to be free of environmental risks*, and the ultimate goal is zero pollution. Thus, the objective should always be to do the best that existing technology will allow.[14]

These basic disputes are one thing that complicates progress in environmental protection. Another is the fact that, for most environmental problems, the effects are not immediate, nor are they readily recognized as such when they appear. The same thing is true of the energy problem itself. It seems either to be an immediate crisis (when oil shipments are cut off, as they were in 1973, or prices rise drastically, as they did in 1979) or a phony issue (when there is a temporary glut or even an adequate supply). To understand the scope of our national energy and environmental problems, we must take a longer-term perspective on both demand and supply.

---

[13]For an account of politics within the government, see Jim Sibbison, "Whose Agency Is It, Anyway? How OMB Runs EPA," *Washington Monthly*, December 1985, pp. 19–22.

[14]These two views are summarized in Clifford S. Russell and Paul R. Portney, "A Policy Foundation for the Future," *Resources*, No. 81 (Summer/Fall 1985), 8–9.

Greenpeace activists returning pollution to its source. (Stoddart-Spooner/Gamma-Liaison)

DEMAND AND SUPPLY IN THE LONG TERM

Demand

You may well be conscious of your need for cleaner air—especially if you live in a city or near a polluting factory. You may also be aware of a desire for good land—especially if you wish to farm. You may not, however, be so conscious of your need for safe water—unless you know that a 1974 government study found that only 60 percent of our public drinking-water systems delivered water of good quality and 10 percent offered very poor quality. Another study of 80 major U.S. cities found 20 organic chemicals known or suspected to cause cancer in the systems.[15] Thus, most of the nation's largest cities have drinking water that has been deemed at least somewhat dangerous to those who drink it. The Clean Water Act of 1972 committed the government to achieve "fishable/swimmable" water quality by 1983 and an end to pollution discharge in all navigable waters by 1985. Neither of these goals has been met. In fact, the United States still injects some 10 billion gallons of sewage,

chemicals, radioactive waste, and brine into the earth each year—and many of these poisons seep into the groundwater we drink.[16]

Even if you feel a need for clean air and safe water, you probably do not feel such a need for adequate energy supplies. The reason is that we all generally expect energy to be available when we turn on a light switch or plug in an appliance or drive up to a gas station. The only exceptions we ever expect to this are electricity "outages" due to storms and gas shortages due to political embargoes. Our only fears about energy seem to be that its price may get so high we can't afford it.

The fact that energy seems always to be available is the biggest obstacle to our understanding the very real coming threats to its adequate and affordable supply. But before we look at supply, we must take note of changing demand.

Until recently, the demand for energy in the United States has been increasing regularly, both for the country as a whole and per capita. The energy crisis of 1973 sent demand down for the first time, but it then began to climb again. However, total energy use per dollar of gross national product has declined every year since 1973. On aver-

---

[15]See Miller, *Living in the Environment*, p. 361.

[16]See Michael Brown, Laying Waste: The Poisoning of America by Toxic Chemicals (New York: Pantheon, 1980); and Jonathan King, *Troubled Water* (Emmaus, PA: Rodale, 1985).

A pro-nuclear-energy demonstration. (Artie Grace/Sygma)

An anti-nuclear-energy demonstration. (Tannenbaum/Sygma)

age, individual householders have decreased their use of energy at home by about 15 percent in recent years. One reason is the fact that many homes are being modified to conserve energy. In addition, declines are occurring outside the home. Corporations have made major improvements. The major factor here is that newer fuel-efficient cars are replacing older "gas guzzlers" in increasing numbers. There are more cars on the road, and more miles are being driven, but gas consumption has been declining since 1978. Most experts now expect most such declines in energy demand to continue.

Supply

These changes have followed upon growing warnings that energy supplies are being depleted, coupled with rapidly rising prices. Most of our current energy sources are in fact old, unused solar energy stored in the ground. We call these nonrenewable resources because there won't be any more of them when these are gone. Most experts now think we'll run out of natural gas and oil in 30 to 80 years and coal in 100 to 300 years—all depending on how fast demand grows. Some hope that nuclear power will fill in once these "fossil fuels" are gone.

At the moment, almost 80 percent of the world's energy comes from fossil fuels, about 20 percent from burning trash and dung, and a very small amount from nuclear plants. The growing public fears about the safety of nuclear reactors—all the stronger since the accident at the Three Mile Island plant in Pennsylvania in 1979 and the catastrophic partial meltdown at the Soviet plant at Chernobyl in 1986—and the skyrocketing costs of nuclear plants and fuels make many doubt how much of a contribution nuclear power will be able to make, at least at the present level of technology. In addition, growing concern about safe disposal of nuclear wastes makes a nuclear solution even less likely. What does that leave as an energy source?

Solar Energy

The sun sends down at the earth 400,000 times as much energy as the entire capacity of all the electric companies of America. You'd think that would be enough to take care of our needs. In fact, it would be enough virtually to vaporize us. But here the earth comes to our rescue, reflecting 30 percent of that energy back into space. Another 47 percent is absorbed by the atmosphere, water, and land. That's what makes life livable on earth. Most of the 23 percent of solar energy that remains makes the water and air on earth move, which gives us tides and winds and rain and tornadoes.

That leaves two hundredths of 1 percent (0.0225 percent) of the incoming solar energy to be absorbed by trees, vegetable plants, grain, grass, and other greenery. These greens then provide the energy for animals and us by producing the food we eat. Much of the rest of the solar energy could be used for heating. More and more people are now using solar energy to heat their homes and water. In theory, we could also gather solar energy and convert it into electricity. But that would require technology we don't yet have because the sun's rays are so diffuse.[17]

Other Energy Sources

There are other likely sources of energy besides solar. *Tides and waves* are very powerful and may be harnessed to drive motors, rather in the way that waterfalls now produce "hydroelectric" power. *Hydroelectric* power too is still largely undeveloped, especially in Western countries. Wind is now making a comeback as cheaper windmills are developed. *Geothermal* ("earth heat") sources such as geysers and steam vents can be used to produce power when they spout steam. And there is room for more progress in one of the oldest types of energy production: *processed waste*, such as garbage and dung, burned to release energy. Finally, some believe that solar collectors in space could orbit the earth, gather solar energy, and transmit it to the earth in concentrated rays.[18]

In a sense, then, the point is not that there is not, or could not be, much more energy then we now have. The point is that all this production of fuel takes time and technology—and, of course, still more energy and more money. You can't make energy without spending energy to produce, store, and transport it. The costs of all this are climbing for a number of reasons. One is that high technology is expensive. Another is that oil-producing countries attempt to get high levels of revenue, anticipating the day when the oil is gone. Yet another is that energy is produced by large companies that can influence prices in their favor. And coupled with these is the fact that everywhere governments are levying special taxes on energy partly to get revenue but also to try to limit consumption and so preserve resources and lessen their vulnerability to possible cutoffs. These are the places where politics and energy become inextricably linked.

THE POLITICS OF ENERGY POLICY

We have seen in previous chapters that policy making always involves more than simply deciding a case on its merits. Special interests intervene. In the instance of energy policy, for example, these have included energy companies, consumer advocates, environmentalists, tax reformers, and civil-rights groups interested in more jobs. As this list suggests, other concerns turn out to be affected by any decisions that might be taken on energy. In other words, there are always trade offs between concerns like energy, environment, and the economy. Recognizing these basic facts, what can we say about the politics of policy making?

National Energy Politics

The federal government has been involved in energy since the 1920s. For decades, its role was to limit the supply of plentiful oil and gas to protect the producers. And when shortages recently became a problem, the government stepped in to allocate energy among businesses and private homes and among parts of the country.

Actually, the government has a double involvement. It continues to influence imports, prices, and allocations by its "national energy policy," which includes subsidies valued at close to $50 billion a year—primarily to nuclear plants and to oil and gas.[19] In addition, it owns most of the remaining energy resources in the country: oil lands under the ocean floor of the Atlantic, Pacific, and Gulf coasts, coal deposits in the western states, and even uranium. What sort of policy has emerged from this?

The Quest for Independence

The Nixon administration was faced suddenly with the Arab oil embargo of 1973 in the midst of the Watergate investigation. It opted for a goal of "energy independence" by 1980, hoping that somehow by then we would no longer need to import oil. When Gerald Ford took over as president, he revised the date of 1985 but retained the objective. Little progress was made in efforts to control consumption, and imports continued to increase. As a result, Carter's efforts had two objectives. One was cutting oil imports. The other was limiting the growth of domestic consumption through more use of coal and incentives for home insulation and use of solar heating, along with restrictions on inefficient cars. U.S. oil imports fell from 50 percent in

---

[17]A splendid survey, on which this account relies heavily, is Earl Cook, *Man, Energy, Society* (San Francisco: Freeman, 1976).
[18]See Gerard O'Neill, *The High Frontier: Human Colonies in Space* (New York: Morrow, 1977).

[19]Richard Heede and Amory B. Lovins, "Hiding the True Costs of Energy Sources," *Wall Street Journal*, September 17, 1985.

Solar panels being installed on part of the White House roof during the Carter administration as part of its effort at cutting energy consumption. (Dennis Brack/Black Star)

1973 to 37 percent in 1986. Table 18.1 shows where U.S. oil comes from.

The Emphasis on Conservation

The reason for this shift in emphasis toward conservation is that America's use of energy is still remarkably inefficient. Figure 18.2 shows that *about half the energy we use is wasted*, in the sense that it doesn't contribute to the end result desired, such as heating or powering transportation. Some of this waste is inevitable because of the limits of efficiency. But many believe that about half the waste—or a quarter of the energy we consume—could be saved by conservation. However, conservation alone seems unlikely to solve our problems—partly because most people are not motivated to conserve actively, for they do not recognize the extent of the challenge.[20]

---

[20]See Pietro S. Nivola, *The Politics of Energy Conservation* (Washington, DC: Brookings, 1986), which focuses on the dispute over gasoline taxes.

TABLE 18.1
Where U.S. Oil Imports Come From

Canada	13 percent
Venezuela	13 percent
Mexico	12 percent
Saudi Arabia	11 percent
Nigeria	7 percent
United Kingdom	6 percent
Indonesia	5 percent
Algeria	4 percent
Virgin Islands	4 percent
Trinidad	2 percent

Source: These figures, for 1986, are from the American Petroleum Institute.

The Return to the Market

The Reagan administration decided to curtail regulation and conservation efforts in the hope that market forces would be more effective. It officially abandoned the hope of energy independence, assuming instead that America would import Middle Eastern oil for at least two decades. It also cut programs intended to foster conservation and renewable sources, although Congress resisted these efforts somewhat.

Reagan succeeded in eliminating some regulations designed to encourage conservation. A case in point is refrigerators. The average family spends about $110 a year to run its refrigerator. Refrigerators in America are not very efficient. The Japanese now have refrigerators that use less than half as much energy. If American consumers wake up to this information, U.S. appliance manufacturers will face the same sort of competition Detroit has over autos. If they don't, the United States will have to spend some $50 billion to build new power plants over the next 20 years—just to produce the amount of energy wasted by inefficient refrigerators, which consume 3 percent of our total electricity.

To increase energy efficiency, the state of California set refrigerator standards in 1976. All U.S. manufacturers met them for all their products sold in all states by 1981 because that was easier than developing different products for different states. Meanwhile, in 1980 the Carter administration's Department of Energy (DOE) proposed much stricter standards. But then Reagan replaced Carter, and the new energy officials withdrew the standards. They preferred to leave things to the consumers and the manufacturers—to the free

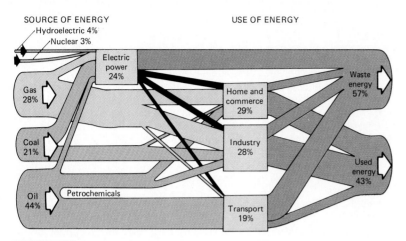

SOURCE OF ENERGY   USE OF ENERGY

Hydroelectric 4%
Nuclear 3%
Electric power 24%
Gas 28%
Coal 21%
Oil 44%
Petrochemicals
Home and commerce 29%
Industry 28%
Transport 19%
Waste energy 57%
Used energy 43%

FIGURE 18.2
Sources, Uses, and Wastage of Energy.

Source: U.S. Energy Information Administration, *Annual Report to Congress 1980* and *Monthly Energy Review*, March 1980, data for 1979. Other energy sources (wood, wind, geothermal, and so on) make up less than 1 percent of total supply.

market. A law passed in 1975 had called on DOE to set such standards, but to protect manufacturers it said that no state could have stricter standards than DOE—even if DOE decided on no standards. When DOE withdrew its proposals, California and other states developed new, tougher ones. But when in September 1983 DOE finally announced there would be no national standards, it meant that the states would have to abolish theirs. In 1986 Congress passed a bill that would require most new home appliances to use 15 to 25 percent less electricity or gas than they now do. Reagan vetoed it, even though it was supported by consumer groups, electric utilities, and appliance manufacturers. The losers are primarily the consumers in the short run. In the longer run, dependence on imported oil might influence foreign policy. And ultimately U.S. manufacturers might suffer from Japanese imports. Such are the possible consequences of deregulation in the realm of energy.[21]

This pattern of efforts to rely on market forces has been characteristic of the Reagan administration in most areas of energy and environmental policy. The efforts by Anne Gorsuch Burford at

EPA and by James Watt at Interior caused so much trouble that they were eventually forced to resign and were replaced by people whose rhetoric and actions were more moderate. Nonetheless, a major reorientation had been achieved. Where Carter had put advocates of the environment in positions of responsibility, Reagan put advocates of the market. Where Carter budgeted for subsidies to conservation and renewable energy sources, Reagan cut regulatory budgets and eliminated most subsidies to all but nuclear power. One consequence was a strengthening of the environmental lobbies described in Action Unit 18.1—supported by a public largely opposed to the new policies. Another was distraction of attention from problems of controlling pollution to controversies over politicized administration.[22] But neither U.S. energy policy nor environmental policy is yet firmly and finally in place. Much remains to be decided.

Future Options

Our energy policy is now a complex consequence of a dozen important laws, summarized in Table 18.2. But despite these laws, fundamental debates

---

[21]See David B. Goldstein, "Refrigerator Reform: Guidelines for Energy Gluttons," *Technology Review*, February–March 1983, pp. 36–46; and Elizabeth Tucker, "Reagan Pulled the Plug on Appliance Standards," *Washington Post National Weekly Edition*, November 17, 1986.

[22]See Norman J. Vig and Michael E. Kraft, eds., *Environmental Policy in the 1980s: Reagan's New Agenda* (Washington, DC: CQ Press, 1984); and Jonathan Lash et al., *A Season of Spoils: The Reagan Administration's Attack on the Environment* (New York: Pantheon, 1984).

TABLE 18.2
The Major Laws that Constitute U.S. Energy Policy

LAW	PURPOSE
Atomic Energy Act of 1954	Authorized private development of nuclear energy and established federal responsibility for disposal of nuclear wastes
Emergency Petroleum Allocation Act of 1973	Authorized president to control prices and allocate available fuel among regions and activities
Energy Supply and Environmental Coordination Act of 1974	Declared that new power plants must use coal and older ones should be encouraged to do so
Energy Policy and Conservation Act of 1975	Created price incentives for new oil discoveries, set fuel-economy standards for autos, and required establishment of a strategic petroleum reserve to stockpile oil
Energy Conservation and Recovery Act of 1976	Required buildings to meet minimum energy-efficient standards and involved government in setting prices for electricity to encourage conservation
Natural Gas Policy Act of 1978	Provided for gradual decontrol of prices of natural gas, now regulated by the federal government, through 1985
Public Utility Regulatory Policies Act of 1978	Required that utility rate structures reflect actual cost of providing power to encourage conservation
National Energy Conservation Policy Act of 1978	Required utilities to help customers learn how to conserve energy at home
Powerplant and Industrial Fuel Use Act of 1978	Strengthened government's power to get utilities to switch from oil or gas to coal
Energy Tax Act of 1978	Created "tax credits" for installation of energy-saving devices or solar equipment in homes and businesses and established tax on "gas-guzzling" autos
Energy Security Act of 1980	Created large subsidies for "synthetic fuels" such as liquid fuels made from coal and oil made from shale
Crude Oil Windfall Profits Tax of 1980	Taxed oil company profits from decontrol of prices and allocated some aid to those who would suffer most from rising prices

continue over what the emphasis should be in coming decades. One interesting characterization of the choice has been developed by energy consultant Amory Lovins.[23] The "hard energy path" the United States and other countries now follow relies on fossil fuels and nuclear power. He characterizes this approach as "strength through exhaustion" because its high costs, growing international conflict over scarce resources, and nuclear dangers threaten the countries following it. The alternative he calls the "soft energy path." It would mean abandoning nuclear power and "synthetic fuels" such as gas made from coal in favor of solar, hydroelectric, and wind energy. The way to achieve this goal would be by user conservation encouraged by government and power companies. The argument over whether or not a soft energy path would be feasible is still raging.[24]

---

[23]See Amory B. Lovins, *Soft Energy Paths: Toward a Durable Peace* (New York: Harper & Row, 1979).

[24]For the text of various attacks on Lovins and his responses, see Lovins et al., *The Energy Controversy: Soft Path Questions and Answers* (San Francisco: Friends of the Earth, 1980).

The Case of Agriculture

The debate over the possibility of relying primarily on conservation rather than new energy sources is starkest in the area of agriculture. The United States has what most people consider by far the most productive agricultural system ever created. However, the main reason why American agriculture is so productive is that we use massive quantities of energy in farming. We use immense amounts of fertilizer, some of which is made from oil and gas. The same is true for pesticides. We use machinery at every stage of farming, and it runs on gas. We use energy to pump water to irrigate and energy to dry grain when it's harvested, and energy to transport the food to factories, and energy to pack it and ship it and store it and sell it. And you and I then use energy driving to the store, energy refrigerating the food we buy, and energy disposing of our wastes.

Energy expert Donald Carr writes:

If we look at farming from the standpoint of calories of food crop delivered to the American table com-

(© 1980 Owen M. L./Black Star)

pared to calories of energy expended in the form of fuel, electricity, chemicals (including pesticides as well as fertilizer), energy tied up in the manufacture of farm tools, transportation devices, supermarket refrigerators, etc., etc., we come to the appalling conclusion that the American food system devours over 9 times as many calories as it produces. Instead of being the most efficient system, it is energetically by far the least efficient system of agriculture that has ever existed or that we can imagine.[25]

Viewed from this perspective, for a soft energy, or conservationist energy policy, to be feasible, there would have to be major changes in American food policy. Some have argued that such changes will be necessary in any event, simply because of the growing world demand for food.[26]

Thus, America's food policy is intimately connected with its energy policy. Just as tightly bound together are U.S. energy and environmental policies. As Walter A. Rosenbaum writes:

> Almost all energy policies become environmental policies, and environmental policies in good part become energy policies. It is virtually impossible for public officials to plan the use of future energy resources and technologies without deciding, if only implicitly, the

nation's tolerance for environmental degradation. Conversely, government can rarely establish environmental pollution standards without deciding, in the process, what levels of energy production and which energy technologies will be tolerated.[27]

This brings us, then, to the underlying question of the principles on which our energy and environmental policies should be based.

SOME KEY PRINCIPLES FOR ENERGY AND ENVIRONMENTAL POLICY

So far, we have looked at problems of energy and environment largely in terms of politics and technology. We have examined various policies and programs as they have been developed by officials or as they have emerged from the political process. Before we end our examination, however, it would be wise to consider briefly some general principles that, according to most experts, should influence the energy and environment policies we adopt in coming years. Each of these principles is complex in its nature and fascinating in its implications.

[25]Carr, *Energy and the Earth Machine* (New York: Norton, 1976), p. 178.
[26]See John Gever et al., *Beyond Oil* (Washington, DC: Carrying Capacity, 1986).

[27]Walter A. Rosenbaum, *Energy, Politics, and Public Policy* (Washington, DC: CQ Press, 1981), pp. 130–31.

Scarcity, Economy, Entropy, Waste, and Conservation

Resources are scarce. This is an assertion most people now accept, but it requires qualification. We noted earlier that most experts believe that we will most likely, for practical purposes, run out of oil in a matter of decades. This does not mean that there will then be no oil left underground. It means instead that the remaining oil will be so expensive to recover that it will not be worth recovering.[28] The same thing is likely to become increasingly true of various minerals. The point is, they are becoming scarcer in the sense that they are more expensive to uncover and obtain.

Debates still rage between those experts who believe that some resources really are running out and those who believe we will find new and cheaper ways to retrieve them or adequate substitutes.[29] Whatever the truth in this argument, it is clear that we cannot consider supply without considering price. Scarcity and economy are closely intertwined.

In energy, scarcity is related to the fact that not all the fuel we use does the work we want it to do. Much of the energy produced by the fuel dissipates into the environment in the form of heat. This tendency of energy to disperse or become dissipated or disordered means that it's no longer available to do work. The tendency of energy to degrade or dissipate is described technically by the law of **entropy**. An everyday example of this law at work is the hot cup of coffee that spontaneously cools off unless you add more heat.[30]

We are living in a "high-energy culture." Most things we use—from cars to electric can openers—require lots of energy to make and more energy to run. In all this energy expenditure, as we saw in Figure 18.2, we waste more energy than we actually use to achieve what we want. That and the decline in readily available energy sources have led to much greater interest in conservation—more efficient use of energy and other resources. We are now making progress in conserving in some areas, as we noted above.

Two Laws of Culture and Evolution

But such progress is difficult precisely because the old way of doing things was so successful for so long that it eliminated most alternative ways, including those that are more energy efficient. This situation is expressed in two laws developed by anthropologists to explain the evolution of cultures. The first is called **the law of cultural dominance**. It states: "[A] cultural system which more effectively exploits the energy resources of a given environment will tend to spread in that environment at the expense of less effective systems."[31] When oil was plentiful and gasoline was therefore cheap, Detroit built large, "gas-guzzling" cars. Because these big cars cost so little to run, small American cars were unmarketable and mass transit declined. The big cars used cheap energy so effectively that they drove out the alternative transportation systems.

Then the price of energy shot up very quickly, primarily because major oil producers banded together and imposed higher prices on us. Suddenly, big cars were no longer efficient. But they were all Detroit knew how to make. So what happened? Factories in other countries, where incomes were lower and energy less plentiful, had long been making high-mileage cars because those were most efficient in their cultures. They exported fuel-efficient cars to the United States, where people were desperate for them. The American auto makers had great trouble adapting to these new energy conditions and this new competition from abroad. Only high tariffs and import limits on Japanese cars gave Detroit the opportunity belatedly to adapt.

This illustrates the second cultural principle, **the law of evolutionary potential**. It states: "The more specialized and adapted a form in a given evolutionary stage, the smaller is its potential for passing

[28]For an account of how estimates of such reserves are made and the controversies surrounding them, see Richard A. Kerr, "How Much Oil? It Depends on Whom You Ask," *Science*, April 24, 1981, pp. 427–29. See also Aaron Wildavsky and Ellen Tenenbaum, *The Politics of Mistrust* (Beverly Hills, CA: Sage, 1981).

[29]For an interesting instance of this debate, see Julian L. Simon, "Resources, Population, Environment: An Oversupply of False Bad News," *Science*, June 27, 1980, pp. 1431–37; and the hostile responses and Simon's rejoinder in the letters section of *Science*, December 19, 1980, pp. 1296–1308. See also Simon's article "The Scarcity of Raw Materials," *Atlantic*, June 1981, pp. 33–41; and his book The Ultimate Resource (Princeton, NJ: Princeton Univ. Press, 1981).

[30]For a discussion of the role of entropy in our energy crisis, see Jeremy Rifkin, *Entropy: A New World View* (New York: Viking, 1980) p. 35. See also Nicholas Georgescu-Roegen, *The Entropy Law and the Economic Process* (Cambridge, MA: Harvard Univ. Press, 1971).

[31]David Kaplan, "The Law of Cultural Dominance," in *Evolution and Culture*, ed. Marshall D. Sahlins and Elman R. Service (Ann Arbor: Univ. of Michigan Press, 1960), p. 75.

to the next stage."[32] In other words, the very fact that efficiency makes one way of doing things dominant in one set of conditions makes it harder for the system to adapt to new conditions.

This may seem rather abstract. However, you should be able to see the relevance to the problems the United States faces in the new world conditions of expensive energy and extensive pollution. The successes of our earlier technological development now hamper our adjusting to new challenges.

Centralization versus Decentralization

One of the clearest ways this problem appears is in the high degree of centralization of so much of our lives. Although there are now auto factories in various parts of the country, cars are still designed in Detroit for a standardized national market rather than for more geographically distinct localized markets. Although there are some 242 million Americans, with 50 state governments and some 78,000 local governments, most of the money we pay in taxes goes to Washington, to our national government. There *it*—not we, not our local government—decides what to spend it on and how much of it to return to local units to solve local problems. We've seen that such centralization has real advantages. We also find increasingly that local units may be more aware of needs and more responsive to particular conditions, as we saw in the chapter on urban problems.

The same thing now seems to be true of energy. Our electricity system is tied together nationally so that if one part of the country needs an unusual amount, it can get it from a part that has a surplus. But this also means that a malfunction in one local unit may cause electrical power in a whole region to break down, as happened in 1965 in the Northeast. Similarly, a nuclear explosion somewhere in the United States—whether in war or by accident—might shut down the entire power grid of the country.[33] Our energy system is highly centralized and, so, vulnerable. We are now concluding that some things are best dealt with in a centralized fashion, but others are best met with local approaches. Energy systems can be decentralized

Greenpeace demonstration to save the penguins. (Gamma-Liaison)

so that each household or neighborhood generates all or at least some of its electricity via windmills or solar systems. This might provide greater security and greater efficiency in the long run. The same might be true of certain aspects of pollution fighting. But in this realm, the problems are rarely localized in their effects, so it seems to require more centralized approaches.

More and more people now fear that this centralization in energy will also jeopardize our civil liberties and even our democratic way of politics. "In an electrical world," writes Amory Lovins,

> your lifeline comes not from an understandable neighborhood technology run by people you know who are at your own social level, but rather from an alien, remote and perhaps humiliatingly uncontrollable technology run by a faraway, bureaucratized, technical elite who have probably never heard of you. Decisions about who shall have how much energy at what price also become centralized—a politically dangerous trend because it divides those who use energy from those who supply and regulate it. Those who do not like the decisions can simply be disconnected.[34]

Thus, there will be decisions about the allocation of energy and of pollution, of costs and benefits—not only among us but also between us and the citizens of other countries that produce energy or experience or pollution and between us and those who come after us. These questions are already being decided, not always with full consciousness of their implications and almost never with real consultation with the populace as a whole. In-

[32]Elman R. Service, "The Law of Evolutionary Potential," in *Evolution and Culture*, ed. Sahlins and Service, p. 97.

[33]See William J. Broad, "Nuclear Pulse: Awakening to the Chaos Factor," *Science*, May 29, 1981, pp. 1009–12.

[34]Lovins, *Soft Energy Paths*, p. 55. See also Lovins and L. Hunter Lovins, *Brittle Power: Energy Strategy for National Security* (Andover, MA: Brick House, 1982); and Dudley J. Burton, *The Governance of Energy* (New York: Praeger, 1980).

stead, once again, as with so many other topics, we see the politics of knowledge at work, and we are forced to rely on authorities to make vital decisions for us.

We shall see in the next chapter, when we examine U.S. relations with the rest of the world, that the situation is often comparable at that level. In world affairs, less wealthy and less advanced countries must rely on the United States, sometimes in cooperation with the Soviet Union and other major states, at other times in conflict with them, to decide important aspects of the fate of the world.

SUMMARY

Environment and energy have only recently become political issues in the United States. The process began with the Clean Air Act Amendments passed in 1970, just after passage of the National Environmental Policy Act, which we examined in Chapter 10. The amendments were intended to lessen pollution by controlling auto exhaust. But exhaust controls decreased fuel mileage. Then the energy crises of 1973 brought questions of energy use to the fore. Efforts were made to lower American dependence on imported oil by making cars lighter and so more efficient. This change increased deaths in wrecks; making cars stronger made them heavier again. These *tradeoffs* illustrate the problems of energy and environmental policy making. So does the case of coal burning and acid rain faced by electric utilities.

To understand the problems, we must understand both demand and supply. People demand or desire a clean environment; they also demand cheap energy. But supplies of both are limited by the impact of industrial society. There are other sources of energy besides fossil fuels, but they have not yet been highly developed.

U.S. energy policy has evolved from a quest for energy independence under Nixon and Ford through an emphasis on conservation and alternate energy sources under Carter to a reliance on market forces under Reagan. Yet efforts to rely on the market can have bad consequences. At this point, many decisions remain to be made. Among them are the choice between "hard" and "soft" energy paths, the question of the role of conservation, and changes in the food system, which is now highly energy intensive. Each of these questions involves an interplay of energy and environment.

The key principles or considerations that should underlie U.S. policy are scarcity and economy, waste and conservation, the laws of cultural dominance and evolutionary potential, and the question of centralization versus decentralization. Decisions to be made will allocate costs and benefits not just among us but between us and citizens of other countries and between us and those who come after us.

Suggestions for Further Reading and Study

The literature on problems of energy and environment and various proposals for their solution is now immense. Some of the most helpful and interesting books are cited in the text or footnotes of this chapter. For a general bibliographical orientation to many key topics, see Kenneth A. Hammond et al., *Sourcebook on the Environment: A Guide to the Literature* (Chicago: Univ. of Chicago Press, 1978).

Two splendid and very well-illustrated introductions are G. Tyler Miller, Jr., *Living in the Environment*, 2d ed. (Belmont, CA: Wadsworth, 1979), and Earl Cook, *Man, Energy, Society* (San Francisco: Freeman, 1976).

To put matters in their long-term global context, see the special report by the Council on Environmental Quality and the State Department, *The Global 2000 Report to the President of the U.S.: Entering the 21st Century*, vol. 1, the summary report, directed by Gerald O. Barney (Elmsford, NY: Pergamon, 1980); Alexander King, ed., *The State of the Planet* (Elmsford, NY: Pergamon, 1980), a report prepared by the International Federation of Institutes for Advanced Study; Kenneth E. F. Watt, Leslie F. Molloy, C. K. Varshney, Dudley Weeks, and Soetjipto Wirosardjono, *The Unsteady State: Environmental Problems, Growth, and Culture* (Honolulu: Univ. Press of Hawaii, 1977); and Barbara Ward, *Progress for a Small Planet* (New York: Norton, 1979).

For regular updates, see the Worldwatch Institute's *State of the World*, ed. Lester R. Brown (New York:

Norton, annual); and see *The State of the Environment* (Washington, DC: Organization for Economic Cooperation and Development, 1985) for studies of the developed world; and World Resources Institute and International Institute for Environment and Development, *World Resources 1986: An Assessment of the Resource Base that Supports the Global Economy, with Data Tables for 146 Countries* (New York: Basic Books, 1986).

Among the helpful studies of various aspects of these problems are two books by Walter A. Rosenbaum: *Energy, Politics, and Public Policy* (Washington, DC: CQ Press, 1981), and *Environmental Politics and Policy* (Washington, DC: CQ Press, 1985). See also William Ophuls, *Ecology and the Politics of Scarcity* (San Francisco: Freeman, 1977); David and Marcia Pimentel, *Food, Energy, and Society* (New York: Wiley, 1979); Earl Finbar Murphy, *Energy and Environmental Balance* (Elmsford, NY: Pergamon, 1980); Sheldon Kamieniecki et al., eds., *Controversies in Environmental Policy* (Albany: SUNY Press, 1985); and the Science Action Coalition, with Albert J. Fritsch, *Environmental Ethics: Choices for Concerned Citizens* (Garden City, NY: Anchor, 1980). For interesting suggestions of what you can do in your daily life, see John McCormick, *The User's Guide to the Environment* (London: Kogan Page, 1985).

19

THE POLITICS
OF GLOBAL RELATIONS:
American Foreign Policy

Our everyday lives are entangled with the lives of other peoples around the world in many ways. For a long time, we have been living with products made in other countries: Japanese clock radios; morning coffee from Brazil or Angola, or tea from Ceylon or China; bicycles, motorcycles, and cars made in Europe or Japan; stereos made in Japan; alcoholic beverages from Scotland or France or Italy or Mexico. . . . The list is endless.

We have long known that we bought these goods from other countries, but few of us have realized the effect of our purchases on those other countries. When we import foreign goods, that creates more jobs for workers in industries abroad that export goods to us and unemployment in countries whose goods we no longer buy—or, as we saw for the case of shoes in Perspective 5, in our own. But our impact on other peoples extends beyond our purchase of foreign goods. When we buy auto insurance or make

a deposit in a local bank, for example, those funds may end up invested in a new factory in Brazil or an apartment complex in Hong Kong. Our contributions to charitable organizations that work abroad also affect the lives of many people.

All of these and many other activities are consequences of American foreign policy. That policy makes it possible for us to do certain things in the world, and it prevents us from doing others. Of course, the wars and crises and foreign military aid that we learn about every day in the media—and that we may some day be a part of—are also affected by American foreign policy. In this chapter, we'll learn what American foreign policy is and how it is made. We'll also learn about some major challenges that the United States faces and what opportunities there are for U.S. foreign policy to make a difference in the world—and for us to make a difference in U.S. foreign policy. ■

OUR EXPERIENCE OF THE WORLD

There are a great many *connections* between peoples of various countries around the world. Those that are *political* are generally conducted by governments and their representatives. Nonetheless, citizens of one country now often sign petitions and write letters to foreign governments protesting violations of human rights, or opposing explosion of nuclear weapons that cause dangerous radioactive fallout to spread quickly across boundaries around the world, or calling for an end to the killing of whales. Those connections that are *economic* are usually undertaken by business corporations and their employees. But governments generally set the political context for these economic relations by controlling currencies and developing trade and aid policies. Still, even citizens can and do get involved by boycotting goods from countries whose policies they disapprove. Those relations that are *cultural* (the exchange of orchestras or rock bands or dance groups, for example), sporting (the Olympics, tennis's Davis Cup, track meets, and so on), or *educational* (foreign-student exchange, importing of books and magazines, and so on) involve governments, businesses, and citizens.

As individuals we decide whether to buy foreign goods, meet foreign individuals, applaud or protest acts of foreign countries, or encounter foreign ideas. In making these decisions, *each of us has his or her own foreign policy*—his or her own set of ideas about what foreign contacts are valuable, what international activities to undertake, such as study or business abroad, what developments in other countries to hope for or to fear, and what to do to perpetuate or change experiences involving peoples and organizations in other countries.[1]

The point is that by now the average American's life is interdependent with the lives of others. Each, in other words, is affected by and affects not only what his or her nation and other nations do but also what organizations and individuals in other nations do. It is still true that the foreign policies or countries are usually very remote from individuals. Wars, trade disputes, international boycotts and embargoes, and the like occur often and without consultation with the people they affect. Consequently, if often seems that we as individuals and citizen groups are powerless to affect the lives of people in other states because we cannot control our own country's foreign policy. But the more interaction between peoples increases, and the more it spreads to new parts of the world, the more we may be able to affect the foreign policies of our country—and of other countries too.

Growing interdependence and what we might call growing penetration of one culture by another, or of individuals' lives by other individuals, are facts in today's world. Today, you can fly from Washington, DC, or New York City to London or Paris in three and a half hours if you take the Concord supersonic airliner. Each year more than 8 million Americans travel overseas, and in three times that number of foreigners travel to the United States. We send about a billion pieces of mail abroad and make over 50 million overseas telephone calls each year. The rest of the world sends about 300,000 students to America to study each year—and almost 200,000 of us go abroad to study. Foreigners also invest billions of dollars in the United States each year, as Americans invest abroad.

All these connections make it all the more important that we as individuals know what the situations of other peoples are and what impacts we have upon them, just as we must continue to know about the relations of our government with other governments. To get a better understanding of the U.S. role in the world, we must take note of how American foreign policy has been and is being made. We must also discover how the rest of the world is changing and the way these changes are transforming our prospects, opportunities, and challenges.

OUR NATION'S EXPERIENCE OF THE WORLD

The nation's founders and our early presidents had a foreign policy of avoiding "entangling alliances" with the traditional—and, in American eyes, corrupt—states of Europe. The reason for this policy was not that America was not interested in the fate of Europe. Rather, it was that the former colonies were not strong enough to influence European developments directly. So they decided instead to in-

---

[1]See Chadwick F. Alger, "Increasing Opportunities for Effective and Responsible Transnational Participation," *Mershon Center Quarterly Report* 1 (Summer 1976), 1–8.

crease their new nation's power while setting an example for their former colonizers. The example they chose to set, they said, was that of a new order so attractive it would lead Europe to reform itself politically, in accordance with the dictates or our Declaration of Independence and our Constitution.

The United States Becomes a World Power

This desire to abide by moral standards and set a moral example for others in foreign affairs has persisted in America to this day, although the actual moral standards have changed considerably. The United States generally stayed aloof from conflicts in Europe until the end of the 19th century. Then, in the Spanish-American War (1898), it defeated Spain and took away Spain's colonies of Puerto Rico, Cuba, Guam, and the Philippines. Following that brief, successful war, the United States returned to isolation until German provocations during World War I (1914–1918) led the country to enter that war in Europe. Once World War I was won, President Woodrow Wilson sought to reform Europe in the Treaty of Versailles. Wilson advocated freedom—**self-determination**, he called it—for the various east European nationalities that had been dominated by Germany and the Austro-Hungarian Empire. He also took the lead in supporting the creation of a League of Nations, which, together with a World Court, under American leadership was supposed to resolve international conflicts peacefully so there would never be another world war.

Return to Isolationism

But American isolationist impulses were so strong that Wilson could not convince the Senate to ratify U.S. membership in the League of Nations, as required by the Constitution. So America withdrew again from European politics. Nonetheless, we continued to use our military forces and political power to dominate much of Latin America in these decades. This policy derived from our proclamation in 1823 of the **Monroe Doctrine**, which attempted to keep European powers from intervening there. But we did not return to the world arena until World War II (1939–1945) was well underway in Europe and the Japanese had bombed the American naval fleet in Pearl Harbor, Hawaii, in December 1941.

The United Nations and the Cold War

Victory over Japan, Germany, and Italy in that war left the United States an industrial and military giant—the only major country in the world whose homeland had not been severely damaged by the war. But this time the American government, with strong popular support, decided to participate actively in the postwar settlement. The United States took the lead in organizing the United Nations, which was composed of the "nations united" against Germany and Japan. Soon thereafter, the United States developed the **Marshall Plan**, a massive program of economic recovery aid to the war-torn countries of Europe, named for the American secretary of state who proposed it, General George Marshall.

During the war, the Soviet Union had been invaded by Hitler's Germany. This brought it into the war as an ally of the Western countries. But after the war, relations between the Soviets and the Western countries deteriorated quickly. Diplomats and historians still disagree about why that happened and about which country was most responsible for it. But everyone agrees that what came to be called the **cold war** (to distinguish it from the "hot war," World War II) drastically transformed world politics.[2]

The Soviets sought protection against the possibility of yet another attack from Germany—something that had happened several times previously. They therefore insisted that Germany be split up among the allies. Berlin, which lay inside the Soviet zone, was also divided. The Soviets then gradually imposed Communist governments in the smaller countries of Eastern Europe, seeking to create a buffer between themselves and the Germans. In the words of the British leader Winston Churchill, an Iron Curtain descended, separating Europe into West and East. Hostility and provocation increased along that border, and the nations

---

[2]The literature on the cold war is by now unmanageably large. For one helpful analysis, see John Lewis Gaddis, *The United States and the Origins of the Cold War* (New York: Columbia Univ. Press, 1972).

on each side rearmed and eventually established alliances to coordinate defenses. Much of the world increasingly became divided into two great blocs confronting each other in central Europe. This situation is generally called a bipolar world—a world of nations organized around two poles—the United States and the Soviet Union.

Global Alliances

First, the United States joined the Western European countries in the North Atlantic Treaty Organization (NATO) in 1949. Then, when the Western countries decided to rearm West Germany in 1954, the Soviets gathered their Eastern European allies into the Warsaw Pact. The U.S. also formed alliances against the Soviet Union with other states around the world. Figure 19.1 depicts the major alliances on both sides. Relations in Europe between the two blocs then remained conflictual and militaristic until tensions were finally relaxed in the period called **détente** (a French diplomatic term for relaxation of tensions) some 15 years later.

Limited Wars

Meanwhile, in Asia lines were also being drawn. China, which had been corruptly ruled as an American ally by Chiang Kai-shek, finally fell to a peasant revolution under the Communist leader Mao Tse-tung in 1949. This led to fears in the West that the Soviet Union and China, united as Communist powers, might come to dominate the rest of the world. And so, when military conflict broke out on the Korean Peninsula in 1950, the United States, with United Nations approval, came to the

FIGURE 19.1
U.S. Military Alliances and the Warsaw Pact.

- NATO (Belgium, Canada, Denmark, France, Great Britain, Greece, Iceland, Italy, Luxembourg, Netherlands, Norway, Portugal, Spain, Turkey, United States, West Germany)
- Inter-American Treaty (Argentina, Barbados, Bolivia, Brazil, Chile, Colombia, Costa Rica, Dominican Republic, Ecuador, El Salvador, Guatemala, Haiti, Honduras, Mexico, Nicaragua, Panama, Paraguay, Peru, Trinidad–Tobago, United States, Uruguay, Venezuela)
- Bilateral treaties with United States (Japan, Nationalist China, Philippines, South Korea)
- ANZUS Alliance (Australia, New Zealand, United States)
- Warsaw Pact (Albania, Bulgaria, Czechoslovakia, East Germany, Hungary, Poland, Rumania, USSR)

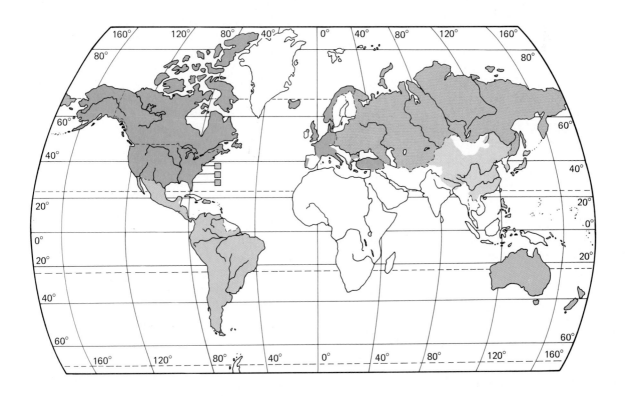

aid of South Korea. The Korean War was fought to a virtual standstill in 1953. In American eyes, the Korean War was fought not just to prevent the spread of communism, but also to teach other states—and particularly the Chinese, who had sent in "volunteers" when American troops approached the Chinese border—that we would refuse to allow military movements that would change the political and military status quo.

If American resistance in Korea had achieved this latter deterrent effect, there might not have been a Vietnam War. But the French, who had previously colonized Indochina, engaged in a losing struggle to hold it in the early 1950s and finally partitioned the region into Cambodia, Laos, North Vietnam, and South Vietnam. The region had been composed of various tribal groupings that rarely got along. The political boundaries the French left behind rarely coincided with traditional divisions. And so over the next decade, turmoil grew and instability increased. The United States chose to take the place of the departed French, supporting the forces in control of Cambodia, southern Laos, and South Vietnam. Finally, in the early 1960s, the American-supported forces found themselves under growing pressure from civil uprisings within their territories. The rebels were aided by Communists to the north and indirectly by the Chinese and the Soviets.

The Vietnam Veterans Memorial in Washington. (Peter Marlow/Magnum Photos)

The War in Vietnam

The stage was now set for the longest war in American history—and the only war the United States has lost. The United States began long-term bombing of North Vietnam and Laos in 1965. We then sent in American combat troops, whose numbers grew regularly from 1965 until they totaled over half a million by 1968. The eventual cost of our presence was some $150 billion and 56,717 American lives.[3] Despite all this effort, the best the United States could finally engineer, when domestic opposition by protesting citizens and Congress forced it to withdraw in 1973, was a cease-fire. That truce deteriorated almost immediately. Finally, in April 1975 America's allies in Cambodia, Laos, and South Vietnam collapsed totally, and the Communists took over.[4]

What had started out as an effort to shape the future of the world in accordance with our interests and what we perceived to be the interests of the people of Indochina had ended in disaster. The disaster led many to a new questioning of the roots of American foreign policy. American policy had come full circle from the years of active, even enthusiastic intervention around the world to the years of the **Nixon Doctrine**, which proclaimed that

---

[3]Of course, most of the costs were borne by Vietnamese, North and South. The war killed 1,535,000 civilians and 1,127,586 Indochinese soldiers. Another 12,100,000 Indochinese had been made into refugees by the war by the time the United States withdrew, and untold millions more were made refugees thereafter. Those still in Indochina are still bearing other costs, such as the consequences of 17 million gallons of herbicide the United States dropped on Vietnam. The United States also dropped 7 million tons of bombs on Vietnam (compared to 2 million tons dropped in World War II). See, for these and other figures, "The Nobility of Napalm," *Inquiry*, October 6, 1980, p. 4.

[4]For a history of the war, see Stanley Karnow, *Vietnam: A History* (New York: Viking, 1983).

other countries would have to bear the military burden of their defense themselves. The world too had changed, from "bipolarity"—organization of states around two poles—into a "multibloc" structure with many blocs, such as NATO, the Warsaw Pact, the Arab bloc, and the Organization of African Unity. The disaster also led to a reexamination of the way American foreign policy is made.

WHO MAKES AMERICAN FOREIGN POLICY?

The United States, we have already seen, has policies to deal with many public problems, from urban affairs to poverty, from energy to inflation. We might therefore expect that foreign affairs would be just another "area" for which policy must be made. But in fact foreign policy is a special case. "What is special about it," George Quester has written,

> is that it is generally seen to have an "enemy," a continuing need to deal with a rational adversary. This supposed need produces not only secrecy, but strategy and a sense of combative solidarity. And in the wake of this, it produces seemingly greater clarity about common goals, and seemingly greater opportunities for optimization and rational policy analysis.[5]

Politics in the formation of foreign policy is less obvious than in domestic policy. Nonetheless, politics is there. We find politics in disputes among individuals in the Department of State, for example, as well as in struggles between the Departments of State and Defense, among other agencies.[6] These political battles may concern either ends or means, objectives or instruments.

The Policy Machinery

Many different individuals and organizations within the government are involved in the making of foreign policy. Because it is the combination of these various actors that finally produces the policy, we often refer to them together as the foreign policy machinery. The most important components, besides the president, are the cabinet departments, the National Security Council, the Central Intelligence Agency, and the Congress.

The Cabinet Departments

The process by which the United States decides what efforts to make to protect its own interests short of resorting to war is an old one but a changing one. It dates back to the establishment of the Departments of State and War in 1789 as two of the first executive departments. Through the centuries, the military component has proliferated: The Department of the Navy was created in 1798, and when an independent air force was created in 1947 the three services were united into the National Military Establishment (renamed the Department of Defense in 1949).

There has always been some question as to the actual roles of the military and the diplomatic components in the making of American foreign policy. The only certainty has been that as both military commander in chief and diplomatic chief of state, the president has ultimate responsibility for developing a unified policy. But as America's role in the world increased, and as economic factors became much more important in policy, that task became much more demanding, regularly involving such other departments as Treasury, Commerce, Agriculture, and even Labor. In recent years, Energy too has become involved.

The National Security Council

To assist the president, a new organization was established in the Executive Office of the President in 1947: the National Security Council. Its function, according to its official description, is "to advise the President with respect to the integration of domestic, foreign, and military policies relating to the national security." Formally, it consists of the president, the vice-president, the secretary of state, and the secretary of defense. In fact its meetings are attended by representatives of many other departments plus the intelligence services and are under the supervision of the assistant to the president for national security affairs, who in turn has several hundred professionals working for him.

Henry Kissinger was appointed to that position while a professor of government at Harvard University, when Richard Nixon became president in

---

[5]George Quester, "Foreign Policy," in *Nationalizing Government: Public Policies in America*, ed. Theodore J. Lowi and Alan Stone (Beverly Hills, CA: Sage, 1978), pp. 393–94.

[6]For an interesting account of conflicts between State and DOD, see the memoirs of Reagan's first secretary of state, Alexander M. Haig, Jr., *Caveat: Realism, Reagan, and Foreign Policy* (New York: Macmillan, 1984).

Henry Kissinger. (Dennis Brack/Black Star)

fessor Zbigniew Brzezinski was National Security Affairs advisor.

The Reagan administration had five different heads of the NSC in its first six years. The Reagan NSC was transformed from an advisory and co-ordinating body into an operational one. Its major **covert action** was arranging the secret sale of arms to Iran in 1986. This sale took place while the president was publicly condemning Iran as a sponsor of terrorism and telling U.S. allies not to send arms. NSC operatives then diverted profits from the arms sales to the Contras—rebels fighting the Nicaraguan government. The Reagan administration was openly supporting the Contras' effort to overthrow Nicaragua's leftist government. However, Congress had passed a law prohibiting military aid to the Contras while efforts at a peaceful settlement were underway. Thus, this secret NSC operation violated both the president's public statements and the judgment of most professional foreign policy experts as to wise policy.

The Central Intelligence Agency

From our perspective on the outside, many of the recent examples of conflicts that have surfaced seem to have involved the CIA. The CIA is the most prominent of 12 bodies that gather information about other countries and world affairs for use by the president and the executive branch. The CIA has tended to operate both autonomously and secretly. The problems such activities have created for those attempting to coordinate American policy could fill a book—and in fact have filled two massive congressional reports and numerous books by investigative journalists.[8] The challenge of these problems has led to renewed efforts to get greater control over "covert" CIA operations. The success of these efforts, however, is not easy to determine or estimate from the outside. The failures—such as its illegal placing of explosive mines in Nicaragua's harbor and its role in the secret sale of arms to Iran and diversion of profits to the Contras—become

1969. In the next eight years, under Nixon and Ford, Kissinger played a major—most observers would say *the* major—role in formulating American foreign policy. It was a period that saw four more years of fighting in Vietnam, ending several years further on with the eventual collapse of our forces there. Before that collapse, Kissinger and his counterpart in North Vietnam had received a controversial Nobel Peace Prize for the interim agreement they had reached. Diplomatic relations with China were resumed for the first time since 1949. In addition, considerable progress was made in arms negotiations with the Soviet Union to stabilize the political situation in Central Europe and to limit the nuclear missiles built by each side (**arms control**, this is called). There was also continuing American mediation in the Middle East conflict between Israel and the Arab states.[7] All these policies were later carried on by the Carter administration, in which former Columbia University pro-

[7]There are by now many books on Kissinger. On his world view, see Stephen Graubard, *Kissinger: Portrait of a Mind* (New York: Norton, 1974). For a favorable "insider" biography, see Marvin Kalb and Bernard Kalb, *Kissinger* (Boston: Little, Brown, 1974). For a somewhat more critical view, see Roger Morris, *Uncertain Greatness: Henry Kissinger and American Foreign Policy* (New York: Harper & Row, 1977). For Kissinger's own view, see his memoirs, *White House Years* (Boston: Little, Brown, 1979), and *Years of Upheaval* (Boston: Little, Brown, 1982).

[8]See Allen Dulles, *The Craft of Intelligence* (New York: Harper & Row, 1963), by the agency's first director; Victor Marchetti and John D. Marks, *The CIA and the Cult of Intelligence* (New York: Knopf, 1974), and Philip Agee, *Inside the Company: CIA Diary* (New York: Stonehill, 1975), both by dissident former agents; and David Wise, *The American Police State* (New York: Random House, 1976), about the agency's domestic transgressions. See also Thomas Powers, *The Man Who Kept the Secrets: Richard Helms and the CIA* (New York: Knopf, 1979).

known only when they are leaked by disgruntled officials or uncovered in infrequent congressional investigations. The successes are even less likely to be publicized.[9]

The Congress

In the years since Vietnam, the Congress has played an increasing role in foreign policy, as we have already seen in Chapter 10. The Constitution gives Congress the power to declare war, and the War Powers Act of 1973 strengthened that power. The Constitution also provides for Senate ratification of treaties and approval of major appointments, as well as congressional appropriation of funds for foreign affairs. And of course Congress can pass laws making policy—something it does more often on economic issues such as trade than on political or military policy. But that document also gives primary responsibility for foreign policy making to the executive branch. Edward S. Corwin observed some 40 years ago that "the Constitution . . . is an invitation to struggle for the privilege of directing American foreign policy."[10] Cecil Crabb and Pat Holt recently surveyed the present status of this struggle and concluded that

> Congress appears to be more decentralized, fragmented, and resistant to unifying influences than in any previous period of American history. To date, Congress has supplied little evidence to show that it is prepared to adapt its own organizational structure and internal procedures to the demands of an active foreign policy role its members are determined to play.[11]

In the early 1980s, with party control of Congress split and a Republican in the White House, there was once again an opportunity for more foreign policy debate *between* the parties. There has been a tradition of bipartisan foreign policy making in American politics—a tradition rarely breached since the start of the cold war. The assertion has always been that "politics stops at the water's edge."[12] Actions of the Reagan administra-

tion—especially on defense and arms control—led to more conflict with Congress than had been seen in decades. When the Democrats regained control of the Senate in 1987, that conflict intensified.

Important Influences on Policy Making

From this brief survey, it is clear that the foreign policy machinery is a complex organization, itself consisting of a collection of complex organizations. As we have seen time and time again in previous chapters, in such policy machinery conflicts often develop. Some of the conflicts arise openly and are resolved by the machinery—questions about whether to give military aid to a particular country, for example, or about whether to sell grain to the Soviet Union. But other conflicts emerge only after a policy has been made and implemented by one cog in the machinery and then turns out to conflict with something another cog is doing or attempting.

It is often hard to know what caused adoption of particular foreign policies. First, as we have just noted, there are many actors involved. Second, the policies, like the world they are designed to cope with, tend to be very complex. And third, secrecy is often a feature of the process.

Still, scholars studying the making of foreign policy generally agree that four major types of factors influence it: external, societal, governmental, and individual. The *external* factors make up the international setting for foreign policy. Included are the policies and actions of other states and international organizations as well as the nation's geographical location. The *societal* factors constitute the domestic nongovernmental setting and include the views of interest groups and public opinion, as well as the economic status of the country. The *governmental* category refers to the policy-making process and includes the role of the bureaucracy and the Congress. The final category is *individual* characteristics of decision makers. The special personality, talents, knowledge, and values of people such as the president, the secretary of state, the secretary of defense, and the national security advisor are likely to be important influences. Just which factors will matter and how important each will be depend on the particular case, and it is hard to generalize about this.

[9]See John Prados, *Presidents' Secret Wars: CIA and Pentagon Covert Operations since World War II* (New York: Morrow, 1987).

[10]Edward S. Corwin, *The President: Office and Powers*, quoted in Cecil V. Crabb, Jr., and Pat M. Holt, *Invitation to Struggle: Congress, the President, and Foreign Policy* (Washington, DC: CQ Press, 1980), p. ix.

[11]Crabb and Holt, *Invitation to Struggle*, p. 215.

[12]See, for example, Cecil V. Crabb, Jr., *Bipartisan Foreign Policy: Myth or Reality?* (New York: Harper & Row, 1957).

WHAT IS AMERICAN FOREIGN POLICY?

National Interests

Foreign policy, we noted in Perspective 5, is the general principle—or collection of principles—concerning how a country will relate to other countries. Foreign policy is usually described as built upon, or designed to achieve, the "national interest" of the country. National interest is usually thought of, in the words of Donald Neuchterlein, as "the perceived needs and desires of one . . . state in relation to the . . . states comprising its external environment."[13] We usually find, however, much dispute over just what the national interest is. This dispute arises among policy makers just as much as it does between policy makers and their critics outside government.

"Traditionally, two conceptions have vied for primacy in U.S. foreign policy," writes Linda B. Miller.

> The first, borrowed from older European roots, stresses the morality of power, and the second, the power of morality. In the first conception, circumstances dictate a relentless quest for advantage in an anarchical world. Power is both a means and an end. Realism absolves statesmen from individual moral responsibility in pursuit of the national interest.[14]

Some 30 years ago, Arnold Wolfers issued a warning that is every bit as appropriate today:

> Statesmen, publicists, and scholars who wish to be considered realists . . . are inclined to insist that the foreign policy they advocate is dictated by the national interest, more specifically by the national security interest. . . . When political formulas such as "national interest" or "national security" gain popularity they need to be scrutinized with particular care. They may not mean the same thing to different people. They may not have any precise meaning at all. Thus, while appearing to offer guidance and a basis for broad consensus, they may be permitting everyone to label whatever policy he favors with an attractive and possibly deceptive name. In a very

vague and general way, "national interest" does suggest a direction of policy which can be distinguished from several others presenting themselves as alternatives. It indicates that the policy is designed to promote demands that are ascribed to the nation rather than to individuals, subnational groups, or mankind as a whole. It emphasizes that the policy subordinates other interests to those of the nation. But beyond this, it has very little meaning.[15]

Miller calls the second conception that has vied for primacy in U.S. foreign policy "the power of morality." According to it, she writes: "Events require responses consonant with moral values. Concerns for justice and equality derived from the American experience are paramount." Policy makers, she argues, have lurched from one extreme, "the morality of power," to the other, "the power of morality . . . usually claiming that their behavior reflects the peculiarities of the international system."[16]

Whatever policy makers may say, however, our study of American politics thus far should help us to recognize that, as Neuchterlein writes, "the determination of a nation's interests is the result of a political process in which conflicting private interests, bureaucratic politics, and the so-called totally dispassionate view of the facts by policy planners play a role—and should play a role."[17]

This political process produces views in the minds of leaders about the national interests. Neuchterlein, like many other analysts, distinguishes between four categories of basic national interests:

- Defense interests: Protection of the state and its citizens against external threats
- Economic interests: Increase in the state's economic well-being via relations with other states
- World-order interests: An international political and economic system allowing for peaceful security and commerce
- Ideological interests: Protection and spreading of a set of values that citizens share and believe to be good for others

A state's interests will cut across all four categories. Groups within the state will tend to emphasize one or another. The intensity with which each interest will be sought may vary over time.

---

[13]Donald E. Neuchterlein, *National Interests and Presidential Leadership: The Setting of Priorities* (Boulder, CO: Westview, 1978), p. 3. See also Stephen D. Krasner, *Defending the National Interest* (Princeton: Princeton Univ. Press, 1978), chap. 9. The concept actually goes back more than three centuries to the earliest stages of the evolution of the modern state. See Joseph Frankel, *National Interest* (New York: Praeger, 1970).

[14]Linda B. Miller, "Morality in Foreign Policy: A Failed Consensus?" *Daedalus* 109 (Summer 1980), 143.

[15]Wolfers, *Discord and Collaboration* (Baltimore: Johns Hopkins Univ. Press, 1962), p. 147.

[16]Miller, "Morality in Foreign Policy," p. 143.

[17]Neuchterlein, *National Interests*, p. 3.

The Recent Evolution
of U.S. National Interests

The Cold War

We can discern several basic U.S. foreign policy objectives during the period after World War II that is generally called the cold war. The first was a rejection of isolation in favor of active involvement in world affairs. The second was the belief that communism was the chief danger to the United States and the rest of the world. The third was the conclusion that American policy should be directed at **containment** of Soviet expansion and limitation of Soviet influence everywhere in the world. Once other countries, and especially China, became Communist, the concern was strengthened and the objective was broadened to the containment of communism anywhere and everywhere.[18]

Détente

Over the decades, Soviet military power inevitably increased. As a result, the United States came to rely less on military containment and more on creating a vested Soviet interest in cooperation and restraint through increased trade, technology transfer, and peaceful exchange of diplomats, scholars, and artists. This policy, which was most strongly developed under Nixon and Kissinger, was called détente. Experts disagree on whether détente was really a new policy.[19] Détente, Charles Kegley and Eugene Wittkopf argue,

> was based on Kissinger's conviction that American power and influence relative to that of the Soviet Union was rapidly diminishing, that Russia was an ascendant power, and its influence was growing. The central problem for the United States, given this predicament, is to create a situation in which American losses would be minimized and the status quo preserved. . . . When in a position of superiority, containment was practiced by coercion and force; from a position of parity, containment continues to be practiced, but now by seduction and cooperation.[20]

Central to Kissinger's concept of détente was the opening to China, which gave the Soviets a greater incentive to cooperate in order to avoid being isolated by its two major adversaries. Among détente's major consequences were important arms-control agreements with the Soviet Union.

The Post-Détente Period

The United States had become less confident of the utility of its armed forces in the so-called developing countries of the Third World after the Vietnam debacle. It had also become newly sensitive to its dependence on Third World countries for oil and other natural resources after the oil embargo of 1973. The consequence of these two new factors was a greater interest in developing new ways of influencing politics in the Third World. The Carter administration was the first to adjust U.S. policy in this direction. It showed new sensitivity to the concerns of black African countries and to the views of Arab states in the Middle East. At the same time, it saw the regime of America's military ally, the Shah of Iran, collapse, to be replaced by a militant Islamic regime. Iranian rebels seized the U.S. embassy in Teheran and held more than 50 American citizens, mostly diplomats, hostage for 444 days before releasing them as Ronald Reagan was being inaugurated.

This experience, widely characterized as "America held hostage," made it harder for Americans to be sympathetic to social and economic revolutions abroad. It also made many Americans be-

American hostages were displayed by their Iranian captors after the seizure and occupation of the U.S. Embassy in Teheran in 1979. (A. Mingam/Gamma-Liaison)

[18]See John Lewis Gaddis, *Strategies of Containment* (New York: Oxford Univ. Press, 1982).

[19]See, for example, Kissinger's speeches saying it was, and Leslie Gelb, "What Exactly is Kissinger's Legacy?" *New York Times Magazine*, October 31, 1976, saying it wasn't.

[20]Charles Kegley and Eugene Wittkopf, *American Foreign Policy: Pattern and Process* (New York: St. Martin's Press, 1979), p. 48. The most comprehensive account is Raymond L. Garthoff, *Détente and Confrontation: American-Soviet Relations from Nixon to Reagan* (Washington, DC: Brookings, 1985).

lieve that the United States needed more military forces in better condition to react quickly to challenges in the Third World. The United States thus began creating a rapid deployment force to be ready for such armed intervention.

At the same time, the Soviet Union had continued its military buildup and in December 1979 invaded neighboring Afghanistan, an ally whose Communist government appeared to be losing to rebels. The result was a new stage in superpower relations. By the time of the 1980 presidential election, surveys showed Americans favoring a tougher stance toward the Soviet Union, more defense buildup, greater willingness to aid allies, and use of trade as a weapon. The Reagan administration seemed to take these wishes to heart. Reagan appointed as his foreign policy makers advocates of a more militant foreign policy. Some people began to refer to this period as cold war II.

Like its predecessors, whatever its objectives, the Reagan administration found its room for maneuver limited by the environment, or the setting, within which it had to operate. This setting for foreign relations creates what can be called a structure of possibilities. These possibilities include challenges from adversaries and opportunities for better relations with allies such as NATO countries and Japan and with that other power sharing strong hostility to the Soviet Union, the People's Republic of China.[21] But the structure of possibilities also includes severe dangers, among them nuclear war and nuclear proliferation. And it sets certain limits to what means can be used in foreign policy as well as what ends can be achieved.[22]

THE EMERGENCE OF NEW ISSUES

Nuclear War and Nuclear Weapons

The cold war was in a sense international politics as usual, but it was at the same time politics with new and different means or instruments. The United States ushered in the nuclear age by developing atomic bombs and dropping them on the civilian populations of the Japanese cities of Hiro-

The underground command post at Strategic Air Command headquarters near Omaha, Neb., from which a nuclear attack would be launched. (UPI/Bettmann Newsphotos)

shima and Nagasaki in August 1945. We claimed that we used the bombs to hasten the end of World War II in Asia, although some experts argue that their use was unnecessary because Japan was ready to surrender. They were weapons of previously inconceivable destructive power.

Once the Soviets developed nuclear weapons, it became difficult for either country to conceive of fighting a nuclear war with the other because both would be largely destroyed in the process. That is the essence of nuclear deterrence.[23] But the nuclear stalemate in a sense once again made smaller-scale wars more possible, and the years since 1945 have seen hundreds of violent conflicts resulting in insurrections, civil wars, armed border conflicts, and even occasional "conventional wars" between various countries.[24]

[21]See Robert C. Gray and Stanley Michalak, eds., *American Foreign Policy since Détente* (New York: Harper & Row, 1984).

[22]See Kenneth A. Oye, Robert J. Lieber, and Donald Rothchild, eds., *Eagle Resurgent? The Reagan Era in American Foreign Policy* (Boston: Little, Brown, 1987).

[23]Among the numerous studies of deterrence, see Alexander L. George and Richard Smoke, *Deterrence in American Foreign Policy* (New York: Columbia Univ. Press, 1974); and Robert Jervis, Richard Ned Lebow, and Janice Gross Stein, *Psychology and Deterrence* (Baltimore: Johns Hopkins Univ. Press, 1985).

[24]See Adda B. Bozeman, "War and the Clash of Ideas," *Orbis* 20 (Spring 1976), 61–102, for a fascinating account of different cultures' conceptions of conflict and violence.

An anti-nuclear demonstration. (Ivan Massar/Black Star)

Two other important developments have further transformed relations among states. The first is the continuing *spread of nuclear weapons capability.* Britain, France, China, and India had all demonstrated this capability by the 1970s, and such states as Israel and South Africa developed the capability shortly thereafter. Experts believe that Canada, West Germany, Italy, Japan, Sweden, Switzerland, Argentina, and Pakistan are now capable of building a nuclear bomb. They also project that by 1990 they could be joined by Australia, Austria, Belgium, Brazil, Denmark, Iraq, South Korea, the Netherlands, Norway, Spain, and Taiwan. We may presume that most of these countries will decide not to join the nuclear club. But whichever ones do may well make the world an even more dangerous place.

New Weapons, Military Reform, and the SDI

The military situation is also complicated by the continuing development of new weapons. Most of the weapons being added to the U.S. arsenal are high tech—they depend on high technology for their impact. In recent years, critics have argued that the U.S. military has become too dependent on weapons that are so complicated that they may break down quickly in combat situations and are so expensive that they prevent the military from buying large enough quantities to equip all forces and retain needed spares. This has been the argument of the **military-reform** movement among some military officers, a fourth of all members of Congress comprising the new Military Reform Caucus, and various specialists. The movement has been spearheaded by former Senator and presidential candidate Gary Hart.[25]

The most expensive and most controversial high-tech program is the **Strategic Defense Initiative (SDI),** popularly known as **Star Wars.** Launched by president Reagan in 1983, SDI is a program intended to seek ways of defending against ballistic missiles. The required technology does not exist, and many experts doubt that it can be developed. Still, the Reagan administration has already spent

---

[25]See Gary Hart with William S. Lind, *America Can Win: The Case for Military Reform* (New York: Adler & Adler, 1986).

Friday... The Day Of

ICBMs taking off from the U.S. to attack the Soviet Union in the TV Drama "The Day After." (John Marmaras/Woodfin Camp & Associates)

many billions of dollars sponsoring research to try to develop the technology for such a shield. The idea is appealing, especially because nuclear war is such an appalling prospect and also because defense always appeals. However, some political analysts believe SDI is a bad idea because if it worked it would destabilize the nuclear "balance of terror" that many think has prevented nuclear war. To answer this objection, Reagan offered to give the technology to the Soviet Union once it was developed. The Soviets, ever suspicious of the United States, have not been impressed by the offer. Instead, they call for a halt to such research. In the summit meeting between Reagan and Soviet chief Mikhail Gorbachev in Rekjavik, Iceland, in 1986, seeming progress on nuclear disarmament was stymied by Reagan's refusal to abandon SDI. The program remains in its infancy—a very expensive and controversial infancy.[26]

Limits on the Utility of Military Force

Another transforming development is a growing sense of *the practical limitations on the effective use of military force* in world affairs. Americans, as the military leaders of the world, have been slow to recognize these limitations. The American suc-

cess in World War II only confirmed a long-held belief that overwhelming force would prevail. The stalemate in Korea led to a new belief in the necessity and promise of military technology—airpower plus counterinsurgency electronic gear and weaponry—as the salvation of those resisting aggression. A study by the Brookings Institution found that the United States deployed its military forces, usually in ways short of war, at least 215 times from 1945 to 1975. The Soviet Union did the same thing at least 115 times.[27]

In Vietnam, the most flagrant and long-lasting American military action, the United States used the most advanced nonnuclear military technology without ultimate success. But we were opposing forces expert in unconventional, generally guerrilla-style war. The Viet Cong and their North Vietnamese allies were so deeply committed to their struggle that they would not give up in the face of massive technological superiority and instead consistently found ingenious ways to get around and through our efforts.

Ultimately, the reliance upon military force to compel an unattractive political solution in Vietnam failed utterly. In addition, it had further bad consequences at home: inflation coupled with recession, student rebellion, disillusion, and a general popular distrust of political authorities.

Mimicry and World Militarization

In addition, however, America's actions in Vietnam and elsewhere have set bad examples for other states. World affairs in our era are often characterized by the phenomenon of *mimicry*—imitation for the sake of imitation, almost regardless of its likely promise. Mimicry is, of course, a common human trait. We see it in fashion, in the arts, and in political campaigns. In these instances it is usually harmless, but in world politics it can be very dangerous. Any nation that fears another is likely to imitate the other. It does so to avert the possibility that its adversary will be able to make a significant breakthrough before it can understand what is happening and take countermeasures. If only one side has a space program, for example, it

[26]The literature on SDI is already voluminous. For a helpful review, see Michael McGwire, "The Ultimate Umbrella," *Times Literary Supplement*, October 31, 1986, pp. 1214–16.

[27]Barry M. Blechman and Steven S. Kaplan, *The Use of the Armed Forces as a Political Instrument* (Washington, DC: Brookings, 1976).

may discover a surprising military use of space, such as spy satellites or orbiting bombs, which could then be a serious threat if the other side hasn't developed its own space capability.[28]

We can see this phenomenon of mimicry at work in American-Soviet relations throughout the cold war years. It occurred not just over military development and space exploration but also over the training of specialized engineers and scientists, foreign aid, cultural-exchange programs, athletics, and so on. Now, as other states become stronger, they too are tempted to imitate the large states in developing their military forces as well as constructing their other foreign activities.

One widespread result of all this is temptations for many states to "go nuclear." Another result is efforts to develop massive military establishments that far exceed local defense needs (such as, for example, those developed by Iran under the Shah, Saudi Arabia, and Libya). In these ventures, the countries have the assistance of the world's leading arms merchants, the United States (which supplied 39 percent of all arms exports from 1981 to 1985) and the Soviet Union (28 percent) along with France (11 percent) and Britain (5 percent).[29]

In fact, the countries of the world now spend well over a million dollars a minute on military forces. About half of that is spent by the United States and the Soviet Union. We might assume that this spending is strictly for deterrence. But since 1960 over 10 million people have died in 65 wars fought on the territories of 49 countries. That works out to more than 1300 dead every day for over two decades.[30] Ultimately, this resort to large military forces has the effect of destabilizing political situations, distorts economies that are in desperate need of capital for economic development, and results in greater political turmoil and repression. This set of effects is not very promising for the future of the world.

---

[28]For a discussion of this phenomenon, see David V. Edwards, *Creating a New World Politics* (New York: McKay, 1973). And for a fascinating study, see Christer Jonsson, *Superpower: Comparing American and Soviet Foreign Policy* (London: Francis Pinter, 1984).

[29]Glenn Frankel, "Weapons: The Global Commodity," *Washington Post National Weekly Edition*, January 12, 1987, pp. 6–7.

[30]"Behind the War Machine: A Consumer's Guide," *New Internationalist*, March 1983, pp. 10–11. The best source of these data is Ruth Sivard, *World Military and Social Expenditure*, published each year. Another useful source is the *SIPRI Yearbook*, published by the Stockholm International Peace Research Institute.

The Continuing Quest for Arms Control

The prospect of more states becoming military powers does not seem to worry the superpowers very much. Any state will tend to be most concerned about the growing military capability of its major adversary, and the superpowers are no exception. Thus, the United States and the Soviet Union have long sought to achieve arms-control agreements.[31] In recent years, progress has been slight because the Reagan administration sought instead to build up American forces. Its argument was that the United States had fallen seriously behind the Soviet Union and that the new weapons would serve as "bargaining chips" and enable it to "negotiate from strength." However, no progress was made in any of the five negotiations:

- Mutual and balanced force reductions (MBFR)—negotiations to limit NATO and Warsaw Pact forces in Europe
- Comprehensive test ban (CTB)—talks among the United States, the USSR, and Britain to ban all nuclear weapons tests
- Antisatellite (ASAT) weapons—talks to limit further development of weapons designed to "kill" satellites in orbit
- Intermediate-range nuclear forces (INF)—talks to limit deployment of new nuclear missiles in Europe
- Strategic arms reduction talks (START)—negotiations between the United States and the USSR to reduce strategic nuclear weapons (a continuation of the SALT negotiations, begun in 1982 under this new name)

Meanwhile, nuclear weapons stockpiles on both sides have continued to mount. Each side claims the other is ahead, and so it must catch up. In fact, both have massive "overkill" capabilities: Each has enough weapons to destroy the other many times over. The Soviets have more land-based missiles than we do, but we have more nuclear-missile submarines and more long-range bombers. Each side can "prove" its claim by focusing on some elements of the military balance, as it is called, and ignoring others.

There is no definite answer overall to who's

---

[31]For more details, see Julie Dahlitz, *Nuclear Arms Control* (Boston: Allen & Unwin, 1983), esp. pp. 24–31.

ahead. The debates on this question, both between the United States and the USSR and between advocates and opponents of the massive Reagan buildup, are political in our sense of the word.[32] They are disputes over claims to the authority to describe and interpret the nature of nuclear force reality.[33] The most important points are that each side has much more than enough to deter the other from attacking, that neither side can afford to use its weapons against the other except for such deterrence, and that these weapons are dangerous.[34]

The Special Case of the Nuclear Freeze

The failure of the superpowers to reach nuclear-arms-control agreements in the Reagan years finally led citizens to propose and push a "nuclear freeze." This plan calls for both sides to cease testing, production, and deployment of new nuclear weapons and to arrange for verification so that each side can be confident the other is keeping its word. We examined the political origins and development of this movement in Chapter 6. It became a major political issue in the 1984 presidential campaign because the Democrats endorsed it (see Perspective 2). It is but one effort of citizens to try to break the deadlock between the superpowers. This effort takes on added importance because world affairs are becoming more complex as new issues and new actors enter the arena. The superpowers, however, tend to be so obsessed with their military relations that they have difficulty attending to these new issues and new actors.

New Concerns about Resources

But there may be grounds for hope in several other developments. One is the spreading recognition that resources such as oil and gas are rapidly di-

minishing as development increases and population grows. Population growth in addition puts greater strain on agriculture and makes hunger and occasional famine a reality for many of the five billion people of the world.

Such fears of shortages seem increasingly likely to compel diversion of more resources toward agriculture and development of domestic energy resources. This in turn will necessarily mean fewer resources for military establishments. But the danger now is that before these trends can take effect, states will be encouraged to use the weapons they already have as a consequence of the bad examples set by the big powers, coupled with the provocations from cartels (like the Organization of Petroleum Exporting Countries, OPEC), multinational corporations (such as the oil companies, General Motors, or Kennecott Copper), or revolutionaries inside or outside their borders.

The New Emphasis on Trade: Protection and Pacific Shift

The combination of resource shortages and internal economic problems has led the U.S. to develop a large trade deficit. When Reagan took office, the United States still exported about $6 billion more a year in goods and services than it imported. But by 1986 that surplus had turned into a deficit of $170 billion a year. The shoe trade (see Perspective 5), is but one small part of this trend. This means that U.S. businesses are losing sales and profits, and U.S. workers are losing jobs. Thus, there is pressure for more government support of ailing industries and subsidies for exports. These policies are intended to increase **competitiveness** with other countries. Also, exporters want government to pressure other countries to lower tariffs and lift import quotas and other trade barriers so that more American exports can enter.

The Reagan administration has been in favor of free trade in principle. Trade has become a major factor in the strength and role of nations.[35] Thus in practice, the government has been less and less able to resist calls for protection of domestic industries and retaliation for barriers imposed by other states.

The major trade imbalance has been with Japan, from which we import autos and electronics,

[32]For an account of the debate through history, see John Prados, *The Soviet Estimate: US Intelligence Analysis and Russian Military Strength* (New York: Dial, 1982). For a useful recent summary, see Sandra Sedacca, *Up in Arms: A Common Cause Guide to Understanding Nuclear Arms Policy* (Washington, DC: Common Cause, 1984), available for $3.50 from Common Cause, 2030 M St. NW, Washington, DC 20036.

[33]See *Ground Zero, Nuclear War: What's in It for You* (New York: Pocket Books paperback, 1982); and Jonathan Schell, *The Fate of the Earth* (New York: Knopf, 1982), for accounts of the weapons and their effects. And for an account of how they are controlled to prevent accident and error, see Paul Bracken, *The Command and Control of Nuclear Forces* (New Haven, CT: Yale Univ. Press, 1984).

[34]See David V. Edwards, *Arms Control in International Politics* (New York: Holt, Rinehart & Winston, 1969).

[35]See Richard Rosecrance, *The Rise of the Trading State* (New York: Basic Books, 1986).

(By MacNally for the *Chicago Tribune*)

among other items. Until 1980 we traded more with Western Europe than with Asia, but by 1986 our trade with Asia had become 30 percent greater than that with Europe and was still rising. This trend toward the Pacific has been manifest in military affairs as well. As the Soviets have increased their navy, so has the United States. These navies are increasingly deployed in the Pacific, where the major trade routes are. At the same time, Americans have become more interested in various aspects of Asian culture—everything from Japanese management styles of worker-boss cooperation, job security, and quality control, to Hindu spirituality and Zen Buddhism. The result, some say, is a **Pacific shift** that will change world politics as it has already changed economics and culture.[36]

THE EMERGENCE OF NEW ACTORS

The notion that the states of the world, which had dominated world politics for centuries, would have to "share" world politics with such "nonstate actors" as cartels and multinational corporations would have shocked most foreign policy makers in

[36]For the cultural dimension, see William Irwin Thompson, *Pacific Shift* (San Francisco: Sierra Club, 1985).

the years of the cold war. International relations have traditionally been just that: relations among nations—nations that have territorial boundaries. Even in the cold war years international relations were being opened up to new "actors"—countries that had been colonies of Britain and France but were insisting on, and winning, independence.

New States

At the close of World War II, there were less than 50 independent states in the world. The State Department today lists 165. Many of the new states remain under the strong influence of a former colonial master such as Britain or France. Others are effectively the clients of one or the other superpower. Nonetheless, most are active members of major international organizations. The United Nations, for example, admitted its 159th member, Brunei, in 1984.

New Economic Actors and Issues

Both the World Bank (which makes loans to developing countries) and the International Monetary Fund (which coordinates national currencies

TABLE 19.1
Selected Measures of National Living Standards for Various Countries

COUNTRY	LIFE EXPECTANCY AT BIRTH (YEARS)	FOOD (CALORIES PER DAY, AND PERCENT FROM ANIMAL SOURCES)	EDUCATION: PERCENT OF POPULATION OVER 15 YEARS OLD ILLITERATE	GNP PER CAPITA (1983 IN DOLLARS)	ENERGY CONSUMED (COAL EQUIVALENT KILOGRAMS PER CAPITA PER YEAR)
Australia	71	3160/45%	1	11,080	7,164
Bolivia	50	1760/14	37	600	n.a.
Brazil	58	2620/15	24	1,967	704
Canada	72	3200/46	2	11,535	9,699
Chad	42	2240/8	80	110	n.a.
China (People's Republic)	50	2050/9	23	376	581
Czechoslovakia	67	3030/27	0	7,511	6,239
Egypt	54	2900/7	62	674	618
West Germany	70	3150/42	1	10,903	5,510
India	46	1950/5	66	248	200
Ireland	69	3460/41	1	5,230	3,183
Ivory Coast	41	2430/6	.35	1,200	n.a.
Jamaica	64	2280/17	4	1,180	n.a.
Japan	74	2450/14	1	9,149	3,503
Nigeria	37	2300/5	75	782	195
Peru	55	2270/14	28	984	611
Saudi Arabia	42	2080/8	48	12,600	3,026
United States	72	3250/40	0.5	13,492	9,431
USSR	64	3180/21	0.2	6,490	5,768

n.a.-information not available

Sources: Life Expectancy: *1986 Information Please Almanac and 1987 World Almanac;* Illiteracy: *United Nations Statistical Yearbook 1983/84* and *1986 Information Please Almanac;* energy consumption: *1986 Information Please Almanac,* figures for 1982; food: George L. Tuve, *Energy, Environment, Populations, and Food: Our Four Interdependent Crises* (New York: Wiley, 1976), pp. 210–15; GNP: *Statistical Abstract of the U.S. 1986* and *World Tables,* 3d ed., vol. 1 (Baltimore: Johns Hopkins Univ. Press, 1983).

in international economic relations) have gained new members. These new states have made international affairs much more complex and much more difficult for the major powers to control. And all the signs suggest that this difficulty will grow as the newer states get more experience in operating effectively in world affairs, and as our needs for their raw materials and cheap labor increase.

This difficulty will be increased by the fact that the world today is characterized by growing disparities in economic development, as Table 19.1 reveals. The newer states are becoming less willing to settle for the status of permanent paupers and are demanding in the United Nations and other international organizations major steps toward creating what a 1974 UN declaration called a New International Economic Order. Meanwhile, many states have borrowed large sums of money from banks in developed countries and are unable to re-

pay the loans. This global debt crisis has become another new challenge.

In the face of economic challenges, older states too have combined to coordinate their economic activities. The most advanced instance of this is the European Community, which joins Belgium, the Netherlands, Luxemburg, France, West Germany, Italy, Denmark, Great Britain, Ireland, Greece, Spain, and Portugal in a *common market* with free trade among members and identical tariff barriers to the rest of the world. The Communist countries of Europe have also combined into a Council of Mutual Economic Assistance (which we usually call COMECON—for Communist and economic). Other regions too are attempting similar collaboration, particularly in Latin America and Scandinavia. Furthermore, 120 countries in the General Agreement on Tariffs and Trade (**GATT**) meet annually to attempt to foster freer trade.

Multinational Corporations and Cartels

Another major complicating factor is the increase in nonstate actors in world affairs. The most familiar of these today are multinational corporations (MNCs). These are major companies like General Motors or the largest oil companies (Exxon, Royal Dutch Shell, British Petroleum, and the others) that have plants scattered around the world and engage in mining, manufacturing, trading, and/or selling wide varieties of products in a great many countries. These MNCs are often so big and so important economically that they can influence the politics as well as the economies of many countries in which they operate. The efforts of International Telephone and Telegraph (ITT) to topple the elected Marxist government in Chile in the early 1970s or the payments made by Lockheed Aircraft to politicians in various countries to get these countries to purchase Lockheed planes may be typical of the illegal activities of some MNCs. Most of what MNCs do to get favorable trade arrangements is quite legal in the countries where they operate. Much of it is welcomed by the "host" countries as contributing to their economic development. But the most important point for our understanding of international relations is that MNCs often act in the world almost as if they themselves were states.

These MNCs have "foreign policies" of their own. Often these corporate foreign policies do not relate to, and may even contradict, the policies of the countries in which their headquarters are located. A revealing example occurred in the fall of 1975, when the United States was supporting a conservative faction in the Angola civil war. Gulf Oil, headquartered in Pittsburgh with major oil-drilling rights in Angola, was at the same time paying millions of dollars in oil royalty fees to Angola's Marxist faction, which controlled the capital city and government, but which the American government was opposing. Gulf suspended these payments only when public outrage at this "unpatriotic" behavior, coupled with the State Department's requests, became too difficult to resist. And as soon as the Marxist faction triumphed, Gulf resumed its payments. Later, Chevron, another U.S.-based MNC, took over Gulf. It continued to pump 70 percent of Angola's oil, even though the Reagan administration was giving $15 million in arms aid to rebels trying to overthrow Angola's government. In this case and generally, MNCs have little or nothing to gain from war. They thus tend to become important forces for peace in many places of political conflict. But they can also be very destabilizing influences.

Political and economic activity of even the largest states can also be heavily influenced by other new nonstate actors. Everyone now knows about OPEC—the Organization of Petroleum Exporting Countries—because of the increases in oil prices and the oil embargo of 1973 by the Arab members of OPEC, which created long lines at American gas stations. A series of oil-price increases decreed by OPEC made almost everything in our daily lives more expensive. These price rises led to a decline in demand for oil, and at this point OPEC has trouble maintaining high prices. By 1987 the price of oil had fallen by about 50 percent, and OPEC was in disarray. But political changes that cut supplies—such as wars and revolutions—could bring the return of a dominant role for OPEC. Like the MNCs, OPEC has acted almost as if it were a state, and it influences the policies of its members and of virtually all oil-consuming states. There is a somewhat similar cartel in industrial and gem diamonds as well as continuing efforts to create cartels for such products as bauxite (the ore of aluminum), natural rubber, copper, and coffee.

Terrorists

Terrorist organizations are yet another type of nonstate actor. There have always been terrorists and assassins, but until recently they tended to confine their occasional activities to civil-war situations. Now they may claim to represent a group of people without a territory (as the Palestine Liberation Organization and its various allied organizations in the Middle East do) or an international revolutionary conspiracy. Examples of their activities include the hijacking of airplanes on international flights, the attacks on Israeli Olympic athletes in Munich in 1972, and the kidnapping of the OPEC oil ministers as they met in their Vienna headquarters in 1974. They are now active in most parts of the globe, from Northern Ireland to Argentina, from Yugoslavia to the Philippines, from the Soviet Union to the United States.

One survey found that in a recent year there were 2838 terrorist incidents, including 119 kidnappings, 1120 bombings, 1231 other attacks on installations, 362 assassinations, and 5 hijackings. Of these, 77 incidents involved the United States—5 assassinations and 54 bombings.[37] Terrorists sometimes take hostages and demand that imprisoned fellow terrorists be freed in exchange for the hostages. But whatever their actions, they too make international relations more dangerous and more difficult for states to control. And should terrorists develop or steal nuclear weapons, their leverage—and the destruction they cause—may become greater.

New Citizen Attitudes

Many terrorists, international bureaucrats working for organizations such as the United Nations, and officers of MNCs have developed allegiances to organizations other than the states in which they were born. In doing so, they become examples of another important new development in the world. It may turn out that the greatest check on the inclination of states to wage war against each other in coming years will be the growth of new attitudes in the citizens of states large and small.

There are signs of a growing antimilitarism (opposition to military adventures and even to military spending) in economically advanced states such as Japan and France. Recent years have seen signs of localism and separatist attitudes in minorities within major states who seek independence or lessened external control over their lives. Examples include Quebecois in Canada, Scots and Welsh in Britain, Bretons in France, and Basques and Catalans in Spain. The spread of these attitudes to minorities in more and more countries may make it more difficult for states to support and conduct military adventures as usual.

Some observers believe that the populations of many developed countries are becoming more interested in local autonomy and preserving their cultural distinctiveness and less interested in dominating other states. The trend toward antimilitarism seems often to be coupled with the emergence of political attitudes that combine a **transnational** concern for the welfare of other peoples with a

growing interest in **subnational** or local ethnic, cultural, religious, and linguistic practices. The citizens of French Alsace and German Baden, for example, have joined to organize resistance to the building of nuclear power plants they consider dangerous. Their feeling of unity across national boundaries is strengthened by the common dialect they speak as well as by their regular trips across the Rhine River—the French to work in Baden factories, the Germans to shop in French markets.

The big question, to many observers, is whether these new attitudes will also emerge in the Communist countries. Both the Soviets and the Chinese have a history of serious nationality problems, as they are called. These difficulties for the Soviet Union are traceable to the fact that the "Great Russians" conquered many smaller Asian and east European nationalities to make the Union of Soviet Socialist Republics out of 125 different nationalities. And the Chinese Han conquered Mongolians and Tibetans among others on their fringes to create the Chinese state. So the major Communist powers, like many Western powers, may increasingly find themselves facing popular attitudes that weaken the state's ability to mobilize its peoples and resources for wars outside its boundaries.

HOW EFFECTIVE IS AMERICAN FOREIGN POLICY?

These various challengers and changes set the context within which American policy makers attempt to formulate an effective foreign policy. It is a difficult task in the best of times, and it is especially complex in two turbulent regions in which the United States has a special interest: the Middle East and Latin America.

The Case of the Middle East

Most of the countries of the Middle East were once colonies of Britain and France. Some of them have large reserves of oil. When they gained independence, politics in the region became increasingly fluid. Many other countries were interested in access to oil. With the establishment of the state of Israel in what had recently been Arab lands, hostilities and even wars became frequent. The United States took an active role in the region, and be-

<hr/>

[37]The study, for 1983, was done by *Risks International*. See David Shribman, "The Textbook Approach to Terrorism," *New York Times*, April 22, 1984.

cause of the cold war sought to keep the Soviets out. (Figure 19.2 shows the strategic location of the states—and their oil—in the region.) Over the years, the United States has vacillated between seeing conflicts there as primarily Arab-Israeli or East-West.

The Carter administration emphasized Arab-Israeli conflict and sought to begin the process of resolving it by helping Israel and Egypt make peace in the Camp David accords. But rather than con-tinue the effort to expand that peacemaking, the Reagan administration redefined the basic conflict as East-West. It therefore sought to exclude the So-viets from influence in the region, and so it op-posed Syria, which was a Soviet ally. The result was the temporary commitment of U.S. Marines to "keep the peace" in Lebanon when Christians and Muslims there attacked each other and Syria and Israel intervened. After those troops suffered large casualties Reagan withdrew them in the spring of

FIGURE 19.2
The Middle East.

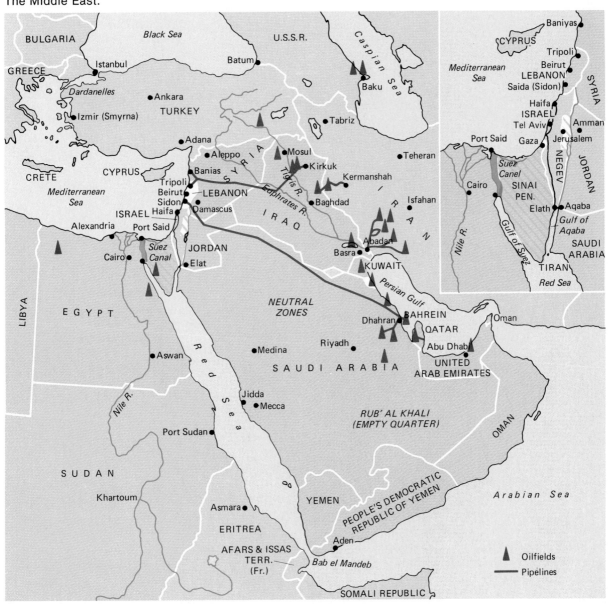

591

1984 without their having achieved success. U.S. policy in the Middle East was once again based primarily on support of Israel, but hostilities between Israel and the Arab states and between states representing various versions of Islam continued unabated. The revelations in 1986 and 1987 of secret U.S. involvement on both sides of the Iran-Iraq war also compromised U.S. efforts in the region.

The Case of Central America

The Reagan administration placed the same general interpretation on the growing conflict in Central America. The United States has always supported dictators in the region. Finally, in 1979 leftists (who called themselves Sandinistas after a patriot) overthrew the dictator Somoza in Nica-

FIGURE 19.3
Central America.

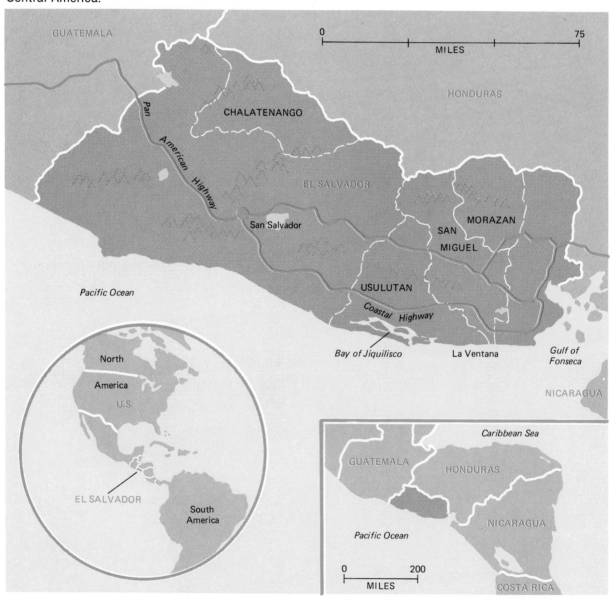

(Ben Sargent © 8/1983 *The Austin American Statesman*)

ragua. Their revolutionary government moved further to the left, and the United States began to support guerrillas, consisting largely of former Somoza soldiers, who were trying to overthrow the government. The United States also supported the military dictatorships in neighboring El Salvador and Guatemala against popular insurrections.

Many experts on the region believe that the underlying cause of leftist insurgency—or at least the condition that generates widespread popular support for these rebels—is the deep poverty of most of the people. For example, 14 wealthy families control El Salvador and its five million people. They do so with the help of the military and right-wing "death squads" that roam about freely, killing suspected rebel sympathizers. Yet the Reagan administration chose to attribute the unrest in the area to Soviet and Cuban meddling. It blamed Nicaragua for funneling arms to the rebels in El Salvador and used that as a basis for its attempt to overthrow the new Nicaragua government. Most experts and journalists question this interpretation and expect the United States to continue to have

grave difficulties fostering stability by military means.[38]

The same criticism is often made of U.S. foreign policy in other parts of the world. Most critics call for a greater emphasis on economic aid and diplomatic negotiation. Their view is that American foreign policy is not now very effective. That view became much more widely held with revelation of the Iran-Contra affair. Our allies in Europe joined many Americans in wondering whether the Reagan administration any longer had a coherent foreign policy.

The Case of South Africa

The same concern has been raised by U.S. policy toward South Africa. The Republic of South Africa since 1948 has had laws requiring racial segrega-

---

[38]See, for example, a book by a *New York Times* El Salvador correspondent: Raymond Bonner, *Weakness and Deceit: U.S. Policy and El Salvador* (New York: Times Books, 1984); and see Lloyd S. Etheredge, *Can Governments Learn? American Foreign Policy and Central American Revolutions* (Elmsford, NY: Pergamon, 1985).

tion and granting political and economic superiority to the 18 percent who are white descendants of Dutch and British colonists. The 68 percent who are black have virtually no rights and no role in governance. Asians (3 percent) and "coloureds" of mixed descent (11 percent) have very limited rights. This policy of separateness, or **apartheid**, has been condemned by the United States and most other countries. However, until 1986 the Reagan administration pursued a policy it called constructive engagement. This involved trying to persuade the government to change apartheid. As the blacks in South Africa became more militant, American companies doing business there began to withdraw. Under pressure from Congress and public opinion, Reagan agreed to impose limited economic sanctions on South Africa. Reagan had feared that serious pressure would weaken the regime, which is both anti-Communist and a major supplier of vital minerals such as uranium, chromite, and platinum. In addition, he argued that economic sanctions would hurt blacks dependent on the economy for whatever jobs and income they had. However, advocates of sanctions argued that strong pressure was the only hope of forcing enough change to prevent an eventual bloody civil war. There is widespread support among American blacks, students, and liberals for much stronger action, including **divestment**—an end to all U.S. investment in South Africa. But the Reagan administration has resisted stronger measures, even though there has been little movement toward liberalization by the racist government. Thus the Reagan policy remains very controversial.

The Difficulty of Assessing Foreign Policy

There are several important reasons for disagreement about American policies and actions. First, there is no clear and public official statement of America's long-term objectives in the world beyond the common platitudes of national security, peace, prosperity, democracy, progress, and the like. Were there such a generally recognized statement, it could be used as a criterion for some evaluation of short-term achievements. Second, things now change so rapidly that what may appear to be success at one moment (a victory in Vietnam, say, or a truce in the Middle East or a trade agreement

with the Soviet Union) may soon seem outdated or inadequate.

And if it is difficult to assess the success or failure of particular policies, it is all the more difficult to assess the roles and contributions of the parties participating. One reason is that deliberations take place in secret, and the full story is hard to discover. Furthermore, the various bodies may have different interests in a given situation. For example, State may want to institute a conservative democratic civilian regime. Defense may want to strengthen the reliable military. Treasury may want to protect private American investment. And the CIA may want to engineer a coup. These various conflicting objectives were approximately those held during the brief rule in Chile of Marxist President Salvador Allende. Allende was overthrown by the Chilean military with encouragement from both the CIA and agents of American multinational corporations. In such situations of different interests, agencies may act at cross-purposes, and praise or blame may be difficult to apportion.

The war in Vietnam may be the clearest case. There the civilian officials tended to blame the military for not succeeding despite massive technological superiority and virtually unlimited spending. The military blamed the civilians for requiring that it fight "with one hand tied behind its back" by prohibiting obliteration bombing and even invasion of North Vietnam. Some observers blamed the Congress for "abdicating its responsibilities in wartime" by allowing the executive to wage an undeclared war despite the constitutional provision that wars must be declared by Congress. Other observers blamed the advisors to Presidents Kennedy and Johnson for misunderstanding the impossible political situation in Vietnam and so being unjustifiably optimistic throughout the war.[39] And many government officials blamed the intelligence agencies for not reporting accurately, while the intelligence agencies blamed the policy makers for not taking their reports and interpretations correctly and seriously.

Vietnam was such a deep and prolonged catastrophe for America that there is probably sufficient blame to go around. But for our efforts to improve upon the past, to learn the lessons of our mistakes

---

[39]See George McT. Kahin, *Intervention: How America Became Involved in Vietnam* (New York: Knopf, 1986).

as well as of our successes, we would like to know more about who did what, and why it produced the outcomes it did, than we are ever likely to learn. Consequently, neither the policy machinery and policy-making process nor the policies themselves are likely to change fast enough to keep pace with the rapid changes in the world.

The Range of Options

One part of the problem of assessing foreign policy, some believe, is a failure to consider a broad enough range of options in formulating policies. It is always tempting for a superpower to rely on military approaches to solve what are essentially political or economic problems. The Reagan approach has from the beginning emphasized buying large quantities of weaponry. This policy of *procurement*, or purchase of weapons, has been supplemented by a focus on *research and development* for SDI. In addition, Reagan has occasionally relied on a third approach, *demonstration*. This approach, also called force projection, involves demonstrating our willingness to use military force if other approaches do not work. Thus, Reagan ordered the bombing of Libya after a terrorist attack said to be sponsored by Libya on Americans in Germany. Similarly, he ordered an invasion of the small Caribbean island of Grenada after a coup by leftists with Cuban support. Such actions, taken where there is little risk of opposition or defeat, are intended to strengthen the deterrent effect of military threats.

We can see, however, that none of these policies—procurement, research and development, and demonstration—has succeeded in pacifying our turbulent world. Terrorism, rebellion, civil war, political instability, economic chaos—all are still very common in much of the world.

The problem is that these situations are usually the result of political conflicts: Communist versus capitalist, authoritarian versus democratic, Arab versus Israeli, and so on. Thus, it seems likely that any real and lasting solutions will have to come out of a fourth approach: *negotiation*. The trouble with negotiation is that it is usually very hard and time-consuming. Furthermore, its successful use requires a kind of fundamental understanding of the adversaries. Experts in and out of government have developed extensive knowledge of how to negotiate

effectively and successfully.[40] But until now governments have tended to prefer other approaches that seem easier—but rarely work as well.

OUR OWN ROLES IN POLICY AND ACTION

Whatever the policies pursued by the United States and other major states, the growing pressure on the world's shrinking supply of vital food, energy, and mineral resources will tend to increase *interdependence*. The effect will be strengthened by the growing threat to the earth's ecosystem from pollution. And the growing tastes for material goods not locally available plus the spread of technology will further intertwine economies.

Recognizing these new developments, one citizen-interest group asked historian Henry Steele Commager to develop a Declaration of *Interdependence* as part of its observance of the Bicentennial. This declaration reads in part:

> When in the course of history the threat of extinction confronts mankind, it is necessary for the people of The United States to declare their interdependence with the people of all nations and to embrace those principles and build those institutions which will enable mankind to survive and civilization to flourish.
>
> . . .
>
> To establish a new world order of compassion, peace, justice and security, it is essential that mankind free itself from the limitations of national prejudice, and acknowledge that the forces that unite it are incomparably deeper than those that divide it—that all people are part of one global community, dependent on one body of resources, bound together by the ties of a common humanity and associated in a common adventure on the planet Earth.[41]

There remain major political threats to peace around the world. There are still risks of major nuclear war or of new imperialist ventures such as an effort by Western industrial powers to seize Middle Eastern oilfields by force—something once hinted at as a possible last resort by Henry Kissinger. But the longer the world survives these risks, the less able major states are likely to be to wage traditional wars, and the less willing populations are

---

[40]For especially valuable studies, see Roger Fisher and William Ury, *Getting to Yes: Negotiating Agreement without Giving In* (Boston: Houghton Mifflin, 1981); and I. William Zartman and Maureen R. Berman, *The Practical Negotiator* (New Haven: Yale Univ. Press, 1982).

[41]Henry Steele Commager, "A Declaration of INTERdependence," prepared for the World Affairs Council of Philadelphia, October 24, 1975.

likely to be to sustain the sacrifices such wars would entail.

In the interim, the effort to avoid major war and renewed imperialism will make major demands on states and nonstate actors alike. Many observers believe it will require a general balance among a great many states. This is what is usually meant by the "balance of power." It will also require, more agree, delicate efforts to sustain restraint in the relations between the superpowers.[42] Given these basic conditions, for stability and progress to be achieved, all states will have to cooperate more than they ever have thus far in a basic restructuring of economic relations between the rich and the poor. This is what is meant by a "new international economic order."

The major states show many signs of appreciating the importance of the balance of power and of mutual restraint. But both of these are *conservative* concepts and *conservative* approaches. The "new international economic order," however, is not. It is, or calls for, a drastic change in world relations—a change that will challenge our democratic political attitudes and our capitalist political interests as never before. Many observers wonder whether American policy makers and the interests that influence them will be able to overcome the conservative tendencies of our foreign policy bureaucracy and our foreign policy process, as well as the vested American economic interests, to develop the needed new departures.[43]

Meanwhile, the almost inevitable conservatism of the foreign policy process puts a greater burden on those most removed from it: the American people. The American people have a tradition of concern for the welfare of peoples in need elsewhere in the world. Their active roles in transnational organizations such as Amnesty International (see Action Unit 12.3) are an example. With memories of Vietnam still in their minds, they are also weary of the sacrifices compelled by mistaken military adventures. Because they hold these attitudes the American people may have to play a growing role in reminding their leaders of the need to work with diligence and imagination to adjust constructively and humanely to a world changing more rapidly

(Tom Sobolik/Black Star)

than policy makers in Washington, immersed in day-to-day responsibilities, may realize.

"In a world where system change is desirable and necessary but where dominant institutions resist change," writes Robert C. Johansen of the World Policy Institute,

> an extraordinary responsibility falls upon the individual citizen, religious communities, and other nongovernmental agencies to bring about the required changes. These groups should make themselves more genuinely transnational and then provide the bridge between the present and the future systems, while pressing institutions with a vested interest in the prevailing structures of power and wealth to join the forces for a humane transformation. . . . The road leading to destruction is easy because it is familiar. The road toward achieving peace, economic well-being, justice and ecological balance is difficult and unfamiliar but promises some hope. Traveling down that road during the remainder of the twentieth century depends upon a popular movement fueled by our own imagination and willingness to act.[44]

[42]See Graham T. Allison, Albert Carnesale, and Joseph S. Nye, Jr., *Hawks, Doves, & Owls: An Agenda for Avoiding Nuclear War* (New York: Norton, 1985).

[43]For suggestions, see Carolyn M. Stephenson, ed., *Alternative Methods for International Security* (Washington: Univ. Press of America, 1982).

[44]Johansen, *The National Interest and the Human Interest* (Princeton, NJ: Princeton Univ. Press, 1980), p. 407. See also Gale Warner and Michael Shuman, *Citizen Diplomats: Pathfinders in Soviet-American Relations—And How You Can Join Them* (New York: Continuum, 1987) and Bruce Stokes, *Helping Ourselves: Local Solutions to Global Problems* (New York: Norton, 1981). And see the occasional articles in *New Options*, a monthly available for $25 a year from P.O. Box 19324, Washington, DC 20006.

This citizen responsibility for influencing policy makers is what energizes the organizations described in Action Unit 19.1, which lobby to influence American foreign policy. At this point, no one really knows what adjustments will be required in our own lifestyles by the growing needs, demands, and requests of the less developed two-thirds of the world's peoples. Some citizens are already posing questions about what they call right sharing of the world's resources—questions that involve conservation of scarce resources by the rich and sharing of them with the poor. These questions, at one extreme, and the public statements of our leaders, at the other, all serve to remind us that in our own small ways we too have foreign policies that will need considerable and regular adjustment in this unstable world of growing interdependence. Time and our efforts will tell whether here, as in race relations and urban affairs, for example, our leaders might learn from, and be inspired by, our own private efforts.

ACTION UNIT 19.1

How to Influence American Foreign Policy

You can, of course, attempt to influence foreign policy by writing public officials, demonstrating, lobbying, and so forth, just as you might on other issues. But you may wish to join with others having similar interests in organizations devoted to study and action on foreign affairs questions. Among the more prominent such organizations are the following, most of which publish newsletters, pamphlets, and other educational materials:

The **Air Force Association** (1501 Lee Highway, Arlington, VA 22209) informs the public of aerospace developments.

The **American Friends Service Committee, Peace Education Division** (1501 Cherry St., Philadelphia, PA 19102) opposes militarism and advocates nonviolent action for change.

American Security Council (499 South Capitol St., Washington, DC 20003) fosters a strong American military posture and a conservative foreign policy by publishing, lobbying, and organizing.

The **Arms Control Association** (11 Dupont Circle NW, Washington, DC 20036) seeks to broaden public interest in arms control, disarmament, and national security policy.

The **Association of the United States Army** (2425 Wilson Blvd., Arlington, VA 22201) informs the public of army-related developments.

The **Center for Defense Information** (1500 Massachusetts Ave. NW, Washington, DC 20005) studies the defense budget, weapons systems, and troop levels to educate the public.

Clergy and Laity Concerned (198 Broadway, New York, NY 10038) emphasizes ethical aspects of U.S. foreign policy.

The **Coalition for a New Foreign and Military Policy** (712 G St. SE, Washington, DC 20003) publishes background materials and legislative updates on foreign policy issues.

Committee on the Present Danger (905 16th St. NW, Washington, DC 20006) supports military strength and an active role for the United States in world affairs.

The **Council for a Livable World** (100 Maryland Ave. NE, Washington, DC 20002) supports political candidates favoring arms control and reduced military spending.

The **Council on Economic Priorities** (84 Fifth Ave., New York, NY 10011) analyzes the impact of American corporations on society and foreign policy.

The **Defense Orientation Conference Association** (1330 New Hampshire Ave. NW, Washington, DC 20036) promotes continuing education through tours of defense installations.

The **Ethics and Public Policy Center** (1030 15th St. NW, Washington, DC 20005) conducts research and public education on public issues.

The **Federation of American Scientists** (307 Massachusetts Ave. NE, Washington, DC 20002) lobbies on questions of the use of science in society, especially for weaponry, and in favor of disarmament.

The **Fellowship of Reconciliation** (Box 271, Nyack, NY 10960) is a pacifist organization supporting nonviolent methods for social and political change.

The **Foreign Policy Association** (345 E. 46th St., New York, NY 10017) fosters public education and nonpartisan discussion of foreign policy issues by publishing books and pamphlets.

The **Friends Committee on National Legislation** (245 Second St. NE, Washington, DC 20002) lobbies Congress and the president on foreign policy questions from a Quaker perspective.

The **Institute for Policy Studies** (1901 Q St. NW, Washington, DC 20009) does research and public education on public issues.

Mobilization for Survival (853 Broadway, Room 2109, New York, NY 10003) emphasizes political organization to protest the militarization of U.S. policy.

National Peace Institute Foundation (110 Maryland Ave. NE, Washington, DC 20002) supports creation of an academy to study peacemaking and its application to world problems.

The **Navy League of the United States** (2300 Wilson Blvd., Arlington, VA 22201) supports strengthening American naval power.

Nuclear Weapons Freeze Campaign (4144 Lindell Blvd., Suite 404, St. Louis, MO 63108) coordinates local efforts to support a nuclear freeze.

Physicians for Social Responsibility (1601 Connecticut Ave. NW, Washington, DC 20009) conducts public education on nuclear war and arms control.

SANE (711 G St. NE, Washington, DC 20003) organizes to mobilize support for American initiatives for peace, arms control and disarmament, reduced military spending, and so on.

Union of Concerned Scientists (26 Church St., Cambridge, MA 02238) studies technical aspects of public policy questions, including arms control.

The **United Nations Association/USA** (300 E. 42nd St., New York, NY 10017) educates the public on the United Nations and its activities and supports American initiatives in the United Nations.

The **Women's International League for Peace and Freedom** (120 Maryland Ave. NE, Washington, DC 20002) is the Washington lobbying office of the national organization that supports human rights, arms control, and reduced military spending.

The **World Federalists Association** (418 7th St. SE, Washington, DC 20003) supports world peace through world law with justice.

The **World Policy Institute** (777 United Nations Plaza, New York, NY 10017) works to transform the international system around four values: redistribution of wealth, redistribution of power, war prevention, and ecological stability.

SUMMARY

Almost all aspects of our lives are affected by world affairs. In effect, we have our individual foreign policies, which we use in deciding what to buy, what to eat, what to use, where to travel, and so on. Our lives are interdependent with those of others around the world.

Earlier in American history, the nation was able to remain free of entangling alliances. It was largely isolationist, with exceptions for World War I and World War II. Then the United States took the lead in establishing the United Nations and the Marshall Plan and made alliances against communism with many nations. It also fought limited wars in Korea and Vietnam to halt the spread of communism. But the Vietnam War became very unpopular and led to a reexamination of American foreign policy and the processes by which it is made.

The foreign policy machinery consists primarily of the cabinet departments, the National Security Council, and the Central Intelligence Agency. The Congress also plays an important role. Other factors influencing policy making are the external setting, the societal factors (interest groups, public opinion, the economy), and individual characteristics of policy makers.

We usually analyze American foreign policy in terms of national interests, although the term is vague. It is usually thought to involve four types of interests: defense, economic, world order, and ideological.

American national interests have evolved from containment in the cold war, through cooperation in détente, to a period of dispute at present. New issues have emerged over the years, among them: nuclear war and nuclear weapons, including proliferation; questions of the limited utility of military force; the role of mimicry in world militarization; the continuing quest for arms control and perhaps a nuclear freeze; and concerns about limited resources. Another important change has been the emergence of new states and of nonstate actors, such as economic unions, multinational corporations, cartels, and terrorists. There have also been new citizen attitudes, including growing antimilitarism and separatism.

Debate continues over how effective American foreign policy is. Among the major topics of dispute today are policies in the Middle East and in Central America. These disputes are so great that it is difficult to get agreement on an assessment of current United States policy.

We citizens may play increasingly important roles in shaping American foreign policy because we now face interdependence not just among states but also among peoples.

Suggestions for Further Reading and Study

Among books that examine the newer developments in world affairs, in addition to those cited in chapter footnotes, are Lester Brown, *The Twenty-Ninth Day* (New York: Norton, 1978); Seyom Brown, *New Forces in World Politics* (Washington, DC: Brookings, 1974); Robert Keohane and Joseph Nye, *Power and Interdependence: World Politics in Transition* (Boston: Little, Brown, 1977); Saul Mendlovitz, ed., *On the Creation of a Just World Order* (New York: Free Press, 1975); Herman Kahn et al., *The Next 200 Years* (New York: Morrow, 1976), which offers a drastically different perspective of optimism; and David A. Baldwin, *Economic Statecraft* (Princeton: Princeton Univ. Press, 1985).

To learn more about the making of American foreign policy, you may find these books helpful: Graham Allison, *The Essence of Decision* (Boston: Little, Brown, 1971); Roger Hilsman, *The Politics of Policy Making in Defense and Foreign Affairs* (New York: Harper & Row, 1971); Morton Halperin, *Bureaucratic Politics and Foreign Policy* (Washington, DC: Brookings, 1974); Richard Barnet, *The Roots of War* (New York: Penguin, 1972); John H. Esterline and Robert B. Black, *Inside Foreign Policy* (Palo Alto, CA: Mayfield, 1975); and James Nathan and James Oliver, *Foreign Policy Making and the American Political System* (Boston: Little, Brown, 1983).

THE FUTURE POSSIBILITIES OF AMERICAN POLITICS

"Politics as usual" in America is "nonparticipatory." As we have seen, barely a majority of those eligible to vote actually does vote in our presidential elections, and a smaller percentage votes in most state and local elections. And while perhaps 1 in 5 will occasionally attend a political meeting or rally, only 1 in 7 ever contacts a political official, and but 1 in 33 ever runs for any political office.

Of course, the country was established two centuries ago not as a democracy but rather as a republic—a government intended to represent the interests of its citizens. But we have seen in previous chapters what many have long argued: that governmental officials in their actions more often represent the interests not of the public as a whole (the "common good") but rather of coalitions of special interests. In this sense, American politics continues to be not only nonparticipatory but also nonrepresentative, in terms of the average citizen. ■

POWER FROM THE PEOPLE— AND POWER AGAINST THE PEOPLE

Our Republic was based, as we have seen, on the principle of popular sovereignty. The Declaration of Independence asserted that "governments are instituted among men, deriving their just powers from the consent of the governed," and the Constitution began with the words, "We the People of the United States . . . do ordain and establish this Constitution. . . . "

Concepts of Democracy

As decades passed, formal or legal obstacles to participation—to voting, and then to campaigning for office—decreased. America was, we have said, becoming more democratic. Such a conclusion presumes, of course, a concept of democracy grounded in the right of the citizens to vote for their leaders. But if the right to vote in free elections is a common definition of democracy, it is far from the only one.[1]

Some people define democracy in terms of **majority rule**—rule by 50 percent plus one of the voters. But in our system, one can generally win an election with less than that—as Nixon did in 1968 with 43.4 percent. So perhaps we should think of democracy as **plurality rule**—rule by whoever gets more votes than any other candidate. Either criteria would allow the Soviet Union to qualify as a democracy, even though in that country there is usually only one candidate for any office.

Perhaps the important point is to have a real *electoral choice among candidates*, whether or not the victor then pays attention to the interests of the voters. Or perhaps, as some say, democracy should be thought of in terms of citizens having a high degree of *access* to, and *influence* upon, their elected officials, whether or not they choose to exercise it.

The concepts of democracy are, as we can see, many and varied. Indeed, one observer suggests that there are perhaps 200 different definitions in

use.[2] By virtually any of the most common definitions, we could say that American government is more democratic now than it was when Americans had slaves and when women and those without property were not allowed to vote.

Democracy in America

But is America continuing to become more democratic? Or is the "power from the people" still frequently "power against the people"? Everyone will answer this question somewhat differently, depending not only on his or her concept of democracy but also on his or her image of contemporary political reality in America. In the same way, we may disagree over just how democratic America actually is today, when compared to our own ideal concept.

One of the most demanding and most thought-provoking sets of criteria for assessing how democratic America is has been offered by historian Howard Zinn. These criteria are listed in the box titled "How Democratic Is America?"

In previous chapters, I have portrayed progress toward greater democracy on many of these dimensions while suggesting serious limitations to the actual "democraticness" of America in terms of these criteria. But can we conclude that America is still on the way toward becoming more democratic when the government remains seriously unrepresentative—both in the types of people who serve in it and in the policies it adopts? And even more, can we discern a trend toward greater democracy in an America of declining popular participation in electoral politics?

The Debate over Political Participation

In the 1960's, as electoral participation declined seriously, less conventional forms of political participation—protest meetings, marches, street dem-

---

[1]See Carole Pateman, *Participation and Democratic Theory* (Cambridge: Cambridge Univ. Press, 1970).

[2]Massimo Salvadori, *Liberal Democracy* (Garden City, NY: Doubleday, 1957). For an interesting and unique distinction between two concepts of democracy—unitary (based on our personal experience of friendship) and adversary (based on the traditional liberal image of conflicting interests), see Jane J. Mansbridge, *Beyond Adversary Democracy* (New York: Basic Books, 1980). And see Giovanni Sartori, *The Theory of Democracy Revisited* (Chatham, NJ: Chatham House, 1987).

How Democratic Is America?

I propose a set of criteria for the description "democratic" which goes beyond formal political institutions, to the quality of life in the society (economic, social, psychological), beyond majority rule to concern for minorities, and beyond national boundaries to a global view of what is meant by "the people," in that rough, but essentially correct view of democracy as "government of, by, and for the people."

Let me list the criteria . . .

1. To what extent can various people in the society participate in those decisions which affect their lives: decisions in the political process and decisions in the economic structure?

2. As a corollary of the above: do people have equal access to the information which they need to make important decisions?

3. Are the members of the society equally protected on matters of life and death—in the most literal sense of that phrase?

4. Is there equality before the law: police, courts, the judicial process—as well as equality with the law-enforcing institutions, so as to safeguard equally everyone's persona and his freedom from interference by others, and by the government?

5. Is there equality in the distribution of available resources: those economic goods necessary for health, life, recreation, leisure, growth?

6. Is there equal access to education, to knowledge and training, so as to enable persons in the society to live their lives as fully as possible, to enlarge their range of possibilities?

7. Is there freedom of expression on all matters, and equally for all, to communicate with other members of the society?

8. Is there freedom for individuality in private life, in sexual relations, family relations, the right of privacy?

9. To minimize regulation: do education and the culture in general foster a spirit of cooperation and amity to sustain the above conditions?

10. As a final safety feature: is there opportunity to protest, to disobey the laws, when the foregoing objectives are being lost—as a way of restoring them?

From Howard Zinn, "How Democratic Is America?" in *How Democratic Is America?* ed. Robert A. Goldwin (Chicago: Rand McNally, 1969, 1971).

---

onstrations, and even riots—increased dramatically. With the proliferation of these new (or, more accurately, revived) forms of participation, there emerged a vigorous public debate over the meaning and value of participation.

The battle cry of "power to the people" mobilized the Left—and especially students—in their movement to gain full civil rights for blacks and then in their opposition to the Vietnam War. The general argument was that too much power had been transferred from the people to the government—or taken from the people by the government. It was time to shift power back to the people so that they could make on their own the important decisions that affected their lives. This movement became known as the New Left because it sought the same objectives of equality, justice, and liberty that the traditional political Left had sought, but it had lost the faith that leftists traditionally had that big, centralized government could

achieve these objectives.[3] Instead, it emphasized "participatory democracy," focused on the local level and extended beyond politics into the economic sphere as well, where it sought greater economic equality and worker democracy.

As this New Left developed, it was joined in its concern for less reliance on big government to solve problems and for more emphasis on individual liberty by what came to be called the New Right.[4] The members of this amorphous group of radical conservatives often termed themselves *libertarians* because of the emphasis on the need for more individual liberty, almost regardless of its cost in decreased governmental power at home and abroad.

---

[3]For interesting accounts of the current views of prominent members of the Left, see "Voices from the Left: A Conversation between Michael Harrington and Irving Howe," *New York Times Magazine*, June 17, 1984, pp. 24–53, and the book edited by Howe, *Alternatives: Proposals for America from the Democratic Life* (New York: Pantheon, 1984).

[4]For an indication of one New Right perspective, see Richard A. Viguerie, *The Establishment vs. the People: Is a New Populist Revolt on the Way?* (Chicago: Regnery, 1984).

Participatory Democracy

We regard men as infinitely precious and possessed of unfulfilled capacities for reason, freedom, and love. In affirming these principles we are aware of countering perhaps the dominant conceptions of man in the twentieth century: that he is a thing to be manipulated, and that he is inherently incapable of directing his own affairs. We oppose the depersonalization that reduces human beings to the status of things—if anything, the brutalities of the twentieth century teach that means and ends are intimately related, that vague appeals to "posterity" cannot justify the mutilations of the present. We oppose, too, the doctrine of human incompetence because it rests essentially on the modern fact that men have been "competently" manipulated into incompetence—we see little reason why men cannot meet with increasing skill the complexities and responsibilities of their situation, if society is organized not for minority, but for majority, participation in decision-making.

Men have unrealized potential for self-cultivation, self-direction, self-understanding, and creativity. It is this potential that we regard as crucial and to which we appeal, not to the human potentiality for violence, unreason, and submission to authority. . . .

We would replace power rooted in possession, privilege, or circumstance by power and uniqueness rooted in love, reflectiveness, reason, and creativity. As a social system we seek the establishment of a democracy of individual participation, governed by two central aims: that the individual share in those social decisions determining the quality and direction of his life;

that society be organized to encourage independence in men and provide the media for their common participation.

In a participatory democracy, the political life would be based in several root principles:

- that decision-making of basic social consequence be carried on by public groupings;
- that politics be seen positively, as the art of collectively creating an acceptable pattern of social relations;
- that politics has the function of bringing people out of isolation and into community, thus being a necessary, though not sufficient, means of finding meaning in personal life;
- that the political order should serve to clarify problems in a way instrumental to their solution; it should provide outlets for the expression of personal grievance and aspiration; opposing views should be organized so as to illuminate choices and facilitate the attainment of goals; channels would be commonly available to relate men to knowledge and to power so that private problems—from bad recreation facilities to personal alienation—are formulated as general issues. . . .

From *The Port Huron Statement* drawn up by a group of young New Left members of the Students for a Democratic Society in 1962. For the story behind SDS and its evolution, see James Miller, *"Democracy Is in the Streets": From Port Huron to the Siege of Chicago* (New York: Simon & Schuster, 1987).

The New Left and the New Right parted company on the extent to which equality was to be valued as well as on the extent to which government at the local level was to be relied upon. But they were in agreement on the call for returning "power to the people."

In this they were at odds with traditional Marxists, who sought state socialism, and with anarchists, who sought to abolish all government. They also found themselves at odds with a new grouping of old liberals and conservatives who were united in the belief that greater popular political participation, both conventional (voting, campaigning, and so on) and unconventional (such as protests and riots), posed a grave threat to the survival of the

state.[5] Their thesis is well expressed in the phrase "the ungovernability of democracies," which is often used by the bankers, business people, and academics who have come to share this view. The boxes titled "Participatory Democracy" and "The Ungovernability of Democracies" contain analyses representative of the basic views of both groups.

The interest in participatory democracy today seems to be fragmenting into several distinct camps. One might be termed "modern populism" or "the new populism." We met the old populism, 1892 vintage, in Chapter 4 as a minor party. To-

[5]See Peter Steinfels, *The Neoconservatives: The Men Who Are Changing America's Politics* (New York: Simon & Schuster, 1979).

The Ungovernability of Democracies

American society is characterized by a broad consensus favoring democratic, liberal, and egalitarian values. For much of the time, the commitment to these values is neither passionate nor intense. During periods of rapid social change, however, these democratic and egalitarian values of the American creed are reaffirmed. The intensity of belief during such creedal passion periods leads to the challenging of established authority and to major efforts to change governmental structure to accord more fully with those values. . . .

Al Smith once remarked, "The only cure for the evils of democracy is more democracy." Our analysis suggests that applying that cure at the present time could well be adding fuel to the flames. Instead, some of the problems of governance in the United States today stem from an "excess of democracy." . . . Needed, instead, is a greater degree of moderation in democracy.

In practice, this moderation has two major areas of application. First, democracy is only one way of constituting authority, and it is not necessarily a universally applicable one. In many situations, the claims of expertise, seniority, experience, and special talents may override the claims of democracy as a way of constituting authority. . . . The arenas where democratic procedures are appropriate are, in short, limited.

Second, the effective operation of a democratic political system usually requires some measure of apathy and noninvolvement on the part of some individuals and groups. In the past, every democratic society has had a marginal population, of greater or lesser size, which has not actively participated in politics. In itself, this marginality on the part of some groups is inher-

ently undemocratic, but it also has been one of the factors which has enabled democracy to function effectively. Marginal social groups, as in the case of the blacks, are now becoming full participants in the political system. Yet the danger of "overloading" the political system with demands which extend its functions and undermine its authority still remains. Less marginality on the part of some groups thus needs to be replaced by more self-restraint on the part of all groups. . . .

Over the years . . . the American political system has emerged as a distinctive case of extraordinarily democratic institutions joined to an exclusively democratic value system. Democracy is more of a threat to itself in the United States than it is in either Europe or Japan. . . . Political authority is never strong in the U.S., and it is peculiarly weak during a creedal passion period of intense commitment to democratic and egalitarian ideals. In the United States, the strength of the democratic ideal poses a problem for the governability of democracy in a way which is not the case elsewhere.

. . . A value which is normally good in itself is not necessarily optimized when it is maximized. We have come to recognize that there are potentially desirable limits to economic growth. There are also potentially desirable limits to the extension of political democracy. Democracy will have a longer life if it has a more balanced existence.

From *The Crisis of Democracy: Report on the Governability of Democracies to the Trilateral Commission* by Michel T. Crozier, Samuel P. Huntington, and Toji Watanuki (New York: New York University Press, 1975), pp. 112–15. © 1975 The Trilateral Commission.

---

day, we would meet the new populism in state and local government offices across the nation. Its unofficial members attack big business, big banks, and agribusiness, in the interests of workers and small farmers. They still argue against large concentrations of economic power.[6]

Another camp is now increasingly called the neoliberals. It received national attention in 1984 because of the impact of Gary Hart's campaign for

the Democratic presidential nomination.[7] This loose grouping includes some Democratic members of Congress and various activists and academics. They are united in the belief that traditional approaches to national problems no longer work and must be replaced by new programs. They have no common program at this point. Most agree, however, that technology has transformed the world and the nation. They oppose protection of the American economy from foreign trade competi-

---

[6]See Harry C. Boyte, Heather Booth, and Steve Max, *Citizen Action and the New American Populism* (Philadelphia: Temple Univ. Press, 1986) and Harry C. Boyte and Frank Riessman, eds., *The New Populism: The Politics of Empowerment* (Philadelphia: Temple Univ. Press, 1986).

[7]See "Baby Boomers Push for Power, and They're Getting It—In Business, in Politics, and in the Marketplace," *Business Week*, July 2, 1984, pp. 52–62.

tion. Instead, they favor reliance on high technology plus more worker involvement in management to increase productivity and economic growth while protecting the environment. They would rely more on decentralization and market forces than traditional liberals would.[8]

Still others place greater emphasis on the role of personal transformation in creating a new politics.[9] More than a thousand of them drafted a new manifesto of 10,000 words in 1984 to express their common concerns and program. The box "At the Crossroads" contains brief excerpts from this manifesto.[10]

Of course, most people do not affiliate with any particular movement. Many, however, do things that advance these changes. Foremost among these things today is the use of computers and other electronic technology to transform work, community, and politics. Apple Computer, for example, has a special division that gives computers to social-action organizations around the nation so that they can set up information networks to share resources. "There are 300,000 non-profit organizations in the U.S. employing 5,600,000 workers," says Mark Vermilion, Apple's manager of community affairs. "Their main function is that of information broker, to provide contemporary information between their client base and society at large. The computers allow them to deliver their product more efficiently."[11]

The same thing is now being done internationally as well, also by computer. For example, an organization called Carinet, established in Africa in 1970 by a group of Quakers, enables Third World citizens to ask technical questions on development and agriculture directly of American experts by computer. Experts on call respond to questions by computer through the New Jersey Institute of Technology—in a day or less.[12] Others are now arranging similar programs elsewhere.[13]

Some people have feared that the spread of electronic technology would prove to be a force for evil in the hands of the state, as it was in George Orwell's famous novel *1984*. There is no doubt that such technology can be misused. But many people are attentive to these dangers while others are using the technology in the service of decentralized expertise. None of this resolves the long debate over democracy and participation. None of it resolves the current conflicts between Left and Right, neoliberal and neoconservative.

These arguments will rage at least as long as the American political system is unable to solve the difficult problems and resolve the fundamental conflicts that continue to challenge it from Right and Left, domestically and internationally. The eventual outcome may be decentralization emphasizing "power *to* the people," whether or not it confirms "the ungovernability of democracies" thesis. Another possibility is restoration of a conventional political status quo of "power *from* the people," whether or not it turns out to be largely "power *against* the people."

Whatever the ultimate outcome, however, the arguments, the theorizing, and the experimentation have brought about significant changes. Some of these changes have been in the way we Americans think about politics. Others have been in the types of actions we take, or believe it appropriate for others to take, in attempting to perform the responsibilities of citizenship in a democracy.

CHANGING CONCEPTS OF CITIZENSHIP

In Politics, Around Politics, and Beyond Politics

Traditionally, most everyone seeking change has focused his or her attention on politics. There has always been, therefore, a *reformist* movement in

---

[8]See Randall Rothenberg, *The Neoliberals: Creating the New American Politics* (New York: Simon & Schuster, 1984), and Gary Hart, *A New Democracy* (New York: Morrow paperback, 1984).

[9]Among the many examples of this decentralist perspective are Marilyn Ferguson, *The Aquarian Conspiracy: Personal and Social Transformation in the 1980s* (Los Angeles: Tarcher paperback, 1980); Fritjof Capra and Charlene Spretnak, *Green Politics: The Global Promise* (New York: Dutton, 1984); Jonathan Porritt, *Seeing Green: The Politics of Ecology Explained* (Oxford: Blackwell, 1984); Bill Devall and George Sessions, *Deep Ecology* (Salt Lake City, UT: Peregrine Smith, 1985); and Harvey Wasserman, *American Born and Reborn* (New York: Collier, 1984). For a more philosophical approach, see Neal Riemer, *The Future of the Democratic Revolution* (New York: Praeger, 1984).

[10]*At the Crossroads* is available for $2 from The Communications Era Task Force, Box 3623, Spokane, WA 99220.

[11]Quoted in Richard Schrader, "Access to Power," *Micro Discovery*, November 1983, p. 40. For other examples, see Susan Chace, "Radical Chip: The Counterculture Discovers Computers," *Wall Street Journal*, January 18, 1983.

[12]See Edward Warner, "Net Provides Third World with Link to U.S. Experts," *Computer World*, April 2, 1984, p. 26.

[13]For a description of a variety of novel approaches to current problems, see Connie Matthiessen and Mark Schapiro, "A Dozen New Ideas," *New Age Journal*, July 1984, pp. 39–49.

At the Crossroads

The magnitude of the changes we will see in our lifetimes is almost overwhelming. A number of forces fuel this change—among them, electronic communications, genetic engineering, computers and robots, the widening gap between rich and poor, changes in the role of women and the family, and our move to outer space.

Our challenge is to understand and use these forces so we can create the more humane world so many of us desire.

Goal: Communications Era

We are *already embarked* on a journey toward this "more humane world."

We are emerging out of what may be called the "industrial era" and entering what may be called the "communications era."

At the heart of this journey is a growing realization of the importance of human skills. We çan and must develop the full potential of people, both individually and in groups. . . .

In the following sections, we discuss the kinds of changes we need to make as we travel to a healthier society in the communications era.

New Traditions

The shifts from the industrial era to the communications era involve a return to past values as well as the recognition of new values.

- We need *honesty, responsibility, humility and love.* In a world with today's productive and destructive power, these "traditional" values have become our most important survival skills!

- We need to develop a common loyalty as *citizens of the world,* without losing our local and national commitments.

- The main human activity needs to be *learning and growing.* The essential human contribution to life will be creative, integrative, and focused on relationships.

New Assumptions

From Separation to Interconnectedness The deeper we probe into inner and outer space, the more we come to realize that everything is interconnected.

Ecology also illustrates how all life on the planet is interdependent; how our attempts to "conquer" and "exploit" nature make us victims of our own actions rather than victors.

From Dependency to Self-Reliance Specialists will no longer be the decision-makers, but will be the creators and communicators of tools, techniques and knowledge. They will teach others how to be more self-reliant.

New Policies

From Courts to Mediation There are other ways to resolve conflicts than by turning them over to lawyers and judges. . . . Mediation . . . is generally cheaper and faster, and the solutions are more creative, more healing, and more meaningful for the parties involved.

From Hierarchy to Participation As we move into the communications era, the demand for repetitive work is decreasing rapidly and many more jobs are requiring creativity and self-direction. Our work structures need to be redesigned to encourage these qualities in a much larger percentage of the work force.

New Directions

From Schooling to Life-Long Learning In the communications era, the goal of education will be to help each person become a skillful independent learner, capable of life-long learning.

From Jobs to Creative Living There are urgent world problems which can absorb huge amounts of human energy. We also need a great deal of socially valuable, productive activity—homemaking, parenting, teaching, and various community activities, as well as all kinds of creative and innovative endeavors in the arts and in social entrepreneurship.

We describe the sum of these activities as the "committed economy" because people do them out of a sense of personal commitment and commitment to society. People don't get paid for doing them.

In the communications era, the committed economy will be on an equal footing with the market economy; in fact, committed activities will account for a *higher* percentage of our time than traditional "jobs."

From the Nation-State to Local Control/Global Cooperation The most dramatic shifts will be required at the local level. The communications era requires that people be creative and develop the capacity for self-reliance and self-direction. People with these qualities will demand greater involvement in government than our present system provides.

Our image of "world government" is usually that of a super-state bureaucracy. As we move into the communications era, we will not create world government, but we will make decisions based on our interconnectedness. Our systems of networks, coalitions, professional societies and international agencies are—even now—bringing us together.

What We Can Do

Fundamental change has always begun at the personal level.

We can begin *talking with the people around us*—spouses, children, parents, neighbors, co-workers—about what is happening in our world. . . .

We can *take a fresh look at the patterns of our own lives.* Each of us plays many roles, parent, spouse, neighbor, consumer, worker, etc. We can make significant small changes in each of these areas. . . .

We can *get together with others who share our concern.* A small group, working together, can be amazingly powerful in creating a cooperative, saving a historical building, bringing about a better school. . . .

We can *use the many "tools" available to us.* We can read one key book, give one key magazine article to a friend, contact one group which is working for positive change. . . .

We can *use this document* to provide a picture of the new world. . . .

In doing these things—all of which we *can* do—we will begin to discover that the visible, apparent breakdown in our society hides an extraordinary range of exciting activities and new directions.

Source: Excerpted from *At the Crossroads* (Spokane, WA: Communications Era Task Force, 1984).

---

politics. In recent years, that movement captured—and later lost—the leadership of the Democratic party. Reformists were able in 1972 to secure the nomination of George McGovern by a convention whose delegates were more representative of the diversity of the American people than those of any other political convention before or since.

Other elements in this political reformist movement active in recent years include the citizen lobby Common Cause, and the Ralph Nader Public Citizen conglomerate of researchers, lawyers, and lobbyists, both of which we examined in Chapter 5, along with numerous other special-interest groups trying to influence elections or legislation.

But while such reformist political activity has continued and even grown in recent years, those same years have seen growing disillusionment with, and rejection of, political approaches and political solutions to human problems. The result has been two other types of approach. One is a general movement *around politics.* This is an effort to circumvent politics carried out by such activist groups as feminists, ecologists, and pacifists, who believe the political system to be too unresponsive and politics too superficial to solve major human problems.

The second alternative approach has been a movement *beyond politics.* This is an effort to transcend politics by reasserting spiritual attitudes and emphasizing spiritual activities. In this cate-gory fall such groups as Scientology, the "Moonies" (followers of Korean Reverend Sun Yung Moon), the Hare Krishna groups often found chanting near college campuses, and the long-lived Campus Crusade for Christ.

The spiritualists often see the same worldly problems as the circumventers and the reformers but generally emphasize faith and spiritual practices as the best way to resolve problems. The circumventers tend to emphasize the importance of heightening people's consciousness. They point to the need for greater understanding of the roots of current problems, which they believe are not in politics or economics but rather in deeper attitudes. The feminists, for example, tend to find the roots of sexism, and perhaps of war and racism as well, in male chauvinist presuppositions of male superiority and of patriarchy—the view that men were made to rule women. Ecologists often trace similar evils to humankind's common desire to dominate rather than live in harmony with nature. And pacificists sometimes trace these problems to the corruption of ethical standards of conduct by resurgent animalistic tendencies, discredited religious doctrines, and a culture of competition.

Distinctive as each of these views is in important ways, they have in common a rejection of the traditional analysis that politics is both the root of the problem and the route to its solution. In the aftermath of the activism of the civil-rights movement and the antiwar movement, important lessons have been learned about the range of effective actions open to "change agents" and about the most appropriate strategies and tactics for maximizing the effectiveness of political action.

New—and Renewed—Types of Action

The underlying sense that seems to be emerging among the advocates of change in America today is that, contrary to appearances, the people have the power. That is, they have it if they really want to exercise it and are prepared to do the hard work of developing effective strategies and organizing those who seek or would benefit from political change.

Conventional Political Action

In a sense, of course, that power has always been there, ever since the right to vote was extended to the vast majority of the American people. Before they got the vote, in fact, most Americans were benefiting little from the way politics was conducted. But it is difficult to get the poor and pessimistic to take seriously the idea that they can resort to the ballot box to change their condition. This is especially so when the candidates in most elections have been selected by "party regulars," who tend to be conservative. The conventional act of *voting* therefore seems less promising today, at least at the federal level. At the local level, election of change-oriented mayors, city councils, and others, more and more of them members of previously excluded groups such as women, blacks, Chicanos, and Puerto Ricans, has recently begun to change this pessimism in some places.[14]

The conventional political act of *lobbying*, which used to be engaged in primarily by representatives of vested interests, has in recent years been undertaken by people who were formerly excluded. The pioneering public venture was the Poor People's Campaign of 1968 organized by the late Reverend Martin Luther King, Jr., and his Southern Christian Leadership Conference, which we discussed in Chapter 13. It set a public precedent for poor people to go to Washington to lobby. This example has since inspired others, especially advocates of welfare rights and Native Americans, to use methods previously left to the vested interests.

Yet another recent expansion of use of conventional political devices has been the movement to institute and use the old Progressive era devices of *initiative*, *referendum*, and *recall*, which we discussed in Chapter 3. But perhaps the most significant recent reinvigoration of conventional political participation has been the growth of *efforts by nonelites to serve* in government. As we saw in Chapter 13, more and more blacks are running for and winning political office, especially at local levels. The same thing, we saw in Chapter 14, is true of women. Such participation by the previously uninvolved and still underrepresented is especially important because its public, visible nature may stimulate others to follow suit. In terms of actual influence on policy, however, more important may be the movement toward what is now being called participatory bureaucracy. This is a bureaucracy staffed with more minority and female government employees, and therefore it is more representative.[15]

Unconventional: Violent Action

The failure of conventional political activities in the 1960s to bring quick success led some on both the Left and the Right to resort to violence. Violence has a long history in America. Early Americans used it against the Native Americans as well as to control their slaves. Business, often with the assistance of the government, sometimes dealt violently with militant labor. The Ku Klux Klan and other racist and anti-Catholic groups often handled those they opposed with violence. And through it all, some police have handled activists and members of minority groups violently. Violence is, in the memorable words of black power activist H. Rap Brown, "as American as cherry pie." Furthermore, our foreign policy, like those of other countries, has always relied ultimately on violence and on the threat of violence to preserve and protect its interests around the world.

Small wonder, then, that it should occur to the downtrodden, the dispossessed, and the angry that violence is the established and effective way to achieve their ends. There are certain arguments

[14]See George Beam and Dick Simpson, *Political Action* (Athens, OH: Swallow Press, 1984), esp. chap. 8, and Byron Kennard, *Nothing Can Be Done, Everything Is Possible* (Andover, MA: Brick House, 1982).

[15]Harry Krantz, *The Participatory Bureaucracy* (Lexington, MA: Lexington Books, 1976). See also Willis O. Hawley, "The Possibilities of Nonbureaucratic Organizations," in *Improving Urban Management*, ed. Hawley and David Rogers (Beverly Hills, CA: Sage, 1976), pp. 209–63.

often made for the resort to violence. Some say it strengthens one's sense of power, self-confidence, and pride to use violence on one's enemy. Others say it instills fear in one's adversary, which makes the adversary more likely to give in and even more likely to treat one with respect.

One major problem with using violence is that it tends to elicit violence in response. Some advocates argue that this effect is good because it shows the weak-willed and tenderhearted whose side the authorities are on and thereby forces them to rally to the cause.

These are all controversial assertions, and no single analysis will ever resolve differences on the question. But several other important points need to be made when the desirability of resorting to violence is considered.

One is the response to the common citation by leftists of Mao Tse-tung's dictum that "all power comes from the barrel of a gun." The point was well put by Saul Alinsky, the organizer we met in Chapter 3 and will meet again shortly. Alinsky was fond of pointing out the absurdity of making and accepting such an assertion when the other side—the police, the armed forces, and the vigilante citizens—has all the guns. In modern times, the state will always have a virtual monopoly on usable military force. The only exception is terrorist activities such as assassinations and bombings. Terrorist activities can cause serious disruption, especially in highly technological societies such as ours. But disruption rarely translates into construction, and so the prospects of achieving positive ends by violence are slight.

The other important negative effect of violence is the impact of means on ends. Most movements for social change in this country are based on a belief in humanized relations among people. But using violence against others is the most dehumanizing act one can commit. Part of the point is that it is difficult for those you use violence against to relate humanly to you afterwards. More important, however, is that it is difficult for one to retain his or her commitment to human ends when using dehumanizing means. We often see evidence of this in the effects of war on soldiers once they return home. We can see the same tendency at work perverting revolutions after they succeed. Most violent revolutions, after all, are carried out in the name of humanity. But few manage to salvage those ends from the rubble of the death and destruction that

quick, violent success seemed at the time to demand.[16]

Unconventional: "Direct Action"

This pessimistic conclusion about the efficacy of violence has led to greater interest in the strategies of "direct action." Saul Alinsky pioneered development of many such techniques, as we saw in Chapter 3. Alinsky and those who work in similar ways are not necessarily opposed to violence on principle. Rather, they find that obstruction, embarrassment, and other techniques of direct action work more effectively in achieving social change. Many community-action groups across the country now train activists in these methods and practice them as well.[17]

Unconventional: Nonviolent Action

Some activists are on principle opposed to the use of violence because they believe it is immoral. These people are *pacifists*—a term meaning "peaceful ones" derived from the Latin word *pax* ("peace"). Many leaders of the civil-rights movement, such as the Reverend Martin Luther King, were pacifists, as were some leaders of the movement against the Vietnam War. Pacifists often serve as the "conscience" of movements for social change, although they are rarely able or willing to take power themselves. That is because political power today still seems to demand of those who exercise it a willingness to use force and violence against other peoples—and even against the people of one's own country.

LESSONS FOR STRATEGY AND TACTICS

We live in an era of "multiple manipulation." There are always people trying to manipulate us— our leaders, advertisers, our enemies, and even our friends. At the same time, we try to manipulate others—our leaders, our adversaries, and even our friends. The world is full of books on how to manipulate others, many of them best-sellers. This book too has been about manipulation, focusing both on how politics and politicians tend to ma-

---

[16]For a thoughtful analysis, see Gordon Zahn, "The Bondage of Liberation," *Worldview*, March 1977.
[17]For an interesting survey, see Judy MacLean, "Training Organizers for the Future," *In These Times*, August 3–9, 1977, pp. 11–14.

nipulate us and on how we might manipulate politics and politicians.

There is no escaping manipulation in the kind of world we live in. But we may be better able to see it coming and prevent it from being successful if we know how to recognize it. And we may also become better able to turn it to the ends we seek—if we have enough confidence in the rightness of those ends.

There are important things to be learned from our experience of politics and from the experience of others, too. Everyone, as we well know, sees the world somewhat differently, so everyone will learn somewhat different lessons from the study of American politics. But three lessons stand out in my mind: (1) the importance of experience, (2) the role of information—and its control, and (3) the wide range of roles people may play in politics.

The Importance of Experience

Each of us has a different experience of the world. We act in accordance with our own experience of the world—we have to because it's all we know. Realizing this has very important implications for social change or even for political success of any sort.

You can make someone do what you want if you have the *power* to force him or her to do it. But the most effective way to affect someone's behavior is to get that person to see the world the way you do. That is what we mean by having *authority:* being able to describe, interpret, or explain reality to others in a way that they will accept.

Ronald Laing, a British psychologist, has put the point well in a little book he calls *The Politics of Experience:*

> All those people who seek to control the behavior of large numbers of other people work on the *experiences* of those other people. Once people can be induced to experience a situation in a similar way, they can be expected to behave in similar ways. Induce people all to want the same thing, hate the same things, feel the same threat, then their behavior is already captive—you have acquired your consumers or your cannon fodder.[18]

Laing speaks of this as a dangerous thing. And it well can be, as we see in the history of white American attitudes toward blacks or male attitudes toward females or the attitudes of the rich toward the poor. But the insight can be put to better ends too. As Alinsky reminds us, "When you are trying to communicate and can't find the point in the experience of the other party at which he can receive or understand, then you must create the experience for him."[19]

That's also what I have been trying to do in this book: to create for you as the reader the experience that will make it possible for us to communicate. My understanding of American politics is built upon what I know about how our leaders live and think and act and about how that affects the lives of others. So as part of our study of the presidency, we looked at the life of the president. And elsewhere we've used quotes from presidents to explain how they saw things. The more you know of what it's like to be president, the more likely you'll be able to understand why presidents act as they do.

If that's *all* you know, it probably won't occur to you to question what presidents do. So to help you get a broader perspective, we look at the experiences and views of other political figures and ordinary citizens. Having a number of different outlooks to examine, you will be better able to develop your own views.

So as author of this book I have relied on the same insight that allowed Alinsky to organize the poor in Chicago and Rochester. But it's also the same insight that allowed Nixon to fool most of the American people for a long time about his actual involvement in Watergate. It is a powerful and potentially dangerous insight—but one that can make the difference between success and failure in a leader or in an activist for political change.

The Role of Information— and Its Control

The most compelling kind of experience is, of course, actually living through something. People who have never fought in a war will never know fully what war is like, no matter how many movies they see or books they read or conversations they have about it. But the actual direct experiences each of us—including presidents—can have are limited. So most of us depend most of the time on

[18]R. D. Laing, *The Politics of Experience* (New York: Ballantine paperback, 1968), p. 95.

[19]Saul Alinsky, *Rules for Radicals* (New York: Vintage paperback, 1972), p. 85.

other people's accounts of their own experience. Another way of putting this is to say that most of our experience consists of getting information from other people.

We may choose to accept or reject the information we get from others. If we accept a certain piece of information, we are recognizing the person who gives (or sells) it to us as an authority. If we find people telling us conflicting things, and they are all trying to get us to agree with them, we are in the midst of a political dispute. That's why in earlier chapters we defined politics as *dispute over claims to the authority to describe, interpret, or explain reality.*

People who can convince us to accept their views, their information, have authority for us. They therefore have effective, recognized political power—at least until they are challenged. E. E. Schattschneider puts this point another way, asserting that "the definition of the alternatives is the supreme instrument of power."

> In the competition of conflicts . . . *all depends on what we want most.* The outcome is not determined merely by what people want but by their priorities. What they want more becomes the enemy of what they want less. Politics is therefore something like choosing a wife, rather than shopping in a five-and-ten-cent store.
>
> The conflict of conflicts explains some things about politics that have long puzzled scholars. Political conflict is not like an intercollegiate debate in which the opponents agree in advance on a definition of the issues. As a matter of fact, *the definition of the alternatives is the supreme instrument of power;* the antagonists can rarely agree on what the issues are because power is involved in the definition. He who determines what politics is about runs the country, because the definition of the alternatives is the choice of conflicts, and the choice of conflicts allocates power.[20]

This observation indicates the important role information plays in politics—and how vital it is to control information. That's why presidents make speeches to the nation and hold press conferences while they're in office—and write their memoirs when they leave office. But it's also why activists for political change hold demonstrations, lobby, or even resort to violence. The object is to control the information other people—from presidents to plumbers, from senators to sanitation workers—get and thereby to shape their experience and

so their behavior.[21] But different people use information differently, and that brings us to the third and final lesson.

The Wide Range of Roles People May Play

You can talk about people's roles in many different ways. For politics, the major roles are these five: organizer, leader, participant, follower, and subject.

The organizer usually works behind the scenes while the leader works in public. Alinsky, himself an organizer, once wrote:

> The ego of the organizer is stronger and more monumental than the ego of the leader. The leader is driven by the desire for power, while the organizer is driven by the desire to create. The organizer is in a true sense reaching for the highest level for which man can reach—to create, to be a "great creator," to play God.[22]

Alinksy asserted that the organizer must have curiosity, irreverence, imagination, a sense of humor, "a bit of a blurred vision of a better world" (so he or she knows where to try to go), "an organized personality" (so that he or she can function in the midst of disorganization and irrationality), ego, and a free and open mind. "Change comes from power," he reminded us, "and power comes from organization. In order to act, people must get together."[23]

We normally expect our presidents to be both leaders and organizers. We have seen in our discussion of the presidency and the bureaucracy that a president has a unique ability to organize the government because he or she alone sits at the information center. But we also noted how difficult it is in practice to act effectively because even the president has no monopoly on information in our system.

Members of Congress, bureaucrats, experts, journalists, and ordinary citizens all have information the government may want or need. Also, each of these groups or individual members may influence the experience of others, including the

---

[20]E. E. Schattschneider, *The Semisovereign People* (New York: Holt, Rinehart & Winston, 1961), p. 68.

[21]For an argument in favor of a new type of democratic system based heavily upon access to information, see Michael Margolis, *Viable Democracy* (New York: Penguin, 1979). See also John G. Kemeny, "Saving American Democracy: The Lessons of Three Mile Island," *Technology Review,* June–July 1980, pp. 65–75.

[22]Alinsky, *Rules for Radicals,* p. 61.

[23]Ibid., p. 113.

president, by the way they act. So potentially, everyone in our system has power. Everyone can be a politician.

A NEW TYPE OF DEMOCRACY IN AMERICA?

The realization that everyone can be a politician in America is not necessarily good news. By now most Americans have become rather skeptical of politicians, for one thing, and some may feel we already have enough. For another, the disappointing rate of participation in politics shown by so many Americans fosters skepticism about the likelihood that people actually will become politicians.

If popular action is to improve our politics and make our system more democratic, three things must be developed: a democratic consciousness, a democratic conscience, and democratic practice. Let's look at each in turn.

A Democratic Consciousness

Everyone has an understanding of political reality. We refer to this understanding as one's "political consciousness," or awareness. Some people's understandings are better than other people's in terms of their contributions to the strength of democracy.

A society in which everyone takes the authority of the leaders for granted, no matter how reliable that authority may be, is not very conducive to strong democracy. The strength of democracy depends on the people's ability to see how dependent they are upon authorities and then develop ways to find multiple authorities.

If there are multiple authorities, there will be political competition. There will also be more opportunities for people to participate in, and to matter in, politics. So by a democratic consciousness, we mean a widespread understanding of the necessity not only for authority but also for competing authorities—for active politics.

A Democratic Conscience

In our culture, children are usually told that their conscience will bother them if they don't behave properly. Conscience refers to our sense of responsibility and the values we have learned, or "inter-

nalized." For a democracy to flourish, its citizens must internalize beliefs that emphasize the value of other people and their views and the usefulness of democratic competition.

A major weakness of American democracy until now has been the pervasiveness of the belief that "everybody gets what he or she deserves"—or, put another way, that we are not responsible for others. The government may try to meet the needs of the minorities and the outsiders in the society. But unless the people themselves share a concern for the welfare of the members of these groups, the government will find it has neither the money nor the personnel to implement such a policy. So a widespread democratic conscience is also essential.[24]

Democratic Practice

Consciousness and conscience are still insufficient. No democracy in our present world can long survive without what we might call *democratic practice*. By this we mean action by citizens that contributes to the transformation of society. It is not enough to understand what needs to be done. One must also be able to figure out how it can be undertaken successfully. That is what we mean by democratic practice—experience in acting effectively to further democratize society and improve the fate of those less fortunate.

Reality Construction and Reality Creation

The social sciences have recently helped us to understand two important fundamental social processes. The first of these is often called *reality construction*. This is the technical term for the notion that each of us has his or her own image of reality. Each of us "constructs reality" in our mind and then acts on the basis of this construction. Much of that construction of reality is a product of the influence of authorities, and much of it is simply learned from our families, friends, and schools.[25]

---

[24]For a thoughtful study, see Robert N. Bellah et al., *Habits of the Heart: Individualism and Commitment in American Life* (Berkeley: Univ. of California Press, 1985).
[25]See Peter Berger and Thomas Luckmann, *The Social Construction of Reality* (Garden City, NY: Doubleday Anchor paperback, 1966), Burkhart Holzner, *Reality Construction in Society*, rev. ed. (Cambridge, MA: Schenkman paperback, 1972), and Owen Barfield, *Saving the Appearances* (New York: Harcourt, Brace, Jovanovich, n.d.).

But we also know that people act in accord with their beliefs and expectations about the nature of reality. And we have research showing that people tend to respond to the expectations others have of them.[26] What this means in practical terms is that neither the world nor other people's behavior is fixed and unchanging. With carefully designed strategies one can change others' behavior by changing their experiences.

What this then means to us is that the range of choices open to us is greater than we are usually led to expect. To put it another way, there is a wider range of *choices openable to us* to reconstruct politics democratically—to create a new political reality. *Reality creation* is the second social process important to understand.

Guidelines for Creating the Future

Everyone must decide for himself or herself how he or she wishes things to change and what he or she believes is important to do. No hard and fast projects can yet be recommended in a book such as this. Still, there are certain guidelines for thinking and acting that emerge from the analysis thus far. Here are some of the more important ones. You can develop more.

- Regenerate the ethical sense that gives us objectives and responsibilities.
- Improve sources of information so that they report the needs, desires, possibilities, and projects of ordinary people and leaders everywhere, not just of government figures.
- Foster creative analysis of problems and opportunities, especially by those most involved.
- Regain the optimism about what we can do that until recently has always been part of the American character.
- Work where it will work in politics—especially locally—in order to achieve successes, however limited, that protect against disenchantment.
- Remember the relevance of the extragovernmental sphere—especially the economic possibilities and the informational opportunities available through the use of the media and education.

- Devise new imaginative strategies and tactics that confront the powers that be where they are vulnerable, but do so in constructive ways, as suggested by Alinsky and other creative activists.[27]

OPPORTUNITIES FOR GUIDING POLITICS

Where can we put these and other guidelines to work? The opportunities are many, once we are willing and able to look beyond conventional politics. The leading opportunity now is in community organization, which we have discussed in previous chapters. But even the young have special opportunities as well in learning, leading, and teaching politics. If you have found this book encouraging—or if you've found it infuriating—then a career in politics may be for you. Most people who work in politics start at the local level. Some then go on to state and even national politics. Most work either in campaigns or in community organizing or as lobbyists, but some, of course, become candidates.

But there are also more strictly pedagogical opportunities for you if you are interested in politics. You might become a teacher of political science in a high school or a college.[28]

Much of what is to be done now, according to the argument of this epilogue, is in a sense pedagogical: working to heighten people's consciousness so that they can learn more about politics as it actually works and then act more effectively in politics. In a sense, then, politics itself is becoming more pedagogical. This also means that we never know enough about politics to stop learning. Or to stop helping others to learn.

---

[26]See, for example, Robert Rosenthal and Lenore Jacobson, *Pygmalion in the Classroom* (New York: Holt, Rinehart & Winston, 1968). See also Russell H. Jones, *Self-Fulfilling Prophesies: Social, Psychological, and Physiological Effects of Expectancies* (Hillsdale, NJ: Erlbaum, 1977). And for a more comprehensive application of this insight to politics, see David V. Edwards, *Creating a New World Politics* (New York: McKay, 1973).

[27]See also, for example, Paulo Freire, *Pedagogy of the Oppressed* (New York: Seabury paperback, 1972); Edgar S. Cahn and Barry A. Passett, eds., *Citizen Participation: Effecting Community Change* (New York: Praeger, 1971); Bruce Stokes, *Helping Ourselves: Local Solutions to Global Problems* (New York: Norton paperback, 1981); and, for a guide to other readings, Michael Marien, *Societal Directions and Alternatives* (Lafayette, NY: Information for Policy Design, 1976). Among current sources of such analyses are *CoEvolution Quarterly* (subscriptions $18 a year from P.O. Box 428, Sausalito, CA 94966); *New Options* (a monthly newsletter of ideas about social change, available for $25 a year from P.O. Box 19324, Washington, DC 20036; and the *Utne Reader* (a bimonthly "alternative reader's digest" available for $18 a year from P.O. Box 1974, Marion, OH 43305).

[28]For a history of the discipline, see Albert Somit and Joseph Tanenhaus, *American Political Science* (New York: Atherton, 1964). Ask your political science or government department for a copy of a booklet by Mary H. Curzan, *Careers and the Study of Political Science: A Guide for Undergraduates*, available from the American Political Science Association, 1527 New Hampshire Ave. NW, Washington, DC 20036.

THE CONSTITUTION OF THE UNITED STATES

(Preamble)

We the People of the United States, in Order to form a more perfect Union, establish Justice, insure domestic Tranquility, provide for the common defence, promote the general Welfare, and secure the Blessings of Liberty to ourselves and our Posterity, do ordain and establish this Constitution for the United States of America.

ARTICLE I

(Legislative powers)

Section 1 All legislative Powers herein granted shall be vested in a Congress of the United States, which shall consist of a Senate and House of Representatives.

(The House of Representatives, how constituted, apportionment, impeachment power)

Section 2 The House of Representatives shall be composed of Members chosen every second Year by the People of the several States and the Electors in each State shall have the Qualifications requisite for Electors of the most numerous Branch of the State Legislature.

No Person shall be a Representative who shall not have attained to the Age of twenty five Years, and been seven Years a Citizen of the United States, and who shall not, when elected, be an Inhabitant of that State in which he shall be chosen.

Representatives and direct [Taxes][1] shall be apportioned among the several States which may be included within this Union, according to their respective Numbers, [which shall be determined by adding to the whole Number of free Persons, including those bound to Service for a Term of Years, and excluding Indians not taxed, three fifths of all other Persons.][2] The actual Enumeration shall be made within three Years after the first Meeting of the Congress of the United States, and within every subsequent Term of ten Years, in such Manner as they shall by Law direct. The Number of Representatives shall not exceed one for every thirty Thousand, but each State shall have at Least one Representative; and until such enumeration shall be made, the State of New Hampshire shall be entitled to chuse three; Massachusetts eight; Rhode Island and Providence Plantations one;

This text of the Constitution follows the engrossed (formally handwritten) copy signed by General Washington and the deputies from twelve states. Original spelling, capitalization, and punctuation have been retained. Brackets within the text indicate passages altered by subsequent amendments.

---

[1]Modified by the Sixteenth Amendment.
[2]Replaced by Section 2 of the Fourteenth Amendment.

Connecticut five; New-York six; New Jersey four; Pennsylvania eight; Delaware one; Maryland six; Virginia ten; North Carolina five; South Carolina five; and Georgia three.

When vacancies happen in the Representation from any State, the Executive Authority thereof shall issue Writs of Election to fill such Vacancies.

The House of Representatives shall chuse their Speaker and other Officers; and shall have the sole Power of Impeachment.

(The Senate, how constituted, impeachment trials)

Section 3 The Senate of the United States shall be composed of two Senators from each State, [chosen by the Legislature thereof,][3] for six Years; and each Senator shall have one Vote.

Immediately after they shall be assembled in Consequence of the first Election, they shall be divided as equally as may be into three Classes. The Seats of the Senators of the first Class shall be vacated at the Expiration of the second Year, of the second Class at the Expiration of the fourth Year, and of the third Class at the Expiration of the sixth Year, so that one third may be chosen every second Year; [and if Vacancies happen by Resignation, or otherwise, during the Recess of the Legislature of any State, the Executive thereof may make temporary Appointments until the next Meeting of the Legislature, which shall then fill such Vacancies.][4]

No Person shall be a Senator who shall not have attained to the Age of thirty Years, and been nine Years a Citizen of the United States, and who shall not, when elected, be an Inhabitant of that State in which he shall be chosen.

The Vice President of the United States shall be President of the Senate, but shall have no Vote, unless they be equally divided.

The Senate shall chuse their other Officers, and also a President pro tempore, in the Absence of the Vice President, or when he shall exercise the Office of President of the United States.

The Senate shall have the sole Power to try all Impeachments. When sitting for that Purpose, they shall be on Oath or Affirmation. When the President of the United States is tried, the Chief Justice shall preside: And no Person shall be convicted without the concurrence of two thirds of the Members present.

Judgment in Cases of Impeachment shall not extend further than to removal from Office, and disqualification to hold and enjoy an Office of honor, Trust or Profit under the United States: but the Party convicted shall nevertheless be liable and subject to Indictment, Trial, Judgment and Punishment, according to Law.

(Election of senators and representatives)

Section 4 The Times, Places and Manner of holding Elections for Senators and Representatives, shall be prescribed in each state by the Legislature thereof; but the Congress may at any time by Law make or alter such Regulation, except as to the Places of chusing Senators.

The Congress shall assemble at least once in every Year, and such Meeting shall [be on the first Monday in December,][5] unless they shall by Law appoint a different Day.

(Powers and duties of the houses of Congress: quorum, rules of proceedings, journals, adjournment)

Section 5 Each House shall be the Judge of the Elections, Returns and Qualifications of its own Members, and a Majority of each shall constitute a Quorum to do Business; but a smaller Number may adjourn from day to day, and may be authorized to compel the Attendance of absent Members, in such Manner, and under such Penalties as each House may provide.

Each House may determine the Rules of its Proceedings, punish its Members for disorderly Behaviour, and, with the Concurrence of two thirds, expel a Member.

Each House shall keep a Journal of its Proceedings, and from time to time publish the same, excepting such Parts as may in their Judgment require Secrecy; and the Yeas and Nays of the Members of either House on any question shall, at the Desire of one fifth of those Present, be entered on the Journal.

Neither House, during the Session of Congress, shall, without the Consent of the other, adjourn for more than three days, nor to any other Place than that in which the two Houses shall be sitting.

(Compensation and privileges of senators and representatives)

Section 6 The Senators and Representatives shall receive a Compensation for their Services, to be ascertained by Law, and paid out of the Treasury of the United States. They shall in all Cases, except Treason, Felony, and Breach of the Peace, be privileged from Arrest during their attendance at the Session of their respective Houses, and in going to and returning from the same; and for any Speech or Debate in either House, they shall not be questioned in any other Place.

No Senator or Representative shall, during the Time for which he was elected, be appointed to any civil Office under the Authority of the United States, which shall have been created, or the Emoluments whereof shall have been encreased during such time; and no Person holding any Office under the United States, shall be a Member of either House during his Continuance in Office.

(Legislative procedures: bills and resolutions)

Section 7 All Bills for raising Revenue shall originate in the House of Representatives; but the Senate may propose or concur with Amendments as on other Bills.

Every Bill which shall have passed the House of Representatives and the Senate shall, before it become a Law, be presented to the President of the United States;

---

[3]Superseded by clause 1 of the Seventeenth Amendment.
[4]Modified by clause 2 of the Seventeenth Amendment.

[5]Superseded by Section 2 of the Twentieth Amendment.

If he approve he shall sign it, but if not he shall return it, with his Objections to that House in which it shall have originated, who shall enter the Objections at large on their Journal, and proceed to reconsider it. If after such Reconsideration two thirds of that House shall agree to pass the Bill, it shall be sent, together with the Objections, to the other House, by which it shall likewise be reconsidered, and if approved by two thirds of that House, it shall become a Law. But in all such Cases the Votes of both Houses shall be determined by yeas and Nays, and the Names of the Persons voting for and against the Bill shall be entered on the Journal of each House respectively. If any Bill shall not be returned by the President within ten Days (Sundays excepted) after it shall have been presented to him, the Same shall be a Law, in like Manner as if he had signed it, unless the Congress by their Adjournment prevent its Return, in which Case it shall not be a Law.

Every Order, Resolution, or Vote to which the Concurrence of the Senate and House of Representatives may be necessary (except on a question of Adjournment) shall be presented to the President of the United States; and before the Same shall take Effect, shall be approved by him, or being disapproved by him shall be repassed by two thirds of the Senate and House of Representatives, according to the Rules and Limitations prescribed in the Case of a Bill.

(Powers of Congress)

Section 8 The Congress shall have Power To lay and collect Taxes, Duties, Imposts and Excises, to pay the Debts and provide for the common Defence and general Welfare of the United States; but all Duties, Imposts and Excises shall be uniform throughout the United States.

To borrow Money on the credit of the United States;

To regulate Commerce with foreign Nations, and among the several States, and with the Indian Tribes;

To establish an uniform Rule of Naturalization, and uniform Laws on the subject of Bankruptcies throughout the United States;

To coin Money, regulate the Value thereof, and of foreign Coin, and fix the Standard of Weights and Measures;

To provide for the Punishment of counterfeiting the Securities and current Coin of the United States;

To establish Post Offices and post Roads;

To promote the Progress of Science and useful Arts, by securing for limited Times to Authors and Inventors the exclusive Right to their respective Writings and Discoveries;

To constitute Tribunals, inferior to the supreme Court;

To define and punish Piracies and Felonies committed on the high Seas, and Offences against the law of Nations;

To declare War, grant Letters of Marque and Reprisal, and make Rules concerning Captures on Land and Water;

To raise and support Armies, but no Appropriation of Money to that Use shall be for a longer Term than two Years;

To provide and maintain a Navy;

To make Rules for the Government and Regulation of the land and naval Forces;

To provide for calling forth the Militia to execute the Laws of the Union, suppress Insurrections and repel Invasions;

To provide for organizing, arming, and disciplining, the Militia, and for governing such Part of them as may be employed in the Service of the United States, reserving to the States respectively, the Appointment of the Officers, and the Authority of training the Militia according to the discipline prescribed by Congress;

To exercise exclusive Legislation in all Cases whatsoever, over such District (not exceeding ten Miles square) as may, by Cession of particular States, and the Acceptance of Congress, become the Seat of Government of the United States, and to exercise like Authority over all Places purchased by the Consent of the Legislature of the State in which the Same shall be, for the Erection of Forts, Magazines, Arsenals, dock-Yards, and other needful Buildings;—And

To make all Laws which shall be necessary and proper for carrying into Execution the foregoing Powers, and all other Powers vested by this Constitution in the Government of the United States, or in any Department or Officer thereof.

(Restrictions on powers of Congress)

Section 9 The Migration or Importation of such Persons as any of the States now existing shall think proper to admit, shall not be prohibited by the Congress prior to the Year one thousand eight hundred and eight, but a Tax or duty may be imposed on such Importation, not exceeding ten dollars for each Person.

The Privilege of the Writ of Habeas Corpus shall not be suspended, unless when in Cases of Rebellion or Invasion the public Safety may require it.

No Bill of Attainder or ex post facto Law shall be passed.

No Capitation, or other direct, Tax shall be laid, unless in Proportion to the Census or Enumeration herein before directed to be taken.

No Tax or Duty shall be laid on Articles exported from any State.

No Preference shall be given by any Regulation of Commerce or Revenue to the Ports of one State over those of another: nor shall Vessels bound to, or from, one State, be obliged to enter, clear, or pay Duties in another.

No Money shall be drawn from the Treasury, but in Consequence of Appropriations made by Law, and a regular Statement and Account of the Receipts and Expenditures of all public Money shall be published from time to time.

No Title of Nobility shall be granted by the United States: And no Person holding any Office of Profit or Trust under them, shall, without the Consent of the Congress, accept of any present, Emolument, Office, or

Title, of any kind whatever, from any King, Prince, or foreign State.

Section 10 No State shall enter into any Treaty, Alliance, or Confederation; grant Letters of Marque and Reprisal; coin Money, emit Bills of Credit; make any Thing but gold and silver Coin a Tender in Payment of Debts; pass any Bill of Attainder, ex post facto Law, or Law impairing the Obligation of Contracts, or grant any Title of Nobility.

No State shall, without the Consent of the Congress, lay any Imposts or Duties on Imports or Exports, except what may be absolutely necessary for exercising its inspection Laws: and the net Produce of all Duties and Imposts, laid by any State on Imports or Exports, shall be for the Use of the Treasury of the United States; and all such Laws shall be subject to the Revision and Controul of the Congress.

No State shall, without the Consent of Congress, lay any Duty of Tonnage, keep Troops, or Ships of War in time of Peace, enter into any Agreement or Compact with another State, or with a foreign Power, or engage in War, unless actually invaded, or in such imminent Danger as will not admit of delay.

ARTICLE II

(Executive power, election and qualifications of the president)

Section 1 The executive Power shall be vested in a President of the United States of America. He shall hold his Office during the Term of four Years, and together with the Vice President, chosen for the same Term, be elected, as follows:

Each State shall appoint, in such Manner as the Legislature thereof may direct, a Number of Electors, equal to the whole Number of Senators and Representatives to which the State may be entitled in the Congress: but no Senator or Representative, or Person holding an Office of Trust or Profit under the United States, shall be appointed an Elector.

[The Electors shall meet in their respective States, and vote by Ballot for two Persons, of whom one at least shall not be an Inhabitant of the same State with themselves. And they shall make a List of all the Persons voted for, and of the Number of Votes for each; which List they shall sign and certify, and transmit sealed to the Seat of the Government of the United States, directed to the President of the Senate. The President of the Senate shall, in the Presence of the Senate and House of Representatives, open all the Certificates, and the Votes shall then be counted. The Person having the greatest number of Votes shall be the President, if such Number be a Majority of the whole Number of Electors appointed; and if there be more than one who have such Majority, and have an equal Number of Votes, then the House of Representatives shall immediately chuse by Ballot one of them for President; and if no Person have a Majority, then from the five highest on the List the said House

shall in like Manner chuse the President. But in chusing the President, the Votes shall be taken by States, the Representation from each State having one Vote; A quorum for this Purpose shall consist of a Member or Members from two thirds of the States, and a Majority of all the States shall be necessary to a Choice. In every Case, after the Choice of the President, the Person having the greatest Number of Votes of the Electors shall be the Vice President. But if there should remain two or more who have equal Votes, the Senate shall chuse from them by Ballot the Vice President.][6]

The Congress may determine the Time of chusing the Electors, and the Day on which they shall give their Votes; which Day shall be the same throughout the United States.

No Person except a natural born Citizen, or a Citizen of the United States, at the time of the Adoption of this Constitution, shall be eligible to the Office of President, neither shall any Person be eligible to that Office who shall not have attained to the Age of thirty five Years, and been fourteen Years a Resident within the United States.

[In Case of the Removal of the President from Office, or of his Death, Resignation or Inability to discharge the Powers and Duties of the said Office, the Same shall devolve on the Vice President, and the Congress may by Law provide for the Case of Removal, Death, Resignation or Inability, both of the President and Vice President, declaring what Officer shall then act as President, and such Officer shall act accordingly, until the Disability be removed, or a President shall be elected.][7]

The President shall, at stated Times, receive for his Services, a Compensation, which shall neither be encreased nor diminished during the Period for which he shall have been elected, and he shall not receive within that Period any other Emolument from the United States, or any of them.

Before he enter on the Execution of his Office, he shall take the following Oath or Affirmation:—"I do solemnly swear (or affirm) that I will faithfully execute the Office of the President of the United States, and will to the best of my Ability, preserve, protect and defend the Constitution of the United States."

(Powers of the president)

Section 2 The President shall be Commander in Chief of the Army and Navy of the United States, and of the Militia of the several States, when called into the actual Service of the United States; he may require the Opinion, in writing, of the principal Officer in each of the executive Departments, upon any Subject relating to the Duties of their respective Offices, and he shall have Power to Grant Reprieves and Pardons for Offences against the United States, except in Cases of Impeachment.

He shall have Power, by and with the Advice and

---

[6]Superseded by the Twelfth Amendment.
[7]Modified by the Twenty-fifth Amendment.

Consent of the Senate, to make Treaties, provided two thirds of the Senators present concur; and he shall nominate, and by and with the Advice and Consent of the Senate, shall appoint Ambassadors, other public Ministers and Consuls, Judges of the supreme Court, and all other Officers of the United States, whose appointments are not herein otherwise provided for, and which shall be established by Law; but the Congress may by Law vest the Appointment of such inferior Officers, as they think proper, in the President alone, in the Courts of Law, or in the Heads of Departments.

The President shall have Power to fill up all Vacancies that may happen during the Recess of the Senate, by granting Commissions which shall expire at the End of their next Session.

(Powers and duties of the president)

Section 3 He shall from time to time give to the Congress Information of the State of the Union, and recommend to their Consideration such Measures as he shall judge necessary and expedient; he may, on extraordinary Occasions, convene both Houses, or either of them, and in Case of Disagreement between them, with Respect to the Time of Adjournment, he may adjourn them to such Time as he shall think proper; he shall receive Ambassadors and other public Ministers; he shall take Care that the Laws be faithfully executed, and shall Commission all the Officers of the United States.

(Impeachment)

Section 4 The President, Vice President and all civil Officers of the United States, shall be removed from Office on Impeachment for, and Conviction of, Treason, Bribery, or other high Crimes and Misdemeanors.

ARTICLE III

(Judicial power, courts, and judges)

Section 1 The judicial Power of the United States, shall be vested in one supreme Court, and in such inferior Courts as the Congress may from time to time ordain and establish. The Judges, both of the supreme and inferior Courts, shall hold their Offices during good Behaviour, and shall, at stated Times, receive for their Services, a Compensation, which shall not be diminished during their Continuance in Office.

(Jurisdiction)

Section 2 The judicial Power shall extend to all Cases, in Law and Equity, arising under this Constitution, the Laws of the United States, and Treaties made, or which shall be made, under their Authority;—to all Cases affecting Ambassadors, other public Ministers and Consuls;—to all Cases of admiralty and maritime Jurisdiction;—to Controversies to which the United States shall be a Party;—to Controversies between two or more States;—[between a State and Citizens of another State;][8]—between Citizens of different States,—between Citizens of the same State claiming Lands under

Grants of different States, [and between a State, or the Citizens thereof, and foreign States, Citizens or Subjects.][9]

In all Cases affecting Ambassadors, other public Ministers and Consuls, and those in which a State shall be Party, the supreme Court shall have original Jurisdiction. In all the other Cases before mentioned, the supreme Court shall have appellate Jurisdiction, both as to Law and Fact, with such Exceptions, and under such Regulations as the Congress shall make.

The Trial of all Crimes, except in Cases of Impeachment, shall be by Jury; and such Trial shall be held in the State where the said Crimes shall have been committed; but when not committed within any State, the Trial shall be at such Place or Places as the Congress may by Law have directed.

(Treason)

Section 3 Treason against the United States, shall consist only in levying War against them, or in adhering to their Enemies, giving them Aid and Comfort. No Person shall be convicted of Treason unless on the Testimony of two Witnesses to the same overt Act, or on Confession in open Court.

The Congress shall have Power to declare the Punishment of Treason, but no Attainder of Treason shall work Corruption of Blood, or Forfeiture except during the Life of the Person attainted.

ARTICLE IV

(Full faith and credit clause)

Section 1 Full Faith and Credit shall be given in each State to the public Acts, Records, and judicial Proceedings of every other State. And the Congress may by general Laws prescribe the Manner in which such Acts, Records and Proceedings shall be proved, and the Effect thereof.

(Privileges and immunities of citizens, fugitives)

Section 2 The Citizens of each State shall be entitled to all Privileges and Immunities of Citizens in the several States.

A Person charged in any State with Treason, Felony, or other Crime, who shall flee from Justice, and be found in another State, shall on Demand of the executive Authority of the State from which he fled, be delivered up, to be removed to the State having Jurisdiction of the Crime.

[No Person held to Service or Labour in one State, under the Laws thereof, escaping into another, shall, in Consequence of any Law or Regulation therein, be discharged from such Service or Labour, but shall be delivered up on Claim of the Party to whom such Service or Labour may be due.][10]

(Admission of new states)

Section 3 New States may be admitted by the Congress into this Union; but no new State shall be formed or

---

[8]Modified by the Eleventh Amendment.

[9]See the Eleventh Amendment.
[10]Superseded by the Thirteenth Amendment.

erected within the Jurisdiction of any other State, nor any state be formed by the Junction of two or more States, or Parts of States, without the Consent of the Legislatures of the States concerned as well as of the Congress.

The Congress shall have Power to dispose of and make all needful Rules and Regulations respecting the Territory or other Property belonging to the United States; and nothing in this Constitution shall be so construed as to Prejudice any Claims of the United States, or of any particular State.

(Guarantee of republican form of government)

Section 4 The United States shall guarantee to every State in this Union a Republican Form of Government, and shall protect each of them against Invasion; and on Application of the Legislature, or of the Executive (when the Legislature cannot be convened) against domestic Violence.

ARTICLE V

(Amending the Constitution)

The Congress, whenever two thirds of both Houses shall deem it necessary, shall propose Amendments to this Constitution, or, on the Application of the Legislatures of two thirds of the several States, shall call a Convention for proposing Amendments, which, in either Case, shall be valid to all Intents and Purposes, as Part of this Constitution, when ratified by the Legislatures of three fourths of the several States, or by Conventions in three fourths thereof, as the one or the other Mode of Ratification may be proposed by the Congress; Provided that no Amendment which may be made prior to the Year One thousand eight hundred and eight shall in any Manner affect the first and fourth Clauses in the Ninth Section of the first Article; and that no State, without its Consent, shall be deprived of its equal Suffrage in the Senate.

ARTICLE VI

(Debts, supremacy, oaths)

All Debts contracted and Engagements entered into, before the Adoption of this Constitution, shall be as valid against the United States under this Constitution, as under the Confederation.

This Constitution, and the Laws of the United States which shall be made in Pursuance thereof: and all Treaties made, or which shall be made, under the Authority of the United States, shall be the supreme Law of the Land; and the Judges in every State shall be bound thereby, any Thing in the Constitution or Laws of any State to the Contrary notwithstanding.

The Senators and Representatives before mentioned, and the Members of the several State Legislatures, and all executive and judicial Officers, both of the United States and of the several States, shall be bound by Oath or Affirmation, to support this Constitution; but no religious Test shall ever be required as a Qualification to any Office or public Trust under the United States.

ARTICLE VII

(Ratification)

The Ratification of the Conventions of nine States, shall be sufficient for the Establishment of this Constitution between the States so ratifying the Same.

Done in Convention by the Unanimous Consent of the States present the Seventeenth Day of September in the Year of our Lord one thousand seven hundred and Eighty seven and of the Independence of the United States of America the Twelfth. *In witness* whereof We have hereunto subscribed our Names.

THE AMENDMENTS

ARTICLES IN ADDITION TO, AND AMENDMENT OF, THE CONSTITUTION OF THE UNITED STATES OF AMERICA, PROPOSED BY CONGRESS, AND RATIFIED BY THE LEGISLATURES OF THE SEVERAL STATES PURSUANT TO THE FIFTH ARTICLE OF THE ORIGINAL CONSTITUTION.

(The first ten amendments—known as the Bill of Rights—were passed by Congress on September 25, 1789. They were ratified by three-fourths of the states by December 15, 1791.)

AMENDMENT I

(Freedom of religion, the press, and assembly, and right of petition)

Congress shall make no law respecting an establishment of religion, or prohibiting the free exercise thereof; or abridging the freedom of speech, or of the press; or the right of the people peaceably to assemble, and to petition the Government for a redress of grievances.

AMENDMENT II

(Militia and the right to keep and bear arms)

A well regulated Militia, being necessary to the security of a free State, the right of the people to keep and bear Arms shall not be infringed.

AMENDMENT III

(Quartering of soldiers)

No Soldier shall, in time of peace, be quartered in any house, without the consent of the Owner, nor in time of war, but in a manner to be prescribed by law.

AMENDMENT IV

(Protection against unreasonable search and seizure)

The right of the people to be secure in their persons, houses, papers, and effects, against unreasonable searches and seizures, shall not be violated, and no Warrants shall issue, but upon probable cause, supported by Oath or affirmation, and particularly describing the place to be searched, and the persons or things to be seized.

AMENDMENT V

(Grand juries, double jeopardy, self-incrimination, due process, and eminent domain)

No person shall be held to answer for a capital or otherwise infamous crime, unless on a presentment or indictment of a Grand Jury, except in cases arising in the land or naval forces, or in the Militia, when in actual service in time of War or public danger; nor shall any person be subject for the same offence to be twice put in jeopardy of life or limb; nor shall be compelled in any criminal case to be a witness against himself, nor be deprived of life, liberty, or property, without due process of law; nor shall private property be taken for public use, without just compensation.

AMENDMENT VI

(Criminal court procedures)

In all criminal prosecutions, the accused shall enjoy the right to a speedy and public trial, by an impartial jury of the State and district wherein the crime shall have been committed, which district shall have been previously ascertained by law, and to be informed of the nature and cause of the accusation; to be confronted with the witnesses against him; to have compulsory process for obtaining witnesses in his favor, and to have the Assistance of Counsel for his defence.

AMENDMENT VII

(Trial by jury in common-law cases)

In suits at common law, where the value in controversy shall exceed twenty dollars, the right of trial by jury shall be preserved, and no fact tried by jury, shall be otherwise reexamined in any Court of the United States, than according to the rules of the common law.

AMENDMENT VIII

(Bail, fines, and cruel and unusual punishments)

Excessive bail shall not be required, nor excessive fines imposed, nor cruel and unusual punishments inflicted.

AMENDMENT IX

(Retention of rights by the people)

The enumeration in the Constitution, of certain rights, shall not be construed to deny or disparage others retained by the people.

AMENDMENT X

(Reserved powers of the states)

The powers not delegated to the United States by the Constitution; nor prohibited by it to the States, are reserved to the States respectively, or to the people.

AMENDMENT XI

(Proposed on March 4, 1794, ratification completed on February 7, 1795; suits against the states)

The Judicial power of the United States shall not be construed to extend to any suit in law or equity, commenced or prosecuted against one of the United States by Citizens of another State, or by Citizens or Subjects of any Foreign State.

AMENDMENT XII

(Proposed on December 9, 1803, ratification completed on June 15, 1804; election of the president and vice-president)

The Electors shall meet in their respective States and vote by ballot for President and Vice-President, one of whom, at least, shall not be an inhabitant of the same State with themselves; they shall name in their ballots the person voted for as President, and in distinct ballots the person voted for as Vice-President, and they shall make distinct lists of all persons voted for as President, and of all persons voted for as Vice-President, and of the number of votes for each, which lists they shall sign and certify, and transmit sealed to the seat of the government of the United States, directed to the President of the Senate;— The President of the Senate shall, in the presence of the Senate and House of Representatives, open all the certificates and the votes shall then be counted;—The person having the greatest number of votes for President, shall be the President, if such number be a majority of the whole number of Electors appointed; and if no person have such majority, then from the persons having the highest numbers not exeeding three on the list of those voted for as President, the House of Representatives shall choose immediately, by ballot, the President. But in choosing the President, the votes shall be taken by states, the representation from each state having one vote; a quorum for this purpose shall consist of a member or members from two-thirds of the states, and a majority of all the states shall be necessary to a choice. [And if the House of Representatives shall not choose a President whenever the right of choice shall devolve upon them, before the fourth day of March next following, then the Vice-President shall act as President, as in the case of the death or other constitutional disability of the President.][11] The person having the greatest number of votes as Vice-President, shall be the Vice-President, if such number be a majority of the whole number of Electors appointed, and if no Person have a majority, then from the two highest numbers on the list, the Senate shall choose the Vice-President; a quorum for the purpose shall consist of two-thirds of the whole number of Senators, and a majority of the whole number shall be necessary to a choice. But no person constitutionally ineligible to the office of the President shall be eligible to that of Vice-President of the United States.

---

[11]Superseded by Section 3 of the Twentieth Amendment.

AMENDMENT XIII

(Proposed on January 31, 1865, ratification completed on December 6, 1865; Abolition of slavery)

Section 1 Neither slavery nor involuntary servitude, except as a punishment for crime whereof the party shall have been duly convicted, shall exist within the United States, or any place subject to their jurisdiction.

(Power to enforce this article)

Section 2 Congress shall have power to enforce this article by appropriate legislation.

AMENDMENT XIV

(Proposed on June 13, 1866, ratification completed on July 9, 1868; Citizenship rights, due process, equal protection of the laws)

Section 1 All persons born or naturalized in the United States, and subject to the jurisdiction thereof, are citizens of the United States and of the State wherein they reside. No State shall make or enforce any law which shall abridge the privileges or immunities of citizens of the United States; nor shall any State deprive any person of life, liberty, or property, without due process of law; nor deny to any person within its jurisdiction the equal protection of the laws.

(Apportionment of representatives)

Section 2 Representatives shall be apportioned among the several States according to their respective numbers, counting the whole number of persons in each State, excluding Indians not taxed. But when the right to vote at any election for the choice of electors for President and Vice-President of the United States, Representatives in Congress, the Executive and Judicial officers of a State, or the members of the Legislature thereof, is denied to any of the male inhabitants of such State, being twenty-one years of age, and citizens of the United States, or in any way abridged, except for participation in rebellion, or other crime, the basis of representation therein shall be reduced in the proportion which the number of such citizens shall bear to the whole number of male citizens twenty-one years of age in such State.

(Persons prohibited from holding office)

Section 3 No person shall be a Senator or Representative in Congress, or elector of President and Vice-President, or hold any office, civil or military, under the United States, or under any State, who, having previously taken an oath, as a member of Congress, or as an officer of the United States, or as a member of any State legislature, or as an executive or judicial officer of any State, to support the Constitution of the United States, shall have engaged in insurrection or rebellion against the same, or given aid or comfort to the enemies thereof. But Congress may by a vote of two-thirds of each House, remove such disability.

(Validity of public debts)

Section 4 The validity of the public debt of the United States, authorized by law, including debts incurred for payment of pensions and bounties for services in suppressing insurrection or rebellion, shall not be questioned. But neither the United States nor any State shall assume or pay any debt or obligation incurred in aid of insurrection or rebellion against the United States, or claim for the loss or emancipation of any slave; but all such debts, obligations, and claims shall be held illegal and void.

(Power to enforce this article)

Section 5 The Congress shall have the power to enforce, by appropriate legislation, the provisions of this article.

AMENDMENT XV

(Proposed on February 26, 1869, ratification completed on February 3, 1870; The right to vote)

Section 1 The right of citizens of the United States to vote shall not be denied or abridged by the United States or by any State on account of race, color, or previous condition of servitude—

(Power to enforce this article)

Section 2 The Congress shall have the power to enforce this article by appropriate legislation.

AMENDMENT XVI

(Proposed on July 12, 1909, ratification completed on February 3, 1913; income taxes)

The Congress shall have power to lay and collect taxes on incomes, from whatever source derived, without apportionment among the several States, and without regard to any census or enumeration.

AMENDMENT XVII

(Proposed on May 13, 1912, ratification completed on April 8, 1913; direct election of senators)

The Senate of the United States shall be composed of two Senators from each State, elected by the people thereof, for six years; and each Senator shall have one vote. The electors in each State shall have the qualifications requisite for electors of the most numerous branch of the State legislatures.

When vacancies happen in the representation of any State in the Senate, the executive authority of such State shall issue writs of election to fill such vacancies: *Provided*, That the legislature of any State may empower the executive thereof to make temporary appointments until the people fill the vacancies by election as the legislature may direct.

This amendment shall not be so construed as to affect the election or term of any Senator chosen before it becomes valid as part of the Constitution.

AMENDMENT XVIII

(Proposed on December 18, 1917, ratification completed on January 16, 1919; National prohibition of liquor)

[Section 1 After one year from the ratification of this article the manufacture, sale, or transportation of intoxicating liquors within, the importation thereof into, or the exportation thereof from the United States and all territory subject to the jurisdiction thereof for beverage purposes is hereby prohibited.

(Power to enforce this article)

[Section 2 The Congress and the several States shall have concurrent power to enforce this article by appropriate legislation.

(Seven-year limit for ratification)

[Section 3 This article shall be inoperative unless it shall have been ratified as an amendment to the Constitution by the legislatures of the several States, as provided in the Constitution, within seven years from the date of the submission hereof to the States by the Congress.][12]

AMENDMENT XIX

(Proposed on June 4, 1919, ratification completed on August 18, 1920; women's suffrage)

The right of citizens of the United States to vote shall not be denied or abridged by the United States or by any State on account of sex.

Congress shall have power to enforce this article by appropriate legislation.

AMENDMENT XX

(Proposed on March 2, 1932, ratification completed on January 23, 1933; Terms of office)

Section 1 The terms of the President and Vice-President shall end at noon on the 20th day of January, and the terms of Senators and Representatives at noon on the 3d day of January, of the year in which such terms would have ended if this article had not been ratified; and the terms of their successors shall then begin.

(Time of convening Congress)

Section 2 The Congress shall assemble at least once in every year, and such meeting shall begin at noon on the 3d day of January, unless they shall by law appoint a different day.

(Death of president-elect, failure of president-elect or vice-president-elect to qualify for office)

Section 3 If, at the time fixed for the beginning of the term of the President, the President elect shall have died, the Vice-President elect shall become President. If a President shall not have been chosen before the time fixed for the beginning of this term, or if the President elect shall have failed to qualify, then the Vice-President elect

shall act as President until a President shall have qualified; and the Congress may by law provide for the case wherein neither a President elect nor a Vice-President elect shall have qualified, declaring who shall then act as President, or the manner in which one who is to act shall be selected, and such person shall act accordingly until a President or Vice-President shall have qualified.

(Congress and the election of president or vice-president)

Section 4 The Congress may by law provide for the case of the death of any of the persons from whom the House of Representatives may choose a President whenever the right of choice shall have devolved upon them, and for the case of the death of any of the persons from whom the Senate may choose a Vice-President whenever the right of choice shall have devolved upon them.

(Effective dates of sections 1 and 2)

Section 5 Sections 1 and 2 shall take effect on the 15th day of October following the ratification of this article.

(Seven-year limit for ratification)

Section 6 This article shall be inoperative unless it shall have been ratified as an amendment to the Constitution by the legislatures of three-fourths of the several States within seven years from the date of its submission.

AMENDMENT XXI

(Proposed on February 20, 1933, ratification completed on December 5, 1933; Repeal of national prohibition of liquor)

Section 1 The eighteenth article of amendment to the Constitution of the United States is hereby repealed.

(Transportation of liquor into "dry" states prohibited)

Section 2 Transportation or importation into any State, Territory, or possession of the United States for delivery or use therein of intoxicating liquors, in violation of the law thereof, is hereby prohibited.

(Seven-year limit for ratification)

Section 3 This article shall be inoperative unless it shall have been ratified as an amendment to the Constitution by conventions in the several States, as provided in the Constitution, within seven years from the date of the submission hereof to the States by the Congress.

AMENDMENT XXII

(Proposed on March 21, 1947, ratification completed on February 27, 1951; number of presidential terms)

No person shall be elected to the office of the President more than twice, and no person who has held the office of President, or acted as President, for more than two years of a term to which some other person was elected President shall be elected to the office of President more than once.

---

[12]Repealed by the Twenty-first Amendment.

But this Article shall not apply to any person holding the office of President when this Article was proposed by the Congress, and shall not prevent any person who may be holding the office of President, or acting as President, during the term within which this Article becomes operative from holding the office of President or acting as President during the remainder of such term.

AMENDMENT XXIII

(Proposed on June 17, 1960, ratification completed on March 29, 1961; Presidential electors for the District of Columbia)

Section 1 The District constituting the seat of Government of the United States shall appoint in such manner as the Congress may direct:

A number of electors of President and Vice President equal to the whole number of Senators and Representatives in Congress to which the District would be entitled if it were a State, but in no event more than the least populous State; they shall be in addition to those appointed by the States, but they shall be considered, for the purposes of the election of President and Vice President, to be electors appointed by a State; and they shall meet in the District and perform such duties as provided by the twelfth article of amendment.

(Power to enforce this article)

Section 2 The Congress shall have power to enforce this article by appropriate legislation.

AMENDMENT XXIV

(Proposed on August 27, 1962, ratification completed on January 23, 1964; Bars poll tax in federal elections)

Section 1 The right of citizens of the United States to vote in any primary or other election for President or Vice President, or for Senator or Representative in Congress, shall not be denied or abridged by the United States or any State by reason of failure to pay any poll tax or other tax.

(Power to enforce this article)

Section 2 The Congress shall have power to enforce this article by appropriate legislation.

AMENDMENT XXV

(Proposed on July 6, 1965, ratification completed on February 10, 1967; Vice-president to succeed president)

Section 1 In case of the removal of the President from office or his death or resignation, the Vice President shall become President.

(Choosing a new vice-president)

Section 2 Whenever there is a vacancy in the office of the Vice President, the President shall nominate a Vice President who shall take the office upon confirmation by a majority vote of both Houses of Congress.

(Presidential disability)

Section 3 Whenever the President transmits to the President pro tempore of the Senate and the Speaker of the House of Representatives his written declaration that he is unable to discharge the powers and duties of his office, and until he transmits to them a written declaration to the contrary, such powers and duties shall be discharged by the Vice President as Acting President.

(Presidential disability)

Section 4 Whenever the Vice President and a majority of either the principal officers of the executive department of such other body as Congress may by law provide, transmit to the President pro tempore of the Senate and the Speaker of the House of Representatives their written declaration that the President is unable to discharge the powers and duties of his office, the Vice President shall immediately assume the powers and duties of the office as Acting President.

Thereafter, when the President transmits to the President pro tempore of the Senate and the Speaker of the House of Representatives his written declaration that no inability exists, he shall resume the powers and duties of his office unless the Vice President and a majority of either the principal officers of the executive department, or of such other body as Congress may by law provide, transmit within four days to the President pro tempore of the Senate and the Speaker of the House of Representatives their written declaration that the President is unable to discharge the powers and duties of his office. Thereupon Congress shall decide the issue, assembling within forty-eight hours for that purpose if not in session. If the Congress, within twenty-one days after receipt of the latter written declaration, or, if Congress is not in session, within twenty-one days after Congress is required to assemble, determines by two-thirds vote of both Houses that the President is unable to discharge the powers and duties of his office, the Vice President shall continue to discharge the same as Acting President; otherwise the President shall resume the powers and duties of his office.

AMENDMENT XXVI

(Proposed on March 23, 1971, ratification completed on July 1, 1971; Lowers voting age to 18 years)

Section 1 The right of citizens of the United States, who are eighteen years of age or older, to vote shall not be denied or abridged by the United States or any State on account of age.

(Power to enforce this article)

Section 2 The Congress shall have the power to enforce this article by appropriate legislation.

PROPOSED DISTRICT OF COLUMBIA VOTING AMENDMENT

(The amendment proposing that the District of Columbia be treated as a state for purposes of

congressional representation and election of president and vice-president was proposed by the Ninety-fifth Congress. It passed the House on March 2, 1978, and the Senate on August 22, 1978.)

Resolved by the Senate and the House of Representatives of the United States of America in Congress assembled (two-thirds of each House concurring therein), That the following article is proposed as an amendment to the Constitution of the United States, which shall be valid to all intents and purposes as part of the Constitution when ratified by the legislatures of three-fourths of the several States within seven years from the date of its submission by the Congress:

ARTICLE

Section 1 For purposes of representation in the Congress, election of the President and Vice President, and article V of this Constitution, the District constituting the seat of government of the United States shall be treated as though it were a State.

Section 2 The exercise of the rights and powers conferred under this article shall be by the people of the District constituting the seat of government, and as shall be provided by the Congress.

Section 3 The twenty-third article of amendment to the Constitution of the United States is hereby repealed.

Section 4 This article shall be inoperative, unless it shall have been ratified as an amendment to the Constitution by the legislatures of three-fourths of the several States within seven years from the date of its submission.

GLOSSARY

Acid rain Rain containing high quantities of acid substances that is said to have pernicious effects on vegetation and bodies of water.

Administrative law Regulations made by bureaucratic agencies that have the binding power of laws passed by Congress.

Affirmative action The policy of making active efforts to recruit more minority and female students or employees to overcome the effects of previous discrimination.

Amicus curiae brief Literally a "friend of the court"—brief or argument filed in court by an outside observer to recommend a particular analysis of, or decision on, a case.

Apartheid The legal system of racial segregation practiced in South Africa.

Appropriation A bill actually granting an agency permission to spend funds in specified amounts for specified purposes, the funds having been first authorized.

Arms control An action or international agreement intended to limit the procurement, deployment, or use of weapons or other instruments of war.

Authority Recognized power.

Authorization A bill establishing a ceiling for spending by an agency.

Bicameral Consisting of two houses or chambers—applied to legislatures.

Bill of attainder A law that declares a person or group to have committed a crime and inflicts punishment for it.

Bill of Rights The first ten amendments to the Constitution.

Bipartisan Characterized by accord and cooperation between two major political parties.

Busing Transporting students of one race from one neighborhood to another, where students are primarily of another race, for schooling.

Cabinet The body made up of the heads of government departments.

Capitalism An economic system in which the means of production are owned by individuals and operated by them and their assistants for a profit, employing the rest of the work force as laborers.

Casework Personalized work that members of Congress do for their constituents.

Categorical grants Financial aid from the federal government to the states that must be spent for specific categories of activities.

Charisma The magnetic appeal of a leader to the people.

Checks and balances, system of The system by which government institutions or branches exercise checks on, and balance the activities of, other government institutions and branches.

Civil law Law that applies to relationships between individuals or groups involving contracts, etc.

Civil liberties Prohibitions against state interference in the lives of its citizens.

Civil rights Regulations permitting state interference to guarantee the rights of full political participation to groups previously excluded.

Clear and present danger A constitutional law standard that holds that one's First Amendment right to speak may be curtailed if the words would "create a clear and present danger that they will bring about the substantive evils that the government has a right to prevent," in the words of Justice Oliver Wendell Holmes's Supreme Court opinion.

Cloture Provision by which the Senate cuts off debate if three-fifths of senators present vote to do so at least two days after at least sixteen senators sign a petition requesting it; once cloture is voted, each member may speak only for one more hour on the measure.

Coalitions A temporary alliance or union of parties or other political actors for the purpose of achieving a common legislative policy or of electing a particular candidate.

Cold War Post–World War II conflict between communist countries and Western countries, not involving the use of arms.

Collective goods Public policies whose benefits may be shared equally by all people, whether or not they join or support the group seeking to pressure the government to adopt the policies.

Commerce clause Clause in the Constitution (Article I, Section 8) giving Congress power "to regulate commerce . . . among the several states."

Committee on the Whole House An arrangement whereby the House of Representatives can meet to discuss and debate legislation with a smaller quorum and different rules.

Common law Customary law or precedent applied to redress harm.

Compact theory The theory that colonies became separate, independent states when they declared independence and won the war that followed.

Comparable worth The doctrine used to oppose discrimination in the pay of women that holds that workers should be paid in terms of the skills required by jobs rather than market forces.

Competitiveness A term for the goal of programs designed to support American business and industry in world trade relations.

Concurring opinion Written explanation of the views of one or more justices voting with the majority but disagreeing on the grounds for, or route to, the decision.

Conference committee A committee composed of members of both houses of Congress whose task it is to agree on a compromise version of a bill when each house has produced a different version of the bill.

Conflict of interest A situation in which someone acts in his or her role as an official in a way that benefits, or might be thought to benefit, himself or herself as an individual.

Congressional oversight The responsibility of Congress to keep an eye on how effectively various parts of the executive branch are fulfilling their responsibilities.

Connecticut Compromise The decision reached at the Constitutional Convention whereby membership of the House would be determined by population, whereas each state would have equal representation in the Senate.

Constitution A written document embodying the rules of a political or social organization.

Constitutional law Law derived from a constitution.

Consumer sovereignty The principle, supposed to operate in capitalism, that the consumer can determine what is produced by his or her purchasing decisions.

Containment A U.S. foreign policy objective to limit Soviet influence everywhere in the world.

Continuing resolutions Temporary laws passed by Congress when appropriations bills have not been decided by the start of the new fiscal year, October 1.

Cooperative federalism The period since the New Deal whereby the states and the national government are regarded as mutually complementary parts of a single governmental mechanism.

Covert action Actions, often illegal or otherwise dangerous, undertaken by governmental bodies in secret.

Cultural pluralism The view that each individual culture does or should survive and flourish within a broader common cultural framework.

Customary law Unwritten practice accepted as binding.

Delegate An agent of the voters who elected him or her.

Delegated powers Under the national theory, a certain, specified, limited authority that is given to each level of government.

Demand-side economic theory The theory that holds that producers will supply goods when people demand them.

Democracy Rule by the people.

Deregulation The act or process of removing regulations or restrictions to free an industry from government regulation.

Desegregation Removing barriers to contact among the races or other segregated groups.

Détente The relaxation of strained relations between nations.

Dillon's Rule The principle of the city's legal dependence on the state for its authority, first stated by Judge John F. Dillon in 1872.

Direct action A type of political participation generally involving obstruction within the limits of the law directed at the vulnerability of political power.

Direct popular election Election by simple popular vote.

Direct primary A preliminary election in which voters nominate a candidate to run in a general election.

Discrimination Prejudicial treatment based on race or some other characteristic.

Disenfranchise (disfranchise) To deprive of the right to vote.

Disinformation Term for false information disseminated, usually by a secret governmental source, as if it were true.

Dissenting opinions Written explanations of the views of one or more justices voting in the minority on a case.

Divestment Term for program of ending all foreign investment in a particular country.

Division of powers The division of ruling power between state and national governments and the people in the American federal structure of government.

Doctrine of implied powers See Implied powers.

Doctrine of "political questions" Used by the Supreme Court in order to decline to rule on controversial issues on grounds that they should be decided by the executive and/or legislative branches.

Domain The territory, subject area, or realm in or over which politics or government does or might occur.

Double jeopardy Being tried a second time for the same crime if previously acquitted.

Dual federalism Doctrine that the Supreme Court mediates between two power centers, the national government and the states.

Due process A course of legal proceedings carried out in accordance with established principles and rules.

Duty A tax on an imported good that is a percentage of the good's value.

Elastic clause Clause in the Constitution (Article I, Section 8) giving Congress power "to make all laws which shall be necessary and proper" for executing its enumerated powers; also called the necessary and proper clause.

Elector A member of the electoral college.

Electoral college The group of presidential electors from all states who meet state by state in December after a presidential election to cast the official votes for president.

Electoral votes Votes cast by presidential electors in the December electoral college meetings.

Electorate All those entitled to vote.

Elitism A view that what happens in American politics is primarily determined by a relatively small collection of powerful individuals.

Elitist theory The theory that power is held and shared by a small group of people, a ruling elite, who dominate the major institutions.

Emancipation The act of freeing a person from servitude.

Eminent domain The right of the government to seize private property for public use.

Entitlements Government programs to which specified citizens are legally entitled.

Entropy The tendency of a system to become disorganized or to run down.

Enumerated powers Those powers explicitly stated in the Constitution.

Equal employment opportunity Personnel practices of employers that guarantee the same opportunities to all individuals.

Equity An element in the law developed by judges to be applied to prevent harm where common law does not apply.

Executive branch The branch of government headed by the president and including the bureaucracy.

Executive order A presidential proclamation requiring agencies or individuals to take specific actions without Congress first having passed a law on the subject.

Executive power The power of the executive officer or the executive branch to execute the laws.

Executive privilege The principle by which the president can withhold sensitive papers from Congress.

Expertise Specialized, or expert, knowledge.

Ex post facto law A law that declares something to be a crime only after it has been done.

Express power A power specifically granted to one of the branches of government by the Constitution.

External representation The way government represents the people and the state outside its borders.

External ruling power Power to represent the United States and the U.S. people to the rest of the world.

Fairness doctrine The rule that major advocates of both sides of political issues should be given fair opportunity to broadcast their views if attacked by political opposition over the airwaves; also called the equal time doctrine.

Federal Reserve System The governmental system by which monetary policy and currency are controlled.

Federalism A system of government in which governing power is divided into levels and shared between a central government and state or regional governments.

Federalists Those who, in the early years of the Republic, favored a strong central government.

Federal system A system of government in which power is shared by a central government with its constituent member states.

Federation An organization of states under a government with power over its member states.

Filibuster A term for the process by which a small group of senators can "talk a bill to death," eventually forcing the bill's withdrawal so that other business can be dealt with.

Fiscal policy Policy relating to taxation, public revenues, public spending, and public debt.

Floor leader A member of a legislative body chosen by his or her party to have charge of its organization and strategy on the floor.

Framers Those who framed, or wrote, the Constitution or the Declaration of Indpendence.

Franchise The right to vote; suffrage.

Freedom of Information Act A law that provides that access and disclosure, rather than secrecy, be the policy in government.

Full faith and credit The requirement in the Constitution (Article IV, Section 1) that each state recognize the public acts, records, and judicial proceedings of every other state.

GATT The General Agreement on Tariffs and Trade, an agreement and organization established by many nations to negotiate lowering of barriers to international trade.

General election An election in which candidates are elected in most constituencies of a nation or state.

General public The people of any society taken as a whole.

Gentrification A process whereby young professionals and upper-middle-class suburbanites move into the city and revitalize it.

Gerrymandering Dividing a territorial unit into election districts to give one political party an electoral majority in a larger number of districts while concentrating the voting strength of the opposition in as few districts as possible.

GOP Initials for "Grand Old Party," a traditional term for the Republican party.

Government The public bodies that direct public affairs.

Grandfather clause A provision that only those who could demonstrate that their father or grandfather had voted were exempt from strict literacy tests and property requirements that limited the franchise.

Grand jury A group of citizens convened to decide whether or not there is enough evidence in a given case to merit a trial.

Granting a rule Process by which the House Rules Committee decides that a bill passed by committee will be allowed to be voted on by the entire House and specifies under what terms such consideration can occur.

Grants-in-aid Financial aid from the federal government to the states, usually for specific purposes.

Greenhouse effect The tendency of air pollution to cause a heating up of the atmosphere.

Gross national product (GNP) The total value of goods and services produced in a nation during a given year.

Guaranteed family income See Negative income tax.

Habeas corpus, writ of Issued by a federal court when it finds that imprisonment violates the Constitution or the laws of the U.S. Prisoner must then be released.

Home rule charter A form of local political autonomy drafted by a city in the form of a "home rule charter" that, when approved by the state, cannot be changed by the state's legislature.

Human rights Rights assertedly belonging to all people because they are human beings.

Ideology A coherent set of beliefs about politics and public policy.

Impeachment The formal charging of a public official with misconduct in office by a competent tribunal; in the case of a president, the charge is brought by the House of Representatives.

Implied powers, doctrine of Argument that certain acts that are consistent with the Constitution are constitutional, because they are implied even though not specifically enumerated. The power of Congress "to make all laws which shall be necessary and proper" for executing its enumerated powers is an example of implied power.

Impoundment Presidential refusal to allow an agency to spend funds appropriated by Congress.

Incrementalism The belief that changes in public policy or budgets occur only in small increments.

Incumbent The holder of an office.

Independent agency A governmental regulatory commission or governmental corporation that is independent of any regular executive department.

Independent regulatory commission A government agency or advisory panel that regulates some commercial activity or sector of the economy and that is independent of any regular executive department.

Indirect primary A preliminary election in which voters elect delegates who then meet to pick a candidate to run in a general election.

Industrial policy Policy of a government to foster its country's industries by subsidy, protection, or other measures.

Inflation Continual rise in prices, generally attributed to an increase in the volume of money and credit relative to the amount of available goods.

Infrastructure The roads, bridges, airports, water and sewer systems, and public transportation systems of the country, which support its economic activities.

Inherent powers Those powers inherent in the federal government by virtue of its being a state or nation.

Initiative A law voted on by the general public after it is proposed by petition.

Injunction A writ granted by a court whereby a person or group is required to do or to refrain from doing a specified act.

Institutional racism The process by which institutions set the context within which some people are kept poor and powerless by being denied real opportunities for education, good jobs, good housing, and political roles, whether or not people hold racist attitudes.

Integration Bringing together people who have been segregated.

Interest group An organized group whose members have common views about certain policies or actions and so undertake activities to influence government officials and policies.

Internal colonialism The treatment of a minority group within a country as if it were a colony.

Internal representation The way government represents the people within its borders.

Internal ruling power Power to govern the people of the United States; representing the government to the people.

Iron triangles Members of congressional committees, lobbyists, and heads of bureaucratic agencies who meet to decide on questions about programs and budgets, often without consulting the president or his assistants. See also Subgovernments.

Jim Crow Laws Legislation designed to discriminate against blacks, especially in the South.

Judicial activism The doctrine that advocates an active role for the Supreme Court in enforcing the Constitution and in using judicial review.

Judicial branch The branch of government consisting of the Supreme Court and the other courts.

Judicial restraint A doctrine that argues that the Court should be very hesitant to use judicial review or otherwise to intervene in the political process.

Judicial review The power of the court to assess the actions of individuals and agencies or the laws of Congress, states, and localities to determine whether or not they are in accord with the Constitution.

Justiciable question Any question that can be decided by the courts, the judicial branch of government.

Keynesianism An approach to economic policy making that emphasizes governmental stimulation of demand, usually through spending.

Kitchen Cabinet An informal group of advisors to the president.

Laissez-faire The policy of governmental nonintervention in the economy.

Lame duck A president unable to run again and so thought to be less powerful; more generally, an official who has been defeated in a bid for reelection but who must serve until the inauguration of the elected candidate.

Law A uniform system of rules to govern or prescribe certain behavior for everyone living within a given area or legal jurisdiction.

Law of cultural dominance The principle that a system that more effectively exploits the energy resources of a given environment will tend to spread in that environment at the expense of less effective systems.

Law of evolutionary potential The principle that the more specialized and adapted a form in a given evolutionary stage, the smaller is its potential for passing to the next stage.

Legislative branch The branch of government consisting of the Congress.

Legislative intent The intention of the Congress in drafting and passing a particular law; this is a doctrine or a ground for interpretation used by the courts in deciding upon the meaning of a law.

Legislative veto Provision in a bill reserving to Congress (two-house veto) or a congressional committee (committee veto) or to the entire House or Senate (one-house veto) the power to veto by majority vote an act by an agency.

Legitimacy Authority accepted as legal or right.

Line-item veto Proposal that the president be allowed to veto individual elements of a budget passed by Congress, rather than vetoing all or none of it.

Lobbyist A representative of a special interest who attempts to influence legislation or policy making.

Logrolling The trading of votes by legislators to secure favorable action on legislation of interest to each one.

Majority More than 50 percent of the votes cast.

Majority leader The leader of the majority party in a legislative body.

Majority opinion Written explanation of the views of court justices voting in the majority on a case.

Majority rule Rule by more than 50 percent of the electorate.

Majority whip The whip of the majority party. See Whip.

Mandamus, writ of A writ that orders a government official or court to perform duties required of it by law.

Marshall Plan The policy of granting economic aid to U.S. allies in Western Europe after World War II.

Merit system Civil service system in which jobs are granted on the basis of competitive testing.

Military-industrial complex President Eisenhower's term for the alleged alliance between the military and the industries that supply its material needs who combine to influence defense spending for mutual gain.

Military reform The movement attempting to deemphasize high technology weapons in favor of more effective and more economical fighting forces.

Minority leader The leader of the minority party in a legislative body.

Minority whip The whip of the minority party. See Whip.

Monarchy A form of government headed by a king or a queen.

Monetarism The policy of controlling the economy by influencing the supply of money.

Monetary policy Primarily, decisions about currency supply and how much credit to extend to banks for use in making loans to business and individuals.

Monroe Doctrine The policy stated by President James Monroe in 1823 that warned European powers against interfering in the Western Hemisphere.

Multinational corporation A company whose operations are conducted in various countries, which can influence the economies and politics of the countries within which they operate.

Multiparty system A political system with three or more major political parties.

National supremacy, doctrine of Argument that states cannot act in ways that effectively render the Constitution less than the supreme law of the land.

National debt The total amount of money owed by the United States government to other governments, organizations, and individuals.

National theory The theory that the people (a single sovereign power) created both the national and state governments.

Natural law A body of law derived from the nature of man and society.

Natural monopoly A monopoly that develops spontaneously because such a system is the most efficient means for providing a specific good or service.

Natural rights Rights to which one is entitled by virtue of being a human being.

Necessary and proper clause Clause in the Constitution (Article I, Section 8) giving Congress power "to make all laws which shall be necessary and proper" for executing its enumerated powers. Also called the "elastic clause."

Negative income tax A proposed welfare reform that would pay money to poor families who receive less than a stated minimum annual income.

Nixon Doctrine The doctrine proclaimed by President Nixon after Vietnam that other countries would henceforth have to bear the military burden of their own defense.

Nonpartisan election An election in which the candidates do not represent or run as members of political parties.

No prior restraint (no prior censorship) A ruling that the press cannot be prevented from publishing something but can be punished afterward if it published something illegal.

Nullification The belief that states can withdraw the authority they granted to the national government when they do not like what it does.

Off-year elections Elections in years in which a presidential election does not occur.

Ombudsman An individual whose office serves as a channel through which a citizen can express his or her grievances over the operation of a bureau or the action of a bureaucrat and seek whatever redress is appropriate.

One man, one vote The principle that one person's vote should be worth as much as another's, used in apportionment of seats in a legislature based on equal population segments.

Open primary A primary in which persons can vote for the candidates of either party regardless of their own party membership.

Oversight, congressional The responsibility Congress has for keeping an eye on how well the various parts of the executive branch are fulfilling their responsibilities to carry out the laws and how effectively they are spending their appropriations.

Pacific shift Term for the new emphasis on the countries bordering the Pacific, especially Japan.

Parliamentary government A system of government in which the head of government is elected by, and responsible to, the legislature.

Participatory democracy A system sought by some in which citizens play increased political roles in deciding the things that affect their lives.

Partisanship The holding of attitudes associated with a particular party, or assertion of affiliation with that party.

Party caucus A meeting of all party members.

Party identification The tendency of a person to say that he or she belongs to (or identifies with) a particular political party.

Party loyalty Voting for the candidates of one's party.

Paternalism A system under which an authority dominates the private lives of individuals by supplying their needs and regulating their conduct on the assumption that such domination is in the best interests of the dominated.

Patronage Government jobs given to political supporters.

Perquisites ("perks") Privileges of office (car, staff, etc.) in addition to regular salary or wages.

Personal racism Racist beliefs held by an individual. See Racism.

Petit jury A jury that is selected to decide on the facts at issue in a single case.

Planning-Programming-Budgeting System A new budgeting approach, resulting from criticism of incrementalism, involving long-range planning.

Platform A declaration of the principles and positions held by a political party or a candidate for office.

Plea bargain A deal made between a defense lawyer and a prosecutor for a defendant to plead guilty to a lesser charge and in return, the prosecutor drops the original charge against the defendent.

Plural executive A system under which two or more people would serve as president.

Pluralism A view that what happens in American politics is primarily determined by a large collection of different groups competing with each other.

Plurality The margin of votes by which one candidate leads the next candidate—not necessarily a majority.

Plurality rule Rule by the candidate who gets more votes than any other candidate, but not necessarily a majority.

Pocket veto An indirect veto of a legislative act by an executive who refuses to sign the act or formally veto it and simply holds it until after the adjournment of the legislature.

Policy A general commitment to the pattern of activity adopted for use in making particular decisions.

Political machine A well-entrenched organization of leaders and followers that is generally able to control nominations.

Political party An organization that runs candidates in an election.

Political socialization The process by which an individual becomes aware of, and more or less active in, the political life of his or her society.

Politico An officeholder who is concerned primarily with reelection or personal advancement.

Politics Disputes over claims to the authority to describe, explain, or interpret some aspects of the nature of reality.

Poll A survey of a few people that is supposed to represent with considerable accuracy how everyone involved thinks.

Poll tax A fee that was to be paid when one registered to vote.

Popular votes Votes cast by the people in the November presidential election.

Populism A political movement designed to unite the interests of farmers and union members that led to the formation of the People's party in 1891.

Pork barrel The projects that incumbents get for constituencies, such as public works projects, federal grants, and government contracts.

Positive law Law established by a legislature or other governmental authority.

Positive rights Rights to the attainment of basic human needs.

Power The capacity to make people act in accordance with one's own wishes when they might rather act differently.

Precedents Any actions or statements that establish a new approach or pattern and set examples for the future.

Prejudice A predisposition, not based on reason, to react unfavorably to a particular individual or group.

Presidential electors Individuals selected by a party and elected by the voters of a given state who then cast a vote for president and vice-president in the electoral college.

President pro tempore The presiding officer of the Senate when the vice-president is not present; presiding officer is always a senator of the majority party.

Pressure group An organized special-interest group that puts pressure on government institutions in order to get what it wants.

Private interests The interests of one or more persons.

Private law A law that deals with a specific matter or individual rather than with general legislative concerns; a law that does not affect the public at large.

Private sector All nongovernmental segments of the economy, such as business and industry.

Probability sample Most major national polls interview about 1500 people to represent the American adult population of about 140 million people. These people form a probability sample.

Probable cause Term for the requirement that one show sufficient reason to suspect someone of an illegal action.

Procedural due process See Due process.

Program A series of related actions designed to implement a policy by bringing about a desired effect.

Progressive tax A tax that takes a larger percentage from those with larger resources.

Protectionism The policy of setting up high tariff barriers or low import quotas in order to protect domestic industry from foreign competition by limiting quantities of imported goods, thus raising the price of these goods.

Public goods Goods such as national defense and police protection that must be supplied to all the people, if they are supplied to any.

Public interest Historically, a belief that there were truths about human beings that existed beyond time and place. Today, these interests must include those of the weak and the strong, the poor and the rich, the women and the men, and the yet unborn as well as the living, according to most views.

Public law A law that deals with general legislative concerns and affects the public at large.

Public opinion The collection of preferences about candidates, policies, and party, plus political knowledge and ideology, held by individuals.

Pure democracy Direct rule by the people.

Quorum The number of members of a body that must be present in order for business to be legally transacted.

Racism Belief that a person's race should be used as a criterion to determine how he or she is treated, implying that some races are, or should be, treated better than others.

Random sample In polls, a group of people in which each individual within the whole population being surveyed has an equal chance of being selected.

Reapportionment Redrawing the boundaries of election districts as populations change.

Recall System by which people sign petitions to get a referendum on whether or not to remove an elected official from office.

Recession A serious economic slowdown.

Referendum A law or resolution voted on by the general public after it is proposed by the legislature or by petition.

Registration The process of enrolling formally as a voter prior to an election in order to be eligible to vote in that election.

Regulatory policy Policy that sets the conditions under which private activities operate.

Reindustrialization The proposal to make changes in basic institutions, in the framework for economic policy making, in order to rebuild America's industrial capacity.

Relative deprivation Being deprived in relation to others, even though one may have more than he or she previously did.

Representative democracy A system in which decisions are made by officials who are elected at regular intervals by the people and who represent the people in making decisions for them.

Representative sample In polling, a group of people that is supposed to represent with considerable accuracy the overall thinking of the entire group from which the sample was chosen.

Reprivatization Turning over to private business functions (such as trash collection) now done by government bureaucrats.

Republic A form of government in which authority derives ultimately from the people, who may or may not be allowed to exercise it.

Republican government A government in which supreme power resides in the people who are entitled to vote and is exercised by elected officers and representatives who are responsible to the people and who govern according to law.

Reserved powers Those powers reserved by the Constitution to the states.

Revenue neutral Term for a change in the tax law that produces the same income for the government as the existing provision.

Revenue sharing Program by which the federal government gives funds to state and/or local governments without specifying the use to which the funds must be put.

Reverse discrimination Discrimination in favor of those previously discriminated against in order to overcome the effects of previous discrimination.

Roll-call vote In Congress, a vote in which a legislator votes and is recorded for or against a measure after his or her name has been called.

Rule of four The Supreme Court's practice of agreeing either to hear oral argument on a case or decide it without oral argument when any four Supreme Court justices agree to review the case.

Runoff election An election held when no candidate in a previous election received the required percentage of the total votes cast.

Safe seat A House or Senate seat for which there is little competition between the parties because the election of the candidate of one or the other party is virtually assured.

Sampling The process by which a pollster picks small numbers of people whose views should be representative of those who are not polled.

Search warrant Permission granted by a court to a law enforcement official to search someone's person or quarters.

Secession The withdrawal of a state from the Union.

Self-determination The principle that a group of people should be able to determine for itself its political governance.

Self-incrimination One's testifying against oneself.

Senatorial courtesy The unwritten rule that the president should consult with senators of a state before appointing a federal judge in that state and should allow a senator of his own party an absolute veto over the nomination.

Seniority system System in Congress whereby first choice of committee positions, etc., goes to the longest-serving member.

Separation of powers Allocation of powers among the branches of government at one level.

Sequestration The practice of the executive in refusing to spend certain appropriated funds.

SES See Socioeconomic status.

Sexism The attitudes, beliefs, practices, policies, laws, and behaviors discriminating against men or women on the basis of their gender.

Sharing of powers The sharing of responsibilities at the national level (through checks and balances) among branches and among the levels of the federal system.

Socialization A process of learning whereby a child gets a sense of other people and of his or her relations with them and feelings toward them.

Socioeconomic status (SES) The various factors such as occupation, income, and social class that determine one's status in society.

Sovereignty Supreme power over a body politic.

Speaker of the House The member of the majority party in the House of Representatives who is selected by the party to preside over sessions of the House.

Special interest An interest shared by only a segment of the community.

Split ticket A ballot cast by a voter who chooses candidates from several parties.

Spoils system Civil service system by which a political victor replaces present officeholders with his or her own supporters.

Stagflation The combination of economic stagnation and inflation.

Star Wars Colloquial term for Strategic Defense Initiative.

Stare decisis Literally, "let the decision stand"; the principle that precedent should govern legal decisions until a particular precedent is overturned.

State A politically organized body of people permanently occupying a specific territory and living under a government; in the federal government of the United States of America, one of the political subunits.

States' rights All rights not granted to the federal government by the Constitution nor forbidden by it to the separate states.

Statutory law Legislation; law made by statutes.

Statutory powers Those powers based on laws, or statutes, passed by Congress.

Strategic Defense Initiative Reagan administration program seeking a defensive shield against a nuclear attack.

Strict construction Literal reading of the Constitution to determine what the Founding Fathers really said.

Subgovernments Members of congressional committees, lobbyists, and heads of bureaucratic agencies who meet informally to decide questions about programs and budgets. See also Iron triangles.

Subnational Smaller than the entire nation.

Subpoena A court order declaring that something must be done under penalty of punishment.

Subsidy A grant of money or special privilege to a person or group to stimulate activity that the recipient would otherwise not be inclined to undertake.

Suffrage The right to vote; franchise.

Sunset laws Laws requiring that an existing program or agency be regularly reviewed for its effectiveness and then terminated unless specifically extended as a result of this review.

Sunshine laws Laws requiring that meetings of agencies or government units be open to the public.

Superfund A fund constituted by contributions from chemical polluters used to clean up toxic waste dumps.

Supergrade High level, bureaucratic manager.

Supply-side economic theory The theory that scarcity of goods is created by lack of incentive for workers and businesses, and by obstacles in the form of regulations.

Tax expenditures See Tax loopholes.

Tax loopholes Tax law provisions that allow someone to escape paying taxes that would otherwise be required on something.

Tax preference A special tax benefit.

Transnationalism A political attitude of interest in, and concern about, the status and welfare of others across national boundaries.

Trustee The legislator who believes that he or she is a free agent to vote according to his or her assessment of an issue and not according to the wishes of his or her constituents.

Unemployment The state of not having a job.

Uncontrollables Those elements in the budget that are legally required and so cannot be controlled without changes in the law.

U.S. Code The government publication that includes the text of all laws currently in force.

Urban enterprise zone An urban area in which firms that build a plant are granted special benefits.

Vested interests Special interests that are benefiting from the way things are and that seek to preserve the status quo.

Veto Power of the president to refuse to sign a bill passed by Congress; it then becomes law only if two-thirds of each house votes in favor of overriding the veto.

Virginia Plan The proposal in the Constitutional Convention to apportion both the Senate and House on the basis of population.

Welfare state A state with a type of government that meets or attempts to meet the various human needs over and above the physical safety of its citizens.

Whip The person in a legislative body who, with deputy whips, is responsible for rounding up, or whipping into line, party members when a vote is coming up.

Whistle blowers Employees who disclose evidence of wrongdoing by the government.

White primary A primary in which only whites could vote.

Writ of certiorari See Certiorari, writ of.

Writ of habeas corpus A court order allowing someone to go free.

Writ of mandamus See Mandamus, writ of.

Zero-based budgeting A system that requires each governmental program or agency to justify itself and each aspect of its budget each year.

INDEX